SEARS, ROEBUCK AND CO.
INCORPORATED.
CHEAPEST SUPPLY HOUSE
ON EARTH
OUR TRADE REACHES AROUND
THE WORLD

CONSUMERS GUIDE

FALL
1900

DBI BOOKS, INC., NORTHFIELD, ILLINOIS
(Formerly Digest Books, Inc.)

This miniature reproduction of Sears, Roebuck & Company's 1900 catalogue is a significant historical document. It describes much of the way of life that existed in the United States at the turn of the century, when the country's people were still unconcerned with the "population bomb" and air pollution, but when its ocean barriers were beginning to shrink.

1900—the beginning of a promising new century—saw the emergence of the United States as a recognized world power. The country's decisive victory over Spain in 1898, its leading roles in the First Hague Conference in 1899 and in putting down the Boxer Rebellion in China in 1900, and its expansion into the Western Pacific through the Philippines all served to establish the United States as a world power of the first rank. Its 76 million people lived in 45 states, and according to a recent survey they paid the lowest prices for goods and services that year that the country would ever see. In politics, McKinley had again overwhelmed Bryan's bid for the Presidency, and the "good life" seemed the order of the day.

In 1900 the country was still strongly rural, with almost 11 million of its population employed in farming. Life expectancy was still under 50 years. However, the burgeoning growth of manufacturing was sparking a trend toward urbanization, with plants and factories claiming over six million workers —at an average wage of 22¢ an hour! Prices may have been low, but money did not come easy—though the government did manage to more than balance its budget that year with a $46 million surplus.

Like the country, Sears, Roebuck & Company entered the new century on a note of prosperity and expansion. Initially a "moonlight" watch selling sideline of railroader Richard Sears, the company under his influence grew in only a dozen years to a million dollar giant, selling thousands of diverse items to tens of thousands of customers across the entire country.

Richard Warren Sears was born in Stewartville, Minnesota in 1863, and while still in his teens learned telegraphy and went to work for the railroad. It was in 1886, while he was serving as Station Agent at North Redwood, Minnesota, that a local jeweler refused a shipment of watches and the shipper offered them on consignment to Sears. The watches sold quickly, and the deal proved so profitable that Sears ordered more watches for resale through other Station Agents. Business prospered and in a few months he quit the railroad to set up a full time mail order business in Minneapolis as the R. W. Sears Watch Company. In 1887 Sears moved the business to Chicago, in order to take advantage of its better transportation facilities and more central location for his burgeoning business. Within a month of his arrival in Chicago, Sears' advertisement for a watch repairman was answered by a slender young man from Hammond, Indiana: Alvah Curtis Roebuck.

The fledgling business continued to prosper, but in 1889 Sears sold off his Chicago operation to return to Minneapolis while Roebuck, now a partner, moved to Toronto to take control of a branch they had established there. In

Minneapolis, Sears returned to the watch and jewelry business as the Warren Company. Although this new venture proved highly profitable, Sears sold it in 1891 to Roebuck, who promptly (at Sears' urging) renamed it the A. C. Roebuck Company. Almost immediately Sears talked Roebuck out of a half interest, and in 1893 the name was changed for the final time to Sears, Roebuck and Company. Late that same year a Chicago office was established, and by January of 1895 the company was back in Chicago to stay.

This series of gyrations took its toll on Roebuck, who decided to sell out and retire in August, 1895. In the meantime Sears, always on the move, had lined up new capital in the persons of Aaron Nussbaum and Julius Rosenwald, two successful Chicago businessmen. The company was reorganized with a capitalization of $150,000, with Sears and his two new partners each a one-third owner. Sears remained as the company president, a post he retained until 1908. Sears was an enthusiastic master salesman whose rural origin had given him the ability to sell effectively to people with similar backgrounds, while his partners and their capital provided him with the base from which he had revolutionized mail order selling.

Sears' first catalogue for the A.C. Roebuck Company appeared in 1891, and consisted of 32 pages of watches with an eight-page insert covering jewelry and sewing machines. The next year saw the catalogue increased to well over 100 pages, about a third of which contained testimonials and other institutional materials, while only a dozen or so pages displayed merchandise not related to watches or jewelry. Bearing the new "Sears, Roebuck & Company" name for the first time in 1893, the catalogue reached nearly 200 pages and covered a much broader line of merchandise. Each subsequent year saw further increases in size for the book, while circulation increased at a comparable rate. The cost of printing and distributing such a monumental tome was naturally a major item in Sears' budget.

This miniature 1900 Sears, Roebuck catalogue surely provides a capsule view of the United States at that time. Here you will find literally everything you would have needed to exist in the rural (or urban) America of the period. Groceries (page 12) for your cupboard (page 1067) or ice box (page 807), silver (page 148) and china (page 1085) for your table (1063), baby clothes (page 691) and baby carriages (page 1120) for your offspring, and tombstones (page 739) for your ancestors, medicines for your animals (page 29) and for you (page 14) are just a sampling of the necessities of life available from Sears. A word about these latter items—until the passage of the pure Food and Drug Act in 1906, anyone could make almost any claim he wished about his patent medicine. Sears' "Drug Department" pages offer a broad spectrum of these nostrums, claiming to cure almost every known ill. Pages 24 and 25 are classic— for 15¢ one can purchase a tube of tablets to "cure" any of 24 diseases, or a "Family Medicine Case" with a dozen assorted cures. Little wonder the average American lived to be only 48!

To facilitate your enjoyment of this pocket-sized bit of Americana, here is a listing of Sears' major "Department" sections in the order of their appearance:

Some additional comment on this reproduction. Richard Sears was a thorough salesman, and in his promotional materials (early Sears catalogues were almost entirely his own personal effort, and he maintained an active interest in their composition until his retirement in 1908) Sears endeavored to make the maximum use of every square inch of page space.

Furthermore, to keep this edition within bounds (the original did weigh four pounds!), a number of the less interesting and/or repetitious pages were edited out. However, not all page number gaps can be blamed on the editor, as the original catalogue was composed with a number of intentional omissions of varying lengths.

Enough of this history and background. The pleasure in this catalogue starts when you turn the page and propel yourself back almost three generations. Sears had something for everyone then, and this book has something for everyone now. Turn the page and it won't take long until you start finding it.

Joseph J. Schroeder, Jr.
Glenview, Illinois
June, 1970

Joseph J. Schroeder, Jr. is the editor of a number of catalogue replicas including the 1908 Sears Roebuck & Co., the 1894 Montgomery Ward & Co., and the 1896 Marshall Field & Co. Jewelry and European Fashions. He is co-author of System Mauser, a pictorial history of the Mauser pistol, and has written many articles for technical electronic publications, firearms magazines and books.

NOTICE TO DEALERS.

MERCHANTS IN ALL LINES, ATTENTION!

OUR PRICES ARE ALIKE TO EVERYONE, and while no merchant, no dealer of any kind can buy any article from us, NO MATTER HOW LARGE THE QUANTITY FOR ONE CENT LESS THAN THE PRICE QUOTED IN OUR CATALOGUE, thousands of merchants in all lines are putting our catalogue to very valuable use.

GENERAL STORES—DEALERS IN DRY GOODS, NOTIONS, BOOTS AND SHOES, MACKINTOSHES OR RAIN COATS, HARDWARE, DRUGS, STOVES, BICYCLES, VEHICLES, SEWING MACHINES, MUSICAL INSTRUMENTS—all classes of merchants who buy to sell again, everywhere, are MAKING HUNDREDS OF DOLLARS in profit every year by SELLING GOODS FROM OUR CATALOGUE which they do not carry in stock, and which otherwise would be bought elsewhere, by taking advantage of our special prices, lower than they can buy elsewhere, in the replenishing of their regular stocks.

THE LIVE MERCHANTS OF THE COUNTRY who at first complained bitterly of the extremely low prices we make and sell to their customers, are now coming to us by the thousands for the many articles we can supply them in every line FOR MUCH LESS than they can BUY elsewhere.

THE LIVE MERCHANT OF TODAY IS INFLUENCED BY PRICE, and not prejudiced by sentiment. He buys where he can buy at the LOWEST PRICE so he can UNDERSELL HIS COMPETITOR. With him PRICE AND QUALITY counts and not terms, time and policy. This class of merchants, the live business men of today, everywhere, ARE BUYING IN LARGE QUANTITIES FROM EVERY DEPARTMENT IN OUR HOUSE, and while our business originally was founded as a mail order business to the consumer, our never ceasing PRICE-CUTTING POLICY, made possible by our enormous buying power has enabled us to furnish almost everything in every line of merchandise at PRICES LOWER THAN DEALERS CAN BUY IN ANY QUANTITY, and the live merchant ever on the alert for values that his competitors cannot show, has been quick to perceive the incomparable values shown on every page of our catalogue.

DEALER—MAKE OUR CATALOGUE HELP YOU TO HOLD YOUR TRADE.

IF YOU WILL MAKE KNOWN to your customers that you will supply them with all their wants, if they are wanting goods you do not carry in stock you will send and get them, you will HOLD TRADE that would otherwise go to others, you will hold customers you would otherwise lose, and you will derive a profit on the sale of goods which you do not carry in stock and you otherwise would not sell; and while it is true our catalogues are distributed in your immediate neighborhood, and

WE WILL SELL ONE ARTICLE TO ANYONE IN YOUR NEIGHBORHOOD AT AS LOW A PRICE AS WE WOULD SELL TO YOU BY THE DOZEN OR BY THE HUNDRED,

every live merchant has many customers who will not send away for goods, no matter what the price inducement may be. In every community there are many people who have always patronized their dealer at home, and by force of habit will continue to patronize their dealer at home if the dealer will supply them with the goods they need in spite of any price offers, no matter how tempting, that may be held out by ourselves or any other catalogue house, and no one is more aware of this fact than the progressive merchant who USES OUR CATALOGUE to take orders from this class of people for goods he does not carry in stock. If he has customers in want of goods which he does not carry—

HARDWARE, VEHICLES, FURNITURE, BICYCLES, CLOTHING, SEWING MACHINES, AGRICULTURAL IMPLEMENTS,

and the thousand and one other items that he does not handle, the merchant refers to our catalogue, for he always finds the article his customer wants, always at the LOWEST possible price, takes the order from his customer at a legitimate profit, orders the goods from us and adds to his net earnings a profit heretofore unknown to him and holds his customer from going elsewhere to buy.

WHAT WE WILL DO FOR MERCHANTS.

AS MANY MERCHANTS, ORDERING GOODS FROM US that ordinarily carry our name plate or trade mark, express a desire to have the goods shipped with our name or trade mark removed, we have arranged in supplying merchants with bicycles, vehicles, stoves, agricultural implements, and in fact, all such goods as bear names, where possible, to ship these goods

WITHOUT OUR NAME OR NAME PLATES OR TRADE MARK.

IN BICYCLES, SEWING MACHINES, STOVES AND MUSICAL INSTRUMENTS OUR PRICES, QUALITY FOR QUALITY, are so very much below the prices quoted by any manufacturer or jobber that our trade from dealers in these lines everywhere has grown to such proportions that there is hardly a city in which some of our goods in these lines will not be found in the stores of one or more of the most progressive dealers of such town or city.

OUR TERMS OF SALE AND SHIPMENT to merchants and dealers are exactly the same as to the consumer; that is, either cash in full with order or C. O. D., subject to examination, upon receipt of our required deposit.

OUR ONLY INDUCEMENT TO MERCHANTS IS QUALITY, LOW PRICE AND OUR ABILITY TO SUPPLY ANYTHING a customer may want either in or out of the merchant's stock, and on the basis of more value for the money than you can possibly get elsewhere. We appeal to the intelligent, careful buyer, the progressive merchant in every line in every state and territory, and invite the careful perusal of this catalogue for the selecting of such goods as he may carry in his regular stock, and for the taking of orders from all his customers for everything they use, not to be found in his regular stock.

OUR BANKING DEPARTMENT.

FOR THE BENEFIT of our customers who wish to deposit money for the purpose of savings and to check against the account when ordering goods, we have a thoroughly organized bank, conducted on the same lines as the best banks and saving institutions in this and other large cities, and in this Banking Department we receive deposits of any amount not under $5.00 and not more than $1,000, and to our customers who wish to avail themselves of the privileges of our Banking Department, we allow

FIVE PER CENT PER ANNUM ON ALL MONEY IN OUR HANDS.

For full information pertaining to the privileges of our Banking Department, how to deposit money, check against it, etc., etc., address us in care of Banking Department.

CHICAGO,

IF NECESSARY TO REPLY, PLEASE STATE THAT
THIS LETTER WAS WRITTEN BY

SHOULD YOU WRITE US CONCERNING A SHIPMENT MADE, BE SURE TO GIVE INVOICE NUMBER.

KIND FRIEND:--
        This catalogue which we have the pleasure of mailing you
is good for one year from date. Please preserve this catalogue
until this month next year, and then write us enclosing 15 cents
to pay part of the postage for catalogue No. 111, which we will be
pleased to mail you at that time.
        For the convenience of our customers, and with a view to
an economy that will help to maintain lower prices, our general
catalogue will be issued once a year instead of twice as we have
done in the past. Please be careful to preserve this book for it
will not be necessary to write us for another catalogue for twelve
months, or until this month next year.
        We have endeavored to make this No. 110 catalogue so very
complete in every department, covering every kind of merchandise
for one year so thoroughly, that the expense of issuing two
catalogues a year, and the necessity of asking our customers six
months later to send postage for another copy, can be avoided.
        Hereafter our catalogue will be revised and issued once a
year, good for twelve months, so when you send 15 cents to pay part
of the postage it will be good to order from for twelve months.
        In this way we hope to be able to reach every one of our
customers with our latest catalogue, without putting them to the
inconvenience and expense of sending twice a year for our book.
At the same time we will save thousands of dollars that will go
direct to our customers in the way of lower prices and better
values.
        Endeavoring as we do to inaugurate the strictest kind of
economy in every branch of our business, that we may give our customers the greatest possible value for their money, we feel in
justice to them that it is necessary we abolish issuing a catalogue
twice a year.
        We feel to a great extent the money spent in issuing a
catalogue twice a year is unnecessary, and whether done by us, or
any other house, the expense must come out of the profit on the
goods sold. We believe you will agree with us that our catalogue
No. 110 is a great improvement over any catalogue previously issued
by us or any other house; that it is complete in every department,
                        (over)

and that, furthermore, for 12 months you can make up your order for everything you wish to buy, and by the inauguration of this line of economy, we hope to send you greater value than ever before, and in so doing we hope to merit not only your continued orders, but your influence among your friends and neighbors.

We would thank you very much if you would show this cata-logue to your friends, telling them it will be mailed to them upon receipt of 15 cents to help pay the 27 cents postage; that the book is issued only once a year; that by sending to us for the catalogue once a year, they will be supplied with the latest and most com-plete general merchandise catalogue from which to make up orders for everything they need the year round.

We shall always aim to make the ordering of goods from us pleasant as well as profitable to the purchaser. Our army of em-ployes are instructed to handle every order and letter with care, in fact, to treat every customer at a distance just as they would like to be treated were they in the customer's place and the cus-tomer in theirs.

We try to make every transaction with us, no matter how small, so pleasant, profitable and altogether satisfactory to the buyer as to encourage continued patronage. Any customer ordering anything from us and not finding it entirely satisfactory, even though it be exactly as represented, is under all circumstances at liberty to return it to us and we will promptly refund the money paid for it, and bear the freight or express charges both ways.

Those who have dealt with us know our methods. To those who have not dealt with us, we refer them to their neighbors and friends who have, and as we have nearly two million customers in the United States, there are quite a number in every town and com-munity to whom we refer them. We also take pleasure in referring by permission to City National Bank and German National Bank of New York and to Metropolitan National Bank and Corn Exchange National Bank of Chicago.

With our most sincere thanks for past favors and solicit-ing your patronage in future, which we promise will always warrant every attention at our command, we are,

Yours very truly,

A3415

SEARS, ROEBUCK & CO. (Inc.)

PARAGRAPH A.

ABOUT OUR PRICES.

HOW WE CAN UNDERSELL ALL OTHER CONCERNS.

SECTION 1. BY REASON OF OUR ENORMOUS OUTPUT OF GOODS we are able to make contracts with representative manufacturers and importers for such large quantities of merchandise that we can secure the lowest possible prices, and in some lines our trade has been so large, as, for example, in vehicles, stoves, cloaks, tailoring, etc., that we have been able to equip our own factories and foundries, thus saving you even the manufacturer's profit; but whether the goods are manufactured by ourselves or bought direct in large quantities, we add the smallest percentage of profit possible to the actual cost to us, and on this economic, one small profit plan, direct from manufacturer to consumer, you can buy a large percentage of the merchandise we handle direct from us at less than your storekeeper at home can buy in quantities.

WE EMPLOY THE MOST COMPETENT BUYERS that money can obtain, men who are experts and have a life-long experience in their particular lines. Our established reputation gives our buyers inside track with all the largest manufacturers, thereby giving us the benefit of first choice in the markets. Manufacturers who are overstocked often come to us and offer their goods for a big discount for cash, knowing that we have a larger outlet for merchandise than any other concern. For this reason many articles in this catalogue are quoted at less money than the actual cost to produce. No matter how cheap we buy, we give our customers the benefit, for we feel that our bargains are our customers' bargains.

SECTION 2. WE BUY AND SELL FOR CASH, and having no bad debts, no traveling men's expenses, no expenses for collecting, securing the manufacturers' lowest spot cash prices, we can sell goods at a smaller margin of profit than any other business house could do and still exist.

WE MAKE NO REDUCTIONS IN OUR PRICES. To those who are inclined to write us for a reduction from the prices quoted in this catalogue, we wish to state that we cannot afford to make any reduction or concession, whether you order in large or small quantities. The price quoted on each and every article in this catalogue is as low as we can possibly make it, and it is out of the question to reduce these prices still further; and we earnestly believe a careful comparison of our prices with those of any other concern will convince you that we can furnish you better goods for less money than you can obtain from any other house in the United States.

IN THIS CATALOGUE you will find only such goods listed as we can save you money on, goods that can be delivered anywhere in the United States for less money than can be bought at your local dealer. The amount of money that we can save you over the prices you pay at home, varies from 15 to 50 per cent, according to the nature of the goods, but there is not an item quoted in this entire catalogue on which the saving is not worth taking into consideration, to say nothing of the fact that our goods are, as a rule, of a higher grade than those carried by the average storekeeper or catalogue house.

THE ILLUSTRATIONS AND DESCRIPTIONS IN THIS CATALOGUE can be depended upon. We aim to illustrate and describe every article with the strictest accuracy. Most all of the illustrations are made from photographs taken direct from the article. They are such as enable you to order intelligently; in fact, with our assortment, correct illustrations and accurate descriptions, you can order from this catalogue with the same ease, confidence and security as though you were personally in our store selecting the goods yourself.

PARAGRAPH B.

ABOUT OUR RELIABILITY.

WE ARE AUTHORIZED AND INCORPORATED under the laws of the State of Illinois, with a cash capital and surplus of over one million dollars paid in full. We refer by special permission to the Metropolitan National Bank and Corn Exchange National Bank of Chicago, the National City Bank and the German Exchange Bank of New York (see fac-simile copies of letters from these banks on page 10), to any commercial agency or to any express or railroad company, or any reliable business house or financial institution in Chicago. Should you write for information to any of the references given be sure to enclose a 2-cent stamp for reply. **Our customers are our best references.** As we have thousands of customers in every state and territory, you will no doubt find one of them a neighbor, who can explain to you how thoroughly we live up to all our representations and how carefully we watch the interests of our customers, and we take the most pleasure in referring to our thousands of satisfied customers.

OUR EMPLOYES ARE INSTRUCTED to treat every customer at a distance exactly as they would like to be treated were they in the customer's place and the customer in ours. If you favor us with your patronage we will do everything in our power to merit your trade, and no matter how small your order may be, it will receive the same prompt and careful attention as if it were ever so large. The courteous and careful attention we pay to our customers invites their continued patronage and we consider that a satisfied customer is the best advertisement a firm can have.

WE EMPLOY NO AGENTS. This catalogue is our sole and only representative. We have no agents, and anyone representing himself as such is a fraud. Our customers deal direct with us through this catalogue. Thus the farmer, miner mechanic, business man, in fact, anyone can send us his order and save all the profit the agent or local storekeeper would make.

THE POLICY OF OUR HOUSE. We hold it as the key note and the fundamental principle of this business that the consumer should not be called upon to pay more than one fair profit over and above the actual cost of any kind of merchandise. We contend that it is not legitimate and in accordance with modern business methods for the farmer, the clerk, the mechanic or the laborer, to pay one-half the price of any article in excessive profits, profits of the manufacturers, the jobber, the wholesaler and the retailer; to give out his hard earned money, won by honest toil, for something that adds nothing to the intrinsic value of the goods, but is only a useless expense caused by faulty business methods. The money received by the consumer for his labor is the actual value of his labor. The price of goods in the ordinary store is not the actual value of the goods but is the price on an inflated basis, a price made by an endless and excessive chain of profits. We believe it is therefore unjust and unreasonable for the consumer to exchange the money received for his labor, which is the true and actual value of his labor, for the goods he needs at the fictitious prices usually asked for such goods. It is an unfair plan.

FOR THESE REASONS and for these reasons alone, we commend this catalogue to the careful consideration of all buyers. If you think we are right in our belief that the consumer should not pay more than the actual cost of goods, with only enough added to cover the expense of conducting a business on the most economical plan, and to allow for one fair profit, we then solicit your patronage. If lower prices than any other concern' can quote are any inducement, then we say send us your orders. If a scrupulous and pains-taking honesty, if strictly correct representations, religious-like in their fidelity to truth, are worthy principles, then you need not hesitate to trust us. If "your money back for anything not satisfactory, transportation charges refunded also" is sufficient guarantee, then you can safely trade with us.

PARAGRAPH C.

TERMS.

SECTION 1. WE HAVE NO DISCOUNTS. We sell for cash only and the prices quoted in this catalogue are absolutely net, from which there is no discount whatever (see paragraph A, section 2), and our prices are alike to one and all.

SECTION 2. OUR TERMS OF SHIPMENT ARE LIBERAL. While most of our customers send cash in full with their orders, thus saving the small charge the express company always make for returning the money to us, a large portion of our merchandise can be shipped by express or freight C. O. D., subject to examination, when a sufficient amount of cash accompanies the order to cover the transportation charges both ways. In such cases, the amount sent with the order will be deducted from the full amount of the order and the balance you can pay upon receipt of goods. (For C. O. D. shipments see paragraph L.).

SECTION 3. IN ALL CASES transportation charges are paid by the customer.

PARAGRAPH D.

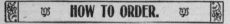

HOW TO ORDER.

Please refer to the sample order on page 11. This illustrates an order made out on one of our regular order blanks.

Always keep supplied with our order blanks as it is more convenient for you to make out your order on our regular order blank than in any other way. If out of them at any time, drop us a postal card and we will be pleased to send you some. Fill out our order blank as shown in the sample order on page 11.

Whether you write your order on our regular order blank or letter paper instead, be sure to observe the following instructions:

Always sign your full name (christian name and surname).

Write your name in full, clearly and distinctly.

Give your postoffice, county, and state, and your shipping point, if different from the postoffice.

Always give catalogue number, description and price of each article ordered.

Always try to mention the number or name of the catalogue or circular from which your order is taken, and be sure to give the size, color, weight and measurements.

We must have your correct size or measurements for such goods as shoes, clothing, ladies' ready-made dresses, cloaks, and the size and color of everything which has size and color.

Be sure to enclose your money with your order and state plainly in your order how much money you enclose and in what form. Sending us money in one envelope and your order in another causes delay and confusion in our office, as they become separated in the mails. For instructions on how to send money see paragraph E.

Be sure you have followed our rules carefully about enclosing the proper amount of money with the order, including enough to pay postage if sent by mail, and insurance fee if sent by insured mail.

Be sure your name and address is written plainly and in full, that your shipping directions are plainly stated, that the exact amount of money enclosed is plainly stated, that you have given us catalogue number, price, description, correct size and measurements and you will seldom if ever have any delay or inconvenience. By carefully observing these rules you will avoid errors and loss of time by our having to write you for further information.

AFTER WRITING AN ORDER, please compare it with these rules, check it over closely and see if you have written your order correctly.

IF YOU WISH TO REFER TO ANY MATTER not concerning the order be sure to write it on a separate sheet. Do not write about it on your order sheet, though you may enclose it in the same envelope with your order. Our orders and letters are handled in separate and distinct departments, and we ask you therefore please do not fail to observe this rule.

Always try to write remarks concerning your order on the same sheet with the order. This will prevent the possibility of such remarks or instructions being separated from the order, Should you have occasion to write us concerning an order which you have already sent us, do not fail to mention the date on which your letter was mailed, also state the nature and value of your remittance and the name and address as given in your order. This information will enable us to promptly locate the matter you refer to.

PARAGRAPH E.

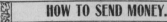

HOW TO SEND MONEY.

REMIT BY POSTOFFICE MONEY ORDER, express money order, bank draft, cash or stamps. We do not accept revenue stamps, foreign stamps and due stamps, as they are of no value to us. Do not send them. Postage stamps will be accepted in any amount as an accommodation to our customers.

WE RECOMMEND THE EXPRESS MONEY ORDER SYSTEM, because it is inexpensive, of less trouble, and is safe. Besides this, if the money order should get lost or miscarry, your loss will be made good by the express company.

DO NOT UNDER ANY CIRCUMSTANCES send money or stamps in a letter except by registered mail. If sent by open mail the letter may never reach us, and in such a case a great amount of trouble and inconvenience is caused, as well as the loss you sustain. If you prefer to remit by registered mail we advise the use of two envelopes, one inside of the other, and the outer one carefully and securely sealed. Do not send gold or silver coin that is defaced, as light-weight coins are worth no more than bullion and bullion is less than the face value of the coin.

TO INSURE SAFETY always register a letter containing money. Be sure to state in your order plainly how much cash you inclose and in what form. You need not be afraid of sending too much, as we always refund when too much money is sent.

PARAGRAPH F.

METHODS OF SHIPMENT.

We can ship goods by mail (see paragraph G about mail shipments), by express (see paragraph H about express shipments), by freight (see paragraph K about freight shipments), C. O. D. shipments by freight or express (see paragraph L). If left to our judgment we will ship goods in the manner which will be the least expense to our customers.

PARAGRAPH G.

MAIL SHIPMENTS.

The mail service affords a convenient method for the transportation of merchandise of small weight and considerable value to points that are distant from express or railroad offices. We require cash in advance with all orders to be shipped by mail and sufficient money, extra to pay postage and insurance or registration, when same is desired. There are three methods of shipping goods by mail.

SECTION 1. OPEN MAIL, which is so called because only the regular amount of postage, according to the classification of goods, is paid and the customer must assume all risk.

SECTION 2. INSURED MAIL. This we consider the best and safest method of shipping by mail. The following is the rate, in addition to the regular postage. For a package valued at $5.00 or under, 5 cents each. For a package valued at $10.00 or under, 10 cents each. For each additional $5.00 in value, 5 cents extra. In case of loss, we duplicate the shipment on receipt of affidavit that goods were not received. We advise insuring everything of value. Insurance is usually less than the cost of registering. If you want your mail package insured be sure to write "insure" in your order, and in addition to your remittance for the order be sure to add enough money to pay postage and insurance fee. To secure adjustment it is necessary to make prompt notification of the failure to receive package.

SECTION 3. REGISTERED MAIL, so called because in such cases the postoffice authorities keep a record of the transaction and are thus enabled to trace your shipment. The amount required to register a package is 8 cents in addition to the regular postage.

A PACKAGE SHIPPED BY MAIL CANNOT EXCEED 4 POUNDS, but any number of packages may be sent at one time, each weighing four pounds or less. If you live at a great distance from the express office, it might be more convenient to send an order by mail in two packages, each weighing four pounds. **One book can be sent by mail, no matter what its weight,** the rate is ½-cent per ounce.

THE RATE ON MERCHANDISE BY MAIL IS 1 CENT PER OUNCE, on books and printed matter, ½-cent per ounce, and you should allow, in addition to the weight of an article, from one to five ounces for packing material, according to size of package shipped. So far as possible we have given the packed weight under each description.

IF YOU ARE NOT SURE AS TO THE WEIGHT OF THE ARTICLE, be sure to enclose enough money for postage; if you send too much we will refund balance.

EXPLOSIVES, POISONOUS OR INFLAMMABLE ARTICLES cannot be mailed under any circumstances whatever.

Liquids over 4 ounces cannot be sent by mail.

SECTION 4. PROFITABLE MAIL SHIPMENTS. ARTICLES SUCH AS WATCHES, JEWELRY and other valuable merchandise of light weight, make profitable mail shipments. In all cases where other goods are not ordered at the same time, we advise that such articles can be sent by mail economically.

CERTAIN MEDIUM PRICED GOODS, which, being weighty, cost considerable postage for transportation, should, if possible be ordered in connection with other needed articles sufficient to make up express or freight shipment, thus reducing the transportation charges to one-quarter or one-eighth of the postage rate and effecting a far greater saving for you.

WITH THE EXCEPTION OF ARTICLES OF SMALL WEIGHT and of some value, sending goods by mail is by far the most expensive means of transportation, but even in cases where the postage may seem out of proportion to the value of the goods, the cost of the goods with the postage added is usually less than if purchased at the local dealer's and frequently the article wanted is not handled by them at all, while our immense stock of merchandise will supply your demands. **PARAGRAPH H.**

EXPRESS SHIPMENTS.

HOW TO FIGURE EXPRESS CHARGES, SEE PAGES 5 TO 10.

SHIPPING GOODS BY EXPRESS is an absolutely safe method of transportation and offers the advantages of quick service. It is the most profitable method of shipping goods when the weight is less than 20 pounds. Frequently a customer is in a hurry for certain goods and is willing to pay the extra cost of express charges over freight, the money we save him making it profitable on such shipments instead of buying the goods at home.

IF YOU HAVE NO AGENT at your station, all C. O. D., and express shipments will be carried to the nearest town where there is an agent. If there is no agent at your station always state in your order at what station you prefer to receive your goods.

A RECOMMENDATION THAT WILL SAVE YOU MONEY. If you live at a far distant point and wish to order some article of merchandise which would weigh about 20 pounds and amount to $6.00 or less, on which the express charges would be from $1.25 to $2.75, and you require nothing further from our catalogue at the time, show the book to your friends, let them add articles they may be in need of and the shipment can go by freight at about the same cost per 100 pounds as by express for 20 pounds, your proportion of the transportation charges being then about 60 cents

PARAGRAPH K.

FREIGHT SHIPMENTS.

FOR FREIGHT CLASSIFICATION AND FREIGHT RATES, SEE PAGES 5 to 10. Heavy, bulky merchandise, such as agricultural implements, household goods, furniture, groceries, hardware, etc., can be shipped most profitably by freight. When a shipment weighs 100 pounds or more, the railroad companies will charge only for the actual number of pounds.

HOW TO SAVE MONEY ON FREIGHT SHIPMENTS Railroad companies usually charge no more for 100 pounds than they do for 20 pounds. While the extremely low prices at which we sell our merchandise would make even an small order by freight profitable, as you would certainly be getting the goods cheaper than you could possibly buy them through your local dealer, at the same time it would be a considerable saving of money if you could make up a larger order, either of your own wants or club together with your neighbors, as the freight charges will amount to comparatively very little more. The saving that may be effected by anticipating your wants and sending one large order instead of five or six smaller orders at different times is quite an item, and therefore should be taken into consideration by our customers.

YOU MUST PAY THE FREIGHT OR EXPRESS CHARGES, but it will amount to very little as compared with what you will save in price.

IF YOU HAVE NO AGENT AT YOUR SHIPPING POINT, we cannot ship C. O. D. and freight charges must be prepaid. In such cases, cash in full must accompany order, and in addition a sufficient amount to cover transportation charges. If you send more than actual amount required we will immediately refund the difference. If you have an agent at your station it is not necessary to prepay charges, as they are the same whether paid by you or by us, as our system for checking rates insures for our customers almost absolute correctness in transportation charges.

OVERCHARGES IN TRANSPORTATION. Whenever a customer suspects an overcharge on the part of the transportation company, we will be pleased to give same our most prompt and careful attention in his behalf, if he will send us the expense bill received from the agent, after he has paid the charges. Complaints for overcharges are very few, as our system of checking the rates on freight and express shipments, insures for our customers almost absolute correctness in transportation charges.

PARAGRAPH L.

C. O. D. SHIPMENTS.

SECTION 1. C. O. D. MEANS COLLECT ON DELIVERY, that is, the goods to be paid for when received at your station. Much of our merchandise can be shipped C. O. D., by express or freight, when a sufficient amount of deposit is sent with the order to cover the transportation charges both ways, or even a smaller deposit, only as an evidence of good faith on the part of the customer. The amount of this deposit will be deducted from our invoice and the balance of the amount will be collected at your station. The express company also makes a small charge on C. O. D. shipments for returning the money to us.

SECTION 2. ORDERS FOR LESS THAN $2.00 CANNOT BE SHIPPED C. O. D. because it would not be profitable for the customer to have goods of less than that value shipped C. O. D., and pay the return charges on the money. We suggest, therefore, that you always send cash in full with small orders as the saving to you will be greater than if sent C. O. D.

SECTION 3. IF YOU HAVE NO AGENT AT YOUR SHIPPING POINT, or if you are located in a town reached only by a boat line, we cannot ship C. O. D. In such cases, cash in full must accompany

see paragraph E

the order, and in addition a sufficient amount to cover the transportation charges. You run no risk by sending too much money, as we always refund any balance in the customer's favor. When shipping goods by express C. O. D., we collect the balance through the express company. When shipping goods by freight C. O. D., we collect the balance through your bank or express agent, as you may request. In all cases we will advise you when the shipment is made, and if by freight, where the freight receipt is sent. Call there, pay the amount of the C. O. D. and collection charges and you will receive the freight receipt; then present this freight receipt to your railroad agent, who will deliver the goods to you upon payment of the transportation charges.

SECTION 4. IF YOU LIVE IN ANY OF THE FOLLOWING STATES, a cash deposit sufficient to cover the transportation charges both ways must accompany your order for a C. O. D. shipment. Arizona, Florida, Louisiana, Nevada, Texas, California, Idaho, Montana, Oregon, Utah, Wyoming, New Mexico and Washington.

SECTION 5. THE FOLLOWING GOODS WE DO NOT SHIP C. O. D. UNDER ANY CIRCUMSTANCES: Powder, etc , seines and fish nets, barbed wire, nails, rubber belting, tents, window glass, steel shafts, pulleys, etc., all kinds of belting, buggy tops, cushions, full backs, etc , when made of a special material or in extra sizes. Goods made to special order, such as engraved jewelry, extra large size suits, etc.

BE SURE TO SEND ENOUGH MONEY. You lose nothing by sending too much, for the amount you send will be credited on your bill, and if you should not send enough we will be obliged to hold the shipment and write for additional cash deposit. Most of our customers prefer to send cash in full with the order instead of having the goods shipped C. O. D., for the following reasons:

YOU SAVE THE RETURN CHARGES ON THE MONEY of 15 to 40 cents, which all transportation companies ask on C. O. D. shipments, you are not bothered with obtaining permission to examine the goods at destination or with waiting for a freight shipment until the bill of lading with draft has been sent to the express office or bank for collection. You run no risk in sending cash in full with your order, for if at any time you receive goods that are not satisfactory, they may be returned to us at our expense and we will immediately refund your money.

PARAGRAPH M.

ABOUT UNPROFITABLE SHIPMENTS

WE FREQUENTLY RECEIVE ORDERS which we term "unprofitable" shipments. For example: A party living far distant may order a dollar's worth of sugar to go by express. The express charges would equal the cost of the sugar. We occasionally get an order for heavy hardware, the order amounting to perhaps less than $5.00. The goods weigh 100 pounds. We are asked to ship them by express. This is usually an "unprofitable" shipment An order for a single pair of heavy cheap boots to go a great distance by express, or for very bulky woodenware or furniture or other merchandise, might be what we term an "unprofitable" shipment.

WE WOULD ADVISE OUR CUSTOMERS to study the freight and express rates as given on the following pages, for we do not wish you to send us a dollar for anything unless we can save you money on the purchase.

ORDERS THAT WOULD BE UNPROFITABLE to ship by mail or express may be very profitable when sent by freight, but as 100 pounds is usually carried by freight for the same charge as 10 pounds, by adding other merchandise to your order, either for yourself or by getting your neighbors to join you in making up a large order, you can make the shipment very profitable.

PARAGRAPH O.

CLUB ORDERS.

TO EQUALIZE OR REDUCE THE COST OF TRANSPORTATION, we advise the sending of club orders. Anyone can get up a club. Simply have your neighbors or friends send their orders in with yours and

advise us to ship all to one person by freight. If each customer writes their order under their own name, it will be a very easy matter for us to keep each one's goods separate, and the freight charges will be next to nothing when shared by several persons.

IF YOU LIVE AT A FAR DISTANT POINT and wish to order some article or articles of merchandise, which together, would weigh about 20 pounds, the value of which may be from $1.25 to $2.75, and there is nothing further in our catalogue that you require at the time, show this catalogue to your friends. Let your friends add 20, 30 or 40 pounds, even 50 or 75 pounds of goods, then the goods can go by freight at about the same rate as the express charges.

PARAGRAPH P.

HOW TO RETURN GOODS.

BEFORE RETURNING THE GOODS to us in any manner, we would ask that you communicate with us in regard to them as we are frequently able to adjust matters in a very satisfactory manner to the customer and avoid the delay occasioned by return of goods.

INVOICE NUMBER. Be sure to mention your invoice number when returning goods.

NEVER RETURN GOODS BY EXPRESS if the weight is more than 25 pounds, as it is cheaper to send heavy packages by freight. When you return goods by express or freight be sure to enclose in the package your letter of instructions and particulars. Don't forget we must always have your invoice number. Never write us about a shipment and omit the invoice number. Don't forget that a letter containing full instructions should be in all express and freight shipments returned. Don't forget we must have your full name and address, exactly as given in the original shipment, in order to properly adjust any matter pertaining to an order returned.

WHEN RETURNING A PACKAGE BY MAIL, write your name, address and invoice number plainly in the upper left hand corner, providing you do not have one of the labels which we furnish when we know goods are to be returned. Send us by separate mail the particulars and instructions.

DO NOT ENCLOSE WRITTEN MATTER of any kind in mail packages, as by so doing you are liable to a fine of $10.00 and double letter rate postage.

THE UNITED STATES POSTAL LAWS AND REGULATIONS require that all packages of merchandise sent in the mails must be wrapped or enveloped in such a manner that their contents may be readily examined by the postmaster without destroying the wrapper. Never seal packages returned by mail, but tie them securely with twine.

DO NOT FAIL TO REGISTER MAIL PACKAGES WORTH $2.00 OR MORE. Merchandise is sometimes lost when sent by open mail. A package can be registered for 8 cents and if necessary can be traced. Do not enclose money with merchandise returned by mail.

DELAYED SHIPMENTS. Always consider the length of time it takes for your order to reach us and for the freight or express company to haul it to your town, allowing us from twenty-four to forty-eight hours to fill the order. You may never have occasion to complain of any delay in transit; but if you should, do not fail to mention the date on which you mailed your order, the name and address as given in the original order, the value and nature of the cash you sent, and, if possible, the invoice number.

ABOUT MISTAKES. If we make a mistake in filling your order, kindly give us a chance to correct it. We try to fill every order absolutely correct; but errors sometimes creep in. They do in all business houses. You will always find us willing to correct ours. Do not fail to write us in case of an error, otherwise we may never know of it.

CHANGE OF ADDRESS. We would kindly request our customers to immediately advise us concerning any change of address, as we keep our records according to states and towns, and should you order from one town and then write from another, we would be compelled to send for further information before we could adjust the matter in question.

This is an Exact Copy of an Order Written on Our Regular Order Blank.

A CAREFUL STUDY OF EACH POINT WILL AID YOU IN MAKING UP YOUR OWN ORDER

A2929
ORDER BLANK OF SEARS ROEBUCK AND CO.

78-96 FULTON ST.
73-87 N. DESPLAINES ST.
13-31 WAYMAN ST.
CHICAGO, ILL.

HOW TO ORDER.

NOTICE TO CUSTOMERS. { Don't fail to read the instructions on this blank before ordering, as a careful observance of our rules will greatly aid us in filling your orders in a satisfactory manner. AND BE SURE TO MENTION, IN SPACE PROVIDED BELOW, THE NUMBER OF CATALOGUE, CIRCULAR, OR NAME OF PAPER FROM WHICH YOU SELECT YOUR GOODS.

PLEASE SEND TO   Feb 3   190 L   (Date of this order.)

NAME   F. M. Horton
(Write very plainly and always sign your full christian name.)

POSTOFFICE   Ruggles

STREET AND NUMBER

COUNTY   Ashland   STATE   Ohio

BELOW GIVE SHIPPING POINT IF DIFFERENT FROM POSTOFFICE.

NAME
(Give name here only when shipment is to be made to another party. If to yourself, leave name blank.)

SHIPPING POINT   New London

COUNTY   Huron   STATE   Ohio

RAILROAD CO.   C. C. & S. L.   EXPRESS CO.

If you will leave method of shipment to our judgment we will ship to best advantage and by cheapest way possible. However if you prefer to state how you want goods shipped put an X in proper space below. READ OUR RULES on pages 1 to 5 of our large catalogue.

FREIGHT   X
EXPRESS
SPEC'L PREPAID EXPRESS
INSURED MAIL
REGISTERED MAIL

TO INSURE SAFETY, ALWAYS REGISTER A LETTER CONTAINING CURRENCY.

Be sure to state how much cash you enclose and in what form, by filling in proper spaces below.

ENCLOSED FIND	DOLLARS	CENTS
Draft or Check		
Postoffice Order	19	00
Express Money Order		
S. R. & Co.'s Check		
S. R. & Co.'s Credit Draft		
Currency		
Postage Stamps		17
TOTAL	19	17

Is there a Freight Agent at Your Shipping Point? Yes (State Yes or No) If not, you must send cash in full to pay for order and also send such freight or express prepay freight charges. WHEN TOO MUCH MONEY IS SENT, WE ALWAYS REFUND THE BALANCE.

ORDERS TO BE SENT BY MAIL MUST BE ACCOMPANIED BY CASH IN FULL, WITH EXTRA FOR POSTAGE AND INSURANCE.

AFTER WRITING YOUR ORDER, CHECK IT OVER CLOSELY TO SEE THAT YOU HAVE WRITTEN DOWN CORRECT CATALOGUE NUMBERS, QUANTITIES, NAME OF ARTICLES WANTED AND CORRECT PRICES.

WHEN ORDERING GOODS, ALWAYS GIVE SIZE, COLORS, ETC., TO AVOID ERRORS AND LOSS OF TIME.

OUR STOCK IS ARRANGED IN THE SAME ORDER AS OUR CATALOGUE QUOTATIONS. PATRONS WILL THEREFORE GREATLY FACILITATE THE HANDLING OF ORDERS BY TRYING, AS FAR AS POSSIBLE, TO ARRANGE THE ARTICLES ORDERED AS THEY ARE IN THE CATALOGUE, OR AT LEAST TO COLLECT ALL GOODS OF A CLASS TOGETHER.

THESE GOODS ARE SELECTED FROM CATALOGUE NUMBER OR NAME   110   CIRCULAR   PAPER

Number of article in Catalogue.	Quantity desired.	NAME OF ARTICLES WANTED	Sizes, Colors, etc.	Price of each, or per dozen Dollars	Cents	Extend totals here and then add this column. Dollars	Cents
49268	2	Mens Cassimere Overshirts	16½		75	1	50
50416	1	Pr Mens Suspenders	medium		25		25
5320	1	" " Gloves			58		58
65456	1	Now X L L Knife			40		40
67106	1	Socket Firmer Chisel	1 ¾ ins		34		34
77503	1	Dietz Side L't Lantern			60		60
99110	1	Burdick Drop Head Sewing Machine		15	50	15	50
						19	17

NOTE. IF ANY OF ABOVE GOODS ARE OUT OF STOCK MAY WE SUBSTITUTE? Yes

IF SO KINDLY MENTION SECOND AND THIRD CHOICE   Use your own judgement

SEE OTHER SIDE OF THIS ORDER BLANK FOR INSTRUCTIONS ON HOW TO TAKE MEASUREMENTS OF EVERY LINE OF WEARING APPAREL.

If You Do Not Use This Order Blank at Once, Preserve It for Future Use, AS WE CAN FILL ALL ORDERS better and quicker if written on our regular order blanks, and they are MORE CONVENIENT FOR YOU. We will be only too glad to send you a new supply when these are gone, if you will drop us a postal card, or will include them in your next order.

SEARS ROEBUCK & CO GROCERY DEPT

SEND FOR OUR FREE GROCERY PRICE LIST

WE ISSUE A GROCERY PRICE LIST EVERY TWO MONTHS WHICH WE WILL MAIL FREE REGULARLY TO ANYONE WHO WILL APPLY FOR IT.

PRICES OF GROCERIES are always fluctuating so rapidly, many articles advancing and declining from month to month, that we do not find it at all satisfactory to quote our complete line of groceries in our general catalogue which holds good for one year, but as all interested to write for our free Grocery Price List, which is completly revised and corrected in price up to the very hour, following the Chicago lowest wholesale prices. WE LIST HEREIN A FEW OF THE MOST STAPLE stayed price articles in groceries, which we invite you to include in making up your order for other merchandise. At the same time we urge you to write for our Free Grocery Price List.

TERMS. As a rule nearly all our customers send cash in full with their grocery orders, but when so desired we will ship groceries to any address by freight C. O. D., subject to examination, on receipt of a sufficient amount of cash with order to cover the freight charges both ways.

UNDERSTAND, we have only attempted in this big book to quote prices on a very few items, and our free Grocery Price List covers everything conceivable in groceries; a 32-page book containing about 600 illustrations and about 6,000 quotations.

READY MIXED HOUSE PAINT IS CARRIED IN OUR GROCERY DEPARTMENT, AND IF YOU ARE INTERESTED IN READY MIXED PAINTS WRITE FOR OUR FREE COLOR SAMPLE CARD. . . .

TEA.

Japan Siftings.

	5-lb. pkgs.	Per lb.
B 30 Best Grade	$0.21	$0.22
B 31 Best grade Japan dust	.20	.21

Sears, Roebuck & Co.'s Acme India Ceylon.

G 7 This is one of the very finest teas grown in Ceylon, a goods we can guarantee. 1 lb. pkgs........ $0.55

Japan Sun Dried Green Tea.

G 12 Extra choicest	$0.44	$0.46
G 13 Extra choice, selected leaf	.41	.43
G 14 Choice	.35	.37
G 15 Bargain	.32	.34

Japan Basket Fired Tea.

G 20 Extra choicest	$0.50	$0.52
G 21 Extra choice	.43	.45
G 22 Bargain	.32	.34

Gunpowder-Moyune.

G 39 Extra choice	$0.42	$0.44
G 41 Good grade	.33	.35
G 38 Extra choicest	.50	.52

Young Hyson Moyune.

G 53 Good grade	$0.32	$0.34
G 51 Extra choice	.40	.42
G 50 Extra choicest	.52	.54

Write for our free grocery price list. Our free color card of mixed paints will be mailed free on application.

Green Coffee.

	125-lb. sack, per lb.	Less than sack, per lb.
G 80 Rio, ordinary grade	$0.13	$0.13½
G 83 Selected Santos	.14	.15
G 87 Maracaibo, extra choice	.19	.20
G 92 Arabian Mocha (genuine), best	.21	.22

Roasted Coffee.

	10-lbs. and up. per lb.	per single lb.
G 110 Good roasted Santos and Rio mixed	$0.12	$0.13
G 108 Golden Rio	.18	.19
G 105 Mocha and Java blend	.20	.21
G 103 Old Government Java	.25	.26

Write for our free grocery price list. Our free color card of mixed paints will be mailed free on application.

Shredded Cocoanut.

	Each
G 180 Our Own Special High Grade, 1-pound package	$0.21
G 133 5-pound box, our high grade shredded cocoanut	.80

Write for our free grocery price list. Our free color card of mixed paints will be mailed free on application.

Doris Brand—Spices.

G 255 Black Pepper, per single pound, 17c; 6 pound boxes, per pound	$0.14
G 258 Cinnamon, per single pound, 25c; 6 pound boxes, per pound	.23
G 260 Ginger, per single pound, 16c; 6 pound boxes, per pound	.13
G 261 Allspice, per single pound, 16c; 6 pound boxes, per pound	.13
G 262 Cloves, per single pound, 16c; 6 pound boxes, per pound	.13

Write for our free grocery price list. Our free color card of mixed paints will be mailed free on application.

Dry Mustard.

G 289 Sears, Roebuck & Co.'s Best Dry Mustard, 1-pound can	$0.23

Prepared French Mustard.

G 298 French Mustard, per gallon jug	$0.35

Baking Powder.

	Per can
G 305 Baking Powder, 1-pound can	$0.10
G 310 Price's, 1-pound can	.42
G 312 Royal, 1-pound can	.42

Write for our free grocery price list. Our free color card of mixed paints will be mailed free on application.

Cream of Tartar.

G 322 Our Own High Grade, Strictly Pure, 1-pound can	$0.38

Write for our free grocery price list. Our free color card of mixed paints will be mailed free on application.

Doris' Double Strength Extracts.
Lemon.

	Doz. Bottle.	Bottle.
G 370 2-oz. panel bottle	$0.75	$0.07
	4-oz. panel bottle	1.50	.14
	8-oz. panel bottle	3.00	.28
	16-oz. panel bottle	6.00	.52

Vanilla.

	Doz.	Bottle.
G 380 2-oz. panel bottle	$0.85	$0.08
	4-oz. panel bottle	1.70	.15
	8-oz. panel bottle	3.40	.30
	16-oz. panel bottle	6.75	.58

Dried Fruits.

G 455 Raisins, loose Muscatels, per pound, 8c; in 50-pound boxes, per pound	$0.07½
G 452 Raisins, California, London Layers, very fine, per lb., 12c; per box of 20 lbs.	2.15
G 457 Currants, English crop, per pound	.07½
G 459 California Dried Prunes, extra fine quality, per lb	.08½
G 481 California French Prunes, medium size, very fine, per pound	.05½
G 452 California Cherry or Ruby Prunes, special price for 20 pounds	1.45

DRIED FRUITS—Continued.

G 464 Fine California Evaporated Apples, our special price for 20-pound box	$1.90
G 468 California Pears, our special price for 20-pound box	2.50
G 470 California Peaches, our special price per 20-pound box	2.00
G 471 California Apricots, our special price per 20-pound box	2.90
G 476 California Figs, good size baskets, per basket	.38
G 478 California Figs, per 10-pound box, $1.00; per single pound	.12

Write for our free grocery price list. Our free color card of mixed paints will be mailed free on application.

Canned Fruits.

All 2½-pound cans unless otherwise specified.

	Doz.	Can
G 490 Apricots, heavy syrup	$1.95	$0.18
G 494 Crawford Peaches	2.25	.20
G 499 White Cherries	2.50	.23
G 501 Green Gage Plums	1.55	.14
G 504 Bartlett's Pears	2.50	.23

The following numbers are in 2-pound cans only unless otherwise specified.

	Doz.	Can
G 516 Blackberries, preserved	$1.20	$0.12
G 518 Strawberries	1.05	.10
G 520 Red Cherries	1.10	.10
G 522 Gooseberries	1.00	.10
G 525 Pineapple	2.90	.9c
G 531 Black Raspberries	1.40	.13
G 534 Apples, 3-lb. cans	.95	.09
G 537 Peaches, 3-lb. cans, pie goods	1.50	.18

Write for our free grocery price list. Our free color card of mixed paints will be mailed free on application.

Canned Vegetables.

	Doz.	Can
G 635 Marrowfat Peas	$1.15	$0.11
G 638 Succotash	1.10	.10
G 639 White Wax Beans	1.10	.10
G 646 Lima Beans	1.20	.11
G 651 Corn	.85	.08
G 656 Tomatoes, 3-pound cans	.90	.09
G 658 Mushrooms, imported	2.75	.34

Write for our free grocery price list. Our free color card of mixed paints will be mailed free on application.

Salted Fish.

G 665 Spiced Herring, per 10-pound pail	$0.80
G 670 Holland Herring, per keg	.80
G 672 Smoked Herring, per box	.17½
G 682 Codfish, per pound	.06½
G 688 Boneless Codfish, per pound	.07
G 703 White Fish, per 10-pound pail	.97
G 708 Trout, per 10-pound pail	.77
G 712 Herring, per 10-pound pail	.48
G 717 Mackerel, per 10-pound pail	1.20

Write for our free grocery price list. Our free color card of mixed paints will be mailed free on

Canned Fish.

	Per doz.	Per can.
G 736 Cove Oysters, 10-ounce cans.	$1.80	$0.16
G 738 Lobsters, extra quality, 5-ounce can.	3.35	.29
G 740 Salmon, 1-pound can, extra fine.	1.40	.13
G 749 Salmon, good quality, 1-pound can.	1.20	.11
G 776 Sardines, domestic.	.85	.08

Write for our free grocery price list.
Our free color card of mixed paints will be mailed free on application.

Meats.

Everything in preserved meats will be found in our free grocery price list, where we follow the lowest market quotations.

Table Sauces.

	Per doz.	Each
G 933 Sears, Roebuck & Co.'s quart bottle Catsup.	$2.00	$0.20
G 936 Our High Grade Catsup in gallon jugs, per jug.		.75
G 980 Pepper Sauce, red or green, small bottle.	.65	.06
G 985 Olives, Extra Queen, 10-ounce bottle.	1.85	.18
G 999 Olive Oil, domestic, 2-ounce bottle.		.05

Write for our free grocery price list.
Our free color card of mixed paints will be mailed free on application.
Pickles of all kinds will be found in our free price list.

Vinegar.

10-gallon kegs, 40, 45, 50 and 60 grain, per gallon, 15, 16, 17 and 18 cents, according to quality. This is our own special apple juice cider vinegar.
Our own special White Wine Distilled Vinegar, 40, 45 and 60 grain at 15, 16, 17 and 18 cents, according to quality.
Write for our free grocery price list.
Our free color card of mixed paints will be mailed free on application.

Salt.

We quote all grades of barrel and table salt in our free grocery price list, following the lowest wholesale market prices.

Flour.

We quote all the standard grades of spring and winter wheat flour, meals, breakfast foods, etc.
Write for our free grocery price list.
Our free color card of mixed paints will be mailed free on application.

Rice.

	25-lb. sack.	Per lb.
G 1300 Japan Prime.	$1.10	$0.05
G 1303 Louisiana Fancy Head.	1.60	.07

Write for our free grocery price list.
Our free color card of mixed paints will be mailed free on application.

Closs Starch.

		Each.
G 1350 Good Laundry Starch, in bulk, in 50-pound box.		$1.70
G 1351 Extra Quality Gloss, in bulk, in 6-pound box.		.33
G 1362 Corn Starch, superior grade, 1-pound package.		.04

Write for our free grocery price list.
Our free color card of mixed paints will be mailed free on application.

Sugar.

We follow the very latest market quotations on sugar in our free grocery list, saving you all the profit your storekeeper would make and more.

Syrup.

	3½-gal. kit
G 1400 Sugar Loaf Syrup.	$0.75
G 1402 Fine Snowdrop Drips.	.70
G 1405 Revere Syrup.	1.00
G 1412 Blackstrap Molasses.	.60
G 1414 New Orleans Molasses.	.95
G 1416 New Orleans Finest Golden.	1.25

Write for our free grocery price list.
Our free color card of mixed paints will be mailed free on application.

Crackers.

	Each
G 1460 20-pound box of Our Own High Grade Crackers in either Soda, Butter or Oyster, as desired, wooden box.	$0.99
G 1461 Soda Crackers, extra fine, 3-pound package.	.19
G 1464 Oyster Crackers, extra fine, 3-pound package.	.20
G 1465 Butter Crackers, extra fine, 4-pound package.	.21
G 1466 Fancy Milk Crackers, 1-pound package.	.09
G 1468 Fancy Graham Biscuit, 1-pound package.	.09
G 1471 Fancy Oatmeal Wafers, 1-pound package.	.13
G 1475 Fancy Fluted Vanilla Cakes, 28-pound wood boxes only, per pound.	.09
G 1476 Fancy Gingersnaps, 1-pound pkge.	.09
G 1479 Grandma's Cookies, 23-pound wood boxes only, per pound.	.09
G 1482 Sweet Creams, 23-pound wood boxes only, per pound.	.09
G 1496 Fancy Sugar Molasses Cakes, 34-pound wood boxes only, per pound.	.09

Write for our free grocery price list.
Our free color card of mixed paints will be mailed free on application.

Candy Department.

In our free grocery price list we quote almost everything conceivable in confectionery at the lowest Chicago wholesale prices.

Soap.

G 1751 Our Own High Grade Family Laundry Soap, per box of 100 bars, 75 lbs. net.	$2.95
G 1756 Our High Grade Mottled German Family Laundry Soap, per box of 60 one-pound bars, 60-pound box.	2.26
G 1760 Our own White Floating Soap, per single 6-ounce cake.	3½
G 1766 Santa Claus Soap, per box of 100 bars.	3.10
G 1768 Proctor & Gamble's Mottled German Soap, per box of 60 one-pound bars.	2.35
G 1769 Proctor & Gamble's Lenox Laundry Soap, per box of 100 15-ounce bars.	3.10
G 1772 Babbitt's Best Laundry Soap, per box of 100 bars.	3.75
G 1788 White Domestic Castile Soap, per lb.	.09
G 1805 Buttermilk Glycerine Soap, per box of 3 cakes.	.12
G 1809 Fancy Castile Soap, per box of 12 cakes.	.45
G 1817 Cocoanut Oil Soap, per box of 12 cakes.	.26

For everything in laundry and toilet soaps, completely illustrated, described and quoted at lowest Chicago wholesale prices, write for free grocery price list.

Matches.

G 1976 Telegraph Matches, 200 matches in each box, 24 boxes in a wooden caddy, making 4,800 matches. Price, per rack of 5 caddies.	$1.50
Per caddy.	.33

For other grades of matches and everything in scouring compounds, candles, seeds, polish, brooms, brushes, etc., write for our free grocery price list.

Miscellaneous.

G 1881 Our own high grade bluing, per quart bottle.	9c
G 1890 Our own high grade Ammonia, per quart bottle.	6c
G 2079 Axle Grease, our special high grade, full 10-lb. pail, (wooden pail).	35c

Chicken Food.

	100-lb.
G 2102 Mica Crystal Grits.	$0.75
G 2105 Cracked Bone.	1.95
G 2108 Ground Oyster Shells.	.55
G 2118 Beef Scraps.	1.80
G 2119 Ground Beef Meal.	1.96
G 2121 Raw Bone Meal.	2.05

For everything in stock foods, cigars, tobacco, oils, everything conceivable in groceries, completely illustrated, fully described and the quotations kept up-to-date at Chicago's lowest wholesale prices.
Write for our free grocery price list.

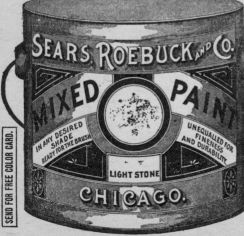

DRUG DEPARTMENT.

OUR PRESCRIPTION DEPARTMENT. OUR PRESCRIPTION DEPARTMENT IS UNDER THE DIRECT CHARGE OF ONE OF THE MOST ABLE CHEMISTS AND PHARMACISTS IN THIS COUNTRY. Every prescription is compounded with the greatest care, only the very best drugs are used and yet we are able to save our customers in nearly all cases more than one-half in price. If you will send your doctor's prescription or any other prescription to us, you can rest assured it will be given professional care. There will not be any substitutions such as local druggists are compelled to make for want of certain drugs, it will be compounded in the most scientific manner and returned to you immediately at a saving in price on an average of more than one-half.

ABOUT STANDARD PATENT REMEDIES. WE CARRY IN STOCK AT ALL TIMES almost every known patent remedy, every remedy of merit, every remedy that is now being or has been advertised to any extent, and our price to you is the lowest wholesale prices on such remedies. We can usually save you from 25 to 50 per cent on any patent medicine of any kind. If there is a known remedy wanted and you do not find it in our catalogue, send your order to us. If it is a dollar article it will be perfectly safe for you to send 75 cents. If it is a 50 cent remedy, it will be perfectly safe for you to send 40 cents. Be sure and send enough. We will fill your order immediately and if you have overpaid us we will return the balance of the money with your order. It will pay you handsomely to order any patent remedies from us. You will be saving all the profit your druggist would make and more.

OUR OWN SPECIAL REMEDIES. IN THIS DEPARTMENT we have endeavored to show a very complete line of our own special remedies, remedies that we have had prepared from prescriptions furnished by the world's highest medical authority. They are prepared in our own laboratory from the very best material that can be obtained, they are to the best of our knowledge the best known remedies for the different ailments for which they are intended, they are prepared without regard to expense that our customers can get the very best that money can buy.

We are daily receiving testimonials from every state and territory telling us of the wonderful cures effected by our many special remedies.

OUR LIBERAL C. O. D. TERMS. SEND US $1.00 WITH YOUR ORDER for any goods from our drug department and the goods will be sent to you by freight or express C. O. D., subject to examination; you can examine them at your express office and if found perfectly satisfactory and exactly as represented, pay the express agent our price and charges less the $1.00 sent with order.

IF YOU WISH GOODS SENT BY MAIL, be sure to enclose enough extra for postage. Four ounce bottles of liquids and smaller sizes can be sent by mail postpaid when packed in our special box which is approved by the postal authorities, but you must remember to allow sufficient to cover postage. If you send too much we will immediately refund your money.

POISONOUS, INFLAMMABLE AND EXPLOSIVE MATERIALS CANNOT BE MAILED.

REGARDING SPIRITUOUS LIQUORS. WE DO NOT DEAL IN SPIRITUOUS LIQUORS OF ANY KIND. We do not believe in the traffic and we allow no liquors to go out of our house except as they are required in our laboratory for compounding remedies and in special cases where fine grade, chemically pure liquors are prescribed by physicians for medicinal purposes, or where we know they are ordered only for such kind. We make this statement for the reason that we are constantly receiving communications from liquor dealers and others for prices on various kinds of liquor. We want it understood not only that we do not deal in spirituous liquors but we are not in sympathy with the traffic.

Sure Cure for the Tobacco Habit.

Our Price, 40 Cents.
Retail Price, $1.00.

WE CURE YOU This is nature's own remedy, entirely harmless. It cures because it builds up and fortifies, rejuvenates the weak and unstrung nerves caused by over indulgence in this poisonous weed. It stops the craving for tobacco by supplying instead a healthy nerve tonic and strengthener; it does more, it eradicates the poisonous nicotine from the system which has accumulated from long continued use of tobacco. Nicotine is a virulent poison and the chief ingredient of tobacco. It is the cause of all the nervous troubles and general debility of smokers. Our sure cure will destroy the effects of this nicotine, chase it from the system and make weak men strong again, and impotent men gain weight and vigor, make the old feel young again. It satisfies the craving for tobacco, and its use brings great health, increasing the appetite for food, strengthens the stomach, enriches and purifies the blood, giving good general health. It is not a drug; it can be chewed the same as tobacco, or taken dissolved in coffee or hot water. It is not only a sure cure for the tobacco habit, but also one of the best tonics for sexual weakness ever made. Give it a trial and be convinced.

No. 5000 Per doz., $4.00; per small box................................. 40c
No. 5001 Per doz., 7.00; per large box.............................. 75c
If by mail, postage extra, per box, small, 2 cents; large, 4 cents.

Somone for Sweet Refreshing Sleep.

Our Price, 75 Cents.
Retail Price, $1.50.

A RELIABLE REMEDY FOR SLEEPLESSNESS. We ask any of our customers who may be troubled with insomnia, who cannot sleep at nights, to give this valuable remedy a trial. No matter from what cause the sleeplessness arises, a sound sleep will be procured by its use, and you will awake in the morning refreshed, strengthened and cheerful; no bad effects from its use. We guarantee it to contain no opium, morphine or poisonous narcotics of any kind whatever. It is a vegetable preparation composed of herbs soothing and healing to the entire system. It can be used in safety by the weakest and most delicate and is a boon to those of nervous dispositions. A single dose will strengthen and invigorate them and cause them to forget their troubles. Ladies troubled with nervous spells should always have a bottle at hand. A dose or two in time will save them many hours of agony and serious discomfort and often prevent total collapse of the nervous system. It has a marvelous effect on those afflicted with nervous prostration, acting like magic in restoring the nerves to their normal condition and causing a strong healthy feeling to prevail throughout the whole body. It quiets the nervous excitement and muscular trembling caused by the excessive use of liquor, and acts as an antidote to the liquor habit. Full directions accompany each bottle how to use it both for sleeplessness and nervous troubles.

No. 5004 Price per dozen, $8.00; per bottle................................. 75c
Cannot be sent by mail on account of weight.

YOU CAN ALWAYS BE SURE OF GETTING THE VERY LATEST STYLES IN CLOTHING when you select your SUIT from our elegant line of samples.

OUR SPECIAL SAMPLE BOOK, No. 5H, COSTS YOU NOTHING. It is mailed postpaid on application.

SEND FOR IT.

Our 50-Cent Liquor Habit Cure.

Every Man can be Permanently Cured of the Habit or Desire for Intoxicating Drink of any Kind.

WE GUARANTEE A COMPLETE CURE.

Our remedy is perfectly harmless, none of the bad effects produced by many so-called liquor cures so widely advertised. That drunkenness is a disease that can be cured by medicine, just the same as other diseases can, is a fact becoming well known. Thousands of cases have been cured by this medicine; in fact, its wonderful curative properties are now well known throughout the entire world. We bring this cure within the reach of everyone. It is now not necessary to go to an Institute for treatment; home treatment is just as successful. The impression has been cultivated by interested parties that cures could not be effected except by hypodermic injections, but nothing is more absurd. Any medicine taken into the stomach will be as effective as if used hypodermically. No medicine has had such a wonderful success in this age of progress as Our Liquor Habit Cure. It creates an appetite for food instead of liquor, it stimulates the whole system to healthy action, it quiets nervous excitement, vertigo, muscular trembling and all the dangerous effects of excessive use of liquor. It improves the appetite and digestion and regulates the bowels. It is, in fact, a perfect cure for the drink habit.

We urge everyone who have accustomed themselves to the excessive use of liquor, and who wish to stop the practice, to send for even a small box as a trial. We know our remedy will cure you. We are sure that after using a few doses you will feel the craving for liquor disappearing and a warm healthy glow spreading from the stomach over the whole system; you will have a desire for food instead of rot gut. This will be the commencement of the cure, and if you will follow it up faithfully for a few weeks it will effect a permanent cure. When you have used a small box we know you will send for 12 more boxes for $5.00, to thoroughly complete the cure.

No. 5009 Price per doz., $5.00; for small box containing 24 doses... $0.50
No. 5010 Price per doz., 9.00; for large box containing 48 doses... 1.00
12 small boxes, per $5.00; 12 large boxes, per $9.00 lot, will cure any case, no matter how severe.

If by mail, postage, extra, per box, small 2 cents; large 4 cents.

Cure for the Opium and Morphia Habit.

Our Price, 75 Cents.
Retail Price, $1.50.

WE HERE OFFER A PERFECTLY SAFE AND RELIABLE CURE to those addicted to the habit of using opium or morphia in any form or manner whatever. We guarantee this preparation to be absolutely harmless, to contain no poisonous narcotics. Can be taken freely without producing any of the deleterious effects on the system, such as are caused by the use of opium and morphia, immediately on taking a dose of this remedy a calming and soothing effect is produced. It acts as a tonic to the nerves; its use will completely destroy that terrible craving for morphine in those who are victims to the deadly habit of taking these poisonous drugs, and free them from their bondage, restoring their health and making them feel like living again. A dose can be taken whenever a craving for morphia or opium exists; it will act at first as a perfect substitute, rendering the patient independent of these poisonous drugs, and after continued use for a short period the nerves will become strong and the general health improved, so that the remedy can be taken at longer intervals and soon afterward discontinued, then the cure is complete.

No. 5014 Price per dozen, $8.00; per bottle................................. 75c
Cannot be sent by mail on account of weight.

Dr. Echols' Australian Auriclo.
A Newly Discovered Cure for Heart Trouble.

WONDER HEART CURE DR ECHOLS' AUSTRALIAN AURICLO PREPARED ONLY BY **SEARS, ROEBUCK & CO., INC. CHICAGO.**

Dropped Dead!

Attention! Every fourth person has a weak or diseased heart.

Our price, 50 cents. Retail price, $1.00.

It is surprising that this most vital portion of the human body should receive so little attention from medical writers and investigators. The duty of the heart is to keep every part of the human frame constantly supplied with the vital fluid called blood, and the moment it ceases to beat, death ensues. It is the hardest worked organ in the body; it works incessantly from the beginning to the end of life. Day and night, it labors without rest, performing such an enormous amount of work as to be almost beyond belief. With every pulsation it exerts a force equal to 50 pounds, which amounts to 3,600 pounds a minute, 216,000 pounds every hour, and the inconceivable number of 5,184,000 pounds in a single day. All this vast amount of labor must be done, and done well, every day; if not, your health will surely suffer in consequence of the least failure of the heart to properly perform its duties. The health of the heart is therefore exceedingly important, and weakness and disorder of this organ are more common than people are aware of. Shortness of breath, palpitation, pain in the chest, fainting spells, etc., are attributed by them in their ignorance to other causes, and even physicians frequently make the same mistake. Every one who reads the daily papers must observe how frequent the words "dropped dead" and "sudden death" occur. Scarcely a day passes without some prominent person being stricken down without warning while apparently in the best of health. We will enumerate a few of the more common symptoms of heart disease:

Shortness of breath, fluttering or palpitation, pain or tenderness in the left breast, side, or under the left shoulder blade between the shoulders, irregular or intermittent pulse, oppressed feeling in the chest, choking sensation in the throat, weak or hungry spells, sleeping on the side, especially the left, is often disagreeable, smothering or sinking spells, fainting spells always indicate a weak heart, difficult or unnatural breathing accompany bad cases, and often cause the patient to sit up in bed, swelling of the feet or ankles, this is a sure sign of heart disease, but not always present, dropsy, a large portion of cases come from heart disease, neuralgia in the chest, on the right or left side, sudden starting in sleep, morbid dreams.

Weak hearts are as common as weak stomachs, lungs or eyes. Every heart that flutters, palpitates, tires out easily, aches, etc., is weak or diseased, and treatment should not be postponed a single day, and there has never been found a remedy so effectual in healing, strengthening and restoring the heart as the newly discovered cure—Dr. Echols' Australian Auriclo. It is daily curing thousands in every stage of heart disease. No one can make a mistake in purchasing a box of this valuable remedy. It is worth its weight in gold a thousand times over. Remember that such simple ailments as cold hands and feet, spots before the eyes, hungry spells, etc., indicate a weak heart or a diseased one. People in their ignorance generally lay the blame elsewhere, and continue to suffer, whilst the heart grows worse and worse. Take a remedy in time and save much suffering, and remember how frequent you read the words "dropped dead" and "sudden death," the result of heart failure. The medicine is in the form of a tablet, can be sent by mail and carried in the pocket without inconvenience.

No. 5018 100 doses for 75c; 50 doses for............................50c

If by mail, postage extra, per box, 2 cents.

Dr. Allan's Asthma Cure.

Retail Price, $1.50. **Our Price $1.00.**

AN IMPORTED REMEDY which is having an immense sale in countries where Asthma prevails. Sears, Roebuck & Co. having received reports through their foreign agents of the wonderful effects of this remedy in relieving and curing Asthma, determined to secure it for the benefit of their customers who might be suffering from this terribly annoying complaint. Through influence and expenditure of money they were able to control the introduction of this valuable remedy to the citizens of the United States, and become sole agents for its sale in this country. Dr. Allan's Asthma Cure is for the instantaneous relief and permanent cure of all forms of Asthma, Phthisis, Hay Fever, Bronchitis, Croup and Nasal Catarrh. It is a scientific combination of oxigenating chemicals with herbs, barks and gums, as have proven themselves effective for the relief of Asthma and other affections of the respiratory organs, attended with short, difficult or spasmodic breathing. It is the result of many years' study and experiment by a German physician who has devoted especial attention to diseases of the lungs and air passages, that has never failed to effect immediate relief or effect a cure when a fair trial was given and used according to directions. This remedy is used by inhalation and as its virtues reach the air passages direct the relief obtained is instantaneous. Plain directions and valuable information is enclosed in each box, and if the sufferer will follow these directions carefully and study what the circular in the box says and act accordingly, mild forms of asthma, hay fever, etc., are often cured in a week or two, but if the disease is old seated and has obtained a firm hold on the system, the treatment ought to be continued for several months, even although the patient may believe himself entirely cured. This great cure for Asthma has heretofore only been sold in $1.50 packages, but we have been enabled to have a quantity of trial packages put up for 50 cents each.

No. 5022 Price, full size box holding 3 of the 50c size for........ $1.00
Per dozen.....................9.00

If by mail, postage extra, per box, small 2 cents; large 5 cents.

Dr. Hammond's Internal Catarrh Cure.

Reduced to 50 Cents.

Formerly sold at $1.00.

A RADICAL CURE FOR CATARRH. If you have Chronic Catarrh order Dr. Hammond's Internal Catarrh Cure and you will get instant relief and a speedy and permanent cure. A great many people cannot understand how our internal remedy can affect catarrh when located in the head, where most people feel the catarrh first, but whether in the head, stomach, bowels, bladder or throat it is all the same. Dr. Hammond's Internal Catarrh Cure will destroy this disease, and make you well again. Catarrh is a chronic inflammation of the mucous surface and it is the same wherever you find it; you cannot completely cure it until the whole system has been put in perfect health. Local treatment will give you relief but cannot cure. When the hearing has become affected we have never failed to give relief and often completely restore it by the use of this great remedy. Full directions accompany each bottle, also fuller particulars concerning it. Cure your catarrh with Dr. Hammond's Internal Catarrh Cure. Try a bottle, and you will surely use it until well again.

No. 5026 Price, per bottle ....$0.5¢
Per doz. 5.00

If by mail, postage and tube, extra, 16 cents

Milto Siberian Catarrh Snuff.

Retail Price, $1.00. **Our Price, 25 Cents.**

The Greatest Catarrh Remedy Known. Immediate relief guaranteed, and a positive cure effected in nine cases out of ten.

SEND US 25 CENTS and stop paying doctor bills. For all catarrhal affections, Headache, Deafness, Cold in Head, Tonsilitis, Quinsy, Sore Throat, nothing acts so quickly as MILTO SIBERIAN CATARRH SNUFF. PERFECTLY HARMLESS. It contains no injurious drugs or chemicals. It has cured in many cases when doctors have pronounced the disease incurable. OUR PRICE FOR THE MILTO CATARRH CURE IS 25 CENTS, complete with blower. If you have friends who have suffered with this great disease—catarrh—tell them of this Siberian Catarrh Cure, that the price has been reduced to only 25 cents. Never sold for less than $1.00 by others.

No. 5029 Our special price..................25¢

If by mail, postage extra, 2 cents.

Dr. Rose's Dyspepsia Powders.
Our Price, 30 Cents.

Retail Price, 50 Cents.

DYSPEPSIA RELIEF SURE FOR 30 CENTS.

A remedy of remarkable efficacy in Dyspepsia and all troubles of like nature. It acts upon the food as a digester and transforms starchy food into soluble and easily digested particles, thus relieving the stomach and allowing rest, and also giving tone to that organ. By taking a powder just before a meal you prevent many of the ills brought on by an irritable stomach, such as dyspepsia, sour stomach, heartburn, indigestion, constipation, distress after eating, belching of wind and, in truth, it can be said that it is a true assistant to digestion. It never fails to relieve, no matter how severe the case may be. A trial is all that is asked for. A single box even will convince any sufferer of the remarkable results obtained from the use of these powders.

No. 5032 Price per dozen, $3.00; per box................30¢

If by mail, postage extra, per box, 2 cents.

Dr. Wilden's Quick Cure for Indigestion and Dyspepsia.

Retail Price, $1.00. **Our Price, 35 Cents.**

THE GREAT STOMACH REMEDY. Dr. Wilden's Tablets for the Speedy and Permanent Cure of Indigestion and Dyspepsia in all its Forms, is without an equal in any known Remedy. No Other Dyspepsia Remedy will compare with Dr. Wilden's. Harmless, a child can take it; it contains no opium, calomel or other injurious substances. Puts your stomach and other digestive organs in perfect condition immediately.

The Greatest Dyspepsia Prescription ever written, the most wonderful dyspepsia remedy ever compounded. Have you Dyspepsia? Very likely you are suffering with Dyspepsia and Indigestion and do not know it. If you are bothered with Constipation, Biliousness, Jaundice, Sick Headache, Liver Complaint; if you are at all distressed after eating, if you have a tired and languid feeling at times, if you are dull, your circulation is poor, weak at times. If you have any of the above or the thousand other disorderly feelings, it almost surely comes from Indigestion and Dr. Wilden's Remedy will do you more good than any other remedy; it will effect a quick and permanent cure, even if all other remedies have failed. Dr. Wilden's Remedy has been introduced into society by us, as the best remedy known for Dyspepsia from the highest authority. Hundreds of Testimonials have been sent us from parties who have doctored for years, treated every where, and taken all kinds of remedies, never to get help until they took Dr. Wilden's Remedy. Put up in tablet form. Easy and pleasant to take and perfectly harmless.

No. 5038 Price, six boxes for $1.90; per box..................35¢
No. 5039 Price, six large boxes at $2.50; for large boxes (hold as much as two small ones)....................50¢

If by mail, postage extra, per box, small 2 cents; large 4 cents.

Fat Folks, Take Dr. Rose's Obesity Powders and Watch the Result.

Our Price, 60 Cents.
Retail Price, $1.00.

TOO MUCH FAT is a disease and a source of great annoyance to those afflicted. It impairs the strength and produces fatty degeneration of the heart, and sudden death results. All people who have obesity are troubled with **sluggish circulation and labored action of the heart.** The patient feels lazy and burdensome. There is a sluggish condition of the whole system; they are not exactly sickly, there is a feeling that all is not right. Nervousness, rheumatism, headache, dropsy and kidney diseases are frequent complications of obesity, and, more cause to be alarmed, the heart is always affected. **Send at once for a box of Dr. Rose's Obesity Cure.** It will reduce corpulency in a safe and agreeable manner, **perfectly harmless.** No bad results follow its use, as is the case with many of the much advertised cures. Explicit directions and valuable information for fat folks enclosed in each box.

No. 5042 Per dozen, $6.00; per box....................60c
If by mail, postage, extra, per box, 2 cents.

Mexican Headache Cure.

Retail Price, 50 cents. **Our Price, 20 Cents.**

A SPLITTING HEADACHE CURED IMMEDIATELY by our **Positive Headache and Neuralgia Cure. Almost everyone is more or less troubled with a headache at some time or other.** Some persons are hardly ever free from them, and suffer martyrdom. We confidently say to our customers that it is not necessary to suffer longer than the time it takes to get a package of our **Mexican Headache cure. We positively guarantee relief within fifteen minutes after the first dose has been taken.** Rarely is a second dose required except **in very obstinate cases.** No matter from what cause, whether a nervous headache, or from the stomach, or a severe case of neuralgia, **we guarantee complete relief.** It is perfectly harmless, no bad results follow its use. Give it a trial when you suffer, and you will be sure to speak of us as your friends.

No. 5046 Dozen, $2.25; box....................20c
If by mail, postage, extra, per box, 2 cents.

Dr. Worden's Female Pills for All Female Diseases.

35 Cents is our Special Price.

This is acknowledged as one of the Greatest Remedies of the age.

A GREAT BLOOD PURIFIER and Nerve Tonic. **Cures all diseases arising from a poor and wasted condition of the blood, such as pale and sallow complexion, general weakness of the muscles, loss of appetite, depression of spirits, lack of ambition, anæmia, chlorosis or green sickness, palpitation of the heart, shortness of breath on slight exertion, coldness of hands and feet, swelling of the feet and limbs, pain in the back, nervous headache, dizziness, loss of memory, feebleness of will, ringing in the ears, early decay. ALL FORMS OF FEMALE WEAKNESS—Leucorrhœa, tardy or irregular periods, suppression of the menses, hysteria, locomotor ataxia, partial paralysis, sciatica, rheumatism, neuralgia. Cures all diseases depending on vitiated humor in the blood, causing scrofula, swelled glands, fever sores, rickets, hip joint diseases, hunchback, acquired deformities, decayed bones, chronic erysipelas, consumption of the bowels and lungs. In invigorating the blood system** when broken down by overwork, worry, diseases, excesses and indiscretions of living, this is a most **wonderful medicine.**

THESE FEMALE PILLS are not a purgative medicine; they are not a cure-all. They contain nothing that could injure the most delicate system but act upon the diseases dependent upon poor and watery blood or a cachetic state of that fluid.

WOMEN CAN BE BEAUTIFUL, their complexion perfect, nervous system normal, circulation perfect. All weakness and disease removed by taking these Pure Vegetable Pills. Thousands of women have been cured by using Dr. Worden's Pills, after all other remedies and physicians had failed.

WE GUARANTEE A CURE in any case from twelve boxes of this remedy; six boxes will cure ordinary cases; one box will furnish great relief, and twelve boxes we positively guarantee to cure in any case of female weakness.

No. 5048 Our special price, per box....................$0.35
Six boxes for $1.90; twelve boxes for....................3.50
If by mail, postage, extra, per box, 2 cents.

Cathartic Pills, Only 10 Cents per Box.

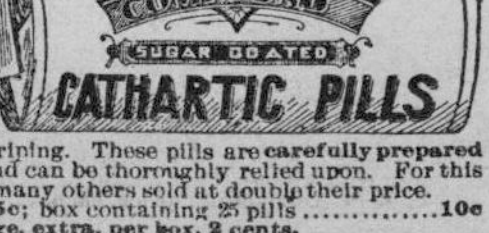

THIS IS THE OLD FASHIONED SUGAR COATED CATHARTIC PILL of the U. S. Pharmacopœia, the same as Ayer's, Brandreth's, Jaynes' and other much advertised pills. They act principally on the liver, and move the bowels gently without griping. These pills are **carefully prepared from fresh vegetable extracts,** and can be thoroughly relied upon. For this reason they are much superior to many others sold at double their price.

No. 5050 Per dozen boxes, 75c; box containing 25 pills....................10c
If by mail, postage, extra, per box, 2 cents.

Our 60-Cent Nerve and Brain Pills.

GUARANTEED THE HIGHEST GRADE ON THE MARKET.

SIX BOXES POSITIVELY GUARANTEED TO CURE ANY DISEASE for which they are intended. This will cure you if you feel generally miserable or suffer with a thousand and one indescribable bad feelings, both mental and physical, among them low spirits, nervousness, weariness, lifelessness, weakness, dizziness, feeling of fullness like bloating after eating, or sense of goneness or emptiness of stomach in morning; flesh soft and lacking firmness, headache, blurring of eyesight specks floating before the eyes, nervous irritability, poor memory, chilliness alternating with hot flushes; lassitude, throbbing, gurgling or rumbling sensations in bowels, with heat and nipping pains occasionally; palpitation of heart, short breath on exertion, slow circulation of blood, cold feet, pain and oppression in chest and back, pain around the loins, aching and weariness of the lower limbs, drowsiness after meals but nervous wakefulness at night, languor in the morning, and a constant feeling of dread, as if something awful was going to happen.

If you have any of these symptoms our **NERVE AND BRAIN PILLS will cure you.** No matter what the cause may be or how severe your trouble is, **DR. HAMMOND'S NERVE AND BRAIN PILLS** will cure you. **These pills have a remarkable effect** on both old and young. They cannot be equaled by any other medicine as a cure for impotence, spermatorrhœa, night sweats, emissions, varicocele (or swollen veins), weakness of both brain and body arising from excesses and abuses of any kind. **They will tone up the whole nervous system,** no matter how much worn out, overworked or depressed you may be; the weak and timid young man made strong and bold again; they will give youthful vigor and a new lease of life to the old.

BEWARE OF QUACK DOCTORS who advertise to scare men into paying money for remedies which have no merit. **Our Nerve and Brain Pills** are compounded from a prescription of one of the most noted German scientists, and are the same as have been used in **German hospitals** for years with marvelous success. **HOW TO CURE YOURSELF** and full and explicit directions are enclosed with every box. All orders and inquiries concerning these pills will be **treated confidentially,** and all shipments made in plain sealed package.

ONLY $3.00 FOR SIX BOXES. Enough to cure any case, no matter how severe, no matter how long standing, whether old or young, no matter from what cause. **Send us $3.00** and we will send you 6 boxes by return mail, postpaid, in plain sealed package, with full instructions, full directions.

No. 5054 Price, 6 boxes (an amount to cure anyone), $3.00; per box, 60c
If by mail, postage, extra, per box, 2 cents.

If you need these pills don't delay, this is the first time the American people have had an opportunity of getting the **genuine Dr. Hammond's Pills,** and the first time they have been sold anywhere at anything like our price.

Wonderful Little Liver Pills.

Bottle, 12c; per dozen, $1.00.

Entirely vegetable in their composition. These wonderful little pills operate without disturbance to the system, diet or occupation.

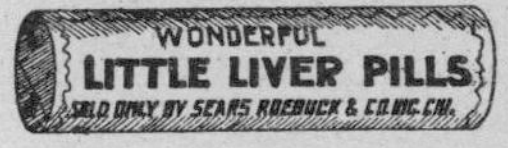

CONSTIPATION, that most hideous and deathly demon of sickness, is an easy enough thing to cure if you will only persist in taking proper treatment. It is one of the commonest troubles and often thought to be a very little thing. Yet we say that nine-tenths of all human sickness is due to this one thing. When the bowels do not move regularly the natural drainage tract in the human system is dammed up, **decomposition ensues and poisonous gases and liquids are carried all through the system. The result is jaundice, torpid liver, biliousness, sallow skin, indigestion, foul breath, coated tongue, loss of appetite, pimples, belching foul gases, blotches, boils, dizziness, headache, cramps, colic, etc.** You can easily avoid all these troubles and keep your system pure and healthy by taking from time to time one or two of our **WONDERFUL LITTLE LIVER PILLS.** Some of our customers call them **"LITTLE GIANTS,"** they are so small in size and so easy to swallow, yet so effective and mild in their operation. Whenever your stomach, liver and bowels get out of order take one or two of our **LITTLE WONDERS** and notice the quick effect and great relief you will experience. Keep a bottle always beside you. Use them occasionally and you will always feel well and look the picture of health.

No. 5057 Per dozen, $1.00; per bottle, only....................12c
If by mail, postage, extra, per box, 2 cents.

Our Famous Blood Pills.

Our Price is 25c per Box.
$2.00 per Dozen.

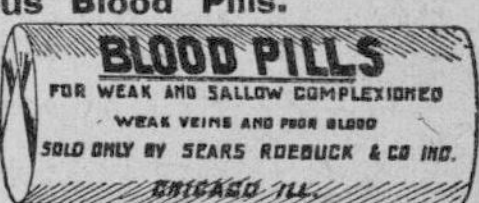

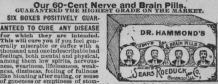

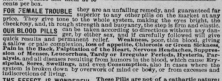

For men and women that require a nerve tonic, blood purifier or builder.

Over one hundred thousand sold last year, which shows what is thought of these pills when known. Others sell them at 50 cents per box.

FOR FEMALE TROUBLE they are an unfailing remedy, and guaranteed far superior to any other pills on the market at any price. They give tone to the whole system, making the eyes bright, the cheek rosy, and, through strength and buoyancy, the step is firm and elastic.

OUR BLOOD PILLS can be taken according to directions without any danger, by either sex, and if carefully followed will give quick results and permanent relief. **Weakness,** poor, thin blood, giving a sallow or pale complexion, **loss of appetite, Chlorosis or Green Sickness, Pain in the Back, Palpitation of the Heart, Nervous Headaches, Suppression of Menses, Leucorrhœa, Tardy or Irregular Periods, Hysteria, Paralysis,** and all diseases resulting from humors in the blood, which cause **Erysipelas, Sores, Swellings, and even Consumption,** also in cases where the system is broken down by overwork of mind or body, or from excesses and indiscretions of living.

THE EFFECT IS WONDERFUL **These Pills are not of a cathartic nature;** they do not, nor are they intended to purge. **They are intended to act on the blood,** and supply what is needed in restoring the tone and lacking constituents, stimulating to activity the sluggish system.

FOR WOMEN in case of **Suppression of Menses, Leucorrhœa or Whites, Chlorosis, Anæmia, Locomotor Ataxia,** a quick and permanent cure can be effected; in fact, it is the greatest remedy known.

FOR MEN these pills stand without a rival. They build up the system and cure **Spermatorrhœa, Impotence, Nervous Despondency, Loss of Memory, Confusion of Ideas, Irritability of Temper, Pain in Back and Perinæum, Draining of Prostatic Fluid. These Pills retail everywhere at 50c to $1.00.** **If by mail, postage, extra, per box, 2 cents.**

No. 5059 Price, per dozen, $2.00; per box....................25c

Do You Sneeze? Camphor Pills, Only 20 Cents.

HAVE BEEN LONG USED BY THE HOMEOPATHIC PHYSICIANS, as a remedy for cold in the head, cramps, colic, diarrhœa and cholera morbus and other annoying troubles resulting from catching cold. Also for menstrual colic. **A bottle of these pills ought to be carried in the pocket continually** by those who are traveling, or outside most of the day exposed to all weathers. Though very effective in performing cures, they are small and can be conveniently kept in the vest pocket. They attained their first reputation many years ago by the remarkable success following their use in **preventing and curing Asiatic cholera.** Since then they have become **a household necessity** with thousands of people.

No. 5063 Doz. vials, $2.00; Small vial........20c

If by mail, postage, extra, small, 2 cents.

Large home vial, containing as much as 4 small vials........50c

If by mail, postage, extra, large, 16 cents.

Ague Cure.

Reduced to 40c.
Retails at $1.00.

For chills and fever this remedy is a true specific. We are selling thousands of boxes to those living in the Southern and Western States, and not a case of failure to cure has as yet been reported to us; we were fortunate to obtain the recipe for this cure from a physician who had used it constantly in his practice for thirty years with great success. It is **an infallible remedy for this disease, and those living in low and swampy localities ought to have it always at hand.** It is much superior and less harmful to the system than quinine. **It acts more promptly and the cure is more complete.** With every package is enclosed a small vial of vegetable liver pills, with explicit directions how to keep the system in condition to guard against malaria.

No. 5065 Per doz., $4.00; per box........40c

If by mail, postage, extra, per box, 2 cents.

Hammond's Sarsaparilla.

GUARANTEED THE BEST ON THE MARKET.

There is no other Sarsaparilla made that will compare with it.

Our price, per large bottle, 59c; Per dozen, $6.00.

Never retails at less than $1.00.

DR. HAMMOND'S SARSAPARILLA combines **in an agreeable form the medicinal properties of the most approved alterative and blood purifying remedies of the vegetable kingdom. Dr. Hammond's Sarsaparilla** will not cure everything, but the fact that on the purity and vitality of the blood depends the vigor and health of the whole system, and that disease of various kinds is often only the sign that nature is trying to remove the disturbing cause, lead to the conclusion that a remedy which gives life and vigor to the blood and eradicates **scrofula** and other impurities, as this preparation undoubtedly does, **must cure and prevent many diseases.** Hence the field of its usefulness is an endless one, and we are warranted in recommending it for all derangements caused by an unnatural **state** of the blood.

FOR SCROFULA **Dr. Hammond's Sarsaparilla is the greatest known remedy** and there is no other disease that is so general among our population. **Almost every individual has this latent poison coursing his veins.** Its alarming fatality is not realized because consumption and other diseases are reported as the causes of deaths, many of which are the result of scrofula. This scrofulous taint weakens the energies of life, and constitutions contaminated by it are more susceptible to disease and have less physical force to withstand it. Persons afflicted with scrofulous sores endure intense suffering which, like the gratitude they feel to a remedy which cures them, cannot be fully appreciated by others. **Scrofulous affection is hereditary,** and may be transmitted, without appearing, through several generations, and then assume its worst forms. The indications of scrofula are many and varied. The following are among its prominent characteristics: Pallid countenance, a bluish white transparent complexion, inflamed eyelids, eruptions on the scalp and various parts of the body, irregular appetite, sometimes keen, at others, dainty; bowels irregular, a general lassitude and debility which takes away all energy or desire for action, business or labor. Scrofula is most dangerous when it seats itself upon the lungs, producing **tubercular consumption.** It is not, however, confined to any part of the body, as it attacks the lungs, liver and kidneys, also the digestive and uterine apparatus, inducing and often resulting in a long train of diseases such as **consumption, ulceration of the liver, stomach or kidneys,** eruptions and eruptive diseases of the skin, **ulcers, tumors, erysipelas, salt rheum, blotches, postules, tetter, pain in the bones, side or head, ring worm, scald head, catarrh, dyspepsia, female weaknesses, leucorrhœa, arising from internal ulceration and uterine diseases aggravated by low condition of the system or impure state of blood, dropsy, emaciation, general debility, and that tired feeling.**

OUR SARSAPARILLA **is a purely scientific preparation. It is carefully prepared from the most powerful, yet perfectly safe and harmless alteratives and blood purifying agents,** selected from the vegetable kingdom. This preparation does not contain mercury or arsenic in any form or combination whatever. **Our Sarsaparilla cures** where all others fail. It combines the merits of all other sarsaparilla compounds with defects of none. **For blood making, blood cleansing, flesh and appetite producing our Sarsaparilla is unequaled. No family can afford to be without it. For infants, children, grown people, it should be taken regularly. Our prices are very low.** **Unmailable on account of weight.**

No. 5068 Price per doz., $6.00; per large bottle........59c

NEVER RETAILED AT LESS THAN $1.00.

Our 70c Positive Rheumatic Cure.

WHAT IS RHEUMATISM? **This dreadful disease, this scourge of humanity, is a blood disease,** always due to one cause, namely the presence in the system of urea, and uric acid, which poisonous elements could not be retained unless there was a defective kidney action underlying the Rheumatic disease.

RHEUMATISM **may be divided into two classes, Acute and Chronic Rheumatism.** Acute, or commonly called inflammatory rheumatism, announces itself through piercing pains in the joints and muscles in the back, the knees, the hips, etc., and generally spreads through the whole body. **Chronic Rheumatism,** on the other hand, is accompanied by no fever, the joints are very painful, swollen, sensitive and often stiff. If this disease is of long duration the joints will swell or expand, and dislocation takes place. The resulting deformity and crippling of the joints; can be cured if correctly treated. **We can say Inflammatory Rheumatism is the most dangerous of the two,** owing to its rapid spreading over the body, implicating certain internal organs and structures, **especially the heart,** often producing **pleurisy, pneumonia, bronchitis, cerebral and spinal meningitis.** If the disease has thus far advanced without receiving proper treatment relapses are frequent and death often results, which is generally due to complications. There is but one satisfactory way to treat rheumatism and that is in a constitutional manner, by giving internal medicines which act on the blood.

OUR POSITIVE RHEUMATIC CURE **will positively cure Rheumatism in all forms,** and in all its different stages, by reason that it removes from the system the urea and uric acid upon which the disease feeds. This remedy has a specific action on the blood, it increases the number of the red blood corpuscles, which are morbidly deficient in cases of rheumatism.

OUR POSITIVE RHEUMATIC CURE is compounded from a prescription of a celebrated **French scientist** who spent the greater part of his life in prescribing for rheumatism in all forms. **Our Remedy Will Cure** when all others fail. If you have rheumatism in any form you should get this remedy at once. **If you have been suffering for years** you will find quick relief and final cure in this remedy. **If your case is chronic order six bottles,** for in severe cases and cases of long standing there is a necessity to use this remedy for a longer period; several months may be needed to fully secure exemption from the disease. **We recommend ordering six bottles,** it will cause a complete reconstruction of the system.

No. 5070 Price, per six bottles, $3.75; per bottle........70c

Unmailable on account of weight.

Brown's Vegetable Cure for Female Weakness.

For Female Weakness, Falling of the Womb, Leucorrhœa, Irregular and Painful Menstruation, Inflammation and Ulceration of the Womb, Flooding, and ALL FEMALE DISORDERS.

It is the Wonder of the Age.

Our special price, very large bottles........60c

6 bottles for........$3.00

This Remedy is Immediate in Effect. It is a blessing to women in pregnancy; saves you a world of suffering. **For all kidney troubles and diseases** it has no equal. For all weaknesses of the generative organs of either sex, it is a wonderful remedy. **WOMEN DO NOT SUFFER SO! Brown's Vegetable Cure** will cure you. In all **female disorders** it is the greatest remedy of the age. **If you have any of the following symptoms** take this remedy at once and be cured: Nausea and bad taste in the mouth, sore feeling in lower part of bowels, an unusual discharge, impaired general health, feeling of languor, sharp pain in region of kidney, backache, dull pain in small of back, pain in passing water, bearing down feeling, a desire to urinate frequently, a dragging sensation in the groin, courses irregular, timid, nervous and restless feeling, a dread of some impending evil, temper wayward and irritable, a feeling of fullness, sparks before the eyes, gait unsteady, pain in womb, swelling in front, pain in breastbone, pain when courses occur, hysterics, temples and ears throb, sleep short and distorted, whites, impaired digestion, headache, trouble with sight or hearing, dizziness, morbid feeling and the blues, palpitation of the heart, nerves weak and sensitive, appetite poor, a craving for unnatural food, spirits depressed, nervous dyspeptic symptoms, a heavy feeling and pain in back upon exertion, fainting spells, difficulty in passing water, habitual constipation, cold extremities. **If you have any of the symptoms send to us for Brown's Vegetable Cure and be cured at once. Doctors may not help you,** other remedies may have failed, but **BROWN'S CURE** will cure quickly, **pleasantly and permanently. Thousands have been cured** who have considered their case incurable. Invalids have been made well and strong. **DO NOT DELAY, one bottle will help and convince you. 6 BOTTLES WILL CURE ANY CASE OF FEMALE WEAKNESS,** no matter how severe or how long standing.

No. 5073 Six bottles for $3.00; large bottle........60c

Unmailable on account of weight.

Just the thing for Our Baby.

Baby's Magic Necklace relieves children from all ailments and pain during teething period. The value of this wonderful discovery cannot be over estimated. No inconvenience is caused the child, who must commence wearing the **Baby's Magic Necklace** at five months of age and wear it constantly during the teething period.

No. 5074 Our special price, each........50c

Dr. Rowland's System Builder and Lung Restorer.
Our Special Price 60 Cents.

Greatest Vegetable Medicine of the Age for the thousand ailments common to the masses.

FOR THE CURE OF COUGHS of all kinds, chronic and lingering, especially Bronchitis, Laryngitis, Consumption, Ulcerated Throat, ministers' or public speakers' Sore Throat, Hoarseness and Suppression or Loss of Voice. It does not nauseate or debilitate the stomach or system, but improves digestion, strengthens the stomach, builds up solid flesh when the system is reduced below a healthy standard, and invigorates and cleanses the whole system.

As a remedy for torpor of the liver, generally termed Liver Complaint or Biliousness, and for habitual constipation of the bowels it has no equal. For loss of appetite, indigestion and dyspepsia, and for general or nervous debility or prostration, in either sex, it has no equal. As an alternative, or blood purifier, this medicine is far superior to any preparation of sarsaparilla, iodide of potassium, or any other medicine now offered for general sale. It is, therefore, very valuable in all forms of scrofulous and other blood diseases, also for all skin diseases, eruptions, pimples, rashes and blotches, boils, ulcers, sores and swellings, arising from impure blood, and cured by the use of a few bottles of this compound. Unlike other alternatives or blood cleansing medicines, it does not debilitate, but strengthens the entire system. This is a very concentrated vegetable extract. The dose is small and pleasant to the taste. Full directions accompany each bottle.

BUILD UP YOUR ENTIRE SYSTEM by using a few bottles of this wonderful remedy. Is your health impaired, are you overworked, do you need a general toning up? If so, order 3 bottles and become a new person.

No. 5076 Our special price, 3 bottles, $1.50; for large bottle.......60c
Unmailable on account of weight.

B. B. B. Dr. Barker's Blood Builder for 75 Cents.

Read Carefully and find out what our B. B. B. Medicine is. These Three Letters Stand for Dr. Barker's Blood Builder.

NATURE'S MOST WONDERFUL REMEDY for destroying poisons in the blood and building up a pure healthy blood, no matter how diseased the system is.

It is universally conceded that seventy-five per cent of the diseases with which the human family suffer today are produced by some poisonous germs in the blood or some derangement of that life giving and sustaining fluid. Physicians tell us that one in every twenty persons is infected with poisonous microbes. It is easy then to understand how blood diseases are so prevalent and needs but little argument to show why a simple vegetable remedy, which destroys and expels these poisonous germs, is the only true blood purifier. It will cure scrofula, cancer, rheumatism, especially that arising from mercurial poisoning; eczema and other skin diseases that arise from the purity of the blood, nasal catarrh, acne or pimples, chronic ulcers, carbuncles, boils. It is a true specific for syphilis in its primary, secondary or tertiary form, eradicating all unclean matter from the blood, removing all taint of this disease. A few bottles taken in the spring will prepare the system to stand the heat and corrupting influence of the hot summer days and ward of sickness. Taken in the fall it braces the system to stand the blasts of winter. As a general tonic and builder up of pure blood DR. BARKER'S BLOOD BUILDER is the most valuable of all medicines, cleansing the system, freeing it from all poisonous germs. It is a powerful remedy, yet no one need be afraid to take it, as it is purely vegetable. It will cure you and make your skin smooth and give to it a healthy appearance.

No. 5080 Large bottles.............................$0.75
            6 bottles..................................3.75
            12 bottles.................................7.00
Unmailable on account of weight.

Cod Liver Oil.
LOOK AT OUR PRICES.

Full Pint Bottles.............................$0.50
Per Dozen......................................5.50
Guaranteed Absolutely Pure. Highest Grade Made.

YOU WILL SAVE ONE-HALF IN PRICE and get the best goods possible to put up if you place your order with us. You can't afford to buy Cod Liver Oil unless you know it is absolutely pure.

If you buy from us you will have our guarantee and know it is absolutely pure and fresh, imported direct from Norway, in original packages, where it is prepared from strictly fresh livers, pure and sweet.

For Consumption, severe Colds, Lung and Throat Troubles, NORWAY COD LIVER OIL should be taken regularly.

No. 5083 Per pint bottle.......................$0.50
            Per dozen.............................5.50
Unmailable on account of weight.

B. B. B.
DR. BARKER'S BLOOD BUILDER
A FAMOUS Blood & Skin REMEDY

PREPARED ESPECIALLY TO DESTROY ALL POISONS IN THE BLOOD PURIFY IT INVIGORATE THE SYSTEM AND GIVE THE SKIN A FINE HEALTHY APPEARANCE

SOLE AGENTS FOR THE UNITED STATES

SOLD ONLY BY SEARS ROEBUCK & CO.
CHEAPEST SUPPLY HOUSE ON EARTH
CHICAGO ILL.

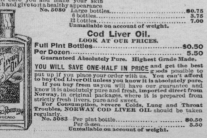

Our Cod Liver Oil Emulsion.
Our Price for Large Bottle, 60 Cents.
Per Dozen, $6.50.

Pure Cod Liver Oil with Hypophosphites of Lime and Soda.

A CONSUMPTION CURE.

60 CENTS is the lowest price at which the highest quality Cod Liver Oil Emulsion was ever sold, and we feel sure our customers will appreciate this opportunity of getting for 60 cents what they have heretofore been compelled to pay $1.00 or more for.

IT IS THE GREATEST REMEDY EVER DISCOVERED for Phthisis or Consumption, Colds and Chronic Coughs, Scrofula in its various forms, Rheumatism, Skin Diseases, Diseases of Children, Anaemia, or poor condition of the blood, and General Debility. In all the above diseases a remedial agent most essential and productive of the best results is a nutrient, an alterative for the body and a tonic for the brain and nervous system. FOR CONSUMPTION there is nothing known to equal our Cod Liver Oil Emulsion, and in the first and second stages will effect a quick and permanent cure. FOR COUGHS AND CHRONIC COLDS there is nothing known to equal our Cod Liver Oil Emulsion, and no family can afford to be without it. Doctor bills can be avoided, often lung fever and other diseases averted by the timely use of Cod Liver Oil Emulsion. We would advise mothers to always have a bottle on hand to give to their children or any member of the family when they have a cold or stubborn cough. AS A CURE FOR SCROFULA in its various forms Cod Liver Oil Emulsion is of the greatest benefit. FOR RHEUMATISM, Cod Liver Oil Emulsion is a valuable remedy, and it has often cured the most stubborn cases when all other remedies have failed. FOR SKIN DISEASES, Cod Liver Oil Emulsion is perhaps on other remedy that exerts so powerful an influence over skin diseases. FOR GENERAL DEBILITY AND EMACIATION our Cod Liver Oil Emulsion, taken regularly after meals, will quickly recuperate and build you up to renewed strength, health and vigor. FOR PURE BLOOD nothing will do so much good as our Cod Liver Oil Emulsion; it will enrich and purify the blood, give it heat and life and tone, and strengthen the entire nervous system. FOR DISEASES OF CHILDREN our Emulsion of Cod Liver Oil should always be used.
No. 5086 Price, 1 dozen bottles, $6.50; for large bottle................60c
Unmailable on account of weight.

Curtis' Consumption Cure.
Guaranteed Cure for Consumption.
Will positively cure Consumption when directions are followed.

CURTIS' CONSUMPTION CURE is compounded after a prescription of one of the highest authorities on the diseases of the lungs, an authority recognizing that the science of medicine has reached a point when they can say Consumption can be cured.

TUBERCULOUS MATTER is nothing more or less than nourishment imperfectly organized. Now if with this remedy we can control the organization of this food material, so that through the process of elective affinity it may take its place in the system, we can cure the disease. This is just what this remedy does. IT ARRESTS AT ONCE THE PROGRESS OF THE DISEASE by preventing the further supply of tuberculous matter, for while the system is under its influence all nourishment is organized and assimilated. It thus controls cough, expectoration, night sweats, hectic fever, and all other characteristics of consumption.

OUR REMEDY WILL CURE YOU, but don't delay; take it in the first stages of the disease; it always yields so much easier to the treatment. PROTECT YOUR LUNGS, don't allow a cold to run. Take this remedy at once, for it cures all kinds of colds with the greatest promptness.

DON'T DELAY A DAY. If you would be cured, send for a trial bottle at once. Comes in 20c and 35c bottles; $1.00 and $1.75 in one-half dozen lots.
No. 5088 Our special price: Small bottles, 20c; six for $1.00; large bottles 35c; six for $1.75.
If by mail, postage and tube, extra, 12 cents; large bottle, 16 cents.

CURTIS CONSUMPTION CURE
A GUARANTEED CURE FOR CONSUMPTION

SOLD ONLY BY SEARS ROEBUCK & CO.
CHEAPEST SUPPLY HOUSE ON EARTH
CHICAGO ILL.

Baby Cough Syrup.
20 Cents Per Bottle.
Retail Price, 50 cents.

WHEREVER THERE ARE CHILDREN YOU ARE NOT SAFE WITHOUT A BOTTLE OF THIS SPECIAL COUGH SYRUP.

MOTHER'S FAVORITE REMEDY. No mother ought to give her child medicine without knowing what it contains. Babies take cold easy, their lungs are weak, and at the first symptom of cold, such as watering at the lips or nose, hoarseness, slight cold, feverish skin, a simple remedy which is known to have healing properties ought to be given, as delay is more dangerous than in adults. Our "MOTHER'S FAVORITE REMEDY," carefully made from the purest materials, thoroughly tested by our chemists, composed of Tolu, Squills, Arabian Healing Gum, Rock Candy, compounded by our chemists from the prescription of a famous English physician, who years ago attended the Royal Family of England, is a good remedy and perfectly harmless.
No. 5092 Price, per doz, $2.25; per bottle......20c
If by mail, postage and tube, extra, 16 cents.

Dr. Hammond's Tar Expectorant.

Only 30 Cents.
Retail price, 75 cents.

MORE CASES OF CONSUMPTION have been cured by the timely use of Dr. Hammond's Tar Expectorant than by all other remedies combined. For the cure of Colds, Coughs, Croup, Influenza, Bronchitis, Quinsy, Laryngitis, Hoarseness, Sore Throat, Night Sweats, Catarrh and for the Immediate relief of Consumptive Patients.

DR. HAMMOND'S TAR EXPECTORANT is the most wonderful remedy ever offered to the public. It wonderfully increases the power and flexibility of the voice, strengthens weak lungs, allays pulmonary irritation and affords the most effectual relief for Whooping Cough and even for Consumption in its advanced stages. It is especially beneficial in those diseases which are too often regarded as simply annoying, such as common colds and coughs, but which are really dangerous in their tendencies and demand prompt and active treatment. For the more serious forms of Throat and Lung Troubles its value cannot be overestimated to anyone worn out with constant coughing and loss of sleep.

DR. HAMMOND'S TAR EXPECTORANT is a blessing, as it gives immediate relief, and sweet rest follows.

WE GUARANTEE that every case of pulmonary disease, not already beyond the reach of human aid, can be relieved and cured by being promptly treated with Dr. Hammond's Tar Expectorant. DELAYS ARE DANGEROUS.

No. 5095 Price per dozen, $3.00; per bottle.................30c
Unmailable on account of weight.

Peruvian Wine of Cocoa.

Our Special Price, 65 Cents.
Retail price, $1.00.

A GENUINE RICH WINE IMPORTED BY OURSELVES and well known throughout Europe for its strengthening and nourishing qualities. It sustains and refreshes both the body and the brain and has deservedly gained its excellent reputation and great superiority over all other tonics. It is more effective and rapid in its action. It may be taken for any length of time with perfect safety, without causing injury to the system, the stomach and gastric juices. On the contrary, Peruvian Wine of Cocoa aids digestion, removes fatigue and improves the appetite, never causing constipation. For many years past it has been thoroughly tested and has received the endorsement of hundreds of the most eminent physicians of the world, who assure us of their utmost satisfaction with the results obtained by using it in their practice. They urgently recommend its use in the treatment of anemia, impurity and impoverishment of the blood, consumption, weakness of the lungs, asthma, nervous debility, loss of appetite, malarial complaints, biliousness, stomach disorders, dyspepsia, languor and fatigue, obesity, loss of forces and weakness caused by excesses, and for similar diseases of the same nature. It is especially adapted for persons in delicate health and convalescents. It is very palatable and agreeable to take and can be borne by the most enfeebled stomach where everything else would fail.

It is used in most of the hospitals in Europe, and many of our American public institutions are adopting it. After many severe tests it has been effectually proven that in the same space of time more than double the amount of hardship and work could be undergone when Peruvian Wine of Cocoa was used and positively no fatigue experienced.

No. 5098 Per dozen, $6.75; 6 bottles, $3.50; 3 bottles, $1.80; bottle, 65c
Unmailable on account of weight.

Nutritive Tonic. Beef, Iron and Wine.

Inferior Grades Sell at 50c to $1.00. Our Price, 35 Cents.

GUARANTEED HIGHEST GRADE ever produced. No family should be without a bottle of Beef, Iron and Wine. This is an old time tonic, universally known for its great strength giving and flesh producing qualities.

THE GREAT TROUBLE with most of the Beef, Wine and Iron found in the market at the present day is the poor quality of materials used in making it. It is often found in a state quite unfit for use on that account. We take great pains with this preparation, using only Liebig's Extract of Beef freshly prepared, the finest imported Sherry Wine and Pure Iron in a form specially prepared for assimilating with and enriching the blood.

THE BEST TONIC KNOWN to be used when suffering from extreme exhaustion, produced by overwork or other causes, brain fatigue, debility of all kinds, blood disorders, salt rheum, eruptions, anemia, scrofula and cancer. It stimulates digestion, improves the condition of the blood. Enriches it and enables it to throw off accumulated humor, and it will give tone and vigor to the entire system. A depraved condition of the blood serves to augment disease. This condition should be a direct warning, and by taking and using as a corrective, much ill health can be avoided.

WE HAVE THOUSANDS OF TESTIMONIALS as to the wonderful good this medicine has done for those that are weak, nervous and debilitated. Our prices are very low. Inferior goods are sold everywhere at two, by double our prices.

No. 5100 Price, for full pint bottles....$0.35
Price, for ¼ doz. pint bottles.... 2.00
Price, for 1 doz. pint bottles.... 3.75
Price, for ½ gallon bottle..... 1.25
Price, for 1 gallon jug........ 2.25

ORDER A GALLON JUG of our Beef, Wine and Iron and you will find it the best investment you ever made.
Unmailable on account of weight.

Our Celery Malt Compound for 55 Cents.

We Sell the Highest Grade Celery Malt Compound for 55 Cents in Large Bottles.

It retails everywhere, even in inferior qualities, at $1.00 and upward.

WE GUARANTEE OUR CELERY MALT COMPOUND to be absolutely pure, unadulterated and superior to any other celery compound on the market, regardless of name or price.

Our Celery Malt Compound is a true nerve tonic, a genuine appetizer, a stimulant both for the young and old. We do not pretend that it is an absolute specific for any chronic disease, but it has a much wider range of usefulness, as it is especially beneficial in hundreds of the ills that flesh is heir to.

A glance at its composition, which we give below, will show any person of ordinary intelligence why it is such a useful preparation and should be kept in every household.

Our Celery Malt Compound contains in a concentrated form the active medicinal properties of the Italian celery seed, well known to physicians as one of the best and most active controlling and strengthening agents for the nerves, also the phosphates in the same state as found in the strong, healthy, vigorous, natural body, and in quantities approved of by the medical profession, the value of which has been so thoroughly demonstrated in all brain and nervous affections and in emaciated conditions. In addition it contains a large percentage of malt, which is very strengthening and fattening.

You will see it is an ideal combination which is not only a most useful tonic and stimulant but a delicious beverage as well.

As a brain and nerve tonic, appetizer and stimulant it is certainly unequaled in the realm of medicine.

For insomnia, nervousness, mental or physical exhaustion, loss of appetite, impoverished blood and for that tired feeling that comes from close confinement or sedentary habits, it is really magical in its effects, infinitely better than all stimulants of an alcoholic nature.

If you are nervous, exhausted, can't sleep, or if the body is poor and your digestion imperfect, and you are out of sorts generally and in a low physical condition, do not fail to try our Celery Malt Compound. It will give you new life and vigor and build up your entire system.

Our Celery Malt Compound is prepared under our special direction by a very able chemist. Every ingredient is carefully tested to know that it is of the very highest quality, and it is sent out under our guarantee that there is no other preparation of the kind that compares with it.

No. 5103— Our special price for large bottles.............$0.55
For half dozen bottles.................................. 3.00
For one dozen bottles.................................. 5.50
Unmailable on account of weight.

Orange Wine Stomach Bitters.

Retail Price, $1.00. Our Price 73 Cents.
Guaranteed Absolutely Pure and the Highest Grade on the Market.

Put up in extra large bottles holding 1½ pints.

DO NOT COMPARE Our Orange Wine Stomach Bitters with the bitters that are being sold by retail druggists generally at $1.00 to $1.50 a bottle, bitters that are made from the very cheapest ingredients. Our Orange Wine Stomach Bitters are made from wine distilled from the fruit of the Seville Orange tree in combination with herbs well known for their tonic and healing effect on the stomach. Order 1 dozen bottles. You can sell them at $1.00 each with profit enough so that several bottles will cost you nothing.

This is a pleasant bitters. As before explained, it is made from a wine distilled from the fruit of the Seville orange tree in combination with herbs well known for their tonic and healing effects on the stomach. As an appetizer there is no bitters made that will equal it, and it is a guaranteed cure for dyspepsia when its use is continued for some time. As a general bracer up of the whole system it has no equal, and the taste is so delicious that the most fastidious enjoy taking it. Owing to the intrinsic and widely established therapeutic value of its chief constituents, which are necessary to good digestion, this preparation stands unequaled. While furnishing admirable means for treating gastric ailments, indigestion, want of appetite, malarial diseases, low spirits, and nervousness, it removes that tired feeling and heals the derangements generally; will purify the blood, the bones, muscles, and the nerves receive new force, brain power is supplied and health and vigor restored. It exerts a wonderful power in sustaining the system during arduous labors and journeys. It stimulates respiration and the brain by increasing the blood supply, increases the heart's action, and under its daily use an extra amount of labor can be borne without suffering. It is an agreeable and wholesome stimulant, and imparts a pleasant taste with an agreeable sense of warmth which permeates the entire system. Don't buy bitters from your local druggist unless you are acquainted with the reputation of the manufacturers, and thus know that the ingredients contained are of the highest grade.

OUR OFFER. Send us 73c for a bottle of our Orange Wine Stomach Bitters, and if you are not greatly benefited, if you do not find it superior to any bitters on the market, return it at our expense and we will cheerfully refund your money. Unmailable on account of weight.

No. 5105 Our special price for bottles holding 1½ pints...$0.75
For half dozen bottles.................................. 4.00
For one dozen bottles.................................. 7.75

Our Homeopathic Remedies.

$1.50 Buys a Family Medicine Case and Remedies.

Retails at Double the Price

OUR HOMEOPATHIC SPECIFICS

are prepared under the supervision of an old experienced Homeopathic physician. Great care is taken in preparing them according to the rules laid down by the highest authorities on homeopathy, and only the purest drugs used. Every one of the following specifics is a special cure for the disease named on it. Adults take 6 pellets children from 1 to 3 according to age, and from two to four doses are to be taken every day, according to the severity of the case. We ask the special attention of all our customers to these high grade remedies. If you have them near at hand, we guarantee they will save you many a doctor's bill, and what is of more consequence, quickly relieve any suffering member of the family and ward off more serious sickness. We make the price as low as we possibly can in order that they may be within reach of every one of our customers, only 18c each bottle, with the exception of three rare ones which of necessity we require to make higher price.

OUR $1.50 FAMILY MEDICINE CASE DR. HAMMOND'S HOMEOPATHIC REMEDIES GUARANTEED HIGHEST GRADE MADE SOLD ONLY BY SEARS ROEBUCK AND CO. INC. CHICAGO ILL.

If by mail, postage, extra, per case, 26 cents.

A SPECIAL OFFER. As an inducement to give these Remedies a thorough trial, we will allow you to select 12 cures, including the 60c ones. Make your own selection, one or more of any kind, and we will put them in a neat case such as we represent here and charge you $1.50. No family can afford to neglect this great offer.

A 12-Box Case will save you many dollars doctor's bills in a year and may save your life. No family should be without a case of our homeopathic Remedies.

		Usual Price	Our Price
No. 5245	Cures rheumatism or rheumatic pains..............	$0.25	$0.18
No. 5247	Cures fever and ague, intermittent fever, malaria etc.	.25	.18
No. 5249	Cures piles, blind or bleeding, external or internal,...	.25	.18
No. 5251	Cures ophthalmia, weak or inflamed eyes............	.25	.18
No. 5253	Cures catarrh, influenza, cold in the head..........	.25	.18
No. 5255	Cures whooping cough, spasmodic cough............	.25	.18
No. 5259	Cures asthma, oppressed or difficult breathing......	.25	.18
No. 5261	Cures fevers, congestions, inflammation............	.25	.18
No. 5263	Cures worm fever or worm diseases................	.25	.18
No. 5265	Cures colic, crying and wakefulness of infants teething	.25	.18
No. 5267	Cures diarrhœa of children and adults............	.25	.18
No. 5269	Cures dysentery, griping, bilious colic...........	.25	.18
No. 5271	Cures cholera, cholera morbus, vomiting..........	.25	.18
No. 5273	Cures coughs, colds, bronchitis...	.25	.18
No. 5275	Cures toothache, faceache, neuralgia............	.25	.18
No. 5277	Cures headache, sick headache, vertigo...........	.25	.18
No. 5279	Cures dyspepsia, indigestion, weak stomach.......	.25	.18
No. 5281	Cures suppressed or scanty menses.............	.25	.18
No. 5283	Cures leucorrhœa, or profuse menses............	.25	.18
No. 5285	Cures croup, hoarse cough, difficult breathing, laryngitis	.25	.18
No. 5287	Cures salt rheum eruptions, erysipelas...........	.25	.18
No. 5289	Cures ear discharge, earache......	.25	.18
No. 5291	Cures scrofula, swellings, ulcers...	.25	.18
No. 5293	Cures general debility, physical weakness, brain fag............	.25	.18
No. 5295	Cures dropsy, fluid accumulations.	.25	.18
No. 5297	Cures seasickness, nausea, vomiting	.25	.18
No. 5299	Cures kidney disease, gravel, calculi.............	.25	.18
No. 5301	Cures nervous debility, vital weakness............	1.00	.60
No. 5303	Cures sore mouth and canker......	.25	.18
No. 5305	Cures urinary incontinence, wetting bed..........	.25	.18
No. 5307	Cures painful menses, pruritis....	.25	.18
No. 5309	Cures diseases of the heart, palpitation..........	1.00	.60
No. 5311	Cures epilepsy, St. Vitus dance..	1.00	.60
No. 5313	Cures sore throat, quinsy or ulcerated sore throat..	.25	.18
No. 5315	Cures chronic congestions, headache..............	.25	.18
No. 5317	Cures grip and chronic colds.....	.25	.18
No. 5319	A strong cardboard case covered with black muslin, containing 12 specifics, your own selection from above list............		1.50
No. 5321	A polished hardwood case, with lock and key, containing 24 remedies...........		4.50
No. 5323	A full line of Humphrey's Munyon's and Ballentine's cures in stock. The size usually sold for...	.25	.20
	The size usually sold for...........	1.00	.80

YOU MAY LIVE MILES FROM A REGULAR PHYSICIAN. If so, you are in danger without these remedies in your home. They are always handy, always convenient, easy to take, act quick, will relieve your suffering and may save your life while waiting a doctor's arrival.

Only $1.50 for a case of 12 bottles, your own selection. Take our warning notice, don't be without them.

If by mail, postage, extra, per bottle, 2 cents.

Homeopathic Medicines.

WE ARE PREPARED TO FURNISH ANYTHING in the line of Homeopathic Supplies, and guarantee them to be full strength and fresh condition. We mention a few of the more prominent. We will be pleased to furnish information on homeopathic medicines if you are in doubt as to what to order. We will also send a copy of Halsey's Manual of (132 pages), a complete homeopathic treatise, free on request. When ordering these medicines please specify what form you wish them in—pills, powder, discs or liquid.

Name.	Strength	Name.	Strength.	Name.	Strength.
Aconite.........	3x	Cuprum met.....	3x	Mercurius viv....	3x
Antimon crud...	3x	Digitalis........	2x	Natrum mur.....	6x
Apismel........	3x	Drosera........	2x	Nitric Acid.....	6x
Arnica.........	3x	Dulcamara......	3x	Nux vomica.....	3x
Arsenic alb.....	3x	Eupatorium p'r	1x	Opium.........	3x
Baptisia........	1x	Ferrum phos....	3x	Phosphorus....	3x
Belladonna.....	3x	Gelsemium.....	1x	Phosphorus aci..	3x
Bryonia alba...	3x	Glonoine.......	3x	Phytolacca.....	0
Calcarea carb..	3x	Graphites......	6x	Podophyllin....	3x
Cantharis......	3x	Hamamelis.....	1x	Pulsatilla......	3x
Carby veg......	3x	Hepar sulphr..	3x	Rhus tox.......	3x
Caulophyllum..	3x	Hydrastis......	1x	Sanguinaria....	3x
Causticum......	3x	Hyoscyamus...	3x	Secale cor.....	1x
Chamomilla....	3x	Ignatia........	3x	Sepia..........	3x
China..........	3x	Iodium........	3x	Silicea........	6x
Chinin, arsen..	2x	Ipecac.........	3x	Spigelia.......	3x
Chimicifuga....	1x	Kali bichr......	3x	Spongia........	3x
Cina...........	3x	Lachesis.......	8x	Staphysagria...	3x
Cocculus.......	3x	Lycopodium....	3x	Sulphur.......	3x
Coffea crud....	3x	Mercurius bnod	3x	Tartar emetic..	3x
Colchicum.....	3x	Mercurius corr.	3x	Veratrum alb...	3x
Colocynthis...	3x	Mercurius sol...	3x		

No. 5330	¼-oz. phials each, 10c; by mail......................	.15c
No. 5332	½-oz. phials each, 15c; by mail......................	.20c
No. 5334	1 -oz. phials each, 20c; by mail......................	.25c
No. 5336	2 -oz. phials each, 40c; by mail......................	.45c

Halsey's Specialties.

		Bottle
No. 5340	Carbo Peptine Wafers................	$0.40
No. 5341	Burn and Frost Liniment............	.25
No. 5342	Camphor Pills.....................	.20
No. 5343	Catarrh Tablets...................	.25
No. 5344	Catarrh Treatment Complete........	2.75
No. 5345	Chestnut Pile Crate...............	.40
No. 5346	Elixir Hydrastic and Cocoa.........	.80
No. 5347	General Debility Specific...........	.50
No. 5348	Goitre Tablets....................	.50
No. 5349	Hensel's Tonic....................	.60
No. 5351	Infant Tablets....................	.40
No. 5351	La Grippe Specific................	.60
No. 5352	Liver Tablets.....................	.40
No. 5353	Nerve Salt.......................	1.60
No. 5354	Neuralgia Cure...................	.25
No. 5355	Rhus and Bryonia Plaster. Small....	.20
No. 5356	Rhus and Bryonia Plaster. Yard rolls	.75
No. 5357	Sore Throat Tablets...............	.25
No. 5358	Tape Worm Remedy................	.75
No. 5359	Uterine Wafers...................	.40
No. 5360	Whooping Cough Syrup.............	.25
No. 5361	Witch Hazel Cream................	.20

Homeopathic Books.

No. 5375 Ruddock's Stepping Stone to Homeopathy and Health. 258 Pages. Price.................... $0.80
No. 5377 Ruddock's Homeopathic Guide, Containing the Stepping Stone and The Ladies' Manual in One Volume. 592 Pages. Price..................... $1.60

Special Homeopathic Cases and Remedies

..AT 85 CENTS UP TO $6.75..

We Make Special Medicine Cases to Order to Contain 12, 24, 36 or 48 Remedies. We will Fill these Cases with any assortment of Remedies you wish, and any size Bottles.

WITH EACH CASE WE SEND A HOMEOPATHIC MANUAL, GIVING FULL DIRECTIONS HOW TO USE THE REMEDIES, ALSO A ...

...GENERAL DESCRIPTION OF DISEASES AND HOW TO TREAT SICK PEOPLE TO GET THEM WELL AGAIN.

OUR PRICES ARE VERY LOW FOR THESE CASES and they are worth from five to six times the amount we ask for them. Send us a description of the remedies wanted and we will send you the cost. There ought to be one in every household, especially where there are children.

THE TWELVE CHIEF REMEDIES DIRECTIONS HALSEY Drug Co.

Our 85c Homeopathic Case.

No. 5380 Contains 12 1-dr. remedies with directions........... 85c

Our $1.50 Homeopathic Case.

No. 5382 Contains 12 2-dr. remedies with directions........... $1.50

Our $5.00 Homeopathic Case.

No. 5384 This is a durable polished hardwood case, containing 24 2-dr. and 4 1-oz. bottles, fitted with lock and key, complete with "Ruddock's Stepping Stone"................ $5.00
No. 5386 Similar to above, containing 36 2-dr. and 4 1-oz. bottles, complete with book...... $6.75

New American Family Physician.

$1.65 For a $4.75 Book.

No. 29130 A popular and authentic guide for the household management of all diseases. It gives the history, cause, means of prevention, and symptoms of all diseases and the most approved methods of treatment. Contains a full description of 64 medical plants. 200 pages are devoted exclusively to diseases of women and children. Handsomely bound in silk cloth, marbled edges. Size, 10¾x8x1 inches. Retail price, $4.75; our special price.... (If by mail, postage, extra, 33 cents.) .$1.65

Nursery Bottle Fittings.

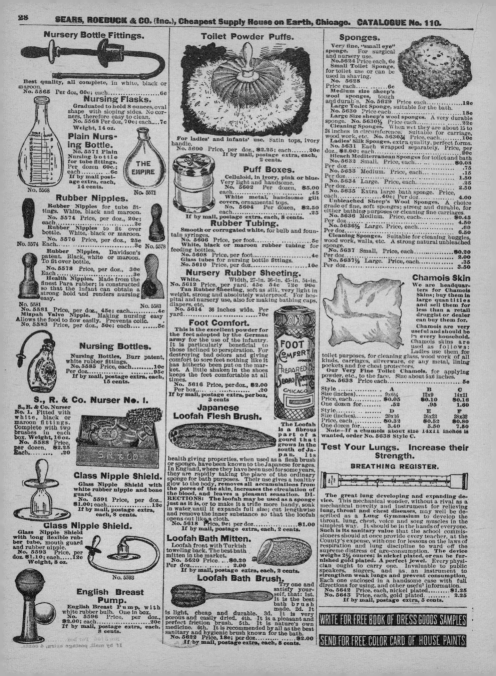

Best quality, all complete, in white, black or maroon.
No. 5565 Per doz, 60c; each...........6c

Nursing Flasks.

Graduated to hold 8 ounces, oval shape with sloping sides. No corners, therefore easy to clean.
No. 5568 Per doz, 70c; each.....7c
Weight, 14 oz.

Plain Nursing Bottle.

No. 5571 Plain Nursing bottle for tube fittings.
Per dozen 60c.;
each...........6c
If by mail postage extra, each, 14 cents.

No. 5568   No. 5571   THE EMPIRE

Rubber Nipples.

Rubber Nipples for tube fittings. White, black and maroon.
No. 5574 Price, per doz., 20c; each...........2c
Rubber Nipples to fit over bottle. White, black or maroon.
No. 5576 Price, per doz., 25c
No. 5578 Each..........3c

No. 5574   No. 5578

Rubber Nipples, Davidson's patent. Black, white or maroon. To fit over bottle.
No. 5578 Price, per doz., 30c
Each...........3c
Health Nipples. Made from the finest Para rubber; is constructed so that the infant can obtain a strong hold and renders nursing easy.

No. 5581   No. 5583
No. 5581 Price, per doz., 45c; each...........4c
Mizpah Valve Nipple. Making nursing easy. Allows the food to flow easily. Prevents colic.
No. 5583 Price, per doz., 50c; each........5c

Nursing Bottles.

Nursing Bottles, Burr patent, white rubber fittings.
No. 5585 Price, each...........10c
Per doz..........95c
If by mail, postage extra, each, 15 cents.

S., R. & Co. Nurser No. 1.

S., R. & Co. Nurser No. 1. Fitted with white, black or maroon fittings. Complete with two brushes in each box. Weight, 16 oz.
No. 5588 Price, per dozen, $2.25
Each...........20

Glass Nipple Shield.

Glass Nipple Shield with white rubber nipple and bone guard.
No. 5591 Price, per doz., $1.00; each........12c
If by mail, postage extra, each, 8 cents.

Glass Nipple Shield.

Glass Nipple Shield with long flexible rubber tube, mouth guard and rubber nipple.
No. 5593 Price, per doz. $1.10; each........12c
Weight, 8 oz.

No. 5593

English Breast Pump.

English Breast Pump, with white rubber bulb. One in box.
No. 5596 Price, per doz., $2.00; each........
If by mail, postage extra, each, 8 cents.

Toilet Powder Puffs.

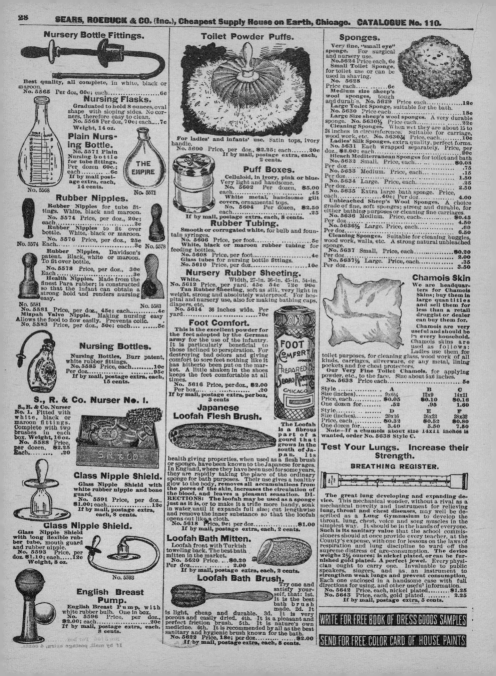

For ladies' and infants' use. Satin tops, ivory handle.
No. 5600 Price, per doz., $2.25; each........20c
If by mail, postage extra, each, 2 cents.

Puff Boxes.

Celluloid, in ivory, pink or blue. Very light and handsome.
No. 5602 Per dozen, $5.00 each...........45
White metal, handsome gilt covers, ornamental tops.
No. 5604 Per dozen, $2.50 each...........25
If by mail, postage extra, each, 8 cents.

Rubber Tubing.

Smooth or corrugated white, for bulb and fountain syringes.
No. 5606 Price, per foot...........5c
White, black or maroon rubber tubing for feeding bottles.
No. 5608 Price, per foot...........4c
Glass tubes for nursing bottle fittings.
No. 5610 Price, per doz...........10c

Nursery Rubber Sheeting.

White.   Width, 27-in. 36-in. 45-in. 54-in.
No. 5612 Price, per yard. 45c 54c 72c 90c
Tan Rubber Sheeting, soft as silk, very light in weight, strong and absolutely waterproof. For hospital and nursery use, also for making bathing caps, diapers, etc.
No. 5614 36 inches wide. Per yard...........70c

Foot Comfort.

This is the excellent powder for the feet adopted by the German army for the use of the infantry. It is particularly beneficial to those inclined to perspiration. For destroying bad odors and giving comfort to sore feet nothing like it has hitherto been put on the market. A little shaken in the shoes keeps the feet comfortable at all times.
No. 5616 Price, per doz., $2.00
Per box...........20
If by mail, postage extra, per box, 3 cents

Japanese Loofah Flesh Brush.

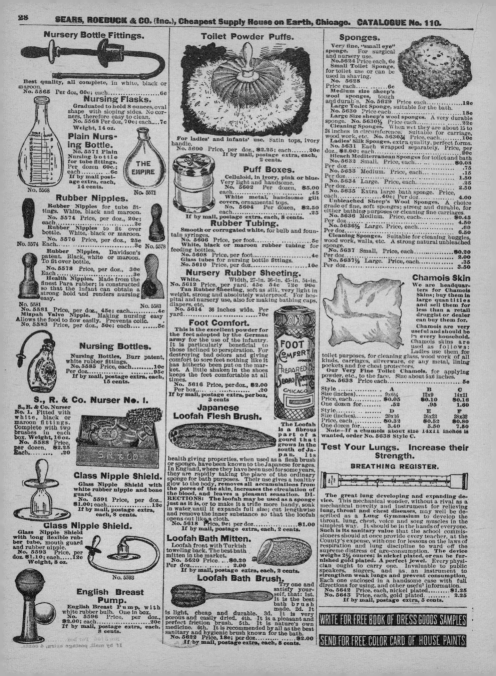

The Loofah is a fibrous gourd that grows in the south of Japan. Its health giving properties, when used as a flesh brush or sponge, have been known to the Japanese for ages. In England, where they have been used for some years, they are rapidly taking the place of the ordinary sponge for bath purposes. Their use gives a healthy glow to the body, removes all accumulations from the pores of the skin, increases the circulation of the blood, and leaves a pleasant sensation. DIRECTIONS: The loofah may be used as a sponge just as it is, or to make it a trifle more handy, soak in water until it expands full size; cut lengthwise and remove the inner substance so that the loofah opens out like a cloth.
No. 5618 Price, 9c; per doz...........$1.00
If by mail, postage extra, each, 2 cents.

Loofah Bath Mitten.

Loofah front with Turkish toweling back. The best bath mitten in the market.
No. 5620 Price...........$0.20
Per doz...........2.00
If by mail, postage extra, each, 2 cents.

Loofah Bath Brush.

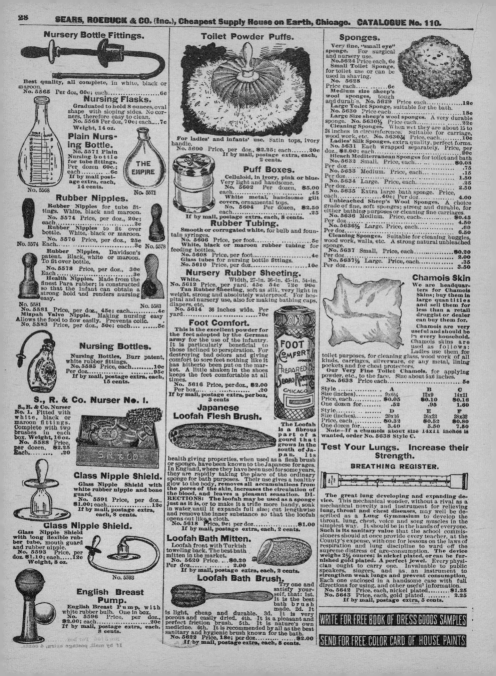

Try one and satisfy yourself, that: 1st. It is the best bath brush made. 2d. It is light, cheap and durable. 3d. It is very porous and easily dried. 4th. It is a pleasant and perfect friction brush. 5th. It is nature's own medicine. 6th. It is recommended by all as the best sanitary and hygienic brush known for the bath.
No. 5622 Price, 18c; per doz...........$2.00
If by mail, postage extra, each, 5 cents.

Sponges.

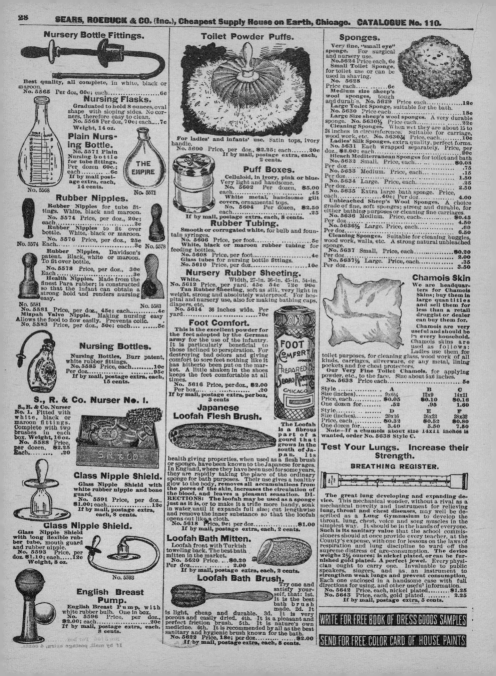

Very fine, "small eye" sponge. For surgical and nursery use.
No. 5624 Price, each...........6c
Small Toilet Sponge, for toilet use or can be used in shaving.
No. 5628 Price, each...........6c
Medium size sheep's wool sponges, tough and durable. No. 5629 Price each...........12c
Large Toilet Sponge, suitable for the bath.
No. 5630 Price each...........18c
Large Size sheep's wool sponges. A very durable sponge. No. 5630½ Price each...........22c
Cleaning Sponges. When wet they are about 15 to 24 inches in circumference. Suitable for carriage, wood work, etc. No. 5630¾ Price, each...........10c
Ladies' Silk Sponges, extra quality, perfect forms.
No. 5631 Each wrapped separately. Price, per doz., $2.00; each...........20c
Bleach Mediterranean Sponges for toilet and bath
No. 5632 Small. Price, each...........$0.05
Per doz...........75
No. 5633 Medium. Price, each...........15
Per doz...........1.50
No. 5634 Large. Price, each...........25
Per doz...........2.50
No. 5635 Extra large bath sponge. Price, each...........40c; Per doz...........4.00
Unbleached Sheep's Wool Sponges. A choice grade of fine, soft sponges; strong and durable, for either bathing purposes or cleaning fine carriages.
No. 5636 Medium. Price, each...........$0.45
Per doz...........4.50
No. 5636½ Large. Price, each...........60
Per doz...........6.50
Cleaning Sponges. Suitable for cleaning buggies, wood work, walls, etc. A strong natural unbleached sponge.
No. 5637 Small. Price, each...........$0.20
Per doz...........2.00
No. 5637½ Large. Price, each...........35
Per doz...........3.50

Chamois Skin

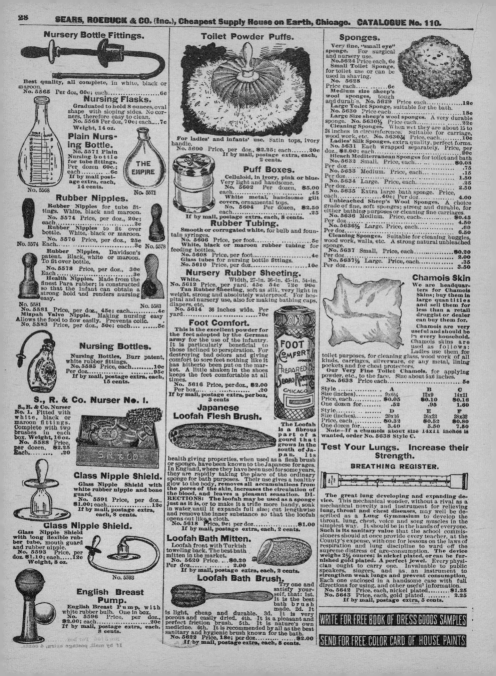

We are headquarters for Chamois Skins; buy them in large quantities and sell them for less than a retail druggist or dealer can buy them for.

Chamois are very useful and should be in every household. Chamois skins are used as follows: Ladies use them for toilet purposes, for cleaning glass, wood work of all kinds, carriages, silverware, or any metal, lining pockets and for chest protectors.

Our Very Fine Toilet Chamois, for applying powder, etc., to the face. Size about 5x6 inches.
No. 5633 Price each...........5c

Style	A	B	C
Size (inches)	9x6¼	12x9	14x11
Price, each	$0.05	$0.10	$0.15
One dozen for	.52	.95	1.60
Style	D	E	F
Size (inches)	20x16	26x23	28x32
Price, each	$0.33	$0.52	$0.80
One dozen for	3.40	5.50	7.50

Note—If a chamois about size 14x11 inches is wanted, order No. 5638 Style C.

Test Your Lungs. Increase their Strength.

BREATHING REGISTER.

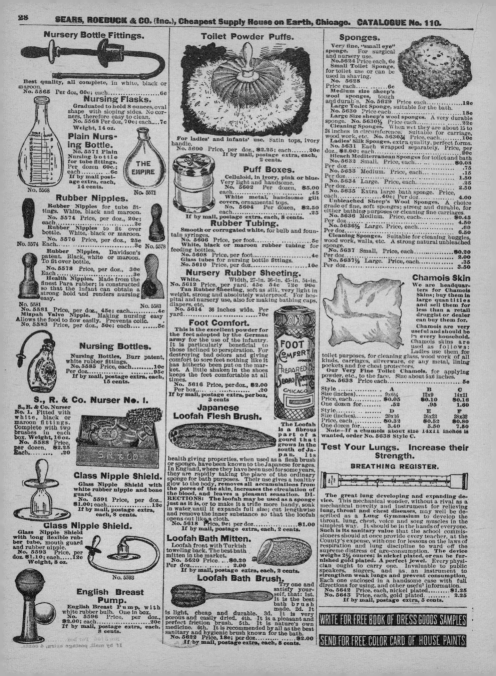

The great lung developing and expanding device. This mechanical wonder, without a rival as a mechanical novelty and instrument for relieving lung, throat and chest diseases, may well be described as a Lung Gymnasium to develop the throat, lung, chest, voice and song muscles in the simplest way. It should be in the hands of everyone. Such is its sanitary value that the school commissioners should at once provide every teacher, at the County's expense, with one for lessons on the laws of respiration and lung discipline to ward off the supreme distress of age-consumption. The device weighs 2½ ounces; is nickel plated, or can be furnished gold plated. A perfect jewel. Every physician ought to carry one. Invaluable to public speakers, singers, and as an instrument to strengthen weak lungs and prevent consumption. Each one enclosed in a handsome case with full directions for using, and other useful information.
No. 5642 Price, each, nickel plated...........$1.25
No. 5643 Price, each, gold plated...........2.25
If by mail, postage extra, each, 5 cents.

VETERINARY DEPARTMENT

Agricultural Department.

Veterinary Medicines and Health Foods for Farmers and Raisers of Stock.

....KEEP YOUR ANIMALS HEALTHY AND SAVE MONEY AND WORRY....

WE PRESENT TO OUR CUSTOMERS a most valuable and complete line of internal and external remedies and health foods for horses, cattle, sheep, hogs, poultry, dogs, and all domestic animals. These have been carefully selected by our Veterinary Surgeon and we guarantee them to be the best preparations of this kind ever offered to the farmer and raiser of stock. You can thoroughly rely on what we say concerning each of them. When your animals are sick and out of condition give these remedies a trial. You will be surprised with the good results. Your animals will soon become well again and feel in better condition than ever. You will find enclosed with each package, complete instructions how to use these remedies, and also valuable information how to treat sick animals.

Veterinary Blister.

A Good Blister for Animals is a Rare and Valuable Article.

We have spent much time and made many experiments in preparing a really practical and thoroughly reliable blister that can be applied easily, and good results follow. We have submitted samples to the best veterinary surgeons in the country and they have approved of it, and are using it daily in their practice. It is unexcelled for bone spavin, ring bone, splint, curb, hog spavin, blood spavin, thoroughpin, etc. Removes wind puffs, calouses, etc., from skin and bruises, thickening of tendons, etc. Full information how to use it and a description of bone spavin, etc., with each package.

No. 5750 Each.............40c
If by mail, postage extra, per box, 8 cents.

Veterinary Fattening Powder.

If your horse is out of condition and getting thin, give him two tablespoonfuls of this powder morning and night, and in a few days he will look like a new animal so that your neighbor will scarcely know him.

Give your cows a dose with each feed of grain, meal or chopped stuff, dampened with water. You will be surprised at the large increase and improvement in quality of the milk as well as the better condition of the animal. Calves, sheep and cattle of all kinds improve in flesh and health when the powder is used occasionally. It is the very best fattening and health giving powder in the market. We guarantee its qualities to our customers. Use this remedy in time; do not wait until your stock is sick, but give it to ward off sickness. It pays for itself, keeping the animal in a strong, healthy condition.

No. 5752 10 lb. package............$1.00   25 lb. package............$2.00
          50 lb. package............ 3.50   100 lb. package........... 6.00

Veterinary Fever Remedy.

Give in all diseases that are accompanied by fever. Give early in lung fever, pneumonia, bronchitis, pleurisy, laryngitis, sore throat, distemper, cold, etc. It is a positive cure, if given promptly, in an attack of laminitis, or founder, and accompanied by hot poultices to the horse's feet, it will remove the congestion and effect a permanent cure in a few hours. In case of inflammation of the bowels, given with Acme Colic Cure, and hot applications to the belly, gives relief to the patient and cures the disease in a few hours.

No. 5756 Bottle, each......40c
Unmailable account of weight.

Veterinary Wire Cut Remedy.

This is a remedy which should always be within reach. It is worth many times its cost when wanted.

It will heal cuts and wounds in all parts of the body without leaving a scar. It is the best remedy for cuts from barbed wire; it heals them the quickest. In using this remedy it is not necessary to sew any cuts: if you have a flap that hangs down, fasten it in place by a bandage, but don't close the sore—give it a free chance to discharge. By applying this remedy it will soon heal. It is an antiseptic destroying all germs and foul odors. It also preserve the sores from flies and insects.

No. 5760 Price, per bottle.................40c
Unmailable on account of weight.

Acme Veterinary Cough Powder.

A sure cure for all coughs, colds, distemper, laryngitis, pneumonia, pleurisy, etc. Full instructions for use with description of the symptoms of distemper on each package.

No. 5764 Price, per box.........25c
If by mail, postage extra, 8 cents.

Gall Cure.

A gall cure that can be depended upon. It will heal collar galls, bit galls, saddle galls, boot galls, and abrasions of the skin, while the animal is at work. Toughens the skin, stains the parts and makes a galled horse look respectable. Quickest cure, most economical and humane treatment.

No. 5766 Per box.................25c
If by mail, postage extra, 4 cents.

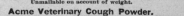

Ground Beef Scraps.

We select and grind the beef scraps ourselves, thus insuring a clean, sweet article. They contain more nutriment than any other article of food, therefore we consider them better to feed to fowl for the market than for eggs. They will fatten a hen wonderfully, and increase its value ten fold. Still many use them and prefer them to anything else as egg producers.

No. 2118   10-lb. bags....30c   50-lb. bags.....$0.95
25-lb. bags....55c   100-lb. bags.. 1.80

Granulated Bone.

A wrong impression exists regarding bone. Fresh bone contains 55 per cent moisture and 12 per cent grease, so that when you buy fresh bone you pay for 65 pounds of useless material in every 100 pounds you buy. Our Granulated Bone is made from fresh, green bones, and the moisture and grease is taken out, leaving nothing but the phosphate of lime and nitrogen. These are the only two feeding properties of the bone, so that when you buy our bone you get all the feeding properties without buying or paying freight on moisture or grease, and you get an article that will keep its any kind of weather if kept dry. Bone is the best producer of egg shells known.

No. 2103   10-lb. bags....30c   50-lb. bags............$1.05
25-lb. bags....55c   100-lb. bags........... 1.95

Ground Oyster Shells.

These are made from bright, clean shells; are a good producer of egg shells, and preferred by many on account of being cheaper than bone. They also make grit necessary. In ordering oyster shells, please state whether you prefer coarse or medium-sized shells. The coarse are as large as kernels of corn.

No. 2106   25-lb. bags............................25c
No. 2107   50-lb. bags............................40c
No. 2108   100-lb. bags...........................55c
MICA CRYSTAL GRITS furnished at same price as Oyster Shells.

Paris Green and London Purple.

In Liquid Form.

For spraying all kinds of fruit trees, vines and plants. Sure death to potato bugs, chinch bugs, curculio, canker and cotton worms, etc. Prompt and pleasing results. Only one trial necessary to convince you. Are much better to handle than the powder and equally effectual when the directions are followed as given on each can. Be sure and use the liquid and avoid the danger of getting poisoned. It mingles freely when put with water and never settles. It being a liquid it discharges freely from the nozzle or sprinkler. We will send a calendar containing full instructions on spraying to any address on receipt of a two-cent stamp. Very useful to farmers, fruit growers and stockmen.

Bigelow's Liquid Paris Green.

For spraying all kinds of fruit trees, vines and plants. Is sure death to potato bugs, chinch bugs, curculio, canker worms, etc. One can is sufficient for 150 gallons of water. Full instructions how to use it on every can.
No. 5860   Price, per can 25c

Bigelow's Liquid London Purple.

For spraying all kinds of fruit trees, vines and plants. Is sure death to potato bugs, chinch bugs, curculio, canker worms, etc. Directions how to use it to the best advantage.
No. 5862   Price, per can 25c

Bigelow's Purple Jack.

Sure death to the worm that eats the head of the cabbage or the fruit of the tomato.
No. 5864   Price, per can 25c

Kerosene Emulsion.

For spraying and washing fruit trees, vines, plants, field crops and domestic animals. Destroys plant lice, red spiders, scales, mealy bugs, lice on cattle and hogs, tick on sheep. One can is sufficient for 50 gallons.
No. 5866   Price, per can 35c

Bordeaux Mixture.

Compounded from the old formula, but by an entirely new process. Prevents blight, rot, mildew and rust. Destroys all fungus growth on vegetation. One can is sufficient to dilute with 35 to 50 gallons of water.
No. 5868   Price, per can 25c

Veterinary Instruments.

In veterinary goods we illustrate only a few instruments that are commonly used by everyone owning a horse, but we are in a position to supply anything made in this line, and will quote prices on application.

Wolf Tooth Forceps, bayonet pattern, length 13 inches, nickel plated.
No. 5900   Price, each $3.00

Wolf Tooth Forceps, curved, nickel plated, length 9 inches.
No. 5902   Price, ea....$2.50

Small Molar Splinter Forceps, nickel plated,13 inches.
No. 5904   Price, each....$3.00

Straight Incisor Cutters
No. 5906   Price...$4.00

Molar Extracting Forceps. Handle extra.
No. 5908   Price, each..............$7.00

Open and Closed Molar Cutters. Handles extra. When ordering mention the kind wanted.
No. 5910   Price, each..............$7.00

Handles for cutters and extractors.
No. 5912   Price, per pair..............$3.00

Dunn's Combined Float consists of one straight float for use on the upper and lower molars, and one Angular Float for use on the first molar teeth, no screws to rust and files cannot drop out.
No. 5914   Price, per set..............$3.75

Palmer's Dental File.
No. 5916   Each..............$1.00

Plain Double File. 10 inches.
No. 5918   Each..............$0.50

Separating Saw.
No. 5920   Each..$1.00

Simmon's Pus Scoops.
No. 5922   Each..............$1.75

Balling Iron. Weight, 1¾ lbs; plain.
No. 5924   Each..............$0.75
Nickel plated.............. 1.50

Castrating Knives.

Castrating Knife. Spring back.
No. 5926   Each.$1.25

No. 5926

Ziegler's Castrating Knife.
No. 5928   Each.$2.00
If by mail, postage, extra, 4 cents.

No. 5928

Horse Flems. Brass handle.
No. 5930   Each, two blades 65c
Three blades....75c
If by mail, postage, extra, 5 cents.

Spring Lancet.

Spring Lancet, guarded.
No. 5932
Price, each $2.25

No. 5932

Seton Needles.

Seton Needles, plain.
No. 5934   Price, 6-inch..............$0.50
Price, 12-inch..............90
Price, 18-inch.............. 1.00
If by mail, postage, extra, 10 cents.

Seton Needles.

Seton Needles, jointed.
No. 5936   Price, 12-inch, 1 joint..............$1.75
Price, 18-inch, 2 joints.............. 2.25
If by mail, postage, extra, 15 cents.

Fetlock Shears.

Fetlock Shears.
No. 5938
Price..............$1.00

Roweling Shears.

Roweling Shears, best quality.
No. 5940   Price...$2.25

Braided Silk.

Braided Silk, 4 sizes on card; white.
No. 5942   Price, per card..............50c

Twisted Silk.

Twisted Silk, one size on card; white.
No. 5944   Price, per card..............10c

Half Curve Needles.

Half Curve Needles in sizes from 2 to 4 inches.
No. 5946   Price, each..............$0.15
Per doz..............1.00

Full Curve Needles.

Full Curve Needles in sizes 2 to 4 inches.
No. 5948   Price, per doz., $1.00; each.....15c

Straight Needles.

Straight Needles, sizes 2 to 4 inches.
No. 5950   Price, per doz., $1.00; each.....15c

Sand Crack Forceps.

Sand Crack Forceps and Cautery Iron.
No. 5952
Price..............$6.00

Hoof Knives.

Hoof Knife, double edge, stiff.

No. 5970 Price, each..........$1.25
If by mail, postage, extra, 5 cents.

Hoof Knife, single edge, folding spring back.
No. 5971 Price, each..........$1.25
If by mail, postage, extra, 5 cents.

Dunn's Improved Ecraseur.

This is one of the latest improved instruments. It can be held in the hand and the slack of the chain can be taken up at once by a simple movement with the thumb and finger without drawing out the screw or lengthening the instrument.
No. 5972 Price..........$11.50

Cattle Trocar and Canula.

Cattle Trocar and Canula, for opening and draining abscesses, etc.
No. 5974 Price..........$1.50
If by mail, postage, extra, 4 cents.

Veterinary Thermometers.

Veterinary Thermometer, 5-inch, sensitive, self registering; in pocket case. No. 5975 Price....$1.25

Veterinary Thermometer, 5-inch, sensitive, self registering; in pocket case.
No. 5977 Price..........$1.50

Veterinary Thermometer fenestrated, case and chain. No. 5978 Price..........$1.50

Perfection Calf Dehorner.

Perfection Calf Dehorner. So simple that it can be operated by anyone. So cheap it is within reach of all.
No. 5980 Price, nickel, $5.00; plain..........$3.50

Keystone Dehorning Clippers.

Keystone Dehorning Clippers. The Latest Improved and most Powerful Instrument for Dehorning Cattle Manufactured.
No. 5983 Price..........$12.00

Haussmann's Mouth Speculum.

The only speculum made by which the pressure of the horse's jaws is brought upon the front teeth instead of the soft tissues of the gums. It is very easily applied, and a special feature of which can be found in no other speculum is the curved side bars, which expose the front molar teeth and afford an unobstructed view of the mouth from either side and the greatest possible space to operate in.
No. 5896 Price..........$9.50

3

Haussmann's Spaying Emasculator.

Haussmann's Spaying Emasculator. This is the simplest, safest and quickest instrument made for castrating. Neither clamps, medicine or cording are required. By means of this instrument the spermatic cord is severed by tortion, completely preventing the loss of blood.
No. 5988 Price..........$9.50

Haussmann's Emasculator.

Haussmann's Emasculator. A simple, strong, safe and quick instrument. No fear of hemorrhage after operations, as the blood vessels are completely closed.
No. 5990 Price..........$9.50

Czar Soft Rubber Drenching Bottle.

Czar Soft Rubber Drenching Bottle. Capacity 1 pint. Will not break.
No. 5900 Price..........$3.00

Drenching Horn.

For administering medicine to horses. Weight, ½ lb.
No. 5995 Price, each..........85c

Drenching Bit.

Burton's Drenching Bit. No longer any trouble to give your horse medicine. One man can do it; used by horsemen throughout the country. Weight 1¼ lbs.
No. 5998 Price each..........$2.75

Dehorning Saw.

No. 6000 Dehorning Saw. Price..........$1.00
No. 6001 Dehorning Saw, nickel plated.
Price..........$2.50

Boss Pig Extractor Forceps.

The Boss Pig Extractor and Tooth Forceps, with a treatise on the raising of the pig. This instrument was given first premium at Iowa State Fair, 1895, and is the newest invention of the kind. The outfit is put up neatly in a box and complete weighs only 18 ounces. Once tried always used, is the general prediction.
No. 6003 Price of outfit, complete..........$1.00

Improved Pig Forceps.

The Improved Pig Forceps has points of excellence which make it a most practical instrument, and may be used upon either small or large sows with equal satisfaction. The instrument is made of malleable iron, tinned to prevent rusting; will not tear the sow or otherwise injure the animal in operation.
No. 6007 Price, each..........75c

Horse Trocar.

No. 6009 Horse Trocar, reversible.
Price..........$1.25

Horse Catheter.

Horse Catheter, best quality.
No. 6012 Price..........$2.00
Horse Catheter, same as above, second quality.
No. 6015 Price..........$1.75

Metal Mare Catheter.

Metal Mare Catheter. No. 6017 Price..........$1.50

Metal Mare Catheter, jointed.
No. 6019 Price..........$2.00

Injection Syringes.

Injection Syringes; metal; 16 ounces. Weight, 1½ lbs.
No. 6022 Price..........$1.04
No. 6024 24 ounces, weight, 2¾ lbs. Price..2.50
No. 6026 36 ounces, weight, 3¼ lbs. Price..2.70

Haussmann's Ball Gun.

No. 6028 Haussmann's Ball Gun, stiff. Price..$2.50
No. 6030 Haussmann's Ball Gun, jointed. Price..........$3.00
No. 6031 Plain Ball Gun. Price..........2.25

Syringes.

Syringes, for administering medicine to horses and other animals. Quittor hard rubber, two pipes.
No. 6035 Price..........$1.50

Syringes, same as preceding, but of metal, nickel plated, quittor, two pipes.
No. 6036 Price, each..........$2.50

Veterinary Hard Rubber Horse Syringes.

Veterinary Hard Rubber Horse Syringes, capacity, 24 ounces.
No. 6040 Price, each..........$3.75

Gouging Forceps.

Gouging Forceps, nickel plated.
No. 6042 Price, each..........$3.50

Probang for Horses and Cattle.

No. 6047 Probang for Horses and Cattle, 6 feet $4.50
No. 6048 Probang for Horses and Cattle, 7 feet 5.00
No. 6049 Probang for Horses and Cattle, 8 feet 6.00

Docking Shears.

Docking Shears. Made of the finest tempered steel, will always keep a good edge.
No. 6052 Price, each..........$7.50

Haussmann's Trephine.

No. 6056. Haussmann's Trephine, with one head..........$3.00
No. 6057 Haussmann's Trephine, with two heads..........$3.50
Made either conical or cylindrical. A most useful instrument and thoroughly reliable.

Dunn's Embryotomy Knife.

Dunn's Embryotomy Knife. Best knife made for removing foal from mare, or calf from cow.
No. 6060 Price, each..........$3.50

Mullen's Sharp Double Embryotomy Hook.

Mullen's Sharp Double Embryotomy Hook, for removing dead foals.
No. 6062 Price, each..........$2.50

Montgomery's Double Blunt Embryotomy Hook.

Montgomery's Double Blunt Embryotomy Hook, for removing foetus from cow or mare.
No. 6064 Price, each..........$2.00

Heidelberg Alternating Current Electric Belts

At $4.00, $6.00, $8.00, $12.00 and $18.00   we sell the new improved and ONLY JUSTLY CELEBRATED HEIDELBERG ELECTRIC

BELTS, guaranteeing them superior to belts that others sell at $10.00 to $40.00 . . . .

...SUPERIOR TO ANY OTHER ELECTRIC BELT MADE...

OUR FREE TRIAL OFFER. Select any belt wanted (state number inches around body at waist), we will send the belt to you by express C.O.D., subject to examination, we will send it in a plain sealed box so the express agent, or no one can else, tell the contents; we will instruct the express agent to collect from you our special price and express charges and HOLD THE MONEY 10 DAYS; you can give the belt 10 days trial, and if at the end of 10 days, you are not perfectly satisfied, if you have reason to believe the belt will not effect a speedy and permanent cure, pack the belt back in the same plain unmarked box it came in and take it back to the express agent and he WILL RETURN YOUR MONEY and will return the belt to us at our expense; otherwise, after 10 days if you do not bring the belt back, he will send the money to us.

10 DAYS' FREE TRIAL gives you every chance to see, examine and try the belt and satisfy yourself that the HEIDELBERG ELECTRIC BELT will do more for you than any belt made; will cure you if a cure by electricity is possible.

OUR NO MONEY C.O.D. TERMS. To show that our Heidelberg Electric Belt is superior to any, that our Heavy Battery $18.00 Belt is superior to belts that sell at $40.00 to $100.00. We offer to send any belt in plain unmarked box to any address (no money in advance) by express C.O.D., subject to examination, and with our 10 days' free trial privilege if desired.

THE ONLY CURE BELT MADE giving a self regulating, alternating, electric current reaching every nerve tissue of the body, giving life and strength instantly in every part of the body.

THE ONLY ELECTRIC BELT that will effectually take the place at once of every other kind of electric appliance and electric treatments for the cure of all the many diseases and weaknesses for which electricity is the only agent.

ARE YOU TIRED OF DRUGS? ARE YOU DISCOURAGED WITH DOCTORS? Have you tried other belts and still failed to get the relief you have been looking for?

ARE YOU SICK, WEAK AND DISCOURAGED? THEN TRY OUR GIANT $18.00 BELT on our FREE 10 DAYS' TRIAL offer. You will get more comfort in the 10 days than all else has given you.

THE ONLY ELECTRIC BELT in which the lightest or heaviest current of electricity is at all times under the instantaneous control of the patient and in which the current is alternating, ever building up those nerve tissues, never reached by the many other belts and appliances.

THE HEIDELBERG ELECTRIC BELTS combine every good, every new and improved feature of any other belt made, and in addition, you have a current of electricity alternating and farther reaching than in any other belt made.

HAVE YOU TRIED OTHER BELTS? If you have tried any other make of belt and you have not received the desired benefit let us send you our Giant Heidelberg $18.00 Belt on 10 Days Free Trial, and if you do not say it is such a belt as is furnished by no other house, if you do not find the alternating current instantaneous in its effect, giving you the sought for relief that no other belt will give you, do not pay one cent but return it at our expense.

HOW THE HEIDELBERG ELECTRIC BELTS EXCELS ALL OTHERS.

FIRST—They are made of the best material that can be procured, regardless of expense.

SECOND—More evenly regulated current of electricity is furnished than in any other electric belt made.

THIRD—Our alternating electric current reaches nerve centers and restores weak parts that can be reached by no other electric appliance.

FOURTH—More distribution, with more and larger electrodes, than on other belts. We give a more evenly distributed current of electricity than can be had from any other belt.

FIFTH—Power Regulator. With the Heidelberg battery you can get from three to five times the power that can be had from any other belt made, and the power regulator attached to the belt is so arranged that by simply moving a lever, without removing the belt, you can instantly change it to six different degrees of power.

SIXTH—Finish. The Heidelberg Electric Belt is the handsomest belt made; easiest adjusted and most convenient electric belt made.

OUR GUARANTEE. Every Heidelberg Electric Belt is covered by a binding one year guarantee, during which time if any piece or part gives out, by reason of defect in material or workmanship, it will be replaced or repaired free of charge. With care it will last a lifetime.

ABOUT OUR PRICES. Our inside prices of $4.00, $6.00, $8.00, $12.00 and $18.00 are less than one-half the price charged by others for inferior belts, in fact, our $4.00 belt will give better satisfaction than any other belt made, regardless of price, while our giant $18.00 belt is much better than other belts you can buy at $40.00 to $50.00, as the difference is the electric current we give. Our special prices are made only to cover our cost from the manufacturer, who gives us the exclusive sale of the Heidelberg Belt in America, with but one small profit added.

WE TOO COULD GET $20.00 TO $50.00 for our belts if we would ask it, for we have the only 20 to 80 gauge electric current electric belt made, the only belt to reach the nerve centers.

FOR NERVOUS DISEASES of all kinds in men and women, to reach the nerve centers for the cure of all nervous disorders the Heidelberg Electric Belt stands alone. For weakness in men and women, nervous exhaustion, bringing back lost strength and power, over brain work, vital weakness, impotency, rheumatism, sciatica, lame back, railroad back, insomnia, melancholia, kidney disorder, Bright's disease, dyspepsia, diseases of the liver, female weakness, poor circulation, weak heart action and almost every known disease and weakness. The constant soothing, alternating, electric current is ever at work touching the weak spots, building up the system, stimulating the circulation. ALL THAT ELECTRICITY WILL DO FOR YOU will be received through the use of our electric belt.

OUR $4.00 HEIDELBERG ELECTRIC BELT.

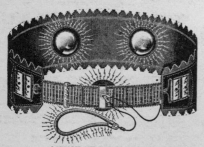

A HUNDRED LITTLE ACHES AND PAINS, HEADACHES, BACKACHES and WEAK-NERVE PAINS, can be saved you by the use of one of these belts.

To Prevent Sickness, Save Doctor's Bills, and Preserve Health DO NOT BE WITHOUT AN ELECTRIC BELT.

THIS Belt produces a 20-gauge current of electricity, and comes complete with stomach attachment and spiral suspensory. This 20-gauge current belt is recommended for mild cases, and yet at 20-gauge, we believe it is superior to any other belt on the market, regardless of price.

Our $4.00 belt will be found in every way superior to other belts that others sell at $15.00 to $40.00. It is the genuine Heidelberg 20-gauge belt full plated electrodes, best insulation, perfect alternating current.

No. 6482   20-Gauge Current Belt.   Our Price. $4.00

OUR $6.00 HEIDELBERG ELECTRIC BELT.

THIS belt produces 30-gauge current of electricity, and comes complete with stomach attachments and spiral electric suspensory.

This 30-gauge current belt is strong enough for all ordinary forms of disease and weakness, and is especially recommended for STOMACH, LIVER AND BLOOD DISORDERS, also for SICK HEADACHE AND DYSPEPSIA; the steady, soothing alternating current of electricity relieves you at once, and a cure in almost every case is soon effected.

IF YOU HAVE TRIED OTHER BELTS

let us send you this 30-gauge belt on

TEN DAYS' FREE TRIAL,

and if you don't find it perfectly satisfactory, such a belt as you could not get elsewhere at any price, return it at our expense.

No. 6484   30-gauge current belt.   Our Price. $6.00

No. 6485
Order by Number

....OUR $8.00 HEIDELBERG ELECTRIC BELT.....

THIS ELECTRIC BELT PRODUCING A 40-GAUGE CURRENT OF ELECTRICITY

comes complete with stomach attachment and spiral suspensory, it also has the automatic lever power regulator for adjusting to six different powers.

OUR $8.00 BELT with its 40-gauge alternating current of electricity is recommended for the electric treatment of all diseases. If you are over worked, nervous and weak, poor circulation and generally run down,

ORDER OUR $8.00 BELT ON 10 DAYS' FREE TRIAL.

and if you do not get immediate relief return it at our expense and

....DON'T PAY ONE CENT....

We give more battery, more current, more evenly divided surface, and a better system of regulation than in any other belt made.

No. 6485   Our price...........................$8.00

ORDER ANY BELT MADE.

TRY BOTH BELTS

and if you do not receive more benefit from our

BELT IN ONE DAY

than from any other belt in ten days, return our belt at

Our Expense, and DO NOT PAY ONE CENT.

OUR......
$12.00 Heidelberg Electric Belt......

NEXT TO OUR 80-GAUGE, $18.00 GIANT POWER, THE MOST POWERFUL BELT MADE.

THIS 60-GAUGE HEIDELBERG ELECTRIC BELT is one of the best electric belts possible to produce. Has all the advantages of all other belts made, with the defects of none. EVERY KNOWN IMPROVEMENT is embodied in this $12.00 belt, and next to our

$18.00 GIANT BELT IS THE BEST ELECTRIC BELT MADE,
For Nervous Diseases of all kinds.
Weakness of any kind . . . .

through the alternating electric current produced by this belt you will find immediate relief, when all others have failed.

No. 6487   Our price

OUR FREE 10 DAYS' TRIAL OFFER

GIVES YOU A CHANCE TO TRY THIS BELT WITHOUT PAYING US ONE CENT, and if it doesn't help you, if it does not prove to be just what you have been looking for, you can return it to us at our expense. No money out.

.............................$12.00

Free 10 Days Trial.

Our $18.00 GIANT POWER ELECTRIC BELT.

OUR GIANT 80-GAUGE CURRENT IS THE HIGHEST POINT OF PERFECTION YET ATTAINED IN ELECTRIC BELT MAKING.

THREE TIMES THE POWER

of any other make of belt, and yet with the alternating current even at 80-gauge can be worn with much greater comfort than any other belt

AT ONE-THIRD THE POWER.

THE LEVER REGULATOR is so arranged that you can reduce the current as much as you like, and when you want THE GIANT STRENGTH you can set it at 80-gauge when

IT WILL PENETRATE EVERY NERVE OF THE BODY.

FOR CHRONIC NERVOUS DISEASES, WEAKNESSES of all kinds, no matter how long standing or from what cause, wear our Giant Belt and you will be surprised at the immediate relief and rapid improvement.

No. 6489   Our price..$18.00

..THE..
MOST POWERFUL BELT MADE . . . .

IF YOU NEED TREATMENT OF ANY KIND let us send you the GIANT HEIDELBERG ELECTRIC BELT on 10 days' free trial, and if it doesn't prove satisfactory YOU NEED NOT PAY US ONE CENT, and the express agent can return it at our expense.

Sears, Roebuck & Co.'s Cologne Water.

Especially prepared by us for the toilet and handkerchief, and equal to the finest colognes in the market. It is very refreshing and of great value in the sick room, where it can be used as a disinfectant by destroying bad odors and rendering the air in the room fresh and pleasant, giving it a nice perfume. No. 6700 Price, 8-oz. bottles, 60c; 4-oz. bottles............35c
If by mail, postage and tube, extra, small, 16 cents.
Large, unmailable on account of weight.

Genuine Florida Water.

This is the finest Toilet Water manufactured. Can be used as a perfume, or mixed with water as a cooling and refreshing lotion for the skin. In the bath it is a luxury only known to those who have tried it. There are many imitations. Send to us and get the only genuine quality.
No. 6702 ½-pint bottles............45c
3-oz. bottles............25c
Unmailable on account of weight.

Atomizer.

The most reliable and useful Atomizer in the world. Has 3 hard rubber tips. Can be used for spraying perfume, or disinfecting a sickroom, or applying medicine to the throat or nthe nose. It is made of the best materials, and with care will last a lifetime. Every household should have one. No better atomizer can be found in the market.
No. 6704 Price........$.85c
If by mail, postage extra, 8c

Genuine Imported Bay Rum.

No. 6708 This is a fine quality of Bay Rum, imported by ourselves from the Island of St. Thomas, in the West Indies. We import it in casks and bottle it as our customers require. Being a pure article it is very useful for toilet purposes. A refreshing lotion for the skin.
4 oz. bottles, each............$0.17
½ pt. bottles, each............ .25
1 pt. bottles, each............ .40
1 gallon bottles, each............ 3.50
Unmailable on account of weight.

Little Puck Lamp.

A Perfume Novelty.

No. 6710 The smallest complete lamp in existence. Only four inches to top of chimney has a polished nickel base, perfect burner and handsome plated shade. Will burn ten hours without refilling. A perfume bottle and night lamp combined, containing choice perfumery in assorted odors. The burner acts as a sprinkler for the perfume, filling the whole house with a nice odor. Price, each............$0.15
Per dozen............ 1.50
If by mail, postage extra, 10c.

English Lavender Smelling Salts.

Refreshing, Invigorating.

For faintness, headache, etc. In pretty glass stoppered bottles, a useful and handsome ornament for the dressing table.
No. 6714 Price, each............$0.20
Per dozen............ 2.00
If by mail, postage and tube, extra, each, 10c

Imperial Perfumed Lavender Salts.

Refreshing and Invigorating.

In pretty glass stoppered bottle, enclosed in handsome leather purse for the pocket. One of the most convenient and useful articles of a ladies' toilet, for headache, faintness, etc. A general bracer. Everybody should have one; will last a lifetime.
No. 6716 Price, each............20c
If by mail, postage extra, 3c.

KAVA KAVA.

A Home Made Temperance Drink of the Purest Ingredients.

No. 6717   MAKE YOUR OWN TEMPERANCE WINE.
GREAT NON-ALCOHOLIC TEMPERANCE WINE.
The most Healthful Wine to Be Had at Any Price.

ADMIRAL DEWEY

WHEN DEWEY SUNK THE SPANISH FLEET AT MANILA a great territory was opened up of which the world knew little; secrets of the medical properties of plants, which were possessed by the natives of Manila, might have remained unknown to the world for ages had not this great American victory thrown the gates wide open for enterprise and investigation.

THE FORMULA FOR MAKING KAVA KAVA, the great non-alcoholic wine, a formula possessed only by Philippine Islanders, is one of inestimable value. We have purchased the entire and exclusive right for use of this formula in the United States, and are prepared to supply the ingredients for this wonderful drink to our customers.

THIS EXTRACT MAKES A MOST DELICIOUS WINE, rich and generous, containing not a drop of alcohol, the finest temperance drink in the world and superior to the highest priced wines on the market. It is exceedingly pleasant to taste, healthful and invigorating. It is of great value as a drink for invalids, children, weak and delicate ladies, in fact, for everyone suffering from nervousness, low spirits or brain fatigue. As a wine for the table it meals it has no equal; it improves the appetite, assists digestion, prevents stomach trouble and is just the article to have in the house when visitors call. Delicious to drink with biscuit or cake, it adds much to the enjoyment of evening parties, picnics, festivals, luncheons, while for general family use it is unexcelled.

WE FURNISH A TRIAL PACKAGE of this extract, sufficient for making one gallon of wine, for $1.25. Full directions are sent with each package, and at a shade more than 30 cents per quart you can make a wine that is superior to imported and domestic wines which sell at 75 cents to $1.25 per quart. Most of our customers buy a larger package, sufficient for making five gallons; not only is it cheaper to do so but it saves delay where only a single package is ordered at a time, and by ordering a larger package you can make a sufficient quantity to last for quite a while.

TAKE NOTICE OF OUR GRAND SPECIAL OFFER.

A FREE WINE SET with each five-gallon package. To get this extract introduced into every community we will, for the present, make this special offer: For each order for one large package, sufficient for making six gallons of wine, the price of $5.00 enclosed with order, we will ship, free of charge, A BEAUTIFUL GLASS WINE SET, as shown in the accompanying illustration. This wine set is made entirely of glass, consisting of large, handsome pressed glass wine cruet, six beautiful pressed glass wine glasses and one large glass tray, in fact, a set such as would scarcely retail at less than $1.50. This beautiful set we give entirely free of charge, packed carefully, and shipped with each large package of Kava Kava extract, for $5.00 cash with order.

COSTS YOU NOTHING.

Scarcely more than 80 cents a gallon for a delicious, healthful temperance wine, and the wine set.

HIGHLY RECOMMENDED TOILET PREPARATIONS.

OUR SPECIAL LINE OF ARTICLES FOR THE TOILET cannot be equaled by any other house, either in this country or in Europe, on account of their good and harmless quality and the magical effects produced. They are prepared by a specialist who has made a lifetime study of the science of improving and beautifying the skin, hair and teeth. It is the nature of the human family from the savage to the most civilized to use the best means obtainable by which they can render themselves more pleasing and attractive to others. Liquids can only be mailed in 4-oz. bottles and no larger, and then only in mailing tube, which costs 5c extra.

Almond Nut Cream.

A cleansing, cooling, excellent face cream; clears the skin from wrinkles, tan, freckles, etc., rendering it soft and white.
No. 6723 Price, each............$0.50
Per dozen............ 5.00
Unmailable on account of weight.

Secret de Ninon.

For freckles. These blemishes are very annoying, especially to those with pretty complexions. This preparation will remove freckles if the directions on the bottle are followed, and will leave the skin in a natural, healthy condition.
No. 6725 Price, each............$0.75
Per dozen............ 8.50
Unmailable on account of weight.

Depilatory.

For removing superfluous hair. Nothing disfigures a woman's face so much as an unnatural growth of hair. This preparation removes all hair from the skin in one or two applications, when the directions on the bottle are carefully followed.
No. 6730 Price, each............$0.75
Per doz............ 8.50
If by mail, postage and tube, each, 16 cents.

Witch Hazel Toilet Cream.

This is an elegant preparation for the skin when it is chapped and rough. A few applications well rubbed in render the skin soft and velvety. It is also good for removing sunburn and freckles. It will prevent the skin from chapping or discoloring when exposed to the cold, if used before going out. It does not leave the skin greasy or sticky. Gloves can be used immediately after using it without soiling them.
No. 6734 Price, each............$0.25
Per doz............ 2.50
If by mail, postage and tube, extra, each, 16 cents.

Camphorated Cold Cream.

Very fine for chapped lips, face or hands. Keeps the skin smooth.
No. 6740 Price, each............$0.15
Per doz............ 1.50
If by mail, postage extra, per bottle, 16 cents.

Rouge.

A harmless preparation for giving color to the cheeks and lips; it gives a perfectly natural, pretty color.
No. 6744 Price, each............$0.50
Per doz............ 5.00
If by mail, postage extra, per box, 2c

Face Powders.

There are a good number of powders for the face on the market, ours we claim to be the superior of any; it is harmless, almost invisible when used rightly, with a very enchanting effect. It is put up in three shades to suit the different complexions, white, pink and brunette.
No. 6748 Price, per doz. $1.50; per box....15c
If by mail, postage extra, per box, 2 cents.

USE VELVET FACE POWDER

WRITE FOR FREE BOOK OF DRESS GOODS SAMPLES.

SEND FOR FREE COLOR CARD OF HOUSE PAINTS.

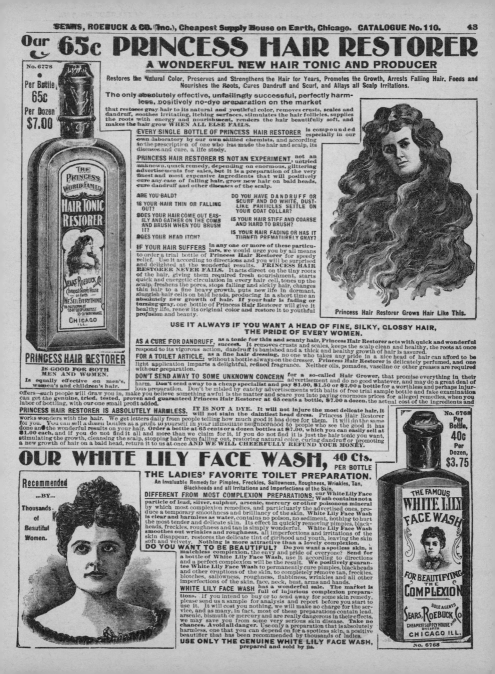

Our 65c PRINCESS HAIR RESTORER

A WONDERFUL NEW HAIR TONIC AND PRODUCER

No. 6778

Per Bottle, 65c

Per Dozen $7.00

Restores the Natural Color, Preserves and Strengthens the Hair for Years, Promotes the Growth, Arrests Falling Hair, Feeds and Nourishes the Roots, Cures Dandruff and Scurf, and Allays all Scalp Irritations.

The only absolutely effective, unfailingly successful, perfectly harmless, positively no-dye preparation on the market that restores gray hair to its natural and youthful color, removes crusts, scales and dandruff, soothes irritating, itching surfaces, stimulates the hair follicles, supplies the roots with energy and nourishment, renders the hair beautifully soft, and makes the hair grow WHEN ALL ELSE FAILS.

EVERY SINGLE BOTTLE OF PRINCESS HAIR RESTORER is compounded especially in our own laboratory by our own skilled chemists, and according to the prescription of one who has made the hair and scalp, its diseases and cure, a life study.

PRINCESS HAIR RESTORER IS NOT AN EXPERIMENT, not an unknown, quack remedy, depending on enormous, glittering advertisements for sales, but it is a preparation of the very finest and most expensive ingredients that will positively cure any case of falling hair, grow new hair on bald heads, cure dandruff and other diseases of the scalp.

ARE YOU BALD?

IS YOUR HAIR THIN OR FALLING OUT?

DOES YOUR HAIR COME OUT EASILY AND GATHER ON THE COMB AND BRUSH WHEN YOU BRUSH IT?

DOES YOUR HEAD ITCH?

DO YOU HAVE DANDRUFF OR SCURF AND DO WHITE, DUST-LIKE PARTICLES SETTLE ON YOUR COAT COLLAR?

IS YOUR HAIR STIFF AND COARSE AND HARD TO BRUSH?

IS YOUR HAIR FADING OR HAS IT TURNED PREMATURELY GRAY?

IF YOUR HAIR SUFFERS in any one or more of these particulars, we would urge you by all means to order a trial bottle of Princess Hair Restorer for speedy relief. Use it according to directions and you will be surprised and delighted at the wonderful results. PRINCESS HAIR RESTORER NEVER FAILS. It acts direct on the tiny roots of the hair, giving them required fresh nourishment, starts quick and energetic circulation in every hair cell, tones up the scalp, freshens the pores, stops falling and sickly hair, changes thin hair to a fine heavy growth, puts new life in dormant, sluggish hair cells on bald heads, producing in a short time an absolutely new growth of hair. If your hair is fading or turning gray, one bottle of Princess Hair Restorer will give it healthy life, renew its original color and restore it to youthful profusion and beauty.

Princess Hair Restorer Grows Hair Like This.

USE IT ALWAYS IF YOU WANT A HEAD OF FINE, SILKY, GLOSSY HAIR, THE PRIDE OF EVERY WOMEN.

AS A CURE FOR DANDRUFF, as a tonic for thin and scanty hair, Princess Hair Restorer acts with quick and wonderful success. It removes crusts and scales, keeps the scalp clean and healthy, the roots at once respond to its vigorous action, dandruff is banished and a thick and healthy growth of hair is assured.

FOR A TOILET ARTICLE, as a fine hair dressing, no one who takes any pride in a nice head of hair can afford to be without a bottle always on the dresser. Princess Hair Restorer is delicately perfumed, and one light application imparts a delightful, refined fragrance. Neither oils, pomades, vaseline or other greases are required with our preparation.

DON'T SEND AWAY TO SOME UNKNOWN CONCERN for a so-called Hair Grower, that promise everything in their advertisement and do no good whatever, and may do a great deal of harm. Don't send away to a cheap specialist and pay $1.00, $1.50 or $2.00 a bottle for a worthless and perhaps injurious preparation. Don't be misled by catchy advertisements with baits of free trial sample bottle and take examination of our preparation. Take no chances. Order our tested, tried, proven and guaranteed Princess Hair Restorer at 65 cents a bottle, $7.00 a dozen, the actual cost of the ingredients and labor of bottling, with our one small profit added.

PRINCESS HAIR RESTORER IS ABSOLUTELY HARMLESS, IT IS NOT A DYE. It will no injure the most delicate hair, it will not stain the daintiest head dress. Princess Hair Restorer works wonders with the hair. We get letters daily from people telling how much good it has done for them. It will do the same for you. You can sell a dozen bottles at a profit to yourself in your immediate neighborhood to people who see the good it has done to the wonderful results on your hair. Order a bottle at 65 cents or a dozen bottles at $7.00, which you can easily sell at $1.00 each, and if you do not find it all and more than we claim for it, if you do not find it is just the hair tonic you want, stimulating the growth, cleansing the scalp, stopping hair from falling out, restoring natural color, curing dandruff or promoting a new growth of hair on a bald head, return it to us at once AND WE WILL CHEERFULLY REFUND YOUR MONEY.

PRINCESS HAIR RESTORER

IS GOOD FOR BOTH MEN AND WOMEN.

Is equally effective on men's, women's and children's hair.

OUR WHITE LILY FACE WASH, 40 Cts. PER BOTTLE

No. 6768 Per Bottle, 40c   Per Dozen, $3.75

THE LADIES' FAVORITE TOILET PREPARATION.

An invaluable Remedy for Pimples, Freckles, Sallowness, Roughness, Wriakles, Tan, Blackheads and all Irritations and Imperfections of the Skin.

Recommended ...BY... Thousands of Beautiful Women.

DIFFERENT FROM MOST COMPLEXION PREPARATIONS, our White Lily Face Wash contains not a particle of lead, silver, sulphur, arsenic, mercury or other poisonous mineral by which most complexion remedies, and particularly the advertised ones, produce a temporary smoothness and brilliancy of the skin. White Lily Face Wash is clear and harmless as water, contains no poison, no sediment, nothing to hurt the most tender and delicate skin. Its effect in quickly removing pimples, blackheads, freckles, roughness and tan is simply wonderful. White Lily Face Wash smoothes out wrinkles and roughness, all imperfections and irritations of the skin disappear, restores the delicate tint of girlhood and youth, leaving the skin soft and velvety. Nothing is more attractive than a lovely complexion.

DO YOU WANT TO BE BEAUTIFUL? Do you want a spotless skin, a matchless complexion, the envy and pride of everyone? Send for a bottle of White Lily Face Wash, use it according to directions and a perfect complexion will be the result. We positively guarantee White Lily Face Wash to permanently cure pimples, blackheads and other eruptions of the skin, to completely remove tan, freckles, blotches, sallowness, roughness, flabbiness, wrinkles and all other imperfections of the skin, face, neck, bust, arms and hands.

WHITE LILY FACE WASH has a wonderful sale. The market is full of injurious complexion preparations. If you intend to buy or to send away for some skin remedy, please send us a sample for analysis and report before you start to use it. It will cost you nothing, we will make no charge for the service, and as many, in fact, most of these preparations contain lead, arsenic, bismuth or mercury and are really dangerous in their effects, we may save you from some very serious skin disease. Take no chances. Avoid all danger. Use only a preparation that is absolutely harmless, one that you can depend on for a spotless skin, a positive beautifier that has been recommended by thousands of ladies.

USE ONLY THE GENUINE WHITE LILY FACE WASH, prepared and sold by us.

THE PRINCESS WORLD-FAMED HAIR TONIC RESTORER — Sears, Roebuck & Co., Cheapest Supply House on Earth, WE SELL EVERYTHING, CHICAGO, ILL.

THE FAMOUS WHITE LILY FACE WASH FOR BEAUTIFYING THE COMPLEXION. SOLE AGENTS SEARS, ROEBUCK & Co. CHEAPEST SUPPLY HOUSE ON EARTH CHICAGO ILL. No. 6768

SEARS ROEBUCK & CO Incorporated

MECHANICAL DEPARTMENT.

...EVERYTHING NEW IN OUR...
WATCH, DIAMOND AND JEWELRY DEPARTMENT.

EVERY ARTICLE IS OF THE LATEST DESIGN, workmanship and finish, and at prices at which such values were never offered before. Confidence must be had when buying watches and diamonds, and to secure for you that confidence we wish to state—emphatically, too—that we guarantee every article to be as represented or money refunded.

OUR LOW PRICES are due to our large purchases for cash. That saving in price for better goods and better designs we give you the benefit of.

OUR DIAMOND PRICES when comparing qualities, will prove that we can save you one-half the prices you would pay elsewhere.

OUR WATCH DEPARTMENT is undoubtedly the largest and most complete in the world, and, as we sell more watches than any other house, it gives us purchasing power over any other. You get the benefit.

SEARS, ROEBUCK & CO.'S Special Watch Movements are the perfection of mechanical skill, made especially for us after our own original design and in such large quantities that we get them at a price which enables us to sell them to you at what other dealers very often ask for cheap and unreliable watches.

WE WANT YOUR ORDERS FOR EVERYTHING IN THE WATCH, DIAMOND AND JEWELRY LINE.

OUR GUARANTEE.
With every gold filled, silver or solid gold watch we give a certificate of guarantee. With gold filled watches the certificate guarantees the case to wear and keep its color for two, five, twenty or twenty-five years, and the movement to be an accurate timekeeper for five years. This guarantee is given in addition to the guarantee which is fitted in the back of the watch case. As to the value of our guaranty, we will refer you to the first page of this book under the head of OUR RELIABILITY.

OUR PRICES.
In Watches, and Jewelry we buy EVERYTHING direct from the manufacturers in large quantities for spot cash. As we sell for cash, having no bad debts, we are satisfied to sell at prices which the retailer pays, and, on a large per cent of goods, for much less money.

YOU CAN MAKE MONEY SELLING WATCHES, ETC., for when you can buy them for the same, or less money, than the retail dealer who sells on from 30 to 100 per cent profit and has large expenses in the way of rent, clerk hire, fuel, light, etc., you can readily see that you could undersell him and still make a handsome profit for yourself.

OUR VERY LIBERAL TERMS.
We desire to make our terms of shipment as liberal as possible, consistent with safety and good business principles. Watches, jewelry and diamonds will be shipped C. O. D. by express when desired, when a deposit of sufficient amount to pay the express charges both ways is sent with the order, the balance to be paid when goods have been received. Goods cannot be sent by mail C. O. D. When to be sent by mail the full amount of cash must accompany the order, also enough to pay postage. Be sure to enclose enough to pay postage, and if any amount remains it will be returned to you. When goods are to be shipped C. O. D. we will require deposits as follows:

AMOUNT OF DEPOSIT REQUIRED.
For Watches and Jewelry, 50 cents must accompany the order; for diamonds, we require $1.00 with the order. We never consign goods to be sold on commission, nor do we sell goods on time. Our terms are strictly cash in full with order, or C. O. D.

MAIL SHIPMENTS.
We recommend sending Jewelry, Watches, etc., by mail as it is perfectly safe and far the cheapest. Postage is 1 cent per ounce. A watch packed for shipment weighs from 6 to 8 ounces; chains, rings and other small articles of jewelry about 2 ounces. Packages amounting to $1.00 or over should be registered, which costs 8 cents extra. We guarantee the safe delivery of all registered mail packages. Be sure to send enough for postage, and if any balance remains we will return it to you.

ENGRAVING.
We charge for engraving in script on jewelry, watches, etc., 2½ cents per letter; in old English, small, 5 cents per letter, small script monograms on jewelry, etc., from 25 to 75 cents. Jewelry and watches to be engraved cannot be sent C. O. D., the full amount of cash must accompany the order.

WATCH REPAIRING.
We have a thoroughly equipped mechanical department, which is fitted with all of the latest tools and appliances for the repairing of all kinds of watches. We have a large force of thoroughly skilled watchmakers under the supervision of a very competent foreman, and any watch sent to us for repairs will receive very careful and prompt attention. We do not solicit for watch repair work, but are willing to accommodate our customers who wish to have work done in a thoroughly first-class manner. Our charges are about half what is usually charged by the retail dealers, but the work will be done in a very superior manner. We cannot give an accurate estimate of the cost of repairs without a thorough examination. Our charges are merely enough to cover cost of manufacture and labor. None but a thoroughly competent watchmaker should ever take a watch to pieces, for the chances are that he will ruin it.

DESCRIPTION OF THE MOVEMENTS WE LIST.

TO SAVE SPACE BY AVOIDING REPETITION WE have adopted the following as the best method of describing movements, because we are able to give a more complete and intelligent description than if inserted in a condensed form on each page. On the following page will be found an explanation of the different terms used. **WE GUARANTEE FOR FIVE YEARS ALL THE MOVEMENTS SOLD BY US.** By this we mean that we will, for five years from date of purchase, correct free of charge any fault which may occur from **DEFECTIVE MATERIAL OR WORKMANSHIP.** Any well made movement will run a lifetime if properly cared for.

THE SETH THOMAS Movements. Nickel damaskeened, 7-jeweled. They have safety pinion and compensation balance. They are made by the old reliable Seth Thomas Clock Co., **whose reputation for fine clocks is a sufficient guarantee** for the quality of the watch movements they make.

THE SEVEN JEWELED Waltham, Elgin and Illinois have compensation balance, patent pinions, and are finished in gilt and nickel.

FIFTEEN JEWELED Elgin or Waltham Movements have compensation balance, patent pinions and patent regulators. The Waltham and Elgin we furnish in both gilt and nickel.

THE G. M. WHEELER Elgin is now made with 17 jewels, safety pinion, train jewels in settings, compensation balance, adjusted; patent Breguet hair spring, patent micrometer regulator and is furnished in either gilt finish or nickel damaskeened, stamped, **"17 jewels adj."**

THE P. S. BARTLETT Waltham is made with 17 jewels, compensation balance, adjusted patent pinion, regulator and Breguet hair spring, hardened and tempered in form, double sunk dial. They come gilt finish or nickel damaskeened.

THE APPLETON, TRACY & CO. Movement of Waltham is now made with 17 ruby jewels in gold settings, compensation balance, adjusted to temperature, isochronism and position, with patent regulator, Breguet hair spring, hardened and tempered in form, patent pinion and double sunk dial. They come gilt finish or solid nickel beautifully damaskeened.

THE B. W. RAYMOND Movement is a grade of the Elgin Watch Co.'s now made with 17 ruby jewels. It has compensation balance, adjusted, safety pinion, patent micrometer regulator, patent Breguet hair spring, double sunk dial. They come in gilt finish or solid nickel, beautifully damaskeened.

THE NEW RAILWAY HAMPDEN Solid nickel, elegantly engraved, 17 extra fine ruby jewels in solid gold settings, 14-karat gold patent regulator, compensation balance accurately adjusted to temperature, isochronism and five positions, Breguet hair spring, patent center pinion, double sunk dial, gilt screws.

THE No. 150 ELGIN is made with 21 fine ruby jewels, compensation balance adjusted to temperature, isochronism and position, gold settings, patent regulator, Breguet hair spring, safety pinion, glass enameled double sunk dial, solid nickel with gilt letter ornaments. **It is a movement built especially to meet the demands of railroad men and others who require a very close timekeeper.**

BUNN, 17 RUBY JEWELS. NICKEL. Made by the Illinois Watch Co. Adjusted to temperature, four positions and isochronism; 17 fine ruby jewels in solid gold settings; compensation balance with solid gold screws: patent regulator; best quality Swiss Brequet hairspring; double sunk dial; handsomely damaskeened plates with gold lettering.

BUNN SPECIAL, 24 RUBY JEWELS. NICKEL. Made by the Illinois Watch Co. Adjusted to temperature, six positions and isochronism; 24 extra fine ruby jewels in solid gold settings; highly polished beveled steel escape wheel with chamfered teeth: compensation balance with solid gold screws; patent regulator; best quality Swiss Breguet hairspring; double sunk glass enamel dial; artistically damaskeened in new style bright fancy rayed pattern with black enameled lettering.

THE VANGUARD WALTHAM Movement made with 21 extra fine ruby jewels in raised gold settings, double roller, exposed pallets, embossed gold patent micrometer regulator, compensation balance adjusted to temperature, isochronism and position, patent safety barrel, exposed winding wheels, patent Breguet hair spring, hardened and tempered in form, elaborately finished nickel plates with gold letters, plate and jewel screws gilded, steel parts chamfered, double sunk dial.

CRESCENT STREET. NICKEL. Made by the Waltham Watch Co.: 21 fine ruby jewels (gold settings), jewel pin set without shellac, double roller escapement, exposed pallets, patent micrometric regulator, compensating balance in recess, adjusted to temperature, isochronism and five positions, tempered steel safety barrel, exposed winding wheels, patent Breguet hairspring, hardened and tempered in form; double sunk dial.

THE HAMPDEN SPECIAL RAILWAY Movement is nickel, has 23 extra fine ruby jewels in solid gold settings, jeweled center, magnificently damaskeened and finished; bevel head screws, 14-karat gold; patent regulator, perfectly compensated and accurately timed to all positions and isochronism; double sunk glass enameled dial, with red marginal minute figures; patent Breguet hair spring, steel work highly polished, patent center pinion, fine escapement, **especially adapted to the requirements of railroad men and others who need a very fine timepiece.**

THE WALTHAM 16-SIZE MOVEMENTS.

The 7 jeweled grade, compensation balance, Breguet hair spring, hardened and tempered in form, exposed winding wheels, and is finished in gilt.

THE No. 28 WALTHAM has 15 jewels in settings, patent regulator, compensation balance, safety pinion, patent Breguet hair spring, hardened and tempered in form, exposed winding wheels, and is made in solid nickel.

THE ROYAL WALTHAM has 17 jewels in settings, center setting raised, exposed pallets, patent regulator, compensation balance, adjusted, patent Breguet hair spring, hardened and tempered in form, exposed winding wheels, and is solid nickel damaskeened.

THE RIVERSIDE WALTHAM has 17 ruby jewels in gold settings, exposed pallets, patent regulator, compensation balance, adjusted to temperature and position, patent Breguet hair spring, hardened and tempered in form, safety pinion, exposed winding wheels, solid nickel plates, finished in gilt and damaskeened.

THE AMERICAN WATCH CO. WALTHAM has 17 fine ruby jewels in gold settings, exposed pallets, patent regulator, compensation balance adjusted to temperature, isochronism and position, patent Breguet hair spring, hardened and tempered in form, safety pinion, exposed winding wheels and fine solid nickel damaskeened plates. A very fine movement and will stand the test of the most rigid railroad inspection.

ILLINOIS 16-SIZE MOVEMENTS........

No. 174 ILLINOIS. NICKEL. 17 jewels; compensation balance; patent regulator; best quality Swiss Breguet hairspring; double sunk dial; handsomely damaskeened.

No. 176 ILLINOIS. NICKEL. Adjusted to temperature and four positions; 17 ruby jewels; compensation balance; best quality Swiss Breguet hairspring; double sunk dial; handsomely damaskeened in gold with gold lettering and gilded steel work.

No. 177 ILLINOIS. NICKEL. Adjusted to temperature, six positions and isochronism; 17 fine ruby jewels in gold settings; highly polished steel escape wheel with chamferred teeth; gold center wheel; compensation balance with gold screws: patent regulator; best quality Swiss Breguet hairspring; double sunk dial; damaskeened in handsome pattern with black enameled lettering.

NO. 179 ILLINOIS. NICKEL. Adjusted to temperature, six positions and isochronism; 21 extra fine ruby jewels in solid gold settings; highly polished beveled steel escape wheel with chamfered teeth; gold train; compensation balance with solid screws; patent regulator; best quality Swiss Breguet hairspring; double sunk dial; finished in two styles of damaskeening, bright rayed pattern, and gold inlaid; black enameled lettering.

THE ELGIN 16-SIZE MOVEMENTS......

THE No. 151 ELGIN is ¾-plate, has 7 jewels, Breguet hair spring, compensation balance, safety pinion is finished in gilt only.

THE No. 152 ELGIN is solid nickel damaskeened ¾-plate, has 15 jewels in settings, patent micrometer regulator, compensation balance, safety pinion Breguet hair spring, and solid damaskeened nickel plates.

THE No. 154 ELGIN is solid nickel damaskeened ¾-plate, has compensation balance, adjusted to temperature, 17 jewels in settings, patent micrometer regulator, Breguet hair spring, moon hands.

THE No. 155 ELGIN is ¾ genuine nickel damaskeened plates, has compensation balance, adjusted to temperature and position, 17 ruby jewels with gold settings, micrometer regulator, patent Breguet hair spring, double sunk dial moon hands, finely finished throughout.

THE No. 156 ELGIN, 21 extra fine red ruby jewels (raised gold settings), adjusted to temperature, isochronism and positions; quick train with gold wheels; straight line escapement with steel escape wheel; pallet arbor and escape pinion cone-pivoted and cap-jeweled; exposed pallets; compensation balance; Breguet hairspring; micrometric regulator; display winding works; patent recoiling click; patent self-locking, setting device; double sunk glass enameled dial; dust ring; beautifully damaskeened plates; closely timed and thoroughly first quality finish throughout,

DESCRIPTION OF 6-SIZE MOVEMENTS

SETH THOMAS movements are ¾-plate, nickel damaskeened, and will be furnished in the 7 jeweled grade. They have patent pinion and compensation balance.

THE SEVEN JEWELED grade of Elgin, Waltham or Illinois, has compensation balance, patent center pinion,and are furnished in gilt and nickel.

THE FIFTEEN JEWELED grade of Elgin, Waltham and Hampden, has compensation balance, patent center pinion, jewels in settings, and is solid nickel, damaskeened.

THE No. 168 ELGIN has 16 ruby jewels, raised settings, compensation balance. Breguet hair spring, fine oval finished patent micrometer regulator with hair spring, hardened and tempered in form, patent center pinion, and is solid nickel, beautifully damaskeened.

THE RIVERSIDE WALTHAM has 17 fine ruby jewels, raised gold settings, exposed pallets, patent center pinion, patent regulator, compensation balance adjusted, patent Breguet hair spring, hardened and tempered in form, and is solid nickel, beautifully damaskeened.

THE HAMPDEN 17 jeweled grade is solid nickel and has 17 fine ruby jewels, raised gold settings, patent center pinion, highly polished center and escape wheels, is beautifully damaskeened in gilt and nickel, Hampden back action mainspring, finest grade hair spring, gilt bevel screws, fine gilt hands, adjusted to five positions and very accurately timed.

THE DESCRIPTION OF 0-SIZE MOVEMENTS is the same as 6-size. The Hampden, Trenton and Seth Thomas are not made in 0-size.

300-SIZE, 16 JEWELS. Solid nickel movement adjustment, highly damaskeened and finished through; 16 genuine ruby jewels in raised solid gold settings; highly polished beveled edge screws; fancy French hard enameled dials.

300-SIZE, 15 JEWELS. Solid nickel movement, 15 jewels in raised gold settings; sunk second, fancy glass dial, finely damaskeened, elaborately finished throughout.

MOLLY STARK, 300-SIZE, 7 JEWELS. Gilt finish with bright flat screws, sunk second, plain hard enameled dial.

DESCRIPTION OF ....

SEARS, ROEBUCK & CO. Open Face, 18-Size.

Solid Nickel through and through. 17 jewel, adjusted. Full plate, fancy solid gold damaskeened finish, five pair gold settings, compensation full double cut expansion balance wheel, adjusted to isochronism and position, patent micrometer regulator, genuine ruby jeweled pin, highly polished beveled edged screws, fully protecting dust band, safety pinion, double sunk, white enameled dial and sunk second hand dial. The superior construction of this movement adapts it to the most exacting service.

SEARS, ROEBUCK & CO. Special, 16-Size.

Solid Nickel, Fancy Gold Damaskeened Finish, consisting of three separate bridges, viz., barrel, train and balance bridges, very artistically arranged. 17 genuine ruby jewels, in solid gold settings. Exposed to view winding apparatus, the steel parts of which are highly polished and chamfered; patent micrometer regulator, five pairs of extra solid gold settings and gold train, genuine ruby pallet jewels, visible to view, and ruby roller jewel, patent safety center pinion and barrel. Compensation, double cut, full expansion balance wheel, adjusted in accordance to variations of the temperature, fully protecting dust band, double sunk, genuine hard French enamel dial. This movement will excel the highest grade movements on the market.

SEARS, ROEBUCK & CO. SPECIAL, 6-SIZE.

Nickel, Very Elaborately Designed, damaskeened finish. 17 jewel, full compensation balance wheel, patent safety center pinion, ruby roller and pallet escapement, blue beveled edge, highly polished screws. Movement consists of three separate bridges, very artistically

arranged, plain white, hard enameled dial and fancy blue steel hands

WATCHMAKERS' TOOLS AND MATERIALS.

THE NUMEROUS INQUIRIES WE HAVE RECEIVED from time to time have induced us to list a line of watchmakers' and jewelers' tools. For want of space we can illustrate only the most useful and desirable, and have been compelled to reduce the cuts in order to illustrate what we do. The goods, however, are all of standard make and size, and of the best quality. If there is anything you want that you do not find illustrated, send us your order, enclosing market price for same, and give an accurate description. If you do not know what the cost is, be sure to enclose enough, and we will return what is left. We guarantee our prices to be as low as any, and you will find that we always furnish goods at lowest wholesale prices. We will be glad, however, to quote you if you desire prices before ordering. When ordering material for repairs, always send a sample, if possible. If not, fully describe the size and make of watch or clock for which parts are intended. When ordering materials you will save both time and trouble by making a remittance of sufficient funds to cover all possible charges for cost of goods and mailing. We will always refund any balance left after paying cost of goods and mailing.

No.		
44	Alcohol cups............................each	$0.35
41	Anvil (Jewelers')......................each	.75
400	Blow Pipes, common brass............each	.25
20	Blow Pipes, with balls................each	.30
101	Blow Pipes, nickel plated, with ball..each	.50
19	Bench Knife (Jewelers')..............each	.50
402	Buffs, Chamois or Felt, round or flat..each	.20
103	Brushes, watch or clock..............each	.30
104	Burnishers, bent...............each, 25 to	.75
5	Broaches, Stub's best quality, assorted sizes from No. 75 to No. 40...per dozen	1.00
6	Broach Handle, adjustable..............each	.25
106	Broaches, Swiss make...............per dozen	.25
26	Caliper, pinion, plain................each	.25
109	Caliper, regular......................each	.50
54	Caliper, nickel plated, with bar and screw..................each	.65
153	Clock Screwdriver....................each	.28
111	Clock wire bender....................each	.50
111	Countersinks, per set of three.........each	1.00
113	Countersinks, adjustable handle, per set..	.75
49	Crucibles, per set of four.............	.50
48	Cups, Oil, for watch or clock.........each	.25
114	Drills, common...................per dozen	.50
116	Drills, Stock, common................each	.50
117	Drill Bow, to use with above stock....each	.50
8	Drill Stock, patent spiral............each	.50
35	Drill Stock, patent guard.............each	1.00
41	Drying Box............................each	1.25
10	Escape Wheel Holder..................each	.40
56	Eyeglass, Watchmakers', common.......each	.10
118	Eyeglass, Watchmakers', with coil spring..	.50
119	Files, three-cornered, round or square, small.................each	.12
10	File, knife.............................each	.35
11	Files, needle, three-cornered..........each	.15
13	Files, needle, knife...................each	.15
14	Files, needle, oblong..................each	.15
16	Files, needle, one-half round..........each	.15
15	Files, needle, square..................each	.15
18	Files, needle, round...................each	.15
12	Files, three cornered, 3½-inch.........each	.30
11	Files, flat, regular...................each	.35
120	Files, screw head.....................each	.35
121	Files, rounding and entering..........each	.30
123	Gauge, Degree, nickel plated, with rule, each	1.00
9	Gravers, according to size, each.......10 to	.75
124	Hammer Handles, ebony................each	.25
125	Hands, Watch, per pair, 10¢; per doz. pair	.80
128	Hands, Second, each, 5¢...per doz.	.50
128	Hands, Clock...........per pair, 5¢; per doz.	.30
129	Handles, adjustable, for graver or small files..................each	
130	Handles, adjustable, for medium files, each	.25
132	Jeweling Tools, Swiss, in box..........each	.15
132	Jewelers' Cement, per bottle...........each	.25
33	Jewel Pin Setter......................each	.88
134	Jeweling Tool, complete...............each	1.50
135	Keys, Watch...............per dozen	.20
136	Keys, Watch, wind any watch..........each	.30

No.		
137	Keys, Watch, for bench use......each	$0.50
138	Keys, Iron or brass, for clocks......each	.10
42	Lamps, Alcohol, patented, large......each	1.75
139	Lamps, Alcohol, faceted glass........each	.88
140	Mainsprings, Watch...each, 25¢; per doz.	1.75
141	Mainsprings, Clock, 1 day............each	.15
142	Mainsprings, Clock, 8 day............each	.45
143	Mainspring Punch, improved..........each	1.25
34	Mainspring Winder....................each	1.50
5	Mallet, Jewelers'.....................each	.20
47	Movement Holder.....................each	.20
36	Oilers, Watch or Clock.........per bottle	.20
25	Oiler, Watch..........................each	.20
144	Oil Stone, best Arkansas, in box......each	1.00
145	Pin Slide, common medium.............each	.15
146	Pin Vise, hollow handle...............each	.75
151	Punch, Mainspring, English............each	.75
1	Punch, Mainspring, (3 punches)....per set	1.25
40	Punches, set of 24, with hollow stake, in hardwood box.......complete set	1.25
36	Plyers, round.........................each	.65
143	Plyers, flat...........................each	.65
33	Plyers, Stubb's best side cutting......each	1.00
21	Plyers, cutting, regular Swiss.........each	.65
38	Polsing tool..........................each	.65
28	Roller Remover.......................each	.75
36	Ruby Pin Setter.......................each	.60
57	Screw Holder and Driver combined....each	.75

No.		
37	Screw Holder..........................each	$0.30
3	Screw Plate.............................	.50
23	Screwdriver, large....................each	.25
22	Screwdriver, Watch, medium..........each	.25
21	Screwdriver, Watch, small............each	.25
24	Screwdriver, Watch, adjustable, 4 sizes, set	.60
8	Second Hand holder, nickel plated....each	.40
153	Stake, Riveting, hard steel............each	.25
43	Saw Frame, Swiss, extra quality, nickel plated.......each	1.10
154	Saws for above.....................per dozen	.15
158	Soldering, copper.....................each	.20
157	Soldering fluid, per bottle............each	.25
158	Solder, silver...................per package	.35
159	Solder, gold....................per package	1.00
4	Screw Stock and Dies............per set	2.00
50	Tweezers, fine........................each	.35
51	Tweezers, medium....................each	.31
153	Tweezers and hand raiser combined...each	.40
46	Vise, Bench...........................each	.70
53	Visc, Hand............................each	.15
48	Watch Cover Glass....................each	.10
161	Watch Glasses, hunting style.........each	.10
162	Watch Glasses, per ¼ dozen of one number	.10
163	Watch Glasses, assorted.............per gross	4.50
164	Watch Glasses, thick, open face, fitted, eac	.10
165	Watch Glasses, thick, open face, per dozen	.50
166	Watch Keys, Birch's...................each	.20

OUR COMPLETE WATCH TOOL SET, PRICE $10.00.

THE TOOLS AND IMPLEMENTS we herewith illustrate are the most necessary in the equipment of a watchmaker's kit. Each and every one of them performs important work, making it absolutely necessary to at least have as great a selection as what we illustrate here in our complete set. The material of which our tools are made is of the very finest procurable; the most expert toolmakers, most skilled in their art, the only ones employed in the production of this merchandise.

EACH AND EVERY TOOL goes through a rigid inspection before leaving our establishment, so that we are assured of them being received by our customers in perfect condition. Our mechanic here who do our watch work use our own manufacture of tools and the work done by us is excelled by none. This set for $10.00 consist of 36 separate and distinct pieces, which we believe the greatest bargain ever offered in tool set. Any man of average mechanical skill can learn to rectify the majority of causes that make a watch stop. The set we not alone include tools necessary for watch repairing, but likewise includes a complete set of tools for silverware, jewelry and clock repairing. We know that you would not fail to be pleased with the results of your purchase if you conclude to favor us with an order for one of these wonderful watchmakers' and jewelers' sets.

No. 100000 Price for complete set, including text book...............$10.00

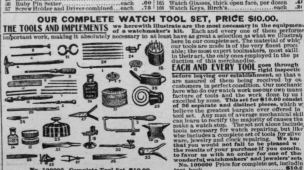

No. 100000   Complete Tool Set, $10.00.

OUR LIBERAL TERMS—viz: Send us 50 cents with your order and we ship by express C. O. D., subject to examination, for the balance—making it possible for you to see and examine the watch you select before you pay for it. **LOOK CAREFULLY** at Our Bargain Pages of watches scattered through this department. Every bargain page is a money saving, money making surprise.

98 CENTS

..98-CENT..

AMERICAN WATCH.

Far better than ever and yet only 98 cents.

A gentleman's stem wind watch for 98 cents.

This is a nickel plated metal watch, stem wind and stem set, regular 18-size, open face case. A patent lever movement, and runs 30 to 36 hours with one winding.

Guaranteed American made and a very good timekeeper; movement is strong in construction, and will stand much rougher usage than a finer and higher priced watch.

Remember your boy with one of these 98-cent watches. Nothing will please him better. 98 cents is little money and far less money than the watch can be bought for elsewhere.

Consider the price, only 98 cents.

No. 100002

ONLY $1.79

$1.79

3500 to be sold at $1.79 each. A $3.00 stem wind watch for only $1.79.

How We Can Do It. We bought a large number of these watches nearly two years ago, before the change in tariff, and we got the lot at the lowest price ever known. Add our one small profit, and the price is $1.79. A nickel stem wind watch. Case is gents' full 18-size, open face, heavy nickel plated, highly polished, stem wind and stem set.

Movement—A nickel cylinder escapement, and while we do not guarantee it, they keep very good time. It's a boy's pride, and as our price is only $1.79, get your boy a watch. He will remember it as long as he lives. $1.79 for this watch will astonish all other dealers and agreeably surprise our customers. $1.79 is our special price until our stock is entirely exhausted.

No. 100003

$2.65 Alaska Silver All-American Open Face Watch.

No. 100006

PHILADELPHIA

$2.65 FOR AN AMERICAN STEM WIND AND STEM SET nickel movement and American case, we believe is a lower price than was ever before quoted by any house in any quantity, and making this price of $2.65 on an all-American watch, one that can be guaranteed for time and for wear, we feel sure will insure us an immense trade. For this reason we have contracted with the manufacturer for a very large number of these watches, which alone makes it possible for us to make this $2.65 price.

DO NOT CONFOUND OR COMPARE THIS ALL-AMERICAN STEM WIND WATCH with any of the many cheap imported nickel watches—watches that are made in Switzerland—made to sell and not for service.

UNDERSTAND, IN THIS WATCH AT $2.65 you have both in the case and in the movement a strictly up to date American Watch—one that is guaranteed for wear guaranteed for timekeeping qualities, and such a watch as has never before been shown at anything like the price.

ALASKA SILVER CASE. THIS HANDSOME CASE AS ILLUSTRATED is what is known as ALASKA SILVER. It is a composition of several metals, giving the watch the appearance of coin silver; and in fact, it is in appearance and in every way except intrinsic value the equal of coin silver. It will wear and retain its coin silver color for a lifetime. It is handsomely finished as shown in illustration, in a CORRUGATED PATTERN with fancy heavy beaded edge. It is open face, full 18-size, stem wind and stem set, and is fitted with a heavy bevel edge crystal.

AT $2.65 WE FURNISH THIS CASE COMPLETE WITH MOVEMENT in what we call snap back and snap bezel. The front and back snap on.

MOVEMENT. WE FURNISH IN THIS WATCH AT OUR SPECIAL PRICE OF $2.65 a 7-jeweled solid nickel stem wind and stem set movement. These movements are made by the Trenton Watch Co., of Trenton, N. J., for export trade. Some are stamped Pan-American; some are stamped Riverside, and some are stamped Trenton. Every movement is guaranteed by the manufacturers for five years, and they issue a five-year guarantee with the watch.

OUR SPECIAL AND HERETOFORE UNHEARD OF PRICE OF $2.65 COMMENDS THIS WATCH to all those who require a reliable timepiece and American case that will not tarnish, for very little money, and $2.65 is a price based on the actual cost to produce, with but our one small profit added.

No. 100009 SAME WATCH AS ABOVE, with the case hinged in front and snap back, $2.90. The 25 cents additional which we charge you is the exact difference in the cost to us, and we believe the watch is well worth the difference. Our special price...$2.90

Coin Silver Filled Dust Proof Watch, $3.95

ONLY $3.95

THIS SCREW BACK AND SCREW BEZEL STEM WIND AND STEM Set, Open Face, Coin Silver Filled American Watch is offered by us as one of our leaders at $3.95, in competition with any watch you can buy elsewhere at nearly, if not fully, double the price, and we are able to offer this watch at $3.95 and a number of other special watch bargains quoted in this catalogue, only by reason of controlling the output of the watch case factory that furnishes us these cases.

ONLY $3.95

No. 100012

A COIN SILVER FILLED, screw bezel, dust proof, stem wind American case, with stem wind movement, at $3.95, is a price heretofore unknown. This case is made of two very heavy plates of solid coin silver, over a stiff inner plate of hard composition metal; and being pure coin silver on the outside and inside over this hard metal you have practically a coin silver case, for it is guaranteed to wear and hold its perfect color for twenty-five years, and in addition the 25-year guarantee accompanies each case. This case is absolutely dust proof. It is screw back and screw bezel.

From the illustration shown you can see the manner in which the front and back fasten to the case by screwing on, thus preventing any possibility of dust or dirt getting into the movement, making the most practical case on the market. As shown in illustration, this case comes only in open face and in plain polished. It has SOLID SILVER CROWN and SOLID SILVER BOW. It is full 18-size and is fitted with a heavy bevel edge French crystal.

At $3.95 we furnish this coin silver filled case complete with a New York Standard solid nickel, 7-jeweled movement, quick train, stem wind and stem set; or we will furnish the case complete with any of the following named movements at the following prices:

7-Jeweled, Elgin, Waltham or Illinois.........................	$6.25
Full 12 Jeweled "Edgemere," Sears, Roebuck & Co.'s, special make...	6.30
Full 15 Jeweled Elgin or Waltham..............................	7.32
Full 17 Jeweled Illinois or Elgin..............................	10.53
Full 17 Jeweled "G. M. Wheeler," Elgin, "P. S. Bartlett," Waltham or Illinois, all adjusted. Special.........................	13.40
Full 17 Jeweled Sears, Roebuck & Co.'s, specially adjusted.......	11.70

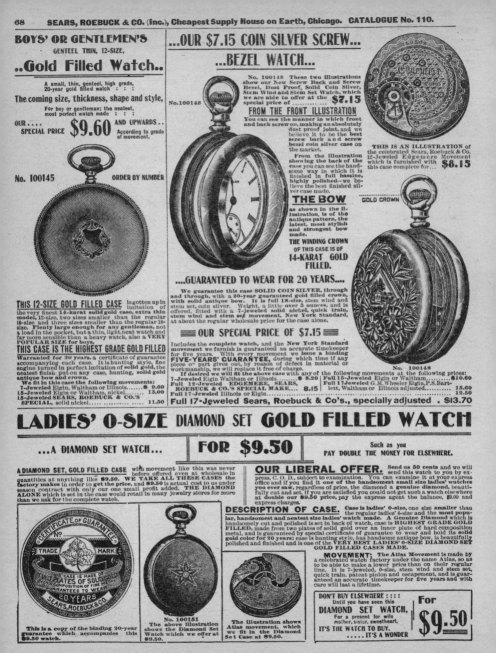

BOYS' OR GENTLEMEN'S

GENTEEL THIN, 12-SIZE,

..Gold Filled Watch..

A small, thin, genteel, high grade, 20-year gold filled watch : : :

The coming size, thickness, shape and style,

For boy or gentleman: the neatest, most perfect watch made : : :

OUR ....
SPECIAL PRICE **$9.60** AND UPWARDS ..
According to grade of movement.

No. 100145   ORDER BY NUMBER

THIS 12-SIZE GOLD FILLED CASE is gotten up in imitation of the very finest 14-karat solid gold case, extra thin model, 12-size, two sizes smaller than the regular 18-size. Plenty large enough for any gentleman, not a load in the pocket, but a thin, light, neat watch and far more sensible than a heavy watch, also a VERY POPULAR SIZE for boys.

THIS CASE IS THE HIGHEST GRADE GOLD FILLED

Warranted for 20 years, a certificate of guarantee accompanying each case. It is hunting style, fine engine turned in perfect imitation of solid gold, the neatest finish put on any case, hunting, solid gold antique bow and crown.

We fit in this case the following movements:

7-Jeweled Elgin, Waltham or Illinois.....$ 9.60
15-Jeweled Elgin or Waltham, nickel.........13.00
15-Jeweled SEARS, ROEBUCK & CO'S
SPECIAL, solid nickel................................11.50

...OUR $7.15 COIN SILVER SCREW...
...BEZEL WATCH...

No. 100148

No. 100148 These two illustrations show our New Screw Back and Screw Bezel, Dust Proof, Solid Coin Silver, Stem Wind and Stem Set Watch, which we are able to offer at the special price of **$7.15**

FROM THE FRONT ILLUSTRATION

You can see the manner in which front and back screw on, making an absolutely dust proof joint, and we believe it to be the best screw back and screw bezel coin silver case on the market.

From the illustration showing the back of the case you can see the handsome way in which it is finished in full basine, highly polished—we believe the best finished silver case made.

THE BOW

as shown in the illustration, is of the antique pattern, the latest, most stylish and strongest bow made.

THE WINDING CROWN
OF THIS CASE IS OF
14-KARAT GOLD FILLED.

....GUARANTEED TO WEAR FOR 20 YEARS....

We guarantee this case SOLID COIN SILVER, through and through, with a 20-year guaranteed gold filled crown, with solid antique bow. It is full 18-size, stem wind and stem set, coin silver. Weight, a little over 3 ounces, and is offered, fitted with a 7-jeweled solid nickel, quick train, stem wind and stem set movement, New York standard, at about the regular wholesale price for the case alone.

OUR SPECIAL PRICE OF $7.15

Includes the complete watch, and the New York Standard movement we furnish is guaranteed an accurate timekeeper for five years. With every movement we issue a binding **FIVE-YEARS' GUARANTEE**, during which time if any piece or part gives out, by reason of defect in material or workmanship, we will replace it free of charge.

If desired we will fit the above case with any of the following movements at the following prices:

THIS IS AN ILLUSTRATION of the celebrated Sears, Roebuck & Co. 12-Jeweled Edgemere Movement which is furnished with this case complete for... **$8.15**

GOLD CROWN

No. 100148

7-Jeweled Elgin Waltham or Illinois.....$ 8.20	Full 15-Jeweled Elgin or Waltham............$10.60
Full 12-Jeweled EDGEMERE, SEARS, ROEBUCK & CO'S SPECIAL MAKE.....8.15	Full 17-Jeweled G.M. Wheeler Elgin, P.S.Bartlett, Waltham or Illinois adjusted.........15.60
Full 17-Jeweled Illinois or Elgin.	12.50

Full 17-Jeweled Sears, Roebuck & Co's., specially adjusted . **$13.70**

LADIES' O-SIZE DIAMOND SET GOLD FILLED WATCH

...A DIAMOND SET WATCH...

FOR $9.50

Such as you
PAY DOUBLE THE MONEY FOR ELSEWHERE.

A DIAMOND SET, GOLD FILLED CASE with movement like this was never before offered even at wholesale in quantities at anything like $9.50. **WE TAKE ALL THESE CASES** the factory makes in order to get the price, and $9.50 is actual cost to us under season contract with only our one small profit added. **THE DIAMOND ALONE** which is set in the case would retail in many jewelry stores for more than we ask for the complete watch.

OUR LIBERAL OFFER. Send us 50 cents and we will send this watch to you by express, C. O. D., subject to examination. You can examine it at your express office and if you find it one of the handsomest small size ladies' watches you ever saw, regardless of price, the diamond a genuine diamond, beautifully cut and set, if you are satisfied you could not get such a watch elsewhere at double our $9.50 price, pay the express agent the balance, $9.00 and express charges.

DESCRIPTION OF CASE. Case is ladies' O-size, one size smaller than the regular ladies' 6-size and the most popular, handsomest and neatest size ladies' watch made. A Genuine Diamond which is handsomely cut and polished is set in back of watch, case is HIGHEST GRADE GOLD FILLED, made from two plates of solid gold over an inner plate of hard composition metal, and is guaranteed by special certificate of guarantee to wear and hold its solid gold color for 20 years; case is hunting style, has handsome antique bow, is beautifully polished and finished and is one of the VERY BEST LADIES' O-SIZE DIAMOND SET GOLD FILLED CASES MADE.

MOVEMENT: The Atlas Movement is made by a celebrated watch factory under the name Atlas, so as to be able to make a lower price than on their regular line. It is 7-jeweled, 0-size, stem wind and stem set, quick train, patent pinion and escapement, and is guaranteed an accurate timekeeper for five years and with care will last a lifetime.

No. 100151
The above illustration shows the Diamond Set Watch which we offer at $9.50.

The illustration shows Atlas movement, which we fit in the Diamond Set Case at $9.50.

This is a copy of the binding 20-year guarantee which accompanies this $9.50 watch.

DON'T BUY ELSEWHERE : : : :
Until you have seen this
DIAMOND SET WATCH,
For a present for wife mother, sister, sweetheart,
IT'S THE WATCH TO BUY.
.....IT'S A WONDER

For **$9.50**

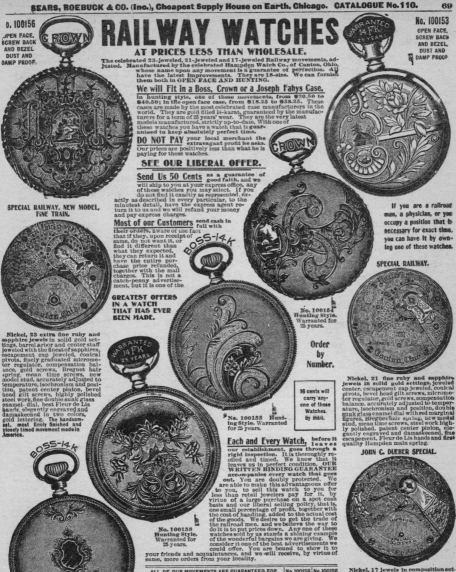

No. 100156 OPEN FACE, SCREW BACK AND BEZEL, DUST AND DAMP PROOF.

No. 100153 OPEN FACE, SCREW BACK AND BEZEL, DUST AND DAMP PROOF.

WARRANTED 14 FK 25 YEARS

RAILWAY WATCHES
AT PRICES LESS THAN WHOLESALE.

The celebrated 23-jeweled, 21-jeweled and 17-jeweled Railway movements, adjusted. Manufactured by the celebrated Hampden Watch Co., of Canton, Ohio, whose name upon any movement is a guarantee of perfection. All have the latest improvements. They are 18-size. We can furnish them both in OPEN FACE AND HUNTING.

We will Fit in a Boss, Crown or a Joseph Fahys Case,

In hunting style, one of these movements, from $20.50 to $40.50; in the open face case, from $18.25 to $38.25. These cases are made by the most celebrated case manufacturers in the world. They are gold filled 14-karat, guaranteed by the manufacturers for a term of 25 years' wear. They are the very latest models manufactured, strictly up-to-date. With one of these watches you have a watch that is guaranteed to keep absolutely perfect time.

DO NOT PAY your local merchant the extravagant profit he asks. Our prices are positively less than what he is paying for these watches.

SEE OUR LIBERAL OFFER.

Send Us 50 Cents as a guarantee of good faith, and we will ship to you at your express office, any of these watches you may select. If you do not find it exactly as represented, exactly as described in every particular, to the minutest detail, have the express agent return it to us and we will refund your money and pay express charges.

Most of our Customers send cash in full with their orders, aware of the fact that if they, upon receipt of same, do not want it, or find it different than what they expected, they can return it and have the entire purchase price refunded, together with the mail charges. This is not a catch-penny advertisement, but it is one of the

GREATEST OFFERS IN A WATCH THAT HAS EVER BEEN MADE.

SPECIAL RAILWAY, NEW MODEL, FINE TRAIN.

Nickel, 23 extra fine ruby and sapphire jewels in solid gold settings, barrel arbor and center staff jeweled with the finest of sapphires, escapement cap jeweled, conical pivots, finely graduated micrometer regulator, compensation balance, gold screws, Breguet hair spring, mean time screws, new model stud, accurately adjusted to temperature, isochronism and position, patent center pinion, bevel head gilt screws, highly polished steel work, fine double sunk glass enamel dial, best Fleur de Lis hands, elegantly engraved and damaskeened in two colors, gold lettering. The handsomest, most finely finished and closely timed movement made in America.

BOSS—14K

No. 100158 Hunting Style. Warranted for 25 years.

No. 100157 Open Face, Screw Back and Bezel, Dust and Damp Proof.

WARRANTED 14 FK 25 YEARS

No. 100155 Hunting Style. Warranted for 25 years.

CROWN

No. 100154 Hunting Style. Warranted for 25 years.

If you are a railroad man, a physician, or you occupy a position that is necessary for exact time, you can have it by owning one of these watches.

SPECIAL RAILWAY.

Order by Number.

16 cents will carry any one of these Watches by mail.

Each and Every Watch, before it leaves our establishment, goes through a rigid inspection. It is thoroughly re-oiled and timed. We know that it leaves in perfect condition. OUR WRITTEN BINDING GUARANTEE accompanies every watch that goes out. You are doubly protected. We are able to make this advantageous offer to you, to sell this watch to you for less than retail jewelers pay for it, by virtue of a large purchase on a spot cash basis and our liberal selling policy, that is, one small percentage of profit, together with the cost of handling, added to the actual cost of the goods. We desire to get the trade of the railroad men, and we believe the way to do it is to put prices down. Any one of these watches sold by us stands a shining example of the wonderful bargains we are giving. We consider it one of the best advertisements we could offer. You are bound to show it to your friends and acquaintances, and we will receive, by virtue of same, more orders from your locality.

Nickel, 21 fine ruby and sapphire jewels in solid gold settings, jeweled center, escapement cap jeweled, conical pivots, bevel head gilt screws, micrometer regulator, gold screws, compensation balance, accurately adjusted to temperature, isochronism and position, double sunk glass enamel dial with red marginal figures, Breguet hair spring, new model stud, mean time screws, steel work highly polished, patent center pinion, elegantly engraved and damaskeened, fine escapement, Fleur de Lis hands and first quality Hampden main spring.

JOHN C. DUEBER SPECIAL.

Nickel, 17 jewels in composition settings, Breguet hair spring, adjusted, micrometer regulator, compensation balance, gilt screws, double sunk dial with red marginal figures, patent center pinion, elegantly engraved and damaskeened, moon hands. Specially guaranteed to be the best timekeeper in the world for the price, and superior to any other full plate watch made outside of the Dueber-Hampden factory. This movement damaskeened in two colors when specially ordered.

ALL OF OUR MOVEMENTS ARE GUARANTEED FOR A TERM OF 5 YEARS. WE PUT ANY OF THESE MOVEMENTS IN THE CASES ILLUSTRATED.	No.100158 No.100154 No.100155	No.100156 No.100157 No.100153
Full 17 Jeweled John C. Dueber Special. Adjusted	$20.50	$18.25
Full 21 Jeweled Special Railway. Adjusted	35.50	33.25
Full 23 Jeweled Special Railway. Adjusted	40.50	38.25

If you want a Watch that will pass Railway Inspection, we can Guarantee the 23 and 21-Jeweled Movement to pass inspection of any railroad in the United States.

LADIES' IMPORTED CHATELAINE WATCHES, Nickel, Silver and Enamel.

PRICE OF EACH COMPLETE

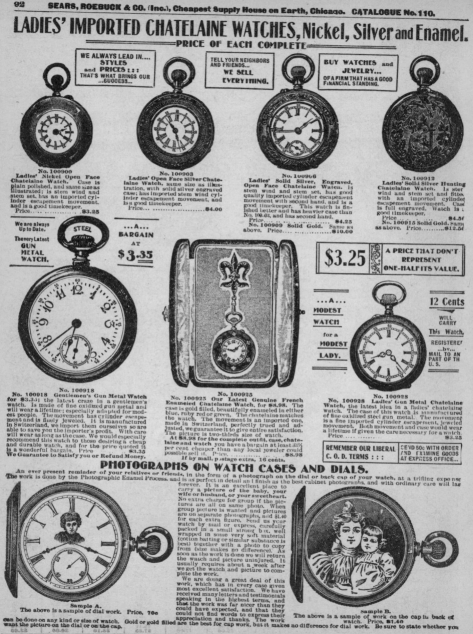

WE ALWAYS LEAD IN....
STYLES
and PRICES : : :
THAT'S WHAT BRINGS OUR
.....SUCCESS...

TELL YOUR NEIGHBORS
AND FRIENDS....
WE SELL
EVERYTHING.

BUY WATCHES and
JEWELRY...
OF A FIRM THAT HAS A GOOD
FINANCIAL STANDING.

No. 100900
Ladies' Nickel Open Face Chatelaine Watch. Case is plain polished, and same size as illustrated; is stem wind and stem set, has an imported cylinder escapement movement, and is a good timekeeper.
Price................................$3.25

No. 100903
Ladies' Open Face Silver Chatelaine Watch, same size as illustration, with solid silver engraved case; has imported stem wind cylinder escapement movement, and is a good timekeeper.
Price....................$4.00

No. 100906
Ladies' Solid Silver, Engraved, Open Face Chatelaine Watch. Is stem wind and stem set, has good quality imported cylinder escapement movement with second hand, and is a good timekeeper. This watch is finished better and has heavier case than No. 100.03, and has second hand.
Price.....................$4.25
No. 100909 Solid Gold. Same as above. Price....................$10.00

No. 100912
Ladies' Solid Silver Hunting Chatelaine Watch. Is stem wind and stem set and fitted with an imported cylinder escapement movement. Case is full engraved. Watch is a good timekeeper.
Price..............$4.5[?]
No. 100915 Solid Gold. Same as above. Price.........$12.5[?]

We are always Up to Date.
The very Latest
GUN METAL WATCH.

...A... BARGAIN AT $3.35

$3.25   A PRICE THAT DON'T REPRESENT ONE-HALF ITS VALUE.

...A... MODEST WATCH for a MODEST LADY.

12 Cents
WILL CARRY
This Watch,
REGISTERE[?] ...by...
MAIL TO AN[?] PART OF TH[?] U. S.

No. 100918
No. 100918 Gentlemen's Gun Metal Watch for $3.35; is the latest craze in a gentlemen's watch. Is made of fine oxidized gun metal and will wear a lifetime; especially adapted for modest people. The movement has cylinder escapement and is finely jeweled. It is manufactured in Switzerland, we import them ourselves so are able to save you the importer's profit. With care it will wear as long as the case. We would especially recommend this watch to those desiring a cheap and durable watch, and for the price quoted it is a wonderful bargain. Price.............$3.35
We Guarantee to Satisfy you or Refund Money.

No. 100925
No. 100925 Our Latest Genuine French Enameled Chatelaine Watch, for $8.98. The case is gold filled, beautifully enameled in either blue, ruby red or green. This chatelaine matches the watch. The movement is an imported one, made in Switzerland, perfectly trued and adjusted, we guarantee it to give entire satisfaction. The picture is two-thirds size of watch.
At $8.98 for the complete outfit, case, chatelaine and watch you have a bargain at least 33⅓ per cent cheaper than any local jeweler could possibly sell it. Price...................$8.98
If by mail, postage extra, 16 cents.

No. 100928
No. 100928 Ladies' Gun Metal Chatelaine Watch, the latest idea in a ladies' chatelaine watch. The case of this watch is manufactured of fine oxidized steel gun metal. The movement is a fine imported cylinder escapement, jeweled movement. Both movement and case would wear a lifetime if given the care necessary for a watch.
Price.....................$3.35

REMEMBER OUR LIBERAL C. O. D. TERMS : : :

SEND 50c WITH ORDER AND EXAMINE GOODS AT EXPRESS OFFICE..

PHOTOGRAPHS ON WATCH CASES AND DIALS.

An ever present reminder of your relatives or friends, in the form of a photograph on the dial or back cap of your watch, at a trifling expense. The work is done by the Photographic Enamel Process, and is as perfect in detail as I finish as the best cabinet photographs, and with ordinary care will last forever. It is an excellent place to carry a picture of the baby, your wife or husband, or your sweetheart. No extra charge for group if the pictures are all on same photo. When group picture is wanted and pictures are on separate photographs, add $1.40 for each extra figure. Send us your watch by mail or express, carefully packed in a small wooden box, well wrapped in some very soft material (cotton batting or similar substance is best) together with a photo to copy from (size makes no difference). As soon as the work is done we will return the watch and picture uninjured. It usually requires about a week after we get the watch and picture to complete the work.

We are doing a great deal of this work, which has in every case given most excellent satisfaction. We have received many letters and testimonials speaking in the highest terms, and that the work was far nicer than they could have expected, and that they could not find words to express their appreciation and thanks. The best work for cap work, but it makes no difference whether you

Sample A.
The above is a sample of dial work. Price, 70c
can be done on any kind or size of watch. Gold or gold filled are the best for cap work, but it makes no difference for dial work. Be sure to state whether you want the picture on the dial or on the cap.

Sample B.
The above is a sample of work on the cap in back of watch. Price, $1.40

Ladies' 6-Size Gold Filled Cases, Guaranteed for 25 Years.

IF YOU WANT TO OWN THE BEST GOLD FILLED WATCH MANUFACTURED, buy one of the celebrated makes we illustrate here. Joseph Fahys, James Boss and Crown cases are positively the best.

THEY ARE GUARANTEED for a term of 25 years, and with care will last a lifetime, the movements the same. We guarantee the movements for a term of five years against defective material or workmanship, but they undoubtedly will wear as long as the cases. You can afford to buy the best.

$9.40 and Upwards is our Price for these Watches.

OUR LIBERAL OFFER. SEND 50 CENTS AS A GUARANTEE OF GOOD FAITH and we will send any watch you select for examination at your express office, and if you do not find it as we describe it and you are not saving money, have the express agent return it immediately, and we will refund the amount deposited. 12 cents will carry any one of these watches to any part of the United States by registered mail. By sending cash in full with your order you save the express charges and the cost of returning money.

☞ THIS IS THE EXACT PICTURE OF THE GUARANTEE JOSEPH FAHYS & CO. give with each one of their 25-year warranted cases.

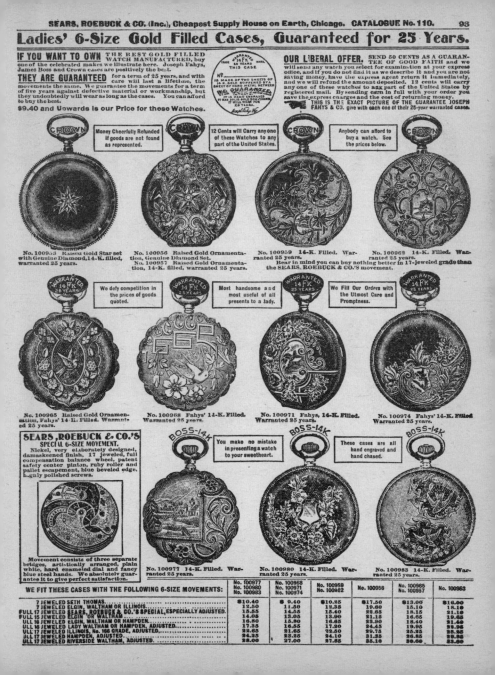

Money Cheerfully Refunded if goods are not found as represented.

12 Cents will Carry anyone of these Watches to any part of the United States.

Anybody can afford to buy a watch. See the prices below.

No. 100953 Raised Gold Star set with Genuine Diamond, 14-K. filled, warranted 25 years.

No. 100956 Raised Gold Ornamentation, Genuine Diamond Set.
No. 100957 Raised Gold Ornamentation, 14-K. filled, warranted 25 years.

No. 100959 14-K. Filled. Warranted 25 years.
Bear in mind you can buy nothing better in 17-jeweled grade than the SEARS, ROEBUCK & CO.'S movement.

No. 100962 14-K. Filled. Warranted 25 years.

We defy competition in the prices of goods quoted.

Most handsome and most useful of all presents to a lady.

We Fill Our Orders with the Utmost Care and Promptness.

No. 100965 Raised Gold Ornamentation, Fahys' 14-K. Filled. Warranted 25 years.

No. 100968 Fahys' 14-K. Filled. Warranted 25 years.

No. 100971 Fahys, 16-K. Filled. Warranted 25 years.

No. 100974 Fahys' 14-K. Filled Warranted 25 years.

SEARS, ROEBUCK & CO.'S SPECIAL 6-SIZE MOVEMENT. Nickel, very elaborately designed, damaskeened finish, 17 jeweled, full compensation balance wheel, patent safety center pinion, ruby roller and pallet escapement, blue beveled edge, highly polished screws.

Movement consists of three separate bridges, artistically arranged, plain white, hard enameled dial and fancy blue steel hands. We absolutely guarantee it to give perfect satisfaction.

You make no mistake in presenting a watch to your sweetheart.

These cases are all hand engraved and hand chased.

No. 100977 14-K. Filled. Warranted 25 years.

No. 100980 14-K. Filled. Warranted 25 years.

No. 100983 14-K. Filled. Warranted 25 years.

WE FIT THESE CASES WITH THE FOLLOWING 6-SIZE MOVEMENTS:	No. 100977 No. 100980 No. 100983	No. 100968 No. 100971 No. 100974	No. 100959 No. 100962	No. 100956	No. 100965 No. 100957	No. 100953
7 JEWELED SETH THOMAS............................	$10.40	$ 9.40	$10.95	$17.50	$13.00	$16.00
7 JEWELED ELGIN, WALTHAM OR ILLINOIS...........	12.50	11.50	12.95	19.60	15.10	18.10
FULL 15 JEWELED ELGIN.............................	15.55	14.55	15.40	22.65	18.15	21.10
FULL 15 JEWELED ELGIN, WALTHAM OR HAMPDEN.....	14.05	13.05	13.90	21.15	16.65	19.65
SEARS, ROEBUCK & CO.'S SPECIAL, ESPECIALLY ADJUSTED	16.50	15.50	16.65	23.90	18.40	21.40
FULL 16 JEWELED LADY WALTHAM OR HAMPDEN, ADJUSTED	17.35	16.55	17.20	24.65	19.95	22.95
ULL 17 JEWELED ILLINOIS, No. 188 GRADE, ADJUSTED	22.65	21.65	22.50	29.75	25.25	28.25
ULL 17 JEWELED HAMPDEN, ADJUSTED................	24.35	23.35	24.10	31.35	26.85	29.85
ULL 17 JEWELED RIVERSIDE WALTHAM, ADJUSTED.....	28.00	27.00	27.85	35.10	30.60	33.60

OUR SPECIAL Ladies's GOLD FILLED Watches

GUARANTEED 20 YEARS.

100984   100989

CERTIFICATE of GUARANTEE
TRADE MARK
TWO PLATES OF SOLID GOLD
GUARANTEED TO WEAR
20 YEARS
SEARS, ROEBUCK & CO.

100985

OUR PRICE IS $9.40

No Retail Dealer Can Sell These Watches.

100991   100987

We control the entire product of the factory for these **CASES** in both Ladies' and Gents' Size.

EVERY CASE MADE TO OUR OWN SPECIFICATIONS AND DESIGNS, under contract by one of the largest and most reliable watch case manufacturers in America; a concern whose enviable reputation for the manufacture of the highest grade gold filled cases is **A GUARANTEE FOR QUALITY.**

WE SAVE YOU ONE-HALF IN PRICE. Our price to you is based on the actual cost of material and labor, with only our one small percentage of profit added. **YOU SAVE THREE PROFITS** and own the watch on the basis of actual cost to make by placing your order in our hands.

WE MAKE THE PRICE AND PROTECT YOU BY A BINDING GUARANTEE.

100993

DESCRIPTION OF CASES. Made of **two plates of solid gold** over fine hard composition metal, are thoroughly well made in every respect and beautifully engraved. They are warranted by certificate of guarantee, which accompanies every case (see copy of guarantee in picture) to wear and retain their color for **TWENTY YEARS.** So far as finish, quality and design are concerned there is nothing made that will surpass them. You must not get the impression on account of the low price that they have an appearance of cheapness, for such is not the case. They are in appearance, style, finish, durability and service equal to any case made.

100995   100998

OUR LIBERAL TERMS OFFER. **SEND US 50 CENTS** (postage stamps taken) and we will send any case and movement selected by express C. O. D., subject to examination. You can examine it thoroughly at the express office, and if found perfectly satisfactory, exactly as represented, one of the handsomest 6-size ladies' watches you ever saw and such value as no other house gives, pay the express agent our price and express charges, less the 50 cents sent with order.

This is a Picture taken direct from our 6-size

SEARS ROEBUCK & CO

17-Jeweled Movement,

a movement we can guarantee to give entire satisfaction.
Price.............................$15.80
Fitted in any case illustrated here.

	NICKEL.
7 Jeweled Seth Thomas............................	$ 9.40
7 Jeweled Elgin, Waltham or Illinois..........	11.95
FULL 15 JEWELED ELGIN OR WALTHAM...........	14.30
FULL 16 JEWELED ELGIN OR HAMPDEN............	19.15
FULL 16 JEWELED LADY WALTHAM OR HAMPDEN, ADJUSTED........	21.00
FULL 17 JEWELED ILLINOIS No. 166 GRADE, ADJUSTED.......	23.00
FULL 17 JEWELED RIVERSIDE WALTHAM OR HAMPDEN, ADJUSTED....	28.00
FULL 17 JEWELED SEARS, ROEBUCK & CO.'S SPECIAL MOVEMENT...	15.80

CONSIDER OUR GUARANTEE. Every case covered by special certificate of guarantee for twenty years. Every movement guaranteed for five years, and so covered by a binding guarantee.

101001

LADIES' 6-SIZE 10-KARAT GOLD FILLED CASES

GUARANTEED BY THE MAKER FOR A TERM OF 20 YEARS.

THE MOVEMENTS we fit in these watches are the best in the land, positively none better. We guarantee them to you for a term of 5 years against defective material or workmanship. James Boss, one of the oldest manufacturers of gold filled cases, claims that a gold filled case such as we illustrate, is equal to any solid gold one manufactured, except in intrinsic value. The name of Lion upon any gold filled case, and signed by the manufacturer is a guarantee of its perfection and durability. Twenty years is practically a lifetime, but we believe with the wear that the average lady gives a watch, they will last 40 years.

FOR TIMEKEEPING QUALITIES, for a watch that is a happy medium size, and for a watch that is recognized as the correct thing, we can recommend the 6-size. Cases manufactured by Joseph Fahys, James Boss and Lion, have no superiors.

OUR WRITTEN BINDING GUARANTEE goes with each and every watch we sell, the manufacturer likewise warrants them to be exactly as represented.

SEE OUR LIBERAL OFFER.

SEND 50 CENTS and we will send any watch you may select, by express C. O. D., subject to examination. You can examine it at your nearest express office, and if you find it exactly as represented, pay the express agent the balance and the express charges

OUR 6-SIZE 17-JEWEL

SEARS, ROEBUCK & CO. movement is the most reliable ladies' size movement made.

12 cents will carry a Lady's Watch to any point in the United States by registered mail; 25 cents to any point by express.

This is the picture taken from the guarantee that JOSEPH FAHYS gives with each of his 20-year cases.

No. 101000 10-K., Gold Filled, 20 years guaranteed.

No. 101003 Diamond Set, 10-K., Gold Filled, 20 years guaranteed.

No. 101006 10-K., Gold Filled, 20 years guaranteed, solid gold ornamentation.
No. 101007 Same as above, set with genuine diamond.

No. 101008 10-K., Gold Filled, 20 years guaranteed.

WE RECOMMEND and advocate 15-jeweled movements. We know that they keep correct time.

You would not be disappointed in the Timekeeping Qualities, of the SEARS ROEBUCK Special Movement.

EVERY CASE GUARANTEED ...FOR... 20 YEARS

No. 101010 10-K., Gold Filled, 20 years guaranteed.

No. 101012 10-K., Gold Filled, 20 years guaranteed, solid gold ornamentation.

No. 101015 10-K., Gold Filled, 20 years guaranteed.

No. 101017 10-K., Gold Filled, 20 years guaranteed.

50 CENTS ...with your Order... BALANCE PAYABLE AFTER RECEIVED..

See our Prices; make no Mistake Any one of these Watches From $9.25 to $30.85 each

Watches will be sent C. O. D., on receipt of 50 cents (cash or stamps) with the order as a guarantee of good faith on your part. The 50 cents will be refunded if goods are not satisfactory.

This is a picture of our 6-Size, Sears, Roebuck & Co.'s Special 17-Jeweled Movement. We guarantee this movement to give you absolute satisfaction. It is the best finished 17-Jeweled movement on the market.

No. 101021 10-K., Gold Filled, 20 years guaranteed.

No. 101024 10-K., Gold Filled, 20 years guaranteed.

No. 101027 10-K., Gold Filled, 20 years guaranteed.

WE FIT THESE CASES WITH THE FOLLOWING 6-SIZE MOVEMENTS. AT $9.25 TO $30.85.

	No. 101000, No. 101008 No. 101010, No. 101015 No. 101017	No. 101003 No. 101006	No. 101007 No. 101012	No. 101021 No. 101024 No. 101027
7 Jeweled Seth Thomas............	$ 9.25	$11.75	$13.75	$ 9.55
7 Jeweled Elgin, Waltham or Illinois.	10.40	12.90	14.90	10.70
17 JEWELED SEARS, ROEBUCK & CO.'S SPECIAL, NICKEL...	13.50	16.00	18.00	13.80
15 JEWELED ELGIN OR WALTHAM....	12.00	14.50	16.50	12.30
16 JEWELED ELGIN OR HAMPDEN...	14.80	17.30	19.30	15.10
16 JEWELED LADY WALTHAM OR HAMPDEN, ADJUSTED..	15.35	17.85	19.85	15.65
17 JEWELED ILLINOIS, No. 106-GRADE, ADJUSTED....	26.85	28.35	26.35	31.15
17 JEWELED HAMPDEN, ADJUSTED....	22.50	25.00	27.00	22.80
17 JEWELED RIVERSIDE WALTHAM, ADJUSTED.....	26.35	28.85	30.85	26.65

...SOLID GOLD, GOLD FILLED AND SOLID STERLING SILVER BRACELETS...

LAST YEAR WE KEPT THE FACTORIES BUSY FILLING OUR ORDERS for BRACELETS.

The demand has not fallen off, but on the contrary is steadily increased, so much so that we have added to our line many new designs beyond competition. The patterns we have illustrated are the latest 1900 designs of the different manufacturers, each piece being perfect in every detail in its make-up. Your order for bracelets would command our careful attention and we know you would be pleased with the result of your purchase in every instance.

IF DESIRED, WE WILL SEND SUCH GOODS AS YOU MAY SELECT C. O. D., subject to examination at your express office, provided you enclose with your order the sum of 50 cents as a deposit, which sum would be refunded to you if the goods were not exactly as we have described them. Most of our customers send cash in full with their orders, thereby saving the express charges and cost of returned money order. If by mail, postage on bracelets, extra, 3 cents; registry and insurance extra.

No. 102078 Child's or Baby Bracelet, gold filled, bright finished, the very latest engraved bangles, soldered links. Price, each.............**$1.75**
No. 102081 Child's or Baby Bracelet, sterling silver, same as above, bright finished. Price, each...**$1.25**

No. 102122 Solid Silver Bracelet, hand engraved and hand chased, six solid silver heart pendants, each set with turquoise and opal. Price, for complete bracelet..**$3.00**

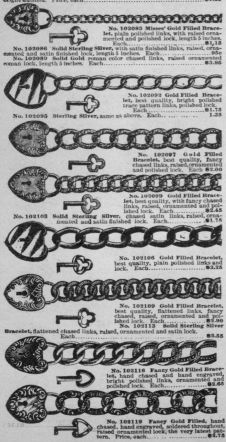

No. 102083 Misses' Gold Filled Bracelet, plain polished links, with raised ornamented and polished lock, length 5 inches. Each...............**$1.15**
No. 102086 Solid Sterling Silver, with satin finished links, raised, ornamented and satin finished lock, length 5 inches. Each..........95c
No. 102089 Solid Gold roman color chased links, raised ornamented roman lock, length 5 inches. Each..............................**$3.95**

No. 102092 Gold Filled Bracelet, best quality, bright polished trace pattern links, polished lock. Each...........**$1.75**
No. 102095 Sterling Silver, same as above. Each..........1.35

No. 102097 Gold Filled Bracelet, best quality, fancy chased links, raised, ornamented and polished lock. Each **$2.00**

No. 102099 Gold Filled Bracelet, best quality, with fancy chased links, raised, ornamented and polished lock. Each..........**$2.45**
No. 102103 Solid Sterling Silver, chased satin links, raised, ornamented and satin finished lock. Each..........**$1.75**

No. 102106 Gold Filled Bracelet, best quality, plain polished links and lock. Each..........**$2.25**

No. 102109 Gold Filled Bracelet, best quality, flattened links, fancy chased, raised, ornamented and polished lock. Each..........**$2.90**
No. 102113 Solid Sterling Silver Bracelet, flattened chased links, raised, ornamented and satin lock. Each..........**$2.55**

No. 102116 Fancy Gold Filled Bracelet, hand chased and hand engraved, bright polished links, ornamented and polished lock. Each..........**$2.65**

No. 102119 Fancy Gold Filled, hand chased, hand engraved, soldered throughout, raised ornamented lock; the very latest pattern. Price, each..........**$4.75**

No. 102125 Gold Filled Bracelet, bright polished square hand chased links, something novel; raised, ornamented, polished lock. Each...........**$2.00**
No. 102128 Solid Silver Bracelet. Same as above, but not chased links; plain satin finished lock. Each...........**$2.35**

No. 102131 Gold Filled Bracelet, loose curb flattened links with chased center, with raised, ornamented and polished lock. Each..........**$1.75**

No. 102133 Solid Silver through and through, soldered links, hand chased and hand engraved, one of the very latest effects. Price, each..........**$2.60**

No. 102136 Gold Filled, hand engraved, roman and bright finished, one of the very latest ideas. Price, each..........**$2.65**

No. 102139 Solid Gold Bracelet, hand chased and hand engraved links, raised, ornamented and polished lock. Each..........**$6.53**

No. 102142 Solid Gold Bracelet, plain flattened links, roman finish, links run to taper at ends, plain satin finish lock. Each..........**$7.50**

No. 102145 Solid Gold Bracelet, bright polished links, bright polished lock. Each..........**$8.50**

No. 102148 Heavy, Massive Solid Gold Bracelet, hand engraved and hand chased links, roman finish; raised, ornamented roman finished lock. Each..........**$15.00**

...Nethersole Bracelets in Gold Filled and Sterling Silver...

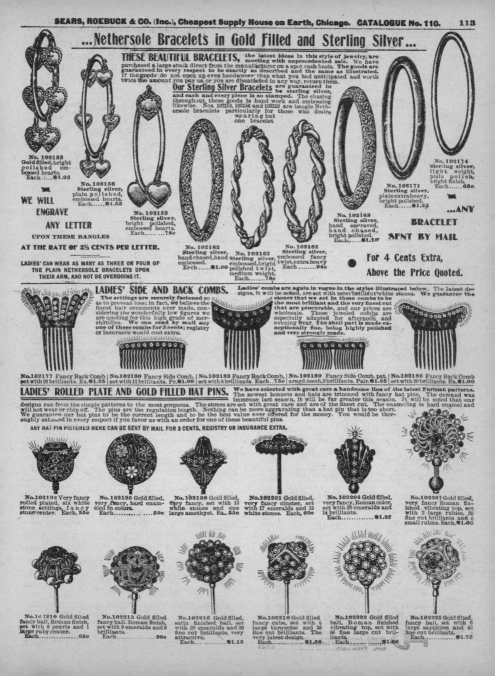

THESE BEAUTIFUL BRACELETS, the latest ideas in this style of jewelry, are meeting with unprecedented sale. We have purchased a large stock direct from the manufacturer on a spot cash basis. The goods are guaranteed in every respect to be exactly as described and the same as illustrated. If the goods do not open up even handsomer than what you had anticipated and worth twice the amount you pay us, or you are dissatisfied in any way, return them.

Our Sterling Silver Bracelets are guaranteed to be sterling silver, and each and every piece is so stamped. The chasing throughout these goods is hand work and embossing likewise. Nos. 102153, 102156 and 102159 are bangle Nethersole bracelets particularly for those who desire wearing but one bracelet

No. 102153
Gold filled, bright polished, embossed hearts. Each....$1.95

WE WILL ENGRAVE ANY LETTER

UPON THESE BANGLES

AT THE RATE OF 2½ CENTS PER LETTER.

LADIES' CAN WEAR AS MANY AS THREE OR FOUR OF THE PLAIN NETHERSOLE BRACELETS UPON THEIR ARM, AND NOT BE OVERDOING IT.

No. 102156 Sterling silver, plain polished, embossed hearts. Each....$1.55

No. 102159 Sterling silver, bright polished, embossed hearts. Each......78c

No. 102162 Sterling silver, hand chased, hand embossed. Each.....$1.00

No. 102163 Sterling silver, embossed, bright polished twist, medium weight. Each......78c

No. 102165 Sterling silver, fancy twist, extra heavy Each.........94c

No. 102168 Sterling silver, hand engraved, hand chased, bright polished. Each......$1.70

No. 102171 Sterling silver, plain extra heavy, bright polished. Each......$1.25

No. 102174 Sterling silver, light weight, plain polish, bright finish. Each......65c

...ANY BRACELET SENT BY MAIL

For 4 Cents Extra, Above the Price Quoted.

LADIES' SIDE AND BACK COMBS.

The settings are securely fastened so as to prevent loss; in fact, we believe the finest hair ornaments ever made, considering the wonderfully low figures we are quoting for this high grade of merchandise. We can send by mail any one of these combs for 3 cents; registry or insurance would cost extra.

Ladies' combs are again in vogue in the styles illustrated below. The latest designs, it will be noted, are set with most brilliant white stones. We guarantee the stones that we set in these combs to be the most brilliant and the very finest cut that are procurable, and our prices are wholesale. These jeweled combs are especially adapted for afternoon and evening wear. The shell part is made exceptionally fine, being highly polished and very strongly made.

No.102177 Fancy Back Comb, set with 28 brilliants. Ea. $1.25 | **No.102180** Fancy Side Comb, set with 11 brilliants. Pr.$1.00 | **No.102183** Fancy Back Comb, set with 8 brilliants. Each.. 75c | **No.102189** Fancy Side Comb, pat. arngd. teeth, 9 brilliants. Pair.$1.25 | **No.102186** Fancy Back Comb set with 20 brilliants. Ea.$1.00

LADIES' ROLLED PLATE AND GOLD FILLED HAT PINS.

We have selected with great care a handsome line of the latest Parisian patterns. The newest bonnets and hats are trimmed with fancy hat pins. The demand was immense last season, it will be far greater this season. It will be noted that our designs run from the simple patterns to the most gorgeous. The stones are set with great care and are of the finest cut. The enameling is hard enamel and will not wear or chip off. The pins are the regulation length. Nothing can be more aggravating than a hat pin that is too short. We guarantee our hat pins to be the correct length and to be the best value ever offered for the money. You would be thoroughly satisfied in every respect if you favor us with an order for one of these beautiful pins.

ANY HAT PIN PICTURED HERE CAN BE SENT BY MAIL FOR 3 CENTS, REGISTRY OR INSURANCE EXTRA.

No.102193 Very fancy rolled plated, six white stone settings, fancy stone center. Each, 35c

No. 102195 Gold filled, very fancy, hard enameled in colors. Each............50c

No. 102198 Gold filled, very fancy, set with 13 white stones and one large amethyst. Ea.. 55c

No.102201 Gold filled, very fancy cluster, set with 17 emeralds and 12 white stones. Each, 60c

No. 102204 Gold filled, very fancy, Roman color, set with 20 emeralds and 14 brilliants. Each..............$1.25

No.102207 Gold filled, very fancy Roman finished vibrating top, set with 2 large rubies, 22 fine cut brilliants and 6 small rubies. Each.$1.60

No.102210 Gold filled fancy ball, Roman finish, set with 8 pearls and 1 large ruby center. Each..............65c

No.102213 Gold filled fancy ball, Roman finish, set with 9 emeralds and 9 brilliants. Each............90c

No.102216 Gold filled, satin finished ball, set with 20 emeralds and 20 fine cut brilliants. Very attractive. Each............$1.15

No.102219 Gold filled fancy cube, set with 6 large turquoise and 36 fine cut brilliants. The very latest design. Each............$1.50

No.102222 Gold filled fancy ball, Roman finished vibrating top, set with 36 fine large cut brilliants. Each..............$1.60

No.102225 Gold filled fancy ball, set with 6 large sapphires and 42 fine cut brilliants. Each............$1.75

...GOLD FILLED RINGS...
AND HOW GOLD FILLED RINGS ARE MADE.

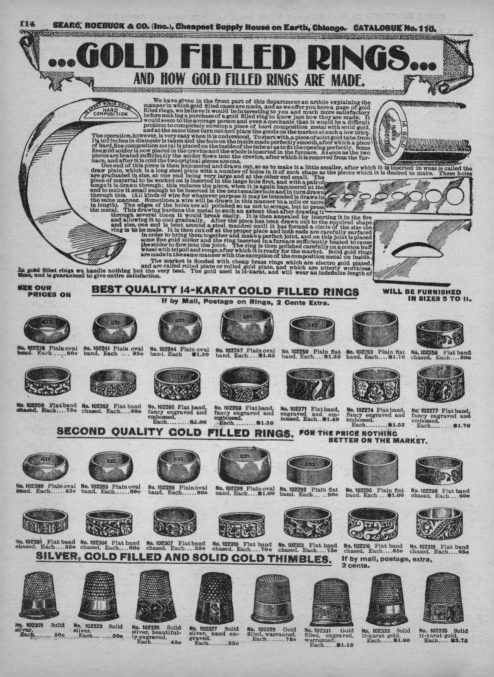

We have given in the front part of this department an article explaining the manner in which gold filled cases are made, and as we offer you here a page of gold filled rings, we believe it would be interesting to you and much more satisfactory before making a purchase of a gold filled ring to know just how they are made. It would seem to the average person and even a mechanic that it would be a difficult problem to completely envelop a piece of hard composition metal with solid gold, and at the same time turn out and place the goods on the market at such a low price.

The operation, however, is very easy when it is understood. To start with, a piece of solid gold tube from 1¼ to 2 inches in diameter is taken and the hole on the inside made perfectly smooth, after which a piece of hard, fine composition metal is placed on the inside of the tube so as to fit the opening perfectly. Some fine gold solder is now placed in the crevice and the whole is inserted in the furnace. As soon as the two pieces are heated sufficiently the solder flows into the crevice, after which it is removed from the furnace, and after it is cold the two original pieces are one.

One end of this piece is then hammered and drawn out, so as to make it a little smaller, after which it is inserted in what is called the draw plate, which is a long steel plate with a number of holes in it of such shape as the pieces which it is desired to make. These holes are graduated in size, at one end being very large and at the other end small. The piece of material to be worked on is inserted in the large hole first, and with a pair of tongs it is drawn through; this reduces the piece, when it is again hammered at the end to make it small enough to be inserted in the next smaller hole and in turn drawn through this. (All kinds of wire for whatever purpose it may be intended is drawn in the same manner. Sometimes a wire will be drawn in this manner to a mile or more in length). The edges of the holes are all polished so as not to scrape, but to press the metal. This drawing hardens the metal to such an extent that after drawing it through several times it would break easily. It is then annealed by inserting it in the fire and allowing it to cool gradually. After the piece has been drawn out to the required shape and size, one end is bent around a steel mandrel until it has formed a circle of the size the ring is to be made. It is then cut off at the proper place and both ends are carefully surfaced in order to bring them together and make a perfect joint, and on this joint is placed some fine gold solder and the ring inserted in a furnace sufficiently heated to cause the solder to flow into the joint. The ring is then polished carefully on a cotton buff wheel with tripoli and rouge, after which it is ready for the market. Solid gold rings are made in the same manner with the exception of the composition metal on inside.

The market is flooded with cheap brass rings which are electro gold plated, and are called rolled plate or rolled gold plate, and which are utterly worthless. In gold filled rings we handle nothing but the very best. The gold used is 14-karat, and will wear an indefinite length of time, and is guaranteed to give entire satisfaction.

SEE OUR PRICES ON

BEST QUALITY 14-KARAT GOLD FILLED RINGS
If by Mail, Postage on Rings, 2 Cents Extra.

WILL BE FURNISHED IN SIZES 5 TO 11.

No. 102238 Plain oval band. Each......60c

No. 102241 Plain oval band. Each 95c

No. 102244 Plain oval band. Each....$1.30

No. 102247 Plain oval band. Each....$1.65

No. 102250 Plain flat band. Each....$1.30

No. 102253 Plain flat band. Each....$1.70

No. 102256 Flat band chased. Each....80c

No. 102259 Flat band chased. Each....75c

No. 102262 Flat band chased. Each....80c

No. 102265 Flat band, fancy engraved and embossed. Each....$1.00

No. 102268 Flat band, fancy engraved and embossed. Each....$1.30

No. 102271 Flat band, engraved and embossed. Each....$1.40

No. 102274 Flat band, fancy engraved and embossed. Each....$1.55

No. 102277 Flat band, fancy engraved and embossed. Each....$1.70

SECOND QUALITY GOLD FILLED RINGS. FOR THE PRICE NOTHING BETTER ON THE MARKET.

No. 102280 Plain oval band. Each....45c

No. 102283 Plain oval band. Each......60c

No. 102286 Plain oval band. Each....80c

No. 102289 Plain oval band. Each....$1.00

No. 102292 Plain flat band. Each....90c

No. 102295 Plain flat band. Each....$1.00

No. 102298 Flat band chased. Each....60c

No. 102301 Flat band chased. Each....55c

No. 102304 Flat band chased. Each....60c

No. 102307 Flat band chased. Each....65c

No. 102310 Flat band chased. Each....70c

No. 102313 Flat band chased. Each....75c

No. 102316 Flat band chased. Each....85c

No. 102319 Flat band chased. Each....95c

SILVER, GOLD FILLED AND SOLID GOLD THIMBLES. If by mail, postage, extra, 2 cents.

No. 102221 Solid silver. Each......20c

No. 102323 Solid silver. Each......30c

No. 102325 Solid silver, beautifully engraved. Each......45c

No. 102327 Solid silver, hand engraved. Each......55c

No. 102329 Gold filled, warranted. Each......75c

No. 102331 Gold filled, engraved, warranted. Each....$1.15

No. 102333 Solid 10-karat gold. Each......$1.90

No. 102335 Solid 14-karat gold. Each....$3.75

BABIES' AND CHILDREN'S GOLD SET AND BAND RINGS.

These rings we have endeavored to embody in simple but durable patterns. We have tried to avoid cutting corners and projecting ornamentation, which have a tendency to catch and tear the laces and embroideries of an infant's clothing. These rings are of solid gold; it would be impossible for the baby to wear it out. The stones we set in our rings are perfect in every detail.

BABY RINGS ARE MADE IN SIZES FROM 0 TO 3. MISSES' RINGS IN SIZES FROM 5 TO 8 ONLY.

For full instructions for measurement of ring size, see bottom of page. When cash in full is sent with order the rings can be sent by mail, postage 3 cents; by registered mail, 8 cents extra.

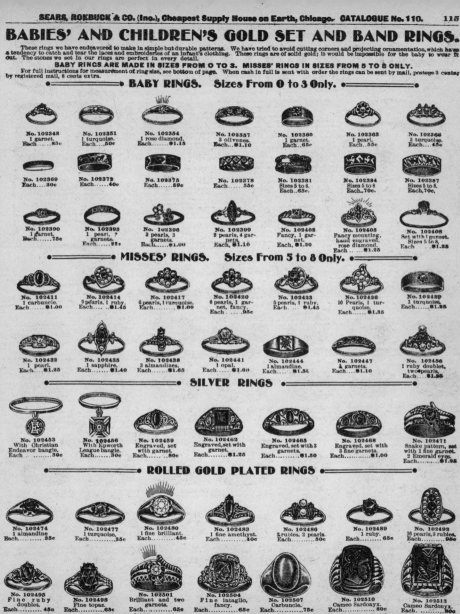

● BABY RINGS. Sizes From 0 to 3 Only. ●

No. 102348
1 garnet.
Each......85c

No. 102351
1 turquoise.
Each...50c

No. 102354
1 rose diamond.
Each........$1.15

No. 102357
3 olivenes.
Each..$1.10

No. 102360
1 garnet.
Each....65c

No. 102363
1 pearl.
Each..55c

No. 102366
3 turquoise.
Each....45c

No. 102369
Each......30c

No. 102372
Each......40c

No. 102375
Each........59c

No. 102378
Each......55c

No. 102381
Sizes 5 to 8.
Each..65c

No. 102384
Sizes 5 to 8
Each..70c

No. 102387
Sizes 5 to 8.
Each, 70c

No. 102390
1 garnet.
Each......75c

No. 102393
1 pearl, ?
garnets.
Each......85c

No. 102396
3 pearls, 3
garnets.
Each....$1.00

No. 102399
2 pearls, 4 garnets.
Each, $1.10

No. 102402
Fancy, 1 garnet.
Each, $1.20

No. 102405
Fancy mounting,
hand engraved,
rose diamond.
Each......$1.25

No. 102408
Set with 1 garnet.
Sizes 5 to 8.
Each......$1.35

● MISSES' RINGS. Sizes From 5 to 8 Only. ●

No. 102411
1 carbuncle.
Each.... $1.00

No. 102414
9 pearls, 1 ruby.
Each.... $1.45

No. 102417
6 pearls, 1 turquoise.
Each.... $1.00

No. 102420
6 pearls, 1 garnet, fancy.
Each.....95c

No. 102423
5 pearls, 1 ruby.
Each... $1.45

No. 102426
10 Pearls, 1 turquoise.
Each... $1.35

No. 10242p
1 turquoise.
Each........$1.25

No. 102432
1 pearl.
Each.. $1.25

No. 102435
1 sapphire.
Each... $1.40

No. 102438
3 almandines.
Each.. $1.65

No. 102441
1 opal.
Each... $1.60

No. 102444
1 almandine.
Each.... $1.50

No. 102447
3 garnets.
Each.. $1.10

No. 102456
1 ruby doublet,
two pearls.
Each... $1.35

● SILVER RINGS ●

No. 102453
With Christian
Endeavor bangle.
Each......30c

No. 102456
With Epworth
League bangle.
Each......30c

No. 102459
Engraved, set
with garnet.
Each......80c

No. 102462
Engraved, set with
garnet.
Each... $1.25

No. 102465
Engraved, set with 3
garnets.
Each.. $1.50

No. 102468
Engraved, set with
3 fine garnets.
Each... $1.00

No. 102471
Snake pattern, set
with 1 fine garnet.
2 Emerald eyes.
Each.......$1.25

● ROLLED GOLD PLATED RINGS ●

No. 102474
1 almandine.
Each.....35c

No. 102477
1 turquoise.
Each......35c

No. 102480
1 fine brilliant.
Each......45c

No. 102483
1 fine amethyst.
Each 40c

No. 102486
2 rubies, 2 pearls.
Each.....50c

No. 102489
1 ruby.
Each......65c

No. 102492
16 pearls, 3 rubies.
Each......95c

No. 102495
Fine ruby
doublet.
Each.... 45c

No. 102498
Fine topaz.
Each.....65c

No. 102501
Brilliant and two
garnets.
Each......65c

No. 102504
Fine intaglio,
fancy.
Each......65c

No. 102507
Carbuncle.
Each......75c

No. 102510
Cameo Sardonyx.
Each........80c

No. 102513
Cameo Sardonyx.
Each......80c

BE SURE TO FOLLOW THESE INSTRUCTIONS in ordering rings, whether Gold Filled or Solid Gold. We must know the size from this scale. Take a narrow slip of paper and measure around the finger, making sure that when both ends meet it will fit exactly as ring should. To get number of size, measure slip on gauge by placing one end of the slip even with the left end of the gauge here illustrated. The figure which the other end meets will indicate the size required. When ordering always write number of size, as slip is sometimes lost and order delayed until another is received.

Secret Society and Emblem Charms. GOLD AND... GOLD FILLED.

These charms are manufactured of the best materials procurable. The enamel is guaranteed a hard enamel, and will not chip or wear off. Warranted to give absolute satisfaction in every particular. Our success as a mercantile firm was only accomplished by honest methods and honest dealings. We know that if you buy once from us you will always be a steady customer.

No. 103975 Blue enameled, gold filled, Masonic. Price.......$1.25
No. 103978 Same as above, solid gold. Price. $3.75

No. 103981 Engraved, gold filled, Masonic and Odd Fellows. Price.........$1.15
No. 103984 Same as above, solid gold. Price........$4.00

No. 103987 Gold filled, enameled and engraved Independent Order of Foresters. Price.........$1.00
No. 103990 Same as above, solid gold. Price.$7.50

No. 103993 Gold filled, enameled, Knights of Pythias, uniformed rank. Price.......$1.25
No. 103996 Same as above, uniformed rank. Price...$1.25

No. 103999 Gold filled, enameled and engraved, G. A. R. Price...$1.25
No. 104005 Same as above, solid gold. Price...........$12.00

No. 104005 Gold filled, enameled and engraved, Independent Order of Odd Fellows. Price...$1.50
No. 104008 Same as above, solid gold. Price........$12.00

No. 104011 Gold filled, enameled and engraved, Sons of Veterans. Price.......85c
No. 104013 Same as above, solid gold. Price.$4.50

No. 104016 Rolled plate, hard enameled, Ancient Order United Workmen. Price 35c
No. 104019 Same style, Masonic. Price.........35c
No. 104022 Same style, Independent Order of Odd Fellows. Price.........35c
No. 104025 Same style, Ancient Order of Pythias. Price...35c

No. 104028 Pearl emblem, onlaid, filled mounting, Independent Order of Foresters Price.........45c
No. 104031 Same style, Woodmen of America. Price. 45c
No. 104034 Same style, Maccabees. Price............45c
No. 104037 Same style, Ancient Order United Workmen. Price..........45c

No. 104040 Pearl, gold filled emblem, Modern Woodmen. Price...........65c
No. 104043 Same style, Masonic. Price...........65c
No. 104046 Same style, Knights of Pythias. Price..65c
No. 104049 Same style, Odd Fellows. Price...........65c

No. 104052 Gold filled, hard enameled and engraved, Improved Order of Red Men. Price......75c
No. 104055 Same style G. A. R. Price............75c
No. 104058 Same style, Odd Fellows. Price......75c
No. 104061 Same style, Catholic Order of Foresters. Price.........75c

No. 104064 Gold filled, enameled, Odd Fellows Encampment. Price.......85c
No. 104067 Same style as above, Odd Fellows. Price..85c
No. 104070 Same style, Ancient Order of United Workmen. Price......85c
No. 104073 Same style, Masonic. Price.....85c

No. 104076 Gold filled emblem, set in black onyx, Masonic. Price......$1.00
No. 104079 Same style, Odd Fellows. Price......$1.00
No. 104082 Same style, Knights of Maccabees. Price......$1.00
No. 104085 Same style, Royal Arcanum. Price...$1.00

No. 104088 Gold filled, hard enameled and engraved, Junior Order United American Mechanics. Price............$1.50
No. 104091 Same style, Knights of Pythias. Price $1.50
No. 104094 Same style, Modern Woodmen. Price.$1.50
No. 104097 Same style, Odd Fellows. Price...........$1.50

No. 104103 Solid gold, hard enameled and engraved, Ancient Order United Workmen. Price.....$3.75

No. 104106 Solid gold, hard enameled, engraved, Odd Fellows. Price.....$3.75
No. 104109 Same style, Masonic. Price......$3.75

No. 104112 Solid gold, Masonic, thirty-second degree. Price...$2.00

No. 104115 Daughters of Rebecca, solid gold. Price........$3.00

No. 104117 gold gold, hard enameled, engraved, Eastern Star. Price.......$3.35

No. 104119 gold, hard enameled, engraved, Knights of Pythias. Price...$2.00

No. 104121 Solid gold, enameled, Odd Fellows. Price...$2.00

No. 104123 Solid gold hard enameled, engraved, Odd Fellows Encampment. Price....$3.75

No. 104125 Solid gold, heavy keystone, Masonic. Price.......$5.50
No. 104127 Same as above, gold filled. Price..........$1.25

No. 104129 Solid gold, Knights of Pythias. Price........$7.00
No. 104131 Same as above, gold filled. Price.......$1.45

No. 104133 Solid gold, hard enameled, engraved, Knights of Pythias. Price......$9.00

No. 104135 Solid gold, hard enameled, engraved, Knights of Maccabees. Price..........$9.00
No. 104137 Same style, Knights Templar, solid gold. Price....$8.00

No. 104139 Solid gold, extra heavy, enameled colors, hand engraved. Price.........$12.00

No. 104141 Solid gold, enameled, hand engraved, Odd Fellows. Price........$9.00

No. 104143 Extra heavy, black onyx 10 rubles, 5 diamonds. Price......$21.00

GOLD AND GOLD FILLED EMBLEM PINS AND BUTTONS.

This year we have added many new society pins to our already immense stock of emblematical goods. We know that an order for these goods would be filled to your entire satisfaction. The goods are exactly as we warrant them in every particular, and if not to your entire satisfaction upon the receipt of same, return them and we will cheerfully refund your money. Two cents will carry any one of these pins to any part of the United States of America by mail. Insurance or registry extra

No 104152 Gold filled, Masonic, engraved.
Each.......40c
No.104154 Solid gold, same as above.
Each.........68c

No. 104156 Gold filled, Masonic, enameled.
Each...........40c
No.104158 Solid gold, same as above.
Each......80c

No.104160 Gold filled, Masonic, enameled.
Each...........55c
No.104162 Solid gold, same as above.
Each.....$1.00

No.104164 Gold filled, Masonic and Odd Fellows, enameled.
Each..........45c
No.104166 Solid gold, same as above. Each..75c

No.104168 Gold filled, Odd Fellows, enameled.
Each 50c
No.104170 Solid gold, same as above. Each......$1.00

No.104172 Gold filled, Odd Fellows, enameled.
Each........40c
No.104174 Solid gold, same as above.
Each....... 75c

No.104176 Gold filled, Odd Fellows, enameled.
Each 45c
No.104178 Solid gold, same as above.
Each 70c

No.104180 Gold filled, Odd Fellows, engraved.........40c
No.104182 Solid gold, same as above.
Each...........90c

No. 104184 Gold filled, Odd Fellows.
Each........35c
No.104186 Solid gold, same as above.
Each.........60c

No.104188 Gold filled, Knights of Pythias.
Each.........55c
No.104190 Solid gold, same as above.
Each 85c

No.104192 Gold filled, Knights of Pythias.
Each..........60c
No.104194 Solid gold, same as above.
Each 95c

No. 104196 Gold filled, G. A. R. enameled. Each.50c
No. 104198 Solid gold, same as above. Each..$1.40

No.104200 Gold filled, Modern Woodmen.
Each.......50c
No.104202 Solid gold, same as above. Each.80c

No.104204 Gold filled, Modern Woodmen.
Each........50c
No.104206 Solid gold, same as above.Each.$1.00

No.104208 Gold filled, Ancient Order United Workmen. Each....40c
No.104210 Solid gold,same as above. Each $1.00

No.104212 Gold filled, Red Men.
Each 45c
No.104214 Solid gold, same as above. Each, 75c

No.104216 Gold filled, Red Men.
Each........50c
No.104218 Solid gold, same as above. Each. 90c

No.104220 Gold filled, Catholic Order of Foresters.Each 55c
No.104222 Solid gold, same as above. Each........$1.35

No. 104224 Gold filled, Independent Order of Foresters.
Each.........65c
No. 104226 Solid gold, same as above. Each....$1.15

No. 104228 Gold filled, Ancient Order of Foresters.
Each........65c
No.104230 Solid gold, same as above. Ea. $1.15

No.104232 Gold filled, Catholic M. B. Association. Each..45c
No.104234 Solid gold, same as above.
Each.......$1.00

No. 104236 Gold filled, Elks.
Each..........75c
No.104238 Solid gold, same as above.
Each.........$1.65

No.104240 Gold filled, Maccabees.
Each.........55c
No.104242 Solid gold, same as above. Each..90c

No.104244 Gold filled, Christian Endeavor.
Each........50c
No. 104246 Solid gold, same as above.
Each........95c

No.104248 Gold filled, Epworth League.
Each......50c
No.104250 Solid gold, same as above. Each, 85c

No. 104252 Gold filled, Daughters of Rebecca.
Each.........60c
No.104254 Solid gold, same as above.
Each.....$1.10

No. 104256 Gold filled, Eastern Star. Each...65c
No.104258 Solid gold, same as above.
Each......$1.30

No. 104260 Gold filled, Daughters of America.
Each.........60c
No.104262 Solid gold, same as above.
Each......$1.50

No.104264 Gold filled, Daughters of Honor.
Each.......37c
No.104266 Solid gold, same as above. Each, 75c

No.104268 Gold filled, Brotherhood of Railroad Trainmen.
Each.........55c
No.104270 Solid gold, same as above.
Each....$1.00

No.104272 Gold filled, Royal Arcanum.
Each 50c
No.104274 Solid gold, same as above. Each, 98c

No. 104276 Gold filled, plain badge.
Each.........50c
No. 104278 Solid gold, same as above.
Each........$1.25

Gold and Gold Filled EMBLEM BUTTONS.

No. 104280 Gold filled, Masonic.
Each.........35c
No. 104282 Solid gold, same as above.
Each.......75c

No. 104284 Gold filled, Odd Fellows.
Each.......35c
No. 104286 Solid gold, same as above.
Each.......75c

No. 104288 Gold filled, Knights of Pythias.
Each.......35c
No. 104290 Solid gold, same as above.
Each....75c

No. 104292 Gold filled, Ancient Order United Workmen.
Each.....35c
No. 104294 Solid gold, same as above.
Each....75c

No. 104296 Gold filled, Maccabees.
Each.....35c
No. 104298 Solid gold, same as above.
Each....75c

No. 104300 Gold filled, Red Men.
Each ...35c
No. 104302 Solid gold, same as above.
Each ..75c

No. 104304 Gold filled, Woodmen.
Each.......35c
No. 104306 Solid gold, same as above.
Each....75c

No. 104308 Gold filled, Elks.
Each.....35c
No. 104310 Solid gold, same as above.
Each.$1.15

No. 104312 Gold filled, Foresters.
Each.....35c
No. 104314 Solid gold, same as above.
Each....75c

No. 104316 Gold filled, Foresters of America.
Each.....35c
No. 104318 Solid gold, same as above.
Each....75c

No. 104320 Gold filled, Catholic Order of Foresters.
Each.....35c
No. 104322 Solid gold, same as above.
Each....75c

No. 104324 Gold filled, Royal Arcanum.
Each.....35c
No. 104326 Solid gold, same as above.
Each....75c

No. 104328 Blank Badge, can be engraved in design suitable for any kind of presentation; border is beautifully engraved by hand. Price, in solid silver, $3.00; in solid gold, $6.00.

No. 104330 Gold filled, Royal Legion.
Each.....35c
No. 104332 Solid gold, same as above.
Each....75c

No. 104334 Gold filled, G. A. R.
Each.....35c
No. 104336 Solid gold, same as above.
Each....75c

No. 104338 Gold filled, Sons of Veterans.
Each.....45c
No. 104340 Solid gold, same as above.
Each....75c

No. 104342 Gold filled, Patriotic Sons of America.
Each.....35c
No. 104344 Solid gold, same as above.
Each....75c

STERLING SILVER ::: NOVELTIES :::

The Demand having increased to such a wonderful extent that it necessitated our putting in a much larger line of these goods, we have with care selected such novelties as are most appropriate for a gift or personal use. In making a gift, we believe that it is always better to give a useful article, so in selecting these novelties we have endeavored to buy only such articles as have utility. All these goods are made of the finest sterling silver, and the prices quoted, it will be noted, are extremely low. It will be seen that the articles, that is a great many of them, can be used as a gift for either a lady or gentleman, as a birthday or holiday present. Bear in mind that our novelties are all 925-1000 fine. The engraving is hand engraved, and the chasing, hand chased. They are sufficiently heavy to be well able to stand continual usage. If you buy once we know that you will continue to be frequent patronizers of our firm. If goods are not exactly as described we always cheerfully refund money.

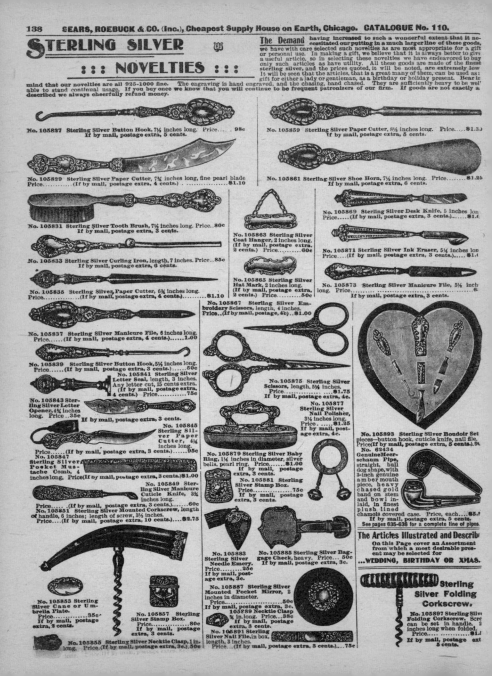

No. 105827 Sterling Silver Button Hook, 7½ inches long. Price...... 98c
If by mail, postage extra, 5 cents.

No. 105829 Sterling Silver Paper Cutter, 7¾ inches long, fine pearl blade
Price............(If by mail, postage extra, 4 cents.) $1.10

No. 105831 Sterling Silver Tooth Brush, 7½ inches long. Price..80c
If by mail, postage extra, 3 cents.

No. 105833 Sterling Silver Curling Iron, length, 7 inches. Price..85c
If by mail, postage extra, 6 cents.

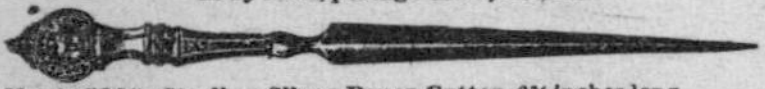

No. 105835 Sterling Silver Paper Cutter, 6¾ inches long.
Price...............(If by mail, postage extra, 4 cents.)..........$1.10

No. 105837 Sterling Silver Manicure File, 6 inches long.
Price......(If by mail, postage extra, 4 cents.)......1.00

No. 105839 Sterling Silver Button Hook, 5½ inches long.
Price......(If by mail, postage extra, 3 cents.)......50c

No. 105841 Sterling Silver Letter Seal, length, 3 inches. Any letter cut, 15 cents extra. (If by mail, postage extra, 4 cents.) Price............75c

No. 105843 Sterling Silver Letter Opener, 4¾ inches long. Price ..35c
If by mail, postage extra, 3 cents.

No. 105845 Sterling Silver Paper Cutter, 4¼ inches long.
Price......(If by mail, postage extra, 3 cents.)......95c

No. 105847 Sterling Silver Pocket Mustache Comb, 4 inches long. Price(If by mail, postage extra, 3 cents.)$1.00

No. 105849 Sterling Silver Manicure Cuticle Knife, 3¾ inches long.
Price...... (If by mail, postage extra, 3 cents.).......60c

No. 105851 Sterling Silver Mounted Corkscrew, length of handle, 6 inches; length of screw, 3½ inches.
Price....(If by mail, postage extra, 10 cents.)....$2.75

No. 105853 Sterling Silver Cane or Umbrella Plate.
Price.............35c
If by mail, postage extra, 2 cents.

No. 105857 Sterling Silver Stamp Box.
Price...............80c
If by mail, postage extra, 3 cents.

No. 105855 Sterling Silver Necktie Clasp, 1 in. long. Price.(If by mail, postage extra, 3c.).50c

No. 105859 Sterling Silver Paper Cutter, 8½ inches long. Price.....$1.3
If by mail, postage extra, 5 cents.

No. 105861 Sterling Silver Shoe Horn, 7½ inches long. Price........$1.25
If by mail, postage extra, 6 cents.

No. 105863 Sterling Silver Coat Hanger, 2 inches long. (If by mail, postage extra, 2 cents.) Price..........60c

No. 105865 Sterling Silver Hat Mark, 2 inches long. (If by mail, postage extra, 2 cents.) Price..........50c

No. 105869 Sterling Silver Desk Knife, 5 inches lon
Price.....(If by mail, postage extra, 3 cents.).......$1.(

No. 105871 Sterling Silver Ink Eraser, 5¼ inches lon
Price....(If by mail, postage extra, 3 cents.)..... $1.(

No. 105873 Sterling Silver Manicure File, 5¼ inch long. Price..6
If by mail, postage extra, 3 cents.

No. 105867 Sterling Silver Embroidery Scissors, length, 4 inches.
Price..(If by mail, postage, 4c)..$1.00

No. 105875 Sterling Silver Scissors, length, 5¼ inches.
Price............... ....$1.75
If by mail, postage extra, 4c.

No. 105877 Sterling Silver Nail Polisher, 3½ inches long, Price. $1.25
If by mail, postage extra, 4c.

No. 105879 Sterling Silver Baby Ring, 1¼ inches in diameter, silver bells, pearl ring. Price.......$1.00
If by mail, postage extra, 3 cents.

No. 105881 Sterling Silver Stamp Box.
Price................75c
If by mail, postage extra, 3 cents.

No. 105883 Sterling Silver Needle Emery.
Price.........25c
If by mail, postage extra, 3c.

No. 105885 Sterling Silver Baggage Check, heavy. Price... 50c
If by mail, postage extra, 3c.

No. 105887 Sterling Silver Mounted Pocket Mirror, 2 inches in diameter.
Price.........................50c
If by mail, postage extra, 3c.

105889 Necktie Clasp ¾ in. long. Price...38c
If by mail, postage extra, 3 cents.

No. 105891 Sterling Silver Nail File, in box, length, 3 inches.
Price...(If by mail, postage extra, 3 cents.)....75c

No. 105893 Sterling Silver Boudoir Set pieces—button hook, cuticle knife, nail file.
Price(If by mail, postage extra, 5 cents.).9(

No. 62434 Genuine Meerschaum Pipe, straight, bull dog shape, with 3-inch genuine amber mouth piece, heavy chased gold band on stem and bowl inlaid, in finest plush lined chamois covered case. Price, each....$5.
If by mail, postage extra, 5 cents.
See pages 635-636 for a complete line of pipes.

The Articles Illustrated and Describ

On this Page cover an Assortment from which a most desirable present may be selected for
...WEDDING, BIRTHDAY OR XMAS.

Sterling Silver Folding Corkscrew.

No. 105897 Sterling Silv Folding Corkscrew. Scre can be set in handle. 2 inches long when folded.
Price.... ....$1.
If by mail, postage ext 5 cents.

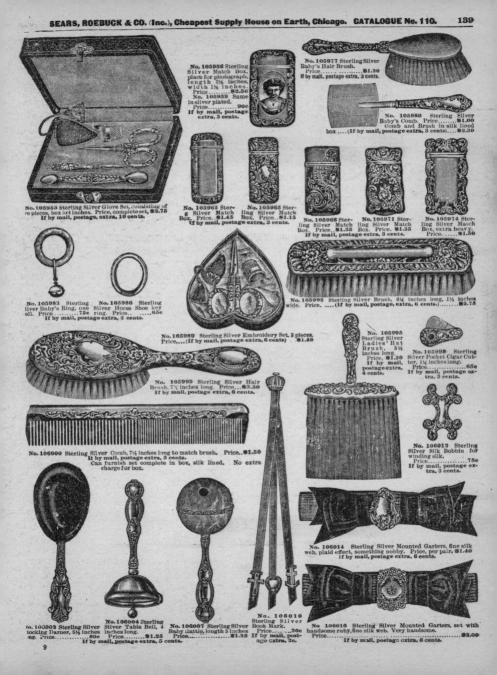

No. 105956 Sterling Silver Match Box, place for photograph, length 2½ inches, width 1¼ inches. Price.........**$2.50**
No. 105959 Same in silver plated. Price.........90c
If by mail, postage extra, 3 cents.

No. 105977 Sterling Silver Baby's Hair Brush. Price.........**$1.20**
If by mail, postage, 3 cents.

No. 105980 Sterling Silver Baby's Comb. Price.........**$1.00**
Comb and Brush in silk lined box ....(If by mail, postage extra, 3 cents.)....**$2.30**

No. 105953 Sterling Silver Glove Set, consisting of re pieces, box 5x4 inches. Price, complete set, **$2.75**
If by mail, postage, extra, 10 cents.

No. 105962 Sterling Silver Match Box. Price...**$1.45**
If by mail, postage extra, 3 cents.

No. 105965 Sterling Silver Match Box. Price...**$1.15**

No. 105968 Sterling Silver Match Box. Price..**$1.35**
If by mail, postage extra, 3 cents.

No. 105971 Sterling Silver Match Box. Price..**$1.35**

No. 105974 Sterling Silver Match Box, extra heavy. Price.......**$1.50**

No. 105983 Sterling Silver Baby's Ring, one Silver Horse Shoe key ell. Price.....75c

No. 105986 Sterling Silver Horse Shoe key ring. Price.......65c
If by mail, postage extra, 2 cents.

No. 105992 Sterling Silver Brush, 6¼ inches long, 1½ inches wide. Price. ....(If by mail, postage, extra, 6 cents.)........**$2.75**

No. 105989 Sterling Silver Embroidery Set, 3 pieces. Price....(If by mail, postage extra, 6 cents) .**$1.40**

No. 105995 Sterling Silver Ladies' Hat Brush. 5½ inches long. Price, **$1.50**
If by mail, postage extra, 4 cents.

No. 105998 Sterling Silver Pocket Cigar Cutter, 1¼ inches long. Price.............65c
If by mail, postage extra, 3 cents.

No. 105999 Sterling Silver Hair Brush, 7½ inches long. Price...**$3.50**
If by mail, postage extra, 6 cents.

No. 106012 Sterling Silver Silk Bobbin for winding silk. Price.............75c
If by mail, postage extra, 3 cents.

No. 106000 Sterling Silver Comb, 7¼ inches long to match brush. Price..**$1.50**
If by mail, postage extra, 3 cents.
Can furnish set complete in box, silk lined. No extra charge for box.

No. 106014 Sterling Silver Mounted Garters, fine silk web, plaid effect, something nobby. Price, per pair, **$1.40**
If by mail, postage extra, 6 cents.

No. 106002 Sterling Silver Stocking Darner, 5½ inches long. Price.............80c

No. 106004 Sterling Silver Table Bell, 4 inches long. Price.............**$1.25**
If by mail, postage extra, 5 cents.

No. 106007 Sterling Silver Baby Rattle, length 5 inches. Price.............**$1.25**

No. 106010 Sterling Silver Book Mark. Price.....30c
If by mail, postage extra, 3c.

No. 106016 Sterling Silver Mounted Garters, set with handsome ruby, fine silk web. Very handsome. Price.............**$2.00**
If by mail, postage extra, 6 cents.

9

PAUL E. WIRT FOUNTAIN PENS.

We are firm believers in the old saying that THE BEST IS THE CHEAPEST.

Before listing a line of fountain pens, we have thoroughly investigated the mechanism of all makes, and have spared no pains to place at the disposal of our customers, the finest fountain pens manufactured. There is nothing more annoying than a fountain pen of poor workmanship and inferior quality. The construction of these pens is of such a simple and practical kind that it is utterly impossible for one of them to become out of order, and cause more trouble to the writer and destroy more copy than the entire thing is worth, instead of being a convenience making it in reality an absolute inconvenience. Better, rather use the old quill of ancient time.

The Paul E. Wirt Fountain Pen stands at the head without a peer, although many imitations have been imposed upon the public. It is most simple and practical in construction as to operation and beauty of workmanship. They have gone into all parts of the world and their popularity rests upon the fact that their ink feed device is the most perfect and simplest ever discovered. Do no buy inferior imitations, but get the original, genuine article. They are elegant, simple, clean and durable; each and every pen fitted with 14-karat gold pen, pointed with a metal called iridium, a metal that is one of the hardest known and more costly than gold. Each and every one is warranted by the manufacturers, and we guarantee them to you personally to be the finest and most practical pen made.

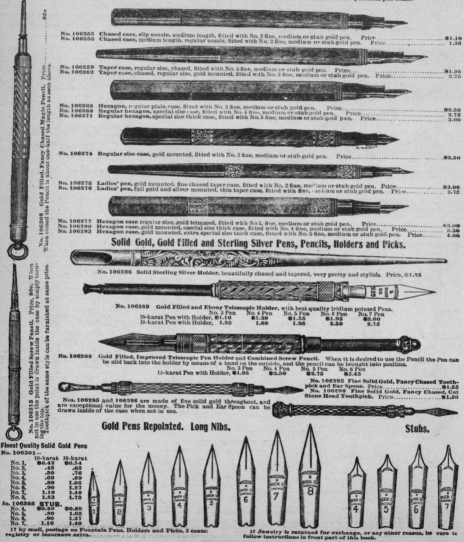

No. 106253   Chased case, slip nozzle, medium length, fitted with No. 2 fine, medium or stub gold pen.   Price............$1.10
No. 106256   Chased case, medium length, regular nozzle, fitted with No. 2 fine, medium or stub gold pen.   Price............1.35

No. 106259   Taper case, regular size, chased, fitted with No. 3 fine, medium or stub gold pen.   Price............$1.95
No. 106262   Taper case, chased, regular size, gold mounted, fitted with No. 3 fine, medium or stub gold pen.   Price............2.75

No. 106265   Hexagon, regular plain case, fitted with No. 3 fine, medium or stub gold pen.   Price............$2.50
No. 106268   Regular hexagon, special size case, fitted with No. 4 fine, medium or stub gold pen.   Price............2.75
No. 106271   Regular hexagon, special size thick case, fitted with No. 5 fine, medium or stub gold pen.   Price............3.00

No. 106274   Regular size case, gold mounted, fitted with No. 3 fine, medium or stub gold pen.   Price............$2.50

No. 106275   Ladies' pen, gold mounted, fine chased taper case, fitted with No. 2 fine, medium or stub gold pen.   Price............$3.00
No. 106276   Ladies' pen, full gold and silver mounted, thin taper case, fitted with fine, medium or stub gold pen.   Price............3.75

No. 106277   Hexagon case regular size, gold trimmed, fitted with No. 3 fine, medium or stub gold pen.   Price............$3.00
No. 106280   Hexagon case, gold mounted, special size thick case, fitted with No. 4 fine, medium or stub gold pen.   Price............3.50
No. 106283   Hexagon case, gold mounted, extra special size thick case, fitted with No. 5 fine, medium or stub gold pen.   Price............4.00

Solid Gold, Gold Filled and Sterling Silver Pens, Pencils, Holders and Picks.

No. 106286   Solid Sterling Silver Holder, beautifully chased and tapered, very pretty and stylish.   Price, $1.25

No. 106289   Gold Filled and Ebony Telescopic Holder, with best quality iridium pointed Pens.

	No. 3 Pen	No. 4 Pen	No. 5 Pen	No. 6 Pen	No. 7 Pen
10-karat Pen with Holder,	$1.10	$1.20	$1.55	$1.95	$2.00
16-karat Pen with Holder,	1.35	1.60	1.95	2.30	2.75

No. 106292   Gold Filled, Improved Telescopic Pen Holder and Combined Screw Pencil.   When it is desired to use the Pencil the Pen can be slid back into the holder by means of a band on the outside, and the pencil can be brought into position.

	No. 3 Pen	No. 4 Pen	No. 5 Pen	No. 6 Pen
16-karat Pen with Holder,	$1.95	$2.50	$3.75	$3.45

No. 106295   Fine Solid Gold, Fancy Chased Toothpick and Ear Spoon. Price............$1.55
No. 106298   Fine Solid Gold, Fancy Chased, Cut Stone Head Toothpick. Price............$1.50

Nos. 106295 and 106298 are made of fine solid gold throughout, and are exceptional value for the money. The Pick and Ear Spoon can be drawn inside of the case when not in use.

Gold Pens Repointed. Long Nibs.   Stubs.

Vertical margin text (left):
No. 106308   Gold Filled, Fancy Chased Magic Pencil.   Price............95c   When closed the Pencil is about one-half the length as seen above.

No. 106315   Gold Filled Screw Pencil.   Price, 80c. When not in use the point is drawn inside the case by simply turning the top. Toothpick of the same style can be furnished at same price.

Finest Quality Solid Gold Pens
No. 106301—

	10-karat	16-karat
No. 1,	$0.42	$0.54
No. 2,	.45	.63
No. 3,	.50	.76
No. 4,	.60	.89
No. 5,	.80	1.05
No. 6,	.90	1.27
No. 7,	1.10	1.40
No. 8,	1.53	1.73

No. 106305 STUB.
No. 4,	$0.60	$0.89
No. 5,	.80	1.05
No. 6,	.90	1.27
No. 7,	1.10	1.40

If by mail, postage on Fountain Pens, Holders and Picks, 3 cents; registry or insurance extra.

If Jewelry is returned for exchange, or any other reason, be sure to follow instructions in front part of this book.

ALASKA SILVERWARE—A NEW DISCOVERY.

THE CHEAPEST AND BEST FLAT WARE MADE **The Alaska silverware is not plated, but is the same solid metal through and through, and will hold** the same color as long as there is any portion of the goods left. Do not be deceived by any dealer who undertakes to sell you any of the numerous imitations of this ware, that are sold on the market for more money than we ask for the genuine. The genuine **Alaska Silverware can be had only of us.**

Before taking hold of this new discovery we left nothing undone to thoroughly investigate the properties of this metal, and to test the same in every conceivable manner, to satisfy ourselves that it was all that it was represented to be. After having made all sorts of experiments, and it stood all tests, we made a contract with the factory to handle the goods. It has now been about two years since we began to handle this line, and it has not only proved from experiment to be as represented, but with two years of actual service in the hands of many thousands of our customers, who send us the most flattering recommendations in praise of these goods, and with the rapidly increasing sales, we feel that we cannot recommend it too highly.

The metal is very dense and tough, is almost as white as genuine silver, takes a beautiful polish and requires no care, as does silver plated ware. You can scrape kettles or pots, or subject it to any kind of service without fear of damage.

We have this year added a beautiful engraved pattern, which is equal in appearance and artistic finish to any of the best silver plated or solid silver goods on the market. The engravings are as fine as can be made, the handles of an oval shape, and will be furnished at only a slight advance over the prices of the plain pattern. The immense quantities of these goods we handle, and the condition of our contract direct with the factory, puts us in a position to furnish this genuine Alaska Silverware at a slight advance over cost to manufacture.

Hereafter all these Goods, except the Knives, will be Stamped "Sears, Roebuck & Co.'s Alaska Silverware."

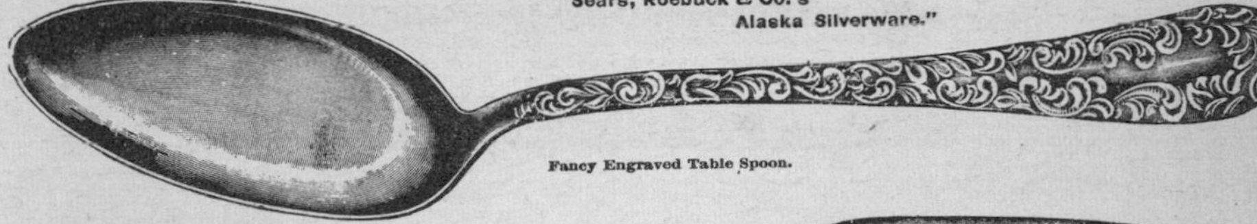

Fancy Engraved Table Spoon.

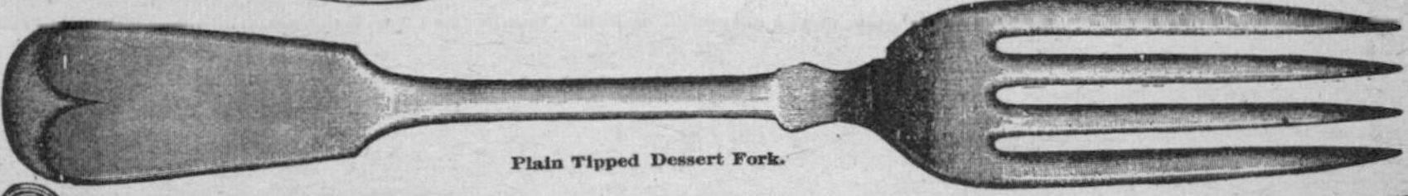

Plain Tipped Dessert Fork.

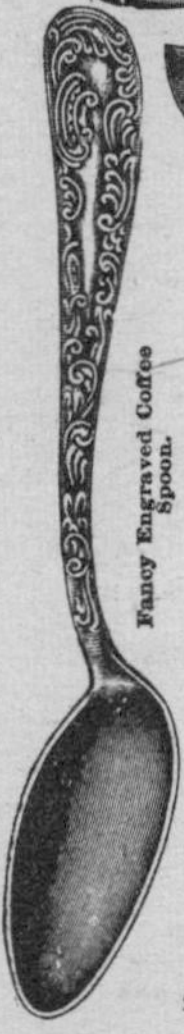

Fancy Engraved Coffee Spoon.

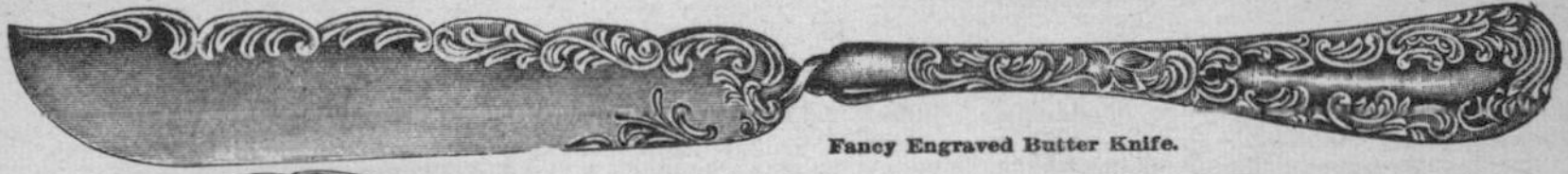

Fancy Engraved Butter Knife.

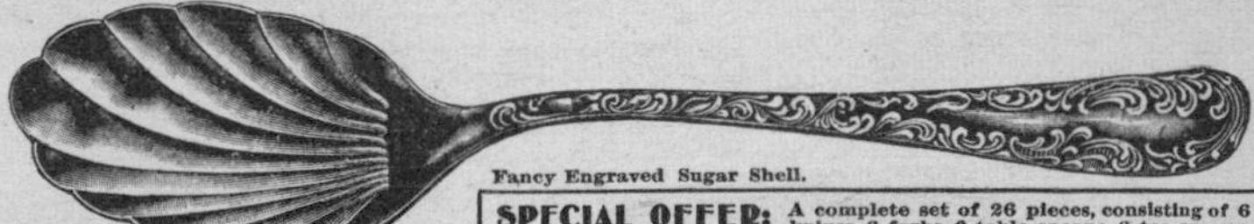

Fancy Engraved Sugar Shell.

SPECIAL OFFER: A complete set of 26 pieces, consisting of 6 knives, 6 forks, 6 table spoons, 6 tea spoons, 1 sugar shell and 1 butter knife. Plain tipped pattern. All in a beautiful lined plush case for **$4.55.** Fancy engraved pattern, **$4.70.**

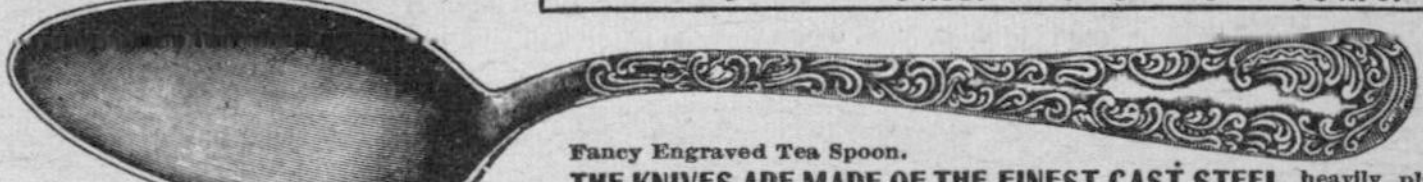

Fancy Engraved Tea Spoon.

THE KNIVES ARE MADE OF THE FINEST CAST STEEL heavily plated with Nickel, then SOLID COIN SILVER and are fully guaranteed. IT IS NOT PRACTICABLE TO MAKE THE KNIVES OF THE ALASKA WARE.

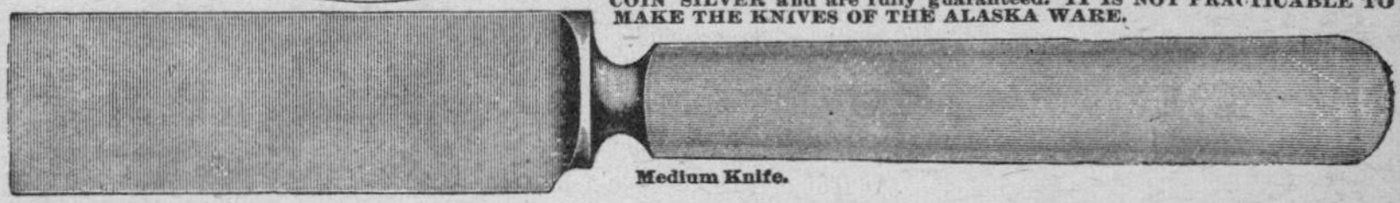

Medium Knife.

Relative Lengths: Coffee spoons, 4⅜ inches; tea spoons, 6¾ inches; dessert spoons, 7¼ inches; table spoons, 8¼ inches; dessert forks, 7 inches; medium forks, 7½ inches, dessert knives, 8 inches; medium knives, 9 inches; sugar shells, 5¾ inches; butter knives, 7 inches.

OUR SPECIAL PRICES.

Any of these goods can be sent by mail on receipt of price and additional amount named to pay postage.

Plain tipped pattern like fork above.

No. 106500	Coffee Spoons	set of ½ doz.,	$0.51
No. 106502	Tea Spoons	set of ½ doz.,	.51
No. 106504	Dessert Spoons	set of ½ doz.,	.85
No. 106506	Table Spoons	set of ½ doz.,	1.02
No. 106508	Medium Forks (regular size)	set of ½ doz.,	1.02
No. 106510	Dessert Forks	set of ½ doz.,	.85
No. 106512	Plain handle Dessert Knives	set of ½ doz.,	1.10
No. 106514	Plain handle medium knives	set of ½ doz.,	1.25
No. 106516	Sugar Shells	each,	.15
No. 106518	Butter Knives	each,	.15

Fancy engraved like all but the fork above.

No. 106520	Coffee Spoons	set of ½ doz.,	$0.56
No. 106522	Tea Spoons	set of ½ doz.,	.56
No. 106524	Dessert Spoons	set of ½ doz.,	.90
No. 106526	Table Spoons	set of ½ doz.,	1.07
No. 106528	Medium Forks (regular size)	set of ½ doz.,	1.07
No. 106530	Dessert Forks	set of ½ doz.,	.99
No. 106532	Sugar Shells	each,	.16
No. 106534	Butter Knives	each,	.16

Postage on the above goods, if to go by mail, will be extra per half dozen as follows: On coffee spoons, 5 cents; tea spoons, 6 cents; dessert spoons or forks, 12 cents; table spoons or medium forks, 15 cents; sugar shells or butter knives, 2 cents; and dessert or medium knives, 18 cents. It is cheaper to send them by express, if you have an express office near by.

The standard of quality and finish of the above goods are guaranteed by the manufacturer to us, and we guarantee them to our customers. You run no risk whatever in purchasing this ware, for if you do not find them to be exactly as represented, they can be returned to us and your money will be refunded. Be sure to state catalogue number and pattern wanted when you order.

We will send any of the above goods by express, C. O. D., subject to examination, providing a deposit of $1.00 as a guarantee of good faith is sent with order.

The best way is to send cash in full and save the charges on the return money order.

AN ASTONISHING SILVER GOODS OFFER

SOLID METAL GOODS AT LESS THAN ONE-THIRD
THE PRICE OF SOLID SILVER ✦ ✦ ✦ ✦ ✦ ✦ ✦

GUARANTEED EQUAL TO SOLID COIN SILVER in appearance, finish, wearing qualities, and in every way except in intrinsic value. **THIS COMPOSITION SILVER** is one solid metal through and through, guaranteed to retain its perfect silver color; wear forever; will never tarnish. SCOUR IT WITH A BRICK, and you can't harm it.

WE ENGRAVE ANY LETTER on every piece you buy FREE OF CHARGE. State the letter you wish engraved on the spoons, forks, butter knives or sugar shells, and we will have it done exactly as illustrated, and free of charge. **FOR 75 CENTS** we furnish a set of TEA SPOONS, every spoon engraved with any letter requested, a set equal to anything of any other make you can buy for $2.00 or more.

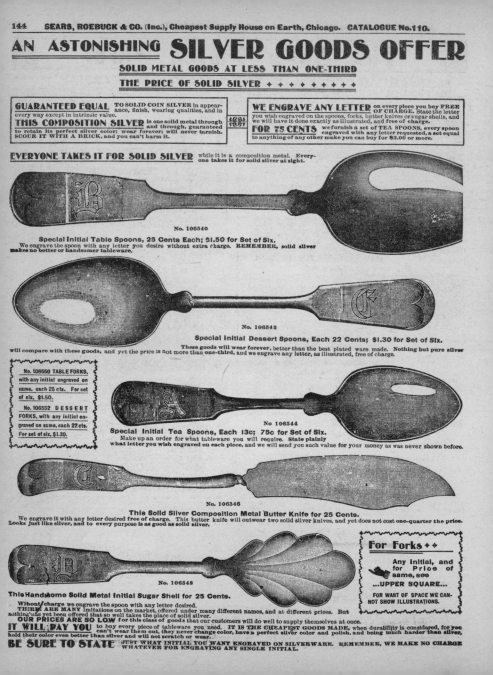

EVERYONE TAKES IT FOR SOLID SILVER while it is a composition metal. Everyone takes it for solid silver at sight.

No. 106540

Special Initial Table Spoons, 25 Cents Each; $1.50 for Set of Six.
We engrave the spoon with any letter you desire without extra charge. REMEMBER, solid silver makes no better or handsomer tableware.

No. 106542

Special Initial Dessert Spoons, Each 22 Cents; $1.30 for Set of Six.
These goods will wear forever, better than the best plated ware made. Nothing but pure silver will compare with these goods, and yet the price is not more than one-third, and we engrave any letter, as illustrated, free of charge.

No. 106550 TABLE FORKS, with any initial engraved on same, each 25 cts. For set of six, $1.50.

No. 106552 DESSERT FORKS, with any initial engraved on same, each 22 cts. For set of six, $1.30.

No 106544

Special Initial Tea Spoons, Each 13c; 75c for Set of Six.
Make up an order for what tableware you will require. State plainly what letter you wish engraved on each piece, and we will send you such value for your money as was never shown before.

No. 106546

This Solid Silver Composition Metal Butter Knife for 25 Cents.
We engrave it with any letter desired free of charge. This butter knife will outwear two solid silver knives, and yet does not cost one-quarter the price. Looks just like silver, and to every purpose is as good as solid silver.

No. 106548

This Handsome Solid Metal Initial Sugar Shell for 25 Cents.

For Forks ✦ ✦
Any Initial, and for Price of same, see ...UPPER SQUARE...
FOR WANT OF SPACE WE CANNOT SHOW ILLUSTRATIONS.

Without charge we engrave the spoon with any letter desired.
THERE ARE MANY imitations on the market, offered under many different names, and at different prices. But nothing has yet been offered that so well takes the place of solid silver.
OUR PRICES ARE SO LOW for this class of goods that our customers will do well to supply themselves at once.
IT WILL PAY YOU to buy every piece of tableware you need. IT IS THE CHEAPEST GOODS MADE, when durability is considered, for you can't wear them out, they never change color, have a perfect silver color and polish, and being much harder than silver, hold their color even better than silver and will not scratch or wear.
BE SURE TO STATE JUST WHAT INITIAL YOU WANT ENGRAVED ON SILVERWARE. REMEMBER, WE MAKE NO CHARGE WHATEVER FOR ENGRAVING ANY SINGLE INITIAL.

Fine Silver Plated Ware.

WE CONGRATULATE ourselves upon the immense increase of business we have had in our silver department, and we know that we have made this grand success solely by giving our many customers and friends the wonderful values we do.

The silverware that we list in our catalogue, both in hollow and flat ware, is the best that is obtainable from the manufacturers. Bear in mind when you buy from us you are buying at strictly wholesale prices; we save you at least 50 per cent in the price of any of the goods illustrated. The goods illustrated upon this page are fine silver plated upon white metal and are guaranteed to give you absolute satisfaction in every particular. We know that if you would favor us with your order for any of these goods that it would not be the only purchase that you would make, but that we would have your steady patronage in the future.

You run no risks, for we will refund all your money if you are not satisfied with your purchase. All the goods listed below, with the exception of the knives and knife handle forks, are made of the fine composition metal mentioned above, beautifully engraved and embossed designs, plated with genuine coin silver. The knives and knife handle forks are made of solid cast steel and plated likewise with pure coin silver.

No. 106562 Salts and Peppers, satin finish, in box.
Price, per set............30c
If by mail, postage extra, 10 cents.

No. 106564 Victoria pattern, very tasty.
Price, per set............30c
If by mail, postage extra, 10 cents.

Butter Knife and Sugar Shell
In Handsome Box Complete for 30 Cents.

Our 40-Cent Child's Set.

No. 106566 Richmond Child's Set, three pieces.
Price................40c
If by mail, postage extra, 12 cents.

Beautiful Child's Set for 20 Cents.

No. 106568 Child's Set, three pieces.
Price................20c
If by mail, postage extra, 12 cents.

Special Value for 95 Cents.

No. 106570 Child's Set, five pieces, very popular.
Price, complete........95c
If by mail, postage extra, 20 cents.

A Rare Bargain.
Complete Silver Plated Carving Set for $3.85.

No. 106572 Carving Set, three pieces, etched handles.............$3.85
No. 106574 Carving Set, three pieces, plain handles............. 3.40
If by mail, postage extra, 35 cents.

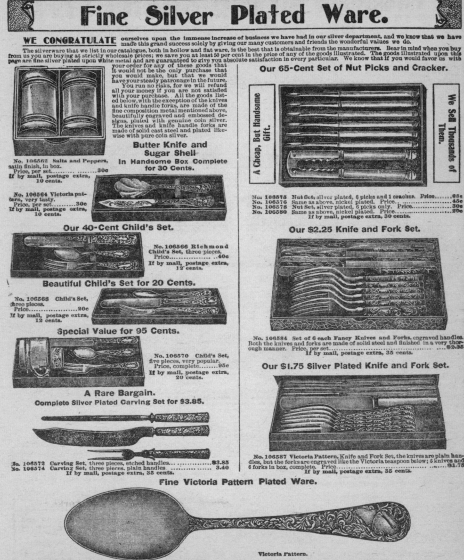

Our 65-Cent Set of Nut Picks and Cracker.

A Cheap, But Handsome Gift.

We Sell Thousands of Them.

No. 106575 Nut Set, silver plated, 6 picks and 1 cracker. Price.....65c
No. 106576 Same as above, nickel plated. Price.....................45c
No. 106578 Nut Set, silver plated, 6 picks only. Price.............30c
No. 106580 Same as above, nickel plated. Price...................20c
If by mail, postage extra, 30 cents.

Our $2.25 Knife and Fork Set.

No. 106584 Set of 6 each Fancy Knives and Forks, engraved handles. Both the knives and forks are made of solid steel and finished in a very thorough manner. Price, per set.....................$2.25
If by mail, postage extra, 35 cents.

Our $1.75 Silver Plated Knife and Fork Set.

No. 106587 Victoria Pattern, Knife and Fork Set, the knives are plain handles, but the forks are engraved like the Victoria teaspoon below; 6 knives and 6 forks in box, complete. Price.................$1.75
If by mail, postage extra, 35 cents.

Fine Victoria Pattern Plated Ware.

Victoria Pattern.

This ware is made of fine composition metal, heavily plated with pure coin silver, is beautifully engraved, well finished and guaranteed to be as represented. We quote this ware in lots of half dozen each, without boxes, and will not sell a smaller quantity than three pieces of any one kind.

No. 106590 Coffee Spoons, per set of six ....40c   No. 106594 Table Spoons, per set of six ....80c   No. 106598 Sugar Shell, each 12c
No. 106592 Tea Spoons, per set of six......40c   No. 106596 Medium Forks, per set of six ....80c   No. 106600 Butter Knife, each 16c

If to go by mail the postage on the Victoria unboxed goods will be extra as follows: Coffee Spoons, 5c; Tea Spoons, 6c; Table Spoons, 15c; Medium Forks, 8c; Sugar Shells, 2c; Butter Knife, 2c.

The illustrations of boxed goods above are all reduced, but the goods are full regular size.

Buy Jewelry and silverware of a reliable concern. We guarantee everything we sell, and what's more we always make our guarantee good. Fine silverware will be sent C. O. D., when desired, on receipt of $1.00 with order. Balance payable after goods have been examined.

C. ROGERS & BROS.' FINE SILVER PLATED WARE IN SILK LINED BOXES.

The reputation of these manufacturers, in fact, all the different Rogers, is so firmly established in the minds of the people as manufacturers whose reputation for honesty in the making of the best goods is beyond question. These goods are of the finest quality, made of solid white metal and very heavily plated with pure coin silver. WE KNOW OF NO GOODS THAT ARE SUPERIOR

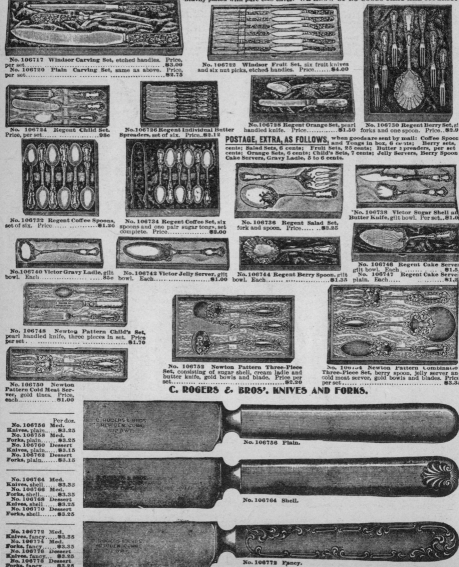

No. 106717 Windsor Carving Set, etched handles. Price, per set................................$3.00
No. 106720 Plain Carving Set, same as above. Price, per set................................$2.75

No. 106722 Windsor Fruit Set, six fruit knives and six nut picks, etched handles. Price......$4.00

No.106728 Regent Orange Set, pearl handled knife. Price............$1.50

No. 106730 Regent Berry Set, six forks and one spoon. Price..$2.90

No. 106724 Regent Child Set. Price, per set......98c

No.106726 Regent Individual Butter Spreaders, set of six. Price..$2.12

POSTAGE, EXTRA, AS FOLLOWS, when goods are sent by mail: Coffee Spoons and Tongs in box, 6 cents; Berry sets, cents; Salad Sets, 6 cents; Fruit Sets, 25 cents; Butter spreaders, per set cents; Orange Sets, 6 cents; Child's Sets, 7 cents; Jelly Servers, Berry Spoons Cake Servers, Gravy Ladle, 5 to 6 cents.

No. 106732 Regent Coffee Spoons, set of six. Price......$1.20

No.106734 Regent Coffee Set, six spoons and one pair sugar tongs, set complete. Price................$2.00

No. 106736 Regent Salad Set, fork and spoon. Price......$2.25

No. 106738 Victor Sugar Shell and Butter Knife, gilt bowl. Per set...$1.00

No.106740 Victor Gravy Ladle, gilt bowl. Each......................85c

No.106742 Victor Jelly Server, gilt bowl. Each................$1.00

No.106744 Regent Berry Spoon, gilt bowl. Each.................$1.35

No. 106746 Regent Cake Server, gilt bowl. Each..........$1.50
No. 106747 Regent Cake Server, plain. Each......$1.25

No. 106748 Newton Pattern Child's Set, pearl handled knife, three pieces in set. Price per set $1.70

No. 106752 Newton Pattern Three-Piece Set, consisting of sugar shell, cream ladle and butter knife, gold bowls and blade. Price per set................$2.20

No. 106754 Newton Pattern Combination Three-Piece Set, berry spoon, jelly server and cold meat server, gold bowls and blades. Price per set............$3.30

No. 106750 Newton Pattern Cold Meat Server, gold tines. Price, each..............$1.00

C. ROGERS & BROS'. KNIVES AND FORKS.

No. 106756 Plain.

No. 106764 Shell.

No. 106772 Fancy.

Per doz.
No. 106756 Med. Knives, plain......$3.25
No. 106758 Med. Forks, plain......$3.25
No. 106760 Dessert Knives, plain......$3.15
No. 106762 Dessert Forks, plain.......$3.15

No. 106764 Med. Knives, shell......$3.35
No. 106766 Med. Forks, shell......$3.35
No. 106768 Dessert Knives, shell......$3.25
No. 106770 Dessert Forks, shell....$3.25

No. 106772 Med. Knives, fancy......$3.35
No. 106774 Med. Forks, fancy......$3.35
No. 106776 Dessert Knives, fancy......$3.25
No. 106778 Dessert Forks, fancy......$3.25

WE HANDLE A COMPLETE LINE OF
ROGERS BROTHERS' 1847 GOODS

But our space will not permit us to list more than a portion of the same. We, however, have represented one of each style of nearly all the styles in which these goods are made, which includes the very

====LATEST AND BEST PATTERNS====

We list the goods in two grades, namely, what is known as the extra plate and the triple plate; the latter of which is the better of the two. Bear in mind that the goods which we quote and describe are exactly as represented. We do not substitute other make of goods, as many unscrupulous firms do.

Tipped

Vesta

Columbia

Berkshire

Shell

PRICES PER DOZEN.

			Tipped	Shell	Vesta	Columbia	Berkshire	Lotus
No. 106792 Tea Spoons.	Extra Plate		$2.25	$2.50	$2.56	$2.56	$2.50	$2.56
	Triple Plate		3.00	3.25	3.30	3.30	3.25	3.25
No. 106794 Dessert Spoons.	Extra Plate		3.85	4.25	4.52	4.52	4.45	4.48
	Triple Plate		5.30	5.75	6.00	6.00	5.70	5.79
No. 106796 Dessert Forks.	Extra Plate		4.00	4.45	4.56	4.56	4.46	4.48
	Triple Plate		5.25	5.65	5.80	5.80	5.75	5.72
No. 106798 Table Spoons.	Extra Plate		4.50	4.90	5.15	5.15	5.00	5.06
	Triple Plate		6.00	6.50	6.62	6.62	6.50	6.54
No. 106800 Medium Forks.	Extra Plate		4.50	5.00	5.18	5.18	5.00	5.06
	Triple Plate		6.00	6.50	6.60	6.60	6.50	6.56
No. 106802 Coffee Spoons.	Extra Plate		not made	2.50	2.60	2.60	2.58	2.58
No. 106804 Sugar Shells.	Extra Plate only. Prices each		.38	.40	.44	.44	.47	.47
No. 106806 Butter Knife.	Extra Plate only. Prices each		.42	.46	.47	.47	.55	.59

No. 106808 Cortland Jelly Knife, in lined box. Price, each, 90c

No. 106810 Savoy Long Pickle Fork, in lined box. Price, each, 70c

BEST QUALITY QUADRUPLE PLATED SILVERWARE.

IS PLATED WITH THE PUREST SILVER ON THE FINEST SOLID WHITE METAL BRITANNIA WARE. WE GUARANTEE EACH PIECE TO GIVE ENTIRE SATISFACTION OR MONEY REFUNDED.

No. 106953 Butter Dish, satin finish, hand engraved, fancy handle. Price, **$1.15**

No. 106956 Butter Dish, satin finish, hand engraved. Price............**$2.50**

No. 106959 Butter Dish, satin finish, hand engraved. Price.................**$1.30**

No. 106962 Berry Set, three pieces, consisting of sugar bowl, berry bowl and cream pitcher, bright polished, raised ornamentation. Height of bowl, 3½ inches; capacity, 5¼ pints. Set boxed weighs ready for shipment about 15 lbs. Price, complete...**$8.25**

No. 106965 Syrup Pitcher, satin finish, hand engraved, plate to match. Height, 4½ inches. Price.........**$1.30**

No. 106968 Syrup Pitcher, satin finish, hand engraved. Price. **$1.50**

No. 106971 Syrup Pitcher, satin finish, fancy handle and spout, hand engraved. Height, 7 inches. Price.........**$1.75**

No. 106974 Syrup Pitcher, satin finish, hand engraved; rococo border; dragon claw feet; absolutely worth double. Each **$2.75**

No. 106977 Butter Dish, hand engraved, satin finish and ornamented border. Height, 7 inches. Each. **$3.30**

No. 106980 Butter Dish, hand engraved, satin finish, raised ornaments, fancy border. Height, 5¼ inches. Each **$3.95**

No. 106983 Butter Dish, satin finish, hand engraved. Each............**$1.50**

No. 109686 Butter Dish, satin finish, hand engraved. Each.................**$2.00**

No. 106989 Butter Dish, satin finish, hand engraved. Each.................**$2.75**

No. 106992 Berry Dish, glass bowl, raised ornamentation. Height, 8 inches. Each, **$2.00**

No. 106995 Berry or Fruit Dish, raised ornamented crystal glass, imitation of cut crystal; very beautiful. Each....**$1.25**

No. 106998 Sugar Bowl and Spoon Rack, satin finish, engraved; very handsome; holds 12 spoons. Each, **$3.25**

No. 107001 Berry or Fruit Dish, bright base, fancy colored bowl, raised ornamented border, fancy handles, very new. Each...**$1.75**

No. 107004 Sugar Bowl and Spoon Rack, holds 12 spoons, satin finish, engraved. Each.................**$1.85**

No. 107007 Berry or Fruit Bowl, fancy glass, with new style base. Price................**$1.60**

No. 107010 Berry or Fruit Dish, fancy handle, raised ornamentation, beautifully scalloped china dish, white on the outside and pink on the inside and beautifully ornamented in raised gold work. Each......................**$5.80**
We cannot give you a description that will fully describe the beauties of this dish nor does the illustration give an idea of it.
Berry dishes weigh about 3½ lbs. each, boxed about 9 lbs.

No. 107013 Fruit Dish, fancy colored glass bowl, fancy ornamented, bright burnished base, very tasty. Height, 9¼ inches. Each.................**$1.60**

No. 107016 Fruit Dish, pink opal bowl, raised ornamentations, bright base, fancy feet, ornamented border. Height, 10 inches. Each........**$3.50**

No. 107019 Fruit Stand, imitation cut crystal glass, bright burnished base. Height, 12½ inches, diameter, 8¼ inches. Each, **$3.25**

NOTE.—The Butter Dishes listed are from 5¼ to 7 inches in width. Silverware takes first class express and freight rate; see front of book for further instructions. You run no risk in sending cash in full with your orders. We guarantee safe delivery of every piece. Butter dishes weigh, boxed ready for shipment, about 2 lbs. Syrups and spoon holders, boxed, about 2½ lbs.

...FINEST QUALITY QUADRUPLE SILVER PLATED WARE...

No. 107043 Pickle Castor and Fork combined, imitation cut crystal glass, height, 10½ inches, fancy feet, fancy handle. Price..................95c

No. 107046 Pickle Caster and tongs combined, burnished base and top, fancy handle. Price..........$2.25

No. 107049 Pickle Caster and tongs combined, ruby decorated glass bowl, fancy handle and fancy feet. Price. $2.75

No. 107052 Breakfast Caster, three bottles, very handsome, genuine cut glass, fancy handle, decorated, raised ornamentation. Price. $3.50

No. 107055 Breakfast Caster, engraved bottles, fancy raised ornamented base, fancy handle and feet, height, 10 inches. Price..............$2.30

No. 107058 Cracker Jar, fancy engraved, satin finished, height, 12 inches. Price..............$1.75

No. 107061 Salt and Pepper, pink and blue decorated bottles, height, 6¾ inches. Price...........$1.45

No. 107064 Salt and Pepper, bright finished stand, crystal bottles. Price..................$1.45

No. 107067 Pickle Caster and Fork combined, ruby glass, height, 9¾ inches, fancy feet and ornamentation. Price..................$1.48

No. 107070 Pickle Caster and Fork combined, fancy handle, ornamented base, height, 11¼ inches. Price......$1.45

No. 107072 Toothpick Holder, gold lined, beaded edge, satin finish........75c

No. 107076 Individual Caster, three bottles, plain base, fancy handle, very serviceable. Price..................$2.75

No. 107079 Caster, five bottles, plain bright burnished, hand engraved, height, 14 inches. Price...........$0.98

No. 107082 Caster, five bottles, bright burnished base, engraved fancy handle and bottles. Price..........$1.35

No. 107085 Caster, five bottles, bright polished base, fancy handle, engraved bottles. Price......$1.70

No. 107088 Very handsome Caster, five bottles, engraved fancy handle, engraved base and center. Price..........$2.00

No. 107091 Caster, five bottles, engraved, very heavy and massive. Price..............$2.50

No. 107094 Caster, five bottles, very fancy handle, hand engraved center, bright and satin finished throughout. Price..............$3.25

No. 107097 Spoon Tray, very fancy, satin finished, ornamented border, length, 8½ in. Price..................$1.75

No. 107100 Fern Dish, very fancy and fashionable, latest craze. Price..................$3.25

No 107103 Mustard Pot, glass lined, raised ornamentation. Price..................$1.10

No. 107106 Toothpick Holder, very fancy embossed gold lined, fancy handle. Price..............$1.50

No. 107109 Salt Set in box with two bowls and spoons, gold lined satin finish, fancy feet. Cut shows one. Price..............$3.00

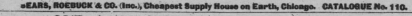

OUR $4.95 INITIAL SILVERWARE SET.

FOR $4.95 we offer a 26-piece set of silverware, stamped with any initial, complete with case, the equal of anything you can buy anywhere at three times the price.

OUR $1.00 OFFER. Send us $1.00 as a guarantee of good faith, state what initial you want on the 26 pieces, we will have the initials put on and send you the complete set of 26 pieces including case by express C. O. D., subject to examination. You

can examine it at your express office and if found perfectly satisfactory, exactly as represented and the equal of anything you can buy elsewhere at three times the price, one of the handsomest sets you have ever seen, pay the express agent the balance $3.95 and express charges. You will find the express charges will amount to next to nothing as compared with what you will save in price. The express charges will average for 500 miles, 35 cents; 1,000 miles, 50 cents; greater or lesser distances in proportion.

THIS SET CONSISTS OF 6 full size table spoons as illustrated, each spoon engraved with any initial desired, as shown in illustration; 6 tea spoons as illustrated, each spoon engraved with any initial desired, as shown on the handle with any initial desired. In illustration; 6 full size forks as illustrated, each fork engraved with any initial, desired, as illustrated; 1 sugar shell, 1 butter knife and 6 heavy silver plated knives.

No. 107300

No. 107300

IN ADDITION TO THE 26 PIECES of silverware as illustrated, we furnish the above handsome blue lined case. Case is 12 inches long, 10 inches wide and 3 inches deep, nicely finished with a fancy metal clasp and so divided as to just hold the 26 pieces in position, as shown in illustration, so that when the tableware is not in use it can be kept in perfect condition in the case, as illustrated.

THIS SOLID SILVER METAL is the nearest approach in composition metal for tableware to the pure coin silver that has ever been attained. This composition silver is one solid metal through and through, guaranteed to retain its perfect silver color and to wear forever. **IT WILL NEVER TARNISH.** It is stronger than silver; more springy; you can scour it with a brick; you cannot harm it. **THIS SILVER COMPOSITION METAL** is made by a process known only to the manufacturer of these sets. It is in appearance, finish and every way (except intrinsic value) equal to coin silver. In appearance it cannot be told from solid coin silver, it must be examined by an expert to detect the difference. **FOR A CHRISTMAS PRESENT,** birthday present, wedding present, for a gift to a friend or a gift for any purpose, nothing is more suitable, nothing at the price will be more appreciated, nothing could be more appropriate than this, our 26-piece set with initial engraved on every piece, except the six knives, all for $4.95.

AT $4.95 WE FURNISH THIS 26-PIECE SET of initial silverware complete with case as the greatest value ever offered in this class of goods; in fact, our $4.95 price is based on the actual cost to us in immense quantities for cash, with but our one small percentage of profit added. We know if you order this case of silverware from us you will be so well pleased with it that you will show it to your friends, recommend our house and other orders will follow from your neighbors. **DO NOT COMPARE THIS,** our composition silver initial ware, with any of the cheap plated ware that is offered in cases. We could furnish a 26-piece set of cheap plated ware with a cheap case similar to the cases that are being furnished by some houses at $1.50 to $2.00, but we believe our customers want a higher grade of good, and we have received so many letters of recommend for this class of goods the past two seasons that we have decided to increase our contracts and offer these goods in sets of 26 pieces at even a lower price than we have ever before been able to sell the same class of goods without the case.

OUR FOUR-PIECE TEA SETS LEAD THE WORLD.

No. 107310 For $10.00 we will sell you this Quadruple Plated Silver Tea Set. Quadruple plate is one plate heavier than triple plate, and we guarantee it to wear and give entire satisfaction. You cannot buy a better quality set even though you paid $20.00 or $25.00. This set is hand engraved, satin finished, has fancy feet and is made extra heavy throughout. The set consists of a coffee or tea pot, capacity, about two quarts; sugar bowl, cream pitcher and spoon holder. These pieces made in proportion to the coffee pot. Price, four-piece set.................$10.00
Syrup pitcher to match, extra............$2.75   Butter dish, extra...........$3.00   Tray, extra.........$2.75

No. 107313 Our $3.75 Four-piece Tea Set, is made of the finest Britannia metal, triple plated, and with care will wear a lifetime; it is hand engraved, hand chased, satin finished or bright burnished throughout. The set consists of four pieces: Tea pot, sugar bowl, cream pitcher and spoon holder. At $3.75 it cannot be duplicated elsewhere. It is made expressly for us in large quantities on a spot cash basis, therefore we are able to quote this remarkably low price.......................$3.75
Can supply butter dish for, extra.................$2.75   Syrup pitcher, extra..................$2.25

No. 107316 Our Wonderful $4.75 Tea Set. We have but a few left, while they last only $4.75 for the four pieces, consisting of tea pot, sugar bowl, cream pitcher and spoon holder; each piece is satin finished and beautifully hand engraved; spouts, handles and other parts fancy embossed. For $4.75 you cannot do better in the way of purchasing a handsome gift. The set is well worth $8.00; we cannot sell you either the syrup pitcher or butter dish, they are all sold, we can procure no more of them. Remember, for the entire set, four pieces, tea pot, sugar bowl, spoon holder and cream pitcher, price..$4.75

CANDELABRA AND ECCLESIASTICAL GOODS.

No. 107320 Crucifix and Holy Water Fount raised ornamentations, satin and bright finish, 15 inches high.
Price, each....$1.60

No. 107323 Candelabrum to hold one candle, nine inches high, raised ornamented feet, satin and bright polish.
Price, each...$1.50

No. 107326 Viaticum Cabinet or Home Altar. The cabinet is a gem of the woodmaker's art. Is constructed of highly polished hardwood, is handsomely trimmed, and has a silver cross on each door. It can only be opened by pressing the spring catch at the top of the doors. The interior of the cabinet is upholstered with a rich shade of purple. In the cabinet, set up and ready for all times and instant use, are the following articles: One silver combination candelabrum, crucifix and holy water fount, gold lined; the crucifix is detachable; one silver cup, gold lined; silver spoon; silver handle holy water sprinkler; glass holy water bottle with cross and crown; two rubrical candles and two linen communion cloths; in fact, absolutely complete. Price, for complete set....$3.50

No. 107328 Combination Crucifix Candelabrum, for 2 candles, and holy water fount, 13 inches high, raised ornaments, bright and satin finish. Each......$1.75

No. 107331 Crucifix, 10 inches high, bright polished base, raised ornaments and embossed cross. Each.........$1.25

CHURCH SERVICE OR COMMUNION SET.

No. 107334 Candelabrum for 3 candles, fancy, bright and satin finished, height 11 inches. Each.........$2.35

No. 107337 Candlestick, height, 7½ inches, satin bright finish. Each............$1.15

No. 107340 Candelabrum for 2 candles, ornamented, satin and bright finish, height, 9½ inches. Each............$1.85

No.107342 Flagon, 3 pints, burnished. Price.................................$5.40
No. 107344 Baptismal Bowl, burnished. Price $2.35.   Same, gold lined, price...........$2.85
No.107346 Goblets, burnished. Price.... 1.75   Same, gold lined.......................... 2.10
The above set is guaranteed to be the best quality made.
No. 107348 Plates to match set, each...$2.00

BEST QUALITY QUADRUPLE PLATED SILVERWARE.

Is plated with pure silver on fine solid white metal, and warranted.

THESE GOODS WERE SELECTED AS BEING APPROPRIATE FOR WEDDING, BIRTHDAY OR CHRISTMAS PRESENTS.

No. 107353 Shaving Mug and brush to match, richly engraved, satin finished, mug gold lined. Each, complete.. **$4.00**
Mug without brush, $1.50 less.
Shipping weight, 1½ to 2 lbs.

No. 107356 Shaving Mug; something neat, new and novel, satin finished, beaded gold border, fancy handle, top lifts out and is used for the soap, the bottom for hot water. Each...... **$1.75**
Shipping weight, 1½ to 2 lbs.

No. 107359 Jewel Box, satin finished, hand engraved. Height, 2½ inches; length, 4½ inches. Each 75c
Shipping weight, 1½ to 2 lbs.

No. 107362 Fancy Box, raised ornamentations, satin finish. Each **$1.15**
Shipping weight, 1½ to 2 lbs.

No. 107365 Soap Box, 4 inches long, satin finished, hand engraved. Each..**$1.85**
Shipping-weight, 1½ to 2 lbs.

No. 107368 Cigar Box, ornamented base and lid, satin finished throughout. Very appropriate gift for gentlemen. Each. (Shipping weight, 1½ to 2 lbs.). **$6.25**

No. 107371 Jewel Box, hand engraved, satin lined, satin finished, burnished throughout. Height, 2½ inches; length, 7 inches. Each. **$3.75**
Boxed ready for shipment, about 3 lbs.

No. 107374 Chafing Dish, ebony trimmings, bright nickel finish, capacity, 3 pints. Complete. **$4.50**
Shipping weight, about 10 lbs.

107377 Stamp Box, raised ornamented border and top, satin finished. Ea.. **$1.00**
If by mail, Postage extra, 4 cents.

No. 107380 Smoking Set, satin finish, hand engraved, gold lined. Height, 3¾ inches; 8½-inch tray. Price, complete, 95c
Shipping weight, about 2 lbs.

No. 107383 Curling Set, burnished throughout. Length, 5¾ inches. Very serviceable. Each **$2.90**
Boxed ready for shipment, about 3 lbs.

No. 107386 Flask; capacity, ¾-pint, satin finish, with screw top.
Each................**$1.90**
Shipping weight, about 2 lbs.

No. 107389 Flask; finely embossed, bright finish, hard metal collapsible cup. Height, 6 inches. Each **$4.25**
Shipping weight, about 2 lbs.

No.107392 Ice Pitcher, hand engraved and chased, inside and satin finished. Each.**$5.50**
Shipping weight, about 10 lbs.

No.107395 Salt and Pepper Set, richly embossed, satin finished and bright polished, fine silk lined box. Height of shakers, 3 inches.
Price, per set in box, **$2.00**
Shipping weight, about 1 lb.

No. 107398 Pepper, Salt Cellar and Spoon in box raised ornamentation, satin finished.
Price, per set, in box, **$2.00**
Shipping weight, about 1 lb.

No. 107401 Ink Stand; beautifully embossed base, flint crystal bottle; height, 2½ inches; width, 5¼ inches. Each.................95c
Shipping weight, about 2 lbs.

No.107404 Ink Stand; fancy top and base, flint crystal bottle; height, 2½ inches; width, 3 inches. Each.................50c
Shipping weight, about 2 lbs.

No 107407 Ink Set; embossed base and top, cut glass bottle; height, 4 inches. Each.....**$2.00**
Boxed ready for shipment, about 3 lbs.

No. 107410 Writing Set; cut glass bottles, very fancy tops; length, 6½ inches; satin finished. Each........**$4.50**
Boxed ready for shipment, about 3 lbs.

No.107413 Ink Stand; cut glass, heavy silver top; height, 3¾ inches. Each........**$1.75**
Shipping weight, about 2 lbs.

No.107416 Cigar Jar; fancy gold filled top, ornamented in enamel; jar of white crystal; height, 7 in.; diameter, 3¾ in. Each **$2.10**

No. 107419 Tobacco Jar; satin finish; imported Bohemian glass, fitted with patent moistener; height, 6½ inches. Each **$2.50**

No.107422 Puff Jar; fancy gold filled top, ornamented with enamel; height, 3¾ in.; diameter 5 inches. Each......75c

No.107425, Puff Jar; gold filled top,ornamented in enamel; height, 4½ in.; diameter, 3½ in. Each.........**$1.25**

No. 107428 Tobacco Jar; latest idea, gold filled; height,7½ in.; diam., 6 in. Each....**$2.50**

No. 107431 Perfume Bottle; fancy gold filled, hard enameled in colors, bottle of pressed flint crystal; height, 4½ in. Each **$1.75**
Shipping weight, about 2 lbs.

BOXED READY FOR SHIPMENT, ABOUT 3 POUNDS.

• OUR CLOCK DEPARTMENT •

IN CLOCKS WE REPRESENT ALL OF THE OLDEST AND MOST RELIABLE MAKERS who have built up a reputation for their goods by making only such clocks as they could guarantee. We list clocks made by the following concerns, namely: **Waterbury Clock Company**, Waterbury, Conn.; **New Haven Clock Company**, New Haven, Conn.; **Ansonia Clock Company**, Ansonia, Conn., and the **Seth Thomas Clock Company**, Thomaston, Conn. Bear in mind that the Waterbury Clock Company has no connection whatever with the Waterbury Watch Company, it is a very much older concern.

EVERY CLOCK THAT WE SELL IS GUARANTEED by the manufacturers and we warrant them to our customers. Any clock bought from us that is not in every way satisfactory can be returned and it **WILL BE EXCHANGED OR THE MONEY REFUNDED.**

WE SELL OUR CLOCKS AT EXTREMELY LOW PRICES. It must be understood that you are buying wholesale, thereby avoiding the retailer's profit. Do no think that the shipping charges will add are our prices to any where near the price you would have to pay your retail dealer, because he likewise must pay express charges and must add same to the cost of the clock when he sells it to you. We wish you to investigate the matter yourself and be convinced that we can save you from 30 to 50 per cent on clocks. It is not necessary for you to pay the shipping charges in advance. The best way is to pay them when you get the goods.

CLOCKS WILL BE SENT C. O. D. to any address when desired providing a deposit of $2.00 is sent with the order. The balance can be paid at the express office after examination, and if the goods are not satisfactory they can be refused and the money advanced will be refunded. You run no risk in sending cash in full, for if the goods are not satisfactory they can be returned at our expense and your money will be refunded.

No. 107500 Imported Nickel Alarm Clock, 4 inch dial, similar to No. 107502, a very good time keeper.
Each 65c
Shipping wt., 2 lbs.

No. 107502 Beacon Nickel Alarm Clock; height, 6½ inches; width, 4½ inches; 4-inch dial; made by the celebrated New Haven Clock Company; lever movement; best grade nickel clock made; warranted.
Each 78c
Shipping wt., 2 lbs.

No. 107502

No.107504 Beacon Luminous Nickel Alarm Clock, with luminous dial, height 6½ inches; width 4½ inches; 4-inch dial, is manufactured the New Haven Clock Company of ... Haven, Conn. ...t grade lever movement.
Each 90c
Shipping wt., 2 lbs.

NOTE—The dial on above clock is luminous, and will show distinctly the time in the dark. The darker it is the brighter it glows.

No. 107504

No. 107509 "MustGet Up," Nickel Alarm Clock; height, 5½ inches; dial, 4½ inches; made by the Waterbury Clock Company. This clock has very large bell on the back of the clock; the alarm runs five minutes with one winding; can be made to run a short, medium, long, or extra long time, and can be stopped at pleasure. The movement is best grade lever escapement and warranted.
Each $1.40
Shipping wt., 2 lbs.

107509

No. 107512 The Fly Alarm Calendar. Height, about 6½ inches; dial 4 inches; ne-day clock with ndar and alarm, nufactured by the Haven Clock mpany. Movent, very fine grade lever; a clock that we know will give entire satisfaction in every respect; has fine large nickel alarm bell on top, entire clock beautifully burnished, the alendar very finely djusted, and thoroughly inspected before leaving our establishment, has extra long alarm ring or can be regulated by winding apparatus for short ring.
Shipping wt., 2 lbs. Each......92c

No. 107512

No.107514 Sears, Roebuck Special. Nickel Alarm Clock. Height, 6¼ inches, dial, 4 inches; made expressly for us by one of the largest clock companies in the United States. It goes through a thorough inspection before leaving the factory and again before leaving our establishment is a clock we can conscientiously recommend to you as being everything that an alarm clock should be.
Each 90c
Shipping weight, 2 pounds.

No. 107514

No. 107518

Celebrated Parker Alarm Clock.

No. 107516 It has the shut off attachment, you can stop the alarm at will. The movement can be taken out without taking the clock apart, one of the very latest improvements.

The alarm runs nearly five minutes with one winding. It is one of the most perfect alarm clocks on the market; it is manufactured by the celebrated **Parker Clock Co.**, of Meriden, Conn. The name of Parker on any clock is a guarantee of perfection. Height of clock 4½ inches; depth of clock 3½ inches. Price..............$1.20
Shipping weight, boxed, about 2 pounds.

Beautiful Oxidized Alarm Clock for $2.75.

No. 107518 The New Long Alarm Clock rings from 20 to 30 minutes, but can be switched off any minute desired. This clock will not tip over; no battery necessary; absolutely no trouble. The case is finished in superfine oxidized copper, hand engraved and hand chased, in fact, making an ornament that would grace any parlor mantelpiece. Height, 10 inches; dial, 5 inches; movement manufactured by the celebrated Seth Thomas Clock Company, and is

GUARANTEED TO GIVE : : ABSOLUTE SATISFACTION IN EVERY RESPECT : : : :

Runs 36 hours with one winding. The steel parts are fish oil hardened, brass parts highly wrought by hand, full conical pivots, patent pinions, agate drawn hair spring, agate drawn main spring, thoroughly timed and adjusted by our expert mechanics, one at the factory and one at our establishment, assuring our customers it being received in perfect condition. It is a clock longed for by thousands. It fills a long felt want. If not exactly as described in every particular return it and we will refund the amount deposited or remitted.
Price...$2.75
Shipping weight, 2 pounds.

A $3.00 CLOCK FOR $1.10.

No. 107520 Sears, Roebuck & Co.'s SEROCO, a clock such as has never been offered before for the money. This beautiful bronze clock, solid metal through and through, standing 12 inches high and 9½ inches broad, weighing when boxed about 7lbs., at the unheard of price, $1.10 in bronze, $1.25 in full gilt. The movement is a fine lever escapement movement, oil tempered steel parts and hand wrought brass parts, conical pivots, the hair spring agate drawn, runs for 36 hours with one winding; in fact, a movement that we guarantee to give absolute satisfaction. The case is a masterpiece representing the emblems of Hope and Plenty, Hope being represented by a heroic figure of a woman with Greek drapery, resting her hand upon a cornucopia that represents Plenty. The base of the clock is made up of three graceful scrolls meeting at a base upon which the figure of Hope stands. The parts are brought out by hand engraving and hand chasing and burnishing. A beautiful wreath of roses in strong relief connects the two designs, that of Hope and Plenty. To sell this clock at this unheard of low price, a price that does not represent one-half its true value, we had to contract with the factory that makes them in such large quantities that the price of a single one is practically lost sight of. The design was executed by ourselves and is copyrighted. It cannot be procured elsewhere. If the clock is not the greatest bargain that you have ever seen or heard of, and if it does not in every way, shape and manner come up to our description and thoroughly satisfy you, return it to us and we will refund you the entire amount of your remittance.
Price, in Bronze...$1.10
Price, in Gilt...$1.25
Shipping weight, 2 pounds.

BRONZE $1.10   GILT $1.25

No. 107520

$1.10
$1.25

FINE CABINET CLOCKS.

MANUFACTURED BY THE GREATEST CLOCK MAKERS IN THE WORLD

WE GUARANTEE EACH AND EVERY ONE OF THEM IN EVERY PARTICULAR, AND IF GIVEN THE CARE THAT ALL CLOCKS SHOULD HAVE, WILL LAST A LIFETIME.

The Jeffrey Clock for $2.75.

No. 107543 THE JEFFREY. Fancy Cabinet Clock; height, 22 inches; dial, 6 inches. Either oak or walnut as desired, handsomely carved and hand engraved. Fine guaranteed 8-day movement, half hour strike; manufactured by the Waterbury Clock Company.
Price.........$2.75.
With gong or alarm, 30c extra.

$3.45 Buys a $5.00 Cabinet Clock.

No. 107555 THE GAINES. Beautiful Cabinet Clock; handsomely carved and decorated in solid oak or walnut, as desired; height, 24 inches; dial, 6 inches; fancy pendulum; decorated glass; 8-day movement; strikes the hour and half hour on a wire bell; manufactured by the celebrated Waterbury Clock Company.
Price....... $3.45
Cathedral gong or alarm, 30c extra.

Our $2.95 Cabinet Clocks

No. 107567 THE TAMPA. One of the most complete clocks ever offered to the public. It has an eight-day movement, guaranteed by the Waterbury Clock Company. Strikes the hour and half-hour on a wire bell. It also has thermometer and barometer attachment. The case is of solid oak or walnut, as desired; beautifully carved, with ornamented door and fancy glass. The pendulum is likewise ornamented and very fancy. Stands 22 inches high and has a six-inch dial. Price.....$2.95
With cathedral gong or alarm, 30c ex[tra.]

Special Value For $3.00.

No. 107546 THE GIRARD. Height; 23½ inches; dial, 6 inches. Very fine movement. Manufactured and guaranteed by the Ansonia Clock Company, frame hand engraved and carved, rich top ornamentation, highly polished throughout. Walnut only.
Price.........$3.00
Alarm 30c extra.

A $5.00 Cabinet Clock for $3.60.

No. 107558 THE HALSTEAD. Handsome Parlor Clock; hand engraved and carved trimmings; fancy top and base; ornamented glass. Black walnut only. Height, 23 inches dial, 6 inches.
Price.......$3.60
For gong or alarm, 50 cents extra.

A Rare Bargain for $3.65

No. 107570 THE BUFFALO. Fancy Cabinet Clock in solid black walnut only; very fancy ornamented and carved case; height, 25½ inches; dial, 6 inches; fitted with fine 8-day movement; made by the Waterbury Clock Company; strikes hours and halves on wire bell; with cathedral gong. Price..$3.65
With cathedral gong, 30c extra.

Nothing Finer for $4.00. Our Price, $2.75.

No. 107549 THE CLARENCE. Fancy Cabinet Clock; 22½ inches high; dial, 6 inches; made in oak only; beautifully carved and ornamented; fine 8-day movement; made by the Ansonia Clock Company; strikes hours and halves on a wire bell.
Price.........$2.75
Gong bell, when desired, 30c extra.

This Elegant Gothic Clock for $3.75.

No. 107561 THE GOTHIC. Manufactured by the New Haven Clock Company; miniature case, like our grandfathers used, but all the style now; handsomely veneered case; 8-day movement; height of clock, 19¼ inches; 6 inch dial; guarantee clock to be a good time keeper; strikes hour and the half hour.
Price.........$3.75

Alarm attachment, 30c extra, if desired.

Our $5.65 Monarch Clock Would Retail for $10.00.

No. 107573 THE MONARCH. Very fancy Cabinet Clock in black walnut only. Fancy carved, with bronze ornament and fancy French sash. Height, 24½ inches; dial, 6 inches with fine 8-day movement; made by th[e] Ansonia Clock Company; strikes hour and halves, with fancy pendulum.
Price.........$5.65
Cathedral gong bell 30 cents extra.

Very Latest and Best Design for $2.00.

No. 107552 THE JARVIS. Latest pattern Cabinet Clock in solid oak or walnut as desired; case finely ornamented with decorated glass; height of clock 22 inches; dial, 6 inches; very fine 8-day movement, guaranteed to keep accurate time; manufactured by the celebrated Waterbury Clock Company; strikes the hour and half hour on a wire bell.
Price.........$2.00
With cathedral gong or alarm, 30c extra.

$2.75 Buys This Beautiful Kingsland Clock.

No. 107564 THE KINGSLAND. Handsome Cabinet Clock in oak or walnut, as desired; latest design; fancy carved and ornamented case; height, 22 inches; dial, 6 inches; fine 8-day movement, guaranteed by the Waterbury Clock Company, strikes the hour and half hour on wire bell.
Price.........$2.75
Gong or alarm, 30c extra.

Such a Clock is Seldom if Ever Seen in a Retail Store.

No. 107576 THE OXFORD. Very fancy Parlor Clock. Can furnish in either oak, walnut or mahogany, as desired. It is 24 inches high; has a six-inch dial, finely carved case, plate glass mirrors and cupids at sides. Has an eight-day movement and strikes the hours and half-hours on wire bell. Manufactured by the Waterbury Clock Co.
Price.........$4.50
Gong or alarm, 30 cents extra.

The Mantel Clocks on this page weigh, boxed, from 22 to 30 pounds. Compare our prices with those you would have to pay in your own town at your retail jeweler's, if you wish to know how much you can save by buying of us.

OUR NEW ACME QUEEN CATHEDRAL GONG CLOCK CUT DOWN TO $5.75

LAST YEAR WE SOLD THIS CLOCK FOR $6.90, BUT ON ACCOUNT OF IMMENSE SALES WE WERE ENABLED GIVE A LARGER ORDER, AND PAYING SPOT CASH WE WERE ABLE TO CUT THE COST THIS AMOUNT. WE ARE GIVING YOU THE ADVANTAGE OF IT.

FROM THIS LARGE ILLUSTRATION, which is engraved by our artist direct from a photograph, you can form some idea of the appearance of this clock and figure, but it must be seen to be appreciated.

No. 107600

At $5.75

we furnish this clock complete with handsome bronze figure exactly as illustrated. At $4.75 we furnish the clock only, without the bronze figure. Send us $1.00, let us send you this clock to examine, and if you do not find it all and even more than we claim for it, such a clock as you could not buy elsewhere even at double the price, you can return it to us at our expense and we will cheerfully refund your money. At $5.75 we offer this big handsome clock, complete, with large bronze figure as illustrated, as the greatest value we have ever offered in a high grade cathedral gong 8-day clock.

THIS OUR SPECIAL $5.75 CLOCK, complete with figure, is a clock that we believe combines the good qualities of all high grade Waterbury mantel clocks, with the defects of none. This clock is covered by a binding guarantee and if any piece or part gives out by reason of defect in material or workmanship, or for the some reason the clock fails to run accurately, it can be returned at our expense and we will cheerfully refund your money

OUR $1.00 OFFER.

SEND US $1.00, as a guarantee of good faith, and we will send you this clock complete with bronze figure by express C. O. D., subject to examination; you can examine it at your express office, and if found perfectly satisfactory, exactly as represented, one of the handsomest clocks you have ever seen and such a clock as was never seen in your section at anything like the price, pay the express agent the balance, $4.75, and express charges.

WHILE WE OFFER MANY RARE BARGAINS in our clock department, offer them at the manufacturers' lowest prices, prices as low, and in many cases even lower than dealers can buy in quantities, this our Special Acme Queen Cathedral Gong 8-day clock, complete with figure, at $5.75 is the greatest clock value in our catalogue, and we recommend this clock in preference to all others. It is a handsome clock for mantel or shelf; for an ornament for the home there is no clock made that will compare with it at anything like the price; as a timekeeper there is nothing better.

GENERAL DESCRIPTION.

SIZE—Height of clock including figure, 20 inches; clock only, 11½ inches; figure only, 8½ inches. Length of clock at base, 17¼ inches; length of clock at top, 15 inches. Diameter of dial, 5½ inches. Length of bronze figure, 9 inches.

This large, handsome bronze, marbleized metal clock is made in two colors, black and green, in imitation of black and Mexican onyx, and it so closely resembles the genuine Mexican onyx that it cannot be detected except by an expert. Better than the genuine onyx, it can be cleaned with a damp cloth without injury and is guaranteed never to warp or crack. This is an 8-day clock—runs eight days with one winding—and strikes the hours and half hours upon a perfect cathedral gong.

This clock stands on large handsome bronze feet. It is ornamented with lion head bronze side ornaments, heavy panel ornaments and bronze center ornaments. It is furnished with a handsome Mosaic dial in heavy gilt, 5½ inches in diameter. This clock is one of the highest grade made by the Waterbury Company. It has blued steel hands, the movement is highly polished wrought brass. All steel parts are oil tempered. Has the latest improved regulator and pinions. safety barrel and escapement.

No. 107600 Price Acme Queen Cathedral Gong Clock................. **$5.75**

OUR PARLOR SPECIAL FOR $3.75

THIS CLOCK AS ILLUSTRATED FOR $3.75 is about one-half what you would pay your local dealer for the same sized clock. A clock as beautifully ornamented, sold by the clock companies to the retail dealers for $4.75. We have made a purchase of an immense quantity, the entire clock is manufactured expressly for us by the renowned Waterbury Clock Company, located at Waterbury, Connecticut, and each and every one of them is thoroughly guaranteed in every respect and we warrant them to give entire satisfaction.

WE WILL SELL BUT ONE TO A FAMILY.

We wish all of our customers to get the benefit of this bargain. Although we have purchased an immense quantity, we do not believe that we can supply all the orders.

DESCRIPTION OF THE CASE.

THIS CLOCK CASE IS MADE OF WOOD, covered with a secret preparation in imitation of black marble. This clock, wiped with a damp cloth at intervals, will always keep it as new. It is guaranteed not to chip, warp or wear off and always retains its appearance of genuine black Italian marble.

THE CLOCK IS ORNAMENTED with four handsome gold plated scrolls. It stands upon beautiful metal feet made to match the balance of the scroll work. The dial of the clock is one of the very latest productions, being fancy rococo embossed pattern. The numerals are Arabic ones. Height of clock is 12½ inches; width of clock, 9¾ inches; depth of clock, 4½ inches.

DESCRIPTION OF MOVEMENT.

THE MOVEMENT FITTED IN THIS CASE is one of the Waterbury guaranteed movements, runs eight days with one winding. It is made of the finest tempered steel and hand wrought brass; it strikes the hour on a cathedral gong and the half hour on a brass bell. You can always know the time without seeing the clock. The hands are very fine hand sawed blue steel of the Fleur de Lis pattern.

THIS PICTURE IS TAKEN DIRECT FROM A PHOTOGRAPH, IN REDUCED SIZE, OF THE ACTUAL CLOCK.

This clock, boxed ready for shipment, weighs about 15 pounds. Remember, our price for this beautiful clock is but $3.75. You cannot have two of them.

No. 107615 Our Special Parlor Clock.................... **$3.75**

No. 107615

Rich Imitation Onyx Clock for $4.50.

No. 107750 THE ARNO. Manufactured by the world famed Seth Thomas Clock Company, of Thomaston, Conn. This clock is finished with the wonderful adamantine finish, equal to the finest genuine onyx or marble clock made. It will not peel or chip off, as cheap enamel on iron or wood clocks at times do. A soft, damp cloth renews it. The top of the clock is the beautiful Queen Anne style, the base beautifully ornamented with fancy Greek feet of solid metal, at the sides the clock has two ornaments of solid bronze representing the head of an African lion holding a ring hanging pendant from its mouth. The sash of the clock is a beautiful French rococo design. The dial is a beautiful plain dial with Arabic figures. The clock itself is one of the finest movements manufactured by the Seth Thomas people and is fully warranted in every particular. It goes 8 days with one winding. Has beautiful cathedral gong upon which is struck the hours and half hours. If not exactly as described and the most wonderful bargain that you ever saw, return it to us and we will refund the amount remitted. Weighs, boxed, about 20 pounds.
Price..................................**$4.50**

No. 107753 POINTER. Fine bronze ornament for mantel or top of mantel clock; height, 4 inches, length, 7 inches.
Price..........93c

Weight, boxed. 2 pounds.

A MOST HANDSOME ORNAMENT

No. 107756

Price, Complete, **$6.65**
Clock, alone - **5.30**

Clock and ornament boxed ready for shipment about 25 pounds.

Rare Value for $5.00.

No. 107759 A beautiful adamantine finished clock manufactured by the Seth Thomas Clock Company. The movement of this clock is a very fine hand wrought brass movement, oil tempered steel parts, agate drawn hair spring and main spring, conical pivots, patent pinions, in fact, a movement such as we know and can warrant to give absolute satisfaction in every respect. The case has a wonderful adamantine finish which never dulls, but is always beautiful as if newly polished. It is guaranteed not to wear or chip off; wipe it with a damp cloth when you wish to renew it and the clock will shine forth as when it left the factory. A beautiful figurehead of Jupiter in solid bronze ornaments the sides, bronze feet molded in the shape of lion's claws, beautifully hand engraved and hand chased. Hand engraved scrolls of various designs ornament the front. The dial is a very beautiful genuine porcelain dial, 5 inches in height, with Roman figures. This clock stands 11 inches high and 14 inches long, and would not fail to give you perfect satisfaction. This clock goes 8 days with one winding; strikes the hours and half hours upon a cathedral gong. Warranted to keep accurate time for 5 years, but with care would last a natural lifetime. Weight of clock when boxed is about 20 lbs.
Price..................................**$5.00**

No. 107762 ORMONDE. Beautiful bronze figure of a horse, for mantel ornament or top of mantel clock; height, 7¼ inches; length, 8 inches.
Price..........**$1.75**

Weight, boxed, 2 pounds.

THE BEAUTY

ONE OF THE FINEST AND MOST BEAUTIFUL CLOCKS EVER MANUFACTURED.

We contracted with the factory to use an immense quantity and we believe we will use three times the number ordered. We quote a price unheard of before, for a clock of this high standard of make. The case is grandly constructed piece of work; height, without ornament, 11 inches; base, 17 inches; with ornament, clock stands 19 inches high. The movement is manufactured by the Seth Thomas Clock Company, of world wide fame, and is guaranteed to keep accurate time. It runs for 8 days with one winding. The parts are made of fine wrought polished brass and oil tempered steel. It strikes the hours and half hours upon a cathedral gong that is toned with the church bells.

The case is adamantine finished and highly polished and can be cleaned without injury with a damp cloth; no other make clocks have this wonderful finish. You can always keep your clock as new. Foot and side ornaments are of highly burnished bronze. It is, in fact, a clock for the price such as you have never seen before.
Price complete with figure..........**$6.65**
Without figure..........**5.30**

Imitation Mexican Marble Clock for $6.50.

No. 107765 THE ZAMORA, the very latest idea in a mantel clock, manufactured by the Seth Thomas Clock Company. This clock is covered by a patent process with a wonderful substance called adamantine, a material closely resembling celluloid, but in fact a much more perfect article. This clock in color is green, imitating the Mexican marble. The clock can always be made as new by the application of a damp cloth. It is guaranteed not to wear, peel or chip off. It is beautifully ornamented with bronze scrolls, beautiful feet finish off the base in an absolutely perfect manner. The length of the entire clock is 13 inches; height 12 inches; dial 5 inches; surrounding the dial is a most beautiful sash. This clock runs 8 days with one winding; strikes the hours and half hours upon a cathedral gong. Weighs, when boxed, about 20 pounds. Price..**$6.50**

Beautiful Mantel Clock for $5.75.

No. 107768 DANDY. A very handsome mantel clock, a most excellent imitation of Mexican onyx, and unless it is examined very closely no one would believe that it was not a real onyx clock. It holds a beautiful polish and with proper care would last a lifetime. If the case gets soiled or dirty it can be wiped off with a damp cloth. Has fancy bronze feet in artistic design and side dragon head metal ornaments. The base is the Corinthian style base. Length of clock 17 inches, height, 11¼ inches. Has an 8-day movement, made by the old reliable Seth Thomas Clock Company of Thomaston, Conn. Strikes hours and half hours on cathedral gong bell; regulated by patent regulator without touching the pendulum. Price..........**$5.75**

A $9.00 Mantel Clock for $6.00.

No. 107781 THE PETREL, manufactured by the Seth Thomas Clock Co., a clock company so well known throughout the United States that to enlarge upon their reliability would be a waste of space. The Petrel is one of the very latest designs; it has the wonderful adamantine finish. The case of this clock measures 17 inches; beautiful bronze ornaments embellish the sides; the base is ornamented with beautiful hand chased bronze feet. The front of the clock is beautifully engraved by hand, and then inlaid with gilt, making a beautiful contrast between the black and the gilt. The top of the clock is made in imitation of beautiful green onyx, so perfect an imitation that it is only by close inspection that one would know the difference. Rubbing with a damp cloth always makes the Petrel a new clock. Strikes the hours and half hours upon a beautiful gong. Price.....**$6.00**
Weighs, boxed, about 90 pounds.

SPECTACLES AND EYEGLASSES.

WE PARTICULARLY CAUTION OUR CUSTOMERS against buying the very cheap grades of spectacles or eyeglasses. The lenses of these cheap goods are made of very poor material, are improperly cut, and almost certain to do untold injury to the eyes. An injury to your clothes can be mended or repaired, but an injury to the eyes may never be cured.

THE PROPER READING DISTANCE for ordinary print is from 12 to 14 inches. If it is necessary to hold the reading nearer the eye than this, glasses for near sight are required. If it is necessary to hold the reading more than twelve to fourteen inches away from the eye, glasses are required for far sight. Practically everybody should wear glasses after reaching the age of forty years, as the eyes at this time commence to be far sighted, and the longer the wearing of glasses is put off the harder it will be to remedy the trouble. Near sightedness is also very common, especially among young people, and should never be neglected, as this trouble is so easily and perfectly relieved by proper eyeglasses or spectacles.

TYPE FOR TESTING THE EYES.

80

Defects of eyesight requiring correction by the use of spectacles are purely mechanical, and can be so corrected by the proper adjustment of perfectly made lenses that their use will be entirely obviated.

60

The smallest size letters on this card should be read easily at fifteen inches from the eye. If you cannot do so you should wear spectacles. It does not pay to buy cheap spectacles.

52

They distort the rays of light, disturb the angles of vision, cause pain and discomfort and injure the eyesight. When it is necessary to hold work or reading matter farther than fifteen inches from the eye

44

in order to see distinctly, it is a sure sign of failing vision, and much annoyance, discomfort and pain will be prevented

36

by having a pair of glasses fitted. Pain in the eyes when wearing spectacles is usually caused

30

either by improperly fitted lenses, or from the centres of the lenses not corresponding with

22

the centres of the eyes. To be perfect, a lens must be made with highly polished surfaces

20

of accurate curvatures. Our crystalline lenses are the best in the market.

They are made from the clearest and finest material obtainable

20

AND ARE WARRANTED TO BE OF ABSOLUTELY

18

PERFECT CONSTRUCTION.

16

BUY NO OTHER KIND.

13

CRYSTALLINE

11

LENSES

10

ARE THE

8

BEST.

INSTRUCTIONS FOR ORDERING SPECTACLES OR EYEGLASSES.

Give the Catalogue number of the style desired, and answer carefully the following questions: 1st. What is your age? 2d. Have you ever worn glasses before, and if so how long? 3d. If you have worn glasses before state, it possible, the number or strength of the lenses. 4 in. Is the bridge of your nose prominent or flat? 5th. What is the distance from the center or pupil of one eye to the center or pupil of the other eye? This measurement may easily be taken with a rule or tape and is usually about 2½ inches. It is never less than 2½ nor more than 2½ inches. 6th. When holding this page in a good light, what is the number of the finest print which you can easily and distinctly read at a distance of from 13 to 14 inches from the eye? 7th. What is the greatest possible distance at which you can easily and distinctly read paragraph No. 207. 8th. Are you nearsighted or farsighted? 9th. Do you desire glasses especially for reading or for distant objects? If glasses are desired for both reading and distant objects, bifocal lenses are sometimes necessary. See paragraph on this page just preceding descriptions of eyeglasses, for prices and descriptions of bifocal lenses.

N. B. Always include 5 cents extra for postage, if spectacles or eyeglasses are to be sent by mail.

OUR $1.90 GOLD FILLED SPECTACLES.

For $1.90 we furnish these fine gold filled Riding Bow Spectacles as the equal of Riding Bow Spectacles that are furnished by opticians at $6.00 to $12.00. 10-YEARS' GUARANTEE. Every pair of our special $1.90 gold filled Riding Bow Spectacles are put out under our binding 10-years' guarantee, and if they wear through, tarnish or in any way change color or give out by reason of defect in material or workmanship within ten years, we will replace or repair them free of charge. The gold filled frame is one of the highest grade gold filled frames made. It is genuine gold filled, made of gold filled stock, two plates of heavy fine solid gold over an inner plate of hard composition metal, beautifully polished and finished, neatly adjusted, the highest grade gold filled frames made.

This illustration will give you an idea of the appearance of our special $1.90, 10-year guaranteed gold filled Riding Bow spectacles. They are made with broad nose piece; they are fitted with the very finest quality of crystalline lenses, accurately adjusted. The lenses are carefully selected to your eye test and order. We send these glasses out on the understanding that if they are not perfectly satisfactory in every way they can be returned to us at our expense and we will return your money. No. 17536 Our special price, per pair............$1.90

GOLD FILLED $1.90

WARRANTED 10 YEARS.

Riding Bow Spectacles.

Riding Bow Spectacles are known also as Hook Bow and are to be preferred in all cases where the glasses are to be worn constantly, or nearly so. The shape of the temples prevents the spectacles slipping off, and also keeps the lenses more exactly in strong position all the time. No. 17528 Steel Frames. Riding bow temples, good quality, blued. With fine crystalline lenses. Price, 75c.

No. 17530 Steel Frames. Riding bow temples, best quality, finely tempered and nickel plated, with finest crystalline lenses. Price............$1.25
No. 17532 Aluminico Frames. Riding bow temples, broad nose piece, light and well finished. Aluminico is a composition metal similar in weight and appearance to aluminum, showy and warranted not to tarnish. Finest crystalline lenses. Price..$1.25
No. 17534 Gold Filled Frames. Riding bow temples, fine quality with broad nose piece and finest crystalline lenses. Price....................$1.45
No. 17541 Solid Gold Frames. Riding bow temples, broad nose piece, heavy weight, solid gold, strong and durable. Nothing better is made. Finest crystalline lenses.
Price, 10-karat, $3.75; 14-karat............$4.90

Straight Temple Spectacles
With Round Eye Wire.

Straight Temple Spectacles are most suitable for those who wear glasses for near work only, and therefore remove them frequently from the eyes.
No. 17504 Steel Frames. Good quality bronzed steel, straight temples with good periscopic lenses. Price...50c
No. 17508 Steel Frames. The very best straight temple steel frame made. Nickel plated and finely finished, perfectly tempered, wide flat nose piece and fitted with finest quality crystalline lenses.
Price...$1.25
No. 17512 Gold Filled Frames. Straight temples, broad nose piece, finest quality, warranted for 10 years. Fine crystalline lenses. Price..........$1.40
No. 17516 Solid Gold Frames, straight temples, broad nose piece, best grade of solid gold with finest crystalline lenses. Absolutely nothing better is made. Price, 10-karat, $3.85; 14-karat......$3.95

Cable Riding Bow Spectacles.

In the Cable Riding Bow frames the temples are slightly larger than the regular style, and owing to their peculiar construction are extremely reliable and thus very comfortable to the wearer.
No. 17542 Steel Frames. Cable riding bow temples, very best quality, finely tempered and nickel plated. Finest crystalline lenses. Price......$1.50
No. 17544 Gold Filled Frames. Cable riding bow temples, broad nose piece, very best quality and warranted for ten years. Finest crystalline lenses. Price...$2.20

Bifocal Lenses.

Cut Showing Appearance of Bifocal Lenses.
A great many people find it necessary to use two pairs of spectacles, one pair for reading and one pair for looking at objects at a distance. Instead of using two pairs of spectacles, however, the same result can be obtained by one pair of spectacles fitted with bifocal lenses. These are lenses in which the lower part, used for near work or reading, is made of a different strength from the upper part, which is used for distant objects.
We furnish these lenses in the style known as cemented bifocal lenses, which are the latest, best and most satisfactory style made.
Any of the spectacles or eyeglasses in this catalogue can be furnished with bifocal lenses for 50c extra, for example, spectacle No. 1708, the regular price of which is $1.25, would be $1.75 with bifocal lenses.

Flexible Guard Eyeglasses.

No. 17575 Steel frames. Flexible cork lined guards, finely finished, nickel plated, with finest periscopic lenses. Price...........................50c
No. 17577 Gold Filled Frames, flexible cork lined guards, finely finished and warranted for 10 years. Finest crystalline lenses. Price............$1.45

Offset Guard Eyeglasses.

No. 17581 Steel Frames, offset guards, cork lined, light weight and finely finished. Best crystalline lenses. Price.............................75c
No. 17585 Gold Filled Frames, offset guards, cork lined, very finely finished and guaranteed for 10 years. Finest crystalline lenses. Price....$1.30

THERMOMETERS.

Our line of thermometers is very large and embraces a great variety for all purposes, indoor or outdoor, scientific work, manufacturing, dairy work, etc. Our thermometers are manufactured by the most representative and reputable concerns, both in this country and abroad, and we handle only such qualities as we can fully guarantee to give entire satisfaction.

Outdoor Thermometers.

No. 18000 Japanned Tin Case Thermometer, ordinary grade, black figures on light metal scale, mercury tube; length, 8 inches. Price......12c
If by mail, postage extra, 7 cents.

No. 18003 Japanned Tin Case Thermometer, good quality, heavier, better made and more accurate than the preceding style, **seasoned tubes of standard size**, mercury only, good reliable thermometers for ordinary use; length, 8 inches. Price......28c
If by mail, postage extra, 8 cents.

No. 18006 Japanned Tin Case Thermometer, best grade made, white figures and graduations upon black oxidized scale, thoroughly seasoned tubes of large size, good material and workmanship throughout, and guaranteed absolutely accurate, mercury only, length, 8 inches. Price......75c
If by mail, postage extra, 10 cents.

No. 18011 Japanned Tin Case Thermometer, with red spirit tubes, graduated to 50 or 60 degrees below zero. Carefully tested for accuracy and perfectly reliable; length, 12 inches. Price....50c
If by mail, postage extra, 13 cents.

Distance Reading Thermometers.

In the Distance Reading Thermometers the scale and figures are large and very distinct, the tube magnifies the column of red spirit, and the temperature is therefore easily read at a distance of from 15 to 25 feet. They **are very convenient and present a handsome appearance.**

No. 18016 Distance Reading Thermometer, enameled metal case, large black figures, red spirit tube, 7¾ inches long. Price......17c
If by mail, postage extra, 6 cents.

No. 18017 Distance Reading Thermometer, same style as No. 18016, but 2¾ inches wide by 9½ long, with extra large and plain figures, easily read at a distance of 25 feet. Price......30c
If by mail, postage extra, 11 cents.

House Thermometers.

No. 18025 Black Wood Thermometer, with white figures and scale, sunken tube, magnifying mercury, nickeled trimmings. Price......20c
If by mail, postage extra, 6 cents.

No. 18026 Boxwood Thermometer, similar to No. 18025, but made of boxwood, better quality and carefully tested. Sunken tube, magnifying mercury, nickeled trimmings. Price......35c
If by mail, postage extra, 6 cents.

No. 18029 Household Thermometer, mounted upon highly polished oak back with white figures on **black oxidized metal plate.** This finish is a permanent black and free from all the defects common to white or silvered scales. **Best materials and workmanship throughout, carefully tested and guaranteed to be accurate.** Seasoned tube of standard size. Suitable for either indoor or outdoor use. Length, 8½ inches. Price......$1.10
If by mail, postage extra, 12 cents.

No. 18031 Household Thermometer, with pure white porcelain scale, mounted on polished wood back, red spirit tube with large flat bulb; 8 inches long. A very handsome thermometer. Price......90c
If by mail, postage extra, 13 cents.

Standard and Self-Registering Thermometers.

Self-Registering Thermometers are very desirable inasmuch as they not only show the exact temperature at the time the observation is made, but also indicate with absolute accuracy the highest or lowest point which has been reached since the last observation.

The Maximum Thermometers show HIGHEST temperature since last observation, and the Minimum Thermometers show LOWEST. These are the same instruments used by the U. S. Signal Service in keeping their records.

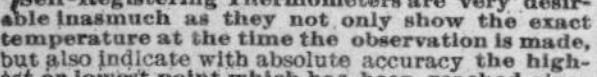

Nos. 18050 to 18052

No. 18050 Standard U. S. Weather Bureau Thermometer, round bulb, white figures and graduations on best grade black oxidized metal plate, 12 inches long, with brass insulating strap for fastening in position. **Absolutely accurate at any temperature** (not self-registering). Price......$2.45
If by mail, postage extra, 15 cents.

No. 18051 Standard U. S. Minimum Thermometer, same style and quality as No. 18050, but self-registering, showing lowest temperature. Price......$2.70
If by mail, postage extra, 15 cents.

No. 18052 Standard U. S. Maximum Thermometer, same style and quality as No. 18050, but self-registering, showing highest temperature. Price...$2.95
If by mail, postage extra, 15 cents.

Storm Glass and Thermometers.

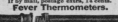

No. 18058 Storm Glass and Thermometer, combined, mounted upon polished wood case, 3 inches wide by 9 inches long. This storm glass foretells the weather with a fair degree of accuracy for 24 hours in advance. Price......19c
If by mail, postage extra, 12 cents.

No. 18060 Antique Oak Storm Glass and Thermometer, combined, mounted upon carved oak back with fancy beaded edge, silvered metal scale to thermometer, with brass mountings; extra large storm glass with etched lettering. A reliable and handsome instrument. Price......68c
If by mail, postage extra, 17 cents.

No. 18061 Copper Case Storm Glass and Thermometer, case made of polished copper, silvered metal scale, high grade thermometer with standard size tube, mercury. A very serviceable instrument for outdoor use. Price......48c
If by mail, postage extra, 14 cents.

Fever Thermometers.

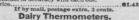

Clinical or fever thermometers are used, as the name implies, for taking the temperature in cases of sickness. **No family should be without a good fever thermometer,** it not only makes it possible to watch more closely the course of a fever or other sickness, but is frequently the means of **saving a doctor's bill,** or of preventing a serious sickness by indicating in time that a physician's services are necessary.

We handle only the highest grade fever thermometers, as a cheap or inaccurate instrument is worse than useless. **Every fever thermometer is accompanied by certificate of accuracy.**

No. 18062 Fever Thermometer, 4 inches long, plain tube, self-registering, in hard rubber case, very accurate. A certificate of accuracy given with each one. Price......75c
If by mail, postage extra, 3 cents.

No. 18064 Fever Thermometer, 4 inches long, self-registering, in hard rubber case, magnifying tube, very carefully tested and guaranteed, each thermometer accompanied by certificate of accuracy. Price......$1.25
If by mail, postage extra, 3 cents.

No. 18066 Fever Thermometer, 4 inches long, self-registering; in black enameled case with gold trimmings, chain and clasp; cannot be lost out of pocket; magnifying tube; very carefully tested and certificate of accuracy with each one. Price......$1.45
If by mail, postage extra, 3 cents.

Dairy Thermometers.

No. 18069 Churn Thermometer, with flange scale, tested at 62 degrees for churning. Each......15c

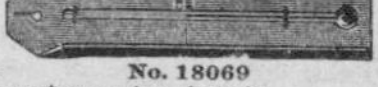

No. 18069

If by mail, postage extra, 4 cents.

No. 18070 Dairy Thermometer, with flange for general dairy use. 8 inches long. Each......15c
If by mail, postage extra, 5 cents.

No. 18071 Dairy Thermometer, same style as No. 18070, but highest grade made; 8 inches long; black oxidized scale; ruby back tube. Absolutely accurate. Each......48c
If by mail, postage extra, 5 cents.

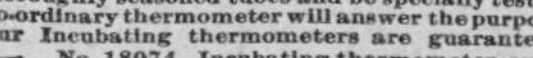

No. 18072 Dairy or Bath Thermometers, all glass. A very desirable instrument and easy to keep clean. Each......20c
If by mail, postage extra, 5 cents.

No. 18073 Dairy Thermometer, all glass. This thermometer floats in the cream in upright position with entire scale exposed to view. **Scale is hand graduated and very accurate. Red spirit,** magnifying tube making it very easy to read. Price, only......48c
If by mail, postage extra, 11 cents.

Incubating Thermometers.

Thermometers for use in Incubators should have thoroughly seasoned tubes and be specially tested. No ordinary thermometer will answer the purpose. Our Incubating thermometers are guaranteed.

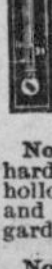

No. 18074 Incubating thermometer, extra large bulb and tube, very sensitive, white graduations on black oxidized metal plate. Absolutely accurate; 6 inches long. Price....50c
If by mail, postage extra, 6 cents.

No. 18075 Incubating thermometer, same style and grade as No. 18074, but 4½ inches long. Price......50c
If by mail, postage extra, 6 cents.

No. 18076 Incubating thermometer, same quality as preceding styles, but triangular in shape, will stand upright among the eggs with scale showing plainly. Price......50c
If by mail, postage extra, 8 cents.

No. 18079 Hot Bed Thermometer, round 15-inch hardwood frame, with handle and sharp pointed hollow brass ferrule to penetrate the soil, red spirit and boxwood scale; is an indispensable article to gardeners or florists. Each......98c
If by mail, postage extra, 16 cents.

No. 18081 Confectioners' Thermometer, heavy copper case, 12 inches long, scale reading up to 350 or 400 degrees, very accurate. Each......$1.75
If by mail, postage extra, 16 cents.

Lactometers.

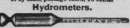

No. 18084 Lactometer, for testing the quality of milk, shows the effects produced by changes in the animal's diet, as different articles of food produce milk of different density; also shows the amount of water contained in milk; complete instructions accompany each instrument. Each......35c
If by mail, postage extra, 13 cents.

Hydrometers.

No. 18085 Hydrometers, for testing specific gravity of liquids, as follows: acids, alkali, ammonia, coal oil, gasoline, salt, spirit, syrup, vinegar, liquids lighter than water, liquids heavier than water. Price, each, any style......45c
If by mail, postage extra, 5 cents.

No. 18087 Hydrometer for wine and must, best quality. Oechles scale. Price......95c
If by mail, postage extra, 5 cents.

No. 18092 Combined Hydrometer and Thermometer, for coal oil, price, $1.25; for spirit, price, $1.25; for milk, price......$1.35;
If by mail, postage extra, 5 cents.

No. 18093 Hydrometer Jars, tall glass jars with foot and pouring spout; height, 12 inches; diameter, 2 inches. Price, each......60c

No. 18097 Moisture Gauge or Hydrometer, for greenhouses, incubators, cigar cases, etc. Indicate exact amount of moisture. Nickel plated metal case, dial 2 inches in diameter. Price......$1.25
If by mail, postage extra, 5 cents.

BAROMETERS.

Barometers are scientific and practical instruments used to foretell the weather, and are of inestimable value to the farmer, gardener, mariner or anybody whose welfare is in any way dependent upon the weather. Complete, carefully written instructions and rules for fortelling the weather by means of the barometer are sent with every instrument.

Aneroid Barometers at $3.45 to $9.60.

No. 18101 Aneroid Barometer, nickel plated case, open face, card dial 4½ inches in diameter, handsomely lettered in red and black, and open in center showing the works. A very pretty instrument. Price......$3.45

No. 18105

No. 18105 Aneroid Barometer, lacquered brass case, beveled edge plate glass front, silvered metal dial 4½ inches in diameter, open in center showing works and provided with **Fahrenheit Thermometer**, as shown in cut. **A very accurate and reliable instrument.** Price, in substantial velvet lined case......$9.60

Barometers should be shipped by express as the delicate mechanism is very liable to injury if sent through the mails.

Pocket Aneroid Barometers for Measuring Heights.

These Pocket Barometers, as now made, not only indicate the varying pressure of the atmosphere just as the barometers described in the preceding paragraphs, but are also provided with a graduated scale showing the exact height above sea level. Their convenience and accuracy make them of great value to engineers, tourists and scientific observers.

No. 18113 Pocket Aneroid Barometer, nickel case, 2 inches in diameter, silvered metal dial, revolving altitude scale, reading to 15,000 feet, compensated for temperature and fitted with Fahrenheit thermometer and compass under heavy glass on reverse side. Price......$12.85

No. 18117 Pocket Aneroid Barometer, heavy oxidized case, 2¾ inches in diameter, revolving altitude scale reading to 12,000 feet. This standard instrument is of the best English manufacture, very carefully tested, compensated for temperature and fully guaranteed. It is provided on the reverse side with a fine jeweled bar needle compass the full diameter of the instrument and contained in strong leather case. Price......$19.90

IMPORTANT.—These instruments should be shipped by express, to avoid liability of injury.

THE PERFECTION COMPLETE VIEWING OUTFIT FOR $15.35

$15.35 ALL THAT IS REQUIRED TO START IN A PLEASANT AND GOOD PAYING BUSINESS.

THERE IS NO OTHER EXPENSE necessary. You can start making money as soon as the outfit is received, as everything is prepared ready for use.

PREVIOUS EXPERIENCE is not necessary, as the work is so thoroughly explained in the instruction book and the operations have been made so simple that an intelligent child can make good pictures.

THERE IS NO RISK as there is no expense. Different from other lines, of business, it is not necessary to rent a place of business, as all the work can be done in any home.

IF YOU HAVE EMPLOYMENT this will afford an opportunity to get started gradually into a business for yourself, and thus satisfy a desire which constantly agitates the mind of every ambitious man.

OUTDOOR VIEW WORK will average about one negative to three pictures (for portrait work it would be less, and from this it will be seen that the average cost of producing pictures in the 5x7 size (including chemicals) is about 5 cents each, thus leaving an average profit of 35 cents on each picture.

$21.00 OUTFIT FOR $15.35 The 5x7 size is the most popular one, both for professional and amateur purposes but the 6½x8½ and the 8x10 are desirable sizes, from the fact that higher prices may be obtained for the pictures, by reason of the larger size.

SUCCESS IS SURE For if perchance there should any difficulty arise, or there should be anything about the manipulation of the outfit which is not understood, write us about it and we would quickly set you to rights.

THE PERFECTION VIEW CAMERA is thoroughly well made and substantial throughout. It is constructed from the best thoroughly seasoned Honduras mahogany, beautifully polished and with all trimmings nickel plated.

IT FOLDS UP compactly, has sliding front for adjusting relative amount of sky or foreground, and is provided with a good swing back, a very valuable feature, especially in photographing buildings.

THE LENS is our Monarch single achromatic, a strictly high grade lens, manufactured expressly for us by the Bausch & Lomb Optical Co., the best achromatic lens that can be made, and suitable for landscapes, buildings, groups or portraits.

THE REVERSIBLE BACK PERMITS THIS CAMERA TO BE USED FOR EITHER VERTICAL OR HORIZONTAL VIEWS AS DESIRED.

A SOLID MAHOGANY CAMERA WITH FINE LENS, CARRYING CASE, TRIPOD, PLATE HOLDER AND COMPLETE OUTFIT, Consisting of Everything Necessary to Commence Work with, For Only

$15.35

THE PERFECTION VIEW CAMERA, COMPLETE, 5x7, WOULD COST, IF PURCHASED AT RETAIL, $14.00. AND THE COMPLETE DEVELOPING, FINISHING AND MATERIAL OUTFIT AS LISTED ABOVE, WOULD COST AT RETAIL $7.10, MAKING THE TOTAL RETAIL VALUE OF THE OUTFIT OVER $21.00.

OUR PRICE,

$15.35

THE COMPLETE OUTFIT CONTAINS:

1 Perfection View Camera, with lens tripod, carrying case and double plate holder.
1 Metal ruby lamp for dark room.
1 Compressed fiber tray for developing.
1 Compressed fiber tray for fixing.
1 Compressed fiber tray for toning.
1 8-ounce graduated glass for measuring liquids. 1 Printing frame.
1 Print roller for smoothing down prints. 1 Heavy 2-inch paste brush.
2 Dozen sheets sensitized paper.
1 Dozen dry plates. 25 Card mounts.
1 Package concentrated developer.
1 Package concentrated toning and fixing solution.
1 Package concentrated intensifier.
1 Package hypo for fixing negatives & prints. 1 Jar mounting paste.
1 Fine gossamer focus cloth.
1 Copy "Complete Instructions Photography."

THE LATEST 1900 MODELS OF THE PERFECTION VIEWING CAMERA are made with cone shaped

bellows and reversible back, improvements never before offered in any but highest priced cameras. A SAMPLE PICTURE MADE WITH THE 5x7 SIZE OF THE PERFECTION CAMERA WILL BE MAILED ON RECEIPT OF 10 CENTS.

OUR SPECIAL PRICES.

No. 18710 The 5x7 Perfection Viewing Outfit, consisting of camera, lens, tripod, carrying case and plate holder, with complete developing, finishing and material outfit as described above ($21.00 worth of goods) all for **$15.35**

No. 18711 The 6½x8½ Perfection Viewing Outfit, consisting of camera, lens, tripod, carrying case and plate holder, with complete developing, finishing and material outfit as described above ($23.50 worth of goods) all for **$21.25**

No. 18712 The 8x10 Perfection Viewing Outfit, consisting of camera, lens, tripod, carrying case and plate holder, with complete developing, finishing and material outfit as described above ($35.00 worth of goods) all for **$26.15**

We can also furnish any of the above outfits with our famous Seroco double rapid rectilinear lens, instead of the single achromatic. See page 188 for description of this lens.

No. 18715 The 5x7 Perfection Viewing Outfit, complete just as described under No. 18710, except that the Seroco double rapid rectilinear lens is included instead of the regular lens. Price................**$19.50**

No. 18716 The 6½x8½ Perfection Viewing Outfit, complete just as described under No. 18711, except that the Seroco double rapid rectilinear lens is included instead of the regular lens. Price................**$25.10**

No. 18717 The 8x10 Perfection Viewing Outfit, complete just as described under No. 18712, except that the Seroco double rapid rectilinear lens is included instead of the regular lens. Price................**$35.60**

PERFECTION VIEW CAMERA WITHOUT THE OUTFIT.

For the benefit of those who already possess the necessary accessories and materials for picture making, and simply desire a first class camera at a moderate cost, we can furnish the Perfection View Camera with either our Monarch single achromatic lens or the Seroco double rapid rectilinear lens at the following reduced prices:

	Sizes, 5x7	6½x8½	8x10
No. 18725 Perfection View Camera with single lens. Price..........	$11.30	$16.35	$19.80
No. 18726 Perfection View Camera with double lens. Price..........	15.75	23.25	29.45

These prices include camera, lens, tripod, carrying case and one double plate holder.

EXTRA PLATE HOLDERS FOR THE PERFECTION VIEW CAMERA.

No. 18728 Each plate holder carries two plates, and it is a great advantage to have a number of extra ones, as more plates can then be carried ready for use.

Size, 5x7.		$1.0
	If by mail, postage extra, 13 cents.	
Size, 6½x8½.		1.2
	If by mail, postage extra, 22 cents.	
Size, 8x10.		1.5
	If by mail, postage extra, 30 cents.	

THE EMPIRE STATE PHOTOGRAPHIC OUTFIT

WITH COMPLETE DEVELOPING, FINISHING AND MATERIAL OUTFITS.

EVERYTHING NEEDED for the BEST AMATEUR or PROFESSIONAL WORK.

A $52.00 OUTFIT FOR $34.65

RAPID RECTILINEAR LENS, DOUBLE VALVE UNICUM SHUTTER.

The Empire State Camera.

3 Sizes:
5 x7
6½x8½
8 x10

THE SPECIAL ADVANTAGES of the EMPIRE STATE CAMERA are many, as it is capable of any class of work that can be done with any view or portrait camera. It is constructed throughout from thoroughly seasoned Honduras mahogany, and all metal parts are of polished brass. FOCUSING is accomplished quickly and easily by a fine rack and pinion movement. The bed is hinged and folds completely under the camera, thus permitting the use of very short focus or wide angle lenses, if desired. THE FRONT has a rising and falling movement, enabling the operator to regulate the relative amount of sky or foreground at will. THE SWING BACK, which is pivoted at the center, can be quickly adjusted to any desired angle and securely clamped into position by turning a milled head screw. THE BACK is reversible, and may be changed instantly from upright to horizontal pictures, without disturbing the camera. The holder is inserted between the spring-actuated ground glass and the camera back, and the slide may be drawn from either side, top or bottom, a great advantage when working in confined situations. THE LENS is our double rapid rectilinear, possessing great depth of focus, giving the finest detail and the most brilliant definition. As it is perfectly rectilinear and works very rapidly, it is splendidly adapted to instantaneous work, groups and portraits, and is unexcelled for landscapes or buildings.

THE UNICUM SHUTTER is one of the features of this outfit, being a wonderfully ingenious piece of mechanism. It is constructed of bronze metal, practically dust proof, and the shutter blades are made of thin, hard rubber, thus avoiding the danger of rust to which metal blades are subject. THE IRIS DIAPHRAGM, with which this shutter is provided, is also made from thin sheets of hard rubber, of the most perfect construction, and affording the best known means for regulating the size of stop or diaphragm. With one pressure of the bulb the Unicum shutter gives automatic exposures of from $\frac{1}{100}$ of a second to one full second. With the indicator set at B, a pressure of the bulb opens the shutter which remains open until the pressure is released, a very convenient and accurate method of making short time exposures. With the indicator set at T, the first pressure of the bulb opens the shutter and it remains open until the bulb is again pressed, the best known method for long time exposures.

The Unicum Shutter.

THE COMPLETE EMPIRE STATE PHOTOGRAPHIC OUTFIT CONTAINS:

- 1 Empire State Camera, with double Rapid Rectilinear Lens, Double Valve Unicum Shutter, Sliding Tripod, one Double Plate Holder, and Canvas Carrying Case.
- 1 Heavy Printing Frame.
- 1 Cone Shaped Graduate for measuring liquids.
- 1 Print Roller for smoothing down prints.
- 1 Heavy 2-inch Paste Brush.
- 1 Dozen Dry Plates.
- 1 Fine Metal Dark Room Lamp, with oil burner.
- 1 Compressed Fiber Tray for developing.
- 1 Compressed Fiber Tray for toning.
- 1 Compressed Fiber Tray for fixing.
- 2 Dozen Sheets Sensitized Paper.
- 25 Card Mounts.
- 1 8-oz. Bottle Concentrated Developer.
- 1 8-ounce Bottle Concentrated Toning and Fixing Solution.
- 1 8-ounce Bottle Intensifier for weak negatives.
- 1 Package Hypo for fixing negatives or prints.
- 1 Jar Photo Mounting Paste.
- 1 Fine Gossamer Focus Cloth.
- 1 Copy "Complete Instruction in Photography."

Taking the 5x7 size as an example, the camera alone, if purchased at retail, would cost $17.00, the lens $15.00, the shutter $9.00, the tripod $2.25, and the developing, finishing and material outfit about $8.80, making the total retail value of the entire outfit over $52.00.

OUR SPECIAL PRICES.

$52.00 WORTH OF GOODS.. FOR **$34.65**

No. 18750 The 5x7 Empire State Photographic utfit, consisting of camera, rapid rectilinear lens, icum shutter, tripod, plate holder and complete tfit, as described above....................$34.65

io. 18751 The 6½x8½ Empire State Photophic Outfit, consisting of camera, rapid rectilin- lens, unicum shutter, tripod, plate holder and plete outfit, as described above...........$43.50

o. 18752 The 8x10 Empire State Photographic fit, consisting of camera, rapid rectilinear lens, um shutter, tripod, plate holder and complete t, as described above.........................$49.75

. 18756 Empire State Outfits without shut- If desired, we can furnish the complete Empire te Outfits, just as described above, without shut-, but fitted with our famous Seroco double rapid tilinear lens, at the following prices: 5x7, $27.50; 6½x8½, $34.95; 8x10, $41.50.

io. 18757 Empire State Outfits with single is. For the benefit of those who do not desire to est in the complete outfit with rectilinear lens l unicum shutter, we can furnish the Empire State tfits, just as described above, without shutter and h our Monarch single achromatic lens, instead he double rectilinear lens, at the following prices: 5x7, $23.25; 6½x8½, $28.50; 8x10, $32.25. rom the profits made with the outfit, the ble rapid rectilinear lens and unicum shut- can be easily added later.

io. 18760 Empire State Cameras without lens, tter or outfit. Empire State Camera, with vas carrying case and one double plate holder, without lens, shutter or outfit:

of View	Weight of Camera	Single Swing	Double Swing
x7	5 lbs.	$14.45	$16.25
½x8½	5¾ lbs.	17.00	18.70
x10	7¾ lbs.	18.70	20.40
x12	8¾ lbs.	23.80	25.50
x14	11½ lbs.	27.20	30.60
x17	23¾ lbs.	36.00	38.25

TRA PLATE HOLDERS. No. 18761 The plate holder used with the Empire State Camera is beyond question the most efficient, most handled and best made holder on the market. In fact, it is one of the features of the . We advise the purchase of a number, as the more holders you have the more plates you can at a time.

Size	Price	Size	Price
5 x7	$1.06	10x12	$2.55
6½x8½	1.37	11x14	3.40
8 x10	1.57	14x17	6.37

JUVENILE MAGIC LANTERN OUTFITS.

The young people not only derive great pleasure from giving MAGIC LANTERN EXHIBITIONS, but the business training which they gain in all the various details connected with the management of an entertainment, putting up advertising posters, selling tickets, etc., gives them ideas of the rudiments of money making which starts them on the highway to business success. REMEMBER that each outfit is complete, containing a fine magic lantern, a splendid assortment of colored views, a large supply of advertising posters, plenty of tickets. INTERESTING, INSTRUCTIVE AND PROFITABLE—You will easily make the original cost of the outfit in your first exhibition; after that it's all profit.

Advertising Posters and Tickets.

No. 19555 Large Size Posters, same as supplied with the outfits, handsomely printed, put up in packages of 25. Price, per package..............15c
If by mail, postage extra, 3 cents.

No. 19556 Admission Tickets, full size, put up in packages of 25. Price, per package..........(If by mail, postage extra, 1 cent.)........10c

NOTE—We cannot make any changes in posters or tickets, or furnish same of special design, as the expense of printing a small lot to order is actually more than we ask for the whole outfit.

The Home Magic Lantern Outfits.

Our illustration gives a very exact idea of the general appearance and construction of the Home Magic Lantern. The body of this lantern is made of metal, japanned in black, handsomely decorated in gilt, and mounted on wood baseboard. Burns ordinary kerosene or coal oil.

No. 19560 The Home Magic Lantern Outfit No. 1, with Home Magic Lantern as described above, using slides $1\frac{3}{16}$ inches wide and magnifying pictures to about one foot in diameter. The complete outfit contains lantern, 6 colored slides, three to four pictures on each slide, 25 advertising posters and 25 admission tickets.
Price, complete..................72c

No. 19561 Home Magic Lantern Outfit No. 2, same as No. 19560, but using slides $1\frac{3}{16}$-inches wide, magnifying pictures to 2 feet and including 12 colored slides instead of 6. Price, complete............................$1.60

No. 19562 Home Magic Lantern Outfit No. 3, same as No. 19561, but using slides 2 inches wide, magnifying pictures to about 3 feet in diameter. Price, complete......$2.48

The Gem Magic Lantern Outfits.

The Gem Magic Lantern, our best grade lantern, is finely finished in Russia sheet iron, lacquered, with brass

lens tube and trimming. The Gem Lantern is provided with a pair of convex condensing lenses, and finely ground projection lens, and has blue glass window in door to protect the eyes from the dazzling light. The lamp with which the Gem lantern is fitted is of the duplex or double burner style, giving a very brilliant illumination. Burns ordinary kerosene or coal oil. A fine instrument for parlor exhibitions.

No. 19570 The Gem Magic Lantern Outfit No. 1, with Gem magic lantern as described above, using slides 2 inches wide and magnifying pictures to about three feet in diameter. The complete outfit consists of the lantern, twelve colored slides, three to four pictures on each slide, one comic slip slide, one movable scenery slide, one brilliantly colored chromotrope or artificial fireworks slide, fifty large advertising posters, and fifty admission tickets.
Price, complete..$6.40

No. 19571 The Gem Magic Lantern Outfit No. 2, same as No. 19570, but using slides $2\frac{3}{8}$ inches wide, magnifying pictures to about four feet in diameter.
Price, complete..$7.90

No. 19572 The Gem Magic Lantern Outfit No. 3, same as No. 19570, but using slides $2\frac{3}{4}$ inches wide, magnifying pictures to about five feet in diameter.
Price, complete..$8.80

View of the Duplex Lamp of the Gem Lantern.

The Brilliant Magic Lantern Outfit.

The Brilliant Magic Lanterns are very handsome instruments of the upright style, finely finished in brass, bronze and nickel plate, with the body of the lantern enameled in bright red. They are provided with double convex condensing lens and finely ground projecting lens. In addition to the regular long glass slides, these lanterns also use a slide in the form of a round disc with six views. Each lantern contained in neat wood box with handle.

Burns Ordinary Kerosene or Coal Oil.

No. 19565 The Brilliant Magic Lantern Outfit No. 1, with Brilliant Magic Lantern as described above, using slides $1\frac{3}{8}$ inches wide, and magnifying pictures to about two feet in diameter. The complete outfit consists of lantern, six long glass colored slides, three to four views on each slide, three glass discs with six colored views on each disc, twenty-five advertising posters and twenty-five admission tickets.
Price, complete..$2.25

No. 19566 Brilliant Magic Lantern Outfit No. 2, same as No. 19565, but using slides $1\frac{3}{4}$ inches wide, magnifying pictures to about three feet in diameter. Price, complete..$3.75

No. 19567 Brilliant Magic Lantern Outfit No. 3, same as No. 19565, but using slides 2 inches wide, magnifying pictures to about four feet in diameter. Price, complete..$4.50

Extra Slides.

Increase your program by adding a few sets of extra slides to outfit.

Plain Colored Slides.

No. 19576 These slides are all highly colored and each slide has from three to four views. They are put up in packages of one dozen slides and each package contains an assortment of both comic and scenic views. We cannot sell less than one package, and we are unable to furnish any special subjects.

Width	Price	Width	Price
$1\frac{3}{16}$ inches, package of 1 dozen..	$0.28	$1\frac{3}{4}$ inches, package of 1 dozen..	$0.60
$1\frac{3}{8}$ inches, package of 1 dozen..	.36	2 inches, package of 1 dozen..	.85
$1\frac{9}{16}$ inches, package of 1 dozen..	.45	$2\frac{3}{8}$ inches, package of 1 dozen..	1.00
		$2\frac{3}{4}$ inches, package of 1 dozen..	1.35

Comic Movable Slides.

No. 19577 These pictures are painted on glass slips, which slide in metal frames, each slide containing two comic views. Very amusing effects are produced by suddenly slipping the second view into the place of the first. Put up in packages of one dozen slides each.

Width, inches	Price, per pkg. of 1 dozen	Width, inches	Price, per pkg. of 1 dozen
$1\frac{3}{8}$	$0.70	2	$1.35
$1\frac{9}{16}$	.85	$2\frac{3}{8}$	1.55
$1\frac{3}{4}$	1.15	$2\frac{3}{4}$	1.75

The Brilliant Slides.

No. 19580 The most economical slides made printed on mica and affording a class of pictures never before offered in anything but high-priced slides. Made in one size only, 2 inches wide, but can be used in any lantern using slides 2 inches or wider. If your lantern uses slides $2\frac{3}{8}$ or $2\frac{3}{4}$-inches wide, we will include, free of charge, a small wooden carrier by means of which you can use these Brilliant slides. Each series of the Brilliant slides contains 12 slides, three pictures on each slide, making a total of 36 views in each series. Order by series.

Series A	Noted Places Around the World.	Price..............50c
Series B	Miscellaneous Views, mostly very comic.	Price..............50c
Series H	Old and New Testament Bible Views.	Price..............50c
Series I	Comic, each good for a laugh.	Price..............50c
Series M	American and Foreign Scenery	Price..............50c

If by mail, postage extra, per set, 1 cent.

Chromotropes.

No. 19585 These Slides, known also as artificial fireworks, consist of two glass discs, painted in bright colors in radiating geometrical patterns, which are revolved in opposite directions by means of the small crank, producing a very brilliant effect. Several different patterns of each size can be furnished.

Width $1\frac{3}{16}$ inches, price, each......32c
Width $1\frac{3}{4}$ inches, price, each......38c
Width 2 inches, price, each......42c
Width $2\frac{3}{8}$ inches, price, each......48
Width $2\frac{3}{4}$ inches, price, each......55

ELECTRICAL GOODS

IN THIS DEPARTMENT we carry a complete line of such electrical goods as are most frequently called for. Upon goods in this line not listed or described in this catalogue, we shall be pleased to submit quotations, and owing to the favorable arrangements we have been able to make with the leading manufacturers, we are in position to quote extremely low prices.

Especial attention is directed to the quality of the electrical goods described herein, every article being the best of its kind and fully guaranteed by us.

TELEGRAPH INSTRUMENTS.

To those who are about to start in life, either ladies or gentlemen, there is nothing at the present time which offers better inducements than telegraphy. The smallest salaries paid are about $35.00 per month, but the salaries usually paid are from $30.00 to $125.00 per month and many even get much more. Besides, the only inducements are not the salary alone, for it opens the way to other and more expansive fields of work.

A large number of the high officials of railroad companies who command salaries from $15,000.00 to $50,000.00 per year started as telegraph operators. Thomas A. Edison, the wonderful inventor, who owns over 600 patents and is immensely wealthy, began as a telegraph operator.

Those who are not familiar with telegraphy are liable to believe that it is something mysterious and difficult to learn, but this is a mistake. It is very easy to learn, can be thoroughly mastered in from two to six months, and with a reasonable amount of care and application it can be learned at home and after a little experience the practice can be made very interesting by constructing a short line between two or more houses, which can be done at a very small expense; all that is necessary is to carefully follow the instructions laid down in this book.

After you have had sufficient practice to enable you to send and read at a moderate speed, a position can be secured as assistant at some railroad office, which will furnish the practical experience, giving an insight into details of the office work, which will fit you to take charge of and manage an office.

The complete Learner's Outfit costs but a trifle, and we advise the purchase of one immediately, no matter if engaged in other work. Telegraphy can be practiced evenings and soon mastered; in fact, the student beginning will make better progress if only a part of the time is devoted to practice.

In addition to our Learner's Instrument, we wish to call special attention to the fact that we list the high grade Standard Western Union Instruments, which need no further recommendation.

Learner's Telegraph Outfit.

No. 19650 Learner's Telegraph Outfit, complete, for telegraphy, consisting of full size sounder and key, mounted on polished cherry base; has full sized battery with wire, chemicals and complete book of instructions, with everything necessary for operating for private practice, complete weight about 10½ lbs. Price............................$2.50

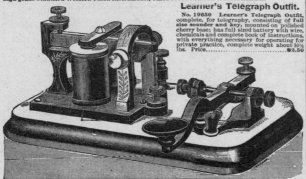

This is the Instrument included with our Learner's Outfit.

Complete Instruments.

Sounder and key mounted on one base.

No. 19652 Learner's Instrument same as above, without battery, weight about 2 pounds.
Each......................................$2.00
No. 19654 Learner's Instrument, mounted on base, as above, but has sounder wound to 20 ohms, for long distance and should be used on line of half mile or more, as it will give better results, weight 2 pounds.
Each......................................$2.25
No. 19656 Private Line Instrument, the highest grade, made with steel lever key, and tubular sounder, same style as Western Union, but one size smaller, on polished cherry wood base, with polished rubber covered coils, wound to 4 ohms resistance. Ea...$3.85
No. 19658 Private Line Instrument, same as above, but wound to 20 ohms resistance...$3.95

Keys.

No. 19667 Steel Lever Key, Standard Western Union, with legs to go through the table. These keys are of the latest and most improved type, the lever and trunions being made of solid steel, nickel plated, instead of brass, as in the old type of instrument. The same strength is secured with much lighter weight and the liability of loose trunions completely avoided. This is without doubt one of the handsomest and best working keys on the market. Its adoption by the Western Union Company is certainly a sufficient recommendation for it. Price......................................$1.50
If by mail, postage extra, 10 cents.

No. 19667 Steel Lever Key, Standard Western Union, legless, with two binding posts to receive the wires. This key is the same as the one described above, with the exception of not having the legs. It is more desirable for screwing on the top of a table. Price, each......................................$1.95
If by mail, postage extra, 10 cents.

Aluminum Sounders.

The perfect construction, fine appearance and loud clear sound yielded make these new Aluminum sounders superior to any other instruments on the market, and we have decided to discontinue all other styles in their favor. The fact that the Western Union Telegraph Co. is now installing these instruments in their offices is sufficient evidence of their quality.

No. 19685 Aluminum Sounder, constructed in best possible manner, mounted on mahogany base, and wound to 4 ohms resistance for short lines.
Price......................................$3.35
No. 19686 Aluminum Sounder, same as No. 19685 but wound to 20 ohms resistance, suitable for lines up to 15 miles in length. Price......................................$3.65

BATTERIES.

Gravity Battery.

The Gravity Battery is a closed circuit battery which is used for telegraphic work, or can be used for operating electric bells, but is not so desirable for bell work on account of evaporation and the necessity for renewing the battery more often.

No. 19746 Gravity Battery, cell complete, size 6x7, weight about 5 pounds.
Each......................................50c
No. 19748 Gravity Battery, cell complete, size 6x8, weight about 7 pounds.
Each......................................60c
No. 19750 Battery Jar, glass, 5x7. Each....25c
No. 19752 Battery Jar, glass, 6x8. Each....30c
No. 19754 Zinc, for 5x7 battery. Each....20c
No. 19756 Zinc, for 6x8 battery. Each....40c
No. 19758 Copper, for 5x7, or 6x8 battery.
Each......................................12c
No. 19759 Blue Vitriol, per pound............8c

Open Circuit Batteries.

For electric bells, burglar alarms, telephone work, etc.

These batteries are intended for use where the circuit is closed only a small portion of the time. If placed on a continuous closed circuit they will soon be exhausted, but for open circuit work such as bells, telephone work, etc., they will last from 12 to 18 months without renewal.
No. 19790 Our Special Battery, a strictly first class open circuit battery, suitable for door bells, telephones, etc., complete with jar, large round carbon, zinc and one charge of sal ammoniac. Price, only............35c
No. 19792 The Le Clede Battery, an old well known, and perfectly reliable battery, complete with zinc carbon, jar and sal ammoniac. Price....35c
No. 19794 The Le Clanche Porous Cell Battery, a very popular style of battery, the porous cup being its distinguishing feature. Price, complete, 40c
No. 19796 Extra Zincs for above batteries. Each, 5c
No. 19797 Sal Ammoniac for recharging above batteries. Per pound............18c

Dry Batteries.

Dry Batteries are largely displacing the wet batteries of La Clede and Le Clanche type for nearly all kinds of work. The principle is the same as Le Clanche. They are clean in every respect and will last from four to eighteen months, depending largely on the amount they are used. They require no attention to keep them in order. When they have run out they are not to be recharged, but must be replaced by a new one. These batteries are largely used for recharging medical batteries.
No. 19865 The Mesco Dry Battery. rice, each............25c

Electric Bells.

No. 19899 Iron Box Bell, with 3 inch nickel plated gong.
Price each......................................35c
No. 19899½ Iron Box Bell, with 4 inch nickel plated gong.
Each......................................45c

Buzzer.

No. 19905 Buzzer, used in place of bells where a loud ringing is not necessary. Makes a buzzing sound heard but a short distance.
Price......................................45c

Electric Door Bell Outfits.

No. 19908 Door Bell Outfit, consisting of 1 cell dry battery, 1 3-inch iron box bell, 75 feet annunciator wire, oak push button, staples for attaching wire, and complete instructions for putting up.
Price, complete............75c
No. 19910 Door Bell Outfit, consisting of 1 cell sal ammoniac battery, 3-inch iron box bell, 75 feet annunciator wire, oak push button, staples and complete instructions for putting up.
Price, complete............95c
No. 19912 Door Bell Outfit, consisting of 2 cells sal ammoniac battery, 3-inch iron box bell, 150 feet annunciator wire, fancy bronze push button, staples and complete instructions for putting up.
Price, complete............$1.65
The instructions sent with these outfits are so simple that anyone without previous experience can put up the bells.

Department of Public Entertainment Outfits and Supplies.

OUR EXPERIENCE in the past has proven to us that public exhibition work is extremely profitable and with a comparatively small investment, affords to the exhibitor, an opportunity for realizing very large profits, and in addition opens up to him a line of business that is pleasant as well as invaluable in the development and building up of a successful business man.

THIS CATALOGUE has been prepared for the information of our friends, and because it has been demonstrated to us that similar outfits which we have put out in the past have been so uniformly successful, as to warrant us in encouraging others to embark in the same line, and while it is an undoubted fact, that until recently, there has been but a limited amount of energy and capital expended in this direction, we believe this to be largely due to insufficient information as to what is required to make up a suitable outfit for the purpose, how the work can be started profitably, how it can be carried on successfully, how it may be made a permanent livelihood, and with ability, energy and push, be the means of enabling the exhibitor to accumulate a fortune.

PUBLIC EXHIBITION WORK is and always has been a pleasant and profitable business, but it has never been brought to the same state of perfection, never been placed within the grasp of the man of limited means, never been represented in such an attractive fashion as now. Our outfits are entirely new, are founded on the newest kind of intensely interesting, new and up-to-date subjects. The business is pleasant because you are independent, and that it is a successful one is demonstrated by the good fortune which has attended the efforts of those who have purchased similar outfits from us in the past. Elsewhere will be found a few selections from the many hundred testimonials we have received bearing upon the same subject, and upon application we will furnish sheets containing a great number of similar testimonials to the beauty, value and profit producing qualities of these outfits; and above all it must not be forgotten that wider fields are now accessible for this work; that the times are more prosperous, and consequently the demand for this class of entertainment has enormously increased. We shall endeavor to outline outfits embracing the wonderful moving or animated picture machine, projecting pictures life size, lifelike and with lifelike motion, the ever popular panoramic stereopticon exhibition, and last but by no means least, the marvel of the century, the graphophone talking machine, reproducing the human voice, the songs of noted vocalists and the strains of the finest bands, with the most astounding accuracy and fidelity.

WHAT MAKES THIS WORK all the more interesting and attractive is that no previous experience is necessary, no ability as a public speaker is required, and some of the most successful entertainers to whom we have supplied outfits in the past had never spoken in public before, but with the outfit we furnished them and by dint of diligence and attention to business have made incomes three, four and five times as much as they did in their previous occupation.

Do not let this money making opportunity pass and when it is too late, say, "I am sorry I did not take hold of it."

WE GUARANTEE every machine, apparatus and appliance sold by us to be exactly as represented, to work perfectly and to give perfect satisfaction.

THIS DEPARTMENT is in charge of an expert, who is constantly in communication with exhibitors all over the country, and while we have endeavored to make everything very plain, and have treated every outfit and each machine very fully, in our book of instructions, which accompanies each and every shipment, we will take pleasure in advising anyone who purchases their outfit from us, or in answering any question from those who are anticipating the purchase of an outfit.

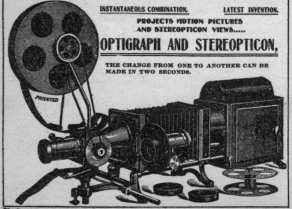

INSTANTANEOUS COMBINATION. LATEST INVENTION.

PROJECTS MOTION PICTURES AND STEREOPTICON VIEWS.....

OPTIGRAPH AND STEREOPTICON,

THE CHANGE FROM ONE TO ANOTHER CAN BE MADE IN TWO SECONDS.

OUR TERMS are most liberal. Any outfit selected will be sent by freight or express, upon payment of a small deposit, C. O. D., and subject to the fullest examination. You can examine it at your nearest station and if you find it perfectly satisfactory, exactly as we represent it, if you are well pleased with the outfit and consider it affords a big opportunity and is a big money maker, you can pay the balance of the C. O. D., with freight or express charges and take up the shipment. If it is not satisfactory, if you do not find it to be just as we represented it, or if you have any reasons to be disappointed with the outfit, it may be returned to us at our expense, and we will promptly refund any money you have paid on it.

OUR MOVING PICTURE DEPARTMENT is one of the most perfectly equipped in our enormous establishment and we frankly assure our customers that we carry in stock a larger selection of necessaries for this work than all other dealers in similar lines in the West combined; If you desire information on any subject in the entire line of Stereopticon and Moving Picture work, write us, or if you contemplate a purchase and live within a reasonable distance of Chicago, see us, and we guarantee to save you the cost of your trip in information and instruction many times over.

A FIRST CLASS....
STEREOPTICON

AND THE ONLY SUCCESSFUL COMBINATION EVER PRODUCED...

No. 21205 Stereopticon with the Improved 1900 Model Optigraph, complete with either calcium burner or electric arc lamp included. Price..................**$64.00**

No. 21206 Stereopticon with 1899 Model Optigraph, complete with either calcium burner or electric arc lamp. Price..................**$54.00**

SEND FOR OUR FREE 128-PAGE CATALOGUE OF ENTERTAINMENT OUTFITS, the most complete, best illustrated catalogue of the kind ever published. The catalogue gives a complete description of everything in the line of lecture outfits, and tells how to make a success of the business. Whether you buy a cent's worth or not, the catalogue will be valuable to you.

The Optigraph or Moving Picture Machine

Is a comparatively New Invention, which projects apparently living and moving figures upon a screen or canvas . . . . . .

Model 1900.

YOU TURN THE CRANK, THE MACHINE DOES THE REST

THE MACHINE FOR HIGH CLASS EXHIBITORS

Successfully Used in Leading Theaters.

The Optigraph Attachment, to be used with any regular Stereopticon or Magic Lantern.

THE MOST PERFECT MOVING PICTURE MACHINE EVER MADE.

PRESENTS A SHARP, CLEAR AND BRILLIANT PICTURE.

Action of the machine is perfectly free from any flicker, and does not wear or tear the films.

WILL RUN FILMS AS READILY BACKWARD AS FORWARD,

with no stop or complicated adjustment. Uses large lenses of three different ranges, with rack and pinion for adjustment of focus.

It represents the highest branch in the art of photography and brings before the eye exact life size reproductions, with all the accompanying effects of light, shadow and expression. Hundreds of interesting and realistic subjects are now being exhibited through the agency of this machine. Our list is practically unlimited, and there is a range from grave to gay, from the sublime to the ridiculous, charges of soldiery in actual engagements, mounted cavalry charging at full speed, acrobatic performances, trains at a great rate of speed, and in fact all kinds of locomotion, from the mule train to the limited express, and from the smallest boat to the Atlantic Liner are shown.

No. 21300

PRICE, - $35.00

WE SHOW HEREWITH AN ILLUSTRATION

...OF OUR...

GREAT COMBINED STEREOPTICON and MOVING PICTURE MACHINE.....

ADAPTED FOR PROJECTING BOTH STATIONARY AND ANIMATED PICTURES, AND COMPLETE WITHIN ITSELF.

Many of our customers, however, are already provided with the lantern or stereopticon, with which the Optigraph or moving picture attachment can be used.

WE SHOW THE TWO LATEST AND MOST PRACTICAL MODELS OF THE MOVING PICTURE MACHINE EVER PLACED UPON THE MARKET IN OUR . . . .

1899 MODEL AT $25.00

...AND OUR...

1900 MODEL AT $35.00

BOTH of these are designed to be used as an attachment to or in connection with the regular professional Magic Lantern or Stereopticon, and while the combination with the stereopticon, as shown above, in connection with the sliding attachment for instantaneous changing from stationary to moving picture or vice versa, is perhaps the most perfect and convenient procurable, perfect work can be attained with either of these two moving picture machines in connection with any regular lantern. These two machines afford chance and an opportunity to make selection which cannot be excelled. The optigraph in both types exceeds all other machines for projecting moving pictures in many of the most essential points and qualifications looked for by the successful exhibitor.

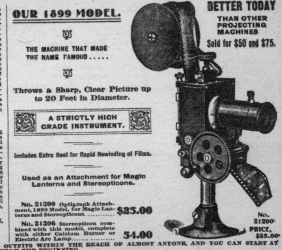

BETTER TODAY

THAN OTHER PROJECTING MACHINES

Sold for $50 and $75.

STEADY PICTURES

are one of the most important and valuable features of these machines, a point which is appreciated and praised by all exhibitors who have used other moving picture machines. This is due to perfect workmanship, superior material and the lightness of parts. The Optigraph is compact, consequently it is easy to handle, easy to move about from place to place and can be carried in a small hand case or satchel. Simplicity is another feature which distinguishes the optigraph from all other machines. It is so simple that a child can run it. The absence of noise is a feature of great value in the Optigraph moving picture machine. It works with a motion so easy, smooth and perfect there is almost no noise at all. There is an entire absence of friction on the picture surface of the film, thus doing away with the marks and scratches which are often seen on films used in other machines. When used in connection with the Enterprise Stereopticon, as shown above, and the instantaneous sliding attachment, the moving picture apparatus can in less than a second be slid out of position, and the machine is at once ready for stereopticon or stationary work. The same is true in changing from stereopticon to animated pictures.

AT PURCHASER'S OPTION

this machine can be fitted with lenses of different range without additional expense. The new 1900 Model No. 3 Optigraph represents the highest point of perfection attained in this class of machine and is the high class exhibitor's standard of excellence. It will run films backwards as well as forwards without stop or complicated adjustment. This will double the length of an exhibition, and is one of the most entertaining and available features in connection with the motion pictures. It has large reels accommodating as high as 500 feet of film, or if provided with special reel 1,200 feet can be handled. In this way a whole exhibition can be placed on reel at one time, dispensing with the necessity of changing films during the exhibition. It can be fitted with an automatic rewind attachment, which will take up and rewind the film as it runs from the reel. This is, however, a feature not regularly supplied.

IT WILL PROJECT PICTURES OF ANY SIZE, AND AT ANY DISTANCE, AND IS GUARANTEED TO DO ANY WORK THAT ANY OTHER MOTION PICTURE MACHINE WILL DO, AND DO IT BETTER.

OUR 1899 MODEL.

THE MACHINE THAT MADE THE NAME FAMOUS . . . . .

Throws a Sharp, Clear Picture up to 20 Feet in Diameter.

A STRICTLY HIGH GRADE INSTRUMENT.

Includes Extra Reel for Rapid Rewinding of Films.

Used as an Attachment for Magic Lanterns and Stereopticons.

No. 21200 Optigraph Attachment, 1899 Model, for Magic Lanterns and Stereopticons. $25.00

No. 21206 Stereopticon combined with this model, complete with either Calcium Burner or Electric Arc Lamp. 54.00

No. 21200 PRICE, $25.00

OUR SPECIAL STEREOPTICON LECTURE DEPARTMENT.

DO YOU WISH TO MAKE MONEY WITH LITTLE EFFORT?

**PLEASANT AND HONORABLE EMPLOYMENT.
SHORT HOURS AND LITTLE EFFORT.
NO SOLICITING AND NO GOODS TO SELL.**

TO THOSE WHO ARE NOT SATISFIED with their present occupation, to those whose income is perhaps less than $1,000 per year, we direct your attention to the unrivaled opportunities presented by our special lecture outfits. Place your order for one of these special outfits. Your first week's work will more than pay for this investment, your first evening's work may pay for it.
NO PREVIOUS EXPERIENCE or no ability as a public speaker is required, as the description of the view is printed and can be read while they are shown with the stereopticon.
A COMPARATIVELY SMALL INVESTMENT will enable you to make a start. For example: $54.50 will buy for you any one of our special lecture exhibition outfits, a few of

which we enumerate. Our lecture on Cuba, the explosion of the Battleship Maine and the War with Spain, which it precipitated, has always been and continues to be very popular, and in the past has made for our customers thousands of dollars. Our somewhat similar lecture on Our New Possessions is perhaps of more interest as dealing with events which have more lately transpired. Our newest lecture on the Boer and English War, with vivid and beautiful scenes, descriptive of life, scenery and incidents in the Transvaal and South African republics, will sweep the country. Along the same line we offer some of the very newest lecture sets produced, "Scenes in Paris and the Exposition," "Around the World in Eighty Minutes," and other lecture sets and miscellaneous slides which we describe fully on the next page.

A COMPLETE PROFESSIONAL STEREOPTICON LECTURE EXHIBITION OUTFIT FOR ONLY $54.50

PROJECTS A CLEAR, BRILLIANT AND PERFECTLY OUTLINED PICTURE 10 FEET SQUARE . . . .

This illustration is made from a photograph of the stereopticon as it appears in operation.

Our Special Stereopticon Offer : : : : :

FOR ONLY

$54.50

we will furnish you with one of our high power, single stereopticons and a special lecture set, complete in every item and detail, ready to go to work, an outfit that is a big money-maker and a

Stereopticon Outfit . . . .

equal to those that have been offered heretofore at $75.00 to $100.00.

OUR REGULAR ILLUSTRATED STEREOPTICON OUTFITS ARE OFFERED FOR $54.50

and represent the greatest bargain in the way of an exhibition outfit ever gotten up.

52 MAGNIFICENT TRANSPARENT PHOTOGRAPHIC VIEWS, **1 POLISHED WOOD CASE FOR THE VIEWS,** **1 SPECIAL HIGH POWER SINGLE STEREOPTICON,** **1 GIANT INCANDESCENT VAPOR ILLUMINATING APPARATUS,** **1 BURNER FOR VAPOR LIGHT, (or, if preferred, and at the same price)** **1 CRITERION GENERATER AND SIMPLEX BURNER FOR ACETYLENE** **ILLUMINATION,**	**ALL FOR** **$54.50** But Worth Twice the Price.	**1 POLISHED WOOD CARRYING CASE FOR STEREOPTICON,** **1 LARGE WHITE SCREEN (120 square feet),** **1 LECTURE, BOUND IN BOOK FORM,** **1,000 LARGE ILLUSTRATED ADVERTISING POSTERS,** **2,000 EXHIBITION ADMISSION TICKETS,** **1 PRINTING OUTFIT FOR FILLING IN DATES, ETC.,** **1 BOOK OF INSTRUCTIONS.**

THE STEREOPTICON provided with this outfit is the Enterprise Stereopticon, with the Giant incandescent vapor light. It is the highest grade of lantern made.
THE INCANDESCENT VAPOR LAMP is the latest invention, many times stronger than kerosene, and will be found fully described on another page.
THE ACETYLENE GENERATER which will be furnished with this lecture set, instead of the Giant lamp where preferred, throws a brilliant picture and is so simple that a child can operate it.
THE 52 MAGNIFICENT PHOTOGRAPHIC VIEWS are made on glass, with glass covers to protect the picture from injury, are each of them works of art, and

when illuminated by vapor lamp or acetylene gas, magnified by the powerful lenses and projected on a screen, they cease to be photographs and have a depth and appearance so true to nature that the audience will almost forget they are not looking upon the original scene.
THE SCREEN is made from fine white material, 12 feet square, provided with ropes and hooks for hanging it.
THE LECTURE is printed in book form, and consists of a short introduction and an interesting description of each view.
THE POLISHED WOOD VIEW CASE is well made, is fitted with brass trimmings, and has dividers for separating the views.

THE ADVERTISING POSTERS are very large, are printed on tinted paper, and illustrated with attractive engravings, with blank spaces left for filling in the place where lecture is to be given, date, prices of admission, etc.
THE ADMISSION TICKETS are printed in good taste on tough cardboard, and the quantity is made large enough to accommodate any size crowd.
THE PRINTING OUTFIT is provided with a case of movable large rubber type, a holder, tweezers and ink pad.
THE BOOK OF INSTRUCTIONS contains full information for the operation of the outfit, showing the pictures, delivering the description of them, and particularly as to the best way to make the business a financial success.

THE ABOVE LECTURE SET COMPRISES A MOST COMPLETE STEREOPTICON EXHIBITION OUTFIT.

ALL THAT REMAINS to be done is the selection of the particular lecture set desired, for which purpose please consider carefully the following description of our various leading lecture sets:
THE SPANISH-AMERICAN WAR AND THE PHILIPPINES—Illustrated.
THE BOER-ENGLISH WAR AND SCENES IN SOUTH AFRICA.
SCENES IN PARIS AND THE EXPOSITION.   SHADOWS OF A GREAT CITY.
CUBA, THE MAINE AND THE CUBAN WAR.   AROUND THE WORLD IN EIGHTY MINUTES.
THE LIFE OF CHRIST ON EARTH.   THE KLONDIKE REGION AND ITS DEVELOPMENT.

THE FIRST FIVE of these sets comprise 52 slides or views, of which 10 are beautifully colored and 42 plain photographic tints. The Life of Christ and the Klondike set each include 50 slides, 10 colored and 40 plain. "Around the World in Eighty Minutes," which is certain to be the most permanent and popular of all our slide sets, is made up either in a set of 52 slides, same as the other lectures, or in full set of 80 slides, of which 30 are colored. Any of these 50 or 52-slide sets may be selected, and the price of the complete lecture outfit will be the same, $54.50.

OUR SPECIAL CONCERT GRAPHOPHONE

..EXHIBITION OUTFIT..

THIS OUTFIT is especially designed for the use of those who wish to engage in public exhibition work. CONCERT GRAPHOPHONE REGULAR $25.00 TALKING MACHINE, and hearing tubes for eleven persons.

No. 21046

The outfit consists of the following:

1 Concert $25.00 Graphophone, with oak carrying-case, recording and reproducing diaphragm.

Hearing Tubes for 11 persons.

24 Musical Records, your own selection.

26-Inch Japanned Horn and Stand.

1,000 Advertising Posters

2,000 Admission Tickets.

1 Rubber Stamping Outfit

ALL ..FOR $45.25

No. 21046

We furnish a very superior canvas covered case for 36 records, with nickel trimmings, lock and key, complete, for $5.00.

COMBINATION ADVERTISING POSTERS AND TICKETS will be furnished when desired instead of Graphophone posters, if the exhibitor has purchased any other exhibition outfit of us.

FOR $10.00 ADDITIONAL we can furnish our genuine brass amplifying horn 42 inches long, with handsome nickel plated stand. This horn will give the loudest and clearest results possible to obtain.

Price of Outfit No. 21046, with 42-inch brass amplifying horn.............**$55.75**

If the hearing tubes for 11 persons are not required they may be omitted, reducing the price of this outfit to.....................................**$38.25**

WITH OUR OUTFITS we furnish 24 of the highest grade, loudest records that can be produced. Nothing is so important in the make-up of an exhibition outfit as the records. Many dealers in these goods cheapen their outfits by using a poor quality of records and this fact is never noted by the purchaser until he gives his first entertainment. We guarantee our records to be the best that can be produced. There are many grades, but in our great special exhibition offer we include none except the highest grade, electrically recorded, new process records. Every record is tested before it leaves our establishment, and only those are sent out which are up to the highest standard, and are absolutely perfect, loud, clear and brilliant.

DO YOU WANT TO MAKE MONEY and with little effort entertain the public. THE GRAPHOPHONE MUSICAL AND TALKING MACHINE will fill the bill, and do all and more than you anticipate. IT IS A WONDER, and with proper management, will draw crowded houses every evening.

A Coin in The Slot Talking Machine for $20.00.

..THE AUTOMATIC MONEY-MAKER..

FURNISHED FOR EITHER PENNIES or 5-CENT PIECES.

Former Price, $50.00 to $75.00.

FOR STORE, OFFICE and **COUNTER WORK.**

No better paying investment can be made than to put a few of these machines into stores and other public places on shares, giving the proprietor of the premises 25 per cent of the receipts, which is customary for his share. The owner of the instruments can go on with his regular duties during the day and he can successfully conduct two different enterprises in this way.

No. 21017

Read what a Druggist in a Small Town in Minnesota writes:

"Gentlemen: I consider one of your graphophones, the style I have, a great investment for a drug store. In two months, one machine took in $75.00, and still does a good business, and in addition has been a great drawing-card."

OPPORTUNITIES WAIT FOR NO MAN! NOW IS THE CHANCE. Invest in one machine at the start, if your capital will admit of no greater purchase, and then add others from the income.

THE PRICE OF $20.00 does not include records, which we can furnish, best quality and particularly adapted to this type of machine, for $5.00 per dozen.

No. 21017 Coin in the slot graphophone..................$20.00

..FOR THE BEST, LATEST AND LOUDEST GRAPHOPHONE RECORDS...

refer to following pages, or better still, send for our free 128-page Special Entertainment Outfit Catalogue which illustrates and fully describes our complete line of records. The most varied assortment shown by any concern. You can make money with the Graphophone.

THE LATEST AND THE GREATEST The Columbia Grand.

USES 5-INCH CYLINDER RECORDS.

Application of new principle, in recording and reproducing. Absolute perfection obtained at last.

Cut represents machine with small recording horn only.

THE MONEY-MAKER OF THE AGE.

.. Will pay for itself in one week ..

The graphophone has been developed step by step, until today the Columbia Grand stands upon the pinnacle of perfection.

FOR REPRODUCING AND CONCERT WORK WE RECOMMEND A LARGER HORN.

ACTUALLY ACCOMPLISHES WHAT HAS HITHERTOFORE BEEN DENIED THE IMPOSSIBLE.

Perfectly reproduces the human voice. Just as loud, just as clear, just as sweet. Duplicates instrumental music with perfect fidelity, tone and brilliancy.

The Columbia Grand Fills the Largest Auditorium or Concert Hall, AND NEVER FAILS TO CHARM ALL WHO HEAR IT.

IT IS THE TALKING MACHINE LONG LOOKED FOR— bringing the singer, the musician or the orchestra, into the audible presence of the listener. Those familiar with other types, but who have never listened to the Graphophone Grand, have no conception of its wonders.

THE PRICE OF THIS MACHINE IS LOW, considering its unique character and the marvelous results which can be obtained from it in sound reproduction. When first produced, less than six months ago, this machine sold readily for $100. We are now able to offer for the first time, the same machine, of the same sterling qualities, the same loudness and beauty of tone, the same wonderfully vibrant and clear reproduction, for the unapproachable price of $50.00, while the five-inch cylinder records will be furnished for $1.00 each.

No. 21050 The Columbia Grand. Price...................**$50.00**

THE SUCCESS OF THE COLUMBIA GRAND has been demonstrated in New York, Washington and Chicago, in some cases to an audience composed of 2,000 people, with the most satisfactory results, even to those in the remote corners of the hall, the reproduction being heard as loudly and plainly as by those in the front seats

For Exhibition Work The COLUMBIA GRAND is Without a Peer.

NOT ONLY AS A TALKING MACHINE, but in its power of entertaining and amazing an audience, and above all as a money getter. It cannot at the present time, be equaled by any other entertainment feature now before the public.

AN UNSURPASSED OPPORTUNITY PRESENTS ITSELF to those who are first in the field, of making not only big wages, but a small fortune in an easy, honorable and pleasant manner.

THE RECORDS FURNISHED BY US with these machines are incomparable. Each and every one is a master or original record, personally tested in our own laboratory by our own special expert. They are 1 foot, 3¼ inches in circumference, and owing to the care exercised in their making and inspection cannot be equaled elsewhere. Cost of Grand Records has heretofore been $2.50. We have reduced price to...**$1.00 Each.**

For list of Grand Records see following pages where all numbers preceded by the letter G are furnished as Grand Records.

OUR COLUMBIA GRAND ENTERTAINMENT OUTFIT.

NO. 21080 IS THE GREATEST WINNER for exhibition work that we have ever been able to offer to our customers. It is especially designed for those who intend to engage in exhibition work as a permanent livelihood and who wish to fit themselves out with the best that money will buy. The outfit includes:

1 Columbia Grand, with handsome oak cabinet.

1 Grand Reproducer.

1 New Style or Perfect Recorder.

1 Grand Shaving knife and adjustable carriage.

1 specially adapted Brass Horn for recording work.

1 42-inch handsome Brass Amplifying Horn, with spun bell and finely nickel plated stand.

12 Grand Records.

1,000 Mammoth Grand Posters, with special illustrations.

1,000 Admission Tickets, 500 adults and 500 children.

1 Hand Rubber Stamp outfit for filling in dates.

All for $75.00

FOR ILLUSTRATED SONG WORK THIS MACHINE IS UNEQUALED.

:: THE SEROCO MAGIC LANTERN. ::

THE SEROCO IS A WELL MADE MAGIC LANTERN. Is constructed expressly for professional work. This and the Enterprise are the only professional lanterns that we list this year, as the two cover the field entirely and will fill the demand for a low priced lantern as well as the highest grade stereopticon money can buy.

THE SEROCO HAS A POLISHED OAK BASE, with planished steel lamp house with hinged door at the rear end, bellows for adjusting the focus, a fine double rectilinear objective lens with rack and pinion for fine adjustment of focus and 4-inch condensing lenses. The front, condenser mountings, rods and brackets are heavily nickel plated, and add much to the beauty and appearance of the lantern. We furnish with this lantern either the 4-wick kerosene lamp, a calcium jet for calcium light, or an acetylene gas burner all complete for **$22.50**
No. 21535   ORDER BY NUMBER.
Electric light can also be used in this lantern. Above prices are for lanterns alone and do not provide for any equipment, such as screens, views, etc.

No. 21535

≡ Profit, Amusement and Instruction for the Young Folks. ≡

By giving Parlor Exhibitions with our No. 21600
Illustrated Lecture Exhibition Outfits . . . .

A $20.00 COMPLETE OUTFIT FOR $10.60. THE OUTFIT CONSISTS OF one good quality magic lantern; 30 fine magic lantern views, choice of 3 sets, either comic pictures, American history or bible history; 1 slide holder, for holding views in place in the lantern; a well written lecture, especially suited to audiences composed of young folks; 100 large advertising posters, 9x12 inches, with 1 rubber printing outfit for filling in places where exhibitions are to be given, dates, etc.; 200 admission tickets; 1 carrying case for outfit and everything needed to successfully conduct a regular exhibition business. This is a plan which will appeal to almost any intelligent youth, and should be encouraged by parents; for by charging a small price for admission, say 5 to 10 cents, the cost of the outfit will be made in a few evenings and all further effort will be rewarded by net profit.

THE EXHIBITIONS WILL BE APPRECIATED AND ENJOYED BY BOTH YOUNG AND OLD, but especially caters to the taste of those from 5 to 10 years old.

COMPLETE FOR $10.60

THE LECTURE CONSISTS OF A SHORT DESCRIPTION OF EACH SLIDE, AND IS TO BE READ ALOUD AS THE VIEWS ARE SHOWN ON THE SCREEN.

Radiants for Use in Illuminating and Projecting from the Stereopticon and Magic Lantern

THE GIANT

Incandescent Vapor Light.

THE NEWEST,
THE BEST,

For the projection of stereopticon pictures this light has produced a complete revolution.

THE GIANT INCANDESCENT LIGHT IS NEXT TO THE CALCIUM, the strongest and most brilliant light for projection purposes known, and is about six times stronger than the best form of kerosene illumination. The apparatus is small, light, perfectly safe, clean to handle, emits no disagreeable odor; it is the most economical form of light made, and will throw a good clear picture up to ten and twelve feet square with an ordinary quarter size lens.

DESCRIPTION OF THE GIANT INCANDESCENT VAPOR LIGHT. The basic principle of this lighting apparatus is similar to the Welsbach gas burner, but the gasoline vapor furnishes a much purer hydrogen gas than is used for house illumination, and the high air pressure adds efficiency, and makes the flow of gas perfectly steady; it has a mantle made on an entirely new principle, of extra heavy material, especially prepared with a chemical preparation of recent discovery. The arrangement and perfecting of this apparatus and its adoption for magic lantern and stereopticon illumination in the latest work of a well known scientist and expert in this line. To operate the apparatus is extremely simple, in fact, is almost as easy to use as an ordinary gasoline stove.
No. 21603   Price, including air pump and burner, complete, two extra mantles **$14.50**
No. 21604   Extra mantles, each .... .25
No. 21605   Extra burner with two mantles and metal chimney for use with double stereopticon.......... **$5.50**
No. 21585   Dissolving key for vapor lamp.......... 7.50

No. 21603

ACETYLENE GAS FOR STEREOPTICON ILLUMINATION........

A REALLY HIGH CLASS LIGHT, FOR THE PROJECTION OF STEREOPTICON PICTURES. PORTABLE, SIMPLE, DURABLE, INEXPENSIVE AND CLEAN. PRODUCES A BRILLIANT LIGHT.

THE NEW SEROCO GENERATOR WITH DRIP CUP ATTACHMENT AND BEST ACETYLENE BURNER. While it has been generally conceded that Acetylene gas provides an almost ideal light for stereopticon work, trouble has sometimes been experienced in keeping a steady light during the entire entertainment, as the gas in generating increases the temperature of the water and more or less steam or vapor is carried into the rubber tube, where it condenses and retards the flow of gas. Various methods have been adopted to overcome this difficulty, but our "drip cup" attachment shown in cut is the only one that has proved entirely satisfactory; any accumulation of water which may form runs at once to the drip cup and the tube is kept free and clear and a brilliant and even flow of gas is the result. The generator outfit consists of generator, rubber tubing, drip cup and five pounds of carbide in tins. (Burner is not included.) The light is strong and very simple to operate, the gas is made automatically as used, and an explosion is therefore impossible.
No. 21605½   Price of generator outfit, complete..........**$8.00**
No. 21587   THE BEST BURNER consists of four tips, each having four air chambers and two gas jets, which unite in one dazzling white flame, giving perfect combustion, and an ideal light. Price..........**$7.00**

No. 21605½

OUR TALKING MACHINE DEPARTMENT.

THE GRAPHOPHONE or Talking Machine.

The Perfect Musical and Talking Machine.   Tried, Tested and Guaranteed.   A Public Entertainer of Unrivaled Merit and a Mint of Money for the Exhibitor.

USED FOR PUBLIC EXHIBITION WORK,

Our Entertainment Outfits described elsewhere, will pay for themselves in from ONE TO THREE NIGHTS.

And by reason of their simplicity, the ease with which they can be operated, the attractiveness of the programme presented, they are the best and most popular form of outfit for parties desirous of embarking in exhibition work on a comparatively limited capital.

THE WONDERFUL HOME GRAPHOPHONE FOR $5.00.

NOT A TOY BUT A HIGH GRADE AND PERFECT TALKING MACHINE. Especially Intended For Home Use.

No. 21036

Louder, more brilliant in its reproduction, and in every way better than the machine which five years ago sold for $50.00. We offer this complete and perfect Graphophone for.... **$5.00**

THIS TALKING MACHINE is not intended for public exhibition outfits. For this purpose, we offer and recommend the larger types of machines already described; but as a home entertainer the Home Graphophone is growing more popular daily, and for this purpose we cannot too strongly recommend it.

No. 21030 Home Graphophone, complete with horn and hearing tube for.... **$5.00** It will brighten the home, entertain and delight yourselves, your family and friends; keep you in touch with the best and latest music by the finest bands and singers, and in a week repay the first trifling expense many times over.

No. 21031 With 12 records you can possess a family concert outfit for.... **$10.00**

1 Home Graphophone,	$5.00
1 Extra Loud Reproducing Diaphragm	
1 Concert Horn	$5.00
1 Hearing Tube	
1 Dozen Best and Loudest Records, your own selection	5.00
Total	$10.00

THE GRAPHOPHONE OR TALKING MACHINE

has proved itself in the past, and we believe always will be a most successful and popular entertainer. The novelty and wonder of the natural reproduction of the human voice as well as band and instrumental music insures preliminary interest, and the performance itself is so wonderfully realistic and the actual reproduction of speech and music of such a quality as could not otherwise be realized.

THEY REPRODUCE WITH STARTLING ACCURACY the productions of the most noted bands, orchestras, vocalists, public speakers and the songs, music or conversation of self or friends. The performance of the Graphophone are not confined to the reproduction of regular factory made records, but, when provided with a recording diaphragm, they will record and reproduce any words spoken to it, or song sung to it, and such records may be preserved and reproduced at any time.

AS A MONEY MAKER or as a home entertainer it has no equal. It is one of the most wonderful of all inventions, and yet its construction is so extremely simple that it causes the observer to wonder that its basic principle did not lead to its discovery long ago.

RECENT IMPROVEMENTS, simplicity of construction, replacing the expensive electric motors, their manufacture, making them in very large quantities, etc., has enabled us to make arrangements with the manufacturers whereby we can now offer this most wonderful little machine, complete with all the necessary accessories, at a price which not only brings them within the easy reach of those of small means, who wish to give public entertainments, but they can be owned by almost any family as a source of home amusement.

AS A MONEY MAKER THE GRAPHOPHONE HAS NO EQUAL.

A MACHINE WHICH WILL RECORD OR MAKE RECORDS AS WELL AS REPRODUCE THEM.

WE ARE OFTEN ASKED by our customers for a machine with which they can make records as well as reproduce those already made. In response to their wishes we have made up and offer at a wonderfully close price

...THE PEERLESS TALKING MACHINE...

New Peerless Graphophone for Only $10.00

RECORDS AND REPRODUCES.

No. 21035

It is the same machine as the HOME GRAPHOPHONE just described, with the addition of a handsome oak base and carrying case, and is provided with a recording as well as a reproducing diaphragm, so that it can be used for making original records as well as reproducing those already made.

THIS MACHINE is both a home entertainer and a money maker. You can play or sing to this graphophone, and it will record and reproduce the same, as many times as desired. Its imitation of the human voice is so perfect as to deceive almost anyone. Anyone can operate it, there is nothing to get out of order and it will never wear out. This machine is specially intended for those who desire an instrument that will afford them the highest class of home amusement and entertainment, and also start them in an easy, pleasant and profitable exhibition business, at which many are now making better money, with less time and labor, than ever before in their lives.

THIS OUTFIT being often used for the smaller class of exhibitions, we have made up a complete and perfect outfit for the purpose, the items of which we give below. Particular attention is directed to the Liqui-Para process included in this outfit without additional charge. This dispenses with the use of an expensive shaving knife, and will completely efface and remove the record from any cylinder in less than a minute, leaving it with a smooth, fine surface, and ready for the recording of any new record which may be desired.

DOING A GOOD BUSINESS.

Colquhoun, Ontario, Canada.

Sears, Roebuck & Co.
Gentlemen: I am doing a good business with my graphophone. People that hear it once, come again, so that I want, and here give you an order for two dozen new selections. With these records I can give a change of program. Ship promptly, because I have a large hall engaged.
Yours truly,
DELBERT CHILEY.

MACHINE PLAINLY HEARD IN HALL 50x100 FEET.

Manitou, Colo.

Messrs. Sears, Roebuck & Co.
Dear Sirs: I received my suit, also the graphophone and records. Everything was all right. I am more than pleased with both the suit and graphophone. I should have written before, but have been too busy playing to my friends. There are several machines in town, some that cost $25.00, but everyone admits mine to be the best they have ever heard. I had the machine in a hall 50x100 feet last evening, and every word was plain at any part of the hall. There are three or four talking as though they would like one of your machines, and as I am so well pleased with the courteous manner in which you have used me, I would like to be able to show up my machine in the best possible manner. Thanking you for your courteous treatment in the past and assuring you of future orders, I remain,
Yours respectfully,
C. H. WALLACE.

SPECIAL OFFER PRICE FOR COMPLETE HOME OR EXHIBITION OUTFIT No. 21036.

1 Peerless Graphophone (No. 21035) with handsome oak carrying case.	
1 Recording Diaphragm.	
1 Reproducing Diaphragm.	
1 Nickel Plated Concert Horn.	
1 Dozen best selected Musical or Talking Records.	
½ Dozen Blank Cylinders for making Records.	**ALL FOR**
1 Substantial Pasteboard Record Carrying Case for 24 Records.	**$18.75**
1 Bottle Liqui-Para for paring blank cylinders.	
500 Advertising Posters.	
1,000 Admission Tickets.	
1 Instruction Book.	

OUR LEADER, THE NEW GEM GRAPHOPHONE TALKING MACHINE.

YOU CAN MAKE $5.00 TO $25.00 every evening by giving public exhibitions in halls, churches, school houses, etc., at 15 to 25 cents admission, or by using with hearing tubes and charging 5 cents for each individual.

No. 21000 Gem Graphophone, with two hearing tubes and concert horn, but without oak base and carrying case...... **$10.00**

No. 21001 Gem Graphophone, with two hearing tubes, concert horn and handsome oak carrying case with handle, as illustrated...... **$12.00**

Above price does not include records. Price of our best musical and talking records is $5.00 per dozen or 50 cents each when ordered in less than dozen quantities.

FROM THE ILLUSTRATION, engraved by our artist direct from a photograph of the outfit, you can form a good idea of the appearance of this, OUR SPECIAL OFFER $23.75 PROFESSIONAL TALKING MACHINE EXHIBITION OUTFIT, but you must see and compare it with other graphophone outfits to appreciate the real value we are offering.

THE GEM GRAPHOPHONE

IS A CONCERT SIZE MACHINE and an exceedingly handsome one, thoroughly well made in every respect, and perfectly finished. It is provided with a powerful spring motor, guaranteed not to get out of order. The gears and pinions are machine cut, insuring perfect accuracy of action. It is provided with governor and tension screw, which effectually regulates the speed. Runs two pieces with one winding. Has the latest automatic, extra loud, aluminum reproducer; new style, extra long bearing record mandrel. The machine is substantially mounted on a handsome oak base, with highly finished bent oak cover, furnished with convenient clamps securing cover to base and carrying handle. It is equipped with all the latest improvements, all the up-to-date points of all high grade graphophones made, with the defects of none. No lighter, more portable, more durable, handsomer or louder graphophone was ever offered; far superior and not to be compared with the old style machines.

GET OUT OF THE RUT

which, perhaps, you are in. If you are making less than $200.00 a month, you cannot afford to lose this opportunity. Start in a business where the way has been paved and everything arranged by those whose wide business experience enables them to place in your hands an outfit perfect and complete in all respects, and ready now to go at once to work.

NO. 21040
Order by Number.

ABOVE ALL DO NOT DELAY

to take advantage of the most liberal offer ever made on the most complete and perfect

talking machine outfit ever gotten together. Every detail of the outfit has been carefully prepared and considered, every item is guaranteed to give satisfaction, and we feel safe in guaranteeing absolute success. Remember, $23.75 is a special offer price; $23.75 is a price that has never been made before on a concert exhibition graphophone and complete outfit such as we are now offering; $23.75 is a price that is intended to secure your order at once; it is a price based on the actual cost of material and labor, with only our one small percentage of profit added; a price that will not be made by any other concern on a complete high grade outfit; a price that means a saving to you on such an outfit of fully one-half.

NEW IMPROVED GEM TALKING MACHINE EXHIBITION OUTFIT.

To those who wish to secure one of our new improved Gem Talking Machines for exhibition purposes, we have made up an exhibition outfit. We furnish the following complete outfit which includes everything needed as follows: For only $23.75 we now offer a complete Talking Machine Exhibition Outfit, including our new large Concert Exhibition Graphophone with the new 26-inch Amplifying Horn. A larger, better and more complete Talking Machine Outfit than has ever been offered before at a great deal more money. No. 21040 Graphophone Outfit Complete:

No. 21001 Gem Graphophone, with oak carrying case, concert horn and hearing tubes for two persons.
This is the popular and perfectly finished Gem Graphophone described above.
1 Automatic extra loud Aluminum Reproducer.
34 best Musical or Talking Records, your own selection.
1,000 Advertising Posters, large size (14x21 inches).

☞ ALL FOR ☜
$23.75

2,000 Admission Tickets.
1 Rubber Printing Outfit, with movable type for filling in date, place where exhibition is to be given, etc.
1 Large-Japanned Tin Amplifying Horn, 26 inches in length, with supporting stand.
1 Instruction Book, complete, with information about operating the outfit, making engagements ahead, etc.

...CONCERT...
EXHIBITION GRAPHOPHONE.
...No. 21010...

Our Concert Exhibition Graphophone is provided with machine-cut gears, and all parts are made with a view to strength, durability and ease of motion. The instrument sets on a polished nickel plated base, which is mounted on the motor and is propelled by a powerful double spring, which is wound up by a detachable crank and runs five or more pieces with one winding. The motor has a governor and a screw for regulating the speed, which may be governed for fast or slow, as may be desired, and automatic screw for tightening and regulating the belt. The motor box, which forms the base of the instrument, is made of the best seasoned oak, beautifully finished and polished. The machine is provided with a top cover made of quarter-sawed oak, which is attached to the base by safety hooks and has a handle for carrying. The base of the box measures 7¼x11¼ inches; total height, including cover, 10½ inches.

THE CONCERT GRAPHOPHONE has recording as well as reproducing diaphragms, so that the original records can be made by the owner and afterwards reproduced. This is a very great advantage and invariably a winner for exhibition work.

OUR PLAN of making up outfits complete in every detail for our customers has met with so much success, and such hearty approval in the past that we have prepared one to include the great Concert Exhibition Graphophone No. 21010. Equipped with this grand outfit the exhibitor has well nigh obtained perfection and is prepared to undertake any engagement. Weight, 21 pounds. Weight, boxed for shipment, about 36 pounds.

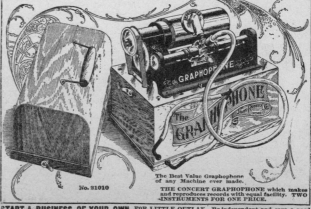

No. 21010

The Best Value Graphophone of any Machine ever made.

THE CONCERT GRAPHOPHONE which makes and reproduces records with equal facility. TWO INSTRUMENTS FOR ONE PRICE.

START A BUSINESS OF YOUR OWN FOR LITTLE OUTLAY. Be independent and earn a good salary. Send for our special entertainment outfit catalogue.

CUBA, THE MAINE AND THE CUBAN WAR.

No. 21190 Price of Stereopticon Lecture Set complete, including 52 views and all the attachments as described on the preceding page.................... **$54.50**

THESE VIEWS as well as the accompanying lecture were carefully revised and brought up-to-date from time to time as the war progressed, and as now made embody a practical

HISTORY OF THE ENTIRE WAR

FROM BEGINNING TO END.

Beautifully illustrated in a manner to insure the interest and appreciation of all who witness it. In addition to this, there are few people but what have near relatives or friends who have been serving in the war, and an entertainment of this kind has only to be advertised, to bring crowded houses, at good prices for admission.

Landing of American Troops in Cuba.

Battleship Maine after its destruction.

FOR VERY COMPLETE DESCRIPTION OF THIS MONEY-MAKING LECTURE OUTFIT, SEND FOR OUR ELEGANTLY ILLUSTRATED 128-PAGE ENTERTAINMENT OUTFIT CATALOGUE.

THE SPANISH-AMERICAN WAR AND THE PHILIPPINES ILLUSTRATED.

No. 21194 Price of Stereopticon Lecture Set, complete, including 52 views, the high grade, high power stereopticon, carrying cases, illuminating apparatus, screen, lecture book, posters and admission tickets, printing outfit, just as described on preceding page........ **$54.50**

PATRIOTIC AND INTERESTING AS WELL AS A MOST POPULAR LECTURE......

OUR NEW POSSESSIONS, our future possibilities, expansion or anti-expansion. These are the all-absorbing topics of the day, and a lecture bearing on these subjects has only to be advertised to bring crowded houses of the best class of people.

INTEREST THE PEOPLE by appealing to popular sentiment. What the people are talking about is the subject to place before them, and the man who is early in the field and the first to secure our latest lecture outfit on the War in Cuba and the Philippines will reap his reward and cannot fail to make big money.

COMPLETE FOR $54.50.

THE LATEST BATTLES and militia engagements, deeds of daring, acts of heroism, beautiful scenery and native customs will interest and inspire every patriotic man, woman and child in the country.

Funston's Two Volunteers Crossing the River. This view represents a famous incident of the Philippine War.

Ingorrote Spearmen Drilling.

FOR VERY COMPLETE DESCRIPTION OF THIS MONEY-MAKING LECTURE OUTFIT, SEND FOR OUR ELEGANTLY ILLUSTRATED 128-PAGE ENTERTAINMENT OUTFIT CATALOGUE.

THE BOER-ENGLISH WAR AND SCENES IN SOUTH AFRICA.

No. 21195 Price of Stereopticon Lecture Set complete, including 52 views and all the attachments as described on the preceding page.......................... **$54.50**

THIS, ALSO, is a magnificent lecture set, dealing with subjects of the greatest present interest and importance, and is made up of vivid and beautiful scenes descriptive of life scenery and incidents in the Transvaal and South African Republic.

THIS LECTURE SET SHOULD SWEEP THE COUNTRY

at the present time, and offers possibilities of a moderate fortune within an incredibly short space of time, to those who are first in the field, and prepared to cater to an almost universal interest in this the second great struggle for liberty of the age. With a set of these most beautiful and valuable pictures, together with the very interesting description of each, every entertainment should be a grand success and serve as an advertisement and a recommendation for future exhibitions.

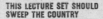

Battle of Elandslaagte.

Descending a Spruit in South Africa.

FOR VERY COMPLETE DESCRIPTION OF THIS MONEY-MAKING LECTURE OUTFIT, SEND FOR OUR ELEGANTLY ILLUSTRATED 128-PAGE ENTERTAINMENT OUTFIT CATALOGUE.

SCENES IN PARIS AND THE EXPOSITION.

No. 21196 Price of Stereopticon Lecture Set complete, with 52 views and including all the attachments as described on the preceding page.......................... **$54.50**

THE EXPOSITION is what everyone wants to see, although only a very small percentage of the people in the United States are in a position to attend it. The exhibitor who has one of these sets to exhibit, with one of Our Wonderful Panoramic Outfits, already described, will make big money and make it easy for a year at least, and probably much longer. The newspapers say much about it. Friends of many are going. All these serve to agitate in the public mind a longing to see it for themselves, and as the entertainment with an outfit of this kind comes the nearest to supplying the desire, the exhibitor will only find it necessary to put up large advertising posters and he will have crowded houses at good prices. Do not work for $15.00 to $25.00 a week, when with an outfit and these views you can make $50.00 to $100.00 per week. 500 posters only included with this set.

FOR VERY COMPLETE DESCRIPTION OF THIS MONEY-MAKING LECTURE OUTFIT, SEND FOR OUR ELEGANTLY ILLUSTRATED 128-PAGE ENTERTAINMENT OUTFIT CATALOGUE.

Sears, Roebuck & Co.

INCORPORATED

MUSICAL GOODS Department

....IN THIS...

OUR DEPARTMENT OF

ORGANS, PIANOS

AND OTHER MUSICAL INSTRUMENTS,

If You Buy From Us

YOU WILL OWN THE GOODS AT EVEN LESS THAN ANY RETAIL DEALER CAN BUY.

We have endeavored to show a Very Complete Line of only Strictly High Grade Goods and at Prices based on the Actual Cost to Produce with only our One Small Percentage of Profit added.

OUR ORGANS AND PIANOS:::

are made by the Largest and Most Reliable Makers in America. . . .

Concerns whose reputation for the manufacture of only strictly high grade instruments is a guarantee for quality; every piece and part that enters into their construction is carefully selected, all wood material is seasoned and everything the highest grade.

25 YEARS' BINDING GUARANTEE accompanies every instrument, during which time if any piece or part gives out by reason of defect in material or labor, we will replace it free of charge. With care our instruments will last a lifetime.

OUR ORGANS, Imperial Grand at $48.50, are all strictly high grade and equal to the best made, regardless of price.

OUR PIANOS from our American Home to our Artists' Cabinet Grand, are strictly high grade, the equal of any instrument made, regardless of price.

WE CAN SAVE YOU SO MUCH MONEY ON ORGANS AND PIANOS that you cannot afford to pay retail dealers' or agents' prices, you cannot afford to buy on time or on the installment plan.

IT WILL PAY YOU TO BORROW MONEY and pay us $98.50 to $155.00 for a piano, rather than pay some local dealer $300.00 to $600.00 and get time payments.

WE WILL SHOW YOU OUR INSTRUMENTS in our store, take you through the factory and show you how they are made, if you can come to Chicago before buying, or if you have friends here we will gladly show them and they can write you about them.

OUR GUITARS AND MANDOLINS we guarantee the highest grade made and our prices astonishingly low. Every guitar and mandolin is American made, warranted never to crack or split, perfect scale, sweetest toned and best finished instrument made.

The MANUFACTURER, EVERY DEALER CONCEDES, IS THE BEST MAKER OF GUITARS and MANDOLINS IN AMERICA.

OUR VIOLINS, BAND INSTRUMENTS and other Musical Instruments and Musical Merchandise, we have made under contract with leading manufacturers, and we import from the most noted European makers, and we base our selling price on the basis of actual cost, freight, duty and our one small profit added, and our prices will in many cases be found less than one-half the price charged by retail dealers.

OUR SPECIAL TERMS OF SHIPMENT.

ORGANS OR PIANOS will be sent to any address by freight C. O. D., subject to examination, on receipt of $1.00 as a guarantee of good faith. You can examine the instrument at your nearest freight depot, and if found perfectly satisfactory and exactly as represented, pay the freight agent our price and freight charges, less the $1.00 deposit. AFTER 30 DAYS TRIAL you can return the instrument and we will refund your money if you are not satisfied.

SMALL MUSICAL INSTRUMENTS, such as Violins, Guitars, Brass and other Instruments will be sent to any address on receipt of ONE DOLLAR as a guarantee of good faith. You can examine the goods at the nearest express office and if found perfectly satisfactory, pay the express agent the balance and express charges.

FIVE DAYS' FREE TRIAL. YOU MAY RETURN THE INSTRUMENT AT ANY TIME within five days from date of purchase if not found entirely satisfactory, and MONEY WILL BE CHEERFULLY REFUNDED.

One Year's Trial

YOU MAY RETURN ANY ORGAN within one year from date of purchase if it is not fully up to the standard as represented by us, and YOUR MONEY WILL BE REFUNDED IN FULL.

ABOUT THE FREIGHT. Organs and Pianos are accepted by railroad companies at first-class freight rate, and under each description we give the weight of each instrument. Refer to freight rates in front of book for first-class rate per 100 pounds to nearest point in your state and you can calculate almost exactly what the freight will amount to.

OUR "NO MONEY IN ADVANCE" PLAN

SPECIAL FREE TRIAL OFFER.

Deposit with your banker the price of the instrument wanted, take his receipt, which should read as follows:

Town....................State....................Date....................

"Received from Mr.....................

....................Dollars,

In payment of Sears, Roebuck & Co.'s....................

We agree to hold this money until the instrument has been received by Mr....................residing

in....................and has had......days' trial, when we shall forward the amount to Sears, Roebuck & Co., Chicago, Ill.

If Mr....................is not perfectly satisfied with the instrument, we will refund money on surrender to us of a bill of lading showing instrument has been reconsigned to Sears, Roebuck & Co.

....

Name of Bank or Express Co.

....

Your Banker or Express Agent should sign his name here.

Send the receipt to us. We will then ship the instrument direct to you. Your banker will hold the money deposited 30 days after arrival of the instrument, during which time you can give it a thorough trial, and if you are not in every way satisfied you can return the instrument to us, and present the railroad company's receipt to your banker, and he will refund all your money.

$98.50
Our Factory-to-Consumer Price.

With every Piano we issue a written, binding, 25 Years' Guarantee.

OUR NEW AMERICAN HOME
UPRIGHT PARLOR GRAND PIANO
ONLY CONSIDER, A FULL SIZE PIANO, MAHOGANY OR BURL WALNUT
FINISH, FOR $98.50. SUCH WAS NEVER KNOWN BEFORE. . . . . . .

$98.50
Retail Dealers ask from $175.00 to $250.00 for Same Grade.

Marvel of Marvels. A Perfect Piano. Guaranteed to last a Lifetime.

ONLY A DOLLAR DOWN. You can have this beautiful piano shipped to you, and you can examine it at your depot without paying a cent more. You be the judge as to the wonderful value we are giving. We only ask that you pass on the merits of the instrument, note its finish and fine appearance, and if you don't think it a wonder at the price, worth far more than our factory-to-consumer price, instruct the agent to return the piano and we will cheerfully return your dollar.

WE CAN GUARANTEE that you will be so well pleased with the instrument that you will pay the balance $97.50 and freight charges, and order it sent up to your home at once.

WE DO MORE. You can use the piano in your own home for 30 days and if you are then not satisfied it is all we represent it to be, you can return it to us and we will refund your money in full and pay all charges.

READ WHAT THE PEOPLE SAY ABOUT OUR MUSICAL INSTRUMENTS
AND ABOUT OUR FAIR AND HONORABLE METHODS.

OUR BINDING 25 YEARS' GUARANTEE.

By the terms and conditions of which, if any piece or part gives out by reason of defect in material or workmanship, we will replace it FREE OF CHARGE. THIS IS THE LONGEST, STRONGEST AND MOST BINDING GUARANTEE GIVEN WITH ANY PIANO.

American Home
Sears,Roebuck&Co.
CHICAGO.

No. 21858 Our $98.50 New American Home Piano, Engraved from a Photograph.

━━━ DESCRIPTION ━━━

SIZE OF PIANO. Height, 4 feet 7 inches; width, 2 feet 3 inches; length, 61 inches; weight, boxed for shipment, about 800 pounds.

THE CASES of these pianos are very pleasing in design, and made of carefully selected hard rock maple, beautifully finished in mahogany or fancy burl walnut. These finishes are so cleverly made that it is with difficulty that you can tell them from the natural wood. This is especially true of our mahogany finish, while the burl walnut is a perfect copy of the natural French burl walnut.

THE ACTION is of a very durable construction, otherwise we could not guarantee our instruments, as we do, for twenty-five years. It is made of well selected material, the hammers and felts being of a superior quality. Has perfect and simple adjustment to take up all possible wear; is very responsive and pleasing to the touch.

WE SEND FREE with each piano a handsome stool and complete instruction book. If you are in need of a good, durable piano at a low price, you had better let us send you one of ours for inspection. REMEMBER, it costs you absolutely nothing if not entirely satisfactory and exactly as represented by us. No one can make a fairer offer than this. Write to us and we will tell you how you can have 30 days' free trial of the piano in your own home before sending us any money.

THE WREST PLANK OR PIN BLOCK is made of several veneers of hard maple, with the grain running in different directions. This makes the tuning pin set firmly in the wood, and renders frequent tuning unnecessary. This wrest plank is securely bolted to our composition metal frame, and its construction makes twisting, warping or otherwise pulling out of shape impossible.

SCALE. Full size, 7½ octaves, overstrung bass, three strings to each note, except wound bass strings. Double cap hammers. The scale is perfectly even and the touch is fine and perfectly repeating.

THE TONE is of course the most important consideration when selecting a piano, at least it is one that should receive careful thought, and in this piano we have used our very best endeavors to produce an instrument at a low figure that would not be lacking in this respect. We can therefore guarantee that this instrument to possess a tone that is full, round and powerful, at the same time sweet and melodious.

OUR NEWEST STYLE COTTAGE ORGAN

GUARANTEED FOR 25 YEARS.

LONGEST, STRONGEST AND MOST BINDING EVER GIVEN WITH AN ORGAN.

THE IMPROVED PARLOR GEM

No. 21924
Order by Number.

A REGULAR ..... $50.00 ORGAN FOR $33.50.

IN DESIGN SO PERFECT, IN STYLE SO NEW, IN TONE SO POWERFUL AND EXQUISITELY PURE, AND IN PRICE SO LOW THAT NO COMPETITION CAN STAND THE TEST OF COMPARISON.

Remember Our 25 Years' Binding Guarantee

OUR $1.00 WITH ORDER PLAN.
You can send us $1.00 with your order and we will ship you our Improved Parlor Gem Organ C. O. D., subject to examination. After examination you can pay the balance and freight charges, otherwise you can return the instrument to us, and we will cheerfully refund your deposit.

OUR FREE TRIAL PLAN.
As fully described in the introduction of this department you can deposit the price of the instrument with your local banker and have the Organ taken to your own home for a free trial. The banker will send us the money at the end of 30 days, unless you have pronounced the Organ unsatisfactory and not as represented, in which case you return the Organ to the freight agent and upon presenting the bill of lading to the banker he will refund your money to you.

DESCRIPTION.
5 Octaves, 11 Stops, 2 Octave Couplers, 1 Tone Swell, 1 Grand Organ Swell, 4 Sets Orchestral Toned Resonatory Pipe Quality Reeds, 1 Set Exquisitely Pure and Sweet Melodia of 37 Reeds, 1 Set Charmingly Brilliant Celeste of 37 Reeds, 1 Set Rich, Mellow, Smooth Diapason of 24 Reeds, 1 Set Pleasing, Soft, Melodious Principal of 24 Reeds

NAMES OF 11 STOPS. Diapason, Principal, Dulciana, Melodia, Celeste, Cremona, Bass Coupler, Treble Coupler, Diapason Forte, Principal Forte and Vox Humana.

THE ACTION
in this Organ consists of the Celebrated Newall Reeds, which are only used in the highest grade instruments. This Organ is fitted with Hammond's Couplers and Vox Humana, also the best Dolge felts, leathers, etc.

THE CASE.
This is one of the handsomest Cases ever used on an Organ at anything like the price. It comes in solid oak or solid black walnut, beautifully carved, ornamented and decorated, as shown in the illustration. It is especially constructed to develop the acoustic properties of the organ, forming a qualifying chamber which gives a pipe like quality to the tone, hitherto unattained in the finest reed organs. The wood used in the case is thoroughly seasoned and will stand any climatic changes. It is highly finished, has a 10x14-inch French bevel plate mirror, nickel plated pedal frames, and every modern improvement. The sides are 1¼-inch lumber, and below the key board it is finished in panels. The new and handsome marquetry designs on each side of the mirror are not found in any other organ.

THE TONE.
That most important quality in an organ is faultless. The depth and breadth, without sacrificing sweetness of tone by the sounding chamber, together with the finely tempered metal used in the reeds, secure a purity of tone which can only be equaled by the soft pipe of the Church Organ. These pipe-like qualities cannot be procured from any other manufacturer at any price.

DIMENSIONS.
Height, 72 inches; length, 42 inches; width, 23 inches.

Weight, boxed for shipment, about 350 pounds.

Our efforts in the past to render greatest possible value in musical instruments have received the commendations of THOUSANDS OF DELIGHTED CUSTOMERS.

BRAINARD'S NEW METHOD ORGAN
SEARS, ROEBUCK & CO.
CHICAGO, ILL.

$1.00 WITH ORDER, balance C. O. D. after satisfactory examination.

REMEMBER OUR LIBERAL TERMS.
SEND NO MONEY. JUST DEPOSIT PURCHASE PRICE WITH YOUR BANKER.

FREE THIRTY DAYS' TRIAL in your home.

A HANDSOME STOOL AND VALUABLE INSTRUCTION BOOK FURNISHED FREE WITH THIS ORGAN.

OUR NEW HOME CABINET ORGAN
A RARE BARGAIN AT $36.75

No. 21928

LATEST STYLE, INCLUDING ALL MODERN IM-
PROVEMENTS. ONE OF THE HANDSOMEST OR-
GANS WE HAVE YET OFFERED FOR THE MONEY

WARRANTED
FOR 25 YEARS.

ORDER BY
NUMBER.

TERMS. As explained in front of book, we will
ship this organ to anyone on receipt of
$1.00. SEND US $1.00 with your order and we will ship
the instrument to you by freight, C. O. D., subject to examination. You can go to the freight depot and examine the
organ; you do not pay one cent more until you are satisfied
that the instrument is just what we claim for it, you then
pay the agent the balance, $35.75 and freight charges, and
the organ is yours.

FREE 30 DAYS' TRIAL OFFER...

Read our Liberal Terms of shipment as
explained in front of book. In all cases of
dissatisfaction we pay the expense of return
and all your money is refunded.

THIS ORGAN IS FURNISHED WITH

1 set beautiful pipe-like Principal reeds of 24 notes.
1 set exquisitely pure and sweet Melodia reeds of 37
notes.
1 set rich, mellow, smooth Diapason reeds of 24 notes.
1 set charmingly brilliant Celeste reeds of 37 notes.

122 REEDS IN ALL.

DESCRIPTION OF THE BEAUTIFUL CASE.

This Beautiful New Home Cabinet Organ is built
in either solid black walnut or quartered oak as
desired. The case is handsomely carved, decorated
and finished, as shown in the illustration, which is
an exact reproduction of the photograph of the
organ. It is 78 inches high, 44 inches long, 23
inches deep.

Only the very best seasoned kiln dried
lumber is used, and the top is ornamented
with a French plate mirror, 10x12 inches
in size, and the carved music desk acts as
a lid for a large and roomy cupboard for
music books, etc. At each side of the
music desk are safety lamp stands.
In addition to the neat and tasty fret-
work, the base of the organ is decorated
with handsome turned pillars and beautiful carvings, and is provided with a
sliding fall cover with lock, rollers for
moving, and in fact, every modern improvement.

THE ACTION. This is the most powerful
double reed action ever
invented, so simple and yet so strongly
constructed that it cannot get out of order.
The tone is powerful, rich, full and sweet,
and by the use of the stops an endless
variety of effects is perfectly at the
organist's command. The metal parts are
of the finest coppered and silvered steel
wire and impervious to damp and rust. It
is especially prepared to withstand all
climatic changes, this being absolutely necessary, owing to our enormous trade in
all climates. It is fitted with 5 octaves,
4 sets pipe-toned reeds, 122 in all; double
octave couplers, 11 necessary stops, 2 knee
swells and Vox Humana, all the latest
improvements, everything up to date
and a perfect parlor organ.

THE BELLOWS. used with this action are
the finest and most pow-
erful possible to construct. The silk rubber cloth is extra heavy, and the bellows
will not leak. The automatic air valve
relieves all surplus pressure so that the
bellows cannot be overstrained.

THE INSIDE FINISH. of this organ is as
neat and perfect
as the outside. Every part is well looked
after and none but the very best mechanics
are employed in building.

FITTINGS. Among the fittings of
this organ you will
find in addition to the heavy bevel
plate mirror, bevel faced celluloid stop knobs, nickel plated
pedal frames with best Brussels
carpet, extension lamp shelf and
candles.

THE SIZE OF ORGAN. This organ
is 78 in-
ches high, 44 inches long, 23
inches deep, and when packed,
ready for shipment, will weigh
about 350 pounds.

HAS OF 11 STOPS. Diapason,
Principal,
Melodiana, Melodia, Celeste, Bass
Coupler, Treble Coupler, Diapa-
son Forte, Principal Forte, Vox
Humana and Cremona.

SEARS
ROEBUCK
AND CO
Organ Instructor

21932 AA GRADE NEW HOME
Same Description as the Regular Grade shown in Illustration, but has 159 REEDS and 13 STOPS. $41.75

GREAT VIOLIN BARGAINS

No. 22159
$7.75

No. 22151
$2.50

No. 22160
$9.60

No. 22153
$4.75

No. 22155
$6.25

No. 22153
$4.75

LIBERAL TERMS

Send $1.00 with order and we will send any violin C. O. D., subject to examination. Pay balance, if pleased, otherwise send it back and we cheerfully refund money. Absolute approval guaranteed whether full cash accompanies order or if shipped C. O. D. **FIVE DAYS' TRIAL FREE** when cash in full accompanies order, violin may be returned at any time within five days, if not found entirely satisfactory and money will be cheerfully refunded.

These instruments are carefully packed in a light strong box and when ready for shipment weigh only 7 pounds.

A Genuine Stradivarius Model Violin for $2.50.

No. 22151 This violin is the Famous Stradivarius Model which is sought after and admired by the world's greatest players. Beautiful rich red varnish elegantly finished, having the appearance of a violin which retailers would ask $10.00 to $12.00 for. Made of specially selected wood, giving it a sweet and powerful tone; a tone seldom found in violins at five times our price. We furnish an extra set of strings, a nice violin bow and a valuable instruction book with this violin. Our special price, $2.50

A Regular $12.00 Violin for $4.75.

No. 22153 For quality and power of tone this violin is one of the finest ever offered. A Genuine Maggini Model, being a direct copy of the violins by that great maker. Made of specially selected and seasoned violin wood. Rich brown varnish, highly polished. It is furnished with an elegant ebony fingerboard and tailpiece well finished in every respect; like the renowned Maggini violins has double inlaid purfling giving it a distinguished and handsome appearance. You should see this violin in order to appreciate its specially fine value. Remit $1.00 with your order and we will send you this genuine Maggini model violin C. O. D., subject to examination. You can examine it at the express office and if entirely satisfied, pay the express agent the balance with express charges and the violin is yours. We furnish a complete instruction book, extra set of violin strings and handsome bow with each instrument. Special price, $4.75

A High Grade Genuine Stainer Model Violin for $6.25.

No. 22155 The Stainer Model is much sought after by all players of the violin on account of this model producing an exceptionally sweet and powerful tone. It is furnished with the best quality ebony trimmings, is handsomely varnished, highly polished and well finished in every respect. You should not fail to examine this genuine Stainer Model before deciding to purchase elsewhere. We furnish a complete instruction book, a handsome violin bow and a set of excellent strings with each instrument. Our special price.................$6.25

Copy of a Genuine Amati for $7.75.

No. 22159 The Amati Violins are noted for their unusually sweet and powerful quality of tone. Are among the finest instruments known to violin players. The violin which we furnish has a beautiful curled maple back and sides, carefully selected top of fine old wood, maple neck and scroll. The varnish is the regular rich Amati color beautifully finished, and the ebony trimmings are of the very best quality. We include with this instrument a handsome violin bow, full set of strings and a valuable instruction book and will send the entire outfit upon receipt of $1.00 C. O. D., subject to examination. You may examine it at the express office and if you find the instrument satisfactory in every respect and by far the greatest value you ever saw or heard of, pay the express agent the balance with express charges and the violin is yours. Our special price, $7.75

$9.60 Buys Our Grand Concert Violin.

No. 22160 A Genuine Stradivarius Model, a fine imitation of an old instrument and a violin of unusual tone, quality, finish and model. It is reddish brown in color, oil varnished, beautifully finished, has ebony fingerboard and tailpiece. An instrument for which purchasers have paid as high as $24.00 to $30.00. At our price we furnish, without extra charge, a nice bow, full set of strings and complete instruction book. We ship on the most liberal C. O. D. terms, allowing you to examine the instrument when $1.00 is sent with the order, and when it is found exactly as we represent it and fully up to our statement, you can pay the express agent the balance and express charges and the instrument is yours. Our special price.................$9.60

SEE LIST OF VIOLIN TRIMMINGS ON PAGES 280 AND 281.

OUR $7.85 GENUINE STRADIVARIUS MODEL.

...SPECIAL
IMPORTATION
DIRECT
FROM EUROPE.

A LIMITED NUMBER
OF THESE OUTFITS
AT OUR SPECIAL
PRICE OF

$7.85

PLACE YOUR ORDER
AT ONCE, AND SEND
CASH IN FULL TO
INSURE PROMPT
DELIVERY.

NOTE THE DESCRIPTION.

A Two-Piece Maple Back, Beautifully
Flamed, as Shown in the Illustration.
Top of resonant spruce, especially selected; reddish brown varnish, beautifully shaded in imitation of an old violin. The neck and scroll are made of curly maple to correspond with the back and sides.

The Fingerboard and Tailpiece of Solid Ebony.
A VIOLIN WHICH WOULD
READILY RETAIL AT $15.00.
NO FINER MODEL IN EXISTENCE THAN THE
..CELEBRATED STRADIVARIUS..

In Addition to the Violin, as Above Described,
WE FURNISH a regular Artists' Tourte Model
Bow, made of genuine Brazil wood, German silver trimmed; ebony frog and button; a solid wood case, American made, beautifully lined and provided with hooks, handle and lock; a piece of artists' rosin and a full set of four strings and one of our most valuable and complete instruction books.

Five Days'
Trial Free.

WHEN CASH IN FULL
ACCOMPANIES ORDER.

SATISFACTION GUARANTEED OR MONEY REFUNDED.

EXAMINE THIS BEAUTIFUL VIOLIN AT YOUR
EXPRESS OFFICE.

Weight, Packed Ready for Shipment, 10 Pounds.

THIS ENTIRE OUTFIT WE ARE OFFERING
AT THE UNUSUALLY LOW PRICE OF

..$7.85..

Complete with the violin, one genuine
Tourte model bow; one large piece of
rosin; one wood case, with lock, handle
and hooks; one full set of strings; one
complete instruction book.

Front View of Violin.

Back View of Violin.

No. 22161
ORDER BY NUMBER
ONLY.

Made Expressly to
us by one of the
GREATEST
MAKERS
according to our
instructions, enabling us to offer
this especially
WELL
MADE
VIOLIN
for an unusually
low price.

WILL SEND THE ENTIRE OUTFIT, SUBJECT TO
EXAMINATION
YOUR APPROVAL, UPON RECEIPT OF $1.00, as
ence of good faith. If you do not find everything expressed as represented by us, and, without doubt, the finest
in ever offered by any dealer at double our price, you
y return it at our expense and your money will be
nded.

GUITARS AT PRICES BEYOND COMPARE.

22330 $3.85

22326 $2.70

22336 $9.60

22328 $3.60

22335 $8.20

LIBERAL TERMS Any guitar sent C.O.D., subject to examination when $1.00 is sent with order.
FIVE DAYS' TRIAL FREE When cash in full accompanies order the guitar may be returned at any time within five days, if not found exactly as represented and entirely satisfactory, and money will be cheerfully refunded in full. WE GIVE WITH EVERY GUITAR A VALUABLE INSTRUCTION BOOK AND FULL SET OF SUPERIOR STEEL STRINGS.

We pack these instruments as carefully as possible in a light, strong box, which insures their reaching you in perfect condition. When boxed for shipment package weighs about 12 pounds.

THE TROUBADOUR.

No. 22326 An instrument of surprising quality and tone. Neat inlaying around sound hole. Fingerboard accurately fretted with raised frets, inlaid position dots, metal tailpiece, highly polished, mahogany finish so near like the genuine wood that most people readily believe it to be the real wood. Genuine American patent head. A complete and desirable outfit, such as no other concern can possibly give at anything like our price.
Our special price, standard size...........$2.70

ThE ENCORE.

No. 22328 A genuine American made instrument of great beauty and immensely popular with every purchaser. Made of the best solid birch, in imitation of rosewood, highly polished. Fingerboard is perfect in scale, accurately fretted with raised frets, inlaid position dots, American patent head, metal tailpiece, celluloid bound top edge, beautiful inlaid strip in back. A regular $8.00 guitar.
Our special price, standard size...........$3.60

THE OAKWOOD.

No. 22330 This beautiful guitar is made of selected quarter sawed oak, highly finished. The top is handsomely finished in orange color, offering a pleasing contrast with the oak back and sides. Beautiful inlaid strip in back. Fancy inlaying around sound hole. Rosewood fingerboard with position dots and raised frets perfect in scale. American screw patent head, metal tailpiece.
Our special price, standard size...........$3.85

THE MARLOWE.

No. 22331 Our special solid mahogany guitar, mahogany neck, rosewood fingerboard, accurately fitted with raised frets and inlaid position dots, orange colored top, handsome inlaying around sound hole, and strip down the back. Best American made brass patent head.
Our special price...........$5.95

Our "20th Century" Bargain.

THE GREATEST VALUE EVER OFFERED.
$16.00 ACME PROFESSIONAL GUITAR FOR $8.20.
No. 22335 is made of selected bird's eye maple, with black edges, beautiful inlaid strip in back; selected cedar front, with beautiful inlaid strip around sound hole. Mahogany neck, with ebony fingerboard, inlaid with three pearl position dots; brass patent head and patent nickel plated tailpiece. Standard size.
Our special price...........$8.20

THE KENMORE.

No. 22336 For $9.60 we offer a solid rosewood guitar of highest merit and retailed at $15.00 to $18.00. A beautifully modeled instrument, with the finest French polish. Popular orange colored front. Best selected cedar neck. Fingerboard absolutely correct in scale with raised frets and inlaid position dots. Genuine American screw patent head. Inlaid around sound hole and beautiful inlaid strip in back. In every respect a superior instrument.
Our special price, standard size...........$9.60
No. 22338 Same guitar as No. 22336, but large concert size.
Our special price...........$10.80

GUITAR CASES AND FURNISHINGS OF ALL KINDS
LISTED ON PAGE 281

❖ OUR $3.95 EDGEMERE MANDOLIN. ❖

A GENUINE EDGEMERE INSTRUMENT

Made by the Celebrated Edgemere Manufacturers (a guarantee for quality), a Grade of Instruments that is sold in Music Stores in Large Cities at 50 per cent More Money.

...OUR $3.95 PRICE...

UPON RECEIPT OF $1.00

IS A PRICE BASED ON THE ACTUAL COST.. of material and labor to make these mandolins, with the narrowest kind of a margin of profit added. Our $3.95 price is only made possible by contracting with the makers of the celebrated Edgemere instruments for an enormous quantity in order that we may offer our customers a genuine Edgemere Mandolin for the small price of $3.95, less than dealers have heretofore been paying wholesale for these instruments.

WE WILL SEND THIS MANDOLIN as described C.O.D., with the privilege of examination. Examine it at your express office, and if you find it exactly as represented, perfectly satisfactory in every respect, pay the express agent our special price, $3.95 (less the dollar sent with order) and express charges. IF THE INSTRUMENT IS NOT IN EVERY WAY UP TO THE DESCRIPTION and representation, return it to us at our expense and we WILL REFUND YOUR DOLLAR.

DESCRIPTION OF OUR $3.95 EDGEMERE.

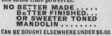

No. 22383
Order by Number
Only.

THIRTEEN RIBS OF MAHOGANY with black stripes inlaid betwen each rib, handsomely finished rosewood cap, highly polished orange colored top, edges beautifully bound with celluloid and inlaying, imitation tortoise shell guard plate with a handsome inlaid floral design in the center, inlaying around the sound hole to correspond with the inlaying of the edges.

OUR $3.95 EDGEMERE has the latest patent nickel plated tailpiece and sleeve protector combined. The mandolin is correctly fretted with raised frets. The tone is sweet, melodious and at the same time powerful.

**NO BETTER MADE . . . . .
BeTTER FINISHED . . .
OR SWEETER TONED
MANDOLIN . . . .
CAN BE BOUGHT ELSEWHERE UNDER $6.00**

WITH EVERY $3.95 EDGEMERE MANDOLIN we include, free of charge, one extra set of Glendon strings, one genuine tortoise shell pick and a book of Guckert's chords.

No. 22383 Back view of mandolin.

SHIPPING WEIGHT (carefully boxed) about 7 pounds. We guarantee safe delivery. Our $3.95 Edgemere Mandolin is a rare bargain and you should send us your order at once.

No. 22383 Front view of mandolin.

These illustrations are taken direct from photographs of the instrument, but it is impossible to show the full beauty of the instrument. It must be seen, tried and compared with other low priced mandolins to understand the full value of our offer.

No. 22383 Our Edgemere Mandolin, price.. **$3.95**

GREAT Banjo Values

BANJOS

No. 2242 $6.90

No. 22432 $2.79

No. 22447 $7.96

No. 22433 $4.35

No. 224325 $3.95

No. 22432 $2.95

LIBERAL C. O. D. TERMS. Send $1.00 with order and we will send any Banjo, except our $1.75 Instrument, C. O. D., subject to examination and approval. **FIVE DAYS' TRIAL FREE.** When cash in full accompanies order we allow you to return the instrument at any time within 5 days, and will cheerfully refund your money if everything is not found exactly as represented and entirely satisfactory.

Our $1.75 Banjo.

No. 22431 The banjo which we show in the illustration under this number has the shell made of maple, with nickel band; the neck is finished in imitation cherry; has 10-inch calfskin head, with six screw brackets. At $1.75 we consider this banjo a wonder. However, we would not recommend it, but would suggest sending for one of our better grades, which we guarantee. Cash in full must accompany order. Weight, boxed, about 10 pounds. Our special price............$1.75

Our Special $2.95 Banjo.

No. 22432 As shown in the illustration, has a genuine nickel shell, wood lined. The neck is stained in imitation cherry, with 7 nickel plated hexagon brackets. Has genuine calfskin head, 10 inches in diameter. Weight, boxed, about 11 pounds. Our special price...............$2.95

Our "Edgemere" at $3.95.

No. 224325 We offer exceptional value in this, our Edgemere Banjo. It has 10-inch head, nickel shell, wood lined, carefully fitted and well made neck, imitation mahogany raised frets, accurately fretted; seven nickel plated hexagon brackets; fine quality calfskin head. Our special price..$3.95

A $7.50 Banjo for $4.35.

No. 22433 This is an 11-inch Banjo, with genuine nickel shell, wood lined; has 17 nickel plated hexagon brackets; raised frets; has birch neck finished in imitation mahogany. Weight, boxed, about 18 pounds. Our special price.... .$4.35

Our Leader.

No. 22438 This banjo has a genuine nickel shell, 11-inch calfskin head; has wired edges, heavy nickel plated strainer hoop and twenty-one nickel plated brackets. The fingerboard is accurately fretted; has raised frets and is inlaid with pearl position dots; birch neck, highly polished. With this banjo we furnish a full set of strings and a valuable instruction book. Our special price...................$5.75

Weight, boxed, about 18 pounds.

A $12.00 Instrument for $6.90.

No. 22442 In offering this banjo we enable good players to secure a first class instrument at a low price. Send for it and after you have tried it for five days you may return it if not found as represented, and your money will be refunded. Has an extra heavy nickel rim, 11-inch best quality calfskin head. Both edges of the rim are wired; has an extra heavy strainer hoop; twenty-one nickel plated brackets with protection nuts; highly polished cherry neck; ebony fingerboard, inlaid with pearl position dots; ebony pegs, patent tailpiece, and is strung with good quality strings. Our special price..................$6.90

Weight, boxed, about 18 pounds.

Wonderful Value.

Your Retail Dealer would ask you $15.00 for this same Instrument.

Our Factory-to-Consumer Plan gives you an opportunity to be the possessor of an instrument such as artists use. In workmanship, finish and tone, it is that of a $15.00 instrument.

No. 22447 This banjo has a genuine nickel, selected maple rim, the edges of which are wired; the head is the best quality opaque, 11 inches in diameter; has twenty-five nickel plated brackets with an extra heavy rabbeted strainer hoop. The neck is made of selected birch, very highly polished, has an ebony fingerboard beautifully inlaid with pearl and metal ebony pegs and patent tailpiece. A metal stay piece is used on the neck which prevents it from coming loose. With this banjo we include a valuable instruction book and full set of strings at our special price of.......................$7.96

Weight, boxed, about 18 pounds.

OUR ACME PROFESSIONAL BANJOS

No. 22452
$9.75

HAVING MADE SPECIAL

rangements with the anufacturers of the mous S. S. Stewart anjos to manufacture or us

OUR ACME PROFESSIONAL BANJOS........

e are enabled to furnish our customers a genuine tewart Banjo, of the same quality that the anufacturer sells under his own name at a much igher price. These arrangements could only be ade by placing a large order under special con- act which enables this celebrated manufacturer o run his factory full force during the dull season. y purchasing an Acme Professional Banjo, ou get the best that can be made. These Banjos are guar- nteed to have an absolutely correct fingerboard and a tone nsurpassed. We pack each banjo in a light strong box nd safe delivery is guaranteed. Shipping weight, about 8 pounds.

....OUR LIBERAL TERMS....

Send $1.00 with order and we will send any Banjo, . O. D., subject to examination and approval.

....FIVE DAYS' TRIAL FREE....

When cash in full accompanies order, we allow you to eturn the instrument at any time within 5 days, and will cheer- ily refund your money if everything is not found exactly s represented and entirely satisfactory.

We furnish with each Banjo an extra set of our Acme rofessional strings, complete instruction book and a Pro- essional Banjo thimble.

THE EMPRESS.

No. 22452 This Banjo has 11-inch genuine nickel shell, latest style brackets with protection nuts. The shell is wood lined and has double wired edge, with finest quality calfskin head and has rainer hoops; highly polished, cherry neck; fitted with best quality ebony egs; ebony fingerboard with pearl position marks. We furnish with this anjo a full set of Acme Professional strings, a Banjo thimble and a valu- ble instruction book. Our special price..........................$9.75

THE REGAL.

No. 22454 Has 11-inch head, 25 latest style brackets with protection nuts; erman silver rim; wood lined; double spun wired edge; finest quality calf- kin head; highly finished; cherry neck; 19¼ inches long; ebony fingerboard; aised frets; fancy inlaid pearl position marks. Best quality pegs and patent ailpiece. Each Banjo is accompanied by a full set of Acme Professional trings, a valuable instruction book and Banjo thimble.
Our special price..........................$12.50

THE GEM.
WONDERFUL VALUE.

No. 22456 This Banjo has heavy German silver covered rim, double pun wire edge, 31 latest style brackets with protection nuts, heavy grooved top oop, all nickel plated. Best quality calfskin head; full length highly polished herry neck; thick ebony fingerboard; rosewood veneered headpiece, all andsomely inlaid with pearl and fitted with best quality patent pegs. Send or this Banjo so that you can hear its wonderful tone and convince yourself f the great bargain we are offering, complete with valuable instruction ook, full set of Acme Professional strings and Banjo thimble.
Our special price..........................$14.50

THE ROYAL.
A STRICTLY PROFESSIONAL BANJO.

No. 22458 Has 11-inch genuine German silver shell; wood-lined, double pun wired edges, 31 latest style nickel plated brackets with protection nuts; eavy rabbeted strainer hoops; best Rogers' head. Polished neck with rose- ood veneered headpiece and thick ebony fingerboard, all elaborately inlaid ith pearl. Patent pegs and tailpiece.
NOTE.—This Banjo is provided with a patent steel neck adjuster, which ives greater strength to the neck and serves as a regulator of the angle of he fingerboard. Our special price..........................$20.00

THE IMPERIAL.
OUR FINEST BANJO—A 3½ OCTAVE INSTRUMENT.

No. 22460 This Banjo is very fine in tone; has a nickel plated German ilver rim 11 inches in diameter and 2½ inches in depth; lined with maple; has ouble over spun wire edges; finest quality Rogers' head; extra heavy grooved trainer hoop; 31 latest pattern brackets with protection nuts, all metal parts ickel plated. The neck is 19 inches in length, handsomely carved at base. he ebony fingerboard is extra thick and elaborately inlaid with pearl. The octaves of frets are absolutely correct. Patent non-slipping pegs and tail- iece. The nickel plated brace shown in the illustration is something new nd fully protected by patents. It gives greater strength to the neck and erves as an adjuster and a regulator to the angle of the fingerboard. You annot afford to purchase elsewhere until you have seen and tried this onderful Banjo. We include free a valuable instruction book, Banjo himble and a full set of Acme Professional strings. The illustration will ive some idea of the front and back views of our finest Banjo. The pur- haser of this magnificent instrument will have the pleasure of owning the very est it is possible to produce—a genuine high grade S. S. Stewart Banjo.
Our special price..........................$25.00

No. 22453
$11.50

No. 22454
$12.50

No. 22456
$14.50

No. 22458
$20.00

No. 22460
$25.00

Back View | Front View

THE AUTOHARP

THE AUTOHARP has become one of the **MOST POPULAR** of small stringed instruments. This popularity is well deserved. Thousands are in use and the sale keeps on increasing at a wonderful rate. **REASONS WITHOUT NUMBER** exist for th universal demand for these high class instruments. **SIMPLICITY.** There are no complicate parts, no mechanism that requires the skilled hand to operate. Anyone—whether he has music ability or not, can play it with very little practice, and play it well. **MUSICAL QUALITY.** Thousands testify to its sweetness of tone, which equals that of the highest grade piano. The mos difficult productions may be played on it, while as an accompaniment for the voice it has no superio. **CHEAPNESS.** Never before has it been possible for the house to be graced with high class music at so small an expense. The prices which we name enable the poorest to possess an instrumen which will produce the sweetest music and give just as much pleasure as would a high priced piano

........OUR MOST LIBERAL TERMS........

Send $1.00 with your order for any autoharp, and we will send it C. O. D. subject to examination and approval. You can examine the instrumen at the express office, and when found just as represented and entirely satisfactory, pay the express agent the balance with express charges, and the instrument is yours. Otherwise return it at our expense and we will refund money.

Our $1.95 Autoharp.

No. 22240 Our $1.95 Autoharp. It has 20 strings, 3 bars, and produces 3 chords. With this instrument the simpler a's and chords may be played. The best steel strings are furnished and the tone is remarkably sweet. Without a single exception, every purchaser has been delighted with this autoharp, and would not part with it at any price if another could not be secured.
Our special price............$1.95
Weight, packed for shipment, 10 pounds.

We carry a full line of

AUTOHARP CASES,

TRIMMINGS, ETC.

For description, see following pages.

$3.10 Buys a $5.50 Autoharp.

No. 22243 Our $3.10 Autoharp has 23 strings, 5 bars and produces 5 chords. The possibilities of this beautiful instrument are unbounded, and while but little practice is needed for the beginner to play nicely, constant practice will enable the performer to produce very difficult music. We ship this Autoharp C. O. D., subject to examination, when $1.00 is sent with order. We give a complete Instructor free with each Autoharp.

OUR SPECIAL PRICE......$3.10
Weight, packed for shipment, 10 lbs.

Our Special Autoharp for $5.45.

No. 22244 For $5.45 we offer an Autoharp that is entirely new, strictly first class in workmanship and susceptible to wonderful manipulation in the hands of a musician, whether artist or amateur. This special Autoharp is complete with 32 strings and is fitted with 8 bars, producing as many different chords. The range of different music is very great, and the possibilities of the instrument are beyond that of any other of similar construction and much higher price. We furnish a very complete instruction book free, and with its use anyone can in a short time become a skilful performer on this most charming of all instruments. We also furnish free with each Autoharp, a ring for playing, music rack, tuning hammer and selections of Autoharp music.

REMEMBER We ship this beautiful instrument C. O. D., subject to examination, when $1.00 is sent with order, and you can see for yourself before paying balance that it is all we claim for it.
Our special price, complete.........................$5.45
Weight, packed for shipment, 12 lbs.

$6.95 for the New Style Autoharp

No. 22247 Autoharp is the very latest product of the manufacturer, and is destined to become the most popular style of their entire list. It has 37 strings and 13 chord bars; these bars are placed closely together, making the manipulation of them exceedingly easy; they produce the major chords of C, D, G and F, with their relative minors. It is strung and tuned in a perfect chromatic scale, making it possible to pick out any tone or melody. The finish is beautiful; highly polished Ebony finish; altogether a handsome, useful, musical instrument
Our special price........................$6.9
Weight, packed for shipment, 12 lbs.

$9.85 Buys a $20.00 Concert Autoharp.

No. 22248 Our $9.85 Concert Autoharp is one of the most desirable in this line which has ever been sold. At this price anyone can readily afford to own a musical instrument, which in every respect will produce the highest grade music. This instrument is constructed on the best principles and every piece and part that enters into its construction is carefully selected, and only the best material is used, and the best workmen employed to make this Concert Autoharp strictly high grade in every respect. It is complete with 28 strings, 5 bars with shifters and produces 13 chords. The case has fancy inlaid edges and imitation rosewood top. It is a beautiful instrument, one that will ornament any home and one that anyone can own at a little expenditure. Our special price, each.......................$9.8
Weight, packed for shipment, 14 lbs.

Our Highest Grade Concert Autoharp for $13.20

No. 22252 This beautiful Concert Autoharp is one of the most desirable of all stringed instruments made. The manufacturers of the world renowned autoharp have taken special pains with this particular style to make it the best that high class material and expensive skilled mechanics can make it. It has 32 strings and 6 bars with shifters, producing 16 chords, as follows: F, C, G, D majors 5 minors and 1 seventh. With this instrument, anyone with sufficient skill and practice can produce any music, no difference how difficult is suitable for all classes of music, sacred, Classical or Popular. It is suitable for accompaniment to the voice, suitable to be played in connection with other musical instruments. The case is unusually handsome, having the finest inlaid edges, imitation rosewood top, and all complete it is polished and finished equal to the finish of a high grade piano. Complete with instruction book, strings, music and music rack. Our special price, each.......................$13.2
Weight, packed for shipment, about 20 lbs.

COLUMBIA ZITHERS.

THE COLUMBIA IS A SIMPLIFIED GERMAN ZITHER and requires no teacher. Our method of instruction is so easy that anyone can learn to play the instrument in a very short time. The bass notes are tuned in groups of chords. This is a very attractive feature, as one has the various chords of the key ready to be plucked without effort. As an accompaniment to the voice these chords are invaluable. In connection with the violin, piano and other musical instruments, the Columbia is delightful. It rewards individual skill more than any other harp in existence. We have produced a musical instrument which charms alike the home circle and the concert audiences. Every instruction book contains a list of music arranged for the instrument in figures easily comprehended. Our repertoire contains nearly everything published in the popular music of the day, besides all standard music which has won the hearts of generation after generation.

CAUTION—Do not confuse the Columbia Zither with anything in the harp line. It is not a harp, a zither, an instrument upon which can be played any class of music as it is without an equal.

OUR LIBERAL TERMS. Send $1.00 deposit and we will send any Columbia Zither you may select, by express, C. O. D., subject to examination. Balance and charges payable after you are satisfied that the instrument is exactly as we represent. If you do not find it so and are not entirely satisfied you can return it at our expense and we will refund your deposit.

FIVE DAYS' FREE TRIAL. If you send cash in full, it will save us considerable time and labor in filling your order, and we agree to refund your money, if after FIVE DAYS' TRIAL you do not find everything as represented, and entirely satisfactory in every respect.

The Columbia Zither, only $1.75.

No. 22552 The Columbia Zither illustrated herewith is 11 inches wide by 19½ inches long, made of maple, finished in imitation ebony, highly polished, has 41 strings, which produce the scale and chords of key of C, also has a chart attached which gives the number and letter of each string. An instruction book, music rack and tuning key free with each instrument. Our special price.......$1.75 Shipping weight, 12 pounds.

Columbia Zither Special No. 2½ at $2.00.

No. 22554 Columbia Zither No. 2½ Special, is similar in appearance to No. 22552, but, as shown in the illustration, is finished in imitation ebony, is beautifully decorated and highly polished, and somewhat larger in size, being 20 inches long by 13 inches wide, has 41 strings, arranged so as to produce scale and chords of key of C. Chart attached to instrument showing number and letter of every string, also arm rest over hitch pins to afford protection to the sleeve. Instruction book, pick and tuning hammer accompany each instrument. Our price.....$2.00 Shipping wei't, 12 pounds.

Only $3.15 for a Regular $5.00 Instrument.

No. 22556 Columbia Zither is 20 inches long by 14 inches wide; finished in imitation ebony, with gilt striping, highly polished; has 38 strings, so arranged as to produce the chords and scales with the relative minor of the keys of C and F; has nickel plated damper, also arm rest over hitch pins.

NOTE. With this instrument we give besides an instruction book, pick and key, three charts for beginners which will enable anyone to play the instrument in five minutes. An invaluable addition. Our special price.......$3.15 Shipping weight, 12 pounds.

A $7.50 Columbia Zither for $5.00.

No. 22558 This Columbia Zither is 21½ inches long by 16 inches wide, finished in imitation ebony with beautiful decalcomanie decorations, pianopolished: 47 strings, arranged so as to produce 6 chords, comprising the scales and major and minor chords of the keys of C and F; has nickel plated damper, also arm rest over hitch pins. Instruction book, pick and tuning key with each instrument. Special price, ...$5.00 Shipping weight, 14 pounds.

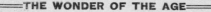

MANDOLIN-GUITAR-ZITHER. THREE INSTRUMENTS COMBINED AT THE PRICE OF ONE.

=THE WONDER OF THE AGE=

THE DEWEYLIN HARP, the greatest musical instrument that has ever been placed before the public. The Mandolin, Guitar and Zither, three of the sweetest toned instruments are combined in this Harp, which is so simply constructed that anyone may become master of it in a very short time, without the aid of a teacher. No picks or rings are required to play the instrument, a patent keyboard being used instead. As you will see in the illustration, the instrument is made after the style of the Guitar Zither, having treble strings on which the air is played and accompaniment strings for the accompaniment. The keyboard which is placed over the strings is the one great feature with which the mandolin effect is produced. The keys, which are made of ebony placed on spiral springs, extend through the cover or keyboard, which is mounted on rubber rollers, actuated by springs on the ends, which, when moved rapidly, trill the strings, imitating the mandolin perfectly; in fact, a better trill can be made than with the hand. This improvement also keeps the instrument in better tune as the strings are picked evenly at all times. The accompaniment or guitar effect is produced with the left hand by picking the strings which are arranged in chords. Any chord or chords of the key of the instruments may be made as well as thirds and sixths. The wonderful simplicity of the instrument together with the numbered music which is published for it, makes it the greatest novelty of the musical world. An instruction book and a tuning hammer accompany each instrument.

A Bargain at $4.50

No. 22563 Deweylin Harp, made of selected material, ebonized with fancy decorated hand rest, exactly as shown in the illustration, has 31 strings, part of which are arranged so as to produce 4 chords as follows: C, G, and F major, and G seventh. Packed in neat pasteboard box with instruction book and tuning key. Weight, packed ready for shipment, 11 lbs. Our special price.......$4.50

No. 22565 Deweylin Harp, made of select material, beautifully ebonized and decorated with decalcomanie ornamentations around the edges; has 41 strings which are so arranged as to give 18 tones and 6 half tones on the keyboard, the balance arranged so as to produce five chords; C, G, D, D and A major. Packed in a neat paper box with instruction book and tuning key. Weight, packed ready for shipment, 16 pounds. Our special price, $6.75

THE CELEBRATED Marceau Band Instruments

23218 $11.31

23209 $7.20

23222 $11.75

23232 $8.95

23237 $13.15

$8.75 23206

SOLO ALTO

TENOR

SLIDE TROMBONE

WE ARE SOLE AGENTS FOR THE UNITED STATES.

We direct the attention of every band leader, every orchestra leader, in fact, every player of a band instrument to the wonderful line which we illustrate and describe on the following pages:

TO MEET A CERTAIN DEMAND for high class band instruments we have secured the sole agency of the Celebrated MARCEAU Instruments. These band instruments are made by Marceau & Co., of Paris, manufacturers with a reputation second to none for high class goods.

THERE ARE MORE EXPENSIVE INSTRUMENTS on the market, but the most of them are mainly expensive by reason of fancy engraving, rich plating or some external expense which adds little or nothing to the tone. These instruments are superior in every respect. They are the Improved short model, the shortest possible consistent with the best musical production. The pattern is graceful and handsome. In tone they are wonderfully perfect and the action is acknowledged by all to be superior in every respect. The finish of these instruments is such as you will find in only the highest class carried by retail dealers.

DO NOT BE DECEIVED by retail dealers who claim to be offering Marceau instruments. No dealer in this country can handle them. They can only be obtained through us as sole agents. Do not be deceived by retail dealers who offer inferior instruments, saying that they are just as good as the Marceau.

WE NOT ONLY COVER EACH INSTRUMENT with a binding guarantee that it shall be perfect in every respect, in tone, quality, model, finish and workmanship, and if any is found not fully up to representation it may be returned to us at our own expense and money refunded, but we furthermore ship on the most liberal C. O. D. terms, the conditions of which you can send $1.00 with order and the instrument selected will be shipped to your express office C. O. D., subject to examination and approval. Pay the balance with express charges to express agent when you have seen and examined the instrument and found it exactly as represented.

FREE WITH EACH INSTRUMENT. We send with each instrument a German silver mouthpiece and music rack as well as a complete instruction book, by the use of which anyone can learn to play without the aid of a teacher. Remember, these instruments are fitted with genuine German silver piston valves and are the best French light action. Bear this in mind when comparing our instruments with others of cheaper make, inferior goods, which are even sold at much higher prices. BEAR IN MIND that most cheap instruments are fitted with the cheapest kind of pump action, an action which no reputable musician will have in his instrument.

FIVE DAYS' FREE TRIAL. To show the confidence we have in the superior quality of the MARCEAU BAND INSTRUMENTS we will allow the instrument to be returned after a five days' trial if not found exactly as represented and entirely satisfactory.

Marceau Eb Cornets.

MARCEAU Eb CORNET. The many musicians who have testified to the wonderfully pure tone of this cornet have not said all that can be said in its praise. An adequate idea of the value which we give can only be had by a personal examination and trial. It is a really high grade brass instrument, short model, fine tone and superior workmanship. Complete with German silver mouthpiece, German silver light action piston valves, music rack and water key. Shipping weight, 7 pounds.

No. 23206 Our special price......................................$6.75
No. 23207 Same as above, finely nickel plated 7.75

Marceau Bb Cornets.

No. 23209 In addition to the German silver mouthpiece, set piece and music rack, this special cornet is fitted with genuine French piston valves, the lightest action made. We ship on our regular liberal C. O. D. terms.
Our special price, all brass.....................................$6.95
No. 23210 The Marceau. Same elegant Bb Cornet as No. 23209 above, but finely nickel plated throughout and elegantly finished.
Our special price..$7.95

Marceau Double Water Key Bb Cornet.

No. 23211 This model is similar to the Cornet No. 23209, but is made of a much better grade of brass, finely tempered; has better joints and braces, the lightest possible French action, German silver piston valves and double water key. Our special price.....................$8.75
No. 23214 Made of brass, same description as above, but finely nickel plated and polished. Our special price.........$9.75
Shipping weight, 7 pounds.

Marceau C Cornet for $7.95.

No. 23215 By using a C Cornet the music does not have to be transposed as with the Bb Cornet. A song with piano accompaniment is played just as written. The improved short model is the most desirable and this pattern is particularly excellent. In workmanship and tone it far excels the cheap instruments sold by retail dealers at often 50 per cent above our price. It is fitted with French light action, German silver piston valves, and is furnished complete with German silver mouthpiece, water key and music rack. The cornet is made of best brass, handsomely finished, and is graceful in pattern. Improved short model and perfect in tone. Our special price....................$7.95
No. 23216 We can furnish the Marceau C Cornet exactly the same as No. 23215 above, but finely nickel plated throughout. Our price..............................$8.95
Shipping weight, 7 pounds.

Artist's Model Double Water Key Bb Cornet.

No. 23218 In addition to the German silver mouthpiece, double water key and music rack, it is fitted with genuine French piston valves, the finest piston valves made. Shipping weight, 7 pounds.
Our special price, all brass...............................$11.25
No. 23219 The Marceau Bb Cornet. Same as No. 23218 above, but expensively nickel plated and finely finished. Our special price.................................$12.25
No. 23220 The Marceau AA Grade Artists' Model. Double Water Key Bb Cornet. In appearance this cornet is like No. 23218 short model, but made of a much better grade of brass, properly tempered, reinforced class joints and braces; has the lightest of action, German silver piston valves, double water key, and is furnished complete with an A set piece, German silver mouthpiece, music rack and instruction book. Our special price $14.35
No. 23221 Same description as No. 23220 but is handsomely nickel plated and polished. Shipping weight, 7pounds. Our special price..$15.35

Marceau Solo Eb Altos.

No. 23222 The Marceau Solo Eb Alto, an instrument that has the very highest reputation with musicians of wide repute. We furnish it complete with German silver mouthpiece and music rack. Price, all brass........$11.75
No. 23223 We furnish the Marceau Solo Eb Alto same as No. 23222 above, but finely nickel plated. Shipping weight, 9 lbs.
Our special price.......................................$13.7

The Marceau Eb Alto Trombones.

No. 23224 This instrument is of the finest French manufacture, extra light action, improved short model. In addition to the German silver mouthpiece and music rack, this instrument is fitted with genuine French piston valves, genuine German silver, the finest and easiest acting piston valves manufactured. It is made of the finest polished brass, beautifully finished, and is an instrument which is sought after by artist and amateur alike.
Our special price in polished brass..................$11.70
No. 23225 The Marceau Eb Alto Trombone, precisely the same as No. 23224 above, but very finely nickel plated and elegantly finished.
Price.........................$13.65

The Marceau Bb Tenor Trombones.

No. 23226 This trombone, in addition to the German silver mouthpiece and music rack, is fitted with the finest French piston valves, which have no superior for lightness of action. The model, pattern and workmanship of these instruments is unrivaled.
Our special price in all brass.....................$13.10
No. 23227 We can also furnish the Marceau Bb Tenor Trombone exactly the same as No. 23226 above, but nickel plated throughout and handsomely polished. Our special price.............$16.10

The Marceau Bb Baritone Trombones.

No. 23228 This trombone is made of all brass, very handsomely finished throughout. It is improved model, of best French manufacture, extra light action, French piston valves, the best piston valves that are made. It is fitted with German silver mouthpiece and music rack. There is nothing in this instrument but what is equal to the best that is made.
Our special price in all brass.....................$15.50
No. 23229 Exactly the same as Bb Baritone Trombone, as above illustrated, the Marceau, but finely nickel plated throughout, and thoroughly finished in the best and most workmanlike manner. Our special price.............$18.50

Marceau Slide Trombones.   Our special prices are as follows:

No. 23230 Eb Alto Slide Trombone, all brass, highly polished	$ 8.25
No. 23231 Eb Alto Slide Trombone, nickel plated	10.25
No. 23232 Bb Tenor Slide Trombone, polished..........$8.95	No. 23233 Bb Tenor Slide Trombone, finely nickel plated..........10.95

Marceau Eb Altos.

No. 23235 Marceau Eb Alto. Best French manufacture, the improved short model and has the light action genuine French piston valves. This instrument is complete with German silver mouthpiece, and music rack. Our special price, in all brass.............$11.65
No. 23236 We also quote the Marceau Eb Alto, exactly the same as No. 23235 but beautifully nickel plated. Our special price.............$13.60

Marceau Bb Tenors.

No. 23237 This Bb tenor is made of finely polished brass, is fitted with nicely finished German silver mouthpiece and music rack, finest French piston valves. Our special price.............$13.15
No. 23238 We likewise furnish this Marceau Bb Tenor, just the same as No. 23237 above, but finely nickel plated throughout.
Our special price.............$16.15

Marceau Eb Bass.

No. 23248 The Marceau Eb bass, exactly like illustration, but as all musicians know, is of much larger size. Fitted with best light action, German silver piston valve complete with German silver mouthpiece and music rack.....$24.45
No. 23250 Same as No. 23248, but nickel plated.. 28.65

WE INVITE Members of bands already formed, and all who contemplate organization, to CORRESPOND WITH US before contracting for their instruments. We can save you money and furnish you better goods. OUR ENORMOUS DEALINGS with the best foreign and American makers of High Grade Instruments are sufficient reasons for a lower price than any dealer can name.

BE SURE TO CONSULT US FIRST.

We Give Herewith a Variety of Combinations for Bands, indicating the Proper Assortment of Instruments.

Marceau Bb Baritones.

No. 23240 We fit the instruments complete with German silver mouthpiece and music rack. Our special price, in all brass.............$15.75
No. 23242 We have this same Marceau Bb baritone, exactly like No. 23240, but finely nickel plated. Our special price.............$18.50

Marceau Bb Bass.

No. 23244 The best French pistons made of German silver. We fit the instrument complete with mouthpiece and music rack. It is made of the best polished brass, is beautiful in appearance and possesses a tone that is rich, powerful and pleasing. Our special price, in all brass, carefully packed and safe delivery guaranteed. Our special price.............$16.95
No. 23246 We can also furnish the Marceau Bb Bass exactly the same as No. 23244 above, but finely nickel plated throughout, instead of plain polished brass. Our special price.............$20.25

BAND OF 6.	BAND OF 7.	BAND OF 8.	BAND OF 9.	BAND OF 10.	BAND OF 11.
1 Eb Cornet.	1 Eb Cornet.	1 Eb Cornet.	2 Eb Cornets.	2 Eb Cornets.	2 Eb Cornets.
2 Bb Cornets.	2 Bb Cornets.	2 Bb Cornets.	2 Bb Cornets.	2 Bb Cornets.	2 Bb Cornets.
1 Eb Alto.	1 Eb Alto.	2 Eb Altos.	2 Eb Altos.	2 Eb Altos.	2 Eb Altos.
1 Bb Tenor.	1 Bb Tenor.	1 Bb Tenor.	1 Bb Tenor.	2 Bb Tenors.	2 Bb Tenors.
1 Eb Bass.	1 Bb Baritone.	1 Bb Baritone.	1 Bb Baritone.	1 Bb Baritone.	1 Bb Baritone
	1 Eb Bass.	1 Eb Bass.	1 Eb Bass.	1 Eb Bass.	1 Bb Bass.
					1 Eb Bass.

BAND OF 12.	BAND OF 13.	BAND OF 14.	BAND OF 15.	BAND OF 16.	BAND OF 17.
2 Eb Cornets.	2 Eb Cornets.	2 Eb Cornets.	3 Eb Cornets.	3 Eb Cornets.	4 Eb Cornets.
2 Bb Cornets.	3 Bb Cornets.	3 Bb Cornets.	3 Bb Cornets.	4 Bb Cornets.	4 Bb Cornets.
2 Eb Altos.	2 Eb Altos.	2 Eb Altos.	2 Eb Altos.	2 Eb Altos.	2 Eb Altos.
2 Bb Tenors.	2 Bb Tenors.	2 Bb Tenors.	2 Bb Tenors.	2 Bb Tenors.	2 Bb Tenors.
1 Bb Baritone.	1 Bb Baritone.	1 Bb Baritone.	1 Bb Baritone.	1 Bb Baritone.	1 Bb Baritone.
1 Bb Bass.	1 Bb Bass.	1 Bb Bass.	1 Bb Bass.	1 Bb Bass.	1 Bb Bass.
1 Eb Bass.	2 Eb Basses.	2 Eb Basses.	2 Eb Basses.	2 Eb Basses.	2 Eb Basses.

23248 $24.45

23240 $15.75

23235 $11.65

Eb BASS

BARITONE

ALTO

VALVE TROMBONE 23224 $11.70

SUBSCRIPTION BOOKS AT MANUFACTURERS' PRICES.

Books that have been sold everywhere by traveling and local book agents, sold by subscription at $2.00 to $5.00, we offer at 75c and $1.00.
OUR PRICES are based on the actual cost of PAPER, PRINTING and BINDING, with but our one small profit added, which means in many cases less than ONE-THIRD the price at which agents have always sold these books.

Story of the Wild West and Camp Fire Chats.

No. 28996 By Buffalo Bill, (Hon. W. F. Cody.) A full and complete history of the renowned pioneer quartette, Boone, Crockett, Carson and Buffalo Bill. Replete with graphic descriptions of wild life and thrilling adventures by famous heroes of the frontier. A record of exciting events on the western borders pushed westward to the sea, massacres, desperate battles, extraordinary bravery, marvelous fortitude, astounding heroism, grand hunts, rollicking anecdotes, tales of sorrow, droll stories, curious escapades and a melange of incidents that make up the melodrama of civilization in its march over mountains and prairies to the Pacific, including a description of Buffalo Bill's conquests in England with his wild west exhibition, where royalty from all the European nations paid him generous homage and made his wonderful show the greatest success of modern times; 250 original illustrations and a beautiful lithographed frontispiece. Handsomely bound in dark red cloth, stamped in gold. Head band. Contains 766 pages.
Retail price, $3.00; our special price..............90c
Weight packed, 52 ounces. See page 4 for postal rates.

AMERICA.

No. 28997 Her patriotism, stories of exciting events, true and thrilling incidents relating to the wonderful progress and achievements of our country. By Prof. Allen F. Fowler. Among other valuable information this book contains a true biographical sketch of Columbus, Penn, Grant, Jackson, Lee, Franklin, Washington, Lincoln and other noted men. Copiously illustrated with handsome engravings. Contains 352 large quarto pages; elegant lithographed frontispiece. Bound in cloth, stamped in colored inks. Subscription price, $2.50; our special price..................75c
If by mail, postage extra, 18 cents.

Twenty Years of Hus'ling.

No. 28998 By John P. Johnson. A book bubbling with merriment, overflowing with fun, full of ridiculous incidents, replete with comic situations. A story of twenty years of a man's life, more interesting than fiction, portraying the peculiar and amusing incidents, laughable situations, failures and successes of a man who tried almost every kind of business. Not a dull page in the book. Illustrated with forty full-page wood cuts. Bound in cloth.
Retail price, $2.50; our price............55c
If by mail, postage extra, 20 cents.
No. 28999 Bound in paper covers. Price....30c
If by mail, postage extra, 6 cents.

United States Secret Service of the Late Civil War.

No. 29000 By Gen. Lafayette C. Baker. Exciting experience in the North and South, peerless adventures, hair-breadth escapes and valuable services of the detectives of the late Civil war. Fully illustrated. Contains 480 pages. Bound in cloth.
Retail price..................$2.50
Our price..........................80
If by mail, postage extra, 16 cents.

Glimpses of America.

No. 29001 Portraying the complete history of the United States and Scenic America by pen and camera, representing the works of the leading artists, both of the United States, Canada and Europe. This work also contains 400 reproductions of photographs. Size, 11¼x14. Subscription price, $4.00. Bound in English silk cloth, stamped in gold. Our price.......98c
If by mail, postage extra, 28 cents.

Story of Stanley and His Travels Through the Wilds of Africa.

No. 29002 A thrilling narrative of this remarkable adventurer's terrible experiences, wonderful discoveries and amazing achievements in the Dark Continent. His explorations to the Congo, the Relief of Emin Bey, with its terrible experiences of slavery, misery and death, are told in a graphic manner. Profusely illustrated. Bound in cloth; size, 7x9x2¼ inches.
Retail price, $3.00; our price....75c
If by mail, postage extra, each, 13 cents.

Makers of Millions;
Or The Marvelous Success of America's Self Made Men.

No. 29004½ Contains thrilling stories of the struggles, trials and triumphs of poor boys who rose to fame and fortune by their perseverance and genius. Among others, **Marshall Field, A. T. Stewart, P. D. Armour, the Vanderbilts, Geo. M. Pullman, Jas. Gordon Bennett, Henry W. Longfellow, Nathaniel Hawthorne, Elias Howe, Colt, Morse, Bonner, Hoe and Fulton.** Most of these famous men were rocked in the cradle of poverty and their struggles with adversity read like fiction. Bound in cloth; size 9x6¼ inches, illustrated; contains 598 pages. Subscription price, $2.00; our price....73c
If by mail, postage extra, each, 21 cents.

Story of American Heroism.

No. 29005 A war gallery of noted men and events, comprising exploits of scouts and spies, forlorn hopes, hand to hand struggles, imprisonments and hair-breadth escapes, perilous journeys, terrible hardships, patient endurance, bold dashes, brilliant successes, clever captures, daring raids, wonderful achievements, magnanimous action, romantic, humorous and tragic, etc. Beautifully illustrated with over 300 original drawings. Bound in cloth; emblematic designs in gold and colors. Subscription price, $4.00; our price....$1.85
Weight, packed, 50 ounces. See page 4 for postal rates.

Story of Cuba.

No. 29006 Her Struggles for Liberty. By Murat Halstead. Cause, crisis and destiny. From the discovery of Cuba by Columbus down through 400 years. Mr. Halstead spent several months in Cuba, and during his stay he was able to get material for this volume that has never before been printed. Complete in one large volume of 625 pages. Size, 6¾x9 inches, printed on extra fine quality of paper, in large clear, perfect type, magnificently illustrated with 40 full page original drawings and photographs, handsomely bound in cloth.
Subscription price, $4.00; our price.............98c
Weight, packed, 42 ounces. See page 4 for postal rates.

Forest and Jungle. Only 90 Cents.

No. 29006½ A rare book, thrilling and instructive, embracing vivid descriptions of the capture and taming of wild beasts, birds and reptiles, together with wonderful adventures in all quarters of the globe. This work is a complete history of the expedition which P. T. Barnum sent to Africa and India in search of curiosities. Contains nearly 250 illustrations, many of them full page. Size 10x8x2 inches, handsomely bound in fine English silk cloth, elaborately stamped. Contains 512 pages.
Subscription price, $3.00; our price.............90c
Weight, packed for shipment, 58 ounces. See page 4 for postal rates.

Napoleon—From Corsica to St. Helena

No. 29007 By John L. Stoddard. A new pictorial work, illustrating the career of the most famous military genius the world has ever known. It contains pictures of all Napoleon's marshals and generals, his relatives, also all the famous places in which Napoleon lived as Emperor, and of the monumen erected to perpetuate his brilliant achievements the battlefields of Europe. Size, 11¼x14 inches, 2 pages, 331 half-tone pictures, with descripti text. Bound in dark green cloth with the Napoleon coat of arms in silver embossed on cover. Subscri tion price, $2.50; our price............................9
Weight, packed for shipment, 74 ounces. See page 4 for postal rates.

Songs That Never Die.

A collection famous words a melodies. This ma nificent book co tains songs of t sea, of home a country, of the Gre Civil War, Nation Airs, Scotch and Iri melodies, lyrics love and sentime songs of the chur a charming collecti of instrumental mus etc. Enriched wi valuable historic and biographic sketches of renown authors and composers, Printed from clear new ty on fine calendered paper and contains over 600 pag with beautiful engravings, bound in cloth, silk finis marble edges.
No. 29009 Retail price, $3.00; our price 9
No. 29010 Bound in extra fine full moroc leather, gilt edges. Retail price, $4.00; our price. $1.
If by mail, postage extra, 26 cents.

Remarks by Bill Nye.

No. 29016 One of the greate works of humor of the 19th ce tury. In the author's preface says: **"It is my greatest and be book; it is the one that will li for weeks after other books ha passed away."** This work contai a selection of the best works of t gifted humorist, embracing 504 pages and containing over 160 illu trations. Bound in cloth, stamp in gold and ink on the side, and bac Size, 8¾x6¼ inches.
Subscription price $2.00; our price................4
Weight, packed for shipment, 50 ounces. See page 4 for postal rates.

Samantha at Saratoga.

No. 29018 By Josiah Allen's wife. The funniest book of all; written amid the whirl of fashion at Saratoga. Take off on fashion, flirtations, low neck dresses, dudes, pug dogs, the water craze, toboggans, etc. In the author's inimitable mirth provoking style. The 100 illustrations by Opper, are "just killing." 600 pages, printed on superior paper, cloth bound. Size, 9x6¼ inches.
Subscription price, $2.50; our price..............8
If by mail, postage extra, 24 cents.

John Sherman's Recollections of For Years in the House, Senate and Cabinet.

No. 29020 Personal Remin cences of the author, including t political and financial history the United States during his pub career as member of Congre United States Senator, Secretary the Treasury, President of the Unit States Senate, etc. Richly illustrat with carefully selected views, cluding places and scenes relati to the author's boyhood; also ma portraits of his contemporaries the cabinet and senate. Bound in cloth, gold si and back stamp, plain edges.
Subscription price, $6.00; our price..........$1.
No. 29021 Bound in half morocco, gold cent back, marbled edges. Retail price, $8.00;
Our price.....................................$2.
If by mail, postage extra, 36 cents.

Illustrated Home Book of the World's Great Nations.

No. 29022 Geographical, Historical, Pictorial. The scenes, events, manners and customs of many nations, ancient and modern, graphically described by pen and pencil. It contains hundreds of well written articles, detailing the knowledge and experience of scores of famous travelers and explorers in the out of the way corners of the earth. Size, 9¾x11x1¼ inches. 670 pages, over 1,000 illustrations. Bound in cloth.
Retail price, $2.00; our price.....................9
Weight, packed for shipment, 5¼ pounds. See page 4 for postal rates.

Shams; or, Uncle Ben's Experience with Hypocrites.

No. 29023 A delightfully humorous and entertaining book, by "Uncle Ben Morgan" It gives a clear picture of everyday life in rural districts. All who have crossed a farm or halted in front of a country school house, will enjoy its reading. **Uncle Ben's trip to the city of Chicago and to California and his amusing experience with the shams and sharpers of the metropolitan** world. Full of funny incidents, combined with good sense, interesting narrative and keen satire. Illustrated with over 100 original illustrations by **True Williams.** Bound in cloth; size of book, 7x8¾ inches, 20 pages. Subscription price, $2.00; our price....**40c**
If by mail, postage extra, 18 cents.

One Thousand Gems of Genius in Poetry and Art.

No. 29024 A vast collection of gems that will live forever, embracing the writings of Will Carleton, James Whitcomb Riley, Eugene Field, Robert Burns, Lord Byron, Tennyson, Moore, Longfellow, Whittier, Bryant and others. This volume cannot fail to prove a great source of entertainment and instruction. To become intimately acquainted with these great authors, through the medium of this book, will exert influence on the reader which cannot be overestimated. Beautifully illustrated. Bound in cloth. Subscription price, $2.50; our price..............**98c**
If by mail, postage extra, 24 cents.

Glimpses of the World.

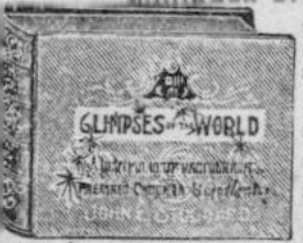

No. 29026 Containing hundreds of full page views, portraying scenes all over the world. This work presents a grand panorama of England, Scotland and Ireland, France, Germany, Russia, Austria, Turkey, Italy, Spain, Asia, Africa and North and South America. Contains 550 pages, printed on the finest quality of heavy book paper, handsomely bound in silk cloth, side and back stamp. Subscription price $5.00; our price............**$1.90**
Bound in full morocco, gold stamped, gilt edges. Retail price, $8.00; our price..................**$3.65**
Weight, packed for shipment 8 lbs.

Indian Horrors; or, Massacres by the Redmen.

No. 29027 By H. D. Northrop. A thrilling narrative of bloody wars with **merciless savages; startling descriptions of fanatic ghost dances; mysterious medicine men; desperate Indian braves; scalping of helpless settlers; burning their houses, etc.** Beautifully illustrated with fine engravings printed in colors. Battles, pictures, and other thrilling scenes among the Indians. Handsomely bound in cloth, marbled edges, size, 6¼x8¼ inches. Retail price, $2.00; our price............**73c**
If by mail, postage extra, 18 cents.

Reminiscences of the War.

This magnificent work contains vivid accounts of personal experiences by officers and men; Admiral Dewey's report of the famous battle of Manila; also account of Admiral Schley of the naval battle near Santiago; glowing descriptions of the battles by officers of the vessels; daring deeds of our brave soldiers at the battles of La Quasina, El Caney and San Juan, to which is added Admiral Cervera's story of his attempt to escape from Santiago; Lieut. Hobson's account of the sinking of the Merrimac; exciting experiences in Porto Rico and at the capture of Manila; battles with the Filipino insurgents, etc. Contains 800 pages, numerous illustrations.
No. 29029 Bound in English silk cloth, marbled edges. Subscription price, $2.50; our special price **85c**
No. 29030 Bound in genuine morocco, gilt edges. Subscription price, $4.00; our special price.....**$1.20**
If by mail, postage extra, 16 cents.

Explorations and Adventures of Henry M. Stanley.

No. 29031 Including Livingstone, Baker, Cameron, Speke, Emin Pasha, Anderson, etc. Contains thrilling accounts of famous expeditions, miraculous escapes, wild sports in the jungle and plain, curious customs of savage races, journeys in unknown lands, graphic descriptions of beautiful scenery, fertile valleys, vast forests, mighty rivers and cataracts, mines of untold wealth, etc. Cloth, Illustrated, library style. Retail price, $2.50; our price.......**90c**
If by mail, postage extra, 24 cents.

Heroic Deeds in our War with Spain.

No. 29033 The most interesting book of the age. **A $2.50 book for $1.35.** A history of the fighting on land and sea by the American soldier and sailor during our war with Spain. Edited by able correspondents who were eye-witnesses. Beautifully illustrated with original drawings designed especially for this work. Handsomely bound in buckram cloth with elaborate side stamp in gold and colors. Size, 9¼x7½x1½ inches. Subscription price, $3.00; our price........................**$1.35**
If by mail, postage extra, 26 cents.

No. 29035 A collection of witty writings by **Mark Twain, Robert J. Burdette, Eli Perkins, Josh Billings, Alexander Sweet, Bill Nye, Petroleum V. Nasby, John B. Gough, Jas. Russell Lowell, Artemus Ward, Proctor Knott, Henry Ward Beecher, Murat Halstead, M. Quad, Geo. W. Peck, Bret Harte, T. De Witt Talmage, Mary Mapes Dodge, Oliver Wendell Holmes, S. S. Cox, Wm. M. Evarts, Will Carleton, Benj. F. Butler, Mrs. Partington,** and nearly fifty others. Humor, wit, pathos, satire, and ridicule, repartee, bulls and blunders, clerical wit and humor, lawyers' wit and humor, anecdotes of great men, puns and conundrums, doctors' wit and humor, political wit and humor, temperance anecdotes, Irish wit, negro wit, women's pathos and humor, children's wit and blunders, railway jokes and anecdotes, charades, riddles, puzzles, etc. **Contains over thirty full page illustrations drawn especially for this work** by leading artists. Contains over 800 pages. Bound in cloth. Subscription price, $2.00; our price.................................**98c**
If by mail, postage extra, 26 cents.

Boers and Britishers in South Africa.

No. 29037 A history of the Boer-British War and the wars in United South Africa, together with biographies of men who have made South Africa. **By John Orimond Neville,** historian, war correspondent and military expert. This volume contains many interesting chapters, among which are the following: How Africa is divided among the nations; facts concerning the people who inhabit it; biographical descriptions of Oom Paul, of Joubert and Cronje. This book is illustrated with many full-page half-tones and other illustrations. Handsomely bound in cloth, stamped in colored inks.
Subscription price, $3.00; our price..................**85c**
If by mail, postage extra, 16 cents.

Uncle Tom's Cabin.

No. 29039 A magnificent edition of this wonderful tale of life among the lowly. Illustrated with over 100 original drawings by celebrated artists and a portrait of the author. The sale of this book has been enormous, reaching nearly two million copies. Bound in cloth, stamped in colored inks. Size, 6x8¾ inches.
Subscription price.... $2.50
Our price................**98c**
If by mail, postage extra, 24 cents.

The World's Brightest Gems of Music.

No. 29041 Contains the richest and most delightful gems from many lands, sacred, patriotic, comic and sentimental. This magnificent book contains the writings of such noted composers as Bennet, Watson, Lesky, Barnby, Adams, Densa and other noted authors. This book is handsomely bound in cloth, stamped in colored inks and gold. Retail price, $3.00; our price............................**$1.15**
If by mail, postage extra, 24 cents.

Beautiful Gems of Thought and Sentiment.

A vast collection of choice productions in Poetry, Prose and Music from the literature of all nations; containing captivating songs of love and romance, narratives and legends, lyrics of heroism and adventure, poems of sentiment and tragedy, beautiful descriptions of scenes in nature; songs for the fireside, melodies, wit and humor, pathos, etc. Printed from clear, new type on calendered paper. Contains 663 pages, embellished with a galaxy of beautiful phototype engravings. **(Postage extra, 21 cents.)**
No. 29043 Bound in fine silk cloth, marbled edges. Retail price, $3 50; our price..................**$1.55**
No. 29044 Bound in full morocco, gilt edges. Retail price. $4.00; our price...................**$1.95**

MEDICAL WORKS.

In this our latest catalogue we have endeavored to offer our customers a selection of the very best medical works as given by the very best authorities.
Every medical book offered is of the highest standard of authority, our prices the lowest ever made on this basis. We earnestly ask for your trade.
Remember, we will ship any book or books C. O. D., subject to examination on receipt of $1.00, balance payable after received.

Every Man His Own Doctor.

No. 29129 A complete family medical adviser. New edition revised and enlarged, **containing knowledge that will promote health, cure disease and prolong life, describing all diseases, and teaching how to cure them by the simplest medicines; Also physiology and functions, diseases of the menstrual function; the womb and its diseases; pregnancy and its disorders; the breast and its disorders;** confinement; abortion; miscarriage. **A chapter for the especial perusal of youths of understanding, as well as for that of fathers and guardians;** on the relations between man and wife, a chapter for the newly married. Contains illustrations and charts, 598 pages, bound in cloth. Retail price, $3.00; our price..............................**98c**
If by mail, postage extra, 20 cents.

New American Family Physician.

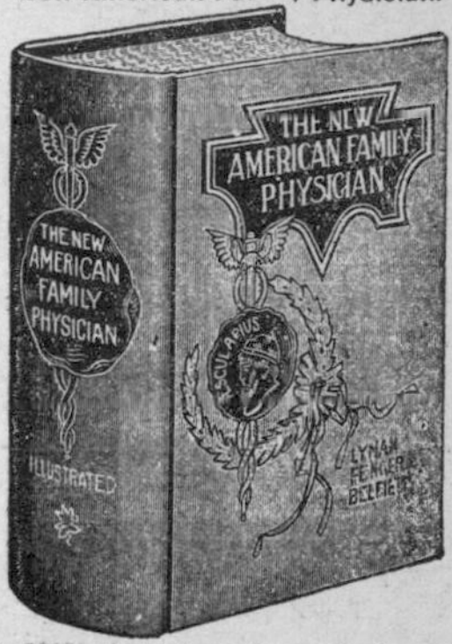

No. 29130 A popular guide for the household management of disease, giving the history, cause, means of prevention and symptoms of all diseases, and the most approved methods of treatment; with plain instructions for the care of the sick, **full and accurate directions for treating wounds, injuries, poisoning, etc.,** also giving a concise account of the structure and functions of the human body, hygiene and rules of health. Written and compiled by **Henry H. Lyman, A. M., M. D.; Christian Fenger, A. M., M. D.; W. T. Belfield, A. M., M. D.; H. W. Jones, A. M., M. D.**
Contains: Exhaustive treatment of all sexual considerations; distinctive traits of the sexes; development of the sexual organs; determining the sex of offspring in advance. **Marriage.**—Factors to be considered in entering the marriage relation; physical basis of marriage; time to marry; the wedding tour, etc. **Pregnancy.**—Rules of conduct during pregnancy; diseases of pregnancy; hygiene of pregnancy; accidents of pregnancy—causes, symptoms and treatment; prevention of pregnancy; to calculate the time of confinement; confinement. **Diseases of Women.**—How caused; unwillingness of women to become mothers; prevention of conception and its effects; special diseases of the organs of generation; sterility and its causes. **Reproductive Organs.**—In addition to over 200 pages of plain talk on the diseases of women and children, this work is supplemented by a thirty-two page pamphlet placed in a pocket made inside the back cover of the book. This pamphlet contains 29 special plates illustrating the female productive organs, each plate being fully described. Bound in art buckram, marbled edges. Size, 10¼x8x4 inches.
Retail price, $4.75; our price.....................**$1.60**
If by mail, postage extra, 38 cents.

Advice to a Wife.

No. 29131 On the Management of Her Own Health and on the Treatment of Some of the Complaints Incidental to Pregnancy, Labor and Suckling. Revised by Fancourt Barnes, M. D., F. R. S. E., consulting physician to the British Lying-In-Hospital. 14th edition. Size, 5¼x7¼ inches. Cloth.
Retail price, $1.25; our price.........................**75c**
If by mail, postage extra, 12 cents.

Advice to a Mother.

No. 29132 On the Management of Her Children and on the Treatment on the Moment of Some of Their More Pressing Illnesses and Accidents. Revised by George Carpenter, M. D. Bound in cloth. Size, 5¼x7¼ inches. Retail price, $1.00; our price..**70c**
If by mail, postage extra, 12 cents.

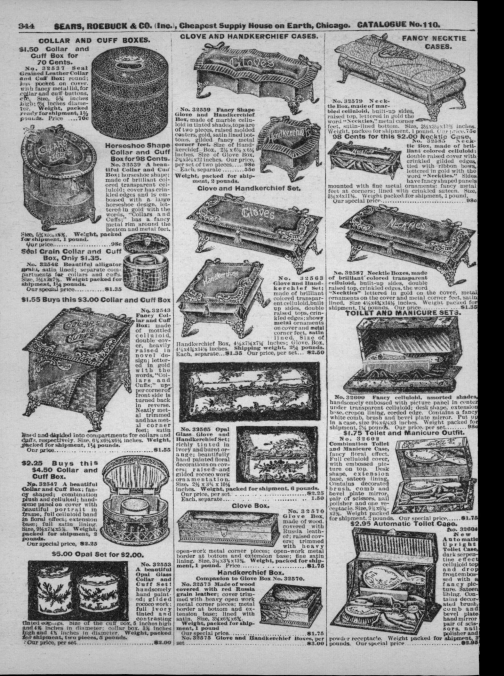

COLLAR AND CUFF BOXES.

$1.50 Collar and Cuff Box for 70 Cents.

No. 32537 Seal Grained Leather Collar and Cuff Box; round; has pocket on cover, with fancy metal lid, for collar and cuff buttons, etc. Size, 5¾ inches high; 6¼ inches diameter. **Weight, packed ready for shipment, 1½ pounds.** Price 70c

Horseshoe Shape Collar and Cuff Box for 98 Cents.

No. 32539 A beautiful Collar and Cuff Box; horseshoe shape; made of brilliant colored transparent celluloid; cover has crinkled edges and is embossed with a large horseshoe design, lettered in gold with the words, "Collars and Cuffs;" has a fancy metal rim around the bottom and metal feet. Size, 5¾x5½x6¾. **Weight, packed for shipment, 1 pound.**
Our price....................................98c

Seal Grain Collar and Cuff Box, Only $1.35.

No. 32542 Beautiful alligator grain, satin lined; separate compartments for collars and cuffs. Size, 5½x7x7⅜. **Weight packed for shipment, 1¼ pounds.**
Our special price............$1.35

$1.55 Buys this $3.00 Collar and Cuff Box

No. 32543 Fancy Collar and Cuff Box; made of mottled celluloid, double cover, heavily raised in novel design; lettered in gold with the words, "Collars and Cuffs;" upper corner of front side is turned back in reverse. Neatly metal trimmed and has metal corner feet; satin lined and divided into compartments for collars and cuffs, respectively. Size, 6⅞x6¼x6½ inches. **Weight, packed for shipment, 1¼ pounds.**
Our price.......................................$1.55

$2.25 Buys this $4.50 Collar and Cuff Box.

No. 32547 A beautiful Collar and Cuff Box; fancy shaped; combination plush and celluloid; handsome panel on cover with beautiful portrait in frame, full celluloid band in floral effect; extension base; full satin lining. Size, 9½x7¼x5⅞. **Weight, packed for shipment, 2 pounds.**
Our special price, $2.25

$5.00 Opal Set for $2.00.

No. 32553 A beautiful Opal Glass Collar and Cuff Set! handsomely hand painted; gilded rococo work; full ivory tinted and contrasting tinted edgings. Size of the cuff box, 5 inches high and 4⅞ inches in diameter; collar box, 3⅞ inches high and 4⅞ inches in diameter. **Weight, packed for shipment, two pieces, 5 pounds.**
Our price, per set.......................................$2.00

GLOVE AND HANDKERCHIEF CASES.

No. 32559 Fancy Shape Glove and Handkerchief Box, made of marble celluloid in tinted shades, tops are of two pieces, raised molded centers, gold, satin lined bottoms, gilded fancy metal corner feet. Size of Handkerchief Box, 2¾ x 6½ x 6¾ inches. Size of Glove Box, 2⅝x5¼x12 inches. Our price, per set of two pieces.....98c
Each, separate..........55c
Weight, packed for shipment, 2 pounds.

Glove and Handkerchief Set.

No. 32563 Glove and Handkerchief Set; made of brilliant colored transparent celluloid, built up sides, double raised tops, crinkled edges; showy metal ornaments on cover and metal corner feet, satin lined. Size of Handkerchief Box, 4½x7¾x7¼ inches; Glove Box, 4¼x4¾x14½ inches. **Shipping weight, 2¼ pounds.**
Each, separate...$1.35 Our price, per set... $2.50

No. 32565 Opal Glass Glove and Handkerchief Set; richly tinted in ivory and burnt orange; beautifully hand painted floral decorations on covers; raised and gilded rococo work ornamentation. Size, 2⅝ x 3¾ x 10⅛ inches. **Weight, packed for shipment, 6 pounds.**
Our price, per set.......................$2.25
Each, separate..............................1.50

Glove Box.

No. 32570 Glove Box, made of wood, covered with Russia leather; raised covers; trimmed with heavy open-work metal corner pieces; open-work metal border at bottom and extension base; fine satin lining. Size, 3½x3⅜x13⅜. **Weight, packed for shipment, 1 pound.** Price.......................$1.75

Handkerchief Box.
Companion to Glove Box No. 32570.

No. 32573 Made of wood covered with red Russia grain leather; cover trimmed with heavy open work metal corner pieces; metal border at bottom and extension base; lined with satin. Size, 3¼x6¾x6¾. **Weight, packed for shipment, 1 pound**
Our special price.......................$1.75
No. 32575 Glove and Handkerchief Boxes, per set.......................................$3.00

FANCY NECKTIE CASES.

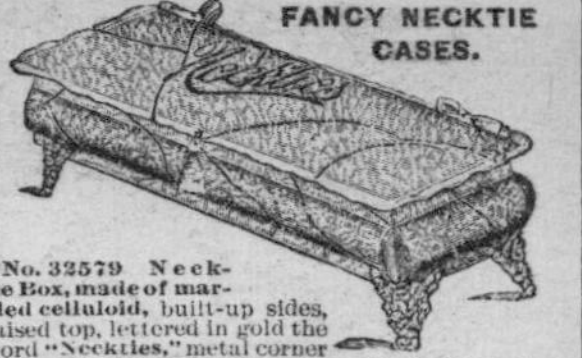

No. 32579 Necktie Box, made of marbled celluloid, built-up sides, raised top, lettered in gold the word "Neckties," metal corner feet, satin-lined bottom. Size, 3½x3½x13⅜ inches. Weight, packed for shipment, 1 pound. Our price.75c

98 Cents for this $2.00 Necktie Case.

No. 32585 Necktie Box, made of brilliant colored celluloid; double raised cover with crinkled gilded edges, tied with ribbon bows, lettered in gold with the word "Neckties." Sides have fancy shaped panels mounted with fine metal ornaments; fancy metal feet at corners; lined with crinkled sateen. Size, 3¾x4x11⅝. Weight packed for shipment, 1 pound.
Our special price.......................................98c

No. 32587 Necktie Boxes, made of brilliant colored transparent celluloid, built-up sides, double raised top, crinkled edges, the word "Neckties" lettered in gold on the cover, metal ornaments on the cover and metal corner feet, satin lined. Size 4½x4¾x14½ inches. Weight packed for shipment, 1½ pounds. Our price..................$1.35

TOILET AND MANICURE SETS.

No. 32600 Fancy celluloid, assorted shades, handsomely embossed with picture panel in center under transparent celluloid; desk shape, extension base, crepon lining, corded edge. Contains a fancy white comb, brush and bevel plate mirror. Put up in a case, size 9½x4½x3 inches. Weight packed for shipment, 2½ pounds. Our price, per set..........98c

$1.75 Toilet and Manicure Outfit.

No. 32602 Combination Toilet and Manicure Case, fancy floral effect. Full celluloid cover, with embossed picture on top. Desk shape, extension base, sateen lining. Contains decorated brush, comb and bevel plate mirror, pair of scissors, nail polisher and one receptacle. Size, 9⅞x6½x3⅜. Weight packed for shipment, 2 pounds. Our special price......$1.75

$2.95 Automatic Toilet Case.

No. 32604 New Automatic Upright Toilet Case, dark serpentine effect celluloid top and drop front embossed with a fancy picture. Sateen lining. Contains decorated brush, comb and bevel plate hand mirror, pair of scissors, nail polisher and powder receptacle. Weight packed for shipment, 3 pounds. Our special price.......................$2.95

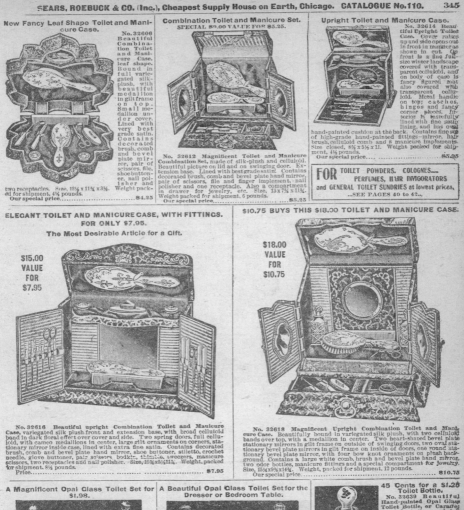

New Fancy Leaf Shape Toilet and Manicure Case.

No. 32606 Beautiful Combination Toilet and Manicure Case, leaf shape. Bound in full variegated silk-plush, with beautiful medallion in gilt frame on top. Small medallion under cover. Lined with very best grade satin. Contains decorated brush, comb and bevel plate mirror, pair of scissors, file, shoe buttoner, nail polisher and two receptacles. Size, 12¾ x 11¾ x 3⅜. Weight packed for shipment, 4½ pounds.
Our special price..................................$4.25

Combination Toilet and Manicure Set.

SPECIAL $9.00 VALUE FOR $5.25.

No. 32612 Magnificent Toilet and Manicure Combination Set, made of silk-plush and celluloid. Beautiful picture on lid and on swinging door. Extension base. Lined with best grade satin. Contains decorated brush, comb and bevel plate hand mirror, pair of scissors, file and finger implement, nail polisher and one receptacle. Also a compartment in drawer for jewelry, etc. Size, 13 x 7⅞ x 11¾. Weight packed for shipment, 6 pounds.
Our special price..............................$5.25

Upright Toilet and Manicure Case.

No. 32614 Beautiful Upright Toilet Case. Cover raises up and side opens out in front in manner as shown in cut. On front is a fine full size winter landscape covered with transparent celluloid, and on body of case is fancy figured mat also covered with transparent celluloid. Metal handle on top; catches, hinges and fancy corner pieces. Interior is tastefully lined with fine satin lining, and has oval hand-painted cushion at the back. Contains fine set of high-grade hand-painted fittings—mirror, hair brush, celluloid comb and 8 manicure implements. Size closed, 8⅝ x 5½ x 11. Weight packed for shipment, 4½ pounds.
Our special price....................................$5.95

FOR TOILET POWDERS, COLOGNES, PERFUMES, HAIR INVIGORATORS and GENERAL TOILET SUNDRIES at lowest prices, ...SEE PAGES 40 to 42...

ELEGANT TOILET AND MANICURE CASE, WITH FITTINGS. FOR ONLY $7.95.

The Most Desirable Article for a Gift.

$15.00 VALUE FOR $7.95

No. 32616 Beautiful upright Combination Toilet and Manicure Case, variegated silk plush front and extension base, with broad celluloid band in dark floral effect over cover and side. Two spring doors, full celluloid, with cameo medallions in center, large gilt ornaments on corners, stationary mirror inside case, lined with extra fine satin. Contains decorated brush, comb and bevel plate hand mirror, shoe buttoner, stiletto, crochet needle, glove buttoner, pair scissors, bodkin, thimble, tweezers, manicure scissors, two receptacles and nail polisher. Size, 15¾x5¾x11¾. Weight, packed for shipment, 8½ pounds.
Price...$7.95

$10.75 BUYS THIS $18.00 TOILET AND MANICURE CASE.

$18.00 VALUE FOR $10.75

No. 32618 Magnificent Upright Combination Toilet and Manicure Case. Beautifully bound in variegated silk plush, with two celluloid bands over top, with a medallion in center. Two heart-shaped bevel plate stationary mirrors in gilt frame on outside of swinging doors, two oval stationary bevel plate mirrors in gilt frame on inside of doors, one round stationary bevel plate mirror, with four bow knot ornaments on plush background. Contains a large white comb, brush and bevel plate hand mirror, two odor bottles, manicure fittings and a special compartment for jewelry. Size, 15¼x9⅝x14¾. Weight, packed for shipment, 12 pounds.
Our special price...$10.75

A Magnificent Opal Glass Toilet Set for $1.98.

No. 32633 A Beautiful Opal Glass Dresser and Toilet Set; consisting of two toilet bottles or caraffes, size 9⅝ inches high and 6 inches in diameter; 1 trinket box, 1¾x2¾x4¼; 1 puff box, 2⅝ inches high and 3⅝ inches in diameter; 1 comb and brush tray, size 8¾ inches wide and 12¼ inches in length; 1 manicure or trinket tray, size 4⅝ inches wide and 9 inches in length. All are decorated with raised and gilded rococo work, neatly hand-painted, tinted edgings. The bottles have wide ribbon bows. **Weight, packed for shipment, 10 pounds.** Our price..$1.98

A Beautiful Opal Glass Toilet Set for the Dresser or Bedroom Table.

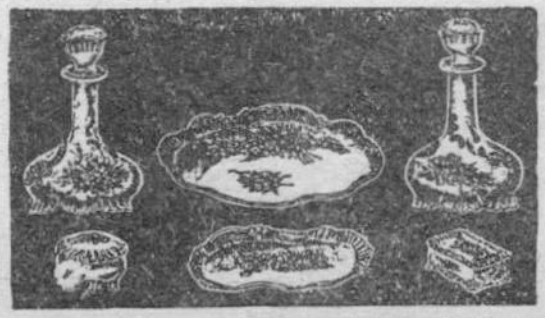

No. 32636 Containing 6 pieces; beautifully hand-painted; full tinted, with contrasting tinted edges; raised and gilded rococo work. This set consists of 2 toilet bottles, or caraffes, size 9⅝ inches high, 6 inches in diameter; 1 trinket box, size 1¾x2¾x4¼ inches; 1 puff box, 2⅝ inches high; 3½ inches in diameter; 1 comb and brush tray, 8¾ inches wide, 12½ inches in length, and 1 manicure or trinket tray, size 4⅝x9 inches long. Our price.............................$2.35
Weight, packed for shipment, 11 pounds.

45 Cents for a $1.25 Toilet Bottle.

No. 32639 Beautiful Hand-painted Opal Glass Toilet Bottle, or Caraffe; floral decorations and full ivory tinted. Size 3½ inches high, 5½ inches in diameter.
Our price...................45c
Weight, packed for shipment, 2 pounds.

Hand-Painted Opal Glass, Puff or Powder Box.

No. 32643 Hand-Painted Opal Glass, Puff or Powder Box, beautifully tinted and neatly hand-painted. Size, 3⅛ x 4¾ inches. **Weight, packed for shipment, 1 lb.**
Our price.........25c

Sears Roebuck & Co.
INCORPORATED
SPORTING
GOODS
DEPARTMENT

WE ARE HEADQUARTERS FOR EVERYTHING IN

Guns, Revolvers, Ammunition, Gun Implements,	Hunters' Clothing, Fishing Tackle,	Lake and River Seines, Tents, Base Ball,	Tennis and other Athletic Goods,

and we can save you money on anything in this line, no matter how little or how much you want to buy.

TERMS

WE WILL SHIP ANY GUN OR REVOLVER TO ANY ADDRESS by Express, C. O. D., subject to examination, on receipt of $1.00 as a guarantee of good faith, and if the goods are exactly as represented, pay the express agent the balance, otherwise return the goods. We would, however, recommend that you send full amount of cash with your order and save the charges collected by all express companies for the return of the C. O. D. money to us. YOU RUN NO RISK by doing this, as all our goods are guaranteed exactly as represented, or your money will be refunded. Guns, rifles, revolvers, etc., made to special order cannot be sent C. O. D.; send cash in full with order.

OUR TERMS on FISH NETS and TENTS of all kinds, are Cash in Full with Order, as these goods are made up specially to your order. This does not delay orders, however, as we always fill these orders in three to six days, according to the number of orders we have on hand when we receive your order.

PARKER BREECH LOADING SHOTGUNS

FOR A SPECIAL CONFIDENTIAL PRICE, a much lower price than was ever printed by anyone, A PRICE THAT WILL SURPRISE YOU, Special Terms and our Free Trial Offer, write us, state the grade wanted by number, length of barrel, weight and get OUR SPECIAL OFFER BY RETURN MAIL.

WE OMIT THE PRICE IN THIS CATALOGUE for the reason that the maker objects to our printing a price as low as we can sell these guns; the price would be so much lower than others sell the Parker gun, so much less than you or others ever heard of, that it would demoralize prices and injure the maker's business.

WE CAN WRITE YOU OUR LOWEST PRICE and our special offer if you will only write us for them. We contracted for an immense number of these Parker guns; we got them at the lowest price ever known on condition that we would not print the low price we can sell them at.

WE CAN'T SELL YOU THE PARKER for as little money as a Davis, Remington or Ithaca, but it will cost so little that it will surprise you. The Celebrated Parker needs no lengthy description from anyone. It stands in the front rank of HIGHEST OF HIGH GRADE for twenty-five years. Every Sportsman, every Professional, every Gun Expert knows the Parker Breech Loader as the leader of all American guns.

The above illustration, engraved from a photograph, will give you an idea of the appearance of the NEW IMPROVED MODEL, V. H. GRADE, GENUINE PARKER HAMMERLESS SHOTGUN. Made by Parker Bros., of Meriden, Connecticut. It comes in 12 or 16 gauge, 30 or 32-inch barrel. Finest Vulcan steel barrels; weight of 12-guage, 7¼ to 8¾ pounds; 2¾ to 3¼ inches drop, finest top lever break, choke bored, imported walnut stock, fancy checkered full pistol grip, handsomely engraved hard rubber butt plate, choke bored by the best known process, to insure the most perfect target, and the greatest possible penetration.

THE PARKER IS MADE OF THE BEST MATERIAL MONEY CAN BUY.

Embodies Every Point of Excellence Known to Gun Making. Every Gun Covered by a BINDING GUARANTEE.

Hammer Guns.

No. 33801 T Grade, twist barrels, extension rib, engraved, American stock, checkered pistol grip and fore end, 12-gauge. List price... $........

No. 33803 R grade, same as No. 33801, 10-gauge. List price..... $........

No. 33805 G grade, Damascus barrels, extension rib, engraved, imported stock, checkered pistol grip and fore end, 12-gauge. Price, $........

No. 33807 E grade, same as No. 33805, 10-gauge. List price..... $. .....

Weight, 12-gauge, 7½ to 8¼ pounds; 30 or 32-inch barrels; 10-gauge, 9 to 10 pounds; length of barrel, 30 to 32 inches; 16-gauge, 28 or 30-inch barrels, 6¾ to 7½ pounds. Any deviation from these dimensions is liable to cause delay, and any guns made to special order will cost extra according to amount of extra work required. Higher Priced Guns made to Special Order.

Hammerless Guns.

No. 33810 D H grade, has very fine Damascus barrels, very fine imported walnut stock, fine checkering and engraving, 12-gauge only. List price.. $........

No. 33812 E H grade, fine Damascus barrels, fine imported stock, nicely engraved. 10-gauge made to special order only. List price $........

No. 33814 G H grade, fine Damascus barrels, fine imported stock, nicely engraved, 12 or 16-gauge. List price........................ $........

No. 33816 P H grade, fine English twist barrels, fine American stock, line engraving, 12 or 16-gauge. List price.......................... $... ....

No. 33818 V H grade, Vulcan steel barrels, fine American stock, plain frame, made in 12 and 16-gauge only. List price.... ... $........

For a Special Price on any grade of Parker Hammer or Hammerless Guns, a lower price than was ever before quoted, a lower price than the manufacturers will allow us to print, or will allow anyone else to print, and for Special Terms and a Special Free Trial Offer, write us.

DON'T FAIL TO WRITE US BEFORE ORDERING A PARKER GUN, or any other high grade American gun, for you will be surprised the amount of money we can save you. If you are about to buy from your dealer at home or order from some other house, a Baker, Ithaca, Hollenbeck, or other grade American gun of the cheaper class, and you are selecting such a gun because it is among the cheaper grade of guns, first write us, and in all probability we will be able to name you a lower price even on the CELEBRATED GENUINE PARKER GUN than you would pay some one else for one of the cheaper makes.

Our Special Price will be a Net Confidential Price, our Offer a Confidential Offer, and the only condition we make is that you treat it as strictly confidential. This the manufacturer exacts from us in allowing us to name the extraordinary low price.

L. C. SMITH BREECH LOADING SHOTGUNS.

OR A SPECIAL PRICE, a lower price than anyone else can name you on an L. C. Smith Gun, select the L. C. Smith Gun anted from the following illustrations and descriptions, state just the kind a gun wanted as to weight, length of barrel, drop, finish, etc., and by turn mail we will quote you a special inside price that will mean a saving you of anywhere from 10 to 33⅓ per cent, a lower price than you can ssibly get from any other house.

E OMIT PRICES ON L. C. SMITH GUNS for the reason that the manufacturer is not willing that we should enly quote these guns at the extremely low price at which we are able sell them. He will allow us to write you our special inside price, which is lower price than you can get elsewhere, but will not allow us to print these ery low prices broadcast to go all over the country.

E L. C. SMITH hammer breech loader and the hammerless and the automatic ejector hammerless are not low priced uns. They cannot be sold in every case as cheap as the very cheapest merican gun, but if you want a really high grade, American made, hammer hammerless shotgun and you write us, you will be surprised at the kind a special price and special offer we can make you on any grade of an C. Smith gun.

HOOTING QUALITIES. The shooting qualities of the L. C. Smith are recognized by the professional sportsen everywhere as the highest of high grades, the greatest ossible penetration, the best target that any gun can make, nd every gun is carefully tested to target, to penetration nd to accuracy in all parts before it leaves the actory.

Special confidential, inside low prices will e named on any grade of L. C. SMITH REECH LOADING SHOTGUNS.

THE L. C. SMITH is made on the very latest principles. It is extra strong at every point, devoid of all complicated mechanism, has the best known mechanical movement for cocking tumblers and strikers; easy to manipulate. The bolting joint check and extractor mechanism are the best known to gun making. The cocking mechanism on the hammerless gun is composed of but two pieces, with no springs, pins or screws.

THE L. C. SMITH hammer and hammerless guns are made from the very best material that money can buy. Only skilled mechanics are employed. There is probably no more popular gun among trap and professional shooters than the L. C. Smith. It has stood the crucial test of years of constant service at the trap and in the field, and it is so strong and so perfect in its action that we have yet to learn of one which has become loose or shaky, and many of them have a record of over one hundred thousand shots, and this is most remarkable when it is considered that the most powerful charges of nitro powder are common to this class of shooting, and this most extraordinary record fully substantiates the claim that the Smith gun is constructed on thoroughly sound mechanical principles, as no gun, no matter how finely made, can stand the test of everyday use unless the metal is properly distributed, the bearings large and well supported and the locking device of the most substantial character.

FINISH. The L. C. Smith Guns are given the highest possible finish and they are put out at our special inside prices in competition with guns that sell everywhere at 50 to 100 per cent more money.

THE L. C. SMITH GUNS are made by the Hunter Arms Company, of Fulton, New York. They have earned a reputation as among the

Write for our.... Special Terms, FREE TRIAL OFFER, and very low confidential price.

Our Special Inside Price, $..................

VERY HIGHEST OF HIGH GRADE AMERICAN HAMMERLESS SHOTGUNS.

Write for our confidential price, special terms and free trial offer.

THE ABOVE ILLUSTRATION, engraved from a photograph, will give you some idea of the appearance of the 00 grade, L. C. Smith hammerless gun. We furnish the L. C. Smith in the various grades as illustrated hereon.

N OUR SPECIAL 00 GRADE illustrated above, we name a very low price, the lowest price ever made on an L. C. Smith hammerless shotgun, and if you wish a genuine L. C. Smith gun at an extremely low price, we would recommend the gun above illustrated and described.

Y OUR SPECIAL ARRANGEMENT with the manufacturer we can quote a price on this gun based on the actual ost of material and labor at the factory, with but one small percentage of rofit added, a price that will surely surprise and please you, and our liberal reatment and free trial offer will interest you.

HIS OUR 00 GRADE is built on the very latest lines for this season. It is made with new Armor high grade steel barrels; oth barrels full choke bored and fully tested; tested for nitro powder. It as a very fine imported English walnut stock, beautifully finished; half pistol grip; fancy checkered and well finished; it has the latest top break; it comes in either 30 or 32-inch barrels: fancy case hardened locks; automatic safety block; heavy breech; narrow muzzles, with all the latest improvements. Weighs from 7½ to 8 pounds.

THE ABOVE ILLUSTRATION will give you a good idea of the appearance of this, our special 00 grade L. C. Smith double barrel hammerless shotgun, but you must see it, examine it and compare it with other high grade guns, and you must write for our confidential price in order to appreciate the value we are giving in these goods.

The above illustration is of the New Armor Steel Smith Hammerless Gun. English walnut pistol grip stock checkered, and checkered fore end, case hardened locks, automatic safety block, heavy breech, narrow muzzles with all the latest improvements, guaranteed for nitro as well as black powders.

No. 33830 No. 00 Grade, 12-gauge, 30 or 32-inch barrels, 7¼ to 8 pounds. WRITE FOR OUR SPECIAL NET PRICES, $.................

BORED FOR NITRO POWDER.

No. 33832

No. 33832 No. 0 Grade Damascus barrels, imported walnut stock, pistol grip, rubber butt plate, case hardened ock plates and action, plain finished but a good gun; very one warranted. 12-gauge, 30 or 32-inch barrels; 7¾ to 8 pounds.
WRITE FOR OUR SPECIAL PRICE $.....................

No. 33834 No. 0 Grade. Same as No. 33832 with patent automatic ejector. 2-gauge.
WRITE FOR OUR SPECIAL PRICE, $.................

BORED FOR NITRO POWDER.

No. 33836

No. 33836 No. 1 quality, fine 2-blade Damascus steel barrels, imported walnut stock, pistol grip and fore end, rubber butt plate, hardened lock plates and action. Plain line engraving, but well made and desirable, and just as good a shooter as a higher priced gun. 12 or 16-gauge, as desired, and 30 or 32-inch barrels. 12-gauge, 7¼ to 8 pounds; 16-gauge, 6¾ to 7 pounds.
WRITE FOR OUR SPECIAL PRICE, $.....................

No. 33838 Same as No. 33836, with automatic ejector. 12 or 16-gauge.
WRITE FOR OUR SPECIAL PRICE, $..

No. 33840 No. 2 Grade Good 3-blade Damascus Steel Barrels, imported walnut stock checkered, rubber butt plate, case hardened lock plates, frame and breech nicely engraved, finely finished, 12 or 16-gauge, 30 or 32-inch barrels; 12-gauge, 7¼ to 8 pounds; 16-gauge, 6¾ to 7 pounds.
WRITE FOR OUR SPECIAL PRICE, $.....................

No. 33842 No. 2 Grade, same as No. 33840, with patent automatic ejector.
WRITE FOR OUR SPECIAL PRICE, $.....................

Nos. 33836, 33838, 33840 and 33842 can also be had with Special Crown Steel Barrels to special order. This would incur some little delay, however. If you wish the Crown Steel Barrels mention it when you order. The price will be the same as for Damascus barrels.

Nos. 33836, 33838, 33840 and 33842 in 10-gauge, 30 or 32-inch barrel, 8½ to 10 pounds, to special order, same price as 12-gauge.

Special High Grade L. C. Smith Guns.

12-gauge, 30 or 32-inch barrels, 7½ to 8 lbs.
16-gauge, 30 or 32-inch barrels, 6½ to 7 lbs.

Bored for nitro powder. Illustration of No. 33844 or No. 3 Grade L. C. Smith.

No. 33844 No. 3 grade fine 4-blade Damascus steel barrels, fine English walnut stock, finely checkered grip and fore end, rubber butt plate, case hardened locks, frame and breech handsomely engraved and finely finished in 12 or 16-gauge.
WRITE FOR OUR SPECIAL PRICE, $.....................

No. 33846 No. 3 grade, same as No. 33844, with automatic ejector in 12 or 16-gauge. WRITE FOR OUR SPECIAL PRICE, $.....................

Nos. 33844 and 33846 can be furnished with special nitro steel barrels, to special order, at the same price as Damascus barrels.

Nos. 33844 and 33846, in 10-gauge, to special order, 30 or 32-inch; 8½ to 9½ pounds, same price as 12-gauge.

The L. C. Smith Pigeon Gun.

No. 33848 The L. C. Smith Pigeon Gun, finest blued finish crown steel barrels, straight grip, highly finished and engraved; bored for nitro powder and made especially for trap shooting, beautifully balanced and made in the highest art of gun making; finely checkered English stock and fore end, matted rib, 2¼ to 3-inch drop for trap shooting, 12-gauge, 30 or 32-inch barrels, 7¼ to 8 lbs. WRITE FOR OUR SPECIAL PRICE, $.....................

No. 33850 L. C. Smith Pigeon Gun, same as No. 33848, in 12-gauge, with automatic ejector. WRITE FOR OUR SPECIAL PRICE, $.................

No. 33852 A1 Grade Ejector, very fine 4-blade Damascus barrel, finished in first class style in every detail, finest quality stock, in fact, as good a gun as can be made, regardless of price, made to special order.
WRITE FOR OUR SPECIAL PRICE, $.....................

L. C. Smith Hammer Gun, 1900 Model.

BORED FOR NITRO POWDER.

No. 33855 Hammer Gun, fine Damascus barrels. Selected walnut pistol grip stock, cross bolted, circular hammers, extension matted rib. Will retail at stores at $35.00 up. 12-gauge only, 30-inch barrels, 7¼ to 7¾ pounds.
WRITE FOR OUR SPECIAL PRICE, $.....................

On Guns made to special order we require full amount of cash with the order and if made according to order cannot be returned under any circumstances.

$17.75 BUYS A CELEBRATED COLTON MANUFACTURING CO.'S DOUBLE BARREL HAMMERLESS SHOTGU

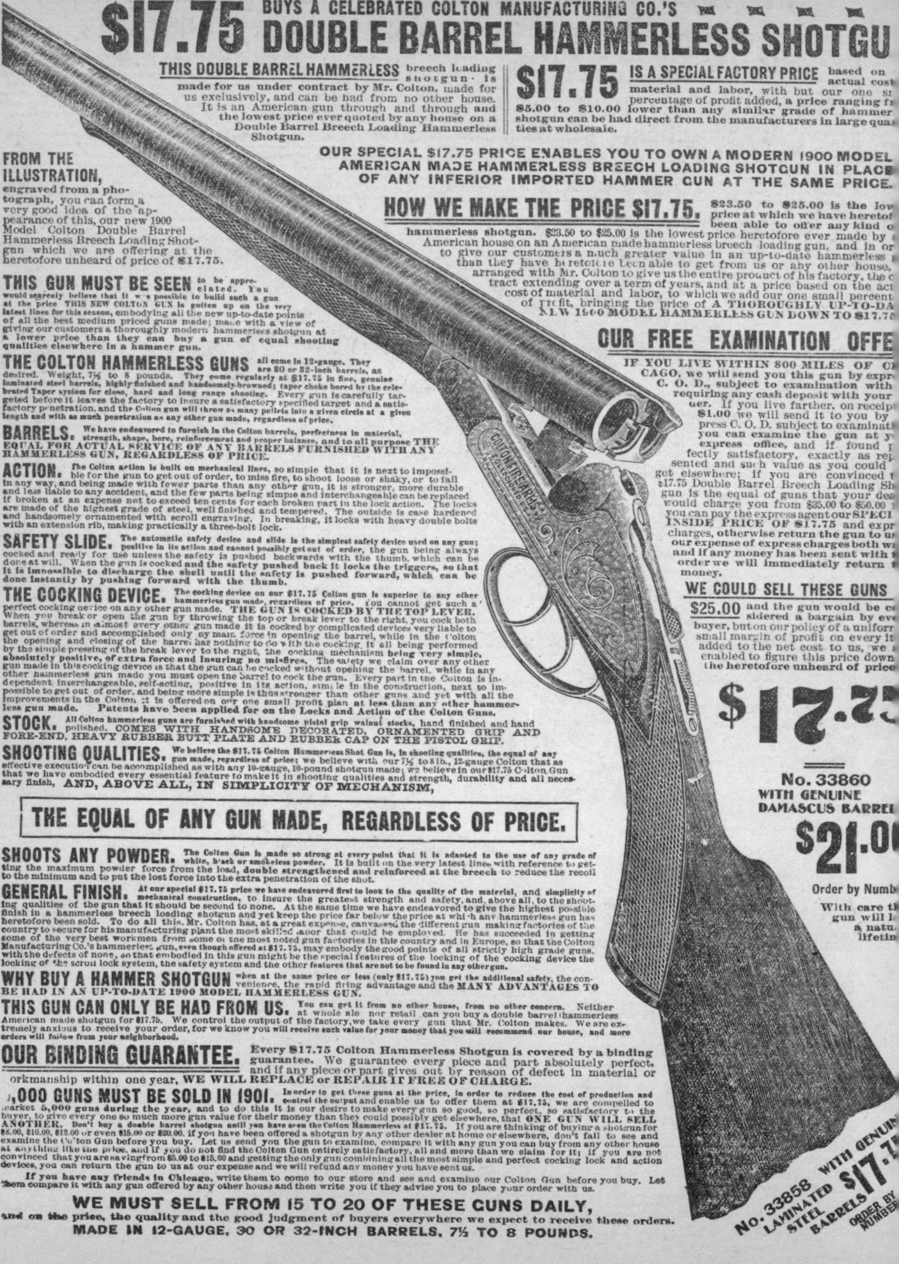

THIS DOUBLE BARREL HAMMERLESS breech loading shotgun is made for us under contract by Mr. Colton, made for us exclusively, and can be had from no other house. It is an American gun through and through and the lowest price ever quoted by any house on a Double Barrel Breech Loading Hammerless Shotgun.

$17.75 IS A SPECIAL FACTORY PRICE based on actual cost, material and labor, with but our one small percentage of profit added, a price ranging from $5.00 to $10.00 lower than any similar grade of hammerless shotgun can be had direct from the manufacturers in large quantities at wholesale.

OUR SPECIAL $17.75 PRICE ENABLES YOU TO OWN A MODERN 1900 MODEL AMERICAN MADE HAMMERLESS BREECH LOADING SHOTGUN IN PLACE OF ANY INFERIOR IMPORTED HAMMER GUN AT THE SAME PRICE.

HOW WE MAKE THE PRICE $17.75.

FROM THE ILLUSTRATION, engraved from a photograph, you can form a very good idea of the appearance of this, our new 1900 Model Colton Double Barrel Hammerless Breech Loading Shotgun which we are offering at the heretofore unheard of price of $17.75.

THIS GUN MUST BE SEEN to be appreciated. You would scarcely believe that it was possible to build such a gun at the price THIS NEW COLTON GUN is gotten up on the very latest lines for this season, embodying all the new up-to-date points of all the best medium priced guns made; made with a view of giving our customers a thoroughly modern hammerless shotgun at a lower price than they can buy a gun of equal shooting qualities elsewhere in a hammer gun.

THE COLTON HAMMERLESS GUNS all come in 12-gauge. They come regularly at $17.75 in bar, desired. Weight, 7¼ to 8 pounds. They come regularly at $17.75 in bar, laminated steel barrels, highly finished and handsomely browned; taper choke bored to the celebrated Taper system for close, hard and long range shooting. Every gun is carefully targeted before it leaves the factory to insure a satisfactory specified target and a satisfactory penetration, and the Colton gun will throw as many pellets into a given circle at a given length and with as much penetration as any other gun made, regardless of price.

BARRELS. We have endeavored to furnish in the Colton barrels, perfectness in material, strength, shape, bore, reinforcement and proper balance, and in all purpose THE BEST AND MOST EQUAL FOR ACTUAL SERVICE OF ANY BARREL FURNISHED WITH ANY HAMMERLESS GUN, REGARDLESS OF PRICE.

ACTION. The Colton action is built on mechanical lines, so simple that it is next to impossible for the gun to get out of order, to miss fire, to shoot loose or shaky, or to fail in any way, and being made with fewer parts than any other gun, it is stronger, more durable and less liable to any accident, and the few parts being simple and interchangeable can be replaced if broken at an expense not to exceed ten cents for each broken part in the lock action. The locks are made of the highest grade of steel, well finished and tempered. The outside is case hardened and handsomely ornamented with scroll engraving. In breaking, it locks with heavy double bolts with an extension rib, making practically a three-bolt lock.

SAFETY SLIDE. The automatic safety device and slide is the simplest safety device and as any gun positive in its action and cannot possibly get out of order, the gun being always cocked and ready for use unless the safety is pushed backwards with the thumb, which can be done at will, when it is cocked and the safety pushed back it locks the triggers, so that it is impossible to discharge the gun until the safety is pushed forward, which can be done instantly by pushing forward with the thumb.

THE COCKING DEVICE. The cocking device on our $17.75 Colton gun is superior to any other perfect cocking device on any other gun made, regardless of price. You cannot get such a THE GUN IS COCKED BY THE TOP LEVER. When you break or open the gun by throwing the top or break lever to the right, you cock both barrels, whereas in almost every other gun made it is cocked by complicated devices very liable to get out of order and accomplished only by main force in opening the barrel, while in the Colton the opening and closing of the barrel has nothing to do with the cocking it all being performed by the simple pressing of the break lever to the right, the cocking mechanism being very simple, absolutely positive, of extra force and insuring no misfires. The safety we claim over any other gun made in this cocking device is that the gun can be cocked without opening the barrel, while in any other hammerless gun made you must open the barrel to cock the gun. Every part in the Colton is impossible to get out of order, and being more simple than the stronger than other guns and yet with all the improvements in the Colton, it is offered on our small profit plan at less than any other hammerless gun made. Patents have been applied for on the Locks and Action of the Colton guns.

STOCK. All Colton hammerless guns are furnished with handsome pistol grip walnut stocks, hand finished and hand polished. COMES WITH HANDSOME DECORATED, ORNAMENTED GRIP AND FORE-END, HEAVY RUBBER BUTT PLATE AND RUBBER CAP ON THE PISTOL GRIP.

SHOOTING QUALITIES. We believe the $17.75 Colton Hammerless Shot Gun is, in shooting qualities, the equal of any effective execution can be accomplished with any 10-gauge, 10-pound shotgun made; we believe in our $17.75 Colton Gun that we have embodied every essential feature to make it in shooting qualities and strength, durability and all necessary finish, and, ABOVE ALL, IN SIMPLICITY OF MECHANISM.

THE EQUAL OF ANY GUN MADE, REGARDLESS OF PRICE.

SHOOTS ANY POWDER. The Colton Gun is made so strong at every point that it is adapted to the use of any grade of white, black or smokeless powder. It is built on the very latest lines with reference to getting the maximum powder force from the load, double strengthened and reinforced at the breech to reduce the recoil to the minimum and to put the lost force into the extra penetration of the shot.

GENERAL FINISH. At our special $17.75 price we have endeavored first to look to the quality of the material, and simplicity of mechanical construction, to insure the greatest strength and safety, and, above all, to the shooting qualities of the gun that it should be second to none. At the same time we have endeavored to give the highest possible finish in a hammerless breech loading shotgun and yet keep the price far below the price at which any hammerless gun has heretofore been sold. To do all this, Mr. Colton has, at a great expense, canvassed the different gun making factories of the country to secure for his manufacturing plant the most skilled labor that could be employed. He has succeeded in getting some of the very best workmen from some of the most noted gun factories in the country and in Europe, so that the Colton Manufacturing Co.'s hammerless gun, even though offered at $17.75, may embody the good points of all strictly high grade guns, with the defects of none, so that embodied in this gun might be the especial features of the locking of the cocking device the looking of the scroll lock system, the safety system and the other features that are not to be found in any other gun.

WHY BUY A HAMMER SHOTGUN when at the same price or less (only $17.75) you get the additional safety, the convenience, the rapid firing advantage and the MANY ADVANTAGES TO BE HAD IN AN UP-TO-DATE 1900 MODEL HAMMERLESS GUN.

THIS GUN CAN ONLY BE HAD FROM US. You can get it from no other house, from no other concern. Neither American made shotgun for $17.75. We control the output of the factory, we take every gun that Mr. Colton makes. We are extremely anxious to receive your order, for we know you will receive such value for your money that you will recommend our house, and more orders will follow from your neighborhood.

OUR BINDING GUARANTEE. Every $17.75 Colton Hammerless Shotgun is covered by a binding guarantee. We guarantee every piece and part absolutely perfect, and if any piece or part gives out by reason of defect in material or workmanship within one year, WE WILL REPLACE or REPAIR IT FREE OF CHARGE.

5,000 GUNS MUST BE SOLD IN 1901. In order to get these guns at the price, in order to reduce the cost of production and control the output and enable us to offer them at $17.75, we are compelled to market 5,000 guns during the year, and to do this it is our desire to make every gun so good, so perfect, so satisfactory to the buyer, to give every one so much gun value for their money than they could possibly get elsewhere, that ONE GUN WILL SELL ANOTHER. Don't buy a double barrel shotgun until you have seen the Colton Hammerless at $17.75. If you are thinking of buying a shotgun for $6.00, $10.00, $12.00 or even $15.00 or $20.00. If you have been offered a shotgun by any other dealer at home or elsewhere, don't fail to see and examine the Colton Gun before you buy. Let us send you the gun to examine, compare it with any gun you can buy from any other house at anything like one price, and if you do not find that the Colton Gun entirely satisfactory, all and more than you claim for it; if you are not convinced that you are paying from $5.00 to $15.00 and getting the only gun combining all the most simple and perfect cocking lock and action devices, you can return the gun to us at our expense and we will refund any money you have sent us.

If you have any friends in Chicago, write them to come to our store and see and examine our Colton Gun before you buy. Let them compare it with any gun offered by any other house and then write you if they advise you to place your order with us.

WE MUST SELL FROM 15 TO 20 OF THESE GUNS DAILY, and on the price, the quality and the good judgment of buyers everywhere we expect to receive these orders. MADE IN 12-GAUGE, 30 OR 32-INCH BARRELS, 7½ TO 8 POUNDS.

$23.50 to $25.00 is the lowest price at which we have heretofore been able to offer any kind of American made hammerless shotgun. $23.50 to $25.00 is the lowest price heretofore ever made by any American house on an American made hammerless breech loading gun, and in order to give our customers a much greater value in an up-to-date hammerless than they have heretofore been able to get from us or any other house, arranged with Mr. Colton to give us the entire product of his factory, the contract extending over a term of years, and at a price based on the actual cost of material and labor, to which we add our one small percentage of profit, bringing the price of A THOROUGHLY UP-TO-DATE NEW 1900 MODEL HAMMERLESS GUN DOWN TO $17.75.

OUR FREE EXAMINATION OFFE

IF YOU LIVE WITHIN 800 MILES OF CHICAGO, we will send you this gun by express C. O. D., subject to examination without requiring any cash deposit with your order. If you live farther, on receipt of $1.00 we will send it to you by express C. O. D. subject to examination; you can examine the gun at your express office, and if found perfectly satisfactory, exactly as represented and such value as you could get elsewhere; if you are convinced $17.75 Double Barrel Breech Loading Shotgun is the equal of guns that your dealer would charge you from $35.00 to $50.00, you can pay the express agent our SPECIAL INSIDE PRICE of $17.75 and express charges, otherwise return the gun to us at our expense of express charges both ways, and if any money has been sent with your order we will immediately return your money.

WE COULD SELL THESE GUNS

$25.00 and the gun would be considered a bargain by every buyer, but on our policy of a uniform small margin of profit on every item added to the net cost to us, we are enabled to figure this price down to the heretofore unheard of price

$17.75

No. 33860 WITH GENUINE DAMASCUS BARREL

$21.00

Order by Number

With care this gun will last a natural lifetime.

NO. 33858 WITH GENUINE LAMINATED STEEL BARRELS $17.75 ORDER BY NUMBER

REMINGTON NEW MODEL DOUBLE BARREL SHOTGUNS.

AT $20.00, $23.00 and $25.00 we furnish the latest New Model, Highest Grade, Guaranteed Double Barrel Breech Loading Hammer Shotguns.

AT $35.00 and $45.00 we furnish the Highest Grade Automatic Remington Double Barrel Hammerless Shotguns.

AT $40.00 and $50.00 we furnish the very latest Self Acting Automatic Ejector Remington Double Barrel Hammerless Shotguns.

SEND $1.00, select the gun wanted by number, state whether you want 10 or 12-gauge, length of barrel and weight wanted, and we will send the gun to you by express C. O. D., subject to examination. You can examine it at your express office and if found perfectly satisfactory, exactly as represented, and you are convinced that you have saved from 25 to 50 per cent in price, pay the express agent our price and express charges, less the $1.00 sent with order.

OUR 10 DAYS' FREE TRIAL OFFER. We give you the privilege of ordering any Remington gun, giving it 10 days' trial, during which time you can compare it as to shooting qualities, strength, durability and finish with any gun made, and if you are not perfectly satisfied with your purchase, you are at liberty to return the gun to us at our expense and we will immediately return all the money you have sent us. All we ask is that you keep the gun in perfect condition.

WE ARE HEADQUARTERS For the Remington double barrel hammer and hammerless self-ejecting shotguns. We buy them direct from the manufacturers, the Remington Arms Company of Ilion, New York, under contract in immense quantities for cash, at a price based on the actual cost to produce, to which our one small percentage of profit is added, making it possible for you to get the highest grade Remington gun direct from us for even less than your dealer can buy in quantities.

$20.00 FOR OUR LATEST MODEL Double Barrel Remington Shotgun.
$20.00 is our price for this the latest double barrel bar lock, pistol grip Remington hammer shotgun. How much we save you in price you can tell by comparing our prices with those asked by others.

THE BINDING GUARANTEE. Every Remington gun is covered by a binding guarantee. It is made on the very latest principles, from the best material that can be secured, by skilled mechanics, and if any piece or part gives out by reason of defect in material or workmanship it will be replaced free of charge. Every Remington gun that goes out of our place is put to a careful test, both as to target, penetration and strength at every point, and each gun bears a tag showing the target that each gun made in its test before shipping.

From the above illustration, engraved from a photograph, you can form some idea of the appearance of this our special $20.00 bar lock, double barrel Remington shotgun. This special $20.00 gun is built on the very latest lines for this season, up-to-date in every piece and part.

BARRELS.—The barrels are made by the Remington Arms Company from blued bar steel, elegantly finished, tested to the highest test and guaranteed in every respect. **STOCK**—The stock is a fine walnut stock, made of thoroughly seasoned selected black walnut, correctly shaped, nicely finished, full pistol grip, handsomely decorated, made with fancy butt plate. **LOCKS**—This gun is fitted with Remington Arms Company decarbonized steel bar action locks, made from the very best material that money can buy, thoroughly tested, accurately fitted and adjusted. **ACTION**—Our $20.00 Remington has the strongest, most simple and nearest perfect action of any similar gun on the market, built with a deep matted extension rib, with two heavy automatic locking bolts; extra heavy, well finished breech; low circular hammers; latest style top snap break; all parts are made interchangeable; the fore end is automatic, self acting; beautifully checkered finish. The gun is built extra strong at every part, made and bored for nitro or black powder.

FOR LONG RANGE SHOOTING, for ducks, geese and other large game, we recommend the 10-gauge Remington as one of the very best long range shooting guns made, and if you order our $20.00 Remington gun and you do not find it as a shooter, the equal of any gun made, regardless of price, you are at liberty to return it to us at our expense and we will refund your money.

OUR $20.00 REMINGTON GUNS come in length of barrel 30 or 32 inches, as desired. 10-gauge guns weigh 8¼ to 8½ lbs; 12-gauge guns, 7¼ to 8 lbs.

OUR REMINGTON GUNS are all the very latest model. There is not an old style or old model gun in our stock all made on the very latest lines. They embody every improvement, are up-to-date, and in comparing our prices with others please bear in mind that we not only save you the difference in price, but we give you the very latest up-to-date, targeted, tested and guaranteed stock.

OUR $20.00 REMINGTON GUNS are furnished with choke bored barrels, bored on the best principles with a view to securing the most perfect long range target possible.

No. 33863 Our No. 1 grade furnished with fine decarbonized steel barrels, as described and illustrated above, 10 or 12-gauge. ... **$20.00**
No. 33865 Our No. 2 grade, same as No. 33863, but with fine laminated steel barrels, 12-gauge, 30 or 32-inch barrels, 7¼ to 8 pounds; or 10-gauge, 30 or 32-inch barrels, 8¼ to 9½ pounds. Our special price ... **23.00**
No. 33867 Our No. 3 grade, same as No. 33863, but with fine two-blade Damascus barrels. 12-gauge, 30 or 32 inch barrels, 7¼ to 8 pounds; or 10-gauge, 8¼ to 9½ pounds. ... **25.00**

REMINGTON DOUBLE BARREL HAMMERLESS SHOTGUNS AT $35.00, $40.00, $45.00, AND $50.00.

AT $35.00 AND $45.00 we offer the highest grade Damascus Steel Barreled Remington Hammerless Shotguns as illustrated and described.

OUR SPECIAL PRICES OF $35.00 TO $50.00 are the lowest prices ever quoted for these high grade guns, and we honestly believe the Remington double barrel hammerless shotgun in any grade is, in shooting qualities and in point of construction, general workmanship, finish and durability, in fact, in every essential point, the equal of any gun made, regardless of price.

OUR SPECIAL $35.00, $40.00, $45.00 AND $50.00 PRICES are prices based on the actual cost under large season contract, with but our one small percentage of profit added, prices that guarantee to you a saving of all the profit your dealer would make and more.

AT $40.00 AND $50.00 we offer the Remington high grade Automatic Self Ejector Remington Hammerless Shotguns as illustrated and described.

THE REMINGTON HAMMERLESS GUNS are strong and durable. The mechanism is very simple, hence it cannot get out of order. In opening the gun, the fore end engages with the cocking levers, which raises the hammers to full cock, when the sears drop into position. The gun can be taken apart by not together with one or both hammers cocked or uncocked. This obviates trouble on the use of special tools in assembling, and does away with the snapping of hammers, or putting the gun away cocked, as required in some actions. The hammers can be let down without snapping, by breaking down the gun, pushing forward the safety slide and closing the action as the triggers are pulled. The cocking mechanism is so arranged that before the gun can be opened sufficiently to admit of a shell being inserted in the chamber

OUR BINDING GUARANTEE Every Remington gun is sent out under our binding guarantee, and if any piece or part gives out by reason of defect in material or workmanship, we will repair or replace it FREE OF CHARGE

No. 33870

From the above illustration, engraved from a photograph, you can form a very good idea of the appearance of the highest of high grade Remington, Double Barrel, Hammerless, Self Acting, Automatic Shell Ejecting Shotguns

BOTH HAMMERS ARE COCKED AND TRIGGERS ARE LOCKED AUTOMATICALLY, which we quote at $40.00 and $50.00, and without the automatic ejector, at $35.00 and $45.00.

THE AUTOMATIC EJECTOR is composed of hammer, sear, center sear, main and sear springs, and is cocked by the action of the extractor when closing the gun. It is operated when the gun is fired by the main spring moving forward and lifting the ejector sear out of the ejector hammer notch. This allows the ejector hammer to fall on the center sear where it remains until the gun is nearly opened, when the joint check engages with the center sear and raises it out of the ejector hammer notch. Then the ejector hammer, moving forward, strikes the ejector stem, causing the fired shell to be expelled from the gun.

QUALITY OF MATERIAL. The Remington Hammerless Guns are made from the best material money can buy. The stock, the barrels, the locks, the working parts, the trimmings and the finishings are from the very best material that can be procured, and only the most skilled mechanics are employed. The fittings are perfection, they are done with all the accuracy of the finest watch mechanism. The action is simple, accurate, strong and almost everlasting.

SHOOTING QUALITIES. The Remington Hammerless Shotgun is in shooting qualities, without doubt, the equal of any gun made, regardless of price. There is no gun made that will give a better target, greater penetration, than will Remington gun at longer range than will the Remington shot guns. They are made by a number of workmen who have had the experience of years; they embody every high point of perfection in every high grade gun, with the defects of none.

AT $35.00 TO $50.00 according to grade, these guns all come with fine Damascus steel barrels as illustrated, all are choke bored to secure the very best possible target and penetration, all have fine imported English walnut stocks, full pistol grip, beautifully finished, polished and checkered; fancy rubber butt plate, fancy checkered fore end, very finest case hardened frame and mountings, latest patent automatic safety, genuine Purdy fore end snap; fore end is beautifully finished and handsomely decorated; extension rib with nitro bite, flat matted rib, and the automatic ejectors on the $40.00 and $50.00 grades are the equal of any ejectors made.

No. 33868 A grade, two stripe Damascus barrels, plain finish. English walnut stock, without ejector, 12-gauge, 30 or 32-inch barrels, 7¼ to 8 pounds. Our special price. ... **$35.00**
No. 33870 AE grade, two stripe Damascus steel barrels, fine line engraving, with automatic ejector, 12-gauge, 30 or 32-inch barrels, 7¼ to 8 pounds. Our special price. ... **40.00**
No. 33872 B grade, extra quality fine three stripe Damascus barrels, fine line engraving, extra fine imported English walnut stock, without ejector, 12-gauge, 30 or 32-inch barrels, 7¼ to 8 pounds. Our special price. ... **45.00**
No. 33874 BE grade, with extra quality 3 stripe Damascus barrels, fine line engraving, extra fine imported English walnut stock, with automatic ejector, 12-gauge, 30 or 32-inch barrels, 7¼ to 8 pounds. ... **50.00**

ON GUNS MADE TO SPECIAL ORDER WE REQUIRE FULL AMOUNT OF CASH WITH THE ORDER, AND IF MADE ACCORDING TO OUR ORDER THEY CANNOT BE RETURNED UNDER ANY CIRCUMSTANCES.

OUR SPECIAL HIGH GRADE AMERICAN GUN WHICH WE QUOTE AT $15.75

WE KNOW IN THESE FIVE HIGH GRADE AMERICAN GUNS we are offering such value as was never before offered, such guns as you could not get elsewhere at less than double the price. We know you would be so well pleased with any one of these guns you order that you would show it to your friends, recommend our house and we will be sure to receive more orders from your neighborhood.

THE GUN IS MADE WITH THE BEST OF MATERIAL THROUGHOUT. It has a strong steel frame, beautifully case hardened steel parts and locks. Every part in this gun is machine made and interchangeable.

THIS GUN HAS THE LATEST TOP SNAP BREAK, fancy laminated steel barrels, strongest bar rebounding locks, barrels are flattened at breech, known as water table; has the very latest concave circular hammers, the best nitro firing pins, full extension rib, capped full fancy pistol grip, handsome checkered walnut stock and fore end, full matted rib. It is fitted with the Deeley & Edge patent fore end, has a fancy rubber butt plate; the left barrel is full taper choke bored, and the right barrel cylinder bored.

The above illustration shows our New High Grade Special $15.75 American Made Gun.

THIS GUN IS HANDSOMELY HAND ENGRAVED AND DECORATED; it is a gun the equal of American guns that sell everywhere at double the price; there is no better shooting gun or stronger gun made at any price.
No. 33961   We furnish this gun in 12-gauge with 30 or 32-inch barrels. Gun weighs 7½ to 8 pounds. Shipping weight, 15 pounds. Price............$15.75

OUR VERY FINEST SPECIAL MADE AMERICAN GUN FOR $17.60.

FOR $17.60 WE OFFER THE HIGHEST GRADE GUN made by the manufacturer on our contract for this year. For $17.60 we have endeavored to furnish you a gun on the basis of the actual cost of material and labor, with but our one small profit added, that will combine the good points of every strictly high grade gun made, with the defects of none. For $17.60 we offer you a gun under our binding guarantee the equal in all essential parts of any gun made, regardless of price, for strength, for safety, for shooting qualities, penetration, pattern, and all, we guarantee this gun equal to any gun made.

MADE IN 12-GAUGE ONLY.

SEND US $1.00, LET US SEND YOU THIS GUN BY EXPRESS C. O. D., subject to examination, examine it at your express office, compare it with any gun you can buy from your storekeeper at home at double the price, and if you are not more than pleased, return it to us at our expense and we will cheerfully refund your $1.00.

FROM THIS ILLUSTRATION, ENGRAVED FROM A PHOTOGRAPH, you can form some idea of the gun we are offering for $17.60. This is a strictly high grade American gun. It has the strongest kind of a steel frame, and the locks, screws, levers and all parts are made of the finest case hardened steel. All are made true to gauge by automatic machinery and are perfectly interchangeable.

THIS $17.60 GUN IS MADE WITH THE LATEST TOP SNAP BREAK, has genuine Damascus steel barrels, has the very best made bar rebounding locks, barrels are flattened at breech, known as water table; is fitted with the very latest concave circular hammers, has the very best nitro firing pins, is made with a strong full extension rib, which is neatly decorated, has a full fancy capped pistol grip, handsomely decorated; fine walnut stock and fore end, is fitted with the celebrated Deeley & Edge patent fore end, has a fancy rubber butt plate; it is elaborately engraved by hand.

CONSIDER, FOR $17.60 YOU GET A GENUINE AMERICAN MADE GUARANTEED DOUBLE BARREL BREECH LOADING SHOTGUN, fitted with the very finest genuine Damascus steel barrels, choke bored by the celebrated Taper system, bored for white or nitro powder; you get a gun covered by a binding guarantee to the effect that it is in all essential parts the equal of any gun made, regardless of price. For $17.60 we furnish this gun in 12-gauge, 30 or 32-inch barrels, a gun weighing 7½ to 8 pounds.

WE ESPECIALLY RECOMMEND THIS OUR HIGH GRADE GUN AT $17.60. We guarantee every penny extra you pay in selecting this our highest grade gun goes into the work. The difference of $10.85 for our cheapest guaranteed American gun and this at $17.60 is the exact difference in cost to us. It is represented by the difference in the cost of material and labor.

WE GUARANTEE THAT IF YOU ORDER THIS GUN FOR $17.60 you will find it equal to any gun you can buy elsewhere for twice the money, equal in all essential parts to any gun at any price. Shipping weight, 15 pounds.
No. 33962   Our special price...$17.60

OUR DIANA PATTERN BREECH LOADER FOR $13.55.

EQUAL TO ANY
$20.00 BELGIUM GUN ON THE MARKET...

12-GAUGE ONLY.
See Our Prices for Loaded Shells.

BAR ⸱⸱ LOCK ⸱⸱ GUN

WITH 2-BLADE DAMASCUS FINISH BARRELS...

Blued at breech, matted extension rib, fancy butt cap, full pistol grip. Stock and fore end handsomely checkered.

No. 33969 12-gauge only, 30 and 32-inch barrels, 7½ to 8¼ pounds.
Our Special Price...$13.55

No. 33969
ONE OF OUR BEST SELLERS.

THE ABOVE ILLUSTRATION is engraved from a photograph, and will give you some idea of the gun. It is one of our best selling Belgian Guns and has all modern improvements. It has engine turned rib, rebounding bar locks, pistol grip, patent fore end, nicely checkered stock and one that will please you. This gun and all our other Belgian guns are thoroughly tested by the Belgian government before we get them. The celebrated Raleigh steel barrels are used in this gun.
—A BREECH LOADER BOXED WILL WEIGH ABOUT 15 POUNDS.—
ON GUNS MADE TO SPECIAL ORDER WE REQUIRE FULL AMOUNT OF CASH WITH ORDER AND IF MADE TO YOUR ORDER THE CANNOT BE RETURNED UNDER ANY CIRCUMSTANCES.

:: OUR CELEBRATED SAM HOLT GUNS FOR $10.45 :::

.. 12-GAUGE ONLY ..   ... CASE HARDENED MOUNTINGS ...

.. BAR LOCKS ..   ... EXTENSION RIB ...

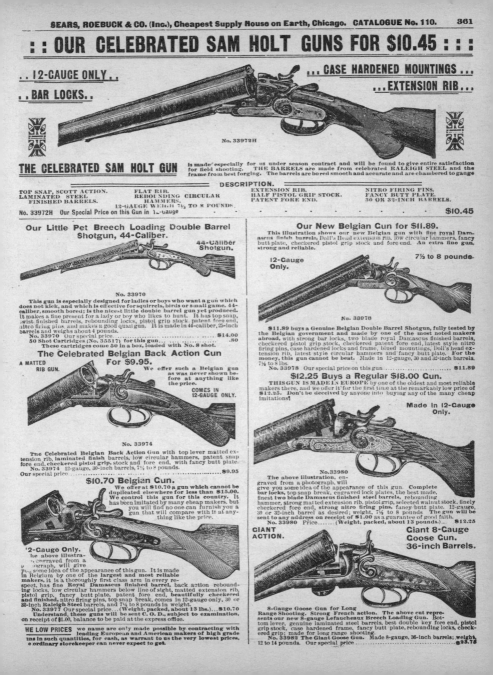

No. 33972H

THE CELEBRATED SAM HOLT GUN

is made especially for us under season contract and will be found to give entire satisfaction for field shooting. THE BARRELS are made from celebrated RALEIGH STEEL and the frame from best forging. The barrels are bored smooth and accurate and are chambered to gauge.

DESCRIPTION

TOP SNAP, SCOTT ACTION.	FLAT RIB.	EXTENSION RIB.	NITRO FIRING PINS.
LAMINATED STEEL	REBOUNDING CIRCULAR	HALF PISTOL GRIP STOCK.	FANCY BUTT PLATE.
FINISHED BARRELS.	HAMMERS.	PATENT FORE END.	30 OR 32-INCH BARRELS.
	12-GAUGE WEIGH 7½ TO 8 POUNDS.		

No. 33972H Our Special Price on this Gun in 12-gauge $10.45

Our Little Pet Breech Loading Double Barrel Shotgun, 44-Caliber.

44-Caliber Shotgun.

No. 33970

This gun is especially designed for ladies or boys who want a gun which does not kick, and which is effective for squirrels, birds or small game. 44-caliber, smooth bored; is the nicest little double barrel gun yet produced. It makes a fine present for a lady or boy who likes to hunt. It has top snap, twist finished barrels, rebounding locks, pistol grip stock, patent fore end, nitro firing pins, and makes a good quail gun. It is made in 44-caliber, 25-inch barrels and weighs about 4 pounds.
No. 33970 Our special price $14.00
50 Shot Cartridges (No. 35517) for this gun 80
These cartridges come 50 in a box, loaded with No. 8 shot.

The Celebrated Belgian Back Action Gun For $9.95.

A MATTED RIB GUN.

We offer such a Belgian gun as was never shown before at anything like the price.

COMES IN 12-GAUGE ONLY.

No. 33974

The Celebrated Belgian Back Action Gun with top lever matted extension rib, laminated finish barrels, low circular hammers, patent snap fore end, checkered pistol grip, stock and fore end, with fancy butt plate.
No. 33974 12-gauge, 30-inch barrels, 7½ to 8 pounds.
Our special price $9.95

$10.70 Belgian Gun.

We offer at $10.70 a gun which cannot be duplicated elsewhere for less than $15.00. We control this gun for this country. It has been imitated by many cheap makers, but you will find no one can furnish you a gun that will compare with it at anything like the price.

'2-Gauge Only.

The above illustration, engraved from a photograph, will give you some idea of the appearance of this gun. It is made in Belgium by one of the largest and most reliable makers, is a thoroughly first class arm in every respect, has fine Royal Damascus finished barrel, back action rebounding locks, low circular hammers below line of sight, matted extension rib, pistol grip, fancy butt plate, patent fore end, beautifully checkered and finished, nitro firing pins, top snap break, comes in 12-gauge only, 30 or 32-inch Raleigh Steel barrels, and 7½ to 8 pounds in weight.
No. 33977 Our special price. (Weight, packed, about 13 lbs.) . . $10.70
Understand, these guns will be sent C. O. D., subject to examination, on receipt of $1.00, balance to be paid at the express office.

THE LOW PRICES we name are only made possible by contracting with leading European and American makers of high grade guns in such quantities, for cash, as warrant to us the very lowest prices, the ordinary storekeeper can never expect to get.

Our New Belgian Gun for $11.89.

This illustration shows our new Belgian gun with fine royal Damascus finish barrels, Doll's Head extension rib, low circular hammers, fancy butt plate, checkered pistol grip stock and fore end. An extra fine gun, strong and reliable.

12-Gauge Only.   7½ to 8 pounds.

No. 33978

$11.89 buys a Genuine Belgian Double Barrel Shotgun, fully tested by the Belgian government and made by one of the most noted makers abroad, with strong bar locks, two blade royal Damascus finished barrels, checkered pistol grip stock, checkered patent fore end, latest style nitro firing pins, case hardened locks and frame, blued mountings, Doll's head extension rib, latest style circular hammers and fancy butt plate. For the money, this gun cannot be beat. Made in 12-gauge, 30 and 32-inch barrels, 7½ to 8 lbs.
No. 33978 Our special price on this gun $11.89

$12.25 Buys a Regular $18.00 Gun.

THIS GUN IS MADE IN EUROPE by one of the oldest and most reliable makers there, and we offer it for the first time at the remarkably low price of $12.25. Don't be deceived by anyone into buying any of the many cheap imitations!

Made in 12-Gauge Only.

No. 33980

The above illustration, engraved from a photograph, will give you some idea of the appearance of this gun. Complete bar locks, top snap break, engraved lock plates, the best made, finest two blade Damascus finished steel barrels, rebounding hammer, strong matted extension rib, pistol grip, selected walnut stock, finely checkered fore end, strong nitro firing pins, fancy butt plate. 12-gauge, 30 or 32-inch barrel as desired; weight, 7½ to 8 pounds. The gun will be sent to any address on receipt of $1.00 as a guarantee of good faith.
No. 33980 Price. . . . . . . (Weight, packed, about 13 pounds.) . . $12.25

GIANT ACTION.

Giant 8-Gauge Goose Gun. 36-inch Barrels.

8-Gauge Goose Gun for Long Range Shooting. Strong French action. The above cut represents our new 8-gauge Lefaucheux Breech Loading Gun. Bottom lever, genuine laminated steel barrels, best made, key fore end, pistol grip stock, case hardened frame, fancy butt plate, rebounding locks, checkered grip; made for long range shooting.
No. 33982 The Giant Goose Gun. Made 8-gauge, 36-inch barrels; weight, 12 to 14 pounds. Our special price $23.75

....CELEBRATED GREENER ACTION BREECH LOADING SHOTGUN, $17.15...

This gun is one we have imported from Europe, at a price which is less than half the price charged by retail dealers for guns of this quality. You will find this gun equal to anything on the market at any price. There is no better shooting gun made.

$17.15 BUYS A $25.00 GUN.

THE BARRELS OF THIS GUN ARE MADE OF WILSON'S BEST STEEL........

..12-GAUGE ONLY..

No. 33985

THIS GUN HAS TOP SNAP BREAK, the best break made, **very beautiful Damascus finished barrels, bar action, rebounding locks,** fancy pistol grip. Patent fore end, extension rib, the **celebrated Greener cross bolt** with engraved locks, nicely checkered stock and fore end, **left barrel modified choke, right barrel cylinder bored. Bar lock, fancy cap on pistol grip, fancy butt plate. Gun comes 12-gauge only, 30 or 32-inch barrels, weighs 7½ to 8 lbs.** We cannot recommend this gun too highly, and we are extremely anxious to receive your order for one of them, for we know it will mean the sale of many more. There is nothing in the market at anything like the price. Under our system of one small profit direct from the manufacturer to the consumer, you will own this gun for less money than your local dealer can buy it in quantities.

No. 33985 12-gauge only, 30 or 32-inch barrels, 7½ to 8 lbs. Our special price,..........................$17.15

Weight, packed in box, about 14 pounds.

OUR ENGRAVED, DIANA STYLE BREECH, DOUBLE BARREL BREECH LOADER FOR ONLY $13.10.

THIS GUN IS MADE IN EUROPE by one of the oldest and most reliable makers there, and we offer it for the first time at the remarkably low price of $13.10. **Don't be deceived by any one into buying any of the many cheap imitations.**

MADE IN 12-GAUGE ONLY.

No. 33986

The above illustration, engraved from a photograph, will give you some idea of the appearance of this gun. **Complete bar lock, top snap break, engraved lock plates, the best made, finest two blade Damascus finished barrels, Diana style steel barrels,** rebounding hammer, strong matted extension rib, pistol grip, selected walnut stock, finely checkered fore end, **strong nitro firing pins,** fancy butt plate. 12-gauge, 30 or 32-inch barrels as desired. Weight, 7½ to 8 pounds. **The gun will be sent to any address on receipt of $1.00 as a guarantee of good faith.**

Weight, packed, about 13 pounds.

No. 33986 Price $13.10

...SEE OUR PRICES ON LOADED SHELLS...

OUR PLAIN BAR LOCK GUN FOR $9.95.

10 AND 12-GAUGE.

No. 33987

Steel barrels, laminated finish, complete double barrel breech loader, top lever, rebounding bar locks, pistol grip, oil walnut stock, **checkered grip and fore end. Case hardened lock plates and mountings,** shell extractor; a plain finished gun, but a good one; solid head strikers; extension rib; **low circular hammers;** patent snap fore end. The browning will wear as long as on a genuine twist barrel, and they are just as good shooters, and sold by many as genuine laminated steel. Barrels polished bright and smooth inside. For a gun for ordinary use this gun will fill the bill every time.

No. 33987 12-gauge, 30 or 32-inch barrels, 7½ to 8 lbs. Price...... $ 9.95
No. 33987 10-gauge, 30 or 32-inch barrels, 8¾ to 9¼ lbs. Price.... 10.30

Weight, packed, about 13 pounds.

"PITTING" OF GUN BARRELS We frequently have complaints from some customers saying that their gun barrels have become pitted (or spotted) inside, and we wish to inform our customers that this is not the fault of the material from which gun barrels are made, nor is it the fault of the gun maker; it is usually caused by carelessness or neglect on the part of the owner of the gun.

If you wish to prevent your gun barrels from becoming pitted, do not leave any burnt powder inside, especially burnt nitro powder. Burnt nitro powder is extremely severe on steel and iron.

When 10, 12 or 16-gauge barrels become pitted, it necessitates having them re-bored and re-polished, which costs from $1.50 to $5.00, according to the condition of the barrels. As we are not responsible for pitting of gun barrels, we must charge for re-boring and re-polishing same.

THE CELEBRATED THOMAS BARKER DOUBLE BARREL BREECH LOADING SHOTGUN FOR $12.59

Made in
16-gauge, 6½ to 7 lbs.
20-gauge, 6¼ to 6¾ lbs.
28 or 30-inch barrels.

10, 12, 16 OR 20 GAUGE.

Made in
12-gauge, 7½ to 8¼ lbs.
10-gauge, 8½ to 9¼ lbs.
30 or 32-inch barrels.

The above illustration will give you some idea of the appearance of this gun. Top snap twist finish barrels, bar action, rebounding locks, matted rib, full checkered pistol grip stock, circular hammers, patent fore end, nitro firing pins, fancy butt plate, **left barrel choked,** extension rib bored smooth and true, inlaid pistol grip. A first-class gun in every respect. **A first-class shooter. None better.** They come in 10, 12, 16 and 20-gauge **(the price is the same for all gauges). One of the best guns made for field shooting.**

No. 33989

....OVER 45,000 NOW IN USE....

Weight, packed, about 13 pounds.

No. 33989 Price, each. See the sizes above and give gauge and length wanted. $12.59

OUR SPECIAL LADIES' OR BOYS' DOUBLE BARREL BREECH LOADER

44-CALIBER SHOTGUN

44-CALIBER.

No. 33991

Has top snap, genuine laminated steel barrels, rebounding hammers, back action locks, extension rib, pistol grip, patent fore end. **An excellent quail gun, 44-caliber, adapted to 44 caliber shot cartridges. Length of barrel, 24 inches. Weight, about 4 pounds. These guns are chiefly intended for ladies and boys, who cannot endure the "kick" of a 12-gauge gun.**

No. 33991 Our special price...$18.00
50 shot cartridges (No. 35682) for this gun, loaded with No. 8 shot..........80c

Weight, packed, about 10 pounds.

THE LOW PRICES we name are only made possible by contracting with leading European and American makers of high grade guns in such quantities, for cash, as warrant to us the very lowest price, prices the ordinary storekeeper can never expect to get.

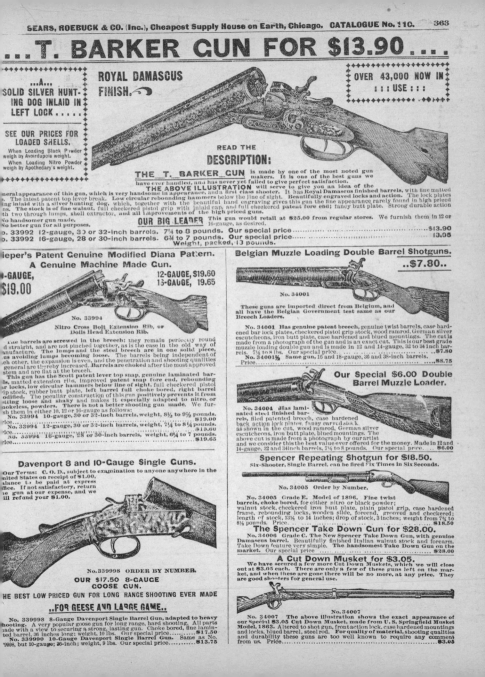

...T. BARKER GUN FOR $13.90...

...A...
SOLID SILVER HUNTING DOG INLAID IN LEFT LOCK.....

SEE OUR PRICES FOR LOADED SHELLS.

When Loading Black Powder weigh by Avoirdupois weight.
When Loading Nitro Powder weigh by Apothecary's weight.

ROYAL DAMASCUS FINISH.

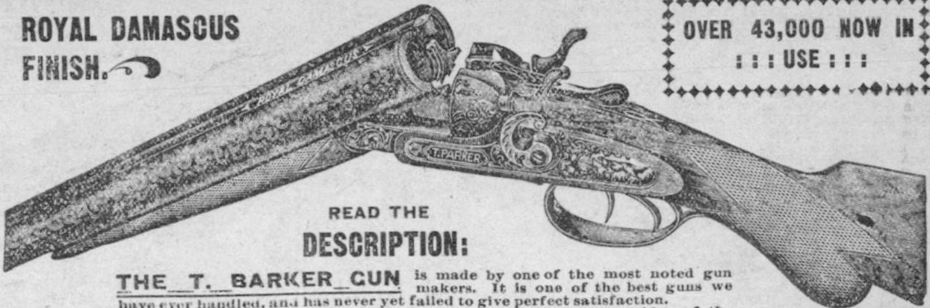

OVER 43,000 NOW IN USE

READ THE

DESCRIPTION:

THE T. BARKER GUN is made by one of the most noted gun makers. It is one of the best guns we have ever handled, and has never yet failed to give perfect satisfaction. THE ABOVE ILLUSTRATION will serve to give you an idea of the general appearance of this gun, which is very handsome in appearance, and a first class shooter. It has Royal Damascus finished barrels, with fine matted rib. The latest patent top lever break. Low circular rebounding hammers below the line of sight. Beautifully engraved locks and action. The lock plates being inlaid with a silver hunting dog, which, together with the beautiful hand engraving gives this gun the fine appearance rarely found in high priced guns. The stock is of fine walnut, full checkered pistol grip with inlaid cap, and full checkered patent fore end; fancy butt plate. Strong durable action with two through lumps, shell extractor, and all improvements of the high priced guns.
No handsomer gun made.
No better gun for all purposes.

OUR BIG LEADER This gun would retail at $25.00 from regular stores. We furnish them in 12 or 16-gauge, as desired.

No. 33992 12-gauge, 30 or 32-inch barrels. 7¼ to 8 pounds. Our special price $13.90
No. 33992 16-gauge, 28 or 30-inch barrels. 6¾ to 7 pounds. Our special price 13.95
Weight, packed, 13 pounds.

Sieper's Patent Genuine Modified Diana Pattern.
A Genuine Machine Made Gun.

10-GAUGE, $19.00

12-GAUGE, $19.60
16-GAUGE, 19.65

No. 33994

Nitro Cross Bolt Extension Rib, or Dolls Head Extension Rib.

The barrels are screwed in the breech; they remain perfectly round and straight, and are not pinched together, as is the case in the old way of manufacture. The lumps and the steel breech are in one solid piece, thus avoiding lumps becoming loose. The barrels being independent of each other, the expansion is even, and the penetration and shooting qualities in general are thereby increased. Barrels are choked after the most approved system and are flat at the breech.

This gun has the Scott patent lever top snap, genuine laminated barrels, matted extension ribs, improved patent snap fore end, rebounding bar locks, low circular hammers below line of sight, full checkered pistol grip stock, rubber butt plate, left barrel full choke bored, right barrel modified. The peculiar construction of this gun positively prevents it from getting loose and shaky and makes it especially adapted to nitro, or smokeless, powders. There is not a better shooting gun made. We furnish them in either 10, 12 or 16-gauge as follows:

No. 33994 10-gauge, 30 or 32-inch barrels, weight, 8½ to 9½ pounds. Price $19.00
No. 33994 12-gauge, 30 or 32-inch barrels, weight, 7¼ to 8¼ pounds. Price $19.60
No. 33994 16-gauge, 28 or 30-inch barrels, weight, 6¼ to 7 pounds. Price $19.65

Davenport 8 and 10-Gauge Single Guns.

Our Terms: C. O. D., subject to examination to anyone anywhere in the United States on receipt of $1.00, balance to be paid at express office. If not satisfactory, return the gun at our expense, and we will refund your $1.00.

No. 339998 ORDER BY NUMBER.

OUR $17.50 8-GAUGE GOOSE GUN.

THE BEST LOW PRICED GUN FOR LONG RANGE SHOOTING EVER MADE

..FOR GEESE AND LARGE GAME..

No. 339998 8-Gauge Davenport Single Barrel Gun, adapted to heavy shooting. A very popular goose gun for long range, hard shooting. All parts made with a view to securing a strong, lasting gun. Choke bored, fine laminated barrel, 36 inches long; weight, 10 lbs. Our special price $17.50
No. 339990 10-Gauge Davenport Single Barrel Gun. Same as No. 339998, but 10-gauge; 36-inch; weight, 9 lbs. Our special price $13.75

Belgian Muzzle Loading Double Barrel Shotguns.

..$7.80..

No. 34001

These guns are imported direct from Belgium, and all have the Belgian Government test same as our Breech Loaders.

No. 34001 Has genuine patent breech, genuine twist barrels, case hardened bar lock plates, checkered pistol grip stock, wood ramrod, German silver escutcheons, iron butt plate, case hardened and blued mountings. The cut is made from a photograph of the gun and is an exact cut. This is our best grade muzzle loading double gun and is made in 12 and 14-gauge, 32 to 34 inch barrels. 7¼ to 8 lbs. Our special price $7.80
No. 34001½ Same gun, 16 and 18-gauge, 36 and 38-inch barrels. Price $8.75

Our Special $6.00 Double Barrel Muzzle Loader.

No. 34004 Has laminated steel finished barrels, filed patented breech, case hardened back action lock plates, fancy carved stock, as shown in the cut, wood ramrod, German silver escutcheons, iron butt plate, blued mountings. The above cut is made from a photograph by our artist and we consider this the best value ever offered for the money. Made in 12 and 14-gauge, 32 and 34 inch barrels, 7½ to 8 pounds. Our special price $6.00

Spencer Repeating Shotgun for $18.50.

Six-Shooter, Single Barrel, can be fired Six Times in Six Seconds.

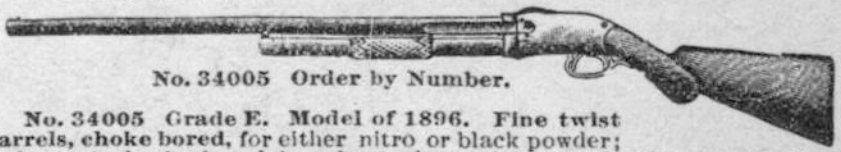

No. 34005 Order by Number.

No. 34005 Grade E. Model of 1896. Fine twist barrels, choke bored, for either nitro or black powder; walnut stock, checkered iron butt plate, plain pistol grip, case hardened frame, rebounding locks, wooden slide, foreend, grooved and checkered; length of stock, 13½ to 14 inches; drop of stock, 3 inches; weight from 7¾ to 8¼ pounds. Price $18.50

The Spencer Take Down Gun for $28.00.

No. 34006 Grade C. The New Spencer Take Down Gun, with genuine Damascus barrel. Beautifully finished Italian walnut stock and forearm. Take Down feature very simple. The handsomest Take Down Gun on the market. Our special price $28.00

A Cut Down Musket for $3.05.

We have secured a few more Cut Down Muskets, which we will close out at $3.05 each. There are only a few of these guns left on the market, and when these are gone there will be no more, at any price. They are good shooters for general use.

No. 34007

No. 34007 The above illustration shows the exact appearance of our Special $3.05 Cut Down Musket, made from U. S. Springfield Musket Model, 1863. Altered to shot gun, front action lock, case hardened mountings and locks, blued barrel, steel rod. For quality of material, shooting qualities and durability these guns are too well known to require any comment from us. Price $3.05

DEPARTMENT OF REVOLVERS.

WE OFFER YOU ALL THE STANDARD MAKES of Revolvers at manufacturers' lowest prices.

When you get our price you are getting the manufacturers' price with only our one small profit added, and owning the revolver for less money than any dealer can buy in quantities. For this coming season we have many special bargains to offer, as our contracts with the different manufacturers have been so very large that we are able to make the very closest prices, and a comparison of our prices with those of any other concern will convince you there is a saving of 25 to 35 per cent.

WHEN ORDERING REVOLVERS BY EXPRESS

most of our customers send cash in full with their orders, as they save the charges of 15 to 5 cents which the express companies charge for returning the C. O. D. money to us.

IN ORDERING SINGLE REVOLVERS

we advise sending by mail. This can be done where enough extra is inclosed to cover postage. The postage is 1 cent per ounce, or fraction thereof. We will ship revolvers by express C. O. D., subject to examination on receipt of $1.00 as a guarantee of good faith. You can examine the revolver at the express office, and if found perfectly satisfactory and exactly as represented, pay the express agent the balance and express charges, and the revolver is yours. We advise sending cash in full, and adding enough to cover postage, insurance or registry fee, and have the revolver sent by mail.

Our New Model Double Action Revolvers.

All full nickel plated and checkered rubber handle.

32 and 38-caliber.

No. 34183 32-caliber, rim fire, 2½-inch barrel. Weight, 16 oz. Using cartridge No. 35352.
Our price......$1.75
No. 34184 38-caliber, rim fire, 2½-inch barrel. Weight, 16 oz. Using cartridge No. 35356.
Our price......$1.75
If by mail, postage extra, 20 cents.
No. 34185 32-caliber, center fire, 4½-inch barrel. Weight, 16 oz. Using cartridge No. 35377. 5 or 6 shot; nickel plated; rubber handles; octagon barrel.
Our price......$1.75
No. 34186 38-caliber, center fire, 2½-inch barrel. Weight, 16 oz. Using cartridge No. 35388. 5-shot; full nickel plated; rubber handles; octagon barrel.
Our price......$1.65
Extra for pearl stock for any of above revolvers.
Our price......$1.15
If by mail, postage extra, 20 cents.

REMEMBER $1.00 MUST ACCOMPANY ALL REVOLVER ORDERS to be sent C.O.D., balance to be paid at express office. For 20 cents extra we will send any revolver on this page by open mail, postpaid. For 28 cents extra we will send by registered mail, postpaid or prepaid express.

Our $2.10 and $2.40 Revolvers.

THESE REVOLVERS ARE STRICTLY FIRST CLASS IN EVERY RESPECT, and made especially for us under season's contract. The quality of material and workmanship is the best. All have rifled barrels and are good shooters; all 5-shot. These are not toys, but good guns. No one can meet our prices on these goods.

ALL FULL NICKEL
PLATED AND
CHECKERED
RUBBER STOCKS.

No. 34189 32-caliber, center fire, 4½-inch barrel, weight, 16 ounces, 5 or 6-shot. Using cartridge No. 35377. Our price......$2.10
Extra for pearl stocks......1.10
No. 34190 38-caliber, center fire, 4½-inch barrel, weight, 16 ounces. 5-shot. Using cartridge No. 35388. Our price......$2.10
No. 34191 32-caliber, center fire, 6-inch barrel, weight, 17 ounces. 5 or 6-shot. Using cartridge No. 35377. Our price......$2.40
Extra for pearl stocks......1.10
No. 34193 38-caliber, center fire, 6-inch barrel, weight, 18 ounces. 5-shot. Using cartridge No. 35388. Our price......$2.40
Extra for pearl stocks......1.10
If by mail, postage extra, 17 to 27 cents.

Our $1.80 Revolver.

DOUBLE ACTION
AUTOMATIC
POLICE
REVOLVER
FOR Home AND POCKET

Forehand & Wadsworth New Double Action, Self Cocking Revolver, full nickel plated, rubber stock, rifled barrel, safe and reliable, accurate, rebounding locks, parts are interchangeable.
No. 34197 32-caliber, 2½-inch octagon barrel; using cartridge No. 35377. Weight, 15 ounces. 6-shot.
Our price......$1.80
If by mail, postage extra, 20 cents.
No. 34198 38-caliber, 2½-inch octagon barrel, 5-shot; using cartridge No. 35388; weight, about 15 ounces. Our price......$1.80
If by mail, postage extra, 20 cents.

Our $1.80 Revolver.

No. 34199 Forehand & Wadsworth safety hammer, double action revolver, full nickel plated, rubber stock, rifled barrel, rebounding lock, safe, reliable and accurate, 32-caliber, 2½-inch octagon barrel, 6-shot, using cartridge No. 35377, weight, 15 ounces. Price......$1.80
No. 34202 38-caliber, 2½-inch octagon barrel, 5-shot, using cartridge No. 35388; weight, 15 ounces. Our price......$1.80
If by mail, postage extra, 20 cents.
These goods are genuine, and new from the factory. Beware of imitations and shop worn goods, which are sold for new goods by some firms. We handle nothing but first class goods.

The Forehand Perfection Automatic 5-Shot Revolver for $3.75.

32-Caliber only.

Forehand Perfection Automatic, small frame, rebounding lock, positive stop on cylinder, and hammer blocked, same as in other Forehand Automatics. Accidental discharge impossible. Using cartridge No. 35377. Weighs but 13 ounces. A fine pocket revolver. Full length, 7¼ inches.
No. 34205 32-caliber, 3-inch nickel plated.$3.75
No. 34207 32-caliber, 3-inch blue steel frame and barrel. Price......$4.10

The Genuine Harrington & Richardson Automatic Revolvers.

32 and 38-Caliber.

Over 2,500,000 Harrington & Richardson Revolvers now in use.

Our $3.75 Automatic.

This revolver would retail in a first class gun store at from $5.00 to $6.00. The celebrated Harrington & Richardson Improved Automatic, self extracting, double action, self cocking revolver, modeled on the Smith & Wesson pattern, beautifully nickel plated, rubber stock, as accurate and durable as any revolver on the market, and equal to the Smith & Wesson in shooting. Weight, 18½ ounces, 3½-inch barrel.
No. 34210 32-caliber, nickel plated, center fire. Using cartridge No. 35377. Our price......$3.75
No. 34211 32-caliber, blued finish, center fire. Using cartridge No. 35377. Our price......$4.15
No. 34212 38-caliber, nickel plated, center fire. Using cartridge No. 35388. Our price......$3.75
No. 34213 38-caliber, blued finish, center fire. Using cartridge No. 35388. Our price......$4.15
Extra for pearl stocks on any of the above revolvers......$1.25

WHEN ORDERING REVOLVERS ALWAYS GIVE CATALOGUE NUMBER, CALIBER AND LENGTH OF BARREL.

Harrington & Richardson's Automatic with 5-inch Barrel.

No. 34215 32-caliber, nickel plated, 5-inch barrel.
Our price......$4.30
No. 34216 32-caliber, blued finish, 5-inch barrel.
Our price......$4.55
No. 34217 38-caliber, nickel plated, 5-inch barrel. Our price......$4.30
No. 34218 38-caliber, blued finish, 5-inch barrel. Our price......$4.55
Extra, for pearl stocks on any of above, $1.25.

Our $3.75 Forehand Automatic.

32 and 38-Caliber

The Celebrated Forehand & Wadsworth Automatic Revolver for $3.75; a revolver that retails at from $5.00 to $6.00. This is the very latest improved model, automatic shell extractor, rebounding lock, double action, self cocking, simple and accurate, interchangeable parts made from drop steel forgings. The frame is cast steel, no malleable iron about it; nickel plated throughout; fancy rubber stock; every revolver is fully warranted, length of barrel, 3¼ inches, weight, 17 ounces, entire length 7¾ inches. The fact that we sold more of these revolvers during the last year than ever before is evidence of the general satisfaction they give.
No. 34219 32-caliber nickel plated, Smith Wesson center fire cartridges, 5-shot, using cartridge No. 35377. Our price......$3.75
No. 34221 32-caliber, blued finish......4.00
No. 34223 38-caliber, nickel plated Smith Wesson, center fire cartridges, 5-shot. Using cartridge No. 35388. Our price......$3.75
No. 34224 38-caliber, blued finish. Our price......$4.00

32 and 38 caliber.

Forehand Automatic. Same as No. 34219 but with 5-inch barrel.
No. 34225 32-caliber, nickel plated, 5-inch......$4.30
No. 34226 32-caliber, blued, 5-inch......4.30
No. 34227 38-caliber, nickel plated, 5-inch......4.30
No. 34228 38-caliber, blued, 5-inch......4.15

The Iver Johnson Bicycle Revolver

32-caliber only.

Made on the same principle as the regular automatic, but has a short barrel—2 inches in length. Expressly designed for cyclists. Can be easily slipped into the pocket and is a sure protection against vicious dogs and highwaymen. Absolutely safe. No explosion till trigger is pulled. 32-caliber only; using cartridge No. 35377. Center fire, 5-shot.
No. 34231 Price......$3.75
If by mail, postage extra, 23 cents.

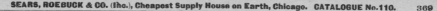

H. & R. Automatic Police Revolver.

AKES CARTRIDGES No. 35377 AND No. 35388.

32 and 38-Caliber. 3¼ and 5-inch barrel.

Nothing like it ever retailed for less than $5.00. The above illustration, engraved from a photograph, will give you some idea of the appearance of this gun. It is the celebrated Harrington & Richardson police, automatic, safety hammer, double action, self cocking, automatic shell extractor, fancy rubber stock, full nickel plated, center fire, 32 or 38-caliber; using cartridge No. 35377.

No. 34232 32-caliber, nickel plated, 6-shot, 3¼-inch barrel, 18 ounces. Our price............ $3.95
No. 34233 32-caliber; blued finish. Our price, 4.30
No. 34234 38-caliber, nickel plated, 5-shot, 3¼-inch barrel, 18-ounces; using cartridge No. 35388. Our price............ $3.95
No. 34235 38-caliber; blued finish, 3¼-inch barrel, 5-shot. Our price............ $4.30
No. 34236 32-caliber, 5-inch barrel, 6-shot, 19 ounces, nickeled. Our price............ $4.45
No. 34237 38-caliber, 5-inch barrel, 5-shot, 19 ounces, nickeled. Our price............ $4.45
Extra for pearl stocks on any of the above, $1.25
If by mail, postage extra, 24 cents.

Our $4.50 Forehand Hammerless.

SMALL FRAME.

32 and 38-Caliber.

AKES CARTRIDGES No. 35377 AND No. 35388.

We offer you at $4.50 a hammerless revolver which has never been retailed at less than $8.00. No other house will meet our price. Make a comparison and decide for yourself. This is the celebrated Forehand & Wadsworth new style hammerless revolver, made by Forehand Arms Co. No better revolver made. Automatic shell extractor, double action, self cocking, rebounding lock, absolutely safe catch to lock hammer, made of best material, beautifully finished throughout, accurate and reliable. All center fire, nicely nickel plated throughout, uses Smith & Wesson center fire cartridges, 32-caliber, 5-shot; 38-caliber, 5-shot; using cartridge No. 35377 and No. 35388.

No. 34240 32-caliber, nickeled; our price.. $4.50
No. 34241 32-caliber, blued; our price..... 5.00
No. 34242 38-caliber, nickeled; using cartridge No. 35388. Our price............ 4.50
No. 34243 38-caliber, blued; our price..... 5.00

Forehand Hammerless, with 5-inch Barrel.

5-INCH BARREL.

No. 34244 32-caliber, nickeled; 5-inch barrel. Our price............ $5.00
No. 34245 32-caliber, blued; 5-inch barrel. Our price............ $5.40
No. 34246 38-caliber, nickeled; 5-inch barrel. Our price............ $5.00
No. 34247 38-caliber, blued; 5-inch barrel. Our price............ $5.40

NOTICE. Owing to the heavy advance in prices on revolvers at the different factories, and which are liable to go much higher,

OUR PRICES ARE SUBJECT TO CHANGE WITHOUT NOTICE.

Place your orders early, while our present stock lasts, as these prices apply only to stock on hand.

The New Harrington & Richardson Automatic Bayonet Revolver.

Made in 38-caliber only, using the same cartridges as the Smith & Wesson Revolvers.

In response to the many inquiries for a bayonet revolver, we are pleased to say that we can now furnish this article.

The Harrington & Richardson New Automatic Bayonet Revolver is made in 38 caliber only, with 4-inch barrel, the bayonet extending 2½ inches forward of the muzzle. They are handsomely nickel plated, all working parts are steel and case hardened, and the bayonet is so constructed that it can be folded under the barrel instantly when desired. When open the bayonet is securely locked. This revolver is fitted with nicely checkered rubber stocks, but can be furnished with pearl stocks when so desired. It is well rifled and thoroughly well made throughout. All parts are interchangeable, so that if you accidentally break any part, it can be duplicated at small cost.

No 34248 38-caliber, 4-inch barrel, 18 ounces. Our special price............ $5.50
No. 34249 38-caliber, 4-inch barrel, 18 ounces, blued finish. Our special price............ $5.90
Extra for pearl stocks............ 1.25
If by mail, postage extra, 27 cents.

Iver Johnson Small Frame Automatic Revolver.

32 and 38-Caliber.

The Iver Johnson Automatic Safety Hammer Revolver, double action, self cocking, 5-shot, 11- and 18 ounce weight, 3-inch barrel, finely nickel plated, neatly finished. Every one warranted. All take center fire Smith & Wesson cartridges.

No. 34257 32-caliber, 3-inch barrel, nickeled. Each............ $3.75
No. 34258 32-caliber, 3-inch barrel, blued finish Each............ $4.15
No. 34259 38-caliber, nickeled. 3¼-inch barrel. Each............ $3.75
No. 34260 38-caliber, blued finish, 3¼-inch barrel. Each............ $4.15
No. 34261 32-caliber, nickeled, 4-inch barrel. Each............ $4.05
No. 34261½ 32-caliber, blued finish, 4-inch barrel. Each............ $4.45
No. 34262 38-caliber, nickeled, 4-inch barrel. Each............ $4.05
No. 34262½ 38-caliber, blued finish. 4-inch barrel. Each............ $4.45
No. 34263 32-caliber, nickeled, 5-inch barrel. Each............ $4.40
No. 34264 32-caliber, blued finish, 5-inch barrel. Each............ $4.80
No. 34265 38-caliber, nickeled, 5-inch barrel. Each............ $4.40
No. 34266 38-caliber, blued finish, 5-inch barrel, Each............ $4.80
If by mail, postage extra, 27 cents.

Hopkins & Allen Hinge Revolver.

22, 32 and 38-Caliber.

The above illustration shows you the Hopkins & Allen shell ejecting, double action self cocking revolver. Very finest forged steel barrels and cylinders, in all respects the best material and finish, guaranteed accurate, safe and reliable, nickel plated, rubber stock. A high grade revolver at a heretofore unheard of price.

No. 34310 32-caliber, nickel plated, 5-shot, 12-ounces, 3-inch barrel. Our price............ $3.75
No. 34311 32-caliber, blued. Our price. 4.15
No. 34312 38-caliber, nickeled, 5-shot, 17-ounces, 3¼-inch barrel. Our price............ $3.75
No. 34313 38-caliber, blued. Our price. 4.15
No. 34314 22-caliber, nickeled, rim fire, 7-shot, 12-ounce, 3-inch barrel. Our price............ $3.75
No. 34315 22-caliber, blued. Our price. 4.15
If by mail, postage extra, 25 cents.

Our Single Action Home Defender, $1.15.

41-caliber rim fire, takes cartridges No. 35360 or 35361. This is a good single action revolver for Home Defense, full nickel plated, 5-shot, fluted cylinder, octagon barrel cylinder check bolt, round or saw handle checkered pattern and we offer it, while our stock lasts, at a bargain. We had a chance to buy a large lot of these below the market prices and we bought them and now we give you the benefit of our purchase.

No. 34316 Our special while they last price, $1.15
No. 34317 Same as the above, 38-caliber, rim fire, imitation ebony, saw handle, taking cartridge No. 35356, our special price............ $1.25
If by mail, postage extra, 18 cents.

Iver Johnson Hammerless Automatic Revolver.

32 and 38-Caliber.

The above illustrated revolver is the celebrated Iver Johnson automatic hammerless double action; high grade finish, fine adjustments. Its trigger locking device makes it one of the safest revolvers to carry in the pocket. Automatic self ejector, rebounding lock, safety trigger locking device, chambered cylinder, rifled barrel. Smith & Wesson small frame, 5-shot, weighs 13 oz., length of barrel, 3 inches; revolver that retails at from $7.00 to $10.00.

No. 34322 32-caliber, nickeled. Our price. $4.35
No. 34323 32-caliber, blued. Our price.... 4.60
No. 34324 38-caliber, nickeled, 3¼-inch barrel. Our price............ $4.35
No. 34325 38-caliber, blued, 3¼-inch barrel. Our price............ $4.60
If by mail, postage extra, 24 cents.
Pearl Stocks, 32-caliber, $1.25 extra; 38-caliber, $1.50 extra.

32-Caliber Only.

A small hammerless Revolver, designed chiefly for bicycle riders.

No. 34327 Iver Johnson Cycle Hammerless Revolver, same as No. 34322, with 2-inch barrel, 32-caliber only, nickel plated. Our special price, $4.25
No. 34328 The same revolver with pearl stocks. Our special price............ $5.50

The Hopkins & Allen Automatic Shell Ejecting Folding Hammer Revolver for $3.95.

32 and 38-Caliber.

The above illustration, engraved from a photograph, gives you an idea of the appearance of this revolver.

Hopkins & Allen automatic shell ejecting, center fire, double action, self cocking, folding hammer revolver, fancy rubber stock, finely made and accurate, 5-shot, 17-ounce.

No. 34330 32-caliber, nickeled, 3-inch barrel. Our price............ $3.95
No. 34331 38-caliber, nickeled, 3¼-inch barrel. Our price............ $3.95
No. 34332 32-caliber, blued, 3-inch barrel. Our price............ $4.35
No. 34333 38-caliber, blued, 3¼-inch barrel. Our price............ $4.35
If by mail, postage extra, 24 cents.

GENUINE SMITH & WESSON REVOLVERS.

Model 1899 Smith & Wesson Military and Police Revolver.

Double action, center fire, 6-shot; with solid frame; swing-out cylinder and hand ejecting mechanism; weight, 30 ounces; 5 and 6½-inch barrel; blued or nickeled frame; using 38-caliber ong Colt DA cartridge No. 35392. **This revolver is Smith & Wesson's latest creation and is a revolverthat is built for business.** It will withstand hard usage and has a movable firing pin on the nose of the hammer, which absolutely closes the firing pin hole and prevents any possible gas from going back of the frame. It is highly recommended for target shooting, and made in blued or nickeled finish; weight, 1¾ to 2 lbs.

No. 34516	Our special price, with 5-inch barrel, nickel plated	$13.00
No. 34516½	Our special price, with 5-inch barrel, blued finish	13.00
No. 34518	Our special price, with 6½-inch barrel, nickel plated	13.50
No. 34519	Our special price, with 6½-inch barrel; blued finish	13.50
	First Quality Pearl Stocks, extra	3.00

If by mail, postage extra, 44 cents.

Smith & Wesson Side Ejecting Revolver.

Solid Frame, side ejecting, rebounding lock, rubber stock, blued or nickel plated; weight, 19 ounces, 3¼, 4½ and 6-inch barrel; 6 shot, using 32-caliber S. & W. long cartridge No. 35376. A fine, strong shooting revolver with a solid steel frame.

No. 34520	3¼-inch barrel, nickel plated	$9.50
No. 34523	3¼-inch barrel, blued finish	9.50
No. 34524	4½-inch barrel, nickel plated	9.75
No. 34525	4½-inch barrel, blued finish	9.75
No. 34526	6-inch barrel, nickel plated	$10.00
No. 34527	6-inch barrel, blued finish	10.00
	First Quality Pearl Stocks, extra	1.50
	Special target sights fitted to the above, (to special order, cash with order) extra	1.75

If by mail or prepaid express, 25 to 30 cents extra.

The Genuine Smith & Wesson Double Action Revolvers.

These revolvers are warranted genuine Smith & Wesson. Manufactured by Smith & Wesson, Springfield, Mass. **Self cocking, double action, automatic shell extractor, fine rubber stocks, nickel plated or blued finish.** Made of the finest material that money can buy and the workmanship is equal in finish, to that of any ordinary watch. If you want the best work for your money buy a Smith & Wesson.

DOUBLE ACTION Revolvers.

No. 34531	32-caliber, 5-shot, 3-inch barrel, nickel plated	$ 9.75
No. 34532	32-caliber, 5-shot, 3-inch barrel, blued finish	9.75
No. 34533	32-caliber, 5-shot, 3½-inch barrel, nickel plated	9.75
No. 34534	32-caliber, 5-shot, 3½-inch barrel, blued	9.75
No. 34535	32-caliber, 5-shot, 6-inch barrel, nickel plated	11.00
No. 34536	32-caliber, 5-shot, 6-inch barrel, blued	11.00
No. 34543	38-caliber, 5-shot, 3¼-inch barrel, nickel plated	10.95
No. 34544	38-caliber, 5-shot, 3¼-inch barrel, blued	10.95
No. 34545	38-caliber, 5-shot, 4-inch barrel, nickel plated	11.25
No. 34546	38-caliber, 5-shot, 4-inch barrel, blued	11.25
No. 34547	38-caliber, 5-shot, 5-inch barrel, nickel plated	11.45
No. 34548	38-caliber, 5-shot, 5-inch barrel blued	11.45
No. 34549	38-caliber, 5-shot, 6-inch barrel, nickel plated	11.95
No. 34550	38-caliber, 5-shot, 6-inch barrel, blued	11.95
	First Quality Pearl stocks for 32 or 38-Caliber, extra	1.25
	Any of the above by mail or prepaid express, 15 to 30 cents.	
No. 34551	44-Caliber, Frontier, 6-shot, 6-inch barrel, chambered for 44-caliber Winchester cartridges, nickel plated	13.75
No. 34552	44-Caliber, Frontier, 6-shot, 6-inch barrel, chambered for 44-caliber Winchester cartridges, blued finish	13.75
	First Quality Pearl handles on 44-caliber revolvers, extra	3.50

If by mail, 40 to 50 cents extra.

NOTICE—On any goods not described or listed in this catalogue and made to order, we must ask cash in full with the order, and they cannot be returned under any circumstances.

Smith & Wesson Hammerless Revolvers.

The GENUINE SMITH & WESSON HAMMERLESS.

Made by Smith & Wesson, Springfield, Mass. Latest type, new model hammerless, automatic shell ejector, patent safety catch self locking rebounding locks, double action, blued or nickel plated finish. This is positively the best hammerless revolver made. "A thing of beauty is a joy forever." If you own one of these revolvers you are certain to own one of the best revolvers made and one which always has a market value.

PRICES OF THE S. & W. HAMMERLESS.

No. 34608	32-caliber, 3-inch barrel, nickel plated	$10.90
No. 34609	32-caliber, 3-inch barrel, blued finish	10.90
No. 34610	32-caliber, 3½-inch barrel, nickel plated	10.90
No. 34611	32-caliber, 3½-inch barrel, blued finish	10.90
No. 34612	38-caliber, 3¼-inch barrel, nickel plated	11.95
No. 34613	38-caliber, 3¼-inch barrel, blued finish	11.95
No. 34614	38-caliber, 4-inch barrel, nickel plated	12.25
No. 34615	38-caliber, 4-inch barrel, blued finish	12.25
No. 34616	38-caliber, 5-inch barrel, nickel plated	12.50
No. 34617	38-caliber, 5-inch barrel, blued finish	12.50
No. 34618	38-caliber, 6-inch barrel, nickel plated	13.00
No. 34619	38-caliber, 6-inch barrel, blued finish	13.00
	First Quality Pearl Stocks, extra	1.25

☞ See our prices on cartridges. **If by mail, postage extra, 18 to 30 cents.**

Harrington & Richardson's Young America, Target Revolver.

Double Action, Reduced Size, 22-Cal., Rim Fire, with 6-inch Barrel.

Young America.

Full nickeled, rubber or pearl stocks, 7-shot, 6-inch octagon barrels.

No. 34627	22-caliber, 7-shot, 6-inch barrel, rim fire, rubber handles, 8-oz.	$2.50
No. 34628	The same, with pearl handles	$3.40

This is the only 22-caliber, 7-shot, target pistol on the market and we are the first to offer it to our customers.

If by mail, postage extra, 15 cents.

Our "16th Century" Flint Lock Pistol for Only $2.75

F is the flint.
C is cover of powder pan.

For $2.75 we offer you our special Flint Lock Pistol. Many people supposed that there were no more of these revolvers to be had, but our European buyer succeeded in finding a small lot of them in Europe, and has sent them to us.

We are always on the lookout for anything that interests our customers, and if you are collecting relics we know that this "16th Century Pistol" will go along with your other antiquities.

This, our special flint lock pistol, is one which our grandfathers and great-grandfathers used to shoot before the advent of modern arms.

Do not think because we offer these pistols cheap, that they can only be used as an ornament, for if you desire you can shoot the pistol; shoot it the same as you would a muzzle loading gun.

The pistol has a 14-gauge barrel, 9 inches long and weighs 2¾ pounds, and is loaded from the muzzle the same as an ordinary muzzle loading gun.

After loading, place a little powder in the powder pan, close down the pan cover (C) to prevent the powder from falling out, pull the hammer to full cock, fire. The flint (F) ignites the powder by sparks caused by striking the pan cover. This pistol has a bright polished barrel, walnut stock, is brass mounted, and has a good, strong, substantial lock.

Do not fail to place your order as early as possible, because the supply is limited and at the present time we do not know of any more to be had anywhere. Show the boys the kind of a pistol which our grandfathers used to shoot, before gun caps were invented.

No. 34629 Our special flint lock pistol, 9-inch barrel, 14-gauge, weight 2¾ pounds, our special price $2.75

AIR RIFLES AND BELONGINGS.

The 1900 Model Chicago Air Rifle shoots regular air-gun darts and bullets. Entire length over all, 33 inches. It will shoot a common BB shot 40 rods, and **kill small game at 50 feet.** No powder or caps, **no noise,** not dangerous to handle. By its use a person **can become a perfect shot. It costs but 1 cent to shoot 100 times.** The barrel, air chamber and all working parts are made of brass and steel. The stock is maple, nicely stained and varnished, **representing rosewood.** The air chamber and barrel are of mandrel drawn brass, **accurately bored and polished.**

No. 34630 Our price **(If by mail, postage extra, 44 cents)** 75c

The New Model King Air Rifle Single Shot.

Our King Rifles we Guarantee the Highest Grade Made.

75 Cents.

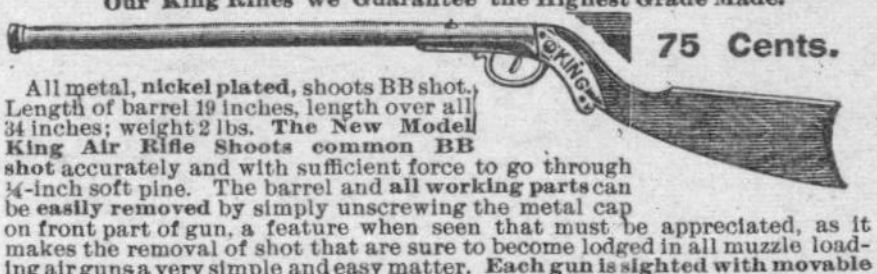

All metal, **nickel plated,** shoots BB shot. Length of barrel 19 inches, length over all 34 inches; weight 2 lbs. **The New Model King Air Rifle Shoots common BB shot** accurately and with sufficient force to go through ¼-inch soft pine. The barrel and **all working parts can be easily removed** by simply unscrewing the metal cap on front part of gun, a feature when seen that must be appreciated, as it makes the removal of shot that are sure to become lodged in all muzzle loading air guns a very simple and easy matter. **Each gun is sighted with movable sights** and packed in paper box.

No. 34632 Our special price **(if by mail, postage, extra, 44 cents)** .. 75c

No. 34633 The New King Repeater. Same style as King single shot. This is one of the **best Repeating Air Rifles** on the market. **Shoots 152 times from once loading.** Our special price $1.10

If by mail, postage extra, 44 cents.

The Improved Daisy Air Rifle for 76 Cents.

Our 76-cent Daisy is the most perfect little all metal gun ever shown. Shoots No. 18-100 darts.

Made entirely of metal, nickel plated, latest improved pattern; length of barrel, 19 inches; **total length, 30 inches.** Weight, 2¼ lbs. Is now fitted with globe sights, each rifle carefully tested before leaving factory. This is the latest model improved Daisy air rifle. Shoots shot or darts.

No. 34634 Our special price, with skeleton wire stock 76c

If by mail, postage extra, 44 cents.

No. 34635 Same as No. 34634 except has **wood stock,** and is more finely finished. Our special price, each 84c

If by mail, postage extra, 45 cents.

The New Cycloid. The Latest Air Rifle.

No. 34640 The Cycloid Single Shot. Made entirely of metal. Barrel finely polished and highly nickeled. Steel stock and balance beautifully finished. Total length, 30 inches; weight 2½ pounds. In the new Cycloid you will find all the old difficulties overcome. **It is a beauty.** Put the shot in at the muzzle and cock the gun to shoot it.

No. 34640 Price, each $1.15

If by mail, postage extra, 45 cents.

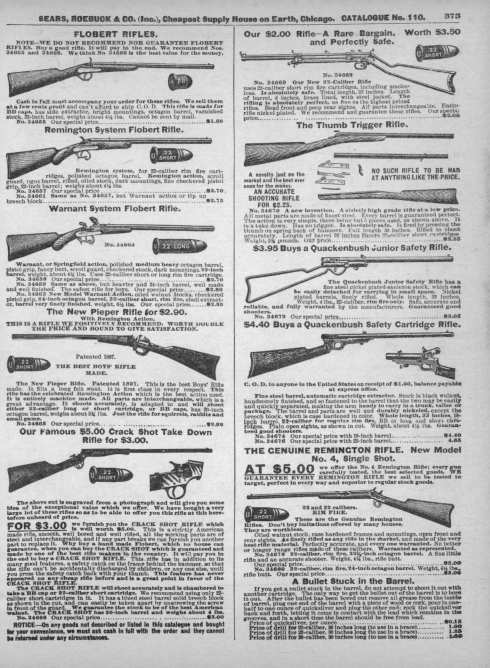

FLOBERT RIFLES.

NOTE—WE DO NOT RECOMMEND NOR GUARANTEE FLOBERT RIFLES. Buy a good rifle. It will pay in the end. We recommend Nos. 34665 and 34666. We think No 34666 is the best value for the money.

Cash in full must accompany your order for these rifles. We sell them at a few cents profit and can't afford to ship C. O. D. This rifle is made for BB caps, has side extractor, bright mountings, octagon barrel, varnished stock, 22-inch barrel, weighs about 4½ lbs. Cannot be sent by mail.
No. 34655 Our special price..........................$1.60

Remington System Flobert Rifle.

Remington system, for 22-caliber rim fire cartridges, polished octagon barrel. Remington action, scroll guard, tight barrel, rifled, oiled stock, dark mountings, fine checkered pistol grip, 22-inch barrel; weighs about 4½ lbs.
No. 34657 Our special price........................$2.70
No. 34661 Same as No. 34657, but Warnant action or tip up breech block...................................$2.75

Warnant System Flobert Rifle.

Warnant, or Springfield action, polished medium heavy octagon barrel, pistol grip, faney butt, scroll guard, checkered stock, dark mountings, 22-inch barrel, weight, about 4½ lbs. Uses 22-caliber short or long rim fire cartridge.
No. 34658 Our special price......................$2.70
No. 34659 Same as above, but heavier and 24-inch barrel, well made and well finished. The safest rifle for boys. Our special price.......$2.80
No. 34663 New Model Warnant Action, oiled walnut stocks, checkered pistol grip, 24-inch octagon barrel, 32-caliber short, rim fire, shell extractor, barrel very finely finished, weight, 6½ lbs. Our special price.....$2.85

The New Pieper Rifle for $2.90.

With Remington Action.
THIS IS A RIFLE WE POSITIVELY RECOMMEND. WORTH DOUBLE THE PRICE AND BOUND TO GIVE SATISFACTION.

Patented 1897.

THE BEST BOYS' RIFLE MADE.

The New Pieper Rifle. Patented 1897. This is the best Boys' Rifle made. It fills a long felt want. It is first class in every respect. This rifle has the celebrated Remington Action which is the best action used. It is entirely machine made. All parts are interchangeable, which is a great advantage. It shoots accurately, is adapted to and will shoot either 22-caliber long or short cartridge, or BB caps, has 20-inch octagon barrel, weighs about 3½ lbs. Just the rifle for squirrels, rabbits and small game.
No. 34663 Our special price..........................$2.90

Our Famous $5.00 Crack Shot Take Down Rifle for $3.00.

The above cut is engraved from a photograph and will give you some idea of the exceptional value which we offer. We have bought a very large lot of these rifles so as to be able to offer you this rifle at this heretofore unheard of price.

FOR $3.00 we present you the CRACK SHOT RIFLE which is well worth $5.00. This is a strictly American made rifle, smooth, well bored and well rifled, all the working parts are of steel and interchangeable, and if any part breaks we can furnish you another part to replace it. Why buy a hand made Flobert, which no house can guarantee, when you can buy the CRACK SHOT which is guaranteed and made by one of the best rifle makers in the country. It will pay you in the end to buy a CRACK SHOT RIFLE. This rifle has in addition to its many good features, a safety catch on the frame behind the hammer, so that the rifle can't be accidentally discharged by children, until you press the safety catch back with your thumb. This feature has never appeared on any cheap rifle before and is a great point in favor of the CRACK SHOT RIFLE.
The CRACK SHOT RIFLE will shoot accurately and is chambered to take a BB cap or 22-caliber short cartridge. We recommend using only 22-caliber short cartridges in it. It has a blued steel barrel and breech block as shown in the cut, and can easily be taken apart by unscrewing the screw in front of the guard. We guarantee the stock to be of the best walnut. The CRACK SHOT has 20-inch barrel and weighs about 4 lbs.
No. 34666 Our special price.............................$3.00

NOTICE—On any goods not described or listed in this catalogue and bought for your convenience, we must ask cash in full with the order and they cannot be returned under any circumstances.

Our $2.00 Rifle—A Rare Bargain. Worth $3.50 and Perfectly Safe.

No. 34669
No. 34669 Our New 22-Caliber Rifle uses 22-caliber short rim fire cartridges, including smokeless. Is absolutely safe. Total length, 33 inches. Length of barrel, 8 inches, brass lined, with steel jacket. The rifling is absolutely perfect, all parts interchangeable. Bead front and peep rear sights. All parts nickel plated. We recommend and guarantee these rifles. Our special price..........................$2.00

The Thumb Trigger Rifle.

A novelty just on the market and the best ever seen for the money.
AN ACCURATE SHOOTING RIFLE FOR $2.25.
NO SUCH RIFLE TO BE HAD AT ANYTHING LIKE THE PRICE.

No. 34670 A new invention. A strictly high grade rifle at a low price. All metal parts are made of finest steel. Every barrel is guaranteed perfect. The action is very simple, there being but 5 pieces used, as shown above. It is a take down. Has no trigger. Is absolutely safe. It is fired by pressing the thumb on spring back of hammer. Full length 36 inches. Rifled to shoot accurately. Length of barrel 20 inches. Shoots 22-caliber short cartridges. Weight, 3½ pounds. Our price..................................$2.25

$3.95 Buys a Quackenbush Junior Safety Rifle.

The Quackenbush Junior Safety Rifle has a fine steel nickel plated skeleton stock, which can be easily detached for carrying in small space. Nickel plated barrels, finely rifled. Whole length, 33 inches. Weight, 4 lbs., 22-caliber, rim fire only. Safe, accurate and reliable, and fully warranted by the manufacturers. Guaranteed good shooters.
No. 34672 Our special price................................$3.95

$4.40 Buys a Quackenbush Safety Cartridge Rifle.

C. O. D. to anyone in the United States on receipt of $1.00, balance payable at express office.

Fine steel barrel, automatic cartridge extractor. Stock is black walnut, handsomely finished, and so fastened to the barrel that the two may be easily and quickly separated, making the arm ready to carry in a trunk, valise or package. The barrel and parts are well and durably nickeled, except the breech block, which is case hardened in color. Whole length, 33 inches, 18-inch barrel, 22-caliber for regular rim fire, BB or long and short cartridges. Plain open sights, as shown in cut. Weight, about 4½ lbs. Guaranteed good shooters.
No. 34674 Our special price with 18-inch barrel...............$4.40
No. 34676 Our special price with 22-inch barrel...............4.65

THE GENUINE REMINGTON RIFLE. New Model No. 4, Single Shot.

AT $5.00 we offer the No. 4 Remington Rifle; every gun carefully tested, the best selected goods. WE GUARANTEE EVERY REMINGTON RIFLE we sell to be tested to target, perfect in every way and superior to regular stock goods.

22 and 32 calibers. RIM FIRE.
These are the Genuine Remington Rifles. Don't buy imitations offered by many houses. They are worthless.

Oiled walnut stock, case hardened frames and mountings, open front and rear sights. As finely rifled as any rifle in the market, and made of the very best rifle material. Perfectly accurate, and every one warranted. No better or longer range rifles made of these calibers. Warranted as represented.
No. 34678 22-caliber, rim fire, 22½-inch octagon barrel. A fine little rifle and an accurate shooter. Weight, 4½ lbs., rifle butt.
Our special price...................................$5.00
No. 34680 32-caliber, rim fire, 24-inch octagon barrel. Weight, 4½ lbs., rifle butt. Our special price.

A Bullet Stuck in the Barrel.

If you get a bullet stuck in the barrel, do not attempt to shoot it out with another cartridge. The only way to get the bullet out of the barrel is to bore it out. After the bullet has been bored out remove all grease from the inside of barrel, plug one end of the barrel with a piece of wood or cork, pour in one-half to one ounce of quicksilver and plug the other end; rock the quicksilver back and forth, letting it come in contact with the lead which remains in the grooves, and in a short time the barrel should be free from lead.
Price of quicksilver, per ounce..........................$0.15
Price of drill for 22-caliber, 30 inches long (to use in a brace)..........1.00
Price of drill for 25-caliber, 30 inches long (to use in a brace)..........1.25
Price of drill for 32-caliber, 30 inches long (to use in a brace)..........1.50

THE NEW MARLIN REPEATING RIFLES, MODEL 1895.

The barrels in rifles of this model are made of nickel steel and guaranteed to fill government tests. The increasing use of nitro powders makes this feature important. The barrels are also slightly tapered, giving extra strength around the chamber and making the balance of the rifle much better.

Rifles of this model have case hardened receivers.

These rifles are identical with Model 1894, but made to shoot large sizes of cartridges; the barrels are made the same as the old Ballard Rifles, of special smokeless steel. The standard rifles will have 26-inch barrels and weigh about 8¾ pounds, and are adapted to 38-56, 40-65, 40-82, 45-70, 45-90 and the magazines will hold 9 cartridges.

With shotgun rubber butt plate and half magazine a rifle will weigh about one-half pound less.

The 38-56 caliber Marlin uses the 38-56-255 cartridge.

The 40-65 caliber Marlin uses the 40-65-260 or the 40-60-260 Marlin cartridges in the same rifle.

The 40-82 Marlin uses the 40-82-260 cartridge. Smokeless cartridges with metal patched bullets can be furnished.

The 45-70 Marlin uses the 45-70-405 Marlin, the 45-70-405 Government, the 45-70-500 Government, the 45-70-330 Gould's Express, the 45-70-350 or the 45-85 Marlin cartridges in the same rifle. Smokeless cartridges with metal patched bullets can also be furnished.

The 45-90 Marlin uses the 45-90-300, the 45-85-350, the 45-82-405, or the 45-85-300 Express cartridges in the same rifle. Smokeless cartridges with metal patched or mushroom bullets can be furnished. All rifles of this model can be furnished with pistol grip, with take down and all other extras except set locks, at extra prices quoted on previous page and below.

No. 34770 Octagon barrel, 26-inch, 38-56 caliber, 9 shots...$14.97
No. 34772 Octagon barrel, 26-inch, 40-65 caliber, 8¾ lbs., 9 shots... 14.97
No. 34774 Octagon barrel, 26-inch, 40-82 caliber, 8¾ lbs., 9 shots... 14.97
No. 34776 Octagon barrel, 26-inch, 45-70 caliber, 8¾ lbs., 9 shots...$14.97
No. 34778 Octagon barrel, 26-inch, 45-90 caliber, 8¾ lbs., 9 shots... 14.97
No. 347815 Carbines in this model, 38-56, 40-65, 45-70 or 45-90 caliber, 20-inch round barrel, 7¾ lbs., 6 shots, made to special order 13.50

MARLIN "TAKE DOWN" ON MODELS 1893, 1894 AND 1895.

In this system the barrel is screwed into the frame exactly as in a solid rifle. No part of the thread is cut away, nor is this union weakened in any way. Can be placed in a Victoria case. As light and compact to carry as a shotgun. Strong as our regular rifle; no looseness; no danger of coming apart owing to accident or carelessness. Cannot become shaky, as all wear is taken up every time the rifle is put together. Made to special order.

No. 348005 Model '94 Take Down. Any caliber made in this model, 24-inch octagon barrel...$16.00
No. 348025 Model '93 Take Down. 25-36 or 30-30 caliber. Octagon barrel 26-inch...$17.50
No. 348045 Model '93 Take Down, 32-40 or 38-55 caliber. Octagon barrel, 26-inch...$16.50
No. 348065 Model '95 Take Down. Any caliber made in this model, 26-inch octagon barrel...$18.50

Cut showing rifle when taken apart ready to be packed.

Cut showing forward end of receiver when rifle is apart.

Cut showing breech end of barrel and magazine when rifle is apart.

OUR LINE OF WINCHESTER REPEATING RIFLES.

WINCHESTER RIFLES. MODEL OF 1873.

Made in 22 Rim Fire.
32-20 CALIBER.
38-40 CALIBER.
44-40 CALIBER.

No. 34780 44-caliber, Octagon Barrel, Winchester Repeating Sporting Rifle, (Model 1873), length of barrel, 24-inch; center fire, 15 shots, weight 8¾ lbs. Price...$12.52

Weight, 8¾ to 9 pounds.

38, 32 and 22-caliber, round barrel...$11.55
No. 34781 44-Caliber, Round Barrel... 11.55
No. 34782 38-Caliber, Octagon Barrel, 24-inch, center-fire, 15-shot, weight, 9 lbs... 12.52
No. 34784 32-Caliber, Octagon Barrel, 24-inch, center-fire, 15-shot, weight, 9 lbs... 12.52
No. 34786 22-Caliber, Octagon Barrel, 24-inch, 25-shot, weight, 9 lbs., 22-caliber rim fire, short only... 12.52
No. 34787 Winchester Carbine, 32 W. C. F., 38 W. C. F. and 44 W. C. F. calibers, with 20-inch round barrels (Model 1873), 15-shot, made to special order, each... 11.55

WINCHESTER MODEL 1892 REPEATER.

25-20 Caliber.   38-40 Caliber.
32-20 Caliber.   44-40 Caliber.

Weight, 6¼ to 7 pounds.

The system is the same as the Model of 1886 now so well known. Manipulated by a finger lever, the firing pin is first withdrawn, the gun unlocked and opened, the shell or cartridge ejected, and a new cartridge presented and forced into the chamber, the firing pin held back until the gun is again locked. The locking bolts are always in sight, and when the gun is closed, support the breech bolt symmetrically against the force of the explosion. The same cartridges are used as in the Model of 1873—44, 38 and 32 Winchester center fire, their widely extended sale having proved their value for general use, and in addition the W. C. F. cartridges. They also take the 25-20 W. C. F. The gun is light, strong, handsome, and simple in construction.

No. 34790 44-caliber, Octagon Barrel, 24-inch, about 7 lbs., 15-shot...$12.52
No. 34791 44-caliber, Round Barrel, about 7 lbs., 6¾ lbs., 15-shot... 11.55
No. 34792 38-caliber, Octagon Barrel, 24-inch, about 7 lbs., 15-shot...$12.52
No. 34793 38-caliber, Round Barrel, 24-inch, 7 lbs., 15-shot... 11.55
No. 34794 32-caliber, Octagon Barrel, 24-inch, 6¾ lbs., 15-shot... 12.52
No. 34795 32-caliber, Round Barrel, 24-inch, 6¾ lbs., 15-shot... 11.55
No. 34796 25-20 W. C. F. caliber, Octagon Barrel, 24-inch 15-shot... 12.52
No. 34797 25-20 W. C. F. caliber, Round Barrel, 24-inch 15-shot... 11.55
No. 34799 Model 1892 Carbine, with 20-inch round barrel, full magazine in 32, 38 or 44-calibers; 6¼ lbs., made to special order. Each, 11.39

WINCHESTER MODEL 1892 "TAKE DOWN" REPEATER.

Made to special order.

No. 348006 Octagon barrel, 24 inches, 32, 38, 44 and 25-20 calibers. Each..$16.00

OUR TERMS ARE VERY LIBERAL. Send us only $1.00 and we will send any gun by express C. O. D., subject to examination. You can examine it at your express office and then pay express agent balance and express charges. This does not apply to goods made to special order.

ALL OUR GUNS ARE CAREFULLY PACKED FOR SHIPMENT.

RIFLE TAKEN APART.

WINCHESTER REPEATING RIFLE, MODEL 1890 "TAKE DOWN" 22-CALIBER.

22-CALIBER ONLY.

Winchester Model 1890, Repeating Rifle. Loads and ejects the shell by the sliding motion of the forearm. All 24-inch octagon barrels are 5¾ pounds weight. New model stock and barrel, can be separated by removing a screw.

NOTE—Only the cartridge mentioned can be used in above rifles, as they are only chambered for one size cartridge and are warranted to be accurate and reliable.

No. 34804 For 22-caliber, rim fire, short only, 15-shot, octagon barrel. Our special price.$10.26
No. 34806 For 22-caliber, rim fire, long only, 12-shot, octagon barrel. Our special price. 10.26
No. 34808 For 22-caliber, rim fire, special Winchester cartridges, No. 35344, octagon barrel, 10-shot. Our special price... 10.26

RIFLE TAKEN APART.

WINCHESTER SINGLE SHOT RIFLES.

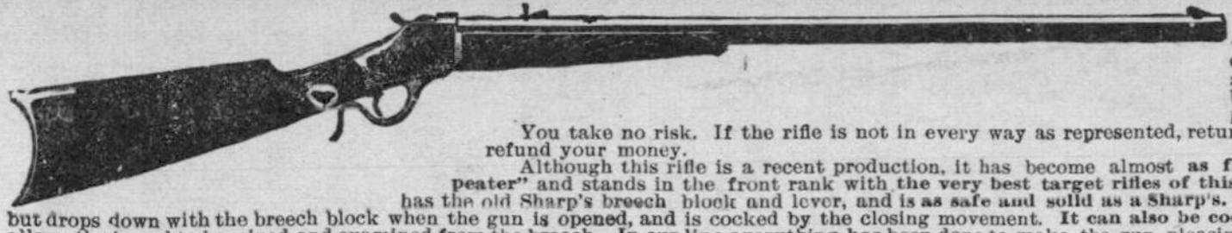

On rifles, our terms are exactly the same as on all other guns, C. O. D. to anyone on receipt of $1.00 as a guarantee of good faith, the balance and express charges to be paid after you receive the rifle.

You take no risk. If the rifle is not in every way as represented, return it at our expense and we will refund your money.

Although this rifle is a recent production, it has become almost as famous as the "Winchester Repeater" and stands in the front rank with the very best target rifles of this and other countries. This gun has the old Sharp's breech block and lever, and is as safe and solid as a Sharp's. The hammer is centrally hung, but drops down with the breech block when the gun is opened, and is cocked by the closing movement. **It can also be cocked by hand.** This arrangement allows the barrel to be wiped and examined from the breech. In our line everything has been done to make the gun pleasing to the eye. **All of these guns have case hardened lock plates** and dark walnut stock. Other styles and calibers made to special order.

Every rifle warranted perfect and accurate. The **double set locks are adjustable** by a little screw in rear of trigger, and can be set to pull as desired or not used at all. Pushing the rear trigger forward places it in the "hair pull" notch, same as working a double trigger. All rifles have sporting rear sights.

No.	Barrel	Weight	Trigger	Caliber	Price	No.	Barrel	Weight	Trigger	Caliber	Price
34810	Octagon, 24-in.	7 lbs.	Plain	22-long or 22-long rifle rim....	$10.75	34820	Octagon, 30-in.	9 lbs.	Set	38-55 Marlin central fire.....	$12.13
34811	Octagon, 26-in.	7 lbs.	Plain	22-long or 22-long rifle rim....	11.60	34821	Octagon, 30-in.	9½ lbs.	Set	40-60 Winchester central fire.	12.13
34812	Octagon, 26-in.	7 lbs.	Plain	32-rim, short or long..........	10.75	34822	Octagon, 30-in.	9½ lbs.	Plain	40-82 Winchester central fire.	10.75
34813	Octagon, 26-in.	7 lbs.	Plain	22 Winchester central fire...	11.35	34823	Octagon, 30-in.	9½ lbs.	Set	40-90 Winchester central fire.	12.13
34814	Octagon, 28-in.	7 lbs.	Plain	25-20 Winchester single shot..	10.75	34824	Octagon, 30-in.	9½ lbs.	Plain	45-70 Winchester central fire.	10.75
34815	Octagon, 28-in.	7 lbs.	Plain	32-20 Winchester central fire.	10.75	34825	Octagon, 30-in.	9½ lbs.	Plain	40-65 Winchester central fire.	10.75
34816	Octagon, 30-in.	9 lbs.	Plain	32-40 Marlin central fire......	10.75	34826	Octagon, 30-in.	9½ lbs.	Plain	45-90 Winch'r C. F., model '86	10.75
34817	Octagon, 30-in.	9 lbs.	Set	32-40 Marlin central fire......	12.13	34827	Octagon, 30-in.	9½ lbs.	Plain	40-70 Winch'r C. F., model '86	10.75
34818	Octagon, 28-in.	8½ lbs.	Plain	38-40 Winchester central fire..	10.75	34828	Spc'l Round 30-in.	9 lbs.	Plain	30 U. S. Army Smokeless......	14.25
34819	Octagon, 30-in.	9 lbs.	Plain	38-55 Marlin central fire......	10.75						

Any additional changes from the above styles will have to be made to order and cause a delay of from one to four weeks, and cannot be sent C. O. D.

WINCHESTER RIFLES, MODEL 1894. 32-40, 38-55, ALSO THE NEW 30-30 CALIBER AND 25-35 CALIBERS.

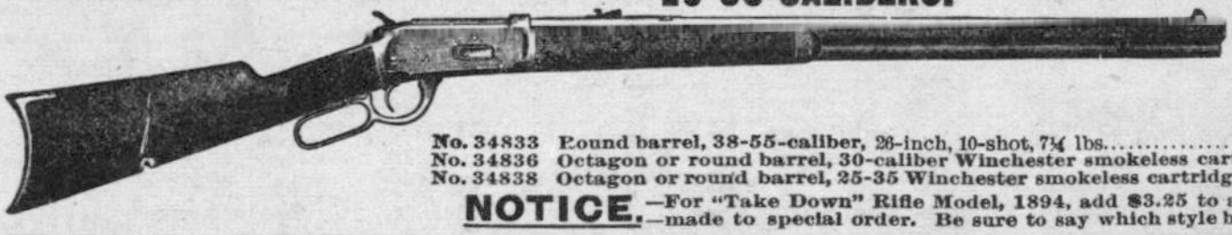

No. 34830 Octagon barrel, 32-40-caliber, 26-inch, 10-shot, 7¼-lbs.................... $10.50

No. 34831 32-40-caliber, Round barrel, 26-inch, 10-shot, 7¼-lbs.................... 11.55

No. 34832 38-55-caliber, Octagon barrel, 26-inch, 10-shot, 7½-lbs.................... 12.52

No. 34833 Round barrel, 38-55-caliber, 26-inch, 10-shot, 7¼ lbs.................... 11.55

No. 34836 Octagon or round barrel, 30-caliber Winchester smokeless cartridges, 26-inch, 10-shot, 7¾ lbs... 14.75

No. 34838 Octagon or round barrel, 25-35 Winchester smokeless cartridges, 26 inch, 10-shot, 7¾ lbs.......... 14.75

NOTICE.—For "Take Down" Rifle Model, 1894, add $3.25 to above prices in any caliber. These are made to special order. Be sure to say which style barrel you wish.

EXTRAS ON RIFLES.

All deviations from standard styles and sizes involve a large proportional outlay for hand labor, and when ordered will be subject to the following charges, and cannot be sent C. O. D. For additional length of barrel and magazine, add to price 75 cents per inch; and on model 1886, add $1.00.

For single set triggers on model 1873, $2.00.

Extra for plain walnut pistol grip stock not checkered, $2.50.

Extra for fancy walnut pistol grip stock and fore end checkered, $12.00.

Sling straps and swivels, $1.50 per set.

WINCHESTER RIFLES. MODEL 1886.

Model . . . 1886.
9 to 9½ pounds.

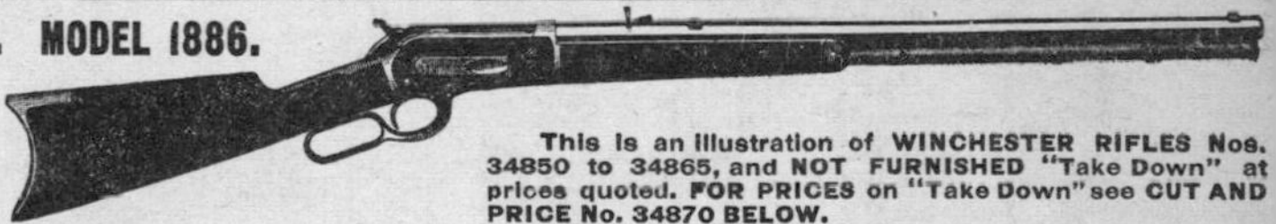

This is an illustration of WINCHESTER RIFLES Nos. 34850 to 34865, and NOT FURNISHED "Take Down" at prices quoted. FOR PRICES on "Take Down" see CUT AND PRICE No. 34870 BELOW.

No. 34850 Octagon Barrel, 26 inches or under, 9½ lbs., 40-82-caliber, 260-grain bullet, 8-shot.................... $14.97

No. 34851 Round Barrel, 40-82-caliber.................... 13.90

No. 34852 Octagon Barrel, 26 inches or under, 9¼ lbs., 45-70-caliber, 405-grain bullet, using a regular government cartridge, 8-shot...... 14.07

No. 34853 Round Barrel, 26 inches or under 9 lbs., 45-70-caliber..... 13.90

No. 34854 Octagon Barrel, 26 inches or under, 9¼ lbs., 45-90-caliber, 300-grain bullet, 8-shot.................... 14.97

No. 34855 Round Barrel, 26 inches or under, 9 lbs., 45-90-caliber..... 13.90

No. 34856 Octagon Barrel, 26 inches, 9½ lbs., 38-56-caliber, 9-shot... 14.97

No. 34857 Round Barrel, 26 inches. 9¼ lbs., 38-56-caliber.............. 13.90

No. 34858 Octagon Barrel, 26 in., 9½ lbs., 40-65-260-caliber, 9-shot.. $14.97

No. 34859 Round Barrel, 26 inches, 40-65-caliber.................... 13.90

No. 34860 Octagon Barrel, 26 inches, 50-110-caliber, Express, 8-shot 14.97

No. 34862 Octagon Barrel, 26 inches, 9½ lbs., 40-70-330-caliber..... 14.97

No. 34864 Octagon Barrel, 26 inches, 9½ lbs., 38-70-255-caliber...... 14.97

No. 34865 Model, 1886, Carbine can be furnished 22 inches, round barrel, in any of the above calibers to special order at............... 13.55

NOTICE.—The standard length of barrel will be 26 inches. Guns taking the **45-70 cartridge** will have the **Sporting Leaf Sight**, and all others the **Sporting Rear Sight.** Each rifle will be accompanied by a **Cleaning Rod FREE. SET TRIGGERS, $2.25 EXTRA.**

WINCHESTER "TAKE DOWN" RIFLES. MODEL 1886.

This cut shows the Model 1886 taken apart so it can be carried in a Victoria style cover.

No. 34870 State caliber wanted. Can be furnished in any of the calibers from No. 34850 to No. 34864. Made to special order 26-inch round or octagon barrels only.................... $17.85.
No other lengths made in "Take Down" style.

THE WINCHESTER BOX MAGAZINE SPORTING RIFLES. MODEL 1895.

30-Caliber Army. 5 Shots.

This is the Gun that Shoots Two Miles.

Velocity, 2,400 Feet Per Second.

No. 34877 The Winchester Box Magazine Sporting Rifle is the first Box Magazine Lever Action gun put on the market, and is one of the strongest shooting guns ever invented. The velocity of a bullet fired from this rifle is 2,400 feet per second. The penetration of this gun is demonstrated by a trial at the factory, at which place the rifle **shot through fifty-eight pine** boards, ⅞-inch each. It is light in weight, **handsome, safe, swift and sure.** The moving parts are few and strong. **It carries five shots in the magazine.** The disposition of the magazine and parts is such that the **gun can be readily used as a single loader**, keeping the loads in the magazine in reserve. This gun is adapted to **smokeless cartridges only**, and will shoot either the **steel jacketed** or **soft point bullets.** The **soft point** gives the best satisfaction for **large game shooting.** The barrel of the 30-caliber army is of nickel steel, and comes only in 28-inch, and only round barrels can be furnished. Our special price.................... $17.84

No. 34879 38-72 275 grains caliber, 26-inch octagon barrel.................... 14.90

WE BOX and EXAMINE ALL GUNS CAREFULLY BEFORE SHIPPING AND GUARANTEE SATISFACTION.

CENTER FIRE MILITARY AND SPORTING CARTRIDGES.

LOADED WITH .....BLACK POWDE

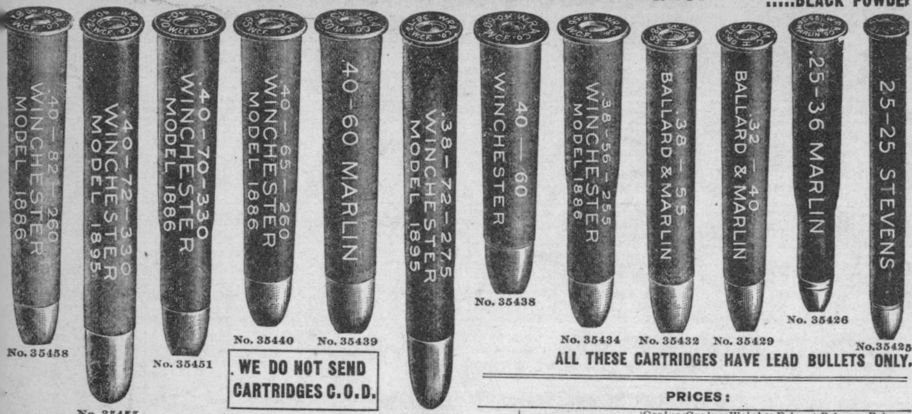

No. 35458 No. 35455 No. 35451 No. 35440 No. 35439 No. 35436 No. 35438 No. 35434 No. 35432 No. 35429 No. 35426 No. 35425

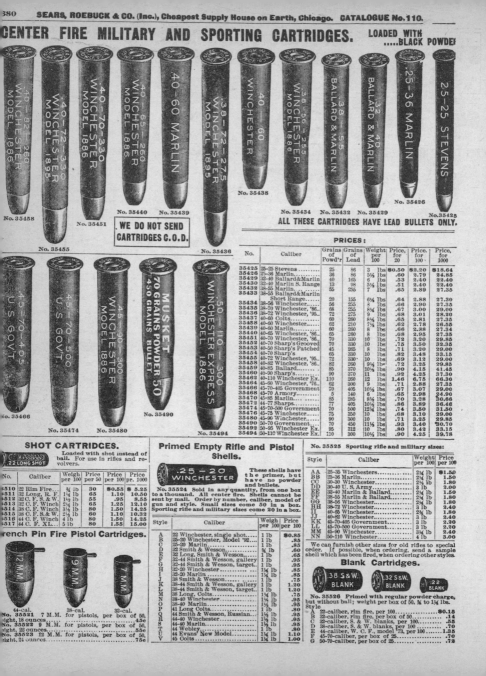

WE DO NOT SEND CARTRIDGES C.O.D.

ALL THESE CARTRIDGES HAVE LEAD BULLETS ONLY.

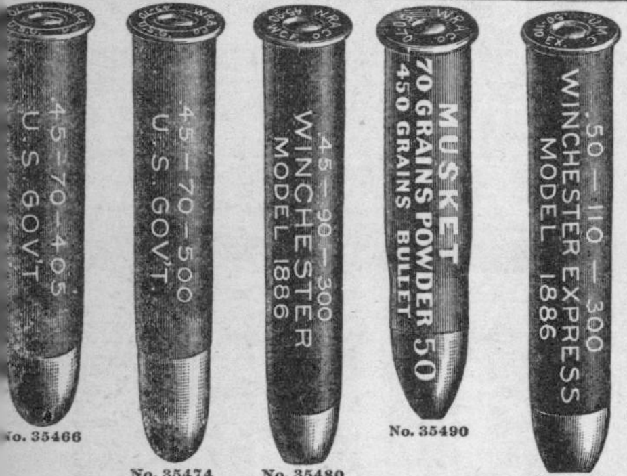

No. 35466 No. 35474 No. 35480 No. 35490 No. 35494

PRICES:

No.	Caliber	Grains of Powd'r	Grains of Lead	Weight per 100	Price, for 20	Price, for 100	Price, for 1000
35425	25-25 Stevens........	25	86	3 lbs	$0.50	$2.20	$18.64
35426	25-36 Marlin..........	36	86	5½ lbs	.60	2.79	24.85
35429	32-40 Ballard&Marlin	40	165	6 lbs	.53	2.40	22.40
35430	32-40 Marlin S. Range	13	98	5½ lbs	.51	2.40	22.40
35432	38-55 Marlin..........	55	255	7 lbs	.65	2.89	27.35
35433	38-55 Ballard&Marlin Short Range......	20	155	6¼ lbs	.64	2.88	27.30
35434	38-56 Winchester......	56	255	8 lbs	.66	2.90	27.35
35435	38-70 Winchester, '86..	68	255	8¼ lbs	.67	3.00	29.00
35436	38-72 Winchester, '95..	72	275	9 lbs	.68	3.01	28.20
35437	40-60 Colts...........	60	260	8½ lbs	.65	2.81	27.35
35438	40-60 Winchester......	62	210	7½ lbs	.62	2.78	26.55
35439	40-60 Marlin..........	60	260	8 lbs	.66	2.38	27.34
35440	40-65 Winchester, '86..	65	260	8 lbs	.68	2.95	27.35
35451	40-70 Winchester, '86..	70	330	10 lbs	.72	3.20	29.85
35452	40-70 Sharp's Grooved	70	330	10 lbs	.75	3.50	32.35
35453	40-50 Sharp's Patched	45	265	8 lbs	.71	3.20	29.00
35454	40-70 Sharp's	65	330	10 lbs	.82	3.48	33.15
35455	40-72 Winchester, '95..	72	330	10 lbs	.69	3.12	29.00
35458	40-82 Winchester, '86..	82	260	9½ lbs	.72	3.25	29.85
35459	40-85 Ballard........	85	370	10½ lbs	.90	4.15	41.45
35460	40-90 Sharp's..........	90	370	11 lbs	.92	4.25	37.30
35462	40-110 Winchester Ex.	110	260	12 lbs	1.46	6.75	66.30
35464	45-60 Winchester, '76..	62	300	9 lbs	.71	2.88	27.35
35466	45-70-405 Government	70	405	10½ lbs	.67	3.07	29.00
35468	45-70 Armory..........	5	140	6 lbs	.65	2.98	24.90
35470	45-85 Marlin....	85	285	8½ lbs	.70	3.28	30.66
35472	44-77 Sharps...........	77	405	10½ lbs	.86	3.89	36.46
35474	45-70-500 Government	70	500	12¼ lbs	.74	3.50	31.50
35476	45-75 Winchester......	75	350	10 lbs	.68	3.10	29.00
35480	45-90 Winchester......	90	300	10 lbs	.71	3.25	29.85
35490	50-70 Government....	70	450	11½ lbs	.93	3.40	30.70
35492	50-95 Winchester Ex.	95	312	10 lbs	.80	3.42	33.15
35494	50-110 Winchester Ex.	110	300	10½ lbs	.90	4.25	39.78

SHOT CARTRIDGES.

Loaded with shot instead of ball. For use in rifles and revolvers.

No.	Caliber	Weigh per 100	Price per 50	Price per 100	Price pr. 1000
5510	22 Rim Fire...	¾ lb	30	$0.55	$ 5.25
5511	32 Long, R. F.	1¼ lb	65	1.10	10.50
5512	32 C. F. S. & W.	1½ lb	55	.95	8.55
5513	32 C. F. Winch	2¼ lb	65	1.25	12.10
5514	38 C. F. Winch	3½ lb	80	1.50	14.25
5515	38 C. F. S. & W.	2½ lb	60	1.10	10.32
5516	44 C. F. Winch	4 lb	80	1.50	14.25
5517	44 C. F. XL...	5 lb	80	1.55	15.00

rench Pin Fire Pistol Cartridges.

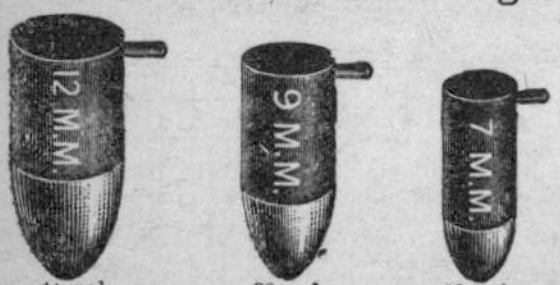

44-cal. 38-cal. 32-cal.

No. 35521 7 M.M. for pistols, per box of 50, ight, 18 ounces......45c

No. 35522 9 M.M. for pistols, per box of 50, ight, 22 ounces......55c

No. 35523 12 M.M. for pistols, per box of 50, ight, 24 ounces......75c

Primed Empty Rifle and Pistol Shells.

These shells have the primer, but have no powder and bullets.

No. 35524 Sold in any quantity, from one box to a thousand. All center fire. Shells cannot be sent by mail. Order by number, caliber, model of gun and style. Small sizes come 50 in a box. Sporting rifle and military sizes come 20 in a box.

Style	Caliber	Weigh per 100	Price per 100
A	22 Winchester, single shot.....	1 lb	$0.85
B	25-20 Winchester, Model '92....	1 lb	.85
C	25-20 Marlin.......	1 lb	.85
D	32 Smith & Wesson............	¾ lb	.60
E	32 Long, Smith & Wesson......	1 lb	.65
F	32-44 Smith & Wesson, gallery	1 lb	.95
G	32-44 Smith & Wesson, target..	1 lb	.95
H	32-20 Winchester	1¼ lb	.85
I	32-20 Marlin	1¼ lb	.85
J	38 Smith & Wesson......	1 lb	.75
K	38-44 Smith & Wesson, gallery	1 lb	1.20
L	38-44 Smith & Wesson, target..	1 lb	1.20
M	38 Long, Colts................	1¼ lb	.75
N	38-40 Winchester.............	1½ lb	.95
O	38-40 Marlin..................	1½ lb	.95
P	41 Long Colts.................	1 lb	.80
Q	44 Smith & Wesson, Russian...	1½ lb	.95
R	44-40 Winchester..............	1½ lb	.95
S	44-40 Marlin..................	1½ lb	.95
T	44 Webley.....................	1 lb	.80
U	44 Evans' New Model..........	1¼ lb	1.10
V	45 Colts......................	1¼ lb	1.00

No. 35525 Sporting rifle and military sizes:

Style	Caliber	Weight per 100	Price per 100
AA	25-35 Winchesters.............	2¼ lb	$1.50
BB	25-36 Marlin..................	2¼ lb	1.50
CC	30-30 Winchester..............	2½ lb	1.80
DD	30-40 U. S. Army..............	3 lb	2.00
EE	32-40 Marlin & Ballard........	2¼ lb	1.50
FF	38-55 Marlin & Ballard........	2¼ lb	1.80
GG	38-56 Winchester..............	2¼ lb	1.80
HH	38-72 Winchester..............	3 lb	2.40
II	40-65 Winchester..............	2¾ lb	1.80
JJ	40-82 Winchester..............	3 lb	2.40
KK	45-70-405 Government..........	3 lb	2.20
LL	45-70-500 Government..........	3 lb	2.20
MM	45-90 Winchester..............	3¼ lb	2.40
NN	50-110 Winchester.............	4 lb	3.00

We can furnish other sizes for old rifles to special order. If possible, when ordering, send a sample shell which has been fired, when ordering other styles.

Blank Cartridges.

No. 35526 Primed with regular powder charge, but without ball; weight per box of 50, ¾ to 1¼ lbs.

Style
- A 22-caliber, rim fire, per 100..................$0.15
- B 32-caliber, rim fire, per box of 50............ .14
- C 32-caliber, S. & W. blanks, per 100.......... .55
- D 38-caliber, S. & W. blanks, per 100 .... .70
- E 44-caliber, W. C. F., model '73, per 100.......1.35
- F 45-70-caliber, per box of 25.................. .70
- G 50-70-caliber, per box of 25........ .... .72

SMOKELESS CARTRIDGES.

Metallic Cartridges, loaded with Smokeless Powder are all the same shape and size as regular Black Powder Cartridges.

THESE TWO CUTS SHOW A SOFT POINT BULLET BEFORE AND AFTER SHOOTING. The soft point bullets have a metal patch or jacket to the point and when the bullet strikes it spreads at the point, as shown in the cut. **The full metal patched bullets have a metal jacket covering the entire bullet and keep their shape after shooting. We recommend soft point bullets for hunting purposes, but for powerful shooting, full metal patched are better;** for instance, a 30-caliber **Army** metal patched bullet will go through 58 pine boards, ⅞-inch thick, 15 feet from the muzzle of the rifle. A 30-caliber Winchester will go through 35 boards ⅞-inch thick in the same distance, while a lead bullet would go through only about one-half as many boards. **DON'T LOAD SHOTGUN SMOKELESS POWDER INTO CARTRIDGE SHELLS.** **In fact, we advise using only factory loaded smokeless cartridges. Factory loaded ammunition is safe, but we have heard of guns bursting** BY LOADING SHOTGUN SMOKELESS POWDER IN RIFLE CARTRIDGES. We do not send Cartridges C. O. D.

No. 35535

No. 35539

No. 35541

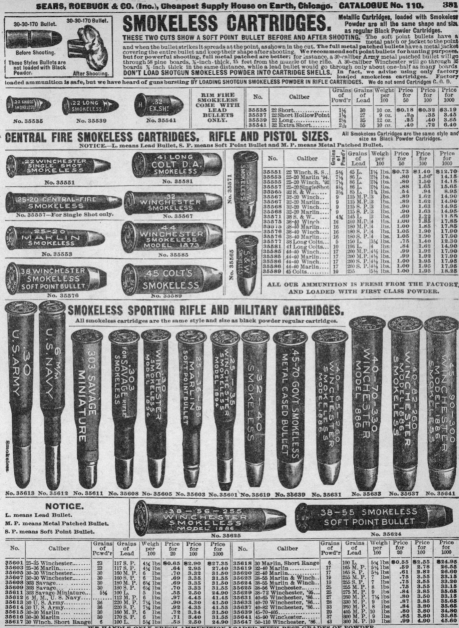

RIM FIRE SMOKELESS COME WITH LEAD BULLETS ONLY.

No.	Caliber	Grains of Powd'r	Grains of Lead	Weight per 100	Price for 50	Price for 100	Price for 1000
35535	22 Short..............	1⅛	30	10 oz.	$0.18	$0.32	$3.19
35537	22 Short Hollow Point	1⅛	27	9 oz.	.20	.35	3.45
35539	22 Long..............	2⅛	35	12 oz.	.25	.40	3.85
35541	32 Extra Short........	2 1/10	55	10 oz.	.40	.72	6.40

CENTRAL FIRE SMOKELESS CARTRIDGES. RIFLE AND PISTOL SIZES.

All Smokeless Cartridges are the same style and size as Black Powder Cartridges.

NOTICE.—L. means Lead Bullet, S. P. means Soft Point Bullet and M. P. means Metal Patched Bullet.

No. 35551

No. 35581

No. 35557—For Single Shot only.

No. 35567

No. 35553

No. 35585

No. 35576

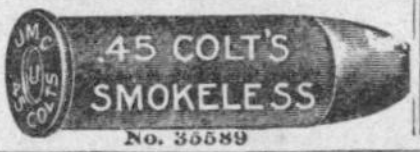

No. 35589

No. 35571

No. 35565

No.	Caliber	Grains of Powd'r	Grains of Lead	Weigh per 100	Price for 50	Price for 100	Price for 1000
35551	22 Winch. S. S..	5⅛	45 L.	1⅛ lbs.	$0.73	$1.40	$12.70
35553	25-20 Marlin '94.	7½	86 L.	2½ lbs.	.80	1.50	14.15
35555	25-20 Winch. '92	7½	86 L.	2⅛ lbs.	.80	1.50	14.15
35557	25-20 Single Shot	8½	86 L.	2⅛ lbs.	.88	1.65	15.65
35565	32 S. & W........	3⅛	85 L.	1¾ lbs.	.54	.94	8.95
35567	32-20 Winch..	9	115 M.P.	3 lbs.	.89	1.62	14.90
35567	32-20 Marlin....	9	115 M.P.	3 lbs.	.89	1.62	14.90
35568	32-20 Winch....	9	115 S. P.	3 lbs.	.90	1.63	14.95
35568	32-20 Marlin....	9	115 S. P.	3 lbs.	.90	1.63	14.95
35571	38 S. & W..	4¾	145 L.	3 lbs.	.69	1.22	11.55
35575	38-40 Winch	16	180 M.P.	4 lbs.	1.00	1.85	17.85
35575	38-40 Marlin....	16	180 M.P.	4 lbs.	1.00	1.85	17.85
35576	38-40 Winch....	16	180 S. P.	4 lbs.	1.05	1.90	17.90
35576	38-40 Marlin....	16	180 S. P.	4 lbs.	1.05	1.90	17.90
35577	38 Long Colts...	5	150 L.	3¼ lbs.	.75	1.40	12.30
35581	41 Long Colts...	10	196 L.	4 lbs.	.84	1.62	14.90
35585	44-40 Winch....	17	200 M.P.	4½ lbs.	.99	1.92	17.90
35585	44-40 Marlin....	17	200 M.P.	4½ lbs.	.99	1.92	17.90
35586	44-40 Winch....	17	200 S. P.	4½ lbs.	1.00	1.95	17.95
35586	44-40 Marlin....	17	200 S. P.	4½ lbs.	1.00	1.95	17.95
35589	45 Colts.........	19	255	5½ lbs.	1.00	1.95	18.25

ALL OUR AMMUNITION IS FRESH FROM THE FACTORY, AND LOADED WITH FIRST CLASS POWDER.

SMOKELESS SPORTING RIFLE AND MILITARY CARTRIDGES.

All smokeless cartridges are the same style and size as black powder regular cartridges.

No. 35613

No. 35612

No. 35611

No. 35608

No. 35605

No. 35603

No. 35601

No. 35619

No. 35639

No. 35631

No. 35633

No. 35637

No. 35641

NOTICE.

L. means Lead Bullet.

M. P. means Metal Patched Bullet.

S. P. means Soft Point Bullet.

No. 35625

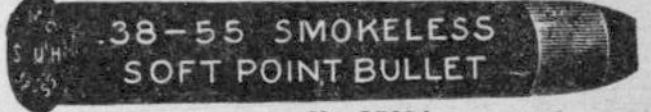

No. 35624

No.	Caliber	Grains of Powd'r	Grains of Lead	Weigh per 100	Price for 20	Price for 100	Price for 1000
35601	25-35 Winchester.........	23	117 S. P.	4¼ lbs	$0.65	$2.90	$27.35
35603	25-36 Marlin..............	23	117 S. P.	4¼ lbs	.64	2.95	27.40
35605	30-30 Winchester.........	30	160 M. P.	6 lbs	.70	3.32	31.50
35607	30-30 Winchester.........	30	160 S. P.	6 lbs	.69	3.35	31.55
35608	303 Savage...	30	180 M. P.	6¼ lbs	.69	3.35	31.50
35609	303 Savage...	30	180 S. P.	6¼ lbs	.70	3.33	31.55
35611	303 Savage Miniature...	5⅛	100 L.	5 lbs	.55	2.50	24.90
35612	6 M. M., U. S. Navy....	....	112 M. P.	6 lbs	.97	4.45	41.45
35613	30 U. S. Army...........	36	220 M. P.	7½ lbs	.90	4.30	41.50
35614	30 U. S. Army...........	36	220 S. P.	7½ lbs	.92	4.35	41.55
35615	30-30 Marlin	30	160 M. P.	6 lbs	.72	3.34	31.50
35616	30-30 Marlin	30	170 S. P.	6 lbs	.71	3.40	31.55
35617	30 Winch. Short Range	6	100 L.	5¼ lbs	.53	2.50	24.90

No.	Caliber	Grains of Powd'r	Grains of Lead	Weigh per 100	Price for 20	Price for 100	Price for 1000
35618	30 Marlin, Short Range	6	100 L.	5¼ lbs	$0.55	$2.55	$24.95
35619	32-40 Marlin	17	165 M. P.	5½ lbs	.59	2.78	26.55
35620	32-40 Marlin.............	17	165 S. P.	5½ lbs	.61	2.82	26.60
35623	38-55 Marlin & Winch..	19	255 M. P.	7 lbs	.75	3.55	33.15
35624	38-55 Marlin & Winch..	19	255 S. P.	7 lbs	.75	3.55	33.20
35625	38-56 Winchester........	25	255 M. P.	8 lbs	.75	3.55	33.15
35629	38-72 Winchester, '95...	25	275 M. P.	9 lbs	.84	3.85	35.65
35631	40-65 Winchester, '86...	27	260 M. P.	7⅛ lbs	.80	3.50	33.15
35633	40-70 Winchester, '86...	28	330 M. P.	9 lbs	.87	3.85	35.65
35637	40-82 Winchester, '86...	33	260 M. P.	8 lbs	.84	3.80	35.65
35639	45-70-405................	29	405 M. P.	10 lbs	.80	3.80	34.80
35641	45-90 Winchester........	37	300 M. P.	9 lbs	.85	3.80	35.65
35647	50-110 Winchester, '86..	43	300 M. P.	10 lbs	.99	4.90	45.60

WE HANDLE ONLY FRESH AMMUNITION LOADED WITH BEST GRADES OF POWDER.

No. 37805 Corbett Pattern. Made of wine colored kid leather, serge lining, stitched fingers, ventilated palm, split wrist with laced wristband and padded cuffs; stuffed with best quality curled hair. Per set of 4 gloves....................$2.00

No. 37806 Corbett Pattern. Made of selected green California Napa leather, with fingers, serge lining, laced wrist, ventilated palm, stuffed with best quality curled hair.
Per set of 4 gloves..................................$2.30

No. 37807 Corbett Pattern. Made of selected wine color kid back and wrist, tan color palm of selected kid, stitched fingers, ventilated palm, split wrist with lacing wristband, serge lining, stuffed with best quality curled hair, stitched fingers, double stitched throughout. Per set of 4 gloves......$3.25

No. 37808 H. A. Steele's Corbett Pattern. Made of selected especially tanned wine color kid, laced wrist, padded cuffs, leather bound best serge lining, ventilated palm, stuffed with extra quality curled hair, stitched fingers, double stitched throughout. Per set of 4 gloves.......................$3.10

Wonderful Value at $3.50 Per Set.

No. 37810 G. Stoll's Corbett Pattern. Made of selected French kid, tan brown color, with grip across center of palm, lined throughout, stitched fingers, double stitched with silk, laced wrist, leather binding, wrist with padded cuffs, ventilated palm, stuffed with best quality curled hair.
Per set of 4 gloves..................................$3.50

No. 37812 Barry Pattern. Made of selected especially tanned French kid leather, green color, with grip in center, thumb well padded on top, affording absolute protection, leather lined and leather binding, laced wrist with tape laces, wrist extra padded, roll hand sewed, stuffed with extra quality curled hair, double stitched throughout with silk. Per set of 4 gloves......$4.75

No. 37813 Our Forster Pattern Men's size Made of best claret colored California kid leather, with grip in center and toe pad, ventilated palm, best serge lining, laced wrist, leather binding; stuffed with best quality curled hair, double stitched with silk throughout. A good sparring glove. Per set of 4 gloves.......$2.85

Our Highest Grade Glove at $5.00 Per Set.

No. 37814 A Quality. Fitzsimmons Pattern with California thumb. Made of selected French kid leather, green color, with grip and side or heel pad leather lined and leather binding, laced wrist with tape laces, wrist made with extra padded roll, hand sewed, stuffed with extra quality curled hair, double stitched throughout with silk. Per set, $5.00

We can furnish this glove in 5 or 6 ounce to order, at the same price as regular.

No. 37815 Our Forster pattern professional Fighting Glove. Made of selected green California Napa leather, with grip in center and toe pad, ventilated palm, lined throughout, laced and leather bound wrist, stuffed with very best quality curled hair, made extra strong for hard usage, double stitched with linen thread, made in 6-ounce only.
Per set of 4 gloves...$2.50

Striking Bag Platform.

No. 37816 Our new steel frame striking bag platform. This is a simple, solid, noiseless platform may be easily attached to any wall in a few minutes. **The strongest, lightest, fastest platform made.** Endorsed by all the champion bag punchers and athletes. Has patent swivel, and sliding adjustment of 6 inches. It should be fastened to the wall so the circle will be about 6¾ feet from the floor. This is the average height to suit most people. Width, 36 inches; height, 24 inches. Weight, packed, 50 pounds.
Our special price, without striking bag..... ..$4.75

Striking Bag Knuckle Gloves.

No. 37817 The celebrated Frazer Striking Bag Knuckle Glove, small, neat, made of the best oil tanned horsehide, heavily padded, thus making a complete protection for the hand. Per pair.....................55c
If by mail, postage extra, 5 cents.

Striking Bag Mitts.

No. 37819 Striking bag mitt, made of kid, with grip in center, padded back, elastic wristband. This is the only punching bag glove to use for bag punching.
Price, per pair..$1.00

STRIKING BAGS.

Our line of bags is the most complete and the finest in the market. All are carefully tested before they are put in stock. Our bags all have the best grade of bladder that money can buy. The buyer of a bag wants a strong, substantial article that can be relied on and a rubber inside that will not burst the first time it is used. All our bags are lined to keep their original shape. 33-inch is the regulation size. **Prices include the bag and bladder, complete, with a piece of rope and screw eye.**

Single End Bags.

No. 37827 Made of Gold Tan with strong loop. Single end, good, desirable and strong, 30-inch circumference when inflated. Price, with bladder..........$1.15

No. 37828 Made of Craven tan leather, with strong loop, very good, strong bag, 33-inch circumference when inflated. Price, with bladder.......$1.35

No. 37829 Best quality claret colored, soft tanned leather, strong loop, triple seams, making an extra strong bag, and one of the best sellers, 33-inches circumference when inflated. Each, with bladder, $1.70

No. 37830 Best quality Craven olive tan leather, strong loop, welted seams, a fine bag and very fast, 33-inch. Each, with bladder....................$2.15

No. 37832 Brown Yucatan leather, triple seams, very strong, durable lively bag, 33-inch circumference when inflated. Each, with bladder.......$2.35

No. 37833 Chrome tan, light and very tough goat skin, triple seams, a beauty and at a low price, 32-inch. Each, with bladder..........................$2.45

No. 37835 Oil tan satin calf, a good, strong, lasting bag. A good article, retails for $4.00. 33-inch circumference when inflated.
Our price, with bladder.........................$2.65

No. 37836 Oil tan, light brown calf skin, very strong and tough. Professional bag, weight 9 ounces very fast, and the finest bag made, 33-inch circumference when inflated. Price, with bladder...$3.00

DOUBLE END BAGS.

Here is a line of double end bags which are lively, good and can be put up anywhere where you can put in 2 screw eyes. The cut shows a bag put up in a doorway. Bore a 1-inch hole in your door sill, turn a screw eye into it so it will be below the sill and out of the way; fasten a hook to the elastic cord and hook it to the screw eye, and you can take down the bag or put it up in a few seconds any time. **These prices include the bag, bladder, a piece of rope, two screw eyes, and a piece of elastic cord.**

No. 37845 Same as No. 37827, but double end, with top and bottom loop. Each, with bladder.................$1.35

No. 37846 Same description as No. 37829, but double end, with top and bottom loop. Each, with bladder.................$2.00

No. 37847 Same as No. 37833, but with double end, top and bottom loop. Each, with bladder....$2.75

Our Pear Shape Bag.

This is the latest thing in punching bags. The Pear Shape Bag has no loop but the rope comes through the top of the bag and is so made that the strain is on all sections of the bag instead of one place. The top and bottom are stitched by hand and the bag is built to withstand constant use—in fact the bag is built for work.

No. 37848 Is made of sheepskin, plain seams, canvas lined, wine color, 30-inch circumference when inflated. Each, with bladder...$2.00

No. 37849 Fine quality Goat Skin, olive green color, napa tanned, bound lips, eyeleted, lace holes, welted triple seams, canvas lined, weight 10 to 13 ounces, 33 inches circumference when inflated.
Price, each, with bladder.................$2.65

No. 37850 Fine quality Satin Calf Skin, craven tan color, bound lips, eyeleted lace holes, welted seams, canvas lined, weight 9 to 12 ounces, 34 inches in circumference when inflated, hand stitched top and bottom with very best quality of rubber bladder that can be had, just the bag for professional bag punchers. Price, each, with bladder..........$3.00

ELASTIC FLOOR ATTACHMENTS.

No. 37851 Elastic Floor Attachments for Double End Bags made of elastic and covered with braided cotton and used for attaching the bottom of the bag to the floor. Price, each...................40c

Rubber Striking Bag Bladders.

No. 37852 10-inch Bladders, made of pure Para Rubber, for 30-inch striking bags.
Price, each.............60c

No. 37853 12-inch Bladders for bags 33 inches. Price, each...............75c

No. 37854 Striking Bag Swivel. The latest out; has all improvements, and none of the defects of the old swivel. Rope can be taken out without unscrewing from platform and permits bag to be knocked in any direction without twisting rope.
Each.............................40c

The Bell Swivel.

No. 37855 An advanced idea in Punching Bag Swivels, the only article of the kind ever invented which thoroughly meets all the requirements of a perfect swivel. When attached to the ceiling has the appearance of a bell. All parts visible being full nickel plated. Saves wear and tear on the rope. The bag will play faster and truer, as the rope is always suspended from a dead center. The bag is quickly put up or taken down without readjusting the length of rope. The revolving cup allows the bag to turn freely, an advantage possessed by no other swivel made. Will never wear out. Used by Corbett, Fitzsimmons, Jeffries, Sharkey and all professional bag punchers. Our special price..............85c

Indian Clubs.

No. 37856 Sold in pairs only and made of the best first quality rock maple, and finely polished. Weight given is the weight on each club. If you order one pair 1-lb. clubs you get two 1-lb. clubs, etc. Per pair

¼-lb.	16c
½-lb.	17c
1-lb.	20c
1½-lbs.	24c
2-lbs.	27c
3-lbs.	38c
4-lbs.	47c
5-lbs.	60c

When ordering state which weight you wish.

WOOD DUMB-BELLS.

No. 37857 Wood Dumb Bells, made of polished maple, of best quality and nicely polished.

Weight	½ lb.	¾ lb.	1 lb.	2 lbs.	3 lbs.	4 lbs.
Per pair	15c	17c	20c	24c	38c	47c

Mention the weight you wish when ordering.

Iron Dumb Bells.

No. 37861 Our Iron Dumb Bells are cast from pure gray iron, and are very much stronger and more durable than those ordinarily sold, which are usually made from scrap iron, tin, etc., and are very brittle and break easily. We make them in weights as follows: 1, 2, 3, 4, 5, 6, 8, 10, 12, 14, 15, 20 and 25 lb. These are the weights of each dumb bell. Sold by the pound. Price, per pound..................6

Quoits.

No. 37865 Japanned Iron Quoits, made of malleable iron; 4½ inches diameter, the weight, per set of 4 is 7¼ pounds. Price, per set............80c
5¼ inches diameter, the weight, per set of 4 is 11¼ pounds. Price, per set.............................$1.10
6 inches diameter, the weight, per set of 4 is 13 pounds. Price, per set.............................$1.25

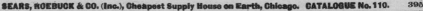

Exercising Rings.

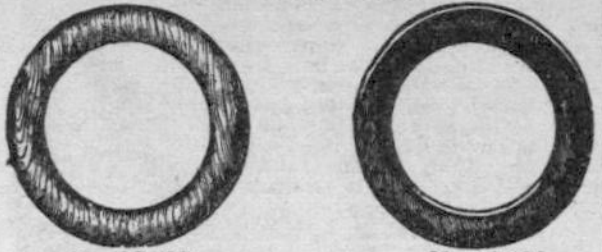

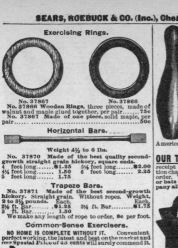

No. 37867 No. 37866

No. 37866 Wooden Rings, three pieces, made of walnut and maple glued together, per pair.......75c
No. 37867 Made of one piece, solid maple, per pair...... ....50c

Horizontal Bars.

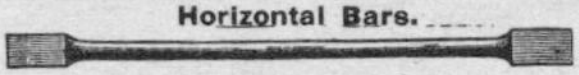

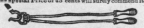

Weight 4½ to 6 lbs.

No. 37870 Made of the best quality second-growth straight grain hickory, square ends.
4 feet long.......$1.25 5½ feet long.......$2.00
4½ feet long....... 1.50 6 feet long....... 2.25
5 feet long....... 1.75

Trapeze Bars.

No. 37871 Made of the best second-growth hickory. Straight grain. Without ropes. Weight, 2 to 3½ pounds. Each. Each.
2½ ft. Bar........$1.25 3½ ft. Bar.........$1.75
3 ft. Bar........ 1.50
We make any length of rope to order, 8c per foot.

Common-Sense Exercisers.

NO HOME IS COMPLETE WITHOUT IT. Convenient, perfect working, the latest and best on the market and our Special Price of 45 cents will surely commend it.

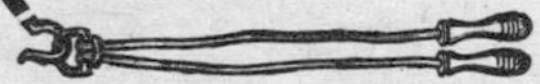

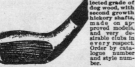

No. 37872 Our New Common-Sense Exerciser, made of heavy elastic cord, the latest and cheapest exerciser yet produced, can be put up in any part of the room. Our price, complete.....................45c
If by mail, postage extra, 12 cents.

Whiteley Exercisers.

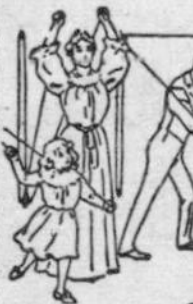

The Whiteley is conceded by all leading gymnasts to be the best exerciser that has ever been produced. Every muscle of the human body may be developed with this simple machine. It is small and compact—can be hung up on any door frame. Is absolutely noiseless. **Is made of elastic cords, running through three cone-bearing pulleys.** All parts guaranteed.
No. 37873 Cheap, but strong and nicely finished......$1.75
No. 37874 Medium quality..........................$2.50
No. 37875 Nickeled trimmings, beautifully finished... 3.25

GOLF CLUBS AND BALLS.

THE VICTOR GOLF CLUBS.

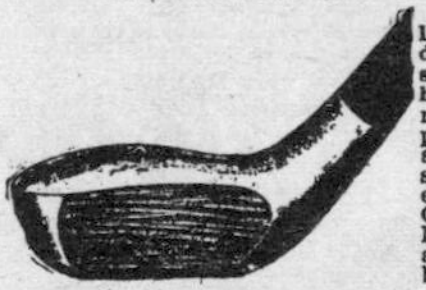

Made of selected grade of dog wood, with second growth hickory shafts, made on approved models, and very desirable clubs in every respect. Order by catalogue number and style number.

No. 38274 Style No. 701, Bulger Driver, each, $1.50; style No. 705, Bulger Brassey, each.....$1.50
The Country Club brand Golf Club. Style No. 801, Bulger Driver, each, $1.25; style No. 805, Bulger Brassey, each...$1.25

VICTOR IRON GOLF CLUBS.

Made of hand-forged heads, straight grain, second growth hickory shafts; rights only. The shafts are made to balance properly by Scotch makers, who are also expert players. Each
No. 38275 Style No. 707, Cleek Club.........$1.50
Style No. 708, Lofting Iron Club................. 1.50
Style No. 709, Niblick Club...................... 1.50
Style No. 710, Gun Metal Putter Club 1.50
Style No. 712, Mashy Club....................... 1.50
Style No. 715, Mid-Iron Club.................... 1.50

GOLF BALLS.

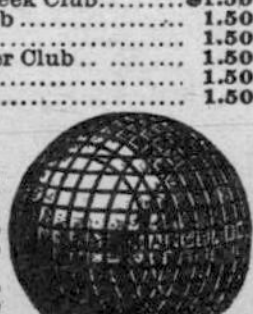

Made of gutta percha rubber, thoroughly seasoned and perfect in flight. We handle only these two styles. Try them. They are all right.
No. 38276 Our Practice Ball, per dozen..........$3.00
No. 38277 Our Craig Park Ball, per dozen...........$3.50

Ten Pins and Balls.

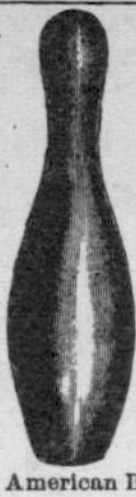

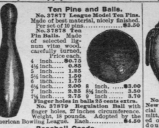

No. 37877 League Model Ten Pins. Made of best material, nicely finished. Per set of 10 pins.......................$3.50
No. 37878 Ten Pin Balls. Made of selected lignum vitæ wood, carefully turned,

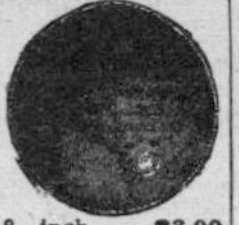

	Price each.		
4 inch	$0.75		
4½ inch	0.85		
5 inch	1.25		
5½ inch	1.50		
6 inch	1.75		
6½ inch	2.00	8 inch	$3.00
7 inch	2.25	8½ inch	3.50
7½ inch	2.75	9 inch	3.70

Finger holes in balls 25 cents extra.
No. 37879 Regulation Ball with finger holes, 27 inches circumference. Weight, 18 pounds. Adopted by the American Bowling League. Each..............$4.50

Baseball Goods.

OUR TERMS on baseball goods. We will send any balls or mitts, masks, etc., C.O.D., on receipt of a sufficient deposit to insure transportation charges. Two dollars should accompany each order. **We do not send uniforms, cheap grade balls or bats C. O. D. Full amount of cash must accompany all orders for these.**

Baseballs.

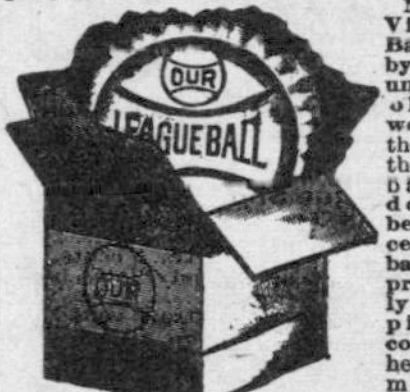

No. 37885 The Victor League Ball, made entirely by hand for us under contract by old, experienced workmen only, thoroughly tried in the science of baseball making; **double covered, best Para rubber center; the best ball that can be produced; specially prepared two-piece horsehide cover, stitched with heavy linen thread, makes this the strongest ball on** the market; the specifications of the National League are rigidly followed. **Guaranteed for nine innings against ripping and shape. No better ball made at any price.** Our special price.......................90c
If by mail, postage extra, each, 7 cents.
No. 37886 For those who wish the Spalding League Balls, we have them at, each.............$1.15
No. 37887 Our National Association, made of best materials exactly in accordance with approved specifications. A regular dollar ball. **Each ball in a separate box and sealed.** Each.........................75c
No. 37888 Our Intercollegiate, a ball made for professionals and minor leagues, and recommended by various leagues throughout the country. Ea..50c
No. 37889 Our High School League. A high grade ball, regulation size, will keep its shape under heavy batting. We recommend it. Each........50c
No. 37890 Our Pitcher's Pride. A beauty, has horsehide cover, well made; each in a separate box, sealed. Each..25c
No. 37891 Our Out of Sight. A fine boys' ball, carefully made and a daisy. Each...................24c
No. 37892 Our Little Victor, the best ball ever offered for the money, well made. Each..........10c
No. 37914 Our Star, an extra well made ball for the money. Not an ordinary ball, but well worth twice our price. Each.................................5c

Baseball Bats.

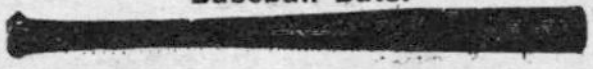

No. 37915 Professional model bat, made of best quality second growth wide grain ash. Guaranteed the best bat on the market. Each.................75c
No. 37916 Made of fine quality ash. An excellent medium grade bat. Men's sizes. Each...50c
No. 37917 Good quality ash. Men's sizes. An extra good bat at a low price. Each..............35c
No. 37918 Boys' professional bat. 31 inches long. Made of selected ash. Each...............25c
No. 37919 Boys' favorite. A good strong, well finished bat. Each...........................10c
No. 37921 Boys' 27-inch bat. A daisy for the money. Each...5c

Baseball Mitts.

No house can compete with us on these goods.

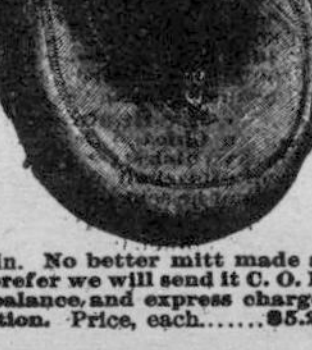

No. 37925 Our Victor Professional Mitt made of the highest grade drab horsehide. This mitt is designed especially for professionals and embodies suggestions received from many of the league catchers. Workmanship the best, material the best. Has patent thumb strap and patent lace. The patent thumb strap forms and keeps a deep pocket in the mitt, thus you buy a mitt that is already broken in. **No better mitt made at any price, and if you prefer we will send it C. O. D. on receipt of $1.00, balance, and express charges to be paid on examination.** Price, each......$5.25

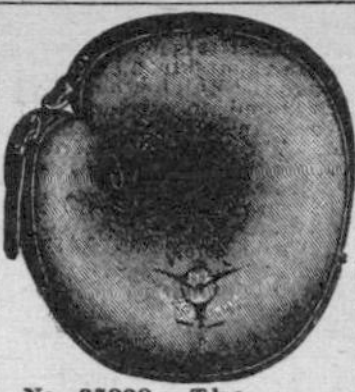

No. 37927 Our Cleveland Mitt. We believe this Mitt superior to any $5.00 mitt that was ever put on the market. The front is of best quality horsehide and the back and trimmings are of calf. Has the patent strap and lace, same as our $5.25 mitt. Made on lines of the professional mitts. Our special price...........$4.25

No. 37929 The New Donahue, special pattern League mitt, made of selected oil tan calfskin; double stitched throughout; sole leather stiffener over top of fingers. **Correctly padded with high grade felt; outer edges full leather bound, thumb reinforced,** and thong leather stitched. Laced bottom, permitting of changing of padding.

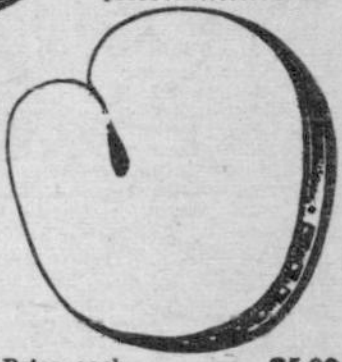

Price, each...................$5.00

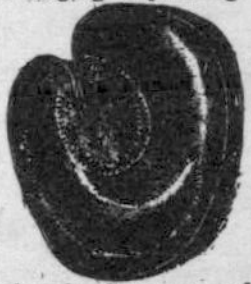

No. 37931 S., R. & Co.'s Men's Mitt, made of fine quality especially tanned selected buck, heavily padded cup shaped palm, with crescent pad; extension quirk, double stitched all around. A fine mitt for little money. Must be seen to be appreciated. Our special price......$3.25
No. 37932 S., R. & Co.'s Chelsea Mitt, palm made of buckskin, back and fingers of selected sheepskin, reinforced thumb; Crescent pad, forming a pocket, well stuffed and well finished, full size. Price..$2.25

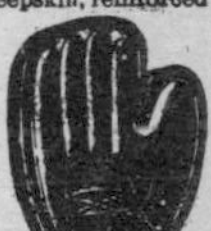

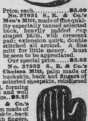

No. 37933 S., R. & Co.'s Men's Buck Mitt, palm made of selected brown buckskin, back made of goat skin, with fingers, thumb reinforced and thong stitched, well finished and well padded. Price, each......$2.75

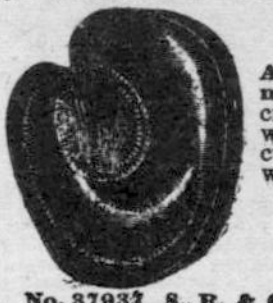

No. 37935 S., R. & Co.'s Amateur Medium size Mitt, made of tan calf leather, crescent pad, sheep skin back, well made and well finished, cup-shaped palm. A fine mitt well stuffed. Each.....$1.95

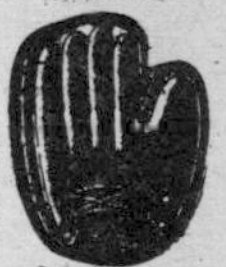

No. 37937 S., R. & Co.'s Medium size Mitt, palm of dark color buck tanned leather, back of colt's skin, reinforced thumb, cup-shaped palm, crescent pad. Each.........................$1.45
No. 37938 S., R. & Co.'s Medium Size, sheepskin finished palm, back of tan color leather, reinforced thumb. Price each...90c
No. 37939 S., R. & Co.'s Medium Size, made of yellow or red leather, well padded, worth 75 cents. Our price...50c
No. 37940 Sears, Roebuck & Co.'s Youth's Mitt, made of selected tan leather, with fingers well padded. **A good strong mitt.** Each...........45c

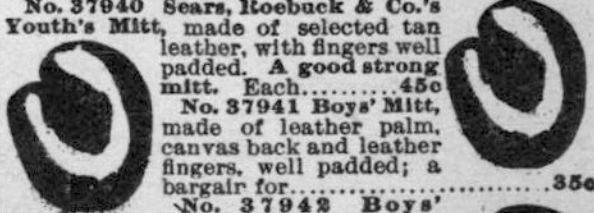

No. 37941 Boys' Mitt, made of leather palm, canvas back and leather fingers, well padded; a bargain for......................35c
No. 37942 Boys' Canvas Mitt. Price, each.........10c

Basemen's Mitts.

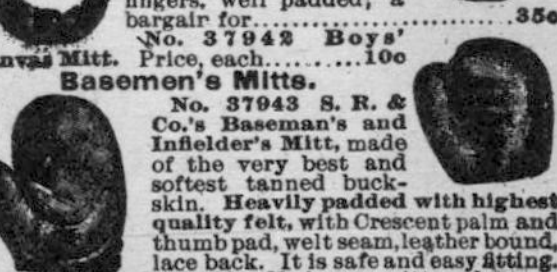

No. 37943 S. R. & Co.'s Baseman's and Infielder's Mitt, made of the very best and softest tanned buckskin. **Heavily padded with highest quality felt, with Crescent palm and thumb pad, welt seam, leather bound, lace back. It is safe and easy fitting.** Very strong and durable. No better mitt made. Our special price.....................................$1.75
If by mail, postage extra, each, 10c

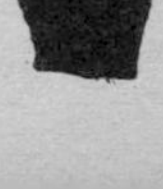

No. 37944 S., R. & Co.'s Baseman's Mitt. Made of select Yucatan goatskin. **Full leather lined. Leather bound all around. With lace back.** Equal in all respects to mitts that sell from $1.50 to $1.75 of other makes. Our price...$1.00
If by mail, postage extra, each, 8c.

Athletic and Swimming Suits.

Our full sleeve and quarter sleeve shirts for all athletic purposes are the highest grade, and the same that are adopted by the highest sporting authorities, and quality considered, are now offered at the lowest prices ever known.

Our standard colors will be black and navy blue, but we are prepared to furnish, on special orders, white, maroon or other solid colors, or stripes, if wanted, but all special orders must be accompanied with cash in full. Any deviation from the standard colors, however, is liable to cause a few days' delay. When ordering be sure to give the measure around the chest for shirts and measure around waist for pants and tights.

Full Sleeve Shirts.

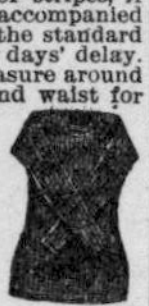

No. 38188 Full sleeve shirts, made of the very best worsted, perfect fitting, black or navy blue color. Give chest measure. Price, each.... **$2.25**
If by mail, postage extra, 15 cents.

No. 38189 Full sleeve fine worsted, shirt, medium quality, black or navy blue color. Give chest measure.
Price, each..**$1.75**
If by mail, postage extra, 12 cents.

No. 38190 Full sleeve, fine cotton shirt, black or navy blue color. Give chest measure. Price, each, **75c**
If by mail, postage extra, 10 cents.

Quarter Sleeve Shirts.

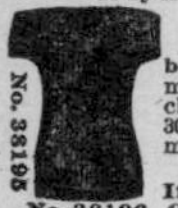

No. 38195

No. 38195 Quarter sleeve shirts, best worsted, solid colors, seamless, made in black or navy blue. Give chest measure when ordering 26, 28, 30, 32, 34, 36, 40 and 42 inches chest measure.
Our special price, each.........**$2.00**
If by mail, postage extra, 15 cents.

No. 38196 Quarter sleeve shirts. Medium quality worsted, solid colors, seamless, made in black or navy blue. Give chest measure when ordering.
Our special price, each........................**$1.50**
If by mail, postage extra, 12 cents.

No. 38197 Cotton shirt, quarter sleeve, good quality. Made in solid colors of black or navy blue. Give chest measure when ordering.
Price, each..**50c**
If by mail, postage extra, 10 cents.

Full Length Tights.

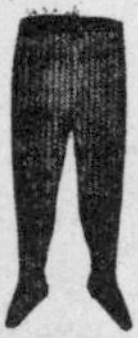

No. 38199 Full length tights, made of best worsted, in solid colors of black or navy blue. Give waist measure. Our special price, per pair, **$2.75**
If by mail, postage extra, 12 cents.

No. 38200 Full length tights, made of medium grade worsted, in solid colors of black or navy blue. Give waist measure when ordering.
Price, per pair..................**$2.25**
If by mail, postage extra, 10 cents.

No. 38201 Full length cotton tights, in solid colors of black or navy blue. Give waist measurement when ordering. Price, per pair........**$1.00**
If by mail, postage extra, 8 cents.

Athletic Knee Tights.

No. 38202 Made of **best quality of worsted** in solid colors of black or navy blue. Give waist measure when ordering. Per pair...........**$1.50**

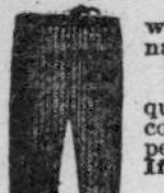

No. 38203 Made of **medium grade** worsted in solid colors of black or navy blue. Give waist measure.
Price, per pair.......... ....**$1.25**

No. 38204 Cotton tights. Good quality cotton tights, made in solid colors of black or navy blue. Price, per pair..............................**50c**
If by mail, postage extra, 6 to 10c.

Velvet Puff Trunks.

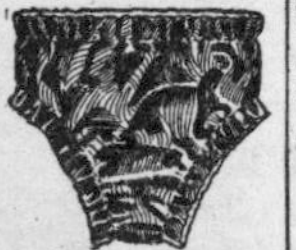

No. 38206 Beautiful velvet puff trunks, made of **the finest** velvet, full puff, either black, navy, green or maroon color for theatrical or athletic exhibitions.
Price, per pair....**$1.00**
If by mail, postage extra, per pair, 7 cents.

BATHING SUITS.

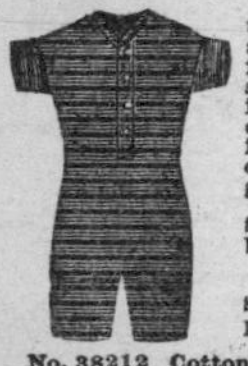

Our one-piece best Cotton Bathing Suit is made like a Union Suit (with buttons in front). It is like an ordinary shirt and knee pants, but all in one piece, made in solid colors and fancy stripes, and ranging in size from 32 to 44 inches chest measure. When ordering give chest measure.

No. 38208 Cotton One-Piece Suit, in solid color black or navy blue; give chest measure.
Price......................................**75c**

No. 38210 Cotton One-Piece Suit, in fancy stripes, assorted patterns; give chest measure.
Price.................................**$1.00**

No. 38212 Cotton One-Piece Suit. Same as No. 38210 for boys, 24 to 32 inch chest. Price...........**75c**

FOR TWO-PIECE BATHING SUITS we recommend knee tights and quarter sleeve shirts quoted above.

TWO-PIECE BATHING SUITS.

Give Chest and Waist Measure.

No. 38216 Two-piece **Bathing Suit,** consisting of quarter sleeve shirt and knee pants, made in black or navy blue colors. Price, per suit.............**50c**

No. 38217 Same, in stripes. Price, per suit. **$1.00**

HAMMOCKS.

The most select line of Hammocks ever placed on the market.

SEE OUR PRICES.

Close-Woven Baby or Child's Hammock.

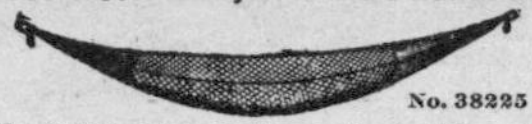

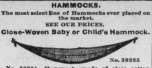

No. 38225

No. 38221 Hammock, made of close cotton weave, fancy mixed colors; with valance on each side; entire length, 6 feet; bed, 36x30 inches with spreader at each end; weight, 2 lbs. **A very fine hammock for the baby with spreaders.**
Our special price...**90c**

No. 38225 Child's Hammock, double cord open mesh, bright colors, entire length from end to end 8 feet 6 inches; bed 4½ feet long; **strong, well made and durable;** weight, 1¼ lbs. Each.............**50c**

Mexican Woven Hammock.

No. 38231

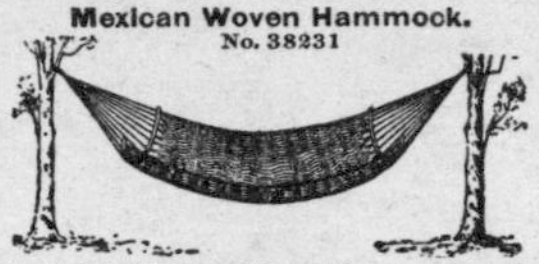

No. 38231 Mexican Woven Hammocks, made of sisal twine, fancy assorted colors; entire length, 12 feet 6 inches; length of bed 6 feet; rope edge.
Each..**90c**

Mexican Hammock with Fancy Valance.

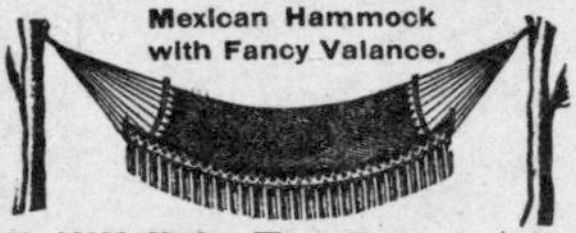

No. 38233 Mexican Woven Hammocks, made of sisal sea grass twine, yellowish white bed, **fancy colored valance on each side,** bright colored end strings, clinch thimble on end, entire length 14 feet, length of bed 6 feet 6 inches, **full width; a fine looking hammock;** weight, 4 lbs. Each...............**$1.75**

Close Woven Hammocks.

No. 38237

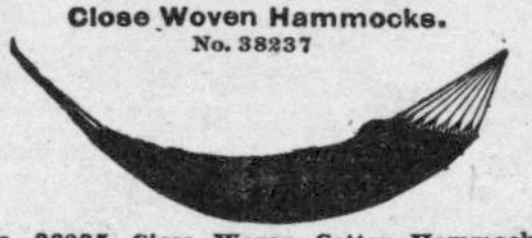

No. 38235 Close Woven Cotton Hammocks. Fine cotton weave, **quarter color, with fancy colored stripes;** size of bed, 6½ feet long, 3 feet wide; **strong and durable;** without pillow or spreader. Our special price..**65c**

No. 38237 Cotton Hammock, with close-woven body, of the best cotton weave, **full fancy colors,** with spreader and pillow; size of bed, 6¼ feet long, 35 inches wide; a hammock that sells regularly at $1.25 to $1.50. Our special price, with fancy pillow, Each..**85c**

No. 38239 Hammock. Made of closest fancy canvas weave, in full fancy bright colors. **Made with four-ply warps,** with fancy colored **pillow and spreader. A very strong hammock.** Retails from $1.75 to $2.00. Size of bed, 6½ feet long, 3 feet wide. Our special price..........................**$1.25**

Special Value for $1.15.

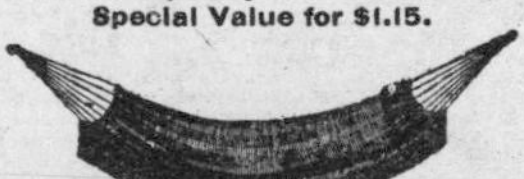

No. 38241 Cotton Hammock, close excelsior weave, with short fancy fringe valance; full fancy bright colors; with **pillow and spreader,** size of bed, 6½ feet long, 35 inches wide. **A first-class hammock in every respect.** Sells regularly at $1.75.
Our special price..**$1.15**

$2.50 Value for $1.75.

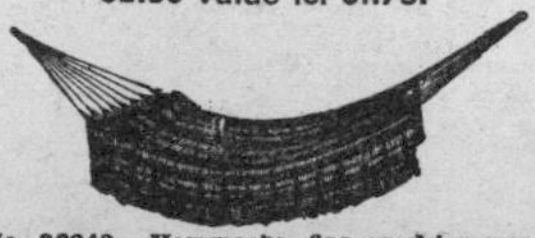

No. 38242 Hammocks, fine excelsior weave with deep woven valance with fringe, full fancy bright colors, with one spreader and one pillow; size of bed, 6½ feet long, 3 feet wide; a beauty for the money; weight, about 4½ lbs. Our special price, **$1.75**

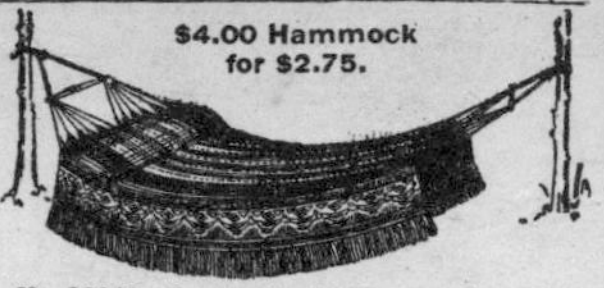

$4.00 Hammock for $2.75.

No. 38243 Our big leader Hammock, made in fancy figured canvas weave, damask pattern, full fancy fluted valance, with fringe and scroll pattern like cut, one strong spreader at head, **with fancy pillow, also two short wood spreaders.** Size of bed, 40x80 inches. One of the most beautiful hammocks ever placed on the market. Strong and durable, and one which generally sells at retail for $4.00.
Our special price..**$2.75**

No. 38245 Hammock, extra heavy, fancy close canvas weave, fine fancy bright colors, extra deep fluted valance with pillow, heavy strong spreader. Two short wood spreaders at each end; size of bed, 40x84 inches. **This is a large size hammock, strong, durable and very showy.**
Our special price...**$3.00**

No. 38247 Hammock, **extra large** for two persons, fancy Grecian weave, has two pillows; **size of bed, 54x90 inches—made of 5-ply warp, fancy delicate colors, strong and durable; will hold two full-grown, heavy persons.** Complete **with spreaders at each end and spreader rings. The strongest and best hammock on the market.** Our special price..**$4.25**

A Wonderful Bargain for $2.45.

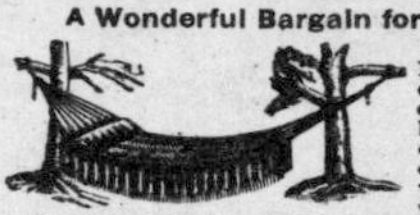

No. 38249 Hammock, close-woven canvas weave body, warp of delicate fancy colors with wide fancy valance on each side, extra deep with fringe, heavy strong spreader, **with two small wood spreaders on each end, fancy pillow,** size of bed 6½ feet, an extra fine hammock for a small price.
Our special price **$2.45**

Canvas Hammocks.

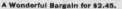

No. 38255

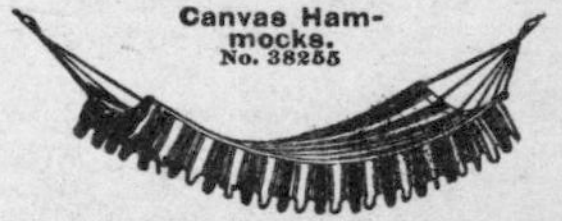

This is the latest thing in Hammocks. These hammocks are made of canvas throughout, are very strong and durable, and we predict a large sale for them. They are made of 8-ounce canvas and will surely become popular. The bed is about 7 feet long and 3 feet wide, and they are similar to hammocks used in the U. S. navy. All have spreaders at each end.

No. 38251 Made of 8-oz. canvas, spreader at each end, **without valance.** Price each........**$1.00**

No. 38253 Made of striped canvas, brown and white stripes, spreader at each end, **without valance.** Price..**$1.35**

No. 38255 Made of striped canvas, brown and white stripes, spreader at each end, **with valance.**
Price... ....**$1.75**

Wire Hammock.

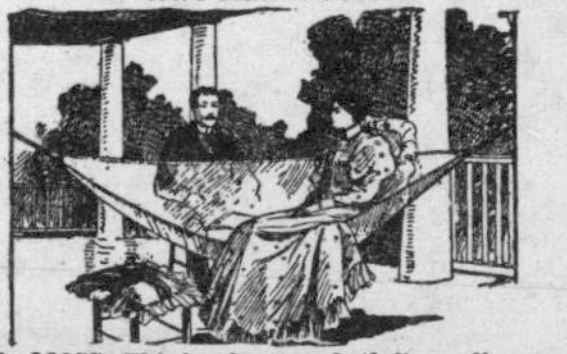

No. 38257 This is a hammock that won't wear out; won't rust; won't break; needn't take it in at night; it is the most springy hammock made. Is made of woven wire and conforms to the shape as easily as a cord hammock. Come with two steel spreaders. Weight, packed, 10 pounds; length, 10 feet. Price, each...**$2.00**

Peerless Hammock Spreader.

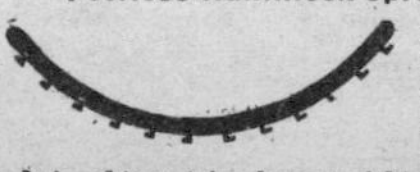

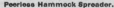

No. 38261 Is made of a solid piece of hardwood, bent bow shape, with hooks on its lower edge. It is designed to sustain a heavy weight, and is so simple in its construction and application that any one will understand how to use it. Weight, about 12 ounces each. Price, each..............................[illegible]

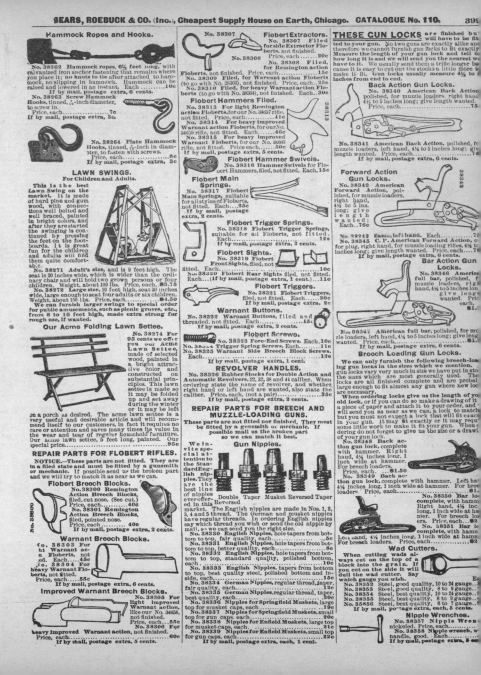

Hammock Ropes and Hooks.

No. 38262 Hammock ropes, 6½ feet long, with galvanized iron anchor fastening that remains where you place it; no knots tie is after attached to hammock, no slipping in hammock. Hammock can be raised and lowered in an instant. Each 10c
If by mail, postage extra, 6 cents.

No. 38263 Screw Hammock Hooks, tinned, ⅞-inch diameter, to screw in.
Price, each..................7c
If by mail, postage extra, 2c

No. 38264 Plate Hammock Hooks, tinned, ⅞-inch in diameter, to fasten with screws.
Price, each.............8c
If by mail, postage extra, 3c

LAWN SWINGS.
For Children and Adults.

This is the best Lawn Swing on the market. It is made of hard pine and gum wood, with connections well bolted and well braced, painted in bright colors, and after they are started the swinging is continued by pressing the feet on the footboards. It is great fun for the children and adults will find them quite comfortable.

No. 38271 Adult's size, and is 9 feet high. The seat is 20 inches wide, which is wider than the ordinary chair and will hold two grown persons or four children. Weight, about 100 lbs. Price, each..$3.75
No. 38272 Large size, 10 feet high, seat 30 inches wide, large enough to seat four adults or six children. Weight, about 150 lbs. Price, each............$4.50
We can furnish larger swings to special order for public amusements, such as picnic groves, etc., from 8 to 16 feet high, made extra strong for rough use, if wanted.

Our Acme Folding Lawn Settee.

No. 38274 For 95 cents we offer you our Acme Lawn Settee, made of selected wood, painted in a bright attractive color and constructed on substantial principles. This lawn settee is made so it may be folded up and set away during the winter or it may be left on a porch as desired. The acme lawn settee is a very useful and desirable article and will recommend itself to our customers, in fact it requires no care or attention and saves many times its value in the wear and tear of regular household furniture. Our acme lawn settee, 5 feet long, painted. Our special price..........95c

REPAIR PARTS FOR FLOBERT RIFLES.

NOTICE.—These parts are not fitted. They are in a filed state and must be fitted by a gunsmith or mechanic. If possible send us the broken part and we will try to match it as near as we can.

Flobert Breech Blocks.

No. 38300 Remington Action Breech Blocks, filed, cut nose. (See cut.)
Price, each............40c
No. 38301 Remington Action Breech Blocks, filed, pointed nose.
Price, each............40c
If by mail, postage extra, 2 cents.

Warnant Breech Blocks.

No. 38303 For light Warnant action Floberts, not filed. Each......45c
No. 38304 For heavy Warnant Floberts, not filed.
Price, each........55c
If by mail, postage extra, 6 cents.

Improved Warnant Breech Blocks.

No. 38305 For light improved Warnant action, like our No. 38468, not finished.
Price, each......55c
No. 38306 For heavy improved Warnant action, not finished.
Price, each.......60c
If by mail, postage extra, 5 cents.

Flobert Extractors.

No. 38307 Filed for side Extractor Floberts, not finished.
Price, each.......20c
No. 38308 Filed for Remington action Floberts, not finished. Price, each........15c
No. 38309 Filed, for Warnant action Floberts (to go with No. 38303), not finished. Price, each..20c
No. 38310 Filed, for heavy Warnant action Floberts (to go with No. 38304), not finished. Each..30c

Flobert Hammers Filed.

No. 38313 For light Remington action Floberts, for our No. 34657 rifle, not fitted. Price, each..........44c
No. 38314 For heavy improved Warnant action Floberts, for our No. 34659 rifle, not fitted. Each.....46c
No. 38315 For heavy improved Warnant Floberts, for our No. 34663 rifle, not fitted. Price each.......50c
If by mail, postage extra, 5 cents.

Flobert Hammer Swivels.

No. 38316 Hammer Swivels for Flobert Hammers, filed, not fitted. Each, 15c

Flobert Main Springs.

No. 38317 Flobert Main springs, suitable for all styles of Floberts, not fitted. Each....25c
If by mail, postage extra, 2 cents.

Flobert Trigger Springs.

No. 38318 Flobert Trigger Springs, suitable for all Floberts, not fitted. Each..................13c
If by mail, postage extra, 2 cents.

Flobert Sights.

No. 38319 Flobert Front Sights, filed, not fitted. Each...................10c
No. 38320 Flobert Rear Sights filed, not fitted. Each....10c
If by mail, postage extra, 1 cent.

Flobert Triggers.

No. 38321 Flobert Triggers, filed, not fitted. Each.......20c
If by mail, postage extra, 2c

Warnant Buttons.

No. 38322 Warnant Buttons, filed and threaded, not fitted. Each.............15c
If by mail, postage extra, 1 cent.

Flobert Screws.

No. 38323 Fore-End Screws. Each..10c
No. 38324 Trigger Spring Screws. Each..11c
No. 38325 Warnant Side Breech Block Screws. Each.................17c
If by mail, postage extra, 1 cent.

REVOLVER HANDLES.

No. 38326 Rubber Stocks for Double Action and Automatic Revolvers, 22, 32, 38 and 44 caliber. When ordering state the name of revolver, and whether right hand or left hand are wanted, also state the caliber. Price, each. (not a pair)...........35c
If by mail, postage extra, 2 cents.

REPAIR PARTS FOR BREECH AND MUZZLE-LOADING GUNS.

These parts are not fitted nor finished. They must be fitted by a gunsmith or mechanic. If possible mail us the broken part so we can match it best.

Gun Nipples.

We invite special attention to the Standard English nipples. They are the best line of nipples ever offered in this market. The English nipples are made in No. 1, 2, 3, 4 and 5 thread. The German and musket nipples have regular threads. In ordering English nipples say which thread you wish or send the old nipple by mail, so we can send you the right size.
No. 38330 English Nipples, hole tapers from bottom to top, fair quality. Each..................3c
No. 38331 English Nipples, hole tapers from bottom to top, better quality. Each............8c
No. 38332 English Nipples, hole tapers from bottom to top, standard quality, polished bottom. Each..........10c
No. 38333 English Nipples, tapers from bottom to top, best quality steel, polished bottom and inside, each.................15c
No. 38334 German Nipples, regular thread, taper, fair quality. Each..................15c
No. 38335 German Nipples, regular thread, taper, best quality. Each............20c
No. 38336 Nipples for Springfield Muskets, large top for musket caps, each......19c
No. 38337 Nipples for Springfield Muskets, small top for musket caps, each........20c
No. 38338 Nipples for Enfield Muskets, large top for musket caps, each..............21c
No. 38339 Nipples for Enfield Muskets, small top for gun caps, each..................22c
If by mail, postage extra, each, 1 cent.

THESE GUN LOCKS

are finished but will have to be fitted to your gun. No two guns are exactly alike and therefore we cannot furnish gun locks to fit exactly. Measure the length of your gun lock and tell us how long it is and we will send you the nearest we have to it. We usually send them a trifle longer because it is easy to cut out the stock a little more to make it fit. Gun locks usually measure 4½ to 5 inches from end to end.

Back Action Gun Locks.

No. 38340 American Back Action, polished, for muzzle loaders. right hand 4½ to 5 inches long; give length wanted.
Price, each................75c

No. 38341 American Back Action, polished, for muzzle loaders, left hand, 4½ to 5 inches long; give length wanted. Price, each...........74c
If by mail, postage extra, 6 cents.

Forward Action Gun Locks.

No. 38342 American Forward Action, polished, for muzzle loaders, right hand, 4½ to 5 inches long; give length wanted. Each..76c

No. 38344 Same, left hand. Each.........75c
No. 38345 C.P. American Forward Action, for plug, right hand, for muzzle loading rifles, 4½ to 5 inches long; give length wanted. Price, each....74c
If by mail, postage extra, 6 cents.

Bar Action Gun Locks.

No. 38346 American full bar, polished, for muzzle loaders, right hand, 4½ to 5 inches long; give length wanted. Price, each................$1.

No. 38347 American full bar, polished, for muzzle loaders, left hand, 4½ to 5 inches long; give length wanted. Price, each..................$1.
If by mail, postage extra, 6 cents.

Breech Loading Gun Locks.

We can only furnish the following breech-loading gun locks in the sizes which we mention. Gun locks vary very much in size we have put in stock the sizes which are most generally used. The locks are all finished complete and are probably large enough to fit almost any gun where new locks are necessary.

When ordering locks give us the length of your old lock, or if you can do so make a drawing of it on a piece of paper and attach it to your order, and we will send you as near as we can, a lock to match, but you must not expect a lock that will fit exactly in your gun. It may be necessary to do some little work to make it fit your gun. When ordering do not forget to give us the size or a drawing of your gun lock.

No. 38348 Back action gun lock, complete with hammer. Right hand, 4½ inches long, 1 inch wide at hammer. For breech loaders.
Price, each......$1.50
No. 38349 Back action gun lock, complete with hammer. Left hand, 4½ inches long, 1 inch wide at hammer. For breech loaders. Price, each......$1.

No. 38350 Bar lock complete, with hammer. Right hand, 4½ inches long, 1 inch wide at hammer. For breech loaders. Price, each......$2.
No. 38351 Bar lock complete, with hammer. Left hand, 4½ inches long, 1 inch wide at hammer. For breech loaders. Price, each......$2.

Wad Cutters.

When cutting wads always cut on the top of a block into the grain. If you cut on the side it will divide the wad cutter. Say which gauge you wish.
No. 38352 Steel, good quality, 10 to 24 gauge..5c
No. 38353 Steel, good quality, 8 to 9 gauge..8c
No. 38354 Steel, best quality, 10 to 24 gauge..7c
No. 38355 Steel, best quality, 8 to 9 gauge..9c
No. 38356 Steel, best quality, 6 to 7 gauge..10c
If by mail, postage extra, each, 2 cents.

Nipple Wrenches.

No. 38357 Nipple Wrench, nickeled. Price, each.....8c
No. 38358 Nipple wrench, with handle, good. Each............5c
If by mail, postage extra, 1 cent.

BROKEN GUN STOCKS.

When stocks of double guns are broken so you can't repair them with glue a new one will have to be fitted by hand and we can do this work all the way from $5.00 to $12.00, according to the quality of wood and amount of labor required. You to pay transportation charges both ways.

Brass Ram Rod Heads.

No. 38359 Rod heads, brass, open end, sizes assorted, ½, ⅝ and ¾-inch each.......10c

No. 38360 Rod heads, brass, solid end, sizes assorted, ½, ⅝ and ¾-inch each.....15c

If by mail, postage extra, 1 cent.

Walnut Gun Stocks.

No. 38361 Rough turned Gun Stocks turned to shape, leaving the square end 1⅞ inches wide and 2 inches from top to bottom, length 16¼ inches, butt measure 5¼x1⅞ inches. Made of good American walnut, not fitted, just shaped. Weight 20 ounces. Each....75c

If by mail, postage extra, 22 cents.

German Worms.

No. 38363 For single guns. Each.......12c

No. 38364 For double guns, reversed, small size. Each..........13c

No. 38365 For double guns, reversed, medium size. Each..........14c

No. 38366 For double guns, reversed, large size. Each..........15c

English Worms, with Cap.

No. 38367 Brass, small size. Each........17c

No. 38368 Brass, large size. Each..........18c

If by mail, postage extra, 2 cents.

Tumbler Pins.

No. 38369 Tumbler Pins, threaded, for muzzle loaders. Each..............7c

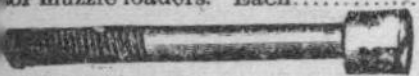

Side Pins.

No. 38371 Side Pins, threaded for Muzzle Loaders. Each..........9c

Cross Pins.

No. 38372 Cross Pins for muzzle loading guns. Each..........15c

No. 38373 Cross Pins, for breech loading guns. Each..........20c

Inside Lock Screws.

No. 38374 Inside Lock Screws, threaded, Each..........20c

Tumbler Swivels.

No. 38375 Tumbler Swivels, filed, single horn, not fitted. Each........9c

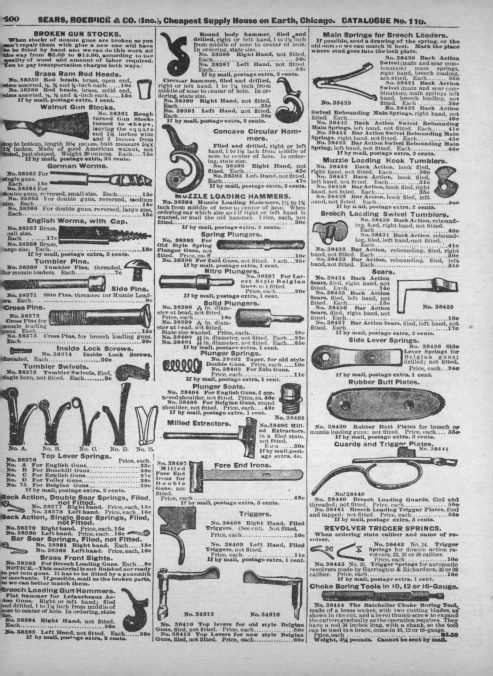

No. A. No. B. No. C. No. D. No. 75.

Top Lever Springs.

No. 38376 Price, each.

No. A	For English Guns......	25c
No. B	For Bonehill Guns......	26c
No. C	For English Guns......	27c
No. D	For Tolley Guns......	28c
No. 75	For Belgian Guns......	29c

If by mail, postage extra, 2 cents.

Back Action, Double Sear Springs, Filed, not Fitted.

No. 38377 Right hand. Price, each, 15c

No. 38378 Left hand. Price, each..16c

Back Action, Single Sear Springs, Filed, not Fitted.

No. 38379 Right hand. Price, each, 15c

No. 38380 Left hand. Price, each..16c

Bar Sear Springs, Filed, not Fitted.

No. 38381 Right hand. Each.....15c

No. 38382 Left hand. Price, each, 16c

Brass Front Sights.

No. 38383 For Breech Loading Guns. Each....8c

NOTICE.—This material is not finished nor ready to put into guns. It has to be fitted by a gunsmith or mechanic. If possible, mail us the broken parts, so we can better match them.

Breech Loading Gun Hammers.

Flat hammer for Lefaucheaux Action Guns. Right or left hand; filed and drilled, 1 to 1¼ inch from middle of nose to center of hole. In ordering, state size.

No. 38384 Right Hand, not fitted. Each..........26c

No. 38385 Left Hand, not fitted. Each......26c

If by mail, postage extra, 2 cents.

Round body hammer, filed and drilled, right or left hand, 1 to 1¼ inch from middle of nose to center of hole. In ordering, state size.

No. 38386 Right Hand, not fitted, Each..........30c

No. 38387 Left Hand, not fitted. Each..........32c

If by mail, postage extra, 2 cents.

Circular hammer, filed and drilled, right or left hand, 1 to 1¼ inch from middle of nose to center of hole. In ordering, state size.

No. 38390 Right Hand, not fitted, Each..........35c

No. 38391 Left Hand, not fitted. Each..........36c

If by mail, postage extra, 2 cents.

Concave Circular Hammers.

Filed and drilled, right or left hand, 1 to 1¼ inch from middle of nose to center of hole. In ordering, state size.

No. 38392 Right Hand, not fitted. Each..........45c

No. 38393 Left Hand, not fitted. Each..........47c

If by mail, postage extra, 2 cents.

MUZZLE LOADING HAMMERS.

No. 38394 Muzzle Loading Hammers, 1½ to 1¾ inch from middle of nose to center of hole. When ordering say which size and if right or left hand is wanted, or mail the old hammer. Price, each, not fitted..........30c

If by mail, postage extra, 2 cents.

Spring Plungers.

No. 38395 For Old Style Spring Plunger Guns, not fitted. Price, each..........10c

No. 38396 For Zulu Guns, not fitted. Each...25c

If by mail, postage extra, 1 cent.

Nitro Plungers.

No. 38397 For Latest Style Belgian Guns, not fitted. Price, each.......20c

If by mail, postage extra, 1 cent.

Solid Plungers.

No. 38398 5/16 in. diameter at head, not fitted. Price, each..........18c

No. 38399 5/16 in. diameter at head, not fitted. State size wanted. Price, each..........20c

No. 38400 11/32 in. diameter, not fitted. Each...22c

No. 38401 13/32 in. diameter, not fitted. Each...25c

If by mail, postage extra, 1 cent.

Plunger Springs.

No. 38402 Taper, for old style Double Guns. Price, each.....10c

No. 38403 For Zulu Guns. Price, each..........11c

If by mail, postage extra, 1 cent.

Plunger Seats.

No. 38405

No. 38404 For English Guns, 6 cornered shoulder, not fitted. Price, ea. 40c

No. 38405 For Belgian Guns, round shoulder, not fitted. Price, each....42c

If by mail, postage extra, 1 cent.

Milled Extractors.

No. 38406 Milled Extractors, in a filed state, not fitted. Each 50c

If by mail, postage extra, 4c.

Fore End Irons.

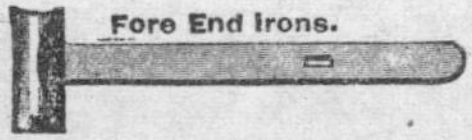

No. 38407 Milled Fore End Irons for Double Guns, not fitted. Price, each..........45c

If by mail, postage extra, 5 cents.

Triggers.

No. 38408 Right Hand, Filed Triggers. (See cut). Not fitted. Price, each..........10c

No. 38409 Left Hand, Filed Triggers, not fitted. Price, each..........11c

If by mail, postage extra, 1 cent.

No. 34812

No. 34810

No. 38410 Top levers for old style Belgian Guns, filed, not fitted. Price, each..........50c

No. 38412 Top Levers for new style Belgian Guns, filed, not fitted. Price, each..........60c

Main Springs for Breech Loaders.

If possible, send a drawing of the spring, or the old one, so we can match it best. Mark the place where stud goes into the lock plate.

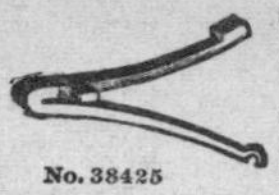

No. 38425

No. 38420 Back Action Swivel (main and sear combination) main springs, right hand, breech loading, not fitted. Each........35c

No. 38421 Back Action Swivel (main and sear combination), main springs left hand, breech loading, not fitted. Each..........36c

No. 38422 Back Action Swivel Rebounding Main Springs, right hand, not fitted Each..........40c

No. 38423 Back Action Swivel Rebounding Main Springs, left hand, not fitted. Each......41c

No. 38424 Bar Action Swivel Rebounding Main Springs, right hand, not fitted. Each..........45c

No. 38425 Bar Action Swivel Rebounding Main Spring, left hand, not fitted. Each..........46c

If by mail, postage extra, 2 cents.

Muzzle Loading Hook Tumblers.

No. 38426 Back Action, hook filed, right hand, not fitted. Each..........30c

No. 38427 Back Action, hook filed, left hand, not fitted. Each..........31c

No. 38428 Bar Action, hook filed, right hand, not fitted. Each..........35c

No. 38429 Bar Action, hook filed, left hand, not fitted. Each..........30c

If by mail, postage extra, 2 cents.

Breech Loading Swivel Tumblers.

No. 38430 Back Action, rebounding, filed, right hand, not fitted. Each..........40c

No. 38431 Back Action, rebounding, filed, left hand, not fitted. Each..........41c

No. 38432 Bar Action, rebounding, filed, right hand, not fitted. Each..........50c

No. 38433 Bar Action, rebounding, filed, left hand, not fitted. Each..........51c

Sears.

No. 38435

No. 38434 Back Action Sears, filed, right hand, not fitted. Each..........14c

No. 38435 Back Action Sears, filed, left hand, not fitted. Each..........15c

No. 38436 Bar Action Sears, filed, right hand, not fitted. Each..........16c

No. 38437 Bar Action Sears, filed, left hand, not fitted. Each..........17c

If by mail, postage extra, 2 cents.

Side Lever Springs.

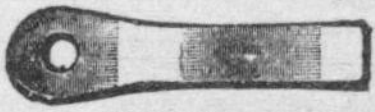

No. 38438 Side Lever Springs for Belgian guns; drilled; not fitted. Price, each...24c

If by mail, postage extra, 1 cent.

Rubber Butt Plates.

No. 38439 Rubber Butt Plates for breech or muzzle loading guns; not fitted. Price, each.... 55c

If by mail, postage extra, 3 cents.

Guards and Trigger Plates.

No. 38441

No. 38440

No. 38440 Breech Loading Guards, filed and threaded; not fitted. Price, each..........50c

No. 38441 Breech Loading Trigger Plates, filed and tapped; not fitted. Price, each..........52c

If by mail, postage extra, 5 cents.

REVOLVER TRIGGER SPRINGS.

When ordering state caliber and name of revolver.

No. 38442 No. 14. **Trigger Springs** for double action revolvers, 22, 32 or 38 caliber. Price, each..........10c

No. 38443 No. 26. **Trigger Springs** for automatic revolvers made by Harrington & Richardson, 32 or 38 caliber. Price, each..........10c

If by mail, postage extra, 1 cent.

Choke Boring Tools in 10, 12 or 16-Gauge.

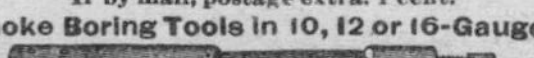

No. 38444 The Batcheller Choke Boring Tool, made of a brass socket, with two cutting blades, as shown in the cut, and a bevel thumb screw to expand the cutters gradually as the operation requires. They have a rod 34 inches long, with a shank, so the tool can be used in a brace, come in 10, 12 or 16-gauge. Price, each..........$5.50

Weight, 2¼ pounds. Cannot be sent by mail.

FISHING TACKLE DEPARTMENT.

OUR FISHING TACKLE DEPARTMENT FOR THIS SEASON Will contain the most complete assortment of high grade tackle on the market. We have dropped all the cheap grades and hereafter will not carry anything but good tackle.

ANY TACKLE BOUGHT FROM US MAY BE RETURNED AT OUR EXPENSE PROVIDED YOU RETURN IT IN PERFECT CONDITION.

WE GUARANTEE EVERYTHING WE SELL IN THIS DEPARTMENT To be exactly as represented and of the best quality. Do not compare our goods with the cheap grades. Descriptions of goods may be just alike, but when you come to compare the goods themselves you will find great difference.

WOOD RODS.

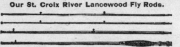

No. 38585 Three jointed Fishing Rod, made of ash with single ferrules, brass mounted. A good rod for light fishing; about 10 feet long. Put up in a neat paper bag. Price, each..............12c

No. 38586 Ash Rod, three joints, brass mounted, single ferrules, ringed for lines, about 10 feet long. Put up in a neat paper bag. Price, each..............18c

No. 38589 Three joints, brass mounted, made of ash, double telescope ferrules, stained, ringed with reel bands and butt caps. A rod that is giving satisfaction all over the country. Length, 10 feet. Price, each..............50c

No. 38593 Four joints, brass mounted, made of ash, double telescope ferrules, ringed and stained, with reel bands and butt cap. Length about 12 feet. Price, each..............80c

Jointed Bamboo Fishing Rods.

The Bamboo rods quoted below are light, handy and strong. Can be used with or without reels. The best trolling rods in the market. The most popular rods on the market are the Japanese and Calcutta bamboo. They may be handled as a high grade one cannot be, will stand a great deal of abuse and are very durable.

No. 38597 Two-piece Japanese Rod, plain straw color, double telescope ferrules, ringed for line, about 8 to 9 feet. Price, each..............20c

No. 38598 Three-piece Japanese Rod, plain double telescope ferrules, straw color, ringed for lines, about 11 to 13 feet long. Price, each..............40c

No. 38599 Three-piece Japanese Rod plain straw color, double telescope ferrules, ringed for lines and reel bands. Price, each..............55c

Calcutta Bamboo Rods.

No. 38601 Our Calcutta Bamboo Rod, made with three joints, double telescope ferrules. Length, 12 to 14 feet. Strong and cheap. Price, each..............50c

No. 38603 Calcutta Bamboo Rod, with three joints, double telescope ferrules, ringed for lines with butt cap and reel bands. Length, 12 to 14 feet. Price, each..............75c

No. 38607 Bamboo Four-piece Rod.

No. 38607 Calcutta Bamboo Rod, four joints, double telescope ferrules, ringed, with butt cap and reel bands. Length, 12 to 15 feet. Price, each..............85c

No. 38610 Five-piece Calcutta Bamboo Rod, with double telescope ferrules, bands, butt cap and guides, scored handle; 15 to 17 feet long. Price, each..............$1.50

Our St. Croix River Lancewood Fly Rods.

No. 38617

No. 38616 Our St. Croix River Lancewood Fly Rod made in three joints, with extra tip, genuine lancewood throughout, nickeled mountings and raised telescope ferrules. Silk wound tie guides and silk whippings at each mounting. Solid reel seat below hand. Zylonite corrugated grip. Length, about 10 feet. Put up in neat partitioned cloth bag. Weight, about 9 oz.; a fine looking rod. Price, each..............$1.25

No. 38617 Our St. Croix River Lancewood Fly Rod, same description as above, with extra silk wrappings. Made of SELECTED Lancewood with corrugated zylonite butt, with extra lancewood tip. Put up on a wood form, in cloth bag. Length, about 10 feet. Weight, about 8½ oz. A fine looking rod. Price, each..............$1.60

Our Twin Lakes Lancewood Bass Rods.

No. 38623

No. 38621 Our Twin Lakes Lancewood Bass Rod, made of genuine lancewood throughout; three joints with extra lancewood tip, nickeled mountings, raised telescope ferrules, silk wound tie guides and silk wrappings at mountings, solid reel seat above hand, with corrugated zylonite grasp, length about 9 feet; weight, about 12 oz. Put up in neat partitioned cloth bag. A fine looking rod and one which will please you. Price, each..............$1.30

No. 38623 Our Twin Lakes Bass Rod, three joints, lancewood throughout, with extra tip, nickel mountings, silk wound tie guides and silk wrappings at mountings, solid reel seat above hand, corrugated zylonite grip; length about 9 feet, weight, about 12 oz., all in cloth bag on a wood form. Price, each..............$1.50

NOTICE:—Fish Rods are too long to be sent by mail, we therefore suggest that you look through our catalogue, make up an order for such goods as yourself and friends may need, and have them all sent by express at a very slight expense.

Our prices are lowest jobbing prices on fishing tackle; this is why the prices made seem low for good goods. Our policy of selling from the maker to the consumer on one small profit makes it possible for us to sell goods cheap.

OUR CLIMAX SPLIT BAMBOO BASS ROD.

NOTE:—Our line of Split Bamboo Rods are of the very best quality. We have taken great care in selecting our rods for the coming season, and our stock is the very best that can be obtained. Our prices on these rods are lower than any retail dealer can possibly sell them. So do not judge the quality by the price. We guarantee them exactly as represented or money refunded. Our Split Bamboo Rods are made of six pieces of bamboo, split, fitted and glued together, making the rod light, flexible and strong. Ten years ago no split bamboo rod could be bought under $7.00 to $10.00. We can now sell them from 98 cents up. This is made possible by our large contract and the small profit we ask above the cost of labor and material.

Split Bamboo Bass Rods.

No. 38630 Our Climax Split Bamboo Bass Rod. Solid reel seat above the hand. This rod is one that we are making a run on at an exceedingly low price and are positive that rod cannot be duplicated for twice the amount anywhere in the country. Split and glued bamboo bass rods. Nickel plated telescope ferrules, silk wound line guides, with alternate silk wrappings, cork or zylonite grasp, nickeled mountings, 3 joints with an extra tip. Put up on a wooden form in a cloth bag. About 9½ feet long, weight, about 11 ounces. Our special price..............98c

Our Acme Split Bamboo Fly Rod.

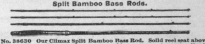

No. 38634 Our Acme Split Bamboo Fly Rod. Solid reel seat below the hand. This rod is the same quality as No. 38630, except that the reel seat is below the hand for trout and light fishing. Has silk wound ring guides, with wrappings of fine silk every few inches; solid reel seat and nickel plated telescope ferrules and mountings; length, about 10 feet, weight, about 9 ounces, with cork or zylonite grasp. Worth $1.75 anywhere. Comes in 3 joints with an extra tip on a wood form and in a cloth bag. Our special price, each..............$1.00

No. 38638 Our Geneseo River High Grade Hexagonal Bamboo Fly Rod. Reel seat below the hand. This rod is of special high grade selected bamboo and finished equal to many of the high priced rods. It has silk wound ring guides, close wrappings of fine silk with reel seat, nickeled telescope ferrules, full nickel mountings. A daisy, with cork grasp. Equal to rods that retail at $3.50 to $5.00 in stores. Comes in 3 joints with an extra tip on a neat wood form and in a cloth bag. Length, about 10 feet, weight, about 8½ ounces. Our special price..............$1.95

Our Chautauqua Lake Split Bamboo Bass Rod.

No. 38640 Our Chautauqua Lake Split Bamboo Bass Rod, solid reel seat above the hand. Made of the best quality selected bamboo, split and glued, hexagonal, with silk wound line guides, cork butt, nickel plated telescope ferrules and mountings; short, heavy, strong and durable. A first class bait casting rod, put up in 3 joints with an extra tip. Length, 7 feet, weight, about 8 ounces. This rod is the coming rod for bait casting. Worth $2.75 anywhere. Our special price..............$1.85

No. 38642 The Hamilton Hexagonal Split Bamboo Bass Rod, solid reel seat above the hand. Made of the best selected split and glued Bamboo, with swelled butt, silk wound line guides, with close wrappings of silk, full nickel plated telescope ferrules and mountings, with cork grasp, 3 joints and one extra tip. Length, about 9½ feet, put up on a neat wood form and in a cloth bag. A rod that retails at $4.50 anywhere. Our special price..............$2.25

Our Special Rio Grande High Grade Split Bamboo Fly Rod.

No. 38646 Special Rio Grande Bamboo Fly Rod. Solid reel seat below the hand. This rod is made of special selected cane, hexagonal in shape, with close wrappings of colored silk, swell butt, full nickel plated telescope ferrules and mountings, white and black zylonite wound butt. Put up in 3 joints with an extra tip on a fine covered wood form and in a neat bag. Length, about 10 feet. A rod that retails at $5.50 in stores. Our special price..............$2.75

No. 38649 The Churchill Hexagonal Split and Glued Bamboo Fly Rod, with patent zylonite or cork grip, full nickeled telescoped ferrules and mountings, solid metal reel seat below hand, welt ferrules, a hand made 7-ounce rod, about 9 feet long. An extra fine, light rod. Put up in 3 joints and an extra tip. Our special price, each..............$3.35

Our Shanley Lake High Grade Bass Rod for $2.95.

No. 38650 Our Special Shanley Lake High Grade Bass Rod. Reel seat above the hand. This rod is made of specially selected bamboo. Split and glued hexagonal, with very close wrappings at short intervals of the finest fancy colored silk, with **nickel plated telescope ferrules and mountings, black and white zylonite wound butt, solid reel seat.** A very handsome and neatly finished rod; strong and durable. Length, about 9 feet. Put up in 3 joints with an extra tip on a fancy covered wood form and cloth bag. Equal to rods that retail in stores at $1.50 to $3.00.
Our special bargain price..$2.95

Our Sand Pond Split Bamboo Bass Rod for $4.00.

No. 38652 **Our Sand Pond Special High Grade Bass Rod. Solid reel seat above the hand.** This rod is made of the very finest quality of specially selected cane, hand made, and equipped with the best German silver mountings, welted ferrules, silk wound line guides, swelled cork grasp. Very close wrappings of fine fancy colored silk, with extra full length tip. Thoroughly hand made throughout, no better rod made for bass fishing. Length, 6 to 8 feet, weight, about 8 ounces, put up with 3 joints and an extra tip, in fancy colored wood form and cloth bag. A rod that cannot be bought at retail for less than $6.00. **This rod will please anybody, and is exceptional value.** Our special price........................$4.00

Our Lake George Special $5.00 Lancewood Bass Rod with Agate Tip.

No. 38653 Our Lake George Fine Special Lancewood Bait Casting Rod, with solid reel seat above hand, German silver mountings, all engraved or milled to make a very handsome appearance. It has an agate tip and solid anti-friction trumpet guides, windings of black and red, beautifully clustered. Put up in 3 joints with an extra tip on a wood form covered with velvet. We cannot recommend these rods too highly. **They are perfection.** Ordinarily retail for $10.00. Weight, 8 ounces; length, 6¼ feet. The Short Rod is the coming Bait casting Rod. Our price........................$5.00

The Beaverkill, a Very Fine Lancewood Fly Rod.

No. 38657 **Our Special Beaverkill Lancewood Fly Rod.** Made up similar to No. 38653 but has German silver guides and a special turned down fly ring tip. Put up same as No. 38653, weight, 6 ounces, 8½ feet long. Our special price........................$4.00

Our 2-Piece Muskallonge and Trolling Rods.

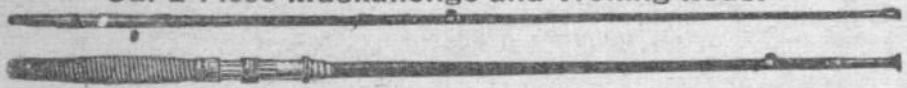

No. 38658 Made of Lancewood, two joints, for heavy trolling, zylonite butt, full nickel plated telescope ferrules and mountings, extra heavy mountings, with double guides on tip, Zylonite grasp, put up in partitioned cloth bag, length 7 feet, strong and good. Each........................$2.40

Our 3-Piece Muskallonge Rods.

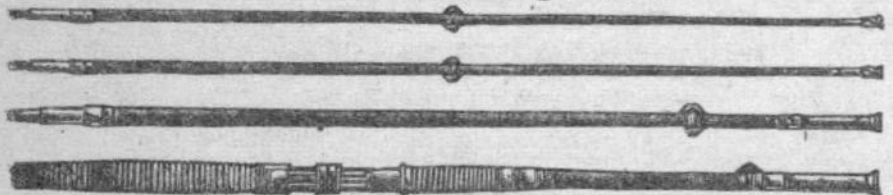

No. 38659 **Muskallonge and Trolling Rod,** extra heavy, made of selected lancewood with zylonite grasp and full nickel plated mountings, 8 feet long, 3-piece with an extra tip, welded telescope ferrules and double guides. Put up in partitioned cloth bag, has grasp above and below hand.
Price, each........................$4.00

OUR LINE OF TRUNK RODS.

These rods are very popular with all those who do much traveling. A rod is a very unhandy thing to carry, unless it is short enough to be carried in a trunk or large size grip. From this the rod gets its name of Trunk Rod.

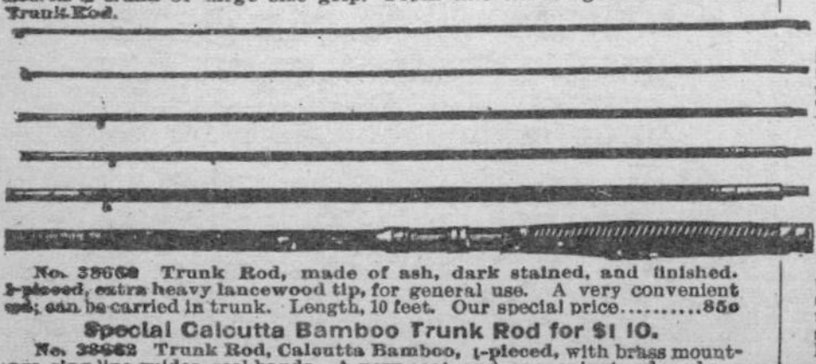

No. 38660 **Trunk Rod, made of ash, dark stained, and finished.** 4-pieced, extra heavy lancewood tip, for general use. A very convenient rod; can be carried in trunk. Length, 10 feet. Our special price........85c

Special Calcutta Bamboo Trunk Rod for $1.10.

No. 38662 **Trunk Rod, Calcutta Bamboo,** 4-pieced, with brass mountings, ring line guides, reel bands. A very neat and convenient rod, and one that will give entire satisfaction; 8 to 9 feet. Our special price......$1.10

Finest Quality of Lancewood Trunk Rods for $2.00.

No. 38666 **Trunk Bass Rod, first quality lancewood.** 4 pieces, nickeled telescope ferrules and mountings, double rim shouldered ferrules, **anti-friction silk wound guides,** covered dowels, **solid metal reel seat above hand,** corrugated zylonite butt, **about 9 feet.** One of the best and most convenient rods on the market Our special price........................$2.00

Our Fox River Split Bamboo Bass Rods, $3.25.

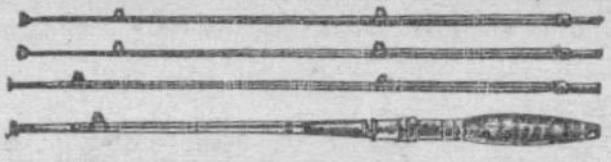

For $3.25 we offer you our Fox River Bamboo Trunk Fishing Rod, made of six pieces selected bamboo, split and glued together, with solid reel seat, standing line guides, fancy silk wrappings at short intervals, nickel-plated mountings, shouldered ferrules and swelled butt. The bamboo is strengthened at the reel seat, by extra inlaying of cedar at the butt, making it very strong and durable. **The rod comes in three joints with an extra tip,** so that if you break one tip you may have the other one at your command. Each piece is about 25 inches long, and when the rod is put together the entire length is about 6 feet. This is undoubtedly one of the best bait casting rods to be had for the money.
No. 38667 **Our Genuine Fox River Bamboo Bait Casting Rod,** about 6 feet long, cork handle. Our special price........................$3.25

Our Celebrated Geneva Lake Bait Casting Rod, $4.10.

For $4.10 we offer our Geneva Lake Split Bamboo Bass Rod. This rod is made of specially selected bamboo, hexagonal shape, wound with fancy colored selected silk at short intervals, has standing line guides, solid reel seat and shoulder ferrules, and the grip is made extra strong with six pieces of inlaid cedar at the butt. The mountings are all solid German Silver and the joints fit perfectly. The rod must really be seen to be appreciated. **It is made in three joints, each about 25 inches long,** and each rod has an extra tip, in case you break one you will have another one at your command. This is one of the best bass rods made and gives universal satisfaction. When put together the entire rod is about 6 feet long.
No. 38668 **Our Geneva Lake Bass Rod,** 6 feet long, German Silver mounted, swelled butt, cork grip, mounted on a flannel covered wood form. This is a swell rod and our special price is only........................$4.10

THE GENUINE BRISTOL STEEL FISHING RODS.

Warranted.

Telescope Fly and Bass Rods, 9½ feet long.

No. 38670 **Steel Telescopic Bass Rod, 9 feet, 6 inches in length, full nickel mounted, with solid reel seat above the hand.** Line runs through the center of the rod. When telescoped, **the rod is 32 inches in length,** all inclosed within the butt length, as shown in cut. Weight, each, 11¾ ounces.
With celluloid handle, our special price........................$3.40

Steel Telescopic Fly Rod.

No. 38672 **Steel Telescopic Fly Rod, 9 feet, 6 inches in length.** Same style as above, but with reel seat below the hand for trout fishing. Line runs through the center of the rod. When telescoped, the rod is 32 inches in length. All inclosed within the butt length. Weight, 11¾ ounces.
With celluloid handle, our special price........................$3.40

Our High Grade 10-foot Jointed Steel Fly Rod.

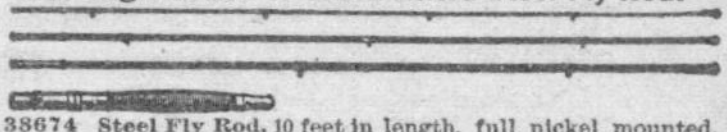

No. 38674 **Steel Fly Rod,** 10 feet in length, full nickel mounted, with solid reel seat below the hand. This rod is jointed, fitted with two ring German silver tie guide and one ring German silver fly tip. Is made with three joints and handle; each joint being 38 inches long. **Does not telescope.** Weight, 9¼ ounces. With celluloid wound handle, our special price....$4.50

The Genuine Henshall 8½-foot Jointed Steel Bass Rod.

No. 38676 **The Henshall Steel Bass Rod. 8 feet, 6 inches in length. Full nickel mounted, with solid reel seat above the hand.** This rod is jointed, fitted with two ring German silver tie guides and German silver three ring tip. Is made with three joints and handle; each joint being 32 inches long. **Does not telescope. This rod is the best bass or pickerel rod made.** Weight, 10 ounces. With celluloid wound handle, our special price......$4.50

The Genuine Expert 6½-foot Jointed Steel Bass Rod.

No. 38680 **The Expert Steel Bait Casting Rod,** 6 feet, 6 inches in length, full nickel mounted, with **solid reel seat above the hand.** This rod is jointed, fitted with two ring German silver tie guides and German silver three ring tip. It is made with three joints and handle; the joints are 24 inches long. This is a fine rod for long casts and for heavy work. **Does not telescope.** Weight, 8¼ ounces. With celluloid wound handle, our special price....$4.50

Genuine Bristol 5½-foot Jointed Steel Bait Casting Rod.

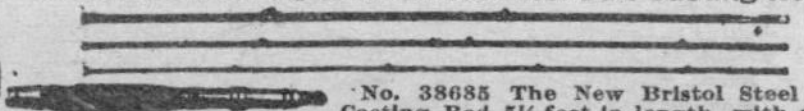

No. 38685 **The New Bristol Steel Bait Casting Rod, 5½ feet in length, with agate tip and one agate guide, the other guides are German silver trumpet style.** This rod is intended for those who prefer a short rod, which is rapidly becoming more popular, being more readily handled and not so severe on the wrist. This rod is not telescopic, but is fitted with celluloid handle. Our special price........................$6.50
No. 38687 **Same as No. 38685, without the agate guides, but has German silver trumpet guides and German silver tip.** Each........................$5.43

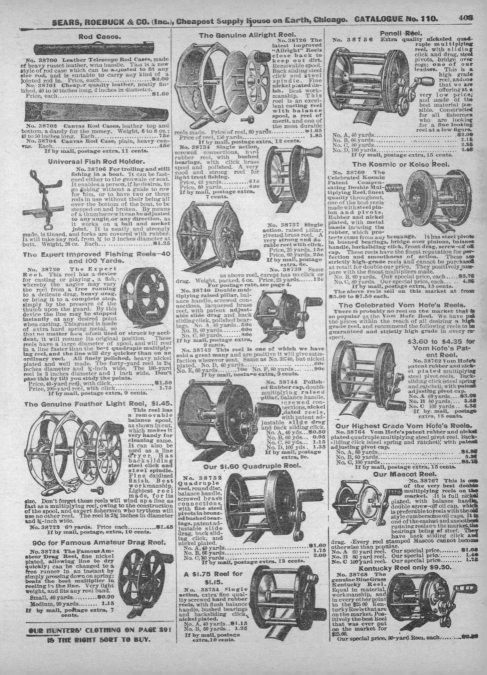

Rod Cases.

No. 38700 Leather Telescope Rod Cases, made of heavy russet leather, with handle. This is a new style of rod case which can be adjusted to fit any size rod, and is suitable to carry any kind of a jointed rod in. Price, each........................$2.00

No. 38701 Cheaper quality leather, neatly finished, 40 to 50 inches long, 2 inches in diameter. Price, each........................$1.60

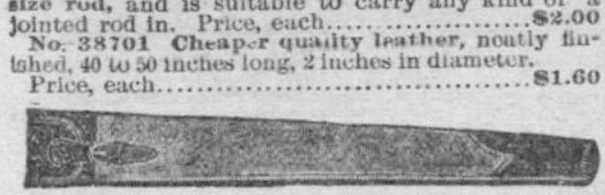

No. 38702 Canvas Rod Cases, leather top and bottom, a dandy for the money. Weight, 6 to 8 oz.; 40 to 50 inches long. Each........................75c

No. 38704 Canvas Rod Case, plain, heavy canvas. Each........................45c

If by mail, postage extra, 11 cents.

Universal Fish Rod Holder.

No. 38706 For trolling and still fishing in a boat. It can be fastened either to the gunwale or seat. It enables a person, if he desires, to go fishing without a guide to row for him, or to have two or three rods in use without their being all over the bottom of the boat, to be stepped on and broken. By means of a thumbscrew it can be adjusted to any angle or any direction, as it works on a ball and socket joint. It is neatly and strongly made, is tinned, and forks are covered with rubber. It will take any rod, from ⅜ to 2 inches diameter at butt. Weight, 26 oz. Each........................$1.25

The Expert Improved Fishing Reels—40 and 100 Yards.

No. 38720 The Expert Reel. This reel has a device for casting or playing a fish, whereby the angler may vary the reel from a free running to a delicate drag, heavy drag, or bring it to a complete stop, simply by the pressure of the thumb upon the guard. By this device the line may be stopped instantly at any desired point when casting. This guard is made of extra hard spring metal, so that no matter how often used or struck by accident, it will resume its original position. These reels have a large diameter of spool, and will reel in a line faster than the best quadruple multiplying reel, and the line will dry quicker than on an ordinary reel. All finely polished, heavy nickel plated and well made. The forty-yard reel is 2¼ inches diameter and ¾-inch wide. The 100-yard reel is 3 inches diameter and 1 inch wide. **Don't pass this by till you study the points.**

Price, 40-yard reel, with click........................$1.50
Price, 100-yard reel, with click........................1.75

If by mail, postage extra, 9 cents.

The Genuine Feather Light Reel, $1.45.

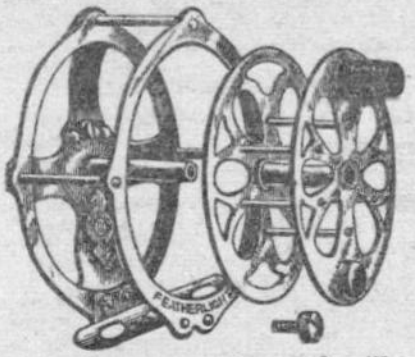

This reel has a removable balance spool, as shown in cut, which makes it very handy for cleaning same. It can also be used as a line dryer. Has backsliding steel click and steel spindle. Fine oxidized finish. Best workmanship. Lightest reel made, for its size. Don't forget these reels will wind up a line as fast as a multiplying reel, owing to the construction of the spool, and expert fishermen who try them will use no other reel. The reel is 2¾ inches in diameter and ¾-inch wide.

No. 38723 60 yards. Price each........................$1.45

If by mail, postage, extra, 10 cents.

90c for Famous Amateur Drag Reel.

No. 38724 The Famous Amateur Drag Reel, fine nickel plated, allowing line to dry quickly; can be changed to a free runner in an instant by simply pressing down on spring; beats the best multiplier in reeling in the line. Very light weight, and fits any reel band.

Small, 40 yards........................$0.90
Medium, 90 yards........................1.15

If by mail, postage extra, 7 cents.

OUR HUNTERS' CLOTHING ON PAGE 391 IS THE RIGHT SORT TO BUY.

The Genuine Allright Reel.

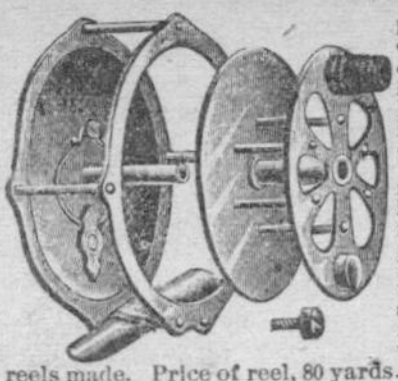

No. 38726 The latest improved **"Allright" Reels close back to keep out dirt.** Removable spool. Back sliding steel click and steel spindle. Fine nickel plated finish. Best workmanship. This reel is an excellent casting reel with balance spool, a reel of merit, and one of the most durable reels made. Price of reel, 80 yards........................$1.65
Price of reel, 150 yards........................1.85

If by mail, postage extra, 12 cents.

No. 38734 Single action, screwed connections, hard rubber reel, with bushed bearings, with click brass spool and polished. A very good and strong reel for light trout fishing.

Price, 40 yards........................41c
Price, 60 yards........................49c

If by mail, postage extra, 7 cents.

No. 38737 Single action, raised pillar, riveted brass reel. **A very strong and durable reel with click.**

Price, 25 yards..15c
Price, 60 yards..25c

If by mail, postage extra, 6c.

No. 38739 Same as above reel, except has no click or drag. Weight, packed, 6 oz. Price, 25 yards......12c

For postage rate, see page 4.

No. 38740 Double multiplying raised pillar, balance handle, screwed connections, lacquered brass reel, with patent adjustable slide drag and back sliding click, polished bearings. No. A, 40 yards..50c
No. B, 60 yards........60c
No. C, 80 yards........80c

If by mail, postage extra, 9 cents.

No. 38742 This reel is one of which we have sold a great many and are positive it will give satisfaction wherever sent. Same as No. 38740, but nickel plated. No. D, 40 yards........................60c
No. E, 60 yards........70c No. F, 80 yards........90c

If by mail, postage extra, 9 cents.

No. 38744 Polished Rubber cap, double multiplying raised pillar, balance handle, **screwed connections, nickel plated reels,** with patent adjustable **slide drag** and back sliding click.

No. A, 40 yds...$0.80
No. B, 60 yds... 0.95
No. C, 80 yds... 1.15
No. D, 100 yds . 1.35

If by mail, postage extra, 9c.

Our $1.60 Quadruple Reel.

No. 38752 Quadruple reel, round disc, balance handle, **screwed brass connections, with fine steel pivots in bronzed bushed bearings,** patent adjustable slide drag, back sliding click; and nickel plated.

No. A, 40 yards........................$1.60
No. B, 60 yards........................1.75
No. C, 80 yards........................2.00

If by mail, postage extra, 13 cents.

A $1.75 Reel for $1.15.

No. 38754 Single action, extra fine quality screwed hard rubber reels, with flush balance handle, bushed bearings and backsliding click, nickel plated.

No. A, 40 yards..$1.15
No. B, 60 yards.. 1.25

If by mail, postage extra, 10 cents.

Penell Reel.

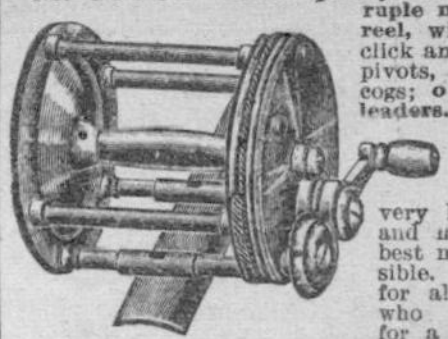

No. 38756 Extra quality nickeled quadruple multiplying reel, with sliding click and drag, steel pivots, bridge over cogs; one of our leaders. This is a high grade reel, and one that we are offering at a very low price; and made of the best material possible. Constructed for all fishermen who are looking for a fine looking reel at a low figure.

No. A, 40 yards........................$2.00
No. B, 60 yards........................2.15
No. C, 80 yards........................2.25
No. D, 100 yards........................2.46

If by mail, postage extra, 15 cents.

The Kosmic or Kelso Reel.

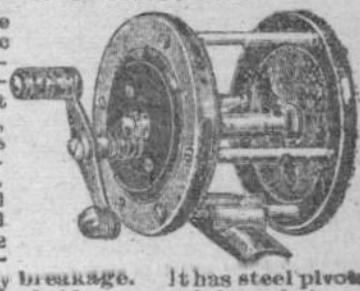

No. 38760 The Celebrated Kosmic Patent Compensating Double Multiplying Reel, finest quality throughout, one of the best reels made with steel pinion and pivots. Rubber and nickel plated, with metal bands incasing the rubber, which protects same from any breakage. It has steel pivots in bushed bearings, bridge over pinions, balance handle, backsliding click, front drag, screw-off oil cap. These reels have the finest reputation for perfection and smoothness of action. These are strictly high-grade reels and cannot be purchased at retail for double our price. They positively compare with the finest multipliers made.

No. B, 60 yards. Our special price, each........$3.75
No. C, 80 yards. Our special price, each........4.25

If by mail, postage extra, 15 cents.

The above reels sell on this market at from $5.00 to $7.50 each.

The Celebrated Vom Hofe's Reels.

There is probably no reel on the market that is so popular as the Vom Hofe Reel. We have put the prices within the reach of all desiring a high grade reel, and recommend the following reels to be guaranteed and strictly high grade in every respect.

$3.60 to $4.35 for Vom Hofe's Patent Reel.

No. 38762 Vom Hofe's patent rubber and nickel plated multiplying steel pivot reels. Back sliding click (steel spring and ratchet), with **patent adjusting pivot cap.**

No. A 60 yards....$3.60
No. B 80 yards.... 3.85
No. C 100 yards.... 4.35

If by mail, postage extra, 15 cents.

Our Highest Grade Vom Hofe's Reels.

No. 38764 Vom Hofe's patent rubber and nickel plated quadruple multiplying steel pivot reel. Back sliding click (steel spring and ratchet), with **patent adjusting pivot cap.**

No. A, 60 yards........................$4.96
No. B, 80 yards........................5.36
No. C, 100 yards........................$5.75

If by mail, postage extra, 15 cents.

Our Mascot Reel.

No. 38767 This is one of the very best double multiplying reels on the market. It is full nickel plated, with balance handle, double screw-off oil cap, which is preferable to reels with the old style cumbersome oil caps. It is one of the easiest and smoothest running reels on the market, the bearings being of steel. They have back sliding click and drag. Every reel stamped Mascot cannot become otherwise than popular.

No. A	60 yard reel.	Our special price........$1.05
No. B	80 yard reel.	Our special price........1.40
No. C	100 yard reel.	Our special price........1.75

Kentucky Reel only $9.50.

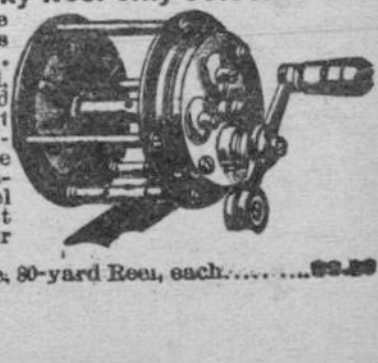

No. 38768 The genuine Blue Grass Kentucky Reel. Equal in material, workmanship, and in every other point to the $25.00 Kentucky Reels that are on the market. Positively the best Reel that was ever put on the market for $25.00.

Our special price, 80-yard Reel, each........$9.50

No. 39020 Genuine Soft Rubber Frogs colored as natural as life. Tied with strong gut loop to treble hook. Colored green and brown. About 1½ inches long.

Price, each 35c

If by mail, postage extra, 3 cents.

Casting Frog.

No. 39021 The most natural Frog, and the most lifelike on the market; weighs one-half ounce, entire length 3 inches, 2 hooks and makes a fine casting frog. Each...(If by mail, postage extra, 4 cents.)...35c

Soft Rubber Angle Worms.

No. 39022 Angle worms; a perfect imitation of red, live worms. Each.............................20c

If by mail, postage extra, 2 cents.

Soft Rubber Froggies.

No. 39024 Made of soft, pliable rubber, with string gut loop and treble hook, about 1 inch long. A good casting bait. Colored natural. Price, each.............20c

If by mail, postage extra, 3 cents.

Rubber Insects.

No. 39024½

No. A. Crickets, each..............16c
No. B. Spiders, each...............15c
No. C. Lady Bugs.................15c
No. D. Beetles, each..............16c

The Celebrated Claflin's Tandem.

No. 39025 A sure bass killer. The cut shows how the bait is attached to remain alive the longest possible time. It may be used with either frog or minnow. It keeps the bait alive and securely. The weighted trailer hook keeps the frog always belly down, and the bait may be made to dive by slackening the line. Try one and you will never want any other kind of bait hook. This Tandem is tied with full length gimp, 3 brass box swivels and dipsey sinker; the weedless and trailer hooks are bright finish, and an extra trailer hook goes with each tandem. Price, each 65c

Weedless Hooks.

No. 39026 The New Weedless Hook, about No. 4-0 size. The only good weedless hook on the market. Cut is about ¾ actual size. For bass, etc.

Price, each............15c

If by mail, postage extra, 1 cent.

Greer's New Lever Hooks.

This cut shows the hook when set and sprung.

No. 39030 Greer's Patent Lever Fish Hook. No more fish lost and baits to reset; no coming home without your largest fish; a dead sure thing on getting your fish if it bites. It is easily adjusted to all kinds of fishing, by sliding the little clamp on the rod. Made of 5-0 and 2-0 Carlisle hooks. Each......................12c

Minnow Gangs.

No. 39031 Minnow Gang, three sets of treble hooks tied on gimp and one sliding No. 1-0 lip hook for live bait. Just the thing to troll for game fish. Nos. 3, 6 and 1-0.

Price, each, No. 6 ....20c
Price, each, No. 3 ....20c
Price, each, No. 1-0 ....30c

No. 39032 The Sockdolager Spring Fishhook. Easy to set and sure to catch any fish that takes it. No. 1 for large fish, No. 2 for medium fish. No. 3 for small fish.

Each..........23c

Postage, 2c.

No. 39034 The snap and catch 'em spring fishhook. Easily set. Fish cannot get away once he is hooked No. 20, small; No. 19, medium; No. 18, large. Say which you want. Each...................16c

If by mail, postage extra, 2 cents.

Fish Stringers.

No. 39036 Fish Stringer, complete with line; very convenient for carrying fish. Each..............8c

If by mail, postage extra, each, 2 cents.

No. 39038 Chain Fish Stringers, brass links, heavy nickel plated, strong and durable; will hold 100 pounds of fish and not break. Each..........20c

If by mail, postage extra, 3 cents.

No. 39044 Acme Frog Spear, 3 tines, 2¼ inches long, with socket to put pole in. Each..........15c

If by mail, postage extra, 6 cents.

Fish Spears.

Lengths given are the entire length of prongs; weight, 8 to 12 ounces each.

No. 39046 Has four tines, 2¼ inches long, with socket for pole. Each..........20c

No. 39047 Has five prongs, 4 inches long, tanged. Each.....25c

No. 39049 has five prongs, 5 inches long, with sockets.

Each........55c

The best spear on the market.

No. 39050 Hand made Fish Spear, all best steel, except socket and wedge; beards of each tine made on solid shank, screws into socket and makes his own thread in wood (of handle); the outside tines can be removed if smaller spear is wanted at any time by putting in larger wedge; width, about 4½ to 4½ inches; entire length of tines, about 6½ inches; entire length, 22 inches. Weight, about 1½ lbs. None better. Price, each $1.50

If by mail, postage extra, 10 to 35 cents.

No. 39052 is same as 39050 but lighter weight, weighing 9 oz. Total length, 14½ inches; length of tines, 4½ inches; width across tines, 4 inches. A good hand made spear with threaded shank to screw into the handle and nickeled ferrule.

Price, each (If by mail, postage extra, 10c.) $1.00

Tackle Boxes.

This is a very practical and ornamental box, made of heavy tin, doubled, seamed and soldered, japanned and lettered, with carrying handle, and will stand hard service.

No. 39060 Single Outfit Tackle Box, has four compartments for tackle. Size, 8 inches long, 4¾ inches wide and 2¼ inches deep. Price, each.........70c

No. 39062 Stock Tackle Box, has 4 compartments, and tray, space for large reel, any amount of lines, hooks, etc. They must be seen to be appreciated. All are made black finish, gilt stripe and ornamentation, with carrying handle. Size, 10¼ inches long, 5½ inches wide and 4 inches deep; price.........$1.25

FLY BOOKS.

No. 39070 Empire City Fly Book; with bar and center clips, 2 heavy envelopes; imitation morocco durable cover, size, 3x3¾ inches and will hold 20 flies. This size will fit any coat pocket.

Our special price, each...35c

If by mail, postage extra, 5 cents.

No. 39071 The Empire City Tackle Book, made for holding Snelled hooks or flies. Imitation morocco durable cover, with bar and centre clips on inside of cover for holding 30 hooks or flies and also 2 long envelopes. This is a very handy and convenient pocket tackle book.

Our special price, each..........................50c

If by mail, postage extra, 5 cents.

No. 39072 Our Pocket Book Style Tackle Book. This book has one metal spring clasp with three celluloid pockets and two leather pockets, also has bar and center clips for holding the hooks or flies. This book has clips for holding 60 Snelled hooks or flies conveniently, and envelopes for holding about three, more. In addition it has two felt leaves for holding flies and leaders to be kept moist. Size, 7x3¼ inches, pocket size, all leaves being made of celluloid and waterproof. Our special price, $1.50

If by mail, postage extra, 10 cents.

Bait Boxes.

All our Bait Boxes are of tin, neatly paint and finished.

Crescent.

No. 39079 The Padlock Bait Box, 3¼ in. wide, 3 in. deep, is shaped very much like a fish basket, with a top cover and a safety Pin on the back so they can be pinned to the coat—no losing of bait or upsetting the bait box.

Price, each..............................15c

If by mail, postage extra, 6 cents.

No. 39081 Crescent shape, as shown in the cut, 6 inches long, and will hold a large quantity of bait. This box is made to strap around the waist—very convenient. Price, each....................20c

If by mail, postage extra, 6 cents.

No. 39082 Bait box straps, leather, ¾-inch wide, 36 inches long. Each........................17c

If by mail, postage extra, 4 cents.

S., R. & Co.'s Celebrated Floating Minnow Buckets.

No. 39085 Handiest, lightest, most noiseless and most complete, minnow bucket ever put on the market. Free circulation of air and water, attracts the fish to it, thereby making good fishing around the bucket. If desired to keep the minnows fresh while in transit put a little tie in the bottom of the bucket. When you arrive at the lake drop the inside bucket into the water, where it can be kept on the surface with a string tied to the boat. The inside bucket is made of wire screening and so open that it affords full flow of fresh water all the time, bringing to your minnows the insect food upon which they exist, as well as attracting other fish to it. Weight, 3½ to 5¼ pounds.

	8 quarts	10 quarts	12 quarts
For holding.....			
Price, each......	$1.35	$1.45	$1.65

Our Universal Live Nets.

No. 39088 These nets are made with wire hoops and tan colored netting, are collapsible and take up very little room. An excellent thing to keep fish alive and fresh when caught. Diameter... 9 in. 12 in. 14 in. Price, each.....40c   45c   50c

If by mail, postage extra, 5 cents.

Minnow Dip Nets.

No. 39089 Linen Minnow Dip Nets

Deep   Price
16 inches...30c
18 inches...30c
20 inches...40c
24 inches...50c
30 inches...73c
36 inches...92c

If by mail, postage extra, 5c.

Linen Landing Nets.

No. 39090 20-inch, 15c; 24-inch, 20c; 30-inch, 30c

If by mail, postage extra, 5 cents.

The Tracy Minnow Dip Net for $1.25.

This is one of the best Minnow Dip Nets on the market. It is constructed so it may be opened very much like an umbrella, and when not in use it may be closed up and folded, as shown in the cut. This Minnow Dip net measures 41 inches in diameter and the net has ¾-inch mesh; Common Sense netting. The handle is jointed and when put together is 60 inches long; the entire net, including the handle and frame, weighs 1½ pounds. This is without doubt one of the best minnow nets upon the market, and the price we name is based on the actual cost of material and labor, with but one small margin of profit added.

No. 39091 Our special price on Tracy Minnow Nets is.......................................$1.25

Crab Nets.

No. 39092 Crab Nets, made of 12-thread cotton seine twine; regulation mesh.

	16 in.	20 in.	24 in.
Deep....			
Price, each......	10c	15c	20c

If by mail, postage extra, 4 cents.

Landing Net Rings.

No. 39093 Tinned Iron Net Rings for landing nets or crab nets.

12 inches diameter..13c
14 inches diameter..16c
16 inches diameter..22c
18 inches diameter..25c

IRON RING TO DRIVE

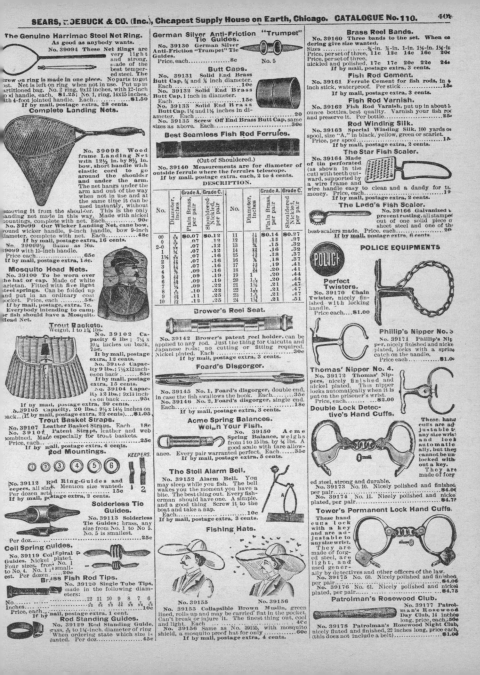

The Genuine Harrimac Steel Net Ring.

As good as anybody wants.

No. 39094 These Net Rings are very light and strong, made of the best tempered steel. The screw on ring is made in one piece. No parts to get lost. Net is left on ring when not in use. Put up in partitioned bag. No. 2 ring, 9x12 inches, with 12-inch wood handle, each, $1.25; No. 1, ring, 14x15 inches, with 4-foot jointed handle. Each..............$1.50
If by mail, postage extra, 28 cents.

Complete Landing Nets.

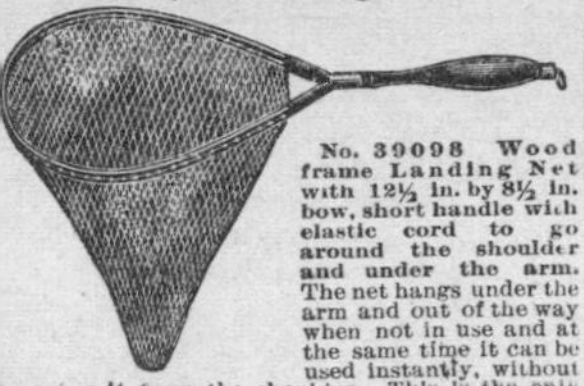

No. 39098 Wood frame Landing Net with 12½ in. by 8½ in. bow, short handle with elastic cord to go around the shoulder and under the arm. The net hangs under the arm and out of the way when not in use and at the same time it can be used instantly, without removing it from the shoulder. This is the only landing net made in this way. Made with nickel mountings, complete with net. Each..............90c
No. 39099 Our Wicker Landing Net, cane bow, round wicker handle, 9-inch handle, bow 9-inch diameter, complete with net. Each..............48c
If by mail, postage extra, 16 cents.
No. 39099½ Same as No. 39099 with 15-inch handle.
Price each....................65c
If by mail, postage extra, 18c.

Mosquito Head Nets.

No. 39100 To be worn over the hat or cap. Made of white tarletan. Fitted with five light steel springs. Can be folded up and put in an ordinary coat pocket. Price, each 58c
If by mail, postage, extra, 7c.
Everybody intending to camp or fish should have a Mosquito Head Net.

Trout Baskets.

Weight, 1 to 1¾ lbs.

No. 39102 Capacity 6 lbs ; 7½ x 10¼ inches on back, 75c.
If by mail, postage extra, 12 cents.
No. 39103 Capacity 9 lbs.; 7½x12inches on back 85c
If by mail, postage extra, 15 cents.
No. 39104 Capacity 12 lbs.; 9x13 inches on back 95c
If by mail, postage extra, 20 cents.
No. 39105 Capacity, 20 lbs.; 9½ x 14½ inches on back..(If by mail, postage extra, 22 cents)....$1.05

Trout Basket Straps.

No. 39107 Leather Basket Straps. Each 18c
No. 39108 Patent Straps, leather and web combined. Made especially for trout baskets.
Price, each............................25c
If by mail, postage extra, 4 cents.

Rod Mountings.

KEEPERS.

1 2

No. 39112 Rod Ring-Guides and Keepers, all sizes. Mention size wanted.
Per dozen sets..............15c
If by mail, postage extra, 2 cents.

Solderless Tie Guides.

No. 39113 Solderless Tie Guides; brass, any size from No. 1 to No 5. No. 5 is smallest.
Per doz...........................25c

Coil Spring Guides.

No. 39119 Coil Spiral Guides. Nickel plated. Four sizes, from No. 1 to No. 4. No. 1 is smallest. Per dozen.....20c

Brass Fish Rod Tips.

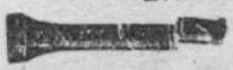

No. 39120 Single Tube Tips, made in the following diameters:

No.	12	11	10	9	8	7	6
Inches	3/32	7/64	3/32	7/64	3/32	5/32	7/32

Price, each..........10c
If by mail, postage extra, 1 cent.

Rod Standing Guides.

No. 39129 Rod Standing Guide, brass, 5/8 to 1¼-inch. diameter of ring When ordering state which size is wanted. Per doz...................45c

German Silver Anti-Friction "Trumpet" Tie Guides.

No. 5

No. 39130 German Silver Anti-Friction "Trumpet" Tie Guides.
Price, each................8c

Butt Caps.

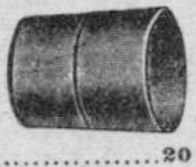

No. 39131 Solid End Brass Butt Cap, ¾ and ⅞ inch diameter.
Each..........................10c
No. 39132 Solid End Brass Butt Cap, 1 inch in diameter.
Each..........................15c
No. 39133 Solid End Brass Butt Cap, 1⅛ and 1¼ inches in diameter. Each...............................20
No. 39135 Screw Off End Brass Butt Cap, same sizes as above. Each..........................30c

Best Seamless Fish Rod Ferrules.

(Cut of Shouldered.)

No. 39140 Measurements are for diameter of outside ferrule where the ferrules telescope.
If by mail, postage extra, each, 2 to 4 cents.

DESCRIPTION.

No.	Diameter, inches	Grade A. Plain Brass, per pair	Grade C. Shouldered Nickled, per pair	No.	Diameter, inches	Grade A. Plain Brass, per pair	Grade C. Shouldered Nickled, per pair
00	5/32	$0.07	$0.12	11	11/16	$0.14	$0.27
0	3/16	.07	.12	12	23/32	.15	.27
2-0	7/32	.07	.12	13	¾	.15	.32
1	¼	.07	.12	14	25/32	.16	.32
1½	9/32	.07	.16	15	13/16	.18	.37
2	10/32	.07	.16	16	⅞	.18	.37
3	11/32	.07	.16	17	15/16	.19	.41
4	⅜	.09	.16	18	31/32	.20	.41
5	13/32	.09	.19	19	1	.20	.44
6	14/32	.09	.19	20	1 1/16	.20	.44
7	½	.09	.22	21	1⅛	.21	.47
8	9/16	.10	.22	22	1 3/32	.21	.47
9	19/32	.11	.25	23	1 3/16	.21	.47
10	12/16	.12	.25	24	1¼	.21	.51

Brower's Reel Seat.

No. 39142 Brower's patent reel holder, can be applied to any rod. Just the thing for Calcutta and Japanese rods; no cutting or fitting required. Nickel plated. Each 30c
If by mail, postage extra, 3 cents.

Foard's Disgorger.

No. 39145 No. 1, Foard's disgorger, double end, in case the fish swallows the hook. Each.........35c
No. 39146 No. 2, Foard's disgorger, single end. Each...18c
If by mail, postage extra, 3 cents.

Acme Spring Balances. Weigh Your Fish.

No. 39150 Acme Spring Balance, weighs from 1 to 15 lbs. by ¼ lbs. A good scale with tare allowance. Every pair warranted perfect. Each......35c
If by mail, postage extra, 5 cents.

The Stoll Alarm Bell.

No. 39152 Alarm Bell. You may sleep while you fish. The bell wakes you the moment you have a bite. The best thing out. Every fisherman should have one. A simple, and a good thing Screw it to the boat and take a nap.
Each..........................10c
If by mail, postage extra, 3 cents.

Fishing Hats.

No. 39155

No. 39156

No. 39155 Collapsible Brown Muslin, green lined, rolls up and may be carried flat in the pocket. Can't break or injure it. The finest thing out, cool and light. Each 40c
No. 39156 Same as No. 39155, with mosquito shield, a mosquito proof hat for only 60c
If by mail, postage extra, 4 cents.

Brass Reel Bands.

No. 39160 Three bands to the set. When ordering give size wanted.

Sizes	¾-in.	⅞-in.	1-in.	1⅛-in.	1¼-in.
Price, per set of three,	11c	12c	14c	16c	20c
Price, per set of three, nickled and polished,	17c	17c	20c	22c	24c

If by mail, postage extra, 3 cents.

Fish Rod Cement.

No. 39161 Ferrule Cement for fish rods, in 4 inch stick, waterproof. Per stick.............................15c
If by mail, postage extra, 3 cents.

Fish Rod Varnish.

No. 39162 Fish Rod Varnish, put up in about 2 ounce bottles, best quality. Varnish your fish rod and preserve it. Per bottle..............................25c

Rod Winding Silk.

No. 39163 Special Winding Silk, 100 yards on spool, size "A," in black, yellow, green or scarlet.
Price, per spool 15c
If by mail, postage extra, 2 cents.

The Star Fish Scaler.

No. 39164 Made of tin perforated (as shown in the cut) with teeth outward, supported by a wire frame and wire handle easy to clean and a dandy for the money. Price, each.......................................12c
If by mail, postage extra, 2 cents.

The Ladd's Fish Scaler.

No. 39166 Galvanized to prevent rusting, all stamped out of one solid piece of sheet steel and one of the best scalers made. Price, each.........................20c
If by mail, postage extra, 6 cents.

POLICE EQUIPMENTS

Perfect Twisters.

No. 39170 Chain Twister, nicely finished with locking handle.
Price each....$1.00

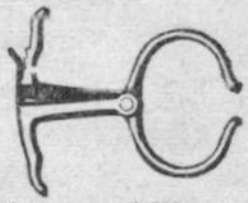

Phillip's Nipper No. 3

No. 39171 Phillip's Nipper, nicely finished and nickel plated, locks with a spring catch on the handle.
Price each............$1.00

Thomas' Nipper No. 4.

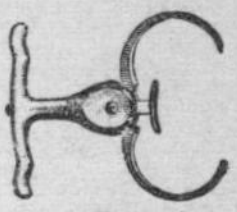

No. 39172 Thomas' Nippers, nicely finished and nickel plated. This nipper locks automatically when it is put on the prisoner's wrist.
Price, each............$2.00

Double Lock Detective's Hand Cuffs.

These hand cuffs are adjustable to any size wrist and lock automatically, but they cannot be unlocked without a key.
They are made of forged steel, strong and durable.
No. 39173 No. 10. Nicely polished and finished per pair..$4.00
No. 39174 No. 11. Nicely polished and nickel plated, per pair...............................$4.75

Tower's Permanent Lock Hand Cuffs.

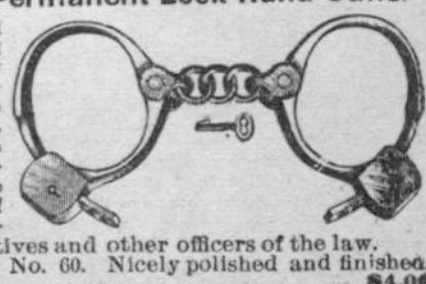

These hand cuffs lock with a key and are adjustable to any size wrist. They are made of forged steel, are light, and used generally by detectives and other officers of the law.
No. 39175 No. 60. Nicely polished and finished per pair..$4.00
No. 39176 No. 61. Nicely polished and nickel plated, per pair...............................$4.75

Patrolman's Rosewood Club.

No. 39177 Patrolman's Rosewood Day Club, 14 inches long, price, each..50c
No. 39178 Patrolman's Rosewood Night Club, nicely fluted and finished, 22 inches long, price each, (this does not include a belt)...............$1.00

Camp Chairs and Stools.

No. 40312 Canvas Top Camp Stool, well made. Price, each................20c
No. 40314 Canvas Top Camp Chair, same as No. 40312, with back. Price, each................30c

The U. S Folding Cot, $1.75.

The U. S. Folding Cot. Just the thing for camping purposes, covered with either white or brown 10-oz. duck. This is the tightest, strongest and most compact folding cot made. It has the only practical pillow ever put on a cot. It is easier opened and closed and folds into less space than any other cot. The duck will wear longer and legs stand more strain, and will stand on more uneven ground because not being stretched with a stretcher. Length, 6 feet, 3 inches. Width, 29 inches. Dimensions, when folded and ready for shipment, 6 feet, 3 inches by 5 inches by 2 inches. Weight, 15 pounds.
No. 40315 Price, complete with pillow......$1.75
No. 40316 Price, complete without pillow.. 1.50

Gold Medal Folding Chair.

No. 40320 Gold Medal Folding Camp Chair. The handiest chair made; the canvas can be taken off instantly and the chair folded as shown in the small cut. Folded, 3 feet long.
Price, each......$1.25

No. 40320

Gold Medal Folding Camp Bed.

No. 40322 Gold Medal Folding Camp Bed, covered with heavy blown canvas, guaranteed to hold 1,000 pounds. Price, each, with pillow, size, folded, 3 feet long by 5 inches square. Price, each......$2.50

BOAT ANCHORS.

No. 40434 Boat Anchors, black wrought iron, regular shape. Per lb. Per lb.
5 to 15 lbs.......12c   30 to 50 lbs.......9c
15 to 30 lbs.......11c   50 lbs. or over......9c

Life Preservers.

No. 40438 Never Sink, Cork Jackets, adopted as standard and the government inspector's stamp on each one; easily put on, durable and has great buoyancy. Weight, 5 lbs. Each...$1.85
No. 40440 Life Belts, in squares, similar to the "Never Sink" and buckles on the same way. One of the best in the market; safe and durable. Each......$1.20

The Mighty Mite Camp Stove.
Pneumatic. Non-Explosive.

THE MIGHTY MITE
CLOSED

No. 40445

IN OPERATION

The only Folding Gasoline Stove made. Boils a gallon of water in four minutes.
The Mighty Mite Folding Stove. Folds up into a small package; covered thoroughly in japanned case, with neat handle; can be carried in the hand or hung from the shoulder with sling straps. This stove is just the thing for hunting, fishing, camping, boating, picnicking, tourists, miners, and prospectors, etc. Made for gasoline. The gasoline stove will burn nine hours without refilling. To cook on this stove requires but a moment to make ready, and will boil a gallon of water in four minutes and cook anything. Full directions with each stove. Single burner. Size of package, 7x7x1 inches; weight, 4¼ lbs.
No. 40445 Price for Single Burner, for Gasoline, each......$3.50

Showing outfit opened.

No. 40454 The Camp Outfit shown in this cut is specially adapted for use in conjunction with the Mighty Mite stove. The chief features of this outfit are compactness, lightness, strength, etc. On wet days a meal may be cooked indoors by using the Mighty Mite stove. The outfit for four persons contains 33 pieces and weighs 6¾ lbs.; and when packed is 9x8½x4 inches. Outfit for six persons contains 45 pieces and weighs 6¼ lbs.; and is same size as for four persons. Contents are as follows: 1 frying pan with detachable handle, one 3-quart pan, 1 coffee pot, 1 sugar box, 1 coffee box, 1 salt can, 1 pepper can, 1 asbestos mat, knives, forks, tablespoons, teaspoons, tin plates, cups. The neatest and best outfit on the market.
Outfit for four persons, our special price...$3.50
Outfit for six persons, our special price......4.25

Camping Outfits Complete at $4.25 and $5.75.

KAMP KOOK'S KIT

No. 40455 Pat. March 10, '96
Cut of kit unpacked.

No. 40455 Wilson's Kamp Kook's Kit. Just the thing for camping out. 53 pieces. Fire Jack, 2 boilers suitable for using as an oven, fry pan, coffee pot and all utensils and tableware for a party of six. Everything first class. Boilers are made of 26-gauge smooth steel. The entire kit nests in small space, and when packed ready for shipment makes a package 24½x 10½x8 inches, all nested together and can be firmly locked up by ordinary padlock. Weight, complete, 20 pounds.
Price complete..........$5.75
No. 40456 20-piece set, containing the stove and complete apparatus without the tableware. Price......$4.25

PAT. MARCH 10.96.

Cut of kit packed for shipment.

Kamp Komfort Heater.
Just The Thing for Heating Tents.

No. 40458 Wilson's Kamp Komfort Tent Heater. The largest and best tent heater on the market. Size, 15½x 12x15 inches, with 9 joints of pipe which telescope and pack inside of the stove for shipping. This stove burns anything, is airtight, with down draught. Holds fire all night. Has spark arrester which insures perfect safety. The pipe nests so closely in this stove, it leaves plenty of room for our Kamp Kook's Kit. Complete with fire Jack. Body made of No. 22 sheet steel. In lid with hasp for padlock, making a secure shipping case with handles ready to check as baggage. One size only. Price, each......$4.30

KAMP KOMFORT
No. 40458
Pat. pending.

FULL LINE OF GAME TRAPS IN
...HARDWARE DEPARTMENT...

Ferguson's (Patent) Universal Reflecting Hunting Lamp.

With Silver Plated Locomotive Reflector.
No. 40481 The Celebrated Ferguson's Hunting and Fishing Lamp. This is the most practical lamp ever invented for hunting, fishing, boating, traveling or driving at night, lighting log cabins, tents or shanties. It will burn the oil from ten to twelve hours without refilling and gives a powerful light by which an object from 40 to 60 yards distant can be readily seen. This lamp burns any ordinary lantern oil. Best results obtained from signal oil, or lard oil mixed with kerosene. The door or cap may be closed when desired, making a dark lantern without extinguishing the light. Black japanned lamp; height, 8½ inches; depth, 2¾ inches; face, 3 inches; weight, 17 ounces.
Price, with head attachment complete, each.$5.

TARGETS AND TRAPS.

Round Iron Figure Target. Figure springs up and rings bell when bull's eye is hit; can be reset with rope from the shooting stand.
No. 40460 12-inch diameter, heavy, for 22-cal rim fire cartridges. Weight 15 to 18 lb.
Each................$2.25
No. 40461 12-inch diameter, steel faced, 4-inch disc Bird is thrown up and bell rings when bull's eye is hit. For guns or cartridges not larger than 22-long. Weight, 12½ lbs
Each................$2.5

The Latest and Best Target Made—Our Special White Flyer.

NOTE OUR PRICES of $2.50 for 500, $4.75 for 1,000, and you will admit our price is below all others. We do not send Target C. O. D. Send cash with order.
No. 40462 This is no doubt the coming target, and will fly from any trap taking the Empire or Blue Rock pigeon. We believe them to be superior in quality to all other targets, and have made arrangements with the manufacturer for an enormous quantity. They having a white rim, make a lighter colored target than the others, which will be a great advantage on dark days. Try a barrel of White Flyers and you will surely want more. Weight, per barrel (500 targets) 148 pounds.
Price, per 1000, $4.75; per barrel (500).......$2.50
We must send targets C. O. D.

Expert Blue Rock Trap.
$6.50 for the Expert Blue Rock Trap is a great reduction in price, made possible by a very large purchase we recently made.
At $6.50 you will be owning this trap for less money than any dealer can buy it.
Our $6.50 Expert is a guarantee the best all around trap on the market. One that is used generally by clubs and trap shooters.
No. 40463 The New Expert Blue Rock Trap, so well known by all trap shooters and considered the best trap on the market. These traps will throw either the Blue Rock or White Flyer targets.
Our price, each, $6.50

Our Special Blue Rock Targets.

We have these Blue Rock Targets specially made so that if only two or three pellets strike them they will break. We do not send Blue Rock Targets C. O. D. Send cash with order.
No. 40464 Price, per barrel (500)......$3.75
Price, per 1,000......5.00
NOTICE—On any goods not described or listed in this catalogue and bought for you or made to order, we must ask cash in full with the order, and they cannot be returned under any circumstances if sent as ordered

Our Special Blue Rock Extension Trap.

No. 40465 Blue Rock Extension Trap. Each......$5.00

White Flyers Work Just as Well as other Targets in Blue Rock Traps.

BICYCLE DEPARTMENT.

AT FROM $11.75 TO $18.00 we offer a Line of New Model Up-to-date High-grade Bicycles as the Greatest Values that Go Out of This or Any Other City.

OUR LIBERAL C.O.D. TERMS.

WHILE NEARLY ALL OF OUR CUSTOMERS SEND CASH IN FULL and thus save express charges on return of money to us, which usually amounts to from 25 to 50 cents, **we will on receipt of $1.00,** send any bicycle to any address east of the Rocky Mountains, by express or freight C. O. D. subject to examination. **You can examine it at your railroad station,** and if found perfectly satisfactory, pay the railroad agent our price and express or freight charges.

OUR FREE TRIAL OFFER.

WE ARE WILLING TO SEND ANY BICYCLE to any address on our regular C. O. D. terms, allow you to give the wheel ten days' trial, during which time you can compare it with other bicycles and if at any time within ten days you have any reason to be dissatisfied with your purchase, you are at liberty to return the bicycle to us at our expense of freight charges both ways, and we will return your money.

THE EXPRESS CHARGES on a bicycle will average about as follows: 400 miles, **$1.00;** 600 miles **$1.50;** 1000 miles, **$2.00. Greater or less distance in proportion.**

THE FREIGHT on two bicycles will average about as follows: 200 miles, **60 cents.** 400 miles, **$1.00;** 600 miles, **$1.50;** 1000 miles, **$2.00. Greater or less distance in proportion.**

WITH EVERY BICYCLE we sell, excepting the Cincinnatus, which is **not guaranteed, we issue a written binding one year guarantee,** by the terms and conditions of which, if any piece or part gives out by reason of defective material or workmanship, we will replace or repair it free of charge. **With care one of our bicycles will last a natural lifetime.** With pneumatic tires, we issue a regular association written binding guarantee by the terms and conditions of which if the tire gives out by reason of defect in material or workmanship within sixty days, it will be repaired or replaced free of charge. **With care our special Seroco tire will give more and better service than any other tire made.**

Our $11.75 Cincinnatus Bicycle.

To meet competition we offer the Cincinnatus bicycle with complete equipment, including tires, pedals, saddle, tools, tool bag, handle bar and grips, for **$11.75. Frame:** The frame is 24 inches. gents'; 22 inches, ladies'; made from common tubing. unguaranteed. **Wheels** are 28-inch front and rear. **Cranks:** Stamped cranks. **Sprockets:** Sprockets and hubs from malleable castings, smooth finished. **Tires:** Low grade, unguaranteed, pneumatic tire. **Bearings:** The bearings are made from finished malleable castings and steel stampings. **Finish:** This bicycle is enameled in black, blue or maroon; highly nickeled ornaments and presents a very bright, showy and gaudy appearance.

At $11.75, without guarantee or recommendation, we furnish this wheel complete, either ladies' or gent's. **As $11.75 is our cash in full with order price,** we do not ship the wheel C. O. D., and do not guarantee it, but we offer it as the equal of bicycles that are being sold largely at $15.00 to $25.00.

Our special price.............................**$11.75**

Our $13.75 New Model Acme Jewel.

No. 41101 **$13.75.**

Our $13.75 Acme Jewel is built in one of the best bicycle factories in this country; of thoroughly reliable material by skilled mechanics and is free from all the earmarks of cheapness common to the cheap wheels that are being sold by department stores and others. **It is a thoroughly reliable bicycle, put out under our written, binding one year guarantee.**

Our $13.75 Acme Jewel comes with 22, 24 or 26-inch frame as desired. Flush joint, 1⅛-inch tubing, extra fine seamless tubing fork sides. Heavy nickel plating, arched prong made with handsome new style one piece hanger.

Good substantial wheel with good rims, with high grade spokes, well finished heavy nickel plated hubs with ball retainers throughout. Good grade heavy nickel plated handle bars with cork grips. Full padded saddle. Good plated ball bearing, ball retaining nickel plated pedals; thoroughly reliable, strong well finished chain. Gear 68 to 84 inches as desired. Finished in black, green or maroon. All usual parts nickel plated. Weighs about 28 pounds, and comes complete with handle bar, saddle, wrench, oiler, quick tire repair outfit and good quality tool bag.

At $13.75 we equip this wheel with our own high grade season guaranteed single tube pneumatic tires.

At $13.75 we guarantee to furnish you such a bicycle as you could not buy elsewhere at anything like the price.

No. 41101 Our special price.................**$13.75**

Ladies' New Model Acme Jewel.

No. 41103 **$13.75.**

Our Ladies' $13.75 Acme Jewel is made in the very latest style for this season.

They come regularly with 22-inch frame flush at every joint; handsomely nickeled arch crowns, very strong, well made frames with extra quality wood rims; good standard grade swaged spokes. Large heavy nickel plate barrel hubs; ball bearing with ball retainers. Well finished bearings with full ball bearing action and ball retainers. Handsome heavy nickel plated combination pedals, full ball bearing, handsome nickle plated sprockets; wheels geared 68 to 84 inches, as desired. **It comes enameled in black, green or maroon,** as desired. We furnish with it our own high grade association guaranteed single tube pneumatic tires, the celebrated Seroco, which we believe to be among the best on the market regardless of price.

It is given a very nice finish; all usual parts heavily nickel plated, and at **our special $13.75 price** comes complete with nickel plated handle bar; good quality full padded saddle, tool bag, all necessary tools and quick tire repair outfit.

No. 41103 Our special price.................**$13.75**

Our New Model Acme Prince.

No. 41105 **$14.75.**

This handsome up-to-date bicycle is built with a diamond flush joint frame, 22, 24, or 26-inch as desired. High grade steel connections, heavy nickel plate fork crown, heavy nickel plate drop or upturned handle bar. Well-made 28-inch wheels with good strong rims and swaged steel spokes, equipped with our own high grade season guaranteed Seroco single tube pneumatic tires, high grade, heavy nickel plated barrel hubs, with ball bearings and ball retainers, good grade, heavy nickel plate ball bearing and ball retaining pedals, late new style one piece crank hanger. **Handsome nickel plated sprockets;** the bearings are all made from fine tool steel, are all ball bearing, accurately true to guage. We use a good quality of chain. Gear 68 to 84 inches as desired. We furnish a high grade, full padded saddle, finish the wheel in either black, green or maroon as desired, with all usual parts nickel plated, and at our special $14.75 price, it comes complete with tool bag, pump, wrench, oiler, and repair kit.

No. 41105 Our special price...............**$14.75**

Our New Model Acme Princess.

No. 41107 **$14.75.**

You will find in this wheel all the up-to-date features of all the modern made bicycles. **It has a very handsome graceful drop curved 22-inch frame** made from the very best cold drawn tubing, steel connections throughout; heavy nickel plated arched crown; neatly curved fork sides; strong nickel plated handle bar; well made 28-inch wheels with extra quality wood rims, swaged spokes, heavy nickel plate barrel, hubs with full ball bearings and ball retainers. Handsome nickel plated sprockets and handsome nickel plated cranks. **Latest style one-piece hanger;** bearings made of tool steel, tempered in oil. All parts ball bearing and ball retaining, fitted with our own high-grade, season-guaranteed, single tube Seroco pneumatic tire; finished either in green, black or maroon enamel, all usual parts highly nickel plated. **And at our special $14.75 price the bicycle comes complete** with handle bar, padded saddle, ball bearing pedals, tool bag, all necessary tools and quick tire repair outfit.

No. 41107 Our special price..................**$14.75**

Our Celebrated Gents' Acme King for $15.75.

No. 41109 **$15.75.**

For $15.75 we offer this strictly high grade new model Acme King bicycle, a flush joint, one piece hanger, up-to-date wheel, put in under our written binding guarantee as the equal of bicycles that retail everywhere at more than double the price.

This is a strictly high grade wheel, the frame 22, 24 or 26-inch as desired, made from the highest grade 1⅛-inch tubing, handsomely finished, made with expander at the seat post, and at the handle bar. The wheels are 28-inch in diameter, made from high grade wood, rims high grade, swaged steel spokes, large tubular hubs heavily nickel plated, fitted with ball bearings and ball retainers. Handsome one-piece hanger, heavy nickel plated cranks and sprockets, the bearings carefully adjusted, all bearings ball bearing with ball retainers. High grade ball bearing pedals. The wheels are flush at every joint, including cluster seat post. They come finished in black, green or maroon enamel. All usual parts nickel plated. **Gear** 68 to 84 **inches** as desired, fitted with our own high grade single tube Seroco pneumatic tire, and at our special $15.75 price are furnished complete; an extra quality tool bag, all necessary tools, oiler, quick repair outfit, up or down turned nickle plated handle bar, high grade padded saddle and high grade pedals.

If you order this wheel at $15.75, and don't find it equal to any wheel you can buy anywhere at double the price, you are at liberty to return it to us at our expense and we will return your money.

No. 41109 Our special price...................**$15.75**

Our $15.75 New Model Ladies' Acme Queen Bicycle.

No. 41111 **$15.75.**

This $15.75 Ladies' Bicycle embodies all the new high grade up-to-date features. Flush at every joint, expander front and rear, cluster seat post, one-piece hanger, ball bearing everywhere, strictly high grade.

This high grade wheel is built with a handsome 22-inch drop curved frame, in the highest grade 1⅛-inch diamond steel tubing. Fork sides, beautifully shaped, heavy nickel plate fork crown, wheels 28 inches in diameter, high grade, made from high grade wood, hubs high grade, swaged steel spokes, Thayer large tubular hubs, turned from bar steel, heavily nickel plated, ball bearing and ball retaining expander at the seat post and handle bars. High grade chain cones and balls. Perfect one-piece hanger, with handsome nickel plated sprockets and cranks. **All bearings are ball bearing, all carefully adjusted.** The pedals a high grade combination, heavily nickel plated, ball bearing and ball retaining; saddle, high grade full padded saddle, and the handle bar drop or upturned high grade, nickel plated. Tires our own high grade guaranteed single tube Seroco pneumatic. They come enameled in either black, green or maroon, highly finished, with all usual parts heavily nickel plated. Gear, 68 to 84 inches, as desired.

At our special $15.75 price we furnish this bicycle complete with handle bars, saddle, dress guard, combination pedals, tool bag, all necessary tools, oiler and quick repair outfit.

Our 15.75 price is based on the actual cost of material and labor, with but our one small percentage of profit added; the best wheel ever turned out at the price.

No. 41111 Our special price.................**$15.75**

Our Daily Sales of from 500 to 1,500 Bicycles

Going into every state and territory in the Union, is made possible by reason of our giving such values in high grade bicycles, that where one wheel goes,

Orders for Others Soon Follow.

Boys' All Steel Velocipedes.

Give the boy all the fun he wants at the expense of a few pennies.

We show an all steel velocipede that will stand a "heap of racket" on the part of the restless youth. **There are no nuts or bolts in the head connections to rattle or come loose.** It is adjustable and can be taken apart in shipping. The coil spring in seat does not sag or get out of repair. **We use the best drive wheel made in this velocipede.** The manner in which the fork and backbone are secured to head and axle is a new method **far superior to any other, and makes them doubly strong.** The handle is of one piece and stationary. The frames are made of malleable iron. Made both with steel tires or rubber tires. Prices as follows:

STEEL TIRES.

No. 41127 Front wheel, 16 in.....$1.35
No. 41129 Front wheel, 20 in.....1.75
No. 41130 Front wheel, 24 in.....2.15
No. 41131 Front wheel, 26 in.....2.55
No. 41133 Front wheel, 28 in.....2.95

RUBBER TIRES.

No. 41135 Front wheel, 16 in.....$2.95
No. 41137 Front wheel, 20 in.....3.45
No. 41139 Front wheel, 24 in.....3.95
No. 41141 Front wheel, 26 in.....4.45
No. 41143 Front wheel, 28 in.....4.95

Tricycles.

Notwithstanding the immense popularity of the bicycle, the tricycle still remains in favor. Many parents prefer them for their children by reason of their safety, convenience, and the ease with which they can be run by the little girl or boy. The tricycle which we illustrate is made for girls or boys from two to fifteen years. **They are constructed with especial care,** and will stand the abuse they very frequently receive. They are very easy running and handsomely finished. The improved spring seat takes all vibration, and being upholstered in plush and finished with back, makes riding easy and comfortable. Frame is enameled black. Quoted with iron tire wheels or C plate rubber tire wheels. The following are our special prices:

IRON TIRE WHEELS.

No. 41145 Rear wheels, 18 in.....$3.35
No. 41147 Rear wheels, 20 in.....4.45
No. 41149 Rear wheels, 22 in.....5.30
No. 41151 Rear wheels, 26 in.....6.35
No. 41153 Rear wheels, 30 in.....7.35

RUBBER TIRE WHEELS.

No. 41155 Rear wheels, 18 in.....$5.75
No. 41157 Rear wheels, 20 in.....6.30
No. 41159 Rear wheels, 22 in.....8.25
No. 41161 Rear wheels, 26 in.....9.95
No. 41163 Rear wheels, 30 in.....11.75

The Dunlop Detachable Tires.

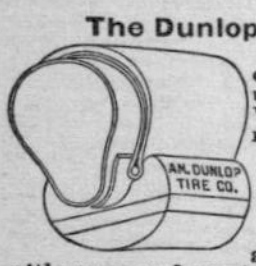

These tires are of the clincher pattern and can only be used on special Dunlop rims. We quote prices on tires and rims separately, as follows:

No. 41814 Dunlop Detachable Tires, 28x1⅝ inch, complete with pump and repair outfit. Price, per pair. .$7.50

No. 41815 Dunlop Detachable Tires, 28x1½ inch, complete with pump and repair outfit. Price per pair...$7.50

No. 41816 Inner tubes, with valve, for Dunlop tire, either 28x1⅝ or 28x1½ inch (always state size wanted). Price, each.....$1.35
If by mail, postage extra, each, 15c.

No. 41817 Dunlop outer casings, either 28x1⅝ or 28x1½ inch, (always state size wanted). Price, each.....$3.25
If by mail, postage extra, each, 25 cents.

No. 41819 Wood rims, for Dunlop tires, 28x1⅝ or 28x1½ inch, drilled 32 and 36 holes, (always state size wanted). Price, per pair.....$1.25

Our Own Single Tube Tires.

A most satisfactory single tube tire, made for us by one of the foremost tire concerns in America. We have used thousands of pairs and can recommend them as being first class. We furnish a pump and repair outfit with every pair. Size, 28x1⅝-inches.

No. 41818 Single Tube Tires. Price, per pair $3.50

Morgan & Wright's Plain Double Tube Tires.

Too well known to require special notice here.

No. 41820 Style S. Size, 28x1¼ inches. Price, per pair.....$6.00
No. 41821 Style D. Size, 28x1⅜ inches. Price, per pair.....$6.00
No. 41822 Style X. Size, 28x1¾ inches. Price, per pair.....$6.00
No. 41823 Style G. Size, 26x1¼ inches. Price, per pair.....$5.00
No. 41824 Style G. Size, 24x1¼ inches. Price, per pair.....4.50
No. 41825 Style G. Size, 20x1¼ inches. Price, per pair.....4.00
No. 41826 Cactus Tires. Sizes, 28x1½ or 1⅝ or 1¾ inches. Price, per pair.....$6.75
No. 41827 Plank Road Tires. Sizes, 28x1½ or 1⅝ or 1¾ inches. Price, per pair.....$6.75
No. 41828 Export Tandem Tires. Sizes, 28x1½ or 1⅝ or 1¾ inches. Price, per pair.....$6.75

Parts of Morgan & Wright's Double Tube Tires.

It is necessary that exact size be stated in order.

No. 41835 Morgan & Wright Outer Casings. Price, each.....$2.05
If by mail, postage extra, each, 25 cents.

No. 41836 Morgan & Wright Plain Inner Tubes. Price, each.....75c
If by mail, postage extra, each, 12 cents.

No. 41837 Morgan & Wright Valve and Stem, complete. Price, each.....15c
If by mail, postage extra, each, 2 cents.

No. 41838 Morgan & Wright Valve only. Price, each.....10c
If by mail, postage extra, each, 2 cents.

No. 41839 Morgan & Wright Stem only. Price, each.....8c
If by mail, postage extra, each, 2 cents.

Morgan & Wright's Single Tube Tires.

We quote only the principal sizes.

No. 41844 Sizes, 28x1½ or 1⅝ or 1¾ inches. Price, per pair.....$6.50

The C. & J. Detachable Tires.

No. 41850 G. & J. Detachable Tires, 28x1⅝-inch, complete including pump and repair outfit. Price, per pair.....$7.50

No. 41851 G. & J. Detachable Tires, 28x1½-inch, complete, including pump and repair outfit. Price, per pair.....$7.50

No. 41852 G. & J. Inner Tubes, with G. & J. valves, for 28x1⅝-inch tire. Price.....$1.35
If by mail, postage extra, each, 15 cents.

No. 41853 G. & J. Inner Tubes, with G. & J. valves for 28x1½-inch tire. Price, each.....$1.35
If by mail, postage extra, each, 15 cents.

No. 41854 G. & J. Outer Casings. Always state exact size wanted. Price, each.....$3.25
If by mail, postage extra, each, 25 cents.

No. 41855 G. & J. Clincher Rims, for any of above listed tires, drilled ready for use. Always state number of holes desired. Price, per pair, $1.00

Vim Tires for 1900.

It is one of the best single tube tires made.

No. 41860 Vim Road Tires, 28x1⅝-inch, complete with pump and repair outfit. Price, per pair..$5.95

No. 41861 Vim Tandem Tires, 28x1⅝-inch, complete with pump and repair outfit. Per pair..$6.95

Hartford Tires.

Hartford tires of the single tube variety require no extended description.

No. 41864 Hartford Tires No. 80, string fabric, 28x1⅝-inch, complete with pump and repair outfit. Price, per pair.....$6.50

No. 41865 Hartford Tires No. 77, woven fabric, 28x1⅝-inch, complete with pump and repair outfit. Price, per pair.....$6.00

No. 41866 Hartford Tires No. 70, medium grade woven fabric, 28x1⅝-inch, complete with pump and repair outfit. Price, per pair.....$5.00

Gents' Padded Saddle, 70 Cents.

Our thoroughly up-to-date Padded Saddle, improved construction, giving a firm and comfortable seat, as well as a handsome appearance. Made of tan colored leather, top and bottom carefully stitched together around the edges. The base is of sheet steel, covered with compressed wool felt, which is acknowledged to be the most suitable material for seating purposes. Saddles are fitted with a finely nickeled spring, and each saddle is accompanied by a good clamp.

No. 41876 Gents' Saddle. Price, each.....70c
If by mail, postage extra, each, 25 cents.

Our Ladies' Padded Saddle.

This is a properly constructed hygienic saddle, the kind recommended by physicians. Made so as to combine perfect comfort with durability and good appearance. Top and bottom coverings are of fine quality, durably stitched on the edges. We furnish these saddles in tan colored leather, as this has proven to be the most popular color the past few seasons. Every saddle is equipped with a finely nickeled spring and clamp.

No. 41878 Ladies' Saddle. Price, each.....70c
If by mail, postage extra, each, 25 cents.

Genuine Christy Anatomical Saddle.

GENTS' MODEL. Metal base, with coil **spring;** hair padding; top covered with maroon colored leather. A most comfortable saddle.

No. 41880 Gents' Christy Anatomical Saddle. Price, each.....$1.45
If by mail, postage extra, each, 30 cents.

LADIES' MODEL. Same construction as above except wider at cantle and a shorter pommel. A very desirable saddle for the ladies.

No. 41882 Ladies' Christy Anatomical Saddle. Price, each.....$1.45
If by mail, postage extra, each, 30 cents.

Our Leader Pedals.

Elegant in design, first class in finish and fully guaranteed. Broken parts will be cheerfully replaced if sent to us prepaid. Made in standard size with ½-inch, 20-thread pedal pins. Mated right and left. **Always state catalogue number of style desired.**

No. 41884 Men's Rat Trap Pedals. Per pair..75c
If by mail, postage extra, per pair, 18 cents.

No. 41885 Men's Combination Pedals. Per pair.....90c
If by mail, postage extra, per pair, 22 cents.

No. 41886 Ladies' Combination Pedals. Per pair.....90c
If by mail, postage extra, per pair, 22 cents.

Perfection Pedals.

So named because they are elegantly constructed, using the best material, embodying a handsome design with a superb finish. In construction, simplicity and durability are the main features. Ball retaining and practically dust proof. We can cheerfully recommend these pedals to the most fastidious, as they will prove a delight to all riders who use them. Made with ½-inch 20-thread pedal pins, both in rat trap and rubber combination.

No. 41888 Gents' Rat Trap. Per pair.....$1.20
If by mail, postage extra, 18 cents.

No. 41889 Gents' Combination. Per pair. 1.35
If by mail, postage extra, 22 cents.

No. 41890 Ladies' Combination. Per pair. 1.35
If by mail, postage extra, 22 cents.

Star Pedals.

Famous the world over. Cannot be beat for quality, durability and finish. These pedals always satisfy the most fastidious and are **fully guaranteed.** Pedal pins are ½-inch, 20-threads. Right and left.

No. 41892 Men's Rat Trap Pedals. Per pair.....$1.25
If by mail, postage extra, per pair, 20 cents.

No. 41893 Men's Combination Pedals. Per pair.....$1.30
If by mail, postage extra, per pair, 25 cents.

No. 41894 Ladies' Combination Pedals. Per pair.....$1.30
If by mail, postage extra, per pair, 25 cents.

Tool Bags.

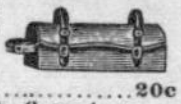

The cut shows our cheapest tool **bag, well sewed, well made and durable.**

No. 41900 Our special price, each.....20c
If by mail, postage extra, each, 6 cents.

Bicycle Tool Bag.

Made of polished grain leather; extra quality; triangular shape; fastened with clasp; **very strongly riveted, and handsomely embossed;** furnished in black or russet. **This is one of the handsomest bags made,** and is the prevailing style.

No. 41902 Our special, each....35c
If by mail, postage extra, each, 8 cents.

High Grade Gents' Tool Bag.

Large and roomy, to accommodate pump, kit, wrench, etc. Sensibly proportioned, elegantly embossed, made of the best quality oak tanned leather, straps to match and patent clasps, which is the most convenient and at the same time the most expensive trimming extant. Edges are well sewed and we are proud of the value we can give you in this article. **You cannot duplicate this bag anywhere else at double our price.**

No. 41904 Gents' High Grade Bag. Price, each.....35c
If by mail, postage extra, each, 7 cents.

The Ladies' Delight Tool Bag.

Just think of it! A swell, handsomely proportioned bag of the desirable **Pistol Pocket** pattern, elegantly embossed, with fine clasp fastening and straps to attach to frame. This bag is really a beauty, made of fine quality oak tanned leather. Now is the time to order, before they are all gone. In size they are roomy, to accommodate pump, wrench, oiler, etc.

No. 41906 Ladies' Fancy Tool Bag. Price, each.....35c
If by mail, postage extra, each, 6 cents.

Bicycle Tourists' Case.

Shaped as per cut, stock size 18¾ inches long, 16¾ inches wide, 5½ inches at head, 3⅛ inches thick. Made of canvas, with leather straps to attach to frame.

No. 41908 Tourist Case.
Price, each..........................**$1.00**

The 20th Century Gas Headlight.

Burns any loose Carbide six to eight hours with one charge. Aluminum Parabola Reflector, which spreads a wonderful light.

A brass Carbide holder accompanies every lamp, together with full directions for handling same. New adjustable lamp bracket, with Gossamer hood to protect lamp from dirt and rain, when not in actual use.

No. 41910 20th Century Gas Headlight. Price, each..........................**$2.25**
If by mail, postage extra, each, 35 cents.

The Solar Acetylene Gas Lamp.

Undoubtedly the most widely known gas lamp on the market. It makes a most beautiful appearance with its large jewel side lights. The lamp is 7 inches high, of very heavy brass elegantly nickel plated. It has a double convex lens 2½ inches in diameter, removable for cleaning. Special bracket fits either on head or fork of bicycle.

No. 41916 Solar Gas Lamp. Price,each....**$2.50**
If by mail, postage extra, each, 40 cents.

The Automatic Gas Lamp.

One of the simplest Gas Lamps on the market, and is actually, as its name implies, automatic. Simply charge it, light it, then leave it alone and you have a steady, bright light until charge of carbide is exhausted. **Burns from six to eight hours according to the amount of carbide used.** Use any loose form of Calcium Carbide. Each lamp packed separately with directions for use.

No. 41918 Automatic Gas Lamp
Price, each..........................**$1.95**
If by mail, postage extra, each, 25 cents.

The Bundy Gas Lamp.

Mechanically correct, of several season's practical service. It generates gas evenly, and purifies it before burning. This lamp uses carbide cartridges. In strength, durability and light-giving quality, **the Bundy lamp is certainly a leader in its class.** The lens and reflector are certainly the most powerful made, and assist greatly in distributing the light produced by the lamp. Every lamp carefully packed in a separate box, complete with brackets and directions.

No. 41920 Bundy Gas Lamp. Price, each, **$2.50**
If by mail, postage extra, each, 40 cents.

The Bundy Lamp burns cartridge charges, prepared to burn from six to eight hours, hermetically sealed. We furnish these charges packed one dozen in a box.

No. 41921 Bundy Lamp Cartridges. Per doz., **40c**

The Solitaire Gas Lamp.

Made of brass, beautifully nickel plated; the smallest good gas lamp before the public. Will burn for four to five hours, gives a very good light and it is certainly the best cheap gas lamp made. Ordinary granulate carbide is used in this lamp. It is fitted with a combination bracket, suitable for head or fork.

No. 41924 Solitaire Gas Lamp. Price, each, **$1.40**
If by mail, postage extra, each, 18 cents.

Calcium Carbide in Bulk.

Packed in 2-pound and 5-pound tin canisters, air tight, suitable for use in any acetylene gas bicycle lamp not requiring specially prepared cartridges.

No. 41926 Carbide, in 2-lb. cans. Price, each, **25c**
No. 41927 Carbide, in 5-lb. cans. Price, each, **50c**

The 20th Century Headlight.

This well known bicycle lamp does not need much description. It is smaller, lighter, and simpler than ever, many improvements being made for 1900, but all with a view to increasing its already **great light-giving capacity.** It has the Parabola reflector, self locking wick, **cannot jar out.**

Rigid bracket, adjustable to fit any angle on fork or head; also has a bail handle, for use as a hand lantern. **Burns kerosene.**

No. 41930 20th Century Oil Lamp. Price, each...**(If by mail, postage extra, 25 cents.)..$1.75**

The Banner Oil Lamp.

Made of brass, riveted wherever there are joints, no solder to melt. Has a hinged front door, wick locking device. Oil fount is removable and reversible. This is a thoroughly satisfactory lamp in every respect.

No. 41932 Banner Lamp. Price, each..........................**$1.45**
If by mail, postage extra, 20 cents.

Our Dandy Lamp.

The best cheap oil lamp made. Entirely of brass, handsomely nickel plated, no solder to melt, no parts to fall apart while riding. Burns kerosene oil, is five inches high and easily kept clean.

No. 41934 Our Dandy Lamp.
Price, each..........................**68c**
If by mail, postage extra, 15 cents.

Handle Bars.

Made in the well known Schinneer pattern, either up or down turn; of best tubing, heavily nickel plated on copper. These bars are 18 or 20 inches wide, as desired, fitted with cork grips. Stem is of standard size, ⅞-inch in diameter. Don't fail to secure one of these handsome bars.

No. 41936 Up Turn Bar, either 18 or 20 inches wide. Price, each..........................**75c**
If by mail, postage extra, 25 cents.
No. 41937 Up Turn Bar, with expander. Price, each....**(If by mail, postage extra, 27 cents)**...**90c**
No. 41938 Down Turn Bar, either 18 or 20 inches wide. Price, each..........................**70c**
If by mail, postage extra, 25 cents.
No. 41939 Down Turn Bar, with expander. Price, each.**(If by mail, postage extra, 27 cts.)**..**85c**

Adjustable Handle Bar.

This bar is strongly made and can be transformed into either a down turn, or an up-turn-bar, as desired, besides any intermediate positions. **Always specify size of stem;** ⅞-inch will be sent unless otherwise ordered.

No. 41942 Adjustable Handle Bar, complete with grips. Price, each..........................**$1.25**
If by mail, postage extra, 27 cents.
No. 41943 Adjustable Bar, with expander. Price, each....**(If by mail, postage extra, 29 cents)**....**75c**

The Sanger Adjustable Handle Bar.

This is the original Sanger bar, which after a thorough test in competition with all styles of patent adjustable bars stands today at the head of this class of equipment. It is made of the best cold drawn seamless tubing with Swedish steel stem head and drop forged arm lugs; ⅞-inch stem, 21 inches wide. Any adjustment from extreme rams style to extreme raised.

No. 41944 Sanger Bar, with grips, plain stem. Price, each..........................**$1.25**
No. 41946 Sanger Bar, with grips, expander stem. Price..**(If by mail, postage extra, each, 30c)..$1.35**

Our 20-Cent Bell.

Electric or double stroke, large gong 2 inches in diameter. Made of pure bell metal. Strong steel base and reliable double screw fastening. **It is handsomely nickel plated** and a beautiful bell at a very low price.

No. 41958 Price, each..........................**20c**
If by mail, postage extra, each, 6 cents.

Decorated Bell for 45 Cents.

A beautiful bell, with gong made from pure metal. Base and all movement parts made of brass, every part being elegantly nickel plated. This bell has that celebrated Rotary Electric Movement, so pleasant to the ear, and is a beauty.

No. 41960 Decorated Bell. Price, each.....**45c**
If by mail, postage extra, each, 6 cents.

The Double Chimes Bell. One bell, with two gongs, of four different tones, harmonioudly blended, making really the most musical sound imaginable. Quadruple stroke, so that one, two, three or four strokes can be made, as desired, at one operation of the lever. Bell 2 inches in diameter.

No. 41962 Double chimes Bell. Price, each..**50c**
If by mail, postage extra, each, 10 cents.

The Continuous Ringing Bell, can be made to ring 5 minutes, works like a watch; by turning the gong to the right, you wind up the continuous ringing mechanism, by simply pressing the lever, the bell will ring for any desired length of time. Gong is of the beaded pattern, 2⅝-inch diameter, made of pure bell metal, base of steel fastened to handle bar by a double screw clamp. All parts elegantly nickel plated, and an ornament to any bicycle.

No. 41964 Continuous Ringing Bell. Price, each..........................**85c**
If by mail, postage extra, each, 12 cents.

Sprocket Lock.

A very handsome appearing lock, steel case, black finish, shackle of brass. Well made and a most remarkable bargain at our price.

No. 41966 Sprocket Lock.
Price, each..........................**12c**
If by mail, postage extra, each, 3 cents.

Yale Sprocket Lock.

Brass spring shackle steel case, finished ivory black. Actual size 2⅝ inches, 2 keys.

No. 41968 Yale Sprocket Lock.
Price, each..........................**19c**
If by mail, postage extra, each, 3c.

A Newly Designed Sprocket Lock.

Every rider needs a lock. This one is intended to be attached to front sprocket, thereby locking same securely, which makes it impossible for anyone to ride the bicycle in the owner's absence. This style is new, lock is neat and elegantly finished, made of real bronze.

No. 41970 Sprocket Lock. Each..**20c**
Postage extra, each, 3 cents.

Emperor Sprocket Lock.

Self Locking Spring. Has rolled bronze metal rod bolts, nickel plated key; a very good lock at a low price.

No. 41972 Emperor Lock.
Price, each..........................**25c**
If by mail, postage extra, each, 5 cents.

BICYCLE WHISTLES.

No. 41976 The Duplex Whistle gives two clear and distinct notes; **made of brass, heavily nickel plated, complete with chain and hook.** Price..........................**15c**
Postage extra, each, 3 cents.

No. 41978 The Gem Whistle; gives a soft, loud alarm, a favorite whistle. Price, with chain........**15c**
If by mail, postage extra, each, 3c.

Single Tube Whistles.

No. 41980 Single Tube Whistle; the strongest and shrillest whistle in use. The slightest effort is all that is required to use it. Price..........................**18c**
If by mail, postage extra, each, 3 cents.

The Security Cyclometer.

No. 41984 The Security Cyclometer for 28-inch wheels. Positively the most durable cyclometer ever presented to the rider. It fits around the barrel of front hub between the flanges and cannot be knocked or broken off in falls. The interference pin is placed on inside of fork, out of danger. Its mechanism is perfect, with a total register of 10,000 miles. It is finely nickel plated and thoroughly first class in every way.

Price, each...**(Postage extra, each, 3 cents.)...90c**

The Veeder Cyclometer.

No. 41986 The Veeder Cyclometer registers 10,000 miles and repeats. So well known to the riding public as to require no special introduction. It is the original barrel cyclometer, very neat and compact, as well as being thoroughly reliable; weighs but one ounce. It is both dust and waterproof, finely nickel plated, every instrument being carefully tested at factory. **Furnished for 28-inch wheels.** Price, each..........................**63c**
If by mail, postage extra, each, 3 cents.

Veeder Double Barrel Cyclometer.

No. 41987 The Veeder Double Barrel Cyclometer is practically two cyclometers set side by side. One registers to 10,000 miles and repeats. The other **is a trip cyclometer,** and registers to 100 miles; but at any moment may be set back to "0," enabling the rider to ascertain his mileage for any trip or hour. Furnished for 28-inch wheels. Price, each..........................**$1.20**
If by mail, postage extra, each, 5 cents.

The U. S. Cyclometers.

No. 41000 The U. S. Cyclometer Model 1 is sure to be one of the leading cyclometers for this year. This model has a total register of **10,000 miles, also an independent recorder of 100 miles.** By turning the end of case the trip can be set to "0" at will, without interfering with the total record. **The trip record shows daily trips or local distances,** while the total keeps **a perfect record of the season's mileage. Perfect mechanism and largest figures.** Made for 28-inch wheels.

Our special price, each..........................**60c**
If by mail, postage extra, each, 6 cents.

Pumps.

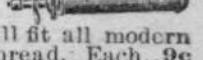

No. 41990 "A very windy Pump," made of good, strong material, and will **last 2 or 3 seasons.** The favorite style and size. **Single action,** including hose connection which will fit all modern valves, having a universal inside thread. Each..**9c**
If by mail, postage extra, each, 6 cents.

Our 40-Cent Giant Foot Pump.

No. 41992 The Giant Foot Pump, will not rust or corrode. Positively the best foot pump ever sold at this price. Sold in many retail stores at double our price. Made of brass, finely nickel plated. Barrel 1¼x12 inches, with a powerful plunger, large wood handle, a pump that will inflate a tire in a jiffy. Hose has a swivel connection that will fit all modern valves having a universal inside thread. You make no mistake in buying this pump.

Price, each..........................**40c**
If by mail, postage extra, each, 18 cents.

Pocket Foot Pump.

"Stand erect and pull the string." Can be carried in tool bag or pocket. Saves time and money and prevents a "crick" in the back. Can be handled by lady or child without exertion. The ideal tire inflator.

No. 41994 Pocket Foot Pump.
Price, each..........................**45c**
Postage extra, each, 10 cents.

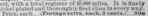

DEPARTMENT OF MEN'S CUSTOM TAILORING

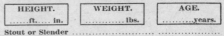

YOUR attention is called to our line of Men's Ready Made Clothing, Boys' Ready Made Suits, Overcoats and Ulsters, our Children's Two-Piece Knee Pants Suits, Reefer Suits, Vestee Suits, Winter Reefer Overcoats and Ulsters.

ON THE FOLLOWING PAGES we call your attention to our new line (MORE COMPLETE THAN EVER BEFORE) of Men's Fine Custom Tailoring, Suits, Overcoats, Ulsters and Pants, which we cut to measure and make to order at prices based on the actual cost of material and labor, with but our one small percentage of profit added, prices lower than are quoted by any other house for similar goods, prices that enable you to have your garments made to your measure at about the price you would be compelled to pay your dealer at home for ready-made garments.

CUSTOM TAILORING DEPARTMENT.

IN OUR CUSTOM TAILORING DEPARTMENT, we make to measure men's garments, employing only expert cutters and expert tailors, a class of mechanics, who turn out for us garments that cannot be equaled by any country tailor, garments in which we guarantee a distinctiveness in workmanship, style and fit not to be had from your tailor at home.

HOW OUR CUSTOM COATS ARE MADE.

EVERY COAT IS CUT BY AN EXPERT COAT CUTTER, made by special coat tailors. We use nothing but strictly high grade coat lining, and in all suits over $5.00 we use a fine grade of genuine imported Italian cloth to match the shade of the cloth. All coats are interlined and stiffened with the best imported canvas, and double stayed by our own patent process to insure lasting shape. All coats are satin piped throughout with fine Skinner satin, back of collar satin lined, stitched and stayed, fitted with fancy sanitary arm shields, sewed throughout with silk and linen. You will find the coat we make for you will fit better, be more shapely, more stylish, better trimmed, and will hold its perfect shape far better than any coat any tailor will make for you.

HOW OUR CUSTOM VESTS ARE MADE.

THE VESTS ARE ALL CUT TO MEASURE, by special vest cutters and made by special vest tailors. We use nothing but strictly high grade linings and trimmings; they are sewed throughout with silk and linen, and we believe, from our tailoring department, we turn out the best made and best fitting vests in this city.

HOW OUR CUSTOM PANTS ARE MADE.

IN OUR TAILORING DEPARTMENT, we employ special pants cutters who work on nothing but pants, special pants tailors who work only on pants, which insures better fitting, more shapely and better made pants than you could have made elsewhere. We use a very high grade of pants linings, facings and trimmings, strictly high grade reamed buttons, safety seamless pockets, pants are all sewed throughout with silk and linen and we guarantee them never to rip. You will find the pants we furnish you better fitting, more shapely and stylish than your local tailor can possibly produce.

HOW OUR OVERCOATS AND ULSTERS ARE MADE.

IN OUR TAILORING DEPARTMENT EVERY OVERCOAT is cut to measure by special cutters who work only on overcoats, made by special tailors who work only on overcoats and ulsters, thus insuring a better fitting, more stylish and better made overcoat than you can get elsewhere. They are lined with a special overcoat lining, stayed and stiffened by our own patent process, fancy satin piped, finished with fancy sanitary arm shields and sewed throughout with silk and linen.

SPECIAL NOTICE TO CUSTOMERS AT FAR DISTANT POINTS.

A SUIT OF CLOTHES can be sent by mail when packed in two separate packages. The postage on a suit is about $1.25. Should the postage be less than $1.25 we will promptly return the difference.
CASH FOR THE FULL AMOUNT must accompany your order, also $1.25 for postage when a suit is sent by mail.
FOR MAIL INSURANCE, 5 cents extra for each package worth $5.00 or under, and 5 cents extra for each additional $5.00 in value.

MEN'S READY MADE CLOTHING.

WE SHOW A VERY COMPLETE LINE of Men's ready made clothing in suits, overcoats, ulsters and pants, garments that are made for us under contract by one of the best makers in this country from strictly high grade fabrics. They are cut in the very latest style, only strictly high grade linings and trimmings are used; you will find the ready made garments we will furnish you will be better made, better trimmed and finished, more stylish and better fitting and at least 33⅓ per cent lower in price than anything you can buy from your dealer at home.

BOYS' AND CHILDREN'S READY MADE CLOTHING.

IN THIS DEPARTMENT WE INCLUDE EVERYTHING in the latest up-to-date styles in boys' and children's ready made clothing, including boys' long pants suits, knee pants suits, vestee suits and reefer suits, heavy storm excluding reefers, overcoats, ulsters, etc., etc., all at prices based on the actual cost of material and labor with but our one small percentage of profit added, prices that will mean a saving to you of from 33⅓ to 50 per cent.

OUR BINDING GUARANTEE.

EVERY GARMENT THAT GOES OUT OF OUR TAILORING AND CLOTHING DEPARTMENT is covered by a guarantee as to quality of material and workmanship, and any garment that you receive from us that is not perfectly satisfactory in every way, you are at liberty to return to us at our expense of express charges both ways, and we will immediately refund your money.

OUR $1.00 C. O. D. TERMS.

SEND US $1.00. SELECT THE GARMENT wanted by number, fill out our regular order blank, follow our rules for measurement, as plainly printed on this page, and we will send you any garment you may select by express C. O. D., subject to examination; you can examine it at your express office, and if found perfectly satisfactory, exactly as represented, and such value as you could not get elsewhere, pay the express agent our price and express charges less the $1.00 sent with order. Nearly all our customers send cash in full. By so doing you save the return charges on money to us, and you take no risk, for we will promptly refund your money if you are not perfectly satisfied.

HOW TO TAKE MEASURE.

IN ORDERING MEN'S TAILORING OR READY MADE SUITS, fill out our regular tailoring order blank, which is plainly printed on the back of every general merchandise order blank, or, if you have no order blank, on a plain sheet of paper state your measure, following printed directions:

HEIGHT.	WEIGHT.	AGE.
....ft.... in.	..........lbs.	..........years.

Stout or Slender ....

In taking measurements, the tape measure should be drawn moderately close but never tight. To avoid error, take each measurement twice and write it in your order blank, before completing other measurements.

WRITE MEASUREMENTS CAREFULLY.

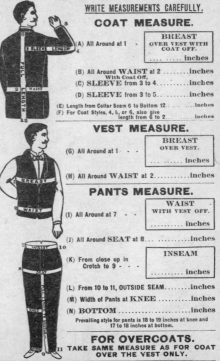

COAT MEASURE.

(A) All Around at 1 — BREAST OVER VEST WITH COAT OFF. ....inches

(B) All Around WAIST at 2 ....inches With Coat Off,
(C) SLEEVE from 3 to 4..........inches
(D) SLEEVE from 3 to 5..........inches
(E) Length from Collar Seam 6 to Bottom 12.......inches
(F) For Coat Styles, 4, 5, or 6, also give length from 6 to 2..........inches

VEST MEASURE.

(G) All Around at 1 — BREAST OVER VEST. ....inches

(H) All Around WAIST at 2 ....inches

PANTS MEASURE.

(I) All Around at 7 — WAIST WITH VEST OFF. ....inches

(J) All Around at SEAT at 8 ....inches

(K) From close up in Crotch to 9 — INSEAM ....inches

(L) From 10 to 11, OUTSIDE SEAM.......inches
(M) Width of Pants at KNEE..........inches
(N) BOTTOM ....inches

Prevailing style for pants is 18 to 19 inches at knee and 17 to 18 inches at bottom.

FOR OVERCOATS.

TAKE SAME MEASURE AS FOR COAT OVER THE VEST ONLY.

FOR MEN'S READY MADE CLOTHING take measure same as above OMITTING measurements (E), (F), (M) and (N), which are only intended for made to measure garments.
TO TAKE MEASURE FOR BOYS' LONG PANTS SUITS, OVERCOATS AND ULSTERS for boys from 12 to 19 years, follow same rules as given above for Men's Ready Made Clothing. Remember, 34 inches breast measure make your selections from men's side.
FOR BOYS' KNEE PANTS TWO-PIECE REEFER AND VESTEE SUITS, REEFER OVERCOATS and ULSTERS, for boys' from 4 to 14. STATE AGE OF BOY and say whether large or small of age, and from our long experience we can guarantee a perfect fit.
FOR FREE CLOTH SAMPLES of men's custom tailoring, including fashion plate, tape measure, rules for measurement, etc., write for free Sample Book No. 2K.
FOR FREE CLOTH SAMPLES of boys' and children's ready made clothing, write for free Sample Book No. 4K.

Style 3

Style 9

Style 2

Style 4

Style 1

Style 1

Style 8

Style 6

Style 5

Style 10

Style 12

CLOTH SAMPLES

of every number ARE FREE, all in Book No. 2K.

WRITE FOR IT

HECHT & CO.'S FANCY DARK, BLACK AND BLUE PLAID ENGLISH WORSTEDS IN SUITS TO MEASURE, $13.50.

No. 44245 FOR $13.50 WE MAKE TO MEASURE MEN'S SUITS from this very fine, heavy weight English worsted cloth. It is a very handsome pattern of black and dark blue in small plaids and it has an invisible chain of red. It is entirely new for this season, is from one of the best English mills, a good heavy weight that we can guarantee for wear; it is the equal of any fabric you will find in tailoring establishments at $25.00 to $30.00.

UNDERSTAND, every garment will be cut to measure and made to order by expert tailors. The coats will be lined with fine imported Italian cloth, interlined, padded, stayed and stiffened by our own present process and sewed throughout with silk and linen.

Price for suit, style 1 or 2	$13.50	Price for coat and vest, style 3, 4 or 5	$10.
Price for suit, style 3, 4 or 5	14.50	Price for coat and vest, style 6 or 8	14.
Price for suit, style 6 or 8	18.50	Price for coat and vest, style 9	16.
Price for suit, style 9	20.50	Price for pants	4.
Price for coat and vest, style 1 or 2	9.00	Price for overcoats, style 10	13.

$2.00 extra for men measuring over 42 inches breast measure.

For cloth samples of our entire line of men's custom tailoring write for Cloth Sample Book No. 2K.

STANTON'S EXTRA FINE IMPORTED DOUBLE DIACONAL FAST BLACK ENGLISH WORSTED CLOTH IN SUITS TO MEASURE, $13.50.

No. 44247 FOR $13.50 WE MAKE TO MEASURE MEN'S SUITS from this heavy weight, firmly woven genuine Stanton black English worsted, superior to any black clay worsted on the market. It is a fine through-and-through all-wool worsted fabric, a cloth that will not wear shiny, the same class of fast black worsted as will be found in the best tailoring establishments at fancy prices, a good black that makes up very stylish in a dress, semi-dress or business suit, suitable for all occasions, seasons and all classes.

THESE WORSTEDS get special attention in the worsted department of our tailoring establishment. We use the very finest of linings, interlinings, padding, staying, trimming and finishings, and we guarantee for you a distinctiveness in workmanship, style, and finish not to be had elsewhere.

Price for suit, style 1 or 2	$13.50	Price for coat and vest, style 3, 5 or 5	$10.
Price for suit, style 3, 4 or 5	14.50	Price for coat and vest, style 6 or 8	14.
Price for suit, style 6 or 8	18.50	Price for coat and vest, style 9	16.
Price for suit, style 9	20.50	Price for pants	4.
Price for coat and vest, style 1 or 2	9.00	Price for overcoats, style 10	13.

$2.00 extra for men measuring over 42 inches breast measure.

For samples of cloth of our entire line of men's custom tailoring, write for Cloth Sample Book No. 2K.

HEAVY WEIGHT PLAIN DARK OLIVE BROWN AUBURN MELTON CLOTH IN SUITS TO MEASURE, $14.00.

No. 44249 FOR $14.00 WE MAKE TO MEASURE MEN'S SUITS from this very fine imported auburn Melton cloth, a very rich shade of dark brown, an extra heavy weight, especially recommended for warm, comfortable suit for fall and winter wear; is a fabric we can guarantee is the equal of anything you can buy elsewhere at double the price. You will find the garments we will make for you from these goods will have a distinctiveness in fit and finish that you would not be likely to get elsewhere.

HOW OUR GARMENTS ARE LINED, TRIMMED AND FINISHED is fully explained in tailoring introductory page.

Price for suit, style 1 or 2	$14.00	Price for coat and vest, style 3, 4 or 5	$10.35
Price for suit, style 3, 4 or 5	15.00	Price for coat and vest, style 6 or 8	14.35
Price for suit, style 6 or 8	19.00	Price for coat and vest, style 9	16.35
Price for suit, style 9	21.00	Price for pants	4.65
Price for coat and vest, style 1 or 2	9.35	Price for overcoat, style 10	14.00

$2.00 extra for men measuring over 42 inches breast measure.

For samples of cloth of our entire line of men's custom tailoring write for Cloth Sample Book No. 2K.

BRADLEY-WELLS & CO.'S HEAVY WEIGHT DOUBLE DIACONAL DARK NAVY BLUE WORSTED SERGE IN SUITS TO MEASURE, $14.00.

No. 44251 FOR $14.00 WE MAKE TO MEASURE MEN'S SUITS from this extra fine, closely woven, heavy weight, fast color navy blue serge cloth. This is a fine imported serge fabric, heavy winter weight, just suitable for your around wear. It makes up very stylish in a dress, semi-dress or business suit. It is a goods you will find only in the representative tailoring establishments, and there at two to three times our price.

How we line, trim and finish these garments is fully explained in tailoring introductory page.

Price for suit, style 1 or 2	$14.00	Price for coat and vest, style 3, 4 or 5	$10.35
Price for suit, style 3, 4 or 5	15.00	Price for coat and vest, style 6 or 8	14.35
Price for suit, style 6 or 8	19.00	Price for coat and vest, style 9	16.35
Price for suit, style 9	21.00	Price for pants	4.65
Price for coat and vest, style 1 or 2	9.35	Price for overcoat, style 10	14.00

$2.00 extra for men measuring over 42 inches breast measure.

For samples of cloth of our entire line of men's custom tailoring, write for Cloth Sample Book No. 2K.

PLAIN SOLID BLACK HEAVY WEIGHT WINSLOW GERMAN VICUNA CLOTH IN SUITS TO MEASURE, $15.00.

No. 44253 FOR $15.00 WE MAKE TO MEASURE MEN'S SUITS from this heavy weight imported German Vicuna, a cloth that is too well known to require any lengthy description from us. You must at least see a sample of the goods to appreciate the value we are offering.

THIS IS A FINE ALL WOOL FABRIC, a velvety surface effect, a heavy wool, wear-resisting goods. For upon for wear, and for garments that will look stylish and dressy, there is nothing more desirable. In making those garments up we will use the very best of trimmings, black Italian cloth lining; the coat will be interlined padded, stayed stiffened, satin piped, fitted with fancy arm shields and every garment will be sewed throughout with silk and linen thread.

Price for suit, style 1 or 2	$15.00	Price for coat and vest, style 3, 4 or 5	$11.00
Price for suit, style 3, 4 or 5	16.00	Price for coat and vest, style 6 or 8	17.00
Price for suit, style 6 or 8	22.00	Price for coat and vest, style 9	19.00
Price for suit, style 9	24.00	Price for pants	5.00
Price for coat and vest, style 1 or 2	10.00	Price for overcoat, style 10	15.00

$2.00 extra for men measuring over 42 inches breast measure.

For samples of cloth of our entire line of men's custom tailoring, write for Cloth Sample Book No. 2K.

WEST OF ENGLAND FANCY GRAY AND BLUE MIXED HEAVY WEIGHT WORSTED IN SUITS TO MEASURE, $15.00.

No. 44255 FOR $15.00 WE MAKE TO MEASURE MEN'S SUITS from this heavy weight, through and through fancy English worsted cloth, a pattern entirely new for this season, a very dark gray relieved from the plain by a very small invisible hairline effect of green and black. It is a rich, modest, this year's pattern, one of the most stylish worsted fabrics that is shown. It is a class of goods that has been bought by city tailors largely and our special $15.00 price is made possible by reason of having contracted for a large quantity of these goods and of our facilities for making the garments up at the very minimum of cost.

HOW THESE GARMENTS ARE CUT, LINED, TRIMMED AND FINISHED is fully explained in tailoring introductory page.

Price for suit, style 1 or 2	$15.00	Price for coat and vest, style 3, 4 or 5	$11.00
Price for suit, style 3, 4 or 5	16.00	Price for coat and vest, style 6 or 8	17.00
Price for suit, style 6 or 8	22.00	Price for coat and vest, style 9	19.00
Price for suit, style 9	24.00	Price for pants	5.00
Price for coat and vest, style 1 or 2	10.00	Price for overcoat, style 10	15.00

$2.00 extra for men measuring over 42 inches breast measure.

For samples of cloth of our entire line of men's custom tailoring, write for Cloth Sample Book No. 2K.

STYLE 4

STANTON'S VERY FINEST, EXTRA HEAVY WEIGHT, PLAIN BLACK DOUBLE DIAGONAL, ALL-WOOL ENGLISH WORSTED CLOTH, $15.00.

No. 44257 FOR $15.00 we make to measure men's suits from this, the very finest black double diagonal heavy weight English worsted cloth woven, a fast black worsted that will give twice the wear of the ordinary clay worsted. For a very fine suit for dress, semi-dress or business, there is nothing that will give better satisfaction, there is no better plain black worsted for men's suitings. It is a fabric we can guarantee for wear, will be made up very stylish and dressy; we will use the very best imported Italian cloth lining, our finest trimmings and finishings, and we will endeavor to give you such garments as you could not get elsewhere.

Price for suit, style 1 or 2............$15.00	Price for coat and vest, style 3, 4 or 5..$11.00	
Price for suit, style 3, 4 or 5.......... 16.00	Price for coat and vest, style 6 or 8.... 17.00	
Price for suit, style 6 or 8.......... 22.00	Price for coat and vest, style 9........ 19.00	
Price for suit, style 9.......... 24.00	Price for pants......................... 5.00	
Price for coat and vest, style 1 or 2.... 10.00	Price for overcoat, style 10............ 15.00	

$2.00 extra for men measuring over 42 inches breast measure.
For samples of cloth of our entire line of men's custom tailoring write for Cloth Sample Book No. 2K.

OUR VERY FINEST PLAIN BLACK IMPORTED MUMMIE CLOTH IN SUITS TO MEASURE, $15.00.

No. 44259 FOR $15.00 we make to measure men's suits from this, our very finest imported plain black, raised pinhead surface effect, French Mummie cloth, one of the finest plain black, through-and-through all-wool worsteds on the market. This plain black pinhead surface Mummie cloth is a good heavy weight, suitable for fall or winter or year-around wear, such a fabric as you will find only in the best tailoring establishments, and there at fancy prices.

Price for suit, style 1 or 2............$15.00	Price for coat and vest, style 1 or 2..$10.00	
Price for suit, style 3, 4 or 5.......... 16.00	Price for coat and vest, style 3, 4 or 5 11.00	
Price for suit, style 6 or 8.......... 22.00	Price for coat and vest, style 6 or 8.. 17.00	
Price for suit, style 9.......... 24.00	Price for coat and vest, style 9...... 19.00	
	Price for pants......................... 5.00	
Price for overcoat, style 10..........		15.00

$2.00 extra for men measuring over 42 inches breast measure.
For samples of cloth of our entire line of men's custom tailoring write for Cloth Sample Book No. 2K.

STANTON'S VERY FINEST PLAIN DARK GRAY ENGLISH DOUBLE DIAGONAL WORSTED, $15.00.

No. 44261 STANTON'S VERY FINEST Plain Dark Gray English Double Diagonal Worsted in suits to measure, $15.00. FOR $15.00, a reduction of $2.00 from last season, we make to measure men's suits from this, our very finest heavy weight dark gray Stanton worsted. This is a plain gray made by the Stanton Mills of England, the finest Clay worsted they make. It is suitable for fall and winter or year-around, suitable in any style, all seasons and for all ages. Understand, our worsted garments are cut by special cutters and made by special tailors who work only on worsteds. We use very fine imported Italian cloth lining, the very best trimmings and finishings and we turn out garments with a distinctiveness in style, fit and finish not to be found elsewhere. $15.00 this season, $17.00 last season. By a favorable contract with the mills we were able to reduce the cost of the cloth and we make the difference in cost to us the difference in price to you.

Price for suit, style 1 or 2............$15.00	Price for coat and vest, style 3, 4 or 5 $11.00	
Price for suit, style 3, 4 or 5.......... 16.00	Price for coat and vest, style 6 or 8.. 17.00	
Price for suit, style 6 or 8.......... 22.00	Price for coat and vest, style 9...... 19.00	
Price for suit, style 9.......... 24.00	Price for pants......................... 5.00	
Price for coat and vest, style 1 or 2.... 10.00	Price for overcoat, style 10............ 15.00	

$2.00 extra for men measuring over 42 inches breast measure.
For samples of cloth of our entire line of men's custom tailoring write for Cloth Sample Book No. 2K.

TITUSVILLE FANCY RAISED PLAID DARK NAVY BLUE WORSTED IN SUITS TO MEASURE, $16.00.

No. 44263 FOR $16.00 we make to measure men's suits from this very fine imported worsted. It is fast dark navy blue in color. It is a ¾-inch plaid, effected by a satin ribbed weave effect, and is given a minute effect by raised worsted dots in the weave. It is a heavy weight for fall and winter and suitable for year-around. It is all fine wool, a through-and-through worsted and one of the handsomest, finest woven plain navy blue worsteds on the market.

Price for suit, style 1 or 2............$16.00	Price for coat and vest, style 3, 4 or 5.$11.70	
Price for suit, style 3, 4 or 5.......... 17.00	Price for coat and vest, style 6 or 8.... 17.70	
Price for suit, style 6 or 8.......... 23.00	Price for coat and vest, style 9........ 19.70	
Price for suit, style 9.......... 25.00	Price for pants......................... 5.30	
Price for coat and vest, style 1 or 2.... 10.70	Price for overcoat, style 10............ 16.00	

$2.00 extra for men measuring over 42 inches breast measure.
For samples of cloth of our entire line of men's custom tailoring, write for Cloth Sample Book No. 2K.

GLASSTON DARK FANCY SILK MIXED WORSTED SUITS TO MEASURE, $16.00.

No. 44265 $16.00 THIS SEASON; $18.00 LAST SEASON; a reduction of $2.00 in price, representing the actual difference in the cost of the material to us, and we give you the benefit by making this suit up on the basis of the actual cost of the material and labor under this season's contracts, with but our one small percentage of profit added. This is a very dark pattern of silk mixed. It is the Glasston weave, a goods we have handled for several seasons; a very dark pattern, almost plain black, with a black background and relieved by a fancy silk mixture of small pinhead effects in green and red.

Price for suit, style 1 or 2............$16.00	Price for coat and vest, style 3, 4 or 5 $11.70	
Price for suit, style 3, 4 or 5.......... 17.00	Price for coat and vest, style 6 or 8.. 17.70	
Price for suit, style 6 or 8.......... 23.00	Price for coat and vest, style 9...... 19.70	
Price for suit, style 9.......... 25.00	Price for pants......................... 5.30	
Price for coat and vest, style 1 or 2.... 10.70	Price for overcoat, style 10............ 16.00	

$2.00 extra for men measuring over 42 inches breast measure.
For samples of cloth of our entire line of men's custom tailoring, write for Cloth Sample Book No. 2K.

ALLARD-LEE & CO.'S FINE DARK DIAGONAL ENGLISH WORSTED CLOTH IN SUITS TO MEASURE, $16.00.

No. 44267 FOR $16.00 we make to measure men's suits from this very fine imported worsted fabric, a very dark pattern in a heavy double ribbed, double diagonal effect of black background, in which is woven a very small plaid, effected by very narrow invisible dotted cross lines of blue and olive and brown. This is one of the handsomest patterns we have seen. It is entirely new for this season, and it is the equal of anything you can buy in any tailoring establishment for all purposes at any price. How these garments are made, trimmed and finished is fully explained in tailoring introductory page.

Price for suit, style 1 or 2............$16.00	Price for coat and vest, style 3, 4 or 5 $11.70	
Price for suit, style 3, 4 or 5.......... 17.00	Price for coat and vest, style 6 or 8.. 17.70	
Price for suit, style 6 or 8.......... 23.00	Price for coat and vest, style 9...... 19.70	
Price for suit, style 9.......... 25.00	Price for pants......................... 5.30	
Price for coat and vest, style 1 or 2.... 10.70	Price for overcoat, style 10............ 16.00	

$2.00 extra for men measuring over 42 inches breast measure.
For samples of cloth of our entire line of men's custom tailoring write for Cloth Sample Book No. 2K.

STYLE 5

STYLE 12

KIEF-CUNTHER & CO.'S EXTRA HEAVY, FINE BLACK IRISH FRIEZE CLOTH IN OVERCOATS TO MEASURE, $8.00.

No. 44309   THIS IS A SOLID FAST BLACK GOODS, an extra heavy weight for heavy ulsters and overcoats, a goods there is practically no wear out to. It is a very firm weave and is intended to take the place of heavy beaver and kersey overcoating where a heavier fabric is wanted. Lined with our double weight overcoat lining, heavily padded, interlined, stayed and stiffened by our own special process, you have one of the warmest, most comfortable winter outer garments you could possibly have made.

Price for men's overcoat, style 10..................................$8.00
Price for men's double breasted, storm excluding ulster, style 12.............. 9.50
Price for pea jacket and vest, style 3............................. 8.00
$2.00 extra for men measuring over 42 inches breast measure.

For samples of cloth of our entire line of men's custom tailoring write for Cloth Sample Book No. 2 K.

N. R. CABE & CO.'S HEAVY WEIGHT OLIVE BROWN IRISH FRIEZE ULSTER CLOTH IN OVERCOATS TO MEASURE, $8.50.

No. 44311   THIS IS THE HEAVIEST IRISH FRIEZE ON THE MARKET, a very dark olive brown with a background of almost solid black. The color is livened with a scattered hairline of dark red. It makes a very modest, rich appearing garment. We have made up thousands of overcoats and ulsters from these goods; in fact, it is the most staple ulster fabric in our entire line. It is a goods there is practically no wear out to, it is a cloth your tailor would make up in ulsters at $20.00 to $25.00.

OUR SPECIAL $8.50 PRICE is based on the actual cost of the cloth bought direct from the mill in large quantities, with but the manufacturing cost and our one small percentage of profit added. While this makes a very comfortable, extra heavy winter overcoat, we especially recommend it for ulsters in style 12.

Price for overcoat, style 10 ....$ 8.50
Price for double breasted, storm excluding ulster, style 12....... 10.00
Price for pea jacket and vest, style 3. .... 8.50
$2.00 extra for men measuring over 42 inches breast measure.

For samples of cloth of our entire line of men's custom tailoring, write for Cloth Sample Book No. 2K.

BLACK AND BLUE MIXED EXTRA HEAVY WEIGHT XXXX BROWN WHARTON IRISH FRIEZE CLOTH IN OVERCOATS TO MEASURE, $9.00.

No. 44313   THIS XXXX WHARTON IRISH FRIEZE is relieved from the plain black by a broken random mixture of bluish effect, giving it a little color, which adds a decided richness to the finished garment. It is one of the heaviest overcoat fabrics woven, a cloth there is practically no wear-out to. It is especially recommended for a very heavy, double breasted, high collar, storm-excluding winter ulster; it also is desirable in a very heavy overcoat for winter wear.

OUR SPECIAL $9.00 PRICE is made possible by reason of a very large purchase of these goods at the lowest price ever made by the mills on the XXXX brand. We have figured the cost of manufacturing at the lowest possible point consistent with the high class of work we do, and we feel confident that if we make you an overcoat or ulster from these goods at our $9.00 price, we will be sure to get your tailoring orders in the future.

Price for men's overcoats, style 10...........................$ 9.00
Price for men's double breasted storm-excluding ulster, style 12.. 10.50
Price for pea jacket and vest, style 3............................ 9.00
$2.00 extra for men measuring over 42 inches breast measure.

For samples of cloth of our entire line of men's custom tailoring write for Cloth Sample Book No. 2K.

WINDOM MILLS HEAVY WEIGHT PLAIN BLACK KERSEY OVERCOATING CLOTH IN OVERCOATS TO MEASURE, $9.00.

No. 44315   FOR $9.00 we make to measure men's overcoats from this extra heavy weight, plain black velvet surfaced Windom kersey cloth in competition with overcoats furnished by the best city tailors at more than double the price.

THE WINDOM MILLS turn out the highest grade of heavy kersey overcoatings made in this country. The cloth can be guaranteed fast color, guaranteed for wear and shape; in fact, for a handsome, dressy, heavy weight winter overcoat in style 10, there is nothing that will compare with this fabric at the price.

IF YOU WANT A HEAVY WINTER OVERCOAT for all purposes, for dress and semi-dress occasions, and later for every-day wear, you will find this coat will have all the appearance of a coat that you would pay your tailor $30.00 to $40.00 for and we guarantee it to give the best of service.

Price for men's overcoat, style 10..............................$ 9.00
Price for men's double-breasted, storm excluding ulster, style 12............... 10.50
Price for pea jacket and vest, style 3............................ 9.00
$2.00 extra for men measuring over 42 inches breast measure.

For samples of cloth of our entire line of men's custom tailoring write for Cloth Sample Book No. 2K.

BAUNDAHL NAVY BLUE CHINCHILLA OVERCOATING CLOTH IN OVERCOATS TO MEASURE, $9.00.

No. 44317.   FOR $9.00 we make to measure Men's Overcoats from this very heavy weight, soft, rough surfaced navy blue Chinchilla cloth, a fabric we can guarantee for wear. It makes a neat, warm, comfortable outer garment. The garments are all cut to measure by expert cutters, made by first-class tailors, lined with double weight overcoat lining, heavily interlined, padded, stayed and stiffened, sewed throughout with silk and linen and guaranteed in every respect.

Price for men's overcoat, style 10.............................$ 9.00
Price for men's double breasted, storm excluding ulster, style 12............... 10.50
Price for pea jacket and vest, style 3............................ 9.00
$2.00 extra for men measuring over 42 inches breast measure.

For samples of cloth of our entire line of men's custom tailoring write for Cloth Sample Book No. 2K.

BREWSTER-HERSEY & CO.'S EXTRA HEAVY WEIGHT PLAIN DARK OLIVE BROWN KERSEY CLOTH IN OVERCOATS TO MEASURE, $10.00.

No. 44319   THIS IS A VERY DARK OLIVE BROWN FABRIC from the Brewster-Hersey & Co.'s mills, one of the heaviest kerseys woven. It has a perfect surface, a fabric we can guarantee for wear, makes a very stylish overcoat in style 10 and at the price is the greatest value ever offered in brown kersey overcoating.

HOW THESE GARMENTS ARE MADE, cut, trimmed and finished is fully explained in tailoring introductory pages.

Price for men's overcoat, style 10.............................$10.00
Price for men's double-breasted, storm excluding ulster, style 12.. 12.00
Price for pea jacket and vest, style 3.............................. 10.00
$2.00 extra for men measuring over 42 inches breast measure.

For samples of cloth of our entire line of men's custom tailoring write for Cloth Sample Book No. 2K.

GOSHEN MILLS HEAVY WEIGHT MEDIUM LIGHT BROWN KERSEY OVERCOATING CLOTH IN OVERCOATS TO MEASURE, $11.00.

No. 44321 $2.00 REDUCTION IN PRICE. We are able to make these goods up in our very best style, with the very best of linings, trimmings and finishings at 00 less than last season's price. We make the difference in price to you the exact difference in the cost of the cloth to us, the lowest price ever attempted on any fabric from the Goshen mills. This is a handsome medium light shade of brown, a velvety surface effect, a fabric that makes up very dressy in style 10.

HOW THESE GARMENTS ARE CUT, made, trimmed and finished is fully explained in tailoring introductory pages.

Price for men's overcoat, style 10...................................$11.00
Price for men's double-breasted, storm excluding ulster, style 12............. 13.00
Price for pea jacket and vest, style 3........................... 11.00
$2.00 extra for men measuring over 42 inches breast measure.
For samples of cloth of our entire line of men's custom tailoring write for Cloth Sample Book No. 2K

EDENTON HEAVIEST WEIGHT DARK BROWN-BLACK IRISH FRIEZE CLOTH IN OVERCOATS TO MEASURE, $11.00.

No. 44323.   REDUCED FROM $12.00. We are able to make this cloth up this season $1.00 lower in price than ever before by reason of a larger purchase and a lower price secured on the piece goods, and the difference in cost to us is shown in the difference in price to you. This is a plain double weight Irish Frieze cloth, almost black, and relieved from the solid black by a solid grayish effect. It is a goods there is practically no wear out to and it is the best fabric we can offer for a very heavy storm excluding winter ulster in style 12.

Price for men's overcoat, style 10...................................$11.00
Price for men's double breasted, storm excluding ulster, style 12...... 13.00
Price for pea jacket and vest, style 3............................. 11.00
$2.00 extra for men measuring over 42 inches breast measure.
For samples of cloth of our entire line of men's custom tailoring write for Cloth Sample Book No. 2K.

DALEVILLE HEAVY WEIGHT MEDIUM LIGHT SHADE BROWN AND GRAY MIXED COVERT OVERCOATING CLOTH IN OVERCOATS TO MEASURE, $12.00.

No. 44325.   REDUCED FROM $13.00. Last fall we were compelled to ask $13.00 for these goods in overcoats and $16.00 in ulsters. This year we are able to make a special inside price of $12.00 and $14.00. We have figured the exact saving in the cost of material and have made the difference in the reduced price.

THIS DALEVILLE COVERT CLOTH is a handsome shade, a brown and gray mixed pin check effect, a very heavy weight. It is the very latest shade for this season and we especially recommend it in a stylish coat in style 10 for fall and winter.

Price for men's overcoat, style 10...................................$12.00
Price for men's double breasted, storm excluding ulster, style 12...... 14.00
Price for pea jacket and vest, style 3.......................... 12.00
$2.00 extra for men measuring over 42 inches breast measure.
For samples of cloth of our entire line of men's custom tailoring write for Cloth Sample Book No. 2K.

NORMAN MILLING CO.'S EXTRA HEAVY DARK NAVY BLUE CHINCHILLA CLOTH IN OVERCOATS TO MEASURE, $11.50.

No. 44327   REDUCED FROM $13.00. This season we are able to make the price $1.50 less for the same grade of goods as we furnished last year, the exact difference in the cost to us.

THIS IS A VERY HEAVY WEIGHT, dark navy blue chinchilla cloth, a soft goods with a very rough surface; is the highest grade chinchilla we carry, one of the best fabrics of the kind in the market.

OUR SPECIAL $11.50 PRICE includes our very best grade of overcoat linings, heavy interlining, padding, staying, stiffening and our very best workmanship throughout.

Price for men's overcoat, style 10...................................$11.50
Price for men's double-breasted, storm excluding ulster, style 12....... 13.50
Price for pea jacket and vest, style 3.......................... 11.50
$2.00 extra for men measuring over 42 inches breast measure.
For samples of cloth of our entire line of men's custom tailoring write for Cloth Sample Book No. 2K.

FINE PLAIN BLACK IMPORTED ENGLISH KERSEY OVERCOATING CLOTH IN OVERCOATS TO MEASURE, $12.50.

No. 44329   THIS IS A VERY FINE IMPORTED HEAVY WEIGHT, perfect surfaced, closely woven, all-wool English kersey overcoating, especially recommended for a fine winter overcoat for dress, semi-dress or everyday wear. How we make, line, trim and finish our overcoats is fully explained in tailoring introductory pages.

Price for men's overcoats, style 10 ....$12.50
Price for men's double breasted, storm excluding ulster, style 12...... 14.00
Price for pea jacket and vest, style 3................. 12.50
$2.00 extra for men measuring over 42 inches breast measure.
For samples of cloth of our entire line of men's custom tailoring write for Cloth Sample Book No. 2K.

STEVENSON IMPORTED ENGLISH NAVY BLUE KERSEY OVERCOATING CLOTH IN OVERCOATS TO MEASURE, $13.50.

No. 44331   REDUCED FROM $15.00. We make a reduction in price of $1.50 over last season, the actual difference in cost to us.

THIS IS THE FINEST plain dark navy blue kersey overcoating we handle, one of the very finest kerseys on the market. If you want a handsome dark navy blue heavy winter overcoat, an all-purpose garment, we are especially anxious to receive your order for a coat from this, our finest blue kersey.

Price for men's overcoat, style 10...................................$13.50
Price for men's double-breasted, storm excluding ulster, style 12....... 15.50
Price for pea jacket and vest, style 3............. 13.50
$2.00 extra for men measuring over 42 inches breast measure.
For samples of cloth of our entire line of men's custom tailoring write for Cloth Sample Book No. 2K.

BROOKS' FINEST GRADE, EXTRA HEAVY WEIGHT, PLAIN FAST BLACK, ENGLISH KERSEY OVERCOATING CLOTH IN OVERCOATS TO MEASURE, $15.00.

No. 44333.   THIS IS THE FINEST KERSEY CLOTH WE HANDLE, one of the very best kerseys on the market. It is the equal of anything you would be likely to find in any city tailoring establishment, regardless of the price you might pay. It is a fine all-wool goods, guaranteed fast color, perfect surface, and with our special making, our fine, heavy weight overcoat lining, heavy interlining, padding, staying, stiffening and finish, we guarantee to furnish you a coat with a distinctiveness in workmanship, fit and finish not to be had elsewhere.

Price for men's overcoat, style 10 ....$15.00
Price for men's double breasted, storm excluding ulster, style 12...... 17.00
Price for pea jacket and vest, style 3.......... 15.00
$2.00 extra for men measuring over 42 inches breast measure.
For samples of cloth of our entire line of men's custom tailoring write for Cloth Sample Book No. 2K.

STYLE 10.

SEND FOR
Book No. 2K.
Our Complete
Line of
CLOTH.....
SAMPLES.

Department of Custom Tailored Trousers

Our special line of Pants Fabrics for this season, ranging in price for the made-to-measure garment from $1.75 to $5.50, embrace almost every new thing desirable, the representative numbers from the best lines that have been shown this season by the best makers.

IF YOU ORDER PANTS MADE BY US they will be made in our special pants department, cut by expert pants cutters, made by special pants tailors; they will be reinforced throughout, the very best of trimmings will be used, sewed throughout, with heavy silk and linen and we will guarantee for you a more stylish, better fitting, more shapely, dressy and altogether satisfactory trousers than you could get from your dealer at home, even at two to three times our price.

GENUINE READING DARK GRAY, NARROW STRIPED PANTS CASSIMERE IN PANTS TO MEASURE, $1.75.

No. 44351 THIS IS A DARK GRAY and black hair line pants cassimere, a genuine Reading fabric. We have cut up thousands of yards of this cloth in the past with general satisfaction to our customers. The cloth is woven in Reading, Pa., by an old German maker, whose reputation for the manufacture of thoroughly first class pants fabrics is the very best guarantee for quality. Originally we were compelled to sell these pants at $1.98, and by reducing the cost of the material we have finally succeeded in producing them in our very best make at the incomparable low price of $1.75. Price, per pair..$1.75

For men measuring over 40 inches waist measure, 50 cents extra.
For samples of cloth of our entire line of men's custom tailoring write to Cloth Sample Book No. 2K.

ANDOVER HEAVY WEIGHT, FANCY STRIPED SPECIAL PANTS CASSIMERE, $2.50.

No. 44353 FOR $2.50 we make to measure men's pants from this dark gray and brown mixed striped special pants fabric. It is a medium light pattern; the stripe is effected by a broken mixture of brown and gray pin head lines and an invisible hairline of blue. It is a good substantial fabric, we can guarantee it for wear, and from our tailoring department you will get a better fitting and more stylish garment at $2.50 than you would be likely to get from your tailor at home at three times this price.

Price, per pair..$2.50
For men measuring over 40 inches waist measure, 50 cents extra.
For samples of cloth of our entire line of men's custom tailoring write for Cloth Sample Book No. 2K.

LEXINGTON FANCY RAISED RIBBED PLAIN DARK NAVY BLUE HEAVY WEIGHT PANTS WORSTED IN PANTS TO MEASURE, $2.50.

No. 44355 FOR $2.50 We make to measure men's pants from this extra heavy weight, dark navy blue worsted. It is a narrow stripe formed by narrow ribbed satin effect lines or stripes. It is a goods we can guarantee for wear and it will give every satisfaction to the purchaser.

Price, per pair..$2.50
For men measuring over 40 inches waist measure, 50 cents extra.
For samples of cloth of our entire line of men's custom tailoring write for Cloth Sample Book No. 2K.

GROTONVILLE EXTRA HEAVY WEIGHT FANCY BLACK AND BLUE STRIPED SPECIAL WEIGHT WORSTED IN PANTS TO MEASURE, $2.75.

No. 44357 FOR $2.75 we make to measure men's pants from this handsome heavy weight, dark striped worsted and we guarantee the garment equal to anything you can get from your tailor at home at double the price. This is a heavy weight, very dark pattern, narrow ⅛-inch stripes of black alternating with broken stripes of blue and black pinhead effects and further relieved by an invisible red silk hairline.

THIS IS A VERY HANDSOME FABRIC, and at $2.75 is the greatest value ever offered by us or any other house in a fancy, heavy weight, wear-resisting worsted fabric. Understand, this garment will be cut by expert pants cutters made by special pants tailors. We will use only the highest grade trimmings, will be sewed throughout with silk and linen to insure never ripping and you will get such trousers as you could not possibly get elsewhere at anything like the price. Price, per pair....................................$2.75

For men measuring over 40 inches waist measure, 50 cents extra.
For samples of cloth of our entire line of men's custom tailoring write for Cloth Sample Book No. 2K.

GOLDMAN HEAVY WEIGHT, FANCY DARK BLUE AND BLACK STRIPED WORSTED, $3.00.

No. 44359 FOR $3.00 we make to measure men's pants from this genuine Goldman pants worsted; a dark narrow ribbed striped pattern of alternating raised worsted stripes of black and herringbone blue and black relieved by a fine invisible red silk hairline. This pattern is entirely new for this season; it is one of the handsomest, medium priced, through and through special pants worsteds on the market and it is such value as can be had from no other house. Price, per pair..$3.00

For men measuring over 40 inches waist measure, 50 cents extra.
For samples of cloth of our entire line of men's custom tailoring write for Cloth Sample Book No. 2K.

AMHERST, DAILY & CO.'S HEAVY WEIGHT FINE ALL-WOOL FANCY BLACK AND GRAY PLAID PANTS CASSIMERES, $3.00.

No. 44361 FOR $3.00 we make to measure men's pants from this heavy weight imported English all-wool pants cassimere. The pattern is entirely new for this season, formed by narrow ⅛-inch alternating squares of dark mixed gray and solid black, and relieved by an invisible green silk hairline. This makes up in one of the handsomest, medium priced plaid effects of anything we have seen. We can guarantee the goods for wear; the same class of cloth is carried by tailors generally. Price, per pair............................$3.00

For men measuring over 40 inches waist measure, 50 cents extra.
For samples of cloth of our entire line of men's custom tailoring write for Cloth Sample Book No. 2K.

BAILEY FANCY HEAVY WEIGHT DARK MIXED ENGLISH WORSTED, $3.00.

No. 44363 FOR $3.00 we make to measure men's pants from this fancy English worsted, a dark fancy invisible striped mixture effected by narrow black satin finished stripes alternating with mixed steel gray and black stripes and relieved with an invisible red silk hairline. This is a very stylish pattern, entirely new for this season, woven expressly for pants. The same class of goods as you will find in the best tailoring establishments and there at two to three times our price. Price, per pair..$3.00

For men measuring over 40 inches waist measure, 50 cents extra.
For samples of cloth of our entire line of men's custom tailoring write for Cloth Sample Book No. 2K.

IN ORDERING FILL OUT OUR TAILORING ORDER BLANK ON BACK OF REGULAR MERCHANDISE ORDER BLANK.

EXTRA HEAVY WEIGHT VERY DARK NAVY BLUE NARROW RIBBED STRIPED GLENSIDE PANTS CASSIMERE, $3.00.

No. 44365 FOR $3.00 we make to measure men's pants from this handsome special pants fabric, a rich dark navy blue raised ribbed and striped effect, a ⅜-inch raised ribbed black, and relieved by dotted invisible hairlines of dark green silk. This is a very rich appearing, extra firmly woven, hard finished goods that we can guarantee for wear and will make up very stylish and dressy.

Price, per pair $3.00
For men measuring over 40 inches waist measure, 50 cents extra.
For samples of cloth of our entire line of men's custom tailoring write for Cloth Sample Book No. 2K.

EXTRA HEAVY BLACK RIBBED STRIPED PANTS WORSTED, $3.00.

No. 44367 FOR $3.00 we make to measure men's pants from this old reliable, and always staple, wear-resisting, ribbed, striped, fast black pants worsted.

THIS FABRIC is woven with a raised herringbone and raised pin headbird's eye effect in alternating stripes, and with very narrow raised satin finished black ribbed hairline stripes. There is nothing more staple woven, it is a goods there is practically no wear out to. It makes up very neat and dressy, and is especially stylish in a suit when worn with a coat and vest of any other pattern.

Price, per pair $3.00
For men measuring over 40 inches waist measure, 50 cents extra.
For samples of cloth of our entire line of men's custom tailoring write for Cloth Sample Book No. 2K.

EXTRA HEAVY FANCY OLIVE BROWN AND GRAY MIXED STRIPED GERMAN WORSTED, $3.50.

No. 44369 FOR $3.50 we make to measure men's pants from this fine imported German worsted goods in competition with anything your tailor will furnish you at double the price.

THIS IS A VERY HANDSOME PATTERN of narrow 1-16-inch alternating stripes of plain dark olive brown and steel gray, with narrow hairlines of dark red silk; is one of the handsomest effects in worsteds that we show, is a very heavy weight, very firmly woven, hard surface goods, woven expressly for trousers, and is such value as you could not possibly get elsewhere.

Price, per pair $3.50
For men measuring over 40 inches waist measure, 50 cents extra.
For samples of cloth of our entire line of men's custom tailoring write for Cloth Sample Book No. 2K.

DOUBLE RIBBED OREGON HAIRLINE PANTS CASSIMERE, $3.50.

No. 44371 FOR $3.50 we make to measure men's pants from this old reliable Oregon Hairline Cassimere, one of the strongest, all-wool cassimeres on the market.

THIS PATTERN is effected by a very dark blue-black background, the hairlines effected by very narrow effectively woven threads of bluish gray, one of the handsomest staple pants cassimeres on the market. It is a fabric you will find in the best tailoring establishments and always at two to three times our price.

Price, per pair $3.50
For men measuring over 40 inches waist measure, 50 cents extra.
For samples of cloth of our entire line of men's custom tailoring write for Cloth Sample Book No. 2K.

BLACK SATIN STRIPED FRENCH WORSTED PANTS FABRIC, $3.50.

No. 44373 REDUCED FROM $4.00. We are able to offer these goods this season at a reduction of 50 cents from last year's prices, the lowest price ever attempted on this class of goods.

THIS IS A SOLID FINE BLACK, all-wool French Worsted, with a raised striped effect of black. There is nothing woven that is more stylish and dressy, nothing that will make up handsomer. It is a goods of which we have cut up thousands of yards with general satisfaction to our customers, a fabric that is carried by the best merchant tailors everywhere, where it is made up at prices ranging from $6.00 to $10.00. If you order a pair of pants from this fabric we will guarantee to furnish you a distinctiveness in style, shape, fit and finish which you could not get elsewhere. Price, per pair $3.50
For men measuring over 40 inches waist measure, 50 cents extra.
For samples of cloth of our entire line of men's custom tailoring, write for Cloth Sample Book No. 2K.

FINE IMPORTED FANCY STRIPED BLACK AND BLUE MIXED ENGLISH WORSTED, $4.00.

No. 44375 THIS HANDSOME SPECIAL PANTS WORSTED is a new effect, and one of the handsomest mixed fancy stripes we have seen. It has a raised pinhead surface effect in alternating dots of steel gray and black satin, the whole pattern relieved by narrow solid lines of alternating reddish olive and dark green. The narrow stripes are alternating stripes of mixed black and steel gray and black and light gray satin finished worsted hairlines. This is a very heavy goods, closely woven, and is from one of the very best English mills. It is one of the handsomest worsteds on the market, will make up very stylish and we guarantee to furnish you such pants as you could not get elsewhere at anything like the price. Price, per pair $4.00
For men measuring over 40 inches waist measure 50 cents extra.
For samples of cloth of our entire line of men's custom tailoring write for Cloth Sample Book No. 2K.

OSGOOD-MENTOR & CO.'S WORSTED, $4.00.

No. 44377 A REDUCTION OF 75 CENTS in price from last year. We give you the benefit of the difference in cost to us.

THIS IS A SPECIAL PANTS PATTERN, a narrow stripe effect, formed by a narrow stripe of solid black and a narrow stripe of broken bluish gray and black, with an invisible reddish solid hairline.

THIS ENGLISH WEAVE has a full heavy back, a very fine surface, is a handsome pattern, entirely new for this season and we offer it in competition with anything your tailor can furnish you, regardless of price.

HOW THESE GARMENTS ARE MADE, trimmed and finished, the style, fit and all will be appreciated after you have allowed us to make you up the garment to your measure. Price, per pair $4.00
For men measuring over 40 inches waist measure, 50 cents extra.
For samples of cloth of our entire line of men's custom tailoring, write for Cloth Sample Book No. 2K.

FANCY IMPORTED RAISED RIBBED DARK NAVY BLUE ENGLISH PANTS WORSTED, $4.00.

No. 44379 FOR $4.00 WE MAKE TO MEASURE MEN'S PANTS from this, one of the very best solid, fast color, navy blue, ribbed pants worsteds on the market. This is a through and through worsted, a hard surface, and the stripe effect is effected by very narrow raised pinhead worsted effects and by very narrow raised black satin ribbed lines.

THIS IS A GOODS THERE IS PRACTICALLY NO WEAR OUT TO, there is nothing woven that makes up more stylish in a plain navy blue pants, and it is a goods we know will please.

Price, per pair $4.00
For men measuring over 40 inches waist measure, 50 cents extra.
For samples of cloth of our entire line of men's custom tailoring write for Cloth Sample Book No. 2K.

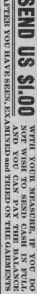

BOYS' LONG PANTS SUITS.

PLEASE NOTICE THAT WITH CERTAIN SUITS WE FURNISH A DOUBLE BREASTED VEST.....

WE CANNOT FURNISH A DOUBLE BREASTED VEST UNLESS SO STATED IN DESCRIPTION.

WE CANNOT FURNISH A SINGLE BREASTED VEST WHEN DESCRIPTION GIVES STYLE AS BEING MADE IN DOUBLE BREASTED.

WE CANNOT FURNISH ANY OTHER STYLE OF COAT OTHER THAN MENTIONED AFTER EACH DESCRIPTION.

DO NOT ORDER A BOYS' SUIT LARGER THAN THE LARGEST SIZE WE MAKE, AS SHOWN BY SCHEDULE ON PAGE 453.

FOR FREE CLOTH SAMPLES of everything in Boys' and children's, also Tape Measure, Fashion Plate, etc., write for Free Book No. 4E.

FOR MEASURE follow same rules as for men, see clothing introductory page, or fill out regular tailoring order blank.

BOYS' UNION AND SATINET CASSIMERE SUITS. Well trimmed and made for the price. We do not recommend buying as cheap a suit, as a better one is cheaper in the end. Dark colors, made in round-cut sack style only.

No. 44501 Price for boys' long pants suit, Style No. 1, only **$2.75**

FOR $3.50 WE OFFER YOU THIS SEASON the best gray union cassimere suit ever made for the money. It will wear better, show less dirt and make a better and warmer winter suit than you can buy elsewhere for $5.00. Coat is made four-button round-cut sack style. three outside pockets and match pocket, single stitched edge; vest cut five-button, notched collar; pants made with two side and one hip pockets, patent buttons, taped through seat and crotch.

No. 44503 Price for boys' long pants suit, Style No. 1, only **$3.50**

MADE FROM VERY DARK, ALMOST BLUE BLACK, MACKINTOSH CASSIMERE interwoven with a dark reddish brown mixture, a smooth surface heavy weight cloth, coat made in round-cut sack style only, body lined with Italian cloth, three outside pockets, including match pocket, one inside pocket, double stitched edge, deep facing, extra buttons on inside of facing. Vest made single breasted, five-button notched collar, four outside, one inside pocket. Pants made with two side, two hip, one watch pocket. Patent never-come-off suspender and fly buttons, double sewed through crotch and seat.

No. 44505 Price for boys' long pants suit, Style, No. 1, only **$4.00**

MADE FROM DUDLEY BATELLE, dark olive and red mixed Melton, a very heavy, smooth and durable material. This mill's goods have always been one of our biggest sellers; our customers know a good thing; you will see the best suit for the money ever offered if you order this number; made in round cut sack style, two lower outside pockets and match pocket in coat, also inside pocket; double stitched edge, extra buttons. Vest made single breasted, five buttons; four outside, one inside pocket. Pants made strong and well trimmed, two side, two hip, one watch pocket; patent buttons.

No. 44507 Price for boys' long pants suit, Style, No. 1, only **$4.50**

MADE FROM SAME MATERIAL AS ABOVE and made and trimmed exactly the same, only coat is made double breasted square cut sack style like our Style No. 3. Vest is made single breasted.

No. 44509 Price for boys' long pants suit, Style, No. 3, only **$5.00**

MADE FROM CLUB CHECK BLACK AND GRAY BASKET WEAVE CASSIMERE a heavy hard twisted goods; a strong suit ready for any and all kinds of wear; dirt and dust proof. We purchased several thousand yards of this cloth for boys' long pants suits only. We have made the suits in our own factory, we know they are honestly made, and we offer you this suit direct from the makers with but one small profit added. Will you save about one-half and give us a trial order? Coat is made in round cut sack style only, like our Style No. 1; well trimmed and finished with usual number of pockets and double sewed edge. Vest made single breasted, five button, notched collar. Pants double sewed and taped through seat and crotch; extra buttons attached to coat facing.

No. 44511 Price for boys' long pants suit, Style No. 1, only **$4.50**

BLUISH VERY DARK MIXED PREMIER CASSIMERE, a black ground with a raised silk stripe effect relieved with a random mixture of light blue, almost invisible; **for good hard wear and general satisfaction we recommend this suit.** Made in two styles, either in round-cut sack like our Style No. 1, or in square cut, single breasted sack like our Style No. 2. **Don't fail to state style desired when ordering.** Coat has usual number of pockets, double stitched edge, extra buttons on facing. Vest made single-breasted, five-button, notched collar. Pants have two side, two hip, one watch pocket, patent buttons on fly and waistband, double sewed crotch stay.

No. 44513 Price for boys' long pants suit in Style No. 1 or 2 . . . .**$5.50**

Don't fail to note style desired in your order.

BLACK FINE ALL-WOOL SMOOTH FINISH THIBET OR VICUNA CLOTH. Seldom made into boys' suits on account of the cloth being too high priced. We buy the cloth direct from the mills at a very low price, quality considered, and can therefore furnish this fine medium weight Thibet suit to our customers at about one-half price. Coat is made in round-cut sack style only—like our style No. 1—double stitched edge, two lower, one match, one inside pocket, Italian cloth body lining, sliesia sleeve lining; vest made single-breasted style, with notched collar; pants have two side, two hip pockets and watch pocket, patent never-come-off buttons on fly and waistband.

No. 44515 Price for boys' long pants suit, Style No. 1, only **$6.50**

UNLESS WE MADE OUR OWN CLOTHING, purchased all of the raw material from the makers for cash, and at a much lower price than is paid by the average wholesale house, we could not offer this fine blue figured worsted suit for $7.00; made from heavy weight cloth, plain navy blue with raised satin effect, half moon figures. Coat is made in round cut sack style like Style No. 1. Well trimmed and tailored, double stitched edge, usual number of pockets and extra buttons attached to facing. Vest is made double breasted style, no collar. Pants are extra well sewed, double through seat and crotch. Patent buttons on fly and waistband, two side, two hip, one watch pocket.

No. 44517 Price for boys' long pants vest in Style No 1 only, vest cut double breasted **$7.00**

THIS SUIT IS MADE FROM AN ALL-WOOL PIN CHECK GRAY READING CASSIMERE. If you like good goods, neat appearance, and to save dollars, **order this number.** We doubt if a suit can be made that will give better all-around satisfaction. Coat is made up like our Style No. 1, round-cut sack, good trimmings and honestly made, double stitched edge, extra buttons attached; vest made single-breasted, with notched collar, two lower, two upper, one inside breast pocket; pants sewed double through crotch and seat, patent buttons on fly and waistband, two side, two hip, one watch pocket.

No. 44519 Price for boys' long pants suit, for boys age 12 to 19, but not over 35 breast measure **$6.00**

MADE FROM SAME CLOTH as above No. 44519, only coat is made a double breasted, square-cut sack style, like our Style No. 3. The vest is made single breasted.

No. 44521 Price for boys' long pants suit, for boys age 12 to 19, but not over 35 breast measure in Style No. 3 only **$6.50**

Style 1

Style 2

Style 3

OUR $6.00 CHEVIOT SUIT.

SCHEFFER, SCHRAM & VOGEL GRAY AND BROWN STRIPE CHEVIOT SUIT, an all-wool heavy weight cloth; a decided stripe effect; very popular; pattern will just strike the boy for a school or everyday nobby suit; guaranteed for wear and color. Coat is made round cut sack style with a double breasted vest without collar, double stitched edge on both coat and vest. Pants cut in the latest style medium width at knee and bottom; two side, two hip, one watch pocket. Your boy likes the new effects and style. Order this number and see how much better he will look.

No. 44523 Price for boys' long pants suit for boys age 12 to 19, but not larger than 35 breast, Style No. 1 only.........................$6.00

GENUINE EWING WORSTED SUIT FOR $6.00.

MADE FROM PLAIN BLACK, satin figured effect. Ewing Worsted, a hard twisted goods that will wear like leather. A suit for the boy for Sunday for one season and then for everyday use. Made up in either round cut sack style like our Style No. 1, or single breasted square cut sack like Style No. 2. Extra buttons on facing, double stitched edge. Italian body lining. Vest made single breasted, five button, two lower, two upper, one inside pocket. Pants made in latest style, double sewed through crotch and seat. Patent buttons on fly and waistband

No. 44525 Price for boys' long pants suit for boys age 12 to 19, not over 35 breast measure, in Style No. 1 or 2..................$6.00
Do not fail to mention style desired in your order.

BLUE SERGE SUIT FOR $8.00.

OUR LINE WOULD NOT BE COMPLETE WITHOUT A BLUE SERGE SUIT.
This one is made from a fine 18-ounce cloth. All pure wool worsted, guaranteed for color and wear; made in either style No. 1 round cut sack or style No. 2 single breasted square cut sack. Coat and vest double stitched. Vest made single breasted, five button, notched collar. Pants made medium width at knee and bottom; two side, two hip, one watch pocket; patent never-come-off buttons on waistband and fly. There is nothing more dressy, no better wearing suit can be had at any price.

No. 44527 Price for boys' long pants suit for boys age 12 to 19, but not over 35 breast measure in Style No. 1 or 2..................$8.00
Do not fail to mention style wanted in your order.

OUR $8.50 MELTON.

PLAIN, DARK BROWN, HEAVY WEIGHT MELTON made from the genuine Baumühl & Co. goods. This cloth is usually to be found in first class tailoring houses by the yard, but not made up into boys' clothing. We can furnish our customers with this fine suit at a low price only on account of our purchasing power and making our own goods. Coat is made in round cut sack style like our Style No. 1, well padded, trimmed and finished, extra buttons on coat facing. Vest is made double breasted style, no collar, two lower and two upper pockets. Pants cut in the latest fashion, well trimmed, patent never-come-off buttons on waistband and fly. If the best is none too good, order this number.

No. 44529 Price for boys' long pants suit for boys age 12 to 19, not over 35 breast measure, Style No. 1.........................$8.50
THIS SUIT IS MADE FROM THE SAME CLOTH AS ABOVE No. 44529, only the coat is cut in a double breasted style like our style No. 3. The vest is also made double breasted, otherwise the suit is made and trimmed exactly the same as Style No. 1.

No. 44531 Price for boys' long pants suits in Style No. 3 only..$9.00

STANTON WORSTED SUIT FOR $8.75.

MADE FROM JET BLACK ENGLISH STANTON WORSTED. It pays to buy a good black suit; this suit is one of them. Made from fine diagonal black pure worsted; it won't get dingy and brown or wear shiny; always looks well and will wear like buckskin. Coat made in round or square cut style, as desired, like style No. 1 or 2. Coat well lined and trimmed, extra buttons on facing, double stitched edge, two lower, one cash, one inside pocket. Vest is made single breasted, five button, notch collar, double stitched edge, two lower, two upper, one inside pocket. Pants made in latest fashion; two side, two hip and watch pocket; patent buttons.

No. 44563 Price for boys' long pants suit for boys age 12 to 19 in Style No. 1 or 2..........$8.75
MADE FROM SAME CLOTH AS ABOVE NUMBER, trimmed and made exactly the same, except coat is made double breasted style like our style No. 3. The extra price is for double breasted coat. The vest of this suit is made single breasted.

No. 44535 Price for boys' long pants suit for boys age 12 to 19, in Style No. 3..................$9.25

MUMMIE CLOTH SUIT FOR $9.00.

OUR BLACK FRENCH MUMMIE CLOTH SUIT has always been one of our leading numbers. We presume it sells fast with us on account of our being able to offer a suit made from this high grade Black Worsted at such a low price. Our order for this cloth stands as a high water mark record for the largest purchase ever made for cloth of any one style by one house. The coat can be furnished in either Style 1 or 2. Style 1 is round cut sack. Style 2 is single breasted square cut sack. Vest made single breasted, 5-button, notched collar. Pants made double sewed throughout crotch and seat. Patent never-come-off buttons, two side, two hip, one watch pocket. You get one of the finest worsted suits possible to make by ordering this number and save at least 33 per cent on your purchase. Don't fail to mention style in your order.

No. 44537 Price for boys' long pants suit, for boys age 12 to 19, in either Style No. 1 or 2.........................$9.00

GREAT VALUE IN SILK MIXED WORSTED AT $10.00.

OUR HIGHEST PRICE BOYS' LONG PANTS SUIT IS $10.00, and for this price we offer a suit made up from the genuine Manton silk mixed worsted. The name is sufficient guarantee that this suit is as good as the best. The color is very dark background covered with a mixture of blue and red silk. Coat is made in round-cut sack style only, elegantly trimmed and tailored, double stitched, extra buttons attached to facing; vest is made double breasted style, no collar; pants are cut, made and trimmed in the very best possible manner, two side, two hip pockets, also watch pocket, double sewed, patent buttons on fly and waistband

No. 44539 Price for boys' long pants suit, for boys age 12 to 19, but not over 35 breast measure, Style No. 1 only...$10.00

Style 1

Style 2

Style 3

HOW TO ORDER. Select suit wanted from description, order by number, follow our rules for measurement as explained on page 436, or for Boys' Long Pants Suits fill out men's regular tailoring order blank, on back of our regular order blank, enclose our price, or if you prefer SEND ONE DOLLAR. We will send the clothing to you by express C. O. D., balance payable after received.

FOR BOYS' LONG PANTS SUITS—If you will state age, weight, height, number of inches around body at breast, waist and hips, and length of leg, inside seam from tight in crotch to heel, we can guarantee a perfect fit.

FOR BOYS' KNEE PANTS, REEFER AND VESTEE SUITS—If you will state age of boy, whether large or small for age, we can guarantee a fit.

FOR FREE CLOTH SAMPLES OF EVERYTHING IN
Boys' and Children's Clothing, Tape Measure, Special Instructions, Etc.,
═══ WRITE FOR FREE BOOK No. 4K. ═══

BOYS' VESTEE SUITS.

Are made for boys, age 3 to 8. No larger or smaller sizes can be furnished. For full information on terms, styles and sizes, see page 453.

No. 44551 Gray Heavy Weight Union Cassimere Vestee Suit, made with large lapels, double breasted style, not all wool but a strong cloth, wool warp and cotton chain. Coat is made as style shows, opposite this description, two rows of buttons, ½-inch black worsted braid on each side under lapels and extends down front to second button on coat. Edged with a narrow black and white silk braid with a rosette opposite last button on coat. Vest made double breasted style of same cloth, dickey made from green broadcloth, with silk braid monogram in center. Pants made closed front, taped and double sewed crotch, patent elastic waistband, three buttons at knee.

Price for boys' vestee suits, for boys age 4 to 8 years..................**$1.75**

No. 44553 Made from Black and White Basket Weave, Ewing Cassimere, a medium gray check pattern. Heavyweight dust and dirt proof cloth, will wear well, and we are sure a better suit than is offered by any other house for 33 per cent more than our price. Coat made double breasted style, large lapels, two rows gray mottled buttons down front, with one-half inch worsted braid on each side extending from collar under lapel to between second and third button, with black and white Grecian figure. Vest is made imitation double-breasted style, two rows buttons. Red flannel dickey with black and white braid rosette. Two watch pockets. Pants made **double seat and double knee,** taped through seat and crotch, closed front, one hip and two side pockets, three buttons at knee, elastic waistband.

Price for boys' vestee suits, for boys age 4 to 8 years..................**$2.00**

WRITE FOR OUR FREE BOOK....

═══ No. 4K ═══

AND GET OUR COMPLETE LINE OF CLOTH SAMPLES OF : : : : :

.....BOYS' AND CHILDREN'S CLOTHING.

No. 44555 Rich Seal Brown Cassimere, relieved from the plain by almost invisible small plaid effect by cross bar thread of yellow. A handsome modest vestee suit; coat is made perfectly plain, double-breasted style, two rows of buttons, large lapels; vest is made imitation double-breasted style, from a brown worsted goods, with light green pin-head silk effect, trimmed with two rows rim buttons and cloth center to match vest; dickey perfectly plain, made from same goods as vest. Pants made double seat and knee, elastic waistband, double sewed and taped through seat, one hip and two side pockets, three buttons and steel buckle at knee.

Price for boys' vestee suits, for boys age 3 to 8 years..................**$2.50**

No. 44557 This number is made from Black and Gray Mixed Cassimere, a partial stripe effect produced by a single thread of reddish brown. Coat is made double-breasted style, with lapels faced with gray satin. Vest is made from same cloth as coat; two rows of buttons, two watch pockets. Dickey made from tan broadcloth, silk embroidered monogram with five stars just below. **Pants made double seat and double knee,** patent elastic waistband; trimmed with buckle and three buttons to match cloth at knee, one hip and two side pockets.

Price for boys' vestee suits, for boys age 3 to 8 years..................**$2.50**

No. 44559 Made from fine All Wool Rich Dark Brown Mixed Scotch Cheviot, a small black and brown check pattern, covered with a large but almost invisible plaid effect, by a single thread of red. This is a very handsome suit. Made double breasted style as opposite cut shows two rows brown buttons to match goods **seal brown satin faced lapels,** vest cut double-breasted fashion from a pure dye dark red corduroy trimmed with two rows ball buttons. Dickey made from red corduroy to match, vest embroidered with blue and white silk, pants made same as all of our knee pants, **with double seat and knees,** elastic waistband, two side, two hip pockets, trimmed at knee with three buttons and steel buckle. Save two dollars on a suit for your boy and order this number.

Price for boys' vestee suits, for boys age 3 to 8 years..................**$3.00**

No. 44561 Made from Genuine Wanskuk Worsted, a hard twisted good weight cloth, noted for its wearing qualities, a snowflake stripe effect on a black ground relieved by a single red thread one-half inch apart, coat is made double breasted fashion trimmed with two rows black ivory buttons, **lapels silk satin faced,** vest cut imitation double breasted style from same cloth, dickey made from dark red flannel, anchor embroidered in center with black silk. Our designer has worked out a very pretty combination in designing this suit, **pants double seat and knee,** silver buckle and three buttons at knee, elastic waistband, one hip and two side pockets.

Price for boys' vestee suits, for boys age 4 to 8 years..................**$3.50**

No. 44563 Navy Blue Heavy Weight Wool Tricot Cassimere. You can tell what the suit is by calling on your local clothing merchant and asking for the best blue Tricot, compare his price with ours and then purchase where you can do the best.

Coat made with double breasted lapels, **silk satin faced,** double stitched edge, two silk cord loops and cluster on each front side of coat, rounding flats on pockets.

Vest cut double breasted fashion of navy blue corduroy trimmed with two rows cream white ivory buttons, dickey made from blue and red plaid "golf pattern" flannel, with white embroidered figure and stars.

Pants made with silver buckle and three buttons at knee, patent elastic waistband, side and hip pockets, **double seat and double knee.**

Price for boys' vestee suits, for boys age 3 to 8 years..................**$4.00**

HOW TO ORDER.

OUR $4.50 FANCY VESTEE SUIT.

No. 44565 This suit is made in the very latest style for this season, and is such a suit as you will find only in the most fashionable city stores at fancy prices. Understand, we guarantee a perfect fit, guarantee every garment, and if not satisfactory in every way you can return it to us and we will immediately return your money. Pure long fibre heavy wool, Navy Blue Cheviot Suit, made from the best Cheviot cloth manufactured by Durkee, Milan & Co.

Coat made with large double breasted lapels **silk satin faced**, trimmed with three clusters and loops instead of buttons, double stitched edge. Vest made double breasted fashion, two rows black ivory buttons, two pockets, dickey made from red twilled flannel. Pants trimmed with buckle and buttons at knee, **double sewed and taped through crotch and seat, double seat and double knee**, elastic waistband. This suit is elegantly trimmed and finished, it will please the most exacting purchaser.

Price for boys' vestee suits, for boys age 3 to 8 years......................**$4.50**

No. 44567 This New $4.50 Vestee Suit for boys from 3 to 8, is offered as one of the handsomest boys' suits made. If you order this suit and you don't find it perfect fitting and in every way satisfactory, you can return it at our expense and we will return your money. The worsted material from which this suit is made we use in our Custom Department, as it is one of the best cloths manufactured. A broken check pattern of Royal Blue, Black and hardly visible Red mixture. Coat is made perfectly plain, double-breasted fashion, trimmed with worsted loops instead of buttons, rounding flaps on pockets. Vest of same cloth, imitation double-breasted style. Dickey made from blue corduroy to match color in suit, with an embroidered anchor of red and white silk. Pants made double seat and double knee, elastic waistband, silver buckle at knee, taped and double sewed through crotch and seat. A high-grade suit at a low price.

Price for boys' vestee suits, for boys age 3 to 8 ....**$4.50**

CHILDREN'S BLOUSE SUITS.

No. 44569 Made from Extra Heavy Quality Ewing Cassimere, neat gray basket weave pattern. Blouse is made with large sailor collar, wide lapels shield of same goods, to button close up to neck. Collar and shield trimmed with red silk braid. Large sleeves, small at wrist, fastened with two buttons. Cord and whistle with each suit.

Pants made double seat and double knees. Blouse suits, for boys age 3 to 8 years, **$2.50**

No. 44571 Boys' Blouse Two-Piece Suit, made from a Hard Twisted Diagonal Worsted. Color is a black ground with raised silk effect in drab and blue, a very handsome pattern. Blouse is made with large sailor collar, blue and white silk star embroidered in each corner. Also silk embroidered figure on left sleeve and center of shield. Cord and whistle with each suit. Large sleeves, pleated down narrow, and button with two buttons at cuff.

Pants made double at seat and knee. Patent elastic waistband, silver buckle and three buttons at knee. Extra well sewed, and fully warranted to give satisfactory wear.

Price for boys' two-piece blouse suits, for boys age 3 to 8 ....**$3.50**

No. 44573 Our Heavy Weight Navy Blue Serge Blouse Suit is an ideal suit for the small boy. Blouse is made with large lapels and deep sailor collar, trimmed in corner with silk embroidered star of red and white. Emblem and crown embroidered with white and red silk on shield, also silk figure on left sleeve. Whistle and cord with each suit. Large sleeve to close at cuff with two buttons. Pants are double sewed through crotch, silver buckle at knee, double seat and double knee, extension waistband with rubber loops.

Price for boys' two-piece blouse suits, for boys age 3 to 8 ....**$4.50**

SPECIAL VALUE FOR $1.50.

No. 44575 Two-piece suits for boys, age 8 to 15, made from a Dark Brown Stripe and Broken Plaid Effect Satinet. A suit that will give good wear if you consider the price; do not expect too much, as we do not **guarantee this suit to give satisfaction if any more is expected of it than good value for the money.** Cut double breasted style, well made pants, made with one hip, two side pockets.

Price for boys' knee pants suits, for boys age 8 to 15 ..**$1.50**

No. 44577 Made from Medium Gray Union Cassimere, good weight, and strong cloth, will not show dirt, a splendid school suit. See fashion figure opposite for style. Coat is sewed well, lined with good quality serge, **deep facing**, three outside pockets, one watch pocket. Pants made **double seat and double knee**, taped and double sewed through seat and crotch, fly front, patent buttons, patent elastic waistband.

Price for boys' knee pants suits, for boys age 8 to 15......**$1.75**

No. 44579 Gray Basket Weave; Black and White Club Check Pattern, heavy weight Cheviot cloth. The best low price suit, we think, ever shown by us. Coat is made as style shown by opposite figure. Italian lined, double stitched edge, four extra buttons on inside facing to replace any that are lost or broken by wear. **Pants made double seat and double knee**, patent elastic waistband, fly front with patent buttons used on fly, taped and double sewed through crotch and seat.

Price for boys' two-piece knee pants suits, for boys age 8 to 15 years........**$2.25**

No. 44615 Does it pay to buy or make a cheap clay worsted suit? We think not if you get a black clay suit for the boy. Take our advice and get a good one, it's money in hand in the end. This suit is made from full 16-ounce heavy pure long worsted, it won't fade, shrink, scuff up, wear shiny, or wear out while it's new, as many of the so-called worsted suits will. We cannot furnish you the best for any less money so we recommend this suit. Made double-breasted style as per opposite cut, honestly tailored, well trimmed, double stitched edge, pants made double seat and knee, taped crotch, fly front, one hip and two side pockets.

Price for boys' two-piece knee pants suits, for boys age 5 to 15 years **$5.00**

No. 44617 In this brown mixed mummie cloth worsted suit we offer you as good or better suit than is sold by regular clothiers at from $8.00 to $10.00. A pure worsted goods, black ground overshot with reddish brown mixture, a very handsome cloth, when made up makes one of the most desirable high priced suits we have ever manufactured. Trimmed, lined and finished in the best possible manner, extra buttons on coat facing, patent buttons on pants, double seat and double knee, taped crotch, side and hip pockets.

Price for boys' knee pants suits, for boys age 8 to 15 years. **$5.50**

TO ORDER, Select Suit wanted from ILLUSTRATION and description, STATE AGE OF BOY, say whether large or small of age, enclose our price and we will send the suit, guaranteeing fit and satisfaction, or you can return the suit to us at our expense and we will return your money.

IF YOU WOULD LIKE TO SEE CLOTH BEFORE ORDERING,
Send us a postal card; just say: SEND ME FREE BOOK No. 4K, and we will send you by return mail our COMPLETE BOOK of Cloth Samples of everything we carry in Boys' and Children's Clothing, also Tape Measure, Fashion Figures, Order Blanks, etc.   **BOOK NO. 4K IS FREE FOR THE ASKING.**

BOYS' THREE-PIECE KNEE PANTS SUITS

Are made for boys, age 10 to 16, or 26 to 32 breast measure. No larger or smaller sizes can be furnished. Suit consists of one round cut sack coat, one vest cut double-breasted style, no collar; one pair knee pants, made double seat and double knee.

No. 44619 Boys' Three-Piece Knee Pants Suits made same style as shown by opposite cut, made from extra heavy Schaffer, Schram & Co. cheviot; a black, white and brown stripe effect, all wool and a splendid wearing goods. Coat is made three-button cutaway sack style, rounding flaps on pockets, Italian body lining, silesia sleeve lining; vest cut double-breasted style, no collar, honestly made and trimmed; pants made double seat and double knee, patent suspender buttons. We especially recommend this suit for school or every day wear.

Price for boys' three-piece knee pants suits, for boys age 10 to 16 years.... **$4.00**

No. 44621 Made from hard twisted worsted, a diagonal pattern of drab and black colors, makes a very handsome suit. Made cutaway sack style; vest double-breasted, no collar; pants extra well made and trimmed, elastic waistband, and suspender buttons, double seat and double knee. Extra buttons on inside facing of coat. This popular style would cost 50 per cent more than our low price if purchased elsewhere.

Price for boys' three-piece knee pants suit, for boys age 10 to 16 years...... **$4.50**

No. 44623 Navy Blue Wanskuk Worsted Suit, relieved from the perfectly plain by raised satin effect figures; a suit that will wear like leather, and is very dressy and neat. Coat made three-button cutaway sack style, well tailored and trimmed. Vest made double-breasted style no collar, two lower and two upper pockets. Pants are made double through seat and knee, elastic waistband, patent suspender buttons, double sewed and taped through crotch and seat. The price is low, but the suit high grade.

Price for boys' three-piece knee pants suit, for boys age 10 to 16 years........ **$5.00**

No. 44625 Is there any cloth more suitable or desirable for a boys' large knee pants suit than a good navy blue serge? We think not. This one is made from heavy, fine all-wool goods. For color, wear and general satisfaction we recommend this suit. Coat is made three-button cutaway sack style. Vest high cut double-breasted without collar. Pants made thoroughly first-class, double through seat and knee, suspender buttons, elastic waistband, taped through crotch and seat.

Price for boys' three-piece knee pants suit, for boys age 10 to 16 years......... **$5.50**

BOYS' SINGLE KNEE PANTS.

They are made from remnants left from our Custom Department. We can, therefore, give much better value than we could if made from regular goods. We also make up a very fine class of goods into boys' knee pants, nothing cheap and shoddy. Boys' single knee pants come in sizes, age 4 to 15. Give age of boy and if large, average or small of age.

No. 44629 Single Knee Pants, made up for boys, age 4 to 15, from dark, heavy weight cassimeres, cheviots, cotton mixed worsteds, etc. All pants are well made, with double seat and double knee, patent elastic waistband, double sewed crotch and seat, two side and one hip pockets. Price.......... **40c**

No. 44631 The next best grade is made from a better quality of cassimere goods, in dark patterns and real heavy weight, good, honest wearing cloth. Made double seat and double knees, patent buttons on fly, elastic waistband, two side and one hip pockets.

Price **50c**

No. 44633 Boys' Knee Pants, made from ends of all-wool cassimeres, cheviots, etc. They are made from ends left over from our Custom Department, and are, therefore, very fine goods and of much better value than can possibly be had in the regular way. Made double seat and double knee, patent elastic waistband, two side and two hip pockets.

Price **75c**

No. 44635 It pays to buy boys' single Knee Pants for $1.00, when you get pants made from ends of the very best worsteds left over from our Custom Department; all shades, in fine heavy weight goods, made double seat and double knee, double sewed through crotch and seat, patent elastic waistband. Price, **$1.00**

BOYS' REEFER JACKETS.

Our boys' reefer jackets are made in sizes, age 4 to 8 for small boys, and from age 9 to 15 for large boys. Do not order reefers larger than is stated after each description, as we have only the sizes mentioned.

No. 44641 Plain reefer with storm collar, made from extra heavy Oxford Gray frieze, double-breasted style, ulster pockets, two lower pockets with flaps, body lining of good quality worsted finish blue, white and tan serge lining, black Italian cloth sleeve lining, for boys age 4 to 8 only.

Price **$2.00**

No. 44643 Plain storm collar reefer, made from same cloth as above number, made and trimmed exactly the same (see fashion figure opposite above description) except we furnish in larger sizes for boys age 9 to 15. Price........ **$2.15**

No. 44645 Made for boys age 4 to 8, from Extra Heavy Blue Gray Shetland Overcoat Cloth. A very warm reefer and one of our best numbers. Made perfectly plain, with large ulster collar and side slanting ulster pockets, two lower pockets with flaps, golf plaid serge body lining, double stitched edge.

Price for boys' double-breasted reefer, for boys age 4 to 8 only. **$2.25**

No. 44647 Made from same cloth as above only for larger boys, age 9 to 15. For fashion figure see cut opposite above number.

Price for boys age 9 to 15 . . . . **$2.50**

No. 44649 Children's Fancy Imitation Double Breasted Reefer for small boys. This is certainly a very handsome coat, made from extra quality very dark red mixed frieze, edge and all seams double stitched, two lower and change pockets, 4-inch military black velvet collar, front made imitation double breasted style, trimmed with white pearl buttons, as shown by opposite cut. Regular fly front to button just the same as a man's fly front overcoat.

Body lined with black Italian. Made in sizes 4 to 8 only.

Price **$2.75**

No. 44651 Made for large boys, age 9 to 15, from same material as above number, Dark Red Mixed Heavy Weight Frieze made perfectly plain in double breasted storm collar. Style as shown by opposite cut. Two lower pockets. Plaid serge lining. A very warm and durable coat.

Price for boys' double breasted reefer jacket, for boys age 9 to 15 only **$3.00**

No. 44653 Boys' Navy Blue. Baundahl Chinchilla Reefer for small boys age 4 to 8. For the money the best chinchilla reefer ever offered. Made double-breasted style with large sailor collar, trimmed with Hercules braid, Soutache trimming at cuff, two lower pockets with flaps, also match pocket, deep facing of black Italian, body lining of plaid serge, edge double stitched.

Price for boys' reefer jacket, for boys age 4 to 8 only . . . **$2.50**

No. 44655 Made from Baundahl Navy Blue Chinchilla, same cloth as above No. 44653, only made double-breasted plain reefer style with storm collar and ulster pockets, for large boys, age 9 to 15. Two lower outside pockets, body lining blue and white golf plaid serge, deep facing. A splendid coat for the money.

Price for boys' double-breasted storm collar reefer, for boys age 9 to 15 only, **$2.75**

No. 44657 Made from Medium Shade Oxford Gray Frieze, a heavy weight cloth that will wear like leather. This is one of the handsomest small boys' reefer jackets ever designed. When the price is lower for this pretty little coat, why buy the ordinary plain out-of-date styles from your local dealer? See fashion figure opposite, it is a perfect illustration of the coat, made fly front, trimmed down front with pearl buttons to imitate double-breasted style, four-inch black velvet collar made military style, two lower and cash pockets, silk embroidered anchor and wheel on left sleeve, turn up cuffs at wrist edged with black velvet, black Italian body lining.

Price for boys' fancy reefer, for boys age 4 to 8 only **$3.00**

No. 44659 This Reefer is made from Oxford Gray Frieze, the same cloth as is used in No. 44657, only that this coat is made plain double-breasted style with large storm collar and ulster pockets, designed for boys, age 9 to 15 only; two lower outside pockets, body lined with Italian. A splendid winter coat, neat, durable and will not show dirt.

Price for boys' double breasted reefer, for boys age 9 to 15 only **$3.25**

No. 44661 This coat is made from a very heavy, long nap Chinchilla, dark navy blue. It pays to buy a good chinchilla reefer, and it will certainly pay you to order this number, made for small boys, age 4 to 8 only. Cut double breasted style, with large sailor collar, artistically trimmed on sleeve and collar with black worsted braid, one cash and two lower outside pockets, black ivory buttons, dark blue and white worsted cloth body lining. A coat that will give you the satisfaction and know that your boy is well dressed. Price for boys' fancy reefer, for boys age 4 to 8 only **$3.50**

No. 44661¼ Made from all-wool heavy weight Navy Blue Chinchilla, same cloth as No. 44661, only made for large boys age 9 to 15, with storm collar, ulster pockets. A plain double breasted reefer, made like opposite cut shows. Economy should be the name of this coat, as a practical lesson is learned by the purchase of one.

Price of boys' double-breasted reefer, for boys age 9 to 15, **$4.00**

FUR COATS.

The fact of our selling more fur coats last season, five times over, than any previous one, was "ot that our prices were any lower, or that we advertised any more extensively. The one reason, and the only one, was because the quality was much higher.

The manufacturer, of our fur coat department says, "Not how cheap can I make a fur coat, but how good can I make it." When we have made a coat that is the very best that good raw material and skilled workmanship can make it, we know positively that it is the cheapest coat on the market.

We claim supremacy as makers of fur coats and it rightfully belongs to us. Our fur coat ideas are original, therefore our coats are different than any other make. Our last year's argument seems too true to omit calling to your attention, namely, that as much care should be taken in selecting and buying a fur coat as in purchasing a diamond. The reputation of a fur coat manufacturer and a diamond merchant is identical; the finest diamonds cannot be had at the lowest price, neither can the best of fur coats. Cheap made and shoddy fur coats bear the same relative value to good coats, such as we make, as the paste diamond to the genuine stone. It is true that while there are hundreds of fur coat manufacturers in the United States, there are fewer than one dozen that make a first-class coat, and one that will give perfect satisfaction.

We solicit your order for a fur coat with the understanding that the coat we ship you will be exactly according to our representations. We are the only house who manufacture our own coats, purchase the raw material in large quantities at the very lowest price (quality considered), and offer the finished coats to consumer direct, with but one small profit added. We are the only house who positively guarantee our coats for wear and workmanship. Every coat has attached our one-year's guarantee, covering workmanship and quality. We are the only house who use the waterproof duck interlining, as shown by skeleton cut. This is certainly a feature that must not be over-looked, as it adds to the wearing quality of a coat and makes it waterproof. A coat made in this way must necessarily be of better value than the ordinary make. The illustrated skeleton cut shows to some extent the thorough and complete manner in which we make our coats. Before any skins are cut, they are tested for strength and durability; any imperfect skins are thrown out and used in cheap coats, such as we do not make or handle. After the skins have been passed by the examiner they are matched and cut into coats. Every coat is double sewed throughout. After this is done it is interlined, as shown in cut, with a ten-ounce waterproof duck. Every seam, with the exception of the seam in the sleeve, is covered with duck and then double sewed through the duck and leather, which makes the sewing so firm that it is utterly impossible for one of our coats to rip. The center seam is covered with a 2¼-inch strip of duck and single stitched on both sides, also double stitched through the center. The front of coat is faced with an 8-inch strip of duck, with three rows of linen sewing on edge of coat. Many of our black coats are also faced down the outside edge with a ⅜-inch worsted tape. Nine-tenths of the work on a fur coat is where you cannot see it; the inside make is just where we take especial pains, and on account of this extra work we can give an absolute guarantee against ripping. Having control of the raw material before it is made up, we can also guarantee our coats for wear.

We hope that our argument in behalf of well made coats will interest you enough to favor us with your order.

SIZES
Sizes on men's fur coats run from 36 to 46 inches breast measure. Our coats are cut full size and run full 52 inches in length. Fur coats should not be worn tight. When ordering, be sure to give your correct height and weight, also the correct measurement around chest under arms, over the coat that you expect to wear the fur coat. Sizes larger than 46 inches breast measure we term as extra sizes, and we make up all extra sizes to special order, for which we charge extra, according to the quality of the goods and size ordered. If you cannot wear a 46-inch breast measure, please let us know the kind of a coat you wish to order and the size desired, and we will take pleasure in quoting your special prices.

TERMS
We recommend cash in full with all orders, as it is more satisfactory in every way to our customers. If the shipment does not meet with your approval, we can just as easily return the full purchase price of the coat as to send back only the deposit. Most of our customers send cash in full with order, as it saves time and trouble and avoids the expense of express charges which the express companies make for the return of money to us. If you do not wish to send cash with order, our terms are as follows: We require a deposit of $2.00 on all fur coats that are listed at $30.00 or less; we require a deposit of $5.00 on all fur coats listed from $42.50 to $50.00. On all fur coats listed above $50.00 we require a deposit of 10 per cent of the price of the coat ordered.

OUR BINDING GUARANTEE.
Every fur overcoat we sell is guaranteed as to quality of the fur, linings, trimmings, workmanship and finish, and any coat not satisfactory when received, can be returned at our expense and we will refund money sent us.

LET US SEND YOU A FUR COAT TO EXAMINE

and if you don't pronounce it the best coat you ever saw at the price, return it at our expense and don't pay a cent.

OUR LINE OF NATURAL BLACK DOGSKIN COATS.

The fashion figure opposite will show you as near as possible the appearance of our Natural Black Dogskin Coats. We could not give you a better description of the numbers listed than to refer you to fashion figure. All of our dogskin coats are made perfectly plain, with plain collar and sleeves. The skins in all coats are thoroughly cleaned and deodorized; they a'' not the cheap kind that are usually sold from $12.00 to $18.00, but fur coats that can be worn at any time or place with perfect satisfaction to wearer.

Natural Black Russia Dogskin Coat.

No. 44711 This coat is made from a jet black Russia dogskin; quilted Italian lined; leather arm shields; one-half interlined with 10-ounce waterproof duck, sewed through the duck and leather as shown in skeleton cut. The skins in this coat are thoroughly deodorized and is one of the handsomest fur coats ever offered. Every coat will have our one-year guarantee attached.
Price.............................$16.00

Natural Black China Dogskin Coat.

No. 44713 This coat is made from best selected natural black China dogskin. The skins are perfectly matched, which gives the coat the appearance of being made out of one hide. Quilted Italian lined; leather arm stays; fur wristers inside of cuffs; has our regular duck interlining as shown in skeleton cut. Coat in appearance does not resemble the ordinary dogskin coat. It is very heavily furred, skins are soft and pliable, and is a coat we recommend very highly. With our one-year guarantee attached.
Price.............................$18.00

Natural Black Japanese Dogskin Coat.

No. 44715 This coat is similar in appearance to our China dogskin coat, except the fur is a little shorter; no one would believe this to be a dogskin coat, as from the appearance one would imagine the coat to be worth double the price that we ask for it. The hide is soft and pliable, and the fur is as fine as silk. It is made with our regular interlined duck process, double sewed, leather arm stays, fur wristers inside of cuffs, and is the best coat of its kind you can possibly buy. Made perfectly plain, as illustration will show. Guaranteed for one year with the privilege of returning it any time if not satisfactory. Price.............................$20.00

This cut represents Nos. 44711, 44713 and 44715.

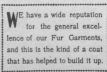

No. 44717

Our Natural Black Bearskin Coat.

THIS HEAVY FUR OVERCOAT

AT $24.50

IS THE EQUAL OF MANY THAT RETAIL AS HIGH AS $40.00 AND EVEN MORE.

No. 44717 This is the same grade of which we sold so many last season. We have prepared for the sale of several hundred more coats than we sold before. The many letters of appreciation that we have received from our customers, and the knowledge that it is the best coat for the money ever placed upon the market, leads us to believe that the sale will be unusually large this year. The Coat is made from natural black bearskin; quilted Italian lined throughout, leather armstays, patent fur wristers, sewed throughout with heavy linen, guaranteed not to rip. It is better this year than ever before.

Our price........$24.50

WE have a wide reputation for the general excellence of our Fur Garments, and this is the kind of a coat that has helped to build it up.

GALLOWAY AND RUSSIAN BUFFALO COATS.

Our Galloway Calf and Russian Buffalo Calfskin Coats, as shown by illustration opposite descriptions below, are the very best coats that we can make. Everyone who is familiar with the fur coat trade knows that Galloway Calfskin Coats and Russian Buffalo Coats are the most popular garments made to day. They take the place of Raccoon coats, so universally worn a few years ago. The fact that they give perfect satisfaction and make one of the handsomest coats possible to produce is the reason of the phenomenal sale of this particular class of coats. The coats listed below are made perfectly plain, collar and sleeves.

Natural Brown Galloway Calfskin Coat.

SPECIAL, PRICE $18.00

No. 44719 We are able to offer our customers this year a genuine Galloway Calfskin Coat at a less price than you could possibly get from any other dealer. The reason is that we purchased enough skin for several hundred coats at a very low price. We give you the benefit of this purchase offering you a coat at less money than you could get it for from any other source. This coat is made up perfectly plain, in a dark brown shade; Albert twill quilted lined; extra well made in every particular. Fully guaranteed.
Price......................$18.00

Extra Quality Seal Brown Galloway Calfskin Coat.
OUR $22.00 FUR COAT.

No. 44721 This coat is made from the very best quality of natural Galloway calfskin; made perfectly plain. Quilted Italian lined; the inside make is exactly the same as shown in skeleton cut.
Price......................$22.00

Black Galloway Calfskin Coat.
OUR $22.50 FUR COAT.

No. 44723 Our natural black Galloway calf is as perfect a coat as we can produce. We guarantee it to be equal, if not better, than any other Galloway coat on the market to day. The coat is made from the very best selected jet black Galloway calfskin, making a light, handsome, and at the same time a warm and durable coat. Has all of our special features, such as duck interlining, quilted Italian lining, leather armstays, fur wristers inside of cuffs. We guarantee it to be the handsomest coat of the kind that you can possibly purchase.
Price......................$22.50

Russia Buffalo Calfskin Coat.
OUR $24.50 FUR COAT.

No. 44725 This is a jet black coat and one of the handsomest fur coats in our entire line. We guarantee it equal to coats usually sold at from $28.00 to $32.00. If taken care of, this coat will last a lifetime. Has all of our special lining, duck interlining, etc. Fully guaranteed in every particular.
Price......................$24.50

Our Bulgarian Lambskin Coat.

No. 44727 Made from best selected stock; fur is very curly and has the appearance of a genuine Astrakhan coat. Do not pay fancy prices for Persian Lambskin coats, as this one is equal in appearance, better made and stronger leather than the average coat you would pay nearly double our price for. Has all of our special features. Written guarantee goes with every coat. This coat is made perfectly plain.
Price......................$24.50
No. 44729 Same as No. 44727, only made with Southern Beaver collar, instead of lamb.
Price......................$26.00
No. 44731 Same as No. 44727, only made in brown instead of black, perfectly plain.
Price......................$23.00

Our Russian Buffalo Calfskin Coat.

No. 44733 This coat is made from the best selected Russian Buffalo Calf stock, with southern Beaver collar, cuffs and pockets, as shown in cut. We sold hundreds of the same kind of a coat last year and we can recommend this number very highly. Skins are evenly matched, jet black in color. Coat is perfect in every particular. Quilted Italian lined. Inside make as shown by skeleton cut.

OUR SPECIAL
$28.00 PRICE

is based on the actual cost of material and labor, with but our profit added.

GUARANTEED THE BEST FUR COAT
ever made for $28.00.

SEND US $2.00 Let us send you this coat to examine; if you find it such a coat as was never before shown in your section at anything like the price, pay the express agent the balance, $26.00, and express charges, otherwise return it at our expense and we will return your $2.00.

Price......................$28.00

First Quality Norway Seal Coat.

No. 44735 This coat is made from a jet black Norway Seal; is a very glossy, short haired coat; fur is thick and it makes one of the handsomest coats possible to produce. We especially recommend this coat for wear, as it is one of the most durable high priced coats we have. Collar, cuffs and pockets trimmed with Southern Beaver. It is made with our special patent interlining, as shown by skeleton cut; edges are bound with mohair binding, worsted loops and olives. Written guarantee with every coat; privilege of returning at any time within one year if unsatisfactory.
SEND $5.00 with your order, and if you do not wish to send cash in full we will send you the coat by express C. O. D., subject to examination; balance and express charges payable after received; if not satisfactory return it at our expense, and we will return the $5.00.
Price......................$32.50

Galloway Kip Coat.

No. 44737 This coat is made from a jet black Galloway Kip. The fur is a little longer than in the Russian Buffalo Calf or Galloway Calf Coats, and is very fine and soft. This is a splendid wearing coat, and one of the most popular fur coats on the market. It is made exactly as shown in illustration except that it has only a Nutria collar instead of Southern Beaver collars and cuffs as illustration shows. Quilted Italian lined; made up with horn buttons and leather loops instead of frog loops as shown in cut.
OUR $25.00 COAT is made with a view of giving our customers such values in a fur coat for $25.00 as never before went out of this or any other market.
Let us send you this coat to examine. You must see it to appreciate the value we are giving.
Price......................$25.00

OUR LIBERAL C. O. D. TERMS

Send $2.00 with order if coat selected is $30.00 or less. We will send the coat to you by express C. O. D. subject to examination. You can examine it at your express office, and if found perfectly satisfactory pay the express agent the balance and express charges.

YOU WILL SAVE express charges on return of money of 25 to 50 cents if you send cash in full with your order, and we will immediately return your money if you are not perfectly satisfied.

OUR BINDING WRITTEN GUARANTEE

**WHICH GOES WITH EVERY GARMENT
PROTECTS YOU ALWAYS.........**

ONE YEAR GUARANTEE If any Fur Coat proves unsatisfactory any time within One Year, return it to us, and we will return your money.

MEN'S MACKINTOSHES OR RAIN COATS

WHEN A MACKINTOSH IS SPOKEN OF AS A WATERPROOF GARMENT, it must be understood that it is a THOROUGHLY RELIABLE WET WEATHER PROTECTOR, except in cases of severe and continuous rain storms.

Our mackintoshes are made from carefully selected waterproof cloth of superior quality, interlined with rubber composition and thoroughly waterproof, except under severe and unusual weather or such extraordinary storms as they will seldom be called upon to withstand. A continuous heavy rain is sometimes known to penetrate the best mackintosh cloth that is made, for mackintosh cloth, it is understood, cannot be made exceedingly stiff by a very thick interlining of rubber, but must be pliable to be used as an overcoat. Where one is liable to be exposed to constant, heavy drenching rains, a rubber surface coat or slicker should be worn.   Let it be understood, however, that our mackintoshes are the best of their class, and the various prices at which they are quoted represent the greatest values in each particular grade.

SHOULD ANY MACKINTOSH NOT GIVE SATISFACTION WE WILL CHEERFULLY MAKE AN ADJUSTMENT which will satisfy you. It must
be understood, however, that as much service cannot be expected of the cheaper grades as of the better qualities.   For this season we show 20 different garments in Men's Waterproof Rain Coats or Mackintoshes.

SEE THE THREE LARGE ILLUSTRATIONS showing the styles in which the garments are made this season, the very latest styles, the same as will be shown by the most fashionable city dealers.

STYLE 20 AS SHOWN IN THE LARGE ILLUSTRATION on this page, is a men's single breasted detachable cape waterproof mackintosh, and all our cape mackintoshes will be made in exactly the same style as shown in this illustration.

STYLE 22 AS ILLUSTRATED BELOW, represents our men's double breasted box coat mackintosh, the exact same coat as is shown in large illustration and all coats listed under style 22 are made exactly as the illustration shows.

STYLE 24 shows our single breasted fly front coat, made much after the style of an overcoat, only it is longer. Looks well worn as a regular overcoat.

HOW THEY ARE MADE. Our mackintoshes are made by the best manufacturers in this country under careful supervision, and cut full size and length, and are not skimped in any part. The proofing and vulcanizing is of the most modern processes, and we warrant every coat to give entire satisfaction.

OUR PRICES are based upon the cost to manufacture, with but one small profit added. You buy them from us at about the price your local dealer pays for them.

OUR LIBERAL $1.00 SUBJECT TO EXAMINATION TERMS OF SHIPMENT.

SEND US YOUR MEASURE AND ORDER. ENCLOSE $1.00 AND WE WILL SEND YOU ANY MACKINTOSH YOU SELECT, BY EXPRESS C. O. D., SUBJECT TO EXAMINATION.   You can examine it at your express office and if found perfectly satisfactory and exactly as represented, pay the express agent our price and express charges, less the $1.00 sent with order.

CLOTH SAMPLES ARE FREE. WE WILL SEND FREE BY MAIL POSTPAID TO ANY ADDRESS on application, cloth samples of our entire line of men's mackintoshes, with illustrations of styles, tape measure, order blanks, rules for measurement, etc.

SIZES FURNISHED. OUR MEN'S MACKINTOSHES COME REGULARLY IN SIZES 34 TO 48 INCHES BREAST MEASURE. ALL STYLES AVERAGE 52 INCHES IN LENGTH.

Extra large sizes, that is above 48 inches breast measure, and all mackintoshes of unusual proportions or styles other than quoted must be made to order, for which we charge $2.00 extra.   Special orders require about two weeks' time for making and we require cash in full with all such orders.

...HOW TO TAKE MEASURE...

ALL AROUND BREAST taken over inside coat, close up under arms.

Correct Height......feet.   Correct Weight ...pounds.
Age......years.

BOYS' OR YOUTHS' MACKINTOSHES. WE FURNISH THE FOLLOWING NUMBERS IN BOYS' SIZES, 24, 26, 28, 30, 32 and 34 breast measure.

No. 45050	Style 20 only, price	$1.00
No. 45051	Style 22 only, price	1.90
No. 45055	Style 20 only, printed plaid lining, price	3.50
No. 45056	Style 22 only, price	5.50

Always Give Height and Weight, and Breast Measure.   In Ordering Always Say that Boys' Mackintosh is Wanted.

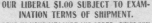

MEN'S FANCY CASSIMERE MACKINTOSH.

No. 45050 MEN'S FANCY CASSIMERE MACKINTOSH.

Made of fancy brown cloth, small check (not loud), equal to most coats sold at $4.00 in retail stores. Not a fine mackintosh, but a special value at our low price.   Made in Styles 20 and 22. Style 22 has fancy woven lining, making a heavier and more durable coat.   Style 20 has light printed lining, and is lighter weight and is made without velvet collar.   Sizes, breast measure, 34 to 48 inches.

STYLE 20   Price......................................$2.00
STYLE 22   Price............................... 2.50
Give style in your order.

OUR $2.00 TAN COVERT BOX COAT.

No. 45051 FOR $2.00 WE FURNISH A BOX COAT,

Style 22, exactly as shown in the large illustration on this page, made from this stylish, heavy weight tan colored Covert Waterproof Cloth.

WE HAVE SOLD THOUSANDS of these coats the past season with universal satisfaction and our price of $2.00 is less than the same goods are offered by jobbers in this city in hundred lots. there is nothing made anywhere that will begin to compare with this tan covert at the price.

THE CLOTH IN THIS COAT is an extra heavy double texture tan covert cloth, with fancy plaid lining, which we can guarantee for wear. It is cut double breasted in the latest box style, cut full size and length.

STYLE 22   Price for men's box coat mackintosh...$2.00
For free cloth samples of our entire line of mackintoshes, write for Sample Book No. 2K.

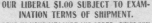

STYLE 20

OUR $2.75 BLACK SILUS CASHMERE CAPE MACKINTOSH.

No. 45052 FOR $2.75 WE OFFER this mackintosh made style 20, single breasted, with detachable cape, exactly as shown in large illustration from this extra fine imported English Silus plain black cashmere cloth.

THIS CLOTH IS WOVEN expressly for mackintoshes, and is made with fancy plaid lining.   The garments are cut full length, they are well sewed, trimmed and finished, seams are double sewed to make them waterproof and we guarantee for you such a coat as you could not get elsewhere at anything like the price.

STYLE 20   Price for men's detachable cape mackintosh coat..$2.75
For free cloth samples of our entire line of mackintoshes, write for Sample Book No. 2K.

FINE WOOL CASHMERE MACKINTOSH.

No. 45053 MEN'S FINE WOOL CASHMERE MACKINTOSH. Navy blue with new design fancy woven plaid lining.   A staple dressy, neat coat, sure to please and give entire satisfaction.   The woven lining adds greatly to its durability and appearance.   Made in two styles, 20 and 22.   Velvet collar and three pockets.   Sizes 34 to 48, breast measure.

STYLE 20   Price, cape coat........................$4.00
STYLE 22   Price, double breasted coat............. 5.00

STYLE 22

OUR $4.25 BLACK WOOL TRICOT CAPE COAT.

No. 45054 FOR $4.25 WE FURNISH Men's Mackintosh Coats in style 20, as shown in large fashion plate, made from this, one of the finest all wool Tricot mackintosh fabrics in the market.

THIS PLAIN BLACK TRICOT is made by the Waller Mills of England, one of the best grades made, and it is lined with medium dark fancy plaid cloth. The garments are cut full length and all size, trimmed with velvet collar, deep facing waterproof, pockets, sanitary arm ventilation, thoroughly first-class work throughout.

STYLE 20 Price for men's detachable cape mackintoshes..........$4.25
For free cloth samples of our entire line of men's mackintoshes, write for Sample Book No. 2K.

OUR $4.50 NAVY BLUE TRICOT DOUBLE BREASTED BOX COAT.

No. 45055 FOR $4.50 WE FURNISH THIS COAT as the equal of coats that retail generally at $6.00. This coat comes in style 22, double breasted box coat, exactly as illustrated. It is cut full length and full size, lined throughout with special mackintosh lining, and is one of the greatest values ever offered by us or any other house. All seams are sewed, strapped and cemented.

STYLE 22 Price for men's double breasted box coat...........$4.50
For free cloth samples of our entire line of men's mackintoshes, write for Sample Book No. 2K.

MEN'S MACKINTOSHES COME REGULARLY IN SIZES 34 TO 48 INCHES BREAST

MEASURE AND AVERAGE 52 INCHES IN LENGTH.
BE SURE TO GIVE CORRECT MEASUREMENTS IN ORDER

OUR $6.00 ALL-WOOL LIGHT TAN COVERT COAT IN STYLES 22 OR 24.

No. 45056 FOR $6.00 WE FURNISH THIS COAT in either double breasted box, style 22, or single breasted fly front, style 24, suitable for all seasons.

THIS IS A VERY HANDSOME MACKINTOSH. It is a medium light shade, a good weight goods, suitable for year around wear, a cloth made by the Winterville English Mills, a fine all-wool fabric. It is lined with a heavy Winter-proof Woven Mackintosh lining, vulcanized by the most improved process. All these garments have sewed, strapped and cemented seams, large velvet collars; all are guaranteed in every respect.

STYLE 22 Price for men's double breasted box coat.............$6.00
STYLE 24 Price for men's single breasted, fly front coat............ 6.00
For free cloth samples of our entire line of men's mackintoshes, write for Sample Book No. 2K.

OUR $5.25 OXFORD ALL WOOL GRAY COVERT MACKINTOSH.

IN STYLES 20 AND 22.

No. 45057 FOR $5.25 WE OFFER YOU one of the neatest cloths made up into mackintoshes. This, like all our covert mackintoshes, is made up in the best possible manner, with fancy plaid lining, large velvet collar, sanitary arm ventilations, two large and one change pocket. Style 20, seams sewed with the duplex water-proof sewed seams, and Style 22 sewed, strapped and cemented throughout. Sizes, 34 to 48 breast measure.

STYLE 20 Price for detachable cape coat.....$5.25
STYLE 22 Price for double breasted box coat 5.25

OUR $6.50 BLACK ENGLISH THIBET SINGLE OR DOUBLE BREASTED MACKINTOSH.

No. 45058 FOR $6.50 WE FURNISH MEN'S MACKINTOSHES from this fine all-wool goods in either style 22, double breasted box coat, or style 24, single breasted, fly front, exactly as shown in the two large fashion figures.

THIS IS A VERY FINE IMPORTED all-wool thibet waterproof mackintosh cloth; a goods that is woven expressly for men's mackintoshes. It is lined with a heavy waterproof woven mackintosh lining, and the proofing is the best.

THE GARMENTS ARE WELL MADE in every respect; all seams are sewed, strapped and cemented, the trimmings are of the very best; in fact, our $6.50 price is based on the actual cost of the material and labor, with but our one small percentage of profit added. Sanitary arm ventilation, velvet collars and three pockets.

STYLE 22 Price for men's double breasted box coat..............$6.50
STYLE 24 Price for men's single breasted, fly front mackintosh.......... 6.50
For free cloth samples of our entire line of men's mackintoshes, write for Sample Book No. 2K.

MEN'S HEAVY TAN ULSTER MACKINTOSH.

No. 45059 MEN'S EXTRA HEAVY ULSTER STYLE MACKINTOSH made of heavy tan Covert with heavy tan color sheeting lining. Tan color, will not show mud and dirt as do other colors. Especially adapted to the requirements of the stockman, farmer, hunter, etc. Made with special storm fly front, closed with ball and cup snap fasteners. Has large, wide, plain ulster collar, draw buckles on sleeves. Length, 54 inches only. Sizes, 34 to 48 breast. If you want the best coat made for storms or rough wear, this is the one you are looking for. No illustration. Price,...... ....$4.50

OUR SPECIAL $5.50 ALL-WOOL COVERT MACKINTOSH IN STYLE 22 OR 24.

No. 45060 FOR $5.50 WE FURNISH THIS COAT made in double breasted box coat, style 22, or single breasted, fly front, style 24. We recommend it in style 24 for either an overcoat or a waterproof coat for all seasons.

THE GOODS USED IN THESE COATS is the celebrated Stinson English Waterproof, all-wool, dark covert mackintosh cloth, a good heavy weight suitable for all seasons. It is exactly the same shade that is used largely in men's overcoats, for Spring, Summer, Fall and Winter. The coat is lined with a heavy special Stinson woven mackintosh lining, thoroughly vulcanized and proofed.

UNDERSTAND, you can have this coat either in style 22 or style 24, as shown in the large fashion figures. These garments could not be made better. They have extra wide facings, large velvet collar, sanitary arm ventilation, all seams are sewed, strapped and cemented, and have three pockets.

STYLE 22 Price for men's double breasted box coat mackintosh...$5.50
STYLE 24 Price for men's single breasted, fly front mackintosh.. 5.50
For free cloth samples of our entire line of men's mackintoshes, write for Sample Book No. 2K.

$7.00 BUYS A FINE MACKINTOSH.

No. 45061 FOR $7.00 WE FURNISH OUR VERY BEST MACKINTOSH, and one of the best mackintoshes handled by any house.

YOU COULD NOT GET A BETTER COAT than we offer you in this, if you paid $10.00. This is an entirely new pattern for this season, an all-wool English cassimere, a new fancy mixed plaid pattern in a dark mixture of brown and black with a diagonal olive effect, something that will give excellent wear, look very neat, is woven expressly for waterproof garments. Special heavy woven waterproof lining. We furnish this only in box coat, style 22, double breasted. It is cut in full length, full size, large velvet collar, sewed, strapped and cemented seams, ventilated arm holes, wide facings, a thoroughly first class coat in every respect.

STYLE 22 Price for men's double breasted box coat $7.00
For free cloth samples of our entire line of men's mackintoshes, write for Sample Book No. 2K.

OUR $11.00 HANDSOME LIGHT COLOR TAN ALL WOOL KERSEY MACKINTOSH, STYLE 22.

No. 45062 AT $11.00 we furnish you one of the handsomest coats of the season. Made up equal to coats selling at double this price. It is made of a very light color tan, all wool Covert cloth, with fancy plaid lining which harmonizes with the outer cloth; wide velvet collar, sanitary arm ventilations, light pearl buttons, two large pockets, one change pocket, sewed, strapped and cemented seams throughout, and you will and that a nobbier coat is made in no establishment. For men wishing a stylish, swell coat, we cannot recommend this one too highly. Sizes, 34 to 48 breast measure.

STYLE 22 Price for men's double breasted box mackintosh...........................$11.00

OXFORD GRAY GOLF LINED MACKINTOSH, $13.50.

No. 45063 MEN'S EXTRA QUALITY AND EXTRA HEAVY MACKINTOSH, made of fine smooth surface Oxford Gray all-wool Covert Cloth, with heavy gray plaid wool lining of light weight golf cloth, which makes up much heavier than a regular mackintosh, and will average six to seven pounds in weight. Velvet collar, sanitary arm ventilation, pearl buttons, two large pockets, one change pocket and inside pocket, sewed, strapped and cemented seams, and fine satin lined sleeves and shoulders.

IT TAKES THE PLACE OF AN OVERCOAT and at the same time proves an efficient protector from rain and wind. A superior high grade mackintosh equal to any you can obtain at retail for $20.00. Sizes, 34 to 48 breast.

STYLE 22 only. Men's double breasted box mackintosh. Each....................... ....$13.50

STYLE 24
Single Breasted Fly Front Mackintosh.

...HOW TO ORDER...

State your height and weight, state number of inches around body at breast, close up under arms, over your outside coat, over the garment you wish to wear the mackintosh.

GIVE US THE ABOVE MEASUREMENT enclose $1.00, (if you do not wish to send cash in full with your order) and thus save the return express charges on money to us; select the coat wanted from the description by number, and we will send the coat to you by express. C. O. D., subject to examination. You can examine it at your express office and if found perfectly satisfactory and exactly as represented and such value as you could not get elsewhere, pay the express agent our price and express charges less the amount sent with order.

NEARLY ALL OUR CUSTOMERS SEND CASH IN FULL. They take no risk, for we immediately return money if they are not perfectly satisfied, and they save the return express charges on money to us, which usually amounts to 15 to 40 cents.

CLOTH SAMPLES ARE FREE.

If you would like to see cloth samples of our ready-to-wear men's mackintoshes or raincoats before ordering a coat, write for Free Cloth Sample Book No. 2K.

IN OUR BOOK OF CLOTH SAMPLES of men's custom tailoring we also include a complete line of cloth samples of our waterproof mackintoshes, showing the different fabrics and linings used in our ready-to-wear men's mackintoshes. This book also contains fashion figures, tape measure, order blanks, return envelopes, etc.

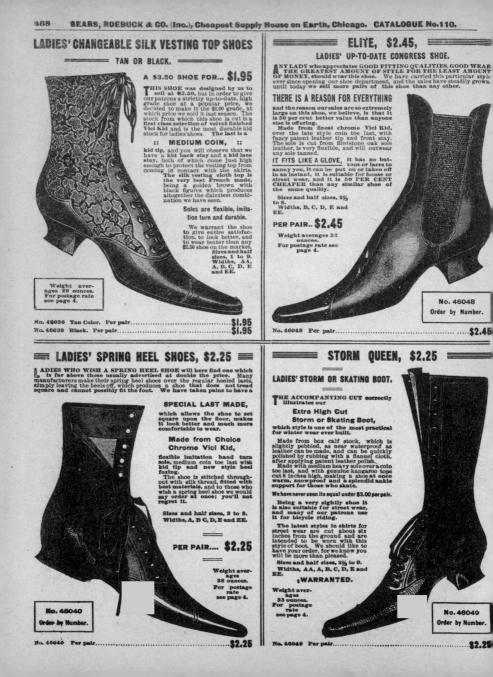

LADIES' CHANGEABLE SILK VESTING TOP SHOES

TAN OR BLACK.

A $3.50 SHOE FOR... $1.95

THIS SHOE was designed by us to sell at $3.50, but in order to give our patrons a strictly up-to-date, high grade shoe at a popular price, we decided to make it the $2.00 grade, at which price we sold it last season. The stock from which this shoe is cut is a first class selection of velvet finished Vici Kid and is the most durable kid stock for ladies'shoes.   The last is a

:: MEDIUM COIN, ::

kid tip, and you will observe that we have a kid back stay and a kid lace stay, both of which come just high enough to protect the vesting top from coming in contact with the skirts.

The silk vesting cloth top is the very best French made, being a golden brown with black figures which produces altogether the daintiest combination we have seen.

Soles are flexible, imitation turn and durable.

We warrant the shoe to give entire satisfaction, to look better and to wear better than any $2.50 shoe on the market.
Sizes and half sizes, 1 to 9.
Widths, AA, A, B, C, D, E and EE.

Weight averages 29 ounces.
For postage rate see page 4.

No. 46036 Tan Color. Per pair...................$1.95
No. 46038 Black. Per pair.........................$1.95

ELITE, $2.45,

LADIES' UP-TO-DATE CONGRESS SHOE.

ANY LADY who appreciates GOOD FITTING QUALITIES, GOOD WEAR & THE GREATEST AMOUNT OF STYLE FOR THE LEAST AMOUNT OF MONEY, should wear this shoe. We have carried this particular style ever since opening our shoe department, and the sales have steadily grown until today we sell more pairs of this shoe than any other.

THERE IS A REASON FOR EVERYTHING

and the reason our sales are so extremely large on this shoe, we believe, is that it is 50 per cent better value than anyone else is offering.

Made from finest chrome Vici Kid, over the late style coin toe last, with fancy patent leather tip and front stay. The sole is cut from flintstone oak sole leather, is very flexible, and will outwear any sole tanned.

IT FITS LIKE A GLOVE, it has no buttons or laces to annoy you, it can be put on or taken off in an instant, it is suitable for house or street wear, and it is 50 PER CENT CHEAPER than any similar shoe of the same quality.

Sizes and half sizes, 2½ to 8.
Widths, B, C, D, E and EE.

PER PAIR.. $2.45

Weight averages 32 ounces.
For postage rate see page 4.

No. 46048
Order by Number.

No. 46048 Per pair..............................$2.45

LADIES' SPRING HEEL SHOES, $2.25

LADIES WHO WISH A SPRING HEEL SHOE will here find one which is far above those usually advertised at double the price. Many manufacturers make their spring heel shoes over the regular heeled lasts, simply leaving the heels off, which produces a shoe that does not tread square and cannot possibly fit the foot. We have taken pains to have a

SPECIAL LAST MADE,

which allows the shoe to set square upon the floor, makes it look better and much more comfortable to wear.

Made from Choice Chrome Vici Kid,

flexible imitation hand turn sole, medium coin toe last with kid tip and new style heel foxing.

The shoe is stitched throughout with silk thread, fitted with best materials, and to those who wish a spring heel shoe we would say order at once; you'll not regret it.

Sizes and half sizes, 2 to 8.
Widths, A, B, C, D, E and EE.

PER PAIR.... $2.25

Weight averages 28 ounces.
For postage rate see page 4.

No. 46040
Order by Number.

No. 46040 Per pair..............................$2.25

STORM QUEEN, $2.25

LADIES' STORM OR SKATING BOOT.

THE ACCOMPANYING CUT correctly illustrates our

Extra High Cut
Storm or Skating Boot,

which style is one of the most practical for winter wear ever built.

Made from box calf stock, which is slightly pebbled, as near waterproof as leather can be made, and can be quickly polished by rubbing with a flannel cloth, after applying patent leather polish.
Made with medium heavy sole over a coin toe last, and with genuine kangaroo tops cut 8 inches high, making a shoe at once warm, snowproof and a splendid ankle support for those who skate.

We have never seen its equal under $3.00 per pair.

Being a very slightly shoe it is also suitable for street wear, and many of our patrons use it for bicycle riding.

The latest styles in skirts for street wear are cut about six inches from the ground and are intended to be worn with this style of boot. We should like to have your order, for we know you will be more than pleased.

Sizes and half sizes, 2½ to 9.
Widths, AA, A, B, C, D, E and EE.

¡WARRANTED.

Weight averages 33 ounces.
For postage rate see page 4.

No. 46049
Order by Number.

No. 46049 Per pair..............................$2.25

JENNESS — FOOT FORM SHOE — $2.65

WE have called this shoe JENNESS from the fact that it is made over the famous Jenness Miller hygienic foot form last, which for comfort, fitting qualities, and stylish appearance excels anything on the market.

THE UPPER STOCK is a special tannage of velvet finished Vici kid which is as soft as a kid glove, will wear like iron, and the sole leather in the bottoms is especially selected for this shoe and is very flexible, notwithstanding the fact that the bottoms are quite plump.

THE SHOE is slipper foxed (mannish style), is a true Goodyear Welt sewn, insuring a perfectly smooth insole, and is fitted with the newest full military heel and custom backstay.

THE UP-TO-DATE WOMAN of today requires a substantial yet stylish shoe, and although it is a hard combination we believe we here offer a shoe that fills the bill, and at a wonderfully low price.

WE WANT YOUR ORDER for a pair of these shoes if you desire the mannish shape and we guarantee to send you such a shoe as you could not possibly get elsewhere under $3.50 to $4.00.

Sizes and half sizes, 2½ to 8. Widths, AA, A, B, C, D, E, and EE.

Weight averages 32 oz.

For postage rate see page 4.

No. 46059
Per Pair, $2.65

LADIES' PATENT LEATHER LACE — $1.95

TO PRODUCE a ladies' genuine patent leather shoe at the small price of $1.95 per pair and still retain the style and fit of the higher grade shoes has been a difficult problem. In order to give our customers such a shoe as we have figured with all of the largest Eastern factories and even then have been compelled to sacrifice the greater part of our profit.

THIS SHOE is made from Riley's best grade of patent leather, which is considered one of the best American makes. It is fitted with a fine black serge cloth top, kid lace stay and backstay, medium concave heel, and light weight sewn soles.

THE STYLE OF LAST is the very latest coin toe, with fancy imitation stitched tip. It is impossible to warrant patent leather shoes, but knowing the maker of this leather as we do, we can recommend it as being generally satisfactory, and those wishing a patent leather shoe at this price will make no mistake in ordering this one.

THIS SHOE is made in our best factory and contains all of the style, good-fitting qualities and good workmanship found in the highest grade shoes.

Sizes and half sizes, 2½ to 8. Widths, C, D, E, and EE.

Weight averages 30 oz.

See page 4 for postal rates.

No. 46068
Per Pair... $1.95

AIDA — LADIES' GOODYEAR WELT LACE — $2.55
...A SPECIAL DRIVE...

THE UPPER STOCK from which these shoes are made is cut from a very fine brand of Vici kid, which was never before put into a shoe to sell under $3.50. The soles are from the best selection of oak tan sole leather, which is flexible and the very best produced. They are sewed on by the Goodyear Welt process; some call them hand sewed, and, as a matter of fact, they are put up in the same manner as the old-fashioned hand made shoes. The inner soles are smooth; no thread or nails to hurt the feet. Outsoles slightly extended, which protects the uppers, and they can be half soled by hand just the same as the hand made shoe.

THE STYLE is the very latest, the toe being round, about the width of a quarter dollar; fancy perforated kid tip; new foxed heel, giving the foot a very graceful appearance, and at the same time very easy and comfortable.

THE PRICE, $2.55, brings them within the reach of all, and we might mention the fact that we know of no concern in existence has ever put out a shoe equal to these for less than $3.50 a pair.

Sizes and half sizes, 2½ to 9. Widths, AA, A, B, C, D, E and EE.

WARRANTED.

Weight averages 33 oz.

For postage rate see page 4...

No. 46064
Per Pair, $2.55

LADIES' BLACK VICI KID BUTTON — $2.00

THE STOCK in this shoe is a good selection of Vici kid, very soft and glove like and at the same time tough and durable. Made over a handsome coin last with fancy kid tip and new style heel foxing. The soles are cut from best Flintstone oak sole leather, and being very flexible, insure comfort and good service. We have these shoes made over the same foot fitting lasts as our finer grades, fitted with outside backstay, and we assure you that you get all of the style, comfort and good wear usually found in the $4.00 kind.

WARRANTED.

Sizes and half sizes, 2½ to 8. Widths, C, D, E and EE. Weight averages 29 ounces.

For postage rate see page 4.

No. 46076
Order by Number.

No. 46076
Per Pair... $2.00

LADIES' WELT BUTTON, $2.55

THIS SHOE is cut from the same Vici kid stock as No. 46064, and having used this stock in our $3.00 shoes for several seasons, we know it will give the best satisfaction. Oak sole leather, which is very flexible and at the same time is the most durable ever produced, is used for bottoms, and being sewed on by the Goodyear welt process, makes the shoe just as easy and durable as the old hand made shoe. They are easy from the fact that they have smooth insoles, no thread or nails to hurt the feet, and when the soles do wear thin, they can be half soled by hand, the same as the old-fashioned custom made shoes. The style of last is the very latest, the toe being slightly wider than No. 46064, and to give the shoe the very best appearance, we fit it with a straight kid tip. We aim to give you more shoe leather, more style and more wear for $2.55 than any other concern can give you for half as much again.

Sizes and half sizes, 2½ to 9. Widths, A, B, C, D, E and EE.

Weight averages 33 ounces.

For postage rate see page 4.

No. 46066
Per Pair, $2.55

THE LATEST STYLE COMMON SENSE... LACE — $2.00

WE make this shoe from a fine soft Vici kid, over a handsome round toe common sense last, and with straight perforated patent leather tip.

THE SOLES are cut from best oak sole leather, therefore imitation hand turn and much more durable than those usually found on a shoe at this price.

THE BACK STAY is of the very latest pattern, extending from heel nearly to top of shoe, making it absolutely rip proof, and to add all the comfort possible, we fit the shoe with the very latest style military heel, which is the most comfortable made.

WARRANTED.

Sizes and half sizes, 2½ to 9. Widths, D, E and EE.

Weight averages 29 ounces. For postage rate see page 4.

No. 46079
Order by Number.

No. 46079
Per Pair... $2.00

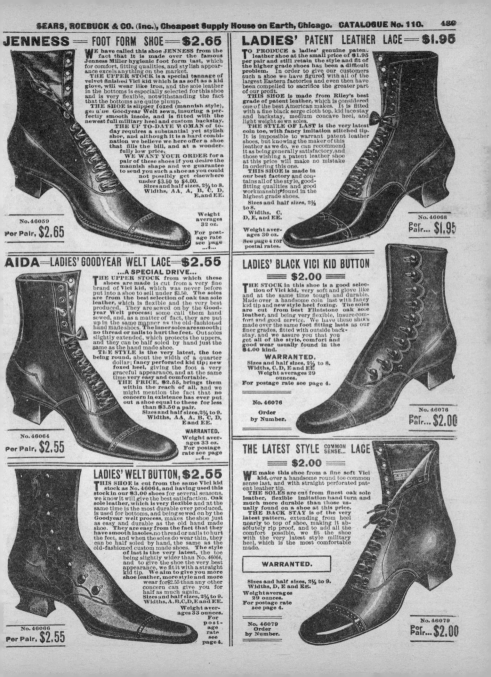

Misses' and Children's Tan Lace, $1.25 and $1.00.

This shoe is one which ... ell at a very close ... n in order to give ou... rons a shoe for little money, which at the same time will give good service and have an attractive appearance. Made from a very good selection of tan colored Vici kid over a medium coin last with tip to match. The shoe has the late heel foxing, carries good bottom stock and will give splendid service.

For postage rate see page 4.

Widths, D, E and EE. Weight averages 22 ounces.
No. 46345 Girls' sizes, 11½, 12, 12½, 13, 13½, 1, 1½ and 2. Price, per pair......$1.25
No. 46347 Child's sizes, 8, 8½, 9, 9½, 10, 10½ and 11. Price, per pair......$1.00

Little Gent's Box Calf Lace, $1.15.

No. 46382 This little gent's shoe is made from a good grade of genuine box calf, over a medium coin toe last, with tip. It is fitted with medium heavy soles, and so built as to insure good service. This shoe is made for children, and can be furnished only in the sizes quoted below. Not intended for men. Sizes and half sizes 9 to 13½. Weight averages 24 ounces.

For postage rate see page 4.
Per pair..$1.15

Shoes for Little Men—Just Like Papa's, $1.00

No. 46384 This little men's shoe is not intended for grown up people but for children, and we cannot furnish it in any sizes not quoted here. Made from satin calf stock over a coin last with tip toe and good dongola tops; the style is almost exactly like that of men's shoes, hence it is liked by the little folks. Sizes and Half Sizes, 9 to 13½. Widths, D, E and EE. Weight averages 22 oz. For postage rate see page 4.

Per pair. $1.00

Misses' and Children's Dongola Oxfords.

$1.20 and $1.00

Weight about 18 ozs.

We have this Oxford made just like our finest Ladies' Oxfords, which gives it a style not ordinarily found in a shoe for this price. Cut from a fine chrome kid, with flexible hand turned soles, spring heel and fancy patent leather tip and lace stays.

Widths D, E and EE.

No. 46510 Sizes, 11, 11½, 12, 12½, 13, 13½, 1, 1½ and 2. Per pair......$1.20
No. 46512 Sizes, 8, 8½, 9, 9½, 10 and 10½. Per pair......$1.00

Misses' and Children's Sandals.

Chocolate Color.

Misses' and Children's Strap Sandals, made from a choice selection of chocolate Vici kid over the narrow coin last, with a plain toe. The soles are hand turned, making them very flexible and easy. Widths, C, D, E and EE. Weight about 10 oz.
No. 46524 Sizes, 11½, 12, 12½, 13, 13½, 1, 1½ and 2. Price, per pair......$1.00
No. 46526 Sizes, 8, 8½, 9, 9½, 10, 10½ and 11. Price, per pair......90c
No. 46528 Sizes, 5, 5½, 6, 6½, 7 and 7½. Price, per pair......80c

For postage rate, see page 4.

Child's Red or Tan Lace, $0.95.

We herewith illustrate our finest Vici Kid, lace shoe for Children, made with fancy inserted vesting top. Made over latest style coin last, straight tip, strictly hand turned soles, and such a shoe as you will find only in the best retail stores, and there at prices fully 50 per cent above ours. We have the latest shade of red or chocolate color as desired. Order by number. Sizes, 4 to 8. Widths, C, D, E, and EE. Weight averages 12 ounces.
No. 46543 Red kid. Per pair......$0.95
No. 46645 Tan kid. Per pair......95

Child's Paris Kid Button, Black or Tan, $0.75.

Child's Fine Shoes, spring heel, made from best selection of Paris kid, black or tan, worked button holes, hand turn, fancy foxed heel, medium toe, with patent leather tip, on the black shoe, kid tip on the tan colored, and suitable for fine dress-wear. Widths, C, D, and E.
Sizes, 4, 4½, 5, 5½, 6, 6½, 7, 7½, and 8. Weight, about 13 ounces.
No. 46550 Black. Per pair......$0.75
No. 46552 Tan color. Per pair......75

Child's Paris Kid Lace Shoes, $0.75.

No. 46554 Child's Very Fine Paris Kid Lace Shoes, made over new coin last, with fancy patent leather tip and lace stays. The shoe is strictly hand turned, flexible soles, has the new fancy heel foxing and for a fine dress shoe is very desirable. Sizes, 4, 4½, 5, 5½, 6, 6½, 7, 7½ and 8. Widths, D, E and EE. Weight, about 13 ounces.
Per pair......$0.75

Child's Fat Baby Shoes at $0.75.

No. 46558 Child's Fat Baby Shoes, made from fine quality of kid skin, spring heel, patent leather tip and cut with extra wide soles and full ankles. The soles are hand turn, flexible, and it has worked buttonholes. Sizes, 4 to 8. Width, EE only. Weight, about 13 oz.
Per pair......$0.75

Child's Kid Button Shoes, $0.65.

No. 46568 Child's Kid Button, made from soft, glove-like stock, spring heel, flexible soles, patent leather tip all solid and durable. Sizes, 5, 5½, 6, 6½, 7, 7½ and 8.

Weight, about 13 oz.

For postage rate see page 4.

Price, per pair, $0.65

Child's Kangaroo Calf Button Shoe.

No. 46570 Child's Kangaroo Calf Button Shoe, cut from good, plump stock; very soft, flexible soles, and a serviceable, stylish shoe for little money.

Sizes, 5, 6, 7 and 8, no half sizes.

Weight, about 15 ounces.

Price, per pair......$0.75

Infants' Tan or Red Kid Button, $0.65.

This Infants' Shoe is made from Fine Chrome Kid, the latest dark chocolate color, or the fashionable red, hand sewed, medium coin toe, with tip, and no heel. Nothing finer made at any price. Sizes, 2, 2½, 3, 3½, 4, 4½ and 5. Weight about 10 ounces.
No. 46574 Tan color, per pair......$0.65
No. 46575 Red, per pair......65

Fat Baby, $0.65.

No. 46580 Infants' Domestic Kid, Fat Baby Shoe, button, no heels, very light and fine, and cut large at ankles, especially for thick, fat feet. Sizes, 2 to 5. Weight is about 10 ounces. For postage rate see page 4.
Price, per pair......$0.65

Infants' Shoes, $0.60

No. 46582 Infants' Glazed Dongola Kid Button, very good stock, latest heel foxing, turn soles, no heel, medium toe, with tip and neat tassel at top. A very dressy shoe. Sizes, 2, 2½, 3, 3½, 4, 4½ and 5. Weight, about 10 ounces. For postage rate see page 4.
Per pair......$0.60

Infants' Kid Button Shoes, $0.45.

No. 46584 Infants' Kid Button, turned sole, patent leather tip, no heel, a neat and well made shoe. Sizes, 2, 2½, 3, 3½, 4, 4½ and 5. Weight, about 10 ounces. For postage rate see page 4.
Per pair... $0.45

Infants' Princess, $0.35.

This is one of the leading novelties in infants' wear for the coming season. It is made from the finest kid, kid sole, handsomely trimmed with silk ribbon and has silk ribbon tie at ankle, which holds it in position. There is nothing nicer for the baby than this shoe. Sizes, 1 to 4. In single cartoon.
No. 46586 Tan color, per pair......$0.35
No. 46587 Wine color, per pair......35
Weight, about 6 ounces.

Infants' Soft Sole Tan and Black, $0.25.

No. 46588 This shoe is made from a choice selection of genuine kid, fancy stitched, has kid sole, and is a very pretty shoe for an infant. Cut very full, so you will have no trouble to put them on. Color, tan. Sizes, 1, 2, 3 and 4.
Per pair......$0.25
No. 46590 The same style, in Black kid. Sizes, 1, 2, 3 and 4. Per pair......$0.25
Weight, about 6 ounces.

Our Special Infants' Moccasin. $0.15.

No. 46598 This Infants' Moccasin is one we have made for our own trade, and we guarantee that it is unequaled for price and quality by any concern in existence. It is made from soft Dongola stock, very full, so you will have no trouble putting it on. Sateen lined, silk stitched, and handsome silk cord laces. Colors, tan and wine. Sizes, 1, 2, 3 and 4. Sold by other houses at 35 cents. Our price, per pair......$0.15
Weight, about 3 ounces.

...THE... MOTORMAN'S BEST.

HIGH CUT. MEN'S BEST BEAVER FELT SHOE.

EXTRA HIGH CUT, lace, medium toe, solid comfort felt insole. This shoe has a

VERY FINE AND SOFT LEATHER FOXING,

long tip toe, and while it is fully as warm as the all felt shoe it is more desirable on account of the leather sole and foxing which enables the wearer to go in the snow the same as if he wore a full leather shoe.

Sizes 6 to 12. No half sizes.

No. 46600

Weight, about 50 ounces. **PER PAIR, - $2.00**
FOR POSTAGE RATE, SEE PAGE 4.

...Men's All Felt Congress...

MEN'S CONGRESS SHOES.

MADE FROM VERY BEST BEAVER FELT THROUGHOUT.

THIS SHOE HAS A HEAVY FELT SOLE, cut from one piece of solid wool felt and treated in such a way as to make it very flexible and at the same time very durable.

NOTHING LIKE IT EVER BEFORE OFFERED AT THIS LOW PRICE.

Sizes, 6 to 12. No half sizes.

No. 46608

Weight, about 40 ounces. **PER PAIR, - $1.50**
FOR POSTAGE RATE, SEE PAGE 4.

.MEN'S ALL FELT SHOES..

THIS SHOE IS MADE FROM the VERY BEST BEAVER FELT THROUGHOUT. The sole is made from one heavy piece of felt, and is very much superior to the two piece soles which are put on the cheaper grades of felt shoes.

WE GUARANTEE THIS SHOE

not only to be warm and comfortable, but to be the BEST EVER OFFERED FOR THE MONEY.

Sizes, 6 to 12.

No half sizes..

No. 46610

Weight, about 40 ounces. **PER PAIR, - $1.50**
FOR POSTAGE RATE, SEE PAGE 4.

LADIES' FELT BUTTON.

MADE FROM FINE BEAVER FELT, and with felt sole from ¼ to ⅜ inch thick.

THIS SHOE WILL WEAR LONGER THAN ANY FELT SHOE WE HAVE EVER SEEN.

If you wear felt shoes do not pass this one, as we warrant it to give entire satisfaction. It is very light, is comfortable, and fits as neatly as any Dongola shoe.

Sizes and half sizes, 2½ to 8.

No. 46616

Weight, about 28 ounces. **PER PAIR, - $1.50**
FOR POSTAGE RATE, SEE PAGE 4.

Men's and Women's Hand Sewed Felt Slippers..

THESE SLIPPERS WE HAVE MADE ESPECIALLY FOR OUR OWN TRADE, and we believe them to be superior to anything ever placed upon the market. Made from a fine beaver felt, all wool, with a felt sole sewed on by hand and a leather outer sole made from harness leather. The outer sole is sewed on by hand, making it very flexible and easy. Don't be surprised if they last three winters. We positively guarantee them to out-wear any felt slipper ever made.

Weight, about 25 ounces. For Postage rate see Page 4

ORDER BY NUMBER.

No. 46612	Men's Sizes, 6 to 12.	Per pair, -	**$0.85**
No. 46614	Ladies' Sizes, 3 to 8.	Per pair, -	**.75**

...MEN'S FELT ROMEO LEATHER SOLE...

THE WAY THIS SLIPPER IS MADE is entirely new, the upper and sole being cut from one piece of black felt, and the leather sole put on after the felt shoe is completed. The sole is sewed to the upper and is

MADE FROM THE FINEST BELTING LEATHER,

which, as you probably know is very flexible and the most durable ever tanned. We have never seen a slipper which insures so much comfort and good wear at such a ridiculously low price.

Sizes, 6 to 11. Widths, E & EE.

No. 46611

Weight, about 28 ounces. **PER PAIR, - $1.00**
FOR POSTAGE RATE, SEE PAGE 4.

MEN'S BOX CALF BLUCHERS, $3.00 TAN OR BLACK.

FASHIONABLE BULL DOG LAST. HAND SEWED.

THE SWELLEST THING in Fine Shoes is the BLUCHER STYLE, and by actual observation we have found that four-fifths of all the swellest dressers in New York, Boston, and the other large eastern cities are wearing this style of shoe.

IT COSTS NOTHING to have the very latest creations, provided you buy your shoes from us. Our shoes are made over the very latest style of lasts, and we are especially anxious to introduce this particular style in your locality.

THE STOCK. The stock from which these shoes are cut is White Bros.' Box Calf, and is one of the most serviceable leathers tanned. It has a slightly pebbled surface, is as near waterproof as leather can be made and can be polished by applying the patent leather paste and rubbing with a flannel cloth. Those who have worn Box Calf Shoes will now have nothing else.

THE WORKMANSHIP is the very best that can be had at any price. The shoe is fitted with fast color hooks and eyelets. It is stitched throughout with silk and linen, fitted with the latest outside backstay and carries the very best California Oak Soles, which being sewed on by hand welt process are very flexible and more comfortable than a machine sewed shoe can possibly be made.

A BETTER SHOE you cannot possibly buy at any price. WE WANT YOU to try a pair of these shoes because we know you will be pleased. You show them to your friends and we will thus sell several pairs of shoes in your immediate vicinity, and every time we do sell a pair of these shoes, we feel sure of a perfectly satisfied customer. We carry this shoe in the latest tan shade as well as black. Order by number.

FOR $3.00

We can furnish you this season, more style, more wear, a better fit and more solid comfort for the feet than it is possible to obtain elsewhere at any price.

SIZES AND HALF SIZES, 5 TO 12.
WIDTHS—A, B, C, D, E and EE.

Weight averages 43 ounces. For postage rate see page 4.

WE WANT YOUR ORDER FOR A PAIR OF THESE HIGH GRADE BLUCHER SHOES for $3.00, and if you send it to us we will guarantee to give you a better shoe than you can possibly obtain anywhere else at any price.

No. 46798 Latest Tan Shade.
Per Pair.................$3.00
No. 46800 Black Box Calf. Per Pair. $3.00

MEN'S BOX CALF HIGH CUT . . .

STORM SHOE.

THE SHOE which we here with illustrate is one of the most desirable of the new styles shown for Fall and Winter wear, and in fact is a splendid shoe at any season to wear hunting. Made from White Bros.' genuine box calf stock, over the latest style bull dog last with fancy full perforated tip, tops cut extra high, and leather outside back stay running from heel to top of shoe. We build this shoe with heavy soles, full outside extension edges and especially for good hard wear, as it is stitched throughout with best silk and linen, making a shoe more durable than any we have ever offered, and at the same time fully as stylish and neat in appearance as our finest shoes. This style was worn largely last season in all Eastern cities, and we predict a large sale for it.
Sizes and half sizes, 5 to 11
Widths, C, D, E and EE.
Weight averages 60 ounces.
For postage rate, see page 4.
Per pair,

$2.75

No. 46813
Order by Number.

MEN'S 9 WIDE LACE, $2.75

GOODYEAR WELT.

This shoe is made from the best Wax Calfskin, plump weight, with plump Dongola top. The soles are cut from best oak sole leather and sewed on by the Goodyear welt process. This shoe is trimmed with bleached calfskin, sewed with best silk and linen thread and is especially desirable for those with fat, wide feet from the fact that it is made on the 9 wide or FFFF last, and low flat heel.

Sizes and Half Sizes, 5 to 12. Width, FFFF, only. Weight averages 60 ounces.

For postage rate see page 4.

Warranted
Equal to any
$5.00 Calfskin
Shoe made.

No. 46802 Lace, pair
$2.75

MEN'S 9 WIDE CONGRESS, $2.75

GENUINE GOODYEAR WELT SOLES.

THIS SHOE, LIKE THE ONE ABOVE, IS MADE FROM FINE WAX CALFSKIN,

Plump weight, genuine Dongola tops, and fitted with best warranted hub gore. Genuine Goodyear welt soles, sewed throughout with best silk and linen and made over the FFFF or 9 wide last especially for thick, fat feet.

. . . WARRANTED . . .

Sizes and Half Sizes, 5 to 12.

For postage rate see page 4.

No. 46804 Per pair,
$2.75

THE BOSTON MEN'S KANGAROO BAL,
$2.50 ┊ Goodyear Welt.

THE LEATHER MARKET is in a very unsettled condition and shoes to-day are worth about 20 per cent more than they were at the time our No. 109 catalogue was issued. We are especially glad, however, through an extraordinary effort, to be able to offer this

Genuine Australian Kangaroo Shoe at the same old price of . . . $2.50.

SUCH SHOE VALUE was never before offered and on the present market would be impossible but for our foresight.

GENUINE KANGAROO leather is very soft and pliable and while it is the ideal leather for summer wear and those with tender feet, it is more durable than many heavier leathers, and makes a splendid dress shoe at any season.

HOW IT IS MADE. We make this shoe alongside of our best goods, over the fashionable Boston last, with tip toe. It is fitted with custom back stay, trimmed in the best possible manner, has white oak soles sewed on by the Goodyear welt process, making them at once flexible and producing a perfectly smooth innersole. Such a shoe bought elsewhere would cost from $3.50 to $4.00.

THE BOSTON last over which this shoe is made, is one which we got out to fit our special trade, and it is really the neatest, most stylish, best fitting and most comfortable round toe last we have ever seen.

WE WANT YOUR ORDER FOR A PAIR OF THESE SHOES, and if you do not consider them the equal of anything you can buy at home for half as much again, send them back and get your money

SIZES AND HALF SIZES, 5 TO 12.
WIDTHS—C, D, E, AND EE.

Weight, averages 40 ounces. For postage rate see page 4.

No. 46817
ORDER BY NUMBER.

Price, per pair, $2.50

MEN'S BOX CALF LACE. LEATHER LINED...... $2.45

TAN OR BLACK.
Box calf stock is fast becoming the most popular of men's shoes, both for summer and winter wear, the stock has a pebbled surface and is as near waterproof as leather can be made. Will outwear any ordinary calfskin, and can be polished with patent leather paste or any liquid dressing. We make this shoe over the new Broadway last, with tip, extra heavy soles, extended edges and with the fashionable English back stay. The shoe has three rows of silk stitches on tip vamp and quarter, is fitted with celluloid eyelets (never turn brassy) and is lined throughout with leather, making a very stylish and practical shoe for general wear. Furnished in Tan color or Black as desired. Warranted.

Sizes and half sizes, 5 to 12. Widths, C, D, E and EE. Weight averages 58 ounces.

For postage rate, see page 4.
Order by... ...Number.

No. 46827 Tan color. Per pair, $2.45
No. 46829 Black. Per pair, $2.45

MEN'S STORM PROOF LACE, $2.15
INVISIBLE RUBBER SOLE.

The stock in this line is a first-class selection of Badger calfskin, medium weight and serviceable. The principal feature of the shoe is a full sheet of rubber which is placed between the inner sole and outer sole, making the bottoms waterproof. Between the vamps and the drill lining which comes next to the foot is placed a waterproof oiled lining, making in all the ideal storm-proof shoe. The bottoms are of the best stock, medium heavy and the shoe has best of Dongola topping. To make this shoe doubly strong we fit it with English back stay, making it practically rip proof. Order by number. Sizes, 6 to 12. Widths, D, E and EE. Wt. averages 58 oz.

No. 46834 Lace, Price, per pair... $2.15
For postage rate see page 4.
Order by Number.

MEN'S KANGAROO CONGRESS $2.50
Genuine Goodyear Welt.

We were the first concern in the United States to offer a genuine Australian Kangaroo shoe at $2.50 per pair, and while the shoe was machine sewed it was very much better than anyone else sold under $3.00 per pair. Determined as we always are to keep in the lead, we offer this season a Genuine Goodyear Welt Kangaroo Shoe for the same small price. This shoe, as you will note by illustration, is made over the globe last, and is especially desirable for those having tender feet. The Kangaroo stock is very soft and pliable and at the same time as tough as any leather tanned. The soles are cut from oak sole leather, being sewed on by the Goodyear Welt process; are very flexible and much more comfortable than it is possible to make a machine sewed shoe.

Sizes and Half Sizes, 5 to 12. Width C, D, E & EE. Weight averages 40 Ounces.

No. 46819 Per pair.......... $2.50

For postage rate, see page 4.

ORDER BY NUMBER.

MEN'S KANGAROO LACE, $2.50
Goodyear Welt.

It is a well known fact that genuine Australian Kangaroo leather is the most comfortable for tender feet and also more tough than many leathers twice as heavy. This shoe is made especially for those who want a soft comfortable shoe, over the plain toe globe last and genuine Goodyear welt oak soles of medium weight. The shoe is stitched throughout with silk and linen, fitted with calf inside lace stay and top band and actually equal to many shoes sold elsewhere at $4.00 per pair.

Sizes and half sizes, 5 to 12. Widths, C, D, E and EE. Weight averages 40 ounces.

No. 46825 Per pair.......... $2.50

Order by Number.

For postage rate, see page 4.

Ladies' Jersey Leggings.

No. 47201 Ladies' Fine imported All-Wool Jersey Leggings, knee length, and with ribbon top. The Jersey cloth legging fits like a stocking, and being all wool, is warm and comfortable. Color, black. Shoe sizes, 1 to 7. Per pair................$0.65 Weight, 8 ounces. For postage rate see page 4.

No. 47203 Ladies' Fine Black All Wool Melton Leggings, knee length, with 9 buttons and buckle at top. Nothing like it ever offered at this price. Shoe sizes, 1 to 7. Per pair......$0.48 Weight, 8 ounces. For postage rate see page 4.

Combination Thigh Legging.
Ladies', Misses' and Children's.

This cut is a very good illustration of our Combination Legging and Overgaiter. It is without a doubt the best fitting, warmest and most comfortable legging that can be produced. Being made from a fine black Jersey cloth, it fits as closely as a stocking, and conforms to every movement of the limb. Has 7 buttons up side, and ribbon top.

No. 47205 Ladies' sizes, 1 to 7. Per pair................$1.00
No. 47207 Misses' sizes, 12 to 2. Per pair................$0.90
No. 47209 Child's sizes, 8 to 11. Per pair................$0.75
No. 47210 Infant's sizes, 4 to 7. Per pair................$0.60
Weight, 9 ounces. For postage rate see page 4.

Ladies' and Men's Overgaiters.

No. 47211 Ladies' Fine Overgaiters made heavy for Fall and Winter wear. Shoe sizes, 1 to 7. Per pair, $0.19
No. 47215 Ladies' 7-button Imported Kersey, Silk Ribbon, Top Facing; the nobbiest and unexcelled. Per pair................$0.59
No. 47219 Men's Heavy 5-button Melton. Per pair................$0.23
No. 47223 Men's Heavy 5-button imported Kersey shoe. Sizes, 6 to 11. Per pair, $0.45 Weight, 8 ounces. For postage rate, see page 4.

RUBBER BOOTS AND SHOES.
We Handle None but the Very Best Rubber Goods Made.

Ladies' Extra Light Buckle Arctics, for Fine Wear.

No. 47318 Ladies' extra light Buckle Arctics, made from pure gum rubber with very fine Jersey cloth tops, suitable for dress wear. Made over a splendid fitting coin last. Sizes, 2¾ to 8; weight, 16 ounces. Per pair $1.00

Men's, Boys' and Youths' Heavy Buckle Arctics.

These Arctics are made extra heavy, dull finish, very heavy cloth top, wool fleece lined and are strictly first quality--suitable for heavy wear. Broad toe only

No. 47300 Men's Arctics, first quality. Sizes 6 to 2½ full width; weight, 39 oz. Per pair.......$1.46
No. 47302 Boys' Arctics, first quality, sizes 2 to 5½; weight, 24 oz. Broad toe only. Per pair....$1.10
No. 47304 Youths' Arctics, first quality, sizes 10 to 1; weight, 20 oz. Broad toe only. Per pair....95c

RUBBER BOOTS AND SHOES.

WHEN COMPARING OUR PRICES ON RUBBER FOOTWEAR with storekeeper's prices, WE WANT YOU TO KNOW that we handle ONLY FIRST QUALITY RUBBERS.

NOT A SINGLE SECOND can find its way into our stock and we give you a full dollar's value for EVERY DOLLAR SPENT IN THIS ESTABLISHMENT.
DO NOT BUY RUBBERS which DEALERS HAVE CARRIED OVER FROM LAST YEAR. They have lost much of their wearing quality. In buying from us YOU ARE SURE OF GETTING NEW, FRESH GOODS since our output is so large that NEW CONSIGNMENTS ARE CONSTANTLY ARRIVING from the factory.
BE CAREFUL TO SEND SIZE of shoes over which rubbers are to be worn. RUBBERS SHOULD NOT BE SENT BY MAIL, but when shipped by freight or express with other goods the cost of transportation is very little.

Ladies', Misses' and Children's Buckle Arctics.

No. 47306 Ladies' first quality Buckle Arctics, heavy cloth top, wool fleece lined and suitable for heavy wear. Sizes, 2½ to 8; full width. Broad toe only. Weight, 20 oz. Per pair...$1.00
No. 47308 Misses' first quality Buckle Arctics, heavy cloth top, wool fleece lined; heel or spring heel; made for heavy wear. Sizes, 11¼ to 2; full width. Broad toe only. Weight, 16 oz. Per pair $0.75
No. 47310 Child's first quality Buckle Arctics, spring heel, wool fleece lined. Sizes, 6 to 10½; weight, 10 oz. Broad toe only. Per pair......$0.55

Men's Extra Light Buckle Arctics, for Fine Wear, $1.45.

No. 47316 Men's Extra light Buckle Arctics, made from first quality of pure gum rubber, very fine Jersey cloth top and suitable for fine wear. Made over a handsome coin last and which fits splendidly. Sizes, 6 to 12; weight, 24 oz.

No. 47316 Pr pair, $1.45
No. 47317 Same as above, broad toe. Pair..$1.45

Men's Light Beacon Gaiters. 4-Buckle, $2.10.

No. 47320 This 4-buckle Shoe is cut extra high, is snow excluding, and being impervious to water over half way up makes it a very dry and warm shoe. It is made from the very best of pure gum rubber, with a heavy cloth top, and over the late style coin last. This is certainly a very comfortable shoe and looks as neat as a light arctic. Sizes, 6 to 11; weight, 42 ounces. Per pair........$2.10
No. 47321 Same as above, broad toe. Per pair........$2.10

Men's All-Rubber Arctics, $1.50.

No. 47298 Men's All-Rubber Arctics, made from heavy duck and covered with rubber, making the most durable arctic yet produced and one that can be cleaned with sponge and water.

Sizes, 6 to 12. No half sizes. Price, per pr..$1.50

Ladies', Misses' and Child's Beacon Gaiters.

No. 47326 Ladies' high cut Gaiter, made from first quality pure gum rubber, Jersey cloth top, and wool fleece lined. This is a neat, durable shoe and very comfortable. It is made especially to fit the coin toe shoes, and the buckles are so easily adjusted that many prefer it to the button gaiter. Sizes, 2½ to 8; weight, 17 oz. Per pair......$1.70
No. 47328 Misses' Extra High Cut, 3-Buckle Gaiter, made from first quality rubbers as above, coin toe only. Sizes, 11 to 2, weight, 14 oz. Pair..$1.40
No. 47329 Child's Extra High Cut, 3-Buckle Gaiter, made from pure gum rubber as above, coin toe only. Sizes, 8 to 10½; weight, 10 oz. Per pair...$1.30

Men's Storm Alaskas, $1.10.

No. 47334 The Men's Storm Slipper Alaska is very desirable, as it protects the front and back of the foot more than the ordinary warm lined Alaska. This shoe is made from pure gum rubber, fine Jersey cloth top, and is very neat appearing when on the foot. This Alaska is made over the new coin toe last. Remember it is the best made at any price. Sizes 6 to 12; weight, 18 oz. Per pair......$1.10
No. 47335 Same as above, broad toe. Pair, $1.10

Ladies' and Misses' Storm Alaskas.

No. 47322 This Storm Alaska differs from the Ordinary Alaska, as it is cut high in front, and protects the front of the foot more. It is made from first quality rubber, has fine cloth top, wool fleece lined, and makes a very desirable shoe for cold weather. Made especially to fit the stylish coin toe shoes. Sizes, 2½ to 8; weight, 13 oz. Per pair......$0.85
No. 47324 Ladies' Spring Heel, as above. Sizes 2½ to 6. Coin toe only. Per pair......$0.85
No. 47323 Misses' Storm Alaskas, made same as the one above, with spring heel, first quality, coin toe only. Sizes, 11 to 2; weight, about 10 oz. Per pair......$0.65

WHEN ORDERING LEATHER SHOES, INCLUDE OVERSHOES OR RUBBERS TO FIT THEM. You save the dealer's profit and by ordering both at one time you are sure of a perfect fit.

Men's Storm Slippers, $0.75.

No. 47336 This is one of the most popular Rubbers ever sold, as it has a very neat appearance and coming up high in back and front, insures dry feet on stormy days. It is made from light, first quality rubber, net lined and comes in the coin toe last.

Weight, 20 ozs. Sizes, 6 to 12. Per pair........$0.75
No. 47337 Same as above, broad toe.
Per pair..75

Men's Self-Acting Rubbers, $0.75.

No. 47340 Men's first quality self acting Sandals, put up exclusively for fine trade, and made to fit the new coin toe shoes. You can't buy a better fitting rubber or a better quality at any price, sizes 6 to 12.

Widths, S, M and F.

Weight, 18 ounces.

Per pair—$0.75

Ladies' Imitation Sandals, $0.45.

No. 47343 Ladies' plain Sandals, medium weight, first quality, made especially to fit heavy shoes and for hard wear. Medium toe only. Sizes, 2¼ to 8; width, W. Weight, 12 to 15 ounces.
Per pair, $0.45

Men's Extra Heavy Rubbers, $0.95.

No. 47344 Made from first quality pure gum, dull finish, extra heavy, net lined and especially designed for hard wear. Broad toe only. Sizes, 6 to 13.
Weight, 28 ozs.
Per pair... $0.95

Ladies', Misses' and Children's Storm Slippers, Heels and Spring Heels.

Ladies' Light Storm Rubbers, first quality, cut high in front and back, and afford good protection for the ankles.

No. 47348 Ladies' Coin Toe, Heels, sizes 2¾ to 8.
Per pair..................................$0.50
No. 47349 Ladies' Wide Toe, Heels, sizes 2¾ to 8.
Per pair..................................$0.50
No. 47349½ Ladies' Coin Toe, Spring Heels. Sizes, 2¾ to 7. Per pair.........$0.50
No. 47350 Misses' Coin Toe, Spring Heels, sizes 11 to 2. Per pair................$0.45
No. 47351 Child's Coin Toe, Spring Heels, sizes 5 to 10½. Per pair................$0.40

Little Gents' Imitation Sandals, $0.42.

No. 47357 Little Gents' Sandal, first quality, made to fit our childs' shoes quoted for little ones.

Sizes and half sizes, 9 to 13½.
Per pair, $0.42

RUBBER BOOTS.

In ordering Rubber Boots be sure to state whether wool or net lining is wanted. We always send cotton lining unless otherwise ordered.

Improved Extra Light Vacation Boot.

No. 47358 This boot is a favorite among sportsmen, from the fact that it can be rolled up closely and takes up little room in a satchel. It is made extra light, weighing only a little over 3 pounds. Net lined, first quality, thigh leg, and is a cool summer boot. Sizes, 6 to 11. Per pair........$4.40

Men's, Boys' and Youths' Pebble Leg Short Boots.

No. 47360 Men's First Quality Pebble Leg Short Rubber Boots, bright finish, handsome 16-inch pebble leg, very light and neat fitting, wool net lined, and will give good service. Nothing better. Sizes, 6 to 12.
Per pair...................$3.30
Shipping weight averages 5 pounds per pair.
No. 47362 Boys' Pebble Leg Boots, first quality. Sizes, 1 to 5. Per pair, $2.25
Shipping weight averages 3½ pounds per pair.
No. 47364 Youths' Pebble Leg Rubber Boots, first quality. Sizes, 10 to 13½.
Per pair...................$1.45
Shipping weight averages 3 pounds per pair.

Men's and Boys' Hip and Thigh Boots, First Quality.

No. 47366 Men's Dull Finish Hip Boots, made from strictly first quality rubber, wool or net lined, and very serviceable. Sizes, 6 to 12.
Per pair...................$4.40
No. 47367 Boys' Dull Finish Storm King Thigh Boots, strictly first quality, net lined. Sizes, 1 to 5. Per pair.....$3.30
No. 47368 Men's Dull Finish Rubber Boots, thigh leg, wool or net lined. Strictly first quality. Sizes, 6 to 12.
Per pair...................$4.40
Shipping weight averages 7½ pounds per pair.

Men's and Boys' Dull Finish Short Rubber Boots.

No. 47370 Men's Dull Finish Rubber Boots, short 16-inch leg, wool or net lined, first quality. Sizes, 6 to 13; weight 81 oz. Per pair..........$3.30

No. 47372 Boys' Dull Finish Rubber Boots, short 16-inch leg, wool or net lined, first quality. Sizes, 1 to 5; weight 58 oz. Per pair......$2.25

Ladies', Misses' and Childs' Pebble Leg Boots.

No. 47374 Women's first quality Rubber Boots, bright finish, fleece lined, pebble leg. Sizes, 2½ to 8. Per pair..$1.75
No. 47376 Misses' first quality Pebble Leg Boot, bright finish. Sizes, 11 to 2.
Per pair................$1.50
No. 47378 Child's first quality Rubber Boot, same style as one preceding. Sizes, 6 to 10.
Per pair................$1.25

Lumbermen's Erie, Rolled Sole, $2.59.

No. 47382 This Lumberman's Erie is made from first quality pure gum, over a heavy imported duck, making it one of the most durable shoes ever sold. It has extra heavy soles, solid heel, front lace, fleece lining, and is snow evcluding to the top. To make it double strong we build it with rolled soles.
Width F, for sock sonly.
Per pair... $2.59

Boys' Combination Felt and Rubbers.

No. 47389 This combination is composed of a strictly first-class wool felt boot which we quote under No. 47186, and the one buckle first quality perfection quoted under No. 47386. Both the felt boot and the rubber are the best we can buy, and we feel sure will please each and every purchaser. When sending your order be sure to state size of shoe worn as we send one size larger. Sizes, 1 to 5. No half sizes, Per pair, $1.80
Weight averages 90 ounces. Postage, see page 4.

Men's Combination Felt Boot and Rubbers. First Quality.

No. 47390 This combination is composed of a strictly all wool felt boot which we quote under No. 46180, made with calf stays, and the lumbermen's one buckle rubber ankle boot quoted under No. 46388. Both the felt boot and the rubber ankle boot are strictly first quality, guaranteed to give perfect satisfaction, and by buying them together in this combination you get them considerably cheaper than we could possibly furnish the same articles if bought separately. When ordering state size of shoe worn, and we will send you the same size wool boot with the Perfection to fit which is one size larger than boot.

Sizes, 6 to 12. Per pair, net.............$2.10
Per dozen pairs................................24.90
Weight averages 95 ounces. For Postage Rate see page 4.

Men's All Wool Knit Boot, Combination, Crack Proof Over, $2.50.

No. 47391 The knit boot No. 46179 which we put in this combination is strictly all wool, is made by the latest improved knitting machinery and then thoroughly shrunk, making a very much more shapely and durable knit boot than we have ever seen. The crack proof rolled sole perfection overshoe we quote under No. 47392, and being made from a heavy duck, covered with first quality pure gum rubber, it is very much superior to those usually sold. The rolled sole is a special feature not usually found and one which adds such wear to the outfit, from the fact that it protects the shoe where the upper and the sole join. We have named an exceedingly close price for this outfit hoping to induce our patrons to buy the best, and should you favor us we guarantee to give you such an outfit as you cannot possibly secure elsewhere for a similar price. When ordering always state size of shoe worn.
Sizes, 6 to 13. Per pair..............$2.50
Weight averages 100 ounces. For postage rate see page 4.

Snag-Proof Perfection, Rolled Sole
No. 47392 Men's one buckle perfection made from heavy snag-proof duck covered with first quality pure gum rubber with heavy rolled sole which protects the uppers and makes the shoe one of the most durable ever sold. Sizes, 6 to 13. For wool boots only. Per pair $2.00 Weight, 65 ounces. For postage rate see page 4.

Lumbermen's Two-Buckle, Captain, Rolled Edge, $2.20.

Weight, 65 ounces. or postage rate see page 4. This shoe is one which we have made special for our own trade.

No. 47394 This shoe is one which we have made specially for our own trade. It has rubber vamp, extra heavy sole and solid heel. The heavy rubber edge is very popular from the fact that it protects the sides. Heavy cloth top, wool lined, snow excluding, and has two adjustable buttons. A good shoe for rough wear. Width. F, for German socks; W, for wool boots. Sizes, 6 to 13. Per pair....$2.20 Shipping weight averages 3 pounds per pair.

Men's Extra Heavy, Rolled Sole.

No. 47396 Arctics. Men's extra heavy buckle arctic. Wool lined, with a heavy rolled edge protecting the uppers, and extra heavy sole and heel; first quality only. Sizes, 6 to 13; full width.
Per pair...$1.60 Weight, 65 ounces. For postage rate see page 4.

Lumbermen's Perfection
1 Buckle.

No. 47398 Men's first quality ankle boot. Made with water-tight fold, tap sole and heel, and to buckle closely around the ankle; can be put on or taken off quickly. When ordering be sure to state width—F for German socks; W for wool boots. Sizes, 6 to 13.
Per pair.. $1.55 Weight, 60 ozs. For postage rate see page 4.

Men's Crack Proof Boot. Rolled Sole to Heel. Warranted.

No. 47402 We herewith show our latest improved crack proof rubber boot, and the only one which we feel can be sold with absolute guarantee that it will not crack or puncture with stones or thorns. The boot is made from a very heavy imported puncture proof duck and covered with best pure gum rubber making it thoroughly waterproof. We put on an extra heavy sole and tap with rolled edge to heel thereby protecting the uppers and making the boot much more durable. We have sold thousands of pairs and have had very few disappointments as to the wear. If you use a rubber boot better try the best as we guarantee every pair for a fair and reasonable amount of service and also guarantee them not to crack or puncture. Sizes, 6 to 13, no half sizes.
Per pair ....$3.45 Weight, averages 96 ounces. For postage rate, see page 4.

Men's Crack Proof Hip Boot, Warranted.

No. 47403 This boot is made crack proof and puncture proof, and in fact, is built exactly the same as No. 47402, but is cut with hip leg and to those who want a hip boot we would recommend it above all others from the fact that it does wear better and consequently is much cheaper in the end than the ordinary rubber boot. We have such confidence in it that we guarantee every pair not to crack or puncture and to be satisfactory in every particular. We want to please every customer and we know of no better way than to urge them to buy goods that we have every confidence in and goods that we warrant. Sizes, 6 to 13 no half sizes. Per pair .. $4.90 Weight averages 115 ounces. For postage rate, see page 4.

Heaton's Patent Button Machine.

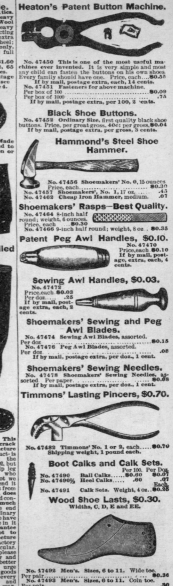

No. 47450 This is one of the most useful machines ever invented. It is very simple and most any child can fasten the buttons on his own shoes. Every family should have one. Price, each....$0.55
If by mail, postage extra, each, 14 cents.
No. 47451 Fasteners for above machine.
Per box of 100 ....$0.09
Per box of 1000 .... .75
If by mail, postage extra, per 100, 2 cents.

Black Shoe Buttons.
No. 47452 Ordinary Size, first quality black shoe buttons. Price, per great gross. 40c; per gross, $0.04
If by mail, postage extra, per gross, 3 cents.

Hammond's Steel Shoe Hammer.

No. 47456 Shoemakers' No. 0, 15 ounces. Price, each...........................$0.30
No. 47457 Shoemakers', No. 1, 17 oz......... .43
No. 47462 Cheap Iron Hammer, medium.... .07

Shoemakers' Rasps—Best Quality.
No. 47464 8-inch half round; weight, 6 ounces. Price, each $0.30
No. 47466 9-inch half round; weight, 8 oz .. $0.35

Patent Peg Awl Handles, $0.10.
No. 47470 Price, each $0.10 If by mail, postage, extra, each, 4 cents.

Sewing Awl Handles, $0.03.
No. 47472 Price, each $0.03 Per doz....... .25 If by mail, postage extra, each, 2 cents.

Shoemakers' Sewing and Peg Awl Blades.
No. 47474 Sewing Awl Blades, assorted.
Per doz $0.15
No. 47476 Peg Awl Blades, assorted. Per doz .... .08
If by mail, postage extra, per doz., 1 cent.

Shoemakers' Sewing Needles.
No. 47478 Shoemakers' Sewing Needles, assorted. Per paper.................$0.08
If by mail, postage extra, per doz., 1 cent.

Timmons' Lasting Pincers, $0.70.

No. 47482 Timmons' No. 1 or 2, each.....$0.70 Shipping weight, 1 pound each.

Boot Calks and Calk Sets.
Per 100. Per Doz.
No. 47490 Ball Calks.....$0.60 $0.07
No. 47490½ Heel Calks..... .60 .07 Each
No. 47491 Calk Sets. Weight, 4 ozs. $0.25

Wood Shoe Lasts, $0.30.
Widths, C, D, E and EE.

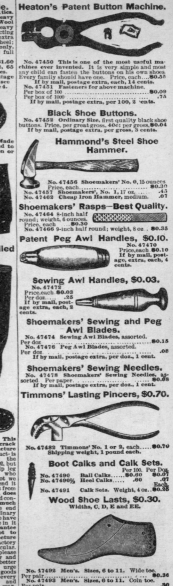

No. 47492 Men's. Sizes, 6 to 11. Wide toe.
Per pair....................................$0.30
No. 47493 Men's. Sizes, 6 to 11. Coin toe.
Per pair.. .30
No. 47494 Ladies'. Sizes, 3 to 7. Wide toe.
Per pair.. .30
No. 47495 Ladies'. Sizes, 3 to 7. Coin toe.
Per pair.. .30
Shipping weight averages 4 pounds per pair.

49305
$2.95

49273
$1.50

49271
$1.00

49276
.95

49275
$1.85

49270
.95

49269
.90

49260
.50

49268
.75

MEN'S WINTER FLANNEL SHIRTS

WE DO NOT SAMPLE SHIRTS.

Sizes are 14½, 15, 15½, 16, 16½, 17. Always order by neck measure.

NOTE THE SAVING TO YOU BY PURCHASING IN QUANTITIES OF THREE OR MORE. It will leave dollars in your pocket to buy your shirts from us. Every shirt is made with full size body and sleeves, and we warrant them to be exactly as represented or YOUR MONEY REFUNDED.

A Good Shirt for 50 Cents.

No. 49260 Men's Winter Weight, Closely Woven Cotton Cassimere Overshirts. They are the best that can be produced at our low price. Yoke back, felled seams and full size. Medium colored plaids and stripes. Sizes, 14½ to 17, only. Per dozen, $5.40; six for $2.76; three for $1.43; each..........................50c
If by mail, postage extra, each, 14 cents.

Our 75-Cent Cassimere Shirt.

No. 49268 Men's Winter weight Cassimere overshirts, made of union twilled wool cloth. A thoroughly good shirt, made full size, in a first-class manner. Yoke back; shaped shoulders; felled seams; pearl buttons and extension neckband. We have large and select assortment of stripes and plaids in medium light colors. Sizes, 14½ to 17, only. Dozen, $8.10; six for $4.24; three for $2.13; each 75c
If by mail, postage extra, each, 15 cents.

Excellent Value for 90 Cents.

No. 49269 Men's Fine Cassimere Shirts, made of fine wool and about 25 per cent cotton. A shirt that never fails to give satisfactory wear; is warm and will wash well. Fancy stripes and plaids, in medium dark colors. Yoke back; pearl buttons; extension neckband; felled seams; gussets, and full size body. The kind that your local merchant must charge $1.25 for. Sizes, 14½ to 17, only. Dozen, $9.72; six for $4.97; three for $2.57; each..........................90c
If by mail, postage extra, each, 16 cents.

No. 49270 Men's Fine Oxford Gray Cassimere Overshirts, full winter weight. Soft finished surface. Made of fine wool with sufficient cotton mixed to prevent shrinkage and add to its durability. Full 36 inches long; large body; felled seams; gussets; shaped shoulders; one pocket, and pearl buttons. A plain shirt that never fails to give satisfaction. Sizes, 14½ to 17. Dark gray only. Dozen, $10.26; six for $5.25; three for $2.70; each..........................95c
If by mail, postage extra, each, 17 cents.

Extra Heavy Shirt, $1.00.

No. 49271 Extra Heavy Dark Gray Overshirt, made of an extra heavy and thick, strong durable cloth, about 60 per cent wool and 40 per cent cotton. A shirt that will stand very rough hard wear. An exceptional value and would cost you $1.35 at your local store. Made full size; yoke back; pearl buttons, and felled seams; one pocket. Average weight, about 22 ounces. Sizes, 14½ to 17, only. What size do you wear? Dozen, $10.80; six for $5.52; three for $2.85; each..........................$1.00
If by mail, postage extra, each, 25 cents.

Fine Cassimere Shirts.

No. 49273 Men's Fine French Wool Cassimere Overshirts, of the latest weave in patterns. Fine smooth surface. Full winter weight. Cloths of this kind are very durable and invariably prove the cheapest shirts in the long run. A large assortment of new stripes and plaids. Made shaped shoulders; felled seams; gussets; pearl buttons; one pocket, and neck to match. Non-shrinking neckband. Full 36 inches long and large body. Sizes, 14½ to 17, only. What size do you wear? Dozen, $16.20; six for $8.28; three for $4.26; each..........................$1.50
If by mail, postage extra, each, 18 cents.

...SEND FOR OUR SAMPLE BOOK NO. 2K OF MEN'S CLOTHING...

Fine Imperial Flannel Shirts.

No. 49275 Men's Extra Quality Fine Imperial Flannel Shirts; all wool of superior quality. A cloth that will not be found in your local store for less than $2.50 a shirt. We offer this quality in neat plaids and stripes, medium dark colors, blue stripes predominating. Medium heavy weight; yoke back; pearl buttons; shaped shoulders; gussets; facings; felled seams; two pockets. High grade in every particular. Sizes, 14½ to 17, only.
Each $1.85
.... 5.28

Pemberton Cotton Shirts.

No. 49276 Men's Pemberton Cotton Cassimere Overshirts. The Pemberton cloth is a heavy, closely twilled cotton, in fancy plaid and stripes effects about the same character as in woolen cashmere shirts. By a special machine the surface is brushed soft, but not fleeced. Very durable and will stand the wear. They are lined with light weight domet flannel to waist, making it extra warm. A new style shirt of much merit. Full size; felled seams; shaped shoulders and pearl buttons; medium colors. Sizes, 14½ to 17. Each ....$ 0.95
Three for 2.70

Extra High Grade Cassimere Shirts

No. 49305 The finest flannel shirt on sale and can be had from but few houses. It represents all that is good in a fine shirt with the defects of none. This grade of cloth is seldom sold by the yd., the entire product being taken by fine shirt manufacturers. The patterns are exclusive, new and neat, in stripes and plaids on medium color background. The handsomest shirt you have ever seen, no loud effects. Made with wide yoke, full size body, faced sleeves, felled seams, finest pearl buttons, button down stay-in-its-place collar, neck tie of same material, two pockets and stitched throughout with silk. Try these shirts and you will have no other.
.......................$2.95

49314
$1.35

49320
$1.00

49324
$2.00

49326
$3.00

MEN'S WINTER OVER-SHIRTS...

Sizes, 14½, 15, 15½, 16, 16½, 17.
Order by neck size.
When ordering shipped by mail,
be sure to include postage.

49312
$.95

Our Leader at $2.00.

No. 49324. Made of fine North Berwick Mills flannel, which is about the quality used in the average shirt at $5.00. Extra fine, soft smooth surface cloth, closely woven, medium heavy weight, shaped shoulders, nonshrinking neck band, felled seams, faced sleeves, gussets, pearl buttons, full 36 inches long, yoke back and silk stitched button holes. Light, medium and dark tan. Sizes, 14½ to 17.
Per dozen, $23.00; six for $11.54; three for $5.70; each $2.00
If by mail, postage extra, each, 17 cents.

Our Special, $2.50.

No. 49304½. Men's Fine High-grade Flannel Shirts, made from North Berwick Mills flannel. Finer quality than the above in light tan and medium gray colors only. Made with coat sleeves, shaped shoulders, non-shrinking neckband, fine pearl buttons, button down collar, two pockets with flaps to button down, wide facing on sleeves, large body, 36 inches long. Sizes, 14½ to 17.
Per dozen, $27.00; six for $13.80; three for $7.13; each $2.50
If by mail, postage extra, each, 22 cents.

Heavy California Flannel Over-shirts.

No. 49307. Men's Extra Heavy All Wool California Flannel Overshirts. Just the shirts for farmers, lumbermen and stockmen. Very warm. Full size, 36 inches long, yoke back, pearl buttons and one pocket, small check designs as shown in illustration. Colors, brown and black, olive and black, blue and black, etc. Average weight, 20 ounces. Our price to you about the cost to your local merchant. Sizes, 14½ to 17.
Per dozen $14.58; six for $7.45; three for $3.55; each $1.35
If by mail, postage extra, each, 23 cents.

Extra Heavy California Flannel Overshirts.

No. 49309. Men's Extra Heavy and Thick All Wool California Flannel Overshirts. Heavier than the above, in fact, one of the heaviest shirts made. For lumbermen, farmers, stockmen or miners they are the best; all wool, thick and warm. Very large full sized bodies, yoke back, non-shrinking neckband and pearl buttons. Regular retail price, $2.50. Three predominating colors, blue, light brown and dark brown. Sizes, 14½ to 17 only. Per dozen, $20.00; six for $10.20; three for $5.21; each $1.85
If by mail, postage extra, each, 25 cents.

SPECIAL EXTRA HEAVY BLUE FLANNEL SHIRTS.

No. 49316. Men's Extra Heavy Blue Flannel Shirts. Average weight, 34 ounces. The heaviest blue flannel shirt made and will outwear two or three shirts of ordinary weight. For stockmen, farmers, hunters and lumbermen, it will be found superior to all others as a cold excluder. A small percentage of cotton gives the shirt additional durability. Made yoke back, shaped shoulders, extension band, non-shrinking neckband, pearl buttons, faced sleeves, two pockets, full size body, 36 inches long. No illustration. Sizes, 14½ to 17.
Price, per dozen, $27.00; six for $13.80; three for $7.13; each $2.50

MEN'S BLUE FLANNEL SHIRTS.

Sizes, 14½ to 17.

49307
$1.35

No. 49312 Men's Fine Winter Weight Blue Flannel Overshirts, made from the best twilled union flannel. Single breasted, felled seams, yoke back, extension neckband and pearl buttons. The best shirt ever offered at our low price. Sizes, 14½ to 17 only. Per dozen, $10.40; six for $5.30; three for $2.75; each 95c
If by mail, postage extra, each, 20 cents.
No. 49314 Men's Fine Blue Flannel Winter Overshirts, made from fine blue flannel with a mixture of cotton sufficient to prevent shrinkage. Shaped shoulders, yoke back, pearl buttons, extension non-shrinking neckband, gussets and faced sleeves. Full sized body, 36 inches long. A special value. Sizes, 14½ to 17 only.
Price, per dozen, $14.58; six for $7.45; three for $3.55; each $1.35
If by mail, postage extra, each, 23 cents.
No. 49315 Men's Genuine California Blue Flannel Shirts. All from pure wool. The California flannels are the best all wool flannels made. They are smooth and even in surface and absolutely fast in colors. Made single breasted, yoke back, shaped shoulders, felled seams, faced sleeves, gussets, non-shrinking neckband, extension band, collar buttons down on each side and pearl buttons. A better shirt is not made. Large body, 36 inches long. Size, 14½ to 17.
Price, per dozen, $21.60; six for $11.04; three for $5.70; each $2.00
If by mail, postage extra, each, 19 cents.

Men's Double Breasted Blue Flannel Shirts.

No. 49320 Men's Double Breasted Full Winter Weight Blue Flannel Overshirts, made from good quality twilled Union flannel. Large pearl buttons, non-shrinking band, yoke back, full size and length. The best value obtainable at this low price. Sizes, 14½ to 17. What size do you wear? Price, per dozen, $11.00; six for $5.60; three for $2.85; each $1.00
If by mail, postage extra, each, 22 cents.
No. 49322 Men's Fine Double-Breasted Blue Flannel shirts made from fine blue flannel with a sufficient mixture of cotton to prevent shrinkage, which also adds to its durability. Yoke back, pearl buttons, full size body, 36 inches long. A special value at our low price. Sizes, 14½ to 17 only. Per dozen, $15.66; six for $8.00; three for $4.14; each $1.45
If by mail, postage extra, each, 23 cents.

Men's California Flannel Double-Breasted Shirts at $2.00.

No. 49324. Men's Genuine California Twilled Blue Flannel. All pure wool California flannels are better than all others, having smooth, even surface and better color. Made yoke back, pearl

49304
$2.00

49304½
$2.50

49309
$1.85

band, full size body, 36 inches long. You will pay $2.50 to $3.00 for this grade in your home town. Sizes, 14½ to 17 only. Per dozen, $22.00; six for $11.50; three for $5.80; each $2.00
If by mail, postage extra, each, 24 cents.

Firemen's Shirts, $3.00.

No. 49326 Firemen's Heavy Weight, Twilled California Blue Flannel Shirts, made up in regulation firemen's style. Double breasted, with wide pearl buttons, extra long pointed collar and double back, deep cuffs trimmed with pearl buttons, warranted first quality in every respect. All wool and cut full size. Sizes, 14½ to 17. Positively unexcelled for wear and service. Retail value, $4.00.

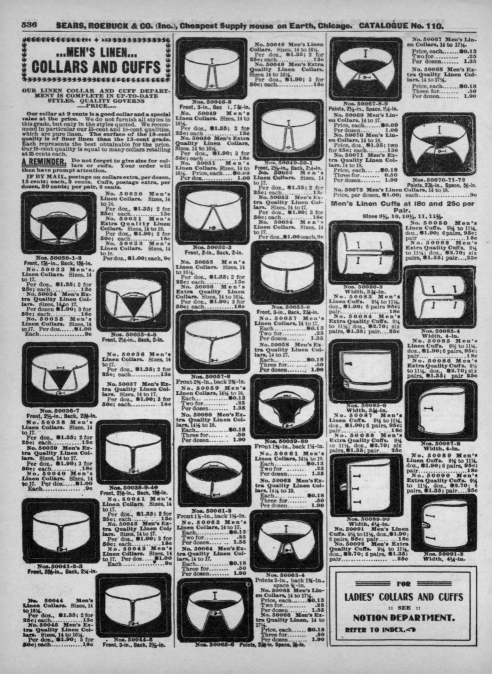

...MEN'S LINEN... COLLARS AND CUFFS

OUR LINEN COLLAR AND CUFF DEPARTMENT IS COMPLETE IN UP-TO-DATE STYLES. QUALITY GOVERNS .....PRICE.....

Our collar at 9 cents is a good collar and a special value at the price. We do not furnish all styles in this grade, but only in the styles quoted. We recommend in particular our 13-cent and 18-cent qualities, which are pure linen. The surface of the 18-cent quality is of finer linen than the 13-cent grade. Each represents the best obtainable for the price. Our 18-cent quality is equal to many collars retailing at 25 cents each.

A REMINDER. Do not forget to give size for collars or cuffs. Your order will then have prompt attention.

IF BY MAIL, postage on collars extra, per dozen, 15 cents; each, 2 cents. Cuffs, postage extra, per dozen, 20 cents; per pair, 2 cents.

Nos. 50030-1-2
Front, 1⅞-in., Back, 1⅝-in.

No. 50030 Men's Linen Collars. Sizes, 14 to 18.
Per doz., $1.35; 2 for 25c; each............13c

No. 50031 Men's Extra Quality Linen Collars. Sizes, 14 to 18.
Per doz., $1.90; 3 for 50c; each............18c

No. 50032 Men's Linen Collars. Sizes, 14 to 18.
Per doz., $1.00; each, 9c

No. 50033 Men's Linen Collars. Sizes, 14 to 17.
Per doz., $1.35; 2 for 25c; each............13c

No. 50034 Men's Extra Quality Linen Collars. Sizes, 14 to 17.
Per dozen $1.90; 3 for 50c; each............18c

No. 50035 Men's Linen Collars. Sizes, 14 to 17. Per doz......$1.00
Each..................9c

Nos. 50033-4-5
Front, 2¼-in., Back, 2-in.

Nos. 50036-7
Front, 2½-in., Back, 2⅜-in.

No. 50036 Men's Linen Collars. Sizes, 14 to 17.
Per doz., $1.35; 2 for 25c; each............13c

No. 50037 Men's Extra Quality Linen Collars. Sizes, 14 to 17.
Per doz., $1.90; 3 for 50c; each............18c

No. 50038 Men's Linen Collars. Sizes, 14 to 17.
Per doz., $1.35; 2 for 25c; each............13c

No. 50039 Men's Extra Quality Linen Collars. Sizes, 14 to 17.
Per doz.. $1.90; 3 for 50c; each............18c

No. 50040 Men's Linen Collars. Sizes, 14 to 17. Per doz.....$1.00
Each..................9c

Nos. 50038-9-40
Front, 2⅛-in., Back, 1⅝-in.

Nos. 50041-2-3
Front, 2⅝-in., Back, 2¼-in.

No. 50041 Men's Linen Collars. Sizes, 14 to 17.
Per doz., $1.35; 2 for 25c; each............13c

No. 50042 Men's Extra Quality Linen Collars. Sizes, 14 to 17.
Per doz., $1.90; 3 for 50c; each............18c

No. 50043 Men's Linen Collars. Sizes, 14 to 17. Per doz......$1.00
Each..................9c

No. 50044 Men's Linen Collars. Sizes, 14 to 16½.
Per doz., $1.35; 2 for 25c; each............13c

No. 50045 Men's Extra Quality Linen Collars. Sizes, 14 to 16½.
Per doz., $1.90; 3 for 50c; each............18c

Nos. 50044-5
Front, 3-in., Back, 2½-in.

Nos. 50046-8
Front, 3-in., Back, 2¾-in.

No. 50046 Men's Linen Collars. Sizes, 14 to 16½.
Per doz., $1.35; 2 for 25c; each............13c

No. 50048 Men's Extra Quality Linen Collars. Sizes, 14 to 16½.
Per doz., $1.90; 3 for 50c; each............18c

No. 50049 Men's Linen Collars. Sizes, 14 to 16½.
Per doz., $1.35; 2 for 25c; each............13c

No. 50050 Men's Extra Quality Linen Collars. Sizes, 14 to 16½.
Per doz., $1.90; 3 for 50c; each............18c

No. 50051 Men's Linen Collars. Sizes, 14 to 16½. Price, each....$0.09
Per doz............1.00

Nos. 50049-50-1
Front, 2½-in., Back, 2¼-in.

No. 50052 Men's Linen Collars. Sizes, 14 to 17.
Per doz., $1.35; 2 for 25c; each............13c

No. 50053 Men's Extra Quality Linen Collars. Sizes, 14 to 17.
Per doz., $1.90; 3 for 50c; each............18c

No. 50054 Men's Linen Collars. Sizes, 14 to 17.
Per doz., $1.00; each, 9c

Nos. 50052-3
Front, 2-in., Back, 2-in.

No. 50055 Men's Linen Collars. Sizes, 14 to 16½.
Per doz., $1.35; 2 for 25c; each............13c

No. 50056 Men's Extra Quality Linen Collars. Sizes, 14 to 16½.
Per doz., $1.90; 3 for 50c; each............18c

Nos. 50055-6
Front, 3-in., Back, 2¾-in.

Nos. 50057-8
Front 2⅝-in., back 2⅜-in.

No. 50057 Men's Linen Collars, 14 to 17.
Each............$0.13
Two for.......... .25
Per dozen....... 1.35

No. 50058 Men's Extra Quality Linen Collars, 14 to 17.
Each............$0.18
Three for....... .50
Per dozen....... 1.90

No. 50059 Men's Linen Collars, 14½ to 18.
Each............$0.13
Two for.......... .25
Per dozen....... 1.35

No. 50060 Men's Extra Quality Linen Collars, 14½ to 18.
Each............$0.18
Three for....... .50
Per dozen....... 1.90

Nos. 50059-60
Front 1⅝-in., back 1¼-in.

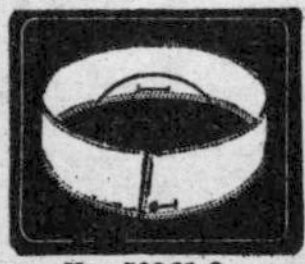

Nos. 50061-2
Front 1⅞-in., back 1¼-in.

No. 50061 Men's Linen Collars, 14½ to 19.
Each............$0.13
Two for.......... .25
Per dozen....... 1.35

No. 50062 Men's Extra Quality Linen Collars, 14½ to 19.
Each............$0.18
Three for....... .50
Per dozen....... 1.90

No. 50063 Men's Linen Collars, 14 to 17.
Each............$0.13
Two for.......... .25
Per dozen....... 1.35

No. 50064 Men's Extra Quality Linen Collars, 14 to 17.
Each............$0.18
Three for....... .50
Per dozen....... 1.90

Nos. 50063-4
Points 2-in., back 1⅝-in., space ⅜-in.

No. 50065 Men's Linen Collars, 14 to 17½.
Price, each......$0.13
Two for.......... .25
Per dozen....... 1.35

No. 50066 Men's Extra Quality Linen, 14 to 17½.
Price, each......$0.18
Three for....... .50
Per dozen....... 1.90

Nos. 50065-6 Points, 2⅜-in. Space, ⅞-in.

Nos. 50067-8-9
Points, 2½-in., Space, 1¼-in.

No. 50067 Men's Linen Collars, 14 to 17½.
Price, each......$0.13
Two for.......... .25
Per dozen....... 1.35

No. 50068 Men's Extra Quality Linen Collars, 14 to 17½.
Price, each......$0.18
Three for....... .50
Per dozen....... 1.90

No. 50069 Men's Linen Collars, 14 to 17.
Price, each......$0.09
Per dozen....... 1.00

No. 50070 Men's Linen Collars, 14 to 18.
Price, doz., $1.35; two for 25c; each..........13c

No. 50071 Men's Extra Quality Linen Collars, 14 to 18.
Price, each.....$0.18
Three for....... 0.50
Per dozen....... 1.90

Nos. 50070-71-72
Points, 2⅞-in., Space, ⅝-in.

No. 50072 Men's Linen Collars, 14 to 18. Price, per dozen, $1.00; each..................9c

Men's Linen Cuffs at 18c and 25c per Pair.

Sizes 9½, 10, 10½, 11, 11½.

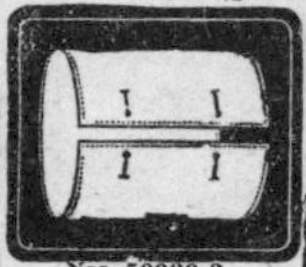

Nos. 50080-2
Width, 3¾-in.

No. 50080 Men's Linen Cuffs. 9½ to 11½, doz., $1.90; 6 pairs, 95c; pair..............18c

No. 50082 Men's Extra Quality Cuffs. 9½ to 11½; doz., $2.70; six pairs, $1.35; pair....25c

No. 50083 Men's Linen Cuffs. 9½ to 11½, doz., $1.90; 6 pairs 95c; pair..............18c

No. 50084 Men's Extra Quality Cuffs. 9½ to 11½; doz., $2.70; six pairs, $1.35; pair....25c

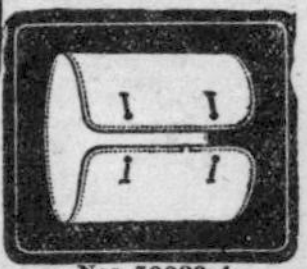

Nos. 50083-4
Width, 4-in.

No. 50085 Men's Linen Cuffs. 9½ to 11½. doz., $1.90; 6 pairs, 95c; pair..............18c

No. 50086 Men's Extra Quality Cuffs. 9½ to 11½, doz., $2.70; six pairs, $1.35; pair 25c

Nos. 50085-6
Width, 3¾-in.

No. 50087 Men's Linen Cuffs. 9½ to 11½, doz., $1.90; 6 pairs, 95c; pair..............18c

No. 50088 Men's Extra Quality Cuffs. 9½ to 11½, doz., $2.70; six pairs, $1.35; pair.... 25c

Nos. 50087-8
Width, 4-in.

No. 50089 Men's Linen Cuffs. 9½ to 11½, doz., $1.90; 6 pairs, 95c; pair..............18c

No. 50090 Men's Extra Quality Cuffs. 9½ to 11½, doz., $2.70; 6 pairs, $1.35; pair....25c

Nos. 50089-90
Width, 4¼-in.

No. 50091 Men's Linen Cuffs. 9½ to 11½, doz., $1.90; 6 pairs, 95c; pair.......18c

No. 50092 Men's Extra Quality Cuffs. 9½ to 11½, doz., $2.70; 6 pairs, $1.35; pair..................25c

Nos. 50091-2
Width, 4¼-in.

FOR LADIES' COLLARS AND CUFFS :: SEE :: NOTION DEPARTMENT.

REFER TO INDEX.

No. 50100
Back, 1¾-in. Points, 2-in.

BOYS' OR YOUTHS' LINEN COLLARS, 10 CENTS.

Sizes, 12, 12½, 13, 13½, 14.

No. 50100 Boys' or Youths' Fine Linen Collars. Sizes, 12 to 14 only. Price, per doz., $1.10; six for 55c; each... .10c

No. 50102
Back, 2⅛-in; front, 2⅜-in

Boys' and Youths' Linen Collars.

No. 50102 Boys' or Youths' Fine Linen Collars. Sizes, 12 to 14 only. Price, per doz. $1.10; six for 55c; each....10c

No. 50103
Front, 1⅝-in; back, 1½-in.

No. 50103 Boys' or Youths' Fine Linen Collars. Sizes, 12 to 14 only. Price, per doz. $1.10; six for 55c; each....10c

Boys' or Youths' Linen Cuffs.

Size 8, 8½, 9, 9½.

No. 50105 Boys' or Youths' Fine Linen Cuffs. sizes, 8 to 9½, doz., $1.65; 6 pairs, 83c; pair.....15c

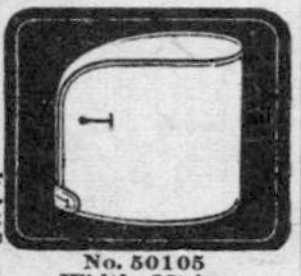
No. 50105
Width, 3⅝-in.

No. 50106 Boys' or Youths' Fine Linen Cuffs. Sizes, 8 to 9½ doz., $1.65; 6 pairs.....83c; pair ...15c

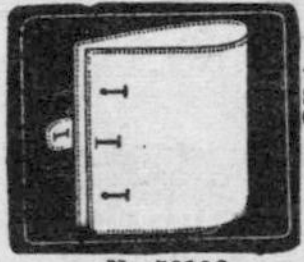
No. 50106
Width, 3¾-in.

No. 50107 Boys' or Youths' Fine Linen Cuffs. 8 to 9½, doz., $1.65; 6 pairs, 83c; pair.................15c

No. 50107 Width, 3¼-in.

Celluloid Waterproof Collars and Cuffs.

The following are the best Waterproof Collars and Cuffs made. Will not break or tear at button holes. Order collars half size larger than shirt worn.

No. 50110 Style Royal Celluloid Collars. Sizes, 12½ to 20 inches. Per doz., $1.35; 2 for 25c; each.............13c

ROYAL.
Front, 1⅞-in.

No. 50111 Style Clerical Celluloid Collars. Sizes, 12 to 19½. Per doz., $1.35; 2 for 25c; each...........13c

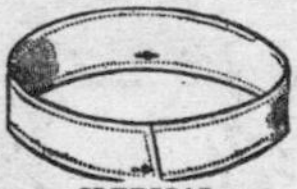
CLERICAL.
Front, 1½-in., Back, 1⅝-in.

No. 50112 Style Sterling Celluloid Collars. Sizes 12 to 18½. Per doz., $1.35; 2 for 25c; each.............13c

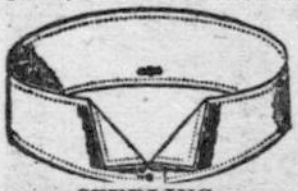
STERLING.
Front, 2-in., Back, 1¾-in.

No. 50113 Style Imperial Celluloid Collars. Sizes, 13½ to 18½. Per doz., $1.35; 2 for 25c; each..............13c

IMPERIAL.
Front, 2-in., Back, 1¾-in.

No. 50114 Style Manhattan. Sizes, 12½ to 18½. Per doz., $1.35; 2 for 25c; each.........13c

MANHATTAN.
Front, 2⅜-in., Back, 1⅞-in.

FIFTH AVENUE.
Width, 3¼ in.

Celluloid Cuffs.

No. 50116 Style Fifth Avenue, Celluloid Cuffs. Sizes, 9½ to 11½.
Price, per pair.........$0.25
Price, per dozen....... 2.70

No. 50117 Style Excelsior Celluloid Cuffs. Sizes, 9 to 11½.
Price, per pair...........$0.25
Price, per dozen......... 2.70

Do not forget size when you order collars and cuffs.

NOTE.—Dozen rates apply where half dozen or more of the same kind of collars or cuffs are ordered.

EXCELSIOR.
Width, 3½ in.

SHORT.
Front 7 In.
Width 6 3/4 In.

Celluloid Shirt Front.

No. 50118 Celluloid Shirt Front, interlined, medium length.
Price, each.................$0.30
Price, per dozen............ 3.25

Celluloid Shirt Front.

No. 50119 Celluloid Shirt Front, interlined, medium.
Price, each.......$0.40
Price, per dozen . 4.30

Medium.
Front, 9¼ in.
Width, 7 in.

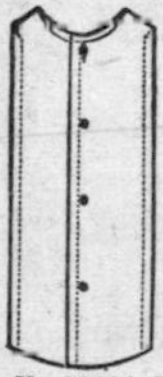

Celluloid Shirt Front.

No. 50120 Long Shirt Front; length, 13 in., width, 6⅝ in.; made of extra quality celluloid, interlined. Price, each..............$0.50
Price, per dozen.............. 5.30

When collars and cuffs are ordered sent by mail, always include extra stamps for postage. If by mail, postage on Collars, extra, per doz., 14 cents; each, 1 cent; on Cuffs, per doz. pairs, 20 cents; per pair, 2 cents.

Men's Rubber Bosoms.

No. 50121 Men's Rubber Bosom, 9¼ inches long, medium length. Price, each.................. $0.60
Price, per dozen.............................. 6.70

White Rubber Collars and Cuffs Made with Smooth Luster Surface.

Wheeler.
Front, 2 in.
Back, 1¼ in,

No. 50130 Style Wheeler Rubber Collar. Sizes 12 to 18½.
Price, each..$0.20
Per dozen..... 2.15

No. 50131 Style Roosevelt Rubber Collar. Sizes, 13½ to 17½.
Price, each..$0.20
Per dozen.... 2.15

Roosevelt.
Front, 2¼ in.
Back, 1⅜ in.

Miles.
Front, 2 in.
Back, 1⅜ in.

No. 50132 Style Miles Rubber Collar. Sizes, 12 to 18½.
Price, each.$0.20
Per dozen.. 2.15

No. 50134 Style Funston Rubber Collar. Sizes, 13½ to 17½.
Price, each...........................$0.20
Per dozen............................ 2.15

Funston.
Front, 2⅜ in.
Back, 2¼ in.

Shafter.
Front, 2⅜ in.
Back, 2¼ in.

No. 50135 Style Shafter Rubber Collars, sizes 13½ to 17½. Price, each. 20c; per dozen..........$2.15

No. 50136 Style Lee Rubber Collars, sizes 13½ to 17½.
Price, each..$0.20
Per dozen.... 2.15

No. 50137 Style Otis Rubber Collars, sizes 12 to 18.
Price, each.$0.20
Per dozen.. 2.15

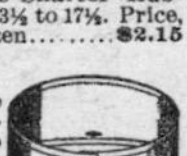
Lee.
Front, 2⅜ in.
Back, 2¼ in.

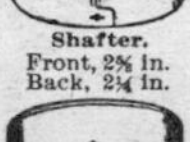
Otis.
Front, 2 in.
Back, 1⅜ in.

Men's Rubber Cuffs.

Watson.

No. 50140 Men's Watson Style Rubber Cuffs. Sizes, 10½ and 11 only.
Price, per pair $0.40
Per dozen............ 4.50

No. 50141 Men's Sampson Style Rubber Cuffs. Sizes. 8½ to 11½.
Price, per dozen, $4.50; per pair...............40c

Sampson.

OUR NECKWEAR DEPARTMENT.

MEN'S AND BOYS'.

For Ladies' Neckwear see Notion Department.

IT IS QUITE POSSIBLE to buy good neckwear at a low price, but it is never possible to be satisfied with poor neckwear. In asking your careful consideration of this department, we need only say that **the goods are good and the prices are right. If you buy of us and do not find that this is so,** we are only too anxious to have you return the goods at our expense and we will refund your money.

Men's Silk Teck Scarfs, 19 and 25 Cents.

No. 50151 Men's Silk Teck Scarfs in large assortment of stripes, plaids and floral designs; also plain black silk or satin.
Price, each......................$0.19
Per dozen.......................... 2.10
If by mail, postage extra, each, 3 cents.

No. 50152 Men's Fine Silk Teck Scarfs in large assortment of floral, Persian, plaid and stripe effects. Also all white.
Price, each.......$0.25
Six for............ 1.35
Per dozen......... 2.70
If by mail, postage extra, each, 3 cents.

Excellent Value at 35 Cents.

No. 50153 Fine Brocaded Silk Teck Scarf, of the latest design and shape. Large assortment of light, medium and dark colors in new patterns. Also plain black silk or satin.
Price, each.......$0.35
Three for......... 1.00
If by mail, postage extra, each, 3 cents.

No. 50155 Men's Fine Silk Teck Scarfs. At this price we furnish a scarf which for quality and style is the best. Full width bands, best linings. The latest assortment in grouped stripe, Persian effect and plaids. **Strictly reliable high grade goods.** Give color preference and we can please you. Also plain white.
Price, each.......$0.45
Three for...... 1.28
Per dozen....... 5.00
If by mail, postage extra, each, 3 cents.

Men's Handsome Silk Teck Scarfs.

No. 50156 Medium dark and light evening shades, latest new shape, in great variety of designs. Persian, Floral Plaids, Etc. In new Effects and colorings. All are made in strictly first-class manner, wide band and fine linings. An exquisite present. Each scarf put up in beautiful box.
Price, each..........$0.55
Three for............ 1.50
Dozen.................. 6.00
If by mail, postage extra, each, 10 cents.

No. 50157 Our new style Teck Scarf, made to hook in the back. Small knot with wide aprons. A stylish strictly high grade scarf in large assortment of new silks.
Price, each..............$0.45
Per dozen................ 5.00

50394
50¢

50396
$1.00

50395
75¢

50397
$1.50

50380
$1.00

50383
75¢

50391 $1.50   **50379 75¢**

50381
50¢

50373
35¢

50382
50¢

50389
$1.25

50371
25¢

50327
60¢

50387
$1.00

50391½
$1.50

SILK and CASHMERE MUFFLERS

If by mail, postage extra, each, 4 cents.

CASHMERE MUFFLERS.

No. 50371 Soft Cashmere Mufflers, large size, dark and medium colors. Plaids, stripes, checks and fancy figures. Price, per dozen, $2.80; each.................25c

No. 50373 Imported Worsted Mufflers, fine soft twill in dark and medium plaids, stripes and checks, in combinations, such as black and white, gray and white, brown mixed, etc. Per dozen, $3.80; 3 for $1.00; each........35c

No. 50377 Cream White Cashmere Mufflers, with dainty interwoven silk stripes of contrasting colors. Will wash and wear well. Price, per dozen, $5.60; each.........60c

No. 50379 Fine Wool Cashmere Mufflers, soft, warm and comfortable. Will wash and wear well. Handsome medium and dark color plaids, checks and stripes. Particularly large assortment in brown and blue.
Price, per dozen, $8.50; each..........................75c

No. 50380 High grade fine all-wool Cashmere Mufflers in newest plaids, rather modest plaid effects in medium and dark colors. Much warmer than silk mufflers. Will wash and wear well. Price, each....................$1.00

No. 50381 Men's Fancy Figured Silk Mufflers, assorted colors and combinations, blue, pink, green in soft shades, also black and cream white. Price, per doz., $5.69; each, 50c

No. 50382 Good quality Silk Muffler, full size; navy blue, white polka-dot. Size, 28 inches.
Price, per dozen, $5.60; each............................50c

No. 50383 Men's Pure Silk Brocaded Mufflers. Rich floral and scroll designs in beautiful combinations, such as blue, red, green, pink, etc., including all black and cream white. All pure silk. Price, per doz., $8.50; each.....75c

No. 50387 Extra Fine Large All Silk Brocaded Mufflers, rich Dresden figures in satin relief. Dark and bright colors, such as red, dark blue, light blue, pink, green, etc. also black and cream white. Price, per doz., $11.00; each, $1.00

No. 50389 Men's Fine New Novelty Silk Plaid Mufflers. Pretty basket weave in entirely new plaid effects never before retailed for less than $2.00. Blue is the predominating color. You will be more than pleased with the exquisite design and quality. Price, 3 for $3.50; each..........$1.25

No. 50391 This Charming Assortment of Fine Mufflers cannot be matched in any regular retail store for less than $2.50. Made of twill silk in a great variety of richly brocaded Persian, Dresden and floral designs in stripes as shown in illustration. Stylish combinations in the latest designs. Also all black or all white. Price, 3 for $4.20; each......$1.50

Ladies' Mufflers.

No. 50391½ While ladies frequently wear the same style and size mufflers that gentlemen do, we present under this number an especially pleasing article of fine quality in raised stripe effect combined with designs as shown in illustration. Light colors, such as delicate pink or blue; also white. Size, 27 inches. Price, each..........$1.50

Oxford Mufflers.

(Worn by gentlemen or ladies.)
If by mail, postage extra, each, 5 cents.

No. 50394 Good quality silk Oxford mufflers, made with fine satin lining, full size, in large variety of scroll designs, plaids and stripes, or plain black. Price, each..........50c

No. 50395 Fine Oxford mufflers, made of stylish neckwear silks, in large variety of plaids and stripes, with pretty colored silk lining, very fashionable and up to date. Give color preference and you will not be disappointed.
Price, each..75c

No. 50396 We offer under this number an especially beautiful Oxford muffler in a new style as shown in illustration. Lower part is of fine black satin, and the part fitting around the neck is made of different designs of silk on each side. Will give better wear and is equal to any muffler offered retail at $1.50.
Price, per dozen, $11.00; each............................$1.00

No. 50397 Fine high grade Oxford Mufflers, made from new patterns in fine neckwear silks. New Persian effects in most fashionable colors and patterns. Fine silk lining or the same on both sides. Special value at our low price.
Price, each..$1.50

...SUSPENDER DEPARTMENT...

OUR LINE IN THIS DEPARTMENT IS THE MOST COMPLETE EVER PUT INTO CATALOGUE form. Our prices range from 8 cents to $1.35 per pair, and each represents the best of its kind. While we quote cheap suspenders, we do not warrant or recommend them. The better qualities are the cheapest in the end.
Be sure to include postage when ordering shipped by mail.

Suspenders and Braces.

No. 50400 Men's 1¼-Inch Elastic Web Suspenders. Dark or medium colors, fancy patterns, metal grip, back, braided ends and strong wire buckles. Per pair....90c.
No. 50403 Men's Fancy Silk Embroidered Suspenders. 1¼-inch elastic web,medium colors, with braided ends and drawer supporters. Nickeled cast-off buckles. Handsomely embroidered with silk in assorted patterns. Price per pair ..$0.15
Per dozen 1.50

No. 50400

If by mail, postage extra, per pair, 5 cents.

Berlin Back Suspenders.

No. 50404 A Great Favorite. Made from heavy, strong 1¼-inch elastic web, cushioned back. Assorted colored patterns. Extra strong non-breakable clasp and buckles. Full length.
'per pair....$0.25
Per dozen, 2.70

If by mail, postage extra, per pair, 5 cents.

No. 50404

Stronghold Cross-back Suspenders.

No. 50406 Men's Heavy Strong Elastic web Cross-Back Suspenders. Web 2 inches wide, heavy leather trimmings and ends. Strong buckles. 40 inches long. High colored stripes.
Per pair....$0.19
Per dozen.. 2.10

If by mail, postage extra, per pair, 5 cents.

No.50406

Extra Heavy Cross-back Suspenders.

No. 50408 Men's Extra Heavy and Strong. Assorted dark and medium stripes, extra heavy, 2-inch elastic web, cowhide ends. Leather trimmings. Sandow wire buckles. 40 inches long. Strongest and best made. Retail value. 35c.
Per pair...$0.28
Per dozen .. 3.00

No. 50408
If by mail, postage extra, per pair, 5 cents.
Order suspenders in quantities. Dozen rates apply to half dozen orders.

Men's Hercules Suspenders.

No. 50409 Men's Extra Heavy and strong Hercules suspenders. Made with self adjusting back; 3-inch elastic web, cow hide ends, wire buckles, length 40 inches. Excels all others for strength and wear.
Each $0.28
Price, doz... 3.00
If by mail, postage extra, per pair, 7 cents.

Lace Back Suspenders.

No. 50410 Men's Fine Elastic Web Suspenders. Self-adjusting lace back, braided ends. Fine strong cast off buckles. Medium colors, fancy embroidered designs in contrasting colors. Drawer supporters with cast off ends. Comfortable and durable.
Per pair ... .25c
Per doz. pairs ..$2.70

If by mail, postage extra,per pair, 7 cents.

No. 50410

Plain Black Suspenders.

No. 50412 Men's Fine Plain Black Suspenders. Close woven 1¼-inch elastic web. Kid trimmings. Ornamental sliding buckles and clasps. Fine black braided mohair ends and drawer supporters, glove snap cast-off. Price, per pair. $0.25
Per dozen pairs 2.70

Plain White Suspenders.

No. 50414 Same as above in plain white. Price, per dozen pairs, $2.70; per pair ....25c.
If by mail, postage extra, per pair, 5 cents.

Our New S., R. & Co.'s Suspender.

No. 50417 A New Suspender designed to equalize the extreme movements of the body, relieves the strain on the shoulders and buttons. No matter what position you assume the strain is practically the same on all buttons. Brings ease and comfort and never pulls buttons off. Made in a large variety of strong elastic webs. The running cord is non-elastic, strong and durable.

No. 50417

Price, per dozen, $2.75; each......25c
If by mail, postage extra, per pair, 6 cents.

No. 50418

Floral Design Suspenders.

No. 50418 Men's Dresden and Floral Pattern Elastic Web Suspenders. New, handsome designs. Ornamental sliding buckles with cast-off. Fancy braided ends and drawer supporters. Leather back and will give lasting satisfaction. Latest novelty. Per pair....$0.25
Per dozen....... 2.70
If by mail, postage extra, per pair, 5c.

Fancy Elastic Web Cross-Back Kid End Suspenders.

No. 50420 Handsomely designed, colors woven in web, glove snap fasteners with metal support adding much to durability. Fancy ornamental sliding buckles. Fine kid ends. Medium and light colors.
Per pair....$0.29
Per doz....... 3.10

If by mail, postage extra, per pair, 5 cents.

No. 50420

Fancy Silk Embroidered Elastic Web Suspenders.

No. 50422 Braided mohair ends, gold sliding buckles and drawer supporters. Very handsome. Medium light and dark colors. Assorted patterns. Very handsome.
Price, per dozen, $3.75; per pair 35c
If by mail, postage extra, per pair, 5 cents.

Extra Fine Silk Embroidered Suspenders.

No. 50426 Men's Extra Fine Silk Embroidered Suspenders. Handsome ornamental gold slides and cast-off. Braided lisle ends and drawer supporters. New exclusive patterns. Light medium and dark colors, artistic and elaborate silk embroidery. Charming and effective contrasts.
Per pair........$0.45
Per dozen......... 4.60

If by mail, postage extra, per pair, 5 cents.

No. 50426

Extra Long Suspenders.

No. 50427 Men's Extra Length Plain White or Slate Color Elastic Web Suspenders, made same style as No. 50420, 40 inches long. Fine and first-class in every particular. Price, per pair.......$0.45
Six pairs for..... 2.60
If by mail, postage extra, per pair, 5 cents.

The Cuyot.

No. 50430 Bretelle's Universelles. The Famous French Sanitary Suspenders. Light weight, strong, linen web, with elastic in back pieces only. Unexcelled for comfort and durability. Light and dark colors. All colors absolutely fast.
Per pair....$0.45
Per doz..... 4.90

If by mail, postage extra, per pair, 5 cents.

No. 50430

New Parisian Suspender.

No. 50435 The New Parisian Suspender. Made of finest imported elastic web in plaids and stripes of medium colors. Full length, cross back, kid trimmed with duplicate rolled and stitched leather ends, one running on the metal, the other on the leather. Thus the strain is equalized, making an unusually attractive and dependable suspender. Regular retail value, 75 cents.
Price, pair...$0.45
Per doz..... 4.90
If by mail, postage extra, per pair, 5 cents.

Men's Mocha Mittens, Plain Wrists.

No. 51082 Men's fine quality Mocha Mittens. Full size, soft and warm, made with wool fleeced lining, elastic wrists and embroidered backs; dark shades only, no blacks. Sizes, 7½, 8, 8½, 9, 9½, 10, 10½. Price, per dozen, **$10.00**; per pair......**90c**
If by mail, postage extra, per pair, 5 cents.
NOTE—For Men's Lamb Lined Mocha Mittens, see No. 51068 on page 551.

WRISTLETS OR PULSE WARMERS.

No. 51090 Men's Plain Black Double Wool Wristlets. Very elastic and will fit well. Price, per dozen, $1.25; per pair......**12c**
No. 51901 Men's Fancy Colored, Striped, Double Wristlets. Good quality. Price, per dozen, $2.10
Per pair......**.20**
No. 51092 Men's Fine Ribbed, Black, All Wool Double Wristlets. Medium weight. Price per dozen, $2.10; per pair......**20c**
No. 51093 Men's Extra Heavy and Thick Warm All Wool Double Wristlets. Plain black. Price, per doz., $2.70; per pair......**25c**
If by mail, postage extra, per pair, 2 cents.
No. 51094 Men's Silk Wristlets. Medium weight. Black only. Price, per dozen, $3.50; per pair...**35c**
If by mail, postage extra, per pair, 1 cent.

Warmpulse Wristlets.

No. 51095 The best patent wristlet ever made to prevent wind from blowing up sleeve. Made of brown fur with elastic through center, can be worn with any glove and will fit any size wrists.
Price per pair......**$0.25**
Per dozen......**2.50**
If by mail, postage extra, per pair, 4 cents.

Ladies' and Children's Warmpulse Fur Wristlets.

No. 51096 Ladies' New Warmpulsers, made of fine imitation sable. Almost as good as fur gloves to keep wind out of sleeves and the hands warm. A practical article, made with elastic in center and is pushed over hand. Price, per doz., $5.40; per pair, 2 cents... ......**50c**
If by mail, postage extra, per pair, 2 cents.

Warmpulse Wristlets for Children 43 Cents.

No. 51097 Snow White Fur Warmpulse Wristlets for children. A new serviceable article, sure to keep hands warm and wind out of sleeves. Select fine white fur. Price, per doz., $4.75; per pair...**43c**
If by mail, postage extra, per pair, 2 cents.

Men's Saxony Yarn Mittens.

No. 51100 Men's Plain Black, All Wool, Double Mittens, made of fine saxony yarn, seamless and fashioned to shape of hand. Usual retail price 35c.
Price, per dozen, $2.75; per pair......**25c**
If by mail, postage extra, per pair, 3 cents.

MEN'S SCOTCH WOOL GLOVES.

No. 51102 Men's All-Wool Scotch Gloves. Full seamless soft and warm, assorted dark and medium colors, heather mixtures or black. Sizes, small, medium and large. Price, per pair...**$0.25**
Per doz......**2.70**
If by mail, postage extra, per pair, 2 cents.

Men's Heavy All Wool Scotch Gloves, 35c.

No. 51103 Men's Heavy All-Wool Scotch Glove, seamless, durable and warm, double wrists. Oxford gray mixed and brown colors, all dark. Sizes, small, medium and large. Price, per pair......**$0.35**
Per doz......**3.80**
If by mail, postage extra, per pair, 2 cents.

McGeorge Gloves, 48c.

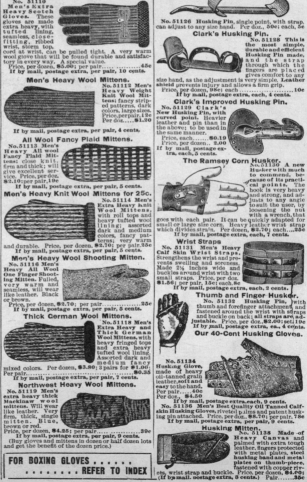

No. 51104 Men's Extra Quality All-Wool Imported genuine McGeorge Scotch Gloves. Full seamless, handsome patterns, assorted colors, dark and medium soft and comfortable.
Price, per pair......**$0.48**
Per doz......**5.25**
If by mail, postage extra, per pair, 3 cents.

McGeorge Gloves, 75c.

No. 51106 Men's Extra High Grade Scotch Gloves, made by J. & D. McGeorge, Dumfries, Scotland, manufacturers of the finest woolen gloves in the world. Handsome plaids in brown, black and mixed colors. Seamless and perfect fitting. Give size. Sizes 7½ to 10.
Price per pair......**$0.75**
Per doz......**8.40**
If by mail, postage extra, per pair, 3 cents.

McGeorge Gloves, $1.00.

No. 51108 Men's extra quality, very heavy McGeorge Bros.'s Scotch gloves, in dark colors only; made with heavy warm wool fleeced lining. A superior seamless glove. One clasp at wrist. Sizes, 7½ to 10. Every pair warranted.
Price, per dozen, $11.00; per pair......**$1.00**
If by mail, postage extra, 3 cents.

Men's Extra Heavy Scotch Gloves, 45c.

No. 51110 Men's Extra Heavy Scotch Gloves. These gloves are made extra heavy, with tufted lining, seamless, close-fitting, ribbed wrist, storm top, cord at wrist, can be pulled tight. A very warm wool glove that will be found durable and satisfactory in every way. A special value.
Price, per dozen, $5.00; per pair......**45c**
If by mail, postage extra, per pair, 10 cents.

Men's Heavy Wool Mittens.

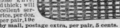

No. 51112 Men's Heavy Weight Knit Wool Mittens; fancy striped patterns, dark colors, large sizes. Price, per pair, 12c. Per doz......**$1.20**
If by mail, postage extra, per pair, 4 cents.

All Wool Fancy Plaid Mittens.

No. 51113 Men's Heavy All wool Fancy Plaid Mittens; close knit, firm and thick; will give excellent service. Price, per doz. $2.10 per pair, 19c
If by mail, postage extra, per pair, 5 cents.

Men's Heavy Knit Wool Mittens for 25c.

No. 51114 Men's Extra heavy knit wool Mittens, with roll tops and heavy tufted wool lining; assorted dark and medium colors, fancy patterns; very warm and durable. Price, per dozen, $2.70; per pair, 25c
If by mail, postage extra, per pair, 5 cents.

Men's Heavy Wool Shooting Mitten.

No. 51116 Men's Heavy All Wool One Finger Shooting Mitten. Fulled, very warm and seamless, will wear like leather. Black or brown.
Price, per dozen, $2.70; per pair......**25c**
If by mail, postage extra, per pair, 5 cents.

Thick German Wool Mittens.

No. 51118 Men's Extra Heavy and Thick German Wool Mittens, with heavy fringed tops and extra heavy tufted wool lining. Assorted dark and medium fancy mixed colors. Per dozen, $3.80; 3 pairs for $1.00. Per pair......**$0.35**
If by mail, postage extra, per pair, 7 cents.

Northwest Heavy Wool Mittens.

No. 51119 Men's extra heavy thick Mackinaw wool mittens. Will wear like leather. Very firm, thick, single mitten. Blue, brown or red.
Price, per dozen, $4.25; per pair......**39c**
If by mail, postage extra, per pair, 9 cents.
(Buy gloves and mittens in four or half dozen lots and get the benefit of the dozen price.)

Wind and Waterproof Mittens.

No. 51120 Men's Wind and Waterproof Heavy Wool Mittens. Heavy thick wool, wool lined, and waterproof interlining. May be wet and cold on outside, but on the inside always warm and dry.
Price, per dozen, $4.90; per pair......**45c**
If by mail, postage extra, per pair, 10 cents.

Extension Roll Wrist Mittens.

No. 51122 Men's Heavy Thick Wool Mittens, with wool linings, thick close-fitting wrists, and an over-wrist which can be rolled up over sleeve to keep out wind. A good driving mitten. Dark colors.
Price, per dozen, $4.90; per pair......**45c**
If by mail, postage extra, per pair, 11 cents.

Husking Gloves and Pins.

If by mail, postage extra, each, 4 cents.

No. 51126 Husking Pin, single point, with strap, can adjust to any size hand. Per doz., 50c; each, 5c

Clark's Husking Pin.

No. 51128 This is the most simple, durable and efficient Husking Pin made, and the strap through which the fingers are placed gives comfort to any size hand, as the adjustment is very simple. Leather shield prevents injury and allows a firm grip.
Price, per dozen, 96c; each......**10c**
If by mail, postage extra, each, 4 cents.

Clark's Improved Husking Pin.

No. 51129 Clark's New Husking Pin, with curved point. Heavier leather and pin than in the above; to be used in the same manner.
Price, each......**$0.19**
Price, per dozen...**2.00**
If by mail, postage extra, each, 5 cents.

The Ramsey Corn Husker.

No. 51130 A new Husker with much to commend, because of its practical points. The hook is very heavy and strong, and adjusts to any angle to suit the user, by loosening the nut with a wrench, that can be quickly adapted for small or large size corn. Heavy leather wrist strap which divides strain. Per dozen, $2.70; each...**25c**
If by mail, postage extra, each, 7 cents.

Wrist Straps

No. 51131 Men's Heavy Calf Skin Wrist Straps. Strengthens the wrist and prevents swelling and soreness. Made 2½ inches wide and buckles around wrist with two small straps. Price, per doz. $1.56; per pair, 13c; each, 8c
If by mail, postage extra, each, 2 cents.

Thumb and Finger Husker.

No. 51132 Husking Pin, with thumb and forefinger attachment, and fastened around the wrist with straps and buckle on back; all straps are adjustable. Price, per doz., $1.00; set, 10c
If by mail, postage extra, ea., 4 cents.

Our 40-Cent Husking Gloves.

No. 51134 Husking Glove, made of heavy oil-tanned grain leather, soft and easy to the hand.
Per pair......**40c**
Per doz., $4.50
If by mail, postage extra, each, 9 cents.
No. 51136 Men's Best Quality Oil Tanned Calfskin Husking Gloves, riveted palms and patent husking pin attached. Price, per dozen, $8.70; per pair, 78c
If by mail, postage extra, per pair, 9 cents.

Husking Mitten.

No. 51138 Made of Heavy Canvas and palmed with extra tough leather, fingers protected with metal plates, steel husking band and metal plates on thumb-piece, fastened with copper rivets, wrist strap and buckle. Price, per dozen, $4.00; Pair......**35c**
If by mail, postage extra, 5 cents.

HAT & CAP DEPARTMENT
FROM
MAKER
TO
WEARER

HOW TO MEASURE FOR A HAT.

Hat size	Inches around head	Hat size	Inches around head	Hat size	Inches around head
5⅞	18¾	6⅝	21	7⅜	23⅜
6	19	6¾	21¼	7½	23¾
6⅛	19⅜	6⅞	21⅝	7⅝	24
6¼	19¾	7	22¼	7¾	24½
6⅜	20¼	7⅛	22½	7⅞	25
6½	20¾	7¼	23	8	25¼

Men's Sizes are 6¾, 6⅞, 7, 7⅛, 7¼, 7⅜ and 7½. Extra sizes are: 7⅝ to 8. **Boys' Sizes** are 6½, 6⅝, 6¾, 6⅞ and 7. **Children's Sizes**, 6¼, 6⅜, 6½, 6⅝ and 6¾. **If you do not have a tape measure at hand, use strip of paper for measuring and attach same to your order.**

MEN'S DERBY OR STIFF HATS.

No. 52160 Young Men's Stiff Hat in fashionable fall shape. A very neat block, not extreme but stylish. Crown 4¾ in.; brim, 1⅞ in. Fine silk band and binding. Colors: Black or brown. Sizes, 6¾ to 7½.
Price:
Each $ 1.50
Doz... 16.50
If by mail, postage extra, each, 34 cents.

A Fashionable Block in Men's Stiff Hats for $2.00

No. 52161 Young Men's Fashionable Stiff Hat. A strictly correct block in a superior quality. A nonbreakable that will wear like a $3 hat. Crown, 4¾ in.; brim, 1⅞ in; fine silk band, binding and sweat. We warrant every hat to give satisfactory service. Sizes, 6¾ to 7½. Colors: Black and dark brown.
Each. $ 2.00
Doz.... 22.50

If by mail, postage extra, each, 34 cents.

Late Style and Excellent Value for $2.25.

No. 52162 Men's medium shape stiff hat, a little larger than the above styles. Medium curled brim. Not an extreme in any respect, but a strictly stylish block. Crown, 5 inches; brim, 1⅞ inches. A very fine hat at our low price that we warrant to give satisfactory wear. Equal to most hats sold at $3.00. Colors, black or dark brown. Sizes, 6¾ to 7⅝.
Each...... 2.25
Per doz... $24.50
If by mail, postage extra, 34 cents.

Very Good Value for $1.49.

No. 52163 Men's medium shape stiff hat of the staple open curl style. An excellent hat that will give good satisfaction. Crown, 5¼ inches; brim, 1⅞ inches. Sizes, 6¾ to 7½. Colors, black or brown.
Price, per dozen, $16.40; price, each $1.49
If by mail, postage extra, 34 cents.

No. 52164 Men's Staple Shape Stiff Hat. Medium crown and brim. We do not recommend a hat at this price for wear, but we will send you the best hat you ever had for such a low price. No illustration. Sizes 6¾ to 7⅜. Black only. **What size do you wear?**
Price, per dozen, $11.50; price, each 98c
If by mail, postage extra, 34 cents.

Dunlap, Knox or Youman Styles.

No. 52165 Men's High Grade Stiff Hat, made of very fine quality of fur, with select silk trimmings, in the Dunlap, Knox or Youman styles; small, medium or large shape. We furnish the latest styles or shapes as issued in the spring and fall. The usual retail price of this quality is $ 0 and combines **all the points of merit and non breakableness of the finest derby hat.** Sizes 6¾ to 7⅝. Price, each, $2.75
If by mail, postage extra, each, 34 cents.

Men's Fashionable Square Crown Hats, $2.00.

No. 52166 At this price we have the new style square crown hat. A very fashionable block. Crown, 5⅛ inches; brim, 2 inches wide. A nonbreakable hat that will not fail to please in style and quality. Fine silk band and binding. Imported leather sweat band. What size do you wear? Sizes, 6¾ to 7⅝. Price, each............................$ 2.00
Price, per dozen.......................... 22.50
If by mail, postage extra, 34 cents.

Men's Large or Full Shape Stiff Hats.

No. 52167 A style particularly suited to large men. A shapely, staple hat, as shown in illustration. Crown, 5⅛ inches; brim, 2¼ inches. Fine silk band and binding. Sizes, 6¾ to 7⅝. Color: Black only. Price, per dozen, $16.50; price each....$1.50

$2.25 Quality.

No. 52168 Men's full shape hat, same style and dimensions as the above, in the high grade nonbreakable stock, with very fine silk band and binding, imported leather sweat band. Color: Black only. Sizes, 6¾ to 7¾.
Price, per dozen, $24.50; price each.........$2.25
If by mail, postage extra, 34 cents.

No. 52362 Cowboys' Extra-Fine Heavy Weight Saxony Wool Sombrero, with 4½-inch crown and 4-inch brim, with wide single-buckle embossed leather band and leather binding. Band is embossed in beautiful floral and novelty patterns in variegated colors. Sizes, 6¾ to 7⅝ only. Colors, belly nutria or light calfskin. **What size do you wear?**
Price, each..**$1.50**
If by mail, postage extra, 20 cents.

COWBOY SOMBREROS.

The Phœnix **$2.50**

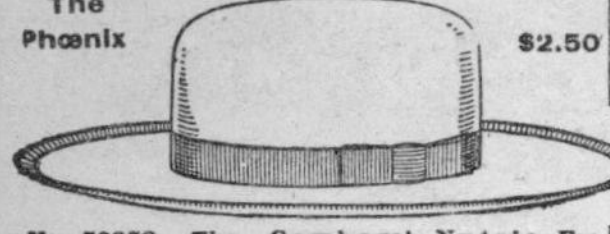

No. 52379 The Cowboys' Nutria Fur Sombrero. 4½-inch crown, 4-inch brim, silk band and binding. Thoroughly durable and never fails to please. Sizes 6¾ to 7½. **What size do you wear?** Price, each..**$2.50**
If by mail, postage extra, 38 cents.

Pine Ridge Scout.

No. 52380 Cowboys' Favorite Sombrero Hat. Belly nutria color; crown, 4 inch; brim, 4 inch; raw edge, flat, stiff, knife-blade brim; 1-inch silk ribbon band; weight, 6 ounces. Sizes, from 6¾ to 7½. **What size do you wear?**
Our price, Each, **$2.75**
If by mail, postage extra, 38 cents.

The Montana.

No. 52384 The Montana. Known throughout the west as a top-notcher for appearance, durability and quality, and made from selected nutria fur of a superior grade. Best imported silk band and binding. Crown, 4½ inches; brim, 4½ inches; weight, 6 oz. Color, belly nutria. The sizes run from 6¾ to 7½. **What size do you wear?**
Price, each..**$3.00**
If by mail, postage extra, 38 cents.

$3.00 **$3.00**

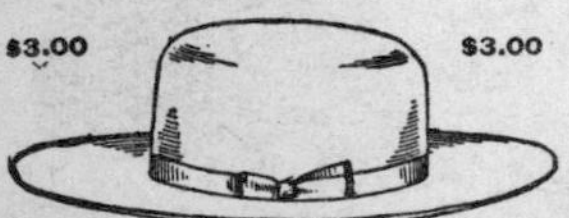

No. 52388 This is the Never Flop Hat. There are many so-called Never-Flop Hats on the market, but there is only one Never-Flop that has proven to be all that its name implies, the raw-edge, scoop brim, 4 inches wide; 4½-inch crown; weight, 8 oz. Color, side nutria. Sizes run from 6¾ to 7½. **What size do you wear?**
Our price, with a guarantee not to flop **$3.00**
If by mail, postage extra, 38 cents.

No. 52390 The Texas Steer style Sombrero hat. Crown, 4½ inches; brim, 5 inches. Fancy leather band with four silver stars. Fine nutria fur, never-flop brim. Weight, 8 oz. Color, side nutria. Sizes, 6¾ to 7½. Price, each..**$3.50**

No. 52391 The Mountaineer Sombrero. A good friend of the cowboy. A fine fur hat with medium stiff brim; sure to be satisfactory. Crown, 4½ inches; brim, 4 inches, with 2-inch embossed leather band. Calfskin color. Sizes 6¾ to 7½. Weight, 8 ounces.
Price, each..**$3.00**
If by mail, postage extra, 38 cents.

No. 52391½ Mexican Sombrero. Crown, 7 inches; brim, 4 inches; bound with silk. Elaborate fancy trimming. Side nutria color. Sizes, 6¾ to 7½.
Each....**$3.00**
If by mail, postage extra, 38 cents.

The J. B. Stetson Sombrero.

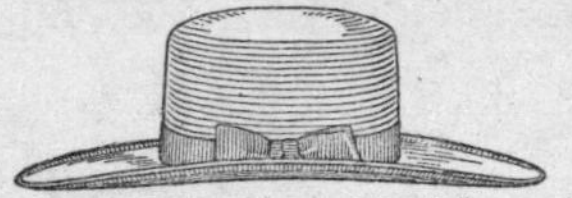

No. 52392 Stetson's Boss of the Plains, most popular Cowboy Hat, made from the finest selected nutria fur. Silk band and binding; crown, 4½ inches; brim, 4 inches; weight, 6 ounces. The sizes run from 6¾ to 7½. Color, belly nutria. **What size do you wear?** Each..**$4.50**
If by mail, postage extra, 38 cents.

The Texan Chief, $5.25.

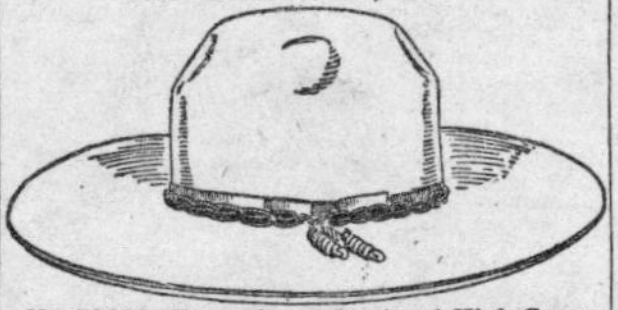

No. 52420 Texan Chief Cowboys' High Crown Mexican Style Sombrero Hat, 5-in. brim and 6½-in. crown; fine leather sweat band, and handsome satin lining; 1-inch silk ribbon band or tassel cord braided band, if desired. Flat, never-flop brim with raw edge. One of the very best as well as the most popular sombreros ever made from best quality clear nutria fur. Full of real goodness and will give excellent satisfaction. Color, belly nutria. Sizes, 6¾ to 7½. Price, each..**$5.25**
If by mail, postage extra, 38 cents.

No. 52421 Pride of the West Sombrero. Made with silver tinsel cloth band braided, four silver tinsel stars on crown and four on underside of brim. A very fine cowboy's fancy hat that is sure to give satisfaction; crown 4 inches, brim 5 inches wide; color, side nutria. Weight, 12 oz. Sizes, 6¾ to 7½.
Price, each..**$6.50**
If by mail, postage extra, 38 cents.

Leather Hat Bands.

No. 52432 Cowboys' 2-in. all leather hat bands. Embossed russet leather, with double straps and two small buckles, will fit any hat. Price, each, **39c**
If by mail, postage extra, 3c.

No. 52434 Russet Leather Embossed Hat Bands, 1½-in. wide, with single strap and buckle. All solid leather, oak tanned. Price, each...... **25c**
If by mail, postage extra, 3 cents.

Imported Silver Tinsel Stars.

For Decorating Cowboys' Hats, Gloves, Etc.

No. 52436 Extra Fine Quality Imported Silver Stars. Largely used for decorating sombreros, gauntlet gloves, masquerade costumes, etc. Per gross, **$7.50**; doz........**70c**
If by mail, postage extra, per dozen, 4 cents.

BOYS' OR YOUTHS' HATS.

Sizes are 6½, 6⅝, 6¾, 6⅞, 7. Always state size in your order. If you do not know the size measure as directed on first page of Hat Department.

No. 52444 Boys' and Youths' Fine Saxony Wool Hats, medium shaped crown and brim. Colors, black, blue or brown. Always state size and color wanted. These hats will give excellent service. They are fine in finish and very durable. Made with ribbon band and leather sweat. Sizes, 6½ to 7 only. **What size do you wear?**
Price, per dozen, **$5.00**; each........................**45c**
If by mail, postage extra, 13 cents.

No. 52445 Boys' Latest Style Fedora Hats. Made from fine Saxony wool, with silk band and leather sweat band. Sizes, 6½ to 7 only. Color, black. Each...**45c**
Per doz....**$5.00**

No. 52446 Boys' Latest Style Saxony and gray Wool Fedora Hats. Same as above in dark brown. Price, each........................**45c**

No. 52447 Boys' Wool Hat, Telescope Style. Very popular hat, becoming to most boys. Wide silk band, leather sweat banding and raw edge. Colors, black brown or blue. Sizes, 6½ to 7 only. Price, per dozen, **$5.40**; each..........**50c**
If by mail, postage extra, 13 cents.

No. 52448 Boys' Fine Fur Telescope Style Hat. Made of good quality fur, that will hold color and shape; fine silk band and binding. Colors, black navy, brown and fawn. Sizes, 6⅝ to 7 only. Price, per dozen, **$10.80**; each..........**95c**
If by mail, postage extra, 13 cents.

Boys' Fine Fedora Hats.

No. 52474 Boys' Handsomest Fedora Hat. Very latest Fedora style, wide silk ribbon band and binding, fine leather sweat band. Soft, fine and very dressy. Made from fine fur felt. Colors, brown and black. Sizes, 6½ to 7⅛ only. A medium shape, suitable for boys up to 16 years of age. Price, each...**$1.25**

The Chester—90c.

No. 52475 Boys' Clear Fur Fedora. Medium wide silk ribbon band and silk binding, leather sweat band; colors, golden dark brown and black. Sizes, 6½ to 7. Extremely nobby. **What size do you wear?**
Price, each..**90c**
If by mail, postage extra, 13 cents.

No. 52477 Boys' Saxony Wool Pasha. Silk ribbon band; leather sweat band. A good value. Colors, brown and black; Sizes, 6½ to 6¾. **What size do you wear?**
Per dozen, **$5.00**; each........................**45c**
If by mail, postage extra, 13 cents.

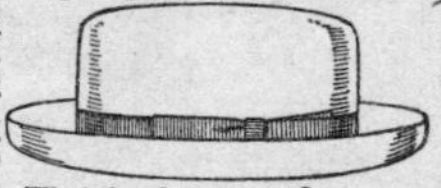

50c—Boys' Cowboy Hat—50c.

No. 52478 Rough and Tumble Saxony Wool Hat. Leather band and binding; leather sweat. Made to stand the rough usage that the school boys' hat is sure to receive. Colors, belly nutria or gray; sizes, 6½ to 7. **What size do you wear?** Price, per doz., **$5.40**; each........................**50c**
If by mail, postage extra, 14 cents.

No. 52479 Child's Fancy Wool Turban nicely trimmed with satin cord braid. Pretty, durable and extremely low in price. Leather sweat; sizes, 6¼ to 6¾; colors, black, blue and brown. **What size do you wear?** Price, per doz., **$4.25**; each..........**39c**
If by mail, postage extra, 11 cents.

LIGHT WEIGHT OR SUMMER CAPS.

Men's sizes, 6¾, 6⅞, 7, 7⅛, 7¼, 7⅜, 7½.

THE SIZE OF A CAP is very important, therefore when you make out your order don't forget to state just what size you want. We can then fill your order promptly and to your entire satisfaction.

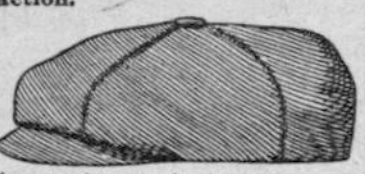

No.52484 One of our specially good values. **Men's Navy Blue Cloth Golf Caps.** Six-piece top. Sizes, 6¾ to 7½.
Price, each, $0.25
Per dozen.. 2.70
If by mail, postage extra, each, 4 cents.

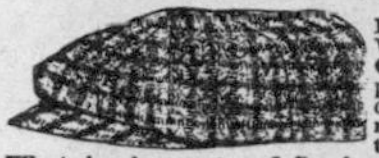

No. 52485 Men's Extra Quality, All Wool Cheviot Golf Caps. Six or eight piece top and hook down front. All neat, dressy patterns. Sizes, 6¾ to 7¼. **What size do you wear?** Per doz., $5.00; each ..45c
If by mail, postage extra, each 6 cents.

No. 52487 Same cap as above, in handsome brown-mixed, all-wool cassimeres. Full satin lined.
Price, per dozen, $5.00; each. ..45c
If by mail, postage extra, each, 6 cents.

No. 52489 Made from a fine quality of navy blue broadcloth, with heavy satin lining and hook-down front. Six-piece top with double stitched seams. They would be cheap in large retail stores at 75 cents. Sizes, 6¾ to 7½. **What size do you wear?**
Our price, per dozen, $5.40; each 50c
If by mail, postage extra, each, 6 cents.

No. 52493 Men's Fancy Mixed Corduroy Golf. Best imported material, beautiful satin lining, gray and brown mixed stripes and plaids. A handsome cap, suitable for all seasons. Sizes, 6¾ to 7½. **What size do you wear?** Per doz., $4.22; each........39c
If by mail, postage extra each, 8 cents.

Men's Golf Yacht Caps.

No. 52495 This Splendid Cap at 25c is an exceptional value. Better than anything we have ever been able to offer before at this price. Plaid and checked cassimeres or plain blue. Sizes, 6¾ to 7¼. **What size do you wear?** Per doz., $2.70; each..25c
If by mail, postage extra, each, 8 cents.

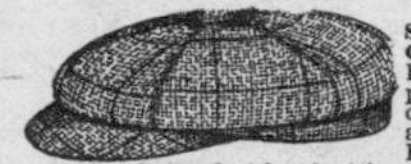

No. 52497 Men's Scotch Cheviot Golf Yacht Cap. Handsome broken plaids and nobby checks in brown and gray. Finest Russian leather sweat band, lined with soft rich satin lining. Sizes, 6¾ to 7½. Price, per doz. $5.40; each............50c
If by mail, postage extra, each, 10 cents.

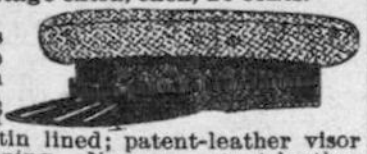

No. 52550 The Latest Men's Yacht; made up in imported Scotch sheviot mixtures, plaids and checks of gray and brown; satin lined; patent-leather visor with green underlining. Narrow patent-leather front band. Trimmed all around with band of 2-inch Black French lattice braid. Sizes, 6¾ to 7½. **What size do you wear?** Per doz., $5.40; each..48c
If by mail, postage extra, each, 12 cents.

No. 52556 Men's Marine Yacht Caps. Made in blue German broadcloth, heavy hercules braid band, black patent leather visor and ornamental front strap, leather sweatband. Decidedly Nobby. Sizes, 6¾ to 7½.
Price, per dozen, $5.40; each. ...50c
If by mail, postage extra, each, 12 cents.

Conductor Caps.

Made with patent wire frame. Never gets out of shape.

Cut Showing Wire Frame.

No. 52564 Conductors' Extra-Fine Navy Blue Broadcloth Caps, with patented wire frame and fine leather sweat band. We guarantee them to be the most practical as well as the best wearing caps of this kind made. Money refunded if not exactly as represented. When lettering is desired we require cash in full with order. Sizes, 6¾ to 7½.
Price, each..............................$1.45
This price is for plain cap without lettering. Gold wire block embroidered letters will cost 10c per letter extra. Allow us one week for delivery.
If by mail, postage extra, each, 18 cents.

No. 52566 Made from finest quality of grosgrain silk or fine blue broad cloth with wire frame. Sizes, 6¾ to 7¾. Where lettering is desired we require cash in full with order.
Price....... $1.45
Price, with Conductor in gold wire block letters.................$2.35
If by mail, postage extra, each, 18 cents.
Gold wire block letters as shown in cut, cost 10 cents extra per letter.

Nickel Plated Cap Badges.

The following badges are made from German silver, handsomely nickel plated.

These badges are made to order with any lettering desired. The full amount of cash must be sent with the order. We do not send these goods C. O. D., and they cannot be returned or exchanged unless we are clearly at fault. Always order by catalogue number and state plainly just what lettering you desire and your orders will receive prompt attention and be filled correctly. Allow about five days for making.

No. 52581 Official Stars, fourteen letters, such as City Marshal, Deputy, etc.
Price,.....................................$1.00
If by mail, postage extra, each, 3 cents.

No. 52582 Nickel Plated German Silver Badge. Size, ¾x3 inches. Conductor, baggageman, porter, news agent, expressman or any words not exceeding fifteen letters. Made to order. Price, each......$0.60
Price, per doz.................................. 6.50
If by mail, postage extra, each, 2 cents.

No. 52586 Nickel Plated German Silver Badge, with fancy oval. 1-inch wide by 3 inches long. Suitable for such words as Hotel Porter, A. T. & S. F. R'y Conductor, City Expressman, B. & O. Baggageman and similar words not exceeding twenty-two letters. Always state what letters you want. Price, per doz., $8.90; each..80c
If by mail, postage extra, 2 cents.

NOTE—Larger badges made to order at from $1.25 to $2.50, according to size and lettering. It requires about 5 days to have these badges made to order.

Black Cotton Shop Caps.

No. 52594 Men's Black Cotton Shop Cap; very light but durable. Sizes, 6¾ to 7½. **What size do you wear?** Price, per dozen, $1.00; each..........9c
If by mail, postage extra, 5 cents.

Engineers' Caps.

No. 52596 Engineers' Black Leather Caps. Standard shape, well made and just the cap to wear on the engine. Sizes, 6¾ to 7½.
Price, each..$0.50
Per dozen.... 5.40
If by mail, postage extra, each 8 cents.

No. 52600 Engineers' Fine Black Silk Caps, with extra wide visor to protect the eyes. Handsomely satin lined. Sizes, 6¾ to 7⅝.
Price, each.......$0.50
Per dozen........ 5.40
If by mail, postage extra, 5 cents.

Silk Pullman.

No. 52601 Men's Fine Silk Pullman or Scull Cap, with fine silk lining. Black only. Sizes, 6¾ to 7⅝.
Price, each.............$0.50
Per dozen............... 5.40
If by mail, postage extra, each, 2 cents.

BOYS' SPRING AND SUMMER CAPS.

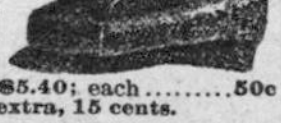

No. 52608 Boys' Finest Navy Blue Broadcloth University Caps. Similar to the golf style, but fuller in the crown, and does not hook down in front; lined with satin. Sizes, 6½ to 7. Warranted first-class in every way. Price, per doz., $5.40; each.........50c
If by mail, postage extra, 15 cents.

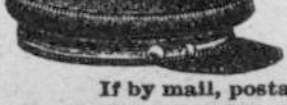

No. 52617 Boys' Cheviot Yacht Caps in mixed and assorted patterns. With cord band.
Price, each........$0.18
Per dozen.......... 1.65
If by mail, postage extra, 8 cents.

No. 52619 Our Special 25c Yacht. Made from fine quality navy blue wove cloth, with wide hercules braid and silk cord trimming. Serge lining.
Price, per dozen, $2.70; each..........................25c
If by mail, postage extra, 8 cents.

Boys' Golf Yacht Caps.

No. 52621 The Dunkirk Boys' New Style Golf Yacht Cap. Made up in all-wool goods in a pretty range of patterns, brown, gray and blue mixtures, patent leather visor, hercules braid trimming. An unusually good value. Sizes, 6¼ to 7. **What size do you wear?** Price, each......$0.35
Per dozen... 4.00
If by mail, postage extra, each, 8 cents.

No. 52625 Boys' Plain Navy Blue Broadcloth Golf Caps. Six-piece top with sateen lining.
Per dozen, $2.70; each.................................25c
If by mail, postage extra, each, 6 cents.

Boys' Harvard Golf Caps.

No. 52627 The Harvard Golf Cap. Made from fine all-wool fancy gray mixed cheviot suitings. Heavy satin lining and patent hook-down front. Sizes, 6½ to 7.
Each..............45c
If by mail, Postage extra, 4c.

No. 52629 The Harvard Golf Cap. Same as above, in rich brown mixtures.
Each...45c
If by mail, postage extra, 6 cents.

Boys' Military Caps.

No. 52633 Boys' Fine Navy Blue Cadet or Military Cap. Made from regulation uniform cloth, with gilt cord and buttons. Always a great favorite with the boys. Sizes, 6⅜ to 7⅛.
Price, per dozen, $5.35; price, each...... ......48c
If by mail, postage extra, each, 10 cents.

Children's Caps.

Sizes, 6⅛, 6¼, 6⅜, 6½, 6⅝, 6¾, 6⅞.

No. 52635 Children's Navy Blue Broadcloth Golf Cap. Silk lined throughout and handsomely embroidered on front of crown in gold and silver. Fancy designs. One of the handsomest and swellest caps we have. Sure to please. You will like them. Price, per dozen, $5.40; each.............47c
If by mail, postage extra, each, 6 cents.

The Midshipman Cap at 50 Cents.

No. 52637 Children's Fancy Midshipman Yacht Cap; Made from navy blue broadcloth, with leather sweat band, one-inch gold band and double gold cord and buttons. Gold ornament on front of crown. **Rich and dressy.** Nothing but fine materials used in this cap. Sizes, 6⅛ to 6⅞.
Price, each $0.50
Per dozen.................. 5.40
If by mail, postage extra, each, 11 cents.

BOYS' OR YOUTHS' WINTER CAPS.

Sizes 6½, 6⅝, 6¾, 6⅞, 7.

No. 52770 Boys' Dark Melton Brighton Caps, with pull down band to protect the ears. Colors, navy blue or dark Oxford gray mixed. Sizes, 6½ to 7. Price, each.... ....$0.25
Per dozen... 2.80
If by mail, postage extra, each, 10 cents.

No. 52772 Boys' Plain Blue Wool Cheviot Caps, turban style, pulls down over ears. Lined throughout. Sizes, 6½ to 7 only.
Each.............$0.25
Per dozen........ 2.70
If by mail, postage extra, each, 8 cents.

No. 52774 Boys' Academy Cap. Made from fine wool yacht cloth, with pull down band to protect the ears. **Nicely lined and well made throughout.** Navy blue, or gray mixed. Size 6½ to 7 only. Price, each.........$0.25
Per dozen.. 2.76
If by mail, postage extra, each, 9 cents.

54666
.89¢

54657
.90¢

54627
43c

54674
$1.50

MEN'S
RIBBED AND FLEECED UNDERWEAR

54664
$1.75

No. 54629 Men's Extra Fine German Imported Balbriggan Underwear, made of fine Egyptian cotton, will always remain soft and pliable, elastic cuffs and silk facing all around. This garment is made especially for those who cannot wear wool, and will be found the most durable and satisfactory of all kinds of cotton underwear. Sizes, 34 to 44 bust measure.
Price, per dozen **$13.00**; each..................**$1.15**
No. 54631 Men's Fine German Ribbed Balbriggan Drawers, to match shirt No. 54629, trimmed with pearl buttons, full fashioned throughout. Sizes, 30 to 42 waist measure.
Price, per dozen **$13.00**; each **$1.15**
If by mail, postage extra, each, 20 cents.

Fine All-Wool Ribbed Underwear.

No. 54657 Men's Fine All-Wool Ribbed Undershirts, trimmed with silk, neck and front, pearl buttons. This is full winter-weight ribbed wool undershirt, that will certainly prove satisfactory, and is one of the greatest values we have ever offered. We have made a special effort to secure the very best underwear in the market to be sold at this price, which represents a special value. Made in a light tan or fawn color. Sizes, 34 to 44 breast measure.
Price, per dozen **$9.90**; each **90c**
No. 54660 Men's Fine All-Wool Drawers to match shirt No. 54657, trimmed with pearl buttons, suspender tapes, and never-rip seams throughout. Sizes, 30 to 42 waist measure.
Price, per dozen **$9.90**; each...............**$0.90**
Three full suits above underwear **4.95**
If by mail, postage extra, each, 19 cents.

WE REMIND YOU again not to forget size, as we can then give your order prompt attention. When ordering shipped by mail always include sufficient for postage.

All-Wool Blue Underwear.

No. 54662 Men's Fine All-Wool Ribbed Undershirts, same quality as No. 54660, and same style trimming, made in light blue fast color, which is a very desirable fancy winter undergarment. Sizes, 34 to 44 breast measure.
Price, per dozen **$9.90**; each...................**90c**
No. 54663 Men's Fine All-Wool Drawers, to match above shirts, suspender taped, pearl buttons, never-rip seams throughout. Sizes, 30 to 42 waist measure. Price, per dozen **$9.90**; each.......**$0.90**
Three full suits of the above underwear.....**4.95**
If by mail, postage extra, each, 19 cents.
No. 54664 Men's Fine All-Wool Ribbed Underwear. A special high grade quality, trimmed with silk, and pearl buttons. In this garment is to be found the result of the experience of thirty-five years in making this particular kind of underwear, and when we offer it to our customers, we are placing before them the very best of this character of goods that can be had for the price. With careful washing this underwear will shrink but a trifle. We recommend it in particular for those who like a neat close fitting garment. The seams throughout are of a special elastic construction, and will out wear the garment itself. We guarantee every garment to prove entirely satisfactory. Color, light blue only, fast color. Sizes, 34 to 44 breast measure. We sample this number.
Price, per dozen **$19.20**; each **$1.75**
No. 54665 Drawers to match shirt No. 54664. Trimmed with heavy sateen waist band, suspender tapes, pearl buttons, and elastic covered seams throughout. Price, per dozen **$19.20**; each...**$1.75**
Two full suits of this underwear............ **6.00**
If by mail, postage extra, each, 19 cents.
For Fine Heavy Medlicot, Morgan Co.'s Underwear see page 568.

Men's Ribbed Underwear.

No. 54625 Men's Regular Winter-Weight Ribbed Balbriggan, undershirts fleeced on the inside, brushed soft and smooth. Collarette neck, satin front, pearl buttons, perfect form fitting. The very best cotton undershirts that can be offered for this price. Color, light blue. Sizes, 34 to 44 breast measure. Price, per dozen **$4.80**; each..........**43c**

No. 54626 Men's Cotton Ribbed Drawers, full winter weight, to match shirt No. 54625. Sizes, 30 to 42 waist measure.
Price, per dozen **$4.80**; each.....................**43c**
If by mail, postage extra, each, 19 cents.

No. 54627 Men's Full Winter-Weight Ribbed Balbriggan Underwear, same style as No. 54625, in trimming, weight and quality, made in light brown color. Sizes, 34 to 44 breast measure.
Price, per dozen **$4.80**; each.....................**43c**

No. 54627½ Men's Full Winter-Weight Cotton Ribbed Drawers, made with suspender tapes, satin waistband. Sizes, 30 to 42 waist measure.
Price, per dozen **$4.80**; each.....................**43c**
If by mail, postage extra, each, 19 cents.

Fine Fleece-Lined Underwear.

For fleeced underwear at 43c, 50c, etc. See page 572.

Dr. Wright's Famous Underwear.
We Sample this Number.

No. 54666 Dr. Wright's Celebrated Sanitary natural gray fleece lined Underwear, silk trimmed, ribbed cuffs, covered non-ripping seams throughout. The special properties and healthfulness of Dr. Wright's underwear is known throughout the world, and especially in this country, they are the most reliable of fleeced underwears, and have warmth and sanitary properties that cannot be excelled. For those who like fleeced lined underwear we recommend Dr. Wright's above all others. They are non-shrinking, better trimmed and more durable than other kinds. Sizes, 34 to 44 breast measure.
Price, per dozen **$9.80**; each.........................**89c**
No. 54668 Dr. Wright's Wool Fleeced Lined Drawers to match above shirt, trimmed with pearl buttons, suspender taped, never-rip seams throughout. Sizes, 30 to 42 waist measure.
Price, per dozen **$9.80**; each............... **$0.89**
Three full suits of the above underwear ... **4.90**
If by mail, postage extra, each, 19 cents.
No. 54672 Dr. Wright's Famous Underwear in extra fine quality. We sample this number. Not quite so heavy as the above, made with a fine soft Australian wool fleecing, and a fine smooth close knit outer surface, silk taped neck, and pearl buttons, and "union special" covered seams throughout, and close ribbed cuffs. This is a superior quality of the Dr. Wright's manufacture, and usually retails at $2.00 each. We especially recommend this quality to persons with a sensitive skin, and as they are non-shrinking they invariably prove satisfactory. Natural mottled gray color. Sizes, 34 to 44 breast measure. Price, per dozen **$16.20**; each. **$1.40**
No. 54673 Dr. Wright's Fine Wool Drawers to match shirt No. 54672, trimmed with pearl buttons, suspender tapes, close ribbed cuffs and never-rip seams throughout. Sizes, 30 to 42 waist measure.
Price, per dozen **$16.20**; each...............**$1.40**
Two full suits of the above underwear **5.50**
No. 54674 Dr. Wright's Fine Fleeced Wool Underwear, made in light blue color. We sample this number. A very durable garment with Australian wool fleecing. Trimmed around neck with silk, silk facing, pearl buttons, and close ribbed cuffs. This is a very beautiful finished garment, containing all the healthful properties of the garment quoted above, the only difference being this is light blue in color, and slightly heavier. The usual retail price is $2.00, and our price represents about the cost to your local merchant. Sizes, 34 to 44 breast measure. Per dozen **$17.00**; each............**$1.50**
No. 54675 Dr. Wright's Fleeced Lined Drawers, to match shirt No. 54674, trimmed with pearl buttons, suspender tapes, never-rip seams throughout. Sizes, 30 to 42 waist measure. Per doz., **$17.00**; each, **$1.50**
Two full suits of the above underwear...... **5.75**
If by mail, postage extra, each, 19 cents.

Men's Silk Fleeced Underwear $1.

No. 54676 Men's Silk Fleeced Undershirts, made with silk trimmed neck and front, close fitting ribbed cuffs. This is a special value, made with silk fleecing that is very soft and non-irritating to the skin. It is durable and at our price will be found a most superior value. Made in light blue color only. Stitched throughout with special covered seams. Sizes, 34 to 44 breast measure.
Price, per dozen **$11.00**; each.....................**$1.00**
No. 54676½ Men's Silk Fleeced Drawers, never-rip seams throughout to match shirt No. 54676. Sizes, 30 to 42 waist measure. Per doz., **$11.00**; each, **$1.00**
Three full suits of the above underwear...... **5.50**
If by mail, postage extra, each, 19 cents.

54698 85¢ 54716 $1.25 54714 $1.50 54706 .95¢

54719 2.00

EXTRA HEAVY WINTER UNDERWEAR.

THE UNDERWEAR quoted under this head is intended for rough wear and usage, for men exposed to the weather, and is designed for durability rather than fineness, and we recommend them in particular for the use of lumbermen, farmers, miners, surveyors, prospectors, etc. For finest extra heavy worsted underwear see page 568 and catalogue No. 54532.

HEAVY UNDERWEAR 45 CENTS.

No. 54690 Lumbermen's Heavy Thick, Natural Gray Wool Undershirts, ribbed, trimmed with silk around neck, and pearl buttons, woolly surface, heavy, thick and warm. For the price this is the best heavy garment that can be offered, but we would recommend the higher grade immediately following as the cheapest in the long run. Weight, about 16 ounces. Sizes, breast measure, 36 to 44 inches.
Price, per dozen, $5.00; each.....(If by mail, postage extra, each, 19 cents.)...45c
No. 54692 Lumbermen's Heavy Wool Mixed Drawers, to match above shirt. Sizes, waist measure, 32 to 42 inches.
Price, per dozen, $5.00; each. (If by mail, postage extra, each, 19 cents.)...45c

TWO STRONG VALUES, 85 AND 95 CENTS.

No. 54698 Lumbermen's or Farmers' Extra Heavy Natural Gray Wool Undershirts, heavy thick, soft surface, silk taped front and pearl buttons. These garments are unexcelled for their warmth and durability, and persons living in a very severe climate requiring a very warm garment will find this quality invariably satisfactory. Our price represents about the cost to your local merchant. Average weight, 17 ounces. Three-quarters wool. Sizes, breast measure, 36 to 46 inches.
Price, per dozen, $9.20; each.....................85c
If by mail, postage extra, each, 20 cents.
No. 54700 Farmers' or Lumbermen's Extra Heavy Natural Gray Ribbed Wool Drawers, to match above shirt. Sizes, waist measure, 32 to 44 inches.
Price, per dozen, $9.20; each.....................85c
If by mail, postage extra, each, 20 cents.

No. 54706 Lumbermen's or Farmers' Extra Heavy Thick Natural Gray Wool Undershirts, made with double breast and back as shown in the illustration, extra warm and durable. Extra thickness on the chest and back make this underwear particularly desirable in severe climates, affording just that much extra protection to the lungs. Weight, 20 ounces. For lumbermen, farmers, railroad men and others exposed to the severity of the weather. The same kind as No. 54700 but double breasted. Sizes, breast measure, 36 to 46 inches.
Price, per dozen, $10.20; each.................95c
If by mail, postage extra, each, 23 cents.
No. 54708 Lumbermen's Heavy Wool Drawers to match above shirts. Sizes, waist measure, 32 to 44 inches.
Price, per dozen, $9.20; each.................85c
If by mail, postage extra, each, 20 cents.

MEN'S PLUSH BACK UNDERWEAR.

By plush back we mean underwear that is brushed up soft on the inside, by a machine made especially for this purpose, leaving a plush like surface.
No. 54709 Men's Heavy Plush Back All Wool Undershirts in light brown or buckskin color, trimmed with pearl buttons, ribbed cuffs and tail. This is a special value we are offering at 88 cents and is seldom retailed at less than $1.25. For the price we believe it excels all other garments offered. You will make no mistake in ordering this quality. Sizes, breast measure, 34 to 44 inches.
Price, per dozen, $9.80; each.....................88c
If by mail, postage extra, 20 cents.
No. 54709½ Men's Heavy Plush Back Drawers, to match above shirts. Made for wear. Sizes, waist measure, 30 to 42 inches.
Price, per dozen, $9.80; each.....................88c
Three suits of above.........................4.90

Plush Back Underwear, $1.25

No. 54711 Men's Heavy Plush Back Undershirts, of superior quality, trimmed with silk front, pearl buttons and close ribbed cuffs. In this underwear is to be found unusual value and we recommend it over any garment of this kind for the price. It is practically non-shrinking, having a single thread of cotton knit into the cloth in such a manner as to reduce shrinkage and increase its durability. An extra soft surface on the inside, extremely warm and the warmest every garment to give satisfaction. We can save you at least 50 cents on the price that you would have to pay your local merchant. You will make no mistake in ordering this quality. Color dark golden brown only. Sizes, breast measure, 34 to 46 inches. Average weight, 20 ounces. WE SAMPLE THIS NUMBER.
Price, per dozen, $13.90; each.................$1.25
No. 54713 Men's Mixed Golden Brown Drawers, to match above shirt, made plush back, pearl buttons, suspender taped and never-rip seams. Sizes, waist measure, 32 to 44 inches.
Price, per dozen, $13.90; each.................$1.25
Three full suits of the above underwear......6.95
If by mail, postage extra, 23 cents.

REMEMBER TO STATE YOUR BREAST AND WAIST MEASURE WHEN ORDERING UNDERWEAR ....

ALL-WOOL PLUSH BACK UNDERWEAR, $1.50.

WE SAMPLE THIS NUMBER.

No. 54714 Men's Plush Back Undershirt, made of fine quality of lambs wool trimmed with silk front and pearl buttons and close fitting ribbed cuffs. Strictly all-wool. We especially recommend this quality. Light brown or buckskin color, and warrant every garment to be perfectly satisfactory. We will save you about 50 cents on each garment over the cost in your own town. Do not confuse qualities of this kind with the ordinary goods sold at $1.50. This quality would cost your local merchant almost this much. Sizes, breast measure, 36 to 46 inches.
Price, per dozen, $16.80; each.................$1.50
If by mail, postage extra, 20 cents.
No. 54715 Men's Heavy Plush Back All Wool Drawers, to match above shirts, made with never-rip seams and pearl buttons. Sizes, waist measure, 32 to 44 inches.
Price, per dozen, $16.80; each.................$1.50
Three full suits of above underwear........8.40
If by mail, postage extra, 20 cents.

ALASKA UNDERWEAR.

No. 54719 Men's Heavy All-Wool Undershirts, made expressly for use in the coldest climates, wind proof and cold proof. Average weight, about 27 ounces. Brushed soft on the inside. This is the strongest and most durable underwear made, and is stitched throughout with covered seams, trimmed with silk tape which extends all around the box front, and is closed with pearl buttons. Color, dark golden brown. In this garment is to be found the extreme of warm under garments, and we would recommend them for wear in the coldest climates. Sizes, breast measure, 36 to 46 inches.
Price, per dozen, $23.00; each.................$2.00
If by mail, postage extra, 30 cents.
No. 54720 Men's Extra Heavy Wool Drawers, plush back, made with the patent covered seams throughout, extra strong and durable. Sizes, waist measure, 32 to 44 inches.
Price, per dozen, $23.00; each.................$2.00
Two full suits of above underwear..........7.70
If by mail, postage extra, 30 cents.

54711 $1.25

EXTRA HEAVY WOOL UNDERWEAR, $1.25.

WE SAMPLE THIS NUMBER.

The kind of underwear to wear in the northwest that will defy the cold and blizzards. Manufactured especially for us and is a special value.
No. 54716 Extra Heavy All Wool Undershirts, with box fronts as shown in illustration, light fawn color, taped all around neck and front with silk and trimmed with pearl buttons; close fitting ribbed cuffs, excelled in wear and durability only by No. 54719, which is the heaviest underwear made. We especially recommend this grade to men who are exposed or live in extremely severe climates. Made throughout with heavy covered seams that are particularly adapted to the rough wear they are sure to get in the outdoor occupations. Farmers will find this quality especially adapted to their requirements. Average weight, 22 ounces. Sizes, breast measure, 36 to 46 inches.
Price, per dozen, $13.80; each.................$1.25
If by mail, postage extra, 26 cents.
No. 54718 Men's Extra Heavy All Wool Drawers, to match above shirts, trimmed with pearl buttons, suspender taped, never-rip seams. Sizes, waist measure, 32 to 44 inches.
Price, per dozen, $13.80; each.................$1.25
Three full suits of above underwear........6.90
If by mail, postage extra, 26 cents.

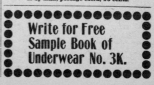

54746
$1.95

GLOVE-FITTING, WARM, COMFORTABLE
UNION SUITS

54743
$1.65

54741
89¢

The Greatly Increased Demand

For this style of garment is due to its warmth and neatness. Particularly comfortable at the waist, because it allows perfect fitting of the outer garments. Ladies' Union Suits are made to fit busts 33 to 40 inches, except where spotted larger.

ALWAYS INCLUDE HEIGHT and WEIGHT IN ORDER.

Allow 20 Cents Extra for Postage when Ordering Suits by Mail.

Ladies' Ribbed Princess Union Suits, $1.95.

No. 54746 Extra Princess Style Union Suits. We sample this number. Buttoned down front; Australian lamb's wool, with small mixture of fine cotton; perfect fitting and dependable; fancy crocheted neck and front; shaped waist; extra finely made and finished; colors; black, white, and light shade of sanitary gray; state color in your order. Be sure to give height, weight and bust measure in order. Bust sizes, 32 to 44.
Price, per dozen, $22.00; per suit..................$1.95

Ladies' Australian Worsted Suits, $2.95.

No. 54747 Ladies' Princess Style Jersey Ribbed Union Suits, made from select Australian yarns; not too heavy, but the regular winter weight. Union Suits are warmer for their weight than old style underwear, as they fit directly against the body, retaining the warmth. Trimmed with crocheted neck and front; shaped waist, and a superior finish throughout. Stitched throughout with the new elastic seam—stronger than the garment itself. Will not irritate the most sensitive skin. Colors: Black or white, or blue gray. Give color, height and bust measure in order. Sizes, bust, 32 to 44 inches. We sample this number. Price, each...................$2.95

Ladies' Extra Size Union Suits.

No. 54749 Ladies' Extra Size Union Suits, made in natural gray or ecru color; Egyptian cotton, fleece-lined, buttoned across bust. Bust sizes, 42, 44, 46.
Price, 3 suits for $2.10; each......................75c
No. 54751 Ladies' Extra Size Natural Gray Wool Union Suits, button across bust; 75 per cent pure wool. A very serviceable, warm garment, fleece-lined. Bust, 42, 44, 46.
Price, 3 suits for $3.50; each....................$1.25

54756
$1.95

THE QUEEN UNION SUIT.

The Queen is the newest and most perfect Union Suit made, and superior to all others in fit. When the front is unbuttoned the full elasticity is permitted across the shoulders and bust, thus making it very easy to get into and out of.

Fleecing: By this we mean that the garment has a soft surface brushed up on the inside of garment, making it soft and non-irritating. No other garment affords more complete protection to the lungs and neck than the Queen.

No. 54731 Ladies' Queen Style Jersey Ribbed Union Suit, made of fine Egyptian cotton and fleeced on the inside. Elastic ribbed cuffs and anklets. Ecru color. Bust, 32 to 40. Price, per dozen, $4.70; each...............43c
No. 54733 The Queen Style Jersey Ribbed Union Suit, same as above in silver gray. Be sure to give height and weight. Bust, 32 to 40.
Price, per dozen, $4.70; each....................42c
No. 54737 The Queen Style Fine Jersey Ribbed Union Suit. Finer yarn than the above, silk trimmed neck and front, fleece lined, elastic ribbed cuffs and anklets. Give height and weight in order. Bust, 32 to 40. Silver gray color.
Price, per dozen, $6.40; each....................58c
No. 54739 The Queen Style Fine Jersey Ribbed Union Suit. Same as above, but made in ecru color. Bust 32 to 40. Price, per dozen, $6.40; each.......58c

Queen Style Wool Union Suits.

No. 54741 The Queen Style Fine Natural Gray Half-Wool Union Suit. Jersey ribbed, elastic cuffs and anklets, silk trimmed front and soft fleeced lined throughout; non-shrinking and thoroughly dependable. Give height and weight in order. Bust, 32 to 40. Price, per dozen, $9.90; each.....................89c

Special Worsted Union Suits, $1.65.

No. 54743 The Queen Style, Extra Quality, Natural Gray Union Suit. Silk ribbed, made of fine worsted yarn, equal to garments usually sold for $2.50. Silk trimmed neck and front, fine elastic ribbed cuffs and anklets. Give height and weight and bust measure. Bust, 32 to 40.....................$1.65

Ladies' Drop Seat Cotton Union Suit.

No. 54743½ Ladies' Very Heavy Egyptian Cotton Union Suits, ecru color, with soft fleeced lining. Made with drop seat, same as children's; buttons down front to waist. Very comfortable and preferred by many. Sizes, 34 to 44 bust measure. Price, per dozen, $8.40; each....................75c

Ladies' Fine Wool Union Suits, Open Down Front.

No. 54746 Ladies' Princess Jersey Ribbed Union Suits. We sample this number. Opened down the front, fancy crocheted neck and front. Regular winter weight and guaranteed to give entire satisfaction. They contain enough cotton to keep from shrinking and will wear longer and better than all-wool, and are fully as warm. Colors, black, white, or natural gray. Be sure to give height, weight, and bust measure in order. Bust sizes, 32 to 44. Price, per dozen $17.50; suit, $1.50

MEN'S FORM FITTING UNION SUITS.

Give breast measure over vest close up under arms, and your height and weight.

A rational garment for men. Try our Union Suits for ease and comfort and you will wonder why you did not wear them before.

Men's Winter Weight Cotton Union Suits.

No. 54753 Men's Silver Gray Heavy Cotton Union Suits. Button down front. A special value at this low price. Finished neck and pearl buttons. Sizes 34 to 44, breast and height in order.
Price, per dozen, $10.00; per suit.................85c

Men's Wool Union Suits.

No. 54756 Men's Natural Gray Ribbed Wool Union Suits. Knit to fit the form perfectly, will not irritate the most sensitive skin. 70 per cent fine lamb's wool, non-shrinkable, serviceable and thoroughly dependable in every way. Regular winter weight, not extremely heavy. Buttons down the front. Lengths, 53, 56, 59, 62 and 65; chest, 34 to 44 inches. Give length and chest measure in order. We sample this number.
Price, per dozen, $22.00; per suit.................$1.95

Our Leader at $2.95.

No. 54758 Men's Fine Natural Gray Ribbed Sanitary Union Suits. Made from Australian lamb's wool. There is a slight mixture of cotton in this yarn which prevents extreme shrinkage and adds much to its wearing properties. We want your order for this quality. You could spend $4.00 per suit at retail and not be better. Don't forget height and weight in order, non-irritating and comfortable. Strictly first-class in every particular: Buttons down the front. Lengths, 53, 56, 59, 62 and 65; chest, 34 to 44 inches. Give length and chest measure in order. We sample this number.
Price, per suit.....................................$2.95
No. 54759 Men's Extra High Grade Sanitary Wool Union Suits. Full fashioned, all seams knit together, fine, soft elastic yarn, non-irritating and high grade in every particular. There is in this garment also about 8 per cent of cotton to prevent shrinkage and improve its permanent wearing properties. By full fashioned we mean knit on hand machines, which produces a more even surface; as all joined parts are knit together, it is practically seamless. Sizes, 36 to 44 breast measure. Regular retail price, $7.00. Price, per suit..................................$5.00

LADIES' WINTER UNDERWEAR.

Always give size.

We would advise careful consideration of our better grades in particular for they are the cheapest in the end.

Ladies' Ribbed Cotton Underwear.

No. 54850 Ladies' Fine Jersey Ribbed Cotton Vests, fleeced lined, bleached or ecru colors, fancy trimmed neck. Sizes, 3, 4 and 5. Busts, 32 to 40 inches.
Price, each.....$0.24
Price, per doz., 2.75

No. 54851 Ladies' Jersey Ribbed Cotton Drawers, ecru color to match above vests. Sizes, 3, 4 and 5.
Price, each.....$0.24
Price, per doz., 2.75

If by mail, postage extra, each, 12 cents.

No. 54852 Ladies' Jersey Ribbed Vests, silver gray color, same quality as above. Sizes, 3, 4 and 5. Busts, 32 to 40 inches.
Price, per dozen, $2.75; each.....24c

No. 54853 Ladies' Jersey Ribbed Drawers, to match above vests. Sizes, 3, 4 and 5.
Price, per dozen, $2.75; each.....24c

If by mail, postage extra, each, 12 cents.

No. 54854 Ladies' Fine Jersey Ribbed Egyptian Cotton Vests, slightly heavier than the above, and finer quality. Sizes, 3, 4, 5; busts 32 to 40. Ecru or bleached colors only. Price, per dozen $3.90; three for $1.00; each.....35c

No. 54855 Ladies' Fine Ribbed Drawers, to match shirt above. Sizes, 3, 4, 5. Price, per dozen, $3.90: three for $1.00; each.....35c

If by mail, postage extra, each, 13 cents.

Ladies' Fine Combed Egyptian Underwear.

No. 54858 Ladies' Fine Combed Egyptian Cotton Ribbed Vests, ecru or bleached color. Silk crocheted neck and front. A very fine vest, heavy winter weight, soft fleecing on the inside, close ribbed cuffs. Sizes, 3, 4, 5; busts 32 to 40. Price, per dozen, $4.80; each.....43c

No. 54859 Ladies' Fine Combed Egyptian Cotton Drawers, to match above vests. Sizes, 3, 4, 5.
Price, per dozen, $4.80; each.....43c

If by mail, postage extra, each, 15 cents.

Ladies' Ribbed Wool Underwear.

No. 54862 Ladies' Natural Gray, Winter Weight, Ribbed Undervests. One-third wool; silk taped neck and pearl buttons; soft fleecing on inside. A special value at our low price. Sizes, 3, 4 and 5; busts, 32 to 40. Price, per dozen, $4.90; each....45c

No. 54863 Ladies' Natural Gray Drawers, to match above vests. Sizes, 3, 4 and 5.
Price, per dozen, $4.90; each.....45c

If by mail, postage extra, each, 15 cents.

Ladies' Worsted Underwear, 75 Cents.

No. 54864 Ladies' Fine Worsted Undervests, natural gray; ribbed. One half fine worsted and the other Egyptian cotton; a fine vest that will not shrink and a special value that will wear and give entire satisfaction. Carefully shaped waist, silk trimmed neck and front. Sizes, 3, 4 and 5. Bust, 32 to 40. Price, per dozen, $8.20; each.....75c

No. 54865 Ladies' Fine Worsted Drawers, to match vests above.
Price, per dozen, $8.20; each.....75c

If by mail, postage extra, each, 15 cents.

Ladies' Fine Worsted Underwear 95c.

No. 54868 Ladies' very fine quality worsted wool undervests, ribbed, silver gray color. We cannot recommend too highly soft, fine underwear of this quality, which retails at a much higher price than asked by us. Practically all-wool worsted, having a single cotton yarn, which adds to its value. Trimmed with silk, crocheted neck and front, pearl buttons. Average weight, 12 ounces. A perfect fitting vest. Sizes, 3, 4 and 5. Bust, 32 to 40.
Price, each.....$ 0.95
Per dozen..... 10.80

No. 54869 Ladies' very fine drawers to match above vests. Sizes, 3, 4 and 5. Price, per dozen, $10.80; each.....95c

If by mail, postage extra, each, 15 cents.

Fine Australian Wool Underwear, $1.40.

No. 54870 Ladies' Fine Australian Wool Ribbed Undervests, soft light gray color. If you want the best fine all Australian wool ribbed underwear this is the one to order. Strictly high grade in every particular, fine, close fitting cuffs, silk crocheted neck and front and pearl buttons. Fine non-irritating elastic seams throughout. Sizes, 3, 4, 5; busts, 32 to 40; average weight, 12 oz. Price, per dozen, $15.80; each.....$1.40

No. 54871 Ladies' Fine Australian Wool Drawers to match above vests. Sizes, 3, 4 and 5.
Price, per dozen $15.80; each.....$1.40

If by mail, postage extra, each, 15 cents.

Let us remind you again that we cannot fill your order correctly without the bust measure for vests and waist measure for drawers.

Ladies' Winter Underwear.

Flat knit. Sizes in ladies' flat knit underwear are bust 30, 32, 34, 36, 38, 40, 42 and 44. The drawers are made to correspond; viz: the drawers to match 36 vests are sized 36, etc.

Natural Gray.

Do not fail to state size in your order.

No. 54880 Ladies' Merino Vests, plain, natural gray, winter weight, good value at a low price. Sizes, 30 to 42 bust.
Per dozen, $3.90; 3 for $1.00; each.....$0.35

No. 54881 Ladies' Merino Drawers to match vests.
Per dozen, $3.90; 3 for $1.00
Each.. (If by mail, postage extra, each, 12 cents.) 35c

No. 54882 Ladies' Flat knit Merino Vests, good winter weight, natural gray color. Taped neck, front, and pearl buttons. A special value at this price. Sizes, 30 to 44 bust. Average weight, 12 oz.
Price, per dozen, $4.90; each.....43c

No. 54883 Ladies' Merino Drawers to match above vests; sizes 30 to 44. If by mail, postage extra, each, 14c
Price, per dozen, $4.90; each.....43c

Ladies' All-Wool Underwear, 75 cents.

No. 54886 Ladies' Fine All-Wool Flat Knit Undervests, natural gray, with silk taped neck and front. You cannot match this quality at home for less than $1.00. The best value ever given at this price. Average weight, 12 ounces; sizes, 30 to 44 bust.
Price, per dozen, $8.40; each.....$0.75

No. 54887 Ladies' Fine All Wool Drawers, to match above vests, sizes 30 to 44.
Price, per dozen, $8.40; each.....$0.75
Three full suits of the above underwear..... 4.20

If by mail, postage extra, each, 14 cents.

Ladies' Fine All-Wool Underwear.

We sample this number.

No. 54888 Ladies' Fine All-Wool Flat Knit Undervests, natural gray color. With us this is a special value which cannot be excelled. Made of fine domestic wool with slight mixture of Australian, which makes the surface very soft. Unmatched in quality or price. Although fine wools have advanced this is better value than ever offered before. Sizes, 30 to 44 inches bust. Average weight, 13 ounces.
Price, per dozen, $9.90; each.....90c

No. 54889 Ladies' Fine All-Wool Drawers, to match above vests. Sizes, 30 to 44 inches.
Price, per dozen, $9.90; each.....$0.90
Three full suits of the above underwear..... 4.95

If by mail, postage extra, each, 15 cents.

Ladies' Pure Australian Wool Underwear.

Send for free sample of this number.

No. 54892 Ladies' Fine Pure Australian Lamb's Wool Undervests. Natural gray color. We mean what we say; pure Australian wool undervest, unmatched in value. Made by one of the oldest mills in this country, whose goods for forty years have been recognized as the best. If you want the finest, equal to garments sold at retail for $2.00 to $2.50, order this one. Soft, fine surface, that will not irritate the most sensitive. Silk trimmed neck and front and pearl buttons. Sizes, 30 to 44 bust. Average weight, 12 oz. If by mail, postage extra, each, 15c
Price, per dozen, $16.00; each.....$1.40

No. 54893 Ladies' Fine Australian Wool Drawers, to match shirts above. Sizes, 30 to 44.
Price, per dozen, $16.00; each.....$1.40
Two full suits of the above underwear..... 5.45

LADIES' CAMEL HAIR WINTER UNDERWEAR. Flat Knit.

No. 54900 Ladies' Fine All Wool Flat Knit Undervests, camel hair color with silk taped neck and front. You cannot match this quality at home for less than $1.00. A value unmatched anywhere at our price; average weight 12 ounces; sizes 30 to 44 bust.
Price, per dozen, $8.40; each.....75c

No. 54901 Ladies' Fine Camel Hair Color all Wool Drawers to match above vests; sizes 30 to 44.
Price, per dozen, $8.40; each.....75c
Three full suits of the above underwear.....$4.20

If by mail, postage extra, each, 14 cents.

No. 54902 Ladies' Fine All Wool Flat Knit Undervests, camel hair color. With us this is another special value which cannot be excelled. Made of fine domestic wool and a slight mixture of Australian which makes the surface soft. Although fine wools have advanced much in price, we offer better values than in previous seasons. Average weight, 13 ounces. Sizes, bust, 30 to 44. Price, per doz., $9.90; each, 90c

No. 54903 Ladies' Fine All Wool Drawers to match above vests, sizes 30 to 44.
Price, per dozen, $9.90; each.....90c
Three full suits of the above underwear.....$4.95

Ladies' Australian Wool Underwear.

We sample this number.

No. 54904 Ladies' Australian Wool Undervests. Camel's hair color, flat knit. Made of 50 per cent. fine Australian lamb's wool and usually sold all Australian. A superior fine high grade underwear; all-wool with soft, smooth non-irritating surface. For 40 years the manufacturers have made fine woolen underwear and are excelled by none in quality and workmanship. Light fawn or camel's hair color. Weight, 12 ounces. Sizes, 30 to 44 bust.
Price, per dozen, $13.80; each.....$1.25

No. 54905 Ladies' Fine Australian Camel's Hair Color Drawers to match above vests. Sizes, 30 to 44. Price, per dozen, $13.80; each.....$1.25
Two full suits of the above..... 4.75

If by mail, postage extra, each, 15 cents.

Write for Free Sample Book, No. 3K, of Fine Underwear.

LADIES' ALL-WHITE UNDERWEAR.

Flat Knit.

No. 54910 Ladies' Fine White Flat Knit Undervests. All cotton, with soft, smooth surface. Usually called merino. Sizes, 30 to 44 bust.
Each.....43c
Per dozen.....$4.90

No 54911 Ladies' Fine White Drawers to match above vests.
Each.....43c
Per dozen.....$4.90

Ladies' Fine White Underwear, 75c.

No. 54912 Ladies' Fine White Wool Undervests, flat knit, with smooth, soft, surface; 80 per cent pure, fine wool. A very fine garment for which your local merchant will ask $1.00 each. They will give good wear and entire satisfaction. Average weight, 12 ounces. Sizes, 30 to 44 bust. Per dozen, $8.40; Each.....75c

No. 54913 Ladies' Fine White Wool Drawers to match above vests. Sizes, 30 to 44. Price, per dozen, $8.40; Each.....75c
Three full suits of the above underwear.....$4.20

If by mail, postage extra, each, 15 cents.

All Wool White Underwear, 90c.

No. 54914 Ladies' fine white all wool flat knit Undervests. Another of our special values which cannot be excelled for the price. Fine domestic wool with some mixture of Australian lamb's wool, which make the surface very soft, and is unmatched anywhere for quality and price. A superior value. Average weight, 13 ounces. Sizes, 30 to 44 bust.
Price, per dozen, $9.90; each.....90c

No. 54915 Ladies' fine white all wool Drawers, to match above vests. Sizes, 30 to 44.
Price, per dozen, $9.90; each.....$0.90
For three full suits of the above underwear.. 4.95

Fine White Australian Wool Underwear, $1.25.

No. 54916 Ladies' fine white flat knit Australian Lamb's wool undervests, made of 50 per cent pure Australian Lamb's wool and fine imported wool; frequently sold for pure Australian. For 40 years the manufacturers of this quality have made goods of this and finer grades, and are excelled by none in skill and workmanship. Strictly high grade. Average weight, 12 ounces. Sizes, 30 to 40 busts.
Price, per dozen, $13.80; each.....$1.25

No. 54917 Ladies' fine white Australian wool drawers, to match above vests. Sizes, 30 to 44.
Price, per dozen, $13.80; each.....$1.25
For two full suits of the above underwear.... 4.75

Ladies' Scarlet Underwear.

No. 54920 Ladies' fine all wool scarlet flat knit Undervests. An excellent value fine all wool garment with silk taped front and neck, pearl buttons. Average weight, 12 ounces.. Sizes 30 to 44 bust.
Price, per dozen, $11.00; each.....95c

No. 54921 Ladies' fine all wool Scarlet Drawers to match above Vests.
Price, per dozen, $11.00; each.....95c

If by mail, postage extra, each, 15 cents.

LADIES' FLEECE LINED UNDERWEAR.

By fleece lined we mean that the inside is especially knit and fleeced by a machine made for the purpose, which makes a soft smooth non-irritating surface.

Size 30 to 44 bust measure. The drawer sizes correspond to vest sizes, viz.: size 36 drawer matches 36 vest.

Always give size.

No. 54926 Ladies' Fine Cotton Fleeced Flat Knit Undervests, natural gray color. Thick and warm. Sizes 30 to 44 bust.
Price, each..$0.45
Per dozen.... 5.00

No. 45927 Ladies' Fine Cotton Fleeced Drawers to match above vests. Sizes 30 to 44.
Price, per dozen, $5.00; each.....45c

Dr. Wright's Fleeced Underwear.

Every garment branded with "Dr. Wright's Health Underwear." We sample this number.

No. 54930 Ladies' Fine Natural Gray Underwear, made by the famous "Dr. Wright Mills"; fine, soft, wool fleecing, and bound all around with silk tape. Not extremely heavy, but thick and very warm. A special leader in value. Sizes, 30 to 44 bust.
Price, per dozen, $10.80; each.....95c

No. 54931 Ladies' Fine Natural Gray Drawers, to match above vests. Sizes, 30 to 44.
Price, per dozen, $10.80; each.....95c
Two full suits of the above underwear.....$3.70

If by mail, postage extra, each 15 cents.

Dr. Wright's Australian Wool Fleeced Underwear, $1.35.

Write for sample of this number.

No. 54932 Dr. Wright's Ladies' Fine Undervests, soft, natural gray color, with fine Australian lamb's wool fleecing. One of the finest fleeced undergarments made for ladies. One of the great advantages of Dr. Wright's underwear is that they will not shrink, and therefore always give lasting service. You might spend $2.00 at home for a garment no finer. Every one has the Dr. Wright trademark. Sizes, 30 to 44. Average weight, 11 ounces.

Price, per dozen, $15.20; each **$1.35**

No. 54933 Ladies' Fine Drawers to match above vests, sizes, 30 to 44.

Price, per dozen, **$15.20**; each **$1.35**

Two full suits of the above underwear **5.20**

Ladies' Extra Size Underwear.

For extra sizes Union suits, see Nos. 54749, 54751.

For large women busts measure up from 42 to 48.

No. 54936 Ladies' Bleached Cotton, Fleeced Jersey Ribbed Undervests, winter weight. Sizes, 42 to 46 bust. Sizes, 6, 7, 8. Each **$0.28**

Per doz. **3.20**

No. 54937 Ladies' Bleached Drawers, to match above vests. Sizes, 6, 7, 8.

Each **$0.28**

Per doz. **3.20**

Extra Size Egyptian Vests, 45 Cents.

No. 54938 Ladies' Fine Bleached Egyptian Cotton Vests, heavy weight, Jersey ribbed, fine soft fleecing on the inside; silk trimmed neck and front. Sizes, 7, 8, 9. 42 to 48 bust. Each **$0.45**

Per doz. **5.00**

No. 54939 Ladies' Fine Bleached Egyptian Cotton Drawers, to match above vests. Sizes, 7, 8, 9.

Price, per dozen, **$5.00**; each, ... **45c**

INFANTS' AND CHILDREN'S UNDERWEAR

TABLE OF SIZES FOR INFANTS' SHIRTS.

Size 1, length, 10 inches, suitable for ... 1 to 3 months
Size 2, length, 12 inches, suitable for ... 3 to 6 months
Size 3, length, 14 inches, suitable for ... 6 to 9 months
Size 4, length, 16 inches, suitable for ... 9 to 12 months
Size 5, length, 17 inches, suitable for ... 1 to 2 years
Size 6, length, 18 inches, suitable for ... 2 to 3 years

The Ruben's Infant Shirt.

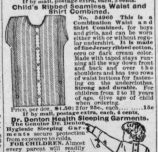

NO BUTTONS
NO TROUBLE
PAT NOV 13 94 NOV 15 95

THE RUBEN'S SHIRT

Is simplicity itself. Is made without any buttons whatever, and is so constructed that

Double Protection

is given to the vital parts, the chest, lungs and abdomen. This is by all odds, **the most sensible and practicable infants' shirt ever made.** The highest medical authorities pronounce it healthful and as being particularly desirable for infants. **If by mail, postage extra, each, 3 cents.**

No. 54945 The Ruben's Infant Shirt. Fine Saxony 66⅔ per cent fine wool with finished neck and double-stitched edges. The straps fasten at back with small safety pin, and can be adjusted in an instant. **Fine Jersey ribbed and very soft.**

Length, inches,	10	12	14	16	17	18
Sizes	1	2	3	4	5	6
Price, each	**25c**	**28c**	**31c**	**33c**	**37c**	**41c**

No. 54946 The Ruben's Shirt. Same as above, but made of all pure, soft cream white Saxony wool. Fine Derby ribbed.

Length, inches	10	12	14	16	17	18
Sizes	1	2	3	4	5	6
Price, each	**32c**	**35c**	**38c**	**42c**	**45c**	**47c**

Ruben's Shirts at 45 cents to 60 cents.

No. 54947 The Ruben's Infants' Shirt. Made from finest and softest all-wool cream white Saxony yarn, fine Derby ribbed with fancy silk braid trimming all around, collarette neck, silk stitching all around straps, skirt, sleeves, cuffs, and over all edges. **A perfect little beauty.**

Length, inches	10	12	14	16	17	18
Sizes	1	2	3	4	5	6
Price, each	**45c**	**48c**	**50c**	**53c**	**56c**	**60c**

Infants' Cotton Vests.

No. 54949 Infants' Fine Cotton Vests or Wrappers, open down the front, light weight, nicely trimmed. Color, white.

Length, inches	10	11	12	13	14
Sizes	1	2	3	4	5
Price, each	**11c**	**12c**	**13c**	**14c**	**15c**

No. 54950 Infants' Heavy Cotton Vests or Wrappers, full winter weight, soft fleecing on the inside; open down front; cream white.

Length, inches ...	10	11	12	13	14
Sizes	1	2	3	4	5
Price, each	**13c**	**14c**	**15c**	**16c**	**17c**

Infants' Wool Vests.

If by mail, postage extra, each, 3 cents.

No. 54952 Infants' Fine Derby Ribbed Cream White Merino Vests, (Wool and Cotton Mixed), buttoned all the way down front with overcast stitching on neck, cuffs and tail. **Soft and comfortable and non-shrinkable.**

Length, inches	10	12	14	16	17
Sizes	1	2	3	4	5
Price, each	**20c**	**22c**	**24c**	**27c**	**29c**

Infants' Fancy Derby Ribbed Vests.

Same style as cut of Wool Vests above.

No. 54953 Infants' Fine Derby Ribbed Cream White Saxony Wool Knit Vest. Button all the way down the front. Very easily put on and taken off. Neck, front and tail all overcast with silk cross-stitch embroidery.

Length, inches	10	12	14	16	17
Sizes	1	2	3	4	5
Price, each	**23c**	**25c**	**27c**	**30c**	**34c**

Infants' Extra Fine Jersey Ribbed Vests.

No. 54955 Infants' Extra-Fine Quality Jersey Ribbed Cream White Lamb's Wool Vests. Button all the way down the front. Fine white pearl buttons and silk trimming down the front, 90 per cent purest lamb's wool.

Sizes	1	2	3	4	5
Length, inches ...	10	12	14	16	17
Price, each	**33c**	**36c**	**40c**	**45c**	**50c**

Infants' Silk Vests.

No. 54957 Infants' High Grade Fashioned Silk Vest. Made of pure spun silk. Fashioned sleeves and cuffs. Silk crocheted around neck and down front. A superior garment for the baby.

Sizes	1	2	3	4	5
Length, inches	10	12	14	16	17
Price, each	**92c**	**$1.02**	**$1.12**	**$1.22**	**$1.30**

Infants' Fine Ribbed Bands.

No. 54958 Infants' Fine Jersey Ribbed Cashmere Wool Bands, with shoulder straps silk crocheted. Will fit perfectly and remain in place without the use of pins. This is accomplished by extra fine rib at bottom of garment. 90 per cent pure lamb's wool and very soft.

Length, inches	8	9	10	11	12
Price, each	**25c**	**28c**	**31c**	**33c**	**36c**

If by mail, postage extra, each, 3 cents.

Child's Ribbed Seamless Waist and Shirt Combined.

No. 54960 This is a Combination Waist and Shirt Combined, for boys and girls, and can be worn either with or without regular undershirt. **It is made of fine Jersey ribbed cotton,** ecru or dark cream color. Made with taped stays running all the way down front and back and over the shoulders and has two rows of waist buttons for fastening on the underclothes. **Strong and durable.** For children from 2 to 12 years of age. Give age of child when ordering.

Price, per doz., **$1.50**; 2 for **25c.**, each **15c**

If by mail, postage extra, each, 4 cents.

Dr. Denton Health Sleeping Garments.

The Genuine Dr. Denton Hygienic Sleeping Garments secure protection from exposure to colds.

FOR CHILDREN. Almost every parent will readily appreciate the value of these garments for their children. They afford such warmth and protection that it makes no difference whether the children kick out of the bed clothing or not. One-half of the ills of children are induced by exposure due to kicking out of the covering at night.

FABRIC. Made of knit merino natural gray cloth, easily washed and will not shrink.

Children's Sleeping Garments.

No. 54962 Dr. Denton's Sleeping Garment for Children, with cuff to roll down over hand and draw cord. Drop seat, moccasin feet, pearl buttons and open down back; made of natural gray knit merino cloth.

Ages	2	3	4	5	6	7	8	9	10
Length in.	28	30	32	34	36	38	40	42	44
Price ea...	**60c**	**65c**	**70c**	**75c**	**80c**	**85c**	**90c**	**95c**	**$1.00**

If by mail, postage extra, each, 15 cents.

Men's and Women's Sleeping Garments.

If by mail, postage extra, each, 30 cents.

No. 54963 Dr. Denton's Men's Sleeping Garment made of natural gray merino, knit cloth and pockets for feet. Comes down to the floor.

Chest 40, 56, 60, 64 inches.
Chest 44, 58, 62, 66 inches.
Price, each **$1.25**

No. 54964 Dr. Denton's Ladies' Sleeping Garment, made of same cloth as children's, made like regular night dress, length to the floor, with pockets for feet.

Bust 38, lengths 52, 56, 60 inches.
Bust 42, lengths 54, 58, 62 inches.
Price, each **$1.25**

U. S. Army Abdominal Bands.

For Men or Women.

No. 54966 This is the standard quality of Abdominal Bands adopted by the United States army and navy. The most scientific band made. Very useful in protecting the bowels and stomach against sudden changes in temperature or climate. For men or women. Made of worsted and wool, good quality. **Summer weight.** Natural gray color. Give waist measure. Sizes 24 to 44.

Price, per doz., **$6.50**; each ... **60c**

If by mail, postage, extra, 6 cents.

No. 54967 U. S. A. Abdominal Band, made fine all worsted regulation weight, heavier than 54966, natural gray, full fashioned, seamless and the best that money can buy. Standard of the world. Sizes 24 to 44. Price, per dozen, **$11.50**; each, ... **$1.00**

If by mail, postage extra, 9 cents.

Ladies' Winter Tights.

No. 54970 Ladies' Fine Ribbed Egyptian cotton Tights. Made ecru color, ankle length, closed seat and draw string tape at top. Size, 3, 4 and 5, which will fit women who wear vests of same size.

Price, per doz., **$5.40**; each ... **50c**

Ladies' Half Wool Tights.

No. 54971 Ladies' Fine Half-Wool Jersey Ribbed Tights. Made with specially ribbed waist and draw tape and closed ribbed ankles. **This is a superior garment and the usual retail price is $1.00.** Colors: natural gray or black. Sizes 3, 4 and 5.

Price, per doz., **$8.20**; each ... **75c**

If by mail, postage, extra, each, 10 cents.

Extra Quality All-Wool Ladies' Tights.

No. 54973 Extra Quality All-Wool Fine Jersey Ribbed Ladies' Tights. Made with fine close ribbed elastic waist and draw tape, close ribbed anklets, double elastic seams throughout. **This article seldom retails for less than $2.00.** Made fast black only. Sizes, 3, 4, 5 and 6.

Price, per doz., **$17.00**; each **$1.50**

Perforated Buckskin Chamois Underwear for Men and Women.

A superior wind, cold proof garment, made of selected skins, dressed expressly for underwear. Being perforated they give sufficient ventilation to the body which the rules of health require. A secure protection against sudden changes in temperature, and is recommended by leading physicians as an excellent cure and preventive of rheumatism.

For shirt and vest, measure around chest, close up under arms. For drawer measurements give waist and inseam. Always wear over other underwear. Should never be worn next to the skin.

Extra Sizes—50c extra will be required for each 2 inches larger than sizes quoted below.

No. 54980 Men's Perforated Buckskin Undershirts, made of the best quality only. Size 32 to 42 Price, **$6.00**

No. 54981 Men's Perforated Buckskin Drawers to match Sizes 28 to 40 waist **$6.00**

No. 54982 Ladies' Perforated Buckskin Undershirts, long sleeves, sizes 28 to 40 bust. Price, each .. **$6.00**

Without sleeves **$5.00**

No. 54983 Ladies' Perforated Buckskin Drawers, inseam 18 to 20 inches; waist, 22 to 36.

Price each **$5.00**

No. 54984 Men's Perforated Buckskin Vest, buttons close to neck Weight 5 oz. Sizes 32 to 42 chest.

Price, each **$4.00**

Men's Canton Flannel Drawers

No. 54985 Men's Bleached White Canton Flannel Drawers (no shirts), well made throughout, full size in seat, elastic cuffs at ankle. Price, per dozen **$5.00**; per pair **45c**

Shipping weight, per pair, 15 ounces.

55014
55010
55018
55034
55050
55044

MISSES' AND CHILDREN'S

≡ WINTER UNDERWEAR. ≡

If by mail, postage extra, per suit, 16 cents.
Table of Sizes for Children's and Misses' Undershirts.

Size 16 is suitable for Infants under..............................3 months old
Size 18 is suitable for child..1 year old
Size 20 is suitable for child.....................................2 to 3 years old
Size 22 is suitable for child.....................................4 to 5 years old
Size 24 is suitable for child....6 to 7 years old | Size 30 is suitable for child..10 to 13 years old
Size 26 is suitable for child....8 to 9 years old | Size 32 is suitable for child..14 to 15 years old
Size 28 is suitable for child..10 to 11 years old | Size 34 is suitable for child........16 years old
Children usually require the same size in Vest and Pants.

No. 55010 Children's Heavy Winter Weight Camel's Hair Color Undershirts, with very soft fleece lining, collarette neck and pearl buttons. Fine Jersey ribbed and perfect fitting. The greatest value ever offered in children's underwear.
Sizes....16 18 20 22 24 26 28 30 32 34
Each....8c 11c 14c 17c 20c 23c 26c 29c 32c 35c
No. 55011 Children's Pantalets to match. Open sides.
Sizes....16 18 20 22 24 26 28 30 32 34
Each....8c 11c 14c 17c 20c 23c 26c 29c 32c 35c
No. 55012 Children's Winter Weight Jersey Ribbed Undershirts, with soft fleeced lining, same as No. 55010, but ecru or bleached color.
Sizes....16 18 20 22 24 26 28 30 32 34
Each....8c 11c 14c 17c 20c 23c 26c 29c 32c 35c
No. 55013 Children's Ecru Pantalets. Open sides.
Sizes....16 18 20 22 24 26 28 30 32 34
Each....8c 11c 14c 17c 20c 23c 26c 29c 32c 35c
No. 55014 Children's Fine Natural Gray Random wool Mixed Undershirts. Silk taped front and neck, fine white pearl buttons and elastic ribbed cuffs. Heavy, soft, and warm. Thoroughly well made and will give the best of satisfaction.
Sizes....16 18 20 22 24 26 28 30 32 34
Each 8c 12c 16c 20c 26c 32c 40c 47c 55c 60c
No. 55015 Children's Fine Natural Gray Wool Mixed Pantalets, to match above vests. Open sides.
Sizes....16 18 20 22 24 26 28 30 32 34
Each 8c 12c 16c 20c 26c 32c 40c 47c 55c 60c
No. 55018 Children's Heavy Flat Fleeced Lined Undershirts, all cotton, natural, gray, heavy and warm. Special value at our low price.
Sizes....16 18 20 22 24 26 28 30 32 34
Each....12c 15c 18c 20c 23c 27c 30c 33c 36c 38c
No. 55017 Children's Pantalets, open sides to match.
Sizes....16 18 20 22 24 26 28 30 32 34
Each....12c 15c 18c 20c 23c 27c 30c 33c 36c 38c
No. 55018 Children's Extra High Grade Pure Australian Lamb's Wool Underwear. The pick of the flock. Nothing finer made. Handsome light fawn color, with fine finished neck and white pearl buttons. Soft and fine, and guaranteed strictly all pure lamb's wool. No adulteration of any kind.
Sizes....16 18 20 22 24 26 28 30 32 34
Each....25c 33c 40c 50c 56c 65c 73c 78c 80c 85c
No. 55019 Children's Pantalets to match.
Sizes....16 18 20 22 24 26 28 30 32 34
Each....25c 33c 40c 50c 56c 65c 73c 78c 80c 85c
No. 55020 Children's Fine White Australian Lambs Wool Underwear, same quality and style as No. 55018, but white. A beautiful under garment.
Sizes....16 18 20 22 24 26 28 30 32 34
Each....25c 33c 40c 50c 56c 65c 73c 78c 80c 85c
No. 55021 Children's Fine White Pantalets, open at sides.
Sizes....16 18 20 22 24 26 28 30 32 34
Each....25c 33c 40c 50c 56c 65c 73c 78c 80c 85c

Boys' and Youths' Winter Underwear.

Boys' sizes are from 24 to 34 inches. Always give chest and waist measure in ordering. Usually the drawer size is 2 inches smaller than chest, but some measure the same. Don't fail to give size.
No. 55022 Boys' Good Weight Ribbed Fleeced Lined Camel's Hair Color Undershirts, with very soft fleece lining, collarette neck, pearl button Jersey ribbed, form fitting, never rip seams and a durable garment.
Sizes....   24   26   28   30   34
Each....   20c   23c   26c   29c   35c
No. 55023 Boys' Drawers to Match, Open Front.
Sizes....   24   26   28   30   34
Each....   20c   23c   26c   29c   35c
No. 55026 Boys' Natural Gray Merino Undershirts, with fancy taped neck and front, and cuffs; well made and finished and warranted good.
Sizes....   24   26   28   30   34
Price....   22c   24c   26c   28c   32c
No. 55027 Boys' Drawers to match; open front.
Sizes....   24   26   28   30   34
Price....   22c   24c   26c   28c   32c

Boys' Fleeced Lined Underwear.

No. 55030 Boys' Plain Natural Gray Fleece Lined Undershirts, made with ribbed cuffs and taped neck and front. Sizes 24 to 34 only.
Sizes....   24   26   28   30   34
Price....25c 27c   30c   33c   36c   39c
No. 55031 Boys' Plain Natural Gray Fleece Lined Drawers, to match above; open front.
Sizes....   24   26   28   30   34
Price....30c 32c   34c   36c   39c
No. 55034 Boys' Fine Australian Wool Undershirts, natural gray color. Fine pure and soft of softest quality. Durable, warm and healthful. It is well directed economy to buy good woolen underwear for your boy. Retail price, 75 cents to $1.00.
Sizes....   24   26   28   30   34
Price....   48c   55c   60c   65c   70c   75c
No. 55035 Drawers to match above, open front.
Sizes....   24   26   28   30   34
Price....   48c   55c   60c   65c   70c   75c

Misses' and Children's Winter Union Suits

NOTE—These garments can be worn by either girls or boys. Order by length. Measure down back from neck to ankle.
No. 55042 Misses' and Children's Natural Gray Jersey Ribbed, Fleece Lined Union Suits. Crocheted neck. Drop seat back.
Length of Suit   28   32   36   40   44
Length of Suit 4   5-6   7-8   9-10   11-12
Price, each....$0.23 $0.25 $0.27 $0.29 $0.31
Price, per doz. 2.60   2.75   2.90   3.05   3.20

No. 55043 Children's Fine Bleached Cotton Union Suits, fine heavy cotton, carefully proportioned and perfect fitting. Soft fleecing throughout. Open down front and drop seat. Order by Length.
Age....   4   5-6
Each, $0.35 $0.38
Dozen, 4.00   4.30
Age.... 7-8   9-10
Each, $0.41 $0.44
Dozen, 4.60   4.90
Age.... 11-12 13-14
Each, $0.47 $0.50
Dozen, 5.20   5.56
Age, 15; Length, 52; per dozen, $5.80; each....$0.53

No. 55044 Misses' and Children's Merino Back Union Suit. Made with double back of merino yarn, which gives extra protection to the lungs, where the child needs it most. Heavy weight, natural gray; fine soft fleeced lined throughout. Open down front and drop seat. Order by length.
Age....   4   5-6   7-8   9-10 11-12 13-14 15
Length, 28   32   36   40   44   48   52
Each, $0.42 $0.46 $0.50 $0.54 $0.58 $0.62 $0.66
Dozen, 4.60 4.90 5.30 5.70 6.10 6.45 6.70
No. 55046 Children's and Misses' Fine Wool Union Suits. Made of 65 per cent pure wool. The best values ever shown in fine children's Union Suits. Buttoned down the front, and made with drop seat. Finely made and finished. Colors: black, white or natural gray. Ages 5 to 14 years.
Length....   28   35   45   48   52
Each, $0.86 $0.92 $0.99 $1.06 $1.13 $1.20 $1.27

No. 55050 Misses' Fine Cotton Vests with Shaped Waist, fleeced lined, crocheted neck and front, regular winter weight. The length of each size in inches.
Sizes..........   2   3   4   5   6   7
Length, inches..   15   18   21   24   27   30
Price, each.... 20c 21c 22c 24c 25c 26c
No. 55051 Misses' Open Side Drawers, to match.
Sizes..........   2   3   4   5   6   7
Price, each.... 20c 21c 22c 24c 25c 26c

TRUNKS AND TRAVELING BAGS.

WE SELL TRUNKS AT ALL PRICES. We can suit you in style and quality. We want your order, because we can sell you GOOD TRUNKS AND BAGS CHEAPEST. In trunks and bags, as in most other kinds of merchandise, we recommend the medium and better grades, they are cheapest in the end. A dollar or two added to the price of a trunk may mean many years of additional usefulness. The particular reasons why we deserve careful consideration and your order, is because we protect you from high prices, from dishonest quality and workmanship. While we sell the cheaper kinds as well as the better grades, each represents the best value of that kind at lowest possible prices. We do not offer one kind of trunk or bag at cost and then ask you to pay too much for another. THERE IS INTEGRITY in trunks as in other merchandise. They should be made to stand the wear and tear, which they are sure to get from time to time.

OUR TRUNKS AND BAGS Are made under careful supervision; every nail, rivet, clamp, hinge and lock is attached with exactness and skill of the thorough workmen. THIS IS WHY WE WARRANT EVERY TRUNK AND BAG to be as represented and the best of its kind at the lowest possible price.

If you do not see what you want, write to us for information and get our prices.

WHEN ORDERING duplicate keys, give catalogue number of trunk or bag, also number of letter on key or lock. Duplicate keys furnished at 5 cents each.

WEIGHT OF TRUNKS AND BAGS. Metal covered trunks will average about 60 pounds; canvas covered, about 55 pounds; gladstones and dress suit cases, from 5 to 12 pounds; club bags average about 3 or 4 pounds.

Crystallized or Fancy Metal Covered Trunks.
Cross Bar Slats, Iron Bottom.

No. 55305 Very substantially made; barrel stave top, iron bound, cross bar slats on top, body slats, set up tray with covered bonnet box, iron bottom.

26-inch	$1.75		
28-inch	2.00		
30-inch	2.25		
34-inch	2.75		
		36-inch	3.00

Crystallized Metal Covered Trunks.
Flat Top.

No. 55309 Will stand the hard knocks that any trunk is sure to receive. Flat top, large shape, iron bound, cross bar slats on top; long slats on body, set up tray with covered bonnet box. Iron bottom.

26-inch	$1.90		
28-inch	2.70		
30-inch	2.50	32-inch	$2.75
34-inch	3.15	36-inch	3.40

Great Bargain $2.50 Trunk.

Extra Quality Crystalized, Metal Trunks.

No. 55313 Full finished cross bar slats, iron bottom, barrel stave top, cross bar slats on top, and upright on front, iron clamps, flat steel key lock, patent bolts, rollers, hinges, etc.; covered tray with bonnet box and side compartments; fall-in top. This is a handsome trunk, very wide and high and extra well made.

26-inch	$2.50	32-inch	$3.40
28-inch	2.80	34-inch	3.70
30-inch	3.10	36-inch	4.00

New Shape Up-to-Date Trunk, Cross Bar Slats, Iron Bottom.

No. 55317 Fancy Metal Covered, flat top, with front and back rounded, hardwood reverse bent slats, metal corner bumpers, clamps, rollers, etc. Monitor lock and patent bolts, heavy strap hinges, tray with bonnet box. Fall-in top and side compartments, all separately covered and four slats on all sizes. Without a doubt this is the handsomest and most substantial trunk ever built for our low price.

28-inch	$3.40	34-inch	$4.20
30-inch	3.70	36-inch	4.60
32-inch	4.00		

Crystallized Metal Covered Trunks.

No. 55321 Cross Bar Slats, Hinge Bottom, Full Finish, with Parasol Case. Barrel stave top, wide iron bound, five cross bar slats on top and upright in front, end slats, malleable iron corners and shoes, etc., stitched leather handles. Excelsior lock, patent bolts, covered tray with bonnet box, parasol case and side compartment, fall-in top, fancy skeleton work, covered tray with bonnet box, parasol case and side compartment, fall-in top.

28-inch	$3.55	34-inch	$4.70
30-inch	3.95	36-inch	5.10
32-inch	4.30	38-inch	5.60

A $7.50 Crystal Covered Trunk for $4.00.

No. 55325 Handsome Silver Crystal Covered Trunk, fitted with parasol case, Excelsior lock, hinge tray and all of the conveniences to be found in high price trunks. Large trunk, flat on top with corners rounded, hardwood slats on top and body, heavy bolts, malleable iron, skeleton work, hinges, etc., full finished tray with hat box, side compartment, fall-in top, four slats on all sizes.

28-inch	$4.00	34-inch	$4.90
30-inch	4.30	36-inch	5.30
32-inch	4.60	38-inch	5.70

Charter Oak Special for $4.00.
Iron Bottom and Oak Finish.

No. 55331 High, wide Trunk, covered with heavy iron, enameled and finished in handsome imitation of quarter-sawed oak. Flat top, iron bottom, round corners. Hardwood bent slats over entire top upright on front and end slats. All protected with heavy metal clamps and bumpers, cross strip clamps and fancy skeleton iron work on ends. Heavy Excelsior lock and side bolts, stitched leather handles, heavy hinges, covered tray, with bonnet and parasol compartments. Handsomely finished and one of the very best values we have ever offered.

26-inch	$4.00	32-inch	$4.60
28-inch	4.30	34-inch	4.90
30-inch	4.30	36-inch	5.30

Black Enameled Iron Trunk for $4.00.

No. 55337 Black enameled iron, round top trunk, large size box covered with black enameled iron, flat top with rounded corners, hardwood bent slats on top to with one extra slat in center full length of trunk, fancy clamps, rollers, leather handles, brass Excelsior lock, patent bolts, full covered hinged tray, with bonnet box, fall-in top, all fancy trimmed, iron bottom.

28-inch	$4.00	34-inch	$4.90
30-inch	4.30	36-inch	5.30
32-inch	4.60	38-inch	5.70

Crystallized Fancy Metal Covered Trunks
Cloth Finish, Hinge Tray and Parasol Case.

No. 55343 Extra barrel stave top, cross bar slats on top, upright on front, malleable iron corner bumpers, heavy hinges, iron bolts, covered tray, bonnet box, stitched leather handles, parasol case, extra dress tray, linen faced. A handy trunk, elegant in appearance.

30-inch	$5.15	
32-inch	5.55	
34-inch	5.95	
36-inch	6.35	
38-inch	6.90	

Fancy Metal Covered Trunk at $5.75 and Up.
Excelsior Lock.

No. 55346 Extra high and wide, barrel stave top, cross bar slats on top, upright on front, malleable iron bumpers, Excelsior lock, fancy chain work, malleable iron bolts, heavy hinges, stitched leather handles, covered tray with bonnet box, parasol case and other compartments, fall-in top, linen faced, crystallized metal, handsomely trimmed and finished.

32-inch	$5.75	36-inch	$6.50
34-inch	6.10	38-inch	7.20

Our $3.55 Steel Bound Trunk.

No. 55349 Cheapest Steel Bound Trunk in the market, large box covered with heavy canvas, four heavy hardwood slats on top and two on body running full length of trunk, heavy japanned corners and steel strip clasp, heavy bolts, monitor lock, hinge tray with hat box and side compartment separately covered cloth faced. An honest, strong trunk at a very low price.

30-inch	$3.55	36-inch	$4.45
32-inch	3.85	38-inch	4.75
34-inch	4.15		

A $6.00 Canvas Covered Trunk for $4.25.

No. 55355 Canvas covered, iron bottom, square top corners double iron bound, four hardwood slats full length of trunk, two slats all around body, japanned steel corners and clamps, large brass plated Monitor lock, heavy bolt locks, extra wide iron center band on top and body, tray containing hat box and packing compartment, fall-in top, all covered. With dress tray.

Sizes, in.	28	30	32	34	36	38
Prices	$4.25	$4.55	$4.95	$5.35	$5.75	$6.25

Flat Top Heavy Duck Cover Trunk.

No. 55359 Flat Top, Heavy Duck Cover Trunk. Double wide iron bound, two center bands, hardwood slat on top and body end slats all protected with heavy iron bumpers, corner shoes, etc. Excelsior lock and patent buckle bolts, heavy hinges, rollers, etc., stitched leather handles, high combination tray, hat box with removable frame, hinged shirt box on side and compartment underneath, all covered, linen finish, iron bottom.

30-inch	$5.75	34-inch	$7.00
32-inch	6.25		

New Steel Bound Trunk.

Special value at $6.00 to $8.00.

No. 55364 Steel bound, brass plated clamps and sole leather straps, Large size box covered with painted canvas, olive colored iron binding, four heavy hard wood slats on top, two slats running full length of trunk on body, with hard wood bottom cleats. Front and back of top and bottom protected with our new steel binding running entire length of trunk, heavy brass plated corner shoes and clamps, heavy brass plated bolts and Monitor lock. Sole leather straps, hinge tray with hat box and side compartment separately covered, with cloth facing. Dress tray. Positively the greatest value in a square top trunk ever offered.

30-inch....$6.00	32-inch....$6.50	34-inch....$7.00
36-inch.... 7.50	38-inch.... 8.00	

Special Canvas Covered Wall Trunk for $4.90.

No. 55367 Canvas Covered, Iron Bottom, Cloth Finish, Excelsior Lock, High and Wide Trunk, covered with heavy canvas duck, flat top, with front and back rounded, hardwood bent slats over entire top, upright on front, end slats; all protected with tinned clamps, bumpers, cross-strip clamps, fancy skeleton iron work on ends, etc., heavy brass locks, patent side bolts, stitched leather handles, heavy hinges, set-up tray, cloth faced.

30-inch....$4.90	34-inch....$5.70
32-inch.... 5.30	36-inch.... 6.10

Sole Leather Straps, Canvas Covered Trunk.

A bargain at $6.50 and upwards, according to size.

No. 55369 Sole leather straps, canvas covered, heavy japanned steel clamps and corners. We have here an article to meet the demand for a cheap strap trunk, large box covered with heavy canvas, painted, wide iron bound, heavy hardwood slats full length of trunk, body and end slats, heavy bumpers and steel clamps, rollers, etc. and brassed Excelsior lock, with heavy bolts, iron bound, all protected with two heavy sole leather straps, high set-up tray with hat box and side compartments all separately covered and cloth faced, extra dress tray.

30-inch....$6.50	36-inch....$8.00
32-inch.... 7.00	38-inch.... 8.50
34-inch.... 7.50	

Full Riveted, Cloth Lined, Heavy Bolts. Ladies' or Gentlemen's Trunk.

No. 55373 Man's ingenuity never contrived a more compact, durable, or thoroughly successful trunk than this—a wonder for strength. Large in shape, covered with heavy duck, painted, bound with heavy iron. Full set of steel trimmings, bumpers, clamps, braces, heavy brass excelsior lock, side bolts, heavy leather handles, strap hinges, set-up covered tray, with hat box. Two extra dress trays. Riveted throughout.

32-inch....$9.50	38-inch....$12.50
34-inch.... 10.50	40-inch.... 13.50
36-inch.... 11.50	

Ladies' Dress or Skirt Trunk With Three Dress Trays, All Cloth Lined.

No. 55377 Large, roomy and especially made for ladies' use. Covered with heavy painted canvas, hardwood slats, all protected with heavy steel clamps, extra heavy corners, bolts and hinges. Heavy sole leather straps, upper tray with sliding partitions, separately covered. About the length of the average skirt. Size 42 inches outside measurement.

Price, each.............$12.00

Leather Bound, All Riveted, Canvas Covered Trunk for $13.00 to $17.00.

OF STAUNCH CONSTRUCTION.

No. 55379 Strength in every feature. Covered with heavy canvas, painted, hardwood slats, all protected with heavy brassed clamps, edges bound with leather, heavy sole leather straps, Brass Excelsior lock, tray with hat box and other compartments, separately covered, edge of tray bound with metal binding, dress tray, cloth lined.

32-inch.........$13.00	36-inch.........$15.50
34-inch......... 14.00	38-inch......... 17.00

Our $13.00 Sole Leather Bound Slatless Basswood Trunk.

No. 55383 Slatless Veneer Top Basswood Trunk, sole leather binding and straps, cloth lined, heavy riveted, large, very light weight and strong, covered with heavy duck, painted, equipped with brassed bumpers, clamps, corner shoes, rollers, extra heavy excelsior lock, side bolts and heavy hinges, bound with leather all around edges, back and front heavy sole leather straps, high set-up tray; with hat box and other compartments, extra dress tray, cloth finished throughout, a quality seldom found in retail stores.

32-inch.........$13.00	36-inch.........$15.00
34-inch......... 14.00	38-inch......... 16.00
40-inch......... 17.00	

Dresser Trunks at $8.25 to $9.50.

(Closed)

(Open)

No. 55384 The best Bureau Trunk for the least amount of money in the market. Covered with heavy canvas, painted, heavy hardwood slats well protected with heavy brassed clamps and corners; large roomy upper trays with hat box and side compartments, separately covered, with two roomy drawers below, equipped with the best excelsior lock, brass plated. A special value medium-priced dresser trunk.

34-inch.........$8.25
36-inch......... 8.90
38-inch......... 9.50

Wonderful Values in Bureau Trunks.

No. 55388 The finest Bureau Trunk made. Steel trimmings, all riveted, Irish linen faced. Basswood box, canvas covered, olive colored steel binding on edges of top and bottom, trimmed with brass clamps and heavy corner bumpers; all riveted; brass excelsior lock. Four steel hinges, Hagney bolts on ends, linen lined, with genuine Irish linen facing; all compartments are separately covered and easy of access, and arranged as shown in cut. A veritable traveling chiffonier of great convenience.

32-inch.........$16.00	38-inch.........$21.00
34-inch......... 18.25	40-inch......... 27.50
36-inch......... 19.60	

Our $9.95 Dresser Trunk.

No. 55391 The most durable and cheapest dresser trunk on the market; being well made, will stand rough usage. Riveted; all space can be utilized, and is accessible at any time; upper part contains three compartments, with three drawers in body. An excellent trunk for skirts and dresses. Covered with heavy painted canvas, hardwood slats on top and around body of trunk, excelsior lock, heavy steel clamps and corners, patent lever bolts on front and heavy lock bolts on ends. A veritable traveling chiffonier of great convenience.

32-inch.........$9.95	34-inch.........$10.75
36-inch......... $11.75	

Ladies' Sole Leather Trunk.

No. 55395 Very elegant in style, made of full weight selected leather, steel ribbed head, new patent roller and clamp combined. Heavy corner clamps, iron frame, heavy dovetailed brass bolts, excelsior lock, large set-up tray with round box, three pockets in front, separate covered secret parasol case underneath, and linen lined. Separate heavy canvas cover, leather bound edges and capped corners. This trunk must be seen to be appreciated. Standard of high grade sole leather ladies' trunk.

32-inch.........$34.00	34-inch.........$37.00
36-inch......... $40.00	

Gentlemen's Fine Sole Leather Trunk.

No. 55397 Made of heavy leather, copper riveted, strong steel ribs. Equipped with excelsior lock, dovetailed side bolts, heavy iron frames, corner clamps and corners combined, extra good quality sole leather straps and buckles, tray with hat box and other compartments. Separate heavy canvas cover with leather bound edges and capped corners.

26-inch.........$21.00	32-inch.........$25.50
30-inch......... 23.00	34-inch......... 28.00

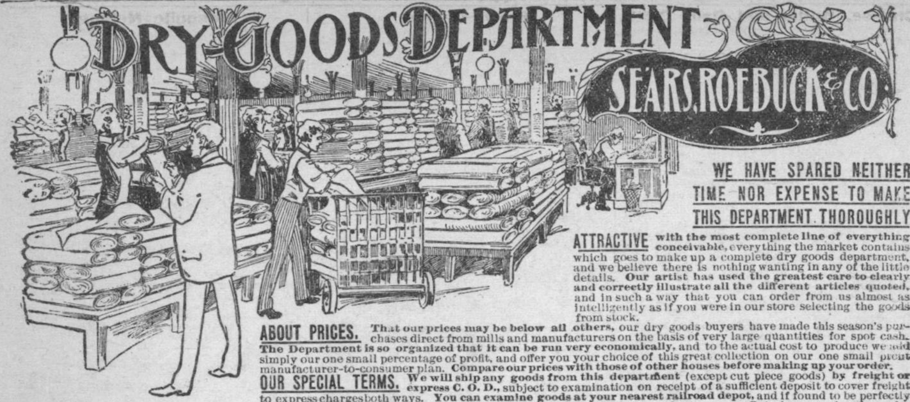

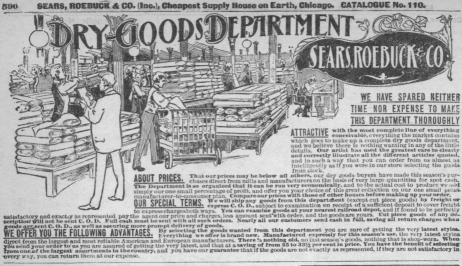

WE HAVE SPARED NEITHER TIME NOR EXPENSE TO MAKE THIS DEPARTMENT THOROUGHLY ATTRACTIVE with the most complete line of everything conceivable, everything the market contains which goes to make up a complete dry goods department, and we believe there is nothing wanting in any of the little details. **Our artist has used the greatest care to clearly and correctly illustrate all the different articles quoted,** and in such a way that you can order from us almost as intelligently as if you were in our store selecting the goods from stock.

ABOUT PRICES. That our prices may be below all others, our dry goods buyers have made this season's purchases direct from mills and manufacturers on the basis of very large quantities for spot cash. **The Department is so organized that it can be run very economically,** and to the actual cost to produce we add simply our one small percentage of profit, and offer you your choice of this great collection on our one small profit manufacturer-to-consumer plan. **Compare our prices with those of other houses before making up your order.**

OUR SPECIAL TERMS. **We will ship any goods from this department** (except cut piece goods) **by freight or express C. O. D.,** subject to examination on receipt of a sufficient deposit to cover freight to express charges both ways. **You can examine goods at your nearest railroad depot,** and if found to be perfectly satisfactory and exactly as represented pay the agent our price and charges, less amount sent with order, and the goods are yours. **Cut piece goods of any description will not be sent C. O. D. Full cash must be sent with all such orders. Nearly all our customers send cash in full, saving all return charges when goods are sent C. O. D., as well as securing more prompt delivery of goods.**

WE OFFER YOU THE FOLLOWING ADVANTAGES. **By selecting the goods wanted from this department** you are sure of getting the very **latest styles. Everything we offer is brand new. Manufactured expressly for this season's use,** the very latest styles direct from the largest and most reliable American and European manufacturers. **There is nothing old,** no last season's goods, nothing that is shop-worn. **When you send your order to us you are assured of getting the very latest, and that at a saving of from 25 to 33⅓ per cent in price. You have the benefit of selecting from one of the largest assortments in the country,** and you have our **guarantee** that if the goods are not exactly as represented, if they are not satisfactory in every way, you can return them at our expense.

SEND FOR SAMPLES OF LADIES' DRESS GOODS

Our Free Sample Booklet, No. 6K, Shows a Line that is Stylish, New and Dressy. The Very Latest Novelties, Silks and Woolens, the Choicest to Be Had at Prices That Cannot Be Surpassed.

We buy all our Domestics direct from the mills and in such large quantities that it enables us to sell them cheaper than your local dealer could buy them for. We only carry the reliable, celebrated brands, which are included in the following list. We will furnish any brand desired, if so requested, and give lowest possible price the day the order is received.

Sheeting, Heavy Unbleached.

No. 56000 Unbleached Cotton, good quality, with a nice even texture, 36 inches wide. Per yd., 5c
Full piece of 50 yards, per yard........................4¾c

No. 56002 Unbleached Cotton, extra strong and **heavy,** full standard muslin of a reliable brand, 36 inches wide. Price, per yard 6c
Full piece of 50 yards, per yard........................5¾c

No. 56003 Unbleached Extra Heavy Muslin. Strong and uniform. Manufactured expressly for us. Full piece about 50 yards. Price, per yard....7c

Sheeting, Fine Unbleached.

No. 56010 Unbleached cotton, the good reliable kind, with a nice soft round thread, this number we **specially** recommend to housekeepers; it washes **easily,** and will bleach out nice and white. 36 inches wide. Price, per yard 7c
Full piece of 50 yards, per yard........................6¾c

No. 56011 Unbleached Sheeting, special value. Perfect fine weave. Width 40 inches.
Price, per yard..........................7½c

No. 56004 Unbleached Sheeting. Fine close **woven; will** bleach properly. 40 inches wide.
Price, per yard..........................8½c

Wide Sheetings, Unbleached, Best Quality.

Where a full piece of 45 yards is purchased, deduct ½ cent a yard from prices below.

No. 56005 Unbleached Sheeting; width, 45 **inches.** Price, per yard..........................12½c

No. 56006 Unbleached Sheeting; width, 54 **inches.** Price, per yard..........................15c

No. 56007 Unbleached Sheeting; width, 68 **inches.** Price, per yard..........................19c

No. 56008 Unbleached Sheeting; width, 80 **inches.** Price, per yard..........................21c

No. 56009 Unbleached Sheeting; width, 88 **inches.** Price, per yard..........................23½c

No. 56009½ Unbleached Sheeting; width, 96 **inches. Price, per yard**..........................27½c

Good Quality Wide Sheeting.

Our Wide Sheetings are made from fine selected stock, and are strictly reliable. We do not carry the very low grade. Where a full piece of 45 yards is purchased, deduct ½ cent per yard from following prices.

		Width.	Price, per Yd.
No. 56013	Unbleached Sheeting;	45 in.	11c
No. 56015	Unbleached Sheeting;	54 in.	13½c
No. 56017	Unbleached Sheeting;	68 in.	17½c
No. 56019	Unbleached Sheeting;	80 in.	19½c
No. 56021	Unbleached Sheeting;	88 in.	21½c
No. 56023	Unbleached Sheeting;	96 in.	23½c
No. 56025	Unbleached Sheeting;	104 in.	27½c

Bleached Cotton.

No. 56036 Bleached Cotton, fair quality, 36 inches wide. Price, per yard 5c
Full piece of 50 yards, per yard........................4¾c

No. 56037 Bleached Cotton, good quality; will give splendid wear; width 36 inches. Price, per yd..6c
A full piece of 50 yards, per yard........................5¾c

No. 56038 Bleached Cotton, full standard, a splendid wearing cotton and nothing better made for the price. 36 inches wide. Price, per yard... 7c
Full piece of about 50 yards, per yard..........6¾c

No. 56040 Bleached Cotton, a nice, soft, even finish, full bleached and will wear like **iron,** this is a good reliable quality. 36 inches wide. Per yard..8c
Full piece of 50 yards, per yard..............7¾c

No. 56042 The Fern Muslin, fully bleached and is manufactured from fine long staple cotton, counting 196 threads to the inch, and is **especially adapted for ladies' and children's fine garments,** and warranted perfect in manufacture and finish. 36 inches wide. Price, per yard..........................10½c
Or a full piece of 50 yards, per yard..............10c

No. 56043 Bleached Sheeting, good quality, width, 42 inches. Price, per yard..11c

No. 56044 Bleached Sheeting, good quality, width, 46 inches.
Price, per yard..........................12½c

No. 56045 Bleached Sheeting, good quality. width, 50 inches. Price, per yard..................14½c

No. 56046 Bleached Sheeting, good quality, width, 54 inches. Price, per yard..................16½c

No. 56047 Bleached Sheeting, good quality, width, 68 inches. Price, per yard..................21c

No. 56048 Bleached Sheeting, good quality, width, 80 inches. Price, per yard..................23c

No. 56049 Bleached Sheeting, good quality, width, 88 inches. Price, per yard..................26c

No. 56049½ Bleached Sheeting, good quality, width 96 inches. Price, per yard..................27½c

Full pieces of 50 yards, ½c per yard less.

Best Qualities.

No. 56050 Bleached Sheeting best quality, width, 42 inches. Price, per yard..................14c

No. 56052 Bleached Sheeting, best quality, width, 46 inches. Price, per yard..................15½c

No. 56054 Bleached Sheeting, best quality, width, 50 inches. Price, per yard..................17½c

No. 56056 Bleached Sheeting, best quality, width. 54 inches. Price, per yard..................20½c

No. 56057 Bleached Sheeting, best quality, width, 60 inches. Price, per yard..................22½c

No. 56058 Bleached Sheeting, best quality, width, 68 inches. Price, per yard..................25½c

No. 56060 Bleached Sheeting, best quality, width, 80 inches. Price, per yard..................27½c

No. 56062 Bleached Sheeting, best quality, width, 88 inches. Price, per yard..................30½c

Full pieces of about 45 yards, ½c per yard less.

Half-Bleached Muslin and Pillow Case Cottons.

No. 56064 36 inches wide soft even finish cotton. Per yard, **8c** or piece of 50 or more yards...7¾c

No. 56065 45-inch Half-Bleached Pillow Case Cotton. A perfect cotton.
Price, per yd., **13c** or full piece of about 50 yds. **12½c**

No. 56066 50 inch Half-Bleached Pillow Case Cotton. Our special make.
Price, per yard, **15c** or piece of 50 or more yds.**14½c**

Wide Sheetings, Half Bleached.

No. 56068 Half Bleached Sheeting, same quality as bleached. A good, substantial and well made cotton, width, 68 inches. Price, per yard............19c

No. 56070 Half Bleached Sheeting, same quality as bleached. A good, substantial and well made cotton, width, 80 inches. Price, per yard............21c

No. 56072 Half Bleached Sheeting, same quality as bleached. A good, substantial and well made cotton, width, 88 inches. Price, per yard............23c

Full pieces of about 45 yards, ½c per yard less.

Twilled Bleached Sheeting.

No. 56078 Twilled Cotton Bleached, especially adapted for night gowns, **a nice soft even texture,** and well made in every respect. 36 inches wide.
Price, per yard..........................11c
Full piece of about 45 yards, per yard.........10½c

No. 56080 Twilled Bleached Sheeting, fully bleached, nothing better manufactured **for wear;** width, 81 inches. Price, per yard..................25c

No. 56082 Twilled Bleached Sheeting, same quality as above. Width, 90 inches.
Price, per yard..........................29c

Full pieces of about 45 yards, ½c per yard less.

White Cambric.

No. 56088 White Cambric. Splendid value for the money; 36 inches wide. Price, per yard............8c

No. 56090 Berkley White Cambric, good standard quality, 36 inches wide. Price, per yard......10c

No. 56092 Jones' White Cambric, the old reliable, 36 inches wide. Price, per yard..............16c

Cheese, Butter and Dairy Cloth.

No. 56100 Unbleached Cheese Cloth; 36 inches wide. Per yard........ 2½c
Full piece, about 60 yards, no less.
No. 56102 Unbleached Cheese Cloth; 36 inches wide. Per yard........ 3½c
Full piece, about 65 yards; per yard........ 3¼c
No. 56104 Bleached Butter Cloth; 36 inches wide. Price, per yard........ 3½c
Full piece, about 65 yards; per yard........ 3¼c
No. 56106 Colored Cheese Cloth; 25 inches wide, comes in yellow, pink, pale blue and white.
Price, per yard........ 4c
Full piece of 50 yards; per yard........ 3¾c
No. 56108 Colored Cheese Cloth; 36 inches wide, comes in yellow, pink, pale blue, nile and white.
Price, per yard........ 6c
Full piece of 50 yards; per yard........ 5¾c

PILLOW SLIPS AND SHEETS

No. 56116 Bleached Muslin Hemmed Pillow Cases. Size, 20½x34 inches. Per pair........ 25c
No. 56118 Bleached Muslin Hemmed Pillow Cases. Size, 22x34 inches. Per pair........ 28c

Bleached Ready Made Sheets.

No. 56124 Bleached Hemmed Sheets, made from cotton manufactured by the celebrated Mohawk Valley Cotton Mills. Following are sizes and prices. The sheets are not quoted in pairs:

Size, inches	63x90	72x90	81x90	90x93½
Price, each	45c	50c	55c	62c

Unbleached Ready Made Sheets.

NAUMKEAG
STANDARD
DRILLING
MANUFACTURED IN UNITED STATES OF AMERICA

No. 56126 Unbleached Ready Made Sheets Hemmed and made same as the bleached sheets. The following are sizes and prices:
Size, in......72x90 81x90 90x90
Price, each..37½c 45c 50c
No. 56129 Unbleached Drilling, used for boat sails, pockets, etc.; extra heavy, 29 inches wide.
Price, per yard........ 6½c
Full piece about 40 yards, per yard........ 6¼c
No. 56132 Unbleached Drilling, 29 inches wide; weight, about 7 oz. to the yard. Per yard........ 9c
Full piece about 40 yards, per yard........ 8½c

Bed Ticking.

These goods are made blue and white stripes only.
No. 56134 Bed Ticking, 30 inches wide. Price per yard........ 6c
Full piece of 55 yards, per yard........ 5¾c
No. 56136 Bed Ticking, 31 inches wide. Price, per yard........ 9c
Full piece of 55 yards, per yard........ 8¾c
No. 56138 Bed Ticking, 32 inches wide. A splendid quality ticking.
Price, per yard........ 12½c
Full piece of 55 yards, per yard........ 12c
No. 56139 Bed Ticking, extra fine quality, with a firm close weave; will wear for years; width, 32 inches. Price, per yard, 15c; per piece 55 yds.... 14c
No. 56140 Bed Ticking. 36 inches wide. This is one of the finest qualities made.
Price, per yard........ 18c
Full piece of 55 yards, per yard........ 17c
No. 56146 Bed Ticking, Tiger Brand, positively the best wearing ticking made. 60 inches wide.
Price, per yard........ 30c

Our 25 Cent Turkey Red Linen Ticking.

No. 56147 German Turkey Red Linen Ticking. warranted to hold feathers and will hold its color. It is oil boiled Turkey red, sateen finished, medium weight, width 35 inches.
Price, per yard........ 25c

Denims.

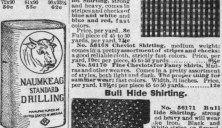

No. 56150 Blue Denim, strong and durable, fast colors, 28 inches wide. Price, per yard, 11c
Full piece of 45 to 50 yards, per yard.... 10½c
No. 56151 Blue Denim, extra heavy, one of the best qualities made, width, 28 inches. Price, per yard,........ 12c
Per piece, 45 to 50 yards........ 11½c
No. 56152 Blue Denim, extra heavy twill and will wear like iron. Width, 28 inches. Price, per yard........ 15c
Full piece of 45 to 50 yards, per yd........ 14½c

Brown Denims.

No. 56154 Brown Denim, good quality and close weave; width, 28 inches. Price, per yard........ 11c
Full piece of 45 to 50 yards, per yard........ 10½c
No. 56155 Brown Denim, good, strong, reliable grade, good weight; width, 28 inches. Price, per yard........ 12c
Full piece, 45 to 50 yards, per yard........ 11½c
No. 56156 Brown Denim, extra quality, strong and heavy; width, 28 inches. Price, per yard.... 15c
Full piece of 45 to 50 yards, per yard........ 14½c

Awning Ticking.

No. 56160 Awning Ticking, twilled and satin finished, comes in Drab and Red and Drab and Blue, wide stripes, fast colors; width, 32 inches.
Price, per yard........ 12½c
Full piece of 45 to 50 yards, per yard........ 12c
No. 56162 Awning Ticking, same width and colors as above but much heavier and better quality. Price per yard.... 18c
Full piece of 45 to 50 yards, per yard........ 17c

Cheviot Shirtings.

No. 56163 Cheviot Shirting, a good wearing cloth, and will hold its color; comes in blue and white checks, also brown and white checks. Price, per yard........ 6½c
A full piece of 45 yards........ 6¼c
No. 56166 Cheviot Shirting, strong and heavy, comes in stripes and checks of blue and white and blue and red, fast colors.
Price, per yard..8c
Full piece of 45 to 50 yards, per yard, 7¾c
No. 56168 Cheviot Shirting, medium weight; comes in a pretty assortment of stripes and checks; a good reliable cloth, strictly fast colors. Price, per yard, 10c; per piece, 45 to 50 yards........ 9½c
No. 56170 Fine Cheviots for Fancy Shirts, Madras and other weaves. Comes in a pretty assortment of styles, both light and dark. The proper thing for summer wear; fast colors. Width, 31 inches. Price, per yard, 12½c; per piece 45 to 50 yards........ 12c

Bull Hide Shirting.

No. 56171 Bull Hide Shirting, strong and heavy and will wear like iron. Black and White stripe or figured.
Price, per yard.... 9½c
A full piece of 45 yards, per yard........ 9¼c
No. 56173 Bull Hide Shirting, same as above, but comes in blue and white striped or figured.
Price, per yard..10½c
Or a full piece of 45 yards, per yard...... 10c
No. 56175 Fleeceback shirting, splendid wearing goods, the proper thing for everyday use, strong and serviceable, comes in neat dark colorings. Is sure to please. Width, 29 inches. Price, per yard...... 12½c
A full piece, 45 to 50 yards........ 12c

Cotton Batting.

Almost all dealers sell Cotton Batting by the roll, and while nothing may be said regarding their weight, people suppose they are getting 16 ounce rolls, as they have always been put up in that way. Almost all dealers have their batts put up today with but 12 ounces, or three-fourths of a pound to the roll, which makes comparisons of prices by the roll obviously unfair, unless weight is taken into consideration.

All our rolls weigh about 16 ounces—1 pound each. We say about 16 ounces, as they are as near that uniform weight as can be put up; some may exceed that, while others may be a trifle under; the average is one pound each. Our batts are patent folded, and are not simply a wad of cotton to be repicked and put into the quilt in bunches; each batt is nicely papered, is folded, and will open up all the same thickness; 36 inches wide and 7 feet long.
Cotton Batting is put up 50 pounds to the bale, and if sold in that quantity an extra discount of 5 per cent will be allowed.
No. 56180 Cotton Batting, fair quality, per roll, 14 oz. to a roll. Each........ 8c
No. 56181 Cotton Batting, good quality, nice and clean and good value for the money. Per roll... 10c
No. 56182 Cotton Batting, nice clean fine rolls, 16 oz. Each........ 12½c
No. 56183 Cotton Batting, one of the finest qualities made, pure and clean. Per roll...... 15c
No. 56184 Snow White Cotton Batting, 16 oz. rolls, used for medical purposes. Price, per roll.. 21c

Mosquito Netting.

No. 56185 Mosquito netting, sold by the piece only; any color desired. Full piece of about 8 yards for.. 40c

Cotton Wadding.

No. 56186 Cotton Wadding, slate color only, good cotton, nicely glazed; size, about 32x36 inches.
Per doz. sheets, 20c; per sheet........ 2c
No. 56188 Cotton Wadding, white, nicely finished, clean and white; size, about 30x36 inches.
Per doz. sheets, 25c; per sheet........ 2½c

Tinted Wadding.

For Fancy Work.

No. 56192 Fancy French Tinted Wadding, in sheets; colors: light blue, pink, Nile, yellow; size, about 28x36 inches. Per doz. sheets, 45c; per sheet.. 4c
No. 56193 Wool Sheet Wadding. Sheets of fine Australian wool; size, 18x36; brown or white. Makes a light and soft filling for comforters; does not become lumpy; has the feeling of a down filling.
Price, per dozen sheets, $2.00; per sheet........ 20c

Carpet Warp.

Our warp is carefully made of good cotton, hard and evenly twisted, of uniform size and long reel; 4-ply No. 8½ yarn, 90-in. reel; 5 pounds will make 25 yards of yard wide carpet. We do not sell less than 5 pounds of white or any one color.
No. 56200 White Warp (sold in 5-lb. bundles only) net weight. Per lb........ 16½c
No. 56202 Colored Cotton Warp (sold in 5-lb. bundles only) net weight. Per lb. 18½c
Colored Carpet Warp comes in brown, orange, red, green, black, medium blue, yellow and slate; one color in each bundle. Special prices will be given on quantities of 100 pounds or more.

SPOOLED
COTTON YARN
SEARS ROEBUCK

Carpet Warp on Spools.

These Spools are ready for the Warper. They save the weaver tedious hand winding. Put up in 5-pound boxes. 20 quarter-pound spools. Exclusive selling agents in Chicago.
No. 56204 Price, colored, per pound........ 20c
No. 56206 Price, white... 19c

Grain Bags.

SEARS ROEBUCK & CO.
CHEAPEST SUPPLY HOUSE ON EARTH
DIRECT TO THE CONSUMER

WE CANNOT GUARANTEE THE PRICES ON GRAIN BAGS as they are subject to change without notice. We will give market value the day the order is received.
No. 56210 Sears, Roebuck & Co.'s Special Grain Bag, made expressly for us and can be obtained only from us; the most satisfactory bag in the world; try them once and you will never use any other. Each.. 15½c
No. 56216 Grain Bags, American A, 2-bushel. Price, per 100, 16¼; each........ 16½c
No. 56218 Grain Bags, Stark A, 2-bushel. Price, per bale 100, $18.50; each........ 19c

White Duck or Canvas.

No. 56223 Extra Heavy Duck, used for tents, awnings, stack covers, harvester aprons, etc.

Width.	Weight per Square Yard about 20 oz. Price per yard.	Weight per Square Yard about 18 oz. Price per yard.	Weight per Square Yard about 15 oz. Price per yard.	Weight per Square Yard about 13 oz. Price per yard.
28 inch	31c	29c	24c	22c
30 inch	33c	30c	26c	24c
34 inch	37c	34c	29c	27c
36 inch	40c	36c	31c	29c
38 inch	42c	38c	33c	....
40 inch	45c	40c	35c	32c
44 inch	49c	45c	38c	35c
48 inch	53c	48c	41c	[illegible]
52 inch	57c	52c	44c	41c
56 inch	62c	56c	47c	45c
60 inch	66c	60c	52c	48c
66 inch	74c	65c	56c	53c
72 inch	80c	72c	60c	57c
84 inch	95c	88c	70c	77c
96 inch	125c	112c	90c	86c
120 in.	160c	142c	121	111c

No. 56225 White Duck or Canvas, 8 oz. weight; width, 29 inches. Price, per yard........ 10c
Full piece of 50 yards, per yard........ 9½c
No. 56226 White Duck or Canvas, 10 oz. weight, 30 inches wide. Per yard........ 14c
Or full piece of 50 yards, per yard........ 13½c

BED BLANKETS AT LOWEST PRICES

...BED BLANKETS...

WE ARE UNDOUBTEDLY HEADQUARTERS FOR BLANKETS.

They are sold in pairs only. A pair is just double the size quoted, which is the size of one blanket only.

White Blankets.

No. 57929 Good Grade White Cotton Blanket, with fancy colored border, 10-4 or regular size. Price, per pair................48c

No. 57931 White Blankets, with fancy colored borders, heavy fleece, 11-4 or full size. Price, per pair................70c

No. 57933 White Blankets, extra heavy and well napped; splendid value for the money. Fancy colored borders. Full 11-4 size.
Price, per pair................95c

No. 57935 White Blankets, excellent value; fancy colored borders; good reliable goods. Extra heavy fleece; full 11-4 size. Weight, 4 lbs.
Price, per pair................$1.35

No. 57937 White Blankets, part wool filled; fancy colored borders. Extra large 11-4 size; splendid values. Weight, 5 lbs. Price, per pair $1.75

No. 57939 White Blankets, all wool filled; extra good value. This blanket will wear better and give far better satisfaction than a cheap all-wool blanket. Full size 11-4. Fancy colored borders. Weight, 5 lbs.
Price, per pair................$2.75

No. 57941 White Blankets. Strictly all pure wool. This blanket is splendid value for the money and one we can strongly recommend. Fancy colored borders and fully 4 lbs. weight. Full 10-4 size. Price, per pair. $2.98

No. 57943 White Blankets. Strictly all wool. This is an extra good blanket and will give thorough satisfaction. Fancy colored borders. Weight, fully 5 lbs. Full 11-4 size. Price, per pair.................$3.05

No. 57945 White Blankets. Extra fine California lambs' wool. These are reliable, well made goods and worth a good deal more than we charge. Fancy colored borders. Full 11-4 size. Weight, 5¼ lbs.
Price, per pair.................$4.98

No. 57947 Extra Fine California White Bed Blankets, very fine texture, made of fine long staple wool, thoroughly shrunk, with fancy colored borders, and mohair bound. Weight, 6 lbs. Extra large 11-4 size, or 72x84.
Price, per pair.................$7.25

No. 57949 Extra Superfine California White Bed Blankets. This is one of the very highest grades made, thoroughly shrunk and reliable, fancy borders and deep mohair binding. Extra large 11-4 size, or 72x84. Weight, about 6 lbs. Worth $12.50.
Our price, per pair.................$8.75

No. 57950 Beautiful Quality Highest Grade White Lambs' Wool Bed Blankets, thoroughly shrunk. This excellent quality blanket must be seen to be appreciated; beautifully finished, fancy colored borders. Extra large size, or 72x84. Price, per pair.................$9.98

No. 57950½ This Blanket is made of the Finest Quality of Selected Saxony Wool, with deep, luxurious fleece, and is of an extraordinary size (76 x 88). Nothing finer shown anywhere. Has a silk binding and handsome colored borders. Price, per pair..............$12.50

SEE PAGE 471 FOR OUR EXTRA HEAVY KLONDIKE AND CAMPING BLANKETS.

BED BLANKETS FOR ALL SEASONS

GRAY BLANKETS.

No. 57951 Gray Blankets, fair quality, with colored borders, 10-4 or regular size. Price, per pair....**48c**

No. 57953 Gray Blankets, with colored borders, heavy fleece, 11-4 or full size. Price, per pair................**70c**

No. 57955 Gray Blankets, extra heavy and well napped. Splendid value for the money. Colored borders, full 11-4 size.
Price, per pair.....................**95c**

No. 57957 Extra Large Size Gray Blankets, wool filled, the best value ever offered in a medium grade blanket. Size 11-4. Weight, 6 pounds. Colored borders.
Price, per pair...................**$1.68**

No. 57959 Excellent Grade Large Size Gray Blankets, wool filled, a good quality mixed blanket and reliable, colored borders, 11-4 size. Weight, 5¼ pounds.
Price, per pair...................**$2.35**

No. 57961 Gray Blankets, Strictly all Pure Wool, this blanket is splendid value for the money and one we can strongly recommend. Colored borders. Weight, fully 4 pounds. Full 10-4 size.
Price, per pair...................**$2.98**

No. 57963 Gray Blankets, strictly all pure wool. This is an extra good blanket and will give thorough satisfaction. Colored borders. Weight, fully 5 pounds. Full 11-4 size.
Price, per pair...................**$3.95**

No. 57965 Gray Blankets, extra fine California wool. These are reliable, well-made blankets and worth a great deal more than we charge. Colored borders. Full 11-4 size. Weight, 5 pounds. Price, per pair..............**$4.98**

No. 57967 Extra Fine California Gray Bed Blankets, made of fine long staple wool, thoroughly shrunk. Colored borders and mohair bound. Weight, 6 pounds. Full 11-4 size or 72x84 inches. Price, per pair.....**$7.25**

No. 57969 Extra Superfine California Gray Bed Blankets. This is one of the very highest grades made, thoroughly shrunk and reliable. Colored borders and deep mohair binding. Extra large 11-4 size, or 72x84. Weight, about 6 pounds. Price, per pair..**$8.75**

No. 57970 This Natural Saxony Wool Gray Blanket is the acme of luxury. It is of the finest texture, finish and quality; beautifully bound, all wool and shrunk, with beautiful colored borders. Size, 76x88 inches.
Price, per pair...................**$9.98**

WHITE CRIB BLANKETS.

No. 57973 Crib Blankets, fine white wool filled, mohair bound and fancy colored borders. Size, 30x40 inches.
Price, per pair................**80c**

No. 57975 White Crib Blankets, extra fine California wool filled; a very fine quality and well worth $2.25 per pair; fancy colored borders. Size, 30x40 inches. A bargain.
Our special price, per pair.....**$1.49**

═══ NOTE—See page 607 for Scarlet Bed Blankets and Camping Blankets ═══

Stair Carpets.

No. 58504 Hemp Stair Carpet, 18 inches wide, comes with a tan mixed center with a red border.
Price, per yard 11c

No. 58505 Ingrain Stair Carpet, wool filled. Comes in medium colors, in tan and red mixed. Width, 22¼ inches. Price, per yard... ....28c

No. 58508 Ingrain Stair Carpet. Much heavier and better quality than the above number. Can furnish any combination of coloring. Width 22¼ inches. Price, per yard,........................39c

Carpet Linings.

No. 58516 Felt Carpet Lining, or paper in rolls of 50 yards. Weight about 31 pounds.
Price, per roll...57c

No. 58518 Sewed Carpet Lining, filled with jute; 36 inches wide. Keeps the floor nice and warm and protects the carpet. Price, per yard......... $0.02½
Full bale of 200 yards...................... 4.50

No. 58520 Carpet Bindings; cotton and wool, carpet binding, 1 inch wide; 12-yard rolls, assorted colors. Price, per roll 11c

The Dantsic Rug.

No. 58783 The Dantsic Rug. This is the very newest in rugs. It is an imitation of Wilton or Axminster; comes in a pretty combination of colors, principally dark. Be sure and order one.
Size, 2 feet 3 inches by 5 feet. Each $1.50

Union Ingrain Art Squares.

We do not carry the very low grade of Art Squares so much on the market. Our Union Art Squares are half wool and will give thorough satisfaction. They come in pretty designs and colorings. It has a fringe of itself and pretty border to harmonize. The predominating colors are red mixed and also green mixed, with pretty contrasting colors. The sizes and prices are as follows:

No. 58785

Size	7½x9	9x9	9x12
Price, each	$2.63	$3.15	$4.20

All Wool Art Squares.

These are the best qualities manufactured in Ingrain Art Squares. Strictly highest grade wool. We can furnish them in green, tan and red, with other pretty colors to harmonize. You will save money by buying your art squares from us. We quote the following sizes:

No. 58789

Sizes,	7½x9	9x9	9x10½	9x12	9x13½	12x12	12x15
Prices,	$4.73	5.67	6.62	7.56	8.51	10.08	12.60

Note reduced prices on above.

White Sheep Rugs.

No. 58791 White Sheep Rug, unlined; size, 30x60 inches. Price, each.............................$2.75

Chinese Goat Fur Rugs.

No. 58793 Fine White Chinese Goat Fur Rug unlined; size, 30x60 inches; thick and heavy.
Price.....$2.65

No. 58795 Fine Gray Chinese Goat Fur Rug, unlined; size, 30x60 inches; same quality as above. Price, each..$2.65

No. 58796 Jet Black Goat Fur Rug; finest quality made; size, 30x60 inches; unlined; thick skin; heavy, long fur. Price, each.........................$3.25

Two-Toned Chinese Goat Rugs.

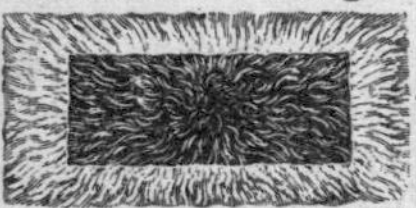

No. 58797 Two-toned Chinese Goat Fur Rugs; white with solid black or gray centers, heavy and thick, finely padded, lined with the finest black Italian cloth; size, 30x60 inches. Price, $4.75

Cocoa Door Mats.

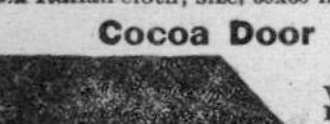

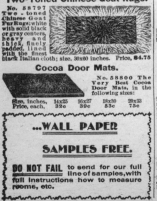

No. 58800 The Very Best Cocoa Door Mats, in the following sizes:

Size, inches,	14x25	16x27	18x30	20x33
Price, each,	32c	39c	53c	75c

...WALL PAPER

SAMPLES FREE.

DO NOT FAIL to send for our full line of samples, with full instructions how to measure rooms, etc.

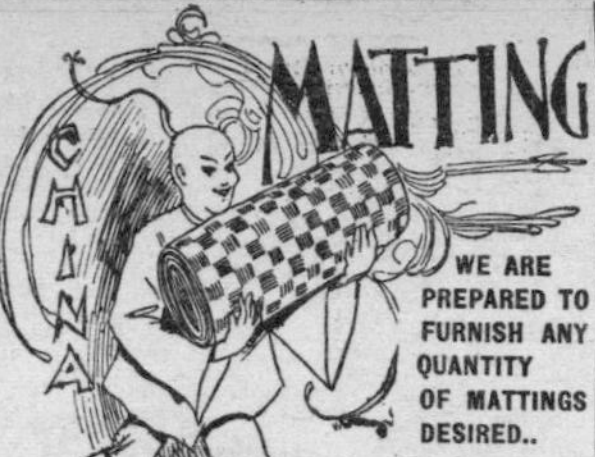

WE ARE PREPARED TO FURNISH ANY QUANTITY OF MATTINGS DESIRED..

As we have purchased these goods in large quantities, which enables us to quote prices exceedingly low, we quote these goods by the yard and also quote prices on full pieces of 40 yards each. **By purchasing full pieces our patrons receive the benefit of the reduction which we make on mattings.** Following you will find full description of same.

No. 58826 Fancy Matting, very good quality, and pretty, 36 inches wide. Colors, medium.
Price, per yard, $0.15; full piece, 40 yards..$5.20

No. 58828 Fancy Check or Plain Straw Color Matting, very fine quality for price, and durable.
Price, per yard, $0.20; full piece, 40 yards..$7.60

No. 58830 The Japanese Straw Matting; nothing its equal. This matting is pure cotton warp very durable; medium colors. **Extra good value.**
Price, per yard, $0.22; full piece of 40 yards.$8.00

No. 58832 The Jointless. A very handsome matting. It wears as well as any matting you would pay double the amount for. Comes in checks and fancy colors, light or dark. Price, per yard....$0.23
Full piece of 40 yards.............................. 8.00

No. 58834 Extra Heavy China Matting, very heavy and the best quality manufactured for the money. Weighs 90 lbs. to the roll. We may not be able to purchase this line at present prices, as the **duties on all grades have advanced, but we have at present on hand a large stock.** This grade comes in check and fancy colors, dark and light.
Price, full piece of 40 yards, $10.00; per yard .30c

Table Oil Cloths.

No. 58851 Best Quality Table Oil Cloths. Marble oil cloth, 45 inches wide. Price, per yard, 17c or full bolt of 12 yards for..........................$1.95

No. 58853 Best Quality Table Oil Cloth. Oak and fancy patterns, 45 inches wide. Price, per yard, 16c or full bolt of 12 yards for..........................$1.80

No. 58855 Shelf Oil Cloth, white or fancy wood patterns, 12 inches wide, scalloped edges, printed with pretty lace effects. Per piece of 12 yards....60c

Brass Stair Rods.

No. 58865 Brass Stair Rods.
24-inch, per dozen..$0.85
26-inch, per dozen....95c 30-inch, per dozen.. 1.15

Vestibule Rods for Sash Curtains.

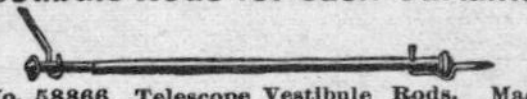

No. 58866 Telescope Vestibule Rods. Made with brackets complete; can be adjusted inside or outside the rods; are made of two brass tubes, one sliding inside of the other, and will extend 24 to 44 inches ⅜ inch rod. Price, per doz., $1.00; each, 10c

No. 58867 Telescope Vestibule Rods. With pretty corrugated ball ends, as per cut; a very fancy rod, complete with screws. Will extend 28 to 54 inches. Price, per dozen, $2.00; each.......... 18c

Stair Pads.

No. 58869 Stair Pads, 22¼ and 27 inches long.
Price, per dozen.......................................$1.20

Curtain Poles.

No. 58870 Wood Trimmed Curtain Poles, 1⅜ inch, finished in California walnut, mahogany, oak and ebony. Price includes two turned wooden ends, two brackets for ends and sufficient quantity of rings for pole. **Don't fail to mention kind of finish wanted.**

Length,	5 ft.	6 ft.	7 ft.	8 ft.	9 ft
Price, each	25c	29c	32c	36c	40c

No. 58871 Wood-Trimmed Curtain Poles, suitable for bedrooms or sash curtains ¾-inch, finished antique oak only. Price includes brackets and ends Length, 4 ft. Price, 12c. Length, 5 ft. Price... 15c

No. 58872 Brass Trimmed Curtain Poles, 1¼-inch poles, finished in oak, mahogany, walnut and ebony, complete with two brass ends, two brass brackets and sufficient quantity of rings for pole.

Length	5 ft.	6 ft.	7 ft.	8 ft.	9 ft.
Pice, each,	19c	23c	26c	29c	32c

Curtain Poles and Sockets.

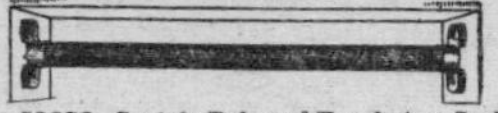

No. 58873 Curtain Pole and Bracket or Socket, complete. As per cut, a brass socket with 1⅜ inch pole, no screws or nails required. It fits on inside of casing and has rubber ends. Cut pole ¾ inch shorter than space between opening and attach brackets.
Price, complete with poles, 5 feet, each.........22c
Price, complete with poles, 6 feet, each.........26c
Price, complete with poles, 7 feet, each.........29c
Price, complete with poles, 8 feet, each.........33c
Price, complete with poles, 9 feet, each.........36c

White Enameled Poles.

No. 58874 White Enameled Corrugated Cottage Curtain Pole. With fancy corrugated ball ends and also fancy rosette screws, as per cut. This is the prettiest rod in the market and is sure to please. ¾-inch rod, 4 feet only. Complete with fixtures, our special price, each...15c

Curtain Loops, Etc.

No. 58884

No. 58890

No. 58884 A White Cotton Curtain Loop, (cord and tassels).
Per pair...........................8c

No. 58886 Curtain Loops, cord and tassels, to be used with tapestry curtains. Per pair......15c

No. 58888 Heavy Chenille Curtain Loops, cord and tassels.
Per pair.................... 19c

No. 58890 Brass Curtain Chain, a good strong chain usually sold for very much more money. Per pair..........7c

No. 58892 Spiral Curtain Chains, pretty, strong and durable. Per pair..............14c

No. 58894 Brass Tassel Hooks, polished. Each,5c

Rug Fringes.

No. 58896 Wool Rug Fringe, with gimp heading 3 inches deep; tan, olive or red combinations, also plain colors. Per doz. yards, 64c; per yard.........6c

No. 58897 Knotted Rug Fringe, 4 inches wide, tan, olive or red, plain or combination.
Per doz. yards, $1.10; per yard.........................10c

Furniture Fringes.

No. 58900 Cotton Furniture Fringe, heavy and durable. Comes in all combinations of colors to match furniture covering. A very pretty fringe for the money. Full width, 7 inches.
Price, per yard................ $0.10
Price, per doz. yards........ 1.00

Worsted Furniture Fringe.

No. 58902 Comes in a very fancy heading and deep fringe, full width in combination of colors to match all furniture coverings. Full width, 7 inches.
Price, per yard....$0.15
Per doz. yards. .. 1.50

Our 20-cent Heavy Furniture Fringe.

No. 58904 Extra High Grade Worsted Furniture Fringe, has beautiful heavy strands and tassels, with fancy deep heading on a good quality of fringe. We can furnish any combination of colors to match furniture coverings. Full width, 7 inches.
Price, per yard....$0.20
Per doz yards..... 2.25

SEND FOR FREE COLOR CARD OF HOUSE PAINTS

TOYS AND GAMES.

Baby Swings.

No. 59000 Baby Swing, has hardwood seat, 11 inches square, upholstered in cretonne; intended to be hung in a doorway; furnished with cotton rope and 2 hooks to hang it on; has no springs.
Price 40c
Shipping weight, 3 pounds.

Jumper Springs.

No. 59001 Springs for Baby Swings; made of heavy steel spring wire, 15 inches long. By adding a pair of these springs to above swing you have a baby jumper. Many people buy these springs and make their own jumper. Springs come in pairs. **Shipping weight, 2 pounds.** Price for springs only, per pair, 50c

Baby Jumpers.

This Jumper combines in one article a baby swing, reclining chair, crib and jumper; strong and large enough for a child 6 years old; child cannot fall out. Should the baby fall asleep while in the chair it can be adjusted to a crib without disturbing the child. **It is light and simple, yet substantial and perfect.**

No. 59002 Baby Jumper, complete, with springs and cotton rope and hooks, with veneer seat and back, not upholstered. **Shipping weight, 12 lbs.** Price, each.. $1.23

No. 59003 Baby Jumper, complete, with springs, rope and hooks, upholstered in cretonne like cut. **Shipping weight, 12 pounds.** Price, each.... $1.75

Patent Swing Horses.

No. 59004 Swing Horse, 19 inches high from floor to saddle, nicely trimmed, has hair mane and tail. **This horse requires very little strength to operate,** and for that reason is a decided improvement over the old style rocking horse. Each........ $1.90
Shipping weight, 20 pounds.

No. 59005 Swing Horse, 21 inches high, from floor to saddle, otherwise same as No. 59004. Each.. $2.75
Shipping weight, 23½ pounds.

No. 59006 Swing Horse, 22 inches high from floor to saddle, trimmed in a superior manner. **Shipping weight, 27 pounds.** Each......... $3.45

Tothill's Baby Tender.

No. 59007 Made on the principle of a reclining chair, is strong and durable, adjusted to any position from chair to crib in a minute by locked ratchet. Child can be placed upright or reclining; has an easy soothing, swinging motion which all the children like—so does mother and nurse; simple and substantial. Price.......... $1.85
Shipping weight, 20 pounds.

Swinging Shoo Fly Rockers.

No. 59008 Swinging Shoo Fly, easy to operate, no danger of child falling out; nicely upholstered in cretonne and painted dapple gray. Each... .... $1.65
Shipping weight, 20 pounds.

Shoo Fly Rockers.

No. 59009 Shoo Fly, 19x38 inches; painted and dappled; has painted hardwood seat, bent rocker and hair tail.
Price............... 74c
Shipping wgt., 10 lbs.

No. 59010 Shoo Fly. Same as No. 59009, but is upholstered in cretonne. **Shipping weight, 12 lbs.** Price......... 88c

No. 59011 Shoo Fly, 22x43 inches, neatly painted and dappled; has box in front to hold childs' toys, and is upholstered in cretonne; hair tail, bent rockers. **Shipping weight, 13 pounds.** Price......... $1.08

Galloping Horse.

No. 59014 A Galloping Horse, nicely painted and ornamented stand, English saddle with enameled cloth; enamel cloth saddle flaps, trimmed with fancy color wool fringe, hair main and tail, stirrups and martingales with reins, heavy breast plating, 6x6 inches, block 32 inches high from floor to head. **Shipping weight, 40 pounds.** Price, $3.45

BOYS' WAGONS.

No. 59015 Iron axles; body, 14x28 inches; wheels, 12 and 16 inches. Hardwood paneled body, landscape painting, scrolled and varnished, hub caps, high seat and dashboard. Iron braced, heavy iron axles in iron thimble skein, oval tires welded and shrunk on. Same as cut. Price, each.......... $2.20
Shipping weight, 28 pounds.

Boys' Farm Wagon.

No. 59016 Boys' Farm Wagon, with pole and shafts. Body, 18x36 inches, with hardwood frame. The sides and ends can be taken off, leaving bed with stakes. The gearing is made like a farm wagon, having bent hawns and adjustable reach; all parts are strongly ironed and braced; wheels are 14 and 20 inches; heavy welded tires; sand boxes and hub caps; has seat, handle and a pair of hardwood shafts for dog or goat. **It is handsomely ornamented with landscapes and scroll work. This wagon is the best in the market.** Price, each........ $5.50
For Goat or Dog Harness, see Index.
Shipping weight, 54 pounds.

Boys' Wagons.

Boys' Steel Wagons. The best and strongest steel wagon made; finely painted and ornamented, steel box, malleable iron gear, tinned steel wheels.

No. 59017 Body, 12x24-inch; wheels, 10 and 12-inch. Price, each........................ $1.20
Shipping weight, 17 pounds.

No. 59018 Body, 13x26-inch; wheels, 10 and 14-inch. Price, each... $1.45
Shipping weight, 18 pounds.

No. 59019 Body, 14x28-inch; wheels, 12 and 16 inch. Price, each... $1.60
Shipping weight, 18 pounds.

No. 59020 Body, 15x30-inch; wheels, 14 and 18-inch. Price each... $1.80
Shipping weight, 20 pounds.

BOYS' SLEDS, COASTERS, SLEIGHS, ETC.

No. 59022 Boys' Hardwood Coaster. A strong, well made, durable sled. Length, 36 inches; width, 11 inches; gear finished on the wood, top painted and decorated, four hand holes, round spring steel shoes.
Price, each... 50c

Great Value for $1.00.

No. 59024 Our Special Bargain Sled. Most excellent value for the price. The general outlines of this sled are admitted by all to be the best in the market. Length, 42 inches; width, 12 inches. Gear nicely finished on the wood. Top painted bright colors and ornamented by hand with landscapes, flowers, etc. Four hand holes. Curved runners. Round spring steel shoes.
Price, each.. $1.00

High Grade Boys' Coaster.

No. 59025 High Grade Boys' Coaster. Length, 42 inches; width, 12 inches. Runners are of polished maple, highly finished, with very high points. Tops painted principally in two colors, neatly paneled and finely decorated with landscapes, flowers, etc. Runners are braced with four angle irons, and points of shoes are scrolled and tinned. Four hand holes. Round spring steel shoes.
Price, each... .... $1.50

50 Cents Buys This Straight Knee Sleigh.

No. 59026 Girls' or Small Boys' Straight Knee Sleigh. Length, 36 inches; width, 12 inches. Three framed knees mortised into runners with square tenons. Top painted various colors, neatly decorated and striped. Flat shoes. Price, each..................................... 50c

Our 68-Cent Bow Runner Sleigh.

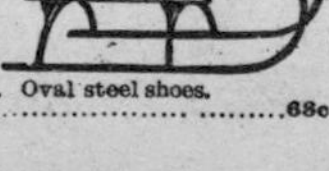

No. 59027 Bow Runner Sleigh; length 33 inches, width 12 inches; two bent knees; gear finished on the wood and has four tinned knee braces. Top highly painted and handsomely hand decorated. Oval steel shoes.
Price, each....................................... 68c

Bent Knee Goose Neck Sleigh.

No. 59028 Bent Knee Goose Neck Sleigh. Length, 36 inches; width, 12 inches. Three bent knees. Braced with six tinned braces. Top painted in bright colors, tastefully decorated and striped. Gear is finely finished on the wood. Flat shoes and goose necks.
Price, each.. 73c

No. 59029 Bent Knee Goose Neck Sleigh. Length, 36 inches; width, 12 inches. Has three bent knees; gear finished on the wood; top handsomely **hand decorated.** Has six tinned braces and tinned malleable goose necks; **oval shoes.** Price, each.......... 98c

$1.25 Buys a $2.00 Fender Sleigh.

No. 59030 Boys' Fender Sleigh, length, 36 inches; width, 13½ inches. Gear finely finished on the wood, and top hands hand painted in two or more varieties of decorations. Has oval shoes, six tinned braces and swan necks. Price, each........... $1.25

Excelsior Fender Sleigh for $2.50.

No. 59032 Excelsior Fender Sleigh. Length, 36 inches; width, 12 inches, gear is made of fine oak or ash, highly finished, with chamfered corners and turned round, fenders are bent to form raves and securely held in position by six tinned braces, tops are decorated in an expensive manner by the best artists, shoes are tinned in front and have fancy ornament on point and heel.
Price, each... $2.50

Bow Runner, Spring Steel Sleigh.

No. 59033 Bow Runner, Self-Equalizing Spring Steel Sleigh. Will carry safely a load of 300 lbs. Tops are hardwood, handsomely painted and decorated by hand, and only the best quality of paint and varnish used, **thus insuring its lasting qualities.** Length, 32 inches, width, 10½ inches. **Finely decorated.** Price, each... .... $1.00

Spring Steel Coaster.

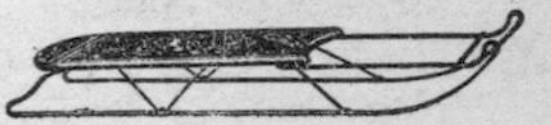

No. 59034 Spring Steel Coasters. Steel and iron are the only cheap materials that will stand the wear and tear of children's use, and it is in accordance with this idea that we present to you our line of this class of sleds. Our coasters are made of $\frac{5}{8}$x$\frac{1}{16}$ oval stock, strongly braced for the roughest use, and they will carry all the load that can be placed on them. **This is undoubtedly the strongest sled ever offered to the trade.** Length, 38 inches; top, 24 inches, with our finest decorations. Runners are strongly braced to stand rough use. **BUT HAS NO BRACE ACROSS POINTS AS SHOWN IN CUT.**
Price, each.. $0.93
Price, with brace (45x28 inches)................... 1.17

Our $2.25 Childs' Cutter.

No. 59041 Children's Cutters. These cutters have a bent dash, high and wide enough to form a protection from the wind. The bodies are nicely painted in pleasing colors, and decorated and striped in a tasteful manner. Length, 38 inches: width, 15 inches. No upholstery.
Price, each... $2.25

No. 59042 Children's Cutter, same as above, except seat and back is upholstered in damask.
Price, each... $3.25

Special Fancy Cutters.

We have had considerable inquiries for a special extra fine cutter and have made preparations to furnish them to our customers. The descriptions are accurate and we can assure purchasers that they will receive excellent value for their money.

No. 59043 Children's Cutters. This model is handsomely finished, decorated and striped. **Gear** made entirely of second growth hardwood, with three bent knees, six tinned knee braces and **oval** shoes. **Painted** in light and dark colors. **Seat only** upholstered. Size, 42x18 inches. Has very large **bent** dash. Price, each.. $4.00

No. 59044 Same as above, except the seat and back is upholstered in damask. Price, each.... $5.50

No. 59045 Our Best Cutter. Larger, deeper and stronger than any we have seen before. Size over all 17x46 inches. **Bent dash** with fenders. **Gear** framed securely and made of the best second **growth** timber. **Knees shaped and ironed like a Portland cutter. Body** has round corners on back, and **entire** cutter finished in both light and dark colors, **artistically** striped and decorated. **Upholstered in plush or corduroy.** Price, each.......................... $8.25

No. 59046 Same as above, except it has **plumes** and plated dash and arm rails. Price, each.. $11.25

Childs' Buggy

No. 59050 Made of the best seasoned wood, nicely painted, body 13x26 inches, with steel wheels 12 and 16 inches in diameter, iron axles, iron tongue draw and 5th wheel. Has hub caps, seat and whip with whip in socket. **These buggies are being more universally used and are a very convenient form for giving the child a ride instead of the baby buggy.**
Price, each **$1.95**
Shipping weight, 28 pounds

Boys' Steel Garden Wheelbarrow.

No. 59054 The body is made of sheet steel, the frame is made of well seasoned material and will stand any amount of knocking around. They are practical and something every boy would like to have. Nicely painted and ornamented. Size of the body 9 inches, box 10½ inches, wheel 6 inches, handles 24 inches.
Price, each **60c**
No. 59055 Steel garden barrow, same style as above. Size of box 13 inches, size of wheel 8 inches, handles 30 inches long. Price, each **70c**

Boys' Tool Chest.

No. 59060 Boys' tool chest with top cover. Contains about eight assorted tools. Size of chest, 9½x4¼x2½ inches. **A chest adapted for small children. Shipping weight, 34 ounces.** Price . . **25c**
No. 59061 Boys' tool chest, contains about 11 assorted tools. Size of chest, 12x6x4 inches. A well made box, adapted for boys' use. Price, each **50c**
Shipping weight, 2½ pounds.
No. 59062 Boys' tool chest, containing about 16 assorted tools. Size of tool chest, 14½x6¾x4¾ inches. A splendid assortment of tools of the better kind in a well made chest and sure to prove interesting to boys. Price, each **75c**
Shipping weight, 3¾ pounds.
No. 59063 Boys' tool chest, better made tools and larger. Contains about 16 assorted tools. Size of chest, 16¾x8¾x6 inches. **This chest is bound to please a boy who will appreciate its worth. Shipping weight, 7 pounds.** Price, each **$1.00**
No. 59064 Youths' tool chest. Contains about 24 assorted tools of the better grade. Size of chest, 17¾x9x7 inches. Put up in well made and handsome chest. **One of the best presents that you might select.** Price, complete **$1.25**
Shipping weight, 8 pounds.
For better grade tool chests see Hardware Department.

Boys' Jumbo Bucksaw and Buck.

No. 59065 Just the thing for Boys. Blade made of good cast steel, well made frame and buck. **A substantial and practical article.**
Price, each **25c**
Shipping weight, 2½ pounds.
No. 59066 Boys' Best Bucksaw and Buck. It makes the sawdust fly and develops the muscles. Steel blade, 20 inches long, painted red, and the metal parts tinned. A well made, very strong and practical article. **The boys' favorite. Shipping weight, 6 pounds.** Price, each **75c**

S., R. & Co.'s Scroll Saw Outfit.

No. 59070 An amusing, instructive and interesting device. The outfit contains 1 S., R. & Co.'s saw frame, 1 V strip with screws, 1 sheet impression paper, 3 saw blades, 1 awl, 3 patterns and 1 piece of bracket wood. **Any boy can make money by making and selling brackets, card cases, handkerchief boxes, photograph frames, doll furniture and other useful and ornamental articles.** Directions with every set. **Shipping weight, 1 pound.** Price for outfit **25c**

The State Safe.

No. 59071 This splendid Bank is made of ornamented steel, back and sides and iron front, all nickel plated and highly polished. Size, 2¼x2¾x4 in. Fastens with a two tumbler combination lock. **Shipping weight, 1¼ pounds.**
Price, each **25c**

Columbus Safe.

No. 59073 Is made of ornamented steel back and sides, round front nickel plated and highly polished. Size, 3¾x4¾x5¼. Fastened with two tumbler combination lock. You have to know the combination to open it.
Price **50c**
Shipping weight, 3 pounds.

Grand Jewel Toy Safe.

No. 59074 Is the best safe made, back, sides and front made of the best cast metal, nickel plated and highly polished. It is fastened with two, two tumbler combination lock, making it equal to a four tumbler lock, and cannot possibly be opened by any one not having the combination. Size, 4x3¾x5¼ in.
Price, each **75c**
Shipping weight, 4 pounds.

The National Safe.

No. 59075 The picture represents our Toy Savings Bank, made the same shape and general design of the National Cash Register. The keys are movable when struck; they ring a bell and open an aperture or slot that allows the coin to drop in the bank. **There are four keys,** and above the keys are four slots representing different denominations of coin, as follows: 25c, 10c, 5c, 1c. **The Bank is locked with a combination, and can only be opened by the combination, and can not be taken apart without unlocking. Made of solid metal, handsomely nickel plated.** Height, 7¼ inches; width, 5¼ inches. **Shipping weight, 7 pounds.** Price, each **83c**

The Penny Saver.

No. 59076 A perfect registering bank; no key, no combination Each time a cent is dropped into the bank the bell rings and the register indicates. Opens automatically at each 50 cents. The total always in sight. **They are attractive and interesting to children.** The mechanism is made of steel, and will not break or get out of order. **It is highly interesting to children, and for this reason will encourage them to save. Shipping weight, 5 pounds.** Price, each **85c**

The Bear Bank.

No. 59077 You place a coin in proper position on the barrel of the rifle press the lever, and the rifle shoots the coin into the bear. Finished in fancy colors. Size, 10½x7¾x3¼ inches
Price, each . . **85c**
Shipping weight, 6 pounds.

The New Artillery Automatic Bank.

No. 59078 Painted in bright fancy colors Size, 6 inches in height and 8 inches in length. The coin is placed in the cannon or mortar; you push back the hammer and press the thumb piece, which fires the coin into the fort or tower. The arm of the artillery man moves up and down.
Price, each **85c**
Unmailable, shipping weight, 6½ pounds.

The Little Gem Dime Savings Bank.

No. 59079 Locks itself and registers the amount deposited. Opens automatically when $5.00 in dimes have been deposited without use of force; nickel plated, and can be carried conveniently in your vest pocket.
Price per dozen, **$1.00**; each **10c**
If by mail, postage extra, each, 2 cents.

Remember the Maine.

No. 59080 The Battleship Bank. Handsomely nickel plated and enameled in colors. Puzzle combination lock. A handsome mantel ornament; large, strong and durable. Length, 10½ inches
Price, each **85c**
Shipping weight, 64 ounces.

No. 59082 Our 25-cent Range is the best value ever offered, well made and furnished with utensils and length of pipe. Length, 4½ inches; width, 4 inches; height, 3½ inches.
Price, each **25c**
Shipping weight, 2½ pounds.

No. 59084 Perfect working toy range, nickel plated and polished edges; furnished with skillet, stewpot, lifter and length of pipe. Length, 8 inches; width, 4½ inches; height, 4½ inches. A model range and sold by many at 75 cents.
Price, each **50c**
Shipping weight, 4½ pounds.

No. 59085 This is an ideal range, and for style, elegance and goodness is hard to beat; finished in nickel; furnished with skillet, pot, shovel, lifter, and length of pipe; in the back is a hot water receptacle. A perfect model toy stove. Length, 8¾ inches; width, 5 inches; height, 5½ inches. Price, ... **90c**
Shipping weight, 7 pounds.

Triumph Toy Sewing Machine.

No. 59088 A first-class machine that will sew perfectly. It has the latest patent feed motion, a perfect stitch regulator, uses the Willcox & Gibbs self-setting needle which has a short blade and long shank and is not easily broken. On account of the simple devices embodied in its construction it runs lighter and quieter than any machine made. **It is fastened to the table with a clamp furnished with each machine. Elegantly enameled and finished in flower designs. Suitable for the little miss, for the nursery maid, for all kinds of plain family sewing and is adapted largely for kindergarten use.** Each machine is packed in a separate box with an extra needle and clamp, thoroughly tested and adjusted, and is sent out with a sample of sewing done on it, showing it leaves the factory in perfect working order. Height, 7½ inches; width, 6¼ inches. Price, each. **$1.50**
Shipping weight, 23 ounces.

Musical and Spinning Tops.

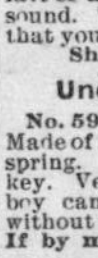

No. 59090 Humming or musical tops with handle, painted in bright colors, changeable tune. Splendid value.
Price, each **10c**
Shipping weight, 9 ounces.
No. 59092 French humming or musical top with handle, very large size, produces a very pretty melody when spinning. Tune changeable. Striped in bright colors. Price, each **20c**
Shipping weight, 16 ounces.
No. 59093 Choral or musical top, painted in bright colors, produces pretty choral changes while spinning. Price, each **20c**
No. 59094 Choral top, similar to above, but larger and handsomer and produces a very loud sound. The best musical top with choral changes that you can buy. Price, each **30c**
Shipping weight, 13 ounces.

Uncle Sam Flag Top.

No. 59096 Uncle Sam Flag Top. Made of hard wood and spins with a spring. Has automatic winding key. Very simple and the smallest boy can wind and spin the top without trouble. Price, each **5c**
If by mail, postage extra, each, 2 cents.

Toy Sad Iron.

No. 59100 The Jewel Toy Sad Iron has a wood handle. The top of iron is bronzed. The body of iron is polished and nickel plated. Packed in pasteboard box with stand.
Price, for iron and stand **10c**
Shipping weight, 10 ounces.

No. 59101 The Baby Sad Iron is a small size of the well known Mrs. Potts pattern, like cut, and has the same artistic finish. Has detachable wood handle. Packed in a pasteboard box with stand.
Price, for iron and stand **15c**
Shipping weight, 18 ounces.
No. 59102 The Lace Sad Iron is a very finely finished sad iron of the Mrs. Potts pattern (see cut 59101). While it is sometimes sold for a toy, **it is a great favorite with the ladies for doing fine work,** such as laces, etc. Has one round end, and **is finely polished and nickel plated.** Has detachable wood handle. **Packed in a pasteboard box with stand.**
Price, for iron and stand **25c**
Shipping weight, 24 ounces.

CHIME BELL TOYS.

The Rough Riders' Chime Toy.

No. 59109 Made of iron, well finished, and is pulled along by a string. As the toy is drawn each revolution of the wheels causes the bell to ring. A very pretty and interesting toy. Price..........50c
Shipping weight, 3 pounds.

Imported Novelty Chime Bell.

No. 59111 Made of white metal, nickel plated; very elegant musical sounding bells. Price, each.........25c
Shipping weight, 8 ounces.

Imported Novelty Chime Bell.

No. 59112 Handsomely constructed toy, nickel plated bell, cushion rubber tires, musical bells. Regular 75-cent toy; will delight and please the children. Price, each..............50c
Shipping weight, 20 ounces.

Toy Passenger Trains.

No. 59115 Toy Passenger Train, Nickel Plated Engine, tender and three coaches, length of train, 20 inches. Price, each..........25c
Shipping weight, 48 ounces.

No. 59116 Passenger Train with locomotive and tender, one freight and one passenger car, similar to above, but large size; enameled in red and black; length of train, 29 inches. Price, each..50c
Unmailable, shipping weight, 5½ pounds.

No. 59117 Passenger Train, consisting of locomotive, tender and two coaches, large size; enameled in red and black; jointed connecting rods on drive wheels. A very strong and handsome toy. Length of train, 40 inches. Price, each.........$1.00
Unmailable, shipping weight, 10 pounds.

Toy Hose Cart and Hook and Ladder.

No. 59120 Hose Cart made of iron, handsomely painted in bright colors with two horses. Length 10¼ inches. Price, each...25c
Shipping weight, 40 ounces.

No. 59121 Hose Cart made of iron, painted in bright, attractive colors, similar to above but much larger in size. Length, 16¼ inches. Price, each..75c
Shipping weight, 56 ounces.

No. 59122 Hook and Ladder, made of iron, painted in bright, attractive colors. Length, 12½ inches.
Price, each..........25c
Shipping weight, 48 ounces.

No. 59123 Hook and Ladder, much larger and handsomer than above, a very strong, interesting and durable toy. Length, 21 inches. Price......75c
Unmailable, shipping weight, 5 pounds.

Toy Ice Wagon.

No. 59124 How would you like to be the ice man? Made of iron, painted in bright colors with two horses and driver. A toy that never fails to please. Length, 16 inches. Price..........80c
Unmailable, shipping weight, 10 pounds.

Standard Toy Scales.

No. 59128 Each one packed in a box with scoop and weights complete. A child finds more real pleasure with one of these toy scales than with many articles costing five times the amount. Price, each..18c
Shipping weight, 1½ pounds.

No. 59129 Toy Scales. Similar to above but finer finished and much larger. Complete in every detail. Shipping weight, 2 pounds. Price......25c

No. 59132 The Canary Bird Whistle. Made of metal. All the pretty notes of the canary can be imitated. Lots of fun for boys and girls. Price, each..........5c
If by mail, postage extra, 3 cents.

No. 59133 The Laughing Camera. A whole passing show. Furnishes more amusement than you would get in a circus. Your friends grotesquely photographed. Stout people look thin and thin people look stout. By getting a focus on passing pedestrians, horses, cars, etc., the most ludicrous pictures are witnessed. The passerby takes on the swinging stride of a grand-daddy longlegs, horses look like giraffes. Price, each..........20c
If by mail, postage extra, 5 cents.

The Climbing Mechanical Monkey.

No. 53134 The Climbing Mechancial Monkey. The greatest novelty of the age. This well known toy is better made than ever. Will climb a string in a lifelike manner, moving arms and legs. Simple and durable. Painted in bright colors.
Price, each..............20c
If by mail, postage each, 8 cents.

No. 59135 The Climbing Mechanical Sailor. A new toy and works in the same manner as the above monkey, moving arms and legs. Made of metal, painted in bright colors. Very interesting at all times.
Price, each..........20c
If by mail, postage extra, each, 8 cents.

Toy Reins.

No. 59141 Toy Reins. Made of good quality webbing, bright, fancy colors, with 3 bells, 50 inches long. Price........10c
If by mail, postage extra, each, 4 cents.

No. 59142 Toy Reins. Made of good quality webbing, one inch wide. Bright, fancy colors. Length, 54 inches. Celluloid front piece, fancy design, and 8 chime bells. This is a particularly good set. Price.......25c
If by mail, postage extra, each, 8 cents.

No. 59144 Toy Reins. Made of fine enameled cloth, 54 inches long, celluloid front piece and 9 chiming bells. This is a very fine set and a bargain at the price. Price..........50c
Shipping weight, 12 ounces.

Wire Jumping Rope.

No. 59145 A toy that always delights the little girls and lots of the boys. Good, healthy recreation and a lot of innocent amusement to be derived from same. Length, 6½, 7 and 7½ feet.
Price, each..........10c
If by mail, postage extra, 7 cents.

Steam Toys.

No. 59147 The Weeden Upright Engine No. 19. A complete steam engine, perfect in all its parts, which are firmly connected together. It is as well and carefully made as the more expensive engines. Richly finished in black, gold and polished brass. Each engine is thoroughly tested, fully warranted and carefully packed in wooden locked corner box, with full directions. Burns alcohol. Each...50c
Shipping weight, 32 ounces.

The Weeden Upright Engine No. 3.

No. 59148 The Weeden Upright Engine No. 3. In construction this engine is simple and sensible. Strong and durable in all its parts. It is made entirely of well tempered polished sheet brass. It has a good water glass, made perfectly tight by means of adjustable nuts, which can be easily tightened or loosened with the little wrench packed in box with each engine. It exhausts steam through the smoke stack, as shown in cut, which no other engine does. The safety valve is lever and ball pattern. Every engine thoroughly tested before packing. Packed securely in wooden lock corner box, with full directions. Burns alcohol. Price, each......75c
Shipping weight, 40 ounces.

The Weeden Horizontal Engine No. 21.

No. 59149 The Weeden Horizontal Engine No. 21. This engine has a highly polished brass boiler, firmly fastened upon substantial base. Finished in colors. The whistle and safety valve are locked on top of boiler, and are made steam tight by means of small rubber washers. If broken these parts can be easily removed and new ones put on. The engine is provided with an extra large balance wheel and nickeled cylinder, running easily and rapidly, and presenting a very fine appearance. Every engine thoroughly tested and warranted. Packed securely in wooden locked corner box, with full directions. Base, 4x6 inches; height, 7½ inches. Burns alcohol. Price, each... 95c
Shipping weight, 36 ounces.

Weeden's Horizontal Engine No. 7.

No. 59150 Weeden's Horizontal Engine No. 7. This engine has a highly polished brass boiler and Russia iron fire box and base. The frame and working parts are also of Russia iron and strongly put together. Every part is finely finished and altogether it is a very substantial and attractive engine. Base, 4¼x5¾ inches. Length of boiler, 4¾ inches. Thoroughly tested and packed in wooden box. Burns alcohol.
Price, each..........$1.35
If by mail, postage extra, 32 cents.

The Weeden Horizontal Engine No. 14.

No. 59151 Has large highly polished brass boiler, trimmed with steam dome whistle and safety valve and connected to steam chest on cylinder by polished brass pipe. The frame case is malleable iron, to which boiler and engine are firmly attached. The cylinder, steam chest and slide rest are cast in one piece and cannot get out of order. Runs rapidly and easily, and is one of the most satisfactory and popular steam toys. Every engine thoroughly tested and packed in wooden box. Burns alcohol. Price, each...$2.35
Shipping weight, 5 pounds.

The Weeden Double Engine No. 18.

No. 59152 Has large polished brass boiler, trimmed with steam dome whistle, safety valve and water gauge. It is connected to the steam chest on cylinder by brass steam pipe. The frame is best malleable iron, to which engine is firmly attached. The cylinder, steam chest and slide rest are cast in one piece and cannot get out of order. The slide eccentric in one connecting rod are all cut from heavy sheet brass and fastened securely together. Runs rapidly and easily. Each engine thoroughly tested and warranted. Packed securely in wooden box, with full directions. Burns alcohol.
Price, each..........$3.50
Unmailable on account of weight.
Shipping weight, 7 pounds.

Weeden's Upright Caloric or Hot Air Engine No. 22.

No. 59154 This is a new engine made this year and is designed to run by the use of hot air entirely. It is nearly all made of brass and decorated in a very attractive manner. The main cylinder and piston are made of accurately drawn brass shells, and the auxiliary cylinder and air pump is also a brass shell and is fitted with air tight plunger. A sheet to protect the parts from being overheated is fastened to the lower end of the main cylinder. No water or steam being used this engine runs indefinitely. Packed in wooden box and fully guaranteed. Shipping weight, 36 ounces. Price, each..........90c

Steam Locomotive and Train.

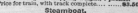

No. 59155 The Weeden Steam Locomotive, Tender and Car is constructed on strictly scientific principles, of the best materials, and has all of its parts properly proportioned and fitted with the nicest accuracy, with track 3¼ feet in diameter made of metal rails and wooden sleepers. This miniature railroad when carefully set up and properly used and well taken care of will prove to be an unfailing source of interest and amusement to old and young. Put up in wooden box with full directions.. Burns alcohol. Unmailable on account of weight. Shipping weight, 7 pounds.
Price for train, with track complete..........$3.50

Steamboat.

No. 59156 This Steamboat has a nicely modeled hull (Torpedo type) with polished brass boiler firmly secured to the thwarts. Steam chest mounted on a nickel frame to which cylinder is adjusted. Length of hull, 15½ inches. Length of boiler, 3¾ inches. The lamp is securely soldered in the bottom of the boat to prevent any sliding about while the boat is in motion. Finely decorated in colors. Burns alcohol. Tested and guaranteed. Shipping weight, 32 ounces.
Price, each..........90c

Malleable Iron Locomotive.

No. 59157 They make good time with clockwork power and are wound up with a key, attractively painted and a toy that is intensely interesting to boys and girls. Length, 8 inches. Price, each.......... 50c
Shipping weight, 3 pounds.

No. 59158 Malleable Iron Locomotive with clock power. Same as above. Length, 10 inches, and much larger throughout. Price, each,....$1.00
Shipping weight, 3¼ pounds.

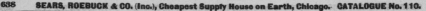

No. 59160 Daisy Printing Press, complete with ink, type, cards, etc; will print forms 2x3 inches.
Price, each, $1.00

No. 59161 The Bonanza Printing Press, complete outfit with ink, type, cards, etc.; will print forms 2¾x3¾ inches; a model press. Price, each.....$1.60

Dry Medical Battery.

No. 59163 A perfect working model of a regular electric battery. You can regulate the power by pulling out the cylinder. It is not only a toy that you can derive much amusement from, but can be used the same as a regular medical battery, to strengthen the nerves. Price, each $1.00
Shipping weight, 6 pounds.

No. 59164 Extra Charged Battery to fit in the above Medical Battery, to replace the battery when used. Price,..........25c

Practical Wash Set.

No. 59165 Wash Set, consists of a wash bench 18 inches long, 10 inches wide and 13 inches high, a twelve inch tub and pail, large wringer, washboard, pulley line outfit and 1 dozen clothespins. The two pulleys, hooks and line are packed in a small box so they cannot get lost. The whole set packed in a large box. **Unmailable on account of weight. Shipping weight, 8 pounds.**
Price 75c

No. 59166 Laundry Outfit similar to above and composed of table, tub, pail, clothes drier, wringer and washboard. All parts to pack inside dimensions of table, 15⅛x8⅛; height, 11¼ inches. **Shipping weight, 64 ounces.** Price, each..........45c

Toy China Tea Sets.

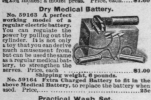

No. 59167 Toy China Tea Set, consists of cups, saucers, teapot, sugar bowl and creamer, about 16 pieces. small 25-cent value packed in paper box.
Per set.......15c
Shipping weight, 10 ounces.

No. 59168 Toy China Tea Set, consisting of decorated plates, cups, saucers, tea pot, creamer, sugar bowl, about 23 pieces. Price, per set..........25c
Shipping weight, 20 ounces.

No. 59169 Toy China Tea Set, consisting of about 17 pieces, decorated plates, cups, saucers, tea pot, creamer and sugar bowl. Larger size, and very interesting for a child. Splendid 75-cent value.
Price, per set..........50c
Shipping weight, 48 ounces.

No. 59170 Toy China Tea Set, consisting of about 25 pieces, finely decorated plates, cups, saucers, tea pot, creamer and sugar bowl. Large size and extra value. Price, per set..........75c
Shipping weight, 56 ounces.

No. 59171 Toy China Tea Set, consisting of about 25 pieces, decorated cups, saucers, plates, tea pot, creamer and sugar bowl. Our larger size set, and suitable for miss up to 14 or 15 years of age. **Unmailable account of weight. Shipping weight, 7 lbs.** Price, per set..........$1.00

No. 59172 Toy China Tea Set. This, our finest set, consists of 23 pieces finely decorated cups, saucers, plates, teapot, creamer, sugar bowl, etc., all larger size and suitable for young miss for an afternoon tea. Equal to any $2.00 value.
Price, per set..........$1.40

Britannia Tea Sets.

No. 59175 Britannia tea set, consisting of about 13 pieces, silver finished teapot, sugar bowl, sugar tongs, creamer plates, cups, etc. Put up in neat pasteboard box. Set..10c
Shipping weight, 7 ounces.

No. 59176 Britannia tea set, consisting of about 17 pieces, silver finished, assortment same as above, but a little larger size. Per set..........20c
Shipping weight, 15 ounces.

No. 59177 Britannia tea set, silver finished, about 17 pieces, and still larger than above. **Shipping weight, 28 ounces.** Per set..........43c

No. 59178 Britannia tea set, consisting of about 17 pieces, silver finished dishes, very handsome filigree design and practical size, assortment about **same as above,** and the largest size we carry. **Shipping weight, 40 ounces.** Price, per set..........75c

Toy Tin Kitchens.

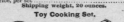

No. 59179 Toy Tin Kitchen consisting of about 18 pieces of kitchen ware. Size 15⅛x7 inches. Always appreciated by the children
Price, per set..........25c
Shipping weight, 20 ounces.

Toy Cooking Set.

No. 59180 Child's Real Toy Cooking Set. The latest novelty and sure to delight the children. This set of toy cooking utensils is made from the best fire clay, and will stand the same amount of heat and wear that the regular large dish will. Consists of 15 pieces, covered meat roaster, covered German coffee pot, covered Boston bean baker, one excelsior crock, and four pudding or gem pans, four pie pans, nicely packed in good pasteboard box. Per set..........50c
Shipping weight, 3 pounds.

No. 59182 Toy Tin Kitchen. A much larger and handsomer set than above, containing about 24 kitchen utensils. Size, 17 x 9 inches.
Per set..45c
Shipping weight 3 pounds.

Harmless Rubber Vacuum Tipped Arrow and Target Pistol.

No. 59183 A Parlor Game. Perfectly harmless and intensely amusing for all ages. Suitable for all seasons of the year. It is not only a game for the boys, as it has been thoroughly tested, and when brought home and hung up in the house it has been found of interest to men, women and children, in fact all members of the family take a lively interest in the game. It has been received with universal favor not only in this country, but throughout entire Europe. It trains the eye and steadies the nerve.
Price for pistol, 1 arrow, target and target holder complete..........55c
Shipping Weight, 16 ounces.

No. 59183½ Extra Vacuum Tipped Arrows for above game. Price, each..........10c

Toy Guns.

Toy guns cannot be sent by mail, on account of length, and liability of breakage.

No. 59185 Toy gun, which shoots a stick, and the best small spring gun for the money to be obtained anywhere. Length of gun, 21¼ inches. **Shipping weight, 12 ounces.** Price 10c

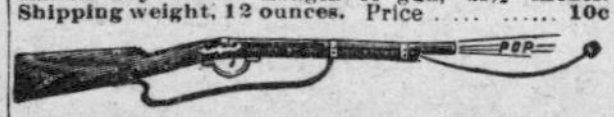

No. 59187 Dangerless Popgun, for shooting corks. A splendid dangerless toy gun for the boy. Length of gun, 26 inches. Price..........20c
Shipping weight, 18 ounces.

No. 59188 Toy Percussion Gun, for shooting paper caps and sticks. A harmless gun and well finished. Length of gun, 26 inches. No bayonet. **Shipping weight, 18 ounces.** Price, each.......... 25c

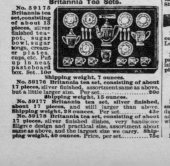

No. 59189 Rubber Ball Popguns, from which small rubber balls may be thrown. There is no danger, no chance of broken windows, especially adapted for indoor amusement, ammunition free with each gun. Length of gun, 31 inches.
Price, each..........50c
Shipping weight, 32 ounces.
Extra Rubber Balls, 12 balls in a box. Per box, 20c

No. 59190 This outfit will certainly please every small boy, being neatly gotten up and attractively arranged on a fancy green glazed card with gold border. The gun is furnished with an elastic spring so arranged that the smallest boy can easily pull back the strap to load it. It will shoot light, hollow wooden projectiles quite a distance without having such a force as to harm anything. Twelve of these in the shape of cartridges are arranged on a belt, together with neatly leather trimmed gun bag.
Price, each..(Shipping weight, 2½ pounds)....75c
Shipping weight, 2½ pounds.

Parachute Gun.

No. 59192 This is a very interesting toy, scientific and instructive. It consists of a parachute painted in gay colors with a handsome gun to shoot it up in the air. A suitable present for a boy or girl and always a source of amusement. Gun, 21 inches long, parachute, 17 inches long.
Price, each..........25c
Shipping weight, 12 ounces.

Snip Snaps.

No. 59193 Snip Snaps or Sling Shot. The boys can have lots of fun with this. Complete with rubber spring, as shown in illustration. **If by mail, postage extra, each, 3 cents,**
Per doz., 75c; each..........7c

No. 59194 Extra Rubbers for the above sling shot. Each.....4c
Per doz..........35c
If by mail, postage extra, per dozen, 2 cents.

The Soldier Camp.

No. 59197 Composed of 30 Soldiers 5 inches high, arranged in 5 companies, each carrying 2 large and 3 small flags, and mounted on an operating base, which, extended to its full length, makes a line 6 feet long. Put together and in a nice labeled box
Price, each (Shipping weight, 2 pounds)......40c

Junior Garden Tool Set.

No. 59200 The material used is of the finest and all the handles are varnished, made of bright steel and nickel plated. Consists of spade, hoe and rake. The latest pattern and a practical set for the boys.
Price per set (Weight, 2 pounds)..........15c
Unmailable, on account of length.

Practical Toy Ice Cream Freezer.

No. 59204 A miniature Peerless Iceland Freezer, an exact model and as well put together as the large Peerless, just as practical in proportion. **Will make ice cream in less than 5 minutes.** All metal parts nickel plated and hoops of brass. Handles finished with two coats of varnish. Size, 6 inches high and 5 inches in diameter. Price, each..........$1.40
Shipping weight, 48 ounces.

No. 59210 Childs' desk, nicely finished in the antique, made from brown ash, handsomely carved, as shown in the cut, furnished with double blackboard, finished with the patent slate surface on which a child can draw with either chalk or slate pencil. Height, 27 inches; width, 21 inches. For shipping, the legs and underwork are taken off and packed closely inside the desk. Price, each..........95c
Shipping weight, 15 pounds.

Slate Surface Blackboards.

Our Blackboards are without question the very best on the market, having a perfect slate surface, and chalk need not necessarily be used—a common slate pencil will work to perfection. The parts are all reversible, and can be used on the other side. Each part is provided with a receptacle for holding the chalk or slate pencil. The frames are nicely molded, and the joints are perfect. **Shipping weight, 32 ounces.**

No. 59212 Size 14x20 inches. Price, each......35c
No. 59213 Size 22¼x30 inches. Price, each.....50c
Shipping weight, 64 ounces.

No. 59214 Is extra quality and finish, and is adapted to school use. Has handsome frame of hardwood, varnished, and has extra large swinging tray for chalk extending across the entire bottom, adjusted to be used for either side of the blackboard. Size, 22¼x30 inches. Price, each..........75c
Unmailable, on account of weight, 10 pounds.

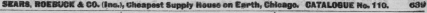

No. 59216 Panorama Blackboard, made of ash handsomely finished in the antique. The Blackboard is reversible—that is, it revolves so that either or both sides can be used. The blackboard is fitted with a panorama arrangement at the top, which revolves, showing different views as copy, including alphabet, musical scale, historical picture views, etc. (map is made of strong cloth—not paper). The blackboard has the best slate surface, on which a slate pencil or chalk may be used. Height, 50 inches; width, 25 inches. Size of blackboard is 15x21¾ inches. **The best ever shown at the money.** Price, each....................**$1.00**
Shipping weight, 10 pounds.

No. 59217 Panorama Desk Blackboard—a combination blackboard and desk. A marvel of convenience and strength. Made from handsomely finished hardwood in the antique. It is fitted with a panorama arrangement at the top, whereby you have only to turn the knob and the map revolves, showing different views for sketching. The map is made of very strong cloth. When the desk is closed the blackboard surface measures 18¼x21⅜ inches, and the extreme height of the blackboard complete is 50 inches. The blackboard is coated with the best patent slate surface, on which a slate pencil or chalk may be used. **A very satisfactory blackboard that will bring much pleasure to the user.** Price, each....................**$1.85**
Unmailable, on account of weight.
Shipping weight, 15 pounds.

Toy Trunks.

No. 59219 Square top, good lock, handles, set up tray.

Size.	Price.
12-inch	.47c
14-inch	.54c
16-inch	.70c

Average shipping weight, 3½ pounds.

Our 70-Cent Saratoga Trunk.

No. 59221 Paper Saratoga. Barrel stave top, good lock, set up tray, with covered bonnet box. 18-inch, 90c; 16-inch 80c; 14-inch 70c
Average shipping weight, 5 pounds.

Crystal Saratoga.

No. 59224 Crystal Saratoga. Fancy metal cover, barrel top, fancy strips, with clamps, bottom rollers, set up tray and covered hat box.
20-inch, $1.05; 18-inch, $1.15; 16-inch..........**$1.00**
Average shipping weight, 9 pounds.

Toy Sweepers.

While these toy sweepers amuse the children they teach them habits of neatness that have an effect in later years. **Help teach the little ones neatness.**

No. 59227 Bissel's Child's Sweeper is 7x4½ inches, having broom action; used on same principle as larger sweeper and useful for taking up light litter. Price, each....................20c
Shipping weight, 20 ounces.

No. 59229 Bissel's Carpet Sweeper, for child. The best medium priced toy carpet sweeper in the world. The case is made of nicely finished selected oak, and the bevels are gracefully rounded, thus giving it a very attractive appearance. Noiseless rubber tired wheels and automatic pans are additional features of merit. It is not so small but that it can be used as a practical little sweeper for taking up light litter from the hearth or carpet. Length of case, 7 inches. Shipping weight, 30 ounces. Price, each 40c

Bissel's Child's Carpet Sweep

No. 59230 Bissel's Little Jewel. The most complete small carpet sweeper ever made. It possesses the practical features of a regular sized Bissel, only they are on a smaller scale. It is nicely finished, has paneled top, pure bristle brush, rubber furniture protector and pans which are automatically dumped by a slight pressure of the finger. Everything about the Little Jewel is strictly first class; length of sweeper, 8 inches.
Shipping weight, 32 ounces. Price, each....60c

Our Doll Beds are made of white enameled reed stock neatly finished, highly polished, and have genuine brass knobs on the posts. Can be trimmed beautifully with colored ribbon, which makes them very ornamental. They are the highest grade goods and delight the little girls. Shipped knocked down, but can be very easily put together.

No. 59231 White Enameled Doll Bed, with extra row of brass ornaments across the top. Size 22 inches long, 17 inches high, and 13 inches wide.
Price, each...(**Shipping weight, 5 pounds**)..**$1.00**

No. 59232 White Enameled Doll Bed, with polished brass knobs of fancy design. Size 18 inches long, 16 inches high, and 10 inches wide.
Price, each...(**Shipping weight, 3 pounds**)....**50c**

Indian Made Doll Cradle.

No. 59236 Indian-Made Trimmed Doll Cradles, something entirely new and must be seen to be appreciated. Handsomely decorated in bright colors, and with mattress complete. Size 16x7 inches. Price, each.......**50c**
Shipping weight, 3 pounds.

Enameled Doll Cradle.

No. 59237 Enameled Doll Cradles, made of strong, durable wood, already set up; no trouble. A very beautiful toy for the children. Can be furnished in pink or blue. Size 17x7 inches.
Price, each..(**Shipping weight, 2½ pounds**)....**25c**

No. 59238 Enameled Wood Doll Cradle, same as above. Size, 20¼x9.
Price, each..(**Shipping weight, 3½ pounds**)...**50c**

Trimmed Wire Doll Bed.

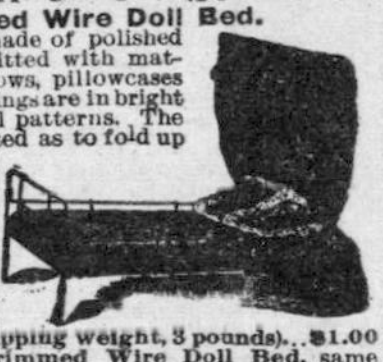

No. 59239 Is made of polished brass wire, fully fitted with mattress coverlet, pillows, pillowcases and canopy. Its fittings are in bright colors and graceful patterns. The bed is so constructed as to fold up and pack in a flat box. It is the best and most elegant doll bed ever placed upon the market. Size, 18 inches long; head, 14½ inches, and width 7 inches. The box is 24x11¼ inches. Price..(**Shipping weight, 3 pounds**)..**$1.00**

No. 59239½ Trimmed Wire Doll Bed, same style as above but larger size, 24 inches long; head, 16¼ inches; width, 8¼ inches. The box and bed, 32x13⅝ inches. This is a nice size and a handsome bed. Price...(**Shipping weight, 4 pounds**)....**$1.40**

No. 59241 Child's folding table, strong, durable and neat. Large enough for the 5 or 6-year old's tea parties, and may be used as a sewing table.
Price, each.........**75c**
Shipping weight, 7 pounds.

No. 59242 Doll furniture, consisting of bed, table and three chairs, finished in fine natural quartered oak, extra well made. Size of bed 6x4½ inches, table top 3x3 inches and 2¾ inches in height. Size of chair 4 inches. Bed has cover made of Swiss, neatly trimmed with lace. **Sure to delight the little ones** Packed in substantial box. Price, per set.........**25c**
Shipping weight, 3 pounds.

Toy China Closet.

No. 59244 A Splendid Toy for the Children, made of fine natural wood, varnished and polished. Two hinge doors, and two drawers below, two glass doors, and three shelves. The closet is 15 inches high, and 12 inches wide. Price..(**Shipping Wt. 4 lbs.**)..**70c**

Child's Bureau.

No. 59251 Child's Bureau, made of highly polished quartered oak. A very attractive and pretty toy, 17½ inches high, 11¼ inches wide, and 6 inches deep, with round mirror, 5x5 inches. Never before sold at this price. Price, each......**50c**
Shipping weight, 8 pounds.

Indian Made Doll Swing.

No. 59255 The best and certainly the handsomest doll swing on the market today. Made by the Indians in all their beautiful shadings and bright artistic colors. Size, 18x9 inches. Price, each..**25c**
Shipping weight, 2¼ pounds.

No. 59256 Indian Made Trimmed Doll Swing, same as above. Size, 23x10 inches. Price, each. **50c**
Shipping weight, 3 pounds.

Indian Made Doll Hammocks.

No. 59258 Original designs, pretty colorings and very beautiful. Simply yet strongly built. Bright colors. Size, 26x7 inches.
Price, each.....**50c**

No. 59260 Indian Made Doll Hammocks, same design as above, but larger. Size 33x9 inches.
Price, each......(**Shipping weight 40 oz.**)......**75c**

No. 59262 Upright Piano, mahogany finish, superior in every respect, a 15-key piano, size 11¼x16x8 inches.
Price, each......**$1.00**
Shipping weight 15 pounds.

No. 59263 Upright Toy Piano, mahogany finish and highly polished, has 18 keys, and you can play a tune on it.
Price, each. (**Shipping weight, 19 pounds**)..**$1.35**

No. 59264 Extra fine upright toy piano, highly polished, having 22 keys, suitable for child to sit up to upon stool or small chair. Size, 13x23¼x9¼ inches.
Price, each..(**Shipping weight, 25 pounds**)..**$1.90**

No. 59267 Upright Toy Piano. This piano is very handsomely finished and is large enough for a child to sit at, has 22 keys, splendid design, and a reliable instrument that will give satisfaction. Size, 23x24x11 inches, each piano packed in a wooden case ready for shipment.
Price, each..(**Shipping weight, 35 pounds**)..**$5.00**

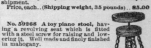

No. 59268 A toy piano stool, having a revolving seat which is fitted with a steel screw for raising and lowering it. Well made and finely finished in mahogany.

Price, each.................... .....**50c**

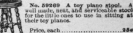

No. 59269 A toy piano stool. A well made, neat, and serviceable stool for the little ones to use in sitting at their toy pianos.

Price, each....................**25c**

Toy Xylophones.

No. 59270 Xylophone. Made of the best seasoned maple wood, 8 notes, clear sounding. Price......**50c**
Shipping weight, 2½ lbs.

No. 59271 Xylophone. Made of fine maple wood, same style as above, but having 15 bars. A practical and sweet sounding instrument, Price, each..(**Shipping wt., 4 lbs**)..**75c**

Our $1.00 Toy Phonoharp.

No. 59275 Phonoharp. Not merely a toy, but a musical instrument, having 15 strings and 3 bars, by the use of which chords are produced to harmonize with sounds obtained by picking the strings as on a common zither. Sheet music with each instrument which can readily be played with very little practice. Price, each...**$1.00**
Shipping weight, 6 pounds.

Toy Phonoharp.

No. 59276 This High Grade Phonoharp has 17 strings, made of the very best materials, only the best piano wire being used, handsomely finished by the best workmen. This harp has a considerable range of music, the tone is deep, very sweet, and is a practical instrument. Price, each..............**$1.75**
Shipping weight, 7 pounds.

Toy Zither.

No. 59277 An attractive Toy Musical Instrument on which the chords may be learned with ease; both instructive and interesting. This zither is handsomely finished, and will be highly appreciated and enjoyed by young people of all ages. They are tuned to concert pitch. Size, 18x9 inches, plain shape, but 5 strings.
Price, each.. ....**50c**
Shipping weight, 3 pounds.

Our 25 and 50-cent Metallophones.

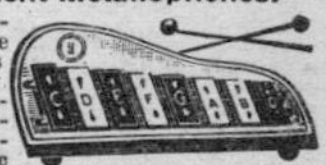

No. 59278 Metallophones. Made of maple wood, with bronzed keys 8 notes and sticks to play Each packed in pasteboard box. New instruction book with each instrument. Each.....**25c**
Shipping weight, 28 ounces.

No. 59280 A Fifteen Note Metallophone, with bronzed keys, clear sounding and an excellent instrument. Each packed in pasteboard box, with new instruction book. Price, each....................**50c**
Shipping weight, 2 pounds.

Toy Violins.

No. 59283 Toy Violin, packed in a neat box, with folding cover and handle for carrying, with bow complete; 20 inches long. Price, each....................**$1.00**
Shipping weight, 2 pounds.

No. 59284 Toy Violin, about 16 inches long, packed one in a box, with bow. Shipping weight, 20 oz. Price, each.......**25c**

No. 59285 Toy Violin, larger size than above, complete with bow. Price, each, **50c**
Shipping weight, 25 ounces.

Comic Vocophones.

No. 59285½ The Vocophones are an imitation in the shape of the different musical instruments used by bands, orchestras, etc. They are made of a composition of paper fabric, wood, etc., giving them extreme lightness combined with durability. As will be seen by the different illustrations, they resemble very much in size and shape the different instruments used by brass bands. The name vocophone is derived from the fact that the tunes they bring forth are produced by the human voice by singing into them, and any person is able to play them without the least difficulty. They are a never ending source of amusement and may be used in burlesque acts, masquerades, serenades, wed. n gs, picnics or surprise parties. They are also an excellent accompaniment for the piano. Have a band of your own. A set consists of 8 pieces, as shown in the illustration, safely packed in wooden case. Price, per set..............................$4.50
Shipping weight, 20 pounds.

Small Music Box.

No. 59286 Plays one tune by turning crank at top. Has 18 teeth, well adjusted and accurate in construction. Round nickel case with fancy chromo top. Our special price 50c
Shipping weight, 15 ounces.

No. 59287 Music Box, plays two tunes by turning crank or top; has 28 teeth, all parts finely adjusted and accurate, round nickel case with fancy chromo top. Our special price..................$1.00

Music Box.

No. 59288 This elegant Music Box winds up with key and runs automatically by spring movement. The box is made of natural maple wood with fancy lithographed chromo top and glass cover over cylinder; has 18 teeth; 1½-inch cylinder; plays two airs and tunes are self changing. Size, 4½x3½x2¼ inches. Price, each..... $2.35
Shipping weight, 22 ounces.

Toy Drums.

No. 59289 Toy Drum. The latest improved pattern, metal shell, finished in red, blue and brass, 7 inches in diameter, with sticks. Price. 25c
Shipping weight, 20 ounces.

No. 59290 Toy Drum. One of the very best styles, with deep and artistic embossing in fancy design. Cord, hook and sling with each drum. 9 inches in diameter. Shipping weight, 28 ounces. Price..50c

No. 59292 Toy Drum. Larger and more durable than above; 11 inches in diameter. Shipping weight, 43 ounces. Price..........................75c

No. 59294 Flat Style Toy Drum. Metal shell, embossed pattern in fancy designs, 8 inch head with hook and belt. Shipping weight, 48 oz. Price...........50c

No. 59296 Flat Style Drum. Same style as above, with 10 inch head. Shipping weight, 43 oz. Price............75c

No. 59297 Flat Style Drum. Same style as above, with 12 inch head. A good big drum for the money. Shipping weight, 48 ounces. Price...........$1.00

Our Finest Kid Body Dolls.

They have double riveted patent joint hip and knees, fine American beauty bisque head, flowing curls, moving eyes and fitted with shoes and stockings. Will sit up or can be adjusted in different positions. The best quality kid and as pretty and perfect a doll as you could wish for. Come in following sizes:

No. 59299 Kid body doll, riveted joints, etc., as described above. Length, 15½ inches. Price, each..........................50c
Shipping weight, 1 pound.

No. 59300½ Kid body doll, riveted joints, etc., as described above. Length, 17½ inches. Price, each..........................75c
Shipping weight, 1¼ pounds.

No. 59301½ Kid body doll, riveted joints, etc., as described above. Length, 19 inches. Price, each. 95c
Shipping weight, 1¾ pounds.

No. 59302½ Kid body doll, riveted joints, etc., as described above. Length, 21 inches. Price, each..........$1.25
Shipping weight, 2 pounds.

No. 59303½ Kid body doll, riveted joints, etc., as described above. Length, 23¼ inches. Price, each $1.75
Shipping weight, 2¾ pounds.

No. 59304 Kid body doll, riveted joints, etc., as described above. Length, 26 inches. Price, each.............................. $2.45
Shipping weight, 4 pounds.

Best Kid Body Dolls.

Biggest Sizes for Least Money.

No. 59305 Kid body doll, straight body, bisque head, with pasted wig. Length, 11¼ inches. Is as good a doll as is usually sold for 25 cents. Price, each..15c
Shipping weight, 14 ounces.

No. 59306 Kid doll, double jointed body, bisque head with flowing curls, steady eyes. Length, 14 inches. Best doll ever sold at the price. Shipping weight, 1¼ pounds. Price, each..25c

No. 59307 Kid doll, double jointed and fat body, bisque head, flowing curls and steady eyes. Length, 17 inches. Splendid value. Shipping weight, 2 pounds. Price, each....50c

No. 59308 Kid doll, double jointed and fat body, bisque head, flowing curls and steady eyes Length, 19 inches. Regular $1.00 value. Shipping weight, 3 pounds. Price, each.. 70c

No. 59309 Kid doll, double jointed body, bisque head, sewed curls, steady eyes. Length 20¾ inches. The greatest value for the price. Shipping weight, 6 pounds. Price, each....95c

Kid Body Dolls with Moving Eyes.

We offer this season exceptional values. We are sure that you will be more than satisfied after receiving same.

No. 59312 Kid Body Dolls, double jointed body, bisque head, flowing curls and moving eyes, length, 17 inches. Shipping weight, 3 lbs. Price, each. 50c

No. 59313 Kid Body Dolls, double jointed body, bisque head, with sewed curls and moving eyes, length, 19 inches. Price, each.............................75c
Shipping weight, 6 pounds.

No. 59314 A Kid Body Doll, double jointed body, bisque head with a full wig, moving eyes, length, 20¾ inches. Shipping w't, 6 lbs. Price, each, $1.00

No. 59315 Kid Body Doll, double jointed body, bisque head, with full wig and moving eyes, length, 22 inches, like many $2.00 dolls sold elsewhere. Price, each...$1.25

No. 59316½ Kid Doll with cork body, double jointed, bisque head and full flowing wig, moving eyes. This high grade kid doll we offer at a very special price, length 23 inches. Price, each....$1.50

No. 59317½ Kid Doll with cork body, double jointed, bisque head, with full flowing wig and moving eyes. This is a very large and handsome doll, 24 inches long. Price, each. $1.95

Dressed Dolls.

Exceptionally pretty; stylishly dressed; better values for less money than you ever bought them for before.

No. 59318 Dressed Doll, Bisque head and flowing hair, steady eyes, jointed body, pretty costume, length, 12 inches. Shipping weight, 28 ounces. Price......................25c

No. 59319 Dressed Doll, jointed body, steady eyes, bisque head, flowing hair, length, 13½ inches, pretty costume and hat. Excellent value. Shipping weight, 36 ounces. Price.......................50c

No. 59320 Stylish Dressed Doll, similar to above, but larger body, steady eye and prettier costume, regular $1.00 value, 15 inches long. Shipping w't, 42 oz. Price....75c

No. 59321 Handsomely Dressed Doll, Bisque head, flowing curls, jointed body and moving eyes, new and pretty costumes, length, 16 inches. Best value ever offered at the price. Shipping weight, 42 ounces. Price 95c

No. 59321½ Handsomely Dressed Doll, Bisque head, flowing curls, jointed body and moving eyes. A very tastefully gotten-up costume, and the highest grade doll that we sell. Length, 17½ inches. Price...$1.50

No. 59322 Infants in long white dresses. Dress and hood embroidered and lace trimmed. Bisque heads with curls, stationary eyes. Something new and pretty. Length, without dress, 8½ inches. Price, each.............25c
Shipping weight, 13 ounces.

Rag Dolls—The American Maid.

Indestructible dolls, something like our grandmother used to make for the baby; serviceable, well designed and planned in every respect. In three sizes.

No. 59323 American Maid Rag Doll. 11¼ inches high. Price.......25c

No. 59324 American Maid Rag Doll. 16 inches high. Price, 50c

No. 59324½ American Maid Rag Doll. 17¼ inches high. Price..95c

No. 59325 Fine kid doll bodies, extra quality kid full stout bodies, shoes and stockings. We are able to quote much lower prices than ever before made.

Style	Length inches	Inches across shoulders	Weight, oz.	Price, each
1	10	3	10	20c
2	12	3½	13	30c
3	13½	4	15	35c
4	16	4½	20	45c
5	19	5½	24	65c
6	23	6	45	95c

Minerva Indestructible Metal Doll Heads.

No. 59327 These doll heads are imported from Germany, they combine the durability of sheet metal and the beauty of bisque, are light in weight, washable, and will not chip; will stand any reasonable wear. Small children cannot injure them, larger ones love them for their unequaled beauty. The eyes are clear and tender, are flexible at the bust, and are fitted with sewing holes, making it easy to adjust and fasten them to body. Come in sizes as follows:

Style	Height inches	Inches across shoulders	Postage extra	Price each
2	3¼	2⅝	3c	25c
3	3⅝	3	4c	30c
4	4	3⅜	4c	35c
5	4½	3⅝	4c	45c
6	5	4	5c	55c
7	5¾	4¼	6c	75c
8	6¼	4¾	7c	90c

Nos. 7 and 8 Minerva Heads have open mouth and showing teeth.

Sewed Wig, Moving Eyes, Metal Doll Heads.

No. 59328 Minerva Indestructible Doll Heads, with moving glass eyes and sewed wig, made of metal same as above; a very beautiful and indestructible head.

Style	Height inches	Inches across shoulders	Postage extra	Price, each
1	3⅝	3	4c	$0.50
3	4⅝	3⅝	5c	.75
5	5¾	4¼	7c	1.25
7	6¼	4¾	8c	1.50

Bisque Doll Heads.

No. 59329 First quality bisque doll heads, the faces are especially beautiful, showing teeth, have stationary eyes, curly flowing wigs, either blondes or brunettes, and full model bust. Sizes:

Style	Height, inches	Inches across shoulders	Shipping weight	Price, each
1	3¾	3	9 oz.	15c
2	4	3½	12 oz.	20c
3	4¾	4	15 oz.	30c
4	5	4½	22 oz.	45c
5	6	5½	25 oz.	55c
6	7	6	30 oz.	80c

Bisque Doll Heads.

No. 59331 Moving Eyes. These pretty Doll Heads have flowing curly wigs same as above, but with the moving eyes, full bust, very handsome.

Style	Height inches	Inches across shoulders	Shipping weight	Price each
1	3¾	3	12 oz.	20c
2	4	3½	15 oz.	25c
3	4¾	4	18 oz.	35c
4	5	4½	21 oz.	50c
5	6	5½	24 oz.	65c
6	7	6	28 oz.	90c

Dressed Sailor Dolls. Boys or Girls.

No 59332 Doll, bisque head, flowing hair, solid eyes, dressed to represent a girl in sailor costume. A very pretty doll. Length, 13 inches. Price, each........ ....50c
Shipping weight, 20 ounces.

No. 59333 Sailor Girl Doll, similar to above, length, 11 inches and smaller body. Price, each 25c
Shipping weight, 15 ounces.

Sailor Boy Dolls.

No. 59334 Sailor Boy Doll dressed to represent a boy in sailor costume, companion doll to sailor girl. Length, 13 inches. Price, each.............................50c
Shipping weight, 20 ounces.

No. 59335 Sailor Boy Doll, similar to above. Length, 11 inches. Price, each.............................25c
Shipping weight, 15 ounces.

Musical Gray Rubber Dolls, Plain.

No. 59336 Something the children can't break and excellent values. Large bodies.

Size 10, length 7 inches. Each, $0.25
Size 20, length 9 inches. Each, .50
Size 30, length 10½ inches. Each, .75
Size 40, length 11¾ inches. Each, 1.00

The size of body increases proportionately to the length.

Allow extra, if by mail, 4c, 6c, 8c and 10c.

No. 59337 Musical Gray Rubber Dolls, with knitted worsted dress and hat. Very desirable doll for small children. The length measurement includes the knitted hat.

Size 01, length 8 inches. Each...25
Size 02, length 10¼ inches. Each...50c
Size 03, length 11¼ inches. Each...70c
Size 04 length 12¼ inches. Each...95c

Allow extra if by mail, 4c, 6c, 8c and 10c.

Rubber Snakes.

Made of gray rubber and fancy decorated to imitate the real. You can have more fun than a bushel of monkeys.

No. 59338 Rubber Snake, 14 inches long. **If by mail, postage extra, 4 cents.** Price, each.......19c

No. 59338½ Rubber Snake, 19 inches long. **If by mail, postage extra, 5 cents.** Price, each.......35c

Fairy Wardrobe.

No. 59339 Teaches little girls how to cut and fit the garments for their dolls. They become their own dressmakers. The cloth to make garments printed in fast colors, with plain directions to fit almost any sized doll, but especially dolls from 14 to 16 inches long, so simple in style that any child can cut and finish the garments. Each set complete in a box. Price, per set....25c

Enamel Reed Doll Perambulator.

No. 58340 Enamel Reed Doll Perambulator. The body is 24 inches long, shellacked, with colored knobs, fancy drop upholstering with ruffled edge, and parasol with ruffled edge to match. Long handle with C springs, 10x12 inches, double spoke iron wheels and iron axle, enameled in pink or pea green. Price, each..$2.75
Shipping weight, 23 pounds.

Doll Reed Go-Cart.

No. 59341 Doll Reed Go-Cart, trimmed with bright colored spindles, 6x10 inches, tinned iron wheels, cretonne mat, trimmed with gimp, and very serviceable. A pretty go-cart at a very low price.
Price, each...............$1.35
Shipping weight, 10 pounds.

Doll Enamel Reed Go-Cart.

No. 59342 Doll Enamel Reed Go-Cart. This is the very finest doll cart we sell. Has a heavy roll body, enameled in assorted colors and gilt, long handle, with C springs; 12-inch double spoke iron wheels in front on iron axle; velour upholstered drop seat. Equal to many $5.00 go-carts sold elsewhere. Price, each. $3 50
Shipping weight, 22 pounds.

Frost's Building Blocks.

No. 58342½ The feature of Frost's Building Blocks is an ingenious system of short wooden hooks upon each block which so fit into the hole of adjacent blocks as to lock firmly. By this means all the principles of masonry are preserved, and bridges, archways, churches, etc., may be built as never before. A book of description accompanies each set. Price...........50c

No. 59357 Fine White Building Blocks, put up in nice wagon box on wheels. The blocks are nicely polished, smooth finish, hard wood. Size of box, 6x9¼ inches.
Price.........25c

No. 59358 Fine White Building Blocks, polished, smooth finish hard wood. Same style as above but much larger. Size, 8¾x15 inches. Price.....50c

No. 59344 Alphabet Blocks, 16 pieces, made of natural wood, with embossed ends, splendid value.
Price, each..............................10c
Shipping weight, 9 ounces.

No. 59345 Alphabet Blocks, consisting of 35 pieces, made of natural wood, with embossed ends, 1¼-inch cubes, giving numerous illustrations as well as all the letters and numerals. Price 20c
Shipping weight, 30 ounces.

No. 59346 Alphabet Blocks, consisting of 16 pieces, 1½-inch cubes, made of natural wood, painted and varnished in colors, previously illustrated, also alphabet and numerals. These blocks are waterproof. **Shipping weight, 34 ounces.** Price, each..25c

No. 59347 Alphabet Blocks, consisting of 20 pieces, made of natural wood, embossed ends, and printed in colors, numerous illustrations, and impressions of each letter and the numerals, packed in wood frame box with fine label. Price, each......40c
Shipping weight, 26 ounces.

No. 59348 Mother Goose Illustrated Blocks, 2½ inch cubes, consisting of 20 pieces. The Mother Goose illustrations and rhymes on blocks with alphabet, complete. Painted, varnished and waterproof. In wood frame box with highly illustrated label. **Shipping weight, 64 ounces.** Price, each........... 75c

No. 59350 Fine White Building Blocks in wagon box 7x4½ inches with real wheels. 36 smooth finished hardwood blocks. Price, each.....................10c

No. 59351 Fine Decorated Building Blocks in wagon box 10x5¼x1¾ inches, with real wheels. 25 embossed whitewood blocks. Price, each........25c

Kite Flying Has Become a Craze.

No. 59363 Horsman's Box Kite. The naval Blue Hill box kite. A sensible and practical pastime for boys, and it pleases the men also. Anyone can fly it and a great deal of amusement can be got out of the sport. A team of two or more can be sent up and will support heavy weights. They are built on scientific principles. (Kite flying is becoming a craze.) Size 30x14x14. It is folded in a small roll and can be mailed. Any child can set it up and fly it. Shipping weight, 1 pound.
Price, per dozen, $2.00; each.......................20c

No. 59364 Blue Hill Box Kite No. 50. This kite has more square inches of surface than the original $1 kites first placed upon the market in 1897. The Blue Hill box kite is the invention of H. H. Clayton, general observer at the Blue Hill observatory near Boston, and is used for sending up recording instruments in making observations. Kites of this kind have attained a height of two miles. Anybody can fly the Blue Hill box kite which goes straight up from the hand like a bird, will fly in a moderate breeze and yet no wind short of a gale is too strong for it. Size, 30x20x10 inches; width of bands 7¾ inches. Shipping weight, 48 ounces.
Price, each......................................60c

No. 59365 Horsman's Blue Hill Box Kite No. 100. This is an improved style and has proved a grand success. Similar to the above No. 50 Blue Hill kite but larger. Size 36x24x10 inches; width of bands 11¾ inches. It does not dive but flies like a bird. Shipping weight, 48 ounces.
Price, each......................................$1.00

No. 59366 Horsman's Blue Hill Kite No. 1. A scientific marvel, a recent and most remarkable achievement in the kite craft. Is constructed to **faithfully represent a full rigged racing sloop,** with jib and mainsail and globe topsail set. The sails are so ingeniously constructed in catching the wind they drive the ship upwards. The kite has great buoyancy and sails on the wind as if riding the waves. Will rise in a very moderate breeze. A very fascinating kite for young and old. Stands 4 feet high. Any child can fly it. Shipping weight, 64 oz.
Price, each $1.75

No. 59367 No. X Fine flax kite line, 300 feet on a spool, for naval kites. Shipping weight, 4 ounces.
Price, per dozen, $1.05; per spool.................10c

No. 59368 No. 11 Flax kite line suitable for flying No. 50 and No. 100 box kites and No. 1. Shipped in one quarter pound balls. Length 400 feet. Shipping weight, 9 ounces. **Price, per ball** $0.22
Price, per dozen 2.40

No. 59369 No. 12 Flax kite line suitable for flying No. 50 and No. 100 box kites and No. 1. Shipped in one-half pound balls. Length 800 feet. Shipping weight 10 oz. Price, per dozen, $4.50; per ball..40c

No. 59370 No. 24 Flax kite line suitable for flying No. 100 box kites in a very strong wind. One-half pound balls, length 400 feet. Shipping weight, 10 oz.
Price, per dozen, $6.00; per ball...................60c

No. 59371 No. 18 Flax line, ½-pound balls, 600 feet to fly No. 100 box kites. Ship kite and Eddy kite.
Price, per dozen, $5.50; per ball...................50c

No. 59372 The Eddy Kite. The Tailless Kite has won not only a national but a world-wide reputation. **The Eddy Kite will fly in a very moderate wind,** and because of its exceedingly light pull is especially suitable for small boys. The Eddy Kite folds compactly into a cloth bag like a fishing rod and is very little larger. Size, 6 feet in height when opened out. Price, each..........................$1.65
Not mailable.

Brower's Building Blocks.

No. 59356 A first-class building block at popular prices which supplies a long-felt want. With Brower's blocks a complete structure may be erected with floors to the rooms and roof to the buildings. They are well finished and in attractive colors, in a handsome box with lithograph label.
Price, per set............45c

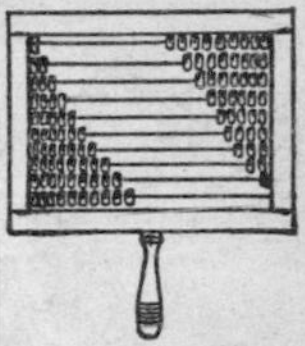

Numeral Frames.

No. 59359 For teaching children to count, teaching the multiplication table, etc. 144 balls, with hardwood frame, 12 colored balls to each wire.
Price..................35c

If by mail, postage extra, 15 cents.

Latest Novelty, Croaking Frog.

No. 59373 By pressing the little rubber bulb, the frog is made to hop and at the same time produce a croaking sound, which is a very correct imitation of the real frog. Bound to be a source of great amusement to the children and grown folks as well, **If by mail, postage extra, 6 cents.** Each.......................25c

Jumping Rabbit.

No. 59374 This interesting toy is worked on the same principle as the frog, by pressing the rubber bulb. It is covered with hair to imitate the rabbit exactly, and its ears move every time it jumps. Entirely new and novel.
Price, each........... 35c
If by mail, postage extra, 6 cents.

Stuffed Felt Covered Rabbit.

No. 59375 Cannot break or get out of order, just the thing for the baby to play with.
Price, each..... .....25c
If by mail, postage extra, 7 cents.

Rattles.

No. 59380 Rattle and Whistle for the baby. Price, each.............3c
Shipping weight, 4 ounces.

Celluloid Baby Rattles and Rings.

No. 59381 Celluloid Rattles, with teething ring, comes in assorted colors (ring pure white). **Shipping weight, 5 ounces.** Per dozen, $2.70; each.......25c

The Rattle Pacifier for 10 Cents.

No. 59382 The Rattle Pacifier, the best rattle, teething ring and plaything ever invented for the babies. It has rubber nipple, bone shields, teething ring and bells. **Made good and strong. If by mail, postage extra, each, 5 cents.** Per dozen, $1.00; each. 10c

No. 59383 Celluloid Rattles (with whistle), 6 inches long, comes in very pretty assorted colors. **If by mail, postage extra, each, 5 cents.** Per dozen, $2.70; each, 25c

Celluloid Teething Rings.

No. 59384 Celluloid Teething Ring, pure white. Far superior to rubber.
1 set of 3 rings.....................................13c
If by mail, postage extra, 2 cents.

Teething Rings.

No. 59385 Rubber Teething Rings, best white rubber. Per dozen, 30c; each.............................3c
If by mail, postage extra, each, 1 cent.

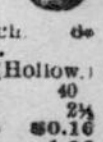

No. 59390 Double Soap Bubble Pipe. An interesting and healthy toy to exercise the lungs. Blows a bubble within a bubble. The only one of its kind. Makes a very strong bubble and furnishes no end of amusement. Price, each 6c
If by mail, postage extra, 4 cents.

No. 59395 White Rubber Bat Balls. (Hollow.)

Size	10	20	30	40
Diameter in inches	1⅝	1⅞	2⅛	2⅜
Each	$0.04	$0.06	$0.08	$0.16
Per dozen	.40	.60	.85	1.06
Weight, ounces	2	3	3	4

No. 59398 White Inflated Rubber Balls.

Size	105	115	130	145	165
Diameter in inches	1⅝	1⅞	2½	3	4
Each	05c	07c	10c	.15	.25
Per dozen	48c	70c	95c	$1.60	$2.50

Hair Switches

JUST AS ADVERTISED.

HUMAN HAIR SWITCHES AT 65 CENTS TO $3.25.

AT 65 CENTS AND UPWARDS WE ARE OFFERING HUMAN HAIR SWITCHES, THE EQUAL OF THOSE THAT RETAIL IN THE BEST HAIR STORES IN ALL LARGE CITIES AT THREE TO FOUR TIMES OUR PRICE.

HOW WE CAN MAKE THE PRICE SO LOW. Our Hair Goods Department is one of the largest in this country. We import all hair from Europe in immense quantities. It is bought for cash and we make it up in the best possible manner in the very latest styles, naming a price to you based on the actual cost to produce with but our one small percentage of profit added.

If you order a hair switch from us and you do not find it equal to anything you could buy elsewhere at three times the price, we ask you to return it to us and we will cheerfully refund your money.

The enormous profit that has heretofore been charged for hair goods has made it impossible for many to own a nice switch, but on our basis of one small profit above the actual cost to produce in quantities, a price which comes within the reach of all, and on this one small profit plan we have established a trade in this line which excels in volume of business any other five houses in America combined.

We guarantee every switch and every article from this department. If you buy a hair switch or any article from our hair goods department and you do not find it exactly as represented and perfectly satisfactory in every way, you can return it to us at our expense and we will cheerfully refund your money.

HOW TO ORDER. Enclose the necessary amount with your order, enclose 5 cents extra to pay postage, send us a good size sample of hair, cut as close to the roots as possible so we can make a perfect match, and we will send you the switch you select by mail, postage paid. We will guarantee it to match perfectly and be in every way satisfactory or we will immediately refund your money.

Every switch is made in three braids. All are strictly high grade, all are guaranteed, and quality considered, the greatest value ever offered by us or any other house.

The illustrations shown on this page will give you some idea of the style of switches we make, the way they are made, and what you can expect in ordering from us.

WHAT WE RECOMMEND. While our 65 and 90-cent switches are wonders in value and the equal of switches that retail at $1.50 to $3.00, in view of the extremely low prices we are making, we especially recommend our 2 and 3-ounce 22-inch switch at $1.25 and $1.50.

Our $3.25 switch is a special leader, the finest switch we make. It is made from carefully selected hair. This switch weighs 3¼ ounces, is 26 inches long, is a handsomer, better made and more stylish switch than you will be likely to get from your dealer at home, even at $5.00 to $10.00 in price. We urge you by all means to select one of our better switches, and especially our leader, our 3¼ ounce, $3.25 switch.

As switches are made to your order, please allow three to five days' time, but it will send sooner if possible.

NOTE OUR FOLLOWING SPECIAL PRICES:

No. 61239 Prices for Ordinary Shades of Hair Switches:

Weight, 2	ounce; length, 20 inches; price, each		$0.65
Weight, 2	ounce; length, 20 inches; price, each		.90
Weight, 2	ounce; length, 22 inches; price, each		1.25
Weight, 3	ounce; length, 22 inches; price, each		1.50
Weight, 3	ounce; length, 24 inches; price, each		2.25
Weight, 3¼	ounce; length, 26 inches; price, each		3.25

The above 65-cent switch is long stem. All other switches are short stem. We advise you to buy the short stem switch and especially those quoted at $1.25 and upwards.

No. 61241 Gray, Red or Blonde Hair Switches are extra in price. They are made of a fine quality of hair, short stem, and finest workmanship.

Weight, 2	ounce; length, 18 inches; price, each		$1.75
Weight, 2¼	ounce; length, 22 inches; price, each		2.50
Weight, 3	ounce; length, 23 inches; price, each		3.90
Weight, 3	ounce; length, 25 inches; price, each		5.45

NOTE—We do not guarantee switches not to fade, as all hair goods will fade more or less; but we will exchange or take back hair goods that are not satisfactory. No oil should be used on switches or hair goods, as it will in time make the hair much lighter.

DO NOT FAIL TO ENCLOSE 5 CENTS EXTRA TO PAY POSTAGE. The 5 cents covers all the postage, the switch will then be sent to you by mail postpaid and if not found a perfect match. If not satisfactory in every way, you can return it to us at our expense and we will cheerfully refund your money.

ALLOW 3 TO 5 DAYS TO FILL ORDERS FOR HAIR SWITCHES.

WAVES, BANGS and WIGS.

All Wigs, Toupees, Waves, etc., being made to order, we ask three to four days' time in filling your order, and we require cash in full with order, guaranteeing satisfaction or refund of money.

BE SURE AND SEND A GOOD SIZED SAMPLE OF HAIR.

No. 61215 Melba Bang. Made of the best quality naturally curly hair, with vegetable lace parting, most suitable for youthful face and a very popular style of hair dressing. If by mail, postage extra, each, 5 cents. Price............$1.50
Gray and blonde color, each............ 2.50

Parisian Bang.

No. 61216 Parisian Bang. Ladies who do not require large, heavy front, will find this a little gem; light and fluffy, ventilated foundation.
Each..............$1.35
Gray and blonde hair, each............$2.00
If by mail, postage extra, each, 5 cents.

Alice Wave.

No. 61218 Alice Wave, invisible hair lace; foundation natural, curly hair; 3-inch part, 12 inches from side to side. Each..........................$3.25
Gray and blonde hair, each............ 4.50
If by mail, postage extra, each, 6 cents.

The Pompadour.

No. 61219 The Pompadour. This style, unlike the old style pompadour, is very light in weight. The soft wavy hair is combed over one's own bald face in which small rolls of crepe hair are placed to produce a puffy effect on sides and top. Price, each...............$3.50
Gray and blonde hair, each............ 5.00
If by mail, postage extra, each, 6 cents.

The Patent Pompadour.

No. 61219½ The Patent Pompadour for simplicity, elegance and style is far superior to anything ever shown. It sits right on, is as dainty as a feminine heart could desire; it reduces the fluffy fullness now so much in vogue and possesses none of the disagreeable qualities of the ordinary roll or pad. It is made on twisted wire, of the best long curly hair and weighs only half an ounce. Can be worn with just the ends concealed under the lady's own hair, or may be used in place of the rolls and the wavy ends coiled in with the natural hair. Send sample of hair. Price, each..............$1.50

The Eugenia Wave.

No. 61221 The Eugenia Wave. This is a new and very becoming wave for middle aged and elderly ladies, made of the best quality natural curly French hair; easily dressed and cared for. 3½-inch parting.
Price, each...........$4.00
Gray and blonde hair, each............$6.00
If by mail, postage extra, each, 8 cents.

Ladies' Wigs—Short Hair.

Send measurement of head.

These wigs are all made of fine selected hair on ventilated open mesh foundation. Absolutely perfect in fit, having that graceful and natural appearance.
No. 61220 Ladies' Curly Dress Wig, made of natural short hair with or without part, mounted on fine open mesh cotton foundation.
Each............$10.00
Gray or blonde hair, each............$15.00

Short Curly Wig.
If by mail, postage extra, each, 8 cents.
No. 61222 Ladies' Wig. Same as above but mounted on silk foundation. Each............$12.00
Gray or blonde hair, each............ 18.00
If by mail, postage extra, each, 8 cents.

Ladies' Wigs—Long Hair.

Can be arranged in many different ways.
No. 61224 Made of the best selected hair on silk foundation, 18-inch hair.
Each..........................$15.00
If by mail, postage extra, each, 10 cents.
No. 61225 Made same as above on silk foundation, 24-inch hair.
Each..........................$18.00
If by mail, postage extra, each, 10 cents.
The above prices are for ordinary shades hair. Red, Blonde and Gray Hair cost 50 per cent more, which please add when you send order. Be sure and send sample of hair. Send measurement of head.

Men's Toupees.

To measure for a Toupee or top piece, cut a piece of paper the exact size and shape of the bald spot, mark the crown and parting, enclose a lock of hair, and state if hair is to be straight or curly.
No. 61228 Men's Toupee, weft foundation. Each, (if by mail, postage extra, each, 8c.)... $5.50
No. 61230 Men's Toupee, ventilated foundation. Each, (if by mail, postage extra, each, 8c.)...$10.00
Red, Blonde and Gray Hair cost extra. Allow one-half more than above prices.
Remember, we guarantee a perfect fit and match if you follow instructions, or your money back.

How to Measure a Wig.

State style of wig, kind of parting, whether for right or left side; price and description as per list; to insure a good fit mention number of inches. Send sample of hair. Inches.
No. 1 Circumference of head.....
No. 2 Forehead to nape of neck....
No. 3 Ear to ear, across forehead....
No. 4 Ear to ear, over top......
No. 5 Temple to temple, round back......

Gentlemen's Wigs.

Gentlemen's Wigs are made of the finest selected hair. We guarantee our work the highest grade, and they cannot be distinguished from the natural growth. If by mail, postage extra, each, 8 cents.
No. 61234 Men's Full Wigs. Weft with crown, cotton foundation. Each..............$8.00
No. 61236 Men's Full Wigs. Gauze or silk parting. Each............$12.00
No. 61238 Men's Wigs. Ventilated with hair net parting. Each............$21.00
Red, Blonde and Gray Hair cost extra; allow one-half more than above prices.

Street Wigs for Colored People.

No. 61240 Street Dress Wig for Colored Women, made of human hair, bang with parting in front, the hair in back is 18 inches long, and done up high in back with a knot. Send measurements as shown in illustration in Rules for Measurement on this page. Price, each..........................$5.50
No. 61241 Street Dress Wig for Colored Men, made of human hair with parting on side, send measurement as per instructions. Price, each, $4.50

Theatrical Wigs and Beards of Every Description.

No. 61250 Mustache on wire spring, common. Each..............10c
Per dozen............75c
No. 61252 Mustache, ventilated. Each............20c
Per dozen............$1.90
No. 61254 Imperials. Each............10c
Per dozen............$1.00
No. 61256 Gontees. Each............10c
Per dozen............$1.00
No. 61258 Whiskers, side. Each............75c
The above come in dark and medium shades only.

Full Beards.
No. 61246 Full Beard on wire. Each............80c
No. 61248 Full Beard, ventilated. Each....$1.75
If by mail, postage extra, each, 3 cents.

Minstrel and Character Wigs.

No. 61251 Minstrel or Plain Black Negro Wigs. Each............75c

Court Wigs, Hair Nets, Imperial Hair Regenerator, Grease Paints, Etc.

No. 61259 Imperial Hair Regenerator, restores gray hair to the color of youth, regenerates bleached hair, gives it new life and vigor, and makes it any color desired; makes it beautiful, natural and healthy. Comes in seven shades: Black, dark or medium brown, chestnut, light chestnut, gold blonde, ash blonde. Absolutely harmless.
Price, per bottle..........................$1.35

Liquids cannot be mailed.

No. 61260 Court Wigs. Made up in first class style. Price, each, $3.25
If by mail, postage extra, each, 6c.
No. 61267 Fright Wigs.
Price, each..........................$3.50
If by mail, postage extra, each, 6c.
No. 61268 Invisible Hair Nets, made of the best quality of best silk netting, all colors. Price, each..............7c
If by mail, postage extra, each, 2c.
No. 61269 Silk Hair Nets, medium size netting, all colors. Price, each...7c
If by mail, postage extra, each, 2c.
No. 61272 Pencils for the Eyebrows, brown or black. Each............20c
If by mail, postage extra, each, 3c.
No. 61274 Blue Pencil for the veins. Each..20c
If by mail, postage extra, each, 3 cents.
No. 61276 Theatre Rouge, in cakes on porcelain tablets, in paper boxes. Per box............20c
If by mail, postage extra, each, 3 cents.
No. 61278 Fard Indien, a preparation for shading the eyelashes artistically, making the eyes appear larger. Colors, light brown, dark brown and black.
Per box..........................50c
If by mail, postage extra, each, 5 cents.
No. 61280 Rusma Depilatory Powder for the removal of superfluous hair from the lips, cheek, chin, arm, etc. Price..95c
If by mail, postage extra, each, 5 cents.
No. 61282 Toupee Paste, which is used to keep Toupee in place; heat and apply. Per stick..........................50c

If by mail, postage extra, each, 5 cents.
No. 61284 Grease Paint, for make-up purposes, eight colors in a box. Per box............70c
If by mail, postage extra, each, 5 cents.
No. 61285 Burnt Cork, in glass jars. Per jar..25c
If by mail, postage extra, each, 5 cents.

The Braided Wire Hair Rolls.

Made of the finest tempered wire, covered with knitted lace to match any shade of hair.

FOR THE LATEST STYLES OF HAIR DRESSING.
No. 61285½ These rolls are most desirable for the pretty pompadour effects now so much in vogue. The only sanitary rolls made to produce fullness in any part of the hair. Can't become musty or damp from perspiration or injure the hair as do the rolls made of hair. No obstruction to hair pins. Comfortable, cool, cleanly and delightful.
No. 61286 4, 6 and 8 inch length. Each....$0.10
Per dozen..........................1.00
No. 61287 10, 12 and 15 inch length. Each....15
Per dozen..........................1.50
If by mail, postage extra, each, 4 cents.

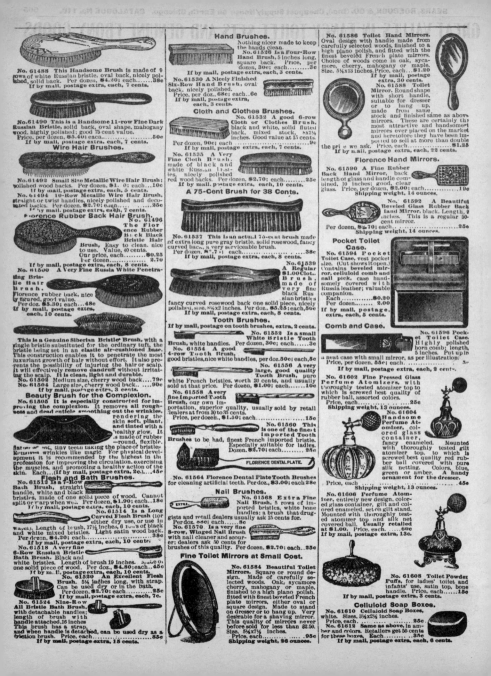

No. 61488 This Handsome Brush is made of 9 rows of white Russian bristle, oval back, nicely polished, solid back. Per dozen, $4.20; each.......38c
If by mail, postage extra, each, 7 cents.

No. 61490 This is a Handsome 11-row Fine Dark Russian Bristle, solid back, oval shape, mahogany wood, highly polished; good 75 cent value.
Per dozen, $5.40; each..........50c
If by mail, postage extra, each, 7 cents.

Wire Hair Brushes.

No. 61492 Small Size Metallic Wire Hair Brush; polished wood backs. Per doz., $1.00; each...10c
No. 61494 10-Row Metallic Wire Hair Brush, straight or twist handles, nicely polished and decorated backs. Per dozen, $2.70; each..........25c
If by mail, postage extra, each, 7 cents.

Florence Rubber Back Hair Brush.
No. 61496 The Florence Rubber Back Black Bristle Hair Brush, Easy to clean, nice to use. Value, 40 cents.
Our price, each......$0.25
Per dozen..........2.70
If by mail, postage extra, each, 8 cents.

No. 61500 A Very Fine Russia White Penetrating Bristle Brush, Florence rubber back, nice figured, good value.
Per doz. $5.30; each......48c
If by mail, postage extra, each, 10 cents.

This is a Genuine Siberian Bristle Brush, with a single bristle substituted for the ordinary tuft, the bristle being set in an elastic air-cushion base. This construction enables it to penetrate the most luxuriant growth of hair without effort. It also prevents the possibility of injuring the hair or scalp. It will effectively remove dandruff without irritating the scalp. It is clean, light and durable.
No. 61502 Medium size, cherry wood back....79c
No. 61504 Large size, cherry wood back......90c
If by mail, postage extra, 8 cents.

Beauty Brush for the Complexion.
No. 61505 It is especially constructed for improving the complexion. It removes all roughness and dead cuticle, smoothing out the wrinkles, rendering the skin soft, pliant, and tinted with a healthy glow. It is made of rubber round, flexible, tiny teeth taking the place of bristles. Removes wrinkles like magic. For physical development it is recommended by the highest in the profession for improving the circulation, exercising the muscles, and promoting a healthy action of the skin. Each....(if by mail, postage extra, 2c.)...45c

Flesh and Bath Brushes.
No. 61511 is a 7-Row Bach Brush, straight handle, white and black bristles, made of one solid piece of wood. Cannot split or warp when wet. Per dozen, $1.90; each...18c
If by mail, postage extra, each, 10 cents.
No. 61514 is a Long Curved Flesh Brush (for either dry use, or use in water). Length of brush, 17½ inches, 6 rows of black and white mixed bristles. Light satin wood back.
Per dozen, $4.20; each.........38c
If by mail, postage extra, each, 10 cents.
No. 61518 A very fine 6-Row Russian Bristle Bath Brush. Black and white bristles. Length of brush 19 inches. Made of one solid piece of wood. Per doz., $4.80; each...45c
If by mail, postage extra, each, 10 cents.
No. 61520 An Excellent Flesh Brush, 5¼ inches long, with strap. Can be used dry or in the bath. Per dozen $2.70; each..........25c
If by mail, postage extra, each, 7c.
No. 61524 Nine-Row All Bristle Bath Brush, with detachable handles; length of brush 5 inches with handle attached, 16 inches. This brush has a strap, and when handle is detached, can be used dry as a friction brush. Price, each..........85c
If by mail, postage extra, 15 cents.

Hand Brushes.
Nothing nicer made to keep the hands clean.
No. 61526 Is a Four-Row Hand Brush, 5 inches long, square back. Price, per dozen, 30c; each..........3c
If by mail, postage extra, each, 3 cents.
No. 61530 A Nicely Finished Hand Brush, oval back, nicely polished. Price, per doz., 68c; each...6c
If by mail, postage extra, each, 3 cents.

Cloth and Clothes Brushes.
No. 61532 A good 6-row Cloth or Clothes Brush, black and white, solid fluted back, mixed stock, 8x2¾ inches. Good value at 15 cents.
Per dozen, 90c; each..........9c
If by mail, postage extra, each, 7 cents.
No. 61535 A Very Fine Cloth Brush, made of black and white bristles, nicely polished red wood backs. Per dozen, $2.70; each...25c
If by mail, postage extra, each, 10 cents.

A 75-Cent Brush for 38 Cents
No. 61537 This is an actual 75-cent brush made of extra long pure gray bristle, solid rosewood, fancy curved back, a very serviceable brush.
Per dozen, $4.71; each..........38c
If by mail, postage extra, each, 8 cents.
No. 61539 A Regular $1.00 Cloth Brush, made of very fine black Russian bristles, fancy curved rosewood back one solid piece, nicely polished, size 8½x2 inches. Per doz., $5.25 each, 50c
If by mail, postage extra, each, 8 cents.

Tooth Brushes.
If by mail, postage on tooth brushes, extra, 2 cents.
No. 61552 Is a small White Bristle Tooth Brush, white handles. Per dozen, 30c; each.......3c
No. 61554 A good 4-row Tooth Brush, good bristles, nice white handles, per doz. 50c; each, 5c
No. 61556 A very large, good quality Tooth Brush, pure white French bristles, worth 20 cents, and usually sold at that price. Per dozen, $1.00; each.......10c
No. 61558 A very fine imported Tooth Brush, our own importation, superior quality, usually sold by retail dealers at from 9 to 15 cents.
Price, per dozen, $1.50; each..........15c
No. 61560 This is one of the finest Tooth Brushes to be had, finest French imported bristle. Especially suitable for ladies. Dozen, $2.70; each..........25c

FLORENCE DENTAL PLATE.

No. 61564 Florence Dental Plate Tooth Brushes for cleaning artificial teeth. Per doz., $3.00; each 28c

Nail Brushes.
No. 61568 Extra Fine Nail Brush, 5 rows of imported bristles, white bone handles; a brush that druggists and retail dealers usually ask 15 cents for. Per doz. 68c; each.......8c
No. 61570 Is a very fine 5-row Winged Nail Brush with nail cleaner and scourer; dealers ask 50 cents for brushes of this quality. Per dozen, $2.70; each..25c

Fine Toilet Mirrors at Small Cost.
No. 61584 Beautiful Toilet Mirrors. Square or round design. Made of carefully selected woods. Oak, sycamore, cherry, mahogany or maple, finished to a high piano polish, fitted with finest beveled French plate mirrors, either oval or square design. Made to stand on dresser or to hang up. Very desirable for a shaving mirror. This quality of mirrors never before sold for less than $2.50. Size, 5⅝x7⅝ inches.
Price, each..........95c
Shipping weight, 26 ounces.

No. 61586 Toilet Hand Mirrors. Oval design with handle made from carefully selected woods, finished to a high piano polish, and fitted with the finest beveled French plate mirrors. Choice of woods come in oak, sycamore, cherry, mahogany or maple. Size, 5⅜x13 inches. Price, each...$1.20
If by mail, postage extra, 30 cents.
No. 61588 Toilet Mirror. Round shape with short handle, suitable for dresser or to hang up, made from same stock and finished same as above mirrors. These are certainly the most attractive and handsomest mirrors ever placed on the market and heretofore they have been impossible to sell at more than double the price we ask. Price, each.......$1.25
If by mail, postage extra, each, 22 cents.

Florence Hand Mirrors.
No. 61590 A Fine Rubber Back Hand Mirror, back length of glass and handle combined, 10 inches; good, clear glass. Price, per dozen, $2.00; each........19c
Shipping weight, 14 ounces.
No. 61592 A Beautiful Beveled Glass Rubber Back Hand Mirror, black. Length, 9 inches. This is a regular 50-cent mirror.
Per dozen, $2.70; each..........25c
Shipping weight, 14 ounces.

Pocket Toilet Case.
No. 61594 Pocket Toilet Case, vest pocket size. (Cut shows it open.) Contains beveled mirror, celluloid comb and nail pick, case handsomely covered with Russia leather; valuable companion.
Each..........$0.20
Per dozen..........2.00
If by mail, postage extra, each, 5 cents.

Comb and Case.
No. 61596 Pocket Toilet Case. Highly polished horn comb; length, 5 inches. Put up in a neat case with small mirror, as per illustration.
Price, per dozen, 55c; each..........5c
If by mail, postage extra, each, 2 cents.

No. 61602 Fine Pressed Glass Perfume Atomizers with thoroughly tested atomizer top to which is screwed best quality of rubber ball, assorted colors.
Price, each..........25c
Shipping weight, 13 ounces.
No. 61604 Handsome Perfume Atomizer, colored glass container, fancy enameled. Mounted with thoroughly tested gilt atomizer top, to which is screwed best quality red rubber ball covered with pure silk netting. Colors, blue, green or amber. A handy ornament for the dresser.
Price, each..........45c
Shipping weight, 13 ounces.
No. 61606 Perfume Atomizer, entirely new design, colored glass container, gilt and enamel enameled, set on gilt stand. Mounted with thoroughly tested atomizer top and silk net covered ball. Usually retailed at $1.00. Price, each..........60c
If by mail, postage extra, 13c.

No. 61608 Toilet Powder Puffs, for ladies' toilet and infants' use, satin top, bone handle. Price, each.......15c
If by mail, postage extra, 3 cents.

Celluloid Soap Boxes.
No. 61610 Celluloid Soap Boxes, white. Sizes, 3¾x2¾ inches.
Price, each..........25c
No. 61612 Same as above, in amber and colors. Retailers get 50 cents for these boxes. Each..........35c
If by mail, postage extra, each, 6 cents.

GREAT VALUES IN FANCY TOILET SETS AND GENUINE EBONY GOODS

Our Special $2.25 Porcelain Toilet Set.

$3.00 Toilet Set for $1.75.

No. 61615 At $2.25 we offer as handsome a Toilet Set as it has ever been our pleasure to quote in our catalogue. The set consists of a brush, comb and French beveled plate mirror. The back of the brush and mirror is made of fine white porcelain, beautifully hand decorated as shown in the illustration. The flowers and figures on the back are in harmonizing colors. The handles and rims of the brush and mirror and the back of the comb are mounted with fine gilt metal, very serviceable and matching perfectly the hand decoration on the porcelain backs. These goods are the newest goods on the market, and compose a toilet set which makes as handsome and tasty a present as one could desire. The brush, comb and mirror are put up in a neat box. Our special price, complete.......$2.25
If by mail, postage extra, 48 cents.

No. 61617 The Handsome Toilet Set shown in the accompanying illustration consists of a brush, mirror and comb, with backs made of genuine ebonite, an exact imitation of real ebony; in fact, it is so near like the genuine ebony that few can tell the difference.
Genuine sterling silver trimmings. Each piece of this toilet set is decorated with genuine sterling silver trimmings as shown in the illustration. The hand mirror is fitted with a genuine French beveled plate mirror. Each of the three pieces is strictly high class and the toilet set complete is a gem and wonderful value for the money. The goods are set up in a neat case.
Our special price, complete, each........$1.75
If by mail, postage extra, each, 46 cents.

We Charge for Engraving
2½ cents per letter Script Style, and 5 cents per letter for Old English Style.

Elegantly Decorated Hand Mirror for $1.25.

No. 61616 The beautiful hand mirror shown in this illustration has a fine white porcelain back, handsomely hand decorated in neat flower designs as shown. The handle and rim are made of aluminum, artistically ornamented, and resembles real silver in appearance. It is fitted with the very best quality

FRENCH BEVELED PLATE MIRROR

and is put up in a neat box.
This hand mirror makes a very tasty and desirable present at a very low price, one of the most popular articles of the kind ever put on the market and the

VERY NEWEST NOVELTY TO BE HAD.

Regular retail price, $2.00.
Our special price, each. $1.25
If by mail, postage extra, 35 cents.

Our 95 Cent Ebonite Brush and Comb Set.

No. 61621 This Handsome Brush and Comb Set is made of real ebonite, an exact imitation of genuine ebony. The brush and comb are decorated with handsome mountings as shown in illustration. Both pieces are strictly high grade and are put up in a neat case. This set is really worth double our price.
Our special price...........................95c
If by mail, postage extra, 35 cents.

Our 25-Cent Gent's Ebonite Dressing Comb.

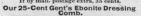

No. 61622 The Handsome Ebonite Dressing Comb shown in above illustration is decorated with handsome sterling silver trimmings as shown. The length of the comb is 6¾ inches, is excellent quality, such a comb as seldom retails at less than 40 to 50 cents.
Our special price, each...................25c
If by mail, postage extra, 4 cents.

Our 20-Cent Ladies' Ebonite Dressing Comb.

The above illustration shows Ladies' Ebonite Dressing Comb, our Ladies' Ebonite Comb.
No. 61623 It is sterling silver trimmed, is 7 inches long and is a very neat and desirable present.
Our special price, each...................20c
If by mail, postage extra, 3 cents.

Our 80-Cent Ebonite Hand Mirror.

No. 61618 The Hand Mirror shown in above illustration is made of real ebonite, an exact imitation of genuine ebony. It has beautiful sterling silver trimmings, as shown in the illustration, and the mirror is a real

FRENCH BEVELED PLATE MIRROR.

This mirror is put up in a neat case. Such a mirror as this ordinarily retails at $1.35.
Our special price, each......................80c
If by mail, postage extra, 35 cents.

No. 61620 We can also furnish the exact same mirror as shown in illustration in

GENUINE EBONY.

This mirror will have the real sterling silver plated trimmings, heavy beveled edge French mirror.
Our special price, each.....................$1.75
If by mail, postage extra, 35 cents.

OUR HIGHEST GRADE GENUINE EBONY TOILET ARTICLES.

No. 61624 Genuine African Ebony Hair Brush, best quality of imported bristle, handsome sterling silver mounting, colonial design. Price, each. .$1.10
If by mail, postage extra, 7 cents.
No. 61625 Real Ebony Hair Brush, smaller size than above, with solid sterling silver mountings, finest quality imported bristle. A brush retailed at your jeweler's for $1.25. Our special price, each..85c
If by mail, postage extra, 7 cents.

No. 61626 Genuine Ebony Military Brush, eleven rows fine white imported bristle, handsome sterling silver mountings, a brush that will give service and last a lifetime. The price has always been more than the average buyer wished to pay. Our price puts them within reach of all. Price, each $1.35
Per pair....(Postage extra, each, 6 cents.)....9.25

No. 61627 Finest Ebony Cloth Brush, for ladies or gentlemen, handsome sterling silver mounted, fine imported white bristle, regular $1.50 value.
Price, each........................$1.15
If by mail, postage extra, 7 cents.

No. 61628 Real Ebony Velvet Brush, with long white imported bristle, for hats and fine cloth, a beautiful present for either ladies or gentlemen, genuine sterling silver mounted. Special value.
Price, each..........................90c
If by mail, postage extra, 7 cents.

No. 61629 Real Ebony Hat Brush, the only style that a gent can reach under the brim, fine soft imported bristle, handsome sterling silver mountings.
Price, each............................65c
If by mail, postage extra, 7 cents.

No. 61632 Fine Ebony Hand or Nail Brush, with handsome sterling silver mounting, best quality imported bristle, a useful article, well worth double the price.
Price, each............................60c

36

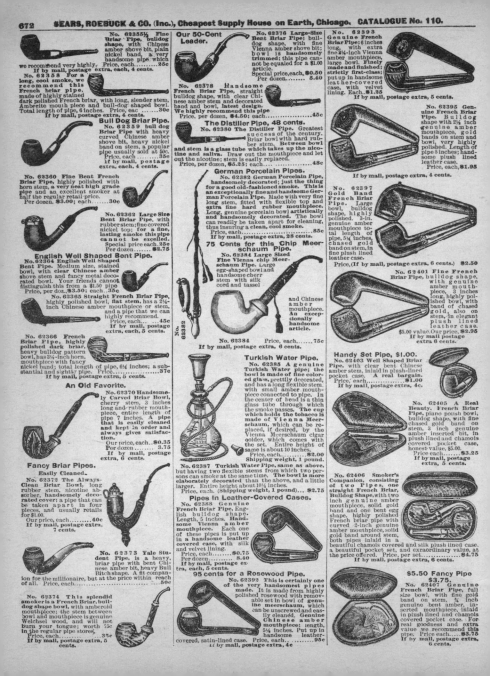

No. 62355½ Fine Briar Pipe, bulldog shape, with Chinese amber shove bit, plain nickel band, a very handsome pipe which we recommend very highly. Price, each..........25c
If by mail, postage extra, each, 4 cents.

No. 62358 For a long, cool smoke, we recommend this French briar pipe, made of highly stained dark polished French briar, with long, slender stem, Amberite mouth piece and bull-dog shaped bowl. Total length of pipe, 6 inches. Price, eac 30c
If by mail, postage extra, 4 cents.

Bull Dog Briar Pipe.

No. 62359 bull dog Briar Pipe with heavy curved Chinese amber shove bit, heavy nickel band on stem, a popular pipe usually sold at 50c.
Price, each 35c
If by mail, postage extra, each, 4 cents.

No. 62360 Fine Bent French Briar Pipe, highly polished with horn stem, a very neat high grade pipe and an excellent smoker at half the regular retail price.
Per dozen. $3.00; each.......30c

No. 62362 Large Size Bent Briar Pipe, with rubber stem; fine covered nickel top; for a fine, lasting smoke this pipe cannot be excelled.
Special price each.25c
Per dozen....... $2.75

English Well Shaped Bent Pipe.

No. 62364 English Well Shaped Bent Pipe. Medium size, stained bowl, with clear Chinese amber shove stem and fancy metal decorated bowl. Your friends cannot distinguish this from a $1.50 pipe
Price, per doz.,$3.50; each..35c

No. 62365 Straight French Briar Pipe, highly polished bowl, flat stem, has a 2½-inch Chinese amber mouthpiece or stem, and a pipe that we can highly recommend.
Price, each... ...45c
If by mail, postage extra, each, 5 cents.

No. 62366 French Briar Pipe, highly polished dark briar, heavy bulldog pattern bowl, has 3¼-inch horn, mouthpiece with fancy nickel band; total length of pipe, 6¼ inches; a substantial and sightly pipe. Price...................37c
If by mail, postage extra, 5 cents.

An Old Favorite.

No. 62370 Handsomely Carved Briar Bowl, cherry stem, 3 inches long and rubber mouthpiece, entire length of pipe 7 inches. A pipe that is easily cleaned and kept in order and always gives satisfaction.
Our price, each..$0.35
Per dozen........ 3.75
If by mail, postage extra, 6 cents.

Fancy Briar Pipes.

Easily Cleaned.

No. 62372 The Always-Clean Briar Bowl, long rubber stem, nicotine absorber, handsomely decorated cover; a pipe that can be taken apart in four pieces, and usually retails for $1.00.
Our price, each.........40c
If by mail, postage extra, 7 cents.

No. 62373 Yale Student Pipe, is a heavy, briar pipe with bent Chinese amber bit, heavy Bull Bitch shape. A fit companion for the millionaire, but at the price within reach of all. Price, each..........................50c

No. 62374 This splendid smoker is a French Briar, bulldog shape bowl, with amberoid mouthpiece; the stem between bowl and mouthpiece is genuine Welchsel wood, and will not burn your tongue; worth 75c in the regular pipe stores.
Price, each.........35c
If by mail, postage extra, 5 cents.

Our 50-Cent Leader.

No. 62376 Large-Size Bent Briar Pipe; bulldog shape, with fine Vienna amber shove bit; bowl is handsomely trimmed; this pipe cannot be equaled for a $1.00 article.
Special price,each, $0.50
Per dozen........ 5.40

No. 62378 Handsome French Briar Pipe, straight bulldog shape, with clear Chinese amber stem and decorated band and bowl, latest design. We highly recommend this pipe
Price, per dozen, $4.50; each..................45c

The Distiller Pipe, 48 cents.

No. 62380 The Distiller Pipe. Greatest success of the century. Briar bowl with hard rubber stem. Between bowl and stem is a glass tube which takes up the nicotine and saliva. Draw out the mouthpiece and let out the nicotine; stem is easily replaced.
Price, per dozen, $5.25; each.... ....48c

German Porcelain Pipes.

No. 62382

No. 62382 German Porcelain Pipe, handsomely decorated; just the thing for a good old-fashioned smoke. This is an exceptionally fine and handsome German Porcelain Pipe. Made with very fine long stem, fitted with flexible top and extra fine hard rubber mouthpiece. Long, genuine porcelain bowl artistically and handsomely decorated. The bowl can readily be taken apart for cleaning, thus insuring a clean, cool smoke.
Price, each..............................85c
If by mail, postage extra, 28 cents.

75 Cents for this Chip Meerschaum Pipe.

No. 62384 Large Sized Fine Vienna chip Meerschaum Pipe. Large egg-shaped bowl and handsome cherr stem with silk cord and tassel and Chinese amber mouthpiece. An exceptionally handsome article.

No. 62384 Price, each.......75c
If by mail, postage extra, 6 cents.

Turkish Water Pipe.

No. 62385 A genuine Turkish Water pipe; the bowl is made of fine colored glass, prettily decorated, and has a long flexible stem, with small amber mouthpiece connected to pipe. In the center of head is a thin glass tube through which the smoke passes. The cup which holds the tobacco is made of Vienna Meerschaum, which can be replaced, if desired, by the Vienna Meerschaum cigar holder, which comes with the set. Entire height of same is about 10 inches.
Price, each..........$2.00
Shipping weight, 1 pound.

No. 62387 Turkish Water Pipe, same as above, but having two flexible stems from which two persons can smoke at the same time. The bowl is more elaborately decorated than the above, and a little larger. Entire height about 10¼ inches.
Price, each. (Shipping weight, 1 pound)... $2.75

Pipes in Leather-Covered Cases.

No. 62388 Genuine French Briar Pipe, English bulldog shape. Length, 5 inches. Handsome Vienna amber mouthpiece. Each one of these pipes is put up in a handsome leather covered case, with silk and velvet lining.
Price, each........$0.75
Per dozen......... 8.40
If by mail, postage extra, each, 5 cents.

95 cents for a Rosewood Pipe.

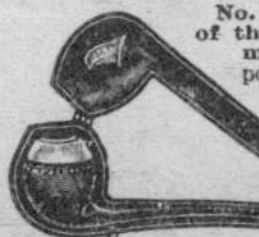

No. 62392 This is certainly one of the very handsomest pipes made. It is made from highly polished rosewood with removable set in bowl of genuine meerschaum, which can be unscrewed and easily cleaned. Genuine Chinese amber mouthpiece; length, 5¼ inches. Put up in handsome leather-covered, satin-lined case. Price, each.. ....95c
If by mail, postage extra, 4c

No. 62393 Genuine French Briar Pipe; 6 inches long, with extra fine 2¼-inch Vienna amber mouthpiece, large bowl. Finely made and finished; strictly first-class; put up in handsome leather-covered case, with velvet lining. Each..$1.25
If by mail, postage extra, 5 cents.

No. 62395 Genuine French Briar Pipe. Bulldog shape with 2¼ inch genuine amber mouthpiece, gold bands on stem and bowl, very highly polished. Length of pipe 5 inches; handsome plush lined leather case.
Price, each,$1.95
If by mail, postage extra, 4 cents.

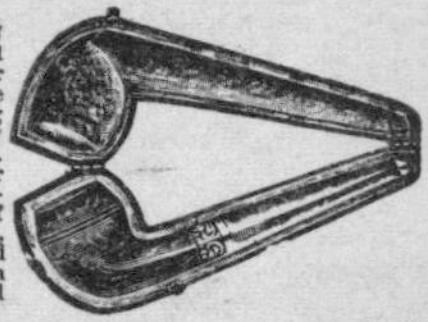

No. 62397 Gold Band French Briar Pipe. Large bowl, bulldog shape, highly polished. 3-in. genuine amber mouthpiece total length of pipe, 5¼ inches, chased gold band on stem, in fine plush lined leather case.
Price,(If by mail, postage extra, 6 cents.) $2.50

No. 62401 Fine French Briar Pipe, bulldog shape, with genuine amber mouthpiece, 3 inches long, highly polished bowl, with band of chased gold, also on stem, in elegant plush lined leather case.
$5.00 value.Our price, $2.95
If by mail postage extra 6 cents.

Handy Set Pipe, $1.00.

No. 62403 Well Shaped Briar Pipe, with clear bent Chinese amber stem, inlaid in plush-lined pocket case. A real bargain.
Price, each................$1.00
If by mail, postage extra, 4c.

No. 62405 A Real Beauty. French Briar Pipe, piano polish bowl, bulldog shape, with fine chased gold band on stem, 3 inch genuine amber inserted bit, in plush lined and chamois covered pocket case, honest value, $5.00.
Price each.......$3.25
If by mail, postage extra, 5 cents.

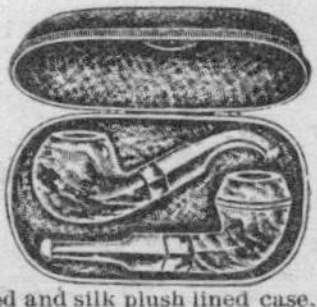

No. 62406 Smoker's Companion, consisting of two Pipes, one straight French Briar, Bulldog Shape, with two inch genuine amber mouthpiece, solid gold band and one bent egg shape, highly polished French briar pipe with curved 2-inch genuine amber mouthpiece, solid gold band around stem, both pipes inlaid in a beautiful chamois covered and silk plush lined case, a beautiful pocket set, and exraordinary value, at the price offered. Price, per set...............$4.75
If by mail, postage extra, 6 cents.

$5.50 Fancy Pipe $3.75.

No. 62407 Genuine French Briar Pipe, full size bowl, with fine gold band on stem, ¾ inch genuine bent amber, inserted mouthpiece, inlaid in plush lined and chamois covered pocket case. For real goodness and extra value we recommend this pipe. Price each.....$3.75
If by mail, postage extra, 6 cents.

Finest Quality French Briar Pipe.

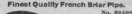

No. 62409 Finest quality French Briar Pipe, Bull Bitch shape pipe. This handsome pipe has a thick curved genuine amber stem, heavily mounted in real gold, such a pipe as you never expect to pay less than $7.50 for elsewhere. Price, each..........$4.85
If by mail, postage extra, each, 6 cents.

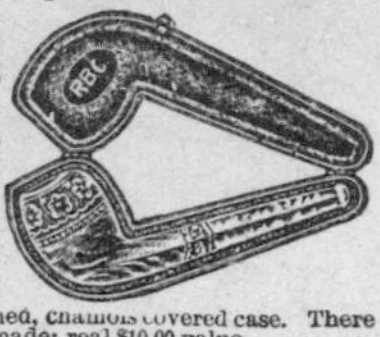

No. 62410 Finest Quality French Briar Pipe, with 3⅛-inch genuine amber mouth piece. The bowl is ornamented with a heavy 14-karat gold band, and a heavy 14-karat gold band also connects the amber mouth piece with the briar bowl. Total length of pipe 6½ inches; inlaid in an elegant plush lined, chamois covered case. There are no finer goods made; real $10.00 value.
Price, each..........$5.50
If by mail, postage extra, 6 cents.

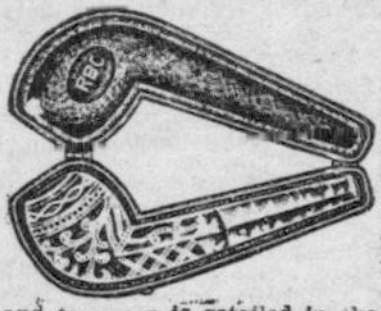

No. 62411 Genuine French Briar Pipe. The bowl is mounted with heavy silver trimming (see cut), genuine amber mouth piece 3 inches long; entire length of pipe about 6 inches. In elegant chamois covered, silk plush lined case. You will find nothing finer on the market, and this pipe is retailed in the pipe stores at from $8.00 to $10.00. Price, each..........$5.25
If by mail, postage extra, 5 cents.

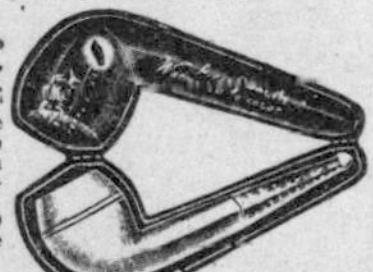

No. 62415 Chip Meerschaum Pipe, bulldog shape bowl, best English amber mouthpiece. We warrant this pipe to color, with satin lined leather covered case.
Price, each, $1.00
If by mail, postage extra, 5 cents.

Genuine Block Meerschaum and Genuine Amber Stem.

No. 62417 Genuine Block Meerschaum Pipe, handsomely carved bowl, assorted designs, such as lions, dogs, deer, etc., amber mouthpiece, 2½ inches long, in a satin-lined case. **Having received a large number of these pipes under particularly favorable circumstances we are able to offer unusual inducements.** Price..........$2.75
If by mail, postage extra, 6 cents.

Our Fine Meerschaum Pipe, with Case, for $3.00.

No. 62419 An extra fine Genuine Meerschaum Pipe, 5⅛ inches long, with fine 3-inch amber mouthpiece. Put up in handsome silk plush-lined leather-covered case. Unexcelled as a smoker.
Price, each..........$3.00
If by mail, postage extra, 5 cents.

Combination Pipe and Cigar Holder.

No. 62421 Combination Pipe and Cigar Holder, fine meerschaum bowl with heavy gold band on stem and fine meerschaum cigar holder with heavy silver band, 2½ inches genuine amber, inserted mouth piece which can be used on both pipe and cigar holder, making a very handsome combination set, the whole inlaid in beautiful plush lined leather covered pocket case.
Price, each..........$3.50
If by mail, postage extra, 6c

No. 62422 Genuine Meerschaum Bowl, finest quality, egg shape. This style of Meerschaum colors quickest, and the only quality and shape that will not break if you drop it; comes in fine chamois-lined case; the finest grade of Meerschaum on the market, in four sizes, as follows:
No. 5 Bowl, each..$4.25 No. 7 Bowl, each..$6.25
No. 6 Bowl, each.. 5.25 No. 8 Bowl, each.. 7.25
If by mail, postage extra, each, 4 cents.

No. 62423 Genuine Weichsel Stem with real amber mouth piece, length six inches. This stem is used in connection with the above meerschaum bowls. Price, each..........60c
If by mail, postage extra, 2 cents.

Our $5.95 Meerschaum Pipe.

No. 62425 Genuine Meerschaum Pipe, straight bulldog shape with 3 inch genuine amber mouthpiece, heavy chased gold band on stem and bowl inlaid in finest plush lined chamois covered case. No better pipe at any price. Price, each..........$5.95
If by mail, postage extra, each, 6 cents.

SMOKERS' SUNDRIES.

No. 62427 Carved Briar Cigar Holder, with horn mouthpiece. Per dozen, $1.22; each..........15c

No. 62429 Chip Meerschaum Cigar Holder, Chinese amber mouthpiece. Each..........$0.10
Per dozen.......... 1.00
Shipping weight, 3 ounces.

Twisted Rubber Cigar Holder.

No. 62431 Twisted Rubber Cigar Holder, something new, to give a nice cool smoke.
Price, each..........$0.10
Per dozen.......... 1.00
Shipping weight, 3 ounces.

No. 62432 Finest Quality Solid Amber Cigar Holder in chamois covered and plush lined case, a very fine article. Come in four sizes as follows:
1½-inch length, each..$1.00
2 -inch length, each.. 1.25
2½-inch length, each.. 1.50
3 -inch length, each.. 1.75
If by mail, postage extra, 2 cents.

Genuine Meerschaum Cigar Holder.

No. 62433 Genuine Meerschaum Cigar Holder, with amber mouthpiece. Comes in leather case.
Price, each..........$0.45
Per dozen.......... 4.75
If by mail, postage extra, 3 cents.

No. 62435 Genuine Meerschaum Cigar Holder, fancy carved, with real amber bit, each in leather case. **Order by number.**
Price, each..........$0.69
Per doz.......... 7.50
If by mail, postage extra, 3 cents.

No. 62434 Genuine Meerschaum Cigar Holder, similar to above, but finer, with fine amber mouth piece. The Meerschaum has carved designs such as horse, dog, deer, etc., inlaid in fine leather case, satin and plush lined. Length, 3¼ inches.
Price, each..........$1.00
If by mail, postage extra, 3 cents.

No. 62436 Genuine Meerschaum Cigar Holder, elegantly carved designs similar to above, but much finer goods, real amber mouth piece, total length of holder 3¾ inches, in finest plush lined case.
Our special price, each..........$1.75
If by mail, postage extra, 3 cents.

Nickeled Match Safe.

No. 62437 Nickeled Match Safe, smooth surface with stamped design, opens with a good spring.
Price, each..........5c
If by mail, postage extra, 2 cents.

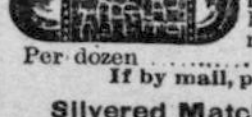

No. 62439 The Charm Match Safe, smooth top and bottom rough sides, opens with a spring like a charm. Made of fine nickel. Our price, each....14c
Per dozen..........$1.25
If by mail, postage extra, 3 cents.

Silvered Match Safe.

No. 62441 Silvered Match Safe, plain center and fancy scroll design, extra strong spring.
Price, each..........20c
If by mail, postage extra, 2 cents.

Pocket Match Safes.

No. 62443 Pocket Match Safe, solid nickel, opens with a spring, something very nice.
Each..........25c
If by mail, postage, extra, 2c.

Old Glory Match Safe.

No. 62445 Old Glory Match Safe handsome, strong and durable, dull finish, silvered or nickel with enameled flag in colors, fancy scroll corners.
Price, each..........25c
If by mail, postage extra, 4 cents.

Rubber Mouthpieces.

No. 62447 2-inch straight rubber mouthpiece. Each..........3c
No. 62449 2½-inch curved rubber mouthpiece. Each..........5c
No. 62451 2-inch square rubber mouthpiece. Each..........5c
No. 62453 2½-inch rubber mouthpiece, with nickel ferrule. Each..........10c

Our 15 Cent Weichsel Pipe Stem.

No. 62455 6½ inch Weichsel Pipe Stem, with curved mouthpiece. Each..........15c
No. 62457 7-inch Cherry Pipe Stem, with curved mouth-piece. Each..........10c

CIGAR CASES.

No. 62458 Real leather cigar case, telescope style; is soft in the pocket, and heavy enough to protect cigars. Price..........25c
If by mail, postage extra, 5 cents.

Our 50-Cent Leather Cigar Case.

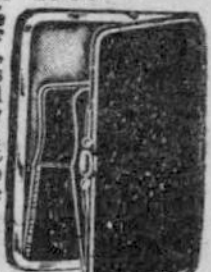

No. 62458½ Fine leather cigar case, plain style, has strong steel frame, highly polished. A very excellent case, which we offer at a special price Each..50c
If by mail, postage extra, 6 cents

No. 62459 Fine embossed leather cigar case, with extra strong steel frame and lock, fancy silk embroidered inside. Suitable as a birthday or holiday gift.
Price..........80c
If by mail, postage extra, 6 cents.

Our Finest Leather Cigar Case for $1.75.

No. 62459½ Genuine Calfskin Leather Cigar Case, very highly polished, with riveted steel frame and lock. A very high grade, and our best cigar case, usually retailed in the regular cigar stores at from $2.50 to $3.00. Price, each..........$1.75
If by mail, postage extra, 6 cents.

No. 62461 A very good calf leather Tobacco or Coin Pouch. Draw strings 5x4 inches. Each, 8c
Per dozen.....75c
If by mail, postage extra, 2 cents.

No. 62463 Prussian or Malsters' Pouch. An excellent pouch for tobacco or coin. An inside pocket for gold. This pouch is manufactured from one solid piece of leather.
Our price, per dozen, $1.46; each..........13c
If by mail, postage extra, 3 cents.

Self-Closing Rubber Pouch.

No. 62465 Raleigh Velvet Rubber Tobacco Pouch. Self-closing, tan color. Diameter, 3⅜ inches. Keeps tobacco moist, clean and sweet. Each..........$0.19
Per dozen.......... 2.10
If by mail, postage extra, 3 cents.

DO NOT FAIL to enclose Extra Stamps for Postage when goods are to go by mail.

GREAT SALE OF REAL OSTRICH FEATHER PLUMES AND TIPS

Fine Demi-Plumes, 35c Each.

ALL OUR...

TIPS AND PLUMES....

are made of THE HARD, GLOSSY, OSTRICH STOCK

We do not handle the poor, fluffy goods.

No. 62795 Our special 9-inch Demi-Plume, made from real ostrich feathers. Excellent quality and warranted to give perfect satisfaction. Black only.
Price, each **$0.35**
Three for.. **1.00**

No. 62796 A very full 10-inch Demi-Plume, made from extra quality real ostrich feathers. Fine fiber and handsome curl. Very rich and glossy, in appearance. Colors: black, cream and white. Always state color desired. Price, each **$0.55**
Two for.. ....**1.00**

No. 62797 Real Ostrich Feather Demi-Plumes, 11 inches long, very heavy and plump, with fine soft curl. Exceptionally handsome. Fine fiber and glossy finish. Colors: black, cream or white. Always state color desired. Price, two for $1.75; each...........**90c**

No. 62798 Fine Ostrich Demi-Plume, 12-inch. Made of fine selected stock, hard finish, long and glossy fibers. Colors: black, cream and white.
Price, two for $2.25; each........................**$1.25**

No. 62799 Finest Quality Real Ostrich Feather Demi-Plume, 13 inches long, full and heavy, with exceptionally fine curl, glossy and beautiful. In fact, these are the richest and finest appearing plumes we have ever imported. Colors: black, cream or white.
Price, two for $2.65; each........................**$1.45**

No. 62799½ Our Highest Grade and Best Quality Genuine Ostrich Feather Demi-Plume, made of glossy, hard fiber, ostrich stock, a rich, glossy black, fine curl, very handsome and plump, length full 14 inches. Colors: black, cream or white.
Price, two for $3.25; each........................**$1.75**

Fine Tips 39 Cents Per Bunch of Three.

No. 62791 Handsome Bunch of Real Ostrich Feather Tips, made of good quality ostrich, some handsome bunch at the price. We can furnish these tips in black only.
Price, per bunch of three....................**$0.39**
Three bunches for........................**1.00**

No. 62792 This Exceptionally Fine Quality Bunch Real Ostrich Feather Tips consists of three tips heavy stock select ostrich. We offer these tips at a special price, a price that you could not possibly duplicate for nearly twice what we ask. Colors: black, white or cream.
Price, per bunch of three........................**59c**

No. 62793 This Elegant Bunch of Real Ostrich Tips, three in the bunch, is made of good, hard glossy ostrich stock. These tips are made for our special use and are unexcelled for beauty and richness. Colors: black, cream or white.
Price, per bunch of three........................**90c**

No. 62794 This Extra Fine Bunch of Rich, Full and Glossy Ostrich Feather Tips consists of three tips and has an exceptionally fine curl and full appearance. We specially recommend this number and you could not duplicate same elsewhere for less than $2.50. Colors: black, cream or white.
Price, per bunch of three........................**$1.50**

No. 62811 Round Top Quill, always desirable; colors, black, brown, cardinal and navy.
Each ...5e
No. 62812 Straight Quills, 9 to 14 inches long; colors,
white, black, pink or purple. Price, each 5c

Stylish Aigrettes.

No. 62813 Sweeping Paradise Aigrettes, long full feathers, six stems. A very handsome ornament. Colors, black or white.
Price, each........................50c

MILLINERY STORES ASK DOUBLE OUR PRICES FOR THESE GOODS . . . .

No. 62814 Ostrich Aigrette, with plumage making the paradise effect, a very stylish trimming, in black only. A real 75-cent Aigrette.
Price........................35c

No. 62815 Angel Wings. This is a padded wing that always retails at 50 cents. Colors, black, white, brown or navy. Price, per pair........................50c
No. 62816 Gray or pearl colored

Angel Wings, padded, very nobby, same shape as above. Special price per pair........................40c

Our 50-Cent Spanish Coque.

No. 62817 Select Spanish Coque, large and full Spanish coques are very popular and add greatly to the beauty as a trimming for hats. These usually retail at 75 and 85 cents.
Price...........50c

Pheasant Tail.

No. 62818 Pheasant Tails, the natural long drooping feathers which make such a beautiful trimming. Colors, brown, tan, myrtle and navy.
Price.........................50c

No. 62819 Fancy Black Jetted Coque Feather, a stylish and showy trimming at a very low price. Price, each........19c

15 Cents for a Fine Black Feather.....

No. 62822 Black Fancy Feather, a trimming for height, very effective.
Price....15c

This is a good quality feather. Our price is very low—as low as MOST DEALERS PAY WHOLESALE FOR THESE GOODS.

We call your especial attention to the fine line of Ready Trimmed Hats we show on pages 678 to 682. Our line this season includes the very latest styles and you can buy from us at much lower prices than such hats will cost you at your home milliner.

No. 62854½ Fine selected quality Black Parrots, rich, glossy and full length, color black. Price, 45c
No. 62855 Fine selected Parrot, same as above in green color.
Price........45c
No. 62855½ Pigeon, best select quality, making a very handsome and full trimming. This quality is retailed at 75 cents and $1.00 elsewhere. Price, each...........59c

No. 62854½. 59c

No. 62856 Black Feather Breast which will be especially good on turbans as well as on hats, splendid value, black only. Price, each, 50c

No. 62857 Jetted Aigrette to be used in connection with other trimming, and very good on bonnets.
Price........................10c

Our 55-Cent Fancy Silk Pon-pon.

A regular 85-cent value.

No. 62858 Fancy Silk Pon-Pon, consisting of two large silk pon-pons, very stylish this season, and make an effective trimming. Black only. Price...........55c

LADIES' TRIMMED OUTING AND UNTRIMMED HATS.

e are showing this season the best sellers and t popular ready-to-wear hats ever shown, hats with wide rims, drooping effect are y stylish this season and the proper thing for by dressers. The assortment we show are only best and most popular styles. Castor and l are very desirable colors for this season.

t 95 cents to $1.75 we offer as choice a line of ing Hats as will be found in any high class inery establishment in large cities.

r Untrimmed Goods are designed after the latest Paris fashions. Our stock is strictly up the times, and you are sure of the best at est prices.

o. 62859 The Wheel, Young Ladies' Soft Felt , specially adapted for wheeling and street wear. y jaunty and pretty. Colors, black, gray, cardi- and castor. Price, each................95c

o. 62859½ Cycle English Felt Hat, for street r as well as for wheel, ribbon trimmed. Colors, rl, castor, cardinal or black. Price, each.....$1.20

o. 62860 Rialto, fine English Felt Street Hat, shed crown on broad brim, ribbon trimming, a ular style, black, pearl, navy or castor. rice, each.................$1.10

o. 62860½ Ladysmith, fine English Wool Felt t with fine quality cloth sash trimming. This hat aving an extraordinary run as it is very stylish l becoming, trimmed in the following combina- s: Castor with red sash trimming, pearl with te sash trimming, pearl with navy blue sash mming. Price...............$1.50

o. 62861 Cambridge, fine English Wool Felt t, with ribbon band trimming, large ribbon bow l gilt buckle at side, one of our most popular sell- : colors, black, navy, castor or pearl. rice.................$1.40

No. 62861½ The Rutland, English Wool Felt Hat t, street or golf, trimmed with plain folded sash, a ry stylish and becoming hat, colors black, pearl or tor. Price, each..................$1.35

No. 62862 Cavalier, this pretty English Wool Felt Street or Golf Hat is trimmed with a broad Roman stripe sash band, which makes a very effective and dressy hat, colors, pearl or castor. Price, each..................$1.75

No. 62862½ Rambler, fine quality Fur Felt, silk cord trimmed, a desirable and popular shape for a Miss; colors, castor, pearl or red. Price, each..$1.10

Untrimmed Hats.

No. 62863 Clermont, English wool felt, large shape, slight droop in front and turned up in back. Comes in black only. Price, each.................75c

No. 62863½ Clermont, velvet covered dress shape, same shape as above, two rows of satin covered wire around edge, black only. Price................70c

No. 62864 Roberts, stylish velvet cov- ered dress hat, droop over face and turned up in back, two rows of satin wire round edge, black only. Price, each..................75c

No. 62864½ Vaudeville, velvet covered dress shape with two rows of satin wire around edge, droops over face and back, trims very stylish, black only. Price, each..................75c

No. 62865 Elysse, velvet covered turban, row of satin wire around brim, this is a very popular and becoming shape, black only. Price, each.........75c

No. 62865½ Corinne, velvet covered bonnet, two rows of satin wire all around, a most becoming style, black only. Price, each................70c
No. 62866 English Wool Felt Bonnet, same shape as per illustration, black only. Price, each................75c

No. 62866½ Short Back Sailor, English wool felt, always becoming and stylish, colors, black, navy, pearl or castor. Price..................75c
No. 62867 Short Back Sailor, velvet covered, with two rows of satin wire around brim, black only. Price, each..................70c

No. 62868 Strat- ford English wool felt dress hat, a very becoming and nobby shape, colors, black, pearl or castor. Price..................85c

No. 62868½ Lady Randolph English wool felt dress hat, a very stylish shape for this season, colors.

black, navy, castor or pearl. Price..................80c

No. 62869 Madrid, fine quality English wool felt, very nobby and popular shape this season. Colors, black, brown, pearl or castor. Price, each.......85c

No. 62869½ Doris, fine quality English wool felt, similar to the short back, but having a slight droop which adds style. Colors, black, pearl, navy or castor. Price, each..................75c

No. 62870 Cam- bridge, fine English wool felt turban. This popular shape is very stylish and extensively worn. Colors, black, pearl or castor.

Price, each..................80c

No. 62870½ Fine English Wool Flat, always in style, very popular and extensively worn, for chil- dren and misses; colors, black, brown, navy, pearl or castor. Price, each..................55c

No. 62871 Ladies' Gingham Sun Bonnet made of best Amoskeag Gingham, laundered, shirred around hood, with exposed bow strings in back. Colors, blue and white and brown and white checks. Price..................25c
No. 62871½ Ladies' Chambray Sun Bonnet, made up nice and full of good Chambray, laun- dered, shirred around hood, with full cape. Extra well made. Colors, navy, light blue, pink and cardinal. Price ... 30c

Plain Hood Sun Bonnets.

No. 62872 Ladies' Chambray Sun Bonnet made of good, fast color Chambray, laundered, bow strings in back, and full cape. Colors, black, navy, light blue, pink, and cardinal. Price..................15c

No. 62872½ Misses' Gingham Sun Bonnet, made up of good quality gingham, laundered, with cape. Colors, blue and white and brown and white checks. Price..................15c
No. 62873 Misses' Chambray Sun Bonnet, made of good grade Chambray, laundered, with full cape. Colors, navy, light blue, pink and cardinal. Price..................18c

No. 62874 A Fine Quality Black English Felt Short Back. On upper and lower edge of brim is a row of fine twisted jet and two rows around crown. A folded trimming of black velvetta is brought around top of side crown. In front is a jaunty trimming of two black jetted quills, with knotted effect and pointed ears of black velvetta. A large gilt buckle and violet trimmed bandeau complete this pretty hat. Can be ordered in black or colors. Price....$1.83

No. 62875 A Very Stylish Velvetta Hat with Tucked Brim, slightly drooping in the front and back, a beautiful crown of velvetta, and trimmed in light blue taffetine rosettes. Two quills on either side complete this very nobby hat. Can be ordered in black and colors.
Price, each.................................$1.55
If you are not pleased with any Hat received from us, send it back and we will refund money.

No. 62876 Black Velvetta Made Hat, "Shepher Style," has large bow of black satin ribbon w loops, two fancy wings with quills completes trimming for the front; on the side is a full of black satin ribbon drawn over the brim and can on the crown with a bow of black satin ribbon. hat is black, but can be ordered trimmed in colors.
Our special price, each....................$

FINE QUALITY FOR $2.65

No. 62877 A Black Fine Quality English Felt Hat, has a pretty tapering crown and brim in "mushroom" shape. Around the hat and crossed under the brim in black is a stylish arrangement of black velvetta, appliqued with polka dots of cream guipure lace. To the left side is a black Russian coque plume. In front and drawn through to form trimming for bandeau is a pretty knotted effect of turquoise blue velvetta. Can be ordered in black or colors.
Price, each.......$2.65

BEAUTIFUL BLACK VELVETTA HAT FOR $1.95.

No. 62878 Hand Made Black Velvetta Dress Shape with full drape arranged gracefully around the crown and broad trimmings in front, consisting of a large bunch of quills on both sides, finished in the center with a large dark cerise stitched taffetta rosette, black velvetta bandeau on side. A very effective and becoming hat. The shape is black, but can be ordered trimmed in all colors.
Price, each.......$1.95

EXCELLENT VALUE FOR $2.60

No. 62879 A Mordore Brown Short Back, has a velvetta bound edge with a band of wide brown felt braid and narrow band of brown velvetta around the crown. Directly in front is a pair of beautifully shaded natural duck wings with chou of brown velvetta caught with handsome steel buckle. The hat is tipped over the face by tab band of purple violets. Can be ordered in all colors, but wings come only natural.

Price, each.......$2.60

OUR $2.00 BLACK FELT AND VELVETTA HAT.

No. 62880 A Black Felt Dress Shape with binding of black velvetta, is richly and simply trimmed with a full drape of black velvetta and large dressy back of black curled quills. A beautiful gilt buckle in front is the only touch of color. The tabs are finished in rosettes of black velvetta. Can be ordered in black or colors.

Price, each.......$2.00

No. 62881 Black Velvetta Made Dress Hat, straight brim, and turned up in back. For trimming it has three large taffeta rosettes, in contrasting colors, on the bandeau, tam crown of fine taffeta silk, with folds of velvetta around the crown, **two black parrots and sweeping aigrettes** complete the trimming for this splendid fitting and stylish hat; especially desirable for middle-aged women. Can be ordered trimmed in any color.

Price, each $2.75

No. 62882 A Large and Extremely Jaunty Hat of Purple Velvetta. Has edge outlined with heavy black satin wire. The shape is an exceptionally becoming one, flaring on the left side and drooping over the hair in the back. Three large bunches of purple violets ornaments the left side, and a folded trimming of purple velvetta is brought around the crown. About the top of this drape is arranged a scarf of heavy cream lace forming scarf ends over the drooping back. A long steel buckle at the front, and one at the back finish the trimming, and a pleasing touch of color is given by a folded bandeau of turquoise velvetta. Can be ordered in black or colors. Price, each **$2.90**

No. 62883 This is a Large Black Dress Hat, with medium broad brim of novelty felt chenille stitched, and a pretty tam crown of black velvetta. It is trimmed full in front, with hemmed bias black silk taffeta, very tastefully trimmed, a very becoming and stylish shape. Can be ordered in all colors.

Price, each........................$2.35

WE GUARANTEE SATISFACTION OR REFUND MONEY.

No. 62334 Handsome Black Velvetta, Hand-Made Dress Shape, one of our most desirable and becoming hats; dips slightly in front and back. It is draped around the crown with black velvetta and faced with yellow-colored taffeta for contrast. **It has two large ostrich feathers, and three sweeping aigrettes** and large rosette of yellow taffeta with fancy ornament makes a full and rich trimming. Two tabs in the back, one taffeta and one velvetta rosette. Trimmed in all colors. Price, each.....**$3.25**

No. 62885 Black Medium Sized Velvetta Hat, with a straight brim, is raised jauntily on one side over a bandeau of purple violets. **Around the crown is a band of three row fish scale.** Two long jetted coques in plume fashion are set in a low, broad effect around the crown and finished with knot and ends of stitched blue taffeta silk and velvetta. A long jet stick pin is passed through the knot. Black only.

Price, each **$3.00**

RARE VALUE FOR $2.95.

No. 62886 Shepherdess Shape Made Hat of pretty castor or tan color silk finished velvetta. The trimming consists of a tastily arranged drape of silk stitched velvetta around the crown. The front trimming consists of a full fold of taffeta with two long pheasant feathers and caught with a very pretty buckle. A side bandeau with full rosette of violet colored satin ribbon complete this very stylish and striking hat. The hat has a jaunty tilt. Castor or tan color is very stylish this season. Trimmed in all colors. Price, **$2.95**

OUR $3.40 GAINESBORO.

No. 62887 This Large Gainesboro Hat is made of turquoise blue silk finished velvetta, has five bias folds of contrasting colors, turquoise and black, around the crown, broad front effect, the trimming consists of velvetta and white taffeta with eight rows of stitching and has two handsome birds, fancy sweeping aigrettes, and finished with knots of velvetta drawn through a handsome rhinestone and jet buckle. This is a very stylish and becoming hat, $5.00 would be a very low price.

Price, each......**$3.40**

4 HOOK SHORT CORSET
62970
50¢

5 HOOK MEDIUM FIGURE
62964
39¢

5 HOOK SUMMER
62965
50¢

HIGH BUST MEDIUM FORM
62968
50¢

MEDIUM FORM SUMMER
62960
25¢

MISSES WAIST 62975
55¢

4 HOOK FANCY SUMMER
62971
60¢

CHILDS WAIST
62973
38¢

MISSES CORSET
62977
40¢

MISSES CORSET
62979
75¢

SUMMER CORSETS.

MISSES' CORSETS AND CHILDREN'S WAISTS.

If you try one of our Corsets we know we will count you a steady Customer. "A Satisfied Customer is our Best Advertisement." If you have heretofore had any trouble with your corsets, let us try to please you.

=== BE SURE AND GIVE YOUR WAIST MEASURE. ===

ALLOW 15 CENTS EXTRA IF YOU WANT CORSET SENT BY MAIL.

GIVE WAIST MEASURE AND NOT YOUR BUST MEASURE.

No. 62960 SINGLE BONE STRIP SUMMER CORSET. Good quality of net and exceptional value for the low price we quote. Sizes, 18 to 30.
Price, each..25¢

No. 62964 FIVE-HOOK MEDIUM FORM SUMMER CORSET, made of an exclusive pattern of fine netting that is decidedly strong. Six side steels and three belts in the zone, which retains the shape of garment. Equal to many 75 cent corsets. Sizes, 18 to 30.
Price, each..39¢

No. 62965 OUR 50-CENT FIVE-HOOK SUMMER CORSET, without a doubt the best that could possibly be produced at the price. Made of good quality netting, with sateen girdle and strips. Reinforced clasps and extra wearing qualities. Sizes, 18 to 30.
Price, each..50¢

No. 62968 HIGH BUST SUMMER CORSET. This is without doubt the most successful corset of its kind. Has the high bust feature which has proven so taking with ladies of slim figure; has four side steels, three bone strips, reinforced bust, inserted zone of extra heavy quality of net to prevent it from breaking out at the waist line. Sizes, 18 to 30.
Price, each..50¢

No. 62970 FOUR-HOOK SHORT SUMMER CORSET. A very popular form-fitting corset; made of fine strong netting, sateen girdle and strips reinforced clasps and corded bust, finished with fine quality lace top. We guarantee it equal to any corset sold for 75 cents. Sizes 18 to 30.
Price, each..50¢

No. 62971 FANCY FOUR-HOOK SUMMER CORSETS, short hip and low bust. This elegant corset is not only slightly, but you will find it a grand wearing and excellent fitting. Made of fine quality Summer netting 12-inch front steels. As shown on illustration, the girdles have pink, blue, or heliotrope bands, which not only adds elegance, but strengthens the corset as well. Sizes, 18 to 30.
Price, each..60¢

No. 62973 "DR. BALL'S" CHILD'S CORSET WAIST will train your child's figure while young. The Dr. Ball's Waist is easy, comfortable and perfect fitting, patent tape fastened buttons and taped button holes, white or drab. Sizes, 18 to 28.
Price, each..38¢
Always give waist measure.

No. 62975 CORONET MISSES' WAIST. We supply a long felt and needed want by the ambitious Miss just blooming into womanhood, when her figure begins to take on the matronly form which this garment so beautifully displays; made of sateen, white or drab. Sizes, 18 to 28.
Price, each..55¢
Always give waist measure.

No. 62977 MISSES' STRIP CORSET, made of good quality corset jeans. This corset has a decidedly advantageous feature, being soft and pliable, which makes it most healthful for growing children. Colors, drab or white. Sizes, 18 to 26. Price, each.....................40¢
Always give waist measure.

No. 62979 "DR. BALL'S" PERFECT FITTING MISSES' CORSET an ideal Corset for growing girls, shaped on scientific principles, made of fine, heavy drill, laced and elastic gored hook, shoulder straps and clasp front lace edging, a perfect Corset, white or drab. Sizes, 18 to 26. Price, each..75¢
Always give waist measure.

4 HOOK MEDIUM FIGURE
62940
85¢

SHORT HIP MEDIUM FORM
62942
$2.50

KABO BUST PERFECTOR
62943
$1.00

HIGH BUST EXTREME LONG WAIST
62944
98¢

SHORT HIP
EXTRA LONG WAIST
FOR SLENDER FORM
62946

ARMORSIDE
NEVER BREAKS DOWN
ON SIDES
62948
85¢

LONG WAIST MEDIUM FIGURE
62950
$1.40

HIGH BUST DRESS FORM
62952
50¢

HIPLESS MEDIUM WAIST FULL FORM
62953
98¢

CORSETS TO FIT ALL FORMS.....

We sell only such Corsets as we can Guarantee and Recommend. They have been tested and tried by thousands of our customers, AND THEY BUY THEM AGAIN. Remember, that if you buy a Corset and it is not entirely satisfactory, YOU CAN HAVE YOUR MONEY BACK, but we know you would rather have the Corset.

THE KABO USED IN THE CONSTRUCTION of the Kabo Corset is of the best and strongest materials, while the loop lacer is a vast improvement on the old brass eyelets which often corrode and soil the under garments, and so thin is the lacing as to be hardly perceptible on the finest silk gown.

DON'T FORGET TO SEND YOUR SIZE, THE WAIST MEASURE, ALLOW 15 CENTS EXTRA FOR POSTAGE IF YOU WISH SENT BY MAIL....

No. 62940 OUR NEW 4-HOOK, 13-INCH FRONT STEEL CORSET, for medium figure; the new medium length waist and medium low bust. Made of very fine quality sateen lined with French coutil, handsome lace trimming both top and bottom with baby ribbon drawn through lace. The best quality and most stylish fitting corset to be had, and the equal of any $1.50 corset today on the market. Colors, black, drab or white. Sizes, 18 to 30. Price, each...............85c

No. 62942 HANDSOME SATIN CORSET, short hips, long waist and medium figure. The new French model 12-inch front steel. Made of the finest quality French sateen with heavy satin stripe, lace and baby ribbon trimming top and bottom, boned with celluloid tipped steels. A very slightly corset and retailed for the finest trade at $5.00. Can be ordered in the following colors, black, white, pink, blue or drab, no brass eyelets. Sizes, 18 to 30 only. Price, each................$2.50

No. 62943 Kabo Bust Protector, designed to be worn with a corset, but can also be worn without if desired, creates a bust of faultless proportion and masks every imperfection of tailored jackets not snug-fitting. Waists are made to set with a degree of smartness unattainable in any other way. Its lightness and ease make it far superior to any padding or other building up, made of the best quality of jeans. Colors: white, drab and black, same size as corset. Sizes, 18 to 30. Price............$1.00

No. 62944 KABO HIGH BUST, extreme long waist, dress form; 6-hook, shaped shoulder straps, sateen covered strips, embroidered edge. Suitable for tall, slender figures, no brass eyelets. Colors, white, drab or black. Sizes, 18 to 30. Price, each.........................98c

No. 62946 KABO CUTAWAY HIPS, extreme long waist for slender figures, an ideal garment. Especially suitable for tailor made gowns. Made of extra quality French sateen, single bone strips and heavily boned bust, heart shaped back, a corset that will give universal satisfaction. Colors, black, white or drab. Sizes, 18 to 30 only. Price, each..........95c

No. 62948 ARMORSIDE. The only corset that never breaks down on the sides, will fit the average figure. It is made of coutil with the sateen strips. Has a vertical boning on the sides which thoroughly supports the figure. We guarantee every pair and for any pair that break at the hips in a reasonable time we will send a new pair or refund the money. Colors, black, drab or white. Sizes, 18 to 30. Price, each......................$0.85
Extra sizes, 31 to 36. Price, each............................1.15

No. 62950 KABO GIRDLE CORSET, long waist and medium form. Made of all fine French sateen, thoroughly boned and handsomely finished with silk flossing and edged with silk embroidery; made with girdle and 5-hook clasps, no brass eyelets. Colors, black, white or drab. Sizes, 18 to 30. Price, each............................$1.40
Extra sizes, 31 to 36, 25c extra. Price, each.....................1.65

No. 62952 HIGH BUST, for medium or slender figure. The best dress reform corset on the market and a very attractive garment. Made of Bedford cord body with sateen strips. This corset will compare in quality and fit with any $1.00 corset. Colors, drab or white. Sizes 18 to 30.
Price, each..........50c

No. 62953 KABO HIPLESS CORSET, medium waist, full form, made of French sateen; single strip, full boned, cut out over hip, with elastic sides. Matchless for athletic purposes and comfort, no brass eyelets. Colors, white, drab or black. Sizes, 18 to 30.
Price, each............................$0.98
Extra sizes, 31 to 36, 25 cents extra. Price, each......................1.23
Always give waist measure.

DEPARTMENT ....OF Ladies', Misses' AND Children's Wearing Apparel.

WE ARE EXTREMELY ANXIOUS TO RECEIVE YOUR ORDER
before, to give you such value for your money as you cannot get elsewhere.

FOR THIS OUR SPECIAL DEPARTMENT OF LADIES', MISSES', AND CHILDREN'S WEARING APPAREL. We know we are in a position this season, better than ever

OUR LIBERAL C.O.D., SUBJECT TO EXAMINATION TERMS.
you may select by express C. O. D., subject to examination; you can examine them at your express office and, if found exactly as represented, perfectly satisfactory and such values as you could not possibly get elsewhere, pay the express agent our price and express charges, less the $1.00 sent with order.

SELECT THE GARMENT WANTED BY NUMBER, FOLLOW OUR RULES FOR MEASUREMENT, and we will send any garment or garments with your order and will send any garment or garments

LADIES' CAPES COME IN SIZES from 32 to 44 inches around the bust. When ordering, please give us your bust and neck measure; measure all around; also state height and weight.

LADIES' JACKETS COME IN SIZES from 32 to 42 inches around the bust. No odd sizes, such as 33, 35, 37, etc. Should you have occasion to order any of the above sizes, order 34, 36, 38, etc., respectively. When ordering, please give us your bust measure, all around the bust under the arms, and all other measurements as indicated below.

LADIES' SKIRTS COME IN SIZES from 37 to 44 inches in length, and from 24 to 30 inches around the waist.

LADIES' WRAPPERS AND TEA GOWNS come in sizes from 32 to 44 inches; no odd sizes, and not over 58 to 60 inches in length. When ordering, state bust measure. If a wrapper sent is a few inches longer than ordered, customers will have to shorten it without any allowance from us.

FUR COLLARETTES. Sizes, from 32 to 44 inches around bust. When ordering, please give us your bust and neck measure.

LADIES' SUITS CONSIST OF JACKET AND SKIRT ONLY. Sizes for jacket 32 to 42 inches; no odd sizes. Sizes for skirt from 37 to 44 inches in length and 21 to 30 inches around the waist. When ordering, please state bust and waist measure and length of skirt.

LADIES' SILK AND CLOTH WAISTS Sizes from 32 to 42 inches around the bust; no odd sizes. When ordering, please give us your bust, neck and waist measure.

INFANTS' LONG COATS FOR INFANTS ONLY.

CHILDREN'S AND GIRLS' REEFER JACKETS SIZES for 4 to 14-year-old children and school girls; no odd sizes. When ordering, please state age, number of inches around the bust, height and weight.

CHILDREN'S AND SCHOOL GIRLS' NEW MARKET. SIZES FOR 4 TO 14 YEARS; no odd sizes. We charge a small advance for each size, as it consumes more material and labor. When ordering, please state age and number of inches around the bust.

MISSES' JACKETS SIZES FOR 14 - 16 - 18 - 20 YEAR-OLD Young Ladies; no odd sizes. The size 20 will correspond with 36 to 38 inches around the bust. When ordering, please state age and number of inches around the bust.

LADIES' MUSLIN AND FLANNEL GOWNS SIZES 14, 15, 16 inches, neck measure.

LADIES' MUSLIN AND FLANNEL DRAWERS SIZES 25, 27, 29 inches in length. When ordering please state open or closed.

LADIES' MUSLIN SKIRT AND PETTICOAT SIZES 38, 40, 42 inches in length; no longer. When ordering, please state the length you desire.

SPECIAL SIZES EVERYTHING DIFFERENT THAN THE SIZES mentioned above, are considered as extra sizes, in which case we require 20 per cent above the price quoted in the catalogue. Also cash in full, as that is required on all special orders.

ALL STYLES ARE SUBJECT TO SMALL CHANGES, SUCH AS SLEEVES BUTTONS, LENGTH, ETC. What we mean by this is that in case the style changes with the advance of the season, we shall make these changes before shipping the goods and thus they will be somewhat different from description and illustration, but always the same in value.

IN ORDER TO AVOID DELAY in shipment, please give us second choice.

IN ORDERING, TAKE MEASURE AS FOLLOWS:

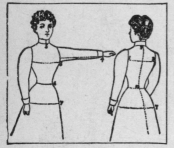

Inches from waist line to bottom of skirt.

BUST MEASURE—All around under the arms, over fullest part in front and well up over the shoulder blades in back. Your weight............pounds.

6 **WAIST**—Around smallest part of waist.

7 **HIPS**—Fullest measure around hips, about 6 inches below the waist line.

1 to 2 **ACROSS BACK**—From shoulder seam to shoulder seam.

9 to 10 **LENGTH OF WAIST IN BACK**—Measure must be taken from the collar seam (9, to waist line (10) in the back.

3 to 4 **SLEEVE LENGTH**—Give the exact measure of the inside sleeve seam from armhole (3 to wrist bone (4), with arm extended.

3 **ARMHOLES**—Around shoulder where sleeve is sewed in.

5 **NECK**—All around neck over dress collar at bottom of collar, not too tight.

NOTE—A correct bust measure will nearly always insure a good fit.

NOTICE CAREFULLY THESE INSTRUCTIONS While filling out the Order Blank, taking the measure over your dress, making no allowance whatever, and there will be no trouble about a fit.

FOR FUR CAPES. Bust and neck measure only are necessary. Use the Order Blanks enclosed and we will send you others.

FOR MISSES' GARMENTS Take measure same as above, but always state age and weight. These garments come in ages 12 to 18 only.

FOR CHILDREN. Garments for children from 4 to 12 years of age, state age of child and say whether large or small for age; no further measurements are necessary.

IN ORDERING SHIRT WAISTS State your height, your weight, number of inches around the body at bust, taken over dress close up under arms, number of inches around the body at neck, and number of inches around the body at waist.

IN ORDERING A SKIRT State your height and weight, number of inches around body at waist, and length of skirt in front from waist to bottom.

IN ORDERING AN UNDERSKIRT State your height and weight, number of inches around the body at waist, and number of inches from waist to bottom—skirt desired length. For 4 to 14 year old girls.

IN ORDERING A DRESS, WRAPPER OR TEA GOWN Take measure exactly the same as for jacket, above explained, and in addition state length of skirt wanted, the number of

Where our rules for measurement are carefully followed a perfect fit is insured.

CHANCE OF A LIFETIME
to buy goods for less money than it costs to manufacture, at the end of every season in order to get rid of the stock and make room for new goods, we sacrifice the carried-over goods and give our customers the full benefit of buying the goods at prices that are less than it costs us to manufacture, in most cases the material alone is worth more than we get for the made-up, first-class ready-to-wear article. Look at the following quotations and be convinced. Send in your orders at once and get the best. These goods are especially good for our patrons from the Southern States.

No. 201H1 Laundered Shirt Waists, made of percales with detachable laundered collars and attached laundered cuffs, in the newest shades; sold as high as 75 cents. Our closing out price at this sale...39c

No. 201H2 Consists of White Lawns, Solid Colored Percales, some trimmed and some plaited; sold as high as $1.25. Our closing out price at this sale, 69c

No. 201H3 Consists of French Percale, Imported Lawns, Tan Grass Cloth, waists with tucks and insertions; sold as high as $2.00. Our closing out price at this sale...98c

No. 201H4 All waists that we sold over $2.00, consisting of French Lawns and Batistes, at the exceptionally low price of...$1.35

LADIES', MISSES' AND CHILDREN'S SPRING JACKETS.
It's a bargain even if you don't need the goods. It would be a sin to miss your chance; we only have 480 in all, and after they are sold, there won't be any more, for we could not think of manufacturing them, at the prices we get for them. Buy them now. They are heavy enough where the CLIMATE IS NOT VERY COLD.

No. 201H5 Children's Reefer Jackets, that sold from $1.25 to $1.75, consisting of navy, red and tan twilled cloth and fancy plaid material, with capes, size from 4 to 14 year old children. All to close at...98c

No. 201H6 Children's Reefers, that sold from $2.35 to $2.98, consisting of good quality cloths in woolen materials, in red, navy, royal blue colors, with fancy trimming, and shoulder capes, thoroughly tailor made, sizes from 4 to 14 years old children. All to close at...$1.75

No. 201H7 Children's Reefers, the best we carry in all wool material, sold from $3.50 to $4.25, in navy blues, royal blues and reds, with fine trimmings or made in the latest box coat effects for 4 to 14 year old children. All to close at...$2.35

No. 201H8 Girls' Shoulder Capes, made in all-wool materials, in tans, reds, navy blues and cadet blues, trimmed with silk or embroidered, sold as high as $2.98. For 4 to 14 year old girls. All to close at...$1.75

No. 201H9 All Misses' Jackets, that sold as high as $3.25, in tans, navys and reds, sizes from 12 to 20 years old young ladies. All to close at......$1.98

No. 201H10 All Misses' Jackets, that sold from $3.98 to $5.25, made of all wool materials in tan only. Sizes from 12 to 20 year old young ladies. All to close at......$2.98

No. 201H12 Misses' Capes, made of all-wool ladies' cloths or checked mixtures, the finest thing to wear to and from school; in tan, red or blue colors, or the newest effects in Scotch plaids. Sizes, from 12 to 20-year old young ladies. All to close at......$2.35

No. 201H13 Ladies' Jackets, made of good quality repellent cloths, in blue or black colors or tan covert cloths. Sold for $2.98 to $3.25. Sizes, from 32 to 42 inch bust measure. All to close at......$1.98

No. 201H14 Ladies' Jackets, made of ladies' cloth, covert cloth or kersey, in tan, navy, black or cadet blue colors. Sizes, from 32 to 42-inch bust measure. Sold from $3.98 to $4.95. All to close for...$2.98

No. 201H15 Ladies' Jackets, made of all-wool kersey and broadcloth, in black, blue or castor colors, tan covert cloth, black clay worsted, in the newest styles; the jackets made of tan covert cloth are made in the new English box coat effects, all thoroughly tailor made; the best trimmings used only. Sold from $5.50 to $9.50. Sizes, from 32 to 42-inch bust measure. All to close at......$4.50

No. 201H16 Ladies' Capes, made of light weight plaid material in dark or light grays, in the newest golf style. Sizes, from 32 to 42 inches. Used to sell for $3.98. All to close at......95c

No. 201H17 Ladies' Light Weight Capes, made of all-wool ladies' cloth, in tan, blue or red colors, 18 inches long. Sold for $2.50. All to close at......98c

IF YOU INTEND TO BUY one of these great bargains it would be advisable to send in your order at once, before we are sold out of them; we could only get them again for the same price, as in most cases the material costs more than we get for the garment.

IT IS NOT ALWAYS THE BEST POLICY TO BUY THE CHEAPEST NUMBERS IN OUR CATALOGUE. While we can positively state that our cheapest numbers equal those that are sold by others at higher prices, at the same time we would advise you to make your selections from the better goods, and then you will be better pleased with your purchase.

GOODS LISTED IN THIS CATALOGUE Are subject to small changes, according to the prevailing styles, such as length of jackets, shape of collar and yoke on waists, the back or binding on skirts.

63760
$1.35

63732
59¢

63742
79¢

63756
98¢

63766
$1.89

63770
$2.25

63768
$1.98

63730
43¢

63756
53¢

63748
98¢

63764
$1.65

LADIES' MUSLIN, NAINSOOK AND CAMBRIC GOWNS

Sizes 14, 15, 16.

No. 63730 LADIES' GOWNS, made of muslin; nine tucks on each side of yoke; neck and sleeves trimmed with cambric ruffles. Price, three for $1.15; each **43c**
If by mail, postage extra, each, 14 cents.

No. 63732 LADIES' GOWN, made of muslin; yoke has two clusters of three tucks and two rows of embroidery insertion; neck and sleeves trimmed with embroidery edge ruffles. If by mail, postage extra, each, 13 cents. Price, three for $1.60; each **59c**

No. 63738 LADIES' EMPIRE GOWN, made of good muslin. Tucked collar trimmed with fine wide cambric ruffling. Wide embroidery in neck.
If by mail, postage extra, each, 14 cents. Price, 2 for $1.25; each **65c**

No. 63742 LADIES' EMPIRE GOWN, made of good muslin. Has V shaped bosom made of three rows embroidery insertion and two rows lace insertion; neck and sleeves trimmed with wide cambric ruffle with torchon lace edge. If by mail, postage extra, each, 15 cents. Price, 2 for $1.50; each **79c**

No. 63748 LADIES' FINE MUSLIN GOWN, EMPIRE STYLE. Collar of embroidery insertions. Bosom has embroidery insertion and wide embroidery edge. Sleeves, collar and neck trimmed with a fine wide Hamburg embroidery.
If by mail, postage extra, each, 17 cents. Price, 2 for $1.90; each **98c**

No. 63756 LADIES' EMPIRE CAMBRIC GOWN. Collar has insertion and lace and ruffle of lawn. Bosom has insertion and embroidery insertion and a lace lawn ruffle. Two ribbon bows and ribbon across bosom. Lace and insertion to match. Price, 2 for $1.90; each **98c**
If by mail, postage extra, each, 15 cents.

No. 63760 LADIES' FINE CAMBRIC GOWN. Yoke has two rows embroidery insertion on each side, with three tucks between and insertion down center. Wide fine Hamburg embroidery trimmed all way round front, and wide embroidery on neck and sleeves to match; entire front of yoke covered with embroidery and insertions. Ribbon bow at neck, fine herringbone braid trimming. Price, 2 for $2.60; each **$1.35**
If by mail, postage extra, each, 18 cents.

No. 63764 LADIES' FANCY NAINSOOK GOWN. Empire style. Collar made of two fancy Valenciennes insertions. Bosom has one row insertion and fine lawn ruffle with lace edge to match the insertion; sleeves to match collar, all trimmed with a fancy open beading and tied with ribbon bow. Price, 2 for $3.15; each **$1.65**
If by mail, postage extra, each, 11 cents.

No. 63766 LADIES' FINE NAINSOOK GOWN. Fancy circular yoke made of solid shirring, fine lawn ruffle and Point de Paris lace insertion and lace set in the ruffles, neck and sleeves trimmed, lace to match. Back has three wide box plaits, neck tied with fine satin ribbon.
Price, 2 for $3.60; each **$1.89**
If by mail, postage extra, each, 11 cents.

No. 63768 LADIES' FINE CAMBRIC GOWN. Empire style. Collar is made of fancy Medici insertion and lace joined with fancy ribbon trimming. Bosom has one row insertion and one row lace and two rows ribbon beading; sleeves have one row insertion and lace and two rows ribbon trimming, ribbon drawn through all the trimming and tied in bows on front and sleeves; back of neck cut square and trimmed to match front.
Price, 2 for $3.75; each **$1.98**
If by mail, postage extra, each, 18 cents.

No. 63770 LADIES' FANCY EMPIRE GOWN. Made of fine Cambric. Fancy collar trimmed all round with fine Point de Paris insertion and lace four inches wide; bosom has one row insertion one row fancy ribbon insertion and 4-inch lace; sleeves have fancy ribbon insertion and lace all trimmed with fancy lace beading; ribbon in bosom and sleeves.
Price, 2 for $4.15; each **$2.25**
If by mail, postage extra, each, 18 cents.

LADIES' WHITE UNDERSKIRTS.

☞ See page (690) for full descriptions and prices of all Long Chemises, Short Chemises and Underskirts shown on this page.

Lengths, 38, 40, 42 inches.

No. 63772 LADIES' MUSLIN SKIRT, with wide belt, trimmed with a 3-inch ruffle and wide lace. Price, 3 for $1.15 ; each **43c**
If by mail, postage extra, each, 10 cents.

No. 63774 LADIES' GOOD MUSLIN SKIRT, with flounce of fine cambric, 5 inches and torchon lace.
Our price only, 3 for $1.55 ; each **55c**
If by mail, postage extra, each, 11 cents.

No. 63778 LADIES' MUSLIN SKIRT, umbrella style. Ruffle of fine cambric and Hamburg embroidery, 5 inches deep, for the small price of 2 for $1.50 ; each **79c**
If by mail, postage extra, each, 13 cents.

No. 63782 FINE MUSLIN SKIRT, with fine lawn ruffle, with torchon lace and insertion set in the flounce. The flounce is 11½ inches deep and 3 yards wide. This is a good $1.00 skirt.
Price, 2 for $1.80 ; each **98c**
If by mail, postage extra, each, 13 cents.

No. 63786 LADIES' FINE MUSLIN SKIRT, with dust ruffle and a fine lawn flounce, with two rows torchon insertion and one row lace to match. The insertion is set in the flounce between 1½-inch bands.
Our price, 2 for $1.85 ; each **98c**
If by mail, postage extra, each, 15 cents.

No. 63792 FINE MUSLIN SKIRT, with a fine dust ruffle of cambric. Lawn flounce has a torchon lace four inches wide and two clusters of two tucks also two clusters of two tucks above flounce on skirt. Price, 2 for $2.35 ; each **$1.25**
If by mail, postage extra, each, 16 cents.

No. 63800 LADIES' CAMBRIC SKIRT, with dust ruffle. Fine lawn flounce, fancy new novelty lace 2½ inches wide connected to a flounce 2¼ inches wide, and 2¼-inch flounce connected to a flounce made of insertions and bands on the bias, the bias flounce connected to a flounce 5½ inches deep, making a flounce 17 inches deep.
Price, 2 for $3.12 ; each **$1.65**
If by mail, postage extra, each, 16 cents.

No. 63802 LADIES' CAMBRIC SKIRT, with dust ruffle. Fine lawn flounce with three rows of open embroidery insertion, covered partly by tucks. A handsome embroidery edge 6 inches deep, makes up a beautiful skirt. Price, 2 for $3.45 ; each **$1.79**
If by mail, postage extra, each, 17 cents.

No. 63804 LADIES' CAMBRIC SKIRT, with fine torchon lace on dust ruffle. A 10-inch lawn ruffle contains 3 rows of insertion to match edge of torchon lace. Price, 2 for $3.75 ; each **$1.98**
If by mail, postage extra, each, 16 cents.

No. 63806 LADIES' HIGH GRADE CAMBRIC SKIRT, with dust ruffle, with 2 fine lawn flounces trimmed with handsome Hamburg 7-inch embroidery on each flounce, making an elaborate double skirt. Price, 2 for $4.15 ; each **$2.25**
If by mail, postage extra, each, 16 cents.

No. 63812 LADIES' BEST QUALITY CAMBRIC SKIRTS, with dust ruffle, having a 5-inch Point de Paris lace. A fine lawn flounce contains 2 rows of Point de Paris lace insertion with 5-inch lace edge to match. This is the latest French style skirt, having the lace run on the bias of the flounce, both inclining and declining. Price, 2 for $5.65 ; each .... (If by mail, postage extra, each, 16 cents.) **$2.98**

63840 98¢

63848 $1.48

63850 $1.65

63820 45¢

63826 55¢

63860

63858 45¢

63854 27¢

63852 65¢

63856 75¢

DRAWERS

SIZES, 23, 25, 27 and 29.

When ordering please state "open or closed."

No. 63814 LADIES' FINE MUSLIN DRAWERS, with a 2-inch hem and cluster of three tucks above hem; unequaled for the money. Price, three for 60¢; each............................**22c**
If by mail, postage extra, each, 6 cents.

No. 63816 LADIES' UMBRELLA DRAWERS, made of good muslin with a large cambric ruffle, trimmed with a fine torchon lace. Price, three for 95¢; each. (If by mail, postage extra, each, 7¢)..**35c**

No. 63820 LADIES' FINE MUSLIN UMBRELLA DRAWERS, trimmed with a neat, showy torchon insertion and edge to match. The ruffle is made of fine cambric. Price, three for $1.25; each....**45c**
If by mail, postage extra, each, 7 cents.

No. 63826 LADIES' LACE TRIMMED UMBRELLA DRAWERS made of fine quality muslin, has two wide insertings of fine torchon lace, with edge to match. Price, two for $1.00; each................**55c**
If by mail, postage extra, each, 7 cents.

No. 63832 LADIES' UMBRELLA MUSLIN DRAWERS, trimmed with open embroidery edge and insertion to match.
Price, two for $1.15; each.. (If by mail, postage extra, each, 7¢)..**65c**

No. 63836 GOOD QUALITY MUSLIN UMBRELLA DRAWERS, trimmed with a cluster of six tucks, above fine embroidery ruffle, made of lawn. Price, two for $1.40; each...............................**75c**
If by mail, postage extra, each, 7 cents.

No. 63840 UMBRELLA DRAWERS with good quality muslin, trimmed with two rows of neat pattern Point de Paris insertion, with edge to match. Price, two for $1.90; each.. (If by mail, postage extra, each, 7¢)..**98c**

No. 63846 LADIES' FINE CAMBRIC UMBRELLA DRAWERS, strikingly trimmed with heavy torchon insertion and edge to match. Pink or blue ribbon inserting at top flounce.
Price, two for $2.40; each...............................**$1.25**
If by mail, postage extra, each, 7 cents.

No. 63848 LADIES' FRENCH PATTERN DRAWERS, made of the best grade lawn, handsomely trimmed with three rows of neat Valenciennes insertion with highly raised edge to match. Two clusters of three tucks adorn the drawer above ruffle.
Price, two for $2.85; each.. (If by mail, postage extra, each, 7¢)..**$1.48**

No. 63850 LADIES' HANDSOME NAINSOOK DRAWERS, with two clusters of four tucks, is trimmed elaborately with a fine Swiss insertion adjoining the ruffle of Hamburg embroidery.
Price, two for $3.15; each...............................**$1.65**
If by mail, postage extra, each, 6 cents.

CORSET COVERS.

32 to 42 inches around bust.

No. 63852 LADIES' MUSLIN CORSET COVERS, with seams in back, made to fit perfect. Price, two for 27¢; each........**15c**
If by mail, postage extra, each, 4 cents.

No. 63858 GOOD QUALITY CAMBRIC CORSET COVERS, V shaped neck, handsomely trimmed with open embroidery insertion around neck with neat edge to match. Between neck and edge is a cluster of five fine tucks. A belt to this corset cover makes it adjustable to any figure. Two rows of herringbone braid trimming makes it neat around the neck.
Price, two for 85¢; each...............................**45c**
If by mail, postage extra, each, 4 cents.

No. 63860 FINE QUALITY CORSET COVERS. Curved neck. Handsomely trimmed around neck with Hamburg embroidery insertion and edge to match, running on both sides of insertion. The armholes are adorned with same pattern embroidery and trimmed off with fine grade herringbone braid trimming. Price, two for $1.20; each...............................**60c**
If by mail, postage extra, each, 4 cents.

No. 63854 FINE MUSLIN CORSET COVERS, V neck, trimmed with wide Hamburg embroidery edge around neck.
Price, two for 50¢; each.. (If by mail, postage extra, each, 4c.)..**27c**

For handsome illustrations of Muslin Chemises, long and short, and short Underskirts, see preceding page.

Short Chemise.

Sizes, 32 to 42 inches around bust.

No. 63863 LADIES' MUSLIN SHORT CHEMISE, square yoke, and trimmed with torchon lace around yoke and armholes. Good value.

Price, two for 55c; each...........................29c

If by mail, postage extra, each, 6 cents.

No. 63864 FINE CAMBRIC SHORT CHEMISE, square yoke, trimmed with neat embroidery around yoke and armholes. Across yoke, chemise is trimmed with a wide Hamburg insertion with a cluster of tucks at either end. Above insertion, a neat embroidery extends across yoke.

Price, two for 95c; each...........................49c

If by mail, postage extra, each, 8 cents.

Long Chemise.

Sizes, 32 to 42 inches around bust.

No. 63866 LADIES' NEAT MUSLIN CHEMISE, trimmed with torchon lace around square yoke and armholes; across yoke is a heavy set 4-inch torchon lace which matches small edge; at the bottom is a cluster of tucks, above an inch hem.

Price, two for $1.00; each...........................55c

If by mail, postage extra, each, 10 cents.

No. 63868 VERY FANCY SQUARE CUT CAMBRIC CHEMISE, has latest style edge, running around the yoke and armholes in ruffle form; across the yoke extends a 4-inch open pattern Hamburg embroidery, a large cambric ruffle at the bottom makes the chemise of good style.

Price, two for $1.20; each...........................63c

If by mail, postage extra, each, 10 cents.

No. 63872 VERY STYLISH ALL-LAWN CHEMISE, trimmed with fine torchon lace around curved neck and armholes; also a very wide lace of same pattern, turned back, runs around yoke. This edge with the narrower one is joined by ribbon run through neat beading. On the bottom is an insertion and edge, very wide to match that around yoke. Price, two for $1.90; each...........................98c

If by mail, postage extra, each, 8 cents.

No. 63878 THE MOST ELABORATE CHEMISE in the market. Has curved yoke, trimmed with very fine torchon lace around sleeves and yoke. The same pattern is joined to lace on yoke, turned back, with ribbon drawn through. Below the neck are artistically arranged 3 rows of insertion to match 3 rows of insertion at the bottom, with an edge of the same pattern at the ruffle.

Price, two for $3.65; each...........................$1.89

If by mail, postage extra, each, 10 cents.

Ladies' White Underskirts, Short.

Length, 27, 29, 31 inches.

No. 63882 LADIES' SHORT MUSLIN UNDERSKIRT, has wide ruffle with 3 fine tucks, above an inch hem. Price, two for 85c; each...........................45c

If by mail, postage extra, each, 8 cents.

No. 63884 LADIES' BEST QUALITY MUSLIN SHORT SKIRT, has cambric flounce, trimmed with wide torchon lace.

Price, two for $1.00; each...........................55c

If by mail, postage extra, each, 9 cents.

Flannel Underwear for Ladies, Misses and Children.

We beg to call your attention to the finish of our goods, which is far superior to anything you can get elsewhere. Our goods all made very full, good length, and as to the fit we have the reputation of having the best on the market. Sizes, 14, 15, 16 inches around neck.

For Muslin Gowns see page 687.

45 Cents Buys a 75-Cent Flannel Gown.

No. 63001

LADIES' FLANNEL GOWN

made in

Plaids and Stripes,

in blue or pink colors.

Turn Down Collar

Yoke in front and back.

Price...........................45c

If by mail, postage extra, 10 cents.

Our 69-Cent Flannel Gown.

No. 63003 Ladies' Gown made of domet flannel, with fancy striped patterns in blue or pink colors. Lay down collar, herringbone braid trimming on yoke and around the flounced cuffs. It is well finished and exceptionally full.

Price.......69c

If by mail, postage extra, 15c.

Ladies' Domet Flannel Gowns for 89 Cents.

No. 63005 Ladies' fine Gown, made of a high grade domet flannel, lay down collar, pointed yoke in front, collar and cuffs trimmed with herringbone braid to match, double yoke in back.

Can furnish in pink or blue colors.

Price.......89c

If by mail, postage extra, 15c.

Ladies' Gowns, Only $1.15.

No. 63007 Very Stylish Ladies' Gown made of a very good quality domet flannel in the newest plaid effects. V shaped yoke in front, plaited and trimmed with herringbone braid to match. Epaulets trimmed with torchon lace on shoulder from yoke in front to yoke in back. Ruffled collar edged with lace, new cuffs and a satin ribbon bow in front.

Price, each.......$1.15

If by mail, postage extra, 22 cents.

Our $1.48 Gown.

No. 63009

Nobby Gown, made of a fine grade of flannel. Fancy yoke in front edged with a ruffle. Three rows of satin ribbon trimming to match gown on ruffle, one around the yoke in front. Six rows of ribbon and three plaits in front, three rows around the collar and three rows around the cuffs. It is gotten up very tastily. It is of an exceptionally good value, serviceable and warm.

Price, each...........................$1.48

If by mail, postage extra, each, 20 cents.

Ladies' Flannel Underskirts.

Sizes, 27, 29 and 31 inches in length. For petticoats and muslin underwear see page 687.

No. 63013   No. 63011

No. 63011 Ladies' Flannel Underskirts striped designs in blue or pink colors. Price, each.......29c

If by mail, postage extra, each, 9 cents.

No. 63013 Ladies' Underskirt, made of domet flannel. Umbrella shape, trimmed with a 6-inch flounce around the bottom. Price, each.......37c

If by mail, postage extra, each, 10 cents.

49 Cents Buys a 75-Cent Flounced Underskirt.

No. 63015 A neat Underskirt. Made of a good quality

DOMET FLANNEL

In striped design in pink or blue colors.

UMBRELLA SHAPED.

Trimmed with 6-inch flounce around bottom, which is edged with torchon lace all around.

Price...........................49c

If by mail, postage extra, 9 cents.

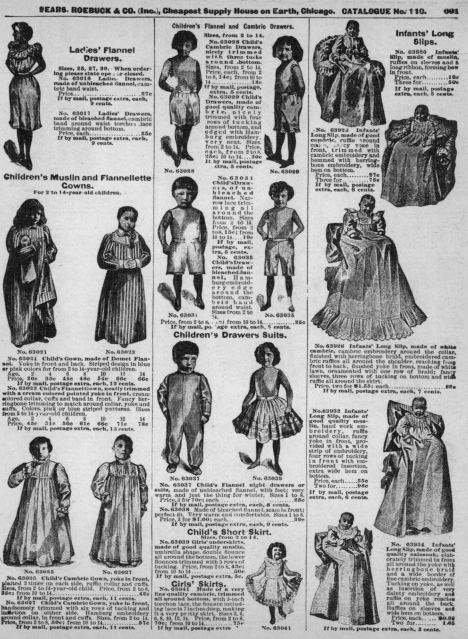

Ladies' Flannel Drawers.

Sizes, 25, 27, 29. When ordering please state open or closed.
No. 63016 Ladies Drawers, made of unbleached flannel, cambric band waist.
Price... ....27c
If by mail, postage extra, each, 9 cents.

No. 63017 Ladies' Drawers, made of bleached flannel, cambric band around waist torchon lace trimming around bottom.
Price, each.............35c
If by mail, postage extra, each, 9 cents.

Children's Muslin and Flannellette Gowns.

For 2 to 14-year-old children.

No. 63021   No. 63023

No. 63021 Child's Gown, made of Domet Flannel. Yoke in front and back. Striped design in blue or pink colors for from 2 to 14-year-old children.
Age,   2   4   6   8   10   12   14
Price, 30c 35c 43c 48c 54c 60c 66c
If by mail, postage extra, each, 12 cents.
No. 63023 Child's Flannel Gown, neatly trimmed with a cream colored pointed yoke in front, cream colored collar, cuffs and band in front. Fancy herringbone trimming to match around collar, yoke and cuffs. Colors, pink or blue striped patterns. Sizes from 2 to 14-year-old children.
Age,   2   4   6   8   10   12   14
Price, 45c 51c 56c 61c 66c 71c 78c
If by mail, postage extra, each, 13 cents.

No. 63025   No. 63027

No. 63025 Child's Cambric Gown, yoke in front, plaited 3 times on each side, ruffle collar and cuffs. Sizes, from 2 to 14-year-old child. Price, from 2 to 8, 35c; from 10 to 14...........42c
If by mail, postage extra, each, 11 cents.
No. 63027 Child's Cambric Gown, yoke in front, handsomely trimmed with six rows of tucking and insertion on either side. Hamburg embroidery around collar, in front and cuffs. Sizes from 2 to 14. Price, from 2 to 8, 56c; from 10 to 14.............57c
If by mail, postage extra, each, 11 cents.

Children's Flannel and Cambric Drawers.

Sizes, from 2 to 14.
No. 63028 Child's Cambric Drawers, nicely trimmed with three tucks around bottom. Sizes, from 2 to 14. Price, from 2 to 8, 14c; from 10 to 14.............18c
If by mail, postage extra, each, 5 cents.
No. 63029 Child's Drawers, made of good quality cambric nicely trimmed with four rows of tucking around bottom, and edged with Hamburg embroidery, very neat. Sizes, from 2 to 14. Price, each, from 2 to 8, 25c; 10 to 14....30c
If by mail, postage extra, 5 cents.

No. 63028   No. 63029

No. 63031 Child's Drawers, of unbleached flannel. Narrow lace trimming all around the bottom. Sizes from 2 to 14. Price, from 2 to 8, 15c; from 10 to 14... 19c
If by mail, postage, extra, 5 cents.
No. 63035 Child's Drawers, made of bleached flannel, Hamburg embroidery edge around the bottom, cambric band around waist. Sizes from 2 to 14.

No. 63031   No. 63035

Price, from 2 to 8.. .c; from 10 to 14.............25c
If by mail, po age extra, each, 5 cents.

Children's Drawers Suits.

No. 63037   No. 63039

No. 63037 Child's Flannel night drawers or suits, made of unbleached flannel, with feet; very warm and just the thing for winter. Sizes 1 to 8.
Price, 3 for 70c each..............25c
If by mail, postage extra, each, 8 cents.
No. 63038 Made of bleached flannel, seam in front; perfect fit. Very warm and comfortable. Sizes 1 to 8.
Price, 3 for $1.00; each,.............39c
If by mail, postage extra, each, 9 cents.

Child's Short Skirt.

Sizes, from 2 to 14.
No. 63039 Girls' underskirts, made of good quality muslin, umbrella shape, double flounce all around the bottom, the lower flounces trimmed with 5 rows of tucking. Price, from 2 to 8, 43c; from 10 to 14.............50c
If by mail, postage extra, 5c.

Girls' Skirts.

No. 63041 Made of a very fine quality cambric, trimmed all around bottom, with 3-inch torchon lace, the flounce including lace is 7 inches deep, making it a very pretty skirt. Sizes 2, 4, 6, 8, 10, 12, 14. Price, from 2 to 8, 70c; from 10 to 14.............75c
If by mail, postage extra

No. 63041

Infants' Long Slips.

No. 63920 Infants' Slip, made of muslin, ruffles on sleeves and a long ribbon, forming bow in front.
Price, each..........19c
Three for...........50c
If by mail, postage extra, each, 5 cents.

No. 63922 Infants' Long Slip, made of good cambric, ruffle around collar, fancy yoke in front, trimmed with cambric embroidery and hemmed with herringbone embroidery, wide hem on bottom.
Price, each.........27c
Three for 75c
If by mail, postage extra, each, 6 cents.

No. 63926 Infants' Long Slip, made of white cambric, cambric embroidery around the collar, finished with herringbone braid, embroidered cambric ruffles all around the shoulder, reaching from front to back, flushed yoke in front, made of white lawn, ornamented with one row of braid; fancy sleeves, three rows of tucking on bottom and wide ruffle all around the skirt.
Price, two for $1.55; each.....................88c
If by mail, postage extra, each, 7 cents.

No. 63932 Infants' Long Slip, made of good quality muslin, hand work embroidery, ruffle around collar, fancy yoke in front, provided with a wide strip of embroidery, four rows of tucking in front with embroidered insertion, extra wide hem on bottom.
Price, each......55c
Two for 98c
If by mail, postage extra, each, 6 cents.

No. 63934 Infants' Long Slip, made of good quality nainsook, elaborately trimmed in front all around the yoke with herringbone braid and a wide border of fine cambric embroidery. Tucking on yoke, as well as insertion of very dainty embroidery and ruffle on yoke reaches all around the back. Ruffles on sleeves and wide hem on bottom.
Price, each.......$0.98
Two for 1.65
If by mail, postage extra, each, 5 cents.

63415
$2.65

63416
$2.75

63411
$1.75

63414
$2.25

63417
$2.98

63418
$3.75

63413
$2.35

63410
$1.48

63412
$1.98

63409
98¢

GIRLS' AND MISSES' CLOTH DRESSES

Sizes From 4 to 14 Years.

WHEN ORDERING PLEASE STATE AGE, HEIGHT, WEIGHT AND NUMBER OF INCHES AROUND BUST. When necessary to make a dress to order, we will charge 20 per cent. extra for material and labor. Special orders must be paid for in advance.

No. 63409 GIRLS' DRESS, made of fancy plaid material. Newest plaids, round yoke in front, trimmed with fancy braid, shoulder capes extending from front to back, pointed at yoke, also trimmed with braid to match, fancy buttons in back. Full front, lined throughout with cambric, wide hem on bottom. Price.........(If by mail, postage extra, 20 cents.)........... **98c**

No. 63410 GIRLS' DRESS, made of fancy plaid material, round yoke in front made of velvet to match, which extends to back, shoulder capes reaching all around in front to back; small button trimming in front; outside part of cuffs made of velvet and trimmed with braid. Very full front, lined throughout with cambric. Sizes, 4 to 14. Price................. **$1.48**
If by mail, postage extra, 32 cents.

No. 63411 GIRLS' DRESS, made of fancy plaid material, fancy front made of red or blue colored serge trimmed with straps made of same material as dress. Braid trimming all around high standing collar, around the sleeves, front and back; large shoulder flaps which add to the neatness of the suit, Very full and effective. Lined throughout with cambric. Wide hem on bottom. Price.........(If by mail, postage extra, 30 cents.)........... **$1.75**

No. 63412 GIRLS' DRESS, made of fancy plaid material, in the newest shades, large collar extending from front to back, trimmed with lace; pointed yoke in front, made of cashmere to match and trimmed with silk gimp. Two rows of silk gimp around sleeves. Very full in front; lined throughout with good quality cambric. Wide hem on bottom. Price........................ **$1.98**
If by mail, postage extra, 32 cents.

No. 63413 GIRLS' DRESS, made of all wool flannel, high standing collar, square yoke in front and shoulder capes which reach from front to back, neatly trimmed with braid to match; similar trimming around the sleeves. The back of the dress is made the same as the front. Lined throughout with good quality cambric. Wide hem on bottom. One of the best bargains on the market, we can highly recommend, as it will wear well and give satisfaction in every respect. Colors, navy blue, red and brown. Price.....................(If by mail, postage extra, 30 cents.) **$2.35**

No. 63414 GIRLS' DRESS, made of good quality fancy plaid material in dark shades, square shoulder capes, high standing collar; the yoke in front, bow and sleeves are neatly trimmed with silk gimp; the yoke, collar, front and outside part of cuffs are made of velvet to match the dress. One of the neatest suits shown this year, for girls going to school there is nothing prettier or neater to be had for the money. Lined throughout with good quality cambric. Wide hem on bottom. Price................If by mail, postage extra, each, 30 cents............ **$2.25**

No. 63415 GIRLS' DRESS, made of the best quality worsted plaid in the very newest combination of shades; high standing collar, yoke in front and shoulder capes as well as the bow in front, are made of good quality cashmere neatly trimmed with fancy silk cording; flaring cuffs as well as belt around the waist are also made of cashmere. A very neat and desirable dress and trimmed throughout with good quality cambric. Wide hem on bottom Price................If by mail, postage extra, each, 31 cents.).......... **$2.65**

No. 63416 GIRLS' DRESS, made of good quality Sicilian cloth, made of two pieces in a sailor suit style, and consists of a blouse which is made with a large sailor collar trimmed with four rows of fancy cord; similar trimming on the sleeves, satin ribbon bow in front and four pearl buttons. The skirt, which is attached to the vestee front is made very full, lined throughout with cambric; wide hem on bottom; the vestee front is trimmed with four rows of cording and four rows of cording around the high standing collar. The suit is very pretty and tasty. Colors, red and blue. Price................. **$2.75**
If by mail, postage extra, each, 28 cents.

No. 63417 GIRLS' DRESS, made of all wool flannel, bolero effect, large collar made of fancy plaid material as well as yoke in front; high standing collar, belt and sleeves are trimmed with fancy silk gimp; satin ribon bow in front; lined throughout with good quality cambric; wide hem on bottom. We can highly recommend this suit, as it is very good value for the money. Colors, navy blue and red. Price................. **$2.98**
If by mail, postage extra, each, 30 cents.

No. 63418 GIRLS' DRESS, made of all wool flannel, Bolero effect, shoulder flaps; the belt and sleeves are neatly trimmed with white cord; very full front; the skirt is made very full and lined throughout with good quality cambric; wide hem on bottom. We can furnish this suit in royal blue and red. Price.................(If by mail, postage extra, 29 cents.)................. **$3.75**

63420 98¢

63424 $2.25

63422 $1.39

63419 79¢

63421 $1.25

63423 $1.65

63426 $2.65

63425 $2.50

INFANTS' AND CHILDREN'S SHORT CLOAKS

The elegant array of goods shown on this page is made in 24, 26, 28 and 30 inches in length, or from 1 to 4-year-old children.

WHEN ORDERING, PLEASE STATE LENGTH DESIRED AND THE AGE OF CHILD.

No. 63419 CHILD'S SHORT CLOAK, made of fancy flannel in red, blue or gray colors. Large sailor collar embroidered and edged with white Angora. Lined throughout with flannel. Sizes, 24, 26, 28 and 30 inches in length. Price, each....................79¢
If by mail, postage extra, each, 17 cents.

No. 63420 CHILD'S SHORT CLOAK, made of good quality Elderdown in fancy striped patterns or figures, in blue, pink or tan. Has a large sailor collar and is trimmed in good quality Angora all around, lined throughout with shaker flannel. We sell this cloak at a special price, and we are certain no one could give one equal to this for the same money. Sizes from 24 to 30 inches. Price, each.....................98¢
If by mail, postage extra, each, 21 cents.

No. 63421 CHILD'S SHORT COAT, made of good quality Elderdown, round collar trimmed with white Angora all around. Lined throughout with shaker flannel. Colors: red, tan, white and light blue. Sizes, from 24 to 30 inches. Price, each.....$1.25
If by mail, postage extra, each, 18 cents.

No. 63422 CHILD'S SHORT CLOAK, made of fancy plaid Elderdown in red and blue, white and red and blue and red plaid. A very neat and stylish cloak; has large pointed collar inlaid with all-wool flannel and embroidered with soutache. A very attractive garment for the money. Lined throughout with heavy flannel. Sizes, from 24 to 30 inches. Price, each.....$1.39
If by mail, postage extra, each, 26 cents.

No. 63423 CHILD'S SHORT CLOAK, made of Boucle cloth, round collar edged with black Angora fur and trimmed with two rows of fancy cording, similar trimming around sleeves. Lined throughout with black sateen and interlined with flannel. It is good value for the money and we can highly recommend it. Colors, red and black, blue and black, and green and black. Sizes, 24 to 30 inches.
Price, each $1.65
If by mail, postage extra, each, 26 cents.

No. 63424 CHILD'S SHORT CLOAK, made of All-Wool Flannel, large collar neatly trimmed with 5 rows of cording as shown in illustration, lined throughout with good quality black sateen and interlined with flannel. Colors, cadet blue, red and navy. Sizes, 24 to 30 inches. Price, each.....$2.25
If by mail, postage extra, each, 24 cents.

No. 63425 CHILD'S SHORT COAT, made of good quality Elderdown, square shoulder capes and collar trimmed with black soutache, similar trimming around sleeves. Double breasted front and trimmed with eight fancy buttons. This coat can be worn by either boy or girl, and good quality sateen to match the coat. This coat can be worn by either boy or girl, and is a very neat and effective garment. Colors, cadet blue or cardinal. Sizes, 24 to 30 inches. Price, each.....(If by mail, postage extra, each, 31 cents.).....$2.50

No. 63426 CHILD'S SHORT CLOAK, made of good quality All-Wool Elderdown, large sailor collar made of velvet and embroidered with white cording, and trimmed all around with white Angora. Lined throughout with cambric. We can furnish this in white with blue, green or red velvet collar, in red with green or dark red velvet collar, and in tan with brown velvet collar. Sizes, 24 to 30 inches. Price, each.....$2.65
If by mail, postage extra, each, 26 cents.

No. 63427 CHILD'S SHORT CLOAK, made of good quality Elderdown, large circular cape faced with good quality sateen, four rows of cording on front, similar trimming on back of collar and on sleeves. This coat can be worn by either boy or girl. Lined throughout. A very attractive garment and a very stylish and desirable cape. We can furnish in light blue, cream or cardinal. Sizes, 24 to 30. Price.....$2.75
If by mail, postage extra, each, 35 cents.

No. 63428 CHILD'S SHORT CLOAK, made of good quality Elderdown, large circular cape trimmed with two rows of Thibet fur and Thibet fur trimming all around collar; it looks as though it had a triple cape. We can highly recommend this as one of the prettiest coats shown. Lined throughout with sateen. We can furnish this in light blue, cream, cardinal, navy or pink. Price, each.....$2.98
If by mail, postage extra, 35 cents.

No. 63429 CHILD'S SHORT COAT, made of good quality Elderdown collar and yoke over large circular collar of white lamb, trimmed with small fur heads. The yoke is edged over the top with Angora. White lamb trimming around the sleeves. A very handsome and desirable garment and one we can highly recommend to the very best people. We can furnish in cream, cardinal or navy. Price, each.....$3.50
If by mail, postage extra, each 36 cents.

No. 63430 CHILD'S SHORT CLOAK, made of all-wool Flannel, large cape edged all around with imitation chinchilla fur trimmed with lace, a very neat and effective garment. This is a garment we highly recommend and one like this usually sells for 15 per cent more than we ask for it, but we make a special leader of this garment and sell it below the average price. We can furnish in navy, cream or red colors. Price, each.....$3.50
If by mail, postage extra, each, 27 cents.

63427 $2.75

63428 $2.98

63429 $3.50

63430 $3.50

63436
$1.65

63442
$3.25

63439
$2.35

63437
$1.98

63434
$1.35

63433
$1.15

63440
$2.50

63441
$2.50

63432
.98¢

63431
.79¢

63435
$1.60

63438
$2.15

INFANTS' LONG CLOAKS.

No. 63431 INFANTS' LONG CASHMERE CLOAK, shoulder cape; embroidered nicely with silk; shirred at collar. Lined throughout with canton flannel. Colors, cream and tan.
Price..............(If by mail, postage extra, 18 cents)............**79c**

No. 63432 INFANTS' LONG CASHMERE CLOAK, handsomely embroidered on shoulder cape, and around the bottom of cloak. Shirred at collar. Bishop sleeves. Imitation pearl buttons. Colors, cream and tan. Price......(If by mail, postage extra, 20 cents)......**98c**

No. 63433 INFANTS' LONG CLOAK, made of Bedford cloth, silk soutache trimming on collar, fancy silk ribbon and silk soutache on shoulder cape, which goes all around cloak in front and back. Bishop sleeves. Canton flannel lining. Very dressy. Cream only.
Price..........(If by mail, postage extra, 23 cents)..........**$1.15**

No. 63434 INFANTS' LONG CLOAK, made of cashmere. Large shoulder cape, elaborately embroidered with silk. Shirred at neck and scalloped with silk all around bottom. Lined throughout with canton flannel. Colors, cream and tan.
Price..........(If by mail, postage extra, 21 cents)..........**$1.35**

No. 63435 INFANTS' LONG CLOAK, made of good cashmere. Shoulder cape beautifully embroidered in a neat flower design. It is scalloped all around with silk. Shirring around collar. The bottom is embroidered in a very wide flower design. Lined throughout with canton flannel. Colors, cream and tan. Price......(If by mail, postage extra, 22 cents)......**$1.60**

No. 63436 INFANTS' LONG CLOAK, made of good cashmere. Large shoulder cape, neatly embroidered and scalloped with silk. It is shirred at the end of the large collar, and neatly trimmed with silk cording. Silk embroidery similar to that on the cape ornaments at the bottom. Imitation pearl buttons. Lined throughout with a good quality of sateen. Interlined with flannel. Very dressy. Colors, cream and tan.
Price..........(If by mail, postage extra, 26 cents)..........**$1.85**

No. 63437 INFANTS' LONG CLOAK, made of a good quality Bedford cloth. Large shoulder cape, handsomely trimmed with three rows of lace insertion all around and one around the bottom and front. It also has three rows of lace insertion running up and down on the cape. Shirring at neck. Lined throughout with a good quality of sateen. Interlined with shaker flannel. Pearl buttons in front. Bishop sleeves. Cream, only.
Price..........(If by mail, postage extra, 26 cents)..........**$1.98**

No. 63438 INFANTS' LONG CLOAK, made of a good quality cashmere. It is very richly embroidered and scalloped with silk on shoulder cape. Shirring at neck. The embroidery in itself is the very newest design, and it almost covers the cape. Similar embroidery to that on the cape trims the bottom of this cloak and is fully 10 inches wide. Bishop sleeves. Lined throughout with cambric and interlined with shaker flannel. Colors, cream and tan. Price..........(If by mail, postage extra, 22 cents)..........**$2.15**

No. 63439 INFANTS' LONG CLOAK, made of a good quality cashmere, very neatly trimmed with silk cording on the collar. Three rows in back, four in front to the pointed yoke. Scalloped shoulder cape with fancy border. Shoulder cape and cuffs also trimmed with silk cording. Cuffs are embroidered and scalloped with silk. Bishops sleeves. Imitation pearl buttons. Lined throughout with a good quality sateen: interlined with shaker flannel. Colors, cream and tan. Price..........(If by mail, postage extra, 26 cents)..........**$2.35**

No. 63440 INFANTS' LONG CLOAK, made of fine Bedford cloth. Double shoulder cape made of same material is very neatly embroidered and scalloped with silk. Round collar trimmed with two rows of silk cording. Shoulder capes extend from this collar. Both capes trimmed with silk. Lined throughout with a good quality sateen. Interlined with shaker flannel. Cream, only.
Price..........(If by mail, postage extra, 30 cents)..........**$2.50**

No. 63441 INFANTS' LONG CLOAK, made of high grade cashmere. Large collar. Large shoulder cape extends from this collar and is neatly embroidered with small designs as well as scalloped with silk. Similar embroidery around the bottom of coat. Lined throughout with a good quality sateen. Interlined with shaker flannel. Imitation pearl buttons in front. Colors, cream and tan.
Price..........(If by mail, postage extra, 26 cents)..........**$2.50**

No. 63442 INFANTS' LONG CLOAK, made of pongee silk. It is washable and very pretty. Large pointed collar is trimmed with satin ribbon and one row of silk cording. Ruffle of silk extends from this collar, which is also trimmed to match collar. Bishop sleeves. Cuffs trimmed with silk. Lined throughout with sateen. Price..........(If by mail, postage extra, 24 cents)..........**$3.25**

63447

63449

63446

63450

63444

63448

CHILDREN'S AND SCHOOL GIRLS' NEWMARKETS.

The garments listed on these pages are made for 4 to 14-year-old girls. A small advance in price will be charged for each size, owing to the fact that it consumes a great deal more material; the advance in price is so very small that it will be hardly noticeable. The goods are far better value than ever shown, and as for style, quality and wear nothing can excel them.

No. 63443   CHILD'S NEWMARKET, made of Wash Satinette, square shoulder capes trimmed with one fold of all-wool flannel. Fold is edged with fancy braid, same around sleeves. Facing in front made of sateen. The belt in back trimmed with flannel and cord. Very full plaited skirt. In dark mixtures.

Age, years	4	6	8	10	12	14
Price	$2.45	$2.65	$2.85	$3.05	$3.25	$3.45

If by mail, postage extra, each, 64 cents.

No. 63444   CHILD'S LONG NEWMARKET, made of Good Quality Melton, shoulder capes edged all around with black Baltic seal. Neatly trimmed with cord around collar, sleeves and belt in back. Double-breasted front with six fancy buttons. Full skirt plaited in back. Pockets on both sides. Lined throughout with black sateen. Facing in front of black sateen. Navy blue and red.

Age, years	4	6	8	10	12	14
Price	$2.95	$3.15	$3.35	$3.55	$3.75	$3.95

If by mail, postage extra, each, 50 cents.

No. 63445   CHILD'S NEWMARKET, made of Good Quality All-Wool Two-toned Boucle. Fancy shoulder capes inlaid with all-wool flannel and neatly trimmed with four rows of fancy cording, similar trimming around the sleeves and on belt in back, very full skirt plaited in back. We can highly recommend this one of the best sellers we have, and judging from the number we have sold already, there is nothing better on the market for the money. Red and black or blue and black. Age, years..

Age, years	4	6	8	10	12	14
	$3.05	$3.85	$4.05	$4.30	$4.55	$4.80

If by mail, postage extra, each, 64 cents.

No. 63446   CHILD'S NEWMARKET, made of Good Quality Melton Beaver, square collar neatly trimmed with black and white braid, as shown in illustration. Similar braid around sleeves. A very effective and stylish garment. It has a loose back according to the very latest automobile style, double breasted, trimmed with eight fancy buttons. Facing in front made of same material as coat. Colors royal blue, and red.

Age, years	4	6	8	10	12	14
Price	$3.80	$4.05	$4.30	$4.55	$4.80	$5.05

If by mail, postage extra, each, 55 cents.

No. 63447   GIRLS' AUTOMOBILE COAT, made of Good Quality Melton Kersey, loose back and front, inlaid velvet collar and lapels. Strictly tailor made. Shirred sleeves, six pearl buttons in front, buttoning up high at the neck. Inlaid velvet on the pocket flaps. Facing in front made of same material as coat. Color, cadet blue only.

Age, years	6	8	10	12	14
Price	$4.00	$4.25	$4.50	$4.75	$5.00

No. 63348   CHILD'S NEWMARKET, made of Good Quality Melton Beaver, large circular shoulder capes trimmed all around with imitation chinchilla fur, also two rows of silk cord trimming finished with small pearl buttons, silk cord trimming on collar, on plait in back and around sleeves. Double plaited front buttoned up high at the neck. This is the very newest and latest style coat. The facing in front is made of the same material. Colors, blue and brown.

Age, years	4	6	8	10	12	14
Price	$5.10	$5.40	$5.70	$6.00	$6.30	$6.60

No. 63449   CHILD'S LONG NEWMARKET, made of Good Quality All-Wool Beaver, has combination cape hood neatly trimmed and piped with all-wool flannel and fancy silk braid, similar trimming around the collar and sleeves. Double breasted front buttoning high at the neck. Facing in front made of same material. Very heavy garment. In blue or brown.

Age, years	4	6	8	10	12	14
Price	$5.70	$6.20	$6.50	$6.80	$7.10	$7.40

No. 63450   CHILD'S NEWMARKET, made of Good Quality All-Wool Fancy Boucle, large double cape of which the upper is made of all-wool Beaver. The cape is bound all around with black mohair braid, trimmed with gilt cord and small round silk buttons. Double breasted front trimmed with six pearl buttons. Facing in front made of same material, very full skirt. Plait in back trimmed with mohair braid and gilt cord, similar trimming around the sleeves. The upper cape is lined throughout with good quality sateen. We can furnish this stylish coat in light green and brown and mixtures. Price, age, 4 years, $6.30; 6 years $6.60; 8 years, $6.90; 1. years, $7.20; 12 years, $7.50; 14 years, $7.80.

63443

63445

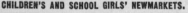

63478
$4.95

63480
$5.75

63479
$5.50

63477
$4.75

63482
$5.35

63481
$4.95

63476
$4.35

63475
$3.75

63474
$2.85

LADIES' JACKETS.

Made in sizes from 32 to 42 inches. NO ODD SIZES.
If you want a 33, 37 or 39, order 34, 38 or 40 respectively.

Goods listed in our catalogue are subject to small changes, according to the prevailing style—such as sleeve length, buttons, etc. We will charge 20 per cent extra if the garment must be made to order. All sizes different than those advertised are considered specials. All Specials must be paid for in advance. When postage is not given, goods cannot be sent by mail.

No. 63474 LADIES' JACKET, made of Beaver, double breasted shield front, high storm collar, facing in front made of same material; trimmed with six horn buttons. Colors: black and navy. Price.... **$2.85**
If by mail, postage extra, 50 cents.

No. 63475 LADIES' JACKET, made of good quality of Raritan beaver, has double breasted front, high storm collar, and large lapels, and jacket buttons up at the neck, fronts lined with good quality silk serge lining and a very good value for the money. We can highly recommend it. Colors: black, navy and castor.
Price..........(If by mail, postage extra, 50 cents.)..... **$3.75**

No. 63476 STYLISH JACKET, made of good quality Boucle cloth, double breasted, front trimmed with six horn buttons, coat shape lapels and velvet collar. Jacket is lined throughout with mercerized sateen; front of jacket is trimmed with Kersey strap trimming and similar trimming on back of jacket, shined sleeves, facing in front made of same material. Color, black only.
Price...........(If by mail, postage extra, 48 cents.)..... **$4.35**

No. 63477 VERY NOBBY JACKET made of all wool covert cloth, double breasted front trimmed with six fancy horn buttons, large lapels, storm collar. The jacket is piped all around with velvet, also piping around pocket flaps. It is lined throughout with mercerized sateen, facing in front made of same material. Very dressy and serviceable. Colors: tan and blueish gray.
Price...........(If by mail, postage extra, 48 cents.)..... **$4.75**

No. 63478 LADIES' NOVELTY JACKET, made of gray covert cloth, has high storm collar, large lapels trimmed with velvet applique and embroidered with fancy black cord. The jacket buttons up high at the neck, is double breasted, trimmed with six horn buttons, lined throughout with black sateen, facing in front made of same material as jacket. New fan back. Color, gray only.
Price.................. **$4.95**

No. 63479 VERY NEAT JACKET made of good quality, light weight Kersey cloth, has high storm collar and coat shape lapels, double breasted front trimmed with four pearl buttons, coat shape sleeves, tight back. Lined throughout with good quality of mercerized sateen, facing in front made of same material as jacket, button holes stitched with silk. Colors: black, royal blue, castor and tan. Price......(If by mail, postage extra, 50 cents.).. **$5.50**

No. 63480 LADIES' JACKET. High storm collar, large lapels and is edged with Black Baltic Seal Fur all around, double-breasted front. Made of a good quality of beaver. Lined throughout with mercerized sateen. It is very heavy and suitable for cold climates. It has shirred sleeves and flaring cuffs. Colors: black, royal blue and castor. Price.... **$5.75**

No. 63481 OUR SPECIAL LEADER FOR $4.95. This jacket is strictly tailor made and is stitched all around five times, five rows of stitching around the sleeves, has large storm collar and lapels, buttoning up at the neck, has double-breasted front and is trimmed with six black horn buttons. The jacket is faced with same material and is lined throughout with blue mercerized sateen. Black and navy blue only. Price....(If by mail, postage extra, 58 cents.)..... **$4.95**

No. 63482 LADIES' JACKET, made of good quality of Kersey, coat shaped collar and lapels, has double-breasted front, trimmed with 4 horn buttons Kersey strap trimming in front, lined throughout with good mercerized sateen, facing in front same material as jacket. Colors: black and blue.
Price ....(If by mail, postage extra, 54 cents.)..... **$5.35**

63489
$6.95

63486
$4.95

63485
$6.35

63491
$7.75

63487
$6.25

LADIES' JACKETS

63484
$5.98

63488
$6.50

63483
$5.95

63490
$7.75

SIZES from 32 to 42 inches. We will charge 20 per cent extra if the garment must be made to order. All sizes different from those advertised are considered special. **SPECIALS MUST BE PAID FOR IN ADVANCE.**

No. 63483 ANOTHER ONE OF THOSE GREAT BARGAINS. Made according to the latest fashion plate, of good quality of Kersey Cloth. It has cost-shape collar, large lapels appliqued with black satin and embroidered with cord, has double-breasted front, trimmed with eight horn buttons. The Jacket is lined throughout with black sateen, facing in front made of same material as Jacket. Colors, black or navy blue. Price, each.......... **$5.95**
If by mail, postage extra, 50 cents.

No. 63484 LADIES STYLISH JACKET, made of good quality, light weight Kersey Cloth, has double-breasted front, trimmed with six fancy buttons, coatshape collar made of velvet, velvet applique on lapels and inlaid velvet on pocket flaps; shirred sleeves. Jacket is stitched three times all around, lined throughout with a good quality of mercerized cotton serge. **We can furnish this Jacket in black, royal blue, castor and tan.** Price, each.. **$5.98**
If by mail, postage extra, 44 cents.

No 63485 THIS EXTREMELY STYLISH, NOBBY JACKET, made of high-grade Diagonal Cloth. The Jacket is 19 inches long, in fact it looks very much like a short Eton Jacket; has a cost-shape velvet collar, and is lined throughout with a guaranteed satin reaching to the edge of the Jacket and turns over on lapels. Has double-breasted front, trimmed with six cloth buttons, strictly tailor-made and perfect fitting. Has coat sleeves with two rows of stitching around the cuffs. Colors, blue and black.
Price, each............ (If by mail, postage extra, 46 cents.)........ **$6.35**

No. 63486 LADIES' JACKET, made of good quality of Boucle Cloth, has shield front and high storm collar, lined throughout with black silk serge, facing in front made of same material as Jacket is made of, interlined with wadding to make it heavy and serviceable for the winter. Elegant Jacket for the money. Color, black only.
Price, each............(If by mail, postage extra, 48 cents.)........ **$4.95**

No. 63487 LADIES' JACKET, made of good quality of Boucle Cloth, has double-breasted front, trimmed with six smoked buttons, large collar and lapels. Bottom of sleeves and pocket flap are bound with kersey strap trimming, stitched three times all around. Very showy garment and inexpensive. It is lined throughout with black silkene, facing in front made of same material as jacket; has coat sleeves and fan back. Color, black only. If by mail, postage extra, 54 cents. Price, each.......... **$6.25**

No. 63488 THIS JACKET is made of very good quality of kersey cloth, we cannot call it all wool, but others do; commercially speaking, it is all wool. It has a high storm collar, large lapels in front, buttoning up high at the neck, is double breasted, and is trimmed with six fancy buttons. Lined throughout with good quality of silk romain lining, facing in front made of same material as Jacket, shirred sleeves and stylish back. Can furnish in black, blue and castor. Price, each.......... **$6.50**

No. 63489 VERY STYLISH LADIES' JACKET, made of all-wool Pebble Cheviot, double-breasted front, trimmed with six fancy smoked pearl buttons. Coat-shape collar and lapels, lapels are faced with rhadame silk and stitched five times. Jacket lined throughout with good quality of satin, thoroughly guaranteed for two seasons. It is lined with material same as Jacket is made of, shirt sleeves, neat cuffs and plaited back. **Very nobby and fashionable garment.** Color, black only. Price, each.......... **$6.95**
If by mail, postage extra, 52 cents.

No. 63490 VERY NOBBY LADIES' JACKET, made of good quality of all-wool Kersey Cloth, coat-shaped collar and lapels, has double-breasted front trimmed with fancy buttons. The collar is made of velvet, is thoroughly tailor-made, and is trimmed with kersey strap trimming in front and on the two back seams, fancy pocket flaps; lined throughout with good quality of mercerized sateen, faced with same material as jacket is made of. Can furnish in black, royal blue, castor and tan. Price, each.......... **$7.75**

No. 63491 VERY STYLISH LADIES' JACKET, made of high-grade of all-wool Boucle, in dark gray color only; has high storm collar, large lapel buttoning up at the neck, double-breasted front trimmed with six horn buttons, thoroughly tailor-made and trimmed with kersey cloth strap trimming in front of lapel and large collar, and on two of the back seams, as well as around the cuffs. The Jacket is lined throughout with good quality of satin. Very serviceable garment and adapted for cold climates. Price, each.......... (If by mail, postage extra, 52 cents.)........ **$7.75**

63548 $13.25

63549 $13.50

63550 $15.00

63551 $15.75

63547 $11.25

63546 $10.75

63545 $9.95

63544 $9.35

PLUSH CAPES

WHEN ORDERING state bust measure, number of inches around the neck, your height and weight. We make these capes from 32 to 44 inches around the bust. Larger sizes must be made to order, for which we charge 20% above the price quoted in the catalogue, and cash in full must accompany the order.

When postage is not given goods cannot be sent by mail.

No. 63544 STYLISH CAPE, made of fine seal plush, neatly embroidered with black soutache and beads. It measures 30 inches in length and 125 inches in sweep. Lined throughout with silk rhadame and interlined with wadding. Bear fur edging around the large storm collar and in front. The embroidery is one of the newest designs. Price, each..$9.35

No. 63545 NOVELTY OF THE SEASON, stylish plush cape appliqued with satin, the very newest thing and copied from an imported garment. It is made of a very good quality plush, 30 inches long and over 100 inches in sweep. Nicely embroidered with black soutache and beads. The large storm collar and front are trimmed with brown bear fur. Lined throughout with good quality silk rhadame in black or lavender colors. Price, each..................................$9.95

No. 63546 LADIES' PLUSH CAPE, 30 inches long, 120 inches in sweep, made of very good quality plush, lined throughout with silk rhadame and interlined with wadding. The large storm collar is made of brown bear fur and the front is trimmed with bear fur. Price, each.............................$10.75

No. 63547 LADIES' CAPE, made of high grade plush, 27 inches long and 100 inches in sweep. Embroidered with black soutache and beads. High standing storm collar and front edged with brown bear fur, lined throughout with good quality black satin and interlined with fiber chamois. Very good value for the money. Price, each...$11.25

No. 63548 LADIES' HIGH GRADE PLUSH CAPE, 30 inches long, 120 inches sweep, embroidered in the very newest and latest style. A perfect wonder, trimmed with black soutache braid and beads. The large storm collar and front are trimmed with brown bear fur, lined throughout with good quality black satin and interlined with fiber chamois and wadding. A very handsome garment. Price, each...$13.25

No. 63549 LADIES' PLUSH CAPE, made of high grade plush, 30 inches long and 120 inches in sweep. The large storm collar is made of South American beaver (nutria) and the front is edged with the same fur. Lined throughout with good quality black satin and interlined with wadding, making the cape heavy, warm and comfortable. On each side of front there is a four-inch facing of plush. We can highly recommend this as one of the best numbers in the catalogue. Price, each..$13.50

No. 63550 LADIES' PLUSH CAPE, made of very fine quality plush, 34 inches long and 120 inches in sweep. The large storm collar is made of genuine black Thibet fur, edged with fur. Each side of front is faced with plush these inches wide. Lined throughout with very good quality black satin and interlined with wadding. A very nobby and neat garment and there is hardly anything better than this on the market, and we would rather sell one of these capes than a cheaper one, knowing they give more satisfaction to our customers. A cape of this kind will last a lifetime and always look nice and neat. Price, each...$15.00

No. 63551 LADIES' PLUSH CAPE, 35 inches long and 120 inches in sweep. The large storm collar is made of brown bear fur and the front is trimmed with the same fur. Is very full and looks like a genuine marten, in fact you could not tell them apart unless you held them alongside of each other, and then only if you were an expert. This cape is lined throughout with all silk rhadame and interlined with wadding. For something exclusive and stylish we can recommend this cape, and for durability there is nothing better. Price, each..................................$15.75

63557
$7.50

63555
$12.50

63561
$11.98

63560
$13.50

63556
$12.75

63559
$12.00

63558
$8.95

63554
$11.50

63553
$10.50

63552
$9.75

LADIES' JACKETS

Made in sizes from 32 to 42 inches, no odd sizes. If you want 33, 37 or 39, order 34, 38 or 40, respectively. Goods listed in our Catalogue are subject to small changes, according to the prevailing style—such as sleeves, length, buttons, etc. We will charge 20 per cent extra if the garment must be made to order and must be paid for in advance.

No. 63552 **VERY SERVICEABLE GARMENT,** made of all-wool Kersey cloth, large collar and lapels of genuine wool seal; looks just like genuine Martin. It buttons up high at the neck, has double breasted front buttoning with loops at one side, lined throughout with Romain silk lining and faced in front with Kersey cloth. It has an inverted plait in the back, plain cuffs and shirt sleeves. Black, royal blue and caster. Price.. (If by mail, postage extra, 31 cents.).. **$9.75**

No. 63553 **JACKET,** made of all-wool Kersey, trimmed with a 1-inch wide satin band around large collar, large pointed lapels in front and bottom. Stitched all around five times with silk, has tight fitting back pointed in the center, double breasted front, trimmed with six fancy pearl buttons. Lined throughout with guaranteed satin fancy facing in front made of same material as jacket. Black, royal blue and tan. Price...... (If by mail, postage extra, 34 cents.).. **$10.50**

No. 63554 **LADIES' JACKET,** made of very heavy all-wool large curl astrakhan. It has large storm collar and large lapels which button up high at the neck; has double breasted front trimmed with six fancy pearl buttons. Lined throughout with a very fine Skinner satin and faced with same material as jacket is made of. Color, black only. Price, each...... (If by mail, postage extra, 55 cents.).. **$11.50**

No. 63555 **THIS ATTRACTIVE AND BEAUTIFUL JACKET** is made of all-wool Kersey; it has large collar and lapels stitched eight times. The collar and lapels are faced with guaranteed satin and there is an extension under this also made of kersey and faced with satin. It is very rich looking and stylish; double breasted front trimmed with six fancy metal buttons; lined throughout with guaranteed satin and faced with same material as jacket is made of. Coat shape sleeves and fancy cuffs stitched eight times. Made by men tailors. Black, caster, gray and royal blue. Price, each...... (If by mail, postage extra, 45 cents.).. **$12.50**

No. 63556 **LADIES' JACKET,** made of all-wool Kersey, large collar and lapels made of genuine black Astrakhan fur; has double-breasted front trimmed with six smoked pearl buttons, coat shape sleeves, plain cuffs, stitched all around three times with silk, lined throughout with Romain silk lining, and faced in front with same material as jacket is made of; new back, fur collar and lapels. Comes in black and caster. Price........... (If by mail, postage extra, 39 cents.)........... **$12.75**

No. 63557 **LADIES' JACKET,** made of good quality silk plush, high storm collar, shield front, lined throughout with black silk lining, faced in front with plush. Price,............... **$7.50**
If by mail, postage extra, 38 cents.)

No. 63558 **LADIES' JACKET,** very nobby and stylish, made of high grade silk plush, has high storm collar, large lapels, double breasted front, buttoning on one side. The jacket is trimmed all around the collar, lapels and front with brown Siberian Marten. It is lined throughout with Romain silk lining and has a wide facing of plush in front. Price............... **$8.95**

No. 63559 **LADIES' NOVELTY JACKET,** made of high grade silk plush, large collar and lapels are appliqued with morsen cloth, beaded and embroidered with astrakhan fur; all around collar. Jacket buttons up high at the neck, is half tight fitting in front and back; facing in front made of same material as jacket and lined throughout with Romain silk lining. (If by mail, postage extra, 50 cents.)Each... **$12.00**

No. 63560 **WINNER OF THE SEASON,** made of fine silk plush. It has large collar and lapels trimmed with brown Siberian Marten, half tight fitting front double breasted style, buttoned with loops; facing in front is made of same material as jacket and is lined throughout with a good quality of satin. Price, each (Postage, extra 42c) **$13.50**

No. 63561 **LADIES' PLUSH SACK,** made of fine plush, has high storm collar and shield front. Lined throughout with Rhadame quilted lining, 3-inch plush facing in front; it is interlined with wadding to make it warm and serviceable for the winter. We can also furnish this sack with around collar, or as shown in illustration ornaments cont and lined with satin. When ordering, please state which one you desire. Price, each.... **$11.98**
If by mail, postage extra, 52 cents.

64821
$3.75

64817
$14.00

64822
$4.95

64819
$15.75

64816
$12.50

64818

64820
$17.50

LADIES' SUITS.

No. 64816 LADIES' SUIT, made of all-wool chevlot serge. The jacket is lined throughout with good quality black satin, reaching up to the front of jacket, covering lapel as shown in illustration; fly front, new sleeves. Skirt is three and one-half yards wide; is lined throughout with good quality percaline and interlined with crinoline; bound with velvet all around the bottom. Colors, black and blue. Price...$12.50

No. 64817 LADIES' TAILOR MADE SUIT, made of all-wool chevlot serge. The jacket is single breasted, tight fitting; small collar and lapels. Jacket is lined throughout with good quality taffeta silk. Skirt is tailor made, plait in back, 3½ yards wide; interlined at the bottom with canvas and bound with waterproof binding. Colors, black and blue. Price.............$14.00

No. 64818 LADIES' TAILOR MADE SUIT, consisting of Eton jacket and skirt. It is made of all-wool Venetian cloth. The jacket is made in the newest Eton style, pointed front, double breasted effect. It is bound in strips of taffeta silk, as shown in illustration, on collar, lapels, in front, all around jacket and on the seams in back. Jacket is lined throughout with good quality taffeta silk; round silk covered buttons. Skirt is tailor made; has one row of silk trimming in front as shown in illustration; is lined throughout with percaline and interlined on the bottom with canvas. It is bound with velvet all around the bottom; plait in back. Colors, black, seal brown and royal blue. Price...$16.50

No. 64819 LADIES' TAILOR MADE SUIT, made of all wool chevlot serge; is fly front style, has coat collar and lapel. The entire suit is lined throughout with taffeta silk. The jacket has light facing on lapel of Peau de Soir. The skirt is 3½ yards wide; is lined throughout with taffeta silk with a taffeta silk band around the waist; interlined with crinoline and bound with corduroy on the bottom. It has a plaited back. We can furnish these suits in black or navy blue colors. Price...$15.75

No. 64820 LADIES' TAILOR MADE SUIT; made of all wool broadcloth; double breasted effect in front, with loops instead of button holes; silk covered round buttons. It has a large collar and lapel, handsomely appliqued with wide taffeta silk. The effect is beautiful and the jacket can be worn open in a blazer effect or closed, as either way it will show the desired effect. It is lined throughout with a good quality taffeta silk. Skirt is tailor made; lined throughout with percaline and interlined on the bottom with canvas and bound with a wide velvet facing; plait in back. It is thoroughly tailor made. A glance will convince you that it is the greatest bargain for the money. Colors, black and royal blue. Price..$17.50

RAINY DAY SKIRTS.

No. 64821 LADIES' RAINY DAY SKIRT; in brown, blue, black or gray. The material is durable and well adapted for the purpose. The skirt is from 37 to 42 inches long, no longer or shorter. It has a band around the waist, stitched four times, and facing of same material and stitching on the bottom. No lining. It has a plait in back. Price...$3.75

No. 64822 LADIES' RAINY DAY SKIRT; made of diagonal plaid back cloth. The skirt has a plait in back, facing of same material on bottom and eight rows of stitching. There is no lining in the skirt, but it has a beautiful fancy plaid back. We furnish these skirts in 37 to 42-inch lengths. It is one of the best skirts on the market for the money. We positively state that there is none better. We will send you samples on request. We can furnish it in black or gray with fancy plaid backs. Price...$4.95

64823 $1.35

64824 $1.48

64828 $2.98

64825 $1.75

64827 $2.75

64826 $2.45

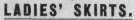

64829 $3.15

64831 $345

64830 $2.98

64832 $3.65

LADIES' SKIRTS.

We can furnish skirts from 37 to 44 inches in length, from 23 to 30 inches around waist. Sizes different from these must be made to order, in which case we require 20 per cent above price quoted in catalogue. All the specials must be paid for in advance.

No. 64823 LADIES' SKIRT, made of figured brilliantine, three yards wide, bound with velveteen all around the bottom. Lined throughout with percaline. Color, black only.

Price, each..**$1.35**

If by mail, postage extra, each, 31 cents.

No. 64824 LADIES' SKIRT, made of fancy plaids, in all the newest shades and colors. Skirt is lined throughout with black percaline, interlined at the bottom with canvas and bound with waterproof binding. It is three yards wide at bottom and has the new plait in back.

Price, each..**$1.48**

If by mail, postage extra, each, 39 cents.

No. 64825 LADIES' SKIRT, made of good quality Manchester cloth, measures 3¾ yards around the bottom, is lined throughout with black percaline, interlined with crinoline. It is bound with velvet all around bottom and has inverted plait in back. Good value for the money.

Price, each..**$1.75**

If by mail, postage extra, each, 35 cents.

No. 64826 STYLISH LADIES' SKIRT, made of twilled cloth, in Oxford, gray color only, has three rows of satin piping on either side of front, with three inverted plaits (as shown in illustration.) This skirt measures 120 inches around the bottom and is bound with waterproof binding, is lined with black percaline and has inverted plait in back. Very good value for the money.

Price, each..**$2.45**

If by mail, postage extra, each, 61 cents.

No. 64827 LADIES' FIGURED SICILIAN CLOTH SKIRT, thoroughly tailor-made, double seams in front, all seams bound, and lined throughout with good quality of black percaline and interlined with crinoline, bound with velvet all around the bottom, has new plait in back and measures three yards around the bottom. Color, black only.

Price, each..**$2.75**

If by mail, postage extra, each, 36 cents.

No. 64828 LADIES' TAILOR MADE SKIRT, made of all-wool cheviot, double seams in front, lined throughout with black percaline and interlined with crinoline, velvet binding all around the bottom, has inverted plait in back, and measures 3¼ yards around the sweep. It is a well made garment and we can highly recommend it. Colors, black and navy blue.

Price, each..**$2.98**

If by mail, postage extra, each, 36 cents.

No. 64829 VERY STYLISH GARMENT, made of good quality of mohair Sicilian, tailor made seams in front, velvet binding all around the bottom, a little over three yards wide, lined throughout with percaline, interlined with crinoline, faced with canvas around the bottom, plait in back. Colors, black and blue.

Price, each..**$3.15**

If by mail, postage extra, each, 34 cents.

No. 64830 NOVELTY SKIRT MADE OF CREPON CLOTH. Crepons have been all the go for the past season and they are the same again this year. Has double seams in front, a little over three yards wide, lined throughout with percaline, interlined with crinoline and bound with velvet around the bottom, has the new plait in back. Can furnish this in all black, blue and black, red and black, and green and black combinations.

Price, each..**$2.98**

If by mail, postage extra, each, 46 cents.

No. 64831 VERY ATTRACTIVE GARMENT, made of good quality repellent cloth, which looks almost as good as a broadcloth. It is neatly trimmed with satin folds stitched six times all around the bottom; it is lined throughout with black percaline and interlined with crinoline, bound with waterproof binding, measures over three yards around the bottom and has the inverted plait in back. Colors, black or blue.

Price, each..**$3.45**

If by mail, postage extra, each, 49 cents.

No. 64832 OUR SPECIAL LEADER FOR $3.65, made of gray Oxford skirting in the latest tunic effect, with knife plaiting all around the bottom. Knife plaiting is made of mercerized sateen, which looks like silk; it also has a dust ruffle made of percaline. Top skirt is scalloped all around and neatly trimmed with three satin bands, has inverted plait in back and measures 3¼ yards around the bottom. Color, gray only.

Price, each..**$3.65**

64920 $5.75

64917 $3.98

64915 $2.65

64923 $6.75

64918 $4.25

64922 $6.50

64925 $7.95

64916 $2.98

64921 $4.98

64919 $4.50

64924 $6.95

LADIES' SILK AND VELVET WAISTS.

Made in sizes from 32 to 42 inches around the bust and from 22 to 29 inches around waist. We do not guarantee taffeta silk. If you desire any other color than the waists are advertised we will make them to order for 20 per cent more than the quotation in the catalogue.

No. 64915 LADIES' WAIST, made of a very good quality of Velvet; High standing detachable collar, flaring cuffs, band in front, four plaits in back. The waist is lined throughout with good quality of cambric. Colors are black, navy, green and garnet.
Price..............(If by mail, postage extra, 22 cents.)..........................$2.65

No. 64916 LADIES' WAIST, made of guaranteed Satin, has high standing detachable collar, corded three times, seven rows of cording on each side of waist in front, French back corded five times; very neat and attractive garment and good value for the money. Can furnish in black, heliotrope and red. Price..........................$2.98
If by mail, postage extra, 18 cents.

No. 64917 LADIES' WAIST. This is positively one of the handsomest and best styles shown in our catalogue. It is our leader, and price and style should be enough inducement to everybody to favor us with an order. This handsome waist is made of a good quality of taffeta silk (Silkina), it is tucked all over, front, back and sleeves, has a high standing detachable collar with five rows of tucking. The waist is lined throughout with good quality of cambric. There is nothing to beat this garment, and if you want the neatest garment of the season, we would advise you to favor us with your order. Colors are black, lavender, old rose, cadet blue and red. Price..........................$3.98
If by mail, postage extra, each, 25 cents.

No. 64918 VERY STYLISH WAIST, made of good quality of Taffeta Silk, it is tucked all over the front and neatly trimmed with black and white silk braid, high standing detachable collar tucked and trimmed to match the waist, similar trimmings on sleeves and on flaring cuffs. French back tucked and trimmed with silk braid to match. Very stylish garment for the money. Can furnish in black, red, old rose, navy and lavender. Price...$4.25
If by mail, postage extra, 20 cents.

No. 64919 HIGH GRADE LADIES' WAIST, made of good quality of Taffeta Silk, with a chemisette front, has high standing detachable collar tucked three times. The inlaid front of the waist is made of white silk, and outside part of the waist made of any color as stated below. It is tucked all over and trimmed with fancy embroidered gimp, sleeves are tucked ten times, French back with five rows of tucking, lined throughout with good quality of cambric lining. Furnished in black, cerise, lavender and royal blue color, with a white inlaid front.
Price..........................$4.50
If by mail, postage extra, 16 cents.

No. 64920 LADIES' HIGH GRADE WAIST, made of very good quality of Taffeta Silk, tucked all over, has high standing detachable collar and flaring cuffs, lined throughout with good quality of cambric. This style of waist has proven to be all the rage since we have been showing it in our catalogue and our machines cannot turn them out fast enough. This alone ought to be sufficient guarantee that it is very popular and the proper style. The materials used are the very best and workmanlike first class in every respect. Colors are black, red, new blue and lavender; any other colors 50 cents extra. Price..........................$5.75
If by mail, postage extra, each, 20 cents.

No. 64921 LADIES' WAIST, made of good quality of Silk Duchess Satin, high standing detachable collar with three rows of tucking, pointed yoke in front, is tucked all over. The style is the very newest revere effect and lapels are tucked and trimmed with fancy gimp around the edges. The entire waist is tucked on the bias, as shown in illustration, in front as well as in the back; has flaring cuffs and is lined throughout with a good quality of cambric. We can furnish this in black, navy, red and lavender colors. Price....[If by mail, postage extra, each, 22 cents]..........................$4.98

No. 64922 VERY NOBBY AND STYLISH WAIST, made of all silk Duchess Satin, has a high standing detachable collar, pointed yoke in front tucked all over, large revers with silk applique and silk cord embroidery. The waist is tucked from shoulder to waist in front as well as in back, cascade ruffle finishing waist in front, trimmed with silk fringe. It is lined all through with good quality of cambric. Can furnish in black, new blue, old rose and red colors. Price..........................$6.50
If by mail, postage extra, each, 18 cents.

No. 64923 VERY NOBBY AND GENTEEL WAIST, made of a high grade of Taffeta Silk; it is tucked and plaited eight times in front and trimmed with fancy black silk braid, similar trimming in back, has detachable crushed collar made of same material and trimmed to match waist, flaring cuffs finished with silk braid, three rows of tucking and black braid around the sleeves; it is a very attractive waist. Waist it is very neat and plain, it is always stylish. Lined throughout with good quality of cambric. Can furnish in black, gray, old rose colors; any other colors, 50 cents extra. Price..........................$6.75
If by mail, postage extra, each, 18 cents.

No. 64924 LADIES' WAIST, made of the very best Taffeta Silk on the market. It is tucked all around, has a revere front, it is also tucked three times on either side, taffeta silk bow in front, has high standing collar, pointed yoke in front made of white taffeta silk, also tucked all over. We cannot do justice to the picture to the waist, and same must be seen to be appreciated. We cannot show the quality, cannot show the workmanship, nor can we show, with justice to the waist, the general appearance. It will be a pleasure to us to send you one of these handsome waists on approval, as we are certain you will be more than pleased with and if you see it. There is nothing better made for the price, and if you want a real stylish, neat, handsome waist, buy this. We can furnish this in black, red, new blue. We can also furnish this for 50 cents extra in sage green, old rose or lavender. These colors are very pretty and with combination of white yoke and collar, it very tasty. Price..........................$6.95
If by mail, postage extra, each, 20 cents.

No. 64925 VERY STYLISH AND ATTRACTIVE WAIST, made of high grade Glossamd Taffeta Silk, has a high standing detachable collar, tucked all over (as shown in illustrations), yoke in front is has applique embroidered with silk cord. From yoke to waist it is tucked all around reaching to the back; part of the sleeves are tucked, and upper part is embroidered with silk cord; it also has a French back. The workmanship is perfect, nothing could excel in style, the quality of materials used are the very best, in fact it is as fine a waist as anyone shows for the money. We can furnish this in black, old rose, turquoise and gray; any other colors but those mentioned, 50 cents extra. Price..........................$7.95
If by mail, postage extra, each, 18 cents.

64934
$1.25

ONLY
MAIL ORDER HOUSE
SELLING
"CORSET
VEST WRAPPER"

64941
$1.59

64936
$1.35

64938
$149

64942
$1.75

64939
$1.55

64937
$1.39

64940
$1.59

LADIES' WRAPPERS.

We furnish Ladies' Wrappers in sizes from 32 to 44 inches around bust. We do not make any odd sizes, such as 33, 35, 37, etc. Should you have occasion to order these sizes always order 34, 36 or 38, respectively. Extra sizes must be made to order, in which case we require 20 per cent. above price quoted in the catalogue.

The figures in material are not always the same as shown in illustration. They are subject to changes in style.

No. 64934 LADIES' HIGH GRADE PERCALE HOUSE DRESS. Guaranteed to be fast colors. Black, blue and red stripes or black or blue polka-dots. One row of plaiting around the collar and three rows on the front. It has the celebrated corset belt with draw string, reaching all around the vest and making it adjustable to any waist, or it can be worn loose. It is very comfortable and very pretty at the same time. You can wear this dress without a corset and look neat. Finished with cuffs on sleeves and wide hem at bottom.
Price, each **$1.25**
If by mail, postage extra, each, 28 cents.

No. 64936 VERY NEAT WRAPPER, made of good quality of flannelette, lay down collar, yoke in front, shoulder epaulets made of solid color percale to match the wrapper. It is trimmed with two rows of fancy braid around yoke, one around the collar and one around the epaulets, collar and shoulder flaps are finished with ruffle, fancy flaring cuffs trimmed with braid. ruffle and belt also trimmed with white braid, good quality cambric vest. Colors: Black, blue, red with white. Price, each **$1.35**
If by mail, postage extra, each, 30 cents.

No. 64937 THIS FLANNELETTE WRAPPER is made in fancy colors such as heliotrope, red or brown with black polka-dots. The yoke is V-shaped in front and is made of fast black sateen. Collar, yoke and front trimmed with white braid. Very neat belt all around with same trimming. Cambric vest inside. A very good quality for the price. Price, each **$1.39**
If by mail, postage extra, each, 29 cents.

No. 64938 LADIES' HIGH GRADE FLANNELETTE WRAPPER, made in blue polka-dot patterns only. It is handsomely trimmed with white cord in front in a plaid effect. Shoulder flaps and sleeves trimmed in a similar manner. Yoke in back of wrapper is same as in front; plaited in back from yoke to waist. Inside cambric vest. Very neat.
Price, each **$1.49**
If by mail, postage extra, each, 31 cents.

No. 64939 LADIES' FLANNELETTE WRAPPER, made in fancy figured or striped design in dark colors with green, blue, rose or gray predominating. It has double shoulder flounces very neatly embroidered with white braid. The large lay-down collar is also embroidered in a similar manner. Pointed yoke in back with plaits to waist. Inside vest made of a good quality cambric It also has the celebrated corset belt. Price, each **$1.55**
If by mail, postage extra, each, 33 cents.

No. 64940 LADIES' WRAPPER, made of good quality flannel in striped patterns, either black, navy blue or red colors. The yoke is made of solid colored flannelette with full flounce around the yoke extending to the back. Large collar finished with narrow flounce and white braid. Shoulder flaps and same trimming as collar. Fancy cuffs finished with small flounce and white braid. Plaited in back from yoke to waist. Price, each **$1.59**
If by mail, postage extra, each, 32 cents.

No. 64941 LADIES' STYLISH WRAPPER, made of high grade flannelette. Colors, black and navy blue polka dots, and black, navy blue and red with small white figures. Double ruffle around upper part of wrapper, reaching from front to back; handsomely trimmed at edges with white torchon lace; two straps of same lace on collar, belt and sleeves. Inside vest of good quality cambric.
Price, each....(If by mail, postage extra, each, 28 cents.).... **$1.59**

No. 64942 A VERY ATTRACTIVE AND STYLISH HOUSE DRESS, made of good quality checked flannelette. It has a lay down collar, finished with velvet ribbon. Yoke in front as well as a straight yoke in back, also made of velvet; has a very full front, extra large skirt and a wide hem on bottom. It has the corset vest arrangement inside, made of good quality cambric and with draw strings. You can adjust it just as you want. Similar arrangements around the waist. Colors: Black and white checks only. Price, each...................(If by mail, postage extra, 32 cents.)...................**$1.75**

64963
$7.50

64960
$9.00

64961
$7.75

64953
$3.40

64955
$5.00

LADIES' SKIRT AND CAPE MACKINTOSH SUITS.

THE NEW CAPE AND SKIRT STYLE MACKINTOSHES are now recognized everywhere as a most practical and useful protection, and in severe storms will save a dress from ruin, which would mean a loss much greater than the cost of the mackintosh. **WE HAVE THE LARGEST LINE** shown by any house, and our prices are the lowest, quality considered.

MEASUREMENTS. FOR CAPE—Bust, all around body, close up under arms in inches. FOR SKIRT—All around waist in inches; length of skirt, down front from waist to bottom. Height and weight.
THE CAPES average 26 inches in length. Double breasted capes average about 150 inches sweep, and are made with one epaulet in back and velvet collars. Double capes average 110 inches sweep and have velvet collars.

WE FIT FROM STOCK. Bust, 32 to 42 inches; Waist, 22 to 30 inches; Length of Skirt, 38 to 45 inches. The skirts are made to button on both sides, are wide sweep and have adjustable waist. By resetting the buttons, any change can be made to suit the figure. Average sweep, 120 inches.

ANY SIZES LARGER than given above, and extreme or unproportionate sizes, must be made to order at an extra cost of $2.00 per suit, or $1.00 extra for either skirt or cape, two weeks' time allowed, and full cash must accompany the order. Always give measurements correctly.

No. 64953 LADIES' SKIRT AND CAPE MACKINTOSH SUIT, made of navy blue cashmere cloth with fancy plaid lining. Made only in the two cape style, as shown in illustration. A good serviceable suit at a low price. Price for either skirt or cape separately, each, $1.70; price for complete suit........ **$3.40**

No. 64954 LADIES' SKIRT AND CAPE MACKINTOSH SUIT. Same quality and style as above. Color black. Price for either skirt or cape separately, $1.70; price for complete suit..................... **$3.40**

No. 64955 LADIES' SKIRT AND CAPE SUIT MACKINTOSH. Made of fine wool Cashmere cloth, navy blue with fancy plaid lining and velvet collar. Double breasted style only. A very serviceable suit. Price for either cape or skirt, separately, $2.50; price for complete suit................................. **$5.00**

No. 64956 LADIES' SKIRT AND CAPE SUIT, same quality and style as above. Color, black. Price for either cape or skirt separately, $2.50; price for complete suit........ **5.00**

No. 64957 LADIES' SKIRT AND CAPE SUIT, made of fine all wool tan covert cloth, with fancy plaid lining. Double-breasted style only. Trimmed with pearl buttons and velvet collar. A very fine high grade garment.
Price for either cape or skirt separately, each, $3.75; price for complete suit................... **$7.50**

No. 64958 LADIES' FINE ALL WOOL COVERT IN DARK BROWN SCOTCH MIXED CLOTH. With fancy woven plaid lining of select design. Very handsome and stylish suit. Made double-breasted style, pearl buttons and velvet collar.
Price for either cape or skirt separately, each $4.00; price for complete suit................. **$8.00**

No. 64959 LADIES' FINE ALL WOOL MACKINTOSH SUIT, made from fancy plaid English cheviot, dark brown in color. A very small plaid figure, modest and stylish and out of the usual range of cloths made into mackintoshes. Dark fancy lining. Pearl buttons and velvet collar. Double-breasted style only.
Price for either skirt or cape separately, each, $3.50; price for complete suit............. **$7.00**

No. 64960 LADIES' FINE GENUINE BANNOCKBURN SCOTCH MIXTURE MACKINTOSH SUIT with very select woven fancy plaid lining. A very dark mixed cloth, equal to any mackintosh you can buy for $15.00. Very high grade in every particular. Trimmed with pearl buttons and velvet collar. Double-breasted style only. Price for either skirt or cape separately, each, $4.50; price for complete suit.... **$9.00**

No. 64961 LADIES' FINE ALL WOOL BLUE CASHMERE MACKINTOSH, lined with bright red plain mercerized silk lining, making a very stylish suit, which cannot be duplicated outside our establishment. Double-breasted style only. Pearl buttons and velvet collar. Price for skirt or cape separately, each, $3.90; price for complete suit.... **$7.75**

No. 64962 LADIES' FINE MACKINTOSH SUIT, made of fine all wool Oxford gray covert cloth with fancy woven plaid lining. A stylish, serviceable suit of high quality. Double-breasted style only. Pearl buttons and velvet collar. Price for either skirt or cape separately, each, $3.90; price for complete suit **$7.75**

No. 64963 LADIES' FINE WOOL ARLINGTON CLOTH MACKINTOSH SUIT, all black in pretty brocaded design; lined with fancy dark red mohair lining of fancy brocaded design. A stylish black suit, sure to please and give entire satisfaction. Double-breasted style only. Pearl buttons and velvet collar.
Price for either skirt or cape separately, each, $3.75; price for complete suit. **$7.50**

MEMORIAL DEPARTMENT

THE WORLD'S BEST ROYAL BLUE VERMONT MARBLE.
IT IS EVERYWHERE CONCEDED TO BE THE FINEST IN THE WORLD. It is of rich, unfading color, and superior to the other blue marbles on the market which lose their color on exposure to the weather. A FINE, CLOSE GRAINED MARBLE.

OUR SUPERIOR FINISHING. We do not use Oxalic Acid, and we employ only skilled artisans. We do not have our work done by the piece, but only employ day labor, thus securing the best possible fineness in finish.

WE OFFER YOU the handsome Marble Markers shown on these pages, with any lettering you desire, at half the prices you can buy them from your nearest marble dealer, and WE PAY THE FREIGHT east of the Rocky Mountains.

OUR LIBERAL $1.00 C. O. D. OFFER. Send us any lettering you may desire carved in the marble, and $1.00 as a guarantee of good faith, and we will send you, freight prepaid, any tombstone you may select from these pages. If it is not exactly as represented and the lettering handsomely engraved according to your instructions, you can return it to us and we will refund the money. Examine it at your freight depot, and if satisfactory, pay the agent our catalogue price less the $1.00 sent with order.

UNHEARD OF VALUE AT $29.00 AND UPWARDS.

LIKE EVERY ONE of our higher grade tombstones this monument is made in the same famous quarry, and, by reason of having been made there, you are guaranteed a quality which you might not expect anywhere else.

The measurements of the smaller size of this tombstone are as follows: Bottom base, 1 foot 4 inches, by 1 foot 4 inches, by 8 inches. Base, 1 foot, by 1 foot, by 6 inches. Shaft, 2 feet 6 inches, by 8 inches. Height over all, 3 feet 8 inches. This tombstone is made in the following variety and qualities of marble:

No. 42755 Dark vein marble.......................$29.00
No. 42756 Florence No. 2........................29.00
No. 42757 Dark mottled marble.................31.25
No. 42758 Extra dark vein marble.............31.25
No. 42759 Average Florence marble...........31.25
No. 42760 Extra dark mottled marble........33.00
No. 42761 Florence No. 1.........................33.00

A LARGER SIZE AT $46.75 TO $52.50.

The next largest size of this handsome monument is as follows: Bottom base, 1 foot 6 inches, by 1 foot 6 inches, by 10 inches. Base, 1 foot 2 inches, by 1 foot 2 inches, by 8 inches. Shaft, 2 feet 10 inches, by 10 inches. Height over all, 4 feet 4 inches. Our special prices on this size are as follows:

No. 42762 Dark vein marble....................$46.75
No. 42763 Florence No. 2........................46.75
No. 42764 Dark mottled marble................50.00
No. 42765 Extra dark vein marble.............50.00
No. 42766 Average Florence marble..........50.00
No. 42767 Extra dark mottled marble........52.50
No. 42768 Florence No. 1.........................52.50

OUR HANDSOME $9.98 MARKER.

JOHN SMITH
Born May 4,1811
Died Jan 6,1871

No. 42800 OUR $9.98 Price includes the Marker and Base complete with any lettering selected, as appears in the illustration, and the price is based on the actual cost of cutting the work out of the quarry with but our one small percentage of profit added. This stone is handsomely polished, has a beautiful surface, and as shown in the illustration, it is trimmed with tracing and beveling. WE PAY THE FREIGHT. Height, with base, 20 inches. Size of base, 16x8x6 inches. Marker, 12x12x4 inches.
No. 42800 Price............................$9.98
For more letters than shown in cut, add for sunk name letters 6c each; for date letters, 2½c each.

OUR FINE $13.75 MARKER.

MARY JONES
Born May 7,1892
Died April 5,1896

No. 42808 AT $13.75 we furnish this Marker, made of the same beautiful Royal Blue Vermont Marble as our $9.98 marker shown above, but a larger size, being 2 inches high and 18 inches wide at the base. It is thicker, heavier, and of different style, shape and carving. It is furnished complete with the base and delivered at your nearest railroad station in good order for $13.75, with the same amount of lettering as shown in the cut, or only a few cents per letter extra for any number of letters you desire. We pay the freight. Height with base, 22 inches; size of base, 18x8x6; size of marker, 14x14x4.
No. 42808 Price.........................$13.75
If more lettering than shown in cut is desired, see prices for extra lettering on No. 42800.

OUR RICH $13.76 MARKER.

HENRY MYERS
Born May 12,1871
Died May 23,1892

No. 42812 THIS $13.76 Marker is the same size and of the same rich unfading Royal Blue Marble as our $13.75 marker, but of a different style of carving, tracing and shape. It is furnished complete with the base, lettered as desired and only costs you $13.76, with the same number of letters as shown in cut. We pay the freight. Height with base, 22 inches; size of base, 18x8x6; size of marker, 14x14x4.
No. 42812 Price.........................$13.76
For more letters than shown in cut, add for sunk name letters 6c each; for date letters, 2½c each.

OUR SUPERIOR $14.98 TOMBSTONE.

BROWN
WM BROWN
Born May 1,1881
Died April 12,1891

No. 42816 AT $14.98 we offer this Royal Blue Marble Marker, made of the same rich, unfading Vermont marble as all the others, but measuring 24 inches high and 18 inches wide at base. Is thicker and of a heavy, dignified style, making a superior looking tombstone. We pay the freight. Height with base, 24 inches; size of base, 18x8x8; size of marker, 16x14x4.
No. 42816 Price.........................$14.98
For extra lettering, see No. 42800.

SEARS ROEBUCK & CO INC

HARDWARE DEPARTMENT.

SO MUCH MONEY CAN BE SAVED by buying your hardware at wholesale prices that you cannot afford to overlook this department. Freight rates are low on this line. Nearly everything in hardware goes at third or fourth class freight, especially the heaviest goods. Consult our table of freight rates on page 4 and you will see the freight will amount to next to nothing as compared with what you will save in price.

QUALITY IS GUARANTEED on everything we offer in this line. We handle only standard goods, the product of well known and reliable manufacturers. We do not handle trashy goods. We believe the best is always the cheapest, and we can save you 25 per cent to 50 per cent on everything in the hardware line.

IF YOU CONTEMPLATE BUILDING a house, barn, granary or other building, consult this catalogue for prices on your hardware, doors, sash, paper, paints, etc., we will save you money. If we don't sell to you we will compel some dealer to sell you the cheapest bill he ever sold in his life. When building, don't buy this class of goods from your dealer until you have compared our figures with his.

CARPENTERS AND BUILDERS are especially requested to consult this catalogue for prices on tools of all descriptions.

OUR LIBERAL TERMS All hardware (except such as must be paid for in advance) will be sent to any address by freight or express, C. O. D., subject to examination, on receipt of one-fourth the amount of purchase, balance and transportation charges payable after goods are received. By reason of our purchasing power we are able to offer goods for this season at prices that are below the market, and which will show even a larger percentage of saving to our customers than heretofore. We reserve the right to refuse orders from dealers. The prices on a few items quoted in this catalogue are subject to market changes. If there is any reduction in cost we will give you the benefit; if any advance, we will charge you the difference. This, however, rarely occurs. and when it does, we make the difference in cost to you the exact difference in cost to us.

CUTLERY DEPARTMENT.

TABLE CUTLERY. Our Table Cutlery is selected from the stocks of the most reliable and well known factories in this country. Our goods are the latest and best patterns possible to obtain. They are made of only the best steel, are fully warranted, and the workmanship cannot be excelled. We do not handle inferior grades known as seconds.

PRICE OF KNIVES ONLY. We will furnish KNIVES ONLY in any of the patterns quoted, (except as noted). The price of 1 dozen Single Bolster Knives only is 10 cents more than the price of the set of same style knives and forks. The price of 1 dozen Double Bolster Knives only is 20 cents more than the price of the set of same style knives and forks. Six knives and six forks constitute a set. Extra, by mail, 25 to 40 cents per set.

ALL ORDERS WILL BE FILLED AT PRICES PRINTED IN LATEST EDITION OF OUR CATALOGUE

No. 65000 Iron handle Knives and Forks. Per set, 6 knives and 6 forks................40c
No. 65001 Iron handle Knives only. Per doz..50c

No. 65002 Cocobolo handle Knives and Forks, no bolster. Per set, 6 knives and 6 forks........40c
No. 65003 Cocobolo handle Knives only. Per dozen..............................50c

No. 65004 White bone handle Knives and Forks, no bolster. Per set, 6 knives and 6 forks........73c
No. 65005 White bone handle Knives only. Per dozen..................................83c

No. 65012 Cocobolo handle Knives and Forks, single bolster. Per set, 6 knives and 6 forks....65c
No. 65013 Ebony handle Knives and Forks, single bolster. Per set, 6 knives and 6 forks....73c

No. 65014 White bone handle Knives and Forks, single bolster. Per set. 6 knives and 6 forks....94c

No. 65021 Fancy ring pattern, cocobolo handle Knives and Forks, swaged Scimiter blades. Per set, 6 knives and 6 forks.........................95c
No. 65022 Same as No. 65021, with ebony handles. Per set, 6 knives and 6 forks......$1.06

No. 65023 Same as No. 65021, with bone handles. Per set, 6 knives and 6 forks.................$1.29

No. 65030 Fancy shape cocobolo handle Knives and Forks, with one cross pattern bolster. Swaged Scimiter blades. Taper point handle. Per set, 6 knives and 6 forks...............................$1.15
No. 65031 Same as No. 65030, with ebony handles. Per set, 6 knives and 6 forks.......$1.30

No. 65032 Same as No. 65030, with bone handles. Per set, 6 knives and 6 forks................$1.65

No. 65039 Double bolstered cocobolo handle Knives and Forks. Per set, 6 knives and 6 forks. 77c
No. 65040 Same as No. 65039, with ebony handles. Per set, 6 knives and 6 forks.............85c

No. 65041 Double bolstered bone handle Knives and Forks. Per set, 6 knives and 6 forks......$1.06

No. 65048 Double bolstered Knives and Forks, cocobolo handles. Scimiter blades. Per set, 6 knives and 6 forks......................83c
No. 65049 Same as No. 65048, with ebony handles. Per set, 6 knives and 6 forks........91c

No. 65050 Same as No. 65048, with bone handles. Per set, 6 knives and 6 forks.... .....$1.12

No. 65057 Double ring pattern Knives and Forks, cocobolo handles. Per set, 6 knives and 6 forks...............................95c
No. 65058 Same as No. 65057, with ebony handles. Per set, 6 knives and 6 forks..........$1.09

No. 65059 Same as No. 65057, with bone handles. Per set, 6 knives and 6 forks..............$1.44

No. 65063 German style, cocobolo handle, Knives and Forks, swaged scimiter blades. Per set, 6 knives and 6 forks................$1.05
No. 65064 German style, same as No. 65063, ebony handle Knives and Forks. Per set, 6 knives and 6 forks $1.20

No. 65065 German style, bone handle Knives and Forks, swaged scimiter blades. Per set, 6 knives and 6 forks.........$1.65

No. 65072 Cross pattern, double bolstered, cocobolo handles, swaged scimiter blades, Knives and Forks. Price, per set, 6 knives and 6 forks, $1.05
No. 65073 Same as No. 65072, with ebony handles. Price, per set, 6 knives and 6 forks $1.20

No. 65074 Same as No. 65072, with bone handles. Price, per set, 6 knives and 6 forks..$1.67

No. 65081 English pattern, double cross, bolstered cocobolo handle, swaged scimiter blades, Knives and Forks. Price, per set, 6 knives and 6 forks.........$1.20
No. 65082 Same as No. 65081, with ebony handles. Price, per set, 6 knives and 6 forks..$1.31

No. 65083 Same as No. 65081, with bone handles. Price, per set, 6 knives and 6 forks..$1.72

No. 65090 Double bolster, swaged scimiter blades, cocobolo handle Knives and Forks. Price, per set, 6 knives and 6 forks.........$1.15
No. 65091 Same as No. 65090, with ebony handles. Price, per set, 6 knives and 6 forks..$1.26

No. 65092 Same as No. 65090, with bone handles. Price, per set, 6 knives and 6 forks..$1.67

No. 65099 French pattern bolster, cocobolo handle Knives and Forks, swaged scimiter blades. Price, per set, 6 knives and 6 forks..$1.45
No. 65100 Same as No. 65099, with ebony handles. Price, per set, 6 knives and 6 forks..$1.65

No. 65101 French pattern bolster, bone handle Knives and Forks. Set, 6 knives and 6 forks..$1.96

No. 65108 Our latest style cross pattern, cocobolo handles, swaged scimiter blades. Price, per set, 6 knives and 6 forks..$1.35
No. 65109 Same as No. 65108, with ebony handles. Price, per set, 6 knives and 6 forks..$1.47

No. 65110 Same as No. 65108, with bone handles. Price, per set, 6 knives and 6 forks..$1.85

No. 65117 Swedish pattern bolster, cocobolo handles, swaged scimiter blades. Price, per set, 6 knives and 6 forks.........$1.65
No. 65118 Same as No. 65117, with ebony handles. Price, per set, 6 knives and 6 forks..$1.77

No. 65119 Same as No. 65117, with bone handles. Price, per set, 6 knives and 6 forks..$2.35

No. 65126 Fancy double bolster, cocobolo handles, Knives and Forks, swaged scimiter blades, swell handles. Per set, 6 knives and 6 forks..$1.54
No. 65127 Same as No. 65126, with ebony handles. Per set, 6 knives and 6 forks....$1.67

No. 65128 Same as No. 65126, with bone handles. Per set, 6 knives and 6 forks.........$2.28

No. 65135 Fancy double link bolster, swelled cocobolo handles, Knives and Forks, swaged scimiter blades. Per set, 6 knives and 6 forks..$1.50
No. 65136 Same as No. 65135, with ebony handles. Per set, 6 knives and 6 forks....$1.67

No. 65137 Same as No. 65135, with bone handles. Per set, 6 knives and 6 forks.........$2.14

No. 65144 Fancy shape blade, cocobolo handles, with fancy double bolster, swaged scimiter blades. Per set, 6 knives and 6 forks.........$1.70
No. 65145 Same as No. 65144, with ebony handles. Per set, 6 knives and 6 forks....$1.82

No. 65146 Same as No. 65144, with bone handles. Per set, 6 knives and 6 forks.........$2.40

No. 65153 Imitation stag handles, double bolster Knives and Forks, swaged scimiter blades. Per set, 6 knives and 6 forks.........$1.35

No. 65160 Hard rubber handles, medium blades. Per set, 6 knives and 6 forks.....$2.65
No. 65161 Hard rubber handle, Dessert Knives and Forks. Per set, 6 knives and 6 forks.....$2.30

No. 65168 Hard rubber handles, medium blades. Per set, 6 knives and 6 forks.........$2.75
No. 65169 Hard rubber handle, Dessert Knives and Forks. Per set, 6 knives and 6 forks.....$2.48

No. 65170 Finest quality steel blades. Nickel plated, four-tined forks. Knives and forks have solid handles. The blades being fastened into the handle with metal, making the blade, handle and bolster practically one solid piece, not affected by hot water, heat or cold. The bolster is heavily nickel plated. The forks are of forged steel, first tinned then nickel plated, guaranteeing almost everlasting wear. Handles are of cocobolo, finely polished. We do not break sets. Set of 6 knives and 6 forks..$1.38

No. 65171 Fancy bolster, cocobolo handle knives and forks, same as previously described, with different pattern handle. We do not break sets. Price, per set of six knives and six forks....$1 40

No. 65172 Fancy bolster, fancy shaped, cocobolo handle. Handle of knives and forks same as described under two preceding numbers. We do not break sets. Per set of six knives and six forks..$1.50

No. 65174 Tinned Steel Knives and Forks. Forged from steel, and are heavily coated with pure block tin to prevent rust. We do not break sets. Price, per set six knives and six forks.........60c
No. 65175 Tinned Steel Table Knives and Forks. Put up in cardboard case as illustrated. Handles of forks are same as knives. We do not break sets. Price, per set six knives and forks....$1.00

Child's Sets.
The blade of knife measures 4½ inches. Entire length is 7½ inches. If by mail allow 5c for postage.

No. 65176 Child's Set, one knife and one fork, on bolster. A strong, well made set, best finish, cocobolo handle. Per set..........10c

No. 65177 Child's Set, one knife and one fork, no bolster, bone handle. A set which will please any child. Per set..........14c

No. 65180 Child's Set, one knife and one Fork. Double fancy ring bolster, cocobolo handles. Price, per set..........20c
No. 65181 Child's Set, one Knife and one Fork. Same pattern as above, with white bone handle. Price, per set..........27c

No. 65182 Child's Set, one Knife and one Fork. Double fancy bolster, swaged scimiter blades, finely finished cocobolo handles. Price per set..24c
No. 65183 Child's Set, one Knife and one Fork. Same pattern as above, with white bone handles. Price, per set..........30c

No. 65670 A Four-Blade strongly made Congress pattern Knife with stag handle, has double bolster and brass lining, length of handle 3¾ inches, length with large blade open 6⅛ inches.
Price, each..50c

No. 65671 Four-Blade, Stag Handle Knife, with double bolster, brass lined, best finish, 3⅝ inches.
Each..50c

No. 65676 Four-Blade, Pearl Handle Knife double bolster and shield, brass lined, 3⅝ inches.
Each..55c

No. 65682 Three-Blade, Stag Handle, Cattle Knife, brass lined, superior finish, 3¾ inches.
Each..80c

No. 65683 The Cattle King, three-blade, brass lined, stag handle and double bolster; large blade has a clip point and cannot be closed until spring in back is pressed. A strong, well made and finely finished knife. Length of handle, 4-inch; length with large blade open, 7⅜ inches. Price, each......$1.00

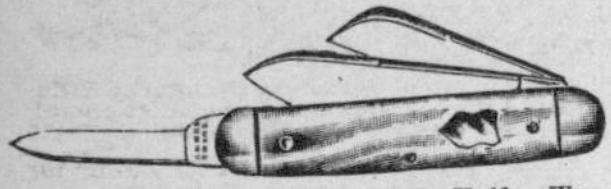

No. 65684 The NON-XLL Cattle Knife. Warranted to be the best English steel; 3 blades and pearl handle, brass lined with solid German silver double bolster and shield. Well made and finely finished; the peer of all cattle knives. Length of handle, 3⅝ inches. Length with large blade open, 6¼ inches. Price, each........................$1.75

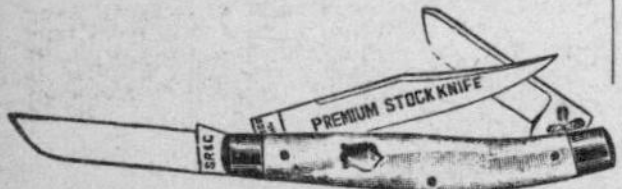

No. 65685 Our Pearl Handle Premium Stock Knife has three blades, as illustrated. Handle is 3¾ inches long, length with large blade open, 7 inches. Has one clip blade, one tobacco blade and one spaying blade. The knife is beautifully finished and polished throughout. Has German silver bolster and shield, brass lined, the blades are fully guaranteed. While this knife is a great favorite with the stock growers of the West, it is a very sensible pattern and will prove a favorite wherever introduced.
Price, each..$1.50

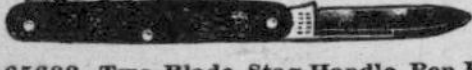

No. 65688 Two-Blade, Stag Handle, Pen Knife, brass lined, our leading leader, 3¼ inches, warranted. Each..30c

No. 65690 Two-Blade, Ebony Handle Pen Knife, brass lined, 3¼ inches, warranted. Each..........40c

No. 65696 Three-Blade, Stag Handle Knife, brass lined, best steel blade and finish, 3⅝ inches, warranted. Each..60c

No. 65698 Three-Blade, Crocus Polished, gray buffalo horn handle knife with bolster, brass lined, 3⅝ inches, warranted. Each..............................75c

No. 65704 Gray Buffalo Horn Handle Pen Knife, three blades, crocus polished, brass lined, **fully warranted**, 3 inches. Each..............................85c

No. 65706 Three Crocus Polished Blades, stag handle, heavy Pen Knife, with bolster, brass lined, **fully warranted**, 3¾ inches. Each..................90c

No. 65708 Three-Blade, Stag Handle Pen Knife, brass lined, **warranted best material and finish**, 3⅝ inches. Each..................................90c

No. 65710 Four Crocus Polished Blades, fine pearl handle knife, German silver tipped, brass lined, fully warranted, 3 inches. Each........$1.00

No. 65712 Four Crocus Polished Blades, stag handle, congress knife, brass lined, one of the neatest and best pen knives made, fully warranted, 3¼ inches. Each..$1.00

Send 5 cents extra for postage when pocket knife is sent by mail.

No. 65714 Stag Handle Pen Knife, with elongated shield, four crocus polished blades, brass lined, fully warranted, 3 inches. Each........$1.00

No. 65716 Four-Blade, Fine Pearl Handle Pen Knife, brass lined, fully warranted, a neat and popular pattern, 3¼ inches. Each......................$1.20

No. 65718 Four Crocus Polished Blades, pearl handle knife, brass lined, a well finished and neat pattern, **fully warranted**, 3 inches. Each.....$1.25

No. 65720 Stag Handle Pen Knife, with elongated shield, four crocus polished blades, brass lined; one of our best sellers. **fully warranted**, 3¼ inches. Each..$1.20

No. 65722 Pearl Handle Knife, one of the neatest and most popular patterns made, three crocus polished blades, brass lined, **fully warranted**, 3 inches. Each..$1.40

No. 65724 One of our best Pen Knives, pearl handle with elongated shield, four fine crocus polished blades, **brass lined**, a prevalent pattern, **fully warranted**, 3½ inches. Each..............................$1.50

Knife Hone.

No. 65726 Pocket Emery Hone. A fine emery knife hone in case. Each..........................10c

Knife Purses.

No. 65727 Knife Purse, will take almost any pe knife. When ordered with knife we send purse to fit knife. They are not large enough for jack knives.
Price, each, without knife...........................8c

Shaving Sets.

THE CHEAPEST SET WE OFFER IS MADE OF GOOD GOODS.

There have been many Shaving Sets gotten up for sale in so-called racket stores or department stores. Quality is no consideration in such cases, the only point being to get up a set at the least possible price. The following sets will be found to be made up of **reliable goods that will give satisfaction in every case.**

No. 65996 Our Bon Ton Shaving Set consists of your choice of any razor quoted in our cutlery department, except our High Art Razor; 1 double swing barber's razor strop; horse hide and linen with metallic end and swivel, 1 barber's shaving brush, white bristles, with buffalo horn ferrule; 1 handsomely decorated shaving mug with partition; 1 cake of the **celebrated Yankee shaving soap (the genuine)**. If you are well posted in qualities of these goods you must admit that this set is **the best that money can buy.**

Make your order for the above shaving set thus: "No. 65996, 1 shaving set with No..........razor," filling in the blank with the catalogue number of the razor you select.
Our price for entire outfit.........................$2.75

No. 65997 Our Acme Shaving Set consists of 1 Sears, Roebuck & Co.'s Acme razor, 1 double swing razor strop (canvas and horse hide with metal ends and swivel), 1 good shaving brush, 1 decorated shaving mug, 1 cake shaving soap. **Remember the razor is fully warranted**
Our price for the complete set.....................$1.75

No. 65998 Our Winner Shaving Set consists of 1 medium hollow ground razor **Warranted**, 1 horsehide swing strop, 1 decorated shaving mug, 1 cake shaving soap, 1 good shaving brush, **all good, reliable goods.** Our price for entire set......$1.25

No. 65999 Our Competition Shaving Set is offered in competition with those sets found in 99-cent stores, and it is far superior to most such goods. It is our intention always to describe all articles exactly as they are, consequently we cannot recommend this set any more than to say it will be found better than you can possibly procure elsewhere at anything like this price. The razor is a good shaver and the strop, etc., will give satisfaction in use. It is wonderful value for the price. The set consists of 1 hollow ground razor, 1 swing strop, 1 shaving brush 1 divided shaving mug, 1 cake shaving soap.
Our price for the entire set..........................75c

REMEMBER THAT SEARS, ROEBUCK & CO.'S RAZORS ARE THE BEST ON EARTH.

See Our Complete Line of
Razors, Razor Brushes, Strops, Mugs Hair Clippers, Etc.
ON FOLLOWING PAGES.

SEARS, ROEBUCK & CO.'S RAZORS

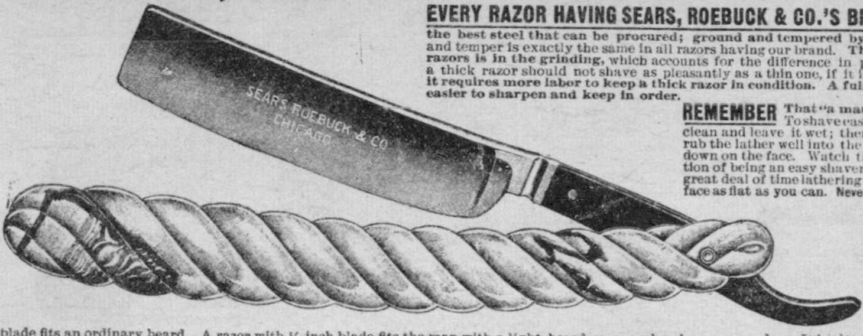

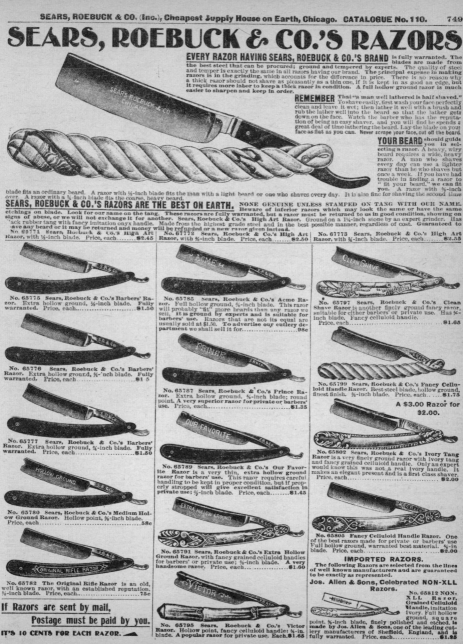

EVERY RAZOR HAVING SEARS, ROEBUCK & CO.'S BRAND is fully warranted. The blades are made from the best steel that can be procured; ground and tempered by experts. The quality of steel and temper is exactly the same in all razors having our brand. The principal expense in making razors is in the grinding, which accounts for the difference in price. There is no reason why a thick razor should not shave as pleasantly as a thin one, if it is kept in as good an edge, but it requires more labor to keep a thick razor in condition. A full hollow ground razor is much easier to sharpen and keep in order.

REMEMBER That "a man well lathered is half shaved." To shave easily, first wash your face perfectly clean and leave it wet; then lather it well with a brush and rub the lather well into the beard so that the lather gets down on the face. Watch the barber who has the reputation of being an easy shaver, and you will find he spends a great deal of time lathering the beard. Lay the blade on your face as flat as you can. Never scrape your face, cut off the beard.

YOUR BEARD should guide you in selecting a razor. A heavy, wiry beard requires a wide, heavy razor. A man who shaves every day can use a lighter razor than he who shaves but once a week. If you have had trouble in finding a razor to "fit your beard," we can fit you. A razor with ⅝-inch blade fits an ordinary beard. A razor with ½-inch blade fits the man with a light beard or one who shaves every day. It is also fine for shaving the second time over. A razor with a ¾-inch blade fits the coarse, heavy beard.

SEARS, ROEBUCK & CO.'S RAZORS ARE THE BEST ON EARTH. NONE GENUINE UNLESS STAMPED ON TANG WITH OUR NAME. Beware of inferior razors which may look the same or have the same etchings on blade. Look for our name on the tang. These razors are fully warranted, but a razor must be returned to us in good condition, showing no signs of abuse, or we will not exchange it for another. Sears, Roebuck & Co.'s High Art Razor. Ground on a 1¼-inch stone by an expert grinder. Has black rubber tang with fancy imitation onyx handle. Made from the highest grade steel and in the best possible manner, regardless of cost. Guaranteed to shave any beard or it may be returned and money will be refunded or a new razor given instead.

No. 65771 Sears, Roebuck & Co.'s High Art Razor, with ½-inch blade. Price, each........$2.45

No. 67772 Sears, Roebuck & Co.'s High Art Razor, with ⅝-inch blade. Price, each........$2.50

No. 67773 Sears, Roebuck & Co.'s High Art Razor, with ¾-inch blade. Price, each........$2.55

No. 65775 Sears, Roebuck & Co.'s Barbers' Razor. Extra hollow ground, ½-inch blade. Fully warranted. Price, each........................$1.50

No. 65776 Sears, Roebuck & Co.'s Barbers' Razor. Extra hollow ground, ⅝-inch blade. Fully warranted. Price, each........................$1 5

No. 65777 Sears, Roebuck & Co.'s Barbers' Razor. Extra hollow ground, ¾-inch blade. Fully warranted. Price, each........................$1.50

No. 65780 Sears, Roebuck & Co.'s Medium Hollow Ground Razor. Hollow point, ⅝-inch blade. Price, each........................58c

No. 65782 The Original Rifle Razor is an old, well known razor, with an established reputation. ⅝-inch blade. Price, each........................75c

If Razors are sent by mail,

Postage must be paid by you.

IT'S 10 CENTS FOR EACH RAZOR.

No. 65785 Sears, Roebuck & Co.'s Acme Razor. Full hollow ground, ⅝-inch blade. This razor will probably "fit" more beards than any razor we sell. It is ground by experts and is suitable for barbers' use. Razors that are not its equal are usually sold at $1.50. To advertise our cutlery department we shall sell it for........................98c

No. 65787 Sears, Roebuck & Co.'s Prince Razor. Extra hollow ground, ⅝-inch blade; round point. A very superior razor for private or barbers' use. Price, each........................$1.35

No. 65789 Sears, Roebuck & Co.'s Our Favorite Razor is a very thin, extra hollow ground razor for barbers' use. This razor requires careful handling to be kept in proper condition, but if properly stropped will give excellent satisfaction in private use; ⅝-inch blade. Price, each........$1.45

No. 65791 Sears, Roebuck & Co.'s Extra Hollow Ground Razor, with fancy grained celluloid handles for barbers' or private use; ⅝-inch blade. A very handsome razor. Price, each........................$1.60

No. 65795 Sears, Roebuck & Co.'s Victor Razor. Hollow point, fancy celluloid handle; ⅝-in. blade. A popular razor for private use. Each.$1.65

No. 65797 Sears, Roebuck & Co.'s Clean Shave Razor is another finely ground fancy razor, suitable for either barbers' or private use. Has ⅝-inch blade. Fancy celluloid handle.
Price, each........................$1.65

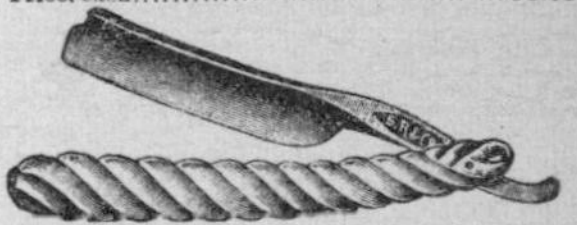

No. 65799 Sears, Roebuck & Co.'s Fancy Celluloid Handle Razor. Best steel blade, hollow ground, finest finish. ⅝-inch blade. Price, each........$1.75

A $3.00 Razor for $2.00.

No. 65802 Sears, Roebuck & Co.'s Ivory Tang Razor is a very finely ground razor with ivory tang and fancy grained celluloid handle. Only an expert would know this was not a real ivory handle. It makes an elegant present and is a first class shaver.
Price, each........................$2.00

No. 65805 Fancy Celluloid Handle Razor. One of the best razors made for private or barbers' use. Full hollow ground, warranted best material. ⅝-in blade. Price, each........................$2.00

IMPORTED RAZORS.

The following Razors are selected from the lines of well known manufacturers and are guaranteed to be exactly as represented.

Jos. Allen & Sons, Celebrated NON-XLL Razors.

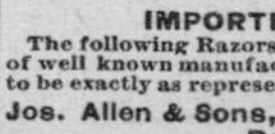

No. 65812 NON-XLL Razor, Grained Celluloid Handle, imitation ivory. Full hollow ground, square point, ⅝-inch blade, finely polished and etched. Is made by Jos. Allen & Sons, one of the leading cutlery manufacturers of Sheffield, England, and is fully warranted. Price, each........................$1.25

MECHANICS' TOOLS.

THE LARGE INCREASE in our sales of Mechanics' Tools shows that our patrons appreciate our efforts to furnish reliable, strictly high grade tools at our usual one-small-profit, factory-to-consumer plan.

WE WISH TO CALL YOUR ATTENTION to the quality of the tools which we sell. We recognize the fact that in order to hold the large tool trade which we have established, it is necessary for us to send out the best goods that it is possible to procure. We wish to emphasize the fact that you will find every article sold by us to be exactly as represented; if not found so it may be returned and money will be refunded.

OUR TERMS ARE LIBERAL. Any goods in this line will be sent to any address by **freight or express** on receipt of a sufficient deposit to cover charges both ways, balance payable when received.

SAWS.

Sears, Roebuck & Co.'s Circular, Cross Cut, Rip, Hand, Panel and Buck Saws are warranted as follows: If these saws do not prove as good or better than any saws you ever had, return them and money will be refunded.

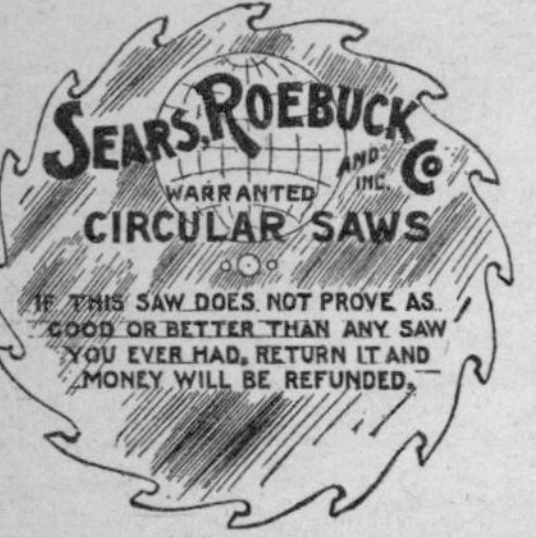
SEARS, ROEBUCK AND CO INC.
WARRANTED
CIRCULAR SAWS
IF THIS SAW DOES NOT PROVE AS GOOD OR BETTER THAN ANY SAW YOU EVER HAD, RETURN IT AND MONEY WILL BE REFUNDED.

Patent ground and tempered solid teeth of extra quality, superior workmanship. Circular saws must not be filed with a square corner in gullet. If so filed any saw will most likely crack. Our guarantee does not cover saws cracked from this cause, or if not kept in proper condition.

No. 66001 Cut Off Saw. Sears, Roebuck & Co.'s, warranted.

No. 66002 Rip Saw. Sears, Roebuck & Co.'s, warranted. **Read remarks following price list before making out your order.**

Diameter, Inches	Thickness, Gauge	Size of hole, Inches	Price, each	Diameter, Inches	Thickness, Gauge	Size of hole, Inches	Price each
4	19	¾	$0.49	20	13	1 5/16	$ 4.20
5	19	¾	.58	22	12	1 5/16	4.90
6	18	¾	.68	24	11	1⅜	5.90
7	18	¾	.83	26	11	1⅜	6.90
8	18	⅞	.98	28	10	1½	7.85
9	17	⅞	1.20	30	10	1½	8.80
10	16	1	1.45	36	9	1⅝	12.75
11	16	1	1.70	40	9	2	17.65
12	15	1	1.80	44	8	2	24.95
14	15	1⅛	2.20	50	7	2	39.00
16	14	1⅛	2.70	54	7	2	48.00
18	13	1¼	3.45	60	6	2	70.00

If you want a saw in any way different from above list, **do not give any catalogue number,** and be sure to give **full specifications.** We aim to carry the above sizes in stock at all times ready for prompt shipment, but can ship saws with odd size holes or made to order with but the usual delay. Any saw made to order will not be taken back or exchanged and order cannot be countermanded after having been placed in work. If saw is wanted with pin holes send a paper pattern giving exact location. Order blanks for ordering saws will be furnished on request.

No. 66003 Circular Saw Mandrels, with pulley on end, of the latest and most approved pattern. **Our Mandrels are made with pulley on right hand side when saw is running toward you with left hand thread, unless otherwise ordered.**

Diam. of Pulley, inches	Face of Pulley, inches	Diam. of Flange, inches	Length of Shaft, inches	Diam. of Shaft, inches	Size of hole in Saw, inches	Price of Mandrel, Complete
2½	3½	2½	16½	1 1/16	1	$ 5.50
3	4	3	19	1 3/16	1⅛	6.00
3½	4½	3½	21½	1 5/16	1¼	6.50
4	5	4	24	1 7/16	1 5/16	7.50
4½	5½	4½	26	1 7/16	1 5/16	8.50
5	6	5	28	1 7/16	1⅜	9.75
5½	6½	5½	30½	1 7/16	1⅜	10.75
6	7	6	32½	1 9/16	1½	13.25
7	8	6	37	1 11/16	1⅝	16.00
8	8	6	41	1 13/16	1⅝	18.75

CROSS CUT SAWS.

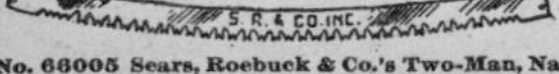
S. R. & CO. INC.

No. 66005 Sears, Roebuck & Co.'s Two-Man, Narrow Cross Cut Saws. Warranted. Champion tooth, without handles.

5½ foot, weight, 3¾ lbs., price, each..........88c
6 foot, weight, 4 lbs., price, each..........96c

SEARS, ROEBUCK & CO. INC.
CHICAGO ILL.

No. 66006 Sears, Roebuck & Co.'s regular width, Champion Tooth, Two-Man Cross Cut Saws. Warranted. Without handles.

Length, feet	Weight, lbs.	Price, each	Length, feet	Weight, lbs.	Price, each
5	5¾	$1.45	6	6¾	$1.74
5½	6¼	1.60	6½	7	1.89

No. 66009 Disston's Plain Tooth, No. 2, Two-Man Cross Cut Saws. Two gauges thinner on back than on teeth. Price quoted is without handles.

HENRY DISSTON & SONS.
SPRING STEEL
WARRANTED.
PATENT GROUND

Length, feet	5½	6	7
Price, each	$1.60	$1.74	$2.03

HENRY DISSTON & SONS.
CAST STEEL
WARRANTED
PHILADELPHIA
PATENT GROUND

No. 66010 Disston's Champion Tooth Two-Man Cross Cut Saw. Two gauges thinner on back than on teeth. Price quoted is without handles.

Length, feet	5	5½	6	6½	7
Weight, pounds	6	7	8	8¾	9
Price, each	$1.35	$1.49	$1.62	$1.76	$1.89

No. 66011 Disston's Great American Tooth Two-Man Cross Cut Saw. Four gauges thinner on back than on teeth and is well adapted for all kinds of timber. 14 gauge on tooth edge, 18 gauge on the back. Price quoted is without handles.

TAKING THIS SAW DAY IN AND DAY OUT
WE CHALLENGE THE WORLD
TO PRODUCE ITS EQUAL
GREAT AMERICAN
HENRY DISSTON & SONS PHILA.

Length, feet	4½	5	5½	6
Price, each	$1.53	$1.70	$1.87	$2.04

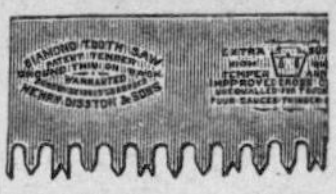
DIAMOND TOOTH SAW
HENRY DISSTON & SONS

No. 66013 Disston's Diamond Tooth Two-Man Cross Cut Saw. Two gauges thinner on back than on teeth. Price quoted is without handles.

Length, feet	4½	5	5½	6
Price, each	$1.40	$1.55	$1.72	$1.86

No. 66015 Toledo Blade Two-Man Cross Cut Saw. This saw is made from the best tough crucible steel and with much care. It is ground four (4) gauges thinner on the back, toothed to end of saw. Aluminum steel is used in this saw and reports say they are giving the best of satisfaction wherever used. Price quoted is without handles.

TOLEDO BLADE
IMPROVED CROSS-CUT SAW
EXTRA HIGH TEMPER
REFINED CRUCIBLE STEEL
FOUR GAUGES THINNER ON BACK

Length, feet	5	5½	6	6½
Price, each	$2.52	$2.73	$2.98	$3.23

HUMBOLDT
IMPROVED CROSS-CUT SAW
FIVE GAUGES THINNER ON BACK

No. 66016 Humboldt Two-Man Cross Cut Saw without handles.

This saw is even gauge on teeth from end to end, and ground five gauges thinner throughout the entire back, and will retain its gauge as the saw wears narrow. The very best tough crucible steel is used in this saw, and each saw is set and sharpened ready for use. This saw is toothed to the ends of the saw for Pacific coast trade.

Length	5 ft.	5½ ft.	6 ft.	6½ ft.	7 ft.
Price, each	$2.50	$2.75	$3.00	$3.25	$3.50

No. 66017 Sears, Roebuck & Co.'s One-Man Cross Cut Saws. Champion tooth; supplementary handle. **Warranted.**

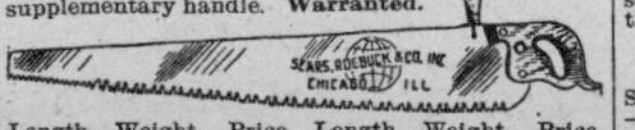
SEARS, ROEBUCK & CO. INC.
CHICAGO ILL.

Length, feet	Weight, lbs.	Price, each	Length, feet	Weight, lbs.	Price, each
3	3¾	$1.05	4	5¼	$1.40
3½	4¼	1.23	4½	6¼	1.58

Saw Handles.

No. 66020 Handle for One-Man Cross Cut Saw. Price, each..........18c

No. 66021 Supplementary Handle for One-Man Cross Cut Saw. Price, each..........9c

No. 66024

No. 66024 Patent Loop Cross Cut Saw Handles. Per pair..........10c

No. 66026 Reversible Cross Cut Saw Handles. Per pair..........11c

No. 66026

SAW TOOLS.

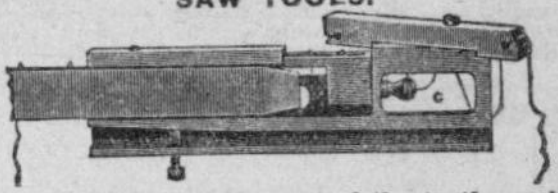

No. 66034 With this saw tool the teeth can be brought to the same amount of set and in perfect condition to cut fast and easy. It insures absolute accuracy in set, side-dressing, jointing and cutting down the rakers; can be used in the woods or shop. **Directions for use packed with each tool.** We consider this the best saw tool ever placed on the market. Price of combination saw tool, complete......$1.37

Swages.

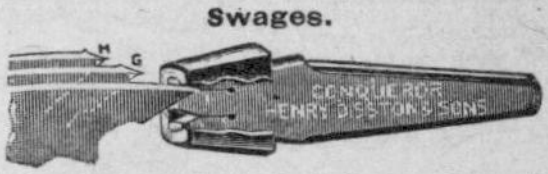
CONQUEROR
HENRY DISSTON & SONS

The Conqueror Swage has always given satisfaction and is indispensable to any sawyer who uses the spread set. Every one sold by us is warranted perfect and to give satisfaction.

No. 66035 Conqueror Swage No. 1, for large circular saws. Price, each..........$2.30
No. 66036 Conqueror Swage No. 2, for small circular and mill saws. Price, each..........$1.88
No. 66037 Conqueror Swage No. 3, for small circular saws. Price, each..........$1.50

Cross Cut Saw Sets.

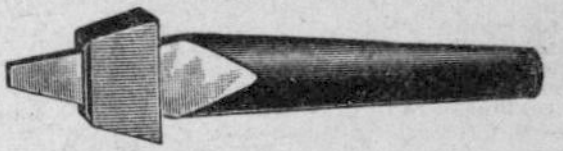

No. 66038 The Whiting Pattern Saw Set for Cross Cut Saws only. Simple and effective and a favorite with lumbermen. Price, each..........45c

Band Saws, Filed and Set.

No. 66039 Band Saws. Not joined.
No. 66040 Band Saws. Joined.

Width	Gauge	Price per foot, not Joined	Extra for Joining
¼-in.	21	6c	20c
⅜-in.	21	7c	20c
½-in.	21	7½c	20c
⅝-in.	21	8c	25c
¾-in.	20	9¼c	25c
⅞-in.	20	10c	25c
1 -in.	20	10½c	30c
1⅛-in.	20	11¾c	30c
1¼-in.	19	12¾c	30c
1⅜-in.	19	14c	40c
1½-in.	19	15c	40c
1¾-in.	19	16½c	75c

No. 66041 Silver Solder for Brazing Band Saws. We do not sell less than one ounce. Per oz..$1.00

Ice Saws.

SEARS ROEBUCK & CO. CHICAGO

No. 66048 Hand Ice Saw, with iron handle.

Length, inches	24	26	28	30
Price, each	78c	85c	98c	$1.08

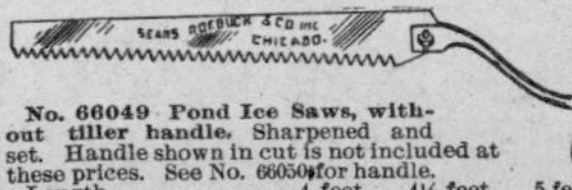
SEARS ROEBUCK & CO. INC.
CHICAGO

No. 66049 Pond Ice Saws, without tiller handle. Sharpened and set. Handle shown in cut is not included at these prices. See No. 66050 for handle.

Length	4 feet	4½ feet	5 feet
Price, each	$1.90	$2.10	$2.30

No. 66050 Extra Tiller Handles, for Pond Ice Saws. Price, each..........60c

WRITE FOR FREE BOOK OF SAMPLES OF ALL KINDS OF BUILDING (SHEATHING) PAPER AND PREPARED FELT ROOFING.

SEARS, ROEBUCK & CO.'S HAND SAWS.

A STRICTLY GUARANTEED SAW. **NO BETTER MADE.**

TRY SEARS, ROEBUCK & CO.'S SAWS AND YOU WILL USE NO OTHER.

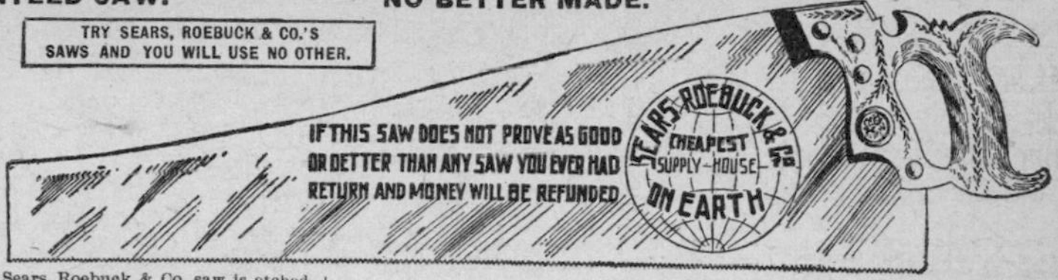
IF THIS SAW DOES NOT PROVE AS GOOD
OR BETTER THAN ANY SAW YOU EVER HAD
RETURN AND MONEY WILL BE REFUNDED
SEARS, ROEBUCK & CO.
CHEAPEST
SUPPLY-HOUSE
ON EARTH

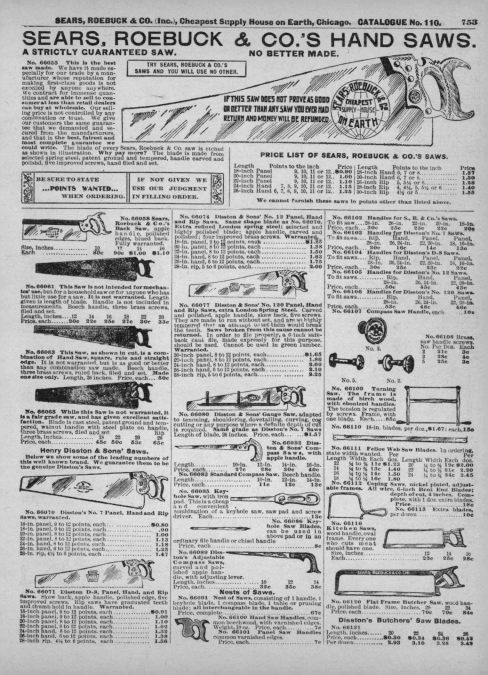

No. 66055 This is the best saw made. We have it made especially for our trade by a manufacturer whose reputation for making first-class goods is not excelled by anyone anywhere. We contract for immense quantities and **are able to sell to consumer at less than retail dealers can buy at wholesale.** Our selling price is not controlled by any combination or trust. We give our customers the same guarantee that we demanded and secured from the manufacturers, and that is **the best, fairest and most complete guarantee we could write.** The blade of every Sears, Roebuck & Co. saw is etched as shown in illustration. **Why pay more?** The blade is made from selected spring steel, patent ground and tempered, handle carved and polishd, five improved screws, hand filed and set.

BE SURE TO STATE ...POINTS WANTED... WHEN ORDERING. | **IF NOT GIVEN WE USE OUR JUDGMENT IN FILLING ORDER.**

PRICE LIST OF SEARS, ROEBUCK & CO.'S SAWS.

Length	Points to the inch	Price
18-inch Panel	9, 10, 11 or 12	$0.90
20-inch Panel	9, 10, 11 or 12	1.00
22-inch Panel	9, 10, 11 or 12	1.10
24-inch Hand	7, 8, 9, 10, 11 or 12	1.15
26-inch Hand	6, 7, 8, 9, 10, 11 or 12	1.25
28-inch Hand	6, 7 or 8	1.37
30-inch Hand	6, 7 or 8	1.50
26-inch Rip	5, 5½ or 6	1.28
28-inch Rip	4, 4½, 5, 5½ or 6	1.40
30-inch Rip	4½ or 5	1.55

We cannot furnish these saws in points other than listed above.

No. 66058 Sears, Roebuck & Co.'s Back Saw, apple handle, polished edges, blued back. Fully warranted.

Size, inches	10	12	14	16
Each	80c	90c	$1.00	$1.10

No. 66061 This Saw is not intended for mechanics' use, but for a household saw or for anyone who has but little use for a saw. It is not warranted. Length given is length of blade. Handle is not included in measurements. Beech handle, three brass screws, filed and set.

Length, inches	12	14	16	18	22	26
Price, each	20c	22c	25c	27c	30c	33c

No. 66063 This Saw, as shown in cut, is a combination of Hand Saw, square, rule and straight edge. It is not warranted, but is as good or better than any combination saw made. Beech handle, three brass screws, ruled back, filed and set. **Made one size only.** Length, 26 inches. Price, each....50c

No. 66065 While this Saw is not warranted, it is a fair grade saw, and has given excellent satisfaction. Blade is cast steel, patent ground and tempered, walnut handle with steel plate on handle, three brass screws, filed and set.

Length, inches	18	22	26	Rip 28
Price, each	45c	50c	53c	65c

Henry Disston & Sons' Saws.

Below we show some of the leading numbers of this well known brand. We guarantee them to be the genuine Disston's Saws.

No. 66070 Disston's No. 7 Panel, Hand and Rip Saws, warranted.

16-in. panel, 9 to 12 points, each	$0.80
18-in. panel, 9 to 12 points, each	.90
20-in. panel, 8 to 12 points, each	1.00
22-in. panel, 8 to 12 points, each	1.13
24-in. hand, 8 to 12 points, each	1.18
26-in. hand, 6 to 12 points, each	1.25
28-in. rip, 4½ to 6 points, each	1.47

No. 66071 Disston D-8, Panel, Hand, and Rip Saws. Skew back, apple handle, polished edge, five improved screws. Rip saws have graduated teeth and thumb hold in handle. **Warranted.**

16-inch panel, 9 to 12 points, each	$0.91
18-inch panel, 9 to 12 points, each	1.00
20-inch panel, 8 to 12 points, each	1.10
22-inch panel, 8 to 12 points, each	1.22
24-inch hand, 8 to 12 points, each	1.32
26-inch hand, 6 to 12 points, each	1.38
28-inch rip, 4½ to 6 points, each	1.56

No. 66074 Disston & Sons' No. 12 Panel, Hand and Rip Saws. Same shape blade as No. 66070. Extra refined London spring steel; selected and highly polished blade; apple handle, carved and polished; four improved brass screws. **Warranted.**

18-in. panel, 9 to 12 points, each	$1.25
20-in. panel, 8 to 12 points, each	1.38
22-in. panel, 8 to 12 points, each	1.50
24-in. hand, 8 to 12 points, each	1.63
26-in. hand, 6 to 12 points, each	1.75
28-in. rip, 5 to 6 points, each	2.00

No. 66077 Disston & Sons' No. 120 Panel, Hand and Rip Saws, extra London Spring Steel. Carved and polished, apple handle, skew back, five screws. They are made to run without set, and are so highly tempered that an attempt to set them would break the teeth. **Saws broken from this cause cannot be returned.** In order to file properly, a 6-inch safe-back cant file, made expressly for this purpose, should be used. Cannot be used in green lumber. **Warranted.**

20-inch panel, 8 to 12 points, each	$1.65
22-inch panel, 8 to 12 points, each	1.86
24-inch hand, 8 to 12 points, each	2.00
26-inch hand, 6 to 12 points, each	2.10
28-inch rip, 5 to 6 points, each	2.25

No. 66080 Disston & Sons' Gauge Saw, adapted to tenoning, shouldering, dovetailing, curving, cog cutting or any purpose where a definite depth of cut is required. **Same grade as Disston's No. 7 Saws** Length of blade, 26 inches. Price, each...$1.57

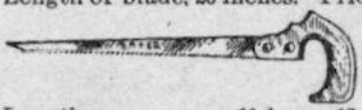

No. 66082 Disston & Sons' Compass Saws, with apple handle.

Length	10-in.	12-in.	14-in.	16-in.
Price, each	27c	28c	30c	40c

No. 66083 Standard Compass Saw. Beech handle.

Length	10-in.	12-in.	14-in.
Price, each	11c	12c	13c

No. 66085 Keyhole Saw, with iron pad. This is a cheap and convenient combination of a keyhole saw, saw pad and screw driver. Each....13c

No. 66086 Keyhole Saw Blades, can be used in above pad or in an ordinary file handle or chisel handle
Price, each....8c

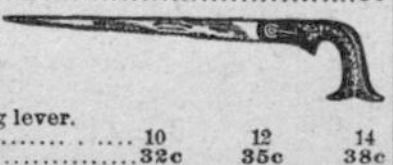

No. 66089 Disston's Adjustable Compass Saws, carved and polished apple handle, with adjusting lever.

Length, inches	10	12	14
Price, each	32c	35c	38c

Nests of Saws.

No. 66091 Nest of Saws, consisting of 1 handle, 1 keyhole blade, 1 compass blade, 1 table or pruning blade; **all interchangeable in the handle.**
Price, complete....67c

No. 66100 Hand Saw Handles, common beechwood, with varnished edges. Weight, 10 oz. Price, each....7c

No. 66101 Panel Saw Handles common varnished edges.
Price, each....7c

No. 66102 Handles for S., R. & Co.'s Saws.

To fit saw	28-in.	26-in.	22-in.	20-in.	18-in.
Price, each	30c	25c	23c	22c	20c

No. 66103 Handles for Disston's No. 7 Saws.

To fit saws	Rip, 28-in.	Hand, 26, 24-in.	Panel, 22, 20-in.	Panel, 18, 16-in.
Price, each	20c	16c	14c	13c

No. 66104 Handles for Disston's D-8 Saws.

To fit saws	Rip, 28-in.	Hand, 26, 24-in.	Panel, 22, 20-in.	Panel, 18, 16-in.
Price, each	30c	25c	23c	22c

No. 66105 Handles for Disston's No. 12 Saws.

To fit saws	Rip, 28-in.	Hand, 26, 24-in.	Panel, 22, 20-in.
Price, each	50c	45c	43c

No. 66106 Handles for Disston's No. 120 Saws.

To fit saws	Rip, 28-in.	Hand, 26, 24-in.	Panel, 22, 20-in.
Price, each	53c	48c	46c

No. 66107 Compass Saw Handle, each....10c

No. 3.

No. 66108 Brass, saw handle screws.

No.	Per Doz.	Each
2	21c	3c
3	28c	4c
5	25c	3c

No. 5.

No. 2.

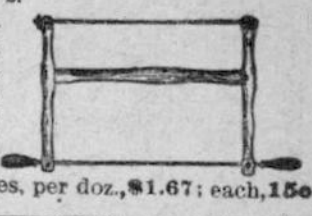

No. 66109 Turning Saw. The frame is made of birch wood, with ebonized handles. The tension is regulated by screws. Frame, with one blade. Each....85c

No. 66110 18-in. blades, per doz., $1.67; each, 15c

No. 66111 Felloe Web Saw Blades. In ordering, state width wanted.

Length	Width	Each	Per doz.	Length	Width	Each	Per doz.
12	¼ to ⅝	11c	$1.23	20	¼ to ⅝	19c	$2.00
14	¼ to ⅝	13c	1.40	22	¼ to ⅝	21c	2.20
16	¼ to ½	14c	1.50	24	¼ to ¾	24c	2.45
18	¼ to ½	16c	1.80				

No. 66112 Coping Saws, nickel plated, adjustable frames. All wire, 6-inch Bent End Blades; depth of cut, 4 inches. Complete, with 1 doz. extra blades.
Price....18c

No. 66113 Extra blades, per dozen....10c

No. 66116 Kitchen Saws, wood handle, oval frame. Every one who cuts meat should have one.

Size, inches	12	14	16
Each	22c	25c	28c

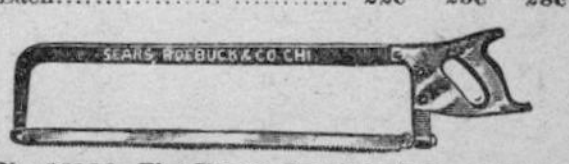
SEARS, ROEBUCK & CO. CHI

No. 66120 Flat Frame Butcher Saw, wood handle, polished blade.

Size, inches	20	22	24
Price, each	70c	79c	84c

Disston's Butchers' Saw Blades.

No. 66121

Length, inches	20	22	24	26
Price, each	$0.30	$0.34	$0.36	$0.42
Per dozen	2.93	3.10	3.25	3.42

No. 66962 Jointer Gauges; an invention to attach to an ordinary jointer plane. It holds the face of the plane at any desired angle, so as to joint edge of board either square or at any bevel desired. No trouble to get edge of lumber "out of wind" when you use this gauge. Weight, 2¼ lbs. Price, each, without plane....$1.18

No. 66963 Cabinet Scraper, a sheet of finely tempered saw steel about 3x5 inches.
Price, each.....6c
Per dozen.....65c

No. 66964 Sand Paper. Nos. 1 and 1½ are commonly used. No. 00 is the finest and No. 3 the coarsest. State numbers wanted when ordering. 24 sheets to the quire.

Nos.	00	0	½	1	1½	2	3
Per sheet	1c	1c	1c	1c	1c	1c	1c
Per quire	15c	15c	15c	15c	15c	16c	18c

Emery Cloth.

No. 66965 24 sheets to the quire.

Nos.	00	0	½	1	1½	2
Per sheet	3c	3c	3c	3c	3c	3c
Per quire	55c	55c	55c	55c	55c	60c

HATCHETS.

All hatchets sold by us have handles, but the weight of handle is not included when we state weight of hatchet.

SEARS, ROEBUCK & CO.'S BRAND OF HATCHETS ARE THE BEST THAT CAN BE PRODUCED FROM THE BEST MATERIALS

that can be found by the very best mechanical skill. Our patrons have found that when SEARS, ROEBUCK & CO.'S name appears on an article it's no use to pay more for some other brand. Before we decide to put our name on any article it is subjected to the most critical examination, practically compared and tested with other goods, and must be able to bear out our guarantee—"as good or better than any you ever had. If not found so return to us and money will be refunded." Every hatchet bearing our name is sold subject to this guarantee.

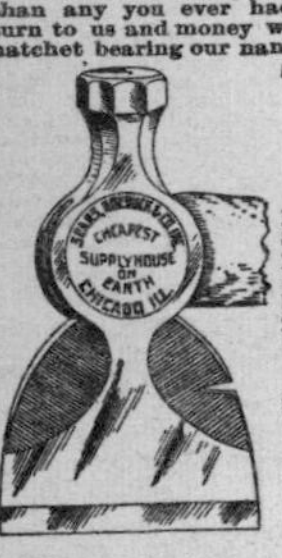

Sears, Roebuck & Co.'s Brand of Hatchets.

No. 66975 Sears, Roebuck & Co.'s Brand Shingling Hatchets, phantom bevel, soft steel body; tool steel bit and poll. Full polished and etched with our name. Warranted.

Size	Weight without handle	Width of bit	Price each
1	1 lb.	3⅛ in.	71c
2	1 lb. 6 oz.	3⅞ in.	74c
3	1 lb. 12 oz.	4¼ in.	76c

The S., R. & Co.'s Half Hatchets.

No. 66976 Sears, Roebuck & Co.'s Brand Half Hatchets, Phantom bevel. Soft steel body. Tool steel bit and poll. Full polished and etched with our name. Warranted.

Size	Weight, without handle	Width of bit	Price each
1	14 oz.	3¼ in.	74c
2	1 lb. 4 oz.	3⅝ in.	77c
3	1 lb. 10 oz.	4 in.	79c

The S., R. & Co.'s Lath Hatchets.

No. 66977 Sears, Roebuck & Co.'s Brand Lath Hatchets, Phantom Bevel. Soft steel body; tool steel bit and poll; full polished and etched with our name. Warranted.

Size	1	2	3
Weight without handle	13 oz.	1 lb.	1 lb. 3 oz.
Price, each	71c	74c	77c

S., R. & Co.'s Claw Hatchets

No. 66978 Sears, Roebuck & Co.'s Brand Claw Hatchets. Phantom bevel. Soft steel body. Tool steel bit and poll. Full polished and etched with our name. Warranted.

Size	1	2	3
Weight, without handle	1 lb. 2 oz	1 lb. 8 oz	1 lb. 14 oz
Width of bit, inches	3¼	3⅞	4¼
Price, each	66c	69c	71c

S., R. & Co.'s Broad Hatchets.

No. 66980 Sears, Roebuck & Co.'s brand, Broad Hatchets. Soft steel body. Tool steel bit and poll. Full polished and etched with our name. Warranted.

Size	Weight without handle	Width of bit	Price each
2	1 lb. 12 oz.	4½ in.	$0.92
3	2 lb. 2 oz.	5 in.	1.00
4	2 lb. 8 oz.	5½ in.	1.11
5	2 lb. 14 oz.	6 in.	1.21

S., R. & Co.'s Brand Bronzed Hatchets.

No. 66990 Shingling Hatchet, S., R. & Co.'s Brand, extra cast steel, bronzed, polished bit, hickory handle, finely finished and carefully tempered. Fully warranted.

	No. 1	No. 2	No. 3
Width, inches	3½	4	4½
Weight	1 lb. 1 oz.	1 lb. 7 oz.	1 lb. 13 oz.
Price, each	42c	45c	47c

S., R. & Co.'s Shingling Hatchets.

No. 66991

No. 66991 S., R. & Co.'s Brand Shingling Hatchet. Adze eye, bell poll, solid cast steel, full polished hickory handles; thin blade; width of bit, 3½ inches. Weight, 1 lb. 4 oz. Warranted.
Price, each.................78c

Lathing Hatchets.

No. 66992

No. 66992 Lathing Hatchet, S., R. & Co.'s brand. Extra cast steel, bronzed, polished bit, common pattern, hickory handle. Fully warranted.

	No. 0	No. 1	No. 2
Width, inches	2	2¼	2½
Weight	10 oz.	14 oz.	1 lb. 1 oz.
Price, each	40c	42c	45c

S., R. & Co.'s Lathing Hatchets.

No. 66994

No. 66993

No. 66993 Full Polished Lathing Hatchet, S., R. & Co.'s Brand. Solid cast steel, thin blade, adze eye, hickory handle. Width of bit, 2¼ inches; weight, 1 lb.; warranted.
Price, each.........73c

No. 66994 The Underhill Pattern Lathing Hatchet, S., R. & Co.'s Brand. Full polished, sold cast steel, extra thin blade, 2¼ inches wide; weight, 15 ounces. Large size head and full grip handle; warranted. Price, each..................78c

Claw Hatchet.

No. 66995 Claw Hatchet, extra cast steel, bronzed, S., R. & Co.'s brand Polished bit, hickory handle. Carefully tempered and finely finished. Warranted.

	No. 1	No. 2	No 3
Width, in.	3½	4	4½
Weight	1 lb. 3 oz.	1 lb. 9 oz.	1 lb. 15 oz.
Price, each	47c	50c	53c

No. 66995

S., R. & Co.'s Broad Hatchets.

No. 66996

No. 66996 Broad Hatchets or Carpenters' Bench Axes, S., R. & Co.'s brand; extra cast steel, bronzed polished bit, hickory handle. Warranted.

Width, inches	Weight	Price, each
4½	1 lb. 12 oz.	56c
5	2 lb. 2 oz.	67c
5½	2 lb. 8 oz.	75c
6	2 lb. 14 oz.	85c

Hatchet Handles.

No. 66997 Hatchet Handles. Length, 14 inches,
Price, each...............4c

No. 66998 Broad Hatchet Handles.

Length	16-in.	17-in.	18-in.
Price, each	6c	7c	8c

No. 66999 Hunters' Hatchet (or Axe) Handles. Length 17 inches. Price, each.......................6c

No. 67000 Carpenters' Broad Axe. S., R. & Co.'s Brand. Western pattern, extra cast steel, bronzed, polished bit; cut 10 to 13 inches. Weight, 6 to 9 lbs. We cannot always fill orders with weight and cut as ordered; we do so as nearly as possible always. If you are most particular about weight, mention weight first; if you are most particular about width of cut, mention cut first, and we will do the best we can for you. Price, each..$1.78

No. 67001 Extra Selected Quality Broad Axe Handle. Reversible for either right or left hand.
Price, each..............................16c

No. 67002 Carpenters' Adze; S., R. & Co.'s Brand, extra cast steel, bronzed, polished bit. Width of cut, 3½ to 4½ inches; weight, 3¾ pounds.
Price, each..$1.25

No. 67004 Selected Quality Carpenters' Adze Handle, 34 inches long. Price, each..............20c

AXES.

Manufacturers no longer warrant Axes—so we are obliged to withdraw our warrant—as given last season.

Special Chemical Process Axe.

Made expressly for Sears, Roebuck & Co.

No. 67003 It is not a difficult matter to make tools of sufficient hardness, but the great trouble heretofore, with the ordinary methods in use, has been in combining toughness with hardness. A practical worker in steel, has at last succeeded in overcoming this difficulty by the discovery of a chemical process for the treatment of steel while being forged. By the use of this Chemical Process it produces hardness and toughness, and greatly improves the quality. Will hold a finer cutting edge. All axes, manufactured by this process superior to any others now manufactured, and INCREASES THE WEARING QUALITIES AT LEAST 100 PER CENT.

This Chemical Process is used in forging as well as tempering. This axe, sold in the regular way, retails at from $1.00 to $1.25. The axe is Michigan pattern, finished black, no polishing to draw the temper. Lumbermen are earnestly solicited to try a sample dozen or more of these axes. Weights are 3, 3¼, 3½, 3¾, 4, 4¼, 4½, 4¾ and 5 pounds. When ordering, state what weight is wanted. Price, per dozen, $7.00; one-half dozen, $3.60; each.......................66c

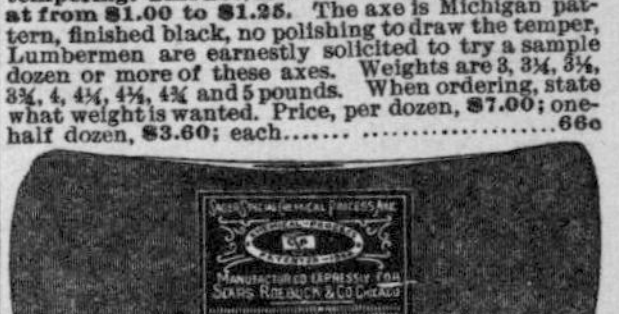

No. 67005 Special Chemical Process Double Bitted Axe, made expressly for Sears, Roebuck & Co.; made of the same material, and by the same process as the single bit axe formerly described under No. 67003. We have this axe in the Wisconsin Pattern, as illustrated. Black finish. We have a large stock and will be able to fill orders promptly. Weights are 3½, 3¾, 4, 4¼ and 4½ pounds.

When ordering state what weight is wanted.

Price, per dozen, $10.00; one-half dozen, $5.25; each.......................88c

No. 67006 The Kelly Perfect Axe. It's the shape and good cutting qualities which have made this one of the most popular axes in the market. It is made of the finest steel, hand hammered, tempered and tested before leaving the factory. The blade is so shaped it will cut deepest but will not bind in the timber. It will burst the chip and will not become stubbed after grinding. It has a taper eye which binds the handle. We have them in all weights, from 3 to 5 pounds. Price, each....$0.70
Per dozen................ 7.75

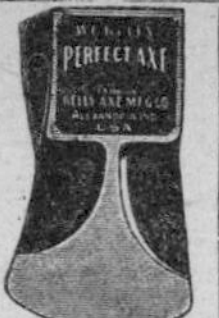

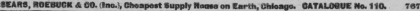

No. 67007 Is another popular pattern of the Kelly Perfect Axe. It differs from the preceding axe only in shape. We have them in all weights from 3 to 5 pounds.

Price, each..............$0.70
Price, per dozen......... 7.75

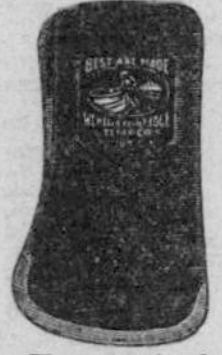

No. 67008 Kelly's Flint Edge Temper Black Axe. In the manufacture of axes, the process of polishing is done with emery, which sometimes heats the steel. This is injurious to highly tempered steel and it is never safe to buy an extremely highly polished axe.

The best axes are those that have a dull finish, or better still are completely black. Of these the celebrated **Kelly Flint Edge Temper Axe is the best made.** These axes show the original temper color which is an absolute guarantee of the toughness and strength of the steel, and the cutting edge is honed so that the axe is ready for use when bought.

We recommend these axes to the trade and the consumer as the very best on the market. We have them in weights from 3¼ to 5 lbs. Price, each..$0.68
Per dozen.......... 7.25

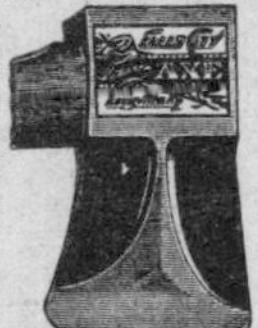

No. 67010 Falls City Handled Axe is a good axe with a good handle put in right. The axe is solid steel tempered by natural gas. The bevel blade will not become stubbed after grinding, will cut deep, and not bind in the timber and will burst the chip. This axe is not sold without handles. Weight of axe only from 3 to 5 lbs.

Price each, handled..$0.75
Price per doz. handled, 8.25

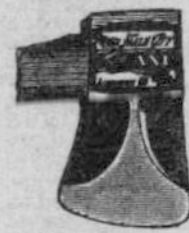

No. 67013 The Falls City Boys' Handled Axe is of the same high grade as are all Falls City axes. The handles are 28 inches, all White Excelsior and put in by workmen who know how an axe should be handled. The axe only (without handle) weighs about 2¼ lbs. Price, each, handled....$0.60
Price, per dozen, handled.. 6.25

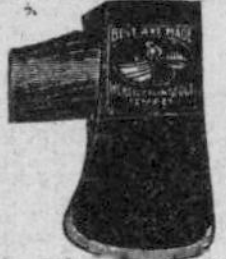

No. 67014 Kelly's Flint Edge Temper Hunters' Hatchet. This pattern is a favorite with hunters and trappers. The handle is 14 inches long. This Hunters' Hatchet is made from same material with the same care as our best grade axes. The bit is natural finish just as it comes from the hammer, and as it is very thin it can be kept in good condition for a long time with an axe stone. It weighs only 1½ pounds with handle. Price, each...50c

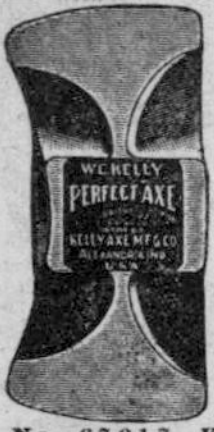

No. 67016 Kelly's Well known Double Bitted Perfect Axe. Same workmanship and material as No. 67007. Weights are from 3¼ to 5½ lbs.
Price, each.............$ 0.95
Per dozen............. 10.75

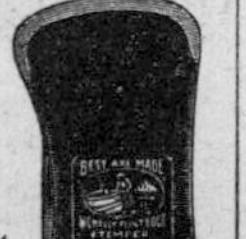

No. 67017 Kelly's Flint Edge Temper Double Bitted Axe. This axe is made of same material and in the same manner as the single bit axe. We have them in weights from 3½ to 5½ pounds.
Price, each.............$ 0.90
Per dozen............... 10.25

Axe Handles.

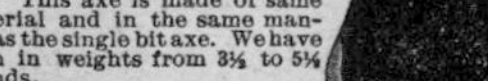

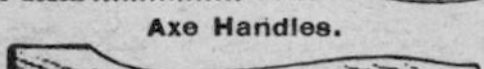

No. 67018 Common Quality Turned Axe Handle, 36 inches long. Price, per doz., $1.08; each..10c
No. 67019 Standard Quality Turned Axe Handle, 36 inches long. Price, per doz., $1.62; each, 15c
No. 67020 Standard Quality Turned Boys' Axe Handle, 28 inches long. Price, each..............15c

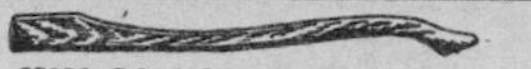

No. 67021 Selected Quality Hand Shaved Axe Handle, 36 inches long. Per doz., $2.16; each..20c
No. 67023 Extra Selected Quality Hand Shaved Axe Handle, 36 inches long. **The best handle we can find.** Per dozen, $2.70; each..............25c

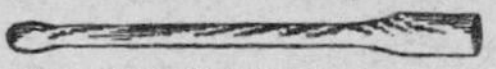

No. 67024 Extra Selected Quality Double Bit Axe Handles, 36 inches long, hand shaved. Excellent value. Price, each 20c

Axe Wedges.

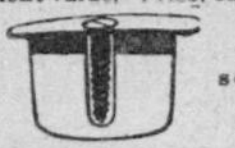

No. 67025 So well known, description is not necessary. Weighs 5 ounces.
Per dozen, 28c; each 3c

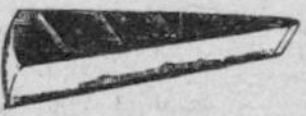

No. 67026 Solid Cast Steel Wood Choppers' Wedges. Weight, 4 lbs.
Price, each..............17c
Weight, 5 lbs., each, 22c

No. 67027 Truckee Pattern Wood Choppers' Wedge, extra tool steel, oil finished.

Weight,	4 lbs.	6 lbs.	8 lbs.
Price, each....	26c	39c	52c

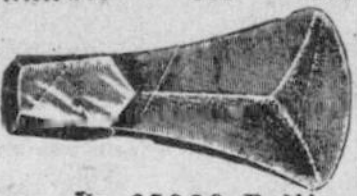

No. 67028 Oregon Pattern Wood Choppers' Wedge, solid cast steel. Oil finished.
Weight, 4 lbs., 31c; 6 lbs., 46c; 8 lbs. 62c.

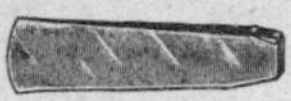

No. 67029 Falling Wedge, solid cast steel, oil finished.
Weights....4 lbs. 6 lbs. 8 lbs.
Price, each, 41c 61c 82c

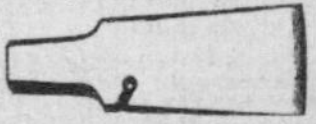

No. 67030 Saw Log Wedge; solid cast steel, oil finished.
Weight, 1½ lb., 15c; 2 lbs., 20c; 2½ lbs., 25c; 3 lbs., 30c.

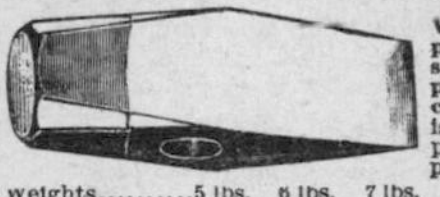

No. 67031 Wood Choppers' Maul, straight cut pattern, solid cast steel. Polished bit and poll, body painted blue.

weights..........	5 lbs.	6 lbs.	7 lbs.	8 lbs.	10 lbs.
Price, each.......	46c	56c	65c	74c	92c

No. 67032 Wood Choppers' Maul. Oregon pattern, solid cast steel, oil finished, polished face. **No better made.** Shape very like No. 67028 with eye for handle.

Weight, pounds..	5	6	7	8	10
Price, each.......	47c	57c	66c	75c	93c

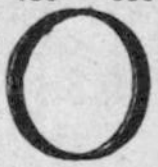

No. 67035 Wrought Iron Beetle Rings. Made of flat iron 1 inch wide, ⅛-inch thick.

Diameter, inches.....	4½	5	6
Weight, pounds.....	1¼	1½	1¾
Price, each..........	10c	12c	14c

Sears, Roebuck & Co.'s Nail Hammers.

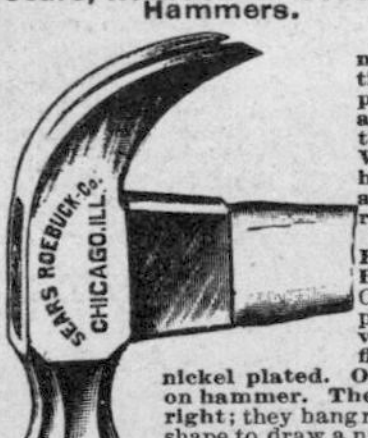

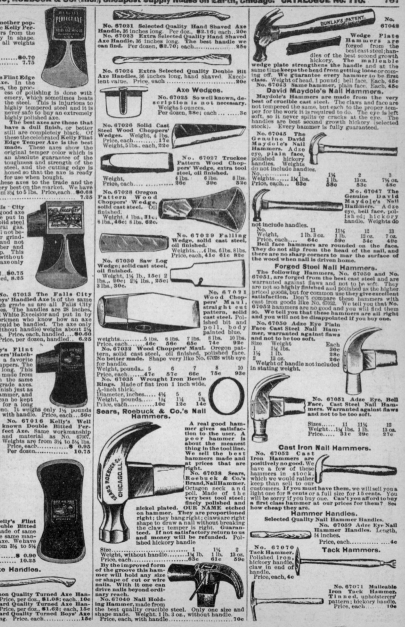

A real good hammer gives satisfaction to the user. A poor hammer is about the meanest thing in the tool line. We sell the best hammers made and at prices that are right.

No. 67038 Sears, Roebuck & Co.'s Brand, Nail Hammer. Octagon neck and poll. Made of the very best tool steel; finely polished and nickel plated. **OUR NAME** etched on hammer. **They are proportioned right; they hang right; claws are right shape to draw a nail without breaking the claw; temper is right. Guaranteed. If not satisfactory return to us and money will be refunded.** Polished hickory handle

Size......................	1	1½	2
Weight, without handle........	1¼ lb.	1 lb.	13 oz.
Price, each..................	63c	61c	59c

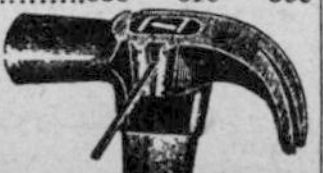

By the improved form of the groove this hammer will hold any size or shape of cut or wire nails. With it one can drive nails beyond ordinary reach.

No. 67040 Nail Holding Hammer, made from the best quality crucible steel. Only one size and shape made. Weight, 1 lb. 3 oz., without handle.
Price, each, with handle..............................70c

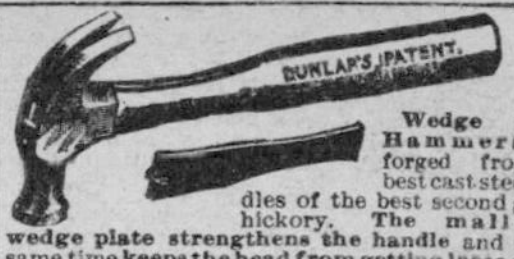

No. 67042 Wedge Plate Hammers are forged from the best cast steel; handles of the best second growth hickory. **The malleable wedge plate strengthens the handle and at the same time keeps the head from getting loose or coming off. We guarantee every hammer to be first class.** Weight of head, 1 pound; bell face. Each, 45c
No. 67043 Same hammer, plain face. Each, 45c

David Maydole's Nail Hammers.

Maydole's Hammers are made from the very best of crucible cast steel. The claws and face are not tempered the same, but each to the proper temper for the work it is required to do. The eye is left soft, so it never splits or cracks at the eye. The handles are best second growth hickory (selected stock). Every hammer is fully guaranteed.

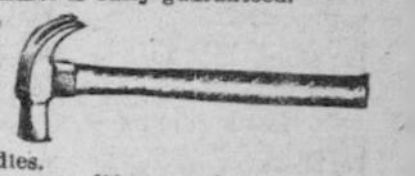

No. 67045 The Genuine David Maydole's Nail Hammers. Adze eye, plain face, polished hickory handles. Weights do not include handles.

No.............	1	1½	2	3
Weights......	1¼ lbs.	1 lb.	13 oz.	7½ oz.
Price, each...	63c	58c	53c	48c

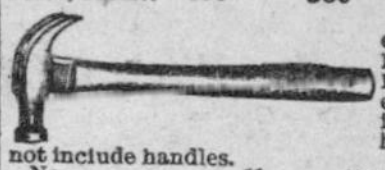

No. 67047 The Genuine David Maydole's Nail Hammers. Adze eye, bell face, polished; hickory handle. Weights do not include handles.

No.	11	11½	12	13
Weight,	1 lb. 3 oz.	1 lb.	12 oz.	7 oz.
Price, each....	64c	59c	54c	49c

Bell face hammers are rounded on the face. They do not slip from the head of the nail, and there are no sharp corners to mar the surface of the wood when nail is driven home.

Forged Steel Nail Hammers.

The following Hammers, No. 67050 and No. 67051, are forged from the best cast steel and are warranted against flaws and not to be soft. They are not so highly finished and polished as the higher priced goods, but for common use they give excellent satisfaction. Don't compare these hammers with cast iron goods like No. 67052. We tell you that No. 67052 hammers are no good and you will find them so. **We tell you that these hammers are all right and you will not be disappointed if you buy one.**

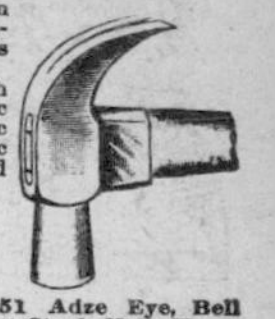

No. 67050 Adze Eye Plain Face Cast Steel Nail Hammer, warranted against flaws and not to be too soft.

Size	Weight	Each
1	1¼ lbs.	30c
1½	1 lb.	28c
2	13 oz.	26c

Weight of handle not included in stating weight.

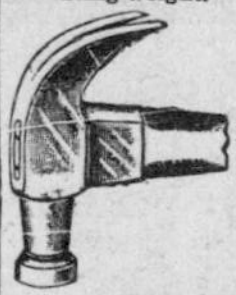

No. 67051 Adze Eye, Bell Face, Cast Steel Nail Hammers. Warranted against flaws and not to be too soft.

Sizes......	11	11½	12
Weight...	1¼ lbs.	1 lb.	13 oz.
Price.....	31c	29c	27c

Cast Iron Nail Hammers.

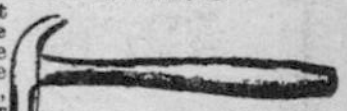

No. 67052 Cast Iron Hammers are positively no good. We have a few of these hammers in stock, which we would rather keep than sell to our customers. **If you must have them, we will sell you a light one for 8 cents or a full size for 15 cents.** You will be sorry if you buy one. **Can't you afford to buy a first class hammer at our prices for them? See how cheap they are.**

Hammer Handles.

Selected Quality Nail Hammer Handles.

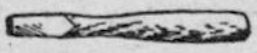

No. 67059 Adze Eye Nail Hammer Handles. Length, 14 inches.
Price, each........... ....4c

Tack Hammers.

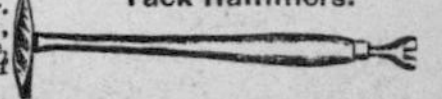

No. 67070 Tack Hammer. Polished iron, hickory handle, claw in end of handle.
Price, each, 4c

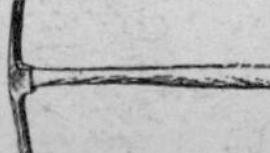

No. 67071 Malleable Iron Tack Hammer, Tinned, upholsterers' pattern; hickory handle.
Price, each.......... 10c

OUR $2.55 EVERY DAY TOOL SET.

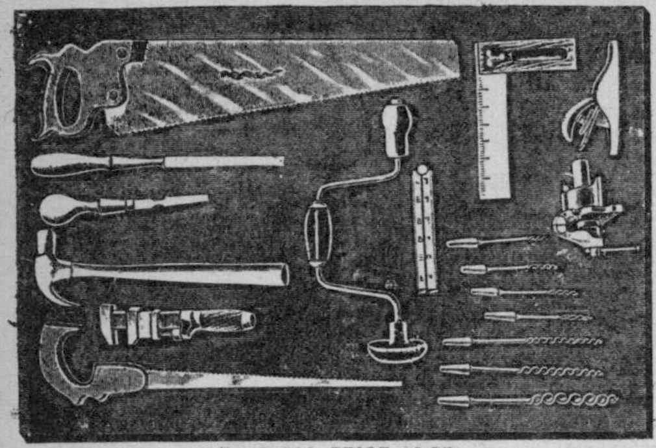

No. 68220 PRICE, $2.55.

AT $2.55 WE OFFER YOU a set of 18 pieces of every day tools, always handy for the home, for the shop, on the farm—and at a price so low that there is no excuse for anyone not being supplied.

$2.55 FOR A SET of tools you could not buy in any market for less than $3.50. Tools that would retail in any hardware store at from $3.50 to $4.50.

IT WILL PAY YOU to take advantage of one of our liberal offers for a complete tool outfit. We make special reductions to those who buy complete, for the reason that it costs us no more to handle the complete set than one item. We are able to buy the goods in larger quantities, thereby reducing the cost, all of which we give you the benefit of in our special reduced price.

OUR EVERY DAY SET of tools for $2.55 is shown in the accompanying illustration, exact representation of the tools arranged on a board as engraved from a photograph.

EACH AND EVERY TOOL in this set is a good practical tool, selected from our regular stock, suitable for all purposes, all kinds of job work and repairing. This is a serviceable household set and will save its cost in a short time.

IT IS A FINE PRESENT for a boy and makes an excellent set of tools for a boy. If your boy manifests any mechanical tendencies, you could not do more for him than to buy him this every day set for $2.55. It will do more to educate him along the lines of practical mechanics than anything you can possibly buy him, and while it is not advertised as a boy's set of tools, and is thoroughly practical for all purposes, we especially urge that you remember your boy with one of our $2.55 every day sets of tools as listed.

THIS SPECIAL SET AT $2.55 CONSISTS OF THE FOLLOWING STRICTLY STANDARD GRADE TOOLS.

1 Hand Saw—Blade 18 inches long.
1 Warranted Nail Hammer.
1 Bit Brace.
4 Double Cut Gimlet Bits, Assorted Sizes.
. Warranted Cast Steel Double Spur Auger Bits; one each 3/8, 1/2 and 3/4 inch.
1 Compass Saw, 14-inch, which can also be used as a Rip Saw.
1 Carpenter's Two-Foot, Four-Fold Boxwood Rule
1 Screw Driver with Forged Steel Blade 5 inches long.
1 Monkey Wrench, length 8 inches.
1 Stanley's Block Plane, length 5½ inches.
1 Warranted Socket Firmer Chisel, ½-inch.
1 Combined Anvil and Vise, 1½ in. jaws opens 1¾ in., weight 1¼ pounds.
1 Stanley's Rosewood Handle Try Square with 6-inch Blade.

TOTAL, 18 TOOLS FOR ONLY $2.55.

OUR FAVORITE TOOL CHEST FOR $11.72

FOR $11.72 WE FURNISH YOU a very complete set of mechanics tools, complete with tool chest, equal to anything offered by others at $18.00. A set of tools complete that would cost you more than double the price were you to buy them singly at retail from any other house in America.

OUR SPECIAL OFFER Send us $1.00 as a guarantee of good faith and we will send you this complete set of mechanics' tools as illustrated, listed and described, together with tool chest, by freight, subject to examination. You can examine them at your freight depot, and, if found perfectly satisfactory and exactly as represented, pay the freight agent balance, $10.72, and freight charges; otherwise return at our expense and we will cheerfully refund your money.

Our Special $11.72 Set Favorite Tool Chest and tools consists of the following first-class tools:

1 Sears, Roebuck & Co.'s Warranted Hand Saw, 26-in.
1 Iron Handle Keyhole Saw.
1 Lever Saw Set.
1 Saw Clamp to hold saw when filing or setting.
2 Saw Files, one each 3 and 5 inch.
1 S., R. & Co.'s Quick Cut Oil Stone, 8x2 inches.
1 Stanley Odd Jobs Combination Tool.
1 Good Boxwood Rule, 2-foot.
1 Steel Square, No. 14.
1 Awl and Tool Set, with hollow Cocobolo handle, containing 10 assorted steel tools.
1 Stanley Wood Jack Plane No. 127, 15 inches long, 2⅛-inch cut.
1 Stanley Wood Fore Plane No. 129, 20 inches long, 2⅜-inch cut.
1 Stanley Double End Iron Block Plane, 8 inches long, 1¾-inch cut. By reversing cutter this plane can be made to plane close to corners.
1 Warranted Adze-Eye Hammer, weight 1 lb.
1 Cast Steel Broad Hatchet, 4¼-inch cut.
1 Square Hickory Mallet, head 6¼x2¾x3¾ inches.
1 Warranted Razor Blade Draw Knife, 8-inch.
1 Cast Steel Screw Driver, 5-inch blade.
1 Iron Handle Spoke Shave, 1¾-inch cutter.
1 Ratchet Brace, 10-inch sweep.
4 Warranted Cast Steel Auger Bits, one each ¼, ½, ¾ and 1 inch.
3 Double Cut Gimlet Bits, one each No. 0, 2 and 4.
2 Warranted Socket Firmer Chisels, one each ½ and 1 inch.
1 Flat Nose Plyer, 5-inch—Tempered Wrought Steel, new pattern.
1 Monkey Wrench, 8 inch.
1 Wrought Iron Bench Screw, Diameter 1 inch.
1 Knurled Cup Point Nail Set.
1 Solid Copper Soldering Iron with Handle, weight ¾ lbs.
1 Glass Cutter, Metal Handle, Steel Wheel.
1 Beech Wood Chalk Line Reel and Awl.
1 Hank Medium Chalk Line.
1 doz. Cakes Carpenter Chalk, assorted colors.
1 Carpenter's Pencil.
1 Polished Steel Wing Divider, 6-inch.

Price of above tools packed in chest as described. $11.72

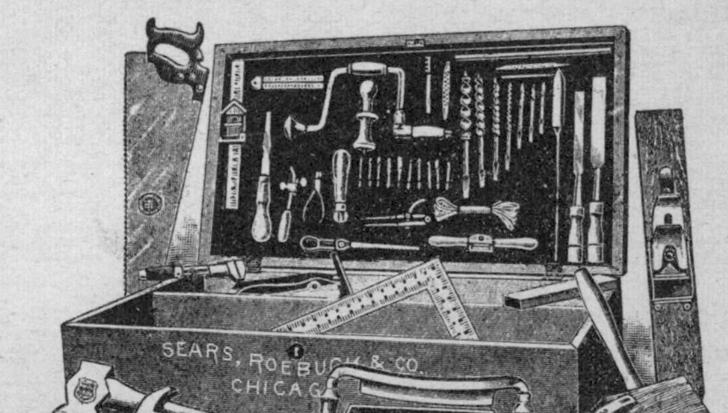

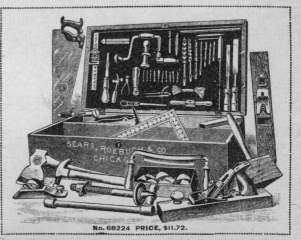

No. 68224 PRICE, $11.72.

From the above illustration engraved by artist from photograph you can form some idea of the great assortment of the big combination, the extraordinary value we are giving. **OUR FAVORITE TOOL CHEST** is a selection of first-class tools suitable for requirements of carpenter, farmer, ranchman, manufacturer, miner, etc. Includes every tool necessary to do any ordinary job. They are not a job lot or cheap tools, but are selected from our regular stock, the same grade of tools on which we have built up our reputation as dealers in reliable tools, which reputation is highly valued by us and we shall ever hope to maintain. **Buy one of these chests of tools for your boy** and let him learn the use of tools. If you will keep an accurate account of what you would have to pay for each job done you will be surprised to find how quickly they pay for themselves. **The tool chest we ship this set of tools in is** made with full sliding tray, well and strongly made, stained and varnished, made with hinges and lock. Outside measurement of chest is 33½ inches long, 17¾ inches wide, 9¼ inches deep. More definite description of each tool will be found under each tool where listed singly in our catalogue.

OUR ACME CARPENTER CHEST OF TOOLS FOR $14.58

$14.58 BUYS A $25.00 OUTFIT.

Each and every article guaranteed to be exactly as described. Every tool good enough for any carpenter or mechanic. Read descriptions carefully. Do you know of better goods at any price? We don't. THERE HAVE BEEN CHESTS OF TOOLS ON THE MARKET, BUT NOTHING LIKE

OUR ACME CHEST OF TOOLS

HAS EVER BEEN OFFERED TO THE PUBLIC.

In sets of tools heretofore offered by others the price has been low, but the quality of tools was much lower in comparison than the price and the set was dear at any price. We have selected every tool that is most commonly used and they are taken from our regular stock. We buy in large quantities, direct from the most reliable manufacturers at the lowest wholesale price for cash, and consequently are in a position to sell you these goods at about the same price your local dealer pays for them and in most cases for less money.

QUALITY. We cannot too strongly emphasize the fact that all these tools are strictly FIRST-CLASS HIGH GRADE GOODS. To build up the enormous tool trade which we have established, it was necessary for us to furnish the best goods we could procure, and to hold and still further increase our tool trade, it is necessary that we continue to deal with our patrons as in the past.

BEWARE OF COUNTERFEITERS who offer WORTHLESS imitations of these sets. Sets that are dear at any price. It has come to our notice that some concerns have attempted to deceive the public by endeavoring to copy our sets at slightly reduced prices. THEY DO NOT HESITATE to sacrifice quality for price. IF THEY WILL COUNTERFEIT OUR OFFER they will counterfeit the goods, and you will not be safe in trusting them. NO ONE WILL MEET OUR PRICES on same quality of goods; we will not sacrifice quality for price, but on our high standard of quality WE DEFY COMPETITION.

READ CAREFULLY THE DESCRIPTION OF GOODS AND REMEMBER THAT EVERY ARTICLE IS GUARANTEED EXACTLY AS REPRESENTED.

No. 68215 ORDER BY NUMBER.

List and Description of Tools in our Acme Chest of Tools.

SAWS. We furnish four saws:

1 RIP SAW, 28 inches long, with walnut handle, with steel plate on handle. It is a fair grade saw, but not warranted.

1 HAND SAW, Sears, Roebuck & Co.'s, 26 inches long, with carved handle, fully warranted.

1 PANEL SAW, Sears, Roebuck & Co.'s, 18 inches long, with carved handle, fully warranted.

1 COMPASS SAW, length, 14 inches.

Every Sears, Roebuck & Co.'s saw is etched on blade: "If this saw does not prove as good or better than any saw you ever had, return it to us and money will be refunded."

PLANES. We furnish 4 planes, all made by the Stanley Rule & Level Co., and no one makes better goods.

1 STANLEY WOOD SMOOTH PLANE. Length, 8 inches with 1¾-inch cutter.

1 STANLEY WOOD JACK PLANE. Length, 15 inches with 2⅛-inch cutter.

1 STANLEY WOOD FORE PLANE. Length, 20 inches with 2⅜-inch cutter.

1 STANLEY IRON BLOCK PLANE. Length, 5½ inches with 1¾-inch cutter.

Remember we guarantee that these Planes are GENUINE, made by THE STANLEY RULE & LEVEL CO.

MISCELLANEOUS TOOLS, SEARS, ROEBUCK & CO.'S IMPROVED MORRILL'S SAW SET. Considered the best made.

SAW CLAMP. To hold saws for filing. Jaws are 9½ inches long, adjustment is by a lever.

2 SLIM TAPER SAW FILES. One 4½ inches long, and one 6 inches long.

1 No. 7 STEEL SQUARE. Guaranteed to be equal to any No. 7 square made by anyone. The body of square is 2 inches wide, 24 inches long. The tongue of square is 16 inches long, 1½ inches wide, marked on both sides, spaced to ⅛ths.

1 CARPENTERS' PINCERS. Best grade, length, 8 inches.

1 COMBINATION WIRE CUTTER AND PLIERS. Length, 5½ inches.

1 KNURLED CUP POINT NAIL SET.

1 SPRING TUBE PUNCH, for cutting holes in leather, etc.

100 SLOTTED RIVETS, assorted lengths, in nice tin box.

1 IRON BENCH SCREW. Length, 13 inches, diameter, 1 inch.

4 IRON CLAMPS. Open, 2¼ inches.

1 BEECHWOOD IMPROVED MARKING GAUGE. Made by The Stanley Rule & Level Co. Will run a gauge line with accuracy, either straight or around curves of any degree, either concave or convex.

1 PAIR OF WING DIVIDERS. Length, 8 inches, polished cast steel, with adjusting screw.

1 CHALK LINE, REEL AND AWL, as shown in illustration.

1 BRAIDED COTTON CHALK LINE. Medium size.

12 CAKES OF CARPENTERS' CHALK. Assorted colors, red, white and blue, and 1 Carpenters' Lead Pencil of good quality.

1 PLUMB AND LEVEL, ADJUSTABLE. Made by The Stanley Rule & Level Co., polished mahogany, arched top plates; two side views. Length, 28 inches.

1 TRY SQUARE. Brass lined with rosewood handle, square inside or outside. Length of blade from inside the handle, 6 inches. It is made by The Stanley Rule & Level Co.

1 SLIDING T BEVEL, with rosewood handle, brass tipped, 8-inch blade, flush adjusting screw so bevel can be used right or left hand, either side up. It is made by The Stanley Rule & Level Co.

1 BOXWOOD RULE. Made by The Stanley Rule & Level Co., two-foot, four-fold, square joints, edge plates, spaced 8ths, 10ths, 12ths and 16ths, with drafting scale, 1 inch wide.

1 SHINGLING HATCHET. Weight, 1 pound 7 ounces, warranted.

1 NAIL HAMMER. Weight, 1 pound, warranted.

1 MONKEY WRENCH. Length, 10 inches.

1 DRAW KNIFE. Length of cut, 8 inches.

1 SPOKE SHAVE, with double cutter, one straight and one concave.

1 SOCKET FRAMING CHISEL. Width, 1-inch with ring on handle to prevent splitting.

3 SOCKET FIRMER CHISELS. 1 each, ⅜, ½ and 1-inch chisels, fully warranted.

1 COLD CHISEL, made by The Vaughan & Bushnell Mfg. Co., of ½-inch octagon steel.

1 SCREW DRIVER, with beech handle and 6-inch blade.

1 RATCHET BIT BRACE, made of 7/16-inch cold drawn steel rod. Head and handle of hardwood 10-inch sweep.

7 AUGER BITS. 1 each size, ¼, 5/16, ⅜, ½, ⅝, ¾ and 1-inch.

3 GERMAN PATTERN GIMLET BITS. 1 each size, 1/8, ⅛ and 3/16-inch.

We pack the ACME set of Carpenters' Tools in a chest, with one tray, well made, stained and varnished, with hinges and lock.

OUR PRICE FOR ALL THE ABOVE TOOLS PACKED IN THIS CHEST IS ONLY $14.58.

ON RECEIPT OF $1.00 as a guarantee that the goods will be called for, we will ship this chest of tools to any address, the balance and freight charges to be paid by purchaser after examination at the depot.

OUR $5.55 WOOD BUTCHERS' SET.

No. 68216 Price, $5.55

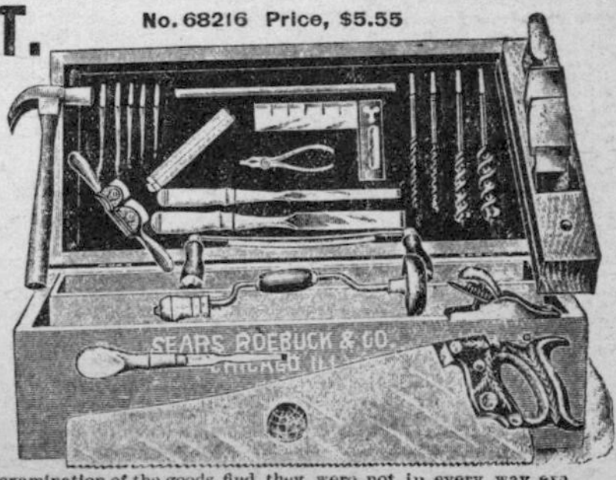

DO YOUR OWN CARPENTER WORK and save five times the cost of this outfit by keeping your property in perfect order, saving time and carpenters' and wagonmakers' bills. The tools included in this set are needed in every family. They are selected from our regular stock and are all STRICTLY HIGH GRADE TOOLS. We pack them in a neat wooden box with one tray well made and nicely finished, with hinges and lock. The box is stained and varnished, and is large enough to hold other articles that you might wish to keep in your tool box. All the tools are not shown in the illustration.

READ THE DESCRIPTION AND FEMEMBER that each and every tool is guaranteed exactly as represented, and if not found so can be returned and money will be refunded without argument. The set consists of the following tools: 1 SEARS, ROEBUCK & CO.'S SAW, 22 inches long, fully warranted. 1 TWO-FOOT RULE, 4-fold, 1-inch wide, made by The Stanley Rule & Level Co. 1 TRY SQUARE, with rosewood handle, brass lined, length of blade 6 inches, made by The Stanley Rule & Level Co. 1 COMBINATION PLIER AND WIRE CUTTER, 5½ inches long. 1 BIT BRACE, 10-inch sweep, like illustration. 4 AUGER BITS, 1 each size, ⅜, ½, ¾ and 1-inch. 5 GIMLET BITS, German Pattern, 1 each size, 1/8, 1/8, 3/16, ¼, 5/16. 1 SOLID STEEL NAIL HAMMER, warranted, weighs 1 pound. 1 DRAW KNIFE, 8-inch cut. 1 SPOKE SHAVE, with two cutters, one straight and the other convex. 2 SOCKET FIRMER CHISELS, 1 each, ½ and 1-inch. 1 SCREW DRIVER, 5-inch blade. 1 BEECH JACK PLANE, 16 inches long, 2¼-inch double iron, made by The Ohio Tool Co. 1 IRON BLOCK PLANE, 5¼ inches long, 1⅓-inch cutter, made by The Stanley Rule & Level Co. 1 GOOD CARPENTERS' PENCIL.

WE FURNISH OUR WOOD BUTCHERS' SET WITH NEAT BOX AS DESCRIBED ABOVE FOR $5.55. At this price, on receipt of $1.00 as a guarantee that goods will be called for, we will ship to any address, the balance and freight charges to be paid after examination at your freight depot. Should you send cash in full with order, and on examination of the goods find they were not in every way as described and perfectly satisfactory, send them back, and your money will be refunded cheerfully and without argument.

When ordering skates give length of shoe in inches.

No. 72080 Full Rocker Skate. As we have had a large number of inquiries from our customers for the old-fashioned rocker skate, we have had these skates manufactured for us by a first-class skate maker, under the direct supervision of an old-time skating enthusiast, and they are correct in every detail. Tops are made of selected beechwood and runners from best rolled steel. All runners are fastened to tops by a brass thimble, which prevents the woods from splitting. We furnish black straps ⅝x20 inches for heel and 1¾-inch broad toe straps with every pair. Sizes, 9½ to 12 inches.
Price, per pair..$1.33

No. 72085 Ladies' Strap Skate. Runner is made of cold rolled cast steel, is highly polished with finely ground cutting edge. The foot and heel plates are made from the best grade of cold rolled open hearth homogeneous steel. The heel and toe straps are of the best oak tanned russet grain leather, tongue buckles and nickel plated heel bands. Sizes, 8 to 10½ inches. Price, per pair.....75c

No. 72088 Ladies' Club Skate. The runner of this skate is made of cold rolled cast steel, which does not lose its edge readily, gives strength and permits a high polish. The foot and heel plates and all clamps are made of the best grade cold rolled open hearth homogeneous steel. Heel strap is the best oak tanned russet grain leather, with tongue buckles and nickel plated heel bands. Sizes, 8 to 10½ in. Price, per pair...............$1.00

No. 72089 Ladies' Club Skate. Same as No. 72080, except that all parts and runners are nickel plated and polished. Sizes, 8 to 10½ inches.
Price, per pair..$1.40

No. 72090 Ladies' Skate. The runners are made from welded iron and steel hardened. Plate clamp and levers of best quality cold rolled steel. All parts polished and nickel plated. Sizes, 8½ to 10½ in.
Price, per pair.......................$2.38
When ordering skates give length of shoe in inches.

$2.90 for Our Best Ladies' Skate.

No. 72091 Our best Ladies' Skate. It has a welded steel and iron runner perfectly tempered. All parts are full nickel plated and full polished on all surfaces. The heel straps have nickel plated tongue buckles and nickel plated heel bands. Sizes, 8½ to 10½ inches.
Price, per pair...$2.90

Ankle Brace.

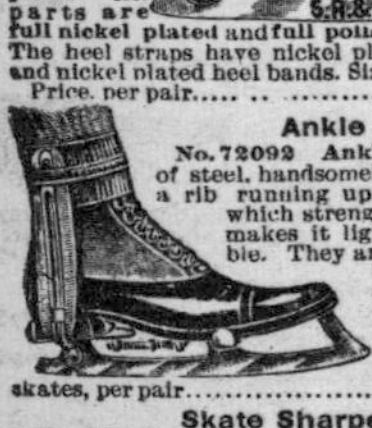

No. 72092 Ankle Brace. It is made of steel, handsomely nickel plated with a rib running up through the center which strengthens the brace and makes it light, strong and durable. They are trimmed with the best quality russet grain leather. Can be attached to any skate by a blacksmith. Price is for brace only without skates, per pair..63c

Skate Sharpener.

No. 72093 Skate Sharpener. This tool is scientific in construction and practical in use. It concaves a skate runner. Its adjustment to any skate is automatic. The only adjustment necessary for the operator to make is when the file is changed to a new side; then the tool opens like a jack-knife and closes as easily. **Not a screw or a bolt is used in its construction. The files are cut on four sides—two flat sides and two convex.** It is nickel plated. Price, each.......................15c

New Extension Rink Skate.

No. 72095 This is a high grade skate, and may be used for sidewalk as well as for rink purposes. Is a better grade sidewalk skate than other shown. For rink use it is the most desirable. Experience has proved this to be a desirable skate, as the adjustment is easily made, is strong and durable and will hold the skate where it is put. The heel and toe plates are of the best homogeneous open hearth steel, and will not break in use. The trucks are oscillating, and have rubber cushions. These trucks have been in use for many years, and have proved to be perfect in every respect. The skate has grain leather heel and toe straps, and the heel band and buckles are nickel plated, and it has boxwood wheels. Only one size required. Price, per pair......$1.75
Write for special prices in lots of 12 pairs or more, stating the quantity wanted.

New Extension Sidewalk Skate.

No. 72096 This is a high grade Sidewalk Skate, which is easily adjusted, and from experience has been proved to be the most desirable extension skate possible. The adjustment, while easily made, is strong and durable, and will hold the skate where it is put and gives no trouble. The heel and toe plates are of the best homogeneous open hearth steel, and will not break in use. The skate is full strapped, with nickel heel band and buckles. Price, per pair....50c

Rink Skate.

No. 72079 This Skate is one which is desirable for rink use. Has oscillating trucks, rubber cushions; the top is of beechwood, the wheels of boxwood, the straps of black pebbled leather and the heel band is nickel plated. We do not carry this skate in stock and cannot sell less quantity than one dozen. We deliver these skates free on board cars at factory in Connecticut.
Price, per dozen pairs...................................$12.00
Price, per 100 pairs.......................................95.00
When ordering, do not fail to state sizes wanted.

No. 72133 Pepper and Spice Mill. To be used as a pepper box on the table or in the kitchen. Buy whole pepper and spice and grind them as used. You will have pure and fresh spices. Height, 3 inches; diameter, 1¾ inches. Made entirely of metal, all handsomely nickel plated. Grinds coarse or fine as desired. With ordinary care will last twenty years. Weight, 9 ounces. Price, each...........20c

Pepper and Spice Mill.

No. 72134 Pepper and Spice Mill. Buy the pure unground pepper and spice, and grind it as you use it, thus preventing adulteration and retaining its full strength. This mill is made of walnut, highly polished, with nickeled top, height, 4¼ inches, diameter 2 inches.
Price, each 23c

Pepper and Spice Mill.

No. 72135 Pepper and Spice Mill. Made of polished maple, barrel shaped; has a regulating screw in bottom, which enables to grind fine or coarse. Remember that the adulterations found in ground spice are frequently injurious to health. Height 3¼ inches, diameter 2⅛ inches. Price, each......................33c

COFFEE MILLS.

No. 72136 The X-Ray Mill, has wood frame and wood hopper with glass front, so coffee is always in sight. A 1-pound wall mill of entirely new design. Easily regulated to grind fine or coarse, as desired. Turns easy. Grinds fast. The mill is well made, strong and durable, and is warranted to give satisfaction.
Price, each.............................$0.43
Price, per case of six mills 2.40

Tin Canister Coffee Mill.

No. 72138 Tin Canister Coffee Mill. Made with japanned tin, canister holding one pound of coffee and cup for catching and measuring the ground coffee. **The canister is practically air tight and by buying the coffee in the bean and grinding it just as you need it, you secure the full strength of the bean,** as it is well known that coffee rapidly loses its strength if allowed to stand after grinding. Price, each.........30c

. . SEND FOR FREE . .
GROCERY PRICE LIST.

A 1-pound Coffee Mill, with Glass Transparent Hopper, transparent receiver; bright and clear; coffee always in sight; easy to grind; easy to clean; easy to see the coffee in hopper or tumbler.

In the Crystal mill both canister and tumbler are made of bright, clear glass, secured to iron frame of mill by clamps and rubber cushions so there is absolutely no danger of breakage, and when mill is fastened to the wall it makes a handsome appearance, and you can always tell at a glance just how you are fixed for coffee. The capacity of the mill is ample for ordinary family use. Fully warranted.
No. 72139 Price, each.......................................75c

No. 72140 New Home Coffee Mill. Wood top, iron cover and side handle. **This mill has large hopper capacity,** holding over a pound of coffee. It is constructed of the best material. **The box is made of hardwood, highly polished and varnished and supplied with our improved grinding burrs, which are warranted to pulverize coffee if desired.** Size, 6¾x6¾x8 inches.
Price, per case of six, $2.85; each...............50c

No. 72141 A Sunk Hopper Mill with hinged cover, hardwood box, with dovetailed corners, highly polished and covered with best copal varnish, nickel plated trimmings. **Very attractive. These mills have a patent regulator and a grinding burr specially constructed so as to pulverize coffee when desired.** Box, 7x7x5¼ inches. Price, per case of six, **$2.75; each....48c**

No. 72142 A Large, Handsome, Sunk Hopper Mill, with an all-iron top, hinged cover and hard wood box, with dove tailed corners, highly finished and covered with best copal varnish. These mills have **a patent regulator and grinding burr specially constructed so as to pulverize coffee if desired. A substantial mill of large capacity.** Box 7x7x5¼ inches.
Price, per case of six, $2.30; each...............42c

No. 72143 A Sunk Hopper Mill, with hinged cover, hardwood top, with dovetailed corners, **highly polished and covered with best copal varnish. Gold bronze trimmings. These mills have a patent regulator and a grinding burr specially constructed so as to pulverize coffee when desired.** Sizes of box, 7x7x5¼ inches.
Price, per case of six, $2.23; each..................39c

No. 72144 Raised Hopper Mill with hinged cover, hardwood box and dovetailed corners, highly polished and covered with best copal varnish, bronzed irons, patent regulator and improved grinding burr that will thoroughly pulverize coffee when desired. This mill has an ornamental top to the box, which makes it strong and durable.
Price, per case of six, $2.25; each 42c

Raised Open Retinned Hopper.

No. 72145 Raised Open Retinned Hopper, with patent shield to prevent coffee from snapping out when crushed. Hardwood box, dovetailed corners, highly polished and covered **with best copal varnish.** Japanned irons, with **patent regulator and improved grinding burr that will pulverize coffee when desired. Size** of box, 7x7x 4¼ inches.
Price, per case of 6, $2.15; each...................$0.36

Favorite Coffee Mill.

No. 72146 Raised Covered Hopper Mill with hinged cover, hardwood box, dove tailed corners, highly polished and covered with best copal varnish, japanned iron, patent regulator and improved grinding burr that will thoroughly pulverize coffee when desired. Size of box, 5½x6¼x4 inches.
Price, each. 38c
Per case of 6.......... $2.10

A Raised Hopper Open top Mill, hardwood box, dove tailed corners, highly polished and covered with best copal varnish, japanned iron, patent regulator and improved grinding burr.
No. 72147 Size of box, 7x7x4½. Each........$0.34
Case of 6........ 1.85
No. 72148 Size of box, 6x6x3¾. Each........$0.28
Per case of 6 ...... 1.50

Our 18-Cent Coffee Mill.

No. 72149 Coffee Mill, whitewood box, 6x6x3¾ inches, **japanned iron.**
Price, each..........$0.18
Per case of 6.......... 1.00

Our 20-Cent Side Coffee Mill.

No. 72150 Side Mill, hardwood board, polished and varnished, iron japanned, medium size.
Price, per case of 6, $1.10; each........20c

Ideal Meat Chopper and Food Cutter.

No. 72151 Ideal Food Cutter. Cutting parts are Steel, not cast iron like other food cutters. Don't you know that Steel Cutters are better than cast iron and much more durable? **The Ideal Food Cutter** is a remarkable invention; it cuts anything and everything you want to use for making **Soups, Hash, Sausages, Croquettes, Salads, Fritters, Pies, Welsh Rarebit, Sandwiches and 319** other dishes which your cook can name. It cuts all kinds of vegetables, celery and onions; all kinds of fruit; all kinds of meat, pork and veal, and it cuts nicely and well. Cuts just as you want—coarse or fine. Clamps securely to table. **Economical, convenient. Cleaned in a minute. Never in the way. Neat as wax. All parts tinned. Two plates are furnished with each machine,** one with 3-16 inch holes, the other with 5-16 inch holes. Cuts 3 pounds of meat per minute. Weight, 4¾ pounds. Price, each........$1.08

No. 72153 Large size, capacity 4 pounds per minute. Price, each........$1.62

No. 72154 Stuffing Attachment to fit family size Ideal Food Cutter. Price, each........22c

No. 72155 Stuffing Attachment to fit large size Ideal Food Cutter. Price, each........25c

No. 72152 The Sterling Meat and Food Chopper will cut meat and any kind of food. Is self sharpening, easy to clean, quickly taken apart, strong and durable. It has a grating attachment not provided with other choppers, that will deliver horseradish and similar articles as well as a grater. Furnished with four cutting plates.
Price, each $1.20

No. 72158 "A Meat Chopper That Chops," simple, durable, handy, cheap, easily cleaned, **can be taken apart** and put together again in less than one minute. **All parts are heavily tinned to prevent rusting.** Runs easily, cuts either **meat or vegetables. Cutters are self sharpening.** No family need be without a meat chopper.
Our price........ 95c

The Enterprise Meat Choppers.

The Enterprise choppers cut the meat as with a pair of scissors, and do not grind or tear it. It is impossible for any strings, sinews or gristle to pass through without being chopped. The small quantity of uncut meat remaining in the machine can be cut by running through some of the already cut meat a second time. **All parts are interchangeable and can be replaced at small cost. The cutting parts being steel, they are vastly superior to the cast iron ones of other makes of choppers.**

By means of the stuffing attachment which we furnish at a small additional cost, they make excellent sausage stuffers.

No. 72158½ Genuine Enterprise Meat Choppers, small family size, with clamp (No. 5) chops 1½ lbs. per minute; weight, 4⅝ pounds.
Price, each.........$1.60

Our $2.40 Meat Chopper.

No. 72159 Family size Enterprise Meat Chopper, with clamp (No. 10) chops 3 lbs. per minute. Weight 8 pounds.
Price, each $2.40

Enterprise Meat Chopper for $1.90.

No. 72162 Family size Enterprise Meat Chopper, with legs to screw on bench or table. (No. 12) chops three pounds per minute.
Price, each......$1.90

No. 72165 Hotel size Enterprise Meat Chopper, with legs to screw to table or bench. (No. 22) chops four pounds per minute; weight, 12 pounds. Price, each........$3.00

No. 72168 Butchers' size Enterprise Meat Chopper, with legs to screw on table or bench. (No. 32) chops 5 lbs. per minute. Weight 18 lbs.
Price, each. $4.80

No. 72169 Butchers' size Enterprise Meat Chopper, with Fly Wheel. (No. 332) chops 5 lbs. per minute. Weight complete, 38 lbs.
Price, each $7.60

Sausage Stuffer.

Lever Sausage Stuffer. Iron japanned. No. 0 for butchers' use; No. 1 for family use.
No. 72170 Size 0. Price, each........95c
No. 72171 Size 1. Price, each........68c

Stuffing Attachments for Enterprise Meat Chopper.

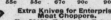

No. 72172 Stuffing Attachments for Enterprise Meat Chopper. After the meat has been chopped, remove the knife and plate place the attachment against the cylinder, screw the ring up moderately tight, and the machine is ready for work. They are made of spun brass, nickel plated, and are very strong and durable. Made in two sizes of tube, viz: ¾-inch and 1¼ inches. When ordering, be sure to give number of chopper for which attachment is wanted.

To fit Chopper, with ¾ inch Tube. Price, each.

No. 5	No. 10	No. 12	No. 22	No. 32	No. 232
30c	35c	35c	45c	55c	55c

To fit Chopper, with 1¼ inch Tube. Price, each.

No. 5	No. 10	No. 12	No. 22	No. 32	No. 332
45c	55c	55c	67c	90c	90c

Extra Knives for Enterprise Meat Choppers.

No. 72173 Knives for Enterprise Meat Choppers.
Price: To fit chopper No. 5, 28c; No. 10, 30c; No. 12, 30c; No. 22, 50c; No. 32, 65c; No. 232, 65c.

Extra Plates for Enterprise Meat Choppers.

No. 72174 Extra Plates for Enterprise Meat Choppers. When ordering, be sure to give number of chopper for which the plate is wanted. The plate having 3/16 inch holes is most commonly used, and is what is furnished with choppers.
With 1/8, ¼, 3/16 or ⅜ inch holes.
Price, each: To fit chopper No. 5, 30c; No. 10, 50c; No. 12, 50c; No. 22, 75c; No. 32, 90c; No. 232, 90c.

Enterprise Sausage Stuffer, Fruit and Lard Press.

Unexcelled for butchers' or farmers' use for stuffing sausages and pressing lard. For kitchen use there is nothing like it for pressing fruit for making jellies, wine, etc. Full directions for use are sent with each press.

No. 72175 Two quart size, japanned, rack movement; weight 21 pounds.
Price, each..........$2.20

No. 72176 Four quart size, japanned, screw movement; weight 30 pounds.
Price, each, $3.80

No. 72177 Eight quart size, japanned, screw movement. Weight 44 lbs.
Price, each........$4.90

Brighton Press.

No. 72178 Brighton Fruit and Lard Press, family size. A simple, effective, quick-acting press for family use for **making jellies, fruit syrups, wines, lard, cheese, etc.** Tinned all over with pure block tin making it free from corrosion. All parts are malleable or wrought iron, no cast iron whatever being used in the construction of these presses. Parts are few in number and simple and press can be taken apart for cleaning and re-assembled by any one in a few moments. Our family press has a capacity of two quarts and a strainer bag is furnished with each one without extra charge.
Price, each........$1.40

Brighton Fruit and Lard Presses.

No. 72179 These are similar in pattern to our Family Press but much larger and stronger and are for use by farmers, hotels, druggists, confectioners, butchers, etc., for making jellies, fruit syrups, wines, extracts, tinctures, lard, cheese, pressed meats and many other purposes that will suggest themselves to the user. The portions of press bearing the greatest strain are made of steel and wrought iron and the balance of malleable iron. They are heavily coated all over with pure block tin which is not affected by ordinary acids and keeps the press pure and free from corrosion. All parts are detachable for cleaning and it is so simple that it can be put together by any one. With care the Brighton press will last a lifetime.
4 quart size, price, each........$3.15
10 quart size, price, each........4.55

Fruit, Wine and Jelly Press.

No. 72180 Combination Fruit, Wine and Jelly Press. Can be used for many purposes, such as making wines, jellies and fruit butter from fruits, the entire substance being extracted in one operation. Weight, 12½ pounds.
Price, each..........$2.67

Henis Fruit Presses.

No. 72182 Henis Fruit and Vegetable Press and Strainer; can be used for a variety of purposes; is especially recommended for mashing potatoes. Potatoes, after being forced through the strainer have a delicious creamy taste that no other method of mashing will impart. Weight, 1 pound, 4 ounces. Price, each........24c

Wrought Steel Meat Hooks.

Our steel hooks will carry one-third more than iron hooks of same size.
No. 72185 Wrought Steel Tinned Meat Hooks, to drive.

Nos.	1	2	3	4	5	6
Size of steel	¼	¼	5/16	⅜	⅜	⅜
Price, per dozen	15c	16c	22c	29c	31c	24c

No. 72186 Wrought Steel Tinned Meat Hooks, to screw in.

Nos.	1	2	3	4	5	6
Size of steel	¼	¼	5/16	⅜	⅜	⅜
Price, per dozen	15c	16c	22c	29c	31c	42c

No. 72188 Wrought Steel Tinned Mutton Hooks, for 2-inch bar, made of 5/16 square steel. Price, per dozen.....40c

No. 72189 Wrought Steel Tinned Beam Hooks, same shape as mutton hook, very heavy, for 2-inch bar, made of 7/16 square steel. Weight, per doz., 3 lbs. 15 oz.
Price, per dozen........66c

No. 72190 Wrought Steel Tinned Beam Hooks, with large round bend, very heavy, for 2-inch bar, made of ½-inch steel. Weight, per dozen, 9¾ lbs.
Price, per dozen........84c

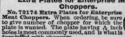

Cleavers.

No. 72195 Family Cleavers, 7-inch cast steel blades forged and hardened. Is a very handy household article and should be in everyone's kitchen. Price, each........30c

Butcher's Cleavers.

Extra cast steel, hickory handles.

No. 72197 7-inch cut, 1¼ lbs. Price, each...75c
No. 72198 8-inch cut, 1¾ lbs. Price, each...87c
No. 72199 Butchers' Cleavers, 9-inch cut, weight, 3¼ pounds. Price, each........96c
No. 72200 Butchers' Cleavers, 10-inch cut, weight, 4 pounds. Price, each........$1.35
No. 72201 Butchers' Cleavers, 12-inch cut, weight, 5 pounds. Price, each........$1.68

Hog Scraper.

No. 72210 Hog Scraper. Will pay for itself the first time used. Wood handle with bolt extending through Scraper. Made of No. 18 sheet steel. Price, each........18c
No. 72211 Hog Scraper, made of No. 20 sheet iron. Price, each........8c

Cork Screws.

No. 72225 Folding Cork Screw, nickel plated. Weight, 2 ounces. Price, each........12c
No. 72226 Pocket Cork Screw. Each in nickel case, case serving as handle, which is passed through ring in screw.
No. 72225 Weight, 2oz. Price, each, 12c No. 72226

Bartenders' Cork Screws.

The screws are made of best quality steel, nickel plated. Polished applewood handles. Special shaped worm, which prevents drawing through the cork. **Every screw tested.**

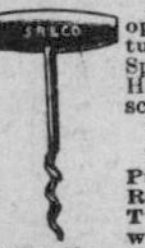

No. 72230 Easiest and quickest operated screw ever made. Three turns screw it into largest corks. Special shape worm. It has no equal. Hall boys and waiters recommend this screw.
Price, each........17c

No. 72232 Self Pulling Cork Screw. Requires no pulling. Twists the cork out with ease. No broken **bottles. No trouble for the smallest child to draw the hardest cork with this screw.** Price, each........23c

Cork Pullers.

No. 72235 The Samson Puller is a complete and simple machine for pulling corks. Takes up but little space. Fastened with screws or clamp. Weight, 2¼ pounds. Price, with clamp........$1.25

No. 72237 Quick and Easy Cork Puller, with bottle clasp attachment. **Clasps the bottle in rubber cushion** while the cork is pulled, which prevents all possibility of injury to the operator. **Cuts the wires when pulling the cork.** Each puller provided with a crown and seal extractor **No springs, no gears, no intricate parts** to get out of order. Weight, 7¼ lbs. Price, each, $3.25

Lemon Squeezers.

No. 72238 Lemon Sqeezer, japanned, with heavy glass cup resting on rubber ring.
Price, each........25c

No. 72239 Lemon Squeezer. Bowls are made of white porcelain; plunger from hardwood, and is detachable. **The frame is of gray iron, japan finish; the handsomest and most complete lemon squeezer** in the market. Price, each........15c

Malleable Iron Lemon Squeezer.

No. 72242 Malleable Iron Lemon Squeezer, fully tinned, strong and durable. Price, each........12c

Glass Lemon Squeezer.

No. 72245 Glass Lemon Squeezer. The best made for privat use; fits any ordinary size tumbler. Each........5c

No. 72248 Acme Lemon Squeezer. No soda fountain complete without it. **Cuts the lemon and squeezes the juice out with one movement of the lever.** Strongly made of malleable iron. Finely nickeled. Cups tinned and easily removed for cleaning. It is small enough to be used on street stands. Weighs 3 lbs. Each........$1.70

SEND FOR OUR LATEST REVISED GROCERY PRICE LIST.

Milk Shake Machines.

No. 72249 Milk Shake Machine, for counter or bar use. Perfectly noiseless, quick and easy; requires but little room. Packed complete with one-half dozen tumblers. Directions for making syrups with each machine. Each...$6.50

Our Best MilkShake Machine for $9.15.

No. 72250 The Imperial Milk Shake Machine, handsomely painted with **nickel plated trimmings.** Glass caps for tumblers. It can be securely fastened to the floor and **does not shake counter. One half-dozen tumblers packed** with each shaker, and directions for making syrups included. Weighs, packed for shipment, 73 pounds. Price, each........$9.15

...DEALERS...
SAVE MONEY
.....BUYING THEIR STOCKS FROM US.

Ice Shave.

No. 72251 Imperial Ice Shave, nickeled legs galvanized top. **Finely finished hardwood base.** Occupies but little space; can be conveniently used on soda counters. Price, $1.70

Ice Cutting Machines.

A small, compact, simple, strong and cheap machine, which cuts the ice into small diamond-shaped pieces with the utmost ease and rapidity. Can be attached by screws to any table, counter or shelf, and occupies a space only eight inches square and about 12 inches high. For iced tea or coffee or ice cream it has no equal.

No. 72252 For bar tops and soda counters. Price, each........$2.92
No. 72253 For family and universal use. Price, each........$4.17
No. 72254 Stands 18 inches high, occupying a space 8x11 inches, weighs about 25 pounds, and will take in a piece of ice weighing 12 pounds. Designed for hotels, confectioners, hospitals and other institutions where crushed ice is used in quantities for table, ice cream or other purposes.
Price, each........$6.67
No. 72257 Stands two feet high, occupying a space 15 inches square, weighs about 85 pounds, and will take in a cake of ice weighing 25 pounds.
Price, each........$16.67

ICE CREAM FREEZERS.

SHEPARD'S LIGHTNING ICE CREAM FREEZERS.

Lightning quadruple motion, automatic scraper, famous wheel dasher, combination hinge top gearing, completely covered. Compared with other freezers, we find: **THIS TUB IS CEDAR,** competitors use pine; has round electric welded wire hoop, galvanized, competitors have flat hoops; can is full size and

MADE FROM ONE SIZE HEAVIER TIN

than is used in other freezers. **Cast iron cover with drawn steel bottom,** competitors have sheet tin cover and bottom; **FREEZES AS QUICKLY AS ANY OTHER IN THE MARKET, WITH MUCH LESS EFFORT. All parts that come in contact with the cream heavily coated with pure block tin.** All other trimmings smoothly galvanized. **Uses 25 per cent less ice and salt than any other freezer**

No. 72255

Size, quarts....	2	3	4	6	8	10	14	With fly wheel, 14	20
Price, each.....	$1.67	$1.92	$2.25	$2.83	$3.72	$4.85	$6.85	$9.51	$13.16

SHEPARD'S BLIZZARD ICE CREAM FREEZER.

No. 72256 The Blizzard Freezer has been made to fill a demand for low price goods and to give at the same time a freezer of superior quality in material and workmanship. It is single action, the can revolving, while the dasher is held in the crossbar or top plate. Its simple construction, fewer parts, less labor and material permit a lower price, and yet, at the same time, to use exactly the same pail and can as in our other freezers. The Blizzard Freezer is unquestionably the best freezer for the money ever put on the market. Pails of best Virginia white cedar, with electric welded wire hoops, guaranteed not to fall off.

Size...........	2-qt.	3-qt.	4-qt.	6-qt.	8-qt.	10-qt.	12-qt.	14-qt.
Price...........	$1.40	$1.60	$.190	$2.52	$3.29	$4.14	$4.88	$5.75

Ice Cream Disher.

No. 72260 Ice Cream Dishers. Has two revolving knives which cut the cream loose. By one half turn of the button the cream slips out a smooth and perfect cone. Sizes designate the number of dishes to the quart.

Sizes........	4s	5s	6s	8s	10s
Each........	14c	13c	12c	11c	10c

Solid Steel Ice Tongs.

Drop forged of Solid cast steel with swell handles. This Ice Tong is far better and stronger than others.
No. 72261 Ice Tongs. No. 1 opens 13 inches, family size. Each......63c
No. 72262 No. 2 opens 17 inches. Each........72c
No. 72263 No. 3 opens 24 inches, wagon size. Weight about 4 pounds. Each........84c
No. 72264 Ice Tongs No. 6, opens 14 inches, with ball top, family size. Weight, about 2¾ pounds. Each........45c

Ice Chippers.

No. 72268 The Star Ice Chipper, iron handle. By the use of this chipper ice can be chipped into small and nearly uniform pieces, the guard projecting beyond the knife making it **impossible to cut off thicker pieces than the space between.** Only a minute's time is required to reduce a 15 or 20 pound block of ice; cuts small pieces. Weight, 1¼ pounds.
Each........18c

No. 72269 Star Ice Picks. Head and pick full nickel plated.
Price, each........9c

No. 72270 Sliding Ice Pick. Japanned, hollow handle, in which is a tempered steel blade 8 inches long. A fine pick for chipping off small pieces. Price, each........12c

No. 72271 Ice Chisel. Polished handle, plain iron head, cast steel blade. Price, each........11c

No. 72272 Ice Chisel. Polished handle, nickel head and blade, cast steel blade. Price, each....15c

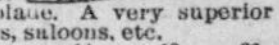

No. 72273 Restauranteurs' Ice Shaves. Black walnut handle, hand forged, steel blade. A very superior article for restaurants, hotels, saloons, etc.

Length inches........	14	18	26
Price, each........	39c	58c	75c

Combined Ice Hatchet, Pick and Chisel.

No. 72275 Combined Ice Hatchet, Pick and Chisel is one of the best combinations we have seen. **Forged from steel, finely polished and nickel plated,** hardwood handle with heavy ferrule; entire length, 14 inches. Price, each........50c

No. 72279 Ice Plane or Ice Shave. Push the blade upon a cake of ice. To produce fine or coarse ice, vary the pressure according to the grade desired. It is not necessary to remove cakes of ice from the refrigerator, as you can shave off from the sides or ends of the cake as well as top. The shaved ice is very desirable for fruits, drinks, oysters on half shell, olives, celery, iced tea, sliced tomatoes, etc. Heavily tinned.
Price, each........30c

Ice Shredder.

No. 72280 Draw the blade upon a piece of ice—the pressure applied producing fine or coarse pieces as desired. Its use will be appreciated for fruits, drinks, oysters and clams on the half shell, olives, celery, radishes, iced tea, sliced tomatoes, etc., and for many purposes in the sick room. It is also adapted for the use in making snow balls, which are variously flavored and sold to children on the streets and at their schools, also to the general public at fairs.
Price, each, tinned........40c

OUR REFRIGERATOR DEPARTMENT.

FROM THIS ILLUSTRATION WE ENDEAVOR TO SHOW the construction of our Michigan Refrigerator. The illustration shows the circulation of the air, arrangement of shelves and drip cup in position. It will be noticed that the air after passing over the ice falls directly under the provision chambers, displacing the warmer and lighter air and forcing it up the flues on either end, where, by contact with the ice it is purified, cooled, and again falls, thus keeping up constant circulation.

PLEASE NOTE that we do not have any condensation on exposed metal plates, but carry the air directly to the ice, which is the greatest purifier known to modern science.

THESE REFRIGERATORS are constructed with an inside case of odorless and tasteless lumber, matched and clamped together with nails and glue, and fastened to hardwood cleats, making it a thoroughly air tight, strong cabinet in itself. The insulator used is charcoal sheathing, which is odorless and tasteless, and a perfect non-conductor.

THE OUTSIDE CASE OF OUR CHEAPEST LINE IS SOLID ASH, The best lumber ever found for Refrigerators; highly polished. It is nailed and glued to the cleats which bind the inside case, thus making it one of the strongest and most durable refrigerators ever built.

The Drip Cup is shown in this cut closed. To empty it pull the rod, and it will throw it over. All the wood in the provision chamber is covered with the metal, and there is no chance for it to become tainted or musty. Our refrigerators are paneled, top, sides, back and bottom, and finished as in no other makes.

OUR BINDING GUARANTEE.

WE GUARANTEE EVERY MICHIGAN Refrigerator to be made of the very best material throughout, to be constructed on the latest improved and most scientific principles, to be found exactly as represented in every respect, and to give universal satisfaction; and if found otherwise than as stated we will refund any money sent us and pay freight charges both ways.

OUR LIBERAL TERMS: We will ship refrigerators to any address anywhere in the United States upon receipt of a sufficient deposit to cover freight charges both ways. You can examine the refrigerator at your freight depot, and if found perfectly satisfactory and exactly as represented, pay the freight agent our price and freight charges, less the amount sent with order.

Michigan Ash Refrigerators.

Michigan single-door Refrigerator from $6.00 to $11.00.

For general description and construction of refrigerator see heading. Understand every refrigerator is guaranteed to be exactly as represented, and if not found so may be returned at our expense and your money will be cheerfully refunded.

It is manufactured of kiln dried ash lumber, beautifully finished antique, brass lock, fancy surface hinges, anti-friction casters. All these refrigerators above $6.00 are fitted with two shelves and provision chambers.

No.	72350	72351	72352
Length, inches.....	24	27	30
Width, inches......	17	18	19
Height, inches.....	39	41	43
Ice Capacity, lbs..	36	45	61
Shipp'g weight, lbs.	100	115	140
Price...............	$6.00	$7.33	$9.00

No. 72353 Same as No. 72351, with porcelain lined water-cooler, and fauct to match trimmings; water-cooler reduces ice capacity to 34 pounds. Price, each................$9.72

No. 72354 Same as No. 72352, with porcelain lined water-cooler and fauct to match trimmings; water-cooler reduces ice capacity to 47 pounds. Price, each...............$11.00

Michigan Refrigerator, Apartment House Style.

This refrigerator is made for the purpose of giving you a refrigerator of large capacity and still occupy small space in a room.

$10.33 IS THE PRICE when sent to any address by freight C.O.D., subject to examination, on receipt of a sufficient deposit to cover freight charges both ways, balance and freight charges to be paid after refrigerator is received.

It is manufactured of the very best kiln dried ash lumber, beautifully finished antique, has solid brass locks, finished surface hinges, patent drip cup.

No. 72370 Length, 28 inches; depth, 19 inches; height 55 inches; ice capacity 65 pounds; shipping weight, 170 pounds. Price..$10.33

No. 72370

Michigan Refrigerator, Extra Large Size, Apartment House Style.

The refrigerator is of same style as one previously quoted, except that it is larger and has a special finish. It is very desirable for those wishing a refrigerator of large capacity and having insufficient space to put it.

No. 72375 Length 31 inches; depth 22 inches; height 54 inches; ice capacity 75 pounds; shipping weight 212 pounds. Price..................$15.00

Inside Measurements of Refrigerators and Ice Boxes.

No.	Inside Measurements of Ice Space.			Inside Measurements of Provision Space.		
	Width	Height	Depth	Width	Height	Depth
72350	15½	9	11¼	16½	15	11¼
72351	18	9½	12	20	16	12½
72352	20¼	10¼	12¼	22½	17¼	13
72353	12	9½	12	20	16	12½
72354	14	10¼	12¼	22½	17¼	13
72360	27	11	15	28½	20¼	14¼
72361	20	11	15	28½	20¼	14¼
72365	26	14	14¼	28½	19	15
72366	27	11¼	16½	12½	21	18
72367	28	12	19	13½	22	20
72368	30¼	12½	20	14½	22½	21
72370	17	16½	13¼	20½	26½	13
72375	19	14	16	22	22	17
72376	21	14	14¼			
72377	26	15	15¼			
72378	31	17	16¼			
72379	27	18	19			
72380	33	21	21			

Our Michigan Double Door Refrigerator at $13.35 and $15.25.

This is a very popular size Refrigerator. The ice chest is very large, will hold artificial ice, and is the only first-class Refrigerator of this size made in which the chest will take in artificial ice. It is manufactured from the very best selected kiln dried ash lumber. Handsomely carved, trimmed and polished.

No. 72360 Dimensions: Length, 36 inches; depth, 21 inches; Height, 46 inches. Ice capacity, 100 pounds. Price, each.........$13.35

Shipping weight, 229 pounds.

No. 72361 Same as No. 72360 with Porcelain Lined Water Cooler and Faucet. Ice capacity, 84 pounds. Price, each.........$15.25

Our Michigan Double Door Refrigerators,

No. 72375

With double doors in front of ice receptacle.

Made from the very best selected kiln dried ash; finished antique, highly polished, beautifully carved. It is trimmed with fancy heavy bronze trimmings throughout. The top is solid and makes a very useful sideboard, besides being a perfect refrigerator.

The upper doors are arranged so that the ice can be placed in the chamber without the inconvenience of raising the upper lid, and when the ice does not fill the large chamber, it serves as a place for storage around the ice. The ice chamber of this refrigerator is made extra large. It is constructed with a view to giving the greatest amount of room possible.

We do not hesitate to guarantee it in every respect, and we are offering it at about one-half the price charged by retail dealers.

Cut Number	Length, inches	Depth, inches	Height, inches	Ice Capacity, pounds	Shipping weight	Price
72365	36	21	50	110	230 lbs.	$16.67
72366	40	24	52	170	290 lbs.	21.00
72367	42	27	54	190	310 lbs.	23.00
72368	45	28	56	220	367 lbs.	26.50

The smallest size in above list has no division in the Provision Chamber.

Our Michigan Hard Wood Ice Chest at $4.00 to $10.00.

We offer the best made Chest in the market at from $4.00 to $10.00 and we would invite you to compare these prices and quality with those of any other house, and if we cannot save you money and furnish you a much better chest we will not ask you to send us your order. Most Ice Chests are not made with walls constructed same as refrigerators and with same insulation. These are made in the same manner and with the same care as our highest priced refrigerators. We do not handle the cheap grade ice chest, for while it may look all right we know it won't satisfy our customers and we must furnish goods that will satisfy our customers.

No. 72376

No.	Length, inches	Depth, inches	Height, inches	Shipping wt., pounds	Price
72376	29	20	25	85	$4.00
72377	32	21	26	93	5.50
72378	35	23	29	118	7.00
72379	37	25	31	130	8.00
72380	41	27	33	176	10.00

Refrigerator Pans.

No.77020 Made of heavy galvanized iron with side handles. Will never rust.

Diameter, 12 inches; depth, 4½ inches. Price, each.........21c
Diameter, 14 inches; depth, 5 inches. Price, each.........25c
Diameter, 16 inches; depth, 5 inches. Price, each.........30c

High Grade Wagon Scales $29.00.

GUARANTEED TEN YEARS. .....FREIGHT PREPAID..... ONLY ONE GRADE—THE HIGHEST.

AT $29.00, $31.50 AND $33.95 for our three, four and five-ton wagon scales we offer the highest grade, 10-year guaranteed wagon scales, and we will ship to any address, all freight charges paid by us, to points east of the east line of North and South Dakota, Kansas, Nebraska, Indian Territory and Texas, and to points further we prepay to the last station east of this line and let the purchaser pay the balance of freight on receipt of scales.

OUR $5.00 OFFER. If you do not wish to send the full amount $29.00, $31.50 or $33.95 with your order, send $5.00 and we will send this scale to any address east of the Rocky Mountains by freight C.O.D., subject to examination. You can examine the scale at your freight depot, and if found perfectly satisfactory and exactly as represented, pay the freight agent our price less the $5.00. **Remember, all freight charges are paid by us to points east of a certain line as mentioned above.**

OUR BINDING GUARANTEE. With every wagon scale we issue a written binding 10 years' guarantee, by the terms and conditions of which if any piece or part gives out by reason of defect in material or workmanship within 10 years, we will replace or repair it FREE OF CHARGE. With care our wagon scales will last a natural lifetime. . . . .

ABOUT THE QUALITY. We offer our wagon scales **as the highest grade wagon scales made**, made of the best material that money can buy, **made by one of the largest and most reliable scale manufacturers in America.** Only skilled mechanics are employed, every piece and part is carefully adjusted and tested, and as they are guaranteed by us to you so they are guaranteed by the manufacturer to us.

EVERY FARMER should own either a set of wagon scales or platform scales. A farmer should not sell a load of grain, a bale of cotton, a hog or a steer that has not been weighed on his own scales. Your scales will check mistakes and detect dishonesty and will pay the cost tenfold in a few years.

WITH EVERY SET OF WAGON SCALES we send building plan and full directions so that you can set the scales up without any trouble whatsoever. The scales come complete with beam box, brass beam, sliding poise and steel pivots.

No. 72600 Capacity, 3 tons. Shipping weight, 500 pounds. Size of platform, 8x14 feet; double beam. Price..**$29.00**
No. 72601 Capacity, 4 tons. Shipping weight, 550 pounds. Size of platform, 8x14 feet; double beam Price..**$31.50**
No. 72602 Capacity, 5 tons. Shipping weight, 600 pounds. Size of plat form, 8x14 feet; double beam. Price..**$33.9**
No. 72603 Fifty-pound sealed test weight which can be used to tes any scale. Price, each..**$2.50**
Remember, we prepay the freight on wagon scales to any railroad station in the United States east of the east line of North and South Dakota, Kansas, Nebraska, Indian Territory and Texas. To points further, we prepay to the last station east of this line and let the purchaser pay the balance of charges on receipt of the scale.

OUR $7.62 PLATFORM SCALES.

Guaranteed 10 Years.

EVERY PLATFORM SCALE is covered by a binding 10 years' guarantee, during which time if any piece or part gives out by reason of defect in material or workmanship, we will replace or repair it FREE OF CHARGE.

OUR PLATFORM SCALES are made for us under contract by one of the best makers in the country, made from the very best of material. They are accurately adjusted, they are very strong and substantial; they are sensitively accurate in weight and any farmer will be repaid a dozen times over in a very short time in the saving effected by weighing everything he sells and everything he buys.

OUR $1.00 OFFER. **If you do not wish to send the full amount, $7.62 to $13.84, according to size,** send us $1.00 and we will send these our high grade platform scales to you by freight C O.D., subject to examination. You can examine it at your freight depot and if found perfectly satisfactory and exactly as represented, pay the freight agent our price and freight charges less the $1.00 sent with order. These scales are securely boxed for shipment and you will find the freight will amount to next to nothing as compared with what you will save in price

WE GUARANTEE SAFE DELIVERY. **These scales are very carefully packed in a strong box and we guarantee them to reach you in the same perfect condition they leave us. From the illustration, engraved from a photograph, you can form an idea of the appearance of our highest grade, 10-year guaranteed $7.62 platform scales.**

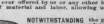

OUR $7.62 TO $13.84 PRICE..... **is based on the actual cost of material and labor,** with but our one small percentage of profit added, and is the lowest price ever named for the highest grade platform scales. We furnish these scales in capacity from 400 to 1,500 pounds at from **$7.62 to $13.84** as quoted below. **With our platform scales** you can weigh every load of grain you sell before going to market, everything on the farm can be weighed and it is not safe to do otherwise.

THESE SCALES **are provided with the best steel pivots,** carefully hardened and finished; have no check rods to bind or get out of place. The platform rests on adjustable chill bearings which takes the wear directly off from the steel pivots, and the pivots remaining sharp, the scales act quick and sensitive. The scales are fitted with heavy, smoothly finished wheels, heavy wood center platform, sliding poise beam, sealed and tested.

	Capacity	Size of Platform	Shipping weight	Price
No 72604	600 pounds	17½x26⅛ inches	150 pounds	......$ 7.62
No. 72605	800 pounds	18x26⅛ inches	160 pounds	...... 8.10
No. 72605½	1,000 pounds	19x26⅛ inches	170 pounds	...... 9.58
No 72606	1,250 pounds	19x26⅛ inches	235 pounds	...... 11.00
No. 72607	1,500 pounds	19x27 inches	245 pounds	...... 13.84

OUR $2.25 PLATFORM COUNTER SCALES.

FOR $2.25 WE OFFER THIS EXTRA LARGE 240-POUND PLATFORM COUNTER SCALES . . . .

as the greatest value in scales ever offered by us or any other house; $2.25 barely covers the cost of material and labor, allowing us one small selling profit.

NOTWITHSTANDING **the great advance in the cost of material and labor,** we are still able to offer this 240-pound capacity platform scale at **$2.25.** We have a large stock on hand, and while they last they will be furnished at the low price, **$2.25.** These 240-pound, $2.25 heavy platform counter scales are made for us under contract by one of the best scale makers in America, made from the very best of material, accurately adjusted and covered by a binding 10 years' guarantee.

OUR GUARANTEE. **Every one of our 240-pound, $2.25 platform counter scales is covered by a 10-years' guarantee,** during which time, if any piece or part gives out by reason of defect in material or workmanship we will replace or repair it free of charge.

THIS OUR SPECIAL $2.25 SCALE **is an all-purpose scale, and unless you have a larger scale or a full standard platform scale do not fail to take advantage of our special $2.25 price,** for you will be repaid many times over during the year.

THESE SCALES WEIGH **from one-half ounce to 240 pounds. They take the place in many ways of the regular platform scale.** They have fine steel bearings, tin scoop, heavy brass beam, weigh boxed for shipment about 43 pounds. You will find the freight will amount to next to nothing, as compared with what you will save in price.

THERE ARE A NUMBER OF SCALES **of from 200 to 250 pounds capacity being advertised at prices ranging very nearly the same as we offer this scale.** We wish to say with reference to scales so advertised that this scale could be cheapened and offered for considerably less money, but if you want **the best single beam platform scale we handle, our 10-year guaranteed scale,** you will get no such platform scale elsewhere at anything like the price.
No. 72612 Our special price, each..**$2.25**

Scale Books.

No. 29957 Fairbank Standard Scale Book. Size, 8½x11 inches. Containing 500 weigh forms. Printed on an extra quality of good paper, with stubs attached. Bound in heavy board, marble paper sides and cloth back. Very durable. Price, per dozen, **$5.00;** our price, each..**48c**
No. 29958 Howe Standard Scale Book. Same style and quality as No. 29957 above. Price, per dozen, **$5.00;** our price, each..**48c**
No. 29959 The United States Standard Scale Book. Same style and quality as No. 29957 above. Price, per dozen, **$5.00;** our price, each.... **48c**

FREIGHT IS NOT PREPAID ON ANY SCALES EXCEPT OUR WAGON SCALES AT TOP OF PAGE.

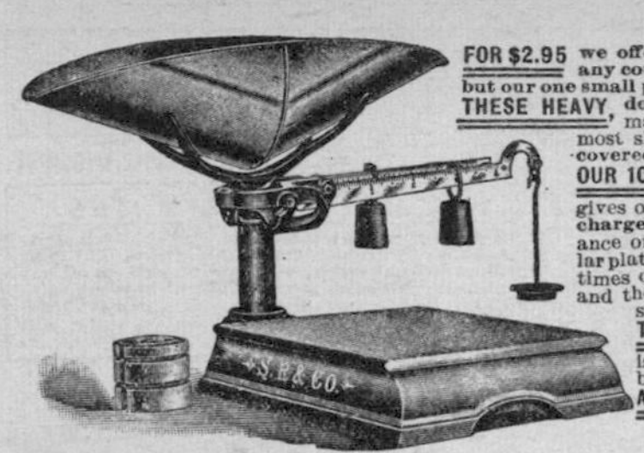

Our $2.95 Double Beam Platform Counter Scales.

FOR $2.95 we offer this high grade, 10-year guaranteed, double brass beam, counter scale as the equal of any counter scale made. $2.95 is a price based on the actual cost of material and labor, with but our one small percentage of profit added. A 240-Pound Platform Counter Scale for only $2.95.

THESE HEAVY, double beam platform counter scales are made for us under contract by one of the best scale makers in this country. They are made from the best material that can be secured, and only the most skilled mechanics are employed. They are carefully tested, accurately adjusted, and are covered by a binding guarantee.

OUR 10-YEAR GUARANTEE. Every special $2.95, 240-Pound Platform Counter Scale is covered by a binding 10-years' guarantee, during which time if any piece or part gives out by reason of defect in material or workmanship, we will replace or repair it free of charge. From the illustration engraved from a photograph, you can form some idea of the appearance of our special $2.95, 240-Pound Platform Counter Scale. If you do not wish to invest in a regular platform scale at $7.50 to $13.84, do not fail to order one of our counter scales. You will be repaid many times over for the $2.95 purchase price, in detecting errors, if not dishonesty, in the goods you buy and the produce you sell. These scales have a capacity of 240 pounds, they are extra large, extra strong and will serve almost any purpose. Boxed for shipment, they weigh about 40 pounds.

THESE SCALES are made with extra heavy brass beam, extra heavy tare beam. This is a great convenience and makes the scale one of the handiest in use. Every scale is tested before leaving the factory, and we guarantee them to be mechanically perfect. The beams are made of solid brass, full polished, accurately graduated.

AT $2.95 the scales come complete with double beam, scoop and extra weights, securely boxed, and we guarantee safe delivery.

No. 72613 Our special price.................................$2.95

Our $1.65 Family Scales.

FOR $1.65 we offer this 25-pound family scale as the best scale of the kind on the market. This scale weighs from ¼-oz. up to 25 pounds. It is made for us under contract by one of the best makers. Every scale is guaranteed, and if it is not found perfect in every respect it can be returned to us at our expense, and your money will be refunded.

IT WILL PAY YOU TO BUY THIS SCALE and weigh your groceries and meat purchases, weigh the butter. Boxed for shipment, they weigh about 20 pounds.

No. 72615 Our special price, each..........$1.65

Our 83-Cent Family Scales.

No. 72609 Our 83-cent price should induce every family in the land to own a pair of these 4-pound scales. You may save the cost in one day's use. Even balance scales. Plain japanned. To weigh 4 pounds, with good tin scoop. Our price..........................83c

Our Household Scale for $1.19.

No. 72626 The Acme Household Scale. A handsome and reliable scale weighs to 20 lbs. by ounces, has tin scoop, brass dial 5 inches in diameter. Guaranteed to be absolutely accurate at all weights, thoroughly tested before leaving the factory. The low price at which we are able to offer this scale will make it a favorite family and household scale. Will save "guess work" in cooking, making mince meat, preserving fruit, etc. Will detect mistakes (intentional or otherwise) in weighing articles you buy. Every farmer and every family should by all means have one or more scales. Our prices place scales within the reach of everyone. Our Acme Household Scales packed ready for shipping, in a wood box, weight of scale, boxed for shipment, 7 lbs. Price, $1.19

Butchers' Scales.

No. 72633 Butchers' Scale. Brass Dial, Large Black Figures. Very sensitive and accurate. Weighs 25 pounds by ounces. Bow and steel pan galvanized. Can be instantly adjusted. Price..............$2.25

No. 72640 Butchers' Scale, marble slab; tested to weigh 32 pounds by ounces; weight, carefully packed in box for shipment, 40 pounds. Price.............$7.60

No. 72641 Same as No. 72640; to weigh 64 lbs. by 2 ounces; weight, carefully packed in box for shipment, 40 pounds. Price..........................$8.15

Spring Balances.

72645

No. 72645 Spring Balance, to weigh 24 lbs. by ½ lbs. Shipping weight, 9 oz. Price, each.........7c
No. 72646 Spring Balance, to weigh 48 lbs. by pounds. Shipping weight, 12 oz. Price, each..........15c
No. 72648 Spring Balance, with round tin dish; weighs 24 lbs. by ½ pound. Shipping weight, 1¾ pounds. Price, each............17c
No. 72649 Spring Balance, with round tin dish; weighs 50 lbs. by pounds. Shipping weight, 2¼ pounds. Price, each...........30c

72648

Finest Straight Spring Scale Made.

These scales are more compact, and have longer dials than other makes. While better in many ways than the old style, comparison will show that our prices are lower.

No.	Weight	Price
72655	50 pounds x ¼ pound.	$0.36
72656	75 pounds x ¼ pound.	.88
72657	100 pounds x 1 pound.	1.05
72658	150 pounds x 1 pound.	1.30
72659	210 pounds x 2 pounds.	1.52

Ice Balances.

No. 72665 Ice Balances, strong and durable; weighs by 5 pounds. Shipping weight, 1¼ pounds. To weigh 200 lbs. $2.52
To weigh 300 lbs. $3.12 To weigh 400 lbs. .. 3.40

72665

Professional Scale.

Every doctor should have one. No family should be without one.

This is a very beautiful and accurate scale, beautifully finished in brass, nickel plated, and offered at about one-half retail price.

No. 72670 10-pound scale.........30c
No. 72671 20-pound scale.........40c

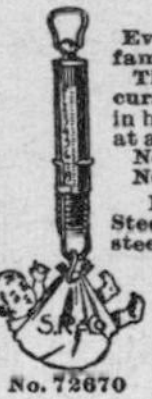

No. 72670

Steelyards.

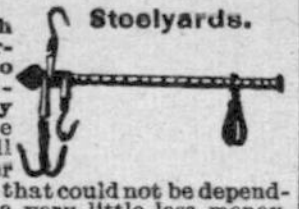

No. 72675 Steelyards with steel bars, guaranteed to weigh absolutely correct. We could sell you cheaper steel yards that could not be depended on, for a very little less money, but we don't care to handle such goods. The 50-lb size weighs by ¼ pounds, larger sizes by ½ pounds.

Cap'cy, lbs..	50	100	150	200	250	300
Price, each,	65c	72c	85c	$1.04	$1.25	$1.45

Scale Beams.

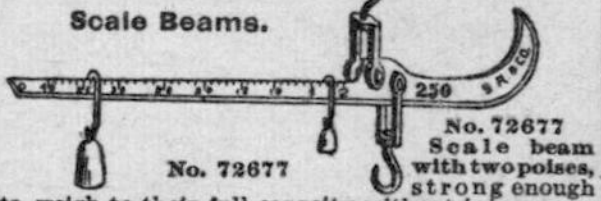

No. 72677

No. 72677 Scale beam with two poises, strong enough to weigh to their full capacity without injury.

Capacity, lbs...	250	400	600	1,000	1,200
Price, compl'e	$1.37	2.10	2.95	4.85	5.85

Our Acme Lawn Mowers at $3.40 to $4.50 Having 4 Cutting Blades.

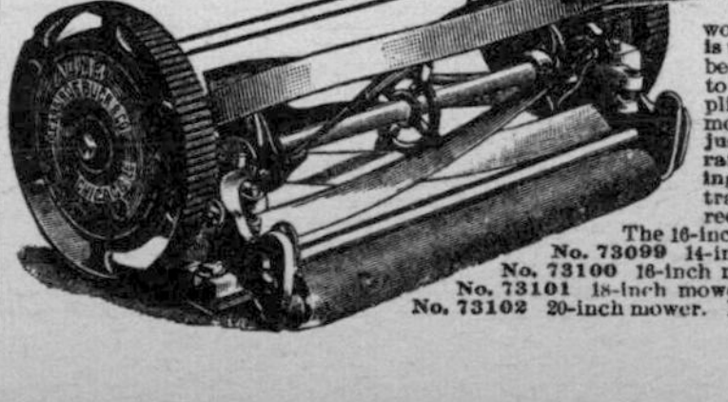

THE ACME MOWERS Have the Latest Patent Micrometer Adjustment. This is our standard high-grade Acme machine and greatly improved for this season. The drive wheels are open for one inch below the tread, though the working parts are completely enclosed. It is the easiest running lawn mower made, because the handle brace is so attached to the drive wheel that the power is applied to the center of motion. This mower has our patent micrometer adjustment solid steel cutter bar, noiseless ratchet, new malleable iron brace, bearings of phosphor bronze. Diameter of traction wheels, 8 inches; diameter of reel, 5½ inches, with four cutting blades. The 16-inch size is most popular.

No. 73099 14-inch mower. Price..................$3.40
No. 73100 16-inch mower. Price..................3.70
No. 73101 18-inch mower. Price..................4.15
No. 73102 20-inch mower. Price..................4.50

Our Acme Lawn Mowers and Sunrise Lawn Mower.

OUR ACME HIGH-GRADE LAWN MOWERS Are guaranteed the best made. We invite a close comparison of our prices with those of any other house on strictly high-grade machines.

In our New Sunrise Lawn Mower we claim to have the easiest running, best made and most complete medium priced lawn mower made. It is made from the best material and all parts are interchangeable. The reel knife shaft is made of solid steel, and runs in split phosphor bronze bushings. It is fitted with large driving wheels, incased gearing, continuous spiral steel reel knives, accurately ground, adjustable handle, self acting and positive pawls, steel handle braces, and a bed knife made from the best lawn mower knife steel, which is finely ground and self sharpening.

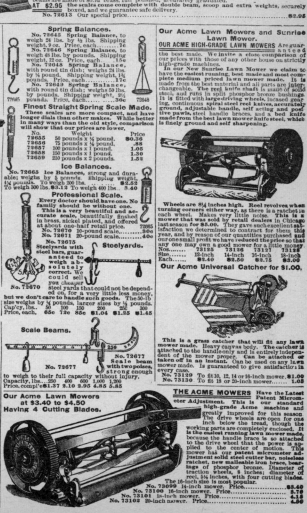

Wheels are 8¼ inches high. Reel revolves when turning corners either way, as there is a ratchet in each wheel. Makes very little noise. This is a mower that was sold by retail dealers in Chicago last season for $5.00. They gave such excellent satisfaction we determined to contract for them this year, and by reason of our quantities purchased and our one small profit we have reduced the price so that any one may own a good mower for a little money.

Nos.......	73125	73126	73127	73128
Size......	12-inch	14-inch	16-inch	18-inch
Each......	$2.40	$2.50	$2.75	$3.00

Our Acme Universal Catcher for $1.00.

This is a grass catcher that will fit any lawn mower made. Heavy canvas body. The catcher is attached to the handle only and is entirely independent of the mower proper. Can be attached or taken off in an instant. Can be used on any lawn mower made. Is guaranteed to give satisfaction in every case.

No. 73129 To fit 10, 12, 14 or 16-inch mower. $1.00
No. 73130 To fit 18 or 20-inch mower....... 1.05

...GREATEST VALUES EVER KNOWN IN WASHING MACHINES...

WE ASK YOUR ORDERS FOR THESE WELL KNOWN AND HIGHEST GRADE MACHINES MADE, BECAUSE WE OFFER THE BEST AND CAN SAVE YOU MONEY.

SEND $1.00 WITH YOUR ORDER AND WE WILL SHIP ANY WASHING MACHINE BY FREIGHT, C. O. D., AND YOU DON'T NEED TO TAKE IT UNLESS YOU FIND IT JUST AS WE SAY.

INSTRUCTIONS FOR USING COMBINATION WASHERS. Fill machine from one-half to two-thirds full of hot strong soap suds, and put in six or seven sheets or the equivalent of these clothes for one washing. Work the machine from ten to twelve minutes, wring out and rinse through clear water, blue and hang on the line. Always keep nuts and bolts on machine tight. A wrench is provided with each machine for this purpose. All bearings should be kept slightly lubricated. Do not allow water to stand in machine. Dry out well after using and keep lid open.

HOW TO USE THE ANTHONY WAYNE, WESTERN STAR, WESTERN CONQUEROR, WAYNE AMERICAN OR COLUMBIA STANDARD WASHERS: Soak your clothes the evening before washday, soaping the dirty spots well with good hard soap. When thoroughly soaked, pass them through wringer and place them in the machine. Do not put over six to eight shirts and about half-dozen towels or handkerchiefs in the machine, then fill the machine with hot, strong soap suds until the clothes are well covered, work the lever about ten minutes, wring, rinse and blue your clothes, and they are ready for the line. If accustomed to it, boil the clothes before rinsing; it is not absolutely necessary when good soap is used.

DIRECTIONS FOR USING THE GOOD LUCK AND ST. LOUIS WASHERS. Soak the clothes and soap the dirty parts well before washing. Put in the necessary amount of clothes to be washed and add a wash boiler full of hot soapy water, or enough to cover the clothes thoroughly. Operate the machine about ten minutes. Take off the dirty water, and fill the machine with clear water. Operate the machine about two or three minutes and the clothes will be rinsed. When through washing, rinse the machine with cold water, hang up lower cylinder on the upper one. Allow the machine to stand open until thoroughly dry.

Anthony Wayne No. 1 Washer.

$4.75

Cut showing inside crate removed.

No. 72843 This machine is our old standby improved, with our patent malleable iron enameled pinwheel. The crate inside is independent of the tub and can be removed after the washing is done. The machine is made out of white pine, painted and grained an ash color and finished in every respect first class. It will wash five shirts at a time clean, without the use of a washboard, and is fully warranted in every respect. Size 23x11 inches; weight 54 pounds. Price, each...$4.75

The No. 22 (formerly No. 2) Anthony Wayne Washer.

Interior view of No. 22.

$2.84

No. 72844 This machine is of the same size and capacity as the No. 1 Anthony Wayne, but instead of the loose crate the staves and bottom of it are corrugated. It is made and finished the same as the No. 1, and warranted to do good work. Parties wanting a cheaper machine will do well to try this before buying any other. Inside dimensions, 23x11 inches; weight, 47 pounds.
Price, each $2.84

$2.90

The Wayne American Washer No. 5.

No. 72846 This machine was gotten up at the special request of some of our customers. It is of the same make and finish as our No. 22 Anthony Wayne. Staves and bottom are corrugated: in fact it is the **No. 22 Anthony Wayne reversed.** Inside dimensions, 23x11 inches; weight, 47 pounds.
Price, each......$2.90

The St. Louis Washer.

$5.75

No. 72847 This machine is made on the rubber principle, the same as used in the No. 8 Good Luck, but has two cylinders working in opposite directions at the same motion of the crank shaft, thus cleaning the clothes quicker and more thoroughly than the former machine. It will not tear the clothes and on account of the balance wheel, the machine will work so easy that a child can work it without being fatigued. We have found that the yellow cottonwood grown in the low lands of Arkansas and Mississippi is the best lumber for washing machines, and we have adopted the same in all the box machines. Well made, well painted and varnished, and all the iron parts coming in contact with the water are heavily tinned or galvanized. Weight, 93 pounds.
Price, each, wringer not included............$5.75

The Genuine Improved Western Star Washer.

The standard family machine. The make up and finish of our Western **Star** will be the same as heretofore, and will not be excelled by any other make. **All of the bolts, washers, nuts, nails,** in fact all iron parts that come in contact with the clothing **are heavily tinned,** absolutely no danger of rust spots on the clothes. Fitted up with our patented round post, and **malleable iron enameled pinwheel,** the greatest invention of the age in washing machines. Made in two sizes—No. 2 and No. 3. The former is the family size.

$2.95

No. 72848 Western Star Washing Machine, size No. 2. Inside dimensions, 17¾x23⅛x10½ inches. Weight, 62 pounds. Price, each.... ....$2.95

No. 72849 Western Star Washing Machine, size No. 3. Inside dimensions, 19¼x25¼x11⅛ inches. Weight, 65 pounds. Price, each..................$3.20

The Western Conqueror.

$2.70

With Wood Post and Galvanized Iron Pinwheel.

The Western Conqueror Washer is same machine as our Western Star, except the finish. We warrant this machine will do the same work as the Star, but on account of the cheaper finish the price is somewhat less. **We have but a few of these machines left, and when these are all sold we can get no more. When ordering state if we shall send some other machine provided these are all sold.**

No. 72850 Western Conqueror, size No. 32. Inside dimensions, 17¾x23⅛x10½ inches. Weight, 62 pounds. Price, each.....................$2.70

No. 72851 Western Conqueror, size No. 33. Inside dimensions, 19¼x25¼x11⅛ inches. Weight, 65 pounds. Price, each.......................$2.95

Columbia Standard No. 113.

$3.15

No. 72856 The advantages of this machine over the well known Western style of washers, are: FIRST—The post pinwheel and pins, which are made of malleable iron and enameled. The post is well riveted into the pinwheel and does not protrude underneath, so that a few pieces of clothing can be washed with the same facility as a machine full, for the weight of the pinwheel and post as well as the spring on top, **will adjust themselves** to the amount of clothes to be washed. **SECOND—In this machine we have discontinued the use of the pins** in each end of the suds box, but have replaced these by corrugated corners, and by changing the size somewhat in making the box a little wider than the No. 2 and a little shorter than No. 3 Western, we get almost a round machine in a square box. This improvement makes the machine easier to clean and saves a great deal of annoyance by reason of the clothes catching and getting tangled into the sticks. Size, 19⅛x22⅛x10½ inches. Weight, 64 pounds.
Price, each..$3.15

The Wayne Combination Washer.

This Machine Is Warranted not to Leak.

In Use **$4.95** Open

The latest and as we believe the best invention in Washing Machines yet made. This machine combines the reciprocal pinwheel motion with an oscillating movement of the whole suds box. The main advantage that we claim for this machine is that **it works fully one-third easier than any other machine** that operates with a pinwheel agitator, that it takes less water (only four pails), and that it is more simple in construction than any other machine now on the market. The machine when open, locks itself, so that a wringer can be attached on the wringer board without tilting it; a small key inserted in the gear will keep it from tilting when full, thereby preventing accidents of any kind. The machine is well made out of the best yellow cottonwood, finished in superior and excellent style, and we can recommend it and will warrant the same as **the best family washer** that we know of. A 30 days' guarantee goes with every machine sold.

No. 72857 Family Size Wayne Combination Washer No. 11. Size, 15½x25¼x10½ inches. Weight, 67 pounds. Price, each...........................$4.95

No. 72858 Family Size Ball Bearing Wayne Combination Washer No. 6. Weight, 73 pounds.
Price, each..$5.45

No. 72859 Large Size Wayne Combination Washer No. 12. Size, 17½x25½x12½ inches. Weight, 71 pounds. Price, each.............................$5.67

No. 72860 Large Size Ball Bearing Wayne Combination Washer No. 7. Weight, 77 pounds.
Price, each..$6.36

No. 72863 By the accompanying illustration we show a machine, which by no means is a new one, but which has for many years been a great favorite in many families. This machine is called the **Good Luck Washer No. 8**, and we are satisfied that by buying this machine every householder will bring good luck into his family and relieve his wife of a great burden. Weight, 43 pounds. Price, each................**$2.45**

Electric Washer.

Constructed of the best Virginia white cedar, and is stronger, more nicely finished, and larger than any round machine on the market. Supplied with our improved gearing, fully galvanized. Inside of machine is fully corrugated, similar to a washboard, there being no nails or blocks of any kind on the inside. The machine is made with large end of tub down, allowing plenty of room for water and clothes. The hoops are made of extra heavy galvanized wire, are electric welded, and are warranted not to break or fall off.

$3.90

Instead of using a square wooden post to work the duty we use a square galvanized iron rod, making it impossible to tear the most delicate fabric, as the dolly and standard are automatically adjusted to the quantity of clothes contained in the machine.

The **Electric** closes tight and retains the heat in the water for a long time, and prevents the odor of foul steam from clothes. The washer can be used on a carpet without soiling same. Large convenient place for holding the wringer, which need not be moved while using the machine. **Shipping weight 50 lbs.**
No. 72865 Price...................**$3.90**

Virginia Rotary Washer.

No. 72866 Virginia Rotary Washer, made with electric welded wire hoops. The balance wheel does the work. The **Virginia Rotary Washer** is the lightest running and easiest working machine on the market. No expense has been spared to perfect this, and by turning the fly wheel, which weighs 18 pounds, the pin wheel or dolly inside the tub is made to rotate in opposite directions. This is the only rotary washer that the dolly rod passes up through the lid, thus giving large space through which to take clothes out. The tubs are made of selected **Virginia white cedar**. The hoops are made of galvanized wire, and are welded by electricity. Price..............................**$5.75**

No. 72868 Cline's Improved Steam Washer has several new features that others do not have. Has a corrugated cylinder, sliding cover and a faucet attached to the boiler for removing the water without lifting the boiler from the stove, which is a decided advantage. Weight, 32 lbs. Price, each..........**$5.75**

55-Cent Washer.

No. 72869 Our **Acme Washer** washes the clothes with less labor than any other washer, and will do a washing in half the time required by the old washboard. No sore fingers, and the operator is at a greater distance from the inhalation of the soap suds. No complications in its manufacture to get out of order. It is noiseless and a child can use it. It occupies but a small space when not in use. A washing can be done in half the time than by any other way. For washing woolens, flannels, blankets, lace curtains, etc., this washer cannot be excelled. Price, each..................................**55c**

WRINGERS.

Rolls in our warranted wringers are made of solid white rubber, and vulcanized immovably to shaft. When we state that a wringer is guaranteed for a certain period, we mean, that should any rolls turn on the shaft, become loose, bulge, or give out because of defects within the time specified, we will replace them free of charge. While we guarantee a wringer for one year, it does not mean that we do not think, and that you cannot expect that the wringer will last longer than that time. If a wringer is defective it will certainly show in one year, and if it does not show within that time, we take it for granted that the wringer is perfect in material and workmanship, and will last, according to the care and usage it receives, from five to twenty years.

No. 72875 The Marvel is an ordinary grade **Wringer**, not guaranteed. It has iron frame, and apron, iron tub clamps, steel springs, rolls are 10x1¾ inches. This wringer is not warranted, and we do not advise its purchase. **Shipping weight, 10 pounds.** Price, each....................**$1.30**

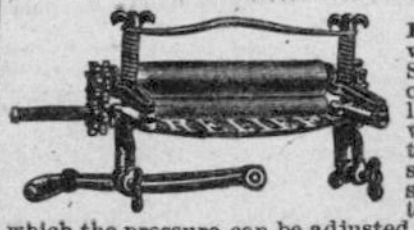

No. 72877 The Dandy Wringer has a frame and apron of the same general appearance as the **Marvel Wringer**, but the rolls are high grade and are warranted for one year. It is furnished with tub clamps that will fasten to galvanized iron, fibre, or wooden tubs. Size of rolls, 10x1¾ inches. **Shipping weight, 10 pounds.** Price, each.................**$1.80**

No. 72879 The Relief Wringer with cog wheels. Special features of merit in the **Relief** iron frame wringers are that they have steel spiral pressure springs and thumb nuts, by which the pressure can be adjusted the same as any wood frame wringer. They are furnished with high-grade rolls, size, 10x1¾ inches, guaranteed for one year. Shipping weight, 10 lbs. Price, each....**$2.63**

No. 72880 The Fowler Wringer has wood frame with two adjusting screws, iron tub clamps as shown in the cut. The rolls are ordinary grade not warranted, and while we believe that our 5-year guaranteed **Curtis wringer** is the cheapest wringer that any one can buy, still there are many people who do not wish to invest so much money in a wringer. Rolls, 10x1¾ inches. **Shipping weight about 10 pounds.** Each....**$1.30**

No. 72882 The Keene wringer is a strictly high grade up to date wringer. It has all the improvements known to wringer manufacturers. It has wheel top screws, tub screws that will fasten to galvanized iron, fiber or wooden tubs, steel pressure springs, double cog wheels. It is guaranteed for one year. Size of rolls, 10x1¾ inches. **Shipping weight about 10 pounds.** Price, each......**$1.90**

No. 72888 Wishing to give our customers a large variety of wringers to choose from, we offer our **Sears wringer** which is a favorite in many localities. This wringer has wheel top screws, tub clamps that will fasten to galvanized iron, fiber or wooden tubs, double cog wheels, spiral steel pressure springs, high grade rolls fully warranted for one year. Rolls, 10x1¾ inches. **Shipping weight about 10 pounds.** Price, each.....**$2.10**

The Seroco Ball-Bearing Wringer.

No. 72887 This wringer has wheel top screws, steel adjustment spring, double gear cog wheels, tub clamps that will fasten to galvanized iron, fiber or wooden tubs. The tub clamp is fastened to the wringer by a bolt, which passes entirely through the wringer, making the strongest fastening known. The ball bearings reduce the friction to a minimum and materially lighten the hardest part of the wash day. There have been wringers placed on the market with roller bearings, and there have been wringers sold with ball bearings, which are to be adjusted and frequently get out of order. The ball bearings in this wringer are so constructed that it is absolutely impossible for them to break or get out of order in any way. We wish to caution users against putting too much pressure against the rolls. This wringer turns so easily that if you have been accustomed to using a wringer with ordinary bearings, you will think that this one is not wringing dry because it turns so easily. You should not put much pressure on the top screws for you will destroy the rolls. If you will simply put enough pressure on the rolls to wring the clothes dry you will find that this wringer will work better than any you can find in the market. The rolls are high grade, guaranteed for one year. Size, 10x1¾ inches. Price, each........**$3.00**
Shipping weight, about 10 pounds.

The Genuine Curtis Five-Year Wringer.
GUARANTEED 5 YEARS.

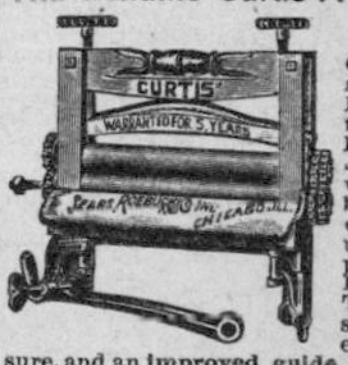

No. 72888 The Genuine Curtis Guarantee Wringer. Rolls guaranteed for five years by Sears, Roebuck & Co. Any roll proving defective within five years will be replaced free of charge. None genuine unless our name appears on the apron. Beware of imitations. This wringer has a steel spring which gives an even and elastic pressure, and an improved guide board, which spreads the clothes as they pass between the rolls, causing the rolls to wear more evenly and lessening the wear on the clothing. You cannot buy a better wringer than this, because better rolls are not made. We have contracted for the entire output of this wringer and must sell them. Our price, combined with our guarantee, should enable us to dispose of them quickly. Size of rolls, 10x1¾ (guaranteed for five years). Price, each..........**$3.50**

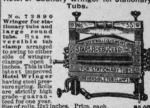

Hotel or Laundry Wringer for Stationary Tubs.

No. 72890 Wringer for stationary tubs and large round tubs. Has a reversible tub clamp arranged to swing to either side of wringer; clamps open 2 inches. This is the latest improved Hotel Wringer having steel pressure spring. Rolls are strictly high grade—guaranteed for one year. Size of rolls, 12x2 inches. Price, each........**$5.00**
No. 72891 The Hotel Wringer for stationary tubs only. Same as above, except is larger. Size of rolls, 14x2 inches. Price, each........**$6.00**

The Alpine Bench Wringer.

No. 72894 The Alpine Bench Wringer. We have often heard said it's more work to hold the tubs than to turn the wringer. Use a Bench Wringer and you don't have to hold the tubs. The bench is strong and durable, large enough to accommodate two large tubs. When not in use bench folds up, taking but little more room than an ordinary wringer and much less than the old-fashioned wash bench. The apron is reversible so clothes can be put in from either side. The wringer is well made. Rolls are guaranteed for one year. Size of rolls 10x1¾ inches. Price, each..........**$3.30**

FIREPROOF SAFES

LARGE, MEDIUM AND SMALL FIREPROOF SAFES FOR BANKS . . . MERCHANTS, PUBLIC INSTITUTIONS PRIVATE USE AND FOR HOME.

AT $6.25 AND UPWARDS, ACCORDING TO SIZE, we offer a line of the highest grade fireproof safes on the market, and we believe our uniformly low prices should attract the attention of every buyer who is interested in saving from 50 to 100 per cent in the purchasing of a safe. IN SPITE OF TRUSTS, POOLS AND COMBINATIONS which have always kept the price of safes at about double their actual worth, and are still succeeding in maintaining exorbitant prices, with our vast purchasing power made possible by the enormous demand for the merchandise we advertise, we are able to control the output of one of the largest and most reliable safe producing factories in America, break the combination or trust price and quote direct to buyer the highest grade work possible to build on the basis of the actual cost to manufacture with but one small profit added, which means that you can buy a thoroughly guaranteed fireproof safe from us for about one-half the price charged by regular safe dealers.

OUR LIBERAL C. O. D. TERMS. Send us $5.00 as a guarantee of good faith, and we will send you any safe you may select by freight C. O. D., subject to examination. On any safe over $6.25 we will letter your name with handsome gilt letters on top of safe, without extra charge. You can examine the safe at your freight depot, and if found perfectly satisfactory, exactly as represented, greatest value you ever saw or heard of, and equal to safes that sell through regular channels at double the price, pay the freight agent our price and freight charges, less the $5.00 sent with order, otherwise you can return to us and we will refund your money.

As a guarantee that these safes are the highest grade made, that they are absolutely fireproof, the equal of any safe on the market, regardless of price, we give the following detailed particulars as to material, construction, etc., and would add that we are constantly in receipt of letters of testimony from parties who have owned these safes, where they have stood the greatest kind of fires and where the contents came out perfectly safe, where it was ruined in other safes. We are at this writing in receipt of letter of testimony from a party who purchased a 300-pound safe, saying that it just went through a raging hot fire for 18 hours, and while it was the smallest safe (the largest weighing 1500 pounds and upward) that was in this fire, it was the only safe in which the contents were in perfect condition, and in which the combination worked perfectly even after 16 or 18 hours red hot test. This is but one sample of the hundreds of testimonials which speak for the satisfactory construction of our special high grade fireproof work.

FIREPROOF MATERIAL. Nothing has been more fully tested and more satisfactorily endorsed than makers cement concrete, which is a first class non-conductor, and becomes perfectly dry until great heat is applied; then a vast quantity of water which this material absorbs in becoming concrete is evolved and converted into steam. By its use we obtain the two great essentials for the composition of fireproof filling. First, entire freedom from corrosion or dampness during the ordinary use of safes without any fear of the discharge of large quantities of water at improper periods. Second, great strength to resist fracture from falling, and a large supply of latent water, to resist the ravages of fire and heat.

CONSTRUCTION. Our Fireproof Safes are constructed by forming outer and inner boxes of wrought steel, between which the concrete filling is introduced in a semi-liquid state, permeating and reaching into every crevice, making the whole structure, when hardened, a solid mass. The filling soon becomes hard and dry as limestone rock, and never corrodes the steel, which is sufficiently thick to cause great strength in connection with the filling, and yet not thick enough to prove injurious as a conductor of heat. The secret of its fireproof qualities is the chemical change that takes place upon being heated to a certain temperature, which generates a vapor that fills all the pores in the concrete, thereby forming a cool, moist wall entirely around the contents during their subjection to the heat. The outside steel box is formed of one continuous plate, bent round at the corners, forming top, sides and bottom. This box is securely attached to heavy front and back angle frames, forming in outline an all round cornered safe. The doors are stepped or flanged in the usual manner, and secured by front and back bolts. We use on all our safes the non-pickable combination lock with "T" handle to operate the bolt work and open door, the dial knob to operate the combination. The lock is a three tumbler lock and set to three numbers, and by operating the dial knob in a certain way in combination with the three numbers, the safe can be opened. Full instructions are sent with each safe, enabling every purchaser of a safe to reset his lock to numbers, so that none will know the combination except himself.

We do not letter name on safe unless it is so ordered. Name should be carefully printed to avoid mistakes.

ABOUT THE FREIGHT. Safes take the lowest rate of freight, or third class. They are shipped from the factory in southern Ohio, from which point the customer must pay the freight, but you will find the freight will amount to next to nothing as compared with what you will save in expense.

For example, fourth class freight will be for 200 miles, 15c to 20c per 100 pounds; 400 miles, 30c to 40c per 100 pounds; 700 miles, 40c to 50c per 100 pounds; 1000 miles, 60c to 75c per 100 pounds from which you can calculate very closely what the freight will amount to.

MEASUREMENTS AND WEIGHTS. All safes are measured from floor to top of safe, including wheels, and approximate weight of safes means we cannot give the exact weight of safes, owing to peculiar process of filling. While the fireproof cementing fluid fills a safe completely, it may weigh more or less, but the fireproof quality is there just the same. We give the average weight; at the same time we guarantee our safes to be absolutely fireproof.

OUR SPECIAL SAFE CATALOGUE SHOWS OUR COMPLETE LINE OF FIRE AND BURGLAR PROOF SAFES, SKELETON SAFES, ETC. IT WILL BE SENT FREE ON REQUEST.

OUR $6.25 FIREPROOF SAFE.

No. 74000

FOR $6.25 WE OFFER OUR FAMILY FIREPROOF SAFE weighing 100 pounds, as a small house safe which should be in every home, as a safe place for holding all valuable papers, etc. While these safes are not positively burglar proof, they are proof against ordinary burglary and petty thieves, and absolutely safe against any kind of fire.

THE ACME AT $6.25 is intended for dwellings and home safe, and is equal to safes sold by other houses at $10.00 to $15.00.

THOUSANDS OF PEOPLE RENT BOXES IN SAFETY DEPOSIT VAULTS, and pay from $5.00 to $15.00 a year as a safe place to hold such valuable papers as insurance policies, deeds, receipts, contracts, etc., when they could by investing $6.25 have the same protection in their own home and save the annoyance of going to the deposit vault whenever it is necessary to consult the contents of the safe.

THIS $6.25 SAFE IS ABSOLUTELY FIREPROOF. It is nicely finished throughout, has a deep fireproof door, latest burglar proof combination lock. It is 16¼ inches high outside, 10 inches inside, 10½ inches wide outside, 6¼ inches inside, 13 inches deep outside, 8 inches inside. Weighs 100 pounds, is offered at $6.25 as the equal of any safe on the market sold by others at $10.00 to $15.00.

No. 74000 Our price..**$6.25**

OUR $12.25 FIREPROOF SAFE.

No. 74001

FOR $12.25 WE OFFER you a single door fireproof safe, the equal of anything you can buy elsewhere at $25.00.

OUR $12.25 ACME SAFE is listed by the different manufacturers at from $25.00 to $35.00 and they seldom give a discount of more than 10%.

$12.25 GIVES YOU the benefit of the actual cost to manufacture, with but one small percentage of profit added, a first-class safe at less money than it can possibly be bought elsewhere. While the safe is intended more as a house safe, we have sold a great many to business men for offices, stores and other places where only a small safe is required as a protection to valuable papers, etc. This safe is beautifully finished, rounded corners throughout, with the very best non-pickable combination lock, highly ornamented with transfer decorations, painting, etc., and finished with your name handsomely lettered in gold, without extra charge.

DIMENSIONS OF SAFE.

Outside measure	24x15x14 inches
Inside measure	13x 9x 8 inches
Approximate weight	300 pounds

DIMENSIONS OF INSIDE SPACE.

One book space	13 x4⅛x8 inches
One iron sub-treasury	4⅜x4⅜x6 inches
One drawer	4⅛x4 x6 inches
One pigeonhole	6 x4⅛x4 inches

No. 74001 Our special price..**$12.25**

No. 74002 Our special price, with inside door........................**13.50**

OUR $16.85 ACME SAFE.

AT $16.85 WE OFFER A REGULAR $35.00 SAFE. This is a safe that retails everywhere at $35.00. Were you to communicate with any safe dealer, he would charge you at least $35.00 for safe of same grade and dimensions, but we are able to make a price of $16.85 by reason of buying these safes in very large quantities direct from the manufacturers, and naming a price to our customers based on the actual cost, with but our one small percentage of profit added.

No. 74003

THIS IS A VERY POPULAR SIZE safe for home, small merchants, and the various places of business where a fireproof safe of limited capacity is required.

IF YOU NEED A SAFE in which the inside dimensions named will hold as much as you require, this, our special $16.85; will be just the safe—will serve you just as well as a safe that costs ten times the price. It is finished with round corners throughout, handsomely ornamented with beautiful gold and ornamented transfers, and we furnish it with your name in gold letters without extra charge.

DIMENSIONS OF SAFE. Outside measure, 28x18x17¼ inches; inside measure, 15x10x10 inches; approximate weight, 500 pounds.

DIMENSIONS OF INSIDE SPACE. (Divided as shown in open cut.) One book space, 14⅞x4⅝x8¾ inches; one drawer, 7⅜x2¾x6¾ inches; two pigeon holes, 4⅛x2¾x8¼ inches; one sub-treasury, 4⅞x5⅞x6¾ inches.

No. 74003 Our special price..**$16.85**

No. 74004 Our special price, with inner door........................**18.25**

Our $20.05 Acme Fire-Proof Safe.

No. 74005

THIS IS A STRICTLY HIGH GRADE FIREPROOF SAFE, one that retails everywhere at $45.00. It is designed for homes, for merchants, for all classes of business men who require a safe larger in dimensions, one with more book room than those previously illustrated.

THIS IS A GOOD SIZED SAFE FOR THE COUNTRY MERCHANT. Weighs 700 pounds. Outside measure, 32x22x20 inches. Inside measure, 18x14x12 inches. Round corners, beautifully ornamented and decorated with handsome transfer landscape views, etc. Furnished with your name handsomely lettered in gold.

DIMENSIONS OF INSIDE SPACE. (Divided as shown in open cut) One book space, 18x8¾x10¾ inches; one drawer, 4⅞x3⅜x9¼ inches; two pigeonholes, 4⅞x3⅞x9¼ inches; one sub-treasury, 5⅞x4⅞x9¼ inches.

No. 74005 Our special price..**$20.05**

No. 74006 Our special price, with inner door........................**21.75**

Our $24.75 Acme Fireproof Safe.

No. 74007

THIS IS A GOOD SIZED SAFE for all business purposes, **weighs 1,000 pounds.** Is offered at **$24.75** in competition with safes that sell everywhere at **$60.00.**

If you order this safe from us at $24.75, you would be saving at least $30.00 in your purchase price, and you will get as high a grade fireproof safe as it is possible to build, **a safe in construction, durability and convenience,** the equal of any safe made, regardless of price. Combination lock is capable of more than a thousand changes. **Made with chilled steel protector door, solid 4-inch cement walls.** It is fitted with iron cash box, book and pigeonhole compartments, made with all the latest improvements known to safe making. **36 inches high, 25 inches wide, 22 inches deep, approximate weight, 1,000 pounds.** Made with round corners throughout, beautifully ornamented and decorated, has handsome gold transfers and landscapes, furnished with your own name handsomely lettered in gold free of charge.

From the illustration below, which shows our $24.75 Acme Fireproof Safe open, you may see the internal arrangement of pigeonholes, etc.

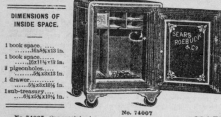

DIMENSIONS OF INSIDE SPACE.

1 book space.......16x5⅝x13 in.
1 book space......16x11⅝x13 in.
3 pigeonholes.........5⅝x3x13 in.
1 drawer.........5⅝x3x10¼ in.
1 sub-treasury.....6⅝x5⅝x10¼ in.

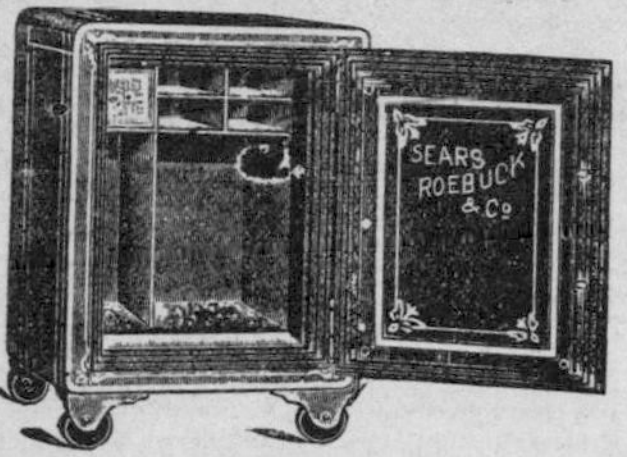

No. 74007

No. 74007 Our special price.................................. **$24.75**
No. 74008 Our special price with inner door..................... **26.40**

Our $28.10 Acme Fireproof Safe.

AT $28.10 WE OFFER the exact same safe that sells everywhere at retail for $75.00. If you order this safe from us, you will get a high grade fireproof safe, a safe combining the good points of every strictly high grade fireproof safe, with the defects of none. You will save over $40.00 in price.

THIS IS A LARGE COMMERCIAL SIZE for stores, business houses of all kinds. Weighs 1,250 pounds. Outside measure, 40x27x22 inches. Inside measure, 26½x18⅜x13¼ inches. Made with iron money chest, pigeonhole and book compartments, best burglar proof combination lock, finished with round corners throughout, highly ornamented and decorated with beautiful transfers and landscape, and your name lettered on the safe in gold, without extra charge.

The illustration below shows our $28.10 Acme Fireproof Safe open. You will note the arrangement of inside space.

DIMENSIONS OF INSIDE SPACE: One book space, 19⅞x13x13¼ inches; one book space, 19⅞x5⅜x13¼ inches; three pigeonholes, 6⅝x3x13¼ inches; one drawer, 6⅝x3x10⅝ inches; one sub-treasury, 6⅝x5⅝x10⅝ inches.

No. 74009 Our special price.............................. **$28.10**
No. 74010 Our special price with inner door.................. **29.75**

WE DO NOT LETTER NAME ON SAFE UNLESS IT IS SO ORDERED.

$64.50 Buys a Regular $135.00 Safe.

$135.00 is the regular price of this strictly high grade, extra large double door fireproof combination safe, and when we offer it to you at $64.50, we have given you the benefit of our contract, which breaks the safe monopoly, the combine to maintain prices, and you will own the safe on the basis of the actual cost to manufacture with but our one small profit added. **You will save $60.00 in the purchase price by getting it from us at $64.50.**

This safe weighs 2400 pounds. You will observe it is sold to you at about 2⅔ cents per pound, and your own judgment will show you that the cost of the raw material represents a good part of our selling price, and you really only pay the cost of material, cost of labor and the smallest kind of a profit added.

THIS IS AN EXTRA LARGE SAFE FOR LARGE STORES, BUSINESS INSTITUTIONS, COUNTRY BANKS, PUBLIC INSTITUTIONS, SOCIETIES, TOWN BOARDS,

and other places where a large roomy, fireproof safe is required. This safe comes complete with large double outside doors, very best combination lock, double inside doors with key lock. Inside measure, 30¼x26⅛x14 inches. Outside measure, 50¼x37½x26 inches. Contains three book spaces, seven pigeonholes, two drawers and one iron sub-treasury with lock. Finished round corners throughout, beautifully ornamented with gold and colored transfers landscape designs, etc., and with your name lettered on the safe in gold without extra charge.

No. 74012 Double Door Safe with inside doors.

DIMENSIONS OF INSIDE SPACES.

Divided as per illustration.

Two book spaces	17 x8¼x14 inches.
One book space	21⅝x8¼x14 inches.
One pigeonhole	8¼x4⅛x14 inches.
Six pigeonholes	4 x4 x14 inches.
Two drawers	8¼x4⅛x11 inches.
One sub-treasury	8⅛x8⅛x11 inches.

No. 74012 Our special price for this regular $135.00 safe with double outside doors, combination lock and double inside doors with key lock................................ **$64.50**

$85.00 Buys a Regular $195.00 Safe.

$195.00 is the price of this safe everywhere, and it is the lowest price at which the manufacturer has ever retailed these safes, and when we are able to quote it at $85.00, a reduction in price of $110.00 from the regular selling price, you can imagine the penalty you are paying for combinations, for the express purpose of holding the goods at fictitious values.

This is a very large safe, weighing 3,000 pounds, and standing nearly 6 feet high, made with double outside combination doors and double inside doors, made expressly for very large business houses, banks, public offices and such institutions as require a safe absolutely fireproof of sufficient size to hold a large number of books, records, papers, etc.

We make the price so very low, only $85.00, that all business houses can afford to have the largest safe we make, and the highest grade turned out. **You would pay $85.00 for a very small single door safe,** if you were to buy it from any safe dealer, but taking advantage of our contract, which has enabled us to break the safe prices monopoly, you can have the biggest safe we make at the price others charge for the very small safes.

This is a safe that combines the good qualities of every strictly high grade safe made, with the defects of none.

THERE IS NOTHING LEFT UNDONE IN THE MANUFACTURE OF THESE GOODS.

This safe stands 68¼ inches high, 37¼ inches wide, 25¾ inches deep. Inside measurements, 48⅛ inches high, 26⅛ inches wide, 14¼ inches deep. Weighs complete, 3,000 pounds.

Our price on this, the finest work we make, is about 3 cents a pound—about 1 cent per pound above the actual cost of the raw material, and less than one-half the price at which the safes are sold; in fact, the lowest inside price with all discounts deducted for this class of work from regular safe houses is 6 cents per lb., making this safe $180.00. We cut the price in two, and offer it at $85.00. **Upon receipt of $5.00 as a guarantee of good faith,** any safe will be shipped by freight, C. O. D., subject to examination, balance and freight charges to be paid after the safe is received, if found perfectly satisfactory and exactly as represented. Safes are shipped from the southern part of Ohio. The freight rate, you will find, will amount to next to nothing as compared to what you will save in price. Remember our special offer price is $85.00.

DIMENSIONS OF INSIDE SPACES.

Divided as per Illustration.

One iron sub-treasury	8¼x8¼x12 inches.
Twelve pigeonholes	4 x4 x12 inches.
Three drawers	3 x8¼x12 inches.
Three book spaces	18 x8¼x14¼ inches.
Two book spaces	20⅝x8¼x14¼ inches.

No. 74013 Our special price, with double folding outside doors, combination lock and double folding inside doors, with key lock... **$85.00**

OUR SPECIAL SAFE CATALOGUE shows our complete line of fire and burglar proof safes, skeleton safes, etc., will be sent free on request.

NAME WANTED SHOULD BE CAREFULLY PRINTED TO AVOID ERRORS.

DEPARTMENT OF STOVES.

WE OFFER THE VERY LATEST DESIGNS IN...

Strictly High Grade Cast Iron Cook Stoves,
Ranges and Heaters,
Steel Ranges,
Air Tight Heaters,
Gasoline and Oil Stoves,

At Prices Heretofore Unknown.

OUR NEW LINE FOR THIS SEASON INCLUDES THE NEW IMPROVED ACME ROYAL SQUARE OVEN LINE. THE VERY LATEST THING IN CAST IRON STOVES,

made from patterns that are new for this season, and offered at about half the price charged by retail dealers. Our line for this season also includes a number of cook stoves from entirely new patterns, stoves molded from patterns that were made under contract for us this season, embracing the good qualities of all strictly high grade stoves, with the defects of none.

OUR STEEL RANGE LINE IS OFFERED TO YOU AS THE.... HIGHEST GRADE WORK ON THE MARKET.

Ranges Combining the Good Qualities OF ALL OTHER STEEL RANGES AND THE DEFECTS OF NONE, and the price is based on the actual cost of material and labor, with but our one small percentage of profit added. Prices so low you can save from 25 to 50 per cent by placing your order in our hands.

How We Make the Prices so Low.

WE ARE ABLE TO NAME A PRICE on any Stove we show direct to the user, which is considerably less than dealers can buy same grade of Stoves in larger quantities. This is made possible by reason of our contracting with several of the best makers in the country for The Entire Product of Their Foundry, having the goods made up during the dull summer and early fall season, figuring the cost on a basis of the raw material, the labor, etc., and charging but one small percentage of profit, which results in our being able to deliver Stoves to your door at prices, quality considered, heretofore unknown.

IF YOU ARE NOT A CUSTOMER OF OURS you possibly may think it impossible for us to sell this class of Stoves at such heretofore unheard of low prices. Do not send us an order if you are in doubt as to our reliability. Investigate, and You Will Find Our Guarantee Is Worth One Hundred Cents on the Dollar.

Our Binding Guarantee with every Stove

WE ISSUE A SPECIAL WRITTEN BINDING GUARANTEE certifying that the Stove is perfect in manufacture, perfect in operation, and unequaled by any other Stove or range of its class for convenience, completeness, durability, economy in the consumption of fuel, and in the practical results that may be obtained by its use.

THAT IT IS PERFECTLY ADAPTED TO THE FUEL, and for the purpose for which it is made. That any defects in material or workmanship will be made good to purchaser without charge.

Our Acme Line of Stoves and Ranges.

EMBODY MORE DISTINCT and Original Features of Merit than are to be found in all other makes combined, and every Acme Stove is made of materials of the highest quality, fashioned by expert mechanics.

Our Guarantee Against Breakage.

SO CONFIDENT ARE WE of the quality of the goods we offer, and that they will invariably reach you in the same perfect condition they leave us, that we make this most liberal offer: Should any stove arrive badly damaged—such as any piece or part broken—you can pay the freight bill, have the agent note the condition of the stove on the freight bill, showing what part or parts are broken and then send the freight bill to us and we will immediately send you, free of charge, new castings to replace broken ones.

Our Liberal $1.00 C. O. D. Terms.

WE WILL SHIP ANY STOVE to any address within one thousand miles of Chicago, by freight C.O.D., subject to examination, upon receipt of $1.00 as a guarantee of good faith. You can examine it at the freight depot, and if it is perfectly satisfactory and exactly as represented, and the greatest value you ever saw or heard of in a strictly high grade stove, pay freight agent our price and freight charges, less the $1.00 sent with order.

What the Freight Amounts to.

THE FREIGHT CHARGES you will have to pay on any stove or range will amount to next to nothing, as compared with what you will save in price. All stoves are accepted by railroad companies at third class freight rate, and by referring to freight classification in front of book, you will see just what the third class freight rate is to different points in every state in the Union, and under the description of every stove we give the weight of the different size stoves, and in this way you can calculate very closely what freight will amount to to your place. For example, you will find third class rates from Chicago to Alabama is from 75 cents to $1.04 cents per hundred pounds, and if a stove weighs 200 pounds the freight rate from Chicago to Alabama will be from $1.50 to $2.06. To all points in Canada, third class freight rate is 55 cents, and the freight on stove weighing 200 pounds would be $1.10. To a point in Indiana the freight on stove weighing 200 pounds, you will observe, will be from 40 to 50 cents; to Iowa, 58 to 90 cents; to Maine, $1.10 to $1.28. A 200-pound stove to any point in Massachusetts, $1.10. To a far distant point, like New Mexico, the freight on a stove weighing 200 pounds would be from $2.74 to $4.14. From this you can calculate, almost to a penny, what the freight rate will be to your place, and you will see it will add next to nothing to the cost, as compared with what you will be compelled to pay your local dealer.

OUR ACME STEEL RANGES AT $18.70 TO $31.05

THE ACME STERLING STEEL RANGES ARE THE LATEST DESIGNS, improved in all points of construction, far surpassing any we have ever made before, and are thoroughly up-to-date 1900 patterns. NOTHING IN THE MARKET CAN COMPARE WITH THEM FOR BEAUTY, ELEGANCE AND EFFICIENCY IN OPERATION.

Beginning at $18.70

FOR A GENUINE STEEL RANGE, 6-hole size with 16-inch oven, to $31.05 for an extra large range with porcelain lined reservoir, high closet and 20-inch oven, we offer such values in strictly high grade thoroughly guaranteed steel ranges as was never before shown by us or any other house.

We not only issue with every Steel Range a written binding guarantee, but so confident are we of our ability to furnish you almost double the value you can get elsewhere, we make this most extraordinary offer:

SEND US $1.00 If you live within a thousand miles of Chicago, and we will send you any Steel Range you may select, by freight, C. O. D., subject to examination.

You can examine it at your freight depot, and if found perfectly satisfactory and exactly as represented, pay the freight agent our special price and freight charges, less the $1.00 sent with order.

How Acme Steel Ranges are Made.

THE ACME STEEL RANGE is made of sheet steel, which is two gauges thicker than that commonly used in Steel Ranges, and, to the best of our knowledge, the steel in these Ranges is one gauge heavier than in any Steel Range manufactured by any other concern in America.

Don't compare these Steel Ranges with any wrought iron ranges on the market which resemble the Acme Steel Range only in appearance.

Oven Plates.

THE OVEN PLATES IN THE ACME STEEL RANGES are wrought steel and held immovably in place by surrounding wrought steel construction. The liability of its being warped or broken from unequal expansion is therefore entirely obviated. The oven bottom is well braced and bolted, and cannot warp. The oven is also ventilated, which adds greatly to the baking and roasting qualities.

Guaranteed Asbestos Lined.

THESE RANGES ARE LINED THROUGHOUT with asbestos, a fireproof material and a nonconductor. Prevents heat from radiating into room and effectually retains it in the range, insuring more comfort and more pleasantness in the kitchen and prevents the japan from being burned off the outside. It also concentrates the heat in the oven, thus economizing fuel and making the oven a quick baker.

Removable Duplex Grate.

WITH EVERY ACME STEEL RANGE we furnish a heavy duplex grate for either hard or soft coal or wood, so arranged that it can be changed to a wood grate instantly. The duplex grate can be drawn out of front of range without disturbing the fire linings. When an Acme Steel Range is used for wood only we furnish an extension fire box, which allows a longer stick of wood to be used in the stove; so in ordering range, do not fail to state whether it is for wood or coal, or both wood and coal.

Do Not Overlook Our Complete Line of Cast Iron Cook Stoves, Heating Stoves, Oil Stoves and Gasoline Stoves.

OUR $18.70 SIX-HOLE ACME STERLING STEEL RANGE. FOR COAL OR WOOD

AT $18.70 TO $23.30 According to size, as listed below, we furnish our Acme Sterling six-hole steel range on the market in competition with any range you can buy elsewhere at 50 per cent more money. We furnish the Acme Sterling steel range, guaranteeing it to be made of heavier sheet steel than any other stove; guaranteeing it to be asbestos lined, thus insuring you economy of fuel; guaranteeing the nickel plating to be of the highest grade; guaranteeing the stove to possess all the good qualities of every strictly high grade steel range, with the defects of none, and offering, if you so desire, to ship to you by freight C.O.D., subject to examination on receipt of $1.00, and if not found perfectly satisfactory and exactly as represented, allow you to return it at our expense and your money will be refunded.

THIS RANGE IS HIGHLY NICKEL PLATED THROUGHOUT Nickel bands on front edges of top of stove, on oven door frame, nickel panel on oven door; nickel clean out door, fire door, nickel front on grate frame; nickel front on ash pan, all highly finished, polished and nickeled, and we believe the handsomest range on the market.

THE OVEN OPENING is the same size as the oven bottom, thus allowing as large a baking pan to enter as the oven will receive.

THIS STOVE IS HIGHLY ENAMELED with the very best quality locomotive black, has highest grade removable Duplex grate, for either coal or wood, or both. We guarantee it to bake quicker, consume less fuel, give better service, and that you will find it the handsomest range on the market, regardless of price.

OUR ACME STERLING STEEL RANGES have been manufactured with a view to furnish our customers the handsomest, most economical, most durable, and in every way the highest grade range possible to produce, and with a view of giving them the benefit of the reduced cost to manufacture where large quantities are turned out on a spot cash basis, and on this basis we quote our price of $18.70 to $23.30 on the sizes listed. If you don't find, when you get the range, that you have saved from $10.00 to $15.00 in price, you are at liberty to return range to us, and we will cheerfully refund the money.

WE FURNISH THIS 6-HOLE ACME STERLING RANGE AT $18.70 TO $23.30 in the sizes and dimensions listed below.

Prices do not include pipe or cooking utensils. See pages 902 to 903.

Price List of the Acme Sterling Six-Hole Steel Range Without Reservoir.

Catalogue Number	Size	Size of Lids	Size of Oven, Inches	Size of Main Top, Inches	Height to Main Top, Inches	Length of Fire Box for Wood, Inches	Size of Pipe to Fit Collar, Inches	Weight, Pounds	Price
74710	8-16	No. 8	16x21x14	34½x28½	30	25	7	310	$18.70
74712	8-18	No. 8	18x21x14	36½x28½	30	25	7	320	20.70
74713	8-20	No. 8	20x21x14	38½x28½	30	25	7	328	22.90
74714	9-18	No. 9	18x21x14	36½x28½	30	25	7	321	20.80
74715	9-20	No. 9	20x21x14	40½x28½	30	25	7	336	23.30

OUR $21.20 TO $25.75 HIGH SHELF SIX-HOLE... ACME STERLING STEEL RANGE

FOR COAL OR WOOD.

AT $21.20 TO $25.75 according to size, as listed, we furnish this, our Acme Sterling six-hole steel range with high shelf, as illustrated, and invite the closest comparison in every little detail on this range with that of any range offered by any other dealer within 50 per cent of the price, and we make you this offer: Order a stove from us and a stove from any other house; let them send their stove to you on the same liberal terms we offer to send the stove, namely, on receipt of $1.00, balance payable after received, and if you do not find our stove not only better, but far cheaper in price, you can return it at our expense.

THIS IS EXACTLY THE SAME STOVE AS ONE PREVIOUSLY ILLUSTRATED at $18.70 to $23.30 under Nos. 74710 to 74715, with the addition of the high shelf, and at the slight difference in cost, we would recommend that you order the high shelf range. It is nickel plated throughout, exactly the same as No. 74710, lined throughout with asbestos, made from the same extra heavy steel plate, covered with the same binding guarantee, and we offer it to you at the heretofore unheard-of price of $21.20 to $25.75. It is the most durable, convenient, economical and handsome steel range on the market.

AT THE PRICES NAMED WE FURNISH THIS RANGE IN THE SIZES AND DIMENSIONS BELOW.

Prices do not include pipe or cooking utensils. See pages 902 to 903.

Price List of the Acme Sterling Six-Hole Steel Range without Reservoir, with High Shelf.

Catalogue Number	Size	Size of Lids	Size of Oven, Inches	Size of Main Top, Inches	Height to Main Top, Inches	Length of Fire Box For Wood, Inches	Size of Pipe to Fit Collar, Inches	Weight, Pounds	Price With High Shelf
74717	8-16	No. 8	16x21x14	34½x28½	30	25	7	339	$21.20
74719	8-18	No. 8	18x21x14	36½x28½	30	25	7	349	23.15
74720	8-20	No. 8	20x21x14	38½x28½	30	25	7	360	25.65
74721	9-18	No. 9	18x21x14	36½x28½	30	25	7	351	23.25
74722	9-20	No. 9	20x21x14	34½x28½	30	25	7	367	25.75

OUR $22.50 HIGH CLOSET 6-HOLE ACME STERLING STEEL RANGE

....FOR COAL OR WOOD....

AT $22.50 TO $27.00 according to size as listed below, we offer you this high closet Six-Hole Acme Sterling Steel Range in competition with ranges that sell at almost double the price.

THIS IS EXACTLY THE SAME RANGE AS THE ONE PREVIOUSLY LISTED at $21.20 to $25.75 under Nos. 74717 to 74722, with the addition of the high closet. As you will see by illustration, the closet is highly ornamented with nickel bands, nickel shelf and nickel handles. It has latest patent roll top, same as roll top desks are made, and at the slight difference in the cost, you will find the addition of a warming closet a very good investment.

SEND US OUR SPECIAL OFFER PRICE, OR IF YOU PREFER, SEND US $1.00 and we will send you C. O. D. by freight subject to your examination, you to pay freight agent balance and charges after received, and if not found exactly as represented, perfectly satisfactory and such value as you could not get elsewhere, you are at liberty to return stove to us at our expense and your money will be refunded. At the prices named we furnish this range in the sizes and dimensions below:

Prices do not include pipe or cooking utensils. See pages 902 to 903.

Price List of the Acme Sterling Six-Hole Steel Range without Reservoir, with High Closet.

Catalogue Number	Size	Size of Lids	Size of Oven, Inches	Size of Main Top, Inches	Height to Main Top of High Closet, Inches	Distance Main Top to Top of High Closet, Inches	Size of High Closet, Inches	Length of Fire Box For Wood, Inches	Size of Pipe to Fit Collar, Inches	Weight, Pounds	Price with High Closet
74724	8-16	No. 8	16x21x14	34½x28½	30	27	33½x14	25	7	356	$22.50
74726	8-18	No. 8	18x21x14	36½x28½	30	27	35½x14	25	7	367	24.50
74727	8-20	No. 8	20x21x14	38½x28½	30	27	37½x14	25	7	382	26.90
74728	9-18	No. 9	18x21x14	36½x28½	30	27	35½x14	25	7	384	24.60
74729	9-20	No. 9	20x21x14	38½x28½	30	27	37½x14	25	7	384	27.00

Water Fronts for Acme Sterling Ranges, each $3.00
Water fronts are used only where there is a water supply furnished with constant pressure through pipes—which can only be obtained in towns and cities having water works.

Our $22.75 6-HOLE RESERVOIR ACME STERLING STEEL RANGE

• • FOR COAL OR WOOD • •

AT $22.75 TO $27.40 WE OFFER THIS LARGE 6-HOLE ACME STERLING STEEL RANGE

WITH PORCELAIN LINED RESERVOIR, WITH ALL THE NICKEL TRIMMINGS, ALL THE IMPROVEMENTS AND THE PATENT FEATURES, THE FINISH, WITH ALL THE GUARANTEES THAT HAVE BEEN NAMED ON ALL THE ACME RANGES PREVIOUSLY DESCRIBED.

THIS RANGE DIFFERS FROM THOSE PREVIOUSLY DESCRIBED ONLY IN THAT THIS RANGE HAS RESERVOIR AS ILLUSTRATED.

WE GUARANTEE THE SIZES WE NAME. Do not take it for granted that stoves marked the same size as ours are actually the same size. In measuring ovens, we measure the actual size of the oven bottom. When you order a range from us, you get exactly the same range that you see illustrated, exactly the same size that we specify, and if you find that any steel range you order from us differs in the slightest degree from the illustration, from the description or from the guarantee, you are at liberty to return it and we will cheerfully refund your money.

THIS RANGE IS NICKEL TRIMMED THROUGHOUT, same as those previously described, contains every good quality of every high grade range with the defects of none, and is offered at the lowest price ever before heard of for a high grade range—is the best range possible to build.

OUR SPECIAL PRICE : : : : $22.75 to $27.40 FOR THE SIZES LISTED BELOW.

PRICES DO NOT INCLUDE PIPE OR COOKING UTENSILS. SEE PAGES 902 TO 903.

PRICE LIST OF THE ACME STERLING SIX-HOLE STEEL RANGE WITH PORCELAIN LINED RESERVOIR.

Catalogue Number	Size	Size of Lids	Size of Oven, Inches	Size of Main Top, Inches	Height to Main Top, Inches	Length of Fire Box for Wood	Size of Pipe to Fit Collar	Weight lbs.	Price
74731	8-16	No. 8	16x21x14	45x28½	30	25 in.	7 in.	370	$22.75
74733	8-18	No. 8	18x21x14	47x28½	30	25 in.	7 in.	381	24.75
74734	8-20	No. 8	20x21x14	49x28½	30	25 in.	7 in.	396	27.30
74735	9-18	No. 9	18x21x14	47x28½	30	25 in.	7 in.	382	24.85
74736	9-20	No. 9	20x21x14	49x28½	30	25 in.	7 in.	397	27.40

Our HIGH SHELF 6-HOLE $25.20 RESERVOIR STEEL RANGE

• • FOR COAL OR WOOD • •

THIS IS EXACTLY THE SAME RANGE AS ABOVE ILLUSTRATED AT $22.75 TO $27.40, UNDER No. 74731 TO 74736, WITH THE ADDITION OF THE HIGH SHELF. THIS RANGE IS HIGHLY NICKEL PLATED THROUGHOUT, ENAMELED WITH THE VERY BEST QUALITY LOCOMOTIVE BLACK, HIGHLY ORNAMENTED, TRIMMED AND FINISHED.

POSSESSES EVERY FEATURE OF EVERY HIGH GRADE RANGE made with the improvements of our Acme Sterling line, guaranteed equal to any steel range on the market at any price, made of heavier steel plate than any other range, lined throughout with asbestos; covered by binding guarantee, and is furnished at

=== $25.20 to $29.75 ===

In any of the following sizes as listed below.

PRICES DO NOT INCLUDE PIPE OR COOKING UTENSILS. SEE PAGES 902 TO 903.

PRICE LIST OF THE ACME STERLING SIX-HOLE STEEL RANGE WITH PORCELAIN LINED RESERVOIR AND HIGH SHELF.

Catalogue Number	Size	Size of Lids	Size of Oven, Inches	Size of Main Top, Inches	Height to Main Top, Inches	Length of Fire Box for Wood	Size of Pipe to Fit Collar	Weight lbs.	Price
74738	8-16	No. 8	16x21x14	45x28½	30	25 in.	7 in.	399	$25.20
74740	8-18	No. 8	18x21x14	47x28½	30	25 in.	7 in.	411	27.24
74741	8-20	No. 8	20x21x14	49x28½	30	25 in.	7 in.	427	29.65
74743	9-18	No. 9	18x21x14	47x28½	30	25 in.	7 in.	412	27.34
74745	9-20	No. 9	20x21x14	49x28½	30	25 in.	7 in.	428	29.75

OUR • • • • • BINDING • • • GUARANTEE • •

WITH EVERY STEEL RANGE WE SELL WE ISSUE A WRITTEN BINDING GUARANTEE. BY THE TERMS AND CONDITIONS OF WHICH IF ANY PIECE OR PART GIVES OUT BY REASON OF DEFECT IN MATERIAL OR WORKMANSHIP, WE WILL REPLACE IT

FREE OF CHARGE;

FURTHER, THAT IT IS STRICTLY HIGH GRADE, EXACTLY AS REPRESENTED, AND SHALL PROVE PERFECTLY SATISFACTORY, OR WE WILL REFUND ALL MONEY PAID US.

OUR RANGES ARE OFFERED AS THE BEST MONEY CAN BUY AND AT PRICES BASED ON THE ACTUAL COST OF MATERIAL AND LABOR, WITH BUT OUR ONE SMALL PROFIT ADDED.

UR ACME STERLING STEEL RANGE AT $26.50 TO $31.05

FOR COAL OR WOOD

This Acme Sterling 6-hole, high closet reservoir steel range, at $26.50 to $31.05, according to size, is our

.SPECIAL LEADER.

We show you this stove with

A LARGE ILLUSTRATION

to give you a better idea of its appearance, and to show you it is the handsomest, best and greatest value ever before offered by us or any other house.

...THIS IS THE POPULAR SIZE...

THE GREATEST VALUE AND OUR SPECIAL LEADER;

highly nickel plated and ornamented throughout, as previously described, with nickel plated bands, shields, doors trimmings, etc. Highly burnished and polished. Contains every good feature of every

HIGH GRADE RANGE

made, with the defects of none. Heavier steel plate, better lining, better interlining, better construction, better trimming, more economical and far more handsome than any other range on the market.

PRICES DO NOT INCLUDE PIPE OR COOKING UTENSILS. SEE PAGES 902 TO 908.

Recommend this Size and Style—This Special $26.50 to $31.05 Model—Above All Others.

RECEIPT OF $1.00 you can see and examine this range at your freight depot, and if found and more than we claim for it, exactly as we illustrate it, greatest value you ever saw, pay the freight agent our e and freight charges, less the $1.00 sent with order.

FURNISH THIS RANGE IN THE DIFFERENT SIZES MENTIONED AT PRICES NAMED.

Price List of the ACME STERLING 6-HOLE STEEL RANGE with Porcelain Lined Reservoir and High Closet.

Catalogue Number	Size	Size of Lids	Size of Oven, Inches	Size of Main Top, Inches	Height to Main Top, Inches	Distance Main Top to top of High Closet	Size of High Closet, Inches	Length of Fire Box for Wood	Size of Pipe to Fit Collar	Weight	PRICE
74745	8-16	No. 8	16x21x14	45x28½	30	27	33½x14	25 in.	7 in.	416	$26.50
74747	8-18	No. 8	18x21x14	47x28½	30	27	35½x14	25 in.	7 in.	428	28.50
74748	8-20	No. 8	20x21x14	49x28½	30	27	37½x14	25 in.	7 in.	444	30.95
74749	9-18	No. 9	18x21x14	47x28½	30	27	35½x14	25 in.	7 in.	429	28.60
74750	9-20	No. 9	20x21x14	49x28½	30	27	37½x14	25 in.	7 in.	445	31.05

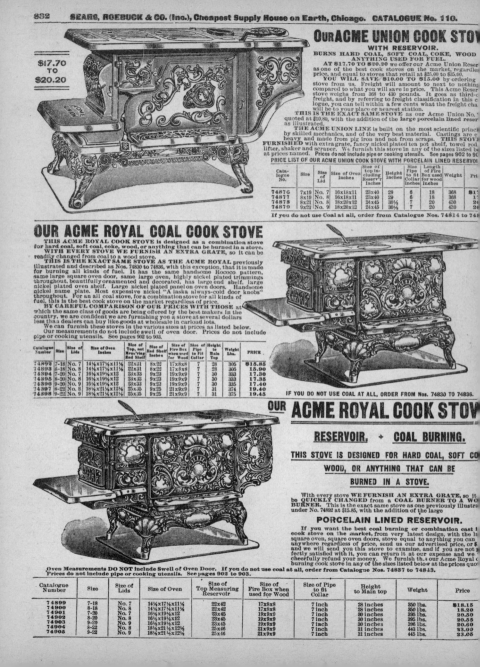

$17.70 TO $20.20

OUR ACME UNION COOK STOV

WITH RESERVOIR.

BURNS HARD COAL, SOFT COAL, COKE, WOOD ANYTHING USED FOR FUEL.

AT $17.70 TO $20.20 we offer our Acme Union Reser as one of the best cook stoves on the market, regardle price, and equal to stoves that retail at $25.00 to $35.00.

YOU WILL SAVE $10.00 TO $15.00 by ordering stove from us. Freight will amount to next to nothin compared to what you will save in price. This Acme Reser stove weighs from 368 to 430 pounds. It goes as third-c freight, and by referring to freight classification in this c logue, you can tell within a few cents what the freight cha will be to your place or nearest station.

THIS IS THE EXACT SAME STOVE as our Acme Union No. quoted at $10.80, with the addition of the **large porcelain lined reser** as illustrated.

THE ACME UNION LINE is built on the most scientific princ by skilled mechanics, and of the very best material. Castings are e heavy and made from pig iron and not from scraps. **THIS STOV FURNISHED** with extra grate, fancy nickel plated tea pot shelf, towel rod, lifter, shaker and scraper. We furnish this stove in any of the sizes listed b at prices named. **Prices do not include pipe or cooking utensils. See pages 902 to 90**

PRICE LIST OF OUR ACME UNION COOK STOVE WITH PORCELAIN LINED RESERVOI

Catalogue No.	Size	Size of Lid	Size of Oven Inches	Size of top including Reserv'r Inches	Height Inches	Size Pipe to fit Collar Inches	Length of Fire Box used for wood Inches	Weight	Pri
74876	7x19	No. 7	16x18x11	23x40	29	6	18	368	$1
74877	8x19	No. 8	16x18x11	23x40	29	6	18	368	1
74878	8x21	No. 8	18x20x12	24x45	30½	7	20	430	2
74879	9x21	No. 9	18x20x12	24x45	30½	7	20	430	2

If you do not use Coal at all, order from Catalogue Nos. 74814 to 74

OUR ACME ROYAL COAL COOK STOVE

THIS ACME ROYAL COOK STOVE is designed as a combination stove for hard coal, soft coal, coke, wood, or anything that can be burned in a stove. **WITH EVERY STOVE WE FURNISH AN EXTRA GRATE,** so it can be readily changed from coal to a wood stove.

THIS IS THE EXACT SAME STOVE AS THE ACME ROYAL previously illustrated and described as Nos. 74830 to 74836, with this exception, that it is made for burning all kinds of fuel. It has the same handsome Rococo pattern, same large square oven door, same large oven, highly nickel plated trimmings throughout, beautifully ornamented and decorated, has large end shelf, large nickel plated oven shelf. Large nickel plated panel on oven doors. Handsome nickel name plate. Most expensive nickel "Alaska always-cold door knobs" throughout. For an all coal stove, for a combination stove for all kinds of fuel, this is the best cook stove on the market regardless of price.

BY CAREFUL COMPARISON OF OUR PRICES WITH THOSE at which the same class of goods are being offered by the best makers in the country, we are confident we are furnishing you a stove at several dollars less than dealers can buy like goods at wholesale in carload lots.

We can furnish these stoves in the various sizes at prices as listed below.

Our measurements do not include swell of oven door. Prices do not include pipe or cooking utensils. See pages 902 to 903.

Catalogue Number	Size	Size of Lids	Size of Oven Inches	Size of Top, not Meas'ring End Shelf	Size of End Shelf Inches	Size of Fire Box when used for Wood	Size of Pipe to Fit Collar	Height to Main Top	Weight Lbs.	PRICE
74892	7-18	No. 7	14½x17½x11½	22x31	8x22	17x8x8	7	28	305	$15.85
74893	8-18	No. 8	14½x17½x11½	22x31	8x22	17x8x8	7	28	305	15.90
74394	7-20	No. 7	16½x19½x12	23x33	9x23	19x9x9	7	30	333	17.30
74395	8-20	No. 8	16½x19½x12	23x33	9x23	19x9x9	7	30	333	17.35
74396	9-20	No. 9	16½x19½x12	23x33	9x23	19x9x9	7	30	335	17.40
74397	8-22	No. 8	18½x21½x12½	25x35	9x25	21x9x9	7	31	374	19.40
74398	9-22	No. 9	18½x21½x12½	25x35	9x25	21x9x9	7	31	375	19.45

IF YOU DO NOT USE COAL AT ALL, ORDER FROM Nos. 74830 TO 74836.

OUR ACME ROYAL COOK STOV

RESERVOIR. ✦ COAL BURNING.

THIS STOVE IS DESIGNED FOR HARD COAL, SOFT CO WOOD, OR ANYTHING THAT CAN BE BURNED IN A STOVE.

With every stove **WE FURNISH AN EXTRA GRATE,** so it be **QUICKLY CHANGED** from a **COAL BURNER TO A WO BURNER.** This is the exact same stove as one previously illustra under No. 74892 at $15.85, with the addition of the large

PORCELAIN LINED RESERVOIR.

If you want the best coal burning or combination cast cook stove on the market, from very latest design, with the la square oven, square oven doors, stove equal to anything you can anywhere regardless of price, send us our advertised price, or $ and we will send you this stove to examine, and if you are not fectly satisfied with it, you can return it at our expense and we cheerfully refund your money. We furnish this our Acme Royal burning cook stove in any of the sizes listed below at the prices quo

Oven Measurements DO NOT include Swell of Oven Door. If you do not use coal at all, order from Catalogue Nos. 74837 to 74843. Prices do not include pipe or cooking utensils. See pages 902 to 903.

Catalogue Number	Size	Size of Lids	Size of Oven	Size of Top Measuring Reservoir	Size of Fire Box when used for Wood	Size of Pipe to fit Collar	Height to Main top	Weight	Price
74899	7-18	No. 7	14½x17½x11½	22x42	17x8x8	7 inch	28 inches	350 lbs.	$18.15
74900	8-18	No. 8	14½x17½x11½	22x42	17x8x8	7 inch	28 inches	350 lbs.	18.20
74901	7-20	No. 7	16½x19½x12	23x45	19x9x9	7 inch	30 inches	395 lbs.	20.50
74902	8-20	No. 8	16½x19½x12	23x45	19x9x9	7 inch	30 inches	395 lbs.	20.55
74903	9-20	No. 9	16½x19½x12	23x45	19x9x9	7 inch	30 inches	396 lbs.	20.60
74904	8-22	No. 8	18½x21½x12½	25x46	21x9x9	7 inch	31 inches	443 lbs.	23.00
74905	9-22	No. 9	18½x21½x12½	25x46	21x9x9	7 inch	31 inches	445 lbs.	23.05

[OUR] NEW 1901 MODEL ACME PRINCESS COOK STOVE

Made With Porcelain Lined Reservoir at $12.50 to $14.25. Made Without Reservoir but with Extension End Shelf at $9.20 to $10.90.

[W]E OFFER THE ACME PRINCESS AS AN ENTIRELY NEW STOVE FOR 1901, MADE IN OUR OWN FOUNDRY FROM THE BEST MATERIAL THAT MONEY CAN BUY, BY THE MOST SKILLED MECHANICS THAT WE CAN EMPLOY.

Our Prices Are Only the Cost of the Material and Labor with but Our One Small Profit Added.

AS ADVERTISED 8X18 SIZE. $13.95.

FROM THE ABOVE ILLUSTRATION, ENGRAVED FROM A PHOTOGRAPH, YOU CAN FORM SOME IDEA OF THE APPEARANCE OF OUR NEW ACME PRINCESS.

[S]END US $1.00 AS A GUARANTEE OF GOOD FAITH, state whether you wish the stove for coal only, or both coal and wood, and we will send the stove to you by freight, C. O. D., subject to examination; you can examine it at your freight depot [an]d if found perfectly satisfactory, exactly as represented, one of the handsomest reservoir cook stoves you have ever seen, and equal to stoves that your [s]torekeeper at home sells at almost double the price, pay the freight agent the balance and freight charges. The freight will amount to next to nothing as [co]mpared with what you will save in price. The stove weighs about 310 pounds and the freight for 200 miles will be about 50 cents; 400 miles, 75 cents; [5]00 miles, $1.00; 1,000 miles, $1.50. Greater or lesser distances in proportion.

[O]UR BINDING GUARANTEE. With every stove we issue a written binding guarantee, [b]y the terms and conditions of which if any piece or part gives out by reason of [d]efect in material or workmanship we will replace it or repair it free of charge.

WE GUARANTEE SAFE DELIVERY Every Acme Princess stove will be carefully crated, and we guarantee it to reach you in the same perfect condition it leaves us, and if upon arrival any piece or part is broken or missing, we will replace the same free of any expense to you.

[W]E WILL ALWAYS HAVE A SUPPLY OF PARTS. If in the years to come any part breaks or gives way we will be prepared to supply you with such part on a short notice, for we shall always have a stock of Acme stove castings on hand which we can supply promptly.

[T]HE ACME PRINCESS BURNS HARD COAL, SOFT COAL, COKE, WOOD OR ANYTHING FOR FUEL.

[G]ENERAL DESCRIPTION. THE ACME PRINCESS is made with very large flues, cut tops, heavy cut centers supported by post, heavy covers, heavy linings with very heavy sectional fire back, large bailed ash pan, slide hearth plate, nickeled outside oven shelf, [t]ouch feed, oven door kicker, nickel plated panel on oven doors, nickel plated name plate on front door, nickel plated door knobs, heavy tin lined oven doors.

When ashes are removed from under the oven they are scraped into the hearth, avoiding all possibility of spilling the ashes on the floor when cleaning [th]e stove. The Acme Princess is furnished with a lifter, shaker and scraper for removing the ashes from under the oven.

It is fitted with a large porcelain lined reservoir, as shown in the illustration, and is furnished on a large, handsome rococo pattern base. It has every [up]-to-date feature of every high grade reservoir cook stove, every improvement up to 1901, and is one of the best reservoir cook stoves on the market.

If you do not burn coal at all, make your selection from Catalogue Nos. 74809 to 74817.

Prices do not include pipe or cooking utensils. See pages 902 to 903.

ALWAYS STATE WHICH FUEL YOU WISH TO BURN.

PRICE LIST ACME PRINCESS COOK STOVE, WITHOUT RESERVOIR.

[C]atalogue Number	Size	Size of Lids	Size of Oven, Inches	Size of top not measuring shelf, Inches	Size of Shelf, Inches	Height, Inches	Pipe to fit Collar, Inches	Fire Box for Wood, Inches	Weight, Lbs.	PRICE
4906	7-16	No. 7	16x14½x10	22x29½	22x7	26½	6	16½	212	$ 9.20
4907	8-16	No. 8	16x14½x10	22x29½	22x7	26½	6	16½	212	9.25
4908	8-18	No. 8	18x17 x11	24x33	24x7	28½	7	18	254	10.85
4909	9-18	No. 9	18x17 x11	24x33	24x7	28½	7	18	254	10.90

PRICE LIST ACME PRINCESS, WITH PORCELAIN LINED RESERVOIR.

Catalogue Number	Size	Size of Lids	Size of Oven, Inches	Size of top including Reservoir Inches	Height, Inches	Pipe to fit Collar, Inches	Fire Box, Inches	Weight, Lbs.	PRICE
74910	7-16	No. 7	16x14½x10	22x40	26½	6	16½	265	$12.50
74911	8-16	No. 8	16x14½x10	22x40	26½	6	16½	265	12.55
74912	8-18	No. 8	18x17 x11	24x44	28½	7	18	310	13.95
74913	9-18	No. 9	18x17 x11	24x44	28½	7	18	310	14.25

$13.95 IS THE POPULAR SIZE, THE 8-18 SIZE; WEIGHS 310 POUNDS AND WE OFFER IT AT $13.95.

OUR ACME ROYAL RANGE,

WITH PORCELAIN LINED RESERVOIR AND HIGH CLOSET.

FOR HARD COAL, SOFT COAL, WOOD OR ANYTHING USED FOR FUEL.

HOW WE TRIM IT

Beautifully nickel plated mountings throughout, including large, handsome nickel plated oven door panel, large nickel panel on draft door; very large nickel oven shelf, large, handsome, fully polished nickel bands on main top, hearth and high closet, nickel hinge pins, nickel tea shelves, nickel plated, patent, fancy (always cold) knobs on all doors.

FANCY NICKEL ORNAMENTATION THROUGHOUT....

highly polished, richly ornamented and decorated, latest Rococo design, and, we believe,

THE HANDSOMEST 1900 RANGE ON THE MARKET.

$25.49 to $30.00 is our price for this, our very finest, completely finished, Acme Royal Range.

This $25.49 Stove is the equal of any range on the market, regardless of price; combines every improvement of every high grade range made, with the defects of none.

Our 20th Century Production. Full square Oven, Duplex Grate, Cut Tops and Centers, Porcelain lined Reservoir, Oven Door Kicker, Large Fire Box, Large Flues, Balled Ash Pan, Slide Hearth Plate, Latest and Handsomest Rococo Design.

Our Gem Grate furnished FREE, makes it a perfect burner for all kinds of fuel, Coal, Wood or Coke.

Our Binding Guarantee makes you perfectly safe and insures for you such a stove as you could not buy elsewhere.

Most stove dealers would say this oven is three or four inches wider than the size we give. We furnish this range just as it is shown in the various sizes at prices as listed below.

Our Binding Guarantee.

With every Acme Royal we issue a written, binding guarantee, by the terms of which if any piece or part gives out by reason of defect in material or workmanship, we will replace it free of charge; further, that it must be received by you in perfect condition, found exactly as represented and perfectly satisfactory, or your money will be refunded immediately.

Our New 1900 Line Factory-to-Consumer Prices and Binding Guarantee, commends our line above all others.

OVEN MEASUREMENTS DO NOT INCLUDE SWELL OF OVEN DOOR

IF YOU DO NOT USE COAL AT ALL, ORDER FROM CATALOGUE Nos. 75206 TO 75218

PRICES DO NOT INCLUDE PIPE OR COOKING UTENSILS. SEE PAGES 902 TO 903.

CATALOGUE NUMBER	SIZE	SIZE OF LIDS	SIZE OF OVEN	SIZE OF TOP MEASURING RESERVOIR	SIZE OF FIRE BOX WHEN USED FOR WOOD	HEIGHT TO MAIN TOP	WEIGHT	PRICE
75242	7-18	No. 7	16x17½x11½	42x25	17x8x8	28 inches	455 lbs	$25.49
75243	8-18	No. 8	16x17½x11½	42x25	17x8x8	28 inches	453 lbs	26.54
75244	7-20	No. 7	18x19½x12	45x27	19x9x9	30 inches	495 lbs	27.70
75245	8-20	No. 8	18x19½x12	45x27	19x9x9	30 inches	497 lbs	27.75
75246	8-22	No. 8	20x21½x12½	46x28	21x9x9	31 inches	538 lbs	29.05
75247	9-22	No. 9	20x21½x12½	46x28	21x9x9	31 inches	540 lbs	30.00

IF DESIRED WITHOUT HIGH CLOSET, SEE PRECEDING PAGE.

OW WE MAKE THE PRICE

$20.00

ur special inside, heretofore unheard of rice of $20.00, $22.50, $25.65 and $29.70, according to size, is made possible by reason f our having contracted with the manuacturer for his entire output of Acme Brilliant Base Burners. The contract rice is based on the actual cost of material nd labor, with pig iron bought at recent educed market quotations, and to the ctual cost of material and labor is added ur one small percentage of profit, mak- price from 15 to 25 per cent ower than inferior base burners f the same size are sold to dealrs in carload lots at wholesale.

WE SHIP ...ON... Most Liberal C. O. D. TERMS ...AND... Guarantee.... Satisfaction.

ENTIRELY NEW DESIGN FOR 1901.

ACME BRILLIANT BASE.... BURNER HARD COAL HEATER FOR $20.00

The finest the world produces, a dream of an artist in design, trimming, finishing, in its construction throughout the highest of high grade base burners the equal of any base burning hard coal heater made by any maker, regardless of price.

THE ACME BRILLIANT BASE BURNER is built on new lines for 1900-01, newly perfected model, and it embodies all the very latest, handsomest and best features of every other high grade base burning hard coal heater made, with the defects of none.

The Acme Brilliant Base Burner excels all others in appearance, in amount of nickel work, in the economic consumption of fuel, and the volume and distribution of heat.

NICKEL FINISH. We believe we put more nickel on the Acme Brilliant Base Burner than is used on any base burning heater made. The nickel finish includes a large handsomely ornamented spun brass nickel urn—we believe the handsomest nickel plated urn that is used on any base burner made; heavy, nickel plated swing top of the very latest design, full nickel dome head of a new design, heavily nickeled corner wings, heavily nickeled hearth plate, heavily nickeled ash door panel, heavily nickeled foot rails, heavily nickeled name plate and the stove stands on a full heavy nickel plate frame with nickel plated legs. The nickel plating is done by the very best process (the XXX Triple Plated Brand), highly polished giving the stove an appearance that must be seen to be appreciated.

IT IS MADE WITH A DOUBLE HEATING FLUE, to which a pipe can be attached for heating an upper room or increasing the heat in the lower room; it is made with the very latest Johnson self-feeding magazine; handsomely finished swing mica doors on three sides; heavy, large, non-destructible fire pot; latest Akron Duplex Grate, with shaking ring; large ash pan; Osgood's patent full base heating flues, tea kettle attachment and cast elbow at back.

OUR BINDING GUARANTEE. Every Acme Brilliant Base Burner is covered by a binding guarantee, as to quality of material, workmanship, finish and burning qualities of the stove, and if it fails to perform its duty, or if it gives out by reason of defect in material or workmanship, we will replace or repair it free of charge.

DELIVERY GUARANTEE. At the price quoted we furnish the Acme Brilliant Base Burner carefully crated and delivered on board the cars in Chicago, and we guarantee the stove to reach you in the same perfect condition it leaves us, and if any piece or part is broken on arrival we will replace it free of any charge to you.

Nothing has been left undone to make the New Model Acme Brilliant Base Burner the highest of high grade burners, the best hard coal stove possible to build.

WE FURNISH THIS STOVE IN THE FOLLOWING SIZES AT THE FOLLOWING SPECIAL PRICES.

Catalogue Number	Stove Number	Size Fire Pot	Floor to Urn Base	Floor Space inches	Size Pipe Collar	Weight (pounds)	Price
75383	12A	12	45	22¼x22¼	6 in.	249	$20.00
75384	13A	13	46¼	23½x23½	6 in.	260	22.50
75385	14A	14	47½	24½x24½	6 in.	293	25.65
75386	16A	16	49	26¼x26¼	6 in.	333	29.70

OUR LIBERAL $1.00 OFFER.

While nearly all our customers send cash in full, and thus save the return express charges on money, which is usually from 25 to 40 cents, we will, on receipt of $1.00, send the Acme Brilliant Base Burner Hard Coal Heater to any address east of the Rocky Mountains by freight C. O. D., subject to examination. You can examine it at your freight depot, and if found perfectly satisfactory, exactly as represented, the handsomest base burner you have ever seen, superior to stoves your dealer at home offers at double the price, such a bargain as you could not get elsewhere, pay the freight agent our price and freight charges less the $1.00 sent with order; otherwise, don't pay a cent, return the stove to us at our expense of freight charges both ways and we will return your $1.00.

ABOUT THE FREIGHT.

The ACME BRILLIANT BASE BURNER weighs from 249 to 333 pounds, according to size as listed. It takes a low freight rate (third class), and the freight will average for 100 pounds for 500 miles about 80 cents, (greater or lesser distances in proportion), so you will find the freight will will amount to next to nothing compared with what you will save in price.

SHEET STEEL AIR-TIGHT HEATING STOVES, $2.72 ...AND...UPWARD

...MOST COMPLETE LINE EVER SHOWN...

OUR LINE OF SHEET STEEL AIR-TIGHT HEATERS INCLUDES THE VERY BEST SELECTION FROM THE BEST MAKERS IN THE COUNTRY, AND DOES NOT INCLUDE ANY OF THE INFERIOR MAKES ON THE MARKET.

No. 75436
20-inch.

$2.72
As Advertised.

WE SOLD OVER THREE THOUSAND AIR-TIGHT SHEET STEEL HEATERS LAST SEASON, and all the time we were far behind on our orders, and, as the indications point to a much larger trade this season, we have made very extensive preparations to not only be able to fill our orders promptly, but with such a line of air-tight heaters as will not be offered by any other house, and at prices so low that our customers can order from us, pay the freight, which will add next to nothing to the cost, and own the best air-tight heater that can be made, at about half the price charged by retail dealers.

IF YOU ORDER AN AIR-TIGHT HEATER FROM US, and you do not find it all we claim for it, and even more, perfectly satisfactory, and far cheaper than you could buy elsewhere, you can return stove at our expense and we will cheerfully refund your money.

The cut on the right shows the interior construction of our **ACME AIR-TIGHT HEATERS.** Nos. 75436 to 75502.

Interior View.

..OUR BINDING GUARANTEE..

WITH EVERY AIR-TIGHT HEATER WE ISSUE A WRITTEN BINDING GUARANTEE that the stove is constructed on the most scientific principles, from the very best material, by most skilled labor, very latest in design, and equal to any similar make of stove on the market regardless of price.

THE HOT BLAST DRAFT HEATS THE AIR BEFORE IT REACHES THE FUEL, THUS PRODUCING PERFECT COMBUSTION . . .

The Lining Extends from the Bottom to the Second Upper Bead

THE COVER TO ASH OPENING IS LOCKED SECURELY TO PREVENT BLOWING OFF.

IT IS HONESTLY CONSTRUCTED OF GOOD MATERIAL, WITH HEAVY LINING, AND CANNOT FAIL TO GIVE SATISFACTION.

THE BODY is made of 26-gauge smooth steel. The lining is 20-gauge. Has fine nickel urn and nickel name plate.

It will burn chunks, knots, chips, straw, cobs, corn, hay or trash, or anything used for fuel EXCEPT COAL.

...THE PIPE SHOULD BE PROVIDED WITH A DAMPER.

Put two or three inches of ashes in bottom of stove before building fire and always leave about this quantity when cleaning the stove.

WILL KEEP FIRE OVER NIGHT.

IN SETTING UP THIS STOVE PUT THE CRIMPED END OF STOVE PIPE DOWN.

IT IS CONSTRUCTED AS FOLLOWS: The body is made of 26-gauge SMOOTH STEEL of a uniform color. The feed opening is 12½ inches in diameter. All sizes take 6-inch stove pipe. It has a check draft in the stove pipe collar. Neat ornament on cover of fuel opening. Nickel plated screw draft supply. The ash opening is 6½ inches in diameter.

PRICES OF SMOOTH STEEL WITHOUT FOOT RAILS.

Catalogue Number	No.	Length inches	Width inches	Height of Body	Total Height	Size of Feed Opening	Size of Ash Opening	Shipping Weight	Price, Smooth Steel
75436	20	20	16	24 in.	43 in.	12½ in.	6½ in.	28 lbs.	$2.72
75437	24	24	17	24 in.	43 in.	12½ in.	6½ in.	32 lbs.	3.08
75438	30	30	18	24 in.	43 in.	12½ in.	6½ in.	40 lbs.	3.96

PRICES OF POLISHED STEEL WITHOUT FOOT RAILS.

Catalogue Number	No.	Length inches	Width inches	Height of Body	Total Height	Size of Feed Opening	Size of Ash Opening	Shipping Weight	Price, Polished Steel
75484	120	20	16	24 in.	43 in.	12½ in.	6½ in.	28 lbs.	$3.30
75485	124	24	17	24 in.	43 in.	12½ in.	6½ in.	32 lbs.	3.70
75486	130	30	18	24 in.	43 in.	12½ in.	6½ in.	40 lbs.	4.55

$3.23 TO $5.30

THE CUT SHOWS

OUR ACME AIR-TIGHT HEATER WITH FOOT RAILS.

It is Constructed the Same as Nos. 75436 to 75486 with Addition of Nickel Foot Rails.

The Hot Blast Draft heats the air before it reaches the fuel, thus producing perfect combustion. The lining extends from the bottom to the next to upper bead. The cover to ash opening is locked securely to prevent blowing off. It is honestly constructed of good material, with heavy lining and cannot fail to give satisfaction. The body is made of 26-gauge smooth steel. The lining is 20-gauge. Has fine nickel urn and nickel screw draft. It will burn chunks, knots, chips, straw, cobs, corn, hay or trash, or anything used for fuel except coal. The pipe should be provided with a damper. Put two or three inches of ashes in bottom of stove before building fire and always leave about this quantity when cleaning the stove. Will keep fire over night. In setting up this stove put the crimped end of stove pipe down. The body is made of 26 gauge smooth steel of a uniform color. The feed opening is 12½ inches in diameter. The ash opening is 7 inches in diameter. All sizes take 6-inch stove pipe. It has a check draft in stove pipe collar. Neat ornament on cover of fuel opening. Nickel plated screw draft adjuster.

PRICE LIST OF THE ACME AIR-TIGHT SMOOTH STEEL HEATER WITH FOOT RAILS.

Catalogue Number	Stove No.	Length Inches	Width Inches	Height of Body	Total Height	Size of Feed Opening	Size of Ash Opening	Shipping Weight	Price Smooth Steel
75494	20[illegible]	20	16	24 in.	43 in.	12½ in.	6 in.	34 lbs.	$3.23
75495	245	24	17	24 in.	43 in.	12½ in.	6 in.	38 lbs.	3.67
75496	305	30	18	24 in.	43 in.	12½ in.	6 in.	46 lbs.	4.69

PRICE LIST OF THE ACME AIR-TIGHT POLISHED STEEL HEATER WITH FOOT RAILS.

Catalogue Number	Stove No.	Length Inches	Width Inches	Height of Body	Total Height	Size of Feed Opening	Size of Ash Opening	Shipping Weight	Price Polished Steel
75502	1205	20	16	24 in.	43 in.	12½ in.	6 in.	34 lbs.	$3.85
75503	1245	24	17	24 in.	43 in.	12½ in.	6 in.	38 lbs.	4.25
75504	1305	30	18	24 in.	43 in.	12½ in.	6 in.	46 lbs.	5.30

WE GUARANTEE ENTIRE SATISFACTION

ON ALL HEATERS. If you are sure that anything you buy from us is not fully up to our representation, send it back

AND WE WILL RETURN MONEY.

...FREIGHT WILL BE VERY LITTLE...

compared with what we save you. Shipping weight on above heaters is only from 35 to 50 pounds. They take low class freight, and it will amount to only a small sum.

POLISHED STEEL $6.70 AND $7.95.

Height of Stove, 45 inches.

Height of Body, 26 inches.

OUR $6.70 AND $7.95 ACME AIR-TIGHT HEATING STOVE.

The cut on the left illustrates our Acme Air-Tight Heating Stove with hot blast draft and hot air circulating system. This stove burns everything (excepting coal) that is used for fuel. The feed opening is 10½ inches in diameter. The ash opening is 7 inches in diameter. Damper has screw adjustment. Ash opening is a cast drop door with a set screw fastening to make it air tight and a screw draft opening in center to make a straight draft when desired. Takes a 6-inch stove pipe. Has nickeled foot rails and nickeled band around the top. The Hot Air Circulating System takes the cold air from the floor, passes it up between the main outer jacket and out at the top, hot. By this system it will warm the furthest corner of the room as well as the space near the stove.

The cut on the right shows the interior construction of our Acme Air-Tight Heating Stove, with hot blast draft and hot air circulating system. For burning any kind of fuel except coal. Cold air enters the flues near the floor, is heated and rises, passing out at the top, thus creating a constant circulation of hot air. Has ornamented cast iron top and corrugated cast iron bottom, polished steel body and heavy sheet steel inner walls made of 20 gauge steel.

SIZE OF PIPE TO FIT COLLAR IS 6 INCHES ON ALL HEATERS...

Price List of the Acme Air-Tight, Polished Steel Heating Stove with Hot Blast Draft and Hot Air Circulating System.

Catalogue Number	Stove No.	Length inches	Width inches	Weight	Price
75505	26	26	17	80 lbs.	$6.70
75506	32	32	18	100 lbs.	7.95

WE CAN ALWAYS FURNISH REPAIR CASTINGS FOR ACMES . . .

THE NEW ERA RADIATOR.

It stops the heat on its way to the chimney and makes it do double duty. You can place a **New Era Radiator** on the stove pipe in the same room with the stove. It will actually save from one-quarter to one-half the fuel. There is no guess work in this statement. Actual tests have proved it time and time again. One ton of coal or one cord of wood will produce nearly as much heat with the **New Era Radiator** as two tons of coal or two cords of wood without it. You can place it in an upstairs room on a pipe running through from below, and it will heat that room without the expenditure of a single extra cent for fuel. It simply uses the heat that is escaping. It is a stove that throws off heat without requiring any fuel or attention at all. **No dust in the room and no ashes to carry out.** No gas escapes from them and they cause no obstruction at all to the draft. They can be as easily cleaned and repaired as a stove pipe. **The New Era Radiator really costs nothing.** It pays for itself in saved fuel in a very short time.

No. 75512

SQUARE STYLE.

This style is only adapted for floors above the stove. They are very handsome in design, and are bought by many who would not otherwise run a stove pipe through their house.

Cannot be used with soft coal.

No. 75512 For 6-inch stove pipe. Body made of Woods' Refined Iron. Cast iron top and base; nickel plated feet. Size of base 17¼ x 13¾ inches; height, with legs, 37 inches; weight, crated, 60 pounds. Price each..... $4.65

No. 75513 Same as above, except the body is made of Woods' patent planished iron. Price, each..... $5.35

CYLINDRICAL STYLE.

To meet the demand for a cheaper Radiator, this style is added. It is smaller but very efficient either on the back of a stove or to heat small upper rooms.

Cannot be used with soft coal.

No. 75514 For 6-inch stove pipe. Made of Woods' Refined Iron. Diameter, 10 inches; height, 28 inches; weight, crated, 24 pounds. Price, each..... $2.17

No. 75514

The Original Round Style.

....HARD OR SOFT COAL....

This style has been successfully sold for many years. They are adapted either for the back of a stove or an upper room or hall.

Furnished with inner tubes for hard coal and without inner tubes for soft coal, for 6-inch stove pipe. Made from Woods' refined iron (sheet steel), with cast iron ends. They are polished, ready to set up, before they leave the factory. Diameter, 12¼ inches; height, with legs, 38 inches; weight, crated, 50 lbs.

No. 75515 For soft coal.. $4.23
No. 75516 For hard coal.. 4.33

Same as above, except it is made of Woods' patent planished iron.

No. 75517 For hard coal. $5.10
No. 75518 For soft coal.. 5.00

75515 to 75518

Peerless Enameled Steel Climax Saucepans.

With patent Climax bottom same as above. Milk and cereals can be cooked in these vessels without danger of scorching or burning.

No. 76321 Peerless Enameled Steel Covered Seamless Climax Saucepans with Retinned Cover. Sizes are actual capacity.

Quarts	2	3	5	7
Inches	6¾x4	8x4¼	9x5	9¾x6
Weight, each, lbs.	1¼	1¾	2½	2¾
Price, each	33c	38c	44c	49c

Peerless Enameled Steel Strong Lipped Saucepans.

No. 76324.

Quarts	1	1½	2	2½	3
Holds, qts.	⅞	1¼	1¼	2⅛	2¾
Inches	6x2½	6½x3¼	7x3½	7¾x3½	8½x3¾
Weight, lbs.	⅝	⅝	⅝	¾	⅞
Price, each	11c	12c	14c	15c	18c
Quarts	4	5	6	7½	
Holds, qts.	3½	4¼	6	7	
Inches	9x4	9¾x4¼	11x5	11½x5½	
Weight, lbs.	1	1¼	1¾	2	
Price, each	21c	24c	27c	33c	

Peerless Enameled Steel Berlin Saucepans.

No. 76325 Peerless Enameled Steel Patent Covered Berlin Saucepans with retinned covers. Sizes are actual capacity.

Quarts	2	3	5	7
Size, inches	6¾x4¼	8x4⅞	8½x5⅝	9¾x6½
Weight, each, pounds	1	1¼	1¾	2¼
Price, each	23c	30c	32c	39c

Peerless Enameled Steel Covered Seamless Berlin Kettles With Retinned Covers.

Sizes are actual capacity.

No. 76327

Quarts	2	3	5	7
Inches	6¾x4¼	8x4⅞	8½x5⅝	9¾x6½
Weight, each, pounds	1	1¼	1¾	2¾
Price, each	23c	30c	32c	39c

Peerless Enameled Steel Lipped Preserving Kettle.

No. 76328 Peerless Enameled Steel Lipped Stewing or Preserving Kettles.

Quarts,	2	2½	3	4	5
Holds, qts.	1½	2	2½	3½	4½
Inches,	7x3¼	7¾x3¼	8¼x3¾	9½x4	9¾x4¼
Weight, lbs.	⅞	¾	⅞	1⅛	1⅜
Price, each,	14c	15c	18c	21c	24c
Quarts,	6	7½	10	12	14
Holds, qts.	5¾	7	9	11	13¼
Inches,	10¾x5	11¼x5¼	12x5¼	13x5¾	14x6¾
Weight, lbs.	1¾	2	2¼	2½	3
Price, each,	27c	33c	39c	50c	59c

Peerless Enameled Steel Seamless Flaring Fruit Preserving Kettle.

No. 76330 Peerless Enameled Steel Seamless Flaring Fruit Preserving Kettles, far superior to brass for preserving purposes. Sizes, from 4 to 14 gallons.

Gallons,	4	6	7½	10	11	14
Holds, qts.	15	23	28	38	42	53
Inches,	13¼x8¾	14¾x9	16¾x10	18¾x13	20x13¼	21x14
Wght., lbs.	3¼	4¼	5¾	5¾	7¼	9
Each,	66c	75c	93c	$1.18	$1.50	$1.83

Peerless Enameled Steel Covered Seamless Stove Pots.

Sizes are actual capacity.

No. 76335 Peerless Enameled Steel Covered Seamless Stove Pots. No. 7, Retinned Covers, Flat Bottom, 9 quarts, 9¼x9 inches. Weight, each, 3 pounds. Price, each 65c

No. 8, 13 quarts, 10¾x9¾ inches. Weight, each, 4¼ lbs. Price, each. 81c

No. 9, 17 quarts, 12x10¾ inches. Weight, each, 5¼ lbs. Price, each 98c

Peerless Enameled Steel Straight Seamed Covered Buckets.

Six quart size holds 5½ quarts, other sizes are actual capacity.

No. 76337 Retinned Covers.

Quarts	½	1	2	3
Weight, pounds	¼	⅜	⅝	⅞
Price, each	13c	13c	16c	21c

With Wood Bails.

Quarts	4	6	8	10	12
Weight, each, pounds	1⅛	1⅜	1⅞	2¼	2½
Price, each	24c	32c	36c	45c	64c

Peerless Enameled Steel Covered Coffee Urns or Soup Stock Pots.

No. 76338 Peerless Enameled Steel Covered Coffee Urns or Soup Stock Pots with Retinned Covers.

Gallons	3	6	9
Holds, gals.	3¼	5¾	9
Inches,	10⅛x10⅛	13⅛x11½	19⅝x13½
Wght., lbs.	9	11½	12½
Price, with ⅝-inch brass faucet. Each	$2.87	$3.43	$4.00
Price with 1-inch brass faucet. Each	$3.37	$3.93	$4.50

Peerless Enameled Steel Straight Pots.

No. 76340 Peerless Enameled Steel Seamed Straight Pots, with two side handles. Sizes are actual capacity.

Quarts	6	8	10	12
Inches	8¾x6½	9⅛x6⅞	9⅞x7¾	10⅞x8½
Weight, each, lbs.	1¾	1⅞	2¼	2½
Price, each	27c	32c	36c	43c

Peerless Enameled Steel Deep Pudding Pans.

No. 76341 Peerless Enameled Steel Deep Pudding Pans.

Quarts	Size, Inches	Holds Qts.	Weight, Each lbs.	Price, each
1	7⅛x2½	1	⅜	9c
2	8⅝x3	1¾	½	12c
3	9⅝x3¼	2½	⅝	13c
4	10¼x3⅜	3¼	¾	14c
5	11 x3¼	4	⅞	16c
6	11⅞x3⅜	5	1	18c

Peerless Enameled Steel Straight Milk Pans.

No. 76342

Quarts	Holds, Qts.	Inches	Weight each, oz.	Price each
¼	¼	5¼x1⅝	2	6c
½	½	6 x1⅝	4	7c
1	¾	7 x1⅞	6	8c
1½	1	7⅞x1⅞	8	9c
2	1½	8½x2	8½	10c
3	2	9¼x2¼	9	11c
4	2¾	10⅜x2½	10	14c
5	3½	11⅜x2⅝	14	15c
6	4¼	12⅜x2¾	16	17c
8	5¼	13¼x2⅞	18	20c
10	6	14¼x3	22	23c
12	6½	15 x3⅛	29	27c

Peerless Enameled Steel Dinner Pails.

No. 76343 Peerless Enameled Steel Oblong Dinner Pail with cup, tray and compartment for coffee. Holds 5 quarts, 9x9x6 inches. Weight, 2⅝ pounds.

Each 92c

Peerless Enameled Steel Water Pails.

No. 76345 Peerless Enameled Steel Seamless Straight Water Pails, flat bottoms.

Quarts,	6	8	10	12	16	20
Holds, qts.	4½	6½	8¼	11½	14	16
Inches	9x6¼	9¼x6¾	10⅛x7¾	11¼x8¾	12x9¾	13x10¾
Weight, lbs.	1½	2	2⅜	3	3¼	3¾
Each.	33c	38c	45c	54c	68c	90c

No. 76346 Peerless Enameled Steel Tubed Cake Pans.

Quarts	1½	2	3	4
Holds, qts.	1¼	1½	2	3
Inches	7¼x2	8¼x2	9¼x2⅝	10¾x2¼
Weight, each, pounds:	⅛	⅜	¾	⅞
Price, each	12c	13c	16c	18c

No. 76348 Peerless Enameled Steel Extra Deep Tubed Cake Pans.

Qts.	Holds, Qts.	Inches	Weight each, lbs.	Price each
2	1¾	8¼x3	⅝	15c
3	2¾	8¾x3¼	⅞	17c
4	3¾	9¾x3⅜	⅞	18c
5	4¾	10¼x3¼	1	22c
6	5¾	11⅛x3⅜	1⅛	25c

No. 76350 Peerless Enameled Steel Pie Plates. Full Size.

Inches	7	8	9
Weight, each, oz.	2	4	6
Each	6c	7c	8c
Dozen	60c	75c	85c
Inches		10	11
Weight, each, oz		8	10
Each.		$0.09	$0.12
Dozen		0.98	1.25

No. 76351 Peerless Enameled Steel Extra Deep Pie Plates. Full size.

Inches	9	10	11	12
Weight, oz.	6	8	10	12
Each.	$0.09	$0.10	$0.12	$0.17
Dozen,	0.39	1.10	1.30	2.00

SEND FOR OUR FREE GROCERY ....PRICE LIST....

No. 76352 Peerless Enameled Steel Soup Plates. Full size.

Inches	8½	9¼	10¼
Weight, oz.	6	8	10
Each	$0.10	$0.11	$0.12
Dozen	1.08	1.23	1.35

No. 76353 Peerless Enameled Steel Flat Bottom Dinner Plates. Full size, 9x1 inches.

Weight, each, ounces 8
Price, each 9c
Per dozen 98c

No. 76354 Peerless Enameled Steel Shallow Jelly Cake Pans. Full size.

Inches	8x½	9x½	10x½	11x½
Weight, each, oz.	5	6	8	10
Price, each	$0.07	$0.08	$0.09	$0.13
Price, per dozen	0.78	0.88	0.98	1.42

No. 76355 Peerless Enameled Steel Deep Jelly Cake Pans. Full size.

Inches	9x¾	10x1
Weight, each, ounces	8	10
Each	$0.09	$0.12
Dozen	0.98	1.37

No. 76356 Peerless Enameled Steel Mountain Cake Pans. Full size.

Inches	8x¾	9x1¼	10x1¼
Weight, each, oz.,	6	8	12
Each	$0.10	$0.11	$0.12
Dozen	1.08	1.20	1.32

No. 76360 Peerless Enameled Steel Seamless Lady Finger Pans.

Cups on frame	6	6
Inches	10x5	12x6
Weight, each, oz	5	6
Each	12c	14c

No. 76362 Peerless Enameled Steel Muffin Pans. Medium sized cups.

No. of cups on frame.	6	8	12
Weight, each, lbs.	½	¾	1⅛
Each	17c	21c	30c

No. 76365 Peerless Enameled Steel Corn Cake Pans. Same as muffin pans except deeper.

Number of cups on frame	6	8	12
Weight, each, pound	½	¾	1⅛
Price, each	18c	22c	32c

Peerless Enameled Steel Cups.

No. 76369 Peerless Enameled Steel Straight Drinking Cups.

Inches	3¼x2¼	4¼x2⅝	5¼x2⅞
Capacity, pints	½	⅝	1
Weight, each, ounces	3	4	5
Price, each	6c	8c	10c
Per dozen	68c	87c	$1.08

No. 76372 Peerless Enamel Steel Flaring Coffee Cups. Holds 1 pint. Weight, each, 6 ounces.

Inches	4½x3
Price, each	$0.09
Per dozen	1.00

Peerless Enameled Steel Saucers.

No. 76373 Peerless Enameled Steel Saucers. Inches, 6⅜x1. Weight, each, 4 ounces. Per doz., 87c; each 8c

Peerless Enameled Steel Bread Raiser.

No. 76375 Peerless Enameled Steel Bread Raiser, with retinned ventilated cover. Sizes are actual capacity. Weight, each,

Sizes, qts.	pounds	Price
10	2¾	$0.70
14	4	0.80
17	4¾	0.94
21	6½	1.24

No. 76377 Peerless Enameled Steel Measuring Cups, marked to measure accurately. Weight, each, 3 ounces.

	½ of a cup.	¼ of a cup
Price, each	9c	10c

Peerless Enameled Steel Coffee Flasks.

No. 76378 1 Pint. Weight, 6 ounces.
Price, each 19c

Peerless Enameled Steel Seamless Water Pitcher.

No. 76380

Size	Holds quarts	Weight, each, pounds	Price
1½ quarts	1	¾	27c
2 quarts	2	1	36c
3 quarts	2¼	1⅛	42c
4 quarts	3	1⅜	48c

No. 76381 Granite Enameled Steel Molasses Pitcher. Size, 1 pint.
Price, each 30c

Peerless Enameled Steel Seamless Oblong Pans.

No. 76382

Inches	13x9x2¼	15x10½x2¼	16x11x2½	17x11¾x2½
Wgt. ea. lbs.	1⅞	2¼	2½	3
Price, each	25c	33c	36c	42c

No. 76383 Granite Enameled Steel Improved Roasters. Seamless, with racks.

Size, inches	Price, each
10½x14¼x7	$0.94
11¾x16½x7½	1.28
12 x18 x9½	2.00

No. 76384 Granite Steel Bread Pans.

Size, inches	9¾x4½x3	10½x5½x3	11½x6x3
Each	18c	23c	27c

Peerless Enameled Steel Milk Kettles.

(Sizes are actual capacity.)

No. 76387

Quarts	1	2	3	4	6
Weight each, lbs.	⅝	1	1¼	1½	1¾
Price, each	18c	22c	27c	32c	36c

Peerless Enameled Steel Funnels.

No. 76388

Capacity	Weight each ounces	Price, each
1 Gill	2	9c
½ Pint	3	10c
1 Pint	3	12c
1 Quart	4	13c
2 Quarts	8	15c
4 Quarts	12	21c

Peerless Enameled Steel Measures.

(Sizes given are U. S. Standard.)

Standard measure	No. 76389 Weight	Price, Each
1 Gill	2 ounces	9c
½ Pint	4 ounces	10c
1 Pint	6 ounces	12c
1 Quart	8 ounces	15c
2 Quarts	14 ounces	22c
4 Quarts	20 ounces	30c

No. 76390 Peerless Enameled Steel Lipped Graduated Measure. 1 Quart. Weight, ½ pound. Price, each.......15c

No. 76391 Granite Steel Handy Strainer, tinned wire bottom. For straining tea, etc. It just fits an ordinary tea-cup. The handiest little strainer made. Size, 4 inches. Price, each.......8c

Peerless Enameled Steel Seamless Milk or Rice Boiler.

No. 76392 Peerless Enameled Steel Seamless Milk or Rice Boiler. With retinned cover that fits both vessels.

Quarts inside boiler	1	2
Holds, quarts	1½	1⅞
Weight, each, pounds	1⅜	2
Each	41c	48c
Quarts inside boiler	3	4
Holds, quarts	3	4½
Weight, each, pounds	2⅝	3⅝
Each	60c	72c

Peerless Enameled Steel Flaring Dippers.

No. 76394 Peerless Enameled Steel Flaring Dippers.

No.	110	No.	112
Size	4½x2	Size	5x2¼
Capacity, pints	⅝	Capacity, pints	⅞
Weight, each, oz.	6	Weight, each, oz.	7
Price, each	10c	Price, each	12c

Peerless Enameled Steel Cocoa Shaped Dippers.

No. 76396 Peerless Enameled Steel Cocoa Shaped Dippers; black enameled wood handle; holds one pint. Weight, 8 ounces, Price, each.......14c

Peerless Enameled Steel Soup Ladles.

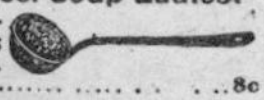

No. 76397 Peerless Enameled Steel Soup Ladles; size, 3½x1⅜. Weight, 4 ounces. Price, each.......8c

Peerless Enameled Steel Flat Skimmers.

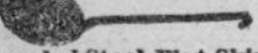

No. 76398 Peerless Enameled Steel Flat Skimmers.

Inches	4⅝	5	5⅜
Weight, each, ounces	5	6	8
Price, each	8c	9c	10c

Peerless Enameled Steel Windsor Dippers.

No. 76400 Peerless Enameled Steel Windsor Dippers.

Quarts	¾	1	2
Holds, qts.	⅝	⅞	1¼
Inches	5x2¼	5½x3	6¼x3¼
Weight, each, ounces	7	8	9
Price, each	15c	17c	18c

Peerless Enameled Steel Basting Spoons.

No. 76401 Peerless Enameled Steel Basting Spoons.

Inches	10	12	14	16	18
Weight, each, ounces	2	2½	3	4	5
Price, each	5c	6c	7c	8c	9c

Peerless Enameled Steel Deep Lip Fry Pan.

No. 76403

No.	3	4	5	6
Inches	9¾x1⅜	10x2	11¼x2	12x2
Weight, each, lbs.	1	1¼	1½	2
Price, each	18c	21c	23c	27c

Peerless Enameled Steel Oval Meat Dishes or Platters.

No. 76405

Inches	12	14	16
Weight, each, lbs.	½	¾	1¼
Price, each	21c	27c	33c

Peerless Enameled Steel Wall Soap Dish.

No. 76407 Weight, each, 4 ounces.
Inches.......6½x4x1½
Price, each.......9c

Peerless Enameled Steel Oblong Soap Dishes.

No. 76408 Weight, each, 4 ounces.
Inches.......4x6x1⅝
Price, each.......9c

Peerless Enameled Steel Chambers.

No. 76409

No.	Inches	Weight	Price, each
1	7 x4⅛	⅝	20c
1½	8½x4⅞	1	25c
2	9¾x5½	1¼	30c

Peerless Enameled Steel Chamber Covers.

No. 76410

No.	01	01½	02
Weight, each, lbs.	¼	⅜	½
Price, each	12c	15c	18c

Peerless Enameled Steel Seamed Chamber Pails.

No. 76411 Capacity, 11 quarts; weight, 2⅝ pounds.
Inches.......11½x11½
Price, each.......54c

Peerless Enameled Steel Bed Pans.

Weight, 2¼ pounds.
No. 76412 Price, each, $1.44

Peerless Enameled Steel Seamless Bed or Douche Pans.

Weight, 3 pounds.
No. 76413 Inches, 15⅜x11⅜x3.
Price, each.......99c

Peerless Enameled Steel Male Urinal.

Weight, ¾ pound.
No. 76415 Price, each.......90c

Peerless Enameled Steel Female Urinal.

Weight, ¾ pound.
No. 76416 Price, each.......99c

Fancy Enameled Pearl Agate Tea Pots.

Fancy Enameled Pearl Agate Tea Pots, in three tints, chocolate, blue and sage. White porcelain inside, enameled covers and handles; a very attractive tea pot, nothing like this ever offered before at so reasonable a figure.

No. 76420 Chocolate Pearl Agate Tea Pot.

Quarts	2	3	4
Holds, quarts	1⅞	2¼	3¼
Weight, each, pounds	1	1½	1⅝
Price, each	69c	78c	87c

No. 76421 Blue Pearl Agate Tea Pot.

Quarts	2	3	4
Weight, each, pounds	1	1¼	1⅝
Price, each	69c	78c	87c

No. 76422 Sage Pearl Agate Tea Pot.

Quarts	2	3	4
Weight, each, pounds	1	1¼	1⅝
Price, each	69c	78c	87c

Fancy Enameled Pearl Agate Coffee Pots.

Fancy Enameled Pearl Agate Coffee Pots, in three tints, chocolate, blue and sage, white porcelain inside; enameled cover and handle. A very attractive coffee pot, nothing like this ever offered at so reasonable a figure.

No. 76423 Chocolate Pearl Agate Coffee Pot.

Size, quarts	3	4	5
Holds, quarts	2¼	3¼	4
Weight, each, pounds	1½	1⅝	1¾
Price, each	77c	86c	96c

No. 76424 Blue Pearl Agate Coffee Pot.

Size, quarts	3	4	5
Weight, each, pounds	1½	1⅝	1¾
Price, each	77c	86c	96c

No. 76425 Sage Pearl Agate Coffee Pot.

Size, quarts	3	4	5
Weight, each, pounds	1½	1⅝	1¾
Price, each	77c	86c	96c

TRUE BLUE ENAMELED WARE.

Each and every piece of this ware is all the name suggests. It is as easily kept clean as crockery or china and is as nearly perfect as possible. Strong and durable. It will not rust and is absolutely pure and safe to use. Made of sheet steel covered with two coats of enamel inside and out. The inside is white, the outside white mottled with dark blue, with a smooth and glossy finish, giving it a handsome and attractive appearance.

.....WE GUARANTEE.....
Each and Every Piece to Give Satisfaction and
TO BE AS GOOD OR BETTER THAN ANY
Enameled Ware in the Market,
. . . Regardless of Price.

No. 76426 True Blue Enameled Tea Pots, with enameled covers.

Trade size, qts.	1	1½	2
Holds, qts.	1	1½	2
Price, each	45c	50c	55c
Trade size, qts.	3	4	
Holds, qts.	2¾	3½	
Price, each	62c	69c	

No. 76427 True Blue Enameled Coffee Pots, with enameled covers.

Trade size, qts.	1	1½	2
Holds, qts.	1	1½	2
Price, each	44c	49c	54c
Trade size, qts.	3	4	5
Holds, qts.	2⅝	3½	4
Price, each	61c	68c	76c

No. 76430 True Blue Enameled Ware Flat Bottom Coffee Boilers, with enameled covers.

Trade size quarts	6	8½	11½
Holds qts.	6	8	11
Each	$ .96	$1.10	$1.24

No. 76432 True Blue Enameled Ware Flat Bottom Tea Kettle.

Size, No.	7	8	9
Diam. of bottom inches	10	11	11¾
Holds, qts.	4½	6	7⅜
Each	$0.96	$1.10	$1.29

No. 76434 True Blue Enameled Ware Wash Basin with patent rings

Number	26	28	30	32	34
Size, inches	10⅜x2¾	11⅜x2⅞	12¼x3½	13x3⅝	14x3⅞
Price, each	22c	24c	29c	34c	39c

No. 76436 True Blue Enameled Ware Deep Dish-pans.

Size, quarts	10	14	17	21	30
Holds, qts.	9	12	15	18	24
Size, inches	14½x5	15⅜x5½	17⅜x5¾	19¼x6	20¾x6⅝
Price, each	62c	74c	86c	$1.00	$1.48

No. 76438 True Blue Enameled Ware Strong Lipped Sauce Pan.

Number	14	16
Size, quarts	1½	2
Holds, qts.	1¼	1½
Inches	6½x3¼	7x3½
Price, each	20c	24c
Number	18	22
Size, qts.	2½	4
Holds, qts.	2½	3¾
Inches	7¾x3¾	9x4
Price, each	27c	36c
Number	24	26
Size, quarts	5	6
Holds, quarts	4¾	6
Size, inches	9¾x4½	11x5
Price, each	41c	48c

CARRIAGE HARDWARE AND SUPPLIES.

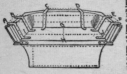

IN CALLING YOUR ATTENTION to this complete department, we are confident that we can supply the great need of thousands of our customers who find it constantly necessary to replace various parts of their vehicles, but who have been paying exorbitant retail prices. We offer a line that has no equal in general excellence of material and finish. At the same time our contracts with manufacturers are so advantageous that we are in a position to make unusually low prices.

IN ORDERING BUGGY TOPS give measurements from center to center of holes in irons, as shown in cut; width from A to F, from B to E, from A to B, from C to D. State whether you want 3 or 4 bows, and give choice of color of lining.

IN ORDERING CUSHIONS give measurements from I to J on bottom of seat; from G to H, width of seat at bottom, and state if square or round corners are wanted.

IN ORDERING CUSHIONS WITH FALL give measurements of cushion as above, and also width of fall at the bottom and distance from bottom of seat to floor of buggy. Our buggy tops are shipped in light but strong crates, and are not liable to injury in transportation.

OUR TERMS OF SHIPMENT ARE LIBERAL.

Any of these goods will be sent by freight C. O. D., subject to examination, on receipt of $5.00, balance and freight charges to be paid after goods are received.

You will save money by buying your own needed repairs direct from us at manufacturers' lowest prices. Freight amounts to nothing compared with what you save in price. Nearly all these goods are taken at second-class rate or lower.

OUR $6.40 COMPLETE BUGGY TOP.

No. 81000

FOR $6.40

We furnish this **BUGGY TOP COMPLETE** with Full Length SIDE AND... BACK CURTAINS with patent shifting rail which adjusts itself to any buggy. The latest style top in every way.

$6.40 IS A SPECIAL PRICE, based on the actual cost of material and labor, with but one small profit added.

MADE IN OUR OWN FACTORY.

WE BUILD THESE TOPS in our own factory here in Chicago; we build them in immense quantities. The bows, bow sockets, shifting rails, joints, prop nuts and finishings are contracted for direct from the largest manufacturers for cash. Our rubber drill, cloth lining and trimming are contracted for in very large quantities, and it is by reason of the low price at which we have been able to buy the material and by reason of our manufacturing them in our own factory that we are able to name this extremely low price of $6.40.

No. 81000

FROM THE TWO ILLUSTRATIONS you can form an idea of the appearance of this, our special $6.40 Buggy Top. The one illustration shows the top, the other illustration shows one of the side curtains. We furnish a pair of side curtains and a full length back curtain.

SEND US $6.40

Or, if you prefer, send $1.00, and we will send this buggy top to you by freight, C. O. D., subject to examination. You can examine it at your freight depot, and if found perfectly satisfactory, exactly as represented, and such value as you could not get elsewhere, pay the agent the balance, $5.40 and freight charges.

IN ORDERING BUGGY TOPS follow our rules for measurement as given above, and we can guarantee the top we furnish you will fit your buggy exactly.

THIS OUR SPECIAL $6.40 TOP IS MADE OF THOROUGHLY RELIABLE MATERIAL. The roof and the quarters are made of good quality extra heavy rubber drill, well padded; roof and back stays lined with No. 14 X cloth, and back stays stiffened with two thicknesses of buckram. Side and back curtains are made of good weight colored back drill. We use nothing but the highest grade tubular steel bow sockets of the latest pattern, full black enameled metal buckle loops, Thomas top props, patent, concealed joints, japanned prop nuts, patent curtain fasteners, wrought iron rail with patent buttons, which makes it adjustable to any buggy. Side and back curtains are full length, large glass fitted in back curtain, patent buttonholes used throughout.

OUR $5.75 DRILL TOP. NO. 81002. At $5.75 we furnish a Drill Top complete with side and back curtains. It is made of light black enameled drill, light material throughout, made to compete with the many cheap tops now being advertised, and while we do not guaranteed it, for a very cheap top it will give good satisfaction.

Our special price..$5.75

The Top weighs, crated for shipment, about 50 pounds, and you will find the freight will amount to next to nothing as compared with what you will save in price.

IN ORDERING BE SURE TO GIVE MEASURE AS PER DIAGRAM ABOVE. ALSO STATE WHETHER THREE OR FOUR BOW TOP IS WANTED.

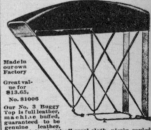

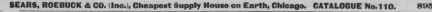

A $20.00 Buggy Top for $12.75

Made in our own Factory.

No. 81012 The accompanying illustration shows our No. 4 Buggy Top, complete with seat, in the white, full back, and cushion, with fall. This top is made of 34-oz. rubber, with seat, wrought rail and joints. Top, back stays and back curtain lined with all-wool fast-color cloth, either blue or green, side curtains indigo-dyed rubber, 18-oz. blue or green cloth on full back and cushion. These are either biscuit or diamond tufted, and filled with selected moss. Front and back valance nailed on. Black nuts and rivets. Three or four steel socket bows, as desired. Our special price on No. 4 top, complete, as described **$12.75**

No. 81014 Our No. 5 Buggy Top complete, with full back and cushion, is made like shown in the picture of our No. 4; 28-oz. rubber drill and leather quarters and stay, and is complete with seat, in the white, wrought rail and joints, three or four steel bows; top, back stays and back curtain lined with all-wool, fast-color cloth. Rubber side curtains, 14-ounce blue or green cloth in full back and cushions. Front valance sewed on. Black nuts and iron rivets. Our special price..............**$15.75**

No. 81016 Our No. 6 Top is the finest Buggy Top made. It has machine buffed leather top and is complete with seat, in the white, cushion and full back. Wrought rail and joints. Lined throughout, except side curtains, with 10-ounce all-wool fast-color cloth. Rubber side curtains, 14-ounce blue or green cloth on full back and cushion. The latter is tufted in biscuit or diamond style, and stuffed with moss. Black nuts and iron rivets. Valance sewed on. Style same as shown in picture of No. 4 buggy top. Three or four steel bows, as desired. Our special price..................**$22.00**

EXTRAS.

No. 81018 Extra rubber back curtains. Each **$1.25**
No. 81019 Extra rubber back stays. Each. **1.00**

Canopy Top Sun Shades.

No. 81020 Canopy Top Sun Shades to use in connection with any Canopy top, furnished complete ready for use. Length 60 inches.
Price each.......................................**75c**
No. 6. Extra Heavy Silesia, color dark blue.
Price each..**75c**
No. 3 Sateen, color fast black............**90c**
No. 1 Austra, color fast black.............**$1.15**
No. 9 Glorious Silk, color dark blue or drab, nickel plated trimmings...................**$1.65**
No. 11 English Cloth, nickel plated trimmings, with silk fringe, colors dark blue........**$2.00**

Canopy Tops.

In measuring for Canopy Top give exact distance from back of back seat to front end of body. Give exact width of seats from outside to outside of top. These canopy tops have drill foot X-cloth, head lining and fringe all around 7 inches deep. Cash in full, must be sent with all orders for canopy top. Weight, crated, about 70 pounds.

No. 81022 Our $7.30 Canopy Top is covered with black drill, lined with all-wool X-cloth, and ornamented with all-wool fringe. Price for 5-foot length or less Top..............................**$7.30**
This price is without standards or curtains. See following measures for ordering measures in ordering Canopy Tops.
For larger sizes over 5 foot, add extra for each additional foot.......................per foot **$1.35**
No. 81023 Complete set side and back curtains, indigo-dyed rubber, for above tops.......**$4.00**

Highest Grade Extension Tops.

In measuring for Extension on Top, give length of seat from outside to outside in top of rim, in widest place. If seat is ironed, give measure across from eye to eye. Also give the distance from the back of front seat to front of back seat on bottom of seats, and state if back seat is higher or lower than front seat.

All tops over 42 inches wide cost from 65c to $2.00 extra, in accordance with the extra width.

No. 81025 Our No. 7 Extension Top, is a 4-bow 26-ounce rubber top, lined throughout with all-wool cloth, except side curtains, which are indigo-dyed rubber. Wrought iron joints, japanned nuts and iron rivets. Front valance sewed on. No rail. Weight, crated, about 65 pounds. Our special price **$12.25**

No. 81027 Our No. 8 Extension Top, just the same as our No. 7, described above, but has leather quarter and stay. Our special price, **$17.00**
No. 81029 Our No. 9 is a full leather Extension Top, otherwise just the same as No. 7, described above. Our special price................**$22.65**

Phaeton Tops.

We can furnish Phaeton Tops of same material as Nos. 81003, 81005 and 81006 at same prices, but, in addition to the measurements required for buggy tops, we must have a paper pattern showing exact shape and size of back of seat.

State how much higher the back goose neck is than the front one. The measurements must be made very carefully, and phaeton top cannot be returned if sent as ordered. Cash in full must accompany orders for Phaeton Tops.

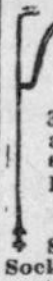

Rolled Steel Canopy Top Standards.

No. 81037 Finished complete, as shown in cut. Made of ⅝-inch round steel; height, 36½ in. hind, 53 in. front. We can send these standards in halves if so desired. Always sent as shown in cut unless otherwise ordered. Price, per set of 2 front and 2 hind pieces..........**$1.65**

Steel Canopy Top Sockets.

No. 81039 Rolled Steel Canopy Top Socket to be used in connection with the above Canopy Top Standards. 
Price, per set of four pieces.................**30c**

Wagon Sunshade.

Especially adapted for express and farm wagons.

This top is furnished complete with irons and bolts, ready to attach to seat. The irons will fit any kind of a seat. The sizes we keep in stock are for seats measuring from 33 to 44 inches. For extra wide tops the additional cost of making will be added. When ordering, give width of seat outside to outside on top of seat at back corner.
No. 81040 Covered with brown duck.
Price..**$2.75**
No. 81041 Covered with awning stripe.
Price **$2.90**
No. 81043 Covered with enameled drill and fringed. Price................................**$3.25**
No. 81043 Covered with rubber and fringed. Price..**$3.75**

Our New 1901 Wagon Umbrella.

No. 81048 If you are looking for a bargain in wagon umbrellas, you will find it in our $1.15 umbrella, which we send out as an advertisement. It is a regular $2.50 article; is made with our new improved steel ribs and notches. Handle is white ash, of good size, oil finished, with patent foot socket and seat fixture. Is covered with fancy striped double faced duck, with removable cover, which can be taken off and repaired in case of an accident. The colors are red, white and orange. Each section having Sears, Roebuck & Co. painted on same, as shown in illustration. It is not a cheap affair, but an umbrella that sells for $2.50 without our name on same. Lettering is done in fast oil, guaranteed not to fade or run. Has six ribs, and a spread of 5 feet and 8 inches. **Only $1.15** for a **$2.50** Umbrella.
Price, each.......................................**$1.15**

Wagon Umbrellas With Fixture Sockets.

Compare our prices on these goods with those of other houses and see if we cannot save you 25 to 50 per cent. on price. These Umbrellas come with best quality heavy steel ribs and fixtures. Handles, 14-inch seasoned white ash, oiled and varnished. Genuine blue, green or buff. Heavy umbrella cloth muslin. Be sure to state color wanted.

The most complete fixtures produced. Made of the best malleable iron, light and strong, quickly applied, and holds the umbrella secure. We furnish all extras complete without extra charge.

No.81050 36-inch, 8 ribs, with fixtures, each.**$1.35**
No.81051 36-inch, 10 ribs, with fixtures, each.**1.43**
No.81052 38-inch, 8 ribs, with fixtures, each.**1.45**
No.81053 38-inch, 10 ribs, with fixtures, each.**1.66**
No.81054 40-inch, 8 ribs, with fixtures, each.**1.75**
No.81055 40-inch, 10 ribs, double face duck, green inside, duck outside, with fixtures, each.**2.18**

$1.70 for the Best Wagon Umbrella Made.

This is the most popular Umbrella on the market, very latest and best. This Umbrella has heavy duck covering, in blue, brown or white. Guaranteed strongest umbrella made, 6 steel ribs, 1¾-inch white ash handles, 5 feet 8-inch spread, cover removable. Price includes all fixtures complete.
No. 81057 This is the Umbrella to buy, and our special price is below all others. Price..........**$1.70**

Buggy Cushions and Falls and Full Backs.

These goods are first-class in all respects. We make strictly inside prices on these goods and can save you a large percentage on each purchase. The price of full back is just the same as that of the cushion with fall. If you want both the full back and cushion with fall, the price will be just twice that of the cushion and fall alone. All these Cushions are based on 34-inch length. All larger sizes we charge 7 cents per inch extra. In ordering cushions, give size of seat. Measure length and width on inside bottom of seat and do not include the flare.

No. 81065 Black drill Cushion and Fall.......**70c**
No. 81066 Black drill Cushion without Fall.**65c**
No. 81070 Rubber Cushion with Fall............**94c**
No. 81071 Rubber Cushion without Fall........**80c**
EXTRAS.—We can furnish any of these cushions with springs for, extra.....................**75c**
Full backs with springs, extra..................**$1.00**

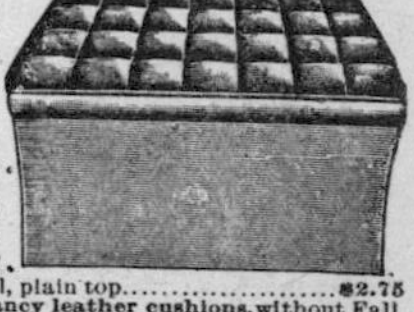

No. 81080 Blue or green cloth Cushion, plain top, with Fall.......................**$1.67**
No. 81081 Blue or green cloth Cushion, with Fall, biscuit or diamond tufted, filled with moss. Price...........**$1.95**
No. 81082 Fancy leather Cushion and Fall, plain top....................**$2.75**
No. 81083 Fancy leather cushions, without Fall, plain top....................**$2.60**
No. 81084 Black leather cushions, with Fall, plain top......................**$2.95**
No. 81085 Black leather cushions, without Fall, plain top....................**$2.60**
No. 81086 Black split leather cushions, with Fall, plain top...................**$2.55**
No. 81087 Black split leather cushions, without Fall, plain top............**$2.00**
No. 81088 Green or black artificial leather cushions, and fall...........**$1.66**
No. 81089 Same as No.81088, without Fall.**$1.35**
No. 81090 Brown corduroy cushions and Fall, plain top....................**$2.00**
No. 81091 Brown corduroy cushions, without fall, plain top................**$1.75**

Oval Foot Tubs.

No. 84765 3X Extra Heavy Tin Foot Tubs, strong and well made, heavy handles, double seamed, etc. Furnished in assorted colors.

1/x13¼ inches, each....................25c
18x14¾ inches, each....................30c
20x16½ inches, each....................35c

Infants' Bath Tubs.

No. 84766 Heavy 4X Tin Infants' Bath Tubs, well made, double seamed, strong rim and handles. Nicely japanned.

27 inches, each $0.70
30 inches, each .... .90
33 inches, each 1.10
36 inches, each 1.30
40 inches, each 1.45

Plunge Bath Tubs.

No. 84767 Extra Heavy Tin Plunge Bath Tubs, double seamed, heavy roll at top, extra wood bottom, waste pipe at end of tub.

Nothing better made in a tin tub.

4 feet, each....................$3.50
5 feet, each....................4.25
6 feet, each....................4.90

Sitz Bath Tubs.

No. 84768 Sitz Bath Tubs, made of heavy 3X tin, heavy base and rim, nicely japanned and finished.

Inches.....17x22x36 18¼x24x37
Price, each $2.94 $4.20

Combination Bath Tub.

No. 84769 Combination Sitz Bath Tub, made of 3-X tin, made extra strong, nicely japanned and finished. Nothing better made in a tin tub. Size, 19x34x36 inches.

Price, each....................$4.25

Hat Shaped Bath Tub.

No. 84770 Hat Shaped Sitz Bath Tub, made of heavy 3-X tin, japanned and varnished outside, has heavy base and legs. Size, 12¼x40 inches.

Price, each....................$4.20

Stationary Zinc Bath Tubs.

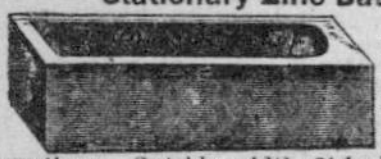

No. 84771 Plain Wood Frame and Box, lined with heavy zinc. A good, serviceable tub. Price does not include plugs or connections. Outside width, 24 inches; outside depth, 19 inches.

Size, 4½ feet. Price, each....................$7.00
Size, 5 feet. Price, each....................7.05
Size, 5½ feet. Price, each....................7.10
Size, 6 feet. Price, each....................7.15

Copper Stationary Bath Tubs.

No. 84772 Stationary Copper Bath Tubs, made of 12-ounce copper. Outside width, at head and foot, 24-inches; outside depth, 19 inches. Prices subject to fluctuation of copper market.

Size, 4½ feet. Price, each....................$9.50
Size, 5 feet. Price, each....................9.75
Size, 5½ feet. Price, each....................10.00
Size, 6 feet. Price, each....................10.25

$10.95 Stationary Bath Tub.

No. 84774 This tub is made of Steel, is very strong and durable. **Just the tub** to make comfortable the home of those in moderate circumstances. No farm house is complete without the luxury of one of our bath tubs. This all steel bath tub is made of No. 20 galvanized sheet steel, coated inside with insoluble **white enamel**, the joints are supported by iron mountings, which terminate in four ornamental feet, the top is capped with polished oak rim, 3 inches wide, 1¼ inches thick, the whole outside polished in a nile green tint, relieved with gold bronze. It is furnished with an overflow, as shown in cut, and **patent connected waste**, which is nickel plated fitting.

Size, 4½ feet. Price, each....................$8.50
Size, 5½ feet. Price, each....................9.50

Our $13.00 Bath Tub.

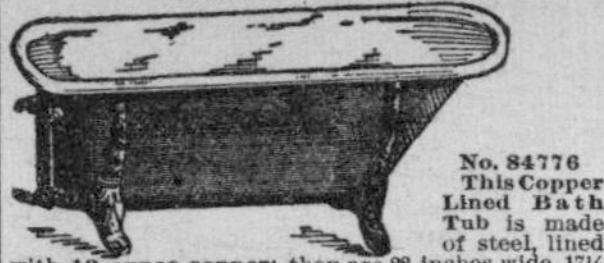

No. 84776 This Copper Lined Bath Tub is made of steel, lined with 12-ounce copper; they are 28 inches wide, 17½ inches deep, 23¾ inches from floor to top of rim, and are furnished with connected waste and overflow, with wood rim.

Length, 4½ feet. Price, each....................$11.00
Length, 5½ feet. Price, each....................12.00

Roll Rim Enameled Iron Baths.

No. 84778 Best Grade Enameled Bath Tub, extra heavy weight enameling put on by a patent process, which we guarantee not to flake or peal off. We furnish the tub with 3-inch wide enameled roll rim; nickel plated overflow and waste plug with strainer; height on legs, 27 inches; width over all, 29 inches; depth inside, 20 inches.

Size tub............	4½ ft.	5 ft.	5½ ft.
Length over rim....	4 ft. 9 in.	5 ft. 3 in.	5 ft. 9 in.
Length over all....	4 ft. 10 in.	5 ft. 4 in.	5 ft. 10 in.
Price, each.........	$20.70	$22.70	$26.50

White Enameled Bath Tub Complete.

No. 84779 Roll Rim White Enameled Bath Tub, complete with No. 4½ Fuller Combination Cock. Has patent overflow, nickel plated plug and chain, ½-inch nickel plated supply pipe and outside nickel plated waste pipes; stands 27 inches high, 29 inches wide over all and 20 inches deep. This is one of the best tubs on the market. Everything about it is new and up-to-date. We guarantee the enameling not to crack or peel off. A first class tub in every respect. Good enough for any residence. Manufactured by one of the largest makers of plumbing goods in the United States and guaranteed to be perfect in every respect. Price includes everything complete, ready for use.

Size, 4½ feet. Price, each....................$27.15
Size, 5 feet. Price, each....................29.25
Size, 5½ feet. Price, each....................32.95

Acme Combination Sink and Bath Tub.

No. 84782 A sink with a bath tub attached for village or country use. It is intended to be placed in kitchen in place of the kitchen sink, with cistern pump placed on right or left end of same, with pipe running through the floor to cistern or well. The frame and box is made of ⅞-inch natural finish oak, sides are matched wainscoting with 5-inch baseboard and round mouldings at top. Length over all, 5 feet 1 inch; height, 32¼ inches; width, 26¼ inches. Back side board made of ⅞-inch oak, 9½ inches wide by 5 feet 2 inches long. **Tub is heavy zinc lined,** regular bath tub shape, square at one end and leaning at the other; length, about 5 feet. **The sink is enameled steel** 18x36 inches, with patent strainer and brass couplings. Bath tub can be filled without opening sink, and with pump attached makes a sink and tub **far ahead of any ever put on the market.** Has waste pipe which carries water to catch basin on the outside.

Be sure and state whether right or left hand tub is wanted—that is, if tub is to go in right or left hand corner of room. Price, each......$12.75

HOT WATER INSTANTLY.

THE ACME INSTANTANEOUS WATER HEATER.

is designed to give hot water instantly, at hour of the day or night, and will give suffici water for a bath in 10 or 15 minutes, owing to h cold the water supply may be.

Acme No. 2 Instantaneous Water Heat

No. 84783 Suitable for baths when small tubs or copper baths are used, and not more than one gallon of water per minute is needed. Also for wash stands, kitchen purposes, etc. Will raise the temperature of one gallon of water per minute 70 degrees, giving a continuous stream at from 100 degrees to 120 degrees, or two gallons per minute at from 85 degrees to 90 degrees. Will heat sufficient water for bath in from 10 to 15 minutes, at temperature given above, at a cost of from ¼ to 2 cents, depending on cost of gas. For washing dishes or ordinary domestic purposes its capacity is ample, and for barber shops or offices where a wash stand is used, i ample; 10 inches in diameter, 36 inches high; ½-i water supply; ½-inch gas supply. Consumptio gas, 1 foot per minute. Flue connection outside ro

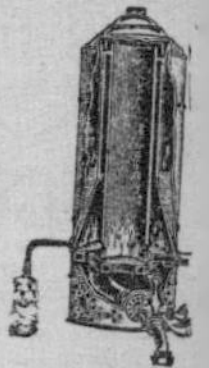

Sectional Cut

Price, No. 2, copper, lacquered, including shelf brackets....................$15
Price, No 2, nickel plated, including shelf brackets....................$19

Acme No. 1 Gas Heater.

No. 84784 Will raise the temperature of gallon of water per minute 95 degrees, givin continuous stream at from 130 to 160 degrees two gallons per minute at about 110 degr Will heat sufficient water for a bath in from 10 t minutes, at a cost of from one-half to two cents, pending on cost of gas or gasoline. The most sim and economical heater ever offered the public an the lowest price. The gas and products of comb tion are entirely separate from the water, whic thus kept pure and sweet. Twelve inches diame 36 inches high, one-half inch water supply, one-h inch gas supply. Consumption of gas, 1½ feet minute. Flue connection outside room.

Price, copper lacquered, including shelf and brackets....................$20
Price, nickel plated, including shelf and brackets....................2(

Instantaneous Water Heater for Gasolin

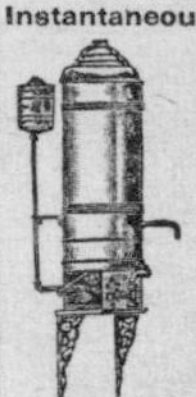

No. 84785 Both the No. 1 a No. 2 heaters are made suita for burning Gasoline as well Gas, and can thus be used a where that water is obtainal and with equally as good resu as with Gas. They are precis the same heater as our Nos. 8 and cut. With the gasoline b ner attachment gasoline makes excellent substitute where gas not to be had. Nothing to get of order—will last a lifetime. **I the heating capacity of th heaters, see gas burners abo** No. 84784 and cut. In lighting gasoline burner it is necessary generate the gas the same as y would an ordinary gasoline sto Size, No. 1—12 inch diameter, 36 inches high. No. 10 inch diameter, 36 inches high.

No. 1—Copper, lacquered, for gasoline......$23.
No. 1—Nickel-plated, for gasoline........26.
No. 2—Copper, lacquered, for gasoline......19.
No. 2—Nickel-plated, for gasoline..........21.
Including shelf and brackets.

GRANITINE LAUNDRY TUBS.

Granitine Combination Kitchen Sink a Laundry Tubs.

No. 84786 With high back, soap cup, strai and painted iron legs. In ordering please st the height of back wanted. Backs higher tha inches will be charged extra. We do not furn faucets unless specially ordered, but 12-inch bac and faucet holes in the backs, will be sent up otherwise ordered. All measurements are outsi

Length	Width	Depth	12-in. ba
4 feet	2 feet	16 inches	$11
4 feet 6 inches	2 feet	16 inches	12
5 feet	2 feet	16 inches	13

o Compartment Granitine Laundry Tubs.

With High Back and Soap Cup.

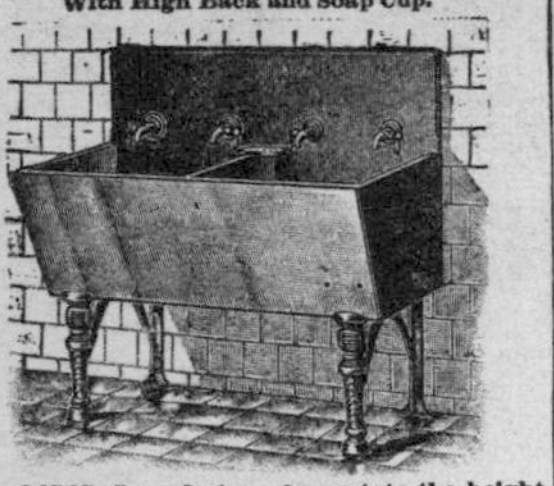

. 84787 **In ordering, please state the height ack wanted.** We do not furnish faucets unless ially ordered. Tubs with 12-inch backs, and et holes in the high backs, will be sent unless rwise ordered. All measurements are outside.

gth	4 ft.	4½ ft.	5 ft.
h	2 ft.	2 ft.	2 ft.
h	16 in.	16 in.	16 in.
e, 16-inch back	$10.70	$12.00	$12.70

Finished Brass Faucets.

For Nos. 84786 and 84787 Laundry Tubs.

No. 84788 **Fuller Wash Tray Bibbs.** with adjustable flange. Price, each...90c

Bath Spray.

No. 84790 **Nickel Plated Bath Spray,** with five feet rubber tubing to attach to faucet, rose is made of brass nickel plated. Price, each 85c

Closet Seat With Cover.

. 84791 **Closet Seat cover,** furnished come, well finished, etc. Fured in oak, natural or ue or light cherry. ice, each $2.35

Bath Tub Plugs.

No. 84793 **Brass Finished Bath Tub Plugs without chains.** 1¼-in... Each 25c 1½-in. Each 30c

Wash Basins.

o. 84794 **Wash Ba-** , crystal enameled; mon overflow; diam- . 14-in., complete stopper; fitted for er lead or iron pipe. ice, each..... $1.00

Enameled Wash Basins.

ast Iron Enameled Wash Basins. Same style as 84794. **Made of the best grade gray iron.** Made ra heavy; will last a lifetime. Common or pat- overflow. Complete with stopper; fitted for er lead or iron pipe. **Diameter 14 inches.**

o. 84795 Price, common overflow, each..$2.50
o. 84796 Price, patent overflow, each ... 2.80

Towel Racks.

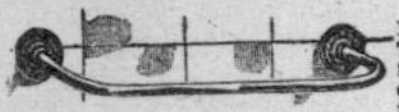

No. 84797 **Nickel Plated Towel Racks.** Strong and durable; finely finished; bar is ach in diameter; projects 2½ inches from wall.

gth, inches.	Price, per dozen.	Price, each.
18	$5.00	45c
21	5.50	50c

Folding Towel Racks.

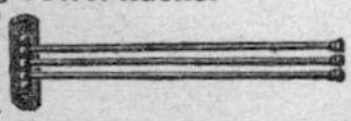

o. 84798 **Three m Nickel Plated wel Racks,** will rust or corrode; e enough for any h room. Diameter bars, ¼ in.; length 12 in. rice, per dozen, $6.50; each......60c

Toilet Paper Holders.

No. 84799 **Solid Brass, Nickel Plated Toilet Paper Holder.** Nicely finished, nice enough for any bath room. Will take roll 5 inches wide by 4 inches diameter. Price, doz., $3.00; each..30c

Bath Seat.

o. 84800 **Here is just at you want to make bath room complete—** bath tub seat. Seat is de of oak, is 18x6 inches, h rounded corners. The porting rods are 5/16-in., ss, nickel plated. Rods hinged under the seat, so they are adjustable to s of different widths. The ends of the rods are ered with rubber, so as not to mar the finish of rim. All parts of the best material and finest sh. **Nothing better made.** Price, each... $1.35

Soap Cups.

No. 84801 **Soap Cups for the rim of the bath, solid brass, nickel plated, finely finished.** Hanging rods can be adjusted so as to fit any tub. Size, 6x3½ inches. Price, each 80c

Solid Brass Soap Cups.

No. 84802 **Shell Pattern solid brass nickel plated Soap Cups,** to be fastened to the wall. **Finest finish, extra fine goods.** Size, 4x3 inches. Price, each....75c

Tumbler Holders.

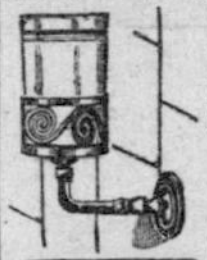

No. 84803 **Solid brass, nickel plated Tumbler Holders,** to be fastened to the wall. **Extra fine.** Price is for holder only; no tumbler furnished. Price, each......90c

Urinals.

No. 84804 **Iron Corner Urinal,** enameled, size, 9 in., fitted for lead pipe. Price, each......$1.50

No. 84805 **Iron Half Circle Urinal,** enameled; size, 12-in.; fitted for lead pipe. Price, each......$1.65

Earthenware Urinals.

No. 84806 **Flat Back Earthenware Urinals.** Furnished without connections as shown in cut.

Size, 12x14, price each........$3.40
Size, 13x15, price each........ 4.10

Sanitary Roll Rim Iron Wash Stands.

No. 84807 **Roll Rim White Enameled Iron Lavatories;** have the appearance of marble. All parts are accessible and carefully fitted together. All exposed surfaces are enameled or bronzed, making it a substantial and perfectly sanitary plumbing fixture, easily kept clean and bright. Wash Stand complete as shown, includes: 18x24-inch counter sunk roll rim slab with soap tray and 12x15-inch oval, patent overflow basin, all cast in one piece; 10½-inch high roll rim back; full length nickel plated brackets; compression basin cocks; overflow strainer, chain and waste plug coupling with rubber stopper, all nickel plated. Price, each......$14.65

If wanted with nickel plated supply pipes add $1.50 to above price.

Rim Roll Iron Wash Stands.

No. 84808 **Roll Rim White Enameled Iron Lavatories** to place in corner of room. For description, sizes, etc., see No. 84807 above. In ordering be sure and state which corner of room stand is to be placed, right or left hand. Price, each.. $15.95

If wanted with nickel plated supply pipe, add $1.50 to the above price.

Open Lavatories.

No. 84809 **Italian Marble Slab, 20x24 inches,** 1¼-inch thick, 10-inch back, 14-inch round patent overflow basin, nickel plated metal plug with rubber stopper, nickel plated S trap; No. 1 Fuller basin cocks, chain and stays, and nickel plated brackets.

Price, as described......$11.50

Open Plumbing Lavatories.

No. 84810 **Open Plumbing Lavatory, furnished complete, as shown in cut.** Back and bottom slabs are made of Italian and Tennessee Pink Marble, highly polished. Back slab is 8 inches high; bottom slab 20x24 inches, with 14-inch earthenware patent overflow bowl; nickel plated No. 1 basin cocks; nickel plated brackets, with nickel plated supply pipe and air chamber; plug and chain nickel plated. A high class Lavatory at a moderate price. It is made by one of the largest manufacturers of plumbing goods in the United States, and we guarantee all parts to be made of the best materials and workmanship to be perfect. Being all nickel plated it does not require the care to keep it clean. Will not rust or corrode. We furnish everything complete, ready for use. Tennessee marble, price, each $17.00
Italian marble, price, each......17.50

Earthenware Basins.

No. 84811 **Patent Overflow White Earthenware Basins for Metal Plugs,** smooth standard goods. Size, 14 inches in diameter. Price, each......85c

Oval Earthenware Basins.

No. 84812 **White Earthenware Oval Basins With Patent Overflow.** Oval in shape. Size, 14x17 inches, for rubber plugs. Price, each...$1.75

Marble Slabs for Above Basins.

No. 84813 **Best Grade White Marble Slabs,** to be used in connection with above basins, finely finished for 14-inch bowl, 20x24 inches, complete ready for use. Size, bottom slab, 20x24 inches.

Price, with 8-inch back, each $4.50
Price, with 10-inch back, each...... 4.75
Price, with 12-inch back, each...... 5.00

Marble Slabs for Corner.

No. 84814 **White Marble Slabs for Corner Basin,** finished and polished complete, ready for use. Price includes two backs for corner. Size, square part, 20 inches.

Price, with 8-in. back, $4.90
Price, with 10-in. back, 5.30
Price, with 12-in back, 5.70

Brackets for Basin Slabs.

No. 840144¼ **Steel Brackets, Nickel Plated,** suitable for Nos. 84813 and 84814 basin slabs. Size, 16x18 inches. Price, per pair......75c

Plugs with Rubber Stoppers.

No. 84815 **Patent Overflow Basin Plugs** with rubber stoppers; made of solid brass, nickel plated.

Size, 1-inch. Price, each......45c
Size, 1¼-inch. Price, each......50c

Safety Chain.

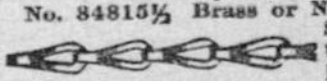

No. 84815½ **Brass or Nickel Plated Safety Chain** to be used on plugs, stoppers, closet pulls, etc.

Size	00	0
Per yard, brass	7c	9c
Per yard, nickel	9c	10c

Range Boilers.

RANGE BOILERS ARE USED only where there is a water supply furnished with constant pressure through pipes—which can only be obtained in towns and cities having water works.

No. 84816 **Galvanized Steel Range Boilers,** tested to 160 pounds pressure. We furnish our boilers complete with inside tubes and brass couplings for lead pipe.

Gallons	Height	Weight	Price, each
30	60 in.	72 lbs.	$ 9.30
35	60 in.	76 lbs.	11.00
40	60 in.	85 lbs.	11.60
52	60 in.	120 lbs.	18.00
63	60 in.	150 lbs.	24.90

Cast Iron Stands.

No. 84818 **Cast Iron Stands for Range Boilers.** Price, each......90c

Elevator Bucket Bolts.

No. 1 Elevator Bucket Bolts, with corrugated flat heads
No. 85935

Size	Per dozen	Per 100
¾x¼-inch	16c	$1.00
⅞x¼-inch	17c	1.10
1 x¼-inch	18c	1.15

Button Head Elevator Bucket Bolts.

No. 85936

Size	Per dozen	Per 100
¾x¼-inch	12c	79c
⅞x¼-inch	13c	82c
1 x¼-inch	14c	84c

Slot Head Elevator Bucket Bolts.

No. 85937

Size	Per dozen	Per 100
¾x¼-inch	12c	$1.05
⅞x¼-inch	13c	1.15
1x¼-inch	14c	1.26

Acme Patent Gate Hanger.

No. 85940 This is the Gate Hanger You Want for the following reasons: It is the most practical device known for hanging and operating a common farm gate. The price is so low and the hanger so simple and perfect in every respect that almost every farmer becomes a purchaser as soon as he sees it. It is designed, as the cut clearly shows, for a style of gate that every farmer has or can make cheaper and easier than any other. It is double pivoted, supports a gate perpendicularly, and is so strong and simple it cannot get out of order. The weight of the gate hangs on the center and at its strongest point. The hanger is made of steel, and is fastened near the center of the post with two lag bolts, and does not project or have weak points.

Price, per set....................................50c

Our $3.25 Truck with Sack Holder.

No. 85950 This is an implement that is almost indispensable on the farm. It is worth its cost a dozen times over every season. We believe it is **the best combination truck and sack holder made.** We can guarantee it superior to those offered by many at from $3.50 to $5.00. The illustration represents the sack placed on the holder and truck ready for filling. The holder is composed of a semi-circular malleable casting, to which is hinged a steel spring bar. The casting has a flange on the outside over which the sack is placed. The spring bar is then brought over the top of the flange and placed directly under it. This holds the sack firmly and cannot injure it in the least.

Our price for truck with combination sack holder, complete....................................$3.25

Trucks.

No. 85951 Warehouse Truck (like cut). Hardwood, well ironed, neatly finished. Axles turned and wheels bored. **Steel nose, side straps, axles and legs. We guarantee this the best truck on the market, and, quality considered, 20 per cent cheaper in price than any other.**

No.	Length handles	Width	Weight	Price
1	3 feet 11 inches	19 inches	44 pounds	$3.10
2	4 feet 4 inches	20 inches	56 pounds	3.60
3	4feet 8 inches	22 inches	77 pounds	5.25

Daisy Truck.

No. 85952 Daisy Truck, with steam bent handles. Length of handle, 46 inches; width at nose, 12 inches; at upper cross-bar, 17½ inches. Weight, 30 pounds.

Price, each....................................$1.35

The Phœnix Barrel Truck.

No. 85953 This Truck is nicely made, strong and durable, and is necessary in every store, warehouse or factory. It is adapted to any size barrel, keg or box. The handiest truck ever made for carrying garbage barrels and ash cans, as by simply setting the nose of the truck against the barrel and dropping the handle-hook over the chine, the barrel is loaded on the truck without being touched by the hands. Price, each....................................$1.35

Wheelbarrows.

This wheelbarrow is well made. Has full sized tray wheel 16 inches in diameter. When packed for shipment wheel is bolted on inside of tray and legs are folded on side of handle. Can be easily set up by any one.

No. 85954 Half Bolted Railroad Wheelbarrow, with wood wheel. Each....................................$1.55

No. 85955 Half Bolted Railroad Wheelbarrow, with steel wheel. Each....................................$1.75

Acme Steel Tray Wheelbarrow.

No. 85957 The handles and frame of these barrows are made of the best selected hardwood. Trays are of heavy sheet steel with edges turned over. Just the thing for canal, firemen, etc. Tray is made of No. 16 sheet steel with No. 1 steel wheels.

Price, each....................................$2.40

Lawn Wheelbarrow.

No. 85959 This is the handsomest and best Lawn Wheelbarrow made. They are fitted with steel wheels, 16 inches in diameter. **These wheels are constructed on the latest improved model of the bicycle.** Size of front, 12 inches by 19 inches; sides 12 inches by 28 inches; bottom, 21 inches by 27 inches. Weight, 40 pounds.

Our special price for this wheelbarrow.......$2.80

Boys' Barrow.

No. 85960 To meet the growing demand for a small well-made barrow, we have placed this barrow on the market. No poor material is used in its construction. It is well made throughout; nicely painted and striped. The legs are braced diagonally across, and have an iron brace around the bottom of the leg, making it very strong and neat in appearance. Put together entirely with bolts and easily set up. Size of bed, wheel end, 14 inches; handle end, 17 inches; length, 22 inches; depth, 9¼ inches; wheel, 17 inches in diameter; height ⅝-inch spokes; tire, ⅞x⅛-inch; axle ⅝-inch; weight, 20 pounds.

Price, each....................................$2.15

Mortar Wheelbarrow.

Tight box for wheeling mortar. Top, iron banded, iron braced and well bolted. Size of box at top, 27 inches wide at wheel; 30 inches long. Size of box at bottom, 19 inches wide, 20 inches long. Box 14 inches deep at wheel, 9 inches deep at handles. Frame is made of selected hardwood, full bolted. Weight, 40 pounds.

No. 85961 Price, wood wheel, each $2.75

No. 85962 Price, steel wheel, each.......... 2.90

Clipper Garden Wheelbarrow.

No. 85964 Clipper Garden Wheelbarrow is strong, well made. **Frame is made of selected hardwood.** Mortised joints. Legs are one solid piece of wood which adds greatly to their strength and beauty. Nicely painted and striped. **The best garden barrow made at any price.** With steel wheel.

Price....................................$3.35

Bent Handle Stone Barrow.

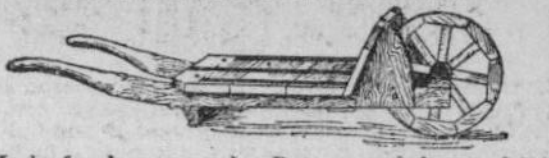

Made for heavy work. Bottom and front of 1¼-inch hardwood, dressed and well seasoned. Barrows painted brown. Size of bottom, 28 inches wide, 27 inches long and 11 inches high in front. Handles 2x3 inches, dressed, made of oak, rock elm or hickory.

No. 83966 Price, wood wheel, each..........$4.25

No. 85967 Price, steel wheel, each......... 4.40

No. 85970 The tray is made of one piece of No. 16 steel of the same thickness throughout. The edges of the trays are flanged and turned over a ³⁄₁₆-inch steel rod. This rod prevents the tray from breaking at the edge and makes it very much stronger. As the steel of the tray is of **uniform thickness, there are no thin corners to give out after using a short time.** These barrows are made to dump forward and are so constructed that at the dumping point they will not run back on the operator. They are well bolted and braced and made of the best material and painted. The wheels revolve on a heavy bolt which also passes through the handles and so materially strengthens the barrow.

Price, each....................................$5.25

Solid Pressed Steel Tray Barrow.

Coal and coke barrow, with one-piece tubular steel frame extending around in front of the wheel. Frame strongly braced and well ironed. The tray is made of best quality of steel, with wired edge. They will carry from 400 to 450 pounds of coal or five bushels of coke. Fitted with our extra heavy No. 4 wheel, 17 inches in diameter, tire 2¼x⅞-inch, nine ⅝-inch spokes, ¾-inch axle.

No. 85972 Gauge of steel in tray, 15; length of tray on top, 41½ inches; width of tray on top, 32 inches; depth at wheel, 12 inches; capacity, 6 cubic feet; weight, 95 pounds. Price, each...........$8.00

No. 85973 Gauge of steel in tray, 13; length of tray on top, 41½ inches; width of tray on top, 33 inches; depth at wheel, 12 inches; capacity, 6 cubic feet; weight, 110 pounds. Price, each..........$8.65

Boss Charcoal Peanut Roaster.

No. 85980 The Boss Peanut and Coffee Roaster is the only successful Roaster on the market. The material used in their construction is the finest grade smooth-rolled sheet steel for the roasters, and XX bright tin and 16-ounce cold-rolled copper for the warmers. Peanuts roasted in the Boss Roaster retain that delicate flavor which is essential to the good peanut, and which is only obtained through perfect roasting.

Prices are F. O. B. Factory.

With Tin Warmer.		With Copper Warmer.	
Size, 1 peck..........	$10.15	Size, 1 peck....	$15.00
Size, ½ bushel.......	12.25	Size, ½ bushel.	17.50
Size, 1 bushel........	16.30	Size, 1 bushel.	21.60

When ordering be sure and state size wanted; also tin or copper warmer.

Boss Gasoline Peanut Roasters.

No. 85981 Our Gasoline Roaster is made of the same material as the Charcoal Burner; has our new improved burners which makes it the most complete machine sold by anyone. No smoke, dust or ashes. So simple a boy can operate them. The fire can be started in a half minute. No more soggy or burnt peanuts, as these machines have steam heaters. 10 cents per day will roast and keep your peanuts or coffee warm and increase your trade 100 per cent.

Price, With Tin Warmer		Price. With Copper Warmer	
Size, 1 peck.......	$13.50	Size, 1 peck..........	$17.50
Size, ½ bushel...	16.85	Size, ½ bushel......	20.50
Size, 1 bushel,.....	23.00	Size, 1 bushel......	24.30

AGRICULTURAL IMPLEMENT DEPARTMENT.

PLOWS. We are headquarters for everything in the line of Plows. Our line of riding and walking plows is for quality, draught and all requirements second to none. Our plows are made for us under contract by several of the largest and most reliable makers in the country, concerns who have devoted their life's work to the manufacture of this class of goods and are turning out the highest grade of work that can be produced. Our line of Riding and Walking Plows for the western prairies is, we believe, without exception the BEST ON THE MARKET.

....THERE IS NOTHING SUPERIOR TO OUR PRAIRIE BREAKING PLOWS....

If indeed there is anything on the market that will equal them. Our Texas and Southern Style Plows are designed and made especially for that territory, and guaranteed to scour in any soil.

WE ISSUE A BINDING GUARANTEE WITH EVERY PLOW

by the terms and conditions of which if it fails to scour and is not found exactly as represented, or if any piece or part gives out by reason of defect in material or workmanship within two years, we will replace it free of charge. Do not pay your local dealer long retail prices when we can save you 33⅓ to 50 per cent. We can sell you a plow for as little or less money than your local dealer can buy in quantities.

PRICES ON ALL OUR PLOWS ARE NET CASH WITH ORDER. NO DISCOUNT.

The S., R. & Co.'s Scotch Clipper Turf and Stubble Plows.

In our S., R. & Co.'s Scotch Clipper we offer the best steel beam walking plow on the market. It is a plow that we guarantee to scour in any soil. It is especially adapted to the prairies of Kansas and Nebraska, Minnesota and the Dakotas, but is used in every state. Our Scotch Clipper Plows are guaranteed to be the lightest, strongest, easiest running and best general purpose plows on earth. The mould-board is made out of the very best soft center cast steel, extra hardened. The points and landsides are soft center steel. This makes a plow suited for all soils and all kinds of plowing. The clevis is a large strong malleable iron clevis, which can be set so that the plow can be used either with two or three horses. In ordering Plows always state kind of soil you wish to use them in and we will send you a plow of the right temper, etc. If we ask is a Trial Order, and if you do not say this is the Best Plow you ever used you can return same at our expense. For an easy running, light, well balanced plow the Scotch Clipper has no equal. Try one and be convinced. Be sure to state whether right or left hand plow is wanted. These Plows have Steel Beams, steel mould-boards, steel points, and land sides. We guarantee them to be the equal of any plow made, or money refunded. Will scour in any soil.

No. 86390 12 in. cut turf or stubble. Price, $11.25
No. 86391 14 in. cut turf or stubble. Price, 11.50
No. 86392 16 in. cut turf or stubble. Price, 11.75
NOTICE.—If you prefer Wood Beam in place of Steel Beam, you can deduct 35 cents from the above prices.

EXTRAS.
No. 86393 13-inch Star Rolling Coulters for above plows. Price, each.............$2.25

General Purpose Plows.

No. 86400 Our General Purpose Plow is an all steel plow that is made with long easy turn to mould-board and is thoroughly a general purpose plow. We can guarantee it for all kinds of work, such as stubble, tame sod, old pastures, etc. Where you have only a limited number of plows this is the one to buy. Mould-board is made of high grade plow steel, the double shin soft center steel, extra heavy landside. They are constructed in a perfect manner and of the best material money will buy. Made right or left hand, wood or steel beam. We always ship right-hand, unless otherwise ordered.

	Wood Beam		Steel Beam
Size, 12 inches.	Price...$11.65	Price...$12.00
Size, 13 inches.	Price...12.15	Price...12.50
Size, 14 inches.	Price...12.65	Price...13.00

EXTRAS.
Size, 12 inch shares. Price, each...........$2.00
Size, 13 inch shares. Price, each........... 2.35
Size, 14 inch shares. Price, each........... 2.50

One Horse Gardener's Plow.

No. 86432 One Horse 8-inch Cut Wood Plow, used mostly by gardeners and for plowing up to corn, potatoes, etc. It has all the improvements of our High Grade Plows, is a very popular plow among gardeners and small truck farmers. Light and strong and well finished. Best white oak beam and handles. Has steel mould-board, cast point and landside. Price, each........................$6.95

All Steel Wood Beam Pony Plows.

WOOD BEAM.

Our light steel plows are guaranteed to do good service in the work they are intended for. They are very durable and are guaranteed against breakage when caused by manifest defects in workmanship or material. They have steel standard and cap, sloping landside and adjustable slip heel. Extra share furnished with each plow.

No. 86433 One-Horse Steel Plow is 7 inch cut, weighs 38 lbs. Will do superior work in cotton and all corn lands. It is also successfully used for gardening purposes. Price, each....................$2.12

No. 86435 One-Horse Plow is, 8-inch cut, weighs 42 lbs. Will do superior work in cotton and corn lands. Also well adapted for gardening purposes. Price, each....................$2.48

No. 86437 One-Horse or Light Two-Horse Plow, is 9-inch cut, weighs 50 lbs. Is designed for either stubble or light sod, doing both kinds of work in the most perfect manner. Very light draft. It does superior work in cotton and corn lands and truck gardens. It does decidedly more work than its width of cut would indicate. Price, each....$2.79

No. 86439 Two-Horse Plow is 10-inch cut. Wood beam steel shares. Weight, 60 pounds.
Price, each.............$3.33

No. 86441 Two-Horse Plow is 11-inch cut, adapted for either light sod or stubble. Weight, 65 lbs. Price, each..................$4.56

$3.02 All-Steel, Steel-Beam Pony Plow.

STEEL BEAM.

Extra Share furnished with each Plow.

No. 86434 One-Horse Steel Plow is 7-inch cut, weighs 38 pounds. Will do superior work in cotton and all corn lands. It is also successfully used for gardening purposes. With steel beam...........$3.02

No. 86436 One-Horse Plow is 8-inch cut, weighs 42 pounds. Will do superior work in cotton and corn lands. Also well adapted for gardening purposes. With steel beam....................$3.33

No. 86438 One-Horse or Light Two-Horse Plow is 9-inch cut. Weighs 50 pounds. Is designed for either stubble or light sod, doing both kinds of work in the most perfect manner. Very light draft. It does superior work in cotton and corn lands and truck gardens. It does decidedly more work than its width of cut would indicate. With steel beam...$3.69

No. 86440 Two-Horse Plow is 10-inch cut, steel shares and steel beams. Weight, 60 pounds. With steel beam....................$4.82

No. 86442 Two-Horse Plow is 11-inch cut, adapted for either light sod or stubble. Weight, 65 pounds. With steel beam...................$5.50

Our $4.00 Full Chilled Plows.

No. 86444 Sears, Roebuck & Co.'s Full Chilled Plows. In all sections where chilled plows are used, our plows will be readily recognized, and our price on plows and repairs appreciated. We use on the same lines as the original Oliver Plows. As a sand soil plow they have no equal. See the following prices:

	Turns for plow, inches	Depth of furrow, inches	Weight pounds	Price
A Right hand only	8	4½	50	$4.00
B Right hand only	10	5	65	4.75
10 Right hand only	11	5¾	70	5.35
13 Right or left....	11	6	85	6.35
19 Right or left....	12	6¼	100	6.50
20 Right or left....	14	7	112	7.00
E1 Right or left....	14	7	125	7.25
40 Right or left....	16	9	130	7.40
Price of jointer, extra.....				1.50
Lead wheel and standard, extra...........				.75

Prices of Repairs for Chilled Plows.

No. 86445 Prices of Repairs. Warranted to fit any of the chilled plows we send out. Be sure and state whether plows or shares are wanted to turn furrow to the right or to the left.

	Standard	Mold'bd	Lan'side	Shares Plain
A Right............	$1.00	$1.00	$0.32	$0.20
B Right............	1.25	1.40	.42	.21
10 Right............	1.35	1.50	.45	.24
13 Right or left....	1.60	1.65	.54	.26
19 Right or left....	1.70	1.90	.57	.27
20 Right or left....	1.80	2.10	.58	.29
E1 Right or left....	1.90	2.25	.59	.30
40 Right or left....	2.00	2.25	.60	.31
Jointer points......				.16
Mould-boards......				.42

Acme Vineyard Plow.

Our Old Reliable One-Horse Chilled Plow is the best plow made for nurseries, orchards, vineyards, and all one-horse work. The beam is adjustable so the horse can walk in the furrow or on the land. The handles can be shifted to right or left, which enables the plowman to walk away from the row of trees or shrubs. The shape of mould-board makes the plow light draft and also cleans out the furrow in loose soil. Will turn a furrow 8 inches to a vineyard plow it is the finest made. As a vineyard plow it is the finest made.
No. 86446 Plain without wheel or coulter..$9.00

EXTRAS. Price, each
No. 86448 Gauge Wheel....................$1.10
No. 86449 Coulters........................ 1.00

Our $10.35 Steel Beam Brush Plows.

We have here a

DOUBLE STEEL BEAM PLOW THAT IS A WORLD-BEATER when you have Rough and Rooty Land to break up.

It is very strong, the beam being double, that is, made of two steel beams placed side by side. This makes a beam much more rigid than a solid piece of steel, also lighter. It has an extra high curve, which allows brush, etc., to pass through—cannot foul or choke up. It also makes an excellent plow for road work, in fact, is a first-class, all-around plow, where strength and durability are required. The braces and handles are extra heavy. In short, we have here a plow that will outlast any wood beam plow made. It does not weigh as much as some of the clumsy plows sold by other firms, and is warranted to give perfect satisfaction, or money refunded. We make this plow straight with wheel and foot coulter, but furnish it with or without, as desired. Has steel mould-boards, cast points, and cuts 13 inches. Made in right hand only.

No. 86456 13-inch cut, without wheel or coulter. Price.................$10.35
No. 86457 13-inch cut, with wheel and coulter, as shown in cut. Price.................$13.00
No. 86458 Extra Gauge Wheels each. .75
No. 86459 Foot Coulters and Clasps, each .90
No. 86463 Knife Coulters and Clasps, each 1.00

Acme Hand-Dump Hay Rake.

At **$13.25 to $15.50**, according to size, we offer **OUR ACME HAND-DUMP HAY RAKE**, under our binding guarantee as the equal of any Hand Dump Rake on the market.

WE CAN SAVE YOU, after paying freight, from **$6.00 to $10.00** on a hand dump rake, and guarantee to furnish you as good a rake as it is possible to build.

SEND US YOUR ORDER, and if you do not find the rake in every way satisfactory, return it at our expense of freight charges both ways and we will refund your money.

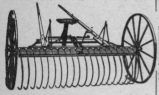

For larger illustrations and more complete descriptions of hay rakes write for Special Hay Rake Circular.

This is a strictly first-class balance hand dump 8 ft. rake, made with 20 steel teeth of the highest grade of steel carefully tempered. It has wrought iron wheel spindles and the axle is stiffened by a truss rod, which prevents any sagging. In operative qualities it will meet the requirements of the farmer, being a perfect lock lever which can be operated with great ease, while teeth cannot raise except when required to dump. The workmanship is first class. 20 teeth, 4¼ inches apart. Weight, 275 lbs.

No.		Price, each
No. 86808	20-tooth rake, wood wheels, 8 feet.	$13.25
No. 86809	20-tooth rake, steel wheels, 8 feet.	$13.90
No. 86810	24-tooth rake, wood wheels, 10 feet.	$14.00
No. 86811	24-tooth rake, steel wheels, 10 feet.	$15.50

Easy Self-Dump Hay Rake.

At **$17.75 TO $19.75**, according to size, we offer our **SELF-ACTING, AUTOMATIC, SELF-DUMP RAKE** as the best rake on the market, regardless of price; a rake combining all the good points of all high grade rakes with the defects of none.

OUR SPECIAL PRICES of **$17.75, $18.25, $18.75 and $19.75** are based on the actual cost of material and labor with but our one small profit added and will mean a saving to you of 25 to 50 per cent.

WE GUARANTEE EVERY RAKE, and if it is not found perfectly satisfactory, we will cheerfully refund your money.

These rakes are models of simplicity and neatness, though light and strong, and the most durable rake on the market, and we claim, the most perfect rake to work, the easiest to ride, the lightest draft and the simplest to operate. They are, in construction, an improvement in each rake from beginning to end; no important features in other rakes being left out, but many valuable ones added. Our patent steel runner tooth which prevents the rake from scratching or taking up grass roots, is connected to the rake head by metal tooth sections, carrying 5 and 6 teeth each and the same can be put on or taken out 1 section at a time. The rake dumps from both wheels, each ratchet being encased, which prevents the wheel from winding with hay; is noiseless in operation and drops back without the least jar. The dumping device is engaged by pressing the foot on the lever; the rake in operation, is entirely under the control of the operator by our improved foot treadle when raking rough or uneven ground. The cleaners or strippers are each oscillating independent of each other, and hold the hay from rolling when the rake is filling; prevents the same from sliding into the wheels. Our seat is one of great comfort, arranged upon an easy steel spring, adjustable to accommodate either a small boy or a man and arranged at a point of balance which prevents weight upon the horse's back. Weight 300 pounds.

No.		Price, each
No. 86812	20-Tooth, Wood Wheel Rake, 8 feet.	$17.75
No. 86813	20-Tooth, Steel Wheel Rake, 8 feet.	$18.25
No. 86814	24-Tooth, Wood Wheel Rake, 10 feet.	$18.75
No. 86815	24-Tooth, Steel Wheel Rake, 10 feet.	$19.75

Acme Hay Tedder.

No. 86816 The tedder forks are made of the very best quality crucible spring steel on our peculiar pattern, and the shape and sweep of the fork are just right to do perfect work. The convenient shifting device has two levers, one for raising and lowering frame, the other for throwing in and out of gear, which can be used easily without dismounting. Complete with shafts and pole attachments. Weight, 450 pounds.

For larger illustrations and more complete descriptions of Hay Tedders, write for Special Circular of Hay Tedders.

No. 1, 6-fork tedder, 8 feet.	Price.	$24.60
No. 2, 8-fork tedder, 10 feet.	Price.	27.10

Six-fork machines furnished with combination pole and shafts, for one or two horses. Eight-fork machine, with pole only, for two horses.

8-Foot Windmill, $16.50.

Acme Steel Windmill.

The **Acme Steel Mill** is the best mill on the market at anything like the price.

There are in this mill many points of superiority over any other. The mill is manufactured to do good service and last for years, instead of cheap affairs made only to sell, which blow to pieces in the first storm. We use a self-oiling oiler on pitman, carrying one month's supply of oil, which is too expensive to be put on cheaper mills made to sell at a less price. We have a positive brake, which effectually prevents the mill from turning when thrown out of gear. The wheel of this mill makes 2¾ revolutions to one stroke of the pump. Every mill is guaranteed, and can be used either on angle tower or wood tower. When ordering, be sure to state what kind of tower mill is wanted to be used on. The prices quoted are for the mills delivered on board the cars at our factory.

For larger illustrations and more complete description of windmills, write for Special Windmill Circular.

Prices include Wheel, Vane, Head, Pull-out Chain and Wire and 32-foot Pump Rod.

If you wish a Windmill sent **C. O. D.**, subject to examination, at our C. O. D. price, which is about 2 per cent higher than our cash-in-full with order price, send $3.00 with your order balance payable after received.

	Diameter of wheel	Weight complete	C. O. D. Price, Painted	Cash in full Price, Painted.
No. 86826	8-ft.	335 lbs.	$16.85	$16.50
No. 86827	9-ft.	375 lbs.	19.10	18.72
No. 86828	10-ft.	425 lbs.	21.40	20.95
No. 86829	12-ft.	765 lbs.	37.10	36.35

	Diameter of wheel	Weight complete	C. O. D. Price, Galvan'd	Cash in full Price, Galvan'd
No. 86826	8-ft.	335 lbs.	$18.53	$18.15
No. 86827	9-ft.	375 lbs.	21.35	20.92
No. 86828	10-ft.	425 lbs.	23.65	23.15
No. 86829	12-ft.	765 lbs.	40.50	39.65

The Acme Hay Loader for $45.00.

No. 86819 We offer this hay loader with the assurance that its possession will place its owner in the best position for taking care of his hay crop in the most economical manner. It is intended particularly as a swath loader, but will work very satisfactorily in windrows; in fact, where the hay is light it is better to rake it in windrows first. Weight, 800 pounds.

For larger illustrations and more complete description of Hay Tedders, write for Special Circular of Hay Tedders.

Our price.. **$45.00**

Our Celebrated Acme Power Windmill

No. 86833 This power mill is used for running machinery as well as for pumping water. We use an adjustable box at upper end of vertical shaft to adjust pinion to bevel gear, which is a grand feature in a power windmill, although much more expensive to make than the ordinary boxing. The prices quoted are for the mills delivered on board cars at our factory. On our power mills the shaft makes 5 revolutions to 1 revolution of the wheel. Prices given below include wheel, vane, head, pull-out chain and wire and 5 feet of vertical shafting. If you wish a windmill sent C. O. D., subject to examination at C. O. D. price, which is about 2 per cent higher than our cash-in-full with order price, send $3.00 with your order, balance payable after received.

Diam. of wheel	12 feet	14 feet	16 feet
Weight, complete, lbs.	900 lbs.	1,200 lbs.	1,700 lbs.
C.O.D. price, Painted.	$32.10	$51.75	$83.25
Cash price. Painted	36.35	50.70	81.55
C.J.D. price, Galvan'd	40.50	56.85	90.00
Cash price, Galvan'd	39.70	55.15	88.20

Acme Wood-Wheel Windmill.

It is made of the very best material possible to be obtained, and put together in such a manner as to combine both strength and durability. It is automatic in all movements. It has an adjustable brake to keep the wheel from turning or running when out of gear.

Prices below.

A reliable mill, at a fair price, is what the purchaser wants. A mill sold cheap must necessarily be made cheap; whereas a mill sold at a reasonable, living price enables the manufacturer to turn out good work. Will regulate and govern itself in any wind that blows, consequently requires no attention from any source. We have a positive brake, which effectually prevents the mill from running when thrown out of gear. When thrown in gear it will head to the wind instantly and when thrown out of gear it instantly turns edgeways to the wind and remains perfectly still. Can be used either on our patent tubular steel tower, angle steel tower or wood tower.

No. 86849 Price for this mill complete, with 10-foot wheel....................................**$25.00**

No. 86850 Price for this mill complete, with 12-foot wheel....................................**$35.00**

Prices for windmill includes all bolts for putting mill together and bolting it to tower; also pitman rod to attach mill to pump. In ordering, state whether mill is to be erected on wood or steel tower.

86849
to
86853

FOR LARGER ILLUSTRATIONS AND MORE COMPLETE DESCRIPTIONS OF WOOD WINDMILLS,
═══ WRITE FOR ═══
SPECIAL WINDMILL CIRCULAR.

WRITE FOR FREE BOOK OF SAMPLES OF ALL KINDS OF BUILDING (SHEATHING) PAPER AND PREPARED FELT ROOFING.

Four-Post Angle Steel Towers.

They are strongly braced with angle steel cross girts, running from corner post to corner post on every side, also by cross-rods running diagonally across each side of the tower. The anchor posts that we furnish with these towers are made of heavy angle steel, and at the bottom are riveted to anchor plates, that they can be secured to the foundation.

Towers for Power Mills are provided with supports for boxes for the vertical shafting, being made so as to attach the timbers for foot gear, pumping jack or feed grinders. **If you wish a windmill tower sent C. O. D., send $3.00 with your order, balance payable after received.**

C. O. D. PRICES.

Height	For 8-foot Pump Mill.		For 9 and 10-foot Pump Mill.		For 12-foot Pump Mill.	
	No. 86834 Painted	No. 86840 Galv'z'd	No. 86841 Painted	No. 86842 Galv'z'd	No. 86843 Painted	No. 86844 Galv'z'd
20 ft	$14.65	$15.75	$16.85	$18.00	$21.35	$22.45
30 ft	20.25	21.35	22.50	23.60	29.30	30.35
40 ft	25.25	27.00	27.55	29.25	37.05	39.35
50 ft	32.62	34.85	34.90	37.10	47.25	50.60
60 ft	40.60	42.75	42.75	45.00	58.50	61.90
CASH WITH ORDER PRICES.						
20 ft	$14.36	$15.43	$16.51	$17.64	$20.92	$22.00
30 ft	19.85	20.92	22.05	23.13	28.71	29.74
40 ft	24.75	26.46	27.00	28.65	36.31	38.56
50 ft	32.00	34.16	34.20	36.36	46.30	49.59
60 ft	39.79	41.89	41.90	44.10	57.33	60.67

Steel Towers for Power Mills.

C. O D. PRICES.

Height	For 12 and 14-foot Power Mill.		For 16-ft. Power Mill.	
	No. 86845 Painted	No. 86346 Galvan'ed	No. 86847 Painted	No. 86848 Galvan'ed
20 feet	$23.60	$24.75	$30.35	$33.75
30 feet	31.50	32.60	39.38	42.75
40 feet	39.35	41.60	51.75	55.10
50 feet	49.50	52.90	65.25	68.60
60 feet	60.75	64.10	78.75	82.10
CASH IN FULL PRICE.				
20 feet	$23.13	$24.25	$29.65	$33.08
30 feet	30.87	31.95	38.59	41.90
40 feet	38.56	40.77	50.72	54.00
50 feet	48.50	51.84	63.95	67.23
60 feet	59.53	63.82	77.17	80.46

Foot Gear for our Acme Power Windmills.

The Foot Gear is designed to transmit power from the vertical shaft of a power windmill to horizontal shafting.

No. 86860 One end of the horizontal shaft is provided with a half clutch to engage with horizontal line shafting; on the other end we furnish a pulley of suitable diameter with a 5-inch face.

The vertical shaft of the Foot Gear projects about 18 inches upward from the horizontal shaft.

We furnish necessary bolts.

For 12 and 14-foot Power Mills, weight 100 pounds with 18x5 inch pulley. C. O. D. price............$7.42
Cash with order price............ 7.27
For 16-foot Power Mill, weight 140 pounds with 24x5 inch pulley. C. O. D. Price............11.25
Cash with order price............11.00

Windmill Feed Grinder.

To attach to mast for power mills.

No. 86862 For use with power windmills. The burrs are conical. An extra set of burrs is furnished with each Grinder. When the Grinder and the mill are running there is no danger of the burrs running together; they will therefore last until worn out by actual grinding of grain. The pulley furnished with this Grinder is 18 inches in diameter by 5 inch face.
Weight, 115 pounds. C. O. D. Price..........$13.50
Cash with order price.... 13.23

Pump Jack.

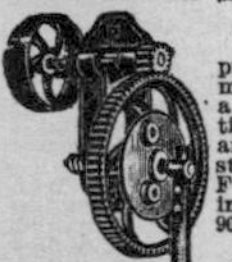

No. 86864 To operate a pump with a power windmill it is necessary to have a jack to convert the rotary motion into an up-and-down. It is arranged for three lengths of stroke, so as to fit any pump. Furnished complete, with a 10x4-inch pulley, bolts, etc. Weight, 90 pounds. C. O. D. price..$7.43
Cash with order price...... 7.28

No. 86868 Our Boss Windmill Grinder can be used in connection with any pumping mill, no matter what size or make. Will grind any kind of grain separate or mixed. The grinder consists of a double metal case and 3 burrs two remaining stationary while the third revolves in the center, producing a double grinding surface which is **double the capacity of any grinder made. We furnish this grinder with an elbow to attach same to connect to pump rod.** It can be changed from grinding coarse to fine by turning one nut.

Price, complete............$8.50

Quadrants.

For Either Pumping or Power Mills.

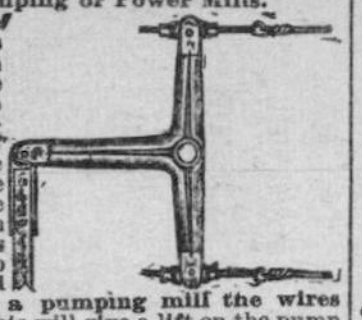

No. 86870 Our Acme Quadrant or Levers are used in connection with mill where same is placed at a distance from pump. We furnish two levers, one of which we show in the cut. These levers are alike in form and are connected with each other by two wires which run from one to the other. **When used in connection with a pumping mill the wires should be crossed;** this will give a lift on the pump with the up stroke of the mill. Price includes two levers and take-up bolts, pump-pole connections and the pivot plates and bolts.
C. O. D. price, per set............$3.35
Cash with order price............ 3.30
C. O. D. price, per 100 feet wire for above..... .67
Cash with order price............ .65

Windmill Guy Rods.

No. 86871 Guy Rods for 12-foot and 14-foot power windmill masts, per set of four rods, each not over 15 feet long, including turn-buckles and end bolts.
C. O. D. price, per set............$4.50
Cash with order price............ 4.40

Windmill Pump Cushion.

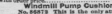

No. 86872 This is the only attachment ever invented that cushions the stroke of the pump. The accompanying cut suggests a cushion spring of the simplest construction, and should be regarded indispensable in every windmill pump connection, **saving the wear and tear of both mill and pump.** It fits all mills, and will attach in the same manner as any common pump connection; directions of attaching sent with each.
Price, each............$1.50

Pumping Jacks.

No. 86873 For Operating Windmill Pump by Horse or Tread Power in times of light wind or calms; can be connected to any horse-power; stroke 4 to 16 inches; **balance wheel, 300 lbs.; complete jack, weight, 600 lbs.**
Price............$16.65

Speeding Jacks.

No. 86873½ Bevel Jacks, used only in connection with a horse-power to increase the speed. Is connected to end of tumbling rod and transmits motion in the same direction. Furnished with 15-inch pulley, made in one size, for 2 or 4 horse-power only; weight, 100 lbs. Price. $10.35

Spur or Bevel Jacks.

No. 86874 This cut represents our Bevel Gear Jack, for increasing speed and transmitting power by belt. The Spur Gear Jack transmits the motion at a right angle with the tumbling rod and the Bevel Gear Jack transmits the motion in a line with the tumbling rod. Be sure and state which style is wanted. **Spur or Bevel.**
Adapted for 2-horse power: pulley revolves to one revolution of tumbling rod 2¼ times.
Price, each............$6.50
Adapted for 4 horse-power; pulley revolves to one revolution of tumbling rod 2¾ times. Price, $10.00

Bevel Jack.

SNo. 86874½ Bevel Speeding Jack; 20 cogs in pinion; speed, to 1; transmits motion by belt in same direction that tumbling rod extends from power; this jack is strong enough for 2 or 4 horse-power; is furnished with pulley, 15 inches in diameter and 5 inch face; weight, 150 pounds. Price, each............$10.25

Iron Frame Bevel-Geared Jack.

No. 86875 This Jack is intended for any 4 or 6 horse-power. Is made extra strong; can furnish either 16, 18 or 24-in. pulleys as desired. Furnished with slip knuckle, complete, ready to receive tumbling rod. Weight, 185 pounds. Price, each............$15.00

The Celebrated Acme Windmill Grinders for $15.00.

No. 86878 The illustration shows this mill with the pulley attachment, and the smaller illustration shows the sprocket wheel attachment. The sprocket grinder was gotten up especially for chain windmills and is adapted to 12 to 14-feet geared wheels. The sprocket wheels are 6 and 10 inches in diameter, fitted with link chain and belting. We can also furnish the link belting and **driving sprocket with spring** clutch complete for line shaft on windmill, which taken together makes a complete outfit at a very reasonable price. **Capacity 8 to 15 bushels per hour according to the velocity of the wind and size of wheel used.** In ordering this kind of a mill be sure to give the diameter of the line shaft if driving sprocket and spring clutch are wanted.

The pulley grinder is similar in all respects to the sprocket grinder, as described above, only it is furnished with a 6 or 9-inch pulley with a 6-inch face.
Price, with 3 sets 6-inch burrs............$15.00
Price of 6-inch burrs, per set............ 1.25
Price of 20 feet of link chain belting............ 6.00
Price for 6 and 10-inch double-driving sprocket with spring clutch complete, with line shaft for windmill............ 3.75

Our $12.00 Grist Mill.

No. 86879 This Mill is the simplest horizontal ring burr mill on the market, with a positive force feed; is superior to burrs running perpendicularly. It is furnished with 6-inch ring burrs, positive auger force feed, strong and compact and is arranged for tumbling rod or belt. The shaft on which the burr rests is flexible and adjustable, thereby avoiding any breakage should nails or any hard substance come in contact with the burrs. Will grind shell corn and all kinds of small grain but not corn on the ear. Capacity ten to twenty-five bushels per hour. Speed required 300 to 250 revolutions per minute. Height, 2 feet, 6 inches, over all 3 feet, 10 inches.
Weight, 135 pounds. Price, each............$12.00

Big Giant Improved Grinding Mills.

A mill with the greatest capacity and most even grinding of all kinds of grain ever offered to the farmer. Automatic in feeding, simple in construction, scientific in principle, looked upon by feeders as the gem of all grinders; requires 2 to 10 horse-power, according to size and speed.

No. 86880 The No. 9 Belt Mill, 6-inch burrs; capacity, 10 to 35 bushels per hour. Weight, 175 lbs.
Price of mill............$17.00
Extra burrs, set............ 1.10

No. 86881 The No. 10 Size, 6-inch burrs geared for attachment to tumbling rod; capacity, 10 to 38 bushels per hour; weight, 225 lbs. Price of mill, $19.75
Extra burrs, per set............ 1.10

No. 86882 The No. 7 size Belt Mill, 8-inch burrs; weight, 250 lbs; capacity, 20 to 30 bushels per hour. Price of mill............$22.00
Extra burrs, per set............ 1.15

No. 86883 The No. 8 size, gear for attaching to tumbling rod; 8-inch burrs; capacity, 20 to 30 bushels per hour; weight, 275 lbs.
Price of mill, $24.90; extra burrs, per set............$1.15

No. 86883

No. 86884

No. 86884 No. 5 Double Mill, has just double the capacity of No. 3 belt mill 2 sets of 8-inch burrs in operation at one time, one on each end of shaft; weight, 400 pounds.
Price of mill............$42.50
Extra burrs, per set. 1.35

Nos. 10 and 8 have 12-inch pulley to connect with corn sheller; 3 sets burrs furnished with each of above mills.

For Larger Illustrations and More Complete Descriptions of

FEED MILLS

Write for Special Feed Mill Circular.

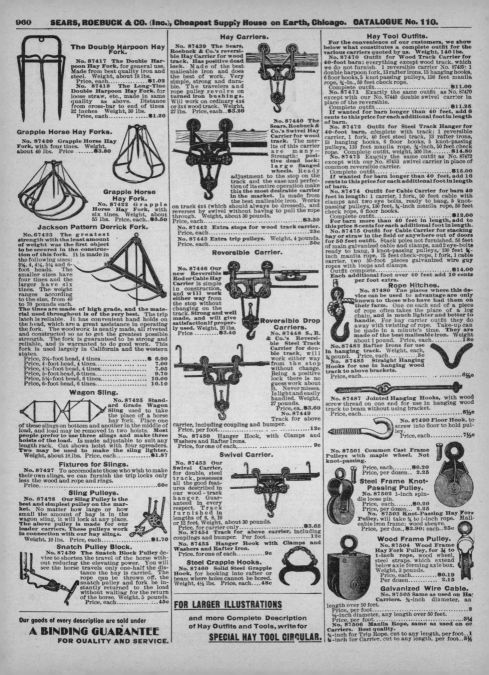

The Double Harpoon Hay Fork.

No. 87417 The Double Harpoon Hay Fork, for general use. Made from best quality iron and steel. Weight, about 18 lbs. Price, each............**$1.02**

No. 87418 The Long-Tine Double Harpoon Hay Fork, for loose straw, etc., made in same quality as above. Distance from cross-bar to end of tines 32 inches. Weight, 30 lbs. Price, each............**$1.20**

Grapple Horse Hay Forks.

No. 87420 Grapple Horse Hay Fork, with four tines. Weight, about 40 lbs. Price **$3.80**

Grapple Horse Hay Fork.

No. 87422 Grapple Horse Hay Fork, with six tines. Weight, about 55 lbs. Price, each..**$5.50**

Jackson Pattern Derrick Fork.

No. 67423 The greatest strength with the least amount of weight was the first object to be secured in the construction of this fork. It is made in the following sizes:
3½, 4, 4½, 5½ and 6-foot heads. The smaller sizes and the larger have six tines. The weight ranges according to the size, from 40 to 70 pounds each.

The tines are made of high grade, and the material used throughout is of the very best. The trip latch is reliable. It has convenient hand holds on the head, which are a great assistance in operating the fork. The woodwork is neatly made, all riveted and constructed so as to get the greatest possible strength. The fork is guaranteed to be strong and reliable, and is warranted to do good work. This fork is used largely in California and the western states.

Price, 3½-foot head, 4 tines...............$ 6.90
Price, 4-foot head, 4 tines............... 7.00
Price, 4½-foot head, 4 tines............... 7.05
Price, 5-foot head, 6 tines............... 9.70
Price, 5½-foot head, 6 tines............... 10.00
Price, 6-foot head, 6 tines............... 10.10

Wagon Sling.

No. 87425 Standard Grade Wagon Sling used to take the place of a horse hay fork. Place one of these slings on bottom and another in the middle of load, and load may be removed in two hoists. Most people prefer to use three slings and make three hoists of the load. Is made adjustable to suit any length rack. Cut shows hoist with four spreaders. Two may be used to make the sling lighter. Weight, about 18 lbs. Price, each........**$1.87**

Fixtures for Slings.

No. 87427 To accomodate those who wish to make their own slings, we can furnish the trip locks only less the wood and rope and rings. Price.........................**60c**

Sling Pulleys.

No. 87428 Our Sling Pulley is the best and simplest pulley on the market. No matter how large or how small the amount of hay is in the wagon sling, it will lock at any place. The above pulley is made for our leader carriers. These pulleys work in connection with our hay slings. Weight, 10 lbs. Price, each............**$1.70**

Snatch Pulley Block.

No. 87430 The Snatch Block Pulley device to shorten the travel of the horse without reducing the elevating power. You will see the horse travels only one-half the distance the hay is carried. The rope can be thrown off, the snatch pulley and fork be instantly returned to the load without waiting for the return of the horse. Weight, 5 pounds. Price, each.................**45c**

Our goods of every description are sold under

A BINDING GUARANTEE
FOR QUALITY AND SERVICE.

Hay Carriers.

No. 87439 The Sears, Roebuck & Co.'s reversible Hay Carrier for wood track. Has positive dead lock. Made of the best malleable iron and does the best of work. Very simple, strong and durable. The travelers and rope pulley revolve on turned iron bushings. Will work on ordinary 4x4 or 3x4 wood track. Weight, 27 lbs. Price, each..**$3.20**

No. 87440 The Sears, Roebuck & Co.'s Swivel Hay Carrier for wood track. The merits of this carrier are many—Strength: positive dead lock; large flanged wheels. Ready adjustment to the stop on the track and the ease and perfection of its entire operation make this the most desirable carrier in the market. It is made from the best malleable iron. Works on track 4x4 (which should always be dressed), and reverses by swivel without having to pull the rope through. Weight, about 30 pounds. Price, each...............**$3.50**

No. 87442 Extra stops for wood track carrier. Price, each...............25c

No. 87443 Extra trip pulleys. Weight, 4 pounds. Price, each...............50c

Reversible Carrier.

No. 87446 Our new Reversible Rod or Cable Hay Carrier is simple in construction, and will work either way from the stop without changing on the track. Strong and well made, and will give satisfaction if properly used. Weight, 20 lbs. Price...............**$3.40**

Reversible Drop Carriers.

No. 87448 S., R. & Co.'s Reversible Steel Track Carrier for double track, will work either way from the stop without change. Being a positive lock there is no guess work about it. Never misses. Is light and easily handled. Weight, 27 pounds. Price, ea...**$3.60**

No. 87449 Track for above carrier, including coupling and bumper. Price, per foot...............12c

No. 87450 Hanger Hook, with Clamps and Washers and Rafter Irons. Price, for one of each...............9c

Swivel Carrier.

No. 87453 Our Swivel Carrier, for double, steel track, possesses all the good features described in our wood-track hanger. Guaranteed in every respect. Track furnished in lengths of 6, 8, 10 or 12 feet. Weight, about 30 pounds. Price, for carrier only...............**$3.65**

No. 87454 Track for above carrier, including couplings and bumper. Per foot...............12c

No. 87455 Hanger Hook with Clamps and Washers and Rafter Iron. Price, for one of each...............9c

Steel Grapple Hooks.

No. 87460 Solid Steel Grapple Hook, for hooking into rafter or beam where holes cannot be bored. Weight, 4½ lbs. Price, each...48c

FOR LARGER ILLUSTRATIONS
and more Complete Description of Hay Outfits and Tools, write for
SPECIAL HAY TOOL CIRCULAR.

Hay Tool Outfits.

For the convenience of our customers, we show below what constitutes a complete outfit for the various carriers quoted by us. Weight, 140 lbs.

No. 87470 Outfit for Wood Track Carrier for 40-foot barn; everything except wood track, which we do not furnish. 1 reversible carrier. No. 87439: 1 double harpoon fork, 13 rafter irons, 13 hanging hooks, 6 floor hooks, 5 knot passing pulleys, 130 feet manila rope, ¾-in., 50 feet check rope.
Complete outfit...............**$11.00**

No. 87471 Exactly the same outfit as No. 87470 except with our No. 87440 double swivel carrier in place of the reversible.
Complete outfit...............**$11.25**
If wanted for barn longer than 40 feet, add 6 cents to this price for each additional foot in length of barn.

No. 87472 Outfit for Steel Track Hanger for 40-foot barn, complete with track: 1 reversible carrier, 1 fork, 40 feet steel track, 13 rafter irons, 13 hanging hooks, 6 floor hooks, 5 knot-passing pulleys, 110 feet manila rope, ¾-inch, 50 feet check rope. Complete outfit, weight, 300 lbs..........**$14.80**

No. 87473 Exactly the same outfit as No. 87472 except with our No. 87453 swivel carrier in place of common reversible carrier.
Complete outfit...............**$15.00**
If wanted for barn longer than 40 feet, add 16 cents to this price for each additional foot in length of barn.

No. 87474 Outfit for Cable Carrier for barn 40 feet in length: 1 carrier, 1 fork, 50 feet cable with clamps and two eye bolts, ready to hang, 5 knot-passing pulleys, 130 feet, ¾-inch manila rope, 50 feet check rope, 6 floor hooks.
Complete outfit...............**$12.00**
For barn more than 40 feet in length, add to this price 8 cents for each additional foot in length.

No. 87475 Outfit for Cable Carrier for stacking hay or straw in the field or anywhere out of doors for 50 feet outfit. Stack poles not furnished. 50 feet of main galvanized cable and clamps, and 2 eye-bolts ready to hang, 3 knot-passing pulleys, 130 feet ¾-inch manila rope. 75 feet check-rope, 1 fork, 1 cable carrier, two 50-foot pieces galvanized wire guy ropes with loops and clamps.
Outfit complete...............**$14.00**
Each additional foot over 40 feet add 10 cents per foot extra.

Rope Hitches.

No. 87480 The places where this device can be used to advantage are only known to those who have had them on their farm. One on each end of a piece of rope often takes the place of a log chain, and is much lighter and better to handle. For hay carrier outfit they do away with twisting of rope. Take-up can be made in a minute's time. They are made of the best malleable iron. Weight about 1 pound. Price, each...............18c

No. 87482 Rafter Irons for use in hanging track. Weight, each, ¾ pound. Price, each............5c

No. 87485 Straight Hanging Hooks for use in hanging wood track to above brackets.
Price, each...............6½c

No. 87487 Jointed Hanging Hooks, with wood screw thread on one end for use in hanging wood track to beam without using bracket.
Price, each...............8½c

No. 87490 Floor Hook, to screw into floor to hold pulley. Price, each...............8½c

No. 87501 Common Cast Frame Pulley, with maple wheel. Not knot-passing.
Price, each..........**$0.20**
Price, per dozen... 2.25

Steel Frame Knot-Passing Pulley.

No. 87502 1-inch spindle loose pin.
Price, each...............**$0.20**
Price, per dozen..... 2.25
No. 87503 Knot-Passing Hay Fork Pulley, will take ¾ to 1-inch rope. Malleable iron frame; wood sheave. Price, per doz., **$2.90**; each..25c

Wood Frame Pulley.

No. 87504 Wood Frame Hay Fork Pulley, for ¾ to 1-inch rope, wood wheel, steel straps, which extend below axle forming axle box. Weight, 3 pounds.
Price, each.........**$0.19**
Price, per dozen..... 2.15

Galvanized Wire Cable.

No. 87505 Same as used on Hay Carriers. ⅜-inch diameter, any length over 50 feet.
Price, per foot...............2
½-inch diameter, any length over 50 feet.
Price, per foot...............3¼
No. 87506 Manila Rope, same as used on our Carriers. Best quality.
¾-inch for Trip Rope, cut to any length, per foot...1
1¼-inch for Carrier, cut to any length, per foot...3½

Sears Roebuck & Co.

INCORPORATED
VEHICLE
HARNESS & SADDLERY
DEPARTMENT

FROM OUR OWN FACTORIES

located at Brighton, Ohio, and Kalamazoo, Michigan, we offer for this season a higher grade of vehicle work than we have ever before been able to show; better made and better finished work throughout than will be offered by any other house, better than anything handled by the local implement and carriage dealer, a class of work such as is offered only in the best city repositories, and there at fancy prices.

IN OUR OWN FACTORY AT BRIGHTON, OHIO, WE BUILD ALL OUR REGULAR PIANO BODY TOP BUGGIES AND SURREYS.

IN OUR MICHIGAN FACTORY AT KALAMAZOO, MICHIGAN, WE BUILD ALL OUR HIGH GRADE OPEN BUGGIES, CONCORDS, PHAETONS, TRAPS AND SPRING WAGONS.

OUR TWO FACTORIES are located where we can take advantage of the lowest possible prices for the highest grades of material that enter into the construction of the different rigs, where we can secure the highest class of mechanical skill at the least possible expense, where the finest work can be made with the greatest economy.

WHY OUR OWN WORK IS BEST AND CHEAPEST.

WE FIRST STARTED OUR OWN VEHICLE FACTORY here in Chicago with a view of supplying our customers a better grade of work than it was previously possible for us to give them. We met with so much encouragement in the manufacture of our work, we found that we could turn out a grade of work that was so much better than anything we could get from the regular makers, would give our customers so much better satisfaction, that we found it necessary to materially increase our manufacturing capacity, for the demand for our work grew so rapidly that our factory in Chicago could not make one-fourth of the work. When it became necessary to greatly increase our manufacturing facilities, we were compelled to consider the advisability of locating a factory at points where the goods could be manufactured at the least possible cost, where skilled labor could be had for the least money, unhampered by any labor influences, where the best material was nearest at hand, and where conditions generally were favorable to the manufacturing of high grade work at the lowest possible cost, and, as a result, we have located our factory for the manufacture of regular top buggies and surreys at Brighton, Ohio, and our factory for the manufacture of open buggies, phaetons, stanhopes and spring wagons at Kalamazoo, Michigan, and from these two factories we turn out a grade of work such as you cannot get from any other house except you buy it from city repositories at fancy prices. We guarantee in our work a distinctiveness in quality and material, style and finish not to be had in anything you can buy from your dealer at home.

IN OUR OWN WORK, SHOWN UNDER SPECIAL HEADING, we use only strictly high grade wheels, only selected hickory gear woods, the best of Norway and wrought iron forgings; we use the highest grade body work, the best of trimmings, including dash, fenders, carpet, leather and cloth stock, the highest grade steel tires, and we set them by the old fashioned hot and cold process and not by cold pressure which ruins so many wheels. In the painting we use only the best of oils, varnish, color and filler. All our own Acme Royal work is given eighteen coats, and our cheaper work is given almost the same finish. We finish the Acme Royal work in the best gray with one body of priming, one putty coat, then sanded off, then a coat of lead, then five coats of filler, then rubbed out of filling with pumice stone, then one putty coat, two coats of color, one coat of rubbing varnish, then rubbed out of rubbing varnish with pumice stone and water, then striped, then a finishing coat of varnish. The gear is finished in practically the same way, and as a result, in our own work we get a surface, a body, a lasting lustre and finish to our work which you will find in none of the ordinary factory work sold by the country dealer.

ABOUT THE FREIGHT.

MOST OF THE RAILROAD COMPANIES accept vehicles by freight at one and one-half times first class. In some cases it is two times first class, and as the shipping weight is given under each vehicle, and the first class freight rate for one hundred pounds from Chicago to the different points in all the different states is listed in the front part of the catalogue, you can calculate very closely what the freight will amount to on any vehicle to your place.

TO MAKE SURE YOU CAN ASK YOUR LOCAL FREIGHT AGENT, OR, IF YOU WISH YOU CAN WRITE TO US AND WE WILL BE PLEASED TO SEND YOU A FREIGHT ESTIMATE FROM THE FACTORY TO YOUR NEAREST RAILROAD STATION ON SUCH A RIG AS YOU WANT.

FROM OUR TWO FACTORIES WE OFFER STRICTLY HIGH GRADE WORK, made of the best material that we can buy, made by skilled mechanics under the direct supervision of our own managers. We offer it at prices based on the actual cost of material and labor, with but one profit added, the manufacturer's profit, the same profit that the wholesale dealer must pay when he buys, to which he must add his profit and the retail dealer his profit before you are allowed to buy.

OUR OWN WORK IS SHOWN IN THIS CATALOGUE under a separate heading and we especially direct you to these numbers, and urge that, when selecting a vehicle, you select one of our highest grade, a rig that is built on honor and sold at a lower price than you could possibly get elsewhere.

TO MEET COMPETITION we have arranged with a number of reputable manufacturers to supply us with the same class of work that is handled by the regular jobber and the retail implement dealer, and advertised by catalogue houses generally. We have gone outside of our own factories to buy this work, for the reason that we find it impossible to build two distinctively different grades of work in the one factory. This work we have made big contracts for. We have secured the lowest prices possible, to which we have added our one small percentage of profit, and if you will compare our prices and descriptions with those of your dealer at home or of any other house, we feel confident you will see where we are from 25 to 50 per cent lower in price.

REGULAR FACTORY WORK IS SHOWN UNDER A SPECIAL HEADING.

AS A MATTER OF ECONOMY OF SPACE we have felt compelled, in order to show a complete line of vehicle work, to use small illustrations and small space, and if in any case you find the illustration so small, or the description so much abridged that you do not get all the information you want, and you will write us, we will be very glad to furnish you with a much larger illustration and a very complete description, and any special information that you may desire.

OUR FREE TRIAL OFFER.

SO CONFIDENT ARE WE OF OUR ABILITY to furnish you a better rig for less money than you can buy elsewhere, that we extend this offer to everyone! Select any rig shown in this catalogue, we will send it to you on our regular terms; you can give it ten days' thorough trial, during which time you can compare it with any rig you can get from your dealer at home or from any dealer or maker anywhere, and, if at any time during the ten days you, for any reason become dissatisfied with our rig, if you, at the expiration of ten days are not still satisfied that you have gotten more value from us than you could get from anyone else, you are at liberty to return the rig to us at our expense of freight charges both ways, and we will immediately refund your money.

OUR BINDING GUARANTEE.

WITH EVERY RIG WE SELL we issue a WRITTEN, BINDING, TWO YEARS' GUARANTEE, by the terms and conditions of which, if any piece or part gives out by reason of defect in material or workmanship, we will replace or repair it free of charge. We extend this guarantee to the outside factory work as well as our own, because it is guaranteed to us, but any of this outside factory work will, at the end of two years, look very old and shabby as compared with the work we build in our two factories, yet nothing may give way to the extent that the guarantee would imply.

Our Fancy Stick Seat Surrey for $69.00.

No. 88859 For $69.00, this Stick Seat Surrey, as illustrated, complete with lamps and shafts, crated and delivered on board the cars at the factory in Southern Ohio. This is a strictly high grade surrey, very latest style body, with handsome stick seats and large, rounded panel backs. The body is very handsomely finished, 30 inches wide by 72 inches long. The gear is strictly high grade, made with 1-1/16-inch axles. Wheels are ⅞, 1-inch or 1⅛-inch, as desired. Highest grade elliptic end springs. Wheels are Sarven's patent or shell band hub, as desired. Trimmings are of fine imported gray English whipcord or dark green body cloth or leather, as desired, full tufted. The job is given a very fine finish in painting; body, black; gear, dark green with suitable striping. At our special price we furnish this rig complete, with carpet, handsome lamps, wrench, anti-rattlers and shafts.

Extra for pole with neckyoke and whiffletree complete in place of shafts..........$1.50
Extra for both pole and shafts..........3.00

Our $118.00 Cabriolet.

With Canopy Top, full length Side and Back Curtains, $115.00.

No. 88861 For $118.00, crated and delivered on board the cars at the factory in Southern Ohio, we offer this new and handsome Tuxedo pattern extension top, cut-under, three-spring carriage, as the equal of carriages that will sell everywhere this season at $200.00 and upwards.

We do not make this rig ourselves, but it is made for us under contract by one of the best makers in Ohio and we guarantee it in every way.

This is a very handsome rig, gotten out on the latest styles for this season. The body is very large and handsome in design, full cut-under, full carriage. Seats are large and roomy, elegantly upholstered. The springs are of the very best oil tempered steel, elliptic front springs, fancy elliptic rear loop springs in back. Gear is strictly high grade and the best of Norway iron and second growth hickory. 1¼-inch axles. Rear axle coached; double bent reach, ironed full length, full braced and bolted. Wheels are a very high grade Sarven's patent. This rig is trimmed with a high grade buffed genuine leather or a very heavy all wool green body cloth, as desired. The top is high grade extension quarters made of high grade buffed leather, heavily lined and finished and comes with full length side and back curtains. The rig is painted in the highest style of the art and only the best oils, colors and varnishes are used. Body is painted black; gear, dark green with suitable striping. It is furnished complete with large, handsome new style lamps, very large full leather fenders, carpet, wrench, anti-rattlers and shafts.

Extra for a strong, high grade, well finished pole with neckyoke and whiffletree complete in place of shafts..........$2.50
For canopy top in place of leather quarter top..........115.00

See Our Acme Royal Big Surreys at

$81.00, $88.50, $88.75 and $94.00...

OUR OWN MAKE Made in our own factory at Brighton, Ohio, the finest Surrey work on the market.

Our $62.50 Fancy Stanhope.

No. 88863 For $62.50 we offer this as the greatest value that will be shown this season in a Stanhope at the price. We do not make this Stanhope and, of course, we recommend you to first consider our **Acme Royal Stanhopes**, but this rig is made by one of the best makers in Southern Ohio. It is covered by a binding guarantee and is equal to rigs that will retail at double the price.

At $62.50 we furnish this Stanhope, delivered on board the cars at the factory in Southern Ohio, from which point you must pay the freight. This is the very latest style doctor's Stanhope. The body is superior in style, the seat is roomy and comfortable, and it has wrought iron sill plates and full length body loops. Axles are 15/16-inch, fantailed, double collar steel, drop front and arched rear. The wheels are ¾, ⅞ or 1 inch, either Sarven's patent or shell band hub, full bolted. It is hung on a high grade gear with elliptic end springs. Springs are 1¼-inch, four-plate front and five-plate rear, graded and oil tempered. Two reaches made of double bent hickory, securely ironed and braced. Is painted in a superior style; gear, Brewster green with gold and red box striping; body, black with bright edgings of bronze green, neatly sprigged with gold. Top is 3-bow leather quarter, well made and finished, comes with full length side and back curtains. Rig is trimmed in a good grade of leather or good weight English body cloth, as desired, Full spring cushion and full spring back.

At $62.50, we furnish this rig complete with full length side and back curtains, toe carpet, wrench, anti-rattlers and shafts.

Extra for pole with neckyoke and whiffletree complete in place of shafts..........$1.50
Extra for both pole and shafts..........3.00

Our $68.00 Milk Wagon.

No. 88865 For $68.00 we furnish this wagon with 1-inch steel axle. At $71.00 we furnish it heavier made throughout, with 1⅛-inch axle. The price quoted is for the wagon crated and delivered on board the cars at Pontiac, Michigan, from which point you must pay the freight.

This is a good, substantial milk wagon. We have sold a great many with universal satisfaction to our customers. The body is made 6 feet 6 inches long by 2 feet 10 inches wide. It is a complete knock down body, put together with twelve iron rods. It stands only 27 inches from the ground and will turn in a circle of 12 feet. The wheels are a good grade Sarven's patent, heavily tired, full bolted and finished. The axles come regularly in 1-inch, but we will furnish 1⅛-inch when desired, as per price named. **We furnish this rig with steel patent sliding doors, with glass panels in upper half of body.** Front is fitted with solid panel at bottom and swinging glass panel at top; front sides are fitted with glass panels or of white enameled oil duck. **This rig is fitted with a special patent short turn wrought iron fifth wheel.** It is painted in a very substantial manner; body, dark blue or dark green with vermilion striping; gear, wine color, nicely striped. The carrying capacity of this wagon is 700 pounds, and the wagon weighs, crated for shipment, about 600 pounds.

At our special prices of $68.00 and $71.00, we furnish the wagon complete with shafts.

Extra for pole with neckyoke and whiffletree complete in place of shafts..........$1.50

SEE OUR ACME ROYAL STANHOPE, No. 88947, at $66.50; Rubber Tired Wheels, $82.50. Made in our Kalamazoo, Michigan, factory. THE STANHOPE OF THE DAY.

Our $37.50 Delivery Wagon

No. 88867 At $37.50 we furnish this wagon crated and delivered free on board the cars at Galion, Ohio, from which point you pay the freight.

This wagon, as shown in illustration, is a good substantial delivery wagon. The body is 8 feet 6 inches long, 38 inches wide and 8 inches deep, made with drop end gate, toeboard and sideboards. Seat is made with 13-inch risers. Trimmed in Keratol leather. Extra heavy, well made, Sarven's patent hickory wheels, full bolted. 1¼-inch tire. Good, substantial gear. 1⅛-inch steel axles. Rear axle coached; front axle fantailed. Springs are oil tempered and graded, made by D. W. Schuler & Son. Front spring 1½-inch, three-leaf; rear spring 1¼-inch, four-leaf. We furnish this wagon body painted black or bronze green, as desired, neatly decorated; gear, green, red or yellow, neatly striped.

At $37.50 we furnish this Delivery Wagon complete with shafts.

Extra for pole with neckyoke and whiffletree complete in place of shafts..........$1.50
Extra for brake..........5.00
Extra for lettering, per letter..........10

$34.50 Delivery Wagon.

No. 88869 At $34.50 we furnish this Light Delivery Wagon, crated and delivered free on board the cars at the factory in Galion, Ohio. This wagon is not made by us, but is made by a good wagonmaker in Galion, Ohio.

This $34.50 Delivery Wagon has a body 7 feet long, 38 inches wide and 8 inches deep, made with drop end gate, toe board and sideboards. The seat is made with 13-inch risers, trimmed with imitation leather. Wheels are good, heavy weight, Sarven's patent, full bolted; 1⅛-inch tires; good, strong gear. Axles are 1-1/16-inch steel. Rear axle coached, front axle fantailed. Springs are oil tempered and graded, made by D. W. Schuler & Son. Front springs 1¼-inch, three-leaf; rear springs 1¼-inch, four-leaf. Body is painted black, amber or bronze green, as desired, neatly decorated; gear, green, red or yellow, neatly striped.

At $34.50 we furnish this rig complete with shafts.

Extra for pole with neckyoke and whiffletree complete in place of shafts..........$1.50
Extra for brake..........5.00
Extra for lettering, per letter..........10

Our $35.50 Three-Spring Wagon.

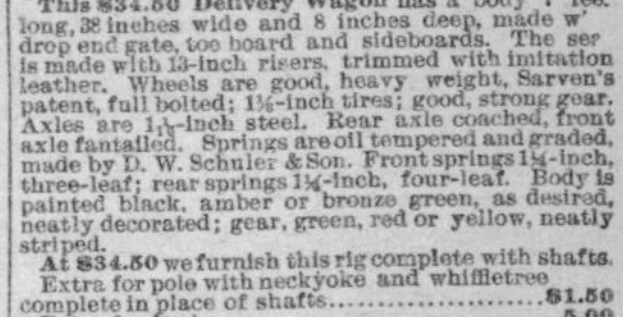

No. 88871 While we offer for $35.50 the best spring wagon that will be shown by anyone at anything like the price, a wagon that will give satisfaction and will mean a saving to you of at least $10.00, we especially recommend our own wagon, which we make at Kalamazoo, Mich., which we offer at $45.75.

This light, three-spring wagon has a body 7 feet long, 32 inches wide and 8 inches deep. Panels bolted to cleats underneath; bottom boards run lengthwise; drop end gate; removable seats. Wheels, Sarven's patent, all hickory, full bolted; 1⅛-inch tire; strong gear. Axles, 1-1/16-inch steel; rear axle coached, front axle fantailed. Springs, oil tempered and graded, made by D. W. Schuler & Son. Front spring, 1¼-inch, four-leaf; rear spring, 1¼-inch, three-leaf. Seats trimmed in imitation leather, whipcord or cloth, as desired. Body, painted black, amber or bronze green, neatly decorated; gear, red, green or yellow, neatly striped. **For $35.50 we furnish this wagon complete with shafts.**

Extra for pole with neckyoke and whiffletree complete in place of shafts..........$1.50
Extra for brake..........5.00

SEE OUR WAGONS Nos. 89105 and 89107 at $45.95. OUR OWN MAKE, from our Kalamazoo factory, the BEST SPRING WAGON MADE.

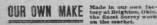

Our $36.00 Combination Wagon.

No. 88873 At $36.00 we furnish this wagon crated and delivered free on board cars at Galion, Ohio.

This wagon is exactly the same as No. 88871 preceding, with the exception of the springs. We furnish this wagon with a combination spring gear. Springs, 1¼ inches wide.

Our price, complete with shafts.............$36.00
Extra for pole with neckyoke and whiffletree, complete in place of shafts............... 1.50
Extra for brake.......................... 5.00

Our $54.50 Full Platform Spring Wagon.

No. 88875 At $54.50 we furnish this surrey, crated and delivered on board the cars at Jackson, Michigan, from which point you must pay the freight.

This is the latest style full platform wagon on the market, a thoroughly substantial rig, covered by a binding two years' guarantee. The body is 7 feet long, 32 inches wide and 9 inches deep; made with drop end gate; strong frame work inside; oval edge irons; one of the best bodies made. Gear is a strictly high grade, strongly constructed gear, made with 1⅛-inch steel axles, coached front and rear. Springs are full platform, 1¾-inch wide in front, 1¾-inch wide in rear, made from oil tempered steel. Wheels are high grade Sarven's patent, 1⅛-inch rim, tired with heavy ⅜-inch steel tire. Wheels are full bolted and full finished. Trimmed in imitation leather, made with full solid panel back, painted in a first class manner. Body and seats, black, with suitable striping and scrolling; gear, Brewster green with suitable striping.

At $54.50 we furnish this wagon complete with pole, neckyoke and whiffletree.

Our Heavy Three-Seat Full Platform Wagon, $59.50.

No. 88877 At these special prices we furnish this heavy three-seat, full platform wagon delivered on board the cars at the factory in Cincinnati, Ohio, from which point you must pay the freight. This heavy wagon is especially recommended for livery trade.

This is a very heavy body made of the very best material; solid ash sills, heavily ironed. It is 8 feet 6 inches long, 3 feet 2 inches wide and has drop end gate. Comes with three large, roomy seats with full backs as shown in illustration. The springs are full platform coupled together with equalizing shackles, strong and durable and the wagon has a guaranteed carrying capacity of 1,800 pounds. The gear is extra strong, has a 1¼-inch double collar steel axle; Norway clips and bolts; heavy Sarven's patent wheels, 1¼-inch rim. It is trimmed regularly in imitation black leather. Body painted black; gear, dark green or carmine, as desired. **At our special $59.50 price, it comes complete with pole, neckyoke and whiffletree.**

With canopy top with full roll up curtains, $72.50
Extra for genuine machine buffed leather cushions and backs in place of imitation leather.................................... 8.00

Heavy Mountain Wagon, $79.00.

No. 88879 At $79.00 we furnish this heavy Mountain Wagon, crated and delivered free on board the cars at the factory in Cincinnati, Ohio, from which point you must pay the freight.

This is a very heavy, strongly built Mountain Wagon. Body is very substantial, 8 feet long, 39 inches wide; ironed all around the top; drop end gate; two removable seats and solid wood panel backs. Will be constructed with toeboard instead of dash, if so desired. Axles are 1⅜-inch, fantailed, double collar steel, coached front and rear. Wheels are 1⅜-inch tread, Sarven's patent, high grade. Heavy, rounded edge tire. Springs are side springs, 1¾-inch wide. Elliptic springs in ends 1¾-inch wide, five-plate front and six-plate rear, made from graded, oil tempered steel. Wagon is made with three heavy reaches running full length, ironed and braced. Is painted in a first class manner; gear, red with black striping; body, green with black moulding and gold striping. Trimmed in Australia leather.

At $79.00 we furnish this wagon complete with two seats, pole, neckyoke and whiffletree.

Extra for brake........ .... $ 5.00
Extra for standing top with curtains........ 12.00

Our $107.00 Extra Heavy, Standing Top, Three-Seat Mountain Wagon.

No. 88881 At $107.00 we furnish this wagon crated and delivered on board the cars at the factory at Cincinnati, Ohio, from which point you must pay the freight.

It is one of the strongest, heaviest and best made mountain wagons on the market. Body is very substantially built, 8 feet long, by 39 inches wide, ironed all around on top. Made with drop end gate; three removable seats with solid wood panel backs. **When ordered, will be constructed with toeboard instead of dash in front.** Axles are 1⅜-inch, fantailed, double collar steel, coached front and rear. Wheels are high-grade, Sarven's patent, 1⅜-inch tread; heavy tire, rounded edge steel; springs of extra high grade steel; 1¾-inch wide elliptic end springs, five-plate front and six-plate rear. Gear is made with three heavy reaches running full length, ironed full length and braced. Top is extra strong standing top with eight standards, heavily ironed and securely fastened to body; heavy roof and full roll-up curtains. Painted, gear, red with black striping; body, green with black moulding and gold striping; trimmed with Evans' leather.

At $107.00 we furnish this rig complete with heavy ratchet brake, pole, neckyoke and whiffletree.

OUR OWN MAKE

ON THE FOLLOWING PAGES

On the following pages we show the entire line of vehicles made in our own factories, our factories at Kalamazoo, Michigan, and Brighton, Ohio. . . . . . .

IN OUR TWO FACTORIES we make a much higher grade of buggy work than goes out of the regular jobbing factory, a much better grade of work than is handled by the wholesale and retail implement and carriage trade, a better grade of work than we have heretofore been able to buy from the regular jobbing makers.

THAT OUR CUSTOMERS MIGHT HAVE A BETTER GRADE OF WORK, better wheels, better gears, better springs, better made bodies and tops, better trimmed and finished, a more lasting and higher finished job of painting, a better rig throughout than is offered by the regular retail dealer or the average catalogue house, we first started our own vehicle factory here in Chicago, and we met with so much encouragement in doing so, we found our customers appreciated a higher grade of work, even to the extent of overtaxing our capacity from the very start, that we were compelled, in order to meet any demands from our customers, to get control of larger manufacturing facilities, and to this end we established a very large factory at Brighton, Ohio, for the manufacture of top buggies and surreys, and another large factory at Kalamazoo, Michigan, for the manufacture of high grade open buggies, phaetons, stanhopes, spring wagons, etc. This our own work, as shown on the following pages, is built on honor from the best material that we can buy, only the most skilled mechanics are employed. Every rig is made under the direct supervision of able managers and superintendents and we turn out such a grade of work as goes out of no regular jobbing carriage factory, a class of work that can be compared only with the highest grade carriage work that is built for fine city trade and will be found only in city repositories at fancy prices.

TO CHEAPEN OUR OWN WORK, to lower the selling price of the work we build in our factories at Brighton and Kalamazoo, we could materially reduce the cost of wheels, gears, springs, body, upholstering, painting and finishing. **It would be an easy matter on a rig we offer at $35.00 to take out $10.00 without materially affecting the general appearance.** Unfortunately, in most all regular jobbing factories this is practiced to a very great extent, but in our factories we do not do this. **Our prices are fixed at the lowest possible cost, quality considered, and only one small profit is added.** If you wish us to make a lower price we will have to build the rig to fit your price and we will do it by telling you in advance just where we will cheapen it.

TO GIVE YOU AN IDEA of the advantage you have in having a rig built in one of our factories, take the item of painting. It is possible to paint an ordinary open buggy, giving it considerable show in outward appearance which will not be at all lasting, at an expense of about $3.00; but in the painting alone all our high grade work from our own factories get the following treatment:

HOW WE PAINT OUR WORK.

BODIES are primed, then a putty coat, then sanded off, then a coat of lead, then five coats of filler, then rubbed out of filling with pumice stone, then a putty coat, then two coats of filler, one coat of rubbing varnish, rubbed out of rubbing varnish, then another coat of rubbing varnish, again rubbed out of rubbing varnish, striped and a final finishing coat of varnish. **The gear is treated in a very similar manner.** In this way we put more than three times the material, more than five times the labor in the painting alone, but as a result we have a finished, lasting job of painting; we have a painting a credit to our factory and a permanent comfort to the owner. In the ironing, trimming, building and general finish of the rig throughout, in a great measure, the same applies as to the painting. **We give you the benefit of all this in our own high grade work from our Kalamazoo and Brighton factories, the carriage work shown in the illustrations on the following pages.**

Our Heavy $59.75 Mountain Wagon.

No. 89151 Complete with heavy brake, end springs and longitudinal spring.

For $59.75 we furnish this wagon delivered on board the cars at the factory at Cincinnati, Ohio, as one of the strongest, heaviest built mountain wagons made. From this illustration you can form some little idea of the appearance of this heavy mountain wagon. Is made on a strong double reach gear, hung on 1⅛-inch double collar steel axles; heavy 1⅛-inch Sarven's patent wheels, with heavy tires; 1⅛-inch three and four-plate elliptic end springs, 36 inches long; heavy longitudinal center spring from front to back axle. Comes complete with foot brake, strong piano box body, 58 inches long by 27 inches wide; made with heavy sills, well-ironed; large seat with full panel spring back; leather boot with straps; big rubber apron; large size four-bow leather quarter top, complete with full-length side and back curtains.

At our special $59.75 price we furnish this heavy mountain wagon complete with brake, full-length side and back curtains, wrench, anti-rattlers and shafts. Our special price.................................$59.75
Extra for pole with neckyoke and whiffletree complete in place of shafts.................. 1.25

Our $42.00 Canopy Top Rig.

No. 89153 At $42.00 we furnish this rig crated and delivered on board the cars at the factory at Cincinnati, Ohio, at the lowest price ever made by any one for a canopy top, two-seated rig of this kind. This rig is made by a reliable maker in Cincinnati, and he guarantees it in every way. From the illustration you can form some idea of the appearance of this two-seated canopy top rig which we furnish at $42.00. The body is 61 inches long, 27 inches wide, made of good material, well ironed and finished. The seats are removable and can be taken out without removing the top. They are well braced and finished. The body is hung on a good strong gear, 1⅛ inch fantailed double collar steel drop axles, 4 and 5 plate; 1⅛-inch elliptic end springs, Sarven's patent wheels. The canopy top is well made and finished. Comes complete with full length curtains. At our special $42.00 price we furnish this rig complete with two seats, trimmed in imitation leather, canopy top, full length side and back curtains, wrench, anti-rattlers and shafts.

Our special price, each..........................$42.00
Extra for pole with neckyoke and whiffletree complete in place of shafts.................. 1.25

Our $30.50 Three-Spring Handy Wagon.

No. 89155 At $30.50 we offer this Three-Spring Handy Wagon delivered on board the cars at the factory in Cincinnati, Ohio, and it is the equal of three-spring wagons that retail at $45.00 to $50.00. This wagon is made by a reliable maker in Cincinnati, and is guaranteed by the maker as regards quality of material and labor, and while we do not issue our own written guarantee with this rig, if any piece or part gives out by reason of defect in material or workmanship, it will be replaced by the manufacturer free of charge. **This open, two-seat light, three-spring, handy wagon at $30.50 is offered at the lowest price at which a reliable three-spring wagon can possibly be furnished.** It is made with a good strong body, 6 feet long, 28 inches wide, outside. It has two full-sized seats, is well-ironed; both seats are made removable; is hung on a good strong gear. The gear is made with 1-inch axles in front and 1⅛-inch axles in rear, ⅞-inch wheels, ¾-inch tires, 1¼-inch elliptic springs. It is well painted and striped; gear, dark green; body, black with neat striping; or at the same price when so desired, we will furnish the rig with body and gear oak-grained. The seats are made with good wide backs as illustrated. At our special $30.50 price we furnish this rig complete, trimmed in imitation leather, and with wrench, anti-rattlers and shafts.

Our special price..................................$30.50
Extra for pole with neckyoke and whiffletree complete in place of shafts.................. 1.25

Our $36.50 Canopy Top Wagon.

No. 89157 For $36.50 we furnish this three-spring, two-seated handy wagon complete, with roll-up canopy top as illustrated. This, our special $36.50 canopy top wagon, is made for us under contract by a reliable wagon-maker in Cincinnati, Ohio, and the price quoted is for the wagon crated and delivered on board the cars in Cincinnati. While we do not send our own written binding guarantee with this rig, the manufacturer guarantees it against defective material and workmanship, and any wagon which gives out in any part, by reason of such defect, will be replaced or repaired by the manufacturer free of charge. **Our special $36.50 price is at least $10.00 below any price quoted by any other house, and is the lowest price ever named by any one for a three-spring canopy top rig.** From the above illustration, engraved from a photograph, you can get an idea of the appearance of this, our special $36.50 three-spring, two-seated canopy-top, all-purpose wagon, a new style for this season. It is a good, strong, substantial rig. The body is 6 feet long, 28 inches wide outside, is well ironed and finished. It has two removable seats with lazy backs, as illustrated, and is hung on a good, strong gear; 1-inch axle in front, 1⅛-inch axle in rear, ⅞-inch Sarven's patent wheels, tired with ¾-inch tire, good, strong 1¼-inch Elliptic springs. The body is painted black with neat striping; gear, dark green with neat striping, or we will furnish the body and gear in oak-grained color, when so desired.

At our special price it comes with canopy top, full size, well braced, with roll-up curtains complete. **At our special $36.50 price,** we furnish the rig trimmed in imitation leather, complete with canopy top, full length roll-up curtains, wrench, anti-rattlers and shafts. Extra for pole with neckyoke and whiffletree, complete, in place of shafts, $1.25.

Our special price..............................$36.50

DON'T order a vehicle of any kind, a buggy, road wagon, surrey, spring wagon or other rig until you have first communicated with us. . . .

If you don't find in our catalogue just the kind of a rig wanted, be sure to write us before ordering elsewhere. In our two factories, the one at Brighton, Ohio, and the other at Kalamazoo, Mich., we are prepared to build almost anything in the vehicle line. We would be glad to figure with you on any special rig you want, figure with you on the basis of the actual cost of material and labor, with but our one small percentage of profit added.

IF YOU WOULD LIKE TO SEE LARGER ILLUSTRATIONS AND MORE COMPLETE DESCRIPTIONS, **if you would like any special information concerning any rig illustrated and described in this book, write us. We will be pleased to communicate with you, send you larger illustrations, more complete descriptions and furnish you any special information you wish.**

Our $34.00 Three Spring Light Delivery Wagon.

WITH SIDE BOARDS.

For $34.00 with regular seat or $36.00 with special high seat as shown in small illustration, we furnish this open, light, three-spring delivery wagon with side boards as the equal of wagons that others sell at 50 per cent more money. **At these special prices cash in full must accompany your order. $2.00 extra if sent by freight C. O. D., subject to examination, on receipt of our regular required deposit.** From the illustration, engraved from a photograph, you can form some idea of the appearance of this wagon. It is made for us under contract by a manufacturer in Cincinnati, and the price quoted is for the wagon crated and delivered on board the cars in Cincinnati, from which point you must pay the freight, but you will find the freight will amount to next to nothing as compared with what you will save in price. This is a strong, well built wagon, guaranteed by the manufacturer. The body is 6 feet long, 31 inches wide, made with drop end gate and side boards. It comes regularly with one seat, with double roll lazy back as illustrated, or, when furnished at $36.00, with high seat as shown in the small illustration. The body is well ironed, braced and bolted, is hung on a good strong gear; 1 inch steel axles, ⅞ or 1 inch Sarven's patent wheels, as desired; three strong elliptic springs, full braced reaches.

Painting: This wagon is well painted; body black with suitable striping; gear, green or red, as desired. We will letter the sides to order, when so desired, at a reasonable charge. At $34.00 and $36.00 we furnish this wagon complete with wrench, anti-rattlers and shafts.

No. 89159 Price of wagon with regular seat as illustrated..................................$34.00
No. 89161 Price of wagon with high seat as illustrated..................................... 36.00
Extra for pole with neckyoke and whiffletree complete in place of shafts.................. 1.25

For same style wagon as above with 1⅛-inch axles and 1⅛-inch Sarven's patent wheels, extra heavy 1¼-inch springs, complete with shafts, **add $4.00 to the above prices.**

Our $36.50 and $38.50 Heavy Platform Market Wagon.

At $36.50 for wagon with regular seat as illustrated, or $38.50 with high seat as shown in illustration, we furnish this half platform market delivery or business wagon as the lowest price made by any house for a rig of this kind. Our special price is based on the actual cost of material and labor, with but our one small profit added. This wagon is furnished delivered on board the cars at the factory in Cincinnati, from which point you must pay the freight. These wagons are made for us under contract by one of the best makers in Cincinnati, who guarantees them to us. They are equal to wagons that sell everywhere at almost double the price. For a delivery wagon for grocers or others there is no better job made. From the illustration, engraved from a photograph, you can form an idea of the appearance of this our special $36.50 and $38.50 delivery or market wagon. At these special prices cash in full must accompany your order. If sent C. O. D. we make an extra charge of $2.00. This is a good, strong wagon, furnished complete with side boards, has an extra strong gear, made with double reach, ironed full length; 1⅛-inch double collar steel axles, 1⅛-inch Sarven's patent wheels, ⅞-inch steel tire, 1¼-inch strong springs, platform spring in the rear. The end spring in front of body is 7 feet long, 36 inches wide; made with drop end gate and side boards; painted regularly body black; gear, dark green or red, as desired, with suitable striping. **At our special $36.50 price we furnish this rig complete with seat with drill cushion and lazy back as illustrated, wrench, anti-rattlers and shafts. At $38.50 we furnish it with high seat as shown in side illustration.**

No. 89163 Price of wagon with regular seat, as illustrated..................................$36.50
No. 89165 Price of wagon with high seat, as illustrated..................................... 38.50
Extra for pole with neckyoke and whiffletree complete in place of shafts.................. 1.25

We will furnish the same wagon with 1¼-inch steel axles, 1¼-inch patent wheels, with heavier springs 1⅛-inch in size, heavier fifth wheel and shafts, heavier rig throughout, at $7.00 extra.

Any lettering on body desired, at a reasonable charge.

DEPARTMENT OF CUTTERS.

WE OFFER FOR THE FALL AND WINTER OF 1900-01 a grade of cutter work built in our own factory at Kalamazoo, Michigan, which in quality of material, workmanship and finish surpasses anything that goes out of any regular jobbing factory. Our prices are based on the actual cost of material and labor, with but our one small precentage of profit added, and will mean a saving to you of from 25 to 50 per cent. The prices quoted are for the cutters delivered free on board the cars at our factory at Kalamazoo, Michigan, from which point you must pay the freight, but you will find the freight will amount to next to nothing as compared with what you will save in price. The cutter weighs about 200 pounds crated for shipment. If you live east, north or south of Kalamazoo, Michigan, the freight will be less than from Chicago; if you live west of Chicago it will add about 60 cents per cutter to the Chicago rate.

YOU CAN EITHER ENCLOSE OUR PRICE, or, if you prefer, and you live east of the Rocky Mountains, you can send $5.00. We will send any cutter to you by freight C. O. D., subject to examination. You can examine it at your freight depot, and if found perfectly satisfactory and exactly as represented, pay the agent the balance and freight charges.

OUR GUARANTEE. Every cutter is covered by a written binding guarantee as to quality of material and workmanship. Any cutter found defective in this regard will be repaired or replaced by us FREE OF CHARGE.

Our $12.95 Swell Body Cutter.

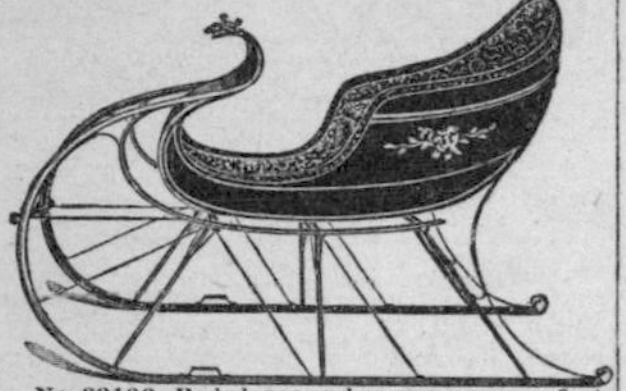

No. 89120 Body large and roomy, very comfortable. Neatly upholstered with Inspector's grade raw silk. Side panels of body are one full piece, ⅝-inch thick; gracefully curved, well painted, striped and ornamented. The gear woods are Rowell's best selected stock, thoroughly seasoned. Gear, ironed throughout with the best grade Norway braces, bolts and clips. **Higgins' best hardened steel shoes, securely bolted to runners. Complete with shafts.**
Extra for pole in place of shafts.............$1.25

Our $16.95 Stylish Portland.

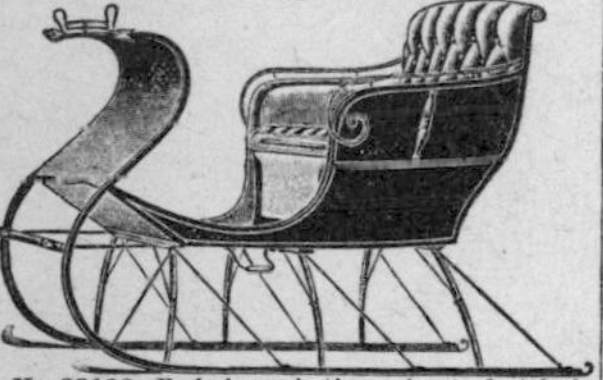

No. 89122 Body is made throughout of strictly A No. 1 air seasoned material; solid panels. All joints are carefully fitted, screwed, glued and plugged. Body is painted in the best possible manner, thoroughly rubbed out with pumice stone, highly polished, neatly striped and ornamented. Gear is made of selected second growth hickory, ironed with best grade of Norway iron. Higgins' best grade hardened steel shoes. Seat is neatly upholstered. Cushions have springs and are removable. **Complete with shafts.**
Extra for pole in place of shafts.............$1.25

Our $18.75 Portland Cutter.

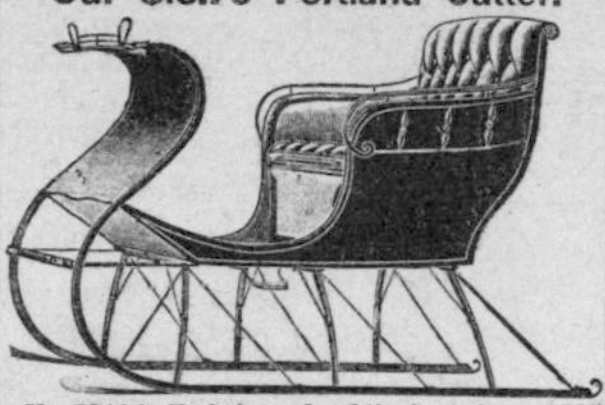

No. 89124 Body is made of the best air seasoned selected timber, solid panels, will not split, warp or crack. Gear is made of selected second growth hickory; double bent knees, braces, bolts and clips best grade Norway iron. Higgins' best grade hardened steel shoes; seat upholstered in the best possible manner with heavy dark green broadcloth, with spring back and spring cushion. Cushions are removable. Painting is first class, thoroughly rubbed out, highly polished and neatly ornamented; dash rail, nickel plated arm rails, steps and nicely trimmed shafts furnished with cutter.
Extra for pole in place of shafts. $1.25

OUR SPECIAL $18.75 PORTLAND.

Our $20.50 Imperial Portland.

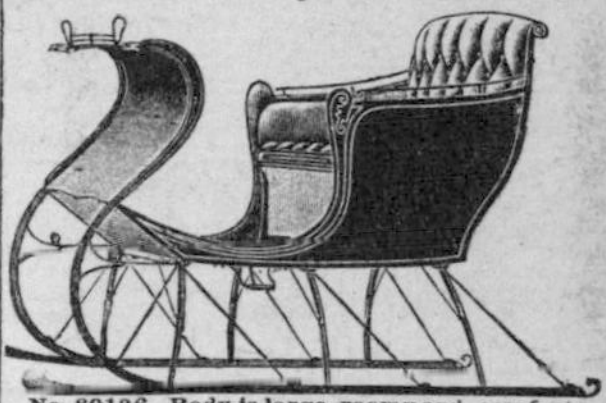

No. 89126 Body is large, roomy and comfortable; made with high panels and extra high back; made of the best air seasoned timber, solid panels. All joints are reinforced, screwed, glued and plugged. Gear is made of the best selected second growth hickory; double bent knees. Braces, bolts and clips from the best Norway iron. Higgins' best grade hardened steel shoes, securely bolted to runners. Painted in the highest style of the art, highly polished, neatly striped and ornamented. Seat upholstered in heavy green broadcloth. Full spring back and spring cushion; cushions are removable; curved dash with side wings and nickel plated dash rail. Nickel plated arm rails; neat foot steps and nicely trimmed shafts.
Extra for pole in place of shafts..............$1.25

Our $22.50 Finest Stanhope Portland Cutter.

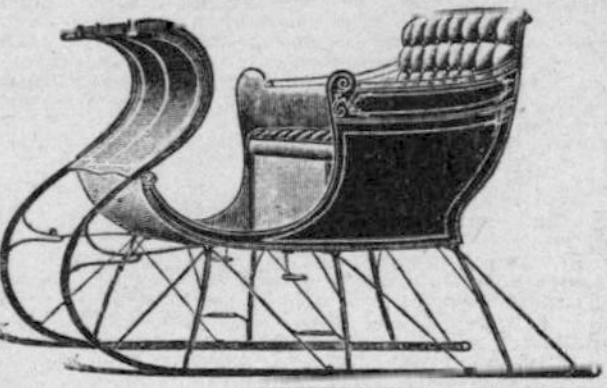

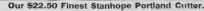

No. 89128 This, our finest Cutter, has a very large body, beautifully designed; solid panels, extra high side panels, with "O G" shaped, handsomely hand carved effect; curved bracket front and round moulding; special constructed and steam bent dash, elegantly proportioned with wings on side and mounted with nickel plated dash rail. Gear made throughout of the best selected air seasoned material; second growth hickory double bent knees; ornamented steps; Higgins' best grade hardened steel shoes, securely bolted to runners. Painted in the best manner known, rubbed out with pumice stone, tastily striped and ornamented. Seat upholstered in the highest style of the art with heavy green broadcloth. Full spring cushion and spring back. Cushions are removable. Nickel plated arm rails; nicely trimmed shafts.
Extra for pole in place of shafts......... ...$1.25

ALL ORDERS FOR FARM WAGONS MUST BE ACCOMPANIED BY CASH IN FULL. THEY WILL NOT BE SHIPPED C. O. D.

Size of skein..................	2½x8	2¾x8	3 x9	3¼x10	3½x11
Size of tire..................	1⅜x7/16	1½x ½	1½x 9/16	1½x ⅝	1⅝x⅝
Depth of bottom box..........	11 inch	12 inch	12 inch	14 inch	14 inch
Depth of top box............	7 inch	8 inch	8 inch	10 inch	10 inch
Capacity of wagon...........	1,500 lbs.	2,000 lbs.	2,500 lbs.	3,800 lbs.	4,800 lbs.
Weight of running gear complete.....................	575 lbs.	625 lbs.	700 lbs.	725 lbs.	750 lbs.
Weight of wagon complete...	790 lbs.	840 lbs.	915 lbs.	1,025 lbs.	1,085 lbs.
Price of running gear complete......................	$33.06	$33.63	$34.20	$34.77	$35.91
Price of wagon complete......	39.75	44.40	45.60	46.74	47.88
EXTRAS.					
Price of bottom box only	7.15	7.80	7.80	7.92	7.92
Price of top box only...	2.43	2.60	2.60	2.92	2.92
Price of spring seat only, with two-leaf springs............	2.60	2.60	2.60	2.60	2.60
Stiff tongue in place of drop tongue, extra................	1.65	1.65	1.65	1.65	1.65
Boot end box, extra,..........	1.20	1.20	1.20	1.20	1.20
Bows and staples, per set, extra......................	.90	.90	.90	.90	.90
Steel skeins instead of cast skeins, extra................	2.95	3.54	4.13	4.72	5.31

Third top box, depth 6 inches, on any size wagon, $2.50. We furnish the third top box in depth as high as 15 inches at 40 cents for each additional inch over 6 inches. Price for heavy wagon is for wagon delivered on board the cars at Jackson, Michigan.

Highest Grade Farm Wagon Made.

WE OFFER AT A PRICE based on the actual cost of material and labor, what we believe to be the best farm wagon made, from one of the best factories in Michigan. We have agreed with the manufacturer not to use his name, but it is a wagon that sells everywhere under the manufacturer's name at $5.00 to $15.00 more than any of the regular standard wagons. **We furnish this wagon in either wide or narrow track, as desired, in either stiff or drop tongue, any width tire.** If you want wider than regular tire add to the price of the wagon **$2.00** for each one-half inch wider than regular; that is, if you want a 3-inch tire on wagon you will add **$2.00** to the price of the wagon; if you want box brake, add **$2.50**; gear brake, add **$5.00**. **At these special prices we furnish these wagons delivered free on board the cars at Jackson, Michigan.**

No. 89141

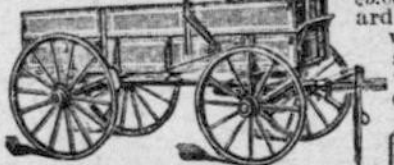

Our $25.25 One-Horse Tubular Steel Axle Wagon.

THIS IS THE VERY BEST SINGLE WAGON ON THE MARKET.

No. 89143

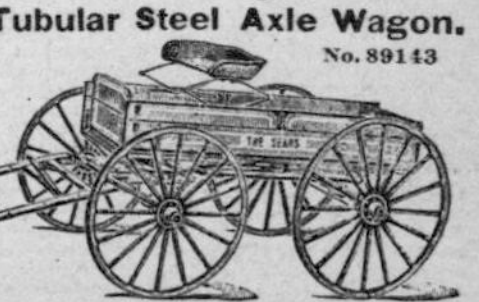

The guaranteed carrying capacity is given in schedule. This wagon is made to supply the demand for a light and strong wagon to be used about the farm. Extra for pole in place of shafts, $2.50. Extra for both pole and shafts, $4.50.

AT OUR SPECIAL $25.25, $29.35, $30.35 and $34.45 PRICES we furnish this wagon complete with double box spring seat and shafts. Brake, $5.00 extra.

Size of Axle.	Height of Wheels. Front.	Height of Wheels. Hind.	Length Box Outside.	Width of Box Outside.	Height. Lower Box.	Height. Top Box.	Size of Tire.	Carrying Capacity.	Shipping Weight.	PRICE, Complete.	PRICE, Gear Only.	When wanted with extra width Tire, add, for Size 2x⅜
1⅜ in.	3 ft. 6 in.	4 ft.	9 ft.	3 ft. 2 in.	9 in.	6 in.	1¼x⅝	1,500 lbs.	525 lbs.	$30.35	$25.25	$ 2.75
1⅜ in.	3 ft. 6 in.	4 ft.	9 ft.	3 ft. 2 in.	11 in.	6 in.	1⅜x7/16	2,200 lbs.	600 lbs.	34.45	29.35	2.75

BE SURE TO GIVE WIDTH OF TRACK, NARROW OR WIDE. ALL ORDERS FOR FARM WAGONS MUST BE ACCOMPANIED BY CASH IN FULL. THEY WILL NOT BE SHIPPED C. O. D.
PRICE FOR ONE-HORSE WAGON IS FOR WAGON DELIVERED ON BOARD CARS AT JACKSON, MICHIGAN.

DEPARTMENT OF HARNESS.

This department is complete with a full line of harness, and our prices are as low as the same goods ever sold by the largest manufacturers to the largest retail trade, and in many cases we have been able to make lower prices than the same class of goods were ever before sold at wholesale. You can save the profit of the retail dealer on everything in this line; in other words, at from 60 to 75 cents you can buy from us what your local dealer would ask you $1.00 for.

WE HANDLE THE VERY BEST OF HARNESS that is possible to be made. Our harness is made of the very best of **high grade leather with fine trimmings.** Our single and double buggy harness is of the **very latest styles** and the trimmings the very best nickel composition or **Davis rubber trimmings. Our Farm, Team and Concord Harness is of the very best that can be made, and we invite the closest comparison of quality and price.**

NOTICE. WE WILL MAKE ANY CHANGE you want in any of our team harness you may order from our catalogue, and only charge you what it costs us to make such changes, except where we say no changes made.

ALWAYS STATE the parts you want in place of the ones which are listed with the harness. **ALWAYS STATE** the size of collar wanted when ordering the harness with collars or in ordering sweat pads, if you want a harness without the collar always state the size of hames it will require to fit your collar. **ALWAYS STATE** the kind of checks wanted, whether overchecks or side checks. **IF YOU DO NOT STATE** the kind of check wanted, we will send you overcheck. **ALWAYS STATE** the style of the harness you want, whether single or double, also the kind of trimmings, whether XC, nickel or imitation rubber. **ALWAYS STATE** the weight of your horse. Give us the measurement of your horse around girth where saddle or pad work, and from gig saddle to horse's tail. The size of bridle from bit ring to bit ring over the head, and state style of horse, if long ranged or short chunky horse.

OUR TERMS AND CONDITIONS OF SHIPMENT. Orders for single harness on receipt of $1.00, and orders for double harness on receipt of $2.00, will be sent to any address by express **C. O. D., subject to examination.** You can examine the goods at your express office, and if found perfectly satisfactory and exactly as represented, pay the express agent the balance and express charges and the goods are yours. **THIS DOES NOT APPLY** to points in California, Washington, Oregon, Idaho, Montana, Utah, Nevada, Arizona, New Mexico, Colorado, Wyoming, Texas or Florida. From these states and territories cash in full must accompany your order.

YOU TAKE NO RISK. If the goods are not perfectly satisfactory and exactly as represented, we will refund your money. Nearly all our customers send cash in full.

WE MAKE NO CHARGE FOR BOXING crating, packing or cartage, **but deliver all goods at any express office or freight depot in Chicago free of charge.**

ANY QUESTIONS you may wish to ask pertaining to goods in this line will be promptly and cheerfully answered by expert saddlery man. Whether you write with a view to purchasing or not makes no difference.

Single Breast Collar Buggy Harness.

WE MAKE NO CHANGES IN THIS HARNESS.

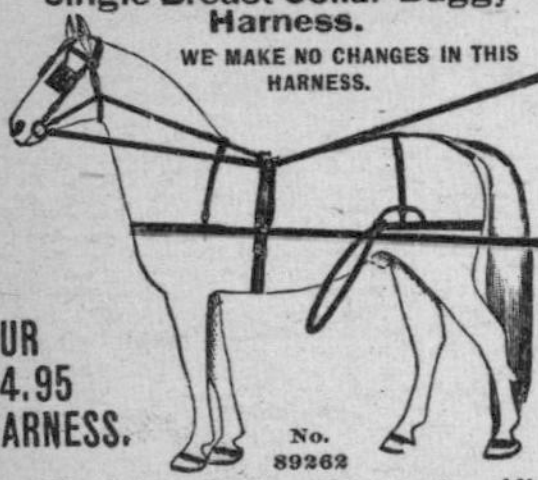

OUR $4.95 HARNESS. No. 89262

Bridle, ⅝-inch checks, patent leather blinds, flat winker brace and check reins, ring bit, fancy front and rosettes, overcheck or side reins, as desired; **lines,** ⅞-inch flat, all black, to loop in bit; **breast collar,** folded and stitched; **saddle,** 2½-inch, enameled cloth bottom, doubled and stitched bearers; **shaft tugs,** 1-inch with ⅞-inch buckles and ⅝-inch belly band billets; **belly band,** ⅞-inch flat; **breeching,** folded and stitched. ⅝-inch flat hip strap, ⅝-inch turn back, lapped and stitched to crupper pieces, folded crupper, docks sewed on breeching straps, ⅝-inch; **traces,** 1-inch doubled and stitched to breast collar. This single buggy harness comes in full XC trimmings, imitation hand sewed.

No. 89262 Price........................$4.95

Our Georgia Single Harness, $7.50.

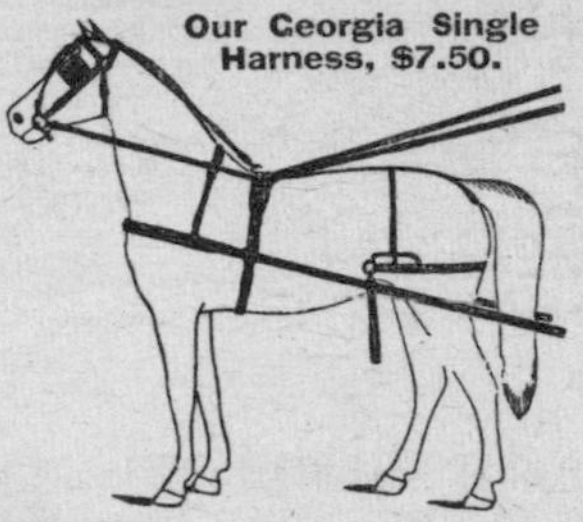

Bridle, ⅝-inch over check, box loops, round winker stay, initial letter rosette; **breast collar,** folded with wide layer and box loops; **traces,** 1-inch, double and stitched, round edge; **breeching,** folded with wide layer; **side straps,** ⅝-inch; **hip strap,** ⅝ inch; **turn back,** ⅝-inch, round crupper; **saddle,** 2¼-inch, single strap, all leather skirts and bottom, patent leather jockey; **belly band,** Griffith style; **lines,** ⅞xl-inch loop in bit, XC trimmings throughout. This harness will fit 900 to 1,250-pound horse.

No. 89272 Price,........................$7.50

No. 89273 Same as the description of No. 89272 with the exception of collar and hames in place of breast collar, 3½-pound iron hames, box loop, hame tugs, kip collars, 1-inch trace, double and stitched with round edge. Price........................$8.50

Weight, about 22 pounds.

Our Ashby Single Harness with Collar and Hames, $9.15.

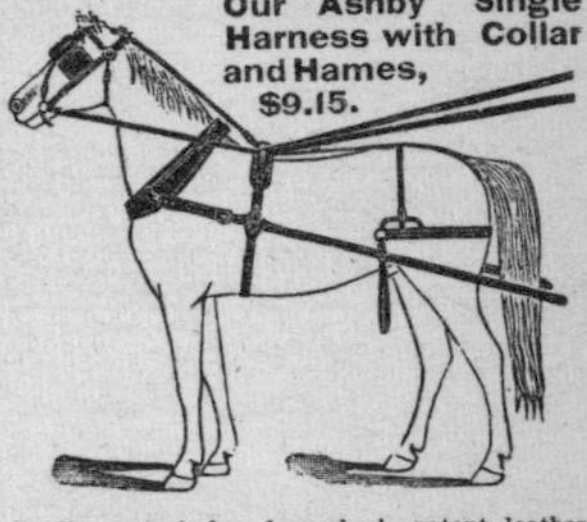

Bridle, ⅝ inch box loop check, patent leather blinds, round winker brace, overcheck or side rein; **lines,** ⅞ inch to loop in bit; **traces,** 1⅛ inch doubled and stitched, round-edge finish, 3½ pound hames, iron hame, full japanned on japanned harness and full XC plate on XC harness; **hame tug** with box loop; **breeching** folded with layer, ⅝-inch single hip strap, ⅝-inch side strap and ⅝ back strap, with crupper sewed on; **gig saddle,** 2½ single strap skirt, leather bottom with iron jockey; **bellyband flat,** Griffith style only. **collar full kip.** We do not make any changes in this harness, only furnish it as described above. This harness made in one size only for 900 to 1,200 pound horse.

No. 89279 Our special price with collar.....$9.15

Weight, boxed, about 35 pounds.

Our Texas Single Harness, $5.25.

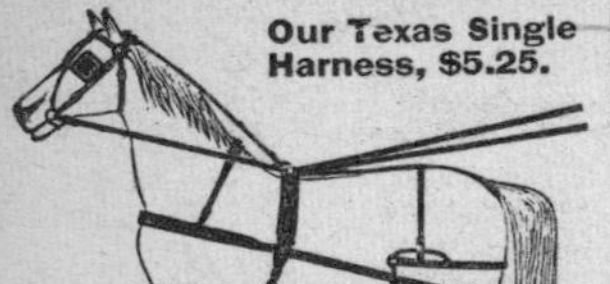

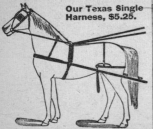

This harness is full size; a cheaper harness must be made smaller size. This harness will be large enough for a 900 to 1,200 pound horse. Don't buy a cheaper single harness than this one. We don't make any changes in this harness.

Bridle, ⅝-inch checks, patent leather blinds, flat winker brace and check reins, ring bit, fancy front and rosettes; over check or side reins, as desired; **lines,** ⅞-inch flat, all black, to loop in bit; **breast collar,** folded and stitched; **gig saddle,** 2½-inch, enameled cloth bottom, doubled and stitched bearers; **shaft tugs,** 1-inch with ⅞-inch buckles and ⅝-inch belly band billets; **belly band,** ⅞-inch flat; **breeching,** folded and stitched, ⅝-inch flat hip strap, ⅝-inch turn back, lapped and stitched to crupper pieces, folded crupper, docks sewed on breeching straps, ⅝-inch; **traces,** 1-inch doubled and stitched to breast collar. This single buggy harness comes in full XC trimmings, imitation hand sewed.

No. 89266 Price (Weight, about 12 lbs.)..$5.25

No. 89267 Same as the description of No. 89266 with the exception of collar and hames in place of breast collar, kip collar, any size, traces attached to hames. Price........................$6.25

State size of collar wanted. Weight, about 18 lbs.

Our Vicksburg Single Harness.

$8.20.

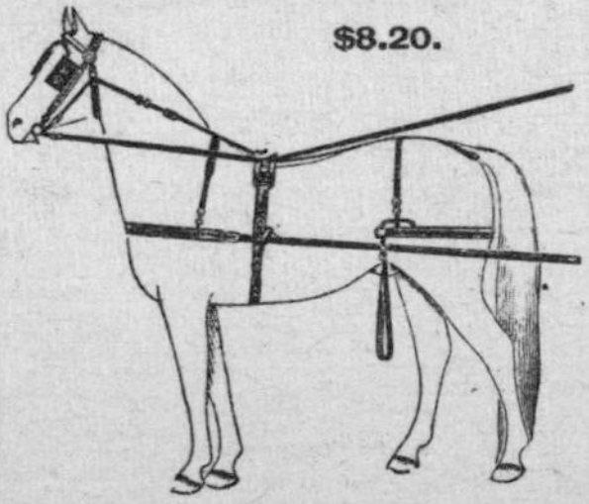

Bridle, ⅝-inch overcheck, box loops, round winker stay or side rim; **breast collar,** folded, with layer, box loops; **traces,** 1⅛-inch, doubled and stitched; **breeching,** folded, with layer, side straps ⅝-inch, hip strap ⅝-inch, turnback ⅝-inch, round crupper sewed on; **saddle,** 3-inch, iron jockey, harness leather skirts, leather bottom, double and stitched shaft rig; **belly band,** Griffith style only; **lines,** ⅞-inch to loop in. Trimming XC or japanned. This harness made for 900 to 1,250 pound horses.

No. 89278 Our special price........................$8.20

Will furnish this harness extra large for 1,400 pound horses for $1.00 extra.

Add for buckle on crupper........................15c

No. 89278½ Same style harness as No. 89278, only made in nickel trimming with **Patent Leather Jocky** saddle, selected quality leather, and smooth hames throughout, always sent with overcheck (unless order flat side rein).

Price, for nickel trimmed harness............$9.00

Our Iowa Single Harness.

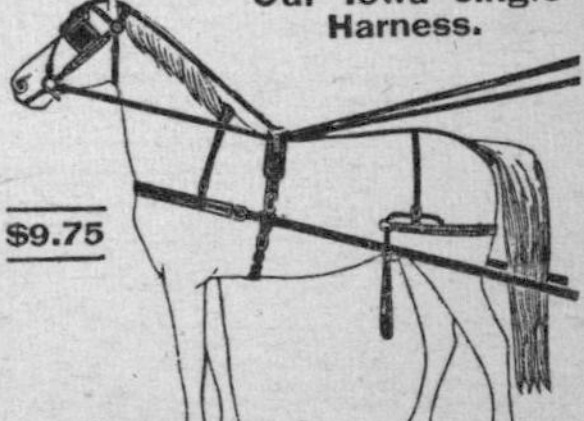

$9.75

Weight, boxed, 23 pounds.

Lines, a very important point about this harness is 1-inch line loop in bit; **extra good stock; gig saddle,** extra good single strap, harness leather skirt, with heavy bearer and shaft tug, **belly band** folds Griffith style, ⅝-inch hip strap, ⅝-inch side strap, ⅝-inch turn back scalloped, with round crupper sewed on; **breast collar,** folded with heavy straight layer and box loops; **breeching,** folded with heavy straight layer double and stitched breeching brace; **traces,** the most important part of this harness, are 1⅛ inches by 6 feet long, extra good stock, well made, smooth round edge to buckle in breast collar; **bridle,** ⅝-inch box loops, round winker brace, patent leather blind, over check or side rein, fancy front and **initial letter rosettes trimmings, fine nickel or Davis imitation rubber.**

No. 89281 Price, as illustrated............$9.7

Add extra to price of harness for buckles on crupper........................1

Will make this harness extra large for 1,400 to 1,60 horse for extra........................$2.0

Our Maine Single Buggy Harness, $11.20

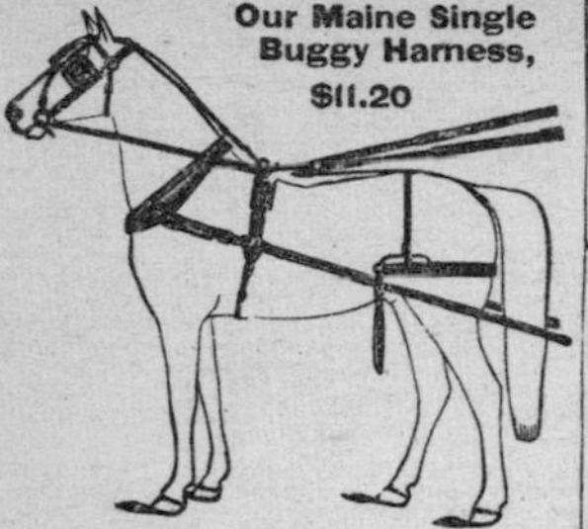

Weight, boxed, about 35 pounds.

NOTICE—This harness made extra large for 1400 and 1600 pound horse, for $2.00 extra to price of harness.

Bridle, ⅝ inch box loop, round winker brace, (**over check or side rein**) (blind or open bridle), patent leather blind fancy front with **initial letter rosette; lines,** 1 inch to loop in bit extra strong and well made; **gig saddle,** good single strap skirts, made of harness leather, double and stitched shaft bearer and shaft tug, belly band folded, **Griffith style or old style belly band; breeching** folded with straight **layers,** ¾ inch single hip strap, ⅝ inch side strap, ¾ turn back with round crupper sewed on; **traces,** the most important of any harness is made of selected **stock,** flat round edge 1⅛x6 feet, to buckle in hame **tug; hame and hame tug,** iron hame, japan body and nickel terret, 1⅛ hame tug box loop; **collar,** fine **kip** collar be sure and state size wanted.

No. 89282 Our special price with collar...	**$11.20**
Our special price less collar..................	**10.35**
Add extra for buckles on crupper...........	**.15**
Add extra for double hip strap, breeching..	**1.75**

Our Kansas Single Harness, $10.50.

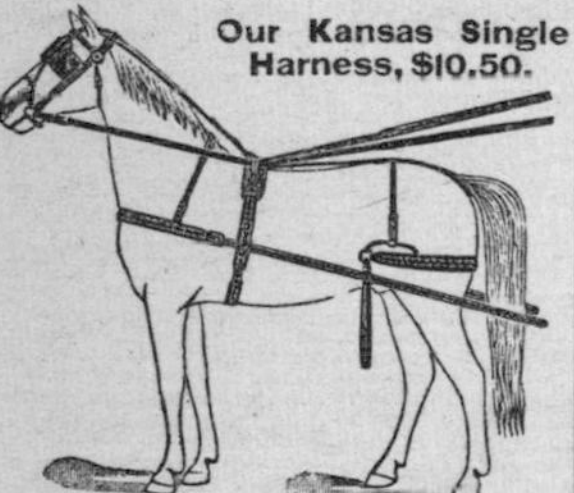

Our Great Bargain in Single Breast Collar Harness, double and stitched. This harness is made **of fine selected stock,** has a fine single strap saddle, with long patent leather jockey with 1 inch swing bearer, with terret and terret post, so you can **change the terret** and **make a low track saddle;** the bridle is made with nose band. The lines are extra fine ⅞x1⅛-inch hand parts, with spring billet.

Bridle, ⅝-inch box loop over check with nose band **or** side rein with initial rosettes, round winker braces, fine patent leather blind; **gig saddle,** fine single strap with patent leather jockey swinging bearer; **lines,** ⅞x1⅛-inch hand parts, black or russet; **breast collars, folded with layer and box loop,** folded neck strap; **turnback,** ¾-inch scalloped, with round crupper sewed on; **breeching,** folded with good layer 3-ring breeching stay, ⅝-inch hip strap, ⅝-inch side strap; **belly band,** Griffith style; **traces, one of the most important parts** about this **No. 89286** harness, they are extra heavy, raised round edges, 1⅛-inch by 6 feet long, **extra good.** This trace is made for service; **trimmings,** fine **nickel** on composition or Davis imitation rubber, fancy pattern.

No. 89286 Our special price............ ..	**$10.50**
Add extra to price of harness for buckles on crupper..................................	**.15**
Add for double hip strap breeching...........	**1.50**

This harness made size only for 900 to 1,250 lb. horse. Weight, boxed, about 24 pounds.

...IF DEALERS CAN BUY OF US...

AND SAVE MONEY

over what they have been paying the jobber,

How Much the More can the Consumer Save.

Our Bradford Single Buggy Harness.

Weight, 30 pounds.

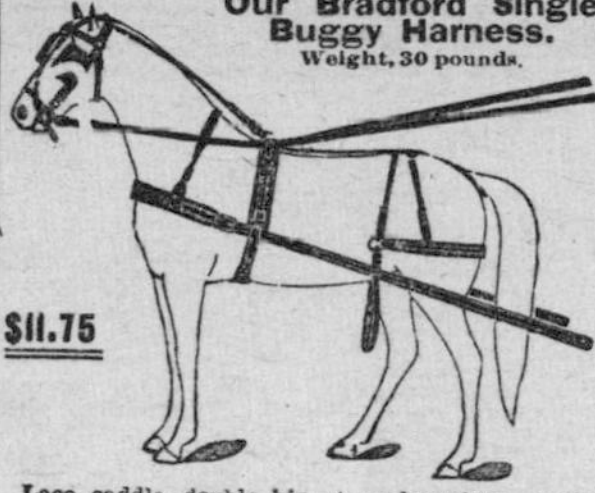

$11.75

Lace saddle, double hip strap breeching, made of extra fine quality of Dundee oak leather, nickel or Davis rubber **trimmings. Bridle,** ⅝-inch, box loop check around winker trace, patent leather blinds, fancy front initial rosettes, overcheck or side rein with tie strap; **lines,** ⅞-inch front with 1⅛-inch hand part and spring billets; **breast collar,** folded with buckle and box loop 1⅛-inch, double stitched, raised round the edge trace. Dee shaft tug with double belly band, or Griffith style if wanted; **gig saddle,** fine patent leather, hand laced leather lined; **breeching,** folded, with layer, ⅝-inch double hip straps, double scallops and stitched back strap with crupper to buckle on, ⅞-inch side strap.

No. 89291 Our special price for **nickel or Davis rubber**....................................	**$11.75**
Add extra for collar and hames in place of breast collar................................	**$2.50**

This harness made for 900 to 1,250 pound horse.

Doctor's Heavy Single Harness.

Notice—If you want 3½-inch full pad, hand buffed, patent leather gig saddle in place of single strap saddle, add $2.00 extra to price of harness. This is an extra fine, full pad saddle.

$16.35

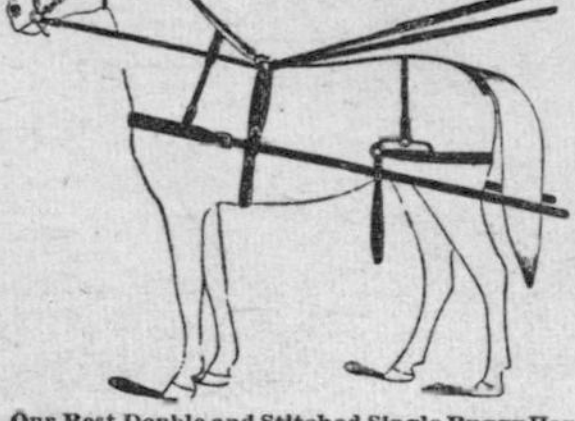

Our Best Double and Stitched Single Buggy Harness. This is a strictly new harness throughout, the call for a fine single harness of this style caused us to make it. Made of the **best of oak tanned harness leather,** well stitched throughout, we have used great care in making the bridle lines, gig saddle and traces. You will find this harness **one of the best** that was ever offered at this price............**$16.35**

Bridle, ⅝-inch box loop with fine patent leather blind, round winker brace, over check with **nose band** or side rein; **lines,** a very important part of a good harness; are made of the **best of leather,** 1 inch by 1⅛-inch hand part, russet or black; **breast collar,** heavy fold, hand finished leather, with fine scalloped raised layer safe under buckle, box loop, small tug box loop. Folded neck strap; **traces,** this is the finest 1⅛-inch by 6 feet raised trace made. We have been very careful to see that they are the best we could make for this grade of harness. Fine round edge finish; **breeching,** heavy fold hand finished, leather scalloped and raised layer, 3-ring breeching stay with box loop tug: **turnback,** ⅞-inch scalloped with round crupper, sewed on ⅝-inch hip strap; **belly band,** heavy fold Griffith style, or **state old style shaft tug if wanted; gig saddle,** this is one of the best gig saddles made, has heavy single strap harness, leather skirt, extra good patent leather jockey, heavy bearer and shaft tugs; **trimmings, full nickel or Davis rubber.**

No. 89300 Price, per set single harness....	**$16.35**
No. 89301 Price, per set **Genuine Rubber Harness**..	**19.45**
No. 89302 Nickel or Davis Rubber Harness, with collar and hame in place of breast collar. Price, complete..............................	**19.75**

No. 89304 Genuine Rubber Harness, with collar and hame in place of breast collar. Be sure and state size of collar wanted.

Price, per set......................................	**24.50**
Add for buckle crupper........................	**.15**
Add for double hip strap breeching..........	**2.25**

NOTE—This harness will be furnished extra large for 1,400 and 1,600-pound horse for $2.00 extra to price of harness.

Weight, boxed for shipment, 30 to 50 pounds.

Our Jones Folded and Stitched Harness $12.75.

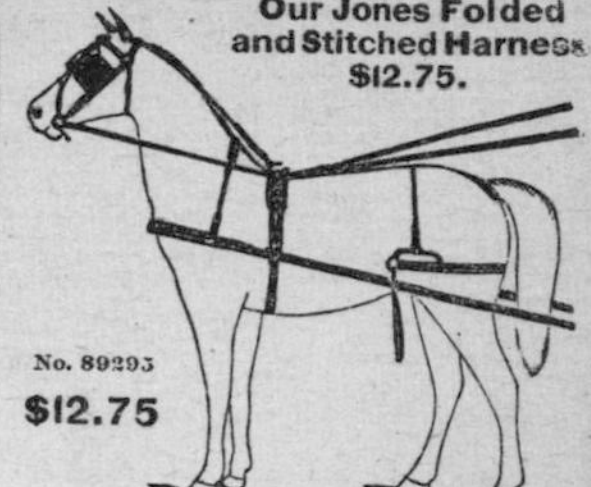

No. 89295

$12.75

We have improved this No. 89295 single buggy harness. We are making this harness this season with a number of changes. You will find this harness strictly first-class throughout.

Bridle, ⅝-inch box loop fine patent leather, blind round winker brace, **over check** with **nose band** or side check. Fancy front with **initial letter rosette; breast collar,** heavy fold with scalloped raised layer safe under buckle with box loop; folded neck strap; **traces,** the **most important** part of this harness, has been selected with great care, 1⅛-inch by 6 feet long, raised round edge finish; **gig saddle,** this is one of the **best** single strap gig saddles made, heavy harness, leather skirts, with long patent leather jockey; heavy bearers, **good shaft tug; belly band,** Griffith style; **turnback,** ¾-inch scalloped with round crupper **hip strap,** ⅝-inch; **breeching,** heavy fold with **fine scalloped layer,** with 3-ring breeching stay well made; **lines,** the lines, together with traces, are **very important,** this line is made from **the best** of leather 1-inch by 1⅛-inch hand parts, black or russet with spring billet; **trimmings,** nickel or Davis imitation rubber.

No. 89295 Price, per set	**$12.75**
For folded russet hand part add...............	**0.75**
For genuine rubber trimming add, extra.....	**2.25**
For collar and hame in place of breast collar, add..	**3.00**

The harness made, size only for 900-pound to 1,250 pound horses.

Weight, 24 pounds.

Our Vermont Single Buggy Harness, $13.95.

Made in collar and hame style only; made size only for 900 to 1,250 pound horse.

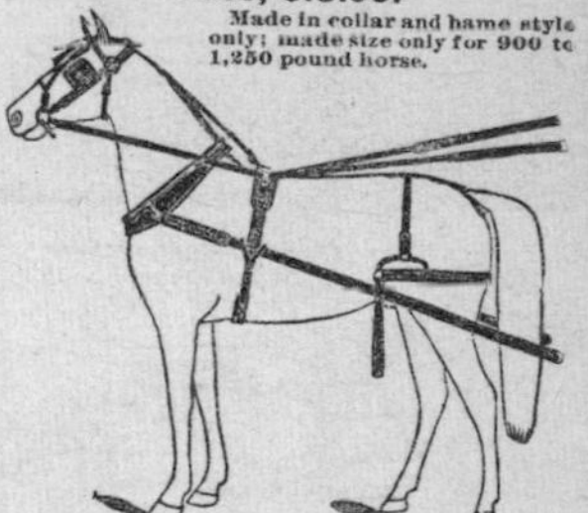

Bridle, ⅝-inch box loop check, patent leather blinds, round winker stay, overcheck with nose band or side check, with layer on crown piece; fancy front initial rosettes and tie strap; **lines,** ⅞-inch front with spring billets to buckle in bit, 1⅛ inch hand parts, russet or black; **collar,** half patent leather, 3½ pound iron hames, box loop hame tug riveted on; **traces,** 1⅛ inch doubled and stitched, raised, round-edge finished; **breeching,** folded with heavy raised layer, ⅝-inch single hip strap, ⅞-inch side strap, ⅞-inch scalloped and stitched back strap, with flaxseed cruppers sewed on; **gig saddle,** 3-inch single strap, harness leather skirt, patent leather jockey, with beaded housing, doubled and stitched shaft bearers, box loop shaft tug, folded belly band, Griffith or old style; **trimmings,** nickel or imitation rubber only. We make no changes whatever in this harness. Sold only as listed above.

No. 89297 Price per set, with collar.......	**$13.95**
If wanted without collar deduct...............	**.85**
Add extra for buckle crupper..................	**.15**

Weight about 37 pounds boxed.

THE USER OF A HARNESS SAVES

Every Profit and Expense

that comes between the making of goods at the factory and their delivery at his door

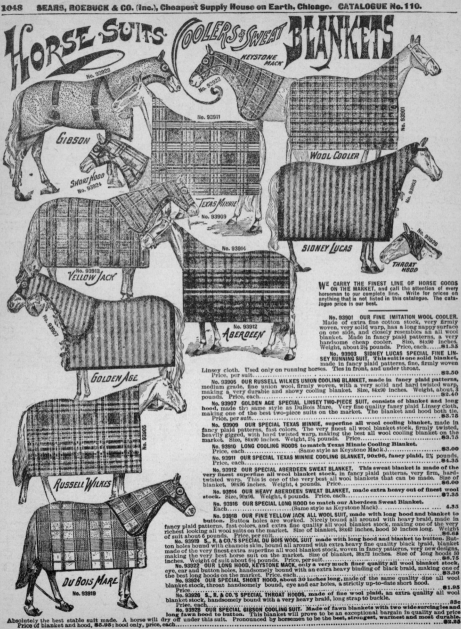

HORSE SUITS, COOLERS & SWEAT BLANKETS

No. 93923

No. 93922   KEYSTONE MACK

No. 93911

No. 93901

GIBSON

WOOL COOLER

SHORT HOOD
No. 93924

No. 93903

TEXAS MINNIE
No. 93909

No. 93914

No. 93926

No. 93913
YELLOW JACK

SIDNEY LUCAS

THROAT HOOD

No. 93907

No. 93912
ABERDEEN

WE CARRY THE FINEST LINE OF HORSE GOODS ON THE MARKET, and call the attention of every horseman to our complete line. Write for prices on anything that is not listed in this catalogue. The catalogue price is our best.

GOLDEN AGE

No. 93901   OUR FINE IMITATION WOOL COOLER. Made of extra fine cotton stock, very firmly woven, very solid warp, has a long nappy surface on one side, and closely resembles an all wool blanket. Made in fancy plaid patterns, a very handsome cheap cooler. Size, 84x90 inches. Weight, about 2½ pounds. Price, each....$1.35

No. 93903   SIDNEY LUCAS SPECIAL FINE LINSEY RUNNING SUIT. This suit is one solid blanket, made in fancy plaid patterns, fine, firmly woven Linsey cloth. Used only on running horses. Ties in front, and under throat.
Price, per suit.....................................$2.50

No. 93905   OUR RUSSELL WILKES UNION COOLING BLANKET, made in fancy plaid patterns, medium grade, fine union wool, firmly woven, with a very solid and hard twisted warp, making a very durable and showy cooling blanket. Size, 84x90 inches. Weight, about 3 pounds. Price, each....................$2.40

No. 93907   GOLDEN AGE SPECIAL LINSEY TWO-PIECE SUIT, consists of blanket and long hood, made the same style as DuBois Mare. Very fine quality fancy plaid Linsey cloth, making one of the best two-piece suits on the market. The blanket and hood both tie.
Price, per suit.....................................$3.75

No. 93909   OUR SPECIAL TEXAS MINNIE, superfine all wool cooling blanket, made in fancy plaid patterns, fast colors. The very finest all wool blanket stock, firmly twisted, heavily gigged, with hard twisted warp, making the best all wool cooling blanket on the market. Size, 84x90 inches. Weight, 2½ pounds. Price..................$3.75

RUSSELL WILKES

No. 93905

No. 93910   LONG COOLING HOODS to match Texas Minnie Cooling Blanket.
Price, each........(Same style as Keystone Mack.)................$3.00

No. 93911   OUR SPECIAL TEXAS MINNIE COOLING BLANKET, 90x96, fancy plaid, 2½ pounds.
Price, each...$4.35

No. 93912   OUR SPECIAL ABERDEEN SWEAT BLANKET. This sweat blanket is made of the very finest superfine all wool blanket stock, in fancy plaid patterns, very firm, hard twisted warp. This is one of the very best all wool blankets that can be made. Size of blanket, 90x96 inches. Weight, 4 pounds. Price............................$6.00

No. 93914   OUR HEAVY ABERDEEN SWEAT BLANKET, made extra heavy out of finest wool stock. Size, 90x96. Weight, 6 pounds. Price, each.......................$7.35

No. 93916   OUR SPECIAL LONG HOOD to match our Aberdeen Sweat Blanket.
Each........(Same style as Keystone Mack)......................4.35

No. 93918   OUR FINE YELLOW JACK ALL WOOL SUIT, made with long hood and blanket to button. Button holes are worked. Nicely bound all around with heavy braid, made in fancy plaid patterns, fast colors, and extra fine quality all wool blanket stock, making one of the very richest looking all wool suits on the market. Size of blanket, 38x42 inches, hood 50 inches long. Weight of suit about 6 pounds. Price, per suit.................................$5.65

No. 93919   S. R. & CO.'S SPECIAL DU BOIS WOOL SUIT, made with long hood and blanket to button. Button holes bound with chamois skin, bound all around with extra heavy fine quality black braid, blanket made of the very finest extra superfine all wool blanket stock, woven in fancy patterns, very new designs, making the very best horse suit on the market. Size of blanket, 38x72 inches. Size of long hoods 50 inches. Weight of suit about 6½ pounds. Price, per suit.........................$8.75

No. 93922   OUR LONG HOOD, KEYSTONE MACK, only a very much finer quality all wool blanket stock, eye, ear and button holes, handsomely bound with an extra heavy binding of black braid, making one of the best long hoods on the market. Price, each...........................$3.30

No. 93924   OUR SPECIAL SHORT HOOD, about 30 inches long, made of the same quality fine all wool blanket stock, throat handsomely bound, eye and ear holes, a strictly up-to-date short hood.
Price...$1.95

No. 93926   S. R. & CO.'S SPECIAL THROAT HOODS, made of fine wool plaid, an extra quality all wool blanket stock, handsomely bound with a very heavy braid, long strap to buckle.
Price, each...83c

No. 93928   OUR SPECIAL GIBSON COOLING SUIT. Made of fawn blankets with two wide surcingles and long fawn hood to button. This blanket will prove to be an exceptional bargain in price and quality. Pronounced by horsemen to be the best, strongest, warmest and most durable. Price of blanket and hood, $5.95; hood only, price, each.....$2.35

DU BOIS MARE
No. 93919

Absolutely the best stable suit made. A horse will dry off under this suit.

SEARS ROEBUCK & CO
INCORPORATED
FURNITURE DEPARTMENT

OUR FURNITURE DEPARTMENT includes almost every modern thing in Furniture. In this book you will find the prices based on the actual cost to manufacture with only one small percentage of profit added, which means you can buy furniture from us cheaper than from any other house, in fact, for less money than local dealers can buy in car lots.

OUR SPECIAL TERMS We will send Furniture to any address by freight C. O. D., subject to examination, on receipt of sufficient deposit to cover freight charges both ways, balance to be paid when received.

OUR GUARANTEE We guarantee every piece of Furniture we advertise to be exactly as represented. Made from selected material in a first class mechanical manner, and, if not found so, you can return it to us and we will refund your money.

OUR DINING ROOM AND KITCHEN
...CHAIRS...

are Green Bay (Wis.) goods, strictly high grade, made for us under contract by one of the best makers in America. Order these chairs from us and you will find for

QUALITY OF WOOD,
STRENGTH.........
STYLE AND FINISH,

you cannot equal them elsewhere at within 50 per cent of our price.

... SPECIAL LEADERS IN ...
KITCHEN AND DINING ROOM CHAIRS.

Our 45-Cent Chair.
No. 94250 Same as No. 94253 only has three spindles in back. We offer this Wood Seat Kitchen Chair at the lowest price ever known for a really first class chair. It has three spindles and bow back, hardwood, finished plain, in antique or dark, as may be desired. Our special price,
Each.................45c

Our 50-Cent Chair.
No. 94252 The Wood Seat Chair shown in the illustration is especially well constructed and is far better than the one preceding. This is a kitchen chair that can seldom be obtained at retail at 65 cents. Our special price is made with a view of proving our ability to render better value than any other house in existence. This chair is made with four spindles, bow back, fancy ornamental stripes. It is made of hardwood and finished in antique. Our special price, each 50c

No. 94250

No. 94252

68 Cents Buys This Handsome $1.00 Dining Chair.

No. 94254 At the above price we are offering a diner which for solid construction, handsome design and style will compare favorably with chairs offered by many dealers at even double our price. Made of select rock elm,carefully seasoned. It is durable; put up by one of the best manufacturers, and is very choice. The workmanship is that which only skilled wood workers can produce. This chair is well finished and the handsome carving adds greatly to its appearance. Fancy spindles in black, solid wood seat and strong, well braced legs. Antique gloss finish. Our special price, each..........68c

85 Cents Buys this $1.25 Dining Room Chair.

No. 94257 Wearable to offer this unusual value, notwithstanding the advance in material and labor, by taking practically the entire output of the factory. 85 cents is practically the manufacturer's cost on this chair. We make the price 85 cents to show how much value can be put into a small price, to show for how little money a really good chair can be furnished, and as an advertisement for this department. One of our newest and most perfect pattern of medium priced chairs, high back, richly carved, fancy turned rope spindles in back, full wood seat, made of rock elm, finished antique.
Price, each.....85c

A Neat High Back Chair

No. 94261 The accompanying cut illustrates one of the handsome dining room chairs made, a chair that you would pay your local dealer at least $1.50 for, but at our special price of 95c, with freight added, if your order amounts to 100 lbs., the chair will cost you $1.00. This chair is made from thoroughly seasoned elm wood, finished antique, made extra high, beautifully carved back, and one of the best chairs in the market.
Price, each 95c

No. 94265 This is a new pattern of high back wood seat chair. The design is one of the handsomest of the many we are showing this season. Made of best quality of rock elm, thoroughly seasoned; high back posts and spindles are of graceful design; the top is large and handsomely carved; it has a comfortable seat and is square; the legs are well braced by nine stretchers of pleasing design. The finish is gloss and is better than most of the so-called polish finishes.
Each....................$1.10
Per set of six.............6.00

Our $1.35 Diner.

No. 94269 This is an unusually attractive wood seat chair; beautifully carved back, seat with fancy shaped legs, has fancy turned spindles in back, and full braced legs. One of the newest and best patterns, and made in best selected elm. Finished antique golden oak.
Price, each..............$1.35

$1.15 Buys a Regular $1.75 Diner.

No. 94271 This is a strictly new and desirable pattern, just put on the market, and the newest thing out for 1900 trade. It has a beautifully embossed high back with six spindles. Woven cane seat, strongly built legs and spindles. The chair is a decided bargain and is offered by us at about half of what you will ordinarily pay for a chair of equal value at retail. Made of solid kiln dried oak.

Our special price................$1.15

No. 94275 This handsome chair is made of solid oak. It has a high back, with an elaborately carved top; the seat is hand woven cane supported to the fancy cane supported bent brace arms. The legs are securely fastened to the seat and are braced by eight stretchers, making it a very strong and beautiful chair. This chair cannot be duplicated by any one, as it is one of our special designs for 1900.
Price, each $1.40

Our Special $2.75 Rocker.

No. 94391 A beautiful high back fully carved Rocker, with full cobbler leather seat. Made of the best selected rock elm, finished antique; broad and roomy and very comfortable. Also made in mahogany finish. Price......$2.75

Our $1.45 Cobbler Seat Rocker.

No. 94393 A Beautifully Carved Rocker, with full wood seat. Made of the best selected rock elm, finished antique; broad and roomy and very comfortable. Price $1.45

Special $3.00 Rocker.

No. 94395 This very handsome Rocker has every high back with upper panel nicely carved; has genuine cobbler leather seat, is very broad and roomy, and guaranteed to be unusually well made and comfortable; made of oak, finished antique. We can also furnish this rocker in mahogany finish. Price....... $3.00

Ladies' $3.45 Parlor Rocker.

No. 94397 This beautiful Rocker, illustrated herewith, is made of solid oak, handsomely finished. Beautifully carved panel back. Full spring bottom. Upholstered in silk plush or brocaline, as desired, and in any color. In ordering, be sure to state color wanted. Price, each $3.45

Latest Design for $2.85.

No. 94403 A beautiful Rocker, large and comfortable; high back, richly carved, has fancy turned rope moulding, rope spindles and posts. Genuine cobbler leather seat. Made of the finest golden elm, hand polished. A rocker that recommends itself for price and quality. Price.....$2.85

Latest Design for $3.25.

No. 94415 A beautiful Rocker, large and comfortable, high back, richly carved, has fancy turned moulding, spindles and posts. Genuine cobbler leather seat. Made in solid antique oak or mahogany finish. A rocker that recommends itself for price, elegance and quality. Price............$3.25

No. 94413 This is a Rocker that is without a doubt elegant enough for the best appointed home. We offer it at a price which brings it within the reach of all. Made of the finest quarter sawed oak or birch with a rich mahogany finish, has beautiful carved back panels of artistic design, fancy turned spindles, broad shaped comfortable arms and fancy illuminated embossed leather seat and is different from the every-day rocker in appearance. Price, each $4.75

65-Cent Child's Rocker.

No. 94431 We show a handsome little Rocker that will delight the children. It is well made and thoroughly substantial. Strongly braced arms, bent back, with turned spindles, wood seat. Finished in antique oak or red. Our special price, each 65c

90-Cent Nursery Chair.

No. 94433 This Chair is really a household necessity, and no family with children should be without one. It is made up handsomely of the best rock elm, handsomely decorated, has full back with three spindles and table in front. It is strongly constructed, handsomely finished either in regular or antique oak or red. Our special price, each...................90c

No. 94435 The Misses' Rocker, we show in illustration, is an entirely new pattern. The back has a beautiful design and carving, the back posts are handsomely turned and arms are securely fastened to the seat posts. Legs are fancy turned and well braced. Rockers securely attached. This rocker is made of the very best rock elm, handsomely finished in antique oak. Our special price, each...................$1.20

No. 94437 Child's Rocker. The comfortable back is beautifully carved and has an elegant appearance. The arms are securely attached to back and seat. Seat is wood, legs are strong and well braced, the rockers are securely attached to them. We make this rocker of the very best kiln dried elm and finish it in antique oak. Our special price, each..............$1.15

No. 94449 This Rocker is made of kiln dried and thoroughly seasoned rock elm, handsomely finished in antique oak, has beautifully carved top, bent arms securely bolted to back and seat; wood seat, strong legs well braced and with rockers thoroughly well attached. A good honest rocker at a good honest price.
Our special price, each............$1.30

No. 94454 A Child's Rocker that is a beauty. Magnificent carving. Fancy turned spindles, and made to stand hard knocks. A bargain. Price...................$1.40

No. 94458 A pretty gift for a child yet very sensible and useful, made of the best reed and rattan, and is very neat and attractive. Price......$1.30

Reed and Rattan Rockers and Chairs.

No. 94485 A Very Neat and Pretty Rocker. Made of the best imported reeds; full braced and supported arms; panel front, medium high back. Perfect in construction and finish. Price..$2.25

No. 94487 One of our best patterns in a medium priced Rocker; has full roll extending over and around back and sides, fancy turned spindles under the arm and also in back; a comfortable sewing rocker and very pretty, made of the best reeds, fancy colors or plain. Guaranteed to give service and satisfaction. In shellac finish. Price...................$3.60

A Beautiful Reed Rocker for $3.50.

No. 94491 Large and exceptionally comfortable Rocker, of the best quality of reeds, made for everyday service and guaranteed to wear equal to wood; is very attractive and the workmanship unexcelled. In shellac or natural finish. Price................$3.50

Our Special $2.55 Reed Rocker.

No. 94493 A very pretty and comfortable Ladies' Reed Rocker made of the best materials in a very attractive design, has a high fancy back well supported with brace arms and is an attractive and useful piece of furniture. In shellac or natural finish. Price.................$2.55

$4.25 Buys $6.50 Reed Rocker.

No. 94495 A comfortable Ladies' Rocker, of handsome pattern. Very pretty arrangement of the design in the back; full roll extending all around and over the arms, made of the best reeds, in the most perfect manner, an d guaranteed to give the best of service and satisfaction; in shellac finish. Price.............$4.25

Plush Upholstered Reed Rocker for $4.45.

No. 94497 A large roomy and ornamental Rocker, consisting of an artistic combination of oak and the finest selected reed, with the seat and back handsomely upholstered in the finest silk plush; this is one of the handsomest medium priced rockers ever offered. Price.......$4.45

$4.40 Buys a $6.50 Reed Rocker.

No. 94501 A large comfortable Rocker, made of best selected reeds, interwoven with fancy colors, full roll arm, graceful outlines and very roomy, and guaranteed for years of comfort and service. Price............$4.40

Worth $7.00. Our Price, $4.60.

No. 94504 A superb comfort Rocker of the finest materials, honestly constructed for service as well as for appearance. Made in combination of plain and colored reeds and is an attractive and desirable addition to the home furnishings. Price.................$4.60

Home Comfort Rocker, only $5.25.

No. 94506 One of our best values; is one of the most comfortable and roomy patterns shown; has full roll arms closely woven, full skirt around the base and made in a combination of plain and fancy colored reeds. A great bargain. Price................$5.25

A Handsome New Design.

No. 94508 This beautiful Rocker is made of selected quarter sawed oak, finished antique and the finest selected reeds. The seat and back are upholstered in the finest silk plush tufted and it is a rich and elegant adornment to the home. Price.....................$5.00

Our Gentlemen's Special Rocker, $5.65.

No. 94510 A large, roomy Rocker for gentlemen; has full roll all around, woven cane seat; back is high so as to afford head rest. Made of finest reeds in combination of plain and fancy colors, very comfortable and handsome. Price....................$5.65

Built for Wear, an Exceptional Value.

No. 94521 One of the best comfort rockers, with full roll arms all around. Made of the best reed and so shaped as to conform to the body. Has full reed basket seat, and will give great comfort and service. Price.................$6.50

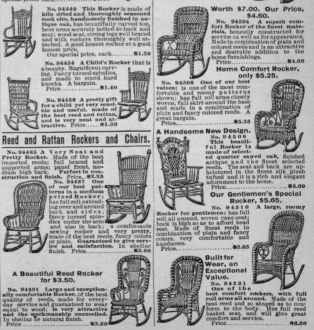

Department of Kitchen and Dining Room Furniture.

We take pleasure in calling your attention to a line of kitchen and dining room furniture, including kitchen tables, dining tables, extension tables, sideboards, buffets, etc., which for quality of material, workmanship and price we feel confident our customers will agree is not equaled by any other line.

Our terms are liberal. Anything in this department, like any other goods, will be sent to any address by freight C. O. D., subject to examination, on receipt of a sufficient deposit to cover freight charges both ways.

Our $1.45 Kitchen Table.

No. 94600 The Kitchen Table which we show in the accompanying illustration is made of basswood, with hardwood legs and large, roomy drawer. It is strongly constructed and has bolt leg fasteners. It can be taken apart for shipping, thus saving very largely on freight. This table is a household necessity and no kitchen is complete without it. Nicely finished. Weighs about 40 lbs. Size of top, 28x42 inches.
Price, each...$1.45

Our $5.40 Handy Kitchen Table.

No. 94602 Among the inventions for assisting the housekeeper, we know of nothing that is more convenient or satisfactory for household uses than the kitchen table we illustrate above. You can gain but very little idea from the illustration of the genuine value of this special table. It saves the tired housewife many a weary step, and keeps all the articles which can be contained therein neat and clean. It is the largest shown and contains, as shown in illustration, two flour bins, one with two compartments and the other with one, all of them large and roomy. Besides, it has two drawers with compartments for cutlery, etc., and two convenient slides. This kitchen table is made of the best hardwood with basswood top and the size of top is 30x48 inches. The table is strongly constructed and will last a lifetime. It is well finished and presents a good appearance. Our special price..................$5.40

Our $2.95 Breakfast Table.

No. 94604 This is one of the most desirable and necessary articles of furniture and one that is convenient for breakfast use or for general kitchen use. This is not an extension table, but the leaves at either side may be dropped so that the table will take up little space when not in use. It is made of selected kiln dried ash with handsome antique finish, and we furnish it in either oval top, as illustrated, or square top, as may be desired. The size of top in either case is 42 inches wide by 52 inches long. The table can be taken apart and shipped knocked down, thus saving freight charges.
Our special price....................................$2.95

Our $3.90 Extension Table.

This Extension Table is made of thoroughly seasoned ash, iron bolted legs, comes complete with best set of casters and is guaranteed in every respect. Size of top closed, 30x42 inches.

No. 94610 Price for 6-foot table	$3.90
No. 94611 Price for 8-foot table	5.25
No. 94612 Price for 10-foot table	6.60

Weight of tables about 75 lbs.

Our $4.90 Extension Table.

The old fashioned Round Drop Leaf Table, which we show in the illustration, is an old time favorite and never goes out of date nor does it lose any of its desirable features. This table is especially well constructed by one of the best manufacturers in this line of goods. It is made of ash, with an oval top, the size of which is 42x42 inches. Can be taken apart and shipped knocked down, thus saving very largely in the freight rate. It comes in three sizes at the following prices:

No. 94616 Price for 6-foot table	$4.90
No. 94617 Price for 8-foot table	6.60
No. 94618 Price for 10-foot table	7.90

Table weighs 100 lbs. Complete with casters.

No. 94621 Price for 6-foot table	$6.25
No. 94622 Price for 8-foot table	7.75
No. 94623 Price for 10-foot table	9.90

For $6.25 we offer you a table that your dealer would ask at least $7.00 for. This pillar extension table is made of solid oak, beautifully finished, nicely carved and ornamented. Size of top, 42x42 inches. Made with bolted legs. Solid molded top rim.

This Pillar Extension Table is made of solid oak, with a heavy molded top rim. It has a beautiful polish finish and good casters. Size of top, 42x42 inches.

No. 94627 Price for 6-foot table	$6.95
No. 94628 Price for 8-foot table	8.90
No. 94629 Price for 10-foot table	10.50

This Pillar Extension Table is made of solid oak, beautifully finished, nicely carved and ornamented. Size of top, 42x42 inches. Heavily molded sides. Weight of table, 100 lbs. All extension tables furnished complete with casters.

No. 94633 Price for 6-foot table	7.50
No. 94634 Price for 8-foot table	9.00
No. 94635 Price for 10-foot table	10.50

Our $5.95 Antique Oak Finished Table.

An unusual opportunity has put in our hands a large consignment of these handsome Dining Tables which we are offering at $5.95. At this price, even, our large stock will be taxed to meet the demand, but we hope to have no trouble in filling every order. This table is made of the best selected and thoroughly seasoned ash, finished in antique oak, as shown in illustration; is very handsome, and just as good as it looks. Size of top, 42x42 inches when closed. The legs are iron bolted and in every way the table is substantial and well finished. Complete with casters. Weight, packed, about 100 pounds.

No. 94640 Price for 6-foot table	$5.95
No. 94641 Price for 8-foot table	7.20
No. 94642 Price for 10-foot table	8.70

Stylish and Handsomely Finished Round Extension Table for $10.90.

Round Extension Tables are very popular at present, and deservedly so. The pattern shown here is one of our new styles and is bound to be a favorite at our price. Made throughout of elegantly finished oak, with five massive 4-inch legs, neatly turned. It is an ornament for any dining room. Size of top when closed, 46 inches in diameter. The leaves are all fitted to the table and numbered in our factory; legs are fitted with latest improved casters. Weight (6 foot) packed, 140 lbs.

No. 94636 Price for 6-foot table	$10.90
No. 94637 Price for 8-foot table	12.90
No. 94637½ Price for 10-foot table	15.50

$7.00 Buys a Regular $10.00 Extension Table.

This Pillar Extension Table is made of solid heavy oak, finished antique, piano polished, carved rim, very fancy carved legs. Size of top, 42x42 inches. Complete with casters.

No. 94666 Price for 6-foot table	$7.00
No. 94675 Price for 8-foot table	$8.90

FANCY SIDEBOARDS.

Our trade in sideboards is such that we are enabled to procure the highest grade goods at an exceedingly low price, and hence make it possible for those of limited means to possess a quality of furniture such as they have heretofore been prevented from buying on account of the high price charged by retail stores and other catalogue houses.

Our sideboards are all guaranteed. We have them made up in special designs with great care by experienced workmen, and from selected material, finished in the best possible manner and put together with special attention to solidity as well as appearance.

Our prices are only made possible by practically taking the entire output of three of the best manufacturers in this line of goods.

When a sufficient amount is sent with your order to guarantee the freight charges both ways, we are only too glad to send any sideboard C. O. D., subject to examination, by freight. Most of our customers prefer to save themselves all the annoyance of C. O. D. shipments and remit money with the order. This is especially true of all our old customers who have dealt with us before and know that the money is as safe in our hands as in the bank.

$12.75 Buys a Regular $15.00 Sideboard.

No. 94700 This handsome Sideboard is made of the best oak, 43 inches long and 20 inches wide. Has full serpentine shaped top drawers, shaped mirror, size, 14x24 inches, one upper drawer lined for silver. It is handsomely carved and finished and has neat, good trimmings. Price........$12.75

Elegantly Carved Sideboard for $15.50.

No. 94702 One of the best Sideboards ever offered that has such good features for so low a price. Made of quartered antique oak; top is serpentine shaped, is 43 inches long and 20 inches wide. All the drawers are serpentine shaped, and has a pretty shaped mirror, size 14x24 inches. In very prettily carved and well made, and finished; upper drawer lined for silver, and has neat, pretty brass trimmings. Weighs about 175 lbs. Price..................$15.50

A $25.00 Sideboard for $19.50.

This is another of our best medium priced sideboards.

No. 94704 Made of the best oak, antique finish, with a graceful serpentine shaped top, 46 inches long and 22 inches wide; swell front drawers, one lined for silver; is handsomely carved and has a shaped bevel French plate mirror 18x30 inches; a real bargain.
Price........................$19.50

No. 94706 A good solid and substantial Sideboard, bevel plate mirror, 28x40 inches; serpentine top, drawers 48 inches long, 18 inches wide; swell front, made of best antique oak richly carved and finely finished; fit to adorn any dining room.
Price..............................$17.50

A $50.00 Combination Bookcase for $33.00.

The Best Type of the Cabinetmakers' Art.

A piece of furniture that is perfect in workmanship and material.

No. 94918

One of the Finest Combination Bookcases Ever Shown.

Bold, rich carvings, and elegantly made of the finest quarter sawed oak; is very roomy and useful; has large plate glass mirror in back, 18x18 inches.

THREE ROOMY DRAWERS......

The interior of the desk is well arranged for paper and other articles necessary for literary work.
Is 5 feet, 6 inches wide, and 6 feet, 2 inches high.

Will Beautify any Parlor or Library.

PRICE, - $33.00

No. 94952 A Neat and Attractive Writing Desk of the finest quartersawed oak. Neat, pretty carvings. Interior arranged for papers, stationery, etc. 27 inches wide. Price...$5.00

No. 94952

Combination Bookcase for $13.75

Combination Bookcase, made of birch and oak; has French pattern bevel plate mirror, 10x14 inches. The inside is very neatly pigeonholed and has a drawer; also a door with a shelf inside. The finish is antique oak or imitation mahogany, with a very high finish; the shelves are adjustable; the back is either a solid oak or birch, neatly paneled, and the case is well finished inside; the glass door is double thick; the size of the case is 4 feet 2 inches high, and 3 feet 4 inches wide; the glass door is double thick; the trimmings, or drawer pulls, are of solid brass.
No. 94927 Price, in oak...$13.75
No. 94928 Price, in imitation mahogany... 13.75

Combination Bookcase, 5 feet 10 inches high, 3 feet 5 inches wide, with a French pattern bevel plate mirror, 12x14 inches; the carving is hand made, the door is of double thick glass, the inside is pigeon-holed and has a drawer. There is one large roomy drawer below the desk. This case is made of solid oak, quarter sawed, with a very fine antique oak finish. Also made in curly birch, finished in imitation mahogany; the back is either solid oak or birch, and drawer pulls are of solid brass, each drawer and door has locks and keys, the shelves are adjustable. Shipping weight, 200 pounds.
No.94931 Price, in oak......$16.20
No. 94932 Price, in imitation mahogany.. 16.20

Beautiful Combination Bookcase for $18.90.

No. 94938 This handsome combination bookcase is made in quarter sawed oak and birch, mahogany finished and is very attractive in design; is richly carved; has shaped bevel mirror, 13x18 inches; has three roomy drawers and cupboard; has four adjustable shelves, large writing lid; interior of desk nicely arranged for stationery; full double glass front; is 73 inches high and 44 inches wide; complete with locks, best trimmings, etc. Price......$18.90

No.94940 A useful and attractive combination Bookcase, made of the finest antique oak, quarter sawed, or birch, with a rich mahogany finish; is 71 inches high and 41 inches wide; has four adjustable shelves, double thick glass door, one swelled drawer and two other roomy drawers; large writing lid and compartment arranged for stationery; has beveled French plate mirror, 12x16 inches; has rich, bold carvings; fitted with the finest brass trimmings. Price......$19.50

No. 94958

No. 94958 This Desk is Solid Oak, Natural or Mahogany Finish. A rare bargain. Freight will be very little, and we can save you from a third to a half. Ladies' Desk, made of solid oak, partly quarter sawed, is also made in birch and is finished in a first class glossy finish, either antique oak or imitation mahogany. Size of desk, 4 feet 5 inches high and 29 inches wide. Inside of this desk is partitioned, pigeonholed and one drawer; it also has one large drawer and shelf, the trimming is of the best brass castings, well finished. Shipping weight, 90 pounds.
No. 94960 Price, in oak...$8.75
No. 94961 Price, in mahogany finish......$9.50

Our $7.95 Solid Oak Desk.

No. 94965 Very popular they are as a house desk, and having reduced the price, we feel sure that the trade will be even greater than ever. This desk is made of thoroughly seasoned quarter sawed oak, finished antique, has three drawers, with drop table to write on. The drawers and drop table are fitted with locks and pulls. It has a cabinet or compartment for books; one small full drawer in center. Height of desk, 4 ft. 8 inches; width, 2 ft. 4 inches. Weight, 75 pounds. Price.$7.95

No Such Desk at Retail for less than $8.00.

No. 94958 A dainty and artistic writing desk in the finest quarter sawed oak, finely made and finished, richly carved writing lid, roomy lower drawer; is 26 inches wide and has French shaped legs. A real beauty for a very low price.
Price, wood back..$4.40
Price, mirror back, 4.95

Our $8.75 Ladies' Desk.

Our Solid Oak Desk. Rare Value for $7.75.

No. 94967 Same as No. 94965, only with large roomy cupboard instead of drawers.
Price......$7.75

Our $9.25 Flat Top Office Desk.

Write for our Special Catalogue of Office Desks.
No. 94976 This Flat Top Office Desk is made of solid oak, beautifully finished, heavy paneled sides and back, imitation leather top. Size, 4 feet 2 inches by 30 inches. Has four drawers, fitted with lock and key, heavy piano legs, well made and finished throughout. Weight, 150 pounds. Price......$9.25

A Fine Office Desk for $10.40.

No. 94978 This is a very sensible and useful Office Desk, made of solid oak, antique finish, and is thoroughly well made and finished. Fitted with three large drawers with locks and keys; is 3 feet 6 inches long, and 2 feet 6 inches wide, heavy, paneled ends. Weight, about 90 pounds.
Price....................$10.40

No. 94980 Large, Roomy Solid Oak Desk, finished antique, polished top; 4 feet 2 inches long. 2 feet 6 inches wide. Drawers on one side, cupboard, with pigeonhole on the other; fitted with locks and keys. Price...$12.50

Double Office Desk For $24.00.

No. 94982 Double Top Office Desk of solid oak, finished antique, polished top; 4 feet 6 inches long and 3 feet 10 inches wide. Full drawers and cupboards, good locks and keys, and is dust proof. Price, $24.00

$15.50 Buys a Solid Oak Desk.

No. 94984 Oak, finished antique, extension slide, finished back. Quarter sawed, sycamore pigeonholes. Combination lock on drawers and spring lock on curtain. Size, 3 feet 6 inches long and 2 feet 6 inches wide. Our special price.....$15.50

Large Curtain Desk for $17.00.

No. 94986 This Desk is made of solid oak. It is nicely finished all around, has two arm slides, card racks and letter drops. It is guaranteed to be built in a first class, workmanlike manner throughout, and is not to be compared with the low priced desks now offered for sale. Size, 4 feet long, 4 feet 6 inches wide. 3 feet 11 inches high. Combination lock on drawers, spring lock on curtains. Price, each....$17.00

No. 94988 Handsome Curtain Top Desk, 5 feet long, 2 feet 6 inches wide; oak, finished antique; extension slides; finished back; quarter sawed, sycamore pigeonhole case; combination lock on drawers, spring lock on curtain; also furnished with closed panel back to order. Price...........$25.00

SPECIAL VALUES IN BEDROOM SUITES.

RECENT ADVANTAGEOUS CONTRACTS have enabled us to make the prices quoted on this and the following pages. Such values in bedroom furniture will not be seen in any retail store or any other catalogue. These values are not merely in the finish of the furniture or in the decoration, but in the substantial workmanship and genuine high class quality of material.

WE PACK OUR FURNITURE WITH GREAT CARE and ship C. O. D., subject to examination, when a sufficient amount is sent with order to guarantee freight charges both ways. We stand back of every article of furniture we sell and agree that if any piece of furniture is not as represented we will cheerfully refund money upon its return. Most of our customers send cash in full, knowing that with us their money is as safe as in the bank, and that we will refund every cent paid us if we do not please the purchaser.

No. 95282 ORDER BY NUMBER.

$10.50 Buys Our Special Two-Piece Bedroom Suite

A Regular $14.00 Suite for $10.50. At $10.50 we offer you a Suite that your Retail Dealer would ask from $12.00 to $15.00 for.

No. 95282 We show in the accompanying illustration a Chamber Suite of two pieces suitable for hotels or for bedrooms that are too small for the larger size three-piece suites. This suite is made of the best selected seasoned elm, is thoroughly well put together and is finished in antique. Is 6 feet high with 4-foot 6-inch slats. Top of headboard is fancy pattern shaped and decorated with heavy molding, giving it a very neat appearance. The Combination Washstand and Dresser is of a style which matches the bed perfectly. The top is handsomely carved. The Dresser is fitted with large roomy drawer and large compartment below. The mirror is of excellent Imported German Plate Glass and is 13x22 inches in size. Weight of suite complete, about 155 lbs.

Our special price...$10.50

No. 95285 In this handsome hardwood suite we offer more value for the money than was ever offered before in the line of Bedroom Furniture. The suite consists of three pieces, finished a beautiful golden oak.

BED. The Bed is 6 feet high and has 4-foot 5-inch slats. The head of the bed is handsomely decorated with heavy molding. Bed sides are thoroughly substantial and the construction of the bed is such as will give great service.

DRESSER. The Square Dresser is very handsome and has beautifully carved top with large square German plate mirror 18x24 inches in size. Fitted with three very large roomy drawers having cast brass handles. The suite throughout is finished very handsomely.

COMMODE. The Commode or Washstand has two drawers and door with splasher back.

Weight of suite complete is about 235 lbs.

Price for the accompanying suite, consisting of three pieces, bed, dresser and commode $13.75

$14.75 Buys Solid Hardwood Bedroom Suite.

No. 95287 Bedroom Suite, made of the best selected golden oak, finished antique. We can recommend it as being good, substantial, well finished and honestly constructed.

This Suite consists of . . . .

BED, DRESSER and COMMODE

and is one of the best values shown this season.

The bed is nicely carved and is 6 feet high and 4 feet 6 inches wide; sides are thoroughly substantial. The construction of the bed is such as will give you years of good honest service.

DRESSER IS VERY HANDSOME, is fitted with extra quality bevel mirror, 20x24 inches; top and sides of mirror frame are artistically carved, dresser top is double and 38 inches in size; drawers are very large and roomy. Commode has 30-inch top, swell front, top drawer and large cupboard.

Price...$14.75

OUR $21.00 BEDROOM SUITE WITH CHEVAL DRESSER.

No. 95289 It is not possible in a mere illustration to give one a very good idea of the genuine value in a bedroom suite.

IT SEEMS SCARCELY POSSIBLE TO FURNISH A STRICTLY FIRST-CLASS BEDROOM SUITE MADE OF HARDWOOD, AT $21.00.

However, a personal examination of this suite will satisfy anyone that it is a wonderful bargain for the money, one seldom sold by retail dealers at less than $28.00 to $33.00. It is handsome in design, beautifully finished, decorated very nicely with tasty carving, and the suite complete consists of bed, cheval dresser and washstand as shown in the illustration. The bed is 6 feet high and 4 feet 6 inches wide. The cheval dresser is fitted with a large mirror, 17x30 inches in size, the mirror being made of bevel plate glass. The drawers on the dresser are extra large, fitted with fancy cast brass handles. The commode has 30-inch top. The entire suite is very substantial in construction and is not to be compared with the cheap $14.00 or $15.00 suites sold by retail dealers. Remember that the cheap bedroom suites sold by retail dealers are usually made of cheap wood and poorly finished. Weight of suite, complete, about 235 pounds.

Our special price..$21.00

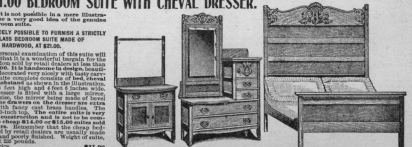

UPHOLSTERED FURNITURE

THE UNUSUAL DEMAND for strictly first class and desirable Upholstered Furniture has compelled us to very largely increase our line. We have recently formed a combination with one of the best known and largest manufacturers of this high grade goods, and by controlling a large portion of his output are in a position to control the price. We have done this to your benefit. A glance at the prices which we have named on the following pages will convince you that nowhere else in the world can you obtain such wonderful values in these desirable goods as you can from us.

UPHOLSTERING. The grades of upholstering are as follows: Grade A, good Cotton Tapestry; Grade B, Corduroy; Grade C, Imported Corduroy or Normandie Plush; Grade D, Crushed Plush; Grade E, Silk Tapestry; Grade G, Silk Brocatelle; Grade H, Satin Damask; Grade I, Silk Damask. In quoting all the various pieces of furniture on the following pages you will note that the upholstering will come in one of the above styles and qualities.

SAMPLES. We will send samples FREE upon application. In asking for samples of upholstering goods, be sure to state the quality you desire, indicating by grade letter, number and stating colors you prefer. By this means we can send you samples of just what you want without putting us to a great deal of expense.

WE UPHOLSTER OUR FURNITURE in the following colors, namely—pink, maroon, crimson, olive, blue, gold, steel, coral, nile, copper, and pomegranate. Leather furniture we can furnish in maroon, dark olive or brown. We furnish our Upholstered Furniture all in one ground color, or the separate pieces in different harmonizing colors, as the customer may select. In ordering Upholstered Furniture, be sure to state what colors or combination of colors you desire. We would recommend, however, that you leave the actual selection of colors, after stating your preferences, to our designer, who is an artist in combining colors in Parlor Furniture so as to harmonize properly.

OUR LIBERAL TERMS. Any Parlor Suite will be sent by freight C. O. D., subject to examination, upon receipt of $5.00, as a guarantee for freight charges both ways. Any single piece of furniture will be sent C. O. D., subject to examination, upon receipt of $2.00, to guarantee freight charges. You can examine the furniture at your freight depot, and if found entirely satisfactory and exactly as represented, pay the agent the balance with freight charges, and the furniture is yours.

WE ARE ONLY TOO ANXIOUS TO RECEIVE YOUR ORDER for some of these goods, as we are positive of our ability to please you so well that you will be glad to tell your friends and neighbors where you have gotten it and how much you have saved on it, and by so doing we have every reason to believe you will greatly increase our furniture business in every neighborhood.

THIS IS OUR $8.00 COUCH

27 inches wide, 76 inches long.

It is deep tufted, made in first class manner, has full spring edge, fringe all around, and guaranteed for comfort and service the equal of couches which

SELL EVERYWHERE AT DOUBLE OUR PRICE.

No. 97213 Our special price, upholstered in Corduroy or three-toned Velours.. $ 8.00
No. 97214 Our special price, upholstered in Silk Tapestry... 10.50

Our $8.90 Rococo Couch.

This, our $8.90 Rococo Couch, is one of the handsomest that is shown by us this season. It is very roomy, 30 inches wide, 72 inches long, made with the very best tempered steel springs, fastened to indestructible bottom, is well filled, nicely tufted and handsomely finished throughout.
No. 97218 Our special price, upholstered in Corduroy or Three-toned Velours. Each............$8.90
No. 97219 Our special price, upholstered in Silk Tapestry or Crushed Plush. Price, each........$9.90

Our $9.75 Couch.

This, our $9.75 Couch, is one of the most attractive couches among our numerous patterns for this season. 32 inches wide, 77 inches long, upholstered throughout with tempered steel springs and full spring edge. Unusually roomy and comfortable.
No. 97256 Our special price, upholstered in Corduroy or three-toned Velours.................$9.75
No. 97257 Our special price, upholstered in Crushed Plush or Silk Tapestry................$11.75

A Handsome Rococo Bed Couch for $16.50.

This handsome Rococo Bed Couch is so constructed that it has nothing about its appearance that would lead one to suspect that it were anything but a handsome parlor couch. Is deeply tufted, has brass beading on outer lines, giving it a very rich and dressy effect. Has a woven wire bed with a cotton top mattress, also extension head, and makes a very comfortable and luxurious bed when open. Is 51 inches wide and 76 inches long and is an elegant and useful article of household furnishing.
No. 97342 Price, upholstered in Corduroy or Velours.................................$16.50
No. 97343 Price, upholstered in Crushed Plush............................$18.00
No. 97344 Price, upholstered in Silk Tapestry.............................$18.50

Wardrobe or Box Couch for $10.50.

No. 97321 This Wardrobe or Box Couch is very roomy, admirably adapted for storing garments, clothing and miscellaneous wearing apparel. It is nicely finished inside; upholstered with the best tempered steel springs. Is comfortable, useful and ornamental; supplying a long felt want. Size, 38x76 inches. Price, Corduroy or Velours..........$10.50

Our $6.00 Lounge.

This lounge has strong oak frame, nicely finished, fancy carved front and top, a very comfortable and beautiful piece of furniture. Prices of lounge, upholstered in tapestry carpet, crushed plush or corduroy and velours.
No. 97304 Price, upholstered in Tapestry Carpet...................................$6.00
No. 97354 Price, upholstered in Grade B Corduroy...........................$6.00
No. 97356 Price, upholstered in Grade D Crushed Plush.....................$6.90

$9.75 Buys a $12.00 Bed Lounge.

This is an extra large and handsome Bed Lounge. The frame and back are of solid oak, beautifully carved, the back is extra high. The bed is fitted with woven wire mattress, cotton top and good quality of ticking. Size when open, 46x70 inches; when closed, 23x70 inches.
No. 97368 Price, Carpet........................$ 9.75
No. 97369 Price, B Corduroy.................. 10.75
No. 97370 Price, D Crushed Plush.......... 11.50

This Beautiful Bed Lounge is 23 inches wide when closed, 46 inches wide when open, 72 inches long. It has a full spring seat, woven wire bed and cotton mattress and good quality of ticking.
IN OAK OR MAHOGANY FINISH.
No. 97375 Price, Carpet......................$ 9.90
No. 97376 Price, Corduroy or Velours........ 10.90
No. 97377 Price, Crushed Plush.............. 11.90
No. 97378 Price, Silk Tapestry.............. 11.90

Bed Lounge, carved and finished oak frame, finished in oak or imitation mahogany as desired. Is extra well upholstered, with tempered steel springs, and all other materials used are the best. Is nicely upholstered in a variety of colors.
No. 97382 Price, B Corduroy...............$12.00
No. 97383 Price, C Normandie Plush........ 12.50
No. 97384 Price, D Crushed Plush.......... 13.00

Bed Lounge, has a full spring seat, woven wire bed and cotton mattress. Size, closed, 23 inches wide; open, 72 inches long; open, 50 inches wide by 74 inches long; height, 43 inches.
No. 97386 In Corduroy or Velours..........$14.40
No. 97387 In Crushed Plush or Silk Tapestry...........................$15.40

OUR GREAT BARGAIN BED LOUNGE

FOR $9.00.

THIS BED LOUNGE is 46 inches wide and 72 inches long when open; it is furnished with a woven wire mattress, made of the best steel fabric, upholstered with a cotton top and a good quality of fancy ticking. The lounge, when closed, is 23 inches wide and 70 inches long, and weighs, ready for shipment, 150 pounds.

No. 97360 Price, upholstered in Tapestry Carpet..........$9.00
No. 97361 Price, upholstered in Grade B Corduroy..........9.75
No. 97362 Price, upholstered in Grade C Corduroy or Normandie Plush..........9.90
No. 97363 Price, upholstered in Grade D Crushed Plush......10.50

No. 97360

No. 97207

THIS OUR $5.95 COUCH

IS ONE OF THE MOST ATTRACTIVE COUCHES AMONG OUR NUMEROUS PATTERNS FOR THIS SEASON.

27 INCHES WIDE, 75 INCHES LONG.
UPHOLSTERED THROUGHOUT, WITH TEMPERED STEEL SPRINGS AND FULL SPRING EDGES.

UNUSUALLY ROOMY AND COMFORTABLE.

No. 97208 Our special price, upholstered in Corduroy, or Three-Toned Velours $5.95

THIS OVERSTUFFED TURKISH COUCH

HANDSOME PATTERN... FRAME MADE OF HARDWOOD, WELL BRACED FULL SPRING SEAT AND EDGES. . . .
UPHOLSTERED IN THREE-TONE VELOURS OR CORDUROY, NICELY TUFTED. ORNAMENTED WITH TASSELED FRINGE.
27 INCHES WIDE BY 74 INCHES LONG.

GOOD VALUE FOR TWICE THE PRICE WE ARE ASKING FOR IT.
No. 97207 Price, upholstered in Corduroy or Velours.............$4.95
Weight, 75 Pounds.

No. 97208

THE GREATEST VALUE EVER OFFERED

IN A MEDIUM PRICE PARLOR SUITE....

At our prices of $13.50 to $18.00 we are offering wonderful value in this beautiful 5-piece parlor suite. There is nothing newer on the market than the designs shown in the illustrations. The suite complete consists of a large sofa, large rocker, large easy chair and two parlor chairs. Both parlor chairs are the same as the one shown in the illustration. This is a very handsome suite, one which will ordinarily retail at from $20.00 to $22.00, for the cheapest up to $30.00 to $35.00 for the highest grade. The frame is constructed by first-class workmen, the materials well selected birch, beautifully finished throughout, and the carvings on the back of each piece are very handsome. We take special pains in the upholstering. We furnish the suite upholstered in a variety of grades at prices in accordance with quality. Each piece has spring seat and spring edges, the springs being of the very best Bessemer steel. In addition to the upholstering of seat and back in the grades below mentioned, each piece has a high back and front handsomely trimmed in silk plush, which does not only add to the appearance, but to the durability. Remember that we will gladly ship this suite to any one on receipt of $5.00 as a guarantee of freight charges, the balance to be paid after you have examined the suite.

No. 97470

No. 97470 Price of complete suite, upholstered in Cotton Tapestry $13.50
No. 97471 Price of complete suite, upholstered in Corduroy or Velours. 15.50
No. 97472 Price of complete suite, upholstered in Crushed Plush....... 19.00

No. 97473 Price of complete suite, upholstered in Silk Tapestry $22.00
No. 97474 Price of complete suite, upholstered in Silk Brocatelle..... 25.00

OUR $10.00 FOLDING BED COUCH.

In the two illustrations we show our Folding Bed Couch, either used as a couch when the sides are dropped and covered with a couch cover, or when opened to be used as

A VERY COMFORTABLE LARGE-SIZE BED.

This couch is made of all steel, making it practically vermin proof, and at the same time strong and durable. It is so constructed that the sides may be lowered, and covered with a mattress and couch cover, it makes a very handsome and comfortable couch, just as shown in the illustration. By the use of a small lever the sides may be raised with ease and the folded couch becomes a very comfortable and extra large size bed. It is convenient, takes up little room, is comfortable and attractive. It lacks the inconvenience attending a folding bed and it is useful when folded up, which cannot be said of a folding bed of any kind. It is entirely free from vermin, nothing to get out of order and one of the most desirable pieces of furniture ever offered by us. The size of the couch when the sides are dropped is 74 inches long by 26 inches wide. The size of the double bed, when opened out to its full extent, is 74 inches long by 50 inches wide.

We furnish this couch either with or without mattress, as shown in the illustration. We do not furnish the couch cover. By referring to our Dry Goods Department you will find a very complete line of draperies which can be furnished at a very small price.

No. 97841½ Steel Constructed Folding Bed Couch, without mattress. Price, each $10.00
No. 97842½ Steel Constructed Folding Bed Couch, with mattress. Price, each 12.50

The freight is very low on this couch, the shipping weight being about 100 pounds. The freight for 100 miles will be about 25 cents; 500 miles, 50 cents. Sent C. O. D., subject to examination, on receipt of $2.00 with order, the balance and freight charges to be paid after receipt of the couch if found exactly as represented and entirely satisfactory.

THIS FIVE-PIECE PARLOR SUITE

OUR $18.50 FIVE-PIECE PARLOR SUITE.

consists of the following pieces, namely: 1 large sofa, 1 large rocker, 1 large easy chair, and 2 large parlor chairs, all of which are shown in the illustrations, excepting the extra parlor chair, which is identical with that shown in the picture. The frames are made of curly birch finished in mahogany.

We upholster each piece in the very best possible manner, with various qualities of coverings at the prices below named. Each piece has full spring seat and spring edge, the springs being made of the best Bessemer steel. We fit the suite complete with the best casters.

Weight of the suite complete, packed in burlap for shipment, about 265 pounds.

Our special prices are as follows:

| No. 97496 | Price of complete Suite in Cotton Tapestry | $18.50 |
| No. 97497 | Price of complete Suite, in Corduroy or Velours | 21.00 |

No. 97498	Price of complete Suite, in Normandie Plush	$20.00
No. 97499	Price of complete Suite, upholstered in Silk Tapestry	23.00
No. 97500	Price of complete Suite, upholstered in Brocatelle	25.00

FIVE-PIECE PARLOR SUITE, $29.00.

THE FIVE PIECES of this suite are as follows: Lage sofa, large arm chair, large rocker and two handsome reception chairs, both of which are alike but only one of which is shown in the illustration. It is made of selected birch richly finished in mahogany. The daintiness of the design is greatly added to by the rich carving with which the backs of the pieces are decorated. Each piece has easy spring seat and spring edge, the springs being made of the best Bessemer steel. The fronts are tufted and the top of the back is finished with a biscuit tufting which gives a wonderfully beautiful effect to the suite.

Our special prices are as follows:

| No. 97605 | Price of Suite, upholstered in Corduroy or Velours | $29.00 |
| No. 97606 | Price of Suite, upholstered in Silk Tapestry | 30.00 |

| No. 97607 | Price of Suite, upholstered in Silk Brocatelle | $31.00 |
| No. 97608 | Price of Suite, upholstered in Silk Damask | 34.00 |

$29.50 BUYS AN ELEGANT MAHOGANY FINISHED PARLOR SUITE.

MADE OF THE BEST SELECTED BIRCH with a rich mahogany finish, handsomely hand polished. This suite complete consists of one large sofa, one large easy chair, one large rocker and two large parlor or reception chairs, as illustrated. Handsome raised carvings on the back of each piece. Each piece is full spring seat and spring edge, the springs being of the best Bessemer steel, hair covered and every piece is soft and comfortable. The back of each piece is finished with full biscuit tufting, and taken all in all is a line of furniture which will ornament any parlor. Weight when packed for shipment about 290 pounds.

OUR SPECIAL PRICES ARE AS FOLLOWS:

No. 97626	Suite complete, in Corduroy or Three-Tone Velours	$29.50
No. 97628	Suite complete, in Silk Tapestry	33.00
No. 97629	Suite complete, in Silk Brocatelle	36.00
No. 97630	Suite complete, in Silk Damask	38.00

A $7.00 Divan for $5.00.

Made in selected birch, neatly carved and finished a rich mahogany; is finely upholstered, with spring seat and edges; is dressy and comfortable.

No. 97456 Price, upholstered in Corduroy or Velours..$5.00
No. 97457 Price, upholstered in Silk Tapestry......$5.50
No. 97458 Price, upholstered in Silk Brocatelle.....$6.25

Our $6.50 Divan.

Selected birch, finished a rich dark mahogany with piano polish, full spring seat and edge, back being trimmed with tufted border; size, 34 inches long, 22 inches wide, 38 inches high.

No. 97463 Price, upholstered in three tone Velours or Corduroy...........$6.50
No. 97464 Price, in Silk Tapestry.............$6.75
No. 97465 Price, upholstered in Brocatelle........$7.50
No. 97466 Price, in Silk Damask........$7.75

Beautiful Divan for $4.50.

Well upholstered, full spring seat with silk plush band, back is nicely biscuit tufted, frame is neatly carved. Made of solid birch with a dark mahogany finish, 33 inches long and 45 inches high. Weight, about 45 pounds.

No. 97635 Price, in Corduroy or Velours.......$4.50
No. 97636 Price, upholstered in Silk Tapestry $5.00
No. 97637 Price, in Silk Brocatelle........$5.05

Wonderful Value at $4.25.

Made of selected birch, nicely carved and ornamented, finished a rich mahogany, full spring seat and edges, silk plush border on front of seat and top of back, 45 inches high and 33 inches long.

No. 97641 Price, in Corduroy or Velours.......$4.25
No. 97642 Price, upholstered in Silk Tapestry. $4.75
No. 97643 Price, in Silk Brocatelle...........$5.25

One of Our Most Attractive Divans.

Richly designed back, beautifully scrolled and inlaid with colored woods, gracefully shaped. Front arm reinforced with shaped spindles, made of selected birch, made of selected birch with a rich mahogany finish; made in the best manner, of the very best materials and all of the features are the latest. 40 inches long and 33 inches high.

No. 97479 Price, in Corduroy or Velours...$12.50
No. 97480 Price, in Silk Tapestry....... 13.50
No. 97481 Price, in Silk Brocatelle.... 13.90
No. 97482 Price, in Silk Damask.......... 14.00

$24.00 Buys a Regular $40.00 FIVE-PIECE PARLOR SUITE

THE ILLUSTRATIONS OF OUR $24.00 PARLOR SUITE are engraved by our artist direct from the photographs of the suite itself and serve you excellently their purpose in showing you the elegance of detail with which this parlor suite is built. The manufacturers of this beautiful furniture are leaders in parlor furniture. They make a specialty of strictly high grade goods, and this suite is no exception to their general rule.

IN OFFERING THIS HANDSOME FIVE-PIECE SUITE TO YOU AT $24.00

we believe that no such value has ever been offered before by us or any concern. The frames are substantially made of the best selected birch with fine mahogany finish. The mahogany finish on birch is very popular. It gives the same general effect as genuine mahogany, and is very much less expensive, at the same time the material is lasting and durable, and you have the same strength as you would have in genuine mahogany furniture. The beautiful carving on the back of each piece is very decorative in effect and adds greatly to the desirability of the furniture. Each piece has extra soft spring seat and spring edge covered with hair and upholstered in the various grades quoted below. The back panels are of artistic design and the upper bands are tufted in silk plush, making a very effective finish.

WE SHIP ON THE SAME LIBERAL C. O. D. TERMS, $5.00 WITH ORDER, BALANCE C. O. D., SUBJECT TO EXAMINATION.

OUR SPECIAL PRICES AS FOLLOWS:

No. 97546 Price of Suite complete, upholstered in Corduroy or Velours $24.00
No. 97547 Price of Suite complete, upholstered in Crushed Plush 26.00
No. 97548 Price of Suite complete, upholstered in Silk Tapestry 27.50
No. 97549 Price of Suite complete, upholstered in Silk Brocatelle 29.50

..The Suite Consists of..

A Large Sofa, 48 inches long;

Large Rocker, 24 inches wide;

Large Easy Chair, 24 inches wide;

and Two Large Parlor Chairs, 18½ inches wide.

We pack the suite with care and use every pains that the goods may reach you in perfect condition.

THE WEIGHT OF THE SUITE WHEN PACKED READY FOR SHIPMENT IS ABOUT 275 POUNDS.

Morris Reclining Chair for $4.90.

Morris Reclining Chair, solid golden oak frame or curly birch, imitation mahogany finish, reversible loose cushions, back adjustable to suit any position desired, makes a most comfortable reading and easy chair.

No. 97595 Upholstered in Denim $4.90
No. 97596 Upholstered in B Corduroy $5.90

$8.00 Upholstered Chair for $5.95.

This illustration represents our Students' Sleepy Hollow Chair. It is shaped so as to afford solid comfort; nicely tufted. It is an ideal reading chair. The frame is made of solid oak, finished antique.
No. 97510 Price, A Cotton Tapestry $5.95
No. 97511 Price, B Corduroy or Velours $7.60
No. 97512 Price, D Crushed Plush $9.15
No. 97513 Price, E Silk Tapestry $9.25
Also furnished as a Rocker for 75 cents extra.

THE BEAUTIFUL ILLUSTRATIONS OF OUR CARPETS IN COLORS, AS SHOWN ON PAGES 619 TO 632, SHOW WONDERFUL VALUES IN BEST GOODS OF THE KIND.
6C

A $10.00 Roman Chair for $6.75.

A Dainty Odd Roman Chair, having graceful, neat lines; at the same time, is a very comfortable chair, back is richly carved and has dainty light open work; is made of 5-ply selected birch and has artistic inlaid center piece; front is also richly carved, and has shaped spindles under the arms; is very strongly made and is finished a rich dark mahogany color; seat is handsomely biscuit tufted; is 35 inches high and 26 inches wide.

No. 97663 Price, Corduroy and Velours $6.75
No. 97664 Price, Silk Tapestry 7.50
No. 97665 Price, Silk Damask 8.00

A Grand Bargain at $15.00 to $20.00.

This is a Chair for solid comfort. It is upholstered in such a manner as to fit the form of a person, giving comfort to all parts of the body; it is handsomely tufted and has a very strong built frame with raised hand carving on the sides. It is a chair that the possessor can be proud of and is fit for any parlor; is 32 inches wide and 40 inches high and is large and roomy. When packed ready for shipment, weighs 105 pounds.

No. 97555 Corduroy or Velours. Price $15.00
No. 97556 Silk Tapestry. Price 16.75
No. 97557 Brocatelle. Price 17.50
No. 97558 Leather. Price 20.00

Our Prices of $4.75 to $6.50 Represent a Saving of Fully 33 1-3 Per Cent.

This Rocker is a very ornamental piece of furniture, built on such lines as to afford not only the greatest amount of strength, but also giving unusual beauty. It has a large spring seat well upholstered. The frame is of solid birch, finished in dark mahogany, a truly artistic creation.
No. 97420 Price, Corduroy or Velours $4.75
No. 97421 Price, Silk Tapestry 5.35
No. 97422 Price, Brocatelle 5.90
No. 97423 Price, Silk Damask 6.50

This Beautiful Rocker for $4.95; $5.25 or $5.90, According to Upholstering.

One of the neatest and most graceful of our new designs. Very attractive in appearance; broad, comfortable, full spring seat, richly carved back, very strong, well built frame, and has features not found in every day rocker.
No. 97427 Price, Corduroy or Velours $4.95
No. 97428 Price, Silk Tapestry 5.25
No. 97429 Price, Brocatelle 5.90

OUR $15.50 5-PIECE UPHOLSTERED PARLOR SUITE.

AT $15.50 we have sold this very serviceable and attractive parlor suite for the past three seasons with great results, not only in the quantity of sales but the satisfaction exhibited by the thousands of people who have purchased it. **$15.50** represents the bare cost of the material and labor, with our one small profit added. During the dull summer season we have had scores of expert upholsterers and cabinet makers busily engaged in making these suites ahead to fill the usual large demand later on in the year. By keeping labor employed during the season when they would otherwise be short of work, and purchasing materials when they are at the lowest market price, we are able to put up a parlor suite for $15.50 which will compare very favorably with anything offered by retailers at as high as $40.00 and even more money.

SEND US $1.00 as a guarantee of good faith if you live east of the Rocky Mountains, or if you live west of the Rocky Mountains, send $5.00 and we will send this

HANDSOME OVERSTUFFED PARLOR SUITE

CONSISTING OF FIVE PIECES

to you by freight, C. O. D., subject to examination. If after receiving the parlor suite you do not consider that it is fully up to our representation and fully worth the price which we ask for it, return it to us at our expense of freight charges both ways and we will cheerfully refund the full amount remitted; otherwise you accept the suite, paying the agent the balance due together with freight charges AND THE SUITE IS YOURS.

THIS BEAUTIFUL PARLOR SUITE CONSISTS OF
A LARGE SOFA, LARGE ARM CHAIR, LARGE ROCKER AND TWO LARGE PARLOR CHAIRS.

WE FURNISH THIS SUITE IN FOUR DIFFERENT GRADES OF UPHOLSTERING AT THE PRICES NAMED BELOW:

THE FRAMES of all the pieces are of the very latest style, made from thoroughly seasoned hardwood, are glued, screwed, and plugged, thoroughly reinforced and one of the strongest and most graceful frames made at anything like the price. **UPHOLSTERING.** These suites are upholstered by the most skilled upholsterers that money will employ, and the result of their high class workmanship is a stylish appearance and thorough ness of finish such as you will find only in the higher priced suites sold by retail dealers. We upholster the different pieces in different colors of the same material, all colors harmonizing and rendering a beautiful effect. Each piece is overstuffed, handsomely decorated and finished with deep fringe, fancy bindings, cords and tassels, and ornamented with rococo brass gimp ornamentation.

FREE CLOTH SAMPLES.

THIS SUITE is made in the following styles of upholstering, namely: Three-tone Velours, Imported Corduroy, Silk Tapestry, Brocatelle or Silk Damask. **WE WILL SEND SMALL SAMPLES OF ANY OF THESE STYLES OF UPHOLSTERING ON REQUEST.**

THE COMFORT of all the pieces of this suite is greatly increased by the strong and easy, steel tempered springs. These springs are the celebrated Eagleton Springs, the best made, springs that do not sag down or weaken, but always retain their elasticity.

IN ORDERING THIS SUITE you may either take advantage of our liberal C. O. D. offer, or send full cash in advance. Most of our customers send cash in full with their order. In any case, if a suite is not found entirely satisfactory and just as represented, return it to us at our expense and we will cheerfully refund your money, and also refund any freight charges that have been paid.

No. 96280   Full five-piece suits upholstered either in three-tone Velours or Imported Corduroy. Our special price.........................$15.50
No. 96281   Complete suite, upholstered in Silk Tapestry.........21.00
No. 96282   Complete suite, upholstered in Brocatelle..........27.00
No. 96283   Complete suite, upholstered in Silk Damask........31.00

The different prices on the different grades represent the actual cost to us of the different grades of upholstering and the extra finish and the extra workmanship required in each case. All grades, however, are packed with the utmost care, thoroughly wrapped in burlap, paper and excelsior insuring safe delivery.

One of Our Most Attractive Divans.

Richly designed back with inlaid woods, beautifully scrolled, gracefully shaped, made of selected birch, with a rich mahogany finish: made in the best manner, of the very best materials and all of the features are the latest. 40 inches long and 33 inches high.

No. 97670   Price, upholstered in Corduroy or Velours.......$10.50
No. 97671   Price, upholstered in Silk Tapestry............$12.00
No. 97672   Price, upholstered in Silk Brocatelle.....14.00
No. 97673   Price, upholstered in Silk Damask   15.50

Beautiful Chair to Match Divan.

No. 97674.   Chair to match Divan.   Price, upholstered in Corduroy or Velours.......$7.50
No. 97675   Price, upholstered in Silk Tapestry   7.75
No. 97676   Price, upholstered in Silk Brocatelle.........$8.90
No. 97677   Price, upholstered in Silk Damask.......... 9.90

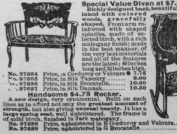

Special Value Divan at $7.75 to $10.50

Richly designed back, beautifully scrolled and inlaid with colored woods, gracefully shaped. Front arm reinforced with shaped spindles, made of selected birch, with a rich mahogany finish; made in the best manner, of the very best materials and all of the features are the latest; 40 inches long and 33 inches high.

No. 97684   Price, in Corduroy or Velours $ 7.75
No. 97685   Price, in Silk Tapestry........ 9.00
No. 97686   Price, in Silk Brocatelle.......10.00
No. 97687   Price, in Silk Damask............10.50

Handsome $4.75 Rocker.

A new design, very ornamental. Built on such lines as to afford not only the greatest amount of strength, but also giving unusual beauty. It has a large spring seat, well upholstered. The frame is of solid birch, finished in dark mahogany.

No. 97688   Price, upholstered in B Corduroy and Velours..............$4.75
No. 97689   Price, upholstered in G Brocatelle.........................5.85

...OUR CROCKERY AND GLASSWARE DEPARTMENT...

WE SHOW ON THIS AND THE FOLLOWING PAGES such an assortment of strictly high-grade ware as will seldom be found in any retail stores, except in large cities, a grade of goods that is made by potteries of world wide reputation, potteries celebrated for making only the best.

WE ARE ONLY TOO ANXIOUS to have these goods compared with any other concern. We are satisfied we can save you 50 per cent in your crockery purchases. Such sets as we sell for $5.25, $6.45, $8.95, $12.75 and other prices, are positively equal to sets that often sell at retail at twice this price; they are the very latest and most attractive designs on the market, none of the old fashioned patterns and styles of decoration such as dealers have been accustomed to carrying on their shelves for years.

IN BUYING ONE OF THESE DINNER SETS FROM US you obtain them at the bare cost of material and labor, with but our one small profit added; you buy them from us under our binding guarantee, that they shall be found as represented or we will cheerfully refund your money.

OUR LIBERAL C. O. D. TERMS. SEND US $1.00 with your order for any dinner set quoted on this and the following pages and we will send the set to you securely packed, by freight C. O. D. Upon receipt of the goods you pay the balance, together with freight charges, and the dinner set is yours, subject to your further approval. Whether you send cash in full with your order (as most of our customers do), or whether the dinner set is sent C. O. D. terms, it is subject to our guarantee that it shall be just as represented or you may return the set to us by freight at our expense and we will cheerfully refund every cent you have paid for it.

WE PACK EACH SET VERY CAREFULLY In barrels or casks and we seldom: if ever hear of any breakage. The freight on a very small item indeed when the great saving in price is considered. Crockery is accepted at first-class freight rate and a 100-piece set weighs, complete with barrel, about 100 pounds. A 56-piece dinner set weighs, when packed for shipment, about 70 pounds.

THE FIRST SET WHICH WE ILLUSTRATE AND DESCRIBE is our highest grade and finest dinner set; in fact, it is the very choicest dinner set we offer and we present it to your attention first of all not only because it is the choicest to be obtained, but because we believe it to be the most wonderful value we have ever been able to secure. We are taking the output of the pottery on this particular dinner set.

IT IS AN EXCLUSIVE PATTERN with us, unusually attractive, the very finest free hand decoration and such a set as you will seldom if ever see at less than $25.00 to $28.00.

Our Very Finest Full Gold Finished 100-Piece Dinner Set for $12.75

IN OFFERING THIS HEAVY GOLD FINISHED DINNER SET AT $12.75, do not confuse it with inferior goods offered by retail dealers at even $16.00 to $18.00. Such a set as we are here offering, would seldom, if ever, be found in stock in retail stores, outside of the most extensive stores in large cities, and such retail dealers as do handle the unusual high grade of goods as we represent in the illustration, never expect to get less than $25.00 and as high as $30.00 for the same goods.

THIS IS THE CELEBRATED MARLIN three-fired, semi-porcelain ware, a ware that is made by a pottery famous for the unusual high quality of goods, superb decorations, beautiful finish and wearing qualities.

THIS MARLIN 100-PIECE DINNER SET is decorated with free hand, filled colored rose decorations, the handsomest decorations shown by any maker. The illustration cannot possibly do this set justice. You can form but a very faint idea of its elegant appearance; heavy, deep, full gold stippled. Each plate and platter has a very deep and heavy gold stippled effect covering the outer edge, all the covered dishes, cups, pitchers, etc., in fact, all pieces with handles, have heavy gold laid decorations and stippled effect on handles and knobs. While we are offering dinner sets at $5.25, $6.45, and other prices much lower than our $12.75 Marlin Set, we recommend and urge that if you can possibly afford it, you should by all means invest in this, our highest grade, most beautiful dinner set.

WE GUARANTEE that you will be delighted with the goods, that you will find them even far greater value than you could possibly expect; in fact, the best value you have ever seen for anything like the price.

SEND US $1.00 we will ship the set C. O. D. by freight, you to pay the balance, with freight charges, when set is received at your depot; or, send us the full amount $11.75, and we will ship the set, securely packed in a barrel by freight, and if you do not find it the best set you ever saw at anything like the price, wonderful value, and if you do not find that you have saved fully 50 per cent in the purchase, you are at liberty to return this dinner set to us at our expense and we will cheerfully refund money.

This 100-piece dinner set comes in the following assortment:

12 Tea Cups with handles	2 Open Vegetable Dishes
12 Tea Saucers	1 Covered Vegetable Dish (2 pieces)
12 Soup Plates	
12 Breakfast Plates	1 Sugar Bowl (2 pieces)
12 Tea or Pie Plates	1 Cream Pitcher
12 Sauce Plates	1 Pickle Dish
12 Butter Plates	1 Slop Bowl
1 Medium Platter	1 Covered Butter Dish (3 pieces)
1 Large Platter	1 Sauce Boat

No. 97695 Our special price for the celebrated Marlin Heavy Gold Finished 100-Piece Dinner Set... **$12.75**

Our $7.45 56-Piece Marlin Pattern Dinner Set.

AT $7.45 WE OFFER THE SAME PATTERN DECORATIONS, same quality of ware as our 100-piece set, illustrated and described above, in a set of 56 pieces. Many of our customers desiring a high grade ware do not want so many as 100 pieces, and hence we are making up this special 56-piece set at a proportionately lower price. It is in every way identical with the 100-piece set above, the only difference being in the number of pieces. We pack it very carefully in a barrel for absolutely safe delivery and ship on the same liberal C. O. D. terms, $1.00 with order, balance with freight charges to be paid upon receipt of goods. Whether you send cash in full or have the set shipped C. O. D., it is forwarded with the express understanding that we guarantee it to be entirely satisfactory, just as represented and a big saving in price, or we will cheerfully refund any amount paid. This 56-piece set consists of the following pieces:

6 Tea Cups	6 4-Inch Fruit Saucers	1 7-Inch Open Vegetable Dish	1 Sauce Boat
6 Saucers	6 Individual Butters		1 Pickle Dish	1 Covered Sugar Bowl (2 pieces)
6 7-Inch Plates	1 8-Inch Platter	1 Covered Butter Dish (3 pieces)	1 Cream Pitcher
6 5-Inch Plates	1 10-Inch Platter	1 8-Inch Covered Vegetable Dish (2 pieces)	1 Slop Bowl

No. 97696 Our Marlin 56-Piece Dinner Set, full gold finished, our special price... **$7.45**

Our $5.25 100-Piece Semi-Vitreous China Dinner Set.

THIS SET is the highest grade genuine vitreous china, as hard as flint; goods that will stand an unusual amount of hard service, in fact, practically indestructible. Pure white in color, and will not turn black when chipped like ordinary ware. Very latest shape, as shown in illustration, making a set in white suitable for any house. From the accompanying illustration you can form some idea of the appearance of this beautiful 100-PIECE WHITE SEMI-VITREOUS CHINA DINNER SET, but you must see it to appreciate the value we are offering. We believe the handsomest shaped white dinner set in the market.

The 100-Piece Set consists of the following pieces:

12 Soup Plates	1 8-Inch Covered Dish (2 pieces)
12 5-Inch Plates	1 Pickle Dish
12 7-Inch Plates	1 Sauce Boat
12 Coffee Cups	1 Covered Butter Dish (3 pieces)
12 Saucers	1 Sugar Bowl (2 pieces)
12 Individual Butters	1 Extra Bowl
12 5-Inch Fruit Plates	1 Large Pitcher
1 8-Inch Dish	1 Medium Pitcher
1 10-Inch Dish	
1 7-Inch Baker	
1 8-Inch Baker	

OUR ONE DOLLAR OFFER. Send us $1.00 as a guarantee of good faith, and we will send the 100-piece set to you by freight, C.O.D., subject to examination.

No. 97698 100-Piece Set... **$5.25**

Special for Hotels, Restaurants, Boarding Houses, etc.

NOTE OUR SPECIAL PRICES FOR BIG HOTEL TRADE

...PRICES BELOW POTTERY JOBBING LIST...

GENUINE STONEWARE WHITE CHINA.

OUR ONLY OPEN STOCK GOODS are the plain white stoneware China shown in the accompanying illustration and quoted below. These are the most durable earthenware made, warranted not to craze, handsome in design and rare value. For hotels this ware is without equal. We have sold thousands of dollars worth of this china to scores of hotels throughout the country and have yet to hear a complaint from any one of them. Our prices are based on the lowest possible cost of production with the smallest possible margin of profit added, and in buying these goods from us you obtain them on the same or a lower basis of price than your local dealer himself can buy them at.

WE WILL MAKE UP ANY ASSORTMENT from the open stock quotations given below, but must decline all orders for open stock amounting to less than $5.00; that is, you can make up your order for $5.00 worth of plates alone if you wish, or the minimum amount of the purchase may include cups and saucers, plates, platters, pitchers or anything you may desire. It is to be understood, of course, that the amount of the purchase is not limited to $5.00. A great many hotels purchase a complete outfit of this china amounting to from $50.00 to $75.00. We pack every assortment very carefully in a cask or barrel and ship by freight.

FULL CASH MUST ACCOMPANY ALL ORDERS FOR OPEN STOCK OF THIS WHITE GRANITE WEAR. SPECIAL PRICES AS FOLLOWS:

No. 97741

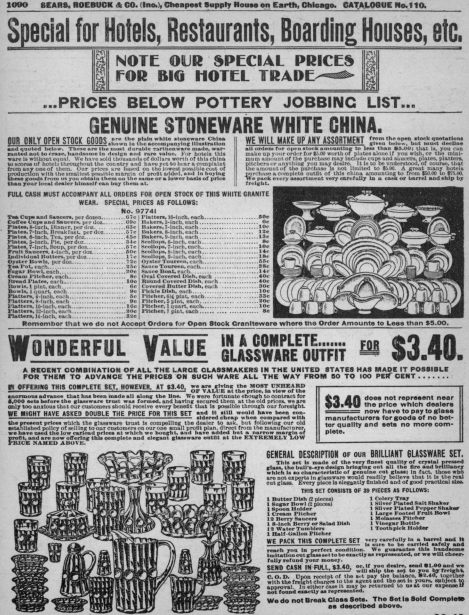

Tea Cups and Saucers, per dozen	67c
Coffee Cups and Saucers, per doz	69c
Plates, 8-inch, Dinner, per doz	63c
Plates, 7-inch, Breakfast, per doz	57c
Plates, 6-inch, Tea, per doz	45c
Plates, 5-inch, Pie, per doz	34c
Plates, 7-inch, Soup, per doz	57c
Fruit Saucers, 4-inch, per doz	50c
Individual Butters, per doz	17c
Oyster Bowls, per doz	72c
Tea Pot, each	32c
Sugar Bowl, each	20c
Cream Pitcher, each	8c
Bread Plates, each	10c
Bowls, 1 pint, each	6c
Bowls, 1 quart, each	9c
Platters, 4-inch, each	5c
Platters, 8-inch, each	9c
Platters, 10-inch, each	16c
Platters, 12-inch, each	20c
Platters, 14-inch, each	32c

Platters, 16-inch, each	50c
Bakers, 5-inch, each	6c
Bakers, 7-inch, each	10c
Bakers, 8-inch, each	12c
Bakers, 9-inch, each	13c
Scollops, 6-inch, each	8c
Scollops, 7-inch, each	14c
Scollops, 8-inch, each	14c
Scollops, 9-inch, each	18c
Oyster Toureen, each	55c
Sauce Toureen, each	25c
Sauce Boat, each	14c
Oval Covered Dish, each	40c
Round Covered Dish, each	40c
Covered Butter Dish, each	30c
Pickle Dish, each	10c
Pitcher, 6½ pint, each	33c
Pitcher, 5 pint, each	20c
Pitcher, 1 quart, each	10c
Pitcher, 1 pint, each	8c

Remember that we do not Accept Orders for Open Stock Graniteware where the Order Amounts to Less than $5.00.

WONDERFUL VALUE IN A COMPLETE GLASSWARE OUTFIT FOR $3.40.

A RECENT COMBINATION OF ALL THE LARGE GLASSMAKERS IN THE UNITED STATES HAS MADE IT POSSIBLE FOR THEM TO ADVANCE THE PRICES ON SUCH WARE ALL THE WAY FROM 50 TO 100 PER CENT......

IN OFFERING THIS COMPLETE SET, HOWEVER, AT $3.40, we are giving the MOST UNHEARD OF VALUE at the price, in view of the enormous advance that has been made all along the line. We were fortunate enough to contract for 5,000 sets before the glassware trust was formed, and having secured them at the old prices, we are only too anxious that our customers should receive every benefit that is possible through our foresight. **WE MIGHT HAVE ASKED DOUBLE THE PRICE FOR THIS SET** and it still would have been considered cheap when compared with the present prices which the glassware trust is compelling the dealer to ask, but following our old established policy of selling to our customers on our one small profit plan, direct from the manufacturer, we have used the low carload prices at which we bought, and have added but a narrow margin of profit, and are now offering this complete and elegant glassware outfit at the EXTREMELY LOW PRICE NAMED ABOVE.

$3.40 does not represent near the price which dealers now have to pay to glass manufacturers for goods of no better quality and sets no more complete.

GENERAL DESCRIPTION OF OUR BRILLIANT GLASSWARE SET.

This set is made of the very finest quality of crystal pressed glass, the bull's-eye design bringing out all the fire and brilliancy which is so characteristic of genuine cut glass; in fact, those who are not experts in glassware would readily believe that it is the real cut glass. Every piece is elegantly finished and of good practical size.

THIS SET CONSISTS OF 39 PIECES AS FOLLOWS:

1 Butter Dish (2 pieces)	1 Celery Tray
1 Sugar Bowl (2 pieces)	1 Silver Plated Salt Shaker
1 Spoon Holder	1 Silver Plated Pepper Shaker
1 Cream Pitcher	1 Large Footed Fruit Bowl
12 Berry Saucers	1 Molasses Pitcher
1 8-inch Berry or Salad Dish	1 Vinegar Bottle
12 Water Tumblers	1 Toothpick Holder
1 Half-Gallon Pitcher	

WE PACK THIS COMPLETE SET very carefully in a barrel and it is sure to be carried safely and reach you in perfect condition. We guarantee this handsome imitation cut glass set to be exactly as represented, or we will cheerfully refund your money.

SEND CASH IN FULL, $3.40, or, if you desire, send $1.00 and we will ship the set to you by freight, C. O. D. Upon receipt of the set pay the balance, $2.40, together with the freight charges to the agent and the set is yours, subject to examination and approval. In either case it may be returned to us at our expense if not found exactly as represented.

We do not Break Glass Sets. The Set is Sold Complete as described above.

No. 97790 Our Brilliant Imitation Cut Glass Set of 39 Pieces. Our Special Price, $3.40

The Choicest Glassware of two Factories.

A BARREL OF GLASSWARE For $1.90 || WHO EVER HEARD OF THE PRICE? || FULL CASH MUST ACCOMPANY ORDER.

....A GREAT CUT IN GLASSWARE....

The price of Glassware has been wonderfully reduced. We are on the bottom. We have two outfits at prices never before heard.

$1.90 ..AND.. $2.75

The above prices are about one-half the retail price. No wholesale house can meet our cut prices of $1.90 and $2.75.

No. 98200 This complete outfit for $1.90. No charge for barrel; we pack and deliver at depot free of charge a complete outfit, consisting of the following 36 pieces: 6 tumblers, 6 goblets, 12 4-inch berry saucers, 1 8-inch berry dish, 1 sugar bowl, 1 butter dish, 1 spoon holder, 1 cream pitcher, 1½-gallon water pitcher, 1 celery dish, 1 pickle dish, 1 tall open fruit bowl and 1 cake stand. The complete outfit for..........$1.90

Freight will be very little. 25 cents will take a barrel 500 miles; 50 cents will pay the freight to most any point. Send $1.90 and the outfit will be sent to you at once.

Decorate your table with one of our sets of glassware and you will surely say: "Never before were such goods sold for so little money."

No. 98200 (Order by number.)

WE PACK OUR GLASSWARE IN BARRELS, EMPLOYING ONLY SKILLED PACKERS, AND WE HAVE YET TO HEAR OF SHIPMENT BEING DAMAGED UNDER ORDINARY CIRCUMSTANCES.

OUR $2.75 GLASSWARE OUTFIT----39 ELEGANT PIECES.

WE MAKE IT A POINT to carry a line that is just as handsome and stylish as the market affords.

Many a rich man's table is decorated with glassware no handsomer than this pattern.

Would retail at $10.00 and upward. OUR SPECIAL CUT PRICE is $2.75. No charge for packing or delivering to depot. We do that free. An expert only could tell it from a $100 glass outfit.

No. 98205 This elegant 39-piece set must be seen to be appreciated. It is an exact reproduction of the celebrated English "Prism" cut glass and is finished so that it requires an expert to detect the difference. The large pitcher, in particular, is a very handsome piece of glass, and, if it were genuine cut, would alone be worth $20.00, but the glass manufacturers have so improved that we are able to sell this assortment at a fraction of the cost of a single item of the genuine cut glass, and very few could possibly tell the difference. Your neighbors will pronounce it genuine cut glass. These goods are very heavy beautifully finished, and each piece is a work of art. This outfit consists of 1 butter dish, 1 sugar bowl, 1 spoon holder, 1 cream pitcher, 12 berry saucers, 1 8-inch berry or salad dish, 12 water tumblers, 1 ½-gallon pitcher, 1 celery tray, 1 silver plated salt shaker, 1 silver plated pepper shaker, 1 large footed fruit bowl, 1 molasses pitcher, 1 vinegar bottle, 1 toothpick holder. Every one who sees this set will want one.

Our price for the complete outfit....$2.75

Just Like Cut Glass, at about 7 Cents a Piece.

No. 98205 (Order by number.)

A COMPLETE LINE OF SILVERWARE IS QUOTED IN OUR SPECIAL JEWELRY CATALOGUE AT PRICES ABSOLUTELY BEYOND COMPETITION IN GOODS OF EQUAL VALUE. SEND FOR SPECIAL JEWELRY CATALOGUE.

FOUR RED HOT BARGAINS

IN GLASSWARE OUTFITS.

WE HAVE MADE ILLUSTRATIONS SMALL TO ECONOMIZE SPACE
BUT EVERY SET ON THIS PAGE IS THE

BIGGEST VALUE FOR THE MONEY EVER OFFERED.

OUR $1.75 40-PIECE GLASS OUTFIT.

No. 98210 Imitation cut glass design. The pattern is the newest produced this year and exceedingly beautiful. We feel confident that you never heard of such a wonderful assortment of glassware for so little money.

SET CONSISTS OF 40 PIECES AS FOLLOWS:

6 Water Tumblers	1 Butter Dish
6 Goblets	1 Sugar Bowl
6 Salt and Pepper Shakers	1 Cream Pitcher
12 Berry Saucers	1 Spoon Holder
1 Large Berry Bowl	1 Pickle Dish
1 Large ¼-gallon Water Pitcher	1 Tall Celery Glass

Price, Complete Outfit..$1.75

SPECIAL 95-CENT GLASS SET.

No. 98212 This outfit is beyond question the greatest bargain ever offered. The design is a copy of a very fine cut glass pattern. The price is so low it seems ridiculous.

SET CONSISTS OF 20 PIECES AS FOLLOWS:

6 Water Tumblers	1 Sugar Bowl
6 Sauce or Berry Dishes	1 Butter Dish
1 Large Berry Bowl	1 Cream Pitcher
1 Large ¼-gallon Pitcher	1 Spoon Holder

Price..95c

33-PIECE GLASS SET FOR $1.45.

No. 98214 Handsome imitation cut glass design. This is a good practical outfit, as we have included a larger quantity of the pieces that are used every day.

SET CONSISTS OF 33 PIECES AS FOLLOWS:

12 Water Tumblers	1 Spoon Holder
12 Sauce or Berry Dishes	1 Sugar bowl
1 Large Berry Bowl	1 Butter Dish
1 Large ½-gallon Pitcher	1 Cream Pitcher
1 Pickle Dish	

Price, Complete Outfit.................................$1.45

$1.20 BUYS A $2.00 23-PIECE SET.

No. 98216 Here is another chance for you to stock your china closet with nice glassware at a price the local storekeeper will charge you for a dozen tumblers. This pattern has met with greater success than any other style of glassware on the market. Pure crystal glass imitation cut glass design.

SET CONSISTS OF 23 PIECES AS FOLLOWS:

6 Tumblers	1 Pepper Shaker
6 Sauce or Berry Dishes	1 Sugar Bowl
1 Large ¼-gallon Water Pitcher	1 Cream Pitcher
1 Large Berry Bowl	1 Butter Dish
1 Pickle Dish	1 Spoon Holder
1 Salt Shaker	

Price..$1.20

::: FOUR BIG LEADERS AT $3.75 TO $6.95 :::

AT FROM $3.75 TO $6.95 we offer you your choice of four new big Banquet Lamps. Very latest for this season. Larger, handsomer and better **AT $3.75, $5.65, $5.90 AND $6.95** Lamps than you would be likely to find in your own town and the equal of Lamps that retail in cities at double the price. we have endeavored to make a selection of the largest, handsomest and best Banquet Lamps made, and to buy them in such large quantities as to enable us to name a price but a trifle above the actual cost to make. Every Lamp is beautifully tinted and colored, as shown in illustrations, flower decorated by free hand work, mounted on beautiful gold plated bases, fitted with very best removable oil founts, and best large No. 2 Royal 100 candle power center draft burner. These large Lamps must be seen to be appreciated. They are so large and handsome that no illustration will do them justice. In ordering you can either send the full amount with order or send $1.00, when we will send any Lamp C. O. D.; balance payable after received.

No. 98677

Our Very Finest Lamp for $6.95.

No. 98677 For $6.95 we offer you one of the largest, handsomest and best Banquet Lamps made, a lamp equal to lamps that retail at double our price, so fine that if you order this lamp you will have such a lamp as was never before seen in your section. This lamp stands 25 inches high, has 12-inch globe and 8-inch bowl, rests on gold-plated stand, is beautifully tinted and elaborately decorated in handsome colored floral decorations, by hand.
Our special price.........$6.95

No. 98675

Our $5.90 Cerise Banquet Lamp.

No. 98675 No description can do this handsome new style lamp justice. It is one of the handsomest banquet lamps made, VERY large, 25 inches high, 12-inch globe, 14-inch bowl.

THIS IS A LAMP THAT RETAILS IN CHICAGO AT $7.50.

A very massive and stylish lamp at $5.90, is a price heretofore unknown.
Our special price...........$5.90

No. 98676

Our Big $5.65 Vase Banquet Lamp.

No. 98676 One of the very largest Lamps made. So large, massive and handsome that it must be seen to be appreciated. Stands 24 inches high, 10½-inch globe, 12½-inch bowl, stands on gold-plated base.

IT IS HANDSOMELY TINTED AND DECORATED BY HAND

in a beautiful floral design. Our $5.65 price means a saving to you of fully 50 per cent.
Our special price............$5.65

Our Big $3.75 Banquet Lamp.

No. 98677½ This Lamp is handsomely tinted and beautifully decorated in hand painted colored floral decorations.

THE BIGGEST, HANDSOMEST LAMP EVER SOLD FOR $3.75.

Stands 30 inches high, has 10½-inch globe, bowl is 8 inches wide, 16½ inches deep.

AT $3.75 IT'S A WONDER OF VALUE.

Our special price.............$3.75

SPECIAL BARGAINS IN NEW STYLE LAMPS.

We show ten new styles in handsome Banquet Lamps at prices based on the actual cost to produce with but our one small profit added. AT THE SPECIAL PRICES QUOTED we furnish each lamp, complete with GLOBE, CHIMNEY, BURNER AND WICK, ready for oil, and at the price we furnish these Lamps, carefully packed, one in a box. THE COLORED ILLUSTRATIONS are exact reproductions in colors, and show you just how each lamp is colored and decorated.

Our $2.10 Lamp.

No. 98673 This handsome Banquet Lamp is 23 inches high, has 9-inch globe, removable oil fount, fitted with the celebrated No. 2 Royal Center Draft Burner of 75 candle power. Beautifully colored and free hand painted, as illustrated.
Our special price.........$2.10

Our $1.95 Banquet Lamp.

No. 98680 This Lamp is 23 inches high, has 9-inch globe, removable oil fount, No. 3 Climax burner, neat hand flower decoration on light background. Wonderful value at $1.95.
Our special price....$1.95

Our $1.50 Banquet Lamp.

No. 98682 One of the handsomest Lamps shown this season, latest and handsomest design decoration. Stands 21 inches high, 9½-inch globe, 8-inch bowl, decorated exactly as shown in illustration and the most wonderful value ever offered at $1.50.
Our special price......$1.50

No. 98678

No. 98680

No. 98682

Our $3.15 Banquet Lamp.

No. 98679 This Lamp is 36 inches high, has 10-inch globe and 9-inch bowl, central draft, removable fount, handsomely decorated in beautiful free hand colorings, gold plated base and mountings.
Our special price....$3.15

No. 98679

Our $1.25 Leader.

No. 98681 For $1.25 we offer in this a Lamp that retails at double the price. It is 19¼ inches high, has 8-inch globe, 7¼-inch bowl, stands on a beautiful metal base. It is handsomely tinted and ornamented.
Our special price....$1.25

No. 98681

Our $1.85 Vase Banquet Lamp.

No. 98683 This handsome Vase Lamp, an entirely new and handsome design, is offered at $1.85 in competition with lamps that sell at double the price. It is 17 inches high, has 9-inch globe, 10-inch bowl. It is beautifully colored and hand decorated as illustrated.
Our special price....$1.85

No. 98683

Our $2.00 Lamp.

No. 98648 Reading Lamp. Nickel plated, 10-inch dome shade. The very best lamp made for use as a reading lamp. Always clean, largest quantity of light, best burner made; this lamp has no equal for actual using.
Price, each..........................$2.00

No. 98650 C. Lamp. This is one of the most staple lamps in the market. Very strong and substantial, and will last a lifetime. You need no chimney with this lamp, the shade and the illuminator taking the place of chimney, and thus saving you from the breakage of chimneys. Price, each..........98c

Perfection Student Lamp.

No. 98652 Perfection Student Lamp. This lamp has been used for so many years that a description of it is unnecessary. It is, without a doubt, the peer of all study lamps. Perfectly safe and reliable. Lamp can be adjusted to any height.
Nickel plated, plain white shades.............................$3.50
Nickel plated, green shades... 3.75

No. 98654 Same as above except lamp has two lights, one on either side of standard, and oil reservoir in center. This is the highest grade student lamp made. Frame is very heavy and finely finished.
Price, nickel plated, plain white shades...............$9.00
Price, nickel plated, green shades............... 9.50

Night Lamps.

No. 98656 Brass Night Lamp. 7¾ inches high, complete Gem burner, chimney and wick. Price each...25c
No. 98658 Glass Night Lamp, with metal handle. Height 7 inches. Complete.
Price, each..........................20c
No. 98660 Glass Night Lamp. This is the most practical night lamp made. The lamp is fitted with a revolving reflector and is a bracket which enables you to hang lamp on wall. Height, 7¼ inches.
Price, complete....................30c

No. 98662 This Very Useful Lamp jumped into popularity at once because of its great utility and low price. It has removable glass fount and reflector, No. 2 Sun burner and chimney. Is made to hang on a wall or rest on a table and reflector can be taken off if desired. Price, each.........35c

No. 98664 Too Well Known to need further introduction. The kitchen bracket lamp still keeps in popular favor. The No. 98664 is finished in French bronze, has glass fount, No. 2 Sun burner and 7-inch silvered glass reflector and No. 2 Sun chimney. Each, 75c

No. 98666 The Most Popular Kitchen and Hall Lamp ever made, and our style is the strongest and best finished on the market. We complete it with No 2 glass fount having outside filler, No. 2 Sun burner and chimney and 8-inch silvered glass reflector.
Price, each....................90c

No. 98668 Glass Stand Lamps, priced with Sun burners, wicks and chimneys. In this grade we show only the heavy plain style having sunk top to catch oil. Five sizes, as follows:
O (height, 9 in.) No. 1 burner......31c
A (height, 9¼ in.) No. 1 burner......35c
B (height, 10 in.) No. 2 burner......40c
C (height, 10¼ in.) No. 2 burner......45c
D (height, 11 in.) No. 2 burner......50c

No. 98670 Glass Stand Lamps,shrunk-on collars; no plaster, collars cannot work loose, and lamps are stronger and heavier than the ordinary grade. Priced with sun burners, wicks and chimneys.
Four sizes, as follows:
O (height, 9¼ in.) No. 1 burner....45c
A (height, 10 in.) No. 1 burner....50c
B (height, 10½ in.) No. 2 burner....55c
C (height, 11 in.) No. 2 burner....60c

Glass Hand Lamp.

No. 98672 Footed Glass Hand Lamp. Just the thing for bedrooms and to carry around the house, into closets, etc.
Price with No. 1 Sunburner, wick and chimney. Each........35c

Footed Hand Lamp.

No. 98674 "Shrunk-on" collar; no plaster. A lamp to last must be made well. On this style the collars are pressed on by machinery and cannot work loose. The lamps are heavier and less liable to break. Price includes No. 1 Sun burner, wick and chimney.
Price, each.......................35c

Center Draught Bracket Lamp.

No. 98676 Where a strong light is needed, we recommend this lamp. Bracket is made of cast iron and is finished in "French bronze." The lamp fount is the celebrated "Royal" and is fitted with burner giving a light equal to 75 candles. Fount is made of brass, highly polished, and will hold enough oil to burn eight hours. The reflector is 10 inches in diameter and is made of silvered glass, and is so arranged that it can be adjusted to throw the light wherever needed. This is the most powerful light giver made.
Price, complete......................$3.50

Hanging Kitchen Lamp.

No. 98674½ Frame is made of heavy wire, japan finish, and is completed with glass oil fount, No. 2 sun burner, chimney and wick. This lamp is just the thing if you want a cheap hanging fixture.
Price, complete....................65c

HANGING LAMPS. Our Leader.

No. 98700 Ball Weight Extension Hanging Lamp, 14 inches plain white dome shade. No. 2 Sun burner and chimney. Frame is gold lacquered finish, equal in every respect to lamps your dealer will ask $3.00 for. Our special price....$1.98
No. 98702 Same lamp as above with automatic spring extension; length closed 25 inches, extended 60 inches.
Price, complete.........$2.48

No. 98704 Has extra heavy frame, handsomely decorated shade and fount to match, automatic spring extension; length closed, 25 inches; extended, 61 inches. Extra large No. 3 burner. Handsomely decorated shade and oil fount to match. The spring extension makes lamp suitable for a high or low ceiling.
Price, complete.......$3.50

No. 98704

No. 98706 Library Lamp. Automatic Spring Extension; length, closed, 25 inches, extended, 61 inches. Plain white 14-inch dome shade. No. 2 Climax burner. Frame is finished in rich gold. Thirty cut glass pendants suspended from shade band.
Price, complete.......$3.75
No. 98708 Same lamp as above trimmed with handsomely decorated dome shade and fount.
Price, complete.......$4.50

No. 98706

No. 98710 Library Lamp, Automatic Spring Extension;

length, closed, 25 inches; extended, 61 inches. The shade and fount are elegantly decorated with a handsome flower design on tinted background. Extra heavy gold lacquered frame No. 2 Climax burner. Shade band is trimmed with thirty elegant cut glass pendants.
Price, complete..$5.25

Our $6.00 Library Lamp.

No. 98712 Library Lamp, Automatic Spring Extension; length, closed, 25 inches; extended, 61 inches. The burner is the celebrated No. 2 Royal center draught, 75-candle power. Oil fount is removable for purposes of cleaning and filling. Elegant decorated shade and fount, genuine hand painted flower design in natural colors on tinted background. Frame is made of brass finished in rich gold. Shade band trimmed with thirty genuine cut glass pendants.
Price, complete.........$6.00

No. 98712

A $12.00 Hanging Lamp for $8.25.

No. 98714 Library Lamp, same general description as No. 98712, with this exception: Extra heavy cast frame gold lacquered finish, and an exceptionally fine hand painted shade and fount. The decorations are chrysanthemums in natural and lifelike colors on a delicately tinted background. This lamp is a beauty and is sure to please.
Price, complete..$8.25

No. 98714

No. 98760 Parlor Extension Lamp fitted with No. 2 royal center draught fount, 75 candle power, removable for purpose of filling. Automatic spring extension. Length, closed, 25 inches; extended 61 inches. Can be used in room with either high or low ceiling. Easy to keep clean as lamp has no prisms. Metal work rich gold lacquer. Vase and globe are decorated to match. Genuine hand painted floral design on rich background of either red, blue or brown. This is the very latest design in parlor hanging lamps, and it is a beauty. In ordering state which color of decoration you desire.
Price, complete.............$7.75

No. 98760

Library Hanging Lamp.

No. 98745½ Ruby and black, made of heavy brass, finished black in imitation of wrought iron; vase is finished in rich ruby enamel and shade, which is 14 inches in diameter, is made of rich ruby glass to match vase; equipped with the celebrated Parker Center Draught Burner, and is guaranteed to give a light equal to 75-candle power; fitted with an automatic spring extension. Length, closed, 30 inches, fully extended, 60 inches.
Price, each............**$6.50**

No. 98747¼ The Globe Hanging Lamp is a new idea; frame is made of heavy brass, finished black in imitation of wrought iron. The vase, which holds oil fount, is finished in rich ruby enamel, and an applied ornament—a Roman torch and wreath in rich gold lacquer. The globe, which is 10 inches in diameter, is richly hand-painted with flowers. The Parker Burner will give a light equal to 75 candles. Automatic spring extension. Length, closed, 25 inches; fully extended, 60 inches.
Price, each.
......**$7.40**

Library Hanging Lamp.

No. 98749½ The frame is made of heavy brass, finished in imitation of wrought iron. The vase, which holds oil fount, is finished in rich green enamel, decorated with an Empire scroll in black; the 14-inch shade is elegantly hand painted. The burner is the celebrated Parker Center Draught, and is guaranteed to give a light equal to 75 candles, fitted with an automatic spring extension. Length, closed, 30 inches; fully extended, 60 inches.
Price, each..........**$7.90**

Zenith Hall Lamp.

No. 98720 Zenith Hall Lamp. Just the thing for a small hall. Ruby, opal or pink globe. This is the cheapest and best hall lamp in the market. In ordering state which color globe you prefer. Price, **$1.75**

Square Hall Lamp.

No. 98722 Square Hall Lamp. This is a larger and better lamp than the Zenith and costs very little more. In two colors, crystal etched or ruby etched glass as desired. Be sure to state color desired. This hall lamp is handsome enough for any dwelling. It is an exact reproduction of the high priced gas lamp that has always been so popular. Length, 36 inches. Complete with burner and chimney
No. 98720 Our price .... **$3.00** **No. 68722**

Store Lamps.

No. 98726 Store Lamp. The best and cheapest in the market. For large areas and where good light is required only the best lamps should be procured. We keep them and guarantee every lamp we sell to give perfect satisfaction. The Juno gives a steady and white light. Just the thing to throw light on a window display. Complete as illustrated, 15-inch tin shade, suitable for store or window lights, 65 candle power. Price, brass finish, **$2.00** Price, nickel finish, **2.25**
No. 98728 Same lamp as No. 98726 only trimmed with 10-inch white porcelain dome shade which makes a much neater lamp without much greater cost. Price, brass finish **$2.50** Price, nickel finish, **3.00**

The Juno Mammoth Store and Hall Lamps.

No. 98734 Juno Mammoth Store and Hall Lamp, 400 candle power. The strongest and best finished lamp on the market. The wick movement is perfect and so simple that a child can rewick the lamp. Patent lock ring to hold fount in ring obviates all danger of fount jarring out of frame. Fount taken out from below for filling. You are taking no chances with this lamp as we guarantee every one to give perfect satisfac-

tion or we will replace them and pay all expenses. The lock ring used to hold the Juno is a great convenience. The fount can easily be taken out from below for refilling. Complete, as illustrated, 14-inch plain dome shade, suitable for churches, halls, stores, etc.
Price, complete, brass finish **$3.75**
Price, complete, nickel finish **4.25**
No. 98736 Same lamp as above only it is trimmed with a 20-inch tin shade, making a cheaper and more suitable lamp for saw-mills, factories, etc.
Price, complete, brass finish **$3.25**
Price, complete, nickel finish........... **3.75**
No. 98740 Same lamp as above, trimmed with 14-inch white dome shade and fitted with an automatic spring extension so as it can be lowered for cleaning or lighting without the use of step-ladder or chairs. Length of lamp, closed, 42 inches; fully extended, 78 inches. Money cannot buy a finer constructed lamp. This makes an ideal lamp for churches, halls and fine stores. Very handsome in appearance.
Price, complete, brass finish **$6.25**
Price, complete, nickel finish **6.75**

PARLOR CHANDELIERS.

Every Detail of **MATERIAL** and **WORKMANSHIP** is given **Close Attention.**	**CHANDELIERS** direct from Manufacturer to Consumer.

Chandelier. With patent automatic extension for raising or lowering. This chandelier, the most popular ever put on the market, still retains its place in general favor. It is finished in rich gold bronze, and the center band has cut glass colored jewels. As shown in the illustration, we trim it with cut glass colored jewels suspended on the oil fount cups, center band, and two rows across the center rod. This gives a very brilliant effect when lighted. The globes are colored opalescent effects, and correspond with the colored jewels. The burner can be lighted without removing globes or chimneys. We furnish the chandelier in three and four lights as follows:
No. 98750 Chandelier, three-light, complete, as shown **$15.75**
No. 98751 Chandelier, 4-light, complete, **18.75**

Our $10.50 Chandelier.

Chandelier, with patent automatic extension for raising and lowering. A handsome chandelier at a price that puts it within the reach of all. This beautiful parlor fixture, useful as well as ornamental, is finished in rich gold bronze, and completed with etched globes of a very popular shape. The burner is of a new design that can be lighted and trimmed without removing the globe or chimney, thus avoiding the possibility of breakage in handling them. We furnish this fixture in the following sizes:
No. 98772 Two-light, complete............ **$ 8.25**
No. 98773 Three-light, complete, as shown **10.50**
No. 98774 Four-light, complete............ **13.50**

Church or Hall Chandelier.

This is an extra large fixture, designed especially for halls and churches. Elegantly finished in rich gold on solid brass. Trimmed with No. 3 Climax burners.
No. 98778 Price, complete, 2 lights **$40.00**
No. 98779 Price, complete, 3 lights......**$45.00**

Patent Extension Chandelier. Length, closed, 36 inches; extended, 57 inches. This chandelier is elegantly finished in rich gold, has colored metal center; trimmed with unique burners, which can be trimmed and lighted without removing chimney or globes. Trimmed with fine etched crystal globes.

No. 98780 Price, complete, 3 lights........**$15.00**
No. 98781 Price, complete, 4 lights........ **18.00**
Church or Hall Chandelier. Same chandelier as above, except burners. This fixture is trimmed with the celebrated B. & H. No. 1 center draft burners, each light 50-candle power.
No. 98782 Price, complete, three lights....**$18.00**
No. 98783 Price, complete, four lights.... **21.00**

Chandelier. Polished Bronze, rich gold finish. The metal ball in center of chandelier is finished in rich enamel, either ruby or green. Length of chandelier, 36 inches, has patent extension, which extends 21 inches, making length of chandelier fully opened 57 in. The globes are crystal glass finished with a handsome etched design. The burners can be lighted and trimmed without removing globes or chimney. We can furnish this chandelier in either 3 or 4-light.
No. 98784 Price, complete, 3 lights **$13.50**
No. 98785 Price, complete, 4 lights........ **16.50**

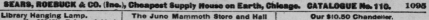

...HIGH GRADE SEWING MACHINES...

WE ARE HEADQUARTERS FOR SEWING MACHINES BOTH IN QUALITY AND PRICE.

OUR MINNESOTA LEADS THE WORLD IN SEWING MACHINES. WE HAVE MACHINES AS CHEAP AS $11.75, AND THE VERY finest High Grade Cabinet with a Minnesota Head for $27.45. We have sold thousands of machines and are represented with one of our sewing Machines in nearly every section of the country.

WITH OUR SUPERIOR FACILITIES
For marketing machines direct from the manufacturer to the consumer, we are able to save the purchaser from $20.00 to $50.00 on a machine. This amount certainly is worth the saving, and it is far more economical to buy for cash than to pay exorbitant profits for the privilege of buying on the installment plan. The price of our machines in many cases about what the agent or average retail dealer would ask for a first payment of a machine on the installment plan. There are many good machines on the market, and, unfortunately for the users of sewing machines, there are many poor ones. We would not handle a poor machine at any price, and as we control the output of the manufacturer, we are able to have our machines made of the very best material, carefully inspected by our own superintendent. Combining, as we do, the good points of all high class machines and protecting our machines with patents, we are able to furnish a machine for the actual cost of labor and material with only one small profit added, that will stand side by side with the highest priced machine sold by agents or retail dealers, do exactly the same work, last as long and, in many cases, longer, run as noiselessly and in every other respect just as good and with many superior features.

WE PRACTICALLY HAVE NO COMPETITORS
as our trade in sewing machines is so large that we are able to make them for less money than any other concern in existence. There are retail dealers, canvassers and various catalogue houses who handle sewing machines, some of which are reliable and many are not, but if we can have one of our sewing machines in any home we know that it will be sure to stay, because it is a better machine than any other concern can afford to sell at our catalogue price, and no better machine can be had at any price. A better machine cannot be made than our Minnesota and we are ready and willing at all times to send it on our regular terms of shipment; and have it returned to us at our own expense if it is not found as represented, and equal to any machine on the market; and with it we send our 20-year binding guarantee which is evidence in itself that if the machine was not as represented and capable of doing everything we claim for it, it would not be policy for us to assume the risk of guaranteeing it for 20 years. But as we have handled the machine for a number of years and have only the most flattering recommendations and testimonials from our customers in its behalf, we know that we cannot say too much for our **Minnesota**.

EVERY PIECE AND PART
of our machines, from the rollers on the floor to the top piece of the cover, is carefully inspected and fully tested before entering into the machine. Every machine is inspected by two inspectors before being packed for shipment; it is threaded and a piece of cloth will be found showing the inspection of sewing and the adjustment to be perfect. Every bearing is carefully oiled and every care given the machine to have to leave our factory in absolutely perfect condition, and reach your home so that you will be able to at once operate it for any purpose required of a sewing machine, from the simplest plain sewing to the most delicate fancy work. With the machine we furnish a set of steel, highly polished nickel plated attachments, the very best made and the same that will be found on any $60.00 or $75.00 sewing machine. The simplicity of our Minnesota makes it superior to the ordinary complicated machine of many parts, as it enables our customers to handle it with very little study and be able to operate it at once without instructions. The instruction book which we send with the machine illustrates the different parts and attachments, and by referring to the instruction book one who has never done sewing before can easily operate our Minnesota machine.

THERE WAS A TIME
when sewing machines were controlled entirely by two or three manufacturers who had patents on the different parts of machines; and this monopoly enabled them to ask unreasonable and exorbitant prices for their machines, these exorbitant high prices do not have to be paid now by the users of sewing machines. A high grade machine with the very latest improvements can be had from us at less than half the price that these same manufacturers now ask for their machines.

WE ARE ABLE to sell our high grade Minnesota machine to the user at factory cost with only one small profit added because we don't employ agents and pay them any part of the selling price for procuring the business.

WE DON'T SELL ON THE INSTALLMENT PLAN and thus run the risk of losing part of the price of some of the machines.

WE DON'T DO BUSINESS IN AN EXPENSIVE and reckless manner and make the purchaser stand the extra cost.

WE DON'T EMPLOY CANVASSERS or peddlers; we don't send out instructors to give lessons at the customer's house, personal instructions not being necessary; thus saving this expense to the customer, which all sewing machine dealers add in the selling price of the machine.

A LITTLE STUDY of our illustrated instruction book will enable the most inexperienced to operate our machines with the utmost satisfaction.

OUR TERMS OF SHIPMENT.

WE SHIP OUR MACHINES on the most liberal terms of any concern and upon receipt of a small deposit of $1.00 we will send any of our sewing machines to you upon receipt of your order, the balance C. O. D. You can call at your freight depot, examine the machine, and if found satisfactory, pay the agent the balance, take the machine to your home, give it a thorough and fair trial, and if you do not find it exactly as represented and equal to our catalogue representation, you can return it to us at our expense and we will promptly and cheerfully refund your money in full. As nearly all our customers send cash in full with the order, we advise everyone purchasing one of our machines to do so, as they save the return charges on the money which is asked on all C. O. D. shipments by the express companies and from one to three days' delay as it requires more time to make a C. O. D. shipment, and when you send cash in full with your order it is with the same understanding that you can return the machine to us if not satisfactory and we will cheerfully and promptly return your money in full and pay the freight charges.

THIRTY DAYS' FREE TRIAL OFFER. BY THIS SPECIAL OFFER YOU ARE PRIVILEGED TO DEPOSIT THE PRICE OF THE MACHINE WITH YOUR LOCAL BANKER, TAKE THE MACHINE TO YOUR HOME FOR 30 DAYS' TRIAL, and after you are satisfied that it is all we represent it to be, instruct the bank to send the money to us. Otherwise, IN ALL CASES OF DISSATISFACTION, we pay all the express, AND ALL YOUR MONEY IS REFUNDED.

IN SENDING YOUR ORDER TO US CONSIDER THESE POINTS:

A first-class high grade sewing machine at manufacturer's prices.
The latest and best set of attachments, all steel.
Liberal terms of shipment. Our binding guarantee.
No risk, money in full refunded if not satisfactory.
Small amount pays the freight charges.

We hope to receive your order and assure you it will command our most prompt and careful attention. In sending your order to us, please be sure to give the catalogue number, name and price of the sewing machine on the order blank.

A FAC-SIMILE OF OUR 20-YEAR GUARANTEE.

SPECIAL HIGH GRADE FEATURES
FOUND ONLY IN OUR
☞MINNESOTA MACHINES☜

Durability,
Ease of Operation,
Light and Noiseless Running,
Simple Construction and Easily Learned,
Positive Feed,
Self-threading Shuttle,
Perfect Tension with Thread Release,
Self Setting Needle,
Positive Take Up,
Automatic Spooler,

Highest Arm,
Hand Rubbed Enamel Finish on Head,
Heavily Nickeled Bright Parts,
Hardened Tool Steel Bearings,
All Working Parts Adjustable,
Latest improved and Best Steel Attachments.

OUR $12.75 HIGH GRADE HIGH ARM Edgemere Machine.

SEND US $1.00

AS A GUARANTEE OF GOOD FAITH, and we will send this our **HIGH GRADE, HIGH ARM 5-DRAWER DROP HEAD EDGEMERE SEWING MACHINE** by freight C. O. D. subject to examination. YOU CAN EXAMINE
If at your freight depot, and if found satisfactory, pay the freight agent the balance, $11.75, and shipping charges. Then after you have used the machine in your own home for three months, if it does not prove exactly as represented and entirely satisfactory in every respect, return it to us and we will cheerfully refund your money in full, including all shipping charges you have paid. The freight charges will amount to nothing as compared with what you save in price.

SPECIAL FEATURES OF OUR $12.75 EDGEMERE.

5-DRAWER DROP HEAD CABINET, a great improvement over the old style upright wood-work, so constructed that when not in use the head may be dropped out of sight, where it is protected from dust and dirt and affords you a handsome desk, stand or table.
HIGH ARM. Our $12.75 Edgemere has one of the highest arms of any sewing machine made, giving ample room for the handling of large and bulky material.
THE EDGEMERE HEAD is one of the very best high arm heads made. Positive four-motion feed, self threading, vibrating shuttle, automatic bobbin winder, adjustable bearings, patent tension liberator, improved nickel plated loose wheel, adjustable presser foot, improved shuttle carrier, patent needle bar, patent dress guard, patent belt controller.
FINISH. Our $12.75 Edgemere is given an extra fine finish throughout. Has a heavy nickel plated face plate, nickel plated hand wheel, very finest full finished enameling with fancy colored decorations and ornamentation.

ATTACHMENTS AND ACCESSORIES FURNISHED.

WITH OUR $12.75 EDGEMERE we furnish a very complete set of attachments free, including one foot hemmer, one tucker, one thread cutter, two screwdrivers, one ruffler, one quilter, six bobbins, one gatherer, one binder, one package of needles, one gauge, one set of plain hemmers of different widths up to ⅜ of an inch, one oil can filled with oil, and an instruction book.

HOW TO COMPARE OUR $12.75 EDGEMERE.

Do not compare our special $12.75 Edgemere Machine with any of the cheap, shoddy sewing machines that are being widely advertised by houses, some of questionable reputation, at prices ranging from almost nothing up to $6.00. If you want to appreciate the difference between the $12.75 Edgemere and the machines advertised by others at the same and higher prices, let us send you one machine at the same time, compare them side by side, and if you do not find the Edgemere cheaper in price and from $10.00 to $30.00 better in quality and finish, you can return the machine to us at our expense.

No. 98990 Order by Number.
From the above illustration, which is engraved from a photograph, you can get an idea of the appearance of our Special $12.75 Edgemere Sewing Machine when open for work, head being raised and in place, and the cover extended as a sewing machine table. No larger, handsomer, more roomy or more convenient cabinet made; no better device for the protecting of a sewing machine head.

OUR NEW 1900 MODEL EDGEMERE has every modern improvement, all the up-to-date points of every high grade machine made. Has the newest style 5-drawer cabinet, made of solid oak, beautifully finished, fine nickel drawer pulls, rests on four casters, has a Saxton adjustable treadle and the full black enameled iron stand.

OUR SPECIAL $12.75 PRICE is based on the actual cost of material and labor, with but our one small percentage of profit added. If you buy an Edgemere Sewing Machine from us at $12.75, you will get one of the handsomest machines that was ever seen in your section, you will get a machine at less than your dealer can buy the same grade machines in carload lots.

THE EDGEMERE MACHINE is not offered by department stores, is not offered by any newspapers as premiums, never sold by scheme houses, can be had only from us and through the manufacturer's regularly appointed agents at two to three times our special $12.75 price.

OUR SPECIAL $12.75 5-drawer, drop head, high arm, Edgemere sewing machine is made for us under contract by one of the best sewing machine manufacturers in America, made from first class material, only skilled mechanics are employed, and every machine is put out under the manufacturer's and our own 20-year binding guarantee.

HAVE YOU A FRIEND IN CHICAGO? If you have friends in Chicago to whom you can write, please tell them to come to our store and see and examine our special $12.75 Edgemere, and then ask them to write you and tell you if they found it such a machine as was never shown at anything like the price, and if they advise you to send us your order.

REMEMBER, IT COSTS YOU NOTHING to see and examine this machine, and compare it with those your storekeepers sell at $40.00 to $60.00, and then if you are convinced you are saving all of this profit, you can pay your railroad agent our special offer price, $12.75, and freight charges, which amount we will agree to return to you at any time within three months if you become dissatisfied.

AS TO OUR RELIABILITY we refer to our customers among your own neighbors. We have many customers in every county, city and town in the United States. Some of them are among your own neighbors. Ask them if they would advise you to send your order to us. We also refer to the National City Bank and German Exchange Bank of New York, to the Metropolitan National Bank and Corn Exchange National Bank of Chicago, to any express company, railroad company, business house or resident of Chicago.

OUR Instruction Book makes everything so plain that even a child without previous experience can quickly learn to operate the Edgemere and do any work that can be done on any sewing machine.

VERY LIGHT RUNNING.

Our Special $12.75 EDGEMERE is one of the Lightest Running, Most Durable and Nearest Noiseless Machines Made.

No. 98990 Order by Number.
This illustration gives you an idea of the appearance of our special $12.75 5-drawer, drop head cabinet Edgemere machine closed, to be used as a writing desk, center table or stand.

OUR 20-YEAR GUARANTEE.

WITH EVERY EDGEMERE SEWING MACHINE we issue a written binding, 20-year guarantee, by the terms and conditions of which, if any piece or part gives out by reason of defect in material or workmanship, WE WILL REPLACE IT FREE OF CHARGE.

OUR $14.95 BURDICK

FOR $14.95 we furnish this Large 7-Drawer, Drop Head, High Grade Burdick Sewing Machine in Competition with Sewing Machines that sell Everywhere at more than Double the Price.

On Other Pages in this Catalogue you will find a Full Description of the Burdick Sewing Machine, the Working Parts Fully Described.

ON ANOTHER PAGE you will find an illustration of our $14.50 5-drawer, Drop Head Burdick Sewing Machine, the one illustration showing the machine open for work exactly as we show in this large illustration; the other showing the machine closed, the head dropped from sight, secure from dust and dirt, and closed forming a handsome piece of furniture, to be used as a desk, center table or stand. When the machine is not in use the head drops down from sight away from dust and dirt, the large extension table folds over the head, closing the machine up completely, as shown in the illustration of our 5-drawer Drop Head $14.50 Burdick

FOR WANT OF SPACE we show one illustration of our $14.95 7-drawer, Drop Head Cabinet. The illustration shows the machine ready for work. For want of space we not only show but the one illustration, but we have been compelled to cut this short. You will observe the drop leaf, which is very large and extends out to take in any kind of work, has, for want of space, been cut off from the illustration.

$14.95 OUR SPECIAL PRICE barely covers the cost of material and labor, with but our one small profit added.

$14.95 IS THE LOWEST PRICE EVER ATTEMPTED BY ANY DEALER.

$14.95 IS A PRICE MADE POSSIBLE ONLY by reason of our handling these machines in immense quantities, controlling the manufacture and therefore able to add but one small profit above the net cost to produce.

WE FURNISH THIS 7-DRAWER MACHINE, EXACTLY AS ILLUSTRATED, THE LATEST STYLE AT... **$14.95**

HIGH GRADE DROP HEAD MACHINE, IN A HANDSOME, BEAUTIFULLY FINISHED OAK CABINET, THREE DRAWERS ON EACH SIDE AND ONE LARGE FULL DRAWER IN THE CENTER, COMPLETE WITH A HIGH GRADE SET OF ATTACHMENTS, THE MOST COMPLETE SET OF ATTACHMENTS FURNISHED WITH ANY MACHINE.

Send us $14.95,

or, if you prefer, send $1.00, and we will send this, our

HIGH GRADE, 7-DRAWER, DROP HEAD BURDICK SEWING MACHINE

to any address by freight C. O. D., subject to examination. You can examine it at your freight depot, and if found perfectly satisfactory pay the freight agent the balance, $14.95, and freight charges. Give the machine three months' trial in your own home, and if at any time during the three months you have reason to be dissatisfied, you can return the machine to us at our expense of freight charges both ways and we will return all your money.

YOUR Home Agent may advise you not to buy a Sewing Machine from us......

To satisfy yourself whether your local sewing machine agent's advice in such cases is wholesome or not, permit us to offer a suggestion: WE WON'T advise you not to buy from your local agent. WE WON'T say that your local agent would not sell you a good machine. WE WON'T even suggest the price he would ask you for how much less we could sell a machine equally as good; but WE WILL presume to offer this suggestion: Before buying a sewing machine from your agent at home, before ordering a sewing machine from any other house, send for one of our machines, compare it with any machine offered by anyone else, regardless of price, call in some thoroughly reliable, disinterested mechanic or sewing machine expert to examine the two machines. Don't take our advice, don't be governed by what we say, and don't be influenced too much by what the local sewing machine agent, who is trying to sell you his machine, says. Use your own judgment and the judgment of the disinterested sewing machine expert or mechanic.

IS THIS A FAIR PROPOSITION?

WE ARE PERFECTLY WILLING TO REST OUR CASE ON THIS SORT OF ACTION.

$14.95

ORDER BY NUMBER 99112

No. 99112 Order by Number

DIRECTIONS FOR USING THE NEW SILENT AND LIGHT RUNNING **BURDICK** Sewing Machine SEARS, ROEBUCK AND CO

On the basis of lower prices than were ever before attempted by any other house on the same high grade machines, we speak for your trade.

FOR COMPLETE DESCRIPTION OF THIS MACHINE SEE PAGE 1102

ANOTHER SUGGESTION: There are at least a few Burdick, Iowa or Minnesota Sewing Machines in every neighborhood, for there is not a town where we have not sold sewing machines during the past year. Go to the people who are using either the Burdick Iowa or Minnesota machines, people in your own neighborhood, friends of yours, perhaps, and possibly relations, ask their advice and their judgment. We don't want you to order from us if they don't advise you to do so.

ANOTHER SUGGESTION: If, perchance, it should happen that you are unable to locate one of our machines in your immediate neighborhood, write some friend in Chicago, tell them to come to our store, see and examine our machines, and don't order from us unless they write you, advising you by all means to order a Burdick, Iowa or Minnesota.

$16.90 BUYS THE BURDICK FULL CABINET MACHINE

FOR $16.90 We offer this FULL SOLID OAK CABINET BURDICK MACHINE as the equal of machines that retail at two to four times the price.

SEND US $16.90 or, if you prefer, send $1.00, when we will send this COMPLETE FULL CABINET BURDICK MACHINE to you by freight C. O. D., subject to examination. You can examine it at your freight depot, and if found perfectly satisfactory and exactly as represented, pay the freight agent the balance, $15.90 and freight charges; give it a three months' trial in your own home, and if at any time during the three months you have reason to be dissatisfied for any cause whatsoever, you can return the machine to us at our expense of freight charges both ways and

We Will Immediately Return Your Money.

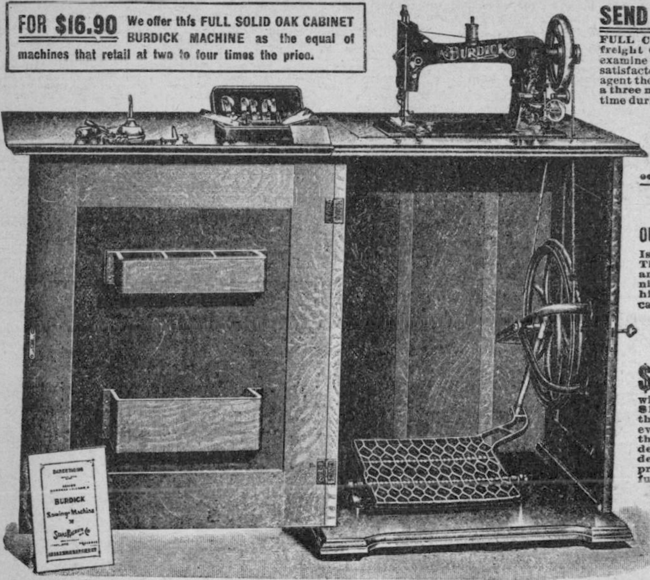

...FULL DESK CABINET...

AS WILL BE SEEN FROM THE TWO ILLUSTRATIONS, THIS.....

OUR HIGH GRADE $16.90 BURDICK MACHINE

Is furnished with a FULL DESK CABINET. The cabinet is made of solid oak finished in antique, made of heavy built up mouldings, nicely ornamented, handsomely carved and highly polished. The one illustration shows the cabinet open ready for use; the other illustration shows the cabinet closed, the head or machine dropped from sight, and closed it makes a handsome piece of furniture to be used as a

Stand, Writing Desk or Table.

$16.90 Is a price based on the actual cost of material and labor, with but our one small percentage of profit added. $16.90 is a lower price than was ever made for this grade of machine with full desk cabinet, even in carload lots to dealers. $16.90 is a price that will save you all the profit your retail dealer would make, all the profit the wholesale dealer would make, and a good part of the profit the manufacturer would make on any full cabinet machine he would offer you.

If every one who knows us and knows our machines don't tell you that we will furnish you a better machine for less money than any one else will furnish you, we will not expect your order.

No. 99114 Open.

THE BURDICK HEAD AND ATTACHMENTS

Are fully described on other pages in this catalogue. By referring to other pages in this catalogue you will find the Burdick head and attachments fully described in all the different parts, and from the description of the head and attachments found elsewhere, and from the illustrations shown hereon of our full sewing machine cabinet, we trust you will be able to form some idea of the value we are offering in our $16.90 machine.

=AT $16.90=

We offer this machine under our BINDING, 20-YEAR GUARANTEE.

WE OFFER TO SEND IT TO ANY ADDRESS C. O. D., SUBJECT TO EXAMINATION, ON RECEIPT OF ONE DOLLAR.

☞ We send it out with the understanding, that you can return it at any time within three months if you are not perfectly satisfied with it, all at our expense, all money paid us, to be immediately refunded.

full set of attachments in this handsome, highly polished, solid oak, full sewing machine cabinet at **$16.90**

ARE YOU ACQUAINTED WITH THE BURDICK MACHINE?

If you are not acquainted with the Burdick Sewing Machine, if you do not know of one in your immediate neighborhood, write us and we will give you the names and addresses of people in your own locality who own these machines which they have bought from us. You can go and see them, examine the machines, talk with the parties who own them and take their advice about ordering from us. If they advise you to order a Burdick Sewing Machine, then consider the most

...EXTRAORDINARY VALUE... we are giving in the HIGH GRADE BURDICK with the

DON'T ORDER A SEWING MACHINE ELSEWHERE,.....

DON'T BUY A MACHINE FROM YOUR LOCAL DEALER AT HOME

Until you have seen, examined and compared our machine with the machine offered by the other party, and if our machine is not better finished, lighter running, better in every way and lower in price than the best offer you can get from any one else, when compared side by side,

Return Our Machine at Our Expense, and We Will Immediately Return Your Money.

No. 99114 Closed.

CLOSED, IT MAKES A BEAUTIFUL DESK, TABLE OR STAND.

BABY CARRIAGE DEPARTMENT OF SEARS, ROEBUCK & CO. Inc.

For this season we offer such values in high-art, up-to-date Baby Carriages, as can be had from no other house.

OUR BABY CARRIAGES

Are made for us under contract by one of the best makers in the country, made of carefully selected material, only the most skilled mechanics are employed and every carriage is covered by a binding guarantee, and if any piece or part gives outby reason of defect in material or workmanship, we will replace or repair it free of charge.

The prices we quote are based on the actual cost of material, with but the labor and our one small percentage of profit added, a price as low as any dealer can buy in quantities.

IF YOU ORDER A BABY CARRIAGE FROM US You will be saved all the profit your local retail dealer and wholesale dealer would make and more; besides, as all our baby carriages are the very latest style for this season, all new and fresh from the factory, you are insured the very latest up-to-date styles, such a carriage as you would get only from the most fashionable city retail stores and there at fancy prices as compared with our prices.

OUR LIBERAL C. O. D., SUBJECT TO EXAMINATION TERMS. While nearly all our customers send cash in full, and we advise you to send cash in full with your order, for we will always return your money, paying the freight or express charges both ways if you are not perfectly satisfied. We will on receipt of $1.00 send any carriage to any address within 100 miles of Chicago, C. O. D., subject to examination. You can examine it at your nearest railroad station, and if found perfectly satisfactory and exactly as represented, pay the railroad agent our price and freight charges.

We require from two to three days for upholstering our Baby Carriages.

Our Famous $6.25 Carriage.

$6.25

This carriage was a big leader with us last season at $6.25. It was shown in our catalogue in a full page colored engraving taken direct from the carriage by the three color photographic process. At $6.25 it was a great leader last season, and notwithstanding the cost to manufacture baby carriages has greatly advanced and all dealers have advanced their prices from 25 to 50 per cent. By reason of our large contract we are able to to maintain last year's price on this famous carriage, namely $6.25.

This is a handsome carriage; body is made extra large and roomy. The frame is made of seasoned maple, mitered, glued, screwed and plugged at joints. The upholstering is a good quality domestic three color velours cloth, trimmed with handsome cords and tassels. The upholstering is removable. It comes upholstered in any of the following colors: Dark peacock blue, cardinal, wine, olive, bronze gold, steel blue, pomegranate or nile green. Highest grade Walker gear, full plated and best quality steel axles, springs, Kinley automatic brake. Parasol is sateen with flounced ruffle, valenciennes lace edge.
No. 99512   Our special price................$6.25
Extra for rubber tired wheels, 75 cents.

Our $7.45 Carriage.

$7.45

The body of this carriage is entirely new for this season, one of the handsomest bodies shown, the equal of bodies that are used in carriages at double the money. The frame is made of the best seasoned maple, mitered, glued, screwed and plugged at corners. Hand woven cane bottom and hand woven rattan work, highly finished. Finest Walker gear, with highest grade wheels, axles, springs, fitted with Kinley Automatic brake. Upholstered in the highest style of the art in the quality Bedford cloth, with fancy silk plush roll, neatly tufted, as shown in illustration, trimmed with handsome cords and tassels. The upholstering comes in the following colors: Dark peacock blue, cardinal, wine, olive, bronze gold, steel blue, pomegranate or nile green. We furnish this carriage complete with sateen parasol, as illustrated, fancy flounced ruffled edge.
No. 99513   Our special price................$7.45
Extra for rubber tired wheels, 75 cents.

Our $3.75 Carriage.

This is the lowest priced carriage we offer. It is made of good material throughout. Heavy maple frame; body is mitered, glued and fitted at corners, well finished. The gear, including the wheels, axles, springs and brake are of Bessemer steel, nicely plated. It is upholstered in a nice shade of cretonne, as shown in illustration, made of a cane embossed good substantial material. It has a cane embossed bent handle with solid brace irons. The parasol is detachable, made of a good quality of silesia, fancy edge, as illustrated.
No. 99500   Our special price................$3.75

Our $5.95 Carriage.

This handsome heavy roll baby carriage is the same style we showed last year, one of the most staple carriages we had. While the cost of material and labor has advanced, we were able, under contract, to procure the goods at last year's prices and we will still maintain our last year's unheard of price of $5.95.

The frame is made of the best seasoned maple, the corners are mitered, glued, screwed and plugged. The body is made of high grade China rattan, very smoothly finished, shellacked by the best process, made with an embossed cane finished bottom. The gear is made of the best material, has long bent handle. The wheels, axles, springs and automatic brake are made of the best Bessemer steel, heavily plated and polished. Upholstered with genuine Bedford cloth, in colors: Dark peacock blue, cardinal, wine, bronze gold, steel blue, pomegranate or nile green. The upholstering is done in the best possible manner. Parasol as illustrated, is made of an extra quality silesia, with neat, scalloped edge, as shown in illustration, is detachable and adjustable.
No. 99503   Our special price................$5.95
Extra for rubber tired wheels, 75 cents.

Our $4.95 Carriage.

This is a new style carriage. Frame is made of seasoned maple; body from a good quality of rattan, woven in a substantial manner as shown in illustration. Upholstered in cretonne which we furnish in dark peacock blue, cardinal, wine, olive, bronze gold, steel blue, pomegranate or nile green, as ordered. The gear is the celebrated Walker Bessemer steel gear, heavily plated and finished, fitted with the Kinley automatic brake. Parasol as illustrated, made of good quality silesia with fancy scalloped edges as illustrated.
No. 99506   Our special price................$4.95
Extra for rubber tired wheels, 75 cents.

$4.95

Our $6.35 Carriage.

$6.35

For $6.35 we offer this carriage as the equal of carriages that will sell at double the price. Is entirely new for this season, one of the handsomest carriages that will be shown by anyone. The body is made of the best quality of reed, hand woven, highly finished, shellacked and polished. Has the celebrated Walker gear, very best Bessemer steel wheels, axles, springs and automatic brake. Is upholstered in genuine Bedford cloth in any of the following colors: Dark peacock blue, cardinal, wine, olive, bronze gold or nile green. Trimmed with handsome cords and tassels. Parasol, as shown in illustration, is made of silesia with handsome lace cover.
No. 99509   Our special price................$6.35
Extra for rubber tired wheels, 75 cents.

Our $7.90 Carriage.

This is a very handsome carriage, entirely new for this season. Body is one of the handsomest made. It is designed by Radcliffe, designer of only the very finest work. The body is full size. Has heavy solid maple frame, closely hand woven cane bottom, beautifully finished throughout. Has the best Walker gear, Bessemer steel springs, wheels and axles, Kinley automatic brake. Is upholstered in extra quality Bedford cloth with fancy silk plush roll, ornamented with handsome cords and tassels. The upholstering is made removable so that it can be instantly removed for cleaning. Comes in any of the following colors: Dark peacock blue, cardinal, wine, olive, bronze gold, steel blue, pomegranate or nile green. The parasol is a handsome sateen parasol with ruffled edge. Parasol is detachable and adjustable.
No. 99514   Our special price................$7.90
Extra for rubber tired wheels, 75 cents.